KING COUNTY LIBRARY

29563384

D1613914

TH IS NO LO ER THE
PROPERTY OF
G COUN LIBRARY TEM

BELLEVUE   JUL 31 '89

SKYWAY   FEB 7   1984

PATHS TO THE NORTHWEST

PATHS
TO THE
NORTHWEST
A JESUIT HISTORY OF THE
OREGON PROVINCE

WILFRED P. SCHOENBERG, S.J.

Foreword by Thomas R. Royce, S.J.

LOYOLA UNIVERSITY PRESS
A Campion Book   CHICAGO, ILLINOIS

Dedicated to

THE LORD JESUS

under whose banner
"we make our paths by walking on them."

Pedro Arrupe, S.J.
May 23, 1980
Spokane

© 1982 Loyola University Press

ISBN 8294-0405-8

Design by Carol Tornatore
Cover: original paper cutout, "Father Modeste
Demers offering the First Mass in the interior
of the Northwest, October 14, 1838," by Sister
Jean Dorcy

Printed in the United States of America

CONTENTS

FOREWORD

Stories about our life and predecessors in the Oregon Province have always been important for us. They have spiced up many sermons, provided recreation-room laughter, and even been an inspiration to prayer during retreats. Who we are as Jesuits and where we will go in the future must be recorded in our story.

We are fortunate, then, in this fiftieth year as a Province to have the present volume written with so much historical research and entertaining human interest. We need not worry that our story will not be retold over and over even though we are no longer required to read the menology at table in our Jesuit houses. The fascination of the present volume will make it a must for all and subject of many conversations (it might even settle some arguments) in the years to come.

So we are deeply grateful to Wilfred Schoenberg, S.J. and his profound love of the province which has produced this work. In spite of a tough deadline and many other demands, his dedicated work has paid off for the province again. We are grateful to all who have helped him, especially Daniel Flaherty, S.J. of Loyola Press and David Leigh, S.J. of St. Michael's Institute. Most especially we are grateful to all the Jesuits of our province in the mold of De Smet and Fitzgerald who struggled to establish the work of the Society of Jesus in the Northwest. May our reading of this volume keep alive the spirit of courage and selfless faith among us and all who work with us. We hope that a book equally exciting can be written after fifty more years of such service as we seek the Greater Glory of God.

February 2, 1982

Thomas R. Royce, S.J.
Provincial
Oregon Province of the
Society of Jesus

ACKNOWLEDGMENTS

It has been my pleasant privilege to present this complete history of the Jesuits in the Northwest for the first time. For accomplishing this task I have benefited from the use of resources, most impressive in volume and detail, that was produced over these last 140 years by my Jesuit colleagues. To these, my brothers, living and dead, I express not only my thanks but my admiration for their incredible accomplishments which were generally regarded by them as only part of the job.

There are others whom I am pleased to acknowledge for their assistance and support. First of all, I wish to thank my provincial, Father Thomas Royce, for providing me an opportunity to conduct my research and writing. I also thank Father Joseph Perri, who was vice-provincial at the time when he assigned me to this task. My thanks to Father Clifford Carroll, Oregon Province Archivist, and to his assistant, Father Richard Sisk, who assisted me with the selection of illustrations; to Father Neill Meany for maps and other props; to Father Robert Grimm, coordinator for the Golden Jubilee Year, for coordinating me, too; Charis Howser for her patience and promptness in typing the manuscript, Father Leo Kaufmann for his suggestions, and the director and staff of the Loyola University Press for their unique professional services, made pleasant by their patience and geniality.

Finally, I thank my Jesuit brothers in Jesuit House at Gonzaga for listening when I talked about our history. They were helpful as sounding boards, and it was not without reason that Father Lee Kapfer, our local correspondent, reported to the *Province News:* "Next best thing to reading at table is sitting next to Schonie."

INTRODUCTION

When Peter De Smet and his five Jesuit colleagues arrived in the Pacific Northwest in 1841, they found themselves committed to a mission which extended then from the Rocky Mountains in the east to the shores of the Pacific, from the Mexican border on the south at the 42° parallel to the Arctic Ocean on the north. This expanse, larger than all of western Europe, had no cities. There was no Seattle, Portland or Spokane, then, not even the thought of building them. San Francisco, the closest settlement, was a small Mexican outpost and mission a thousand miles away. There were no roads. There were only Indian trails and rivers which served as highways in most American frontiers.

There was no government. The borders of the United States ended with the Rockies. In 1818, England and the United States had signed a Treaty of Joint Occupation. Both countries hoped to get the lion's share of this territory for its own expansion. The Hudson's Bay Company of England *de facto* ruled the area through its chief factor, Dr. John McLoughlin, who resided beyond bastions at Fort Vancouver. Through a network of fur trading posts, McLoughlin retained order, controlling even the passage of missionaries from Canada.

There was no church in the area, in the sense of a structured vicariate or diocese. There was no hierarchy. In 1838 two secular priests from Canada, responding to appeals for priests from French-Canadian settlers in the Willamette Valley, had come in the canoes of the fur brigade with the qualified blessings of McLoughlin. Francis Norbert Blanchet and Modeste Demers, supplied with spiritual faculties from Bishop Joseph Provencher, auxiliary of the bishop of Quebec and vicar apostolic for the district of the Northwest, had agreed to establish no mission south of the Columbia River.

During the time between De Smet's arrival and today, the Rocky Mountain Mission slowly matured until it was designated formally as a province on September 8, 1909, and again, after a division, as the Oregon Province on February 2, 1932. By this time the territory consisted of four states: Oregon, Washington, Idaho, and Montana, and the Territory of Alaska, more than one million square miles stretching over five time zones, thinly populated, and largely unchurched.

The Province of Oregon is uniquely distinct, a province with strongly individual characteristics formed by isolation and vast distances, and a tough, pioneering spirit. Its history reflects these qualities and others—some as clean and bracing as the Northwest environment; some as frail as human nature. Thus it is a robust history with elements of Indians and cowboys, cattle wars, train robbers, and even murder. More happily it is a history also of the holy nuns, heroic laymen as well as Jesuits, and the progress of God's people from log cabins to universities and cathedrals.

De Smet's clarinet, which he played to attract Indians around the campfire, was made in Belgium about 1840. It was kept in Young Ignace's family for over a century and was then presented to Father Louis Taelman for safekeeping in the Jesuits' archives.

Peter De Smet, Founder of the Rocky Mountain Mission, shown here at St. Louis University.

Cross and chain presented to Young Ignace by De Smet at St. Joseph's Mission, Council Bluffs, in 1839.

Fragment of De Smet's buffalo robe in which he slept while on the trail.

Aeneas, or Young Ignace, accompanied Peter Gaucher to St. Louis in 1839. He remained in St. Louis during the winter and directed Father De Smet to the Flathead country the following spring. This drawing by Gustavus Sohon was executed on May 16, 1854.

Insula, or Red Feather, a Flathead chief as drawn by Gustavus Sohon on April 26, 1854. He was a great favorite of the Jesuits.

Pierre Kar-so-wa-ta as drawn by Gustavus Sohon on May 16, 1854. Sohon said of him "He is the most industrious Indian in the valley." According to Sohon he spoke "mountain french, and english, besides several indian languages."

1

BEGINNINGS
1831–1840

On the Columbia Plateau, the Salish, or Flatheads, dwelled together with many tribes that were related to them by tongue and perhaps by blood as well.[1] The Kamu'inu, or Nez Perces, although they spoke a different tongue, were especially identified with the Flatheads, and many of them came to live in the valley watered by the Ootlashoots, where the Flatheads lived most of the year.* The Flatheads were the envied aristocrats of the northern plateau. Their language was the *lingua franca* of the entire area and their maidens were much sought after in marriage. In about 1725, they had obtained horses from their southern neighbors, which they learned to breed so well that other tribes coveted them.† This was especially true of the Blackfeet to the northeast.

The possession of fine horses had presented all tribes with much greater mobility. One immediate consequence of this was an acceleration of confrontations between traditional enemies over disputed land in greatly expanded areas. Another consequence was that methods of hunting were radically changed. *Before the horse*—a very meaningful phrase to the Indians—a large team of men had to drive the buffalo over a cliff, or *pushkin*. Other Indians at the base of the cliff would be ready to strike the broken animal with arrows or beat its skull with stone clubs. This strategy greatly reduced the possible sites for hunting. But with a horse that could outrun a shaggy, ponderous buffalo, which might weigh as much as a full ton, a single hunter equipped with arrows could bring one down.

Until the Blackfeet acquired guns from the white Canadians to the north, the Flatheads had enjoyed the use of their ancestral hunting grounds without serious challenge.[2] The buffalo had become extinct on the plateau long ago, so the Flatheads and their friendly neighbors were dependent for food and robes on the buffalo that ranged beyond the continent's divide where the Blackfeet, as soon as they had guns, had the advantage. One could not fight guns with arrows. The Flatheads consequently were forced to take refuge in their mountain valley of the Ootlashoots, the Bitterroot, where they could be approached only from the north through a narrow opening which was called the Gate of Hell by the

---

*The Bitterroot Ootlashoots means "red willows," referring, no doubt, to the willows along the creek.

†Flathead horses were regarded as the best. When Capt. Meriwether Lewis and Lt. William Clark met the Flatheads on September 4, 1805, they estimated each man owned from twenty to one hundred fine horses. Father Gregory Mengarini considered the young Flatheads' preoccupation with their horses as one of the reasons for closing St. Mary's.

trappers. Here they formed with their neighbors a loose kind of alliance to challenge those beyond the east mountains where game abounded. When the Flatheads, too, were successful in obtaining guns, the pursuit of game by small parties became a simple matter, and the Blackfeet were hard pressed to keep the Flatheads and their friends from invading Blackfeet hunting grounds, some of which had been taken from the Flatheads.

The Indians of the vast plains of the northern plateaus, mountains, and coastline of western America had many gods. Some of them believed in a Supreme Being, the Great Spirit, somewhere in the sky, but they had no common revelation. Occasionally rumors of the Christian revelation drifted along ancient trails and waterways between the east and west. Strange, intriguing reports flowed westward with the parfleches* of Indian commerce about exotic men who were white skinned, instead of colored, who wore black dresses like women, and who spoke from "talking leaves." It was said that they carried *high medicine*, a power that overcame all medicine as surely as water from the river snuffed out the coals Indians carried in their stone, fire barrels.†

The Flatheads as a group believed that God was *Spakani*—the sun and the moon.[3] They yearned to live forever, but their elders had nothing to say to them about a future life. They were people without a Happy Hunting Ground. Their dark color meant death, final and forever. It was rumored that white men lived forever—that white meant life.[4] Perhaps the white men with black robes could somehow show them the way to the Happy Hunting Ground. What they needed was the white man's *strong medicine*, as it was commonly called, for survival. Without it, they feared they were doomed. The possession of this strong medicine not only would produce buffalo for the hunt but it would protect one from those who would interfere. Having strong medicine was like having a strong brother . . . but it cost dearly. One could gather his own, if he experienced a propitious dream, or he could buy it either with robes or horses, or with beads that arrived with the fur traders.

If the reports were true that the men in black robes had strong medicine, it would be most desirable to have them as allies. The Flatheads and their neighbors would then have a great advantage over the Blackfeet, perhaps a lasting one.

There was a tradition among the Flatheads that many years before, even before the horse, a tribal visionary called Shining Shirt had foretold the coming of "Black Robes." Shining Shirt had lived in Sinielman, "the Surrounded Place," now called Mission Valley. Like one of the heralds of Old Coyote,‡ he had spoken to his people, so it was alleged, and he had described the Black Robes so vividly that few, if any, doubted his message. "These Black Robes," he said, "would teach the people religion, would give them new homes and would make laws for their conduct. When the time came, the Black Robes would change the lives of the people in ways which they but little dreamed."[5]

It is not likely that Shining Shirt had a special revelation from Old Coyote or from God either. There is reason to believe, however, that he spoke with the conviction of factual

*Trunk-like containers made from hides of buffalo, elk, or deer. Later, cowhide was used.

†Before the use of matches, some Indians carried live coals in a tubular shaped stone about eight inches long and hollowed out. Mud was used to enclose the coals. For air, a straw was inserted in the mud at one end.

‡"Old Coyote" for many tribes of the Plateau, including Shining Shirt's people, was the creator, or "Maker of Things," according to Mengarini. Old Coyote's legendary counterpart on the high plains was called Napi. Unlike Amotkan, both Napi and Old Coyote were rather amusing semi-deities.

knowledge, gathered by report from Indians who had *seen* a Black Robe and discoursed with his companions.

In 1743, three generations before the appearance of Capt. Meriwether Lewis and Lt. William Clark, on a crisp wintry New Year's Day, not only horses had come to Montana, but palefaces as well. Two Canadian Catholic fur traders, Pierre and François La Verendrye reached the Belt Mountains near present Helena, and what is more significant, they continued for *seven days* to travel west before turning back to Fort La Reine on the site of present-day Winnipeg.[6] Father Claude Coquard, a Jesuit missionary had accompanied the expedition at least as far as North Dakota. Though it is unlikely that Coquard was with the explorers when they discovered the "Shining Mountains" (the Rockies), there appears to be little doubt that news of his presence in the West had reached the Mission Valley. Shining Shirt, a medicine man as well as a chief, would have been the first to hear these details from friendly Indians, who were no more capable of keeping to themselves such shocking intelligence than General Custer could ignore Sitting Bull.

Whatever the source of Shining Shirt's information, twenty-four Iroquois Indians "from the Great Lakes area" arrived to live among the Flatheads in the year 1816.[7] They had come with some familiarity of the area, as well as of their own Christian backgrounds, and they lost no time in sharing the latter with their adopted tribesmen.[8]

These were descendents of the Iroquois who had shed Jesuit blood in the seventeenth century. Father Lawrence Palladino, the first of our Northwest Jesuit historians asks a rhetorical question that can be answered only when we meet him: "Did [Father Isaac Jogues] ever imagine, in the midst of his trials and sufferings, that he was preparing apostles for the unknown regions of the Northwest, and that the seed he was planting and fertilizing with his blood on the banks of the St. Lawrence would be borne beyond the Mississippi, across the Rockies and even to the Pacific Coast?"[9]

The leader of this Iroquois emigration to the west was Ignace La Mousse, "better known to the Indians as Big Ignace or Old Ignace." He soon became what missionaries today would call a Prayer Leader, for he often spoke to his companions about "the Catholic religion, its teachings, its prayers and its rites, the conclusion of all his discoveries being always the same, the advantage and necessity of having Black Robes." The best part of his message was this: there was a Great Spirit who loved us all and took our spirits when we died to another land called heaven, and the Black Robes who spoke for the Great Spirit could lead everyone to heaven. This announcement appealed to the deepest yearnings of the Flathead people, especially the older ones. Under the guidance of Old Ignace, the Flatheads learned to pray in common, morning and night. They observed Sundays as special days of prayer when the flag, the *S'chazens,* was raised on a pole. They baptized their infants and placed a cross on the graves of their dead. For some, this was high medicine, indeed, the deep secrets of the spirit world.

It should be noted that by this time the woods were full of fur traders and voyageurs, many of whom were of Iroquois descent. Three major fur companies were competing with each other for the furs of the plateau: the English Hudson's Bay Company, Canada's Northwest Company, and America's Pacific Fur Company of John Jacob Astor. Indians were exposed to all kinds of religious influence: Episcopalian and Presbyterian from England and Scotland, and almost anything from the eastern United States. The significance of the Iroquois *emigres* and their new residence among the Flatheads was this: they systematically taught Catholic doctrine and practice, and literally Christianized an isolated tribe buried in a mountain valley a thousand miles from so-called civilization. In the history of Christianity there are few parallels.

One wonders why it took them so long to form a plan for seeking Black Robes to live among them. "Gradually," Palladino said, "a strong desire to have in their midst some of the Black Robes spoken of by Old Ignace took hold of them." In 1831, they finally made a decision in council: they would send a delegation, not to Caughnawaga, whence Old Ignace had come, nor to Montreal where their furs were usually marketed, but to St. Louis, whence had come white men called the *Sēma*, the explorers with Lieutenant Clark.

Four braves volunteered to make the perilous journey.[10] They left their lodges in the valley of the Ootlashoots when the snow had melted on the meadows, and they eagerly turned the noses of their horses into the gentle south winds. Like young males everywhere they exulted in the challenge, their strong hearts beating with excitement as they raced into the unknown. Theirs was a twofold mission: they were seeking Black Robes who would show them the way to heaven, and they were seeking the high medicine that would render them indestructible before the Blackfeet and immortal before the Great Spirit.

The journey required almost five months. They arrived in St. Louis in October, weary, lean, and hungry enough to eat bark. All four of them were ill because of the hardships of their passage. Two, sensing the approach of death, asked to see a Black Robe and when a pair of them appeared they earnestly beseeched them for baptism with signs and gestures. Clutching a crucifix, and covering it with devout kisses, each died.[11] "Narcisse," according to his baptismal name, was buried in the little parish cemetery on October 31, and "Paul," on November 17. Their two companions recovered and left St. Louis the following spring for the valley of the Ootlashoots, but they never arrived. Their fate has been buried in mystery.

Only one trace of them has ever appeared. In the spring of 1832, George Catlin, the renowned wilderness artist, sketched, during a trip on a Missouri riverboat, two of his fellow passengers—young braves whom he called *Hee-ob'ks-te-kin*, which means "Rabbit-skin-leggins," and *H'co-a'cotes-min*, which means "No-horns-on-his-head."[12] Horns or no horns, the two were the Indian delegates returning home, in high style on a riverboat. Unfortunately, the boat was bearing them into the very heart of Blackfeet dominions. Their families would never see them again.

The missing men were discussed often and long in the tribal council. Four braves were lost, no Black Robes gained. The expedition had been a failure, but it had called attention to a need. The presence of the Flatheads in St. Louis had been highly publicized. Articles appeared in the Protestant press, and the American Methodist Episcopal Church rallied to the cause. In 1834, the Reverend Jason Lee of Stranstead, Canada, and his nephew, the Reverend Daniel Lee, with three laymen were sent to found a mission among the Flatheads.[13] They arrived and left abruptly, having been spurned by the Flatheads who wanted nothing less than the Black Robes they had sought. With less tact than fervor, the Lees were informed that men of God wore long black robes, carried crucifixes, never married, and prayed the great prayer, the Mass.

During the late spring of 1835, the Indians on the Ootlashoots received reports that another group of missionaries were enroute from the east, headed for Flathead country. Prompted by hope that these were the expected Black Robes, the Council dispatched Insula, known as "Little Chief," or "Great Warrior," to meet the newcomers at Green River Rendezvous in southwestern Wyoming. Insula, accompanied by several members of his tribe, were attacked by hostiles, but they fought their way through and reached the Rendezvous where the Reverend Samuel Parker, W.H. Gray, a mechanic, and Dr. Marcus Whitman of the Protestant American Mission Board awaited them. Insula and his companions were not satisfied with the looks nor the message of these missionaries. They would have nothing to do with them and they returned quickly to their valley to inform the council that the Black Robes had not yet appeared.

Shortly after Insula's return, another deputation to St. Louis was planned. Old Ignace offered to go. Taking with him his two sons, Charles and Francis, ten and fourteen years of age, he set out in late summer of the same year, intending first to go to Caughnawaga to place his sons in school there.* Learning, however, that there were Jesuits and a college in St. Louis, he changed his plans. He went the southern route through dangerous Sioux country, instead of the northern route, and arrived in St. Louis "after many privations and sufferings" in late autumn, when the winds were blowing cold from the north. On December 2, his sons were solemnly baptized in the chapel of the Jesuit college by Father Ferdinand Helias while other members of the Jesuit community assisted. "The two youths were then brought to the refectory while Father Helias remained alone in the Church with Ignace, who confessed to him and edified him greatly by the fervent devotion with which he adored on his knees the Holy Sacrament of the altar. He told Father Helias there were seven nations who had asked him to bring a priest . . . in all about six thousand souls. Having partaken of a frugal meal, and carrying with them a load of presents from Father Rector, and a rosary and medal from Father Helias, they returned to Liberty, Missouri, on the frontier of the state, where they counted on spending the winter with their [own] people."[14]

Before leaving the Fathers, Ignace offered Father Helias a dollar, which Helias refused. Ignace made the same offer to father rector with the same result. "Then having earnestly recommended himself to our prayers and sacrifices," said Helias, "he took affectionate leave of the Fathers, walking out of the house without stopping through curiosity to look at anything on the way."

Ignace also pleaded his cause at the cathedral with Bishop Joseph Rosati who assured him that Black Robes would be sent as soon as possible. No doubt Rosati meant it, yet no one had appeared by the spring of 1837. Eighteen months had gone by since the return of Old Ignace. Uneasy about Protestant mission activity in the lower Columbia, Old Ignace persuaded the council to send a third delegation for Black Robes. In the summer of 1837 this group—consisting of Old Ignace as leader, three Flatheads and one Nez Perce—left the valley of the Ootlashoots, never to return. At Fort Laramie, W.H. Gray who had accompanied Whitman and Parker, joined Old Ignace. He, too, was heading for St. Louis "to obtain Presbyterian missionaries to settle among the Flatheads." While passing through Sioux country at a point on the South Platte River called Ash Hollow, Old Ignace and his party were attacked by a large war party. Greatly outnumbered by the foe, all five Indians were killed. Old Ignace, dressed as a white man, had been shoved aside, ordered to stand with the Whites, but he refused to be spared. Declaring himself to be the leader of the Flatheads, he died with them.[15]

News of this latest disaster soon reached the valley of the Ootlashoots and the whole tribe went into mourning. Two of the Iroquois, Peter Gaucher, called "Left-handed-Peter," and Young Ignace, who could speak three languages, offered themselves for another attempt to obtain Black Robes, proposing an alternative route via the northern river. They left their lodges in the summer of 1839, joined "a large company of American beaver hunters" and accompanied them in canoes down the Yellowstone River to the Missouri and down the latter to Council Bluffs to confer with Black Robes who had established St. Joseph's Mission there the previous year. They arrived at St. Joseph's on September 18 and met for the first time the Jesuit who has been called "the greatest missionary of the nineteenth century," Peter John De Smet.

De Smet was impressed by his visitors. Indeed, he was quite overwhelmed by these "savages so fervent in religion." One can see him seated with them in a rude log hut,

---

*Francis was baptized Francis Xavier, but the Indians could not say Xavier, so he was called Francis Saxa. His last name, like his father's, was La Mousse. He lived as an exemplary Christian for many long years in the Mission Valley, dying in 1919 at the age of 97.

speaking in French, probing for specific information about the tribe, its size and location, and the various routes between Council Bluffs and the Bitterroot. He was destined to be their Black Robe, at least for awhile, and he seemed to feel it in his bones.

As for his bones one must assume they were uncommonly strong, for they carried more than ordinary weight with more than ordinary speed. In the prime of his life, thirty-eight years old, De Smet was short and stocky. Once in the mountains he had to fast for thirty days before he could travel, because the snowshoes could not sustain his weight. At this time he was as strong as an ox, like most Flemish of peasant origins. He had a great head of hair which flowed down his neck and covered his ears, after the manner of frontier trappers. De Smet on several occasions grew a heavy beard, which gave his face a droopy appearance. His heavily lidded eyes, topped by bushy eyebrows, missed nothing when he sat astride a horse and surveyed his surroundings.

It is said that he had uncommonly strong teeth which were excellent for chewing jerky, one of his luxuries on the trail. His first biographer notes that when he left Belgium, at the age of twenty, one of his companions requested a keepsake. De Smet took a coin from his pocket, bent it crossways with his teeth and gave it to his friend. He might have presented his twin sister Colette with another, but since he was leaving for America without his father's knowledge or consent, it is unlikely that Colette would be on the ship's quay when this feat was performed.[16]

De Smet as a lad had left a prosperous, tidy, little village. Termonde was in East Flanders at the confluence of the Sheld and Dender rivers, a flat, gentle land in contrast with the flamboyant landscapes of his adopted country. He had lived a life as quiet as the gently flowing rivers there, attending mostly local schools until he entered a junior seminary. Subsequently, inspired by a missionary from America, and probably bored by his orderly life, he offered himself for the missions, like many seminarians from Europe who would succeed him.

If anything, De Smet was impetuous. As his brother commented, "He could not settle down anywhere long." According to his horoscope he was an Aquarius, "a Water Carrier," having been born on January 30. The constellations at that time, if they had any effect on his personality at all, contrived to present him as pragmatic, vain, and lacking in common sense. He should have had fickle health, also, and "weak ankles." Perhaps the constellations were uncertain, the stars and planets in the wrong places in 1801.

De Smet was no pragmatist. Characteristically, as a born optimist he had not given much thought about how he would pay back his borrowed passage money when he scrambled aboard the ship. Like most optimists he experienced great ups and downs of the spirit and like many rugged men he became discouraged when illness tied him down or imprisoned him at a desk job. He was ordained at the age of twenty-six. Perhaps this was a mistake. Plagued by his mysterious illness and bored with paper work—what missionary is not—he requested permission to return to Europe five years after ordination. Leaving St. Louis in 1833, he returned to Belgium; and two years later at his own request he was released from his vows as a Jesuit. In this, it appears, he resembled a number of restless Jesuits of the twentieth century.

Time and his native air rejuvenated De Smet's body and healed his soul. But "a feeling of frustration and of self-reproach haunted him." He wanted to return to the Indian missions of America. Fortunately for him and all of us as well, the general of the Jesuits at that time, Father Johann Roothaan, had liberal views about readmitting ex-Jesuits. By November 1837, when Old Ignace lay dead in an unmarked grave at Ash Hollow, De Smet was back at Florissant, where he had made his first novitiate. A year later he was assigned to open a mission for the Potawatomies at Council Bluffs, an Indian crossroads on the broad Missouri, where the city in Iowa bears the same name today.

Like many of De Smet's foundations, St. Joseph's Mission was short lived. But it served a lofty purpose, first in De Smet's consciousness as a springboard for adventurous journeys to the west, searching for Indians who were as exotic to him as they were to artists like Karl Bodmer and George Catlin. St. Joseph's also served as the unexpected rendezvous for Indians from "beyond the Shining Mountains" and De Smet. The fact is, Peter Gaucher and Young Ignace beat De Smet to the draw. They found him first.

Since they were an answer to prayer, no great effort was required by them to extract from De Smet a willing promise to come to their country. It was all settled in a twinkle. Gaucher, taking De Smet at his word, which in view of all that had occurred was most extaordinary—left with his colleague, as soon as possible, to visit the bishop and the Jesuits at St. Louis. Assured again that a missionary would be dispatched during the following spring, Gaucher hastily departed on October 20 for the valley of the Ootlashoots to announce the glad tidings. Little did he realize how fragile was De Smet's commitment, unconfirmed by overburdened superiors and lacking the conviction of hard cash.

Autumn and winter were bitterly cold that year. Soon winter's heavy snow buried the plains. Peter had one companion, a Nez Perce. Together they galloped up the Platte River, making frequent detours to avoid hostile tribes, with blizzards snapping at their backs. They had left without provisions. "The Nez Perce could not long sustain the hardships of the trip; consumed by exhaustion and hunger, he died.

"Peter continued his journey living on an occasional wild root which he pulled with difficulty from the frozen snow-covered ground. Soon his horse also perished. Peter found himself alone and on foot without any provisions to sustain life, and still a great distance from the Flathead village."[17]

Famished and almost naked he appeared unexpectedly in the camp on Eight Mile Creek, more dead than alive.[18] The snow in the valley had already melted. Buttercups were blossoming on sunny hillsides. Without taking food, scarcely able to stand, Peter announced that the Chiefs of the Black Robes had listened to their request and that a Black Robe would soon be on his way. Young Ignace had remained behind to show the Black Robe the way.[19]

The news Peter brought aroused the whole Flathead Nation from the Surrounded Place in the north to the Big Hole in the south. The great chief of the Flatheads, Big Face, who later received the name of Paul in baptism, "at once detailed ten of his warriors to go ahead to meet the man of God and escort him into their camp."

Young Ignace, as Peter had said, remained in the east. While De Smet set about the troublesome business of getting himself appointed in order to keep his, and the bishop's, word and attended to the more distasteful business of begging and borrowing the money for his passage with the American Fur Company brigade, Young Ignace lived at the novitiate in Florissant. No doubt he edified the novices there, creating no little sensation among the young men who would have regarded a journey west with him and De Smet as a once-in-a-lifetime holiday.

If the matter had rested with Father Roothaan, who seemed always to have one of his skeptical eyes cast on De Smet, there would have been no journey. Roothaan had received a full report from His Lordship, the bishop. Rosati had written to him on October 20, the same day the two Iroquois had visited the bishop's "palace," and Peter Gaucher had left for the west.[20] Rosati needed no one to remind him that the bishops of America assembled in the Second Provincial Council of Baltimore, October 20, 1833, had solemnly recommended to the Holy Father, Pope Gregory XVI, that the Indian missions of the United States be confined to the care of the Society of Jesus. Gregory in the following year issued a decree, confirming this recommendation, and Father General Roothaan had formally accepted the charge on behalf of the Society. Now he must fish or cut bait. Roothaan wrote at the end of 1839 to inform Father Peter Verhaegen, vice provincial of the Missouri Vice Province, that he had already replied to the bishop and that he would make every effort to comply with His Lordship's request. "Perhaps," he wrote, "there are Fathers among you much better fitted to go on such an expedition than those who recently came to you from Europe."[21] This was grudging consent and possibly an oblique reference to De Smet, who had proved himself, heretofore, rather unstable. Roothaan raised another ugly objection: money. Writing to one of many who had volunteered to go west, Father Roothaan said he was pleased with his "Reverence's desire" of going to this new mission of the Rocky Mountains, "nor have I anything against it, if only the business accounts of your Vice Province permits it."

Word was getting around. Even volunteers in Rome clamored to be sent. Some regarded the assignment as an opportunity for a succession of outdoor barbecues and relief from the boredom of correcting student papers. Two scholastics finally selected were directed to prepare for an early ordination, but the order was suddenly rescinded. De Smet, not content with his application by letter, especially when such a hullabaloo was being raised after he thought he had it in the bag, abruptly appeared in St. Louis, saying he required medical attention. Like many after him, seeing the doctor was as good an excuse as any for getting into town.

De Smet was finally appointed, officially that is. He had been self-appointed for some weeks. Time was running out. Only one thousand dollars, like ten thousand today, could be raised for his fare and expenses, thus Verhaegen decided he should go alone. It was well and good for the general to talk about two priests for the expedition, but he did not have to pay the bill. It was understood by all, however, that this first journey was for the purpose of reconnaissance only. Two or more would be sent if on his return De Smet's report proved to be favorable.*

On March 19, 1840, De Smet visited Florissant. In a delightful spiritual pact made on the occasion, he demonstrates the simplicity of his soul. An account appears in the Novitiate House Diary:

"We were privileged to have again in our midst that strenuous worker, Father De Smet, so that we might bid him goodbye, not, however, for the last time, as far as the novices are concerned, for they hope to obtain permission some day to go to the Rocky Mountains. The Father entered into a contract with our Reverend Father Rector and through him with the entire community, by the terms of which the priests are to say a Mass every week for him and his new mission, while two of the scholastics are to recite the rosary every day for the same intention. He, on his part, has pledged us, not vocal prayers, but a share in the fruit of his hard labors and a recompense in heaven. The contract was mutually sealed by the religious embrace."[22]

Eight days later, on March 27, 1840, De Smet set out on his first trip to the Rockies. The keeper of the diary at the University of St. Louis, enchanted with the romantic nature of De Smet's departure, wrote with an ecstatic pen: "The day eagerly desired of the Indians that dwell beyond the Rocky Mountains has dawned at last! For today Rev. Father De Smet departed alone to carry to them the light of the faith and announce to them the way of salvation. . . . Fortunate Indians! Twice fortunate Father to be chosen by God from all eternity as the instrument of his mighty work! He will make smooth and open up the way not only, as I hope, for myself, slight and unworthy thing that I am, but for such others also as may be aflame with zeal for the honor and glory of God and the salvation of souls."[23]

---

*Roothaan later sent a rebuke to Verhaegen for allowing De Smet to go alone. The latter was not much disturbed by this. What better excuse than lack of cash?

The first leg of the journey was as smooth as the Missouri River in summer, as the diarist suggested. It required one week on a freight-bearing riverboat to reach Westport, which is Kansas City today. At Westport, "the jumping-off place," the annual expedition to the Green River Rendezvous of the American Fur Company was assembled. In 1840 the party numbered about thirty and was in charge of a well-known fur trader and mountain man, Captain Andrew Drips.*

De Smet had purchased seven horses, one for Young Ignace, one for himself and five for provisions. Mounted nervously on his gentle animal, probably attired in a black frock coat that reached to his knees and a white cravat at his throat, in accordance with the decree on clerics' attire by the council of Baltimore, he waited on the morning of April 30 for the great adventure to begin. At last the captain shouted, and the long procession of horses and men jerked unsteadily into motion, then picked up a rhythm that was to last two months.

About halfway to South Pass the caravan passed Ash Hollow, where Old Ignace had met his death. Several weeks later, on June 23, experiencing heavy breathing due to the thin air at an elevation of 7,489 feet, the horses bore their burdens over the pass and into the Pacific Watershed. Only a week later the travelers reached their goal, the Rendezvous.

The Green River Rendezvous, greatest of western "flea markets" in the history of the early fur trade, took place in a vast grassy meadow about one hundred miles south and east of an area later known as Jackson Hole, Wyoming.† The Wind River Range towers in the northeast, its sharply pointed crags crowned with snow even in summer. The meadow which extends for miles in all directions is criss-crossed with numerous creeks which have an abundance of willow bushes along their banks. As many as three thousand Indians from tribes all over the west arrived during late June to participate in the rendezvous, which provided them an opportunity to trade furs for guns, gun powder, knives, beads, and other articles much sought after. Sometimes participants were given to great and many excesses—the superfluous use of whiskey, promiscuity in sex, and violence in intertribal encounters. Many braves did not return to their wives or mothers.

Ten Flathead warriors met De Smet to escort him to the Flathead camp. "Our meeting," says De Smet, "was not that of strangers, but of friends. They were like children, who, after a long absence, run to meet their father. I wept for joy in embracing them, and with tears in their eyes they welcomed me with tender words, with childlike simplicity."[24]

When among the Indians, De Smet always wore his cassock, or black robe, even when riding horseback. He used an interpreter, Gabriel Prudhome, for conversation, which sometimes proceeded very slowly because his words had to pass through three or four different languages. Only four of the original Iroquois, who spoke French, were still alive and it is likely they were all present for the arrival of the Black Robe, for which they had yearned for twenty-four long years.‡

For several days De Smet and the Indians remained at the Green River Rendezvous, feasting, sleeping, and discussing the Great Spirit, while their horses rested and grazed in the soft green meadows. On Sunday, July 5, Father De Smet offered Holy Mass on a stone altar which he had decorated with wild flowers. This was the first Mass celebrated in this vast part of the world. "I preached in French and English to the American and Canadian

*Drips was a Pennsylvanian, fifty-one years old. He had been in the fur trade most of his life. The fact that he was still alive in 1840 testified to his ability to survive. He died without his shoes on, in 1860, at the age of seventy-one.

†The rendezvous was not always held at Green River, but this was the most frequently used site. The rendezvous occurred there in 1833, 1835, 1836, 1837, 1839, and last of all in 1840, when De Smet was present.

‡Gabriel Prudhome was a half-breed who could speak French. He was a friend of many Whites for whom he served as a guide and interpreter. He died at Fort Owen (St. Mary's) on January 16, 1856.

hunters and then through an interpreter addressed the Flatheads and Snakes. The Canadians sang some hymns in French and Latin while the Indians chanted in their own tongue. The service was truly *Catholic*. The place where the Holy Sacrifice was offered has since been called by the trappers 'the prairie of the Holy Sacrifice.' "[25]

On the next day the Indians broke camp and De Smet, accompanied by his Flatheads, traveled north across great precipices and rivers to the main Flathead camp at Pierre's Hole at the foot of the Three Tetons. They arrived here on July 12. De Smet was overwhelmed by what he saw, an Indian encampment of over sixteen hundred Indians, which is probably more genuine Indians that most of us have seen in a decade of television. Flatheads, Nez Perces, and Pend d'Oreilles, some of whom had come eight hundred miles to see the Black Robe, crowded around him to shake his hand and bid him welcome in their best guttural accents. According to De Smet's own account, the old men wept with joy, and the children expressed their gladness by gambols and screams of delight. When the excitement had subsided De Smet was escorted to the tepee of the great chief called Big Face. Surrounded by his stoical-looking councilors, Big Face welcomed the Black Robe in the most solemn way possible. "Black Gown," he said in Salish, the language of the Flatheads, "welcome to my nation. Our hearts rejoice, for today the Great Spirit has granted our petition. You have come to a people poor, plain, and submerged in the darkness of ignorance. I have always exhorted my children to love the Great Spirit. We know that all that exists belongs to Him and everything we have comes from His generous hands. From time to time, kind white men have given us good advice, which we have striven to follow. Our ardent desire to be instructed in what concerns our salvation had led us on several occasions to send a delegation of our people to the great Black Robe at St. Louis to ask him to send a priest. Black Gown, speak! We are all your children. Show us the path we must follow to reach the place where abides the Great Spirit. Our ears are open, our hearts will heed your words. Speak, Black Gown! We will follow the words of your mouth."

Big Face meant what he said. He was up every morning at daybreak. Mounting his horse he made a tour of the camp. "Come," he harangued his people, "courage, my children. Tell Him you love Him and ask Him to make you charitable. Courage, the sun is rising. Come, bathe in the river. Be punctual and at the Black Gown's tent when the bell rings."

De Smet preached four times a day, and each time the Indians ran eagerly to get good places. Those who were sick were carried to his tent. He translated Christian prayers through an interpreter, promising to give a medal of the Blessed Virgin to the first one who could recite the *Pater, Ave, Credo* and Ten Commandments. A chief arose. "Black Gown," he grunted, "your medal belongs to me," and to De Smet's great surprise he recited all the prayers without missing a word.

De Smet had the happiness of baptizing three hundred Indians. All the others begged baptism and manifested the best possible disposition, but because of the dangers of apostasy in the wilderness he deferred the administration of the sacrament from them until the following year.

For several days these holy activities occupied the Black Robe. Then the Indians broke camp again and started north, advancing slowly. On July 22 they reached the divide which separates the watersheds of the Missouri from the watersheds of the Columbia. On the following morning while the Indians rested to relieve their weariness from the long, hard climb, De Smet looked over the peaks rising above the pass and selected one of them for the day's excursion. He climbed for five hours, crossed snowfields twenty feet deep but was yet far from the summit. Seating himself on a bench-like rock he gazed out over the panorama below him, first eastward where his companion Jesuits labored throughout the great Mississippi Valley. He thought of them and thanked God he shared in their life.

Looking westward his eye stretched to range upon range of mountains and he tried to measure the vast area between himself and the ocean, an area many times the size of his native country, larger than France, even. He wondered how soon it, too, would be occupied by priests who would help him in his compelling urge to make it all Christian. These thoughts stirred him deeply and filled him with great consolation. Seeing a soft surface of a large flat rock he wrote in large letters: *"Sanctus Ignatius Patronus Montium. Die Julii 23, 1840."*

The winds and rains have long since effaced the inscription on Father De Smet's rock but the blessing has remained. In that very region dedicated so simply yet so profoundly to St. Ignatius, approximately seven hundred Jesuits labor in the twentieth century for the same goals St. Ignatius sought in the sixteenth and De Smet in the nineteenth. Without realizing it, De Smet's eye, roving over the great wilderness, westward from the continental divide to the sea, encompassed what is now the heart of the Oregon Province of the Society of Jesus.

Still under the spell of great spiritual consolation, the Black Robe descended like Moses from his mountain. "I said a Mass of Thanksgiving," he wrote, "at the foot of this mountain, surrounded by my Indians, who chanted canticles of praise to God, and took possession of the country in the name of our Holy Founder."

The next day the Indians took the trail again and De Smet went with them. Like the Indians he lived on roots and wild game and slept on a bed of buffalo hide, wrapped in a blanket. Toward the end of August, he decided to leave for St. Louis to seek help in his great and noble enterprise. All arrangements were concluded by August 26. Long before the next sunrise all of the Flatheads had assembled to see him off. No word was spoken, but sadness was written on every countenance. Morning prayers were repeated amidst the sobs of the Indians. The Black Robe gave a brief sermon, exhorting his Indians to be faithful to the lessons he had taught them and promising to return when the flowers bloomed in the spring. Then, escorted by seventeen warriors who were assigned to see him safely past enemy tribes, he bade farewell to the great chief. Old Big Face arose from his buffalo robe and spoke: "Black Gown! May the Great Spirit accompany you on your long and dangerous journey. Morning and night we will pray that you may safely reach your brothers and we will continue to pray thus until you return to your children in the mountains. When the snows of winter will have disappeared from the valleys and when the first green of spring begins to appear, our hearts, which are now so sad, will once more rejoice. As the meadow grass grows higher and higher, we will go forth to meet you. Farewell, Black Gown, farewell!"

Seldom, if ever, in the history of the Society of Jesus has a Province been inaugurated with such dramatic and auspicious beginnings.

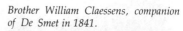
Brother William Claessens, companion of De Smet in 1841.

Brother Joseph Specht spent forty years at the Montana mission.

Point's sketch of "the Reduction of St. Mary's," a village plan that was never realized.

Adrian Hoecken, founder of St. Ignatius Mission.

Point's sketch of the first Sacred Heart Mission which Point himself founded in 1842.

Unknown artist's sketch of original St. Mary's Mission on the Bitterroot.

2

THE FIRST ROCKY MOUNTAIN MISSION
1840–1843

The Missouri Vice Province, which had been a mission of Maryland, was formally established on September 28, 1830 as an independent vice province directly under father general of Rome.[1] Its superior, or vice provincial, Father Peter Verhaegen, who sometimes also served as a substitute for Bishop Rosati, had received De Smet's report on the Indians of the mountains with some misgivings. Nothing would ever be the same. De Smet, like the Pied Piper, had stirred up all of Verhaegen's subjects and rendered them so excited that no one wanted to stay home and take care of the cat. Wherever De Smet went there was a storm of speculation.

On January 15, 1841, Verhaegen took up the matter with his consultors.[2] There seemed to be no doubt in anyone's mind that the time was ripe for establishing a mission "in the mountains." With so many volunteers it was difficult to decide who and how many could be spared for the venture. A decision was postponed, but on March 4 the matter came up again. There was no time for further delays because the last boat for meeting western caravans at Westport would leave the following month.

Verhaegen finally made his decision. He appointed De Smet "Superior of the New Mission in the Rocky Mountains," named two priests and two brothers to accompany him and offered De Smet his choice of one more brother. Since at this time there were only twenty-four priests in the entire vice province who were responsible for more than half of the United States—from the Appalachians on the east to the Rockies on the west; and from the Canadian border on the north to the Mexican on the south—Verhaegen was going the last mile in generosity for the mission in the far west.*

The appointed priests were Father Nicolas Point, an irascible Frenchman who had already been kicked out of two countries, Spain and Switzerland, because of his status as a Jesuit, and Father Gregory Mengarini, a young Jesuit of twenty-nine years, of precocious spirit, who had been recommended by father general himself. De Smet had met Point in 1840 at Grand Coteau, Louisiana where Point was regarded as founder of the novitiate. He was in fact rector, but exposure to De Smet's bewitching charms compelled him to resign this position to become a missionary to the Kickapoo Indians in and around Westport.[3]

---

*In the Missouri Vice Province in 1841 there were 24 priests, 28 brothers, and 28 scholastics; a total of 80 Jesuits. At that time the land beyond the Rockies was claimed jointly by England and the United States in the Treaty of Joint Occupancy negotiated in 1818. There was no operative government in the vast Oregon territory which extended from the Rockies to the Pacific Ocean and from the 42 parallel to the boundary of Alaska.

17

Among the brothers assigned was Joseph Specht, an Alsatian, aged thirty-two, known as "a tinner" or blacksmith, and designated in general as the mission factotum. There is a photograph of him, taken in his later years when photography was available. He appears to have been a little, old German, with twinkling eyes full of curiosity and a wide, firm mouth which showed immense satisfaction with life. He had a German's chin and nose, and, no doubt, the German's sense of order. Another brother assigned was a Belgian, William Claessens, who was a skilled carpenter. Claessens appears to have been of French origin. His open features and concerned-about-others appearance reminds one of a conscientious maître d' in an expensive restaurant. Both brothers were excellent choices.

For a third, De Smet chose George Miles, who had been with him at Council Bluffs. For some reason concealed in the vice provincial's noble head, Charles Huet was assigned instead. Also a Belgian, Huet, thirty-five years old, was said by De Smet to be "a carpenter," though as a "tinner" he had done notable work on the St. Louis Cathedral and courthouse.[4]

There was precious little time for all to prepare for the long journey, and only one fly in the cream, lack of money. As De Smet noted: "Each missionary needs a good horse which costs from sixty to eighty dollars. Then pack horses are needed to carry provisions."[5] There was no need to worry about hay for the animals, but hams, bacon, flour, beans, coffee, sugar and soap for the Jesuits would add up to a pretty sum. De Smet had been scrounging again in New Orleans, where his little mission society of nice young ladies gathered $1,100 in cash and "six boxes full of various and most useful articles," some of them "trinkets such as earrings, bracelets and ornaments of every description."[6]

Only half of the required money had been gathered and De Smet began to panic. A friend, he said, suggested that he appeal to Catholics in Philadelphia. He contacted the coadjutor bishop, Francis Kenrick, who assured him of a warm welcome and directed the priests of the city to take up a special collection for this mission. De Smet was elated. "To the generous people of Philadelphia, who so liberally responded to the call of their pastors, I return my sincere thanks. . . ."[7]

It should be noted here, perhaps, that support for the establishment of the mission, which eventually became the Oregon Province, came especially from the Association of the Propagation of the Faith, through father general's intervention, and four American cities where the church of America had already taken root: New Orleans, Philadelphia, Baltimore and St. Louis.*

As the deadline for the departure of the missionaries approached, Verhaegen began to get cold feet. On April 15 he wrote to Roothaan, saying that members of the expedition were anxiously waiting, but he doubted whether guides and hunters could be employed "owing to the snares and treachery of the Indians."[8] He suggested a postponement.

A few days later, it appears, everything was worked out to Verhaegen's satisfaction. He presented De Smet with a formal directive on the administration of the new mission and supplied him with faculties from the bishops of the dioceses of St. Louis and, as an afterthought, Dubuque, which was about as relevant as faculties from Dublin.† On April

---

*Boston and New York became Catholic strongholds following Ireland's famine in 1845, at a time when the Rocky Mountain Mission was still in its tender years.

†Faculties are formally delegated authority to exercise jurisdiction in certain church matters. They could be presented by bishops only for their own dioceses or vicariates. In the Oregon Territory matters of jurisdiction were unclear until Francis Blanchet was officially appointed vicar apostolic in 1843. From 1838–43 Blanchet and his co-worker, Modeste Demers, had faculties from Bishop Joseph Provencher, an auxiliary of the bishop of Quebec, in residence at St. Boniface, Manitoba. De Smet and the Jesuits received their faculties from the bishop in St. Louis; the diocese of Dubuque, west of St. Louis, was included in the formality of jurisdiction because it was "out west." The missionaries never entered it.

24, 1841, De Smet, Mengarini, Huet, and Specht boarded a riverboat at St. Louis and made themselves comfortable in their cabins as the vessel churned its way north and west for seven days.* On April 30 they reached Westport where Point and Claessens awaited them. A mad nine days of planning and packing followed and then on May 10 they departed for the west. The three priests were in their saddles, the brothers on the carts and wagons. "The wagons started off in single file, the four carts and one small wagon of the missionaries; next eight wagons drawn by mules and horses, and lastly five wagons drawn by seventeen yoke of oxen."[9]

With the Jesuits were Thomas Fitzpatrick, a noted mountain man and trail guide, who had conducted Marcus Whitman and his wife across the plains in 1836; John Gray, a hunter and trapper, whom Mengarini called an Iroquois; Jim Baker, another noted trapper; a young Englishman named simply "Romaine," and five teamsters. At the Kaw River in Kansas, the wagon train was joined by another of fifty members, captained by John Bidwell, with whom the Jesuits were to travel. The group now numbered seventy, most of whom carried rifles. Later another straggler with a small group of pious folk joined them, bringing the total to seventy-seven people in twenty wagons, "the first immigrant train to California."[10]

The leader of the newcomers was Joseph Williams, a Protestant missionary from Indiana, whom De Smet described as "a man of ingenious simplicity."[11] Williams, who was righteous as well, disliked Fitzpatrick. "Our leader, Fitzpatrick," he scribbled in his journal, "is a wicked worldly man and is much opposed to missionaries going among the Indians."[12]

On May 16, De Smet wrote to one of his colleagues: "I hope that the journey will end well; it has begun badly. One of our wagons was burned on the steamboat; a horse ran away and was never found; a second fell ill, which I was obliged to exchange for another at a loss. Some of the mules took fright and ran off leaving their wagons; others, with the wagons, have been stalled in the mud. We have faced perilous situations in crossing steep declivities, deep ravines, marshes, and rivers."[13]

Mengarini had begun to miss the Tiber. "Plains on all sides!" he lamented. "Plains at morning; plains at noon; plains at night. And this day after day."[14]

All of the men in the train, except Fitzpatrick and De Smet, were required to take turns at watch. Early one morning an American by the name of James Shotwell, apparently on watch, reached for his rifle. Taking it by the muzzle, he was accidentally shot at close range and died a few hours later. A brief funeral was conducted and the victim's body was buried by the trail.

On July 30, the wagon train traveled only five miles, then halted in a grassy meadow where De Smet performed a wedding service between "Widow Gray" and "Cocrum," a trapper with one eye. So far, Mengarini reported, there had been plenty of game. De Smet, however, was more interested in miracles, which seemed to appear to him as often as he meditated. The brothers, he believed, were saved from death frequently, and he added: "Those on horseback were accorded the same divine protection. During the journey Father Mengarini was six times thrown from his horse, Father Point almost as often, and once in full gallop, I was pitched over my horse's head; yet none of us had so much as a scratch."[15]

While De Smet occupied his spare time by writing letters to Roothaan and Verhaegen, Nicolas Point was busy painting or drawing. Appropriately, as an artist, he had grown a beard, which fascinated friendly Indians, who, perchance, crossed their paths.

According to De Smet's schedule the wagon train was about two weeks behind

---

*A fifth Jesuit, Father Anthony Eysvogels, accompanied the group as far as Council Bluffs where he took De Smet's former place as missionary.

schedule. He had expected to arrive at the Green River Rendezvous about July 1, where by previous arrangements an escort of Flatheads were to meet the missionaries. On June 2 members of the train held a meeting during which complaints were made that the missionaries were moving too fast. The Jesuits, some said, were too much in a hurry, which sounds familiar. However, as Fitzpatrick, the guide, had been employed by the Jesuits, the rest of the train had little choice except to keep in line.

De Smet's apprehensions and impatience with the wagon train's progress was justified. The Indians had kept their appointment, but after sixteen days of waiting, when their food supplies were depleted, they departed to the mountains to hunt, leaving three of their number behind to await the Black Robes. There is some obscurity about what followed.* Apparently, when De Smet arrived at the rendezvous he found the three Indians, then dispatched John Gray to go north into the mountains in search of the Flathead vanguard, which he suggested, should meet him farther west at Fort Hall.

On the evening of August 10 the members of the wagon train had a parley at Soda Springs, about one hundred miles west of the present Wyoming border.[16] The Jesuits now wanted to turn north to get food and supplies at Fort Hall as well as to meet the Indians there. The fort, a Hudson's Bay Company post, was about fifty miles distant, or four days' travel time for the train. While this change of course served the Jesuits' convenience, it would be an impractical detour for the other two units of the train.

Part of the Bidwell contingent decided to break with the caravan and go south to the Bear River, into the desert of Utah and eventually to California via Nevada. Others, in addition to the Williams party, wanted to continue directly west toward Fort Boise and beyond to settle at last in the Willamette Valley. Their decisions were made with friendship intact, and De Smet that same evening immediately after the parley, left with his three Indians to advance on Fort Hall. He was anxious to meet the rest of the Flatheads.

The wagon train broke up on the following morning with many expressions of mutual respect and affection. While the Jesuits had converted no one, they left their companions with a new tolerance toward Catholics, and with this they were content.

De Smet arrived at Fort Hall one day ahead of the other Jesuits, on August 14, the vigil of the Feast of the Assumption. Presumably he had departed from the direct trail, seeking his Indians. He and his three companions made camp outside the fort, "in the bushes," where swarms of mosquitoes tormented them all night.†

The following day was joyful. The missing Flatheads came in whooping with excitement one after the other, having traveled three hundred miles in a brief time to make their debut. Young Ignace had been running his horse for four days, taking neither food nor drink, in order to be the first to greet the missionaries. Simon, the eldest member of the tribe, was also in the advance guard. Scarcely able to sit in the saddle, he whipped his horse with one hand and held a cane with the other, and he was often heard to shout, "Courage, my children, remember we go to meet the Black Robes."[17]

The Jesuits and their party which now numbered thirty-four, expected to find adequate food supplies at the fort, but in this they were disappointed. The fort's chief factor was Francis Ermantinger, who gave them all a most cordial welcome. The only food he would sell them, however, was two bags of *toro*, or pemican, at one dollar a bag. This was a mixture of dried buffalo meat, grease and berries. Mengarini, whose tastes had been corrupted already by hunger and bad food, commented, "Though this was our first experience of it, it was far from unpleasant."[18] But two bags could not last long as the Indians

---

*Accounts about the period are vague and several versions appear, each contradicting the other.

†They doubtlessly remained outside the fort because they expected the Flatheads to arrive at any moment.

20

were the Jesuits' guests. "We had already faced hunger so often, we found its visage as ugly as ever."

At this point Francis Saxa, who was part of the vanguard, contrived an unbaited hook and going to a hole in the creek, a tributary of the Snake, he switched his line back and forth, a very simple procedure which seems to have been overlooked by the others. In a few minutes he landed a great number of fish, some caught by their fins, some by the tail and some by the belly. "All danger of starvation was quickly dispelled."[19]

From Fort Hall the weary travelers proceeded farther north, and on August 30 they met the main band of the Flatheads who were hunting buffalo in the upper Beaverhead Valley. They were greeted with enthusiasm and remained for a few days "of rest and happy intercourse" during which the site of the new mission was discussed and agreed upon."[20]

These were the first wagons to cross western Montana, one circumstance of the journey which added but little glamour and relieved no one of a heavy burden. There would be many more Jesuit wagons, usually driven by the brothers, over many trackless parts of the Northwest, but none were so crucial to the mission's survival as the first ones, a fact not lost on any of those guiding them.

As if the wretched trails were not trouble enough, the travelers also met with hostile Indians who sniffed around like bears and made everyone except De Smet nervous. De Smet was more curious about the intruders than fearful, but he made no attempt under Fitzpatrick's stern eye to convert them. Mengarini, donning his cassock, like an ancient bishop preparing to meet Attila the Hun, urged De Smet to do the same. When someone asked him where his gun was he replied by showing him his reliquary with bones of the saints. This crisis passed after a few days, when the Bannocks, their curiosity satisfied, drifted away like morning mists.

On September 9, the last stage of the Jesuits' journey began. Accompanied by some of the Flatheads, they moved ponderously toward Hell's Gate. "If the road to the infernal regions," wrote Mengarini, "were as uninviting as that to its namesake, few I think would care to travel it."* Indeed the road was less than a trail, so steep that often the missionaries were required to attach ropes to the wagons to keep them upright. Sometimes they had to unhitch the mules to drag the wagons by long ropes and often they held their breath while their precious cargoes were eased over critical ledges. They had an upright organ in one wagon, an awkward testimonial to Mengarini's determination. Later De Smet himself carried a clarinet with which he regaled his Indian companions around wilderness campfires. But Mengarini, an accomplished musician, doted on his organ and would have nothing less. Little did he know that after all his anxious moments, worrying it across the continent and over the narrow ledges of the Rockies, it would soon be destroyed at his mission, when two husky braves were to sit upon it.

After the missionaries arrived at Hell's Gate, which is contiguous to present Missoula, Montana, they made camp for two days, during which they undertook several scouting expeditions to confirm the Indians' recommended site for a permanent mission. Having performed this duty, they accepted the Flatheads' invitation and chose a tract on a lovely little stream, the Ootlashoots, or Bitterroot, in a broad, protected valley of the same name. Hitching up their squeaking carts and wagons for the last time, they rolled through the valley into their promised land, about twenty-seven miles south of Hell's Gate. They could not have done better, for despite the oft repeated complaints of Mengarini about the bitter

---

*OPA ms. Mengarini, "Personal Memoirs." Hell's Gate on the north of the Bitterroot Valley was sometimes declared to be an ambush where the Blackfeet or other hostiles awaited the Flatheads or trappers to emerge. It was regarded by the latter, who named it *Porte d'Enfer*, as the most dangerous trap on the frontier.

cold, the valley has been nicknamed the Banana Belt by envious neighbors, because of its relatively mild and salubrious climate.

The day of their arrival was Friday, September 24, 1841, the Feast of Our Lady of Mercy, a circumstance which appeared to be providential. They put up their tents that night with some misgivings, for they had no food to cook for dinner. "What will I cook?" one of the brothers wailed in dismay and Mengarini piously replied: "God will provide. Wait." Indians soon began to arrive, each bearing a load of buffalo meat. "Did I not tell you?" Mengarini cried triumphantly. The Jesuits doubtlessly enjoyed their meals of buffalo on that abstinence Friday, the first night in their new mission.*

Father De Smet liked to eat, but at this point he was more concerned about raising a large wooden cross in the center of the chosen area. On the first Sunday in October, as soon as the Indians gathered around, more curious than settlers around a drummer selling snakebite, he preached a little sermon, urging all, from the chief to the youngest child, to come forward and press their lips reverently "upon the emblem of our salvation" and to swear upon their knees to die a thousand deaths rather than abandon their religion. This was heavy stuff. One by one they came up, as solemn as Baptist deacons and they kissed the cross and they swore.

"We soon set to work," Mengarini wrote later in his memoirs, "to erect a log cabin and a church, and built around them a sort of fort protected by bastions. The earth was already frozen and the trench for the foundations had to be cut with axes. Trees had to be felled and trimmed in the neighboring forest, and hauled to the place destined for the buildings. . . . Let not my readers, accustomed to grander buildings, sneer at the first church and missionary residence among the Rocky Mountains. The walls were of logs interlacing one another, the cracks being filled with clay. The partitions between the rooms were of deerskin. The roof was of saplings covered with straw and earth. The windows were 2 × 1, and deerskin with the hair scraped off supplied the place of glass. Small as these windows were, the cold of winter crept in through them so persistently that we found them abundantly large."

The solemn dedication of the mission took place on the feast of Our Lady of the Rosary. The mission was placed under the special patronage of the Mother of God and was called St. Mary of the Rocky Mountains. "Look," said the Indians, when the ceremony had been completed, "the house of prayer stands over the place where little Mary is buried."[21]

This bit of intelligence provoked certain inevitable questions and the Indians, somewhat excited now, like children with a secret, explained who Mary was. They said she was a Flathead child who had died during Father De Smet's absence. Our Lady had appeared to her, standing on the floor where the sick child lay. "I see Mary, our Mother!" she had exclaimed to Peter, the Iroquois who had baptized her. "She says a house of prayer will be built here." They had forgotten the incident until they saw the mission church. Old Big Face assured the Jesuits that it stood exactly on the spot where the vision occurred.

News about the mission and little Mary's prediction spread in all directions. On a single day in October Indians from twenty-four tribes came to St. Mary's seeking Black Robes. De Smet yearned to go to all of them simultaneously, and it must be admitted that he tried his level best to do just that. He was often away on the trail either following Indians into their distant camps or journeying to Fort Colville for needed supplies like seeds, plows, and farm animals.

---

*At this time Catholics normally observed the church law of abstinence from meat on Fridays. The law, however, did not apply when one had good reason to be excused; for example, the lack of substitute food for meat. Most Jesuits in the early Indian missions refrained from promulgating the law of abstinence since the Indians had too little food, often nothing else to eat except meat.

The Indians were persuaded to work at splitting rails so that a garden could be enclosed in the spring. A mission band was organized by Father Mengarini, "a conglomerate affair," he wrote modestly, "but at the same time the wonder and admiration of the non-musicians. We had a clarinet, flute, two accordians, a tambourine, piccolo, cymbals and a bass drum. We played according to notes, for Indians have excellent eyes and ears, and our band, if weak in numbers, was certainly strong in lungs; such as had wind instruments spared neither contortions of the face nor exertions of their organs of respiration to give volume to music."[22]

The Indians made a pre-Christmas gift of seventy bales of dried meat to the Jesuits. This was nearly three tons, a lot of buffalo—whether they ate it with grease and berries, or berries and grease. Sometimes to escape the monotony they had fresh game, birds, deer, or trout, and later in the spring, after the ground had thawed, fresh roots, which were not really so bad under the circumstances, though they would have been left for the pigs in any other.

The order of the day at the mission went something like this: rising at daybreak; prayers, Mass, breakfast, an instruction for about an hour, work until midday. In the afternoon: catechism from two to half-past three, work until sunset, prayers, instruction, singing of hymns, then to bed. There were occasional games. "After catechism on Sundays and holydays," wrote Mengarini, "came sports. The people collected together, and the Indian boys brought their bows and arrows. Standing in their midst I would throw in the air, sometimes a ball of cotton, sometimes a thin stick; and the boys would shoot at it. To win a prize, the ball or stick had to be pierced in its ascent; but no matter how swiftly I threw, the arrows, guided by unerring hands, flew swifter, and the ball would be seen in mid-air, pierced, as if by magic, by a dozen arrows."

The Flathead language, too, was cultivated. Often far into the night Father Mengarini painstakingly rewrote his notes which he had gathered during the day. He soon mastered the language and composed a learned grammar which has become a great classic. Sometimes he sought out the older Indians and, seating himself in the middle of them, he questioned one on the ancient beliefs of his people. The others made great grunts of approval, and in this way Mengarini was able to obtain important anthropological data for subsequent publications.

The mission hummed with activity. The brothers were putting up fences, building barns and plowing fields, while Mengarini was directing the Indian village like a nineteenth-century novitiate. Nicolas Point was busy with his pen and drawing board, using his special talents at De Smet's insistence to lay out a plan for a "reduction," similar to those of Paraguay. De Smet, it seems, was captivated with the idea of the reductions. Naive in this, as in other respects, he fully expected to establish reductions for Indians throughout the interior of the Northwest and he carried with him at all times a copy of Father Luigi Muratori's classic book on the subject.[23] So Point, caught up in De Smet's dream laid out a reduction-like village of St. Mary's, neglecting nothing on paper, not even a cemetery for the dead.

Point preferred to paint Indians. With Mengarini's approval he accompanied the Flatheads on their winter hunt of 1841–42. This was a mistake, since no young hunters wanted the chaplain hanging around while they killed animals and indulged in traditional sports like torturing their captives. It spoiled the fun. Point nearly froze to death. There were sixty warriors in the party and one day they surrounded a small band of seventeen Blackfeet braves, leaving them no chance of escape. In their plight the Blackfeet appealed to the Black Robe for mercy. Point pleaded their case and the Flatheads yielded ungracefully, muttering angrily among themselves because the Black Robe had meddled in their affairs.[24]

Summing up the spiritual results of the first months, De Smet wrote triumphantly:

"On my return, the 8th of December, I continued instructing those of the Flatheads who had not been baptized. On Christmas day I added one hundred and fifty new baptisms to those of the 3rd of December, and thirty-two rehabitations of marriages; so that the Flatheads, some sooner and others later, but all, with very few exceptions, had, in the space of three months, complied with everything necessary to merit the glorius title of true children of God."[25]

As superior of the Jesuits in the far west, De Smet had engaged in a periodic exchange of letters with Father Francis Norbert Blanchet, who had come to the Oregon country three years earlier. With Father Modeste Demers as his assistant, he had responded to petitions from French-Canadian settlers in the Willamette Valley. Reports of their presence had been a major reason for Verhaegen's decision to allow De Smet to go west alone in 1840.[26] Like eastern people nowadays and unaware of the vast distances in the west, Verhaegen had suggested to De Smet that he visit the two priests "while you are in the neighborhood." De Smet, too, until he learned on his first trip west that Blanchet was almost as far from the Green River Rendezvous as the Rendezvous was from St. Louis, expected to drop in on the prelate to pay his respects. This, of course, had not been possible. While he was in the mountains with the Flatheads, De Smet received a letter from Demers, dated August 6, 1840, and addressed to the *Reverendes Pretres Missionaires Catholiques Aux Tetes-Plates.*" This much, at least, we learned from Demers's letter: It is difficult to hide a priest even in the Rocky Mountains. Word gets around.

Four days after Demers wrote, De Smet, too, sat down to write a letter to Blanchet to announce his arrival in the west and to state his purpose in coming. Blanchet's flowery response, hand-delivered to De Smet before he left the mountains, attempted to lure De Smet or other Jesuits to the lower Columbia "where we should have a college, convent and schools."[27] Dr. John McLoughlin, the chief factor of the Hudson's Bay Company with headquarters at Fort Vancouver also sent a letter to De Smet, urging him to assist Blanchet in the establishment of the church in Oregon "among the settlers—as the Indians will join themselves in what they see done by the whites."

This was the first appeal made to De Smet to provide Jesuits for working with the Whites. It would not be the last.

In the spring of 1842, De Smet undertook, at last, the journey to Fort Vancouver, partly to obtain supplies for the mission, but mostly to discuss the future of the Church in the Northwest with Blanchet and Demers. He arrived at the fort on June 8, after a boat accident on the Columbia River in which he witnessed the drowning of five boatmen. He had left the boat only moments before "to walk along the shore," to stretch his legs.

At Fort Vancouver, still shaken by the experience, he greeted Demers first, then Blanchet at St. Paul's. "No sooner had Father De Smet descried the Vicar General than he ran to prostrate himself at his feet, imploring his blessing; and no sooner had the Very Rev. Blanchet caught sight of the valiant missionary than he also fell on his knees imploring the blessing of the saintly Jesuit."[28] What a sight for the angels! Blanchet, who could be autocratic and irascible and De Smet the dreamer, both full of faults and both heroic missionaries kneeling before each other on the wet clay of old Oregon, each recognizing in the other a holiness that came with their jobs.

Many pious devotions, broken by long, weighty consultations followed at Fort Vancouver. During these, Blanchet used persuasive arguments for a Jesuit residence on the Willamette. This could serve, he said, as a headquarters and base for supplies. At least intrigued with the concept, De Smet accompanied Demers to the proposed area on the Willamette.

At this time at St. Paul, there were approximately twenty-six Catholic families of French-Canadian descent, scarcely a suitable potential for a college. On Cowlitz Prairie north of the Columbia, there were four families, among whom was old Simon Plamondon, an indestructible patriarch who outlived many wives.

In Blanchet, De Smet had met his match. He agreed finally to the vicar general's proposal that he return to St. Louis to seek his superior's approval, then to sail to Europe to obtain supplies and recruits. He also agreed with Blanchet on another significant point: they must persuade the pope to provide a bishop for this British-American territory west of the Rockies. Both stressed the urgency of the matter, and De Smet added ingenuously his hope that Blanchet would be appointed. Blanchet disagreed with this.

Following appropriate expressions of regard, De Smet, accompanied by Demers, who was making a missionary safari into the upper Columbia area, left Fort Vancouver by boat. The two priests parted at Fort Walla Walla, Demers continuing by boat up the river and De Smet by horseback over the mountains to St. Mary's. According to a primitive map submitted later to father general by Father Joseph Joset, this journey required about twenty days in all, seven days by boat from Vancouver to Walla Walla and the rest by horse and Indian trail over the mountains, passing first through the lands of the Coeur d'Alenes.

For De Smet the trail was longer. He stopped frequently to discourse with wandering bands of Indians, never failing to promise them resident Black Robes, though he had no knowledge of reinforcements. On the other hand, he had specific orders from Verhaegen that no new residences were to be attempted among the tribes unless two Jesuits, never less, could be assigned to the new mission, leaving St. Mary's with no less than two priests in addition to the brothers. Under no circumstances should more than one mission be added to St. Mary's. It must be admitted that these instructions were very specific, but despite them, De Smet promised the Coeur d'Alenes, as well as the Kalispels, a mission each in the immediate future. Apparently De Smet had more faith in God's Providence than did the rest of us.

When he reached St. Mary's he prepared to leave for St. Louis and directed Mengarini as follows: Father Point, when he returned from the summer hunt, should take Brother Huet and start a mission for the Coeur d'Alenes before winter set in. The Kalispels, too, were to have a mission as soon as new missionaries arrived from the east. De Smet had no doubts that some would arrive by autumn. He reckoned that he himself would be gone for over one year, possibly two.

Having attended to these instructions, De Smet sallied forth from St. Mary's, escorted by ten Flatheads, including Young Ignace. Keeping a close watch they proceeded directly through the country infested by the dreaded Blackfeet. They crossed two mountain chains, progressing 150 miles in three days without sighting the enemy. They paid a prolonged visit with the Crows, to whom De Smet also promised a Black Robe, then entered the Yellowstone Valley where they passed the site of a massacre which had occurred only three days earlier. The bloody remains of ten Assiniboines, partly devoured by wolves, were grim reminders of their vulnerability and filled them with terror. They reached the Missouri River at last, and after a brief respite at Fort Union, they found a small boat in which Young Ignace and De Smet embarked. On the third day of their river voyage, they heard a steamboat whistle. Soon the boat appeared and stopped while the captain welcomed De Smet aboard. Young Ignace bade him goodbye and returned alone up the river, into hostile territory. De Smet's remaining journey by boat required forty-six days. He reached St. Louis on the last Sunday of October.[29]

Verhaegen was pleased. He approved of De Smet's plan to go to Europe and wrote to father general to request arrangements for De Smet to meet the Holy Father. He also requested Roothaan to send some more Jesuits for the Rocky Mountain Mission.

Back at St. Mary's, Point returned from the hunt bearing his sketches, his box of Mass vestments and buffalo robe, in which he slept, and sat down with Mengarini and the three brothers to a square meal—his first in many weeks. In De Smet's absence only two priests were left. Mengarini, who disliked being alone, informed Point, with a touch of sadness, no doubt, that the superior had directed him to prepare for his new assignment, the Coeur d'Alene Mission. Brother Huet was to accompany him. Toward the end of October, while De Smet was still on the riverboat writing innumerable letters, Point reluctantly supervised the loading of pack horses, and the gathering of a small collection of domestic animals. With Huet at his side and escorted by several Chiefs of the Coeur d'Alenes he resolutely set his face toward Hell's Gate, where the party turned west and followed the Indian trail through the mountains, through forests and endless obstacles of brush and fallen logs, and across icy rivers and creeks for the next eight days.

The saddle-weary travelers arrived in Coeur d'Alene territory on the first Friday of November, an accident of time which fostered Point's religious devotion, since Catholics the world over, even in a wilderness, gave special honor to the Sacred Heart of Jesus on the first Friday of every month. Filled with consolation, Point dismounted from his horse, fell upon his knees and devoutly dedicated his mission.

It was a pious beginning, but Point was under no illusions about the future. Some of the Coeur d'Alenes had a bad reputation even among the Indians for thievishness and usually bad moral conduct. Fur company employees had refused to settle among them, and from the very beginning, Point found it quite impossible to secure an interpreter. No one had taken the trouble to learn the language, wanting nothing to do with the Coeur d'Alenes, the people "with hearts as big as an awl."[30]

Father Point had not long to wait before his misgivings were realized. One chief, Stellam, who had been a "consummate knave" with De Smet, greeted him with the words: "How much tobacco have you brought us?" Others, besides the medicine men who could always be counted upon to make trouble, remained coldly aloof. They did their best to wreck the mission and almost succeeded at least twice.[31]

The Coeur d'Alenes were a mere handful, not more than five hundred at the time of Point's arrival.* They lived along several rivers and a lake which bore the tribal name. On the north bank of one of the rivers, given the name St. Joseph by the Jesuits, a mission site was selected, and Brother Huet began construction of buildings.[32]

Father Point joined the main body of the tribe, which moved frequently from river to river. He spent the winter with them at their fish camp on Coeur d'Alene Lake, preaching when he could, sketching and painting what he saw when he could not.[33] In the spring he returned to the developing mission and directed the construction of the first church, a long, low hut of logs and moss. A village was laid out on the plan of the Jesuit "reductions." Point liked to make plans. He had made plans for St. Mary's on the Bitterroot, now in the spring of 1843 he was designing some more, his enthusiasm for it driving him on to countless inspection tours and consultations with Huet.

His plans never materialized. Apparently the site was badly chosen, an error no fine buildings or fine plans could remedy. Very attractive in the autumn when Point first saw it, in the spring it lay under water. To make matters worse the lake backed up in flood season. Roads and fields became impassable bogs. Mosquitoes swarmed over the sloughs created by flood waters. Huet, plagued by these pests, took to bed "with a fever." Sooner or later the mission on this site would have to be abandoned and the sooner the better.

But during those first years there were more compelling problems. The lack of food was one of them. Many times the Jesuits, like their Indian companions, were reduced to eating roots and moss. Other troubles instigated by hostile Indians within the tribe almost

*This represented a considerable decline from the time of Lewis and Clark, thirty-six years earlier, when there were reportedly two thousand in the tribe.

drove Point to desperation. On one occasion he took the hazardous trail to St. Mary's for advice, and Mengarini, who was experiencing his own problems with the Flatheads, sent a newly arrived Jesuit, Father Adrian Hoecken, to take his place. Hoecken, too, had troubles. He threatened to close the mission entirely.

This kind of spiritual cunning had the desired effect. Despite the failings of some individuals, the tribe made great progress during those first struggling years. Two out of three had accepted Christian baptism, which implied a renunciation of polygamy, stealing, and excessive gambling for which they had an almost insatiable passion.[34] Point, who described them on his arrival as having "an habitual inclination to cheating, gluttony and every mean vice," wrote less than two years later that for a period of more than four months "there had not been committed to my knowledge in the village of the Sacred Heart a single fault that could be styled grave."[35] In the end it was the Coeur d'Alenes who proved to be most faithful with the missionaries.

There was still the problem of the bishop for Oregon. Bishops Joseph Rosati of St. Louis and Joseph Signay of Quebec took up the matter with early dispatch, the latter urging the appointment of De Smet and adding that "Mr. Blanchet, who might be considered in this connection, earnestly begs to be passed over."[36] Bishop Peter Kenrick, Rosati's new coadjutor, responded to Signay that he doubted any Jesuit could be assigned. Signay replied in detail. Blanchet, he said, would be required to consent, if necessary, but they should wait for a decision of the Fifth Council of Baltimore. Signay proposed that "the diocese should include all the territory between the arctic circle on the north, California on the south, the Rocky Mountains on the east and the Pacific Ocean on the west."[37] Obviously Kenrick did not know what he was talking about.

When the Fifth Council of Baltimore assembled in May 1843, it recommended to the Holy See the erection of the vicariate apostolic west of the Rocky Mountains, and despite the well-known aversion of Jesuits to accept the honor, proposed three names, all Jesuits, for the selection of a bishop: De Smet, Point and Father Peter Verheyden. The fathers of the council were wary, perhaps, of a British subject as bishop; and Signay, a Canadian, equally uncomfortable with the prospect of an American in disputed territory, which in 1843 was commonly expected to become British, continued to support Blanchet.[38]

On December 1, 1843, Pope Gregory XVI in an apostolic brief created the Vicariate Apostolic of Oregon, embracing "all the territory between the Mexican Province of California on the south and the Russian Province of Alaska on the north" and extended "from the Pacific Ocean to the Rocky Mountains." The terna, submitted by the council, was forwarded to the Sacred Congregation in Rome, where Jesuit superiors soon made much of it, opting for Blanchet. By then De Smet, too, was in Rome and he appealed directly to Roothaan to save him. Letters were flying back and forth among the bishops and Rome, while both Blanchet and De Smet waited impatiently for news that would get them off the hook.

The decision was finally made. Under date of April 12, 1844, Signay sent news of his appointment to Blanchet, adding: "If I deserve any blame for having sought to have you made the recipient of a dignity which you are so far from ambitioning, the good Father deserves much more, for he has worked harder than myself to have it conferred on you. As he is on the ground you can show your resentment over it at your convenience."

While all these ecclesiastical fireworks were being celebrated in Quebec and St. Louis, with Canadian or American flags, as well as prayers to heaven, De Smet had not been idle. He prepared his first book for publication, made a brief begging tour of the large cities, picking them as clean as police regulations allowed, and recruited three new missionaries, Father Peter De Vos, the Novice Master at Florissant, Father Adrian Hoecken whose family had given seven children to the Church, one of whom was Father Christian Hoecken, a missionary to the Potawatomies, and Brother Michael McGean. In April, De Smet personally conducted these chosen ones to Westport. Before he returned to St. Louis to pack his bags again for his trip to Europe, he appointed De Vos, with whom he had corresponded for years, as acting superior of the Rocky Mountain Mission, conveyed additional instructions regarding the Kalispel Mission and expressed his goodbyes tearfully, a little bit envious that he could not share their adventures across the Oregon Trail.

All three recruits became excellent missionaries. As founder of St. Ignatius Mission, Hoecken was probably the most famous. A Hollander with a nearly bald head, which he kept covered with a "beanie," he had deeply set eyes and a broad firm mouth which gave him the appearance of a stern schoolmaster. He was, on the contrary, very gentle and a favorite with the Indians, probably second to De Smet. He was only twenty-eight when he left St. Louis, having been ordained there the previous year. Later, in 1861, he was forced to leave the mission because of ill health.

Of Brother McGean there is little to record except that he was of Irish descent and that he was born in 1812. It was customary in those days to reduce brothers to an anonymous state of mission helpers, hidden away but active, like electrons inside the atom. McGean was usually called "McGinn" and when he died on October 28, 1877, having served the Coeur d'Alene Mission well in farming and tending stock, he was respected by all.

The three Jesuits left Westport during the great emigration of 1843 in the wagon train with three other celebrities: Peter Burnett, later converted to the Church (by De Vos) and first Governor of California; Jesse Applegate, one of the founders of the State of Oregon, and Marcus Whitman, returning to his mission at Waiilatpu after his celebrated race to the east to save his mission from closure.[39] With his nose very much out of joint, Whitman wrote to friends in the east about his Jesuit companions: "Two papal priests and their lay helpers are along and De Smet has gone back in order to go to Europe and bring others by ship."[40]

De Vos had sent word ahead to Mengarini at St. Mary's, requesting him to meet the party and to conduct it during the last stages of the journey. Enroute to this rendezvous De Vos and Hoecken according to Bancroft "discovered a new pass through the mountains to Soda Springs by way of Fort Bridger, on the Black branch of the Green River, a cut-off which saved considerable distance."[41]

Mengarini responded to the appeal of De Vos, taking with him as his guide the ubiquitous Young Ignace who seems to have been living a charmed life in his ridings to and fro upon his horse. Mengarini crossed the Rockies at a point where the Columbia watershed split with that of the Missouri. About this he was almost ecstatic. He met the newcomers on schedule, almost casually in the middle of the continent, like travelers meeting at a well-known landmark. He tells about it in his memoirs:

"The next day I met Fr. De Vos, who with Fr. Hoecken and several novice brothers, was coming to the mountains. I remained with them for a few days, and then reminding Fr. De Vos that I had left the mission without a priest, I asked his permission to hasten back. This he readily granted, and I returned with all speed to make what little preparation I could for his reception. He traveled leisurely and upon his arrival several days later the whole village turned out to give him a welcome. A great traveler, though already advanced in years, and in poor health, he was no sooner over the fatigues of his journey, than, in company with two Indians, two Canadians, a brother and myself, he started for the Calispels [Kalispels]."[42]

Mengarini, characteristically Roman in this passage focused all his attention on the superior, neglecting any mention of the other arrivals. As for De Vos's "advanced age," he had been born in Ghent, Belgium in 1793, indicating that he was forty-six years old—scarcely beyond his prime.

Like a Belgian, too, De Vos settled down to studying the language as soon as he returned from "the Calispels." "I have never seen another man apply himself so diligently in learning another language as Father De Vos . . . he has stolen my dictionary and God knows when he will return it." Thus Mengarini complained to Roothaan.[43]

Roothaan had other reports to consider. De Smet was on his doorstep and would not leave him in peace until he sent more Jesuits to the Rocky Mountain Mission. Prompted by the importunities of Father Verhaegen, the general had already assigned four more Jesuits: Father Joseph Joset, a delightfully innocent little Swiss who became the butt of blame for everything that went wrong; Father Peter Zerbinatti, a Neopolitan whom Roothaan appointed superior for the passage; Father Tiberius Soderini, a Roman; and Brother Vincent Magri, a Maltese. Each of these men was to play a significant role in our history, for good or evil, as the sequel will show.

Joset met the Italians at Lyons, whence all proceeded to Le Havre and on March 20, 1843, they embarked for New Orleans.[44] They reached St. Louis by riverboat, a seven day journey up the Mississippi, on May 18—too late to join the annual wagon train west. They remained in St. Louis until the following year, departing on April 23, 1844, over the Oregon Trail "to the mountains." If everything turned out as De Smet scheduled it, they would meet him at the Green River Rendezvous in mid-summer. No one had given them an alternate plan in the event De Smet was delayed or changed his plans.

Though Zerbinatti had been appointed as superior of this group, it was Joset who assumed the role as leader. Like De Smet he fraternized with other members of the wagon train. During the journey he assisted three people among the emigrants to die as Catholics. At this time Joset was thirty-four years old, having been born in 1810 in the French canton of Berne, Switzerland. He was the youngest of five children, all boys. All but the oldest became priests or religious: one, a Capuchin; one, a diocesan priest; and two, including the youngest, Jesuits. Short of stature with a round open face, thin eyebrows, and rosy cheeks, Joset presented the appearance of a child. With the simplicty of a child he had wondrous faith in divine Providence. When De Smet did not appear at the Rendezvous in mid-summer, as all expected, Joset made the decisions.

In truth, he and his colleagues were stranded, strangers without a guide in an endless wilderness. Joset tried to employ a guide before the wagon train went its way without them, but the price demanded was more than he was able to pay. Thus the Jesuits with their teamsters, seven in all, traveled alone for several weeks. On the eighth day of September, Joset's faith was rewarded. Going a little distance ahead of his caravan to select a site for camping that night, he saw a stranger, who was clothed like a white man but with long, black hair like an Indian. Joset approached the stranger and spoke to him in broken English.

I asked him, Joset said later, whether he was Canadian.

"I am Iroquois."

"Do you know St. Mary's?"

"I have just come from it."

"Your name?"

"Ignace."[45]

It was Young Ignace again, the Raphael for the Jesuits "in the mountains." He became Joset's guide, directing the way to Fort Hall, which they reached in a brief time. While there, Soderini parted company with his confreres, going over the hill, as they say.[46]

Young Ignace now had three Jesuits and three teamsters to smuggle through Blackfeet country to the north. Even Ignace shrank from the uncertain prospects of the immediate future. But Joset stated it, as his view, that it was God's affair, after all, and there was nothing to do but go ahead and leave matters in His hands. Thus, without incident, they traveled through the dangerous territory unnoticed and finally, on October 5, passed Hell's Gate into the valley of the Bitterroot. Two days later they were at St. Mary's.

The roster of the Rocky Mountain Mission at this point, October 7, 1844, comprised a total of seventeen Jesuits, as follows: Father Peter De Smet, general superior; Fathers Nicolas Point and Gregory Mengarini; and Brothers Huet, Specht, and Claessens, all of the original contingent of 1841; Fathers Peter De Vos and Adrian Hoecken and Brother McGean, who arrived by the overland route in 1843; Fathers Joseph Joset and Peter Zerbinatti and Brother Magri, recent arrivals by the overland route; and finally the five Jesuits who came with De Smet by sea, also recent arrivals in Oregon.

Thus the Rocky Mountain Mission began its fourth year of existence with a brave little troop isolated from their colleagues by two thousand miles of mountains and plains, and with many thousands of hostile Indians, scattered and hiding behind the rocks and trees.

It was never by numbers that the Jesuits challenged the raw and boundless wilderness.

Point's sketch of St. Ignatius Mission on the Bay of the Kalispels, founded in 1845.

St. Paul, Oregon, from De Smet's Oregon Missions. Number five locates the Jesuit residence, St. Francis Xavier.

Father Anthony Ravalli, born at Ferrara, Italy, in 1812, spent twenty-six years in the Jesuit missions of Montana. Noted mission architect and Montana's first doctor, he compounded his medicines from materials at hand. In the 1840s, he devised a still for producing alcohol from roots and a kind of sugar from potatoes.

3

THE EARLY YEARS
1843–1850

If De Smet was anxious about his failure to keep his appointment at the Rendezvous he did not reveal it. He had been regaled as a great celebrity in Europe wherever he went and he had not wasted his time in frolicking or in frivolous gadding. On the other hand he had used every opportunity to advance the missions.

He had sailed from New York on June 7, 1843, in the company of Archbishop John Hughes, who introduced him to many of the aristocracy in Ireland and on the continent. Having visited his countrymen, he descended in November upon Rome, where his appeals, confirmed by letters from Verhaegen, brought a tolerable but grudging response. In his net this time he collected five more Jesuits for his mission, all of them volunteers. The general had been deeply moved by De Smet's recital of his adventures and needs, and he arranged for him a special audience with the Holy Father, Gregory XVI. The pope rose from his throne and embraced the sentimental De Smet and plied him with many questions about Indians.

Having enjoyed these triumphs, De Smet returned to Belgium and Holland to undertake his task of begging. The homily was over, it was time for the collection. Within a few weeks he had gathered 125,000 francs [$30,000] mostly from the wealthy who would never miss it. After sweet-talking the superior of the Sisters of Notre Dame de Namur, and obtaining the bishop's reluctant approval, he also added six sisters to his team. It was then that he began negotiating to charter a ship, for it was unthinkable to transport six sisters over the Oregon Trail. By ship they would be safe, or at worst they would only drown.

The acquisition of the sisters, a brilliant stroke, had changed his plans, of course. He would never make it to the Rendezvous. Summoning his five Jesuits to Antwerp, where the sisters had already gathered, he chartered a vessel called the *L'Indefatigable* and arranged for the loading of the mission's supplies.

On December 17, 1843, elated with his progress, De Smet gathered his troop of five Jesuits and six sisters on the deck of the ship and ordered the captain to set his sails. The winds, however, did not cooperate and the sturdy little brig could not clear the harbor to enter the North Sea for nearly three weeks. De Smet used the interval to teach his new missionaries the English language. Finally, on January 9, the winds were favorable and the *L'Indefatigable* with its precious burdens raced through the waves into the sea.[1]

De Smet's Jesuits were handpicked. There were four priests and one brother. Fathers John Nobili, Michael Accolti, Anthony Ravalli, and Louis Vercruysse, and Brother Francis

Huybrechts, a trained mechanic, who was especially adept at making furniture for the missions. None had sea legs, and all, as De Smet noted, paid their tribute to Neptune. The sisters, too, suffered the same indignity.

The *L'Indefatigable* had a prosperous voyage around Cape Horn and up the coast of South America. After crossing the perilous bar on the Columbia it cast anchor off the banks of Astoria. The next day the six sisters went ashore to visit the home of Mr. James Birnie who welcomed them warmly and introduced them to his family of many daughters. These were the first sisters to set foot in Oregon.[2]

De Smet, characteristically impatient to be moving, found several Indians who were willing to take him to Fort Vancouver in a dugout canoe. He hurried away with them while the more cumbersome *L'Indefatigable* proceeded cautiously up the river. Five days later, when the ship arrived at the fort, he was on hand to welcome it. With him was Dr. John McLoughlin, the doctor's wife, Dr. Forbes Barclay, and many others, Indian and White, who gaped with wonder while the sisters led by their superior, Sister Loyola, stepped daintily ashore.[3]

After a respite of nine days, made pleasant by the hospitality of Dr. McLoughlin, the excited little group prepared themselves for the last stretch of their journey. Blanchet had come from St. Paul to escort them, and his attention to their needs was exceeded only by his anxiety to get the sisters to their destination.[4]

On August 14, they set forth again in four canoes and a small sloop. Like swans, the little flotilla coasted down the Columbia and entered the Willamette charily, the wet oars flashing in the late afternoon sunshine. When dusk fell, they camped on the bank of the river on the present site of Portland.[5] That night mosquitoes kept them awake, but the next morning after Blanchet had said the Mass of the Assumption and all had received Holy Communion, they were eager to embark again. Two days later, on August 17, 1844, their voyage ended. The flotilla arrived at St. Paul on the Willamette at 11:00 A.M. This marked an end and a beginning, but the former fades away in the blazing glory of the latter, the beginning of convent schools in Oregon and the arrival of the Jesuits.[6] Little did anyone realize then that the glory, too, would fade away, and the sisters had but a few short years to enjoy their adventure in Oregon.

After a *Te Deum* had been sung to thank God for the biscuits and salt pork of their journey, as well as for their safe deliverance from the perils of the sea, the sisters were dispatched by horse-drawn cart to their partly-completed convent some five miles distant. The Jesuits accepted Blanchet's gracious hospitality and, during the following week, selected a site offered them for their mission. Their choice, made after considerable discussion, was a pleasantly wooded tract near St. Paul on the bank of the river. De Smet gratuitously assumed that Blanchet was making a gift of the property, but such was not the case. Blanchet did not own it. It was still "government" land, though there was no government yet and the Jesuits had to establish title to it years later.[7] Unaware of this, De Smet was in ecstasies over his section of land. "In no part of this region," he wrote, "have I met with more luxurious growth of pine, fir, elm, ash, oak, buttonball, and yew trees. The intervening country is beautifully diversified with shadowy groves and smiling plains, whose rich soil yields abundant harvests, sufficient for the maintenance of a large establishment."[8]

The Methodists, having arrived in the vicinity ten years earlier, were about to abandon their mission called "Place of Rest," and offered its two-to-three thousand acre spread, acquired by squatter's rights, to De Smet for a bargain price. According to Bancroft they had spent a quarter of a million dollars on it.[9] De Smet would have no part of it. He wanted a luxuriant growth "of oak, button-ball, and yew trees" and on the site chosen he surely had got them, with a river nearby and a small lake to boot.

Dedicating this new mission to a brother Jesuit, St. Francis Xavier, De Smet ordered work to be started on it without delay. With the aid of French Canadians, brush was cleared away, three shops were erected, and, lastly, a two-story house was begun, measuring forty-five feet by thirty-five feet and containing fifteen rooms which De Smet hopefully expected to fill with novices and new missionaries.

De Smet then summoned Gregory Mengarini from St. Mary's to attend the annual consultation to be held on the Willamette, and Peter De Vos to supervise the new foundation. De Vos, enroute to Oregon, was directed to meet Hoecken in the territory of the Kalispels, where the two Jesuits were to select a site for a mission there.

Mengarini arrived at Fort Vancouver, after traveling eleven days. Finding McLoughlin absent, he awaited him for another five days, then persuaded him to go along to St. Paul, which occupied three more days. De Smet, when Mengarini and the chief factor arrived, was suffering from dysentery. One would imagine he had no time for such tedious matters. He kept his guests waiting for several days, after which he stoically accepted the news that Michael Accolti, who had come with him on the *L'Indefatigable* was also sick at Oregon City, where he had gone to serve the spiritual needs of white people. Mengarini, out of compassion, though he detested traveling in these unfamiliar dark forests, joined him for eight days. Finally, when De Smet was well enough to travel, Mengarini paired up with him again and together they sailed by canoe to Fort Vancouver. All of this chasing to and fro was very expensive; for example, the passage by Hudson's Bay Company canoe from St. Paul to Fort Vancouver, one way, was sixteen pre-war, silver dollars.[10]

At Fort Vancouver, De Smet spent a great deal more money for supplies for St. Mary's, which did not distress Mengarini, though he complained bitterly later that the prices had been outrageous.[11] Having gathered what they had purchased, the two left by boat for Fort Walla Walla, "with six Kanackes [Canukes]."* As soon as the boat arrived there, De Smet bought some horses and mules for the overland route, then leaving Mengarini with the baggage, he dashed off to the north to see what Hoecken and De Vos were doing with the Kalispel Mission.

As he trotted along he had much to ponder. He had made certain concessions gracefully for the spiritual case of the Whites, many of whom had arrived in Oregon during the great emigration of 1843. If he felt uneasy about the subtle shifting of Jesuit priorities from work with Indians to work with Whites, he did not regard it wise to express it. He was more concerned, at this point, about the Kalispel Mission, long since promised, which was finally under way.

He had other problems in mind—Nicolas Point, especially. When Point, who was moody and easily disheartened, departed angrily from the Coeur d'Alene in 1843, Hoecken had been sent to replace him for a time. But in the summer of 1844 Hoecken, too, fell amiss with the Coeur d'Alenes in a dispute over the sale of some potatoes and some Indian girl's romance, or lack of it. De Smet had dispatched Point to return to the Coeur d'Alenes temporarily, relieving Hoecken to keep the rendezvous with De Vos in the land of the Kalispels.

In early September, in accordance with De Smet's directives, the two met on the banks of the Clark's Fork River where they hastily agreed on the site of the new mission, a meadow-like flat along the stream.† They gave to the new mission the name of St.

---

*Canadian voyageurs for the Hudson's Bay Company.

†The exact site of this mission is uncertain, but it appears to have been on what is now called the Pend d'Oreille River, northwest of present Newport, Washington. The Pend d'Oreille is a continuation of the Clark's Fork, which enters Pend d'Oreille Lake under this name and emerges as the Pend d'Oreille. De Smet regarded both streams as the Clark's Fork.

Michael's. This was probably the first Jesuit foundation in what is now the state of Washington.* As Hoecken began work on the buildings for the mission, De Vos continued his journey to St. Francis Xavier's on the Willamette.

De Smet arrived at St. Michael's on November 6, intending to make a brief visit, then to continue on to St. Mary's. Winter came early that year. With the weather closing in, he was forced to leave sooner than he expected. Proceeding up the Clark's Fork in a fragile canoe, he encountered ice on the river and heavy snow in the mountains. Thus he returned to the Kalispels where plans were formed in great haste to erect temporary mission quarters on the river near Albeni Falls.†

"The place for wintering being determined, the first care of the Indians was to erect a house of prayer. While the men cut down fir trees, the women brought bark and mats to cover them. In two days this humble house of the Lord was completed—humble and poor indeed, but truly the house of prayer.[12]

Christmas was celebrated with the firing of pistols and a general discharge of other guns, midnight Mass, baptisms, renewal of marriage vows, and other unforgettable solemnities, which gave De Smet more grain for his mill, to be ground into the flour of countless letters.

At his first opportunity in February when the snow began to melt, De Smet left the Kalispels for the Flatheads. He spent Easter at St. Mary's, then returned to the Clark's Fork to get things going again. The original site, selected in a hurry by De Vos and Hoecken, appeared in the spring runoff to possess fewer charms than in the autumn. A raging river now flooded most of it. De Smet and Hoecken with some of the chiefs selected a new site on higher land, on the "Bay of the Kalispels," which De Smet prematurely described as "perfect."

"We found a vast and beautiful prairie, three miles in extent, surrounded by cedar and pine, in the neighborhood of the cavern of New Manresa and its quarries, and a fall of water more than two hundred feet, presenting every advantage for the erection of mills. I felled the first tree."[13]

Having performed this ceremony with befitting pomp, like a mayor turning over the first shovel for a civic auditorium, he declared the new name of the mission to be St. Ignatius. He bade Hoecken to complete the construction with all dispatch and mounted his horse for another journey to Fort Vancouver and the Willamette. As Hoecken saw De Smet disappear through the trees he doubtlessly reflected with some chagrin that this was his third construction start in seven months.‡

On the Willamette De Vos had matters well in hand. He had arrived the previous autumn and since he was the only Jesuit there who knew more than a smattering of English, he had become a teacher for all. They studied English while they built their house and barns. They also spent part of their time in apostolic work, each in his own way. Ravalli, a skilled doctor of medicine, visited the lodges of Indians throughout the entire area, treating them for a mysterious "bloody flux," which had struck every family. Father Vercruysse preached and said Mass for the French Canadians at Grand Prairie where he supervised the building of the church at St. Louis, ". . . the most beautiful and grandest in Willamette." Father Nobili worked among the Whites and Indians at Fort Vancouver,

---

*The Washington State Line runs due north of Albeni Falls and the river moves approximately 12 to 15 miles west leaving a corridor west of the state line all the way to Canada.

†Albeni Falls, on the present Idaho-Washington border, has been transformed into a major hydroelectric project. The Jesuit's wintering place was probably in Idaho.

‡This first mission of St. Ignatius, founded in the spring of 1845, was certainly in the present state of Washington, about 14 miles west of the Idaho border.

preaching there the first laymen's retreat in the Northwest during the month of June.[14] De Vos also undertook the spiritual care of English-speaking Catholics at Oregon City. The sisters had finished their convent and opened a school for Catholic children. Certain people in the east who called themselves "Know Nothings" would have been dismayed to see so much Catholic activity on the Willamette.

Since De Vos was extraordinarily successful in Oregon City, De Smet decided that he should take up his residence there. Accolti succeeded him as superior of St. Francis Xavier's in May, 1845. Before his departure two years later De Vos built the first Catholic church in Oregon City, which he called St. John's, and converted two prominent Americans to the Catholic faith: Peter Burnett, who had been on the wagon train west with several Jesuits, and Dr. J.E. Long, secretary of the Oregon provisional government.

De Smet was back on the Bay of the Kalispels in July. He had arrived with eleven horses laden with plows, pickaxes, spades, scythes, carpenter tools, and other supplies which he had freighted all the way from St. Paul with the help of two half-breeds and Brother McGean.[15] Hoecken had not been idle. Since April and with the help of the Indians, he had built fourteen houses and a large barn, besides gathering the materials for a large church and enclosing a field of three-hundred acres for growing potatoes, wheat, and barley. High water from the river, however, had washed out the patotoes planted that spring and some of the grain. Only enough wheat and barley were reaped in the summer for seed in the following spring.[16] One might say that despite De Smet's optimism, it was an inauspicious beginning, a warning of worse to come.

At St. Mary's, Mengarini was recovering from a dreadful experience which occurred during his return to the mission from the Willamette. He had got caught in the same early winter storms that had blocked De Smet and in the struggle had lost most of his horses in the high-mountain snows. They had died from frosts, fatigue, and hunger, and possibly, too, from their heavy burdens, among which were two buhrstones, twelve inches in diameter, for a gristmill. At Fort Vancouver Mengarini had employed a Canadian mechanic Peter Biledot for setting up the mills, and Peter had shared Mengarini's ordeal in the mountains.[17]

The flour mill, powered by water conducted through a millrace, with a capacity of eight bushels daily, was in operation in May, but the construction of the sawmill proved to be a greater challenge. "The first saw mill in Montana," Palladino wrote, "was constructed by the Jesuit Fathers here at St. Mary's. It was, however, a most primitive affair, four wagon tires being welded together and formed into a crank, to work the saw. A fifth tire, flattened out and hardened into a steel blade by dint of hammering, and then toothed by means of a cold chisel and long filing, made the saw. A sledge hammer from melted tin cans was also a curious and useful piece of work of Brother Joseph Specht."[18]

The sawmill, intended to produce lumber to replace the ramshackle church, was finally completed on September 15 and was tested with some satisfaction on the same day. Mengarini reported on this eventful day, which ended in disaster, "The afternoon for setting the mill in motion came; the whole day passed in earnest labor, when I returned to the house in the evening Father Zerbinatti was not there."[19]

The bell for evening devotions had not been rung. Even though all the congregation searched energetically, the missing priest could not be found. By torchlight, at last, his body was found on the bank of the river whither he had gone to bathe. The cause of his death, said Mengarini, was drowning.

Zerbinatti was the first Jesuit to die in the Rocky Mountain Mission, a sad and melancholy reflection for the survivors, who sorely missed him. He was buried at St. Mary's, among the Indians he had come to serve. During the period in which St. Mary's was closed, his grave became confused with others and a curious sequence of events followed.

"With the help of some Indians, who had assisted at the Father's funeral and asserted that they knew the exact spot of his grave, the body was then exhumed by Fathers Giorda and Van Gorp and brought to St. Ignatius.

"But as no indication was ever discovered by which it could be ascertained that the remains removed were really those of Father Zerbinatti, their identity has ever been a matter of doubt, even in the minds of the two Fathers who had disinterred and brought them to St. Ignatius.

"The writer himself [Palladino] buried those very remains some nine years after, placing them in the same grave with the body of Brother Joseph Specht, the same day the latter was laid to rest, June 19, 1844. They had been lying in a corner of the sacristy, apparently forgotten."[20]

Greater disasters were to follow Zerbinatti's death. It will be recalled that the Flatheads, like most Indians of the plateau, possessed no knowledge of immortality before the advent of the missionaries. The Black Robes' gift of high medicine, or "the power," many thought, would render them immortal. "The Indian readily accepted the practices outlined by the missionary, believing that the *manna*, or sacred bread, of Catholicism would make him immortal. In addition to the obvious confusion over the Christian meaning of immortality, the Indians probably associated black with the color of death and white, the complexion of the European missionaries with the color of life."[21]

The appearance of Father Zerbinatti in death was a greater shock to young Indians than the Jesuits realized.

One godsend in the wake of these dour events was the arrival of Father Anthony Ravalli at St. Mary's, whither he had been sent to replace Zerbinatti. Like De Smet's, his presence brought cheer and hope to the weary Jesuits, understaffed and tense behind their palisade of logs, raised ominously around the mission in their fear of the Blackfeet raiders.

Ravalli was a rare genius. Born in Ferrara, Italy, in 1812, he had entered the Society at the age of fifteen. While studying theology, with the cordial approval of his superior, he added courses in medicine and mechanics. He was Montana's first doctor, far advanced in his procedures for setting bones and for artificial respiration.[22] He was also an architect with considerable knowledge of his profession's history. However brilliant in these disciplines, he was never able to master an Indian language. He simply had no knack for it.

At extant photograph of Ravalli in his later years reminds one of other upper-class Italians of the same period. Almost bald, his head had tufts of gray hairs covering each ear. His arched thin eyebrows, widely spaced brown-green eyes, sharp nose, and firm mouth suggest the appearance of a scholar—perhaps a professor of history. Like Italians of his class, he was the epitome of gentility—a sensitive, disciplined man, who had an enormous capacity for compassion. His twenty-seven years in the missions of Montana so deeply endeared him to the people of the state that they named a county for him and raised a lofty monument to his memory. This is at Stevensville near the second St. Mary's where he died on the Feast of the Holy Angels, October 2, 1884.

A month before Ravalli arrived at St. Mary's he had been assigned to build a church on the upper Columbia, near Kettle Falls. Called St. Paul's this proto-mission had to be abandoned temporarily when Zerbinatti met his fate by drowning. The raids of Blackfeet for Flathead horses, not to mention personal vengeance, made it advisable to have two priests at St. Mary's in addition to the brothers. Ravalli doubtlessly was happy with his new assignment, for like most Jesuits he disliked being alone and his work at Kettle Falls had not been entirely pleasant. The Hudson's Bay Company Fort located on rocky bench above the river, just a pleasant stroll from his mission, made little or no difference to him other than its convenience. But the Indians in the vicinity were notorious for their gambling and lack of devotion to anything like work. It was commonly said that the women worked always and the men only one day a year. They put up the nets for the fishing season.

Ravalli soon learned to love his "dear Flatheads," but dwelling at St. Mary's was like living in an eleventh-century Normandy village. An attack was always imminent, especially when the Flatheads were on a buffalo hunt, leaving the mission defenseless. "At times," Palladino states, "even as much as to venture out of the stockade which they had built for their protection, was unsafe, as the missionaries were in danger of being shot at by some Bannock or Blackfoot Indian prowling about or lurking in the brush. The environs of the mission were covered with a thick underbrush, and frequently hostile Indians would lie ambushed for days, biding their chance to come out, murder and scalp some Flatheads and run away with their ponies."[23]

Two Blackfeet were killed in a local skirmish. One, before his death, asked for and received baptism from Father Ravalli. The homicide incensed the other Blackfeet, who were determined to have revenge. "Hence the well grounded fear that they would soon come in force and wreak their vengeance, not only on the Flatheads but also the Mission and missionaries."

Food, always a subject of interest to Jesuits and their boarding students, was plentiful at St. Mary's and reasonably good, considering its isolation. The main diet was dried buffalo meat and its tallow mixed with berries. There was also venison and elk meat, birds and fish, which they had in abundance. They had vegetables from their garden. Old standbys like potatoes, carrots, beets, onions, cabbage, lettuce, parsnips and beans. After the gristmill was in operation they had products made from grain, like bread and pancakes, the latter without syrup. The Indians were fond of most of these foods, especially the pancakes and carrots. The children often sneaked into the garden in early summer to nibble on young carrots, and the Jesuits, usually very protective of their gardens on which they depended for survival, winked at this kind of pilfering. The children, they said, were so incapable of restraining their craving for carrots "they were not even committing venial sins."* But the Indians did not like onions. There were always plenty of these for the Italian-born missionaries who could get along without carrots.

At the new mission of St. Ignatius, the gardens were not successful because of floods. In 1846 more than one hundred acres were sown, but high water reduced the fields to the condition of a marsh. "Summer floods have deprived [the Indians] of roots and the snowless winter had not given them a single deer." The village was reduced "to eating pine moss cooked with a little *gamache*, a meal of which no beggar would care to taste."[24] Another year of high water would bring disaster.

The following year the water was very high in Lake Roothaan, one of the sources of the Clark's Fork which De Smet had discovered and named in honor of the general.[25] The Jesuits and the Indians prayed. Every Saturday they sang litanies in honor of the Mother of God. They waited anxiously. Their simple faith was answered and the mission fields, left undamaged by water, produced such a bumper crop that Brother had to entice even the small children to help with the harvest by giving them rides on a farm wagon. The famine was now over. In addition to an abundance of wheat and barley, gathered in hastily built barns, fifteen hundred carcasses of venison were brought in from a tribal hunt. Though the mission was out of danger, seeds of doubt about the practicality of its location had been sown. The odds of one crop in three years were not good ones. Hoecken knew in his heart that sooner or later a new site would be required.

De Smet had come and gone during their crises. Wherever he found willing subjects, he had established mission stations, which were convenient locations designated for visits by missionaries at regular intervals. In April, 1845, he established St. Francis Borgia Mis-

*The children craved sugar. Carrots, high in sugar, were like candy to them.

sion, for the Upper Pend d'Oreilles, northeast of St. Ignatius. In early August he opened St. Francis Regis Mission at the present site of Chewelah, Washington. Later in the same month he reached Tobacco Plains and dedicated a mission there to the Immaculate Heart of Mary, for the Kootenais. In November he dispatched Father Joset to the Coeur d'Alenes with orders to move their mission to another site as soon as possible. The second site on the St. Joe River had proved to be undesirable for the same reasons that St. Ignatius Mission was faltering—fields flooded by the spring runoff and mosquitoes so thick they drove the brothers out of the fields.

Joset complied with De Smet's directive, of course; though, at this time, he, not De Smet, was actually the general superior of the Rocky Mountain Mission. In a letter dated in Rome on August 5, 1845, Roothaan appointed Joset, a decision which he seemed to regret within a brief time. But mail from Rome to the mountains via Fort Vancouver required a whole year; sometimes two.[26]

Joset, with Brother Huet, abandoned the mission on the St. Joe in the spring of 1846 and selected a new site on a knoll surrounded by wooded hills and mountains and over-looking a vast alluvial meadow to the west, with a trout-filled and navigable river at its base.* Huet erected a temporary bark chapel, then a bark barn and finally three log cabins. The new Sacred Heart Mission was open for business, but it would be several years before the construction of a permanent church could be completed.

During these domestic activities another Jesuit had been dispatched to seek the wandering tribes of western Canada, called at this time New Caledonia. Father John Nobili had not yet pronounced his last vows when De Smet sent him into the vast wilderness, this "sea of mountains," in the summer of 1845. At that time New Caledonia was both British and American territory under the Treaty of Joint Occupation, but in the following year, 1846, "The Year of Decision," the two governments agreed to the 49th parallel as the dividing line between the two nations. This arbitrary decision, of course, meant little to the Indians involved; it was something they could never understand. Nor, at first, did it mean anything to the Jesuits. Nobili, encountering incredible hardships, penetrated as far north as Fort Kilmars near the Alaskan border. He had left the Willamette with a novice, Battiste, who did not last long, and their three pack horses, which did not last long either.[27] Having lost his companion and provisions, Nobili was forced to eat dogs and wolves, and sometimes moss off the trees. Three years of extraordinary success followed, but his health was shattered. Though he lived long enough to become the illustrious founder of Santa Clara University, he died prematurely as a result of his hardships in New Caledonia.

Travels on a horse for De Smet, as well as for his subjects, was not as romantic as De Smet's letters seemed to indicate. Despite Roothaan's complaints that his Jesuits in the mountains traveled too much, an old complaint and a continuing one in the Society, no one, except De Smet, enjoyed the rigors of the trail. Indeed they often complained in their reports that they had no alternative, yet too much time was spent in coming and going. Joset estimated that he spent three months of each year in the saddle. "In this country," he wrote, "there is neither stagecoach nor inns, nor bridges nor highways, nothing except prairies, woods, swamps and broad rivers. I had fancied to myself that, being a good pedestrian, I would not tire my horse overmuch; but apart from the circumstances that traveling on foot would be singularity here, you would merely use up your time and wear out your shoes; and afterwards you would have much greater difficulty replacing your shoes than your horse."[28]

---

*This is the present site of the "Old Cataldo Mission." It should be noted that the Coeur d'Alêne Mission name has undergone change. On the first site Point dedicated the mission in honor of the Sacred Heart. When it was moved to the St. Joe River site, it was called St. Joseph, whereby the river took its name. On the third site, Joset's Knoll, the name Sacred Heart was restored.

Isolated in almost inaccessible valleys, the Jesuits had to thread the labyrinth of mountain passes and waterways that separated one mission from another. Where the trail was good, which was not often, pack animals might cover some thirty-five to forty miles a day. Between St. Mary's and the Coeur d'Alene Mission, a distance of about 240 miles, which one could scarcely traverse in eight days from sunup to sundown, there were seventy-two river crossings. The terrain was so rugged that the horses' hooves were worn out during one trip. Between the Coeur d'Alene Mission and the second St. Ignatius, there were eighty river crossings. Winter brought deep snows to the trails; spring runoffs brought floods.

By the autumn of 1846 there was for De Smet only one priority, peace with the Blackfeet. A subtle change was beginning to appear in his favorites, the Flatheads, like the symptoms of mumps, and De Smet rightfully attributed its cause, at least in part, to the bloody wars with the Blackfeet. There would be no domestic serenity at St. Mary's until he had settled with them.

Thus in the autumn of 1846, accompanied by Nicolas Point, who had become increasingly disenchanted with life in the Rocky Mountains, he joined some Flatheads when they left for the buffalo hunt, expecting quite reasonably to meet war parties of the Blackfeet. Neither he nor the Flatheads were uncomfortable with their prospects. The Flatheads had recently won a decisive victory over the Crows and it was common knowledge that the Blackfeet, who had experienced a disasterous year, wanted to form an alliance with the Flatheads against the Crows.

The Blackfeet, De Smet had reported, had lost twenty-one warriors in two skirmishes with the Flatheads and Kalispels. "Six hundred horses had been stolen, and twenty-seven men scalped by the Crees; fifty families massacred by the Crows, and one hundred and sixty women and children led into captivity."[29]

"The religion of the Black Robes," the Blackfeet said, "is more powerful than ours."[30]

De Smet during the previous year had first encountered Blackfeet warriors at Rocky Mountain House, a Hudson's Bay post in what is now Alberta, Canada. He had met thirteen, including a powerful chief who saw new hope in an alliance with the Black Robe. De Smet had promised them gifts of tobacco and other favors, which readily disposed them for further discussion regarding an armistice.

Point, who had a special rapport with Indians through the use of his paintings, agreed to spend the winter of 1846–47 at Fort Lewis, where he could await a response to his request that he be transferred to a mission in Brazil. On occasion he had become so eccentric in his relations with other Jesuits that De Smet had an explicit directive from the general to dismiss him. On one occasion De Smet used his authority and asked Point to go; the latter however, begged for another chance and was given it. Roothaan, painfully aware of Point's lack of stability, as well as of De Smet's weakness for romanticizing in his reports, had mailed from Rome in 1844 formal orders for Point's removal to the Canadian mission. Due to distance and other factors, Point did not receive this mandate for three years.

As for posterity, this was a happy defect in communications. Point at Fort Lewis busied himself in making paintings of Indians, which have come down to us and have appeared for the most part in a celebrated book called *Wilderness Kingdom*.[31] Male Indians of the period were quite vain. They loved to preen themselves in front of mirrors, which were now plentiful at the fur trading posts, and they were fascinated with Point's brush and oils which created such sensational likenesses of their companions that they yearned to sit for their portraits.*

---

*Mirrors like beads became a staple trade item. Mirrors were used to flash signals over long distances, replacing traditional smoke signals.

Point did not spend all winter at his easel. He lived in a room provided by the American Fur Company and conducted a kind of school, teaching mostly catechism in his characteristic French manner, a narrow kind of dogma which smacked triumphantly of the Religious Wars and St. Bartholomew's Day Massacre. Point tended to see Huguenots under every bush. However he baptized 651 Blackfeet Indians that winter, dutifully recording each rite with its particulars and finally sending this unique record to Rome where it still rests. In composing his memoirs he maintained his style of rigid orthodoxy, thereby preventing their publication for something like eighty years.[32]

When Point finally left Fort Lewis on May 21, 1847, for his new assignment, via St. Louis, he had become immortal for more than one achievement: he had produced early paintings of Indians, like Karl Bodmer; he had founded Indian missions that have survived to this day, like Peter De Smet; and he had produced memoirs like the Whitmans, one-sided, lugubrious, even censorious, but significant. Deprived of his desire to work in Brazil, he passed out of our history obediently and spent the remainder of his life in humble tasks in the parishes and missions of Quebec, dying piously there in 1858. At least his had a happy ending.*

Meanwhile, De Smet had departed again for St. Louis. On September 28, 1846, he embarked in a small canoe with two Indian guides and sailed down the Missouri for two months, stopping frequently to visit employees of the forts or to instruct bands of Indians along the river. Among these were some Sioux who urged him to return to establish missions among them. Arriving at Westport, De Smet discharged his boatmen and made the rest of his journey to St. Louis by horse. He arrived at his destination on December 10, mercifully unaware that his life would never be the same. No longer superior of the Rocky Mountain Mission, he soon received another assignment as procurator for the Missouri Vice Province, and though he enjoyed an interlude in the west now and then, he life was cast into a different mould. He was no longer an empire builder; he became a bookkeeper instead.†

His new assignment, at least, spared him the agony of witnessing the collapse of his dreams. The mission he had founded, for which he had labored so intensely for seven difficult years, disintegrated rapidly after his departure. He himself had partly been to blame, at least Roothaan and Mengarini and others said so, and one should be willing to admit that this was true, without diminishing the glory which is his forever.

The trouble began with the Flatheads. When they returned from the buffalo hunt in late 1846 they appeared to Mengarini to be transformed, a different people from those who had left the village in early fall. Some said they had changed because De Smet, who had promised them tobacco, gave it to the Blackfeet, their enemies, instead. Others, who had placed great value on the Black Robes' medicine, had learned that it sometimes failed them, and they called the Black Robes liars like other white men. The faithful old men and women had all died off, all but one called Lolo, and he was soon mauled by a grizzly bear and his flesh was devoured. This, too, was a bad omen. There were none left to defend the Black Robes' reputation, but there were many who attacked it. It was unthinkable that St. Mary's, a mission renowned throughout the Christian world and as far away as China, known to popes and kings and dukes and cardinals as the pearl of all missions, the brightest star in the heavens, the miracle of grace in the mountains, had somehow gone sour.[33]

---

*After his departure from the Rocky Mountain Mission, Point requested permission to return, an indication that his memories had mellowed before his death.

†Soon after his return to St. Louis, De Smet accompanied the new vice provincial, Father John Elet, to Europe. After his return to America he was assigned the task of procurator, or "treasurer."

The gentle, compassionate Father Ravalli, who found it hard to speak ill of anyone, was the first to blow the whistle. On June 29, 1847, he wrote to Father Roothaan:

"In my letter before this one I wrote to your Paternity what deep consolation the Indians were giving us by their piety, their attachment to the missionaries and their unselfish labors for the new church and house. Things stood thus and we blessed the Lord. . . . But we were not a little astonished when on their approaching this reduction last fall, their camp, which was broken up in various bands, took different courses. Part of the Indians were unwilling or afraid to come up to their village, while the others on entering the village took up again their old-time barbarous yells, which had not been heard since we came among them. They gave a chilly salute to the missionaries and then drew off with their lodges (tipis) far from the latter nor did they show themselves to see the priest except rarely and then only to smoke in his cabin. They sold us grudgingly a little dry meat and that of the worst quality. We heard a little later that on Father De Smet's departure from their hunting camp to descend the Missouri they had given themselves up to their old war dances, to savage obscenity and to shameless excesses of the flesh. . . . We knew that we were not to blame for such a change and we bewailed it all the more when we saw that they went on constantly getting worse."

For Father Roothaan this news was shattering. He had been led to believe that another missionary enterprise like the reductions of Paraguay was in the making at St. Mary's. How was it possible that collapse would occur so suddenly? If he had been critical of De Smet in the past, he became in time even more caustic. "More than one person assures me," he wrote to poor De Smet, who was getting it from all sides, "that your relations published with so much *eclat*, are products of imagination and poetry."[34]

Three more years would pass before St. Mary's was formally closed. During these years the fickle Indians at one time were cooperative and docile to the teachings of the Black Robes, at another defiant and threatening. Mengarini and Ravalli, bewildered by these ups and downs of behavior, gradually lost their confidence in the mission's future and even came to the point where they felt threatened by the Flatheads.

Matters toward the end of 1847 reached a dangerous crisis. Mengarini described this as the "Little Faro Rebellion" in a letter to Rome, February 21, 1848.[35] Little Faro, a Flathead brave, influenced by disaffected non-Indians and half-breeds from other areas, rose up in church several times and openly castigated the fathers, shouting at them "like a man possessed." A local interdict had to be imposed before order was restored.

What Mengarini did not report was worse, though the Jesuits were not directly involved. Three months earlier, on November 29, 1847, Cayuse Indians went on a rampage at Waiilatpu, the Whitman Mission near Fort Walla Walla. Fourteen white people were murdered in cold blood, vivid evidence of Indian resentment and an attempt at reprisals against the Whites, who were pouring into the Oregon country in ever-increasing numbers. So inflamed with violence was the interior of the Northwest that hastily summoned army officials ordered all non-Indians out of the area except the Jesuit missionaries, an exception not taken lightly by the Protestant clergy. Although nothing else was required to spark anti-Jesuit agitation, there were other causes soon at hand to turn Oregon's new white citizens against priests, especially the Jesuits. The Whitman Massacre precipitated what is known as the Cayuse Indian War and there were irresponsible, Protestant charges, especially by the Reverend Henry Spalding, that Jesuits had masterminded the Indians' attack. It is true that when Oregon's Territorial Legislature had passed a law forbidding the delivery of all firearms to Indians, Joset, appalled by the consequences of this legislation, hastened to Oregon City to protest. He asserted before the deeply prejudicial, pioneer, lawmaking body that Indians of the mountains had been loyal and needed their firearms for survival. This was especially true of the Flatheads who, without gun-powder, would be helpless before the Blackfeet. At this point a considerable shipment of arms destined for the missions arrived at Fort Vancouver. This annual supply consisted of 1,080 pounds of powder, 1,500 pounds of balls, 300 pounds of buckshot and 36 guns. Joset ordered Accolti to forward the shipment to Sacred Heart Mission. At The Dalles a certain Lieutenant Rodgers intercepted the shipment and confiscated it, leaving others with the impression that Jesuits were supplying arms to the militant Indians.[36]

Despite the pandemonium raised, the Jesuits were isolated and felt little of the sting of persecution, which was now directed against the Catholics of the lower Columbia. The truth is the bigots of that area were so ignorant they did not know what a Jesuit was, except by name, and they confused Jesuits with priests in general.

There were now six residences of Jesuits in the Northwest under Joset, the general superior. There was, of course, St. Mary's, which was in a bitter struggle for survival. On Joset's Knoll the Sacred Heart Mission was beginning to shape up. St. Ignatius on the Clark's Fork had enjoyed a prosperous year before this, but Hoecken, its superior, was torn with doubts about its future. At St. Francis Regis Mission a number of Crees from Canada had gathered under the spiritual care of Father Louis Vercruysse, who had been removed from the prestigious St. Louis Church on French Prairie in Oregon because of the opposition of his parishioners—former trappers and voyageurs. Some had described Father Louis as "brusque and irritable," but the worst charge against him had been his fiery exhortations on temperance. His sermons on this subject, it was said, "were enough to make the devil himself shudder." This was too much for trappers and voyageurs who had lived for four decades on daily rations of four pounds of meat and rum. So their priest was moved, as often happens, and he rendered his sermons to the Crees instead.

Perhaps the Crees found him too righteous also. We will never know. When the Gold Rush news from California reached the valley of the Chewelah Indians in the spring of 1849, most of the Crees scurried south to dig for gold. The mission was closed, Vercruysse packed his frugal belongings and rode his horse over the "Flowery Trail" to St. Ignatius on the Clark's Fork.*

The fifth residence was St. Paul's on the upper Columbia near Kettle Falls, where Ravalli had remained a month before going to St. Mary's. The Skoyelpi Indians, who had not changed much, had the advantage of a major fishery in their backyard, where the salmon jumped the rapids during the summer of every year, and also the Hudson's Bay post called Fort Colville. So determined was Joset to have a priest in residence there he transferred De Vos from Oregon City, where he was extremely popular with the Whites, to St. Paul's on the Columbia.

For three years De Vos, unassisted by any other Jesuits, conducted a strenuous ministry at St. Paul's. Vercruysse said of him in 1851, "Alone as he was for three years everything changed face . . . He is loved and respected and no longer makes use of an interpreter. Of all the missions, this is the one where most is done for the instruction of Indians."[37]

De Vos, like Nobili, overextended himself until his health was broken. He had to leave St. Paul's and like Nobili before him, he eventually took the long, painful road to California, doubtlessly losing somewhere on the way, his precious manuscripts on the Skoyelpi language.

St. Francis Xavier's on the Willamette was, of course, the sixth residence of the Jesuits. It had already outlived its usefulness, if indeed, it ever enjoyed any. Blanchet and De Smet, always bosom friends and always capable of much flattering conversation with one another, had conceived of the Jesuit residence on the Willamette as a motherhouse, a kind

*Vercruysse returned to Belgium and died at Coutrai in 1867.

of novitiate, supply center and think tank, where the Superior could reside and be at the beck and call of the bishop. If De Smet ever really believed this possible, which I doubt, he was sorely mistaken. The truth is, the motherhouse, far remote from Jesuit activity in the interior, was a white elephant, at least in the nineteenth century. A novitiate with fifteen rooms and no novices, a supply center on the wrong river, further from the source of supplies than usual, an extensive farm with no one to farm it, and a think tank without ideas because no one had time to stay there, just about sums up the situation. As early as 1846 the General had said, "Get rid of the place," but Accolti who succeeded Joset as General Superior on February 18, 1849, argued that if he could hire someone to farm the place he would net $2,000 annually and be able to pay off the $6,000 debt which the mission owed the Hudson's Bay Company. You can see by this that expedience played an important role then, as now, and that our Province history began with debts and still has them.[38]

Accolti was not so wedded to the Willamette farm as might be supposed. When the Gold Rush fever struck Oregon, he readily convinced himself that California gold was a brighter solution to the mission's financial plight than the farm. The Picpus Fathers of the Sandwich Islands [Hawaii], so he had heard, had dispatched two of their lay brothers incognito to work, under the protection of the French Consul, in the gold mines for money to pay their debts.[39] Accolti now proposed that he himself go to California with two brothers, Magri and McGean, who would take up mining claims somewhere and work them, while he, Accolti, engaged himself in the sacred ministry. He urged De Vos to use his influence with Joset for permission to implement this bizarre scheme.

Roothaan had given specific orders that no one was "to go on far-away excursions, to California in particular." On February 17, 1849, he had written to Father John Elet, the new vice provincial in St. Louis, *Nemo in Californiam mittendus*," no one should be sent to California. But Accolti had a meaty bone in his teeth and he would not let go.

Perhaps Joset was influenced by the example of Archbishop Blanchet, who had sent to California Father John Baptiste Brouillet, vicar general of the new Walla Walla Diocese, to beg or borrow $50,000 to pay off a debt to the Hudson's Bay Company. Whatever—he finally yielded to Accolti, "very reluctantly."

This was ironic because at this point, in March, 1849, Accolti himself, not Joset, was the general superior. News of this fact had not reached Oregon, so it was Joset who made the decision and Joset who took the heat when Roothaan, quite angrily, scolded him for disregarding orders.

Michael Accolti could charm a cobra into singing hymns. Originally from southern Italy, he entered the Jesuit Order. He was now in the prime of life, in his forty-third year, and physically as tough as a mule. His broad, amiable face with its high forehead was framed by receding black hair, which, like Ravalli's, formed heavy tufts over his ears. An open, exuberant personality, he seems to have been a dreamer with his feet on the ground. Given to much singing like an opera star, he could fill a vast church with his powerful voice. He tended to be very verbose in letter writing, prompting his superior to complain about "the big thick letters," to which he responded lightly and at some length, "ever since I gave up the study of my dear Tacitus, I have got to be more and more prolix."

Father Nobili, broken in health if not in spirit, had been recalled from New Caledonia to pronounce his solemn vows at St. Ignatius and to engage in some "R and R." Father Joset presided over the vow ceremony on May 13, 1849. Later, on September 29 of the same year, Nobili presided over a similar ceremony "at St. Paul's Cathedral" on the Willamette when Accolti pronounced his solemn vows in the Society. The two, now solemnly professed Jesuits, were formally designated to go to California, not to work in the mines for gold, but to confer with the bishop and to explore the needs of the church, with particular reference to the Society's future there. For reasons unknown they did not board ship for their journey until October 30, the Feast of St. Alphonsus Rodriguez. Contrary winds kept them in port another four days; then, at last, they stood on the prow of the ship as it plowed through the cold waters of the Columbia, westward into the Pacific. As they plunged toward the southern coasts, the tiny ship bobbing in early winter's heavy seas, Nobili had his last sight of Oregon. He would never return. Five days later, the two priests arrived in San Francisco, and disembarked on the following day, December 9, 1849. No one knew it yet, but the California Mission of the Rocky Mountain Mission of the Vice Province of Missouri, had just been inaugurated.

Accolti's first view of the city by the Golden Gate did not impress him favorably. He was at a loss, he said, to regard the city as "Madhouse or Babylon . . . so great in those days was the disorder, the brawling, the open immorality and the reign of brazen-faced crime on a soil not yet under the sway of human laws."[40]

If this first impression had not been altogether promising, Accolti soon discovered countless positive reasons why he and Nobili should remain. He dispatched long, glowing letters to Roothaan and Elet, both of whom were surprised to hear from him in this forbidden territory, at least until Joset's letters of explanation got through. Given faculties for the Diocese of Monterey and urged by the new bishop to start a college in San Jose, both priests were somewhat bewildered by the complexity of their status and the overwhelming amount of work to be done. Nobili's health was still an occasion of concern. In San Francisco, doctors, after examining him carefully, informed Accolti that the patient was suffering from pericarditis, and some serious blood disease besides, and that it would be impossible for him to go back to the Indian missions. "He has conceived a complete aversion for the missions," Accolti wrote, "and does not wish even to speak of them."

In March, 1850, a bomb fell. A certain Judge Pratt of Oregon, a friend of Accolti's, had received permission from postal authorities to examine the Oregon mail pouches for documents he expected from Washington. As he probed the contents of the pouches, he discovered a letter addressed to Accolti and took it upon himself to deliver it personally. The letter from Elet in St. Louis informed Accolti that he had been appointed general superior of the Rocky Mountain Mission by father general in February of the previous year. The letter, in effect, also contained Elet's long-delayed response to Accolti's request for approval of the California project.

"We were uncertain," Accolti wrote to De Smet, "of the approbation of our superior, Father Joset, who reluctantly had sent us thither to comply with my very warm and earnest sollicitations [sic]. My nomination to the superiorship arrived timely indeed for our circumstances, but one year after its date."[41]

During this same windy month of March, Father Roothaan had written to Joset, lamenting the abandonment of New Caledonia. "I had decided and so written more than once that the new mission taken in hand with so much success by Father Nobili was to be kept up by assigning him at least one Father for a companion. Goetz after being dissatisfied at first was beginning to get along with Father Nobili. But you have recalled both of them. Father Nobili himself in California! All my letters lost! It is distressing."[42]

But Accolti, the new superior, had to move on. In July, 1850 he returned to Oregon alone, to discharge his new duties. His presence, especially in view of his current status, was sorely needed to resolve the continuing crisis at St. Mary's. The situation there had gone from bad to worse. Whatever hopes the Jesuits had of saving the mission vanished by the summer of 1850.

Mengarini had kept Joset informed, but he received no instructions on procedures to be followed. Most of the Indians had become increasingly insolent and defiant. Encouraged by former employees of the fur companies, they spread lies about the Jesuits and passively watched as the Jesuits were subjected to taunts and threats. When they left for the summer buffalo hunt they deliberately ignored the need for protection of the village, including fifty of their old people and children, whom Ravalli invited into the mission compound, behind the barricade.

In desperation Mengarini left for the Willamette, nine hundred miles distant, to seek help from Accolti. Left alone with Brother Claessens and the fifty helpless Indians cringing behind the palisade, Ravalli was hard pressed to provide food for his wards. His precautions were not without purpose. On September 7, a Blackfeet war party suddenly appeared and filled the air with savage war whoops. They withdrew, however, after stealing "about sixty horses" and killing a fine young Flathead who had remained true to the Jesuits.

Passing Sacred Heart Mission, Mengarini was fortunate in finding Joset at home. Joset agreed that immediate action had to be taken to protect Ravalli and Claessens. He dispatched two Indian couriers to Ravalli, directing him to start packing whatever could be salvaged. Then having mustered a party of twelve Coeur d'Alenes to accompany him, he left in great haste to rescue those he believed to be in mortal danger. The decision to abandon the mission, at least temporarily, was now taken.

When the Flathead hunters returned, they were greatly surprised to find that the Jesuits were still alive. They took no notice of Joset's presence nor of Mengarini's absence. They maintained a posture of haughty indifference as Joset and Ravalli loaded four wagons and three carts with the accumulation of nine years, the mission records, altar supplies, books, medicines, tools and other items purchased at great cost or made by the brothers.

On November 5, 1850, Joset signed a deed, one of the earliest in Montana history, conveying all rights of improvements to one Major John Owens for the sum of $250. Joset retained certain rights to the land and to the mills, in the event the Jesuits should return.[43] Major Owen, whose titular status was as phony as he was fickle, converted the buildings into a trading post.

Having concluded this sad business in a hasty manner, the Jesuits now mounted their horses and wagons and formed a procession which slowly turned north toward the Gate of Hell, whither they had entered the beautiful valley of the Ootlashoots, seemingly many decades before.

Ravalli with badly damaged health went on to the Coeur d'Alene Mission. Leaving the wagon train beyond the Gate, he turned west, accompanied by an escort of the twelve Coeur d'Alenes, and Joset with his entourage of Brother Claessens and friendly Flatheads proceeded farther north, expecting to reach St. Ignatius before heavy snows blocked their paths. Their progress was slow, for they were driving three milk cows, as well as "work cattle" [oxen] and their course was steep and circuitous. When they reached the south bank of the Flathead River, they decided to pitch their tents for the winter. Thirty lodges of loyal Flatheads soon joined them and camped on the same broad meadow until spring.*

Having tasted the rigors of travel by wagon, Joset now determined to undertake the remaining part of the journey on the rivers which coiled through the mountains and across the northern end of Pend d'Oreille Lake for almost two hundred miles. Thus, he and Claessens spent much of the winter building rafts and disassembling the wagons and carts for storage aboard, in preparation for the voyage. At last, when spring came, they made their final arrangements and plunged their rafts into the foaming current, swollen by spring runoffs. They were not the first, nor the last, to attempt this foolish procedure. The rivers, alas, had many rapids, and on the first, near Horseplains, these amateur boatmen lost one raft with all of its baggage. On the second, at Thompson Falls, they lost everything they had, including their clothing and all of the records from St. Mary's. They were lucky enough to escape with their lives.

*This site is near present-day Plains, Montana.

Many months after this mishap an Indian found on the river bank a wooden box that had survived. He pried it open, quickly closed it again, wrapped it in a blanket and hastened down the river to St. Ignatius Mission. "Black Robe," he said, "here are Brother's little people. They got drowned and speak no more." These were Brother Natalis Savio's puppets which he used for entertaining the children. These were the only relics saved from the disaster.[44]

In the meantime, Mengarini had reached the motherhouse on the Willamette, where he informed Accolti that he would like to be sent so far away that he would never hear again any news about St. Mary's or the Indians. He remained for a brief time on the Willamette and eventually left for California, where he died many years later.* From the Willamette, Accolti, who did not approve of the mission's closure, wrote to De Smet:

"You know perhaps that the Flathead Mission no longer exists. . . . Father Mengarini is with me. The state of his health and especially his morale is badly affected. This makes him quite unfit just now (and I believe forever) for the missions. They write me the same with regard to Father Ravalli."[45]

The loss of St. Mary's had a demoralizing effect upon all the Jesuits of the west. Some, like after-the-game quarterbacks, denounced the decision or offered solutions that should have been applied. "Mysterious indeed is the fall of the Flathead Mission," Roothaan complained from Rome. He blamed Joset for it because, he said, Joset had not sent help to St. Mary's in time. Father Vercruysse was especially vocal. "Our Fathers in China have more to fear from the sword of the Mandarin," he cried. "Still they stand firm."[46] Vercruysse probably would have stood his ground, but one can only speculate what good that would have accomplished.

Most tragic of what followed were the doubts. Had Jesuits run from danger? Could the mission have been saved with a stand of force, a change of personnel? To these and other nagging questions, no replies were ever provided. The questions without answers plagued two very heroic and sensitive Jesuits, Mengarini and Ravalli, as long as they lived.

*Gregory Mengarini, full of years and merit, died in his 76th year at Santa Clara College on September 23, 1886.

Interior of Sacred Heart Mission, 1926.

Steamboat at the landing of Sacred Heart Mission on St. Ignatius River, now called Coeur d'Alene River, about 1900.

Chief Alexander, one of the principal chiefs of the Upper Pend d'Oreilles, led the Jesuits to the site of the present St. Ignatius Mission in 1854. Gustavus Sohon drew this picture of him on April 21, 1854.

Sketch by John Mix Stanley of Sacred Heart Mission or Old Mission, as it was called, near Cataldo, Idaho. Construction of this mission was begun in 1849. This sketch appears in Reports of Explorations and Surveys to Ascertain the Most Practicable and Economical Route for a Railroad from the Mississippi River to the Pacific, 1855-1860.

First St. Ignatius Mission in Mission Valley, Montana, built in 1854.

Joseph Menetrey, who built the first church in Missoula. He died at St. Ignatius in 1891.

St. Ignatius Mission as drawn by Sohon in 1862.

4

THE GATHERING STORM
1850–1858

The new superior could not get California off his mind; it was like having a scruple that would not go away. He had demonstrated his concern for the Indian missions by objecting to the closure of St. Mary's and some day he would get around to visiting them.* Now a greater concern occupied his thoughts when petitions from the new bishop of Monterey came in and when other reports from California indicated that the handful of priests in the west could be more useful to the church in the south than in the north. The latter was being abandoned by the Whites anyway. They were all rushing off to the gold mines. Jesuits desperately needed in California were spending their time with the few tribes in the interior, settling squabbles, building barns, using weeks of time in endless travels between missions. On any profit-and-loss sheet little progress could be shown. Not one single mission could demonstrate that it would survive as a permanent stone in the foundation of the Northwest church. After nine years of sweat and tears at St. Mary's, the life of one Jesuit lost, only aged thirty-six, the spirit of two others broken, there was not one tangible thing left of the mission except what Mengarini carried out with him; not even the mission records.

In the gloomy light of the Willamette winter, so different from the sparkling brightness of his native Italy, Accolti counted the Jesuits that were left for him to shift around when required. Of the original three priests, none were left: Point had departed for Canada; De Smet was no longer attached to the mission; and Mengarini, in shattered health, was convalescing at the motherhouse awaiting a new assignment. Of those who came later, Zerbinatti was dead; Nobili, a broken man in San Jose, was awaiting means to return to Italy, as the general had ordered him;† De Vos at Kettle Falls had burned out at the age of fifty-three; Soderini had gone; and Ravalli was recovering at Sacred Heart Mission. In addition to the brothers, who had proved to be sturdier than the priests, only four of the pioneering Jesuits were left: Hoecken, who was showing signs of wear; Vercruysse, who had a loud voice and strong back, but was hard to live with; Joset, who was regarded as impractical because he was impetuous; and Accolti himself.

*Accolti visited the Indian missions of the interior only once and that was before he became superior. *See* Gilbert J. Garraghan, S.J., *The Jesuits of the Middle United States,* 3 vols. (New York, 1938), 2:434.

†*Ibid.,* p. 413. Nobili had requested the general's permission to return to Europe. Roothaan ordered him to do so, but while he waited for means to obey he changed his mind and decided to remain in California. Despite very poor health, he served admirably as an administrator until his death, March 4, 1856.

There had been reinforcements when Archbishop Blanchet returned from France by ship in August, 1847, just before the Whitman Massacre and the Cayuse Indian War. But these six Jesuits, already reduced to four, were like drops of water in the small lake behind the motherhouse. There were three priests: Joseph Menetrey, a Swiss of thirty-four years, who could endure like an oak; Gregory Gazzoli, scion of a highly placed Roman family, aged thirty-three, another sapling oak; and Anthony Goetz, a German, who was the same age as Gazzoli. Goetz, Accolti knew, had already spent a very difficult year in New Caledonia with Nobili, who had refused to accept Vercruysse in the same mission.

Three brothers had arrived with Blanchet: Natalis Savio and two others. "We need not mention the two others," Palladino caustically reported, "who fell by the wayside and proved untrue to their calling shortly after their arrival in this country."[1] The names of the two were Aloysius Bellomo and Macarius Marchetti. Judged harshly by their contemporaries, they were really not all that bad. Nor were they the only brothers to abandon the mission shortly after their arrival.* The fact is that the brothers who survived those very difficult years—Huet, Specht, Claessens, McGean, Magri, Huybrechts, and Savio—were like saints. Even Accolti, who lived in a bright cloud of euphoria would agree that they were overworked and deprived, sometimes even of daily Mass and the sacraments.

Reports indicated that the health of Father De Vos was beginning to crack. He had beat a tired horse too long. The final straw breaking his back was the defection of a head chief of the Skoyelpi Indians at Kettle Falls. The chief "had refused to punish his daughter's scandalous behavior and in his last illness had recourse to a pretended sorcerer."[2]

Later it would be said that the principal reason for the early failure of the Rocky Mountain Mission was lack of manpower.[3] Too much had been attempted. If Accolti agreed with this diagnosis of the anatomy of failure, he certainly did not reveal it. Mostly he was conscious of his own dilemma: either provide for the needs of the Whites in lower Oregon and California, where he correctly saw visions of huge population centers in the future, or continue to serve the needs of the Indian missions, for which the Jesuits had been called by a mysterious Providence. The Jesuits could not do both.

It had to be a question of priorities; in fact, it would be a question of priorities for many years. Simply expressed: should Jesuits, with their limited manpower resources, place greater emphasis on mission work with the Indians or on parish and school work with the Whites, who were far greater in number and concentrated in relatively small areas? To those who advocated an apostolate with the Whites, the Indian missionaries responded with force: the Second Provincial Council of Baltimore had laid the responsibility for American Indians on Jesuit shoulders and our superiors had formally accepted the burden with the approval of the Holy Father. Furthermore, they added, responsibility for the Whites belonged to the bishops of the dioceses, not to religious orders. One must admit the missionaries had compelling arguments to bolster their position. On the other hand, the critical need for priests and their effectiveness in getting results when they worked with Whites on the frontier could not be ignored. In the lower Columbia, De Vos and others had spectacular success in parish and retreat work among the employees of the Hudson's Bay Company and emigrants from the east "who were mostly Irish and American."† While they worked with Indians as far away as the Chinooks on the coast, they raised permanent churches only for the non-Indians; for example, at Fort Vancouver, Oregon City, and French Prairie.

---

*Ibid., p. 429. Three other brothers left the Society in addition to several novices. The brothers were: Thomas Burris, Daniel Lyons, and Daniel Coably.

†De Vos preached the first retreat for religious women in the Northwest at the sisters' convent at St. Paul, starting November 7, 1844. Edwin V. O'Hara, *Pioneer Catholic History of Oregon* (Portland 1911), p. 127.

In California while the bishop of Monterey, his vicar general, and the only priest in San Francisco, pleaded for priests to help them, thousands of Catholics were pouring in from all nations.

There was some strange irony in the situation. The new bishop was Joseph Alemany, a Dominican, whose order had taken over the Indian missions of lower California when the Jesuits were suppressed there. The vicar general was Father José Gonzales, a Franciscan, whose order had developed the Indian missions of upper California. And the pastor of San Francisco, vicar general for northern California, was Father Antoine Langlois, a Canadian who had frequently appealed to Accolti to enter the Society.* If later a clergy drawn largely from Ireland tended to disapprove of parish activities by the clergy from religious orders, they had little historical precedent to support their views. The point here, however, is that the church hierarchy in California, drawn from religious orders that had been identified with Indian missions, were now urging Jesuits to leave the Indians and come to their aid with their awesome problems in California.

On March 28, 1850, Accolti had written to Roothaan: "No schools except those of the Protestants, who make every effort to show the inadequacy and sterility of Catholicism. Churches are lacking everywhere and yet everybody wants them, everybody offers to put them up, provided only there are priests. The people are preponderantly Catholic. They cry aloud for priests, but the only response one can give them is a sigh from the heart. The French number at least twelve thousand. . . . Almost eight or ten thousand Germans, three or four thousand Italians, an uncounted number of Spaniards coming from the various Republics of South America. With this concourse of people from all the nations, the number of families goes on increasing and so there is a great host of children needing the benefits of an education without anybody being in a position to satisfy their need."

And later he added, "The town of San Francisco is the leading commercial place of California and will soon be such of the entire world."†

When confronted with dilemmas, men usually compromise. Perhaps this is the way God intended it all along. It is doubtful, had Accolti not compromised, whether the great Jesuit institutions in California would exist today.

Even Roothaan, grumpily—as often happened—admitted that California should be accepted and its mission status formalized, though he continued to object to our casual indifference to New Caledonia.‡ As early as December 6, 1849, Roothaan wrote to the new vice provincial in St. Louis, poor Father John Elet, who was caught in the middle: "As to California he [Elet] may send suitable Fathers there if he has them; but nobody will be sent from Europe. The two Spanish Fathers whom he would like to have are no longer available. In accepting an establishment in California, care must be taken to proceed with great prudence and especially to avoid infringing on anybody's rights."[4]

Accolti, it is true, never had doubts about the decision. He had spent his spare time studying Spanish, which nominates him, I suppose, as the first of our province to study the language of the conquistadores for apostolic reasons. He had realized from the beginning that the acceptance of California involved a decision from St. Louis as well as from Rome, and he had corresponded frequently with Elet. The latter was being converted gradually to Accolti's urgings, and when the daily paper in St. Louis announced that a railroad costing

*Blanchet sent Father Langlois, as a kind of chaplain, to accompany the French Canadians to the gold mines. Garraghan, *Jesuits of Middle U.S.*, 2:399.

†*Ibid.*, 407. One must not think that Accolti was ready to understate his views about San Francisco.

‡New Caledonia or western Canada was taken over by a new religious congregation, The Oblates of Mary Immaculate, who have served the church splendidly in this area.

twenty-seven million dollars would be completed in seven years between St. Louis and San Francisco, he joined forces with the former in the conversion of the general.*

So the ball was now in the vice provincial's court. He favored California so long as he could keep his own men in his own vice province. "The Vice Province alone," he wrote to Roothaan, "cannot charge itself with California so I give it up with the greatest regrets."[5] He wanted Spanish Jesuits, but Accolti, warming up to his subject, now that he had a little encouragement, had bigger ideas. "I know the Swiss Province was anxious to have some sort of establishment of its own on the Pacific. Behold here, Reverend Father, a whole region where not one establishment, but ten, if you wish, can be found in less time than one can think."[6]

By August, 1851, Roothaan capitulated. He ordered the Spanish Jesuits to send two of their number to California, enough to hold the fort in some little corner. By December, Nobili, now disposed to remain where he was, acknowledged that his assignment in San Jose had the unreserved approval of the general.

"But by this time," an observer remarked, "the Oregon Missions together with their offshoot, California, had been completely severed from St. Louis and placed by Father Roothaan in immediate dependence on himself."[7]

One gets the impression that Roothaan, who had, by this time, one foot in the grave, was beginning to get fed up. Accolti's boundless energy and verbose reports could wear one's patience rather thin. On October 30, 1851, Roothaan simply cut off the Rocky Mountain mission from the Missouri vice province, which could scarcely support it anyhow, removing by this stroke one party in the process of decision making and reserving to himself greater control over the rather volatile situation. He left Accolti in charge and ordered him to report directly to him. The California mission, while its existence was recognized implicitly, was still just an incidental part of Oregon.

A year after this, Accolti was still agitating for a separate mission in California. He wrote to De Smet, urging him to use his influence with Roothaan to attach California to "some" American province. "Without that I fear—humanly speaking—that all our hopes will fall short and our projects vanish."[8] Since he knew that there was only one American province, Maryland, in addition to the vice province of Missouri, he was casting for fish in a barrel, where he could see them all.

If tradition serves us well, he had gone to the wrong surrogate to plead his cause, for it was not one bit likely that De Smet, who watched developments in California warily, would do anything to weaken the cause of the Indian missions. Later, when disaster struck, survivors of the early years were heard muttering among themselves about "De Smet's curse" on California. While it is unlikely that De Smet cursed anything, much less anything so attractive as California, he certainly favored the Rocky Mountain mission and continued to support it actively to the day he died.

On May 8, 1853, John Roothaan, the best friend in Rome that the Rocky Mountain mission ever had, breathed his last. As general he was succeeded on July 2 by Father Peter Beckx, who was not an amateur superior. Beckx was already fifty-eight years old and a Jesuit of wide administrative experience. His rule as general for thirty-one years was probably the most difficult in Jesuit history. He himself spent twenty-two of those years in exile.

Beckx inherited as general a prickly problem that had been developing in Oregon—a minor feud between Accolti and the archbishop over church jurisdiction. Frustrated in his plans and tempted to lash out, Accolti had been indiscreet in his comments about Oregon. "Far from being favorable to our missions," Bishop Demers complained to Propaganda in

*Delayed in part by the Civil War, the railroad was not completed until 1869.

Rome, "he has such dislike for Oregon in general that he cannot refrain from expressing it on every occasion; but this way of thinking, is far from being that of all the Fathers."[9]

Beckx ordered Accolti to withdraw from Oregon City, where he was regarded as the most popular preacher of any religious group, and to proceed at once to New York City. A short time after his arrival there, he embarked on a voyage to Rome to plead his cause and that of California with father general. In particular he requested that the Oregon and California missions be adopted by one of the European provinces. Beckx agreed with him. On May 16, 1854, Father Alexander Ponza, provincial of the Turin Province since 1850, wrote to Father Nicholas Congiato, rector at that time of St. Joseph's College, Bardstown, Kentucky, announcing that Beckx was about to assign to the Turin Province the care of "the Mission of California." He continued, "after a few days I must start for Rome, where I shall arrange the affair with Father General and Father Accolti."[10]

Accolti, strongly prejudiced against Oregon and the Rocky Mountain missions by this time, had succeeded at last. His persistence over a period of six years had finally borne fruit: the grapes of California, which proved to be bitter ones for some of the pioneers who were still building barns in some lost valley in the inaccessible mountains.

On August 1, 1854, Father Congiato, a college man, was appointed superior of both the Oregon and California missions, "which became on the same day a joint dependency of the province of Turin." The new superior took up his residence at Santa Clara and the title of the new mission was formalized: California Oregon Mission. The Rocky Mountains, older and longer than either, had somehow got lost in the bureaucratic shuffle.[11]

The appointment of Congiato was bad news, for if Accolti acted with cool aloofness toward the missions and never bothered to visit them, Congiato appeared to be more than frosty, a man of ice, though a very efficient one. Sometimes he dispatched sympathetic reports to Father Beckx, but his actions spoke more eloquently than his words. No one doubted where his real interests lay.

When Congiato became superior there were only three active missions left in the entire Northwest: Sacred Heart, St. Ignatius, and St. Paul's near Kettle Falls. Of these, only two, St. Ignatius and Sacred Heart served as mission centers from which Jesuits emerged like rays from the sun, radiating into the gloom in all directions, covering vast areas as frequently as possible. These were the Dark Ages for the missions in general and yet during them both St. Ignatius and Sacred Heart rose to new heights in their influence on the frontier.

In a real sense this was a Golden Age for Sacred Heart Mission. With a saintly genius like Anthony Ravalli in residence, it could not have been otherwise. Ravalli was the local superior, and Gregory Gazzoli, his assistant. Gazzoli's portrait reminds one of a nineteenth-century European statesman, his eyes, tired and bored looking, but his whole demeanor one of dignity and pride in accomplishment. Actually, he was a gentle, paternalistic Roman with a strong streak of Latin piety. Both he and Ravalli formed a close relationship with the three brothers, all of whom earned the highest praise from Congiato. "Old, sickly and broken down as they are the poor men work with a zeal and an energy that astonish and edify everybody." And later Congiato wrote of them: "For the last fifteen years they have labored like martyrs and suffered great privations as true religious and worthy sons of the Society."[12] Huet, "old and sickly," at this time was actually only forty-nine years old, but the hardships of mission life had given him the appearance of bare survival after a hard winter.

Brothers Huet and Magri were the Indians' special friends. Fortunately they were there, because at this time Ravalli was directing the construction of the new mission church, no small undertaking in the circumstances. Ravalli had designed the edifice in Roman Doric, of huge timber and adobe, ninety feet in length, forty in width and twenty-five in height. Joset, who had replaced De Vos at Kettle Falls when the latter was furloughed out—eventually to California—kept in touch with the details of construction. Writing later in "Sketch of the Sacred Heart Mission Church," he described it:

"Large quantity of heavy timbers were to be hewed, 24 posts over 25 feet long, squared 2½ by 2½ feet, some 3 by 3; sills, joists, wall plates, rafters, etc. All in proportion: 20,000 feet of boards to be manufactured at the saw-pit, to be dressed by hand, 50 thousand shingles, (30,000 cubic feet) of stones for the foundation to be dug from the mountains; then the whole to be brought to place on the top of the hill; the stones ½ mile distant, timbers, some more than a mile; large quantity of clay to serve as mortar and filling between the posts. Trucks with block wheels were roughly made and for want of sufficient teams were drawn mostly by hand. They gathered from the prairies a sufficient amount of fibres to make all the ropes needed, and made all other preparations for they were left entirely to their own industry."[13]

To expedite these wonders, Magri succeeded in persuading the Indians to work on the project for no other recompense than rations of bowls of meal. "No one else besides Brother Magri," declared Joset, "would have been equal to such an undertaking." The Indians soon came to regard the labor on the Church as a reward for good Christian living and "the worst punishment that could be inflicted on them was to be forbidden to take part in the construction of their house of prayer."

At least seven years of intermittent work was required to complete the structure, which became one of Idaho's landmarks, "The Old Mission Church."*

It was a landmark in Ravalli's time also. Peace treaties were signed nearby. This was headquarters for the survey and construction of the Mullan Road. Emigrants crossing the mountains either way found it a haven, as well as a great wonder of the wilderness. For the Indians it was a rallying place, a convenient rendezvous after weeks of wandering in the eternal quest for food. Gradually the Coeur d'Alenes came to regard the mission as their tribal home. First a few, then greater numbers built log huts near the church and began to cultivate plots of ground. Father Joset had once said that the extreme poverty of these Indians would bring them more easily to the labor of agriculture. He was right, of course, and when it did they cultivated their first fields within the sound of the bell of the Old Mission Church, for the bell represented a whole way of life, not simply the teaching of dogma.

Meanwhile, Congiato, like Joset, was keeping a sharp eye on the developments taking place on the knoll. In 1857 after the Indians' fervor—occasioned by labor on the house of prayer—had cooled somewhat, Congiato wanted to close the mission. Joset rose stoutly to the defense of the Coeur d'Alenes and convinced the superior general from Santa Clara that these Indians were not lacking in piety, as alleged, rather that other circumstances had rendered them somewhat passive. One had to know Indians, who were very sensitive and easily hurt. Father Ravalli, unintentionally had neglected them, partly because of his preoccupation with construction at the mission and partly because he was unable to learn their language.†

"It stands on record," Palladino states, "that even the Coeur d'Alene Mission would have been closed but for the remonstrances and entreaties of Lieut. John Mullan, U.S.A."[14] Mullan, who was related to Father Elden Mullan, the first American assistant to father

---

*The Old Mission Church was restored twice: once during a four-year period 1926–30 at which time Henry Day, Sr. was chairman of the funding drive; secondly in 1976, the bicentennial year, when Henry L. Day, Jr. was chairman of the funding project.

†Despite his rare genius in several professions, Ravalli simply could not learn Indian languages, even Coeur d'Alene, which Joset said was the easiest to learn. Joset learned only Coeur d'Alene. De Smet, like Ravalli, learned none. He had to use an interpreter at all times.

general, ramrodded work on the road, which bore his name and which extended from old Fort Walla Walla on the Columbia to Fort Benton on the Missouri.[15] This was in part a military road uniting the headwaters for navigation on the two major river arterials in the Northwest, but it served also to open up the area to settlement.

Mullan had befriended the Jesuits on many occasions; for example, by supplying ropes and pulleys to the brothers for the construction projects. "I know not," Hoecken wrote to Father De Smet on October 18, 1855, "how to acquit the debt of gratitude I owe to this excellent officer."[16]

Military awareness had become rather suddenly a government priority after the Whitman Massacre and the Cayuse War of 1848. Following the latter there had been two other Indian wars, rather minor events except for the handful of people killed during them. The Rogue River War (1849–54) in Oregon had alerted authorities in the still young and fickle Bureau of Indian Affairs to the long obvious fact that all was not well. The restlessness of the Cayuse was symptomatic of a general condition, not merely an isolated grudge. The Yakima War in 1855–56, occasioned by frequent violations of Indian rights, added to the concern of those in high places and crystallized Indian opposition to the Whites, including, in some cases, the missionaries. While it was still much safer for men to roam the forests and streams of the Northwest in 1855 than to walk in New York's Central Park six generations later, outsiders like Congiato tended to panic and rationalize the closing of the missions because of Indian militants or alleged lack of response to the efforts of missionaries.

The Coeur d'Alenes, too, would soon be involved in a war against Whites. Fortunately for them, as well as for the scattered settlers in the area, Joset and Mullan had been able to persuade Congiato to let sleeping dogs lie.

St. Ignatius on the Clark Fork had been somewhat isolated from these events. Their time for disillusionment in the word of the palefaces had not yet come. Hoecken with what white contemporaries called his "neophytes" was more concerned with problems that appeared to be even more basic than Indian rights—daily survival. The river fed by the swollen water of Lake Roothaan had not behaved itself. Farming conditions certainly had not improved, and the big game hunting, on which the tribe had depended heavily for food, gradually vanished. The Kalispels had been accused "of wanton killing" of deer, which sounds like the generalization of a well-fed critic. The Indians themselves wanted to move the mission. Victor, one chief of the tribe was quoted as saying: "The Superior does not love us, since he wants us to die here of starvation."[17]

Hoecken's response, says Joset, was that the "Indians should go and look for a better situation."

It is difficult to explain Hoecken's reluctance to take the initiative. He knew that sooner or later they had to make the leap; that is, move the mission. In the summer of 1854, with Accolti out of the country, there was no red tape to cut, no risk of the mission being eliminated, just a decision to be made by himself and his Jesuit colleagues, and a new place to occupy.

In the end it was an Indian who took the initiative. Alexander, another chief of the Kalispels, who had served as a companion for De Smet on many of his mountain journeys, offered to lead the Jesuits to another site beyond the mountains of the east to a place called by the Indians *Sinielman,* which means meeting place or rendezvous. It served, Alexander explained, as a place for bartering and gaming when several tribes came together. In a valley between the mountains and not far from a great lake, Sinielman was regarded as common ground by all the adjacent tribes.

Menetrey and Brother McGean accompanied Alexander to the proposed location. They knew at first sight that this was perfect for a mission. It was a broad meadow-like plain crossed by sweet-water rivers, bountiful in grass for ponies and cattle, protected in the winter and easily accessible to the four tribes for whom the new St. Ignatius would be built. Fish, game, and berries were plentiful, and an abundance of wood for council fires was within reach of the keepers of tepee fires.

The two Jesuits lost no time in conveying their impressions to Father Hoecken. After several councils of their own the Jesuits decided to move without delay. Hoecken sold the cattle for $2,000, McGean built five barges and many packing cases. The mission's possessions were packed and loaded at the river's edge. At the last moment the Kalispels changed their minds and wanted to stay where they were, but it was too late for Hoecken to change his plan. With a certain sadness and uneasiness about the future, the Indians joined their missionary leaders at the old chapel for the last time, and after suitable prayers had been offered for safety in the journey, the great migration began. It was already late summer. The morning air was cool, almost frosty. The waters of the river, lapping gently in the bay, conveyed a melancholy sound, like the waters of Lake Roothaan in the autumn, when the forests were silent and the lake was dark and cold.

Father Hoecken wrote a report to De Smet on what followed:

"Having set out from the Kalispel Mission on the 28th of August, 1854, I arrived at the place designated on the 24th of September and found it such as it had been represented—a beautiful region, evidently fertile, uniting a useful as well as pleasing variety of woodland and prairie, lake and river—the whole crowned in the distance by the white summit of the mountains, and sufficiently rich withal in fish and game. I shall never forget the emotion of hope and fear that filled my heart, when for the first time I celebrated Mass in this lovely spot, in the open air, in the presence of a numerous band of Kalispels, who looked up to me, under God, for their temporal and spiritual welfare in this new home. The place was utterly uninhabited—several bands of Indians live within a few days travel, whom you formerly visited, and where you baptized many . . . In a few weeks we had erected several frame buildings, a chapel, two houses, carpenter's and blacksmith's shops; wigwams had sprung up at the same time all around in considerable numbers, and morning and evening you might still have heard the sound of the axe and the hammer, and have seen newcomers, rudely putting together lodges."[18]

Alexander and his companions had taken care to seek the approval of other tribes for the establishment of the mission in the Sinielman. This, however, lacked legal force, and the Jesuits were required to establish their claim to the mission lands at a later date. Eventually this became a celebrated controversy between the tribes and the Jesuit order. The circumstances, however, under which the Jesuits occupied the land for this second and final St. Ignatius Mission should not be overlooked.

"About Easter of this year, 1855," Hoecken added in his letter, "over one thousand Indians of different tribes from the Upper Kootenais and Flat-Bow Indians, Pend d'Oreilles, Flatheads and Mountain-Kalispels, who had arrived in succession during the winter when they heard of the arrival of the long desired Black Gown made this place their permanent residence."[19]

During this same spring and summer of 1855, Isaac Stevens, governor of the Washington Territory, was engaged in the solemn and very subtle profession of making treaties with the Indian tribes of his jurisdiction. He had spent eighteen sweltering days at Walla Walla, May 24 to June 11, while some five thousand Indians had camped in the adjoining valley, many of them plotting a war against the white men who had invaded the interior.

Their spokesmen were resisting Stevens' proposals stubbornly, saying openly that the government was taking too much land and giving too little in return."*

Jesuit participation in the council was almost negligible. However, like the Oblate missionaries who were engaged in mission efforts with the Cayuse and Yakimas, they regarded themselves as compromised by the government's attitude. "We find ourselves in a very difficult position," Joset wrote later, "the Americans fancy that the priest completely controls the spirit and heart of the natives, and I think that the natives suspect the priest of leaning to the side of the Americans." The Oblates complained that government officials "oblige us to speak for them, to accompany them and even serve as their interpreters," which is exactly what Stevens expected the Jesuits to do.

The Jesuits, because of circumstances painfully clear to all sides, were not opposed to the concept of special reservations for Indians. They objected to being used in one of the greatest land swindles of all time, a loss to the tribes of 174 million acres. There was a limit to which the priests could go in preserving the peace by advising Indian accommodation, but there was also certain knowledge on what would occur if the Indian resisted.

At Walla Walla the fiercely intense disputations, witnessed by two Jesuits, Ravalli and Menetrey, and non-involved Indian observers from the Flathead and Coeur d'Alene Missions convinced most Indians, at least, that war was inevitable. The refusal of many Indians to accept gifts of tobacco, the unyielding harangues of the chiefs in council, and the conspiracies and plots afoot in many of the lodges provided evidence to everybody except the Americans of what was really happening. When suddenly the opposition to the treaty collapsed, with the Indians giving up forty-five thousand square miles of land, Stevens and his staff felt elated. "The Chiefs agreed to a mock treaty," Joset warned, "in order to gain time and prepare for war."[20]

On June 16, the governor with his thirteen-year-old son and staff left Walla Walla for the Coeur d'Alene Mission in bright sunshine, which reflected his triumphant spirits. In nine days he reached the mission, and on the day following, June 26, administered the oath of allegiance to the United States to all of the Jesuits at the mission. His subordinate, Henry Crosbie, acting as the administration clerk, or recorder, reported that the Jesuits subscribed the naturalization papers and "seemed much pleased with the idea of becoming American citizens."[21]

At the mission, Stevens held a council with the Coeur d'Alenes, urging some to attend the impending Flathead Council, which they refused to do, and promising that he would return after seeing the Blackfeet in mid-September, to hold a combined council for the Coeur d'Alenes, Spokanes, Okanogans and Skoyelpi tribes. Ominously Stevens added, "We wish you to have your Missionaries; the President likes to have Missionaries among you who will do their duty."[22] A more threatening greeting could not have been offered by Bolsheviks.

As Stevens struggled over the twisted trail to Hell's Gate, where he planned on negotiating another land give-away, Indian runners behind his back were racing across the plateau, busily engaged in preparing for war. It was only a question of timing, or possibly an unforeseen incident that would set off the explosion, like putting a match to the fuse.

At Hell's Gate on July 16, the Walla Walla scenario was played again. At Stevens's insistence, Father Hoecken of St. Ignatius Mission, which was now being built about fifty miles north of Hell's Gate, attended the council and served as one of the signers of the treaty on behalf of the Confederated Tribes of Flatheads, Pend d'Oreilles and Kootenais. The government demanded that the Indians cede their land extending from approximately

*". . . in the space of less than three years, beginning in 1853, over fifty treaties were to be signed involving nearly a hundred tribes in western America. Thus in one sweep the Whites confiscated 174 million acres." Robert Ignatius Burns, S.J., *The Jesuits and the Indian Wars of the Northwest* (New Haven, 1966), p. 75.

the 42° parallel north to 46°, except for the reservation carved out north of Hell's Gate on the Jocko River, including Sinielman. To this, the Flatheads objected. Chief Victor and his whole nation refused to cede any land in the Bitterroot, in the valley of the Ootlashoots. Eventually Stevens yielded. A special clause had to be inserted into the treaty to this effect, and then Victor and other leading men of the tribe signed the treaty.

"Be it noted, however," Palladino adds, "that the concession made in favor of the Flat Heads was conditional; in other words it authorized them to occupy the Bitter Root Valley so long as the Government did not require them to move to the general reservation on the Jocko."[23] The full meaning of this clause was not understood by the Flatheads.

According to the treaty, the Flatheads were to receive schools, teachers, a blacksmith, a carpenter, wagons, a ploughmaker's shop, a saw mill, a flour mill, a complete hospital and many other benefits. The tribes would receive $120,000 in cash in installments and the chiefs would receive comfortable homes and annual salaries of $500. The tribes and the mission, too, would be prosperous, indeed.

Palladino reports on the government's performance. "The Fathers and brothers at the mission were instructed to carry out, in the name of the Government, this part of the agreement. They did so cheerfully, and continued to do the same for a long time; but theirs was the privilege only of doing the work, whilst remuneration seemed to be entirely lost sight of, or stranded on the way."[24] In other words the government made the promises and expected the Jesuits to redeem them.

Hoecken wrote to De Smet, "We have done and shall continue to do all in our power for the government officers; our brothers assist the Indians and teach them how to cultivate the ground; our blacksmith works for them—he repairs their guns, their knives, and their axes; the carpenter renders them great assistance in constructing their houses, by making the doors and windows; in a word, all we have and all we are is sacrificed to their welfare. Still, our poor Mission has never received a farthing from the Government."[25]

And so it happened that the Hell's Gate Treaty, conducted in an atmosphere of distrust and disorder, helped to sow dragon's teeth that would bite again; the Flatheads' removal from the Bitterroot would be a scandal to a nation beginning to respond to its conscience; and the Jesuits, after covering up for the government's criminal neglect by fulfilling the conditions of the treaty as best they could, created profound misunderstandings with the tribes, especially an impression that the missionaries *owed* to the tribe the services they rendered. While the former was resolved with force, the latter has never been resolved.

As early as 1855, Hoecken turned to Father De Smet in St. Louis for help. He requested that De Smet send two dozen spelling books with the next year's supplies. Though neither De Smet nor the vice province of Missouri were formally responsible for the Rocky Mountain mission, both continued to provide support whenever possible. This was partly due to the fact that the best route for supplies lay via St. Louis and up the Mississippi and Missouri rivers to Fort Benton, a distance of 2,500 miles.

"The itemized orders were sent by the superiors of the missions to De Smet, who made the purchases and saw them packed and safely placed on board some upstream Missouri River steamer or else personally accompanied the cargo. The bills for the purchases made were either charged against the missions or else were met by De Smet out of funds gathered by him in Europe and America on behalf of the Indians. Often the articles ordered by the missions were begged by him from St. Louis merchants while his wide acquaintance with steamboat officials generally enabled him to ship the cargoes free of charge."[26]

Several years later, for example, when Hoecken was establishing a new mission for the Blackfeet on the Sun River near Fort Shaw, he received a shipment from De Smet, "contained in about 40 boxes, 24 bags and bales, bundles of spades, hoes, shovels, axes and handles, cross cut shaws and whip saws, four ploughs, etc.—with a large trunk of chasibles, albs, etc. I hope I shall be able to pay the whole from charitable contributions—the amount may come to near $1,300."[27]

The American Fur Company which controlled a considerable portion of the fur trade in the Northwest during this period operated a number of boats. The company was managed by Pierre Choteau, Jr., whose son Charles was the first to register at St. Louis College when it was taken over by the Jesuits. Charles became the confidant of De Smet and captain of one of the riverboats, the *Spread Eagle*. Because of these fortuitous connections, the American Fur Company not only carried Jesuit freight free of charge at enormous savings but provided company men and wagons to transfer the freight to the missions, even to St. Ignatius, which was 350 miles from Fort Benton. The round trip for the wagons required thirty-six days.* At times the brothers from the mission made the long trip to meet the steamer at the fort, presumably taking the route through present Missoula, up the Blackfeet River and over Rogers Pass.

In 1863 the American Fur Company terminated its business in furs and transportation, retaining only its trading post at Fort Benton. Later De Smet wrote, "[Choteau] has sold out his whole concern in the trading posts on the Missouri River except at Fort Benton. He may even sell that post before long. . . . Should Choteau cease running on the Missouri, some other kind friend might step in his footsteps."[28] De Smet was concerned about freight bills, which in one instance he reckoned to have been approximately $1,000, contributed by Choteau to the mission.

It was not long before another friend stepped in. Captain Joseph La Barge became an intimate friend of De Smet and provided free of charge many services besides freighting the missions' supplies.[29] La Barge named his boat *De Smet* and maintained a special stateroom which was for the exclusive use of De Smet in his travels from St. Louis to Fort Benton. During the last month of De Smet's life, La Barge requested him to bless a new steamboat to replace the old one. This, too, was named *De Smet*. Rising from his sick bed, the old missionary acceded to his friend's request, not wishing to offend one who had so often obliged him and other Jesuits in the work of the missions.[30]

Despite the emptiness of government commitments, this second St. Ignatius in what is now called the Mission Valley, became a vibrant force for civilization in Montana and far beyond. At St. Mary's the first flour, and lumber, mills in Montana had been erected; the first wheat, and oat, fields had been cultivated; the first cattle, hogs, and chickens had been bred; the first medical doctor, Ravalli, had practiced his skill; the first musical band had been organized and the first classes, taught.

Likewise, at St. Ignatius there were in the course of time many firsts; for example, St. Ignatius had the first Catholic sisters in Montana; the first mission printing press, the first resident school for Indians, and the first industrial or trade schools in the Northwest. For civilization in Montana, the influence of St. Ignatius has been uniquely great, far greater than the mills, wagons, cows, and chickens of St. Mary's. In time, even in the early years, St. Ignatius had all of these also. The flour mill and whipsaw mill were built with materials of local origin, "the power for both plants being obtained from the stream close by, through a race over one thousand feet long and five feet wide, made, bottom and sides, of hewn tamarack timbers. . . . The whipsaw mill," Palladino continued, "though of limited capacity, furnished all the material for the construction of the large church forty by one hundred feet with a belfry over one hundred feet high—a real marvel—if we consider the scantiness of means at hand for its construction. The structure, frame, roof and all, was held together

---

*Garraghan, *Jesuits of Middle U.S.*, 2:363, et seq. The American Fur Company, besides providing these gratuities, "presented at intervals acceptable gifts like flour, dried meat, and in one instance '60 buffalo tongues,'" a great delicacy.

by wooden pins, nails in those days being still out of reach, and if obtainable, their cost would have been prohibitive. The columns of the nave, six on each side, were solid timbers, eighteen inches in diameter and fifteen feet high and were turned by hand, the power being furnished by the strong arms of stalwart Indians. In this Church there was a life-size crucifix carved by Father Ravalli."*

This church, when a new and grander one was constructed thirty years later, was converted into a sister's hospital. It served in the interim, however, not only as a temple of God, but as a fitting competitor for the Sacred Heart Mission Church, which had become the St. Peter's Basilica for the tribes of the interior.

By this time it was clear that unless some radical development occurred somewhere between Rome and the Indian missions, the latter would cease to exist. There were only three residences left, five Jesuit priests and seven Jesuit brothers. The motherhouse on the Willamette had long since been vacated, not formally or officially, but after the manner of its occupants leaving and not coming back. Its land was put up for sale.

St. Paul's on the Columbia, too, was on Congiato's hit list. Joset had replaced De Vos there in 1851, and later he was joined by Vercruysse. The proximity of the fort had made farming unnecessary, so no brothers were in residence. De Vos had left a devout congregation, but soon after his departure events beyond Joset's control devastated the mission.

First, during the year 1853–54 there had been a dreadful smallpox epidemic which decimated the tribe. An Indian infected with the disease had brought it into camp and the two Jesuits battled night and day to save the lives of their people. Joset described his efforts, using the third person with reference to himself:

"There was no doctor in the country and no vaccine to be had; as the man was of a very good constitution, the father took the matter from him and inocculated first his wife and children and everyone escaped the infection; the father had never done such [a] thing before [since] he was no doctor; but a missioner in such circumstances must improvise himself a doctor. Camp after camp, succeeding one another to the church the sickness lasted almost one year; generally those who would mind the recommendation of the priest escaped and bear the signs of the pox; but many would not listen and paid with their life."[31]

During this same period the upper Columbia was inflamed by the sensational revelations of Smoholla, a Wanapum Indian who had commenced to intrigue his countrymen about 1850. Described as an odd, little wizard, almost hunchbacked and bald-headed, he was given to cataleptic trances during which, when he spoke, he had a mysterious power over his listeners.[32] Chief Moses, a powerful figure on the plateau, fearing Smoholla, provoked a fight with him and left him for dead. Smoholla survived somehow. He crept into a boat, drifted down the Columbia and was rescured by Whites. More wily and treacherous than ever, he claimed that he had returned from the dead.

Smoholla was especially opposed to the Whites who were drifting into the area, first in search of gold, then in search of farmland in the fertile Colville Valley. The Whites brought whisky with them, and in about 1854 two of them built a saloon on the Indians' route to the church. The effect of this was worse than the smallpox or Smoholla.

"The settlers continued to come to church every Sunday," Joset reported, "but they began to pretend that their horses could not well stand the wait for the afternoon service, but they stood well at the door of the saloon, and the Indians soon followed the example; and what was worst, some of the more influential chiefs began, too, to drink. It was a great drawback."[33]

---

*Lawrence B. Palladino, S.J., *Indians and Whites in the Northwest: A History of Catholicity in Montana 1838–1891*, 2d ed. (Lancaster, Pa., 1922), p. 98. In a footnote, Palladino states that the price of 60 penny nails at a considerably reduced price some years later were still $1.00 per pound.

Not all of Congiato's problems appeared to be Indian-related. In California where most of the Jesuits were now assigned, there was much agitation about the superior's preoccupation with Oregon, meaning the Indian missions. Though some of the Jesuits in the north grumbled about "the hijacking of Jesuits in San Francisco and Santa Clara," it was the complaint of Jesuits in the south that prompted Father Beckx to separate the two missions on March 1, 1858, giving each its own general superior. Both missions remained formally attached to the Turin Province, a great disappointment, I suspect, to Father Accolti who was still agitating as late as 1870 for California's annexation to Missouri.*

Perhaps Congiato was disappointed also. He remained as superior of the northern half, called the Rocky Mountain Mission, in confirmation of the prevailing attitude that the northern mission was still the original from which California had sprung. In obedience, Congiato took up his residence in one or another mission of the Northwest, which was a far cry from San Francisco and Santa Clara. At this point the northern missions could now count six priests, including Congiato, to serve an area of more than 60,000 square miles.

One of Congiato's first major decisions in his new capacity was to close St. Paul's. He had already transferred Joset to the Coeur d'Alene Mission to relieve Ravalli there of the office of local superior. Before his departure in February, 1857, Joset wrote to De Smet, on whom everyone laid his burdens. "The hearts of our poor people are upset;" he said, "within two years what a change! They have become deaf to good advice . . . we are afraid lest some violence on the part of the miners push them over the edge; all are like mice keeping watch on the movements of the cat; they appear to mistrust all whites."[34]

In the Yakima War that spring, one of the Oblates, Father Charles Pandosy, had been seized and whipped by aroused Indians. Later, American soldiers threatened to shoot him and he was forced to abandon the Yakima Mission and take refuge with the Jesuits at Sacred Heart Mission.

The Jesuits themselves did not feel threatened. At best, though, they felt uncertain about their future in the missions. They felt equally uncertain about the Whites moving into the interior. What was expected of the Jesuits, as the only priests available in this empty wilderness? It was one thing for Jesuits to be transferred to California to serve the spiritual needs of Whites, but a much more serious matter for the missionaries to build churches for Whites and assist them on lands which the Indians regarded as their own, the treaties notwithstanding. If the Jesuits had felt uncomfortable in the middle ground between the government and the Indians, they now felt worse, caught as they were between the Indians and an ever-increasing number of belligerent Whites who sought their ministrations. White men had souls too. But the Whites in the minds of the Indians were the aggressors and it was difficult to identify with them without alienating Indians.

It was appropriate under the circumstances for Father Congiato to come to grips with this problem for the first time, a kind of poetic justice. The settlers in the Colville Valley wanted a church of their own. Since Joset was transferred to the Coeur d'Alene Mission to take Ravalli's place, it seemed opportune to send Ravalli to St. Paul's to reside with Vercruysse and to build a church specifically for Whites in the Colville Valley.

Sometime during the latter part of 1857, Ravalli moved to St. Paul's. On some undetermined site he began construction of the edifice, an historic undertaking, since this would be the first church for Whites in the entire interior of the Northwest. Before he completed it, however, he was recalled by Congiato and dispatched to California.

*Fathers Michael Accolti, Joseph Bayma, Aloysius Varsi, and Paul Raffo, mission consultors, appealed in 1870 to Beckx for the separation of the mission from Turin and annexation to Maryland. Garraghan, *Jesuits of Middle U.S.*, 2:420.

Only Vercruysse was left at old St. Paul's, and Vercruysse doubted his own usefulness. On November 13, he had written to a colleague in Europe: "Since these hordes of foreigners have arrived in search of gold the Indian is no longer the same man. Demoralized by bad language and bad example, they no longer heed us. Gambling, stealing, illicit dealings, divorce and sorcery have again begun and reduced them to the condition they were in before the arrival of the Fathers."[35]

In October, 1858, Vercruysse, too, packed his meager personal belongings on the back of his horse and rode disconsolately south through the beautiful Colville Valley, splendid now in autumn colors. He passed the old Chewelah Mission, which had been burned in contempt by settlers, and rode briskly on to Sacred Heart Mission. St. Paul's, he had been told, would be closed temporarily, like St. Mary's. Not all of the grim years of the Dark Ages were spent. Mercifully Vercruysse did not know the future. His little world on the plateau would soon be engulfed in a racial war.

St. Peter's Mission near Bird Tail Rock, Boys' School in the foreground.

St. Peter's Mission near Bird Tail Rock.

Joseph Giorda, second founder of the Missions.

5

A SECOND START
1858–1866

On May 17, 1858, the explosion which had been awaited with cheerless suspense for so long a time took place unexpectedly in a small ravine between the rolling, grass-covered hills, about halfway between Forts Walla Walla and Colville. An army column of 158 men under the command of Lt. Col. Edward Steptoe was fired upon by trigger-happy young braves in a tribal coalition of nearly one thousand warriors. Father Joset was in the company of the so-called hostiles, attempting to convince them that a violent protest would gain nothing and lose all. The coalition, comprised of warriors of at least ten different tribes, included some of Joset's Coeur d'Alenes. They had not attacked on the previous day because it was Sunday, the day of prayer.[1]

In a last, desperate effort Joset had parleyed before the battle with the American commander, but his attempts to change the course of events were useless. After he raced back to a position behind the Indians' lines, the firing, directed at the rear guard, began with sporadic shots followed by a volley.

As these tragic events gained momentum, the troops took to the hills on the east, keeping their formation and covering their pack train at considerable risk to their own lives. Many animals were shot. The advance soon became a scramble for favorable positions on the hills, while the Indians, clinging as firmly as leeches to the backs of their ponies, darted in and out like gnats on a windless day. After losing two of his officers, Steptoe ordered his command to occupy an eminence on which they could take a stand. It was like being treed by a pack of angry wolves, but there seemed to be no other course for survival. There, lying in the tall grass which partially concealed them, they formed a perimeter on the hill, an island of safety as long as their supplies lasted. No one doubted what would happen after that: torture by frenzied Indians, who would take out their frustrations on their captives.

When night fell, the campfires of the Indians encircled the besieged. There were many celebrations beside these fires, and though one of the Yakima chiefs, Kamiakin, had expressed a warning that their prey might escape in the darkness, no one took him seriously.

The American command, Joset wrote later, was surrounded "by an army of ferocious beasts, hungry after their prey, of Indians sufficiently numerous to relieve each other, and who had always means of procuring fresh horses. It appeared impossible that the troops could escape."[2]

Desperate in their plight, the Americans decided to attempt an escape under cover of darkness, their only ally. A party of scouts sent down the hill to the south found a corridor between the enemy lines, and as soon as they reported this to Steptoe, preparations for the flight were made. Cannons were spiked and cached. The hooves of horses, silenced; and light-colored horses, blanketed. After the dead were decently buried, horses were led over the ground to conceal their graves. Fifteen wounded men were mounted and lashed to their saddles. All extra animals were picketed, the supplies, abandoned. Then, in dark-ness, all crept furtively away from their lofty prison, descending the hill in breathless silence. Filing cautiously through the complacent, triumphant Indians, they slipped away into the night. By midnight, when their absence was discovered, it was too late to overtake them.

Known as the Steptoe Disaster, this humiliating defeat for the United States Army had far-reaching repercussions. Settlers, scattered over the entire frontier and conscious of their fragile defense, trembled with fear and joined in hushed meetings to plan their flight or to make preparations to take a stand. Two generals responded to the call for help: first, Gen. Newman S. Clarke, who arrived from San Francisco almost immediately, and later Gen. William S. Harney, who was engaged in a campaign to extricate federal troops in Utah from Morman entrapment. One member of Harney's entourage was Father De Smet who was chaplain, or more accurately, peacemaker.

Skirmishes between the Indians and troops, usually called battles by the War Depart-ment—though no one ever got hurt—lasted all summer. Both Congiato and Joset spent these months riding hither and yon, gathering their recalcitrant neophytes and negotiating with Clarke and his assistant, Col. George Wright, who had few scruples when it came to punishing Indians. The latter, it was clear, had lost the "rebellion" so they were rebels all of them, and Wright often taunted them, boasting that he could hang them all as traitors.

He first threatened the Spokanes with extermination. One Spokane suspected of mur-der was tried, found guilty, and hanged on the same day. Wright's troops captured eight hundred of the Indians' horses and corralled them along the Spokane River near the Coeur d'Alene's tribal border. Wright then detailed two companies to shoot them all, "except one hundred which were retained for Army use." This bloody task took two days to complete. After the noise of the shooting no longer echoed through the hills to the south, the Spokane River was so glutted with carcasses that the tainted water spread beyond its banks. Wright's troops also destroyed the Indians' caches of wheat, vegetables, and camas, their only winter food supply, leaving even many innocent women and children in the state of near starvation. As an Indian nation, the Spokanes were ruined.

While this inhumane strategy was being carried out, a message from Joset arrived, requesting Wright's presence at the mission. The Coeur d'Alenes wanted peace. Most of them were in hiding and it took much urging by Chief Vincent, Joset, and Congiato to bring them back. In a council in the Jesuit's cabin on September 17, Joset served as interpre-ter and peacemaker. The Indians acknowledged their guilt and agreed to the demands of the government, which were twofold: the surrender of the men who started the attack on Steptoe, and the giving of hostages. Doubtlessly due to the entreaties of the Jesuits, no Coeur d'Alenes were executed. A peace treaty was signed between the Indians and the United States. Then a group of Indians, very much relieved by their escape from the hangman's noose, accompanied Wright and his detachment to the river where they ferried them across on their canoes and scows.[3]

Wright was not so easily pacified regarding other tribes. In his report for September 24, he wrote, "Qualchan [a Yakima outlaw] came to me at 9:00 and at 9:15 he was hung." On the following day, September 25, many Palouse Indians entered Wright's camp to declare their rejection of Kamiakin, who was also on the government's wanted list. Wright arrested fifteen of these Palouses, hanged six on the spot and took the others along with him in irons.

Threatening the Palouses with extermination, Wright demanded the surrender of six others who had captured army cattle. The six were turned in. While the colonel continued his *peace talks* with the rest of the Indians, three of these and another Indian who was accused of murder were hanged on a nearby tree. The victims were swinging in the breeze while the conference proceeded. Afterwards the usual quota of hostages was taken from the Palouses: one chief and four men with their families.

General Harney had come mostly to bring peace, not reprisals. He arrived in late October and took up his residence as the new commandant of Fort Vancouver, which included under his jurisdiction all of the Northwest. Influenced by De Smet, he favored leniency toward the Indians and he encouraged the priest to visit the tribes to comfort and reassure them.

The Indians, it was said, "were vanquished but not reconciled." Scattered and humiliated by their stunning defeat, they needed someone like De Smet to help them recover horses, food, their self-respect, and—above all—their confidence in the missionaries. De Smet, an incurable romanticist in some respects, was also a realist about "the insurmountable barriers between the two races." Unlike others who were in a state of shock following the *rebellion,* he was ready psychologically to accept the consequences and to face the Indians honestly. He was also prepared to accept the Indians as equals despite their historic failures to conform to the white man's life-style, and despite their inability to cope with a dominant culture that was destroying them. In the end it was De Smet's strength that the Indians needed, a strong man who would not scold them nor remind them of their deficiencies.

De Smet left Fort Vancouver on October 29; at Walla Walla he met the hostages who had been taken two months earlier. Well-fed by their standards, but unhappy, they proved the old adage that not even honey tastes sweet in captivity. De Smet requested their release. Impossible, the colonel said. Using his influence with Harney, De Smet soon arranged for their freedom and they set out with him as companions and guides "happy as souls escaping from Limbo."

They traveled first to Sacred Heart Mission where De Smet was welcomed with great bursts of enthusiasm. Wherever he went he was greeted as the greatest hero in the lives of his admirers. For the Indians, his presence was like the presence of the pope; indeed, for them he was the pope.

There was something mysterious about all this, a Jesuit priest who could do more to restore peace in the country than the military power of the United States. Hoecken, Joset, Huet, Magri, and other Jesuits lived among the Indians, learned their language and gained their respect, even their love. But all these lacked the mystique that De Smet conveyed to almost all Indians everywhere, including the non-Christians. De Smet had never lived with Indians for any length of time, though he traveled often with them. He had never learned their language. But they were bound to him, and he to them, by bonds that could never be explained. One might say that De Smet, coming and going from far, exotic places, presented the image of some mysterious guru who had dropped from heaven. Deeper than this was his love and loyalty that showed through his aging, peasant-like face.

He remained with the Coeur d'Alenes until mid-February, then despite the bitterness of an uncommonly severe winter, he set off with guides for St. Ignatius, the apple of his eye. His journey thence, he reported, was perilous, which it doubtlessly was, though De Smet in his writings used *perilous* as often as any adjective. He went up the Clark Fork in a frail canoe, skirting ice along the shores and bucking the dangerous current of the angry winter waters. He arrived at last in Mission Valley as excited with his welcome as though it were his first. Many Kootenais appeared a short time later, having walked through deep snow for days to come and shake De Smet's hand. The Flatheads from old St. Mary's came also, filled with regrets and strong words for the return of the missionaries. The old Flatheads deplored the blindness of the tribe and described how their chief had traversed the whole country of Oregon in search of Father Mengarini, who was not there.

On April 16, De Smet left St. Ignatius with nine prominent chiefs from various tribes of the interior to visit Gen. Harney at Fort Vancouver. His objective was to demonstrate the futility of Indian resistance to the Whites by displaying the power of the white man. During the journey a photograph of the chiefs with De Smet was taken by a pioneer photographer from the village of Portland across the river. This became a poignant testament to the late confrontations between the two cultures.* The visit convinced the Indians that additional military action against the Whites was useless. All thought of pursuing the war was rejected and an uneasy peace descended upon the plateau. Other clashes in the process of painful adjustment were inevitable, but thanks to De Smet and, later, other Jesuits, most people on the frontier were able to follow an orderly path without being threatened with widespread violence between the Indian and his conquerors.†

On June 15, De Smet departed from Vancouver with the chiefs to return to the mountains. At St. Ignatius he learned that Father Hoecken and Brother Magri had left the mission for an expedition to the Blackfeet, where, it was hoped, a mission could be built before the snow fell. De Smet was requested to visit these people to renew his friendships there and to confirm their recent good behavior and thus prepare the way for Hoecken. Accompanied by Congiato, De Smet, with six horses and several guides, passed through Blackfeet territory, dispensing handshakes, many blessings, and religious medals, especially crosses. From Father Point's time, De Smet had noted, the Blackfeet had a special veneration for the cross and it was said that any White in danger of being attacked by the Blackfeet would be spared if he made the sign of the cross.[4] The Black Robes who carried crosses on their rosaries were particularly safe now with the southern Blackfeet, or more properly the Piegans, though the northern Blackfeet continued to be a deadly threat.

Congiato and De Smet parted at Fort Benton. A small skiff was built, three rowers and a pilot were engaged, and on August 5 the greatest Black Robe of them all embarked on the Missouri River for St. Louis.[5]

The new mission for the Blackfeet was established finally on the Teton River near present Choteau, Montana in the autumn of 1859. Congiato hailed the event with an uncharacteristic compliment to the missions. Perhaps his exposure to the interior in the company of Joset and De Smet had mellowed, or influenced, him. "This takes the missions," he said, "out of the stationary condition in which they have been for ten years and opens up a vast field for the salvation of souls."[6] Built by Hoecken with the aid of Brother Magri, this new mission consisted of three squat log cabins, hastily assembled to provide winter quarters for the two Jesuits and a haven for the study of Blackfeet nouns and verbs. It lasted only five months, a record for its brevity even in the early period when it was not uncommon for a mission to be moved several times.[7] Today a rocky promontory but a short distance from Choteau bears the name Priest's Butte, a lasting reminder, if not an elegant one, to recall the mission's existence in that foreboding wilderness.

The mission was moved, it was said, because there was an Indian burial ground near the rocky butte. Frequently mourners gathered here, as was the custom, and there followed an uncommonly loud chorus of lamentation, which disturbed even the unflappable Father Hoecken.

*OPA original photograph. Several versions of this photograph appear, one of which is so basically doctored up to impress benefactors one would assume that the Indian chiefs had been fitted with suits in a fashionable haberdashery.

†Wars broke out several times after De Smet's death. Only one of these which took place on the plateau was a major event. This was the Nez Perce War of 1877.

72

Another Jesuit had joined the two before their departure—Father John Baptist Camillus Imoda, who had a list of talents as long as his name. Only thirty years old, he had come from Turin, Italy, by way of Cape Horn and California, escaping somehow the snares laid for him in the latter.[8] His brother was for a time the superior of the California mission. Imoda, who soon became proficient in the Blackfeet language, indicating his yen for languages, also enjoyed a practical joke, like certain Jesuits of our own generation, Frank Duffy and Gordon Toner. He was known among his colleagues to be a gentleman of refinement and good humor.

This second Blackfeet mission called St. Peter's was built on the banks of the Sun River near the site later occupied by the army and called Fort Shaw. During March, 1860, a couple of cabins were constructed. The study of Blackfeet was undertaken again with fervor and determination, and wandering Indians were instructed and many children, baptized. After five months this mission, too, was closed. Congiato on August 9 ordered a suspension of further developments there for reasons that not even Palladino could learn. Imoda and Magri were ordered to St. Ignatius; and Hoecken, who had served the Rocky Mountain Mission with distinction for sixteen years, was directed to return to the Missouri Province.*

Further progress on the Blackfeet Mission appeared to be hopeless, mostly for lack of Jesuits. Many new priests were arriving from Europe, but California was swallowing them up like grapes in September.

Then almost like a miracle another Jesuit, with a charisma like De Smet's, arrived on the scene. Father Joseph Giorda, former seminary professor and brilliant intellectual, aged thirty-eight, first appeared at Sacred Heart Mission in the autumn of 1861. Congiato assigned him to the Blackfeet mission at once. With Imoda and a new brother, Francis De Kock, he took up his residence at Fort Benton, spending the winter there with the traders and local Indians, and seeking, when time allowed, a suitable location for a permanent foundation.

They arrived at Fort Benton on October 25 and by late winter agreed to build on a site on the Marias River. Several chiefs, however, objected to this, tactfully explaining that a mission there would drive the game away from the best of buffalo ranges. At this point Menetrey joined Giorda and these two continued the search.

"Finally," says Palladino, "they struck a place alone the north bank of the Missouri, some six miles above the mouth of the Sun River, which seemed to answer every purpose. There the new mission was located on February 14, and received the name of St. Peter. Cabins were soon constructed; a number of Indians came around and, taking up places to their liking, pitched their tepees here and there in the vicinity."[9]

Father Giorda was on hand to supervise the details of construction. Not an ordinary man in any sense, he presented the silent reposeful appearance of a scholar rather than energetic frontiersman. He spoke a soft, broken English that sounded more Italian than Anglo-Saxon. The Indians came to call him *Mil'Kokan*, which means "Round Head," for despite Palladino's defense that "he was a remarkably square-headed man," his facial features were the shape of a pie. Under a high forehead and bushy eyebrows his dark eyes were set far apart. Oddly, his mouth tended to curve down, giving the impression that perhaps he could be very stubborn. Unlike the Puritan fanatics of English history who were called Round Heads, Giorda was as meek and gentle as Francis De Sales. He was an uncommonly tolerant man and as he became accustomed to his adopted land he threw his enormous energies into a quiet, orderly service of both Indians and Whites, wherever he found them.

---

*Father Adrian Hoecken was assigned to St. Gall Church in Milwaukee where he died peacefully on Easter Monday, April 19, 1897, at the age of 82.

SECOND START

There were five Jesuits at St. Peter's now, Giorda with Imoda and Menetrey and the two brothers, Francis De Kock and Lucian D'Agostino. Giorda kept a sharp eye on his subjects. It was not that he lacked confidence in any of them—they were his spiritual sons, his responsibility. They lived in great danger, from the northern Blackfeet who swooped down from Canada, as well as from other roving bands of Indians who despised the invading white men and regarded the Jesuits as such. How long would St. Peter's on the Missouri last? Giorda could not even guess, but he knew the mission's fate was precarious.

A few days after their arrival on this sharp bow in the river, still anxious about the safety of his men, Giorda ventured across the ice on the river. If this were a foolish thing to do in the month of February, he did not realize it. He was merely interested in examining the new mission's surroundings, the lay of the land. Though a stocky man, he was not heavy, and the already softening ice bore his weight until he moved so far out that the current was strong beneath the ice. Quite suddenly he felt the ice give way. Just a small portion broke off and he instinctively extended his arms so that he sank no lower than his arm pits. There he was, in a most undignified position for a superior, clinging to the ice with his hands, his feet carried up to the surface of the ice by the swift current. The two brothers heard his shouts for help, and an Indian, who had pitched his tepee near the new mission, saw the situation and hurried for his lariat. While the brothers experimented with the ice that broke at every step, the redskin skillfully cast his rope around Giorda's shoulders and dragged him to safety.

Realizing that after God he owed his life to this Blackfeet Indian, Giorda there and then made a solemn vow to devote the rest of his life to the salvation of these Indians, should his superiors approve of his doing so. To the best of his ability he kept this vow.

Palladino relates another account of Giorda's introduction to the Wild West: "Scarcely a couple of weeks after his narrow escape from drowning, the same Father met with another experience no less trying, though of an entirely different kind. About the close of the same month, February, 1862, he set out with his interpreter to visit the Gros Ventres, and fell in with a war party belonging to the camp of Bull Lodge, one of the chiefs of the tribe. Both he and his companion were made prisoners, but the latter managed, somehow, to escape. The marauders took from the missioner his mount and packhorse, provisions and all, and not content with this, they stripped him of the clothes on his back, to his very undergarments. Having relieved him of the cassock, the red flannel shirt he wore caught their fancy, and this, too, he had to surrender to his captors. No sooner had one of the band gotton it, than he put it on himself; but he was considerate enough to offer his own habiliment, a vermin-infested something without a name, in exchange. It is stated that the thermometer at the fort marked at this time forty degrees below zero; and how under such conditions, Father Giorda did not perish with cold is truly remarkable.

"He managed, however, to make his way into the presence of Bull Lodge, who handed him a buffalo skin for a covering. The chief could hardly believe that he who stood naked before him and half frozen was a Black Robe. Not long after, horses, saddle, and some personal effects—namely, breviary, cassock, and a pair of blankets—were returned to the missionary, but he was not permitted to remain in camp."[10]

Every story should have a moral. At least this one does. Palladino triumphantly reports that the leader of the war party who ill-treated Giorda, "died as he had lived, like a devil."[11]

More edifying perhaps is that Giorda appealed to officials in Fort Benton on behalf of the rowdies who had mugged him. Though he earnestly requested that the matter be overlooked, there is no indication that his appeal was honored.

Gradually the new mission of St. Peter's took shape. Built of cottonwood logs with the bark still in place, the structure consisted of a series of seven rooms, mostly twelve feet by

74

sixteen feet, in the form of an "incipient rectangle," with a porch five feet wide along the whole length. Its poverty was appalling, simply seven, dark, smoky cabins with ceilings seven-and-one-half feet high, earthen floors, ill-furnished, ill-supplied with food, and ill-supplied with medicines. Even clothing was lacking and these missionaries, accustomed as they were to the refinements of their native Europe, were required to wear not only buckskin trousers and shirts but buckskin underclothing as well; and if this were not bad enough, it was worse keeping lice from making a home of their buckskin clothing or starving wolves from devouring it, should any of it be put out into the cold to freeze the lice out. When, thanks to a thoughtful benefactor, they were provided with conventional clothes, curious Indians lurked about, eager to steal them.

The passage of time did not diminish St. Peter's problems but rather increased them. During the winter of 1865 a gold stampede attracted vast numbers of miners into the Sun River area. This stirred and fanned glowing embers of Indian hatred for the Whites. The subsequent tension on the frontier prompted Giorda to prepare a new mission site in the Little Belt Mountains near the Indian landmark called Bird Tail Rock. He dispatched the brothers to erect buildings on this location, and during the early spring of 1866 the new mission of St. Peter's took shape.

During this period Giorda was appointed general superior of the Rocky Mountain Mission, succeeding Congiato, on January 21, 1862. At that time, he had exactly fifteen subjects in the entire mission, not more than a corporal's guard, while his counterpart in California claimed fifty-five, almost four times as many. One of Giorda's first projects as general superior was a trip to California to recall to the mountains the Jesuits who had been "borrowed" for California's colleges. He managed to recover five Jesuits, including Father Anthony Ravalli, who had been Master of Novices at Santa Clara. With his reinforcements, Giorda was able to inaugurate a renaissance of the Rocky Mountain Mission which earned for him the time honored title of Second Founder of the Mission.

Giorda served as general superior of the mission from 1862 until 1877, except for a three-year interval of poor health, 1866–69, during which time Father Urban Grassi was vice-superior. Thus the rebirth of the Rocky Mountain Mission occurred during two periods, 1863 to 1866 and 1869 to 1877 and it involved three steps in its progress: the establishment of a ministry to the white settlers; the re-opening of Indian missions that had been closed; and finally, the opening of new missions for Indians. Giorda's successor, Father Joseph Cataldo, followed the same policies, extending them somewhat to place new stress on schools for both Indians and Whites.

It will be recalled that among the western immigrants a large proportion were Catholics. The earliest of these were French Canadians who had retired from the service of the fur companies. These occupied the Willamette Valley and other parts of western Oregon and Washington. In the gold rush in California, as previously noted, the area, originally Catholic in character because of its identity with Spain, attracted large numbers of people of foreign origin, at least half of whom were Catholic. Now in the interior of the Northwest a new Catholic migration was occurring. This began in Ireland with the potato famine that was coextensive chronologically with the Indian Wars and the American Civil War. A large number of soldiers of Irish descent acquired American citizenship in the United States Army, many of whom served in the west and settled there when their martial duties were terminated. Thus in areas like Walla Walla and Colville there were among the settlers a highly disproportionate number of Irish ex-soldiers who sought the benefits of a resident priest. One should add to these a large number of other Catholic immigrants, many of them from the gold diggings in California, who swarmed into the mining camps of eastern Washington, Idaho, and Montana during the 1860s when Giorda was superior.

At first Giorda was the Solomon who offered to split in half the number of his Jesuits who would work on either side of the road, with either the Indians or the Whites. He gradually produced a compromise without antagonizing either group though it must be admitted that later Cataldo reaped an unsavory harvest that followed in the wake of this delicately balanced policy. Perhaps the principal difference in the degree of acceptance of policy could be attributed to the personalities of these two men. Giorda, who was suave and gentle, could induce his own horse to eat sawdust, judging it to be oats. Cataldo, as shall be seen, was autocratic, a demanding man who was hard on himself but also hard on everybody else.

The mission of St. Paul on the Columbia had been closed temporarily by Congiato in 1858. In the following year a group of soldiers at Fort Colville began to build a church at Pinkney City for Whites principally, with the approval of Father Joset, who visited St. Paul's periodically from the Coeur d'Alene Mission. Pinkney City at this time, a small village near the fort, was regarded as the seat of non-military authority for the interior; for example, one obtained a license to marry at the territorial office there. It was perhaps a logical place for a church, given the limited vision of its promoters, but when the village disintegrated as the town of Colville prospered, the soldier's church disintegrated also. Called the Church of the Immaculate Conception, it was opened for services in October 1862, the first of Jesuit parishes for Whites in the entire interior of the Northwest. In the years to follow there would be many more.

Giorda had decided to send a full-time pastor to this parish and to reopen St. Paul's Mission. In the autumn of 1863 he sent Joset to St. Paul's, and Menetrey to Pinkney City.[12] A new spirit was sweeping the Rocky Mountain Mission at this time, and with it there quite suddenly appeared a new stream of missionaries from Europe: Urban Grassi from Italy, via California where he had taught for six years; Joseph Caruana from Malta; later, Joseph Cataldo from Sicily, via California where they tried to keep him "to protect his fragile health;" and Lawrence Palladino, from Italy, also via California where he had taught for three years. One might call this the second wave of missionaries. A third and longer one came during the 1870s and early 1880s, confirming the view that "God usually provides what we deserve."

As additional Jesuits were available Giorda moved about the area like the Vigilantes, who suddenly appeared everywhere in search of the lost sheep, with different intent, however. In the spring of 1863 he showed up in Cottonwood [later called Deer Lodge] and performed baptisms. He was at Alder Gulch for Easter, then at Silver Bow, and elsewhere as eager to bring the sacraments to the scattered settlers as he was to serve the Indians, for whom he had come across the sea.

He had assigned Father Grassi to St. Ignatius Mission. Born in Girola, a small village in Italy in 1830, Grassi came to America as a young Jesuit in 1853 and to Rocky Mountain Mission in 1861. In the course of time he became the trusted trouble-shooter, the man for all times and all jobs, however disagreeable or difficult.

It will be remembered that when the Jesuits arrived in 1841 to establish St. Mary's Mission they passed first through "The Gate of Hell," or Hell's Gate, at the north end of the Bitterroot Valley. Lewis and Clark had camped near the entrance on July 4, 1805, as they noted in their journals.[13] A little creek, presently called The Rattlesnake, flows into the Missoula River nearby and the two discoverers slaked their thirst in either one, for both were mountain cold. The Indian word for the spot *Lm-i-sul-a* pronounced something like Missoula, means "beside the chilling waters," which some interpret as a reference to the site by the rivers. But others say this is an Indian metaphor meaning "by the fearful waters," a reference no doubt to those devilish Blackfeet who lurked beyond the Gate of Hell.[14]

Early Jesuits often had passed through the Gate. They had camped there and dipped water from the same streams that Lewis and Clark had used before them. When the Mullan Road was finally built from Fort Walla Walla to Fort Benton, it passed right through the Gate and up the canyon road toward buffalo country, where two small settlements developed. One was about five miles west of the Gate, taking its name from the ominous landmark. The other, fourteen miles farther west, at the far end of a level bed of some prehistoric lake, became known as Frenchtown for the obvious reason that many French Canadians settled there.

The mission road from old St. Mary's to St. Ignatius, running more or less south to north, struck evenly between the settlements, making the distance equally one day's ride from either place to St. Ignatius. Both settlements, which were the first in Montana, frequently served as hosts for priests on their travels.

Father Grassi decided to build a little church at Hell's Gate, since it was easier for a priest to go there than for all the people to come to St. Ignatius. Accordingly he purchased from one of the Whites there a piece of land on the brow of the north bank of the river. During the summer of 1863, he sent Brother Claessens to build a church on the site. A skilled carpenter, brother did his job well. He set up a church of hewn logs, and Grassi came to give it a name. He called it St. Michael's which was very appropriate since it guarded the Gate of Hell from the outside. What is perhaps more significant is that this was the first church for Whites in the state of Montana, the beginning of a religious epic.

The residents of Hell's Gate were naturally quite pleased with their log church, but now people in Frenchtown began to complain that it was too far to Hell's Gate for church. When could Brother Claessens build them a log church?

Father Grassi was an understanding man, so he patiently considered the situation, deciding at length to do as they asked. In 1864 he bought another piece of land at Frenchtown on the elevated plateau, a little northeast of town. Brother constructed a church of hewn logs like the first, and Menetrey, who had been a companion for him, said the first Mass in it. They called it St. Louis because this saint was a very holy French king whom the trappers would do well to imitate. More specifically, perhaps, this saint was chosen rather than another because Louis Brun, or *Brown* was the first settler in the area, and though he was not ready for canonization he was a good man who supported the Church.[15] The French Canadians now liked their little church better than St. Michael's and it was very pretty on the little plateau above the valley against the smoke-blue mountains.

At first neither church had a resident priest, but when St. Peter's Mission was closed in 1866, Fathers Ravalli and Imoda were assigned to Hell's Gate. Their pact was duly recorded in the St. Peter's records and a waggish Jesuit, as sometimes happens, felt compelled to write a commentary below the entry. He wrote: "A porta inferi erue, Domine, animas eorum," which means, "From the gate of Hell, O Lord, deliver their souls!"

The prayer was apparently heard in the case of Imoda for he was scarcely a week at Hell's Gate when he was recalled and sent to Helena. This left Ravalli who may be rightly given the credit for being that region's first resident missionary. He spent three years at Hell's Gate serving his townsmen in the double role of priest and physician. Ravalli's abode, a small log cabin near the church, was frequently turned into an infirmary where he set bones and performed minor operations. When he was not occupied at Hell's Gate he made missionary excursions to "dear old St. Mary's" and to Frenchtown.

But this was 1866. Other significant events had taken place earlier, especially in 1864 when the first sisters came to Montana. Giorda with Gazzoli had gone to meet them in Walla Walla in September of that year. The four Sisters of Providence, whose names sounded more masculine than feminine, had left their motherhouse in Montreal on June 1, and had sailed via New York and the Isthmus of Panama to Vancouver, Washington Territory. Thence they sailed by riverboat to Walla Walla, where the Jesuits met them.[16]

When Giorda was introduced to them he learned their names were as follows: Sister Mary of the Infant Jesus, Superior; Sister Mary Edward, Sister Paul Miki and Sister Remi. Sister Paul Miki, the Superior added, was very "delicate." Giorda was doubtlessly concerned, but he bluntly informed the sisters that not only would their journey be an arduous one but that after they arrived at St. Ignatius Mission their troubles would really begin. With that he informed them they would start as scheduled on the morning of the seventeenth, despite the sisters' desire of an additional day at Walla Walla. They were ready to go when he was. He made the sign of the cross and set out, leading the way.

The Jesuits had picked up another greenhorn, a young priest from the Missouri Province, Father Francis X. Kuppens, who would later attract some notice as a friend of Sitting Bull. So Kuppens took his place with Giorda at the head of the procession, the four sisters, on horseback like the priests, followed, and, bringing up the rear, there was a large prairie schooner loaded with luggage, provisions, and freight for the Coeur d'Alene Mission, all in the care of two Irishmen whose tongues were much inhibited in the presence of such holy company.

The journey lasted exactly one month. It was memorable for many adventures: for the wagon getting stuck in mud holes, for heavy rains, for one of the sisters getting a swift kick by her horse, and for their horses straying away during the night. Gazzoli hurried off in advance of the caravan, expecting to obtain boats at the Coeur d'Alene Mission and to meet the sisters on the lower end of the Coeur d'Alene Lake. But his horse, too, strayed away when he least expected it, and he had to walk two full days, arriving at the mission after a perplexed Giorda did, so tired and hungry that he might have eaten horsemeat with pleasure.

The sisters finally arrived by water. As their boats came up the river to the mission dock they were met by rows of curious Indians along the banks, all very eager to get a first glimpse of the long-expected "Lady Black Robes." After two days' rest the sisters set off for the most difficult passage over the mountains. Apparently they kept their composure and retained their sunny dispositions, for at the end of the day Giorda, overhearing their chatter, was want to say: "Birds chirping in the evening bring fair weather in the morning."

On October 15, the caravan reached Frenchtown. On Sunday, the day following, they all attended Mass in the little log church Brother Claessens had just finished, and then they left on the trail for St. Ignatius. When they camped that night Giorda had a special message, not about birds, but about crosses. "We are nearing the end of our journey," he told the sisters, "the trials and crosses you have thus far encountered and endured are not to be compared with those that await you." Many times in the years that followed, the brave sisters were to agree that Father Giorda had been a true prophet.

Their troubles began when they arrived at the government agency enroute to St. Ignatius. The agent, almighty representative of the sovereign United States Government, received them "with worse than coldest indifference." He was surly and rude, Palladino added, and they quickly left his "ungentlemanly" presence. This is strong language for pious Palladino, so the encounter, left to our imagination, must have been deplorable. By evening of the same day, exactly one month from their departure from Walla Walla, the travelers reached St. Ignatius. "When the Sisters arrived," says the chronicler, "they found all the Indians assembled to bid them welcome." If our government agent could not be a gentleman, the Indians certainly could.

While the sisters scrubbed and cooked and built a mission school, Giorda, too, kept busy, taking no time at all for a break from his tiresome life on the trail. Packing his Mass kit; his pancake flour, bacon, and beans—the staples of travel in the wilderness—and with the newcomer Father Kuppens in tow, he set out at once for St. Peter's Mission on the Missouri, about four hundred miles distant.[17] On October 30 they stopped at Silver Creek,

78

which was about twelve miles northwest of Last Chance Gulch where four miners had recently struck gold. They rode up to Jake Smith's place (Jake was a son-in-law of Buffalo Bill) and announced that evening services would be held as soon as settlers, miners, and Indians in the vicinity had gathered. The good word spread. Father Kuppens led the recitation of the Rosary and night prayers for the Whites and Giorda had evening devotions for the Indians in their own language. These were the first Catholic services in the present vicinity of Helena.

On the following morning, Kuppens said Mass for the Indians, while Giorda preached in their language. Then the latter said Mass for the Whites and preached again in half-English, half-Italian. After the ceremonies the two Jesuits continued their journey, quite blissfully unaware that history books would some day record their recently performed deeds.

Apparently they were impressed by the size and generosity of their congregations, for Giorda returned to Silver Creek within a month. After saying Masses here and there in the general area, he proceeded west, across the mountains to Deer Lodge Valley and then went on to St. Ignatius Mission where he spent the winter. Kuppens returned to Silver Creek, also about Christmastime, and while there he selected a site for a small chapel, "about a mile and a half from the town, as most miners had their cabins along the upper part of the creek." Kuppens said the first Mass in it at Eastertime, 1865. After that, priests periodically came from St. Peter's to say Mass for the approximate one hundred members of the pleased and gratified congregation.

Once during the father's absence it happened that most of the miners were absent, too, and while they were gone, certain unscrupulous persons occupied the church as though it were their own. When the miners returned there was a great hubbub. They fetched their revolvers and rifles, but before any shots were fired, Kuppens galloped up dramatically, and the show ended there. Since not many people get away with stealing churches, there was not much hope for the intruders. They were soon dislodged with Kuppen's honey words, though you may be sure the miners would have preferred to dislodge them with their own buckshot.

All this was very well, but it so happened that the diggings at Silver Creek were presently exhausted and the miners abandoned the place. The little church was ignominiously used for firewood.

But this was not the end of the trail for Kuppens. At Eastertime in 1865, after blessing the little Silver Creek Church and saying Mass in it, he had covered the whole countryside, saying Mass in Montana City, Boulder Valley, Helena, and many other uncivilized places. In Helena he said Mass in an unfinished log cabin which was located near the present intersection of State and Warren. He used this occasion to examine various sites for a permanent church in Helena and his choice fell upon a stony and somewhat desolate looking hill. Having no means or authority to acquire the site, he filed it away in his memory as a possible future development. He soon returned to St. Peter's.

After St. Peter's at Bird Tail Rock was closed in April 1866, Kuppens accompanied other Jesuits to await their new assignments. Three days after his arrival, a messenger from Gen. Thomas Meagher at Helena (who later became governor) galloped up to the mission with the urgent request that either Giorda or Kuppens come without delay for the purpose of conveying to the United States Military the Missouri site of St. Peter's. Kuppens, a hard man on a horse, raced back to Helena, a distance of two hundred miles, in less than twenty-four hours. At least that's what they say. With Meagher he then traveled to Fort Benton, then by boat to Camp Cook on the Judith River, where the military council was being held. The boat perished enroute but both Jesuit and general reached shore on their blindfolded horses, which they had had with them on the boat.

Apparently while in the company of the general, Kuppens discussed the proposed church in Helena and suggested that steps be taken to acquire the property on the hill. There is no actual record of this discussion, but Meagher, after returning from Camp Cook, either with or without Kuppen's help, staked off a piece of ground on the hill for the specific use of a Catholic church. Soon after this, a meeting of Helena Catholics took place, during which church construction was discussed. A contract was finally awarded to one John M. Sweeney "who desired the work not for the money he could make out of it, but that he might gladden his old mother's heart by building a Catholic Church."

The contract having been awarded, a committee proceeded to Catholic Hill to stake off the exact dimensions of the church. They found their way barred by a fence and when inquiries were made, the procession formed again, this time to Judge Wilkinson's home, for the fence was his. The judge listened impatiently and long enough to grasp the situation and before the speaker had finished, he snorted, "Is that all?" With an axe he demolished the fence for seventy-five feet and pausing to get his breath he said, "Now you will have free passage to your church."

The church was built where they wanted it; and besides the gladness in his mother's Irish heart, John Sweeney received $2,500 for it.

There was another well-known mining camp similar to Helena's, which became a capitol city of Montana before the latter, and this was named Virginia City. Like the strike in Last Chance Gulch, the discovery of gold on May 26, 1863, by a small party of prospectors, became a deep secret, about which everybody soon learned. Within a year uninvited placer miners took ten million pre-Civil War dollars in gold out of Alder Gulch as it was first called, and a town of ten thousand eager humans of all kinds had assembled to sieze a share. It was unthinkable that Jesuits be indifferent about all this. Father Giorda made his first appearance at Alder Gulch on October 31, 1863. He said the first Mass in the vicinity on the next morning, feast of All Saints. Apparently quite naive about the ways of mining camps, he boarded at a hastily established hotel and took his time about his spiritual business, entirely oblivious of the greatly inflated costs of living. He baptized and married and said many Masses, and the days went by quickly while the innkeeper kept strict accounts for his bill. This problem did not escape certain kind and thoughtful miners who could see how unconcerned the holy priest was. They made the rounds of their confreres, taking up gifts of gold dust for him and when they presented the little bag to him, Giorda's eyes widened innocently and he exclaimed, "I didn't come here for gold!" He thanked them most cordially but refused to take the bag of gold.

A few days later as he prepared to leave, the innkeeper, very alert no doubt, presented his bill. Giorda's eyes widened again. The bill demanded many hundreds and he had scarcely a dollar in his possession. Fortunately for everyone concerned and especially for Giorda, the miners were standing by with the bag of gold. This was one lesson Giorda learned well and he never repeated the mistake.

During the following year Father John B. Raverdy, a secular priest from Denver found his way to Virginia City. Remaining about a month, he returned whence he had come and the camp was again without a priest until Giorda rode in during early summer, 1865. More wary about his bills he did his work quickly and departed across the mountains to St. Ignatius. Having observed that the camp had ten-thousand people, many of them Catholics, he promised to send another priest; and he kept his word. Father Kuppens soon arrived. He remained several weeks and passed on to other camps where each time he started all over again in the interminable business of recovering spiritual derelicts.

At Christmastime, 1865, Giorda returned to Virginia City, with a specific plan in mind; he intended to secure property for a permanent church. After conferring with the leading Catholics in town, he purchased an old opera house and converted it into a church, calling it All Saints, which no doubt referred to the building, not to the congregation. Since the conversion had required more than holy water, Gov. Thomas Francis Meagher (who had not disappeared yet) consented to deliver a benefit lecture. Judging from historical accounts of this performance, it was attended by a huge throng who listened to eloquent allusions to "that noble and heroic missionary, our own dear Father Giorda," and applauded thunderously. Afterwards, while the glow was still on the audience, the hat was passed for the priest who bowed his head toward each donor, saying "Thank you" in broken English. They filled his box with loose gold and money; exactly how much has not been recorded.

Poor Giorda, he must have seemed a pathetic figure as he stood there, the weariness and worries of all his missionaries stamped on his wistfully smiling countenance. It had been too much for him, the endless struggle against space in his long journeys, the struggle for the bare essentials of a livelihood, and the anxiety about the safety of his men. They were so few and the needs, so many. Now the Flatheads at St. Mary's were pressing their demands for the reopening of the mission. What did one do in such circumstances?

In the early spring of the following year, March 7, 1866, when Montana's Territorial Legislature convened for the first time, its membership elected Father Giorda as its first chaplain. On the plea that he did not speak English well enough Giorda begged off, but he was installed anyway.* He appeared at subsequent sessions to start proceedings with a prayer. For the legislators it was like having a spaghetti dinner on the fourth of July.

Giorda was still in Virginia City for Holy Week, to offer the many miners an opportunity to fulfill their Easter duties. Easter that year was on April 1. When Giorda's Alleluias had all been sung and their echoes lost in the lonely mountains, a messenger from St. Peter's Mission galloped into town. His news was shocking. John Fitzgerald, the mission herder, had been murdered within sight of the mission and ten head of cattle had been killed as well. Frenzied Indians, seeking vengeance on the Jesuits for giving shelter to a squawman who had incurred their wrath, threatened the lives of everyone.[18]

Giorda reached St. Peter's on the evening of April 26, and when he had acquainted himself with all details, he wept. What about developments at Bird Tail Rock? The new St. Peter's there was almost ready. Good. The superior was greatly relieved. That night, after a sad meal, he addressed his subjects in the chapel. He spoke briefly but earnestly. Prudence, he said, demanded that their mission be abandoned. They would leave on the morrow. The next day, after Mass and breakfast, the Jesuits gathered their scanty belongings. Kneeling on the bank of the Missouri where the Indian had once rescued him, Father Giorda said a long prayer. Then with his Jesuits following him, he firmly set his face to the southwest toward Bird Tail Rock.

All arrived the same evening. The next morning the four priests said Mass and prayers for the aid of the Holy Spirit. They joined the brothers in a frugal breakfast, then heard their superior's new decision. The new St. Peter's would also have to be abandoned. With so many missions in the Northwest needing Jesuits, with countless miners pouring into the country and with innumerable requests for help coming in on all sides, the superior could not risk the loss of his men. They would have to leave St. Peter's temporarily, but they would be back. They left that morning, April 28, 1866, for St. Ignatius across the mountains.

*Ten votes were cast for Giorda and one vote each for several other candidates. *House Journal, Second Session of the Montana Legislative Assemby, Virginia City, March 5–April 13, 1866, 3d day, March 7.*

Joseph Caruana, first Jesuit among Spokanes and Yakimas.

The second St. Mary's Mission near Stevensville, Montana, built in 1868.

The interior of the second St. Mary's Mission, designed and built by Ravalli.

6

PROGRESS THROUGH ADVERSITY
1866–1876

Fatigue had seeped into Father Giorda's bones. Doubts, too, about his strength to lead his brother Jesuits had invaded his customary common-sense thinking and he longed for nothing more than an opportunity to pray in peace. He requested, at last, that he be relieved of his burdens as general superior of the mission.

It is unlikely that he knew at this time that his name had recently appeared on a *terna* to make him a bishop.[1] On February 10, 1866, Archbishop Kenrick of St. Louis dispatched a letter to Archbishop Odin of New Orleans, informing him that he had asked the Sacred Congregation of the Propaganda in Rome to erect "the territories of Idaho and Montana" into a vicariate-apostolic. He submitted the names of three Jesuits as suitable candidates for consecration as vicar apostolic: Peter De Smet, Joseph Giorda and Urban Grassi.[2] De Smet, who had got wind of the archbishop's recommendation, protested eloquently to his own superiors, and another, Father Louis Lootens of San Rafael, California, was appointed instead. It was better that way anyhow, for De Smet was too old, Giorda could not speak English without sounding like an Italian menu, and Grassi was needed desperately elsewhere.

The new vicariate of Idaho Territory was finally erected on March 3, 1868. This included all of Idaho and Montana west of the Rockies. On the same day, Pius IX established the vicariate of Montana east of the Rockies and appointed Father Augustine Ravoux of the diocese of St. Paul as the first vicar apostolic there. Ravoux declined, offering poor health as his reason. The pope accepted his refusal and deferred his plan for a vicariate in eastern Montana, which remained under the vicariate of Nebraska.[3]

Meanwhile in the late summer of 1866, Urban Grassi was appointed as vice superior of the missions to replace Giorda temporarily, a notable departure in protocol which indicated the general's unwillingness to let Giorda off the hook.[4] Giorda's last act as superior, it was said, was the re-establishment of St. Mary's Mission, and with the approval of Grassi, he assigned himself to this task, taking with him Father Ravalli and Brother Claessens, the cream of the crop. Perhaps it was his hankering for a quiet little parish in the country, a peaceful twilight after the thunderstorms of administration, the same kind of pious dreaming his successors would entertain in the years to come. In Giorda's case he would have his country parish even if he had to make one.

Menetrey had written to De Smet, "I think Father Mengarini would be pleased to learn that the Flatheads have been converted anew." He could have spared himself, for already

85

Mengarini had received at Santa Clara a delegation of Flatheads who had gone all the way to California to beg him to return. There was something reminiscent about this, and a departure from the past as well. Instead of traveling the dangerous route to St. Louis, this latest Flathead delegation seeking Black Robes experienced mostly a pleasant interlude in the embracing warmth of the Golden State.

If the Flatheads could travel that far for Mengarini, who was not available, they could accept Giorda, whose benign disposition exceeded that of his colleague. Actually they had gone south for prickly pear and had got peaches instead from a tree in their own backyard. Giorda with his companions, like late peaches, arrived in September. They found Old St. Mary's in ruins.

They built new quarters while they lived in an Indian's old cabin, near the site of the original church. Gradually with Ravalli's professional directives and Claessens's endless labors, they assembled a new church of hewn logs. Major Owens, who had paid $250 for the original St. Mary's building, kept a watchful eye on them from his trading post which had survived the ravages of time and weather. "The Jesuit Fathers," he wrote in his journal, "are putting up a Chapel near here for the use of Inds. and others who desire to hear divine service."[5]

On Wednesday, October 17, Giorda visited the Major whose honorific title had helped to gain for him a controversial reputation. Considering his origins and his business, which was somewhat in opposition to the missionaries, he was friendly to the Jesuits, especially to Giorda. The Father needed glass for windows in the new church? Owens provided them gratuitously with a patronizing flourish of his hand and Giorda invited him to the dedication Mass.

On October 28, 1866, Giorda presided over the simple ceremonies referred to as the dedication. Owens noted the event in his journal: "witnessed dedication of the New Chapel and the Solemn Ceremony of the Elevation of the Host. Father Giorda—assisted by a Lay Bro.—officiating—it truly reminds one of the preparation necessary before being called by our Great Father to leave this Terrestrial Sphere."[6]

In the course of time, Claessens built a small workshop, which still stands, several log huts for farm use, like blacksmithing, and a residence for the three Jesuits. Father Ravalli designed and built an elegant new altar, which is currently a museum piece also. He formed from plaster an almost life-size statue of St. Ignatius and dressed it in a canvas cassock, which he soaked in tar, a somber Jesuit black. Giorda acquired farm animals. Soon mission life took up where it had left off sixteen years before.

Grassi, the vice superior, continued to live at St. Ignatius, where he was also the local superior. It is significant that Grassi, like Giorda, accepted the responsibility for the care of Whites in Montana, though he himself was committed to the work of the Indian missions. In October, while Ravalli and Claessens were putting the finishing touches on the new St. Mary's, he assigned Father James Vanzina to Virginia City, and two other Jesuits, Francis Kuppens and Jerome D'Aste to build the church in Helena, where they became the first resident priests.

Perhaps the most promising of Grassi's subjects was Joseph Cataldo, who was in the process of seasoning at Sacred Heart Mission, still enjoying the exhilaration of his escape from Santa Clara, where he was warned of an early death if he dared to live in the Rocky Mountains. He had been dashing about on a horse, visiting the scattered dwellings of the mission's flock, determined to survive, despite the gloomy predictions about him. Only twenty-nine years in age he had already been a Jesuit for fourteen years, and during this relatively brief period he had experienced more bumps and bruises than most receive in a lifetime. Sent home from the Novitiate at Palermo, because his infallible doctor had declared him consumptive, he talked his way back six months later. Then he was kicked out of Palermo by Garibaldi's terrorists, was sent to Louvain where he studied theology and was finally ordained at the precocious age of twenty-five by Bishop D'Argenteau who had been an officer in Napoleon's army. Later he studied theology at Boston where he could learn English, then he went to Santa Clara and the battle over the possession of his person began. Father George Weibel commented on the situation with wry humor: "We all know of undertakers' competition when they seek possession of a corpse, but hardly ever heard of contention for the possession of a consumptive."[7]

The fact is that Cataldo had proved to be so brilliant in his *Ad Gradum* exam at Santa Clara that California Jesuits were determined to keep him there to teach scholastics philosophy. Giorda, however, would hear none of it. The general himself had assigned Cataldo to the Rocky Mountain Mission, and even if he was half dead, a half dead Jesuit was better than none at all. Early in 1865 Beckx dispatched a curt note, "very short and very dry," to the California superior to assign Cataldo to his final year of studies, called "Tertianship," and when it was completed to send him to the Rocky Mountain Mission.[8] Father Giorda traveled to Portland in the autumn of 1856 to claim his prize. With the latter in tow Giorda took the boat from Portland up the Columbia to Wallula, then the two Jesuits rode horseback to Sacred Heart Mission, stopping enroute for a brief day in Walla Walla to obtain provisions. As the days passed Cataldo's appetite for food improved until as, he said, "I was eating like a wolf;" and Giorda remarked that "he saw perfectly well, that I was affected by consumption—not passive but active."

"We were traveling by what we called in those times the Mullan Road and one day about 1:00 P.M. we emerged from the woods, into the Spokane Prairie.

"We traveled some few miles up the river, and there we found a camp of Seltis (or Seltees), the chief of the Coeur d'Alene Indians, whose mother was a Spokane. Seltees said many things about the Spokane Indians and added that the Spokane Indians should be attended by the Fathers, because several of them were well disposed towards the Catholic religion.

"I took that word in my heart, and began to think, to pray, and then to speak about the Spokane Indians."[9]

The Santa Clara Jesuits who pronounced him as good as dead when he departed, did not know much about the Northwest. They certainly knew little about the patient. If somewhat diminutive and accident prone, Cataldo was tough in spirit, a kind of Duns Scotus voluntarist who regarded his body as Brother Ass, to be disciplined and beat into submission. Even his facial features expressed great determination. His high forehead, crowned by stubborn hairs combed sideways, was overlooked easily because his intense dark Sicilian eyes and his mouth and chin, like carved marble, caught one's attention and held one in docile submission. One did not disagree lightly with Joseph Cataldo, even when he was less than three times ten years in age. Nor could one doubt his Italian origins nor his clerical status. He was never seen without his black clothes and Roman collar, which had come into general use at that time.

Cataldo arrived at the Coeur d'Alene Mission in its Golden Age. Its superior was Joseph Caruana who had come but three years earlier in his twenty-seventh year of age, tall for a Maltese and slender, with a tough, stubborn disposition like Cataldo's and a burning zeal for the Indians' salvation like De Smet's. Like most men of great zeal, he was not a relaxed man to live with, and while the Indians respected him, it is questionable whether they loved him. Cataldo, on the other hand, won both the love and respect of the Indians, if not always of his brother Jesuits.

Throughout the winter months, Cataldo struggled with Indian nouns and verbs. At Santa Clara he had taken his first lessons in Kalispel, or Salish, from Father Mengarini. He soon surpassed his companions in his ability to speak Kalispel and by the spring of 1866 he was ready to go forth and preach the gospel to the Spokanes. Caruana sent him, instead, to celebrate the Easter liturgy with Whites in Lewiston, Idaho, and to examine the possibilities of a mission among the Nez Perce.[10] It will be remembered that this was the same Easter when a worn out and sickly Father Giorda at Virginia City was summoned hastily to his Blackfeet Mission, where the herder had been murdered.

When Cataldo returned to the Coeur d'Alene Mission he requested again to be sent to the Spokanes to build a church. He was under no illusions about the difficulties he would encounter, nor about his role as a late-comer in his attempts to convert the tribe. Other Jesuits, including De Smet had long since visited the Spokanes, over a twenty-year period with only modest results.[11] Nicolas Point had been impressed, it seems, by the fervor of some of the Spokanes, and among his now immortal portraits of Indians he included a very edifying vignette of a Spokane Indian of 104 years, who had walked twenty miles through a snowstorm to seek baptism in the lodge of the Black Robe.[12]

From the Coeur d'Alene Mission, Point made occasional safaris to visit the Spokanes, despite the opposition of the tribe's head chief, Ilumhu-Spokani, who was called Spokane Garry by the Whites. Garry had been educated in a Protestant school near Winnipeg, where he developed his strong antipathy toward Catholics. This should surprise no one for it was currently fashionable to be strongly for or against Catholics, but never lukewarm. When Garry returned to his people in 1831, he taught a Presbyterian form of Protestantism, which was introduced to the Flatheads in the time of Old Ignace, but was rejected. Garry, it appears, used religion to strengthen his control over the tribe which was becoming less authority-centered because of mobility acquired with the horse, and the influence of Whites. He objected even to the presence of Protestant missionaries but curried the favor of Whites who could bolster his prestige.

Despite Garry's open hostility, Father Joset had met with the Spokanes in February 1859. As usual he used the third person to describe himself and his success:

"[He] visited three camps: one situated on the Little Spokane River, a tributary of the Spokane, one at the mouth and another at the falls of the Spokane. Everywhere he was well received, found the Indians well disposed, and baptized several. At the camps on the Little Spokane in particular, he met with a warm reception, and conceived great hopes of success among these 'People of the Creek,' as they were styled in their own tongue."[13]

Joset continued to visit the Spokanes, placing his little tent beside theirs and remaining among them for several weeks at a time.[14]

During late October, 1862, Father Giorda with Father Joseph Caruana, who had arrived on the scene that very year, visited Spokane Falls together to instruct those who were fishing there. It was Caruana's introduction to mission life, and the experience left him spiritually elated. Referring to himself in the third person, like Joset, he later wrote about it: "We remained there about one month and through Fr. Giorda's kindness, Fr. Caruana administered the Sacrament of Baptism to 17 (seventeen) Indian children and five adults at the large Indian camp situated where is now the N P Depot in Spokane City. Not a single shanty could I see then on either side of the Spokane River."* Since Spokane Falls did not exist until at least eleven years later, it is no wonder that Caruana saw no shanties.†

Apparently Caruana derived much pleasure from his work with the Spokanes. He continued to visit them from the Coeur d'Alene Mission. "I was accustomed to visit very often Peone's Prairie, where I would pitch my tent for two or three weeks at a time among

*Oregon Province Archives, Caruana Papers, "Notes on Early Missionary Labors in Spokane." The Northern Pacific Depot mentioned here was on the site presently occupied by the Burlington Northern Depot.

†Spokane Falls was actually incorporated with a city charter in 1881, but the first settlers appeared in 1873.

those Spokane Indians under the direction of their Chief Baptiste Peone whom I baptized in 1864 along with his wife, children and others."[15]

During that same year, 1864, Caruana built "a kind of shanty" on Peone Prairie, the first Catholic house of worship in the Spokane area. This rustic hut was hastily assembled and soon abandoned. The opposition expressed by Garry had become more intimidating to the Upper Spokanes where Peone was chief, and the Jesuits were unable to establish a permanent residence.

In the summer of 1866 Caruana relented and agreed to Cataldo's proposal for an expedition to the Spokanes. With the assistance of an Indian guide, Cataldo began to make preparations. Then Father Paschal Tosi appeared and he, too, wanted to go. Caruana objected to this, saying that it would not be proper since Tosi did not know the Indian language. A short time later Grassi arrived and Tosi applied to him for the required permission. Cataldo recorded Grassi's response: "Fr. Grassi, our General-Vice Superior (instead of Fr. Giorda who was sick), came to visit us at Coeur d'Alene Mission. Fr. Tosi applied to him for permission to accompany me, and Fr. Grassi asked me whether Fr. Tosi knew much of the Indian language. I answered that he knew a great many words, and could teach the first three chapters of the Catechism. Very well, said Fr. Grassi, let him go, and we'll call him the Father of the Three Chapters. So we started both Fathers with our Indian companion from the Coeur d'Alene Mission to go down to Spokane."[16]

The Father of the Three Chapters, Cataldo, and their Indian guide took the Mullan Road to the west, forded the Spokane River near the present St. Joseph's Children's Home, and rode downriver to the north side of the falls where the Indians were encamped. Both Coeur d'Alenes and Spokanes were there and the latter urged Cataldo to spend the winter with them.

Promising to do this if he were permitted, Cataldo explained that he had been given orders to return to the mission before snowstorms closed the mountain passes. When he and Tosi returned to the mission in late autumn Grassi was there again. He listened to Cataldo's report on the Spokanes and said: "Very well, go."

The Upper Spokanes, camping on Peone Prairie north of the present city, welcomed him warmly, but they became vague and defensive when Cataldo urged the building of a permanent mission. They were worried about Garry, who was away on a buffalo hunt. At last the Indians agreed to help Cataldo build a mission and the latter agreed to burn it down if Garry objected to it when he returned. Shouldering an axe, Cataldo led the way to a grove of bull pines where he felled the first tree while the Indians watched him, their dark eyes expressionless, their faces like stone. They soon joined him in his labors, however, and in a few days a log cabin measuring eighteen feet by twenty feet was roofed over with poles and mud. "Then we built a little fireplace with sticks and mud," Cataldo boasted. On December 8, he blessed it in honor of St. Michael and offered the first Mass in it. This mission was located on the southwest perimeter of Peone Prairie, about one hundred yards from the Treaty Tree, which still stands.*

On March 4, 1867, Cataldo received word from Caruana that he was to return to the mission. Before his departure he spoke to Chief Peone and the Spokanes, who now called him S'Chiluisse, "Dried Salmon," because he was so lean from the hardships of his winter. "I had to promise," he told them, "that after 3 or 4 months, when I should leave we would destroy the house. . . . So now let me go and you burn the house."

---

*According to an ancient tradition, the Spokanes smoked the pipe of peace under this tree, pledging their friendship for Whites. "For more than two decades a white flag of truce was flown from the topmost branches of the treaty tree—a clause in the deed to the ranch now on file at the Courthouse stipulates that no hand of man shall harm the treaty tree." *Spokane Chronicle,* January 19, 1923.

"No," said Peone, "We are not going to burn the house. We want the church to remain for good, until we build a better one."[17]

The snow was still deep in the passes and Cataldo had to cross them on snowshoes. The Indians had told him it had snowed for two days and left the trail impassable. Some miles out they left the trail and took to Coeur d'Alene Lake, which was solidly frozen. Cataldo fell and in falling struck his head so violently on the ice that he lost consciousness. "Tagog!" said the two companions, "He is dead." In a few minutes he opened his eyes and quietly replied, "Lut tagog," "He is not dead." When he finally arrived at the mission, justifiably proud of his achievement, he was assured by Caruana that he could return to the Spokanes for Easter.[18] He did return, but he was recalled soon and was ordered to Montana, whereby hangs a tale and a new name for "Dried Salmon."

It will be remembered that this had been a very hard winter throughout the plateau. The route to St. Ignatius was still closed when Cataldo returned to Sacred Heart Mission, so he waited for the spring thaw to open up the mountain passes. While he waited, a hunting party of Colville Indians on their way to the buffalo range arrived at the mission, and with them was Father Leopold Van Gorp, *Kutenalko*, or "Tall-Man," who had orders, like himself, to report to St. Ignatius. Cataldo eagerly joined Tall-Man and the Colvilles. While they were passing through the panhandle of Idaho an Indian appeared and asked for a priest to accompany him to a dying man. Cataldo offered himself and rode off into the forests with the stranger. When he returned he was limping due to a fall from his horse, and the Indians immediately changed his name to *Kaoushin*, "Broken Leg," which stayed with him only until his Indians had reason to change it again.*

The journey to St. Ignatius required seventeen difficult days. When the two Jesuits finally arrived there they learned that Cataldo had been sent by mistake. The superior, Father Grassi, was there, however, and Cataldo had an opportunity to plead the cause of the Spokanes. Grassi promised to send a priest to St. Michael's every winter.

Grassi kept his promise. First he sent Father Joseph Bandini, a recent arrival who was at this time very frail. Bandini was more interested in learning Indian languages than in anything else. Although later Bandini changed and became almost an ordained cowboy who was capable of breaking in more wild horses than most Indians, he did not last long at St. Michael's because he was too timid. Within a few weeks he was replaced by Tosi, the Father of the Three Chapters, who could by this time teach the whole book.

As the number of Grassi's subjects increased—he had twenty-five by late 1867—he spent more time in administration, using Helena as a residence part of the time and moving about frequently, as fiercely dedicated to directing and admonishing his Jesuits as he had been in everything else. He hastily wrote letters, when required, in a tiny script to save paper, no doubt, often using three languages in the same dispatch. He usually began in English then lapsed into Italian and Latin as the spirit moved him.

Grassi was left-handed, a characteristic not overlooked by the Indians who called him *Chizikne*, meaning "Lefty." He also had a booming voice, which proved to be useful when he was hallooing in the forests.[19] He feared nothing and when need arose he could do as much physical work as any frontiersman. Short in stature like most Italians, he presented a square jaw like Giorda's, but he had more hair. When he wore one of those old style hats that came down over one's ears, his thick straight hair extended beneath the rim.†

---

*Cataldo's leg on this occasion was not broken, but within a year he was to earn this new name. George J. Weibel, S.J., *Rev. Joseph M. Cataldo, S.J., A Short Sketch of a Wonderful Career*, p. 11.

†Details of Grassi's appearance have been taken from an interview with Ignatius Dumbeck, S.J. on May 9, 1981. Father Dumbeck did not know Grassi, who was dead before the narrator's birth, but older missionaries pointed out to him Grassi's portrait in a group photograph fifty years ago.

He was much concerned with even the smallest details in management. From Hell's Gate on November 7, 1867, for example, he wrote to Palladino at St. Ignatius: "I received yesterday night a letter from Fr. Joset, telling me that they at Colville have no wine for Mass." Palladino, he added, should send Mass wine at once and there followed specific instructions on how to do it.[20]

A few weeks later he wrote to Palladino again: "When we do our best on anything, we have done God's will, and in this consists all perfection. I have bought a melodeon for St. Ignatius Mission. . . . I think Sisters Remi and Paul Miki know something of music, and a melodeon will give them a chance to practice."[21] Later that month he wrote to say that he had a "magnificent letter" from Tosi who had visited the Kootenais. It was so edifying that he was going to send it to the Provincial in Turin. Tosi did not have a good horse, but Grassi said there were three at St. Ignatius and "these I present him."

In the spring of 1868, taking Brother Campopiano and several workmen from St. Ignatius, he journeyed to St. Michael's in Spokane County and built a new church and residence there. Cataldo's first log church was then abandoned.[22] Built of logs, its floor was the cold ground and its furnishings, the most primitive imaginable.*

From this frontier hut, Tosi sallied forth to labor among the Spokanes, baptizing some of them that Cataldo had missed. When he was able, he tilled the rich soil, planting a garden to grow his own food. The Spokanes became very fond of him, giving him an honored name, *Kuailks-Paschal,* which simply meant "Black-Robe-Paschal." This seems to indicate that Tosi presented no warts or other oddities for a more picturesque title.

It was evident from all this that Grassi meant business. He had on his mind several more fields that needed plowing; the Nez Perce Mission especially required additional attention, and the upper Columbia had tribes of Indians who had been seeking a resident missionary for years.

Cataldo was already entrenched at Lewiston, a miner's supply center near the Nez Perce reservation, but he was experiencing opposition to his efforts, mostly government bureaucratic nonsense. Specifically he presented plans for a school for the Nez Perce. While the Indian Agent, James O'Neil, stalled, presumably for consultation with Indians, Cataldo and his companion, Brother Achilles Carfagno, cooled their heels in Lewiston, frustrated but resolute. Catholics in Lewiston, taking advantage of their presence, raised funds for a church, which was completed by the winter of 1867. This first church for Whites in all of northern Idaho eventually became the mother church of innumerable parishes throughout this region.

No progress appeared on the reservation. Chief Lawyer, a dyed-in-the-wool Protestant, who was suspect to even some of his co-religionists, had spread rumors that if the priest were allowed to teach on the reservation he would sell the Indians' land to the Whites, leaving the Indians in poverty. Thus a majority of the Nez Perce in council turned down Father Cataldo's proposal.[23] The pro-Catholic minority, however, objected to this and demanded the right to retain the services of a priest. A long dispute followed, during which O'Neil was replaced by another agent called Dr. J. Newell. The latter gave Cataldo permission for his mission; then, yielding to hostile pressures, he withdrew it. Finally he compromised by allowing Cataldo to build a log cabin off the reservation at a place called Arrow, beyond the Clearwater River and a mile above the agency. This was on the land of *Stuptupmin,* "Hair-Cut-Short."†

---

*OPA, Cataldo Papers, "Sketch of the Spokane Mission," p. 44. This second St. Michael's Church was destroyed by fire in 1908, some 20 years after the mission had been moved to a new site in a little valley east of Mount St. Michael's.

†Weibel, *Cataldo,* p. 14. Stuptupmin was not a Catholic but he had expressed the desire to become one.

Having achieved this much, Cataldo hurried back to Lewiston, and there he persuaded three miners to help him build a mission for the Nez Perce. Armed with axes instead of picks, the miners accompanied Cataldo to Hair-Cut-Short's camp where another argument with Chief Lawyer's faction threatened the mission's construction.

Cataldo took his last shot. "I will tell you," he said, "that you must consent here and now to have the cabin begun tomorrow, otherwise I'll take my horse, ride back to Lewiston this very evening, never to visit you again."[24] The ultimatum had its intended effect and all sat down "to an Indian supper."

The next morning construction began. The miners cut pine trees on a nearby island. With ox teams borrowed from the reluctant agent, the logs were dragged to the site, notched, and laid in place with frantic haste lest additional opposition be encountered. A heavy mud roof was provided for cover. In February, 1868, the first Catholic church for the Nez Perce Indians was ready for divine service.

Cataldo now had two churches—one in Lewiston called St. Stanislaus, and one at Arrow for the Nez Perce—each requiring a very different type of pastor. At Arrow, for example, he was expected to speak Nez Perce, a highly inflected language as different from Kalispel as Greek is from Swahili. Cataldo was the first Jesuit to study it and he learned it so well that he later published a translation of the New Testament in it.[25]

Father Giorda, during this period of rapid expansion of the Rocky Mountain Mission, was still at St. Mary's, reportedly convalescing but, in fact, busily engaged in restoring the Bitterroot Flatheads to their former position of first among equals. He had not hesitated on occasion to advise Grassi, nor even to use some rather strong language when St. Mary's was threatened by the proximity of the Church at Hell's Gate, a mere thirty miles distant. Giorda seemed to have his strength back, an illusion perhaps, or another case of wishful thinking by his former subjects.

Like Giorda, when he was superior, Grassi had received unrelenting orders from Rome to sell the Willamette property. For two decades the general had complained about delays. He wanted it sold, which was a little like telling his Jesuits to hold up some one at gun point. He wanted them to demand money for their land when there was free land for the taking all over the west. Father Menetrey, now classified as the procurator of the mission, was still in residence there, in effect the waste of one man who was sorely needed in Montana, where things were getting out of hand.

Grassi finally sold the land "to those Germans" who, as things turned out, were not nearly as ignorant about such matters as they first appeared to be. With his own hand, and no doubt with considerable relief, Grassi wrote out the contract conveying title to St. Francis Xavier's on the Willamette to the new owners. Since this document contains some historically significant details it is given here in full:

"This Indenture made the 26th day of September A.D. 1868 between Michael Niebler, George Niebler, Francis Niebler and Michael Schultheis of the first part, and Rev. Father U. Grassi (Superior of the Jesuits Missions in the Rocky Mountains) of the second part, Witnesseth that the said parties of the first part for and in consideration of the sum of six thousand Dollars, doth grant, bargain sell and confirm unto the said party of the second part and to his heirs and assigns, all that tract of land known as *the fathers farm* situated near St. Paul in the County of Marion, State of Oregon and bounded as follows: On the west by the Willamette river and Mullony's farm; on the East by the Catholic Church Mission land; on the North by Flinn's farm; and on the South by the Catholic Church Mission land and Mullony's farm; containing about four hundred and Sixty acres of land, together with the tinements, hereditaments and appurtenances thereunto belonging, being the same premises this day conveyed to the said, Michael Niebler, George Niebler, Francis Niebler, and Michael Schultheis by the said U. Grassi. . . ."[26]

Six thousand dollars was a lot of money in 1868. Eight dollars had to be yielded promptly to purchase federal stamps for appending to the document, as a form of tax on the transaction. Michael Schultheis, one of the purchasers, grandfather of Henry Schultheis, fifth provincial of the Oregon Province, later sold his equity to the Nieblers and homesteaded in eastern Washington Territory near the future town of Colton.[27]

This was also near Lewiston where Cataldo was still holding the fort. During Holy Week of 1869, he was called to attend to a dying woman, a "Mrs. Ryan," at Oro Fino, as it was called then, a mining camp some sixty miles east of Lewiston up the Clearwater. Enroute home, on Holy Thursday, his horse slipped on the ice and fell on its unfortunate rider, fracturing his leg badly and leaving him in a frosty wilderness, unable to move. Now in fact *Kaoushin,* he waited for help, which eventually arrived. He was brought back to Oro Fino, where two good, old Presbyterians took him into their home and cared for him with the greatest kindness for forty days.

Cataldo had missed Easter at Lewiston, much to his chagrin. Even after forty days his hosts insisted that he remain longer, but word arrived that Brother Magri, whom Tosi had brought to Lewiston in exchange for Carfagno, was greviously ill and without a priest. Cataldo hastened to Lewiston, arriving on time to administer the Last Sacraments to poor Magri, who had begun to pray for a "miracle," a priest at his deathbed. Happy with an answer to his prayers, Magri died on June 18, 1869, worn out by labor and hardships in his fifty-ninth year, his thirty-sixth as a Jesuit. What followed is recorded by Palladino, whose reputation as an accurate historian has long been honored in Montana.

"There lived at St. Ignatius an old Kalispel Indian by name, *Quilquilso'm,* which means 'White Bones,' and who most likely had been called so because of his complexion, which was as fair as a white man's. We never saw a nobler mien and a more prepossessing appearance than this venerable old Indian's. . . . He was a man of singular piety, for he measured the distance between places by the number of Rosaries he could recite in going from one to the other, and never pitched his tepee, save close to the Church, if this were possible. 'The House of Prayer' was ever uppermost in his mind. The Fathers employed him in the capacity of catechist, to lead in prayer, watch over the children at church and the like, tasks which he dearly loved to perform.

"While fishing one day at the foot of Flat Head Lake he saw an unusual sight. It burst on him all of a sudden, and as he expressed himself, it seemed to take, together with his breath, his very soul away from him. He dropped his line and hastened to the Mission. 'I saw Sinze Chitas,' he said abruptly and with great emphasis on entering the room where the writer and Father J. Bandini happened to be sitting together. He raised his eyes and both his arms toward the sky, and all aglow with animation; 'I saw him,' he continued, 'riding a most beautiful thing.'

"The only description he could give of the 'beautiful thing' in which he had seen the Brother (Magri) ride through the skies, was that it resembled a two-wheel vehicle, the like of which he had never seen before, and that it was all resplendent and of surpassing beauty."

Several days later, Palladino added, they received word of Magri's death at Lewiston, Idaho, "some four hundred miles away from St. Ignatius" at precisely the time of the vision.[28]

Magri had come to the Rocky Mountain Mission with De Smet. Now he was gone, but De Smet in his sixty-ninth year was still toiling for the benefit of his Indians, like a tired old man seeking the dream of his youth. He was almost deaf now. During the weeks of Magri's last illness he had kept to his own bed, more dead than alive. He had completed travels of more than ten thousand miles during the previous year, mostly in the west, persuading the Sioux to accept the government's invitation for a great council at Fort Rice. The council had been a success because of De Smet's intervention, but now a year later, in June, 1869, the old Black Robe had doubts about his role as peacemaker. Already broken in spirit by reports that his adopted country had been indifferent about keeping its word with Indians, he was spared, for a time at least, any knowledge of the disasters that lay in the future.

Nor did Grassi or Giorda realize how soon a fickle and discriminating government policy would destroy the choicest fruits of their labors. Sometimes one got the impression there was no government policy. Greed for land, oppression and cheating of many Indians, and a wishy-washy bureau in Washington had led most missionaries to believe that their struggle was with the Whites and the whiskey they brought rather than with the devil and the shamans or medicine men of the tribes. Government policy at this time was rooted in a kind "of revivalism, do-goodism and the idea of benevolence," which left the frontier almost defenseless for the Indians.[29] The source of this "humanistic view that influenced government policy from the beginning to the 1930s was Evangelical Protestantism, an attempt to turn them (the Indians) from their tribal allegiance to an American allegiance for their own good." Even in a perfect world this would have been unrealistic. In freedom-obsessed America it created chaos.

If Grassi accepted the prevalent spirit of Jesuit opposition to the influence of the Whites, he did not overlook the behavior of hostile Indians. Still vice-superior in the summer of 1869, he was deeply concerned about the tribes along the upper Columbia where St. Paul's had functioned almost from the beginning. With the removal of the Hudson's Bay Company, and Fort Colville scheduled for removal in the immediate future, the usefulness of St. Paul's would no longer exist.* Grassi regarded the founding of a new mission in that area as a high priority. During the summer of 1869, taking Bandini the scholar with him, he established a mission fifteen miles downstream from St. Paul's, at a place called Stlaken. This proved to be an unsuitable site and it was soon abandoned.[30]

About the same time, Grassi established another mission, which he named St. Francis Regis in recognition of the first mission by that name founded by De Smet near Chewelah. This second St. Francis was first located near Colville, about half-way between St. Paul's and Pinkney City. Grassi purchased forty acres of land from a French Canadian, Francois Lagourtre by name, and there he supervised the construction of several log cabins for the use of the missionaries. He assigned four Jesuits, including Tosi as local superior, to this new mission, revealing the sudden increment in man-power as well as the importance of this development in the mind of the vice-superior.

Grassi wrote to Tosi from Helena on August 30: "F. Joset will mind the Sjoielpi, F. Vanzina the Whites of the Valley, your portion is the Spokanes, the Kalispels and the Kootenais.

"Brother Carfagno is a splendid cook and then knows some things of the Carpenter's trade. He will help you greatly in fixing up St. Francis Regis where all the community will have its residence.

"You are still young to be made a Superior, still if you pray much for the virtue of humility you may possibly do sufficiently well."[31]

As one can judge for himself, Grassi was not given to flattery.

Thirteen days later, on September 12, 1869, Giorda, like a friendly bear returning from hibernation, again became the general superior and Grassi slipped back into his former role. He would begin a new career in central Washington that would occupy most of his remaining years.

Giorda's first crisis was the Nez Perce Mission. He was disappointed in reports he received from Cataldo regarding the Indians' lack of cooperation. While many baptisms of

---

*Fort Colville was moved in 1871. This should be distinguished from Fort Colville, the United States military base.

94

infants had been performed, there were few, if any, adult conversions. Bishop Augustine Blanchet, brother of the archbishop and a rather testy old prelate who spent too much time bickering with the Oblate missionaries, had requested Giorda to provide Jesuits for the Yakima mission. The two got along reasonably well, partly because Giorda sneezed whenever Blanchet snuffed. Giorda pondered his dilemma. Should he transfer Cataldo from the Nez Perce to the Yakima mission?

The Yakima mission, St. Rose, had experienced more ups and downs than a roller coaster. It was founded in October, 1847, the year of the Whitman Massacre, by Bishop Blanchet and the Oblate priests and seminarians from France. It was located on a barren spot where the Yakima meets the Columbia.[32] In January of the following year, Aourrhai, a Yakima chief, visited St. Rose and requested a mission among his people far to the north-west. Two Oblates, Father George Blanchet (no relation to the bishop) and Brother Celestine Verney, constructed a mission chapel on the banks of Mnassatas Creek near present-day Ellensburg.[33] They dedicated this to the Immaculate Conception, but it was usually called St. Mary's. Charles Pandosy, an Oblate seminarian ordained in 1848, was assigned to St. Mary's where he resided until the Yakima Indian War.*

During that same year, the Oblates, induced by Kamiakin, the most famous of Yakima chiefs, built a third mission at a place called Aleshecas. Completed in the spring of 1849 and dedicated to St. Joseph, this mission produced the first garden crops in the now renowned Yakima Valley.[34] Two years later the busy Oblates opened another mission called Holy Cross in the lower Attanam Valley. Finally in April, 1852, Pandosy and Father Louis d'Herbonez founded the second St. Joseph's Mission in the Yakima country on the upper Attanam Creek. This was destroyed three years later by volunteer soldiers who falsely accused the Oblates of supplying gun powder to the Indians.[35] The Oblates, escaping the fury of these soldiers, made their way to St. Paul's where they were welcomed by the Jesuits.

It should be noted that the Oblates were dedicating their many missions in central Washington while the Jesuits were closing theirs in Montana and elsewhere, and were retrenching in their Indian mission development to divert their resources into California. The Jesuits' Dark Ages were contemporaneous with the Oblates' Golden Age. Ironically the occasion of Oblate prosperity, the Yakimas, suddenly became the instrument of their destruction. If the bishop's high-handed manners and constant interference could not drive them out, the Indian wars could and did, and their departure left a huge vacuum which was promptly filled by "Father Wilbur," a rather notorious Methodist minister who was also the government-appointed Indian agent. J. H. Wilbur, it has been alleged, fortified his role as a successful agent by systematically exaggerating his accomplishments in official government reports.[36]

The Oblates diverted their resources to British Columbia. Bishop Blanchet now had Wilbur to contend with, a man he could not order about and, what is worse, a heretic, according to His Lordship, and a bigot to boot. He temporized for some years, hoping perhaps that the Oblates would change their minds, then he appealed to the Jesuits, who turned him down, protesting their lack of men.

In September, 1867, Father J. N. St. Onge, a secular priest from New York State, volunteered to take over the Yakima Mission. A saintly old man with a long, white beard remindful of pictures of St. Jerome, St. Onge left Vancouver on the lower Columbia and made his way over Satus Pass to the Yakima Valley, bringing with him "a chapel chest, carpenter tools, shoemaking tools and nine dollars." Having arrived at the site of St. Joseph's on Attanam Creek he built a temporary hut for a dwelling, then a log cabin

*During the war this mission was destroyed, but on July 18, 1856, Pandosy returned to rebuild it.

measuring sixteen by twenty-four feet for a church and residence.[37] St. Onge soon felt the need for help. In March, 1868, he returned to Vancouver and persuaded a seminarian, John Baptist Boulet, who wanted to take a break in his studies, to return with him to St. Joseph's. Lacking horses, the two men walked to the mission, carrying on their backs a small printing press and fruit trees which they set out that spring. During this same summer they opened a school for Indian children in a shed covered with branches of green trees.[38]

Though the mission was not on the reservation, St. Onge soon began to feel the adverse influence of Father Wilbur, who used his office to reward people of his own faith and to punish Catholics. Disheartened by occasional confrontations with Wilbur and Boulet's decision to return to the seminary, St. Onge appealed directly to the Jesuits to replace him. Meanwhile, on a visit to Rome for his *ad Limina* visit to the pope, Blanchet appealed to Father General. Beckx wrote to Giorda: "The Bishop implored me on his knees and I could not refuse him. Take over the Yakima Mission, even if you have to give up some other place."[39]

In the summer of 1870 Cataldo was ordered by Giorda to visit the Yakima Mission. He remained there for several weeks, returning to Sacred Heart Mission by August 28, when he and Caruana pronounced their final vows as Jesuits. Caruana left almost immediately to take up his new assignment at Attanam Creek.

St. Onge and Boulet remained at the mission until July 15, 1871. They helped Caruana with the language and introduced him to Catholic Indians. On his last day, St. Onge blessed the new St. Joseph's Church, performed a baptism, after which he and his young companion started their long journey back to Vancouver, leaving Caruana to face the bitter struggle which now developed between Father Wilbur and himself.

The law was on Wilbur's side, for in recent months the president of the United States, distinguished for his role in freeing the slaves, had signed into law Grant's Peace Policy, which, in effect, deprived Indians of their free choice of religion.* President Grant had announced the policy to Congress on December 5, 1870: "Indian agencies being civil offices, I determined to give all the agencies to such religious denominations as had heretofore established missionaries among the Indians, and perhaps to some other denominations who would undertake the work on the same terms, i.e., as missionary work."[40] Representatives of the different denominations would henceforth enjoy the privilege of naming the agents in the reservations where they had missions, subject to approval by the president.

This appeared to be a triumph for reason and order. The Catholic church, especially, could be content with it, since the greater number of the agencies had been evangelized by its missionaries. Over one hundred thousand Indians were regarded as Catholic, as contrasted with less than fifteen thousand belonging to other Christian religions. Great, therefore, was Catholic consternation when three days later a Jew was appointed to be superintendent of Indian Affairs in Oregon.

In January, 1871, De Smet was named by the American Catholic bishops to represent them and the church at a conference called to implement the terms of the Peace Policy. Despite his anxieties about being party to a great injustice soon to be perpetrated, De Smet traveled to Washington for the conference. He found himself in the company of about thirty ministers of the Protestant church, likewise summoned for their advice on the agencies. They made it clear that they intended to receive the lion's share of the reservations.

---

*For a complete account of Grant's Peace Policy, *see* Peter J. Rahill, *The Catholic Indian Missions and Grant's Peace Policy 1870–1884* (Washington, 1953).

De Smet's worst fears were realized. "Neither my presence," he wrote, "nor my demands on behalf of the Catholic missions, produced any effect. The plan for civilizing and evangelizing the Indians had already been decided upon by the President and approved by the Senate."[41] Of forty nominations to which the Catholics were entitled by terms of the Policy, only eight were accorded to them. The remainder were divided among the different sects. The president especially favored his coreligionists, the Methodists, to whom he allocated one-third of the agencies.

"The Superintendent of Indian Affairs began the discharge of his new functions by making over the Catholic schools and churches to his Protestant friends, and, in the case of the Yakimas, forbade Catholic missionaries to enter the reservation. At one stroke, eighty thousand Indians, without being consulted, found themselves torn from the Church or exposed to apostasy. But this was not all. Large sums of money due the Indians in exchange for their land were held by the government, and the interest on this was used for the upkeep of the schools. Henceforth this money would be expended on the salaries of Methodist, Presbyterian, and Quaker school teachers, employed to teach the children of Catholic Indians. In this manner did the government repay the services rendered their country by Catholic missionaries."[42]

Feeling betrayed, De Smet went back to St. Louis to carry on the battle "that justice will be done." His letters to Washington went unanswered.

The Indians, finding it difficult to get along with their new masters sent frequent messages to the Great Father in Washington, requesting the return of the Black Robes and their Catholic schools. These petitions "received scant recognition at the White House, the religious convictions of the Indians being of as little importance in the eyes of the Government as their lives and property."[43]

Cataldo, who had remained at the Coeur d'Alene Mission after pronouncing his last vows, was more determined than ever to save the Indians from the baneful effects of the policy. Most Indian reservations on the plateau had been allocated to Catholic agencies. It would be here, then, that Catholic force and enterprise should be stressed. The Nez Perce had been assigned to the Presbyterians; the Blackfeet, like the Yakima, to the Methodists. Jesuit ingenuity would have to be employed in all three places; no one was going to abandon the Catholic Indians because the government decreed it. Did not the Constitution provide for religious freedom in fact as well as in theory?

Pope Pius IX in Rome, popularly called Pio Nono, had his own problems and these had a familiar ring to the Rocky Mountain Jesuits, most of whom had suffered at the hands of Garibaldi's nationalists. Pio Nono under siege had become a voluntary prisoner in the Vatican. Cataldo knew exactly what to do.

The Coeur d'Alenes, distinguished for their devotion to the Church and to the Holy Father, sent him a long letter expressing their loyalty and offering their services to set him free. "We have a number of soldiers," they wrote, "not trained for war, but to keep order in our camp. If these men can be of service to the Pope, we offer them joyfully, and they will esteem themselves fortunate in being able to spill their blood and give their lives for our good Father Pius IX.

"Notwithstanding our poverty, to our great surprise we have been able to collect $110.00." This was enclosed. A request was made for a kind word from the Holy Father, and the letter was signed as follows:

"Vincent, of the Stellam family.

"Andrew Seltis of the family of Emote."[44]

Father Peter Beckx presented this letter to Pio Nono, who read it with amazement and great consolation. He responded by sending the first papal brief ever addressed to an Indian chief:

"Beloved Sons, *Salutations and Apostolic benediction!*

"The devoted sentiments which you, in the simplicity of your hearts express, have caused us great joy. Your sorrow over the attacks made against the Church, as well as your devotions and filial love of the Holy See, is a striking proof of the faith and charity that fill your hearts, attaching you firmly to the center of unity. For this reason we feel certain that your prayers and supplications which rise unceasingly to God will be efficacious for us and for the Church, and we accept with deep feelings of gratitude the offering of your generous charity. The hand of God protects those who seek Him sincerely, and we believe that your good words will obtain the grace to resist the dangers of corruption that threaten you, and the spiritual help which you desire for your daughters. We beg God to complete in you the work of grace, and to fill you with his choicest blessings. As a presage of this and a token of our gratitude and paternal favor, we give you from our heart the apostolic benediction.

"Given at Rome, near St. Peter's, July 31, 1871, in the twenty-sixth year of our pontificate.

Pius IX, Pope[45]

The arrival of this brief in the wilderness created as much excitement as an apparition of the Blessed Virgin. Runners were dispatched in all directions to summon large delegations from all the tribes for the reception of the papal blessing. On August 15, 1872, Father Cataldo convoked the solemn assembly of Indians who, at the appointed hour formed a procession, "headed by twelve acolytes in surplices with tapers in their hands. Then came the missionaries in copes and dalmantics. . . . To the right and left of the statue (of the Blessed Virgin) walked two lines of Indian soldiers in full dress and armed. Then followed an immense concourse in serried ranks, reciting the rosary and chanting litanies."[46]

One of the missionaries read the pontifical letter in Latin and it was then translated into the languages of the Coeur d'Alenes, Kalispels, Kettles, Nez Perces and Yakimas. Every head was bowed to receive the Holy Father's benediction, and from that time on the Indians felt they had been ennobled in some mysterious manner.

These pious fireworks were described and discussed in almost every Indian camp on the plateau. Some very basic need of the Indians was satisfied, and, for the time being at least, the Catholic missionaries held their own against the storm of opposition occasioned by the Peace Policy.

Neither Grassi nor Caruana were much intimidated by Father Wilbur, who objected to their presence on the Yakima reservation. The fathers wasted no time in bellicose confrontations. In November, 1871, Caruana was on the site of present Wenatchee, where he baptized eight children. Soon Grassi visited the Simpesquensi Indians on the Wenatchee River. Winning over Chief Patoi, he was permitted to baptize many of the tribe. On subsequent visits he baptized others and erected a small church called St. Xavier's on the Wenatchee River, about eleven miles west of Wenatchee near present-day Cashmere.[47]

Grassi had his hands full. President Grant on July 2, 1872, established the Colville reservation west of the Columbia, six miles beyond St. Francis Regis Mission, placing the homes of the Indians whom the mission served on the wrong side of the great river and many miles distant from the mission. Thus Grassi was required to cover a vast area hitherto unexplored and unsettled. Jogging along on his horse, with scant provisions in his saddle bags, he covered most of north central Washington, discovering shamans or devilish medicine men behind many rocks, almost as many as De Smet had discovered miracles behind the trees. Grassi kept in touch with his home base, St. Joseph's on the Creek, and St. Francis Regis, where Tosi, too, was busily making changes.

Tosi had moved the mission one-half mile west of the previous site and with characteristic determination had assembled a new crop of mission buildings.* It must be admitted that he had selected the best possible location. The new St. Francis Regis crowned a ridge of extending hills, facing to the south the fertile Colville Valley, with its lovely river meandering through the lush green meadows. Back of the mission, only a walking distance to the north, was a small, fresh-water lake, a convenient place for fishing or taking a bath on a hot day. Though the temperature in winter there sometimes dipped to thirty below, no one minded it much, for the skies were sunny and a limitless supply of fuel for heat lay at hand.

Giorda, meanwhile, with an eye to the future, established a Novitiate for brother-candidates for the Rocky Mountain Mission at St. Joseph's near the Yakima reservation.[48] He appointed Caruana as Novice Master, a logical choice since novice masters in those hard days were expected to be more severe than amiable. This novitiate was not the first, of course, an earlier one having been established on the Willamette, nor was it the last. In point of fact it had only two novices. The first, Nicholas Malony, who entered the Novitiate on October 28, 1872, did not persevere. The second, however, made up for this. He was John Dunninham, alias John Dunnigan, alias John Donnegan, a hard-rock miner from Diamond City, Montana, who entered the Society on September 8, 1873, and persevered to the end, twenty-eight years later.†

Father De Smet, the greatest Black Robe of them all, had died the previous spring.[49] On May 23, 1873, weakened by a long illness and brokenhearted by news of disasters on the reservations following the Peace Policy, his great spirit left this world at a quarter past two in the morning. Up to the last moment he was alert and calm. The news of his death caused universal sorrow, and those who had failed to respond to his appeals for justice for the Indians were among the first to praise him. At his funeral the army was represented by three generals, an irony that would not have been lost on him.

A few days later the new steamboat that De Smet had blessed before his death paddled up the Missouri. Named for him, the *De Smet* arrived in Indian country where the redskins flocked to the landings, emitted wails of grief and covered their heads with dust. "Not only Christians," Father Joseph Guidi wrote, "but pagans as well wept over the loss of their beloved Father, and many Indians regarded his loss as a calamity to their tribe, which alas! is but too true!"[50]

But life went on. Giorda reopened St. Peter's Mission at Bird Tail Rock, which he had closed in 1866 during the Blackfeet war on Whites. Jesuits had visited St. Peter's periodically from Helena, with hopes of its restoration. In the spring of 1874, completely unaware of the government's plan to move the reservation farther north, Father Camillus Imoda together with a greenhorn missionary, Father Philip Rappagliosi, and Brothers Francis De Kock and John Negro, moved into the old buildings and announced his intention to stay. In April, however, the government's action left St. Peter's mission sixty miles distant from the southern border of the reservation. Since this had been assigned to the Methodists neither Imoda nor Giorda shed many tears over the change, though they doubtlessly speculated on the reasons for it, and in particular on the injustice of it toward the Indians. De Smet's death and all of the florid oratory that had followed it had changed nothing. The government was yielding to expedience as much as ever.‡

---

*March 1873. This then was the third St. Francis Regis Mission site. OPA, St. Francis Regis Diary.

†*Catalogues Dispersae Provinciae Taurinensis societatis Jesu.* The catalogue of the Turin Province for various years has Donnigan (correct) listed under different names.

‡St. Peter's was transformed into a mission school.

Two final events, both notable achievements in the twilight years of Giorda's tenure as superior, should be recorded at this point. The first concerns Cataldo's final victory in building a church on the Nez Perce reservation.

Dr. Newell had been succeeded by the Reverend J. B. Monteith, whose egocentric theology was more radical than that of his colleagues. "Agent Monteith's is a numerous family—all of whom take a hand in Indian management," reported the *Lewiston Teller* for September 1, 1873. "The elder Monteith is a minister of extreme views who insists on Indians being saved by his plan. The Indians do not take to the medicine."

The Catholic church at Arrow had been washed away when the Clearwater flooded over its banks. Cataldo applied to officials in Washington for permission to build a replacement on the property of Zimchiligpusse, the first Catholic chief among the Nez Perces, whose name had been corrupted to the simple form of Slickpoo. The latter supported Cataldo's request, but bureaucrats in the capitol refused to allow a Catholic church on the reservation. When this violation of something as basic as religious freedom for two hundred Nez Perce became widely known throughout the west, the fat was in the fire. Catholics and non-Catholics became aroused. Meetings were held and protests made. Delegations were dispatched to Cataldo to urge him to build his church without government approval. When Cataldo replied he had no money for it the cash poured in. Over $400 was raised in one evening by miners, some of them the poor, despised Chinese, who gleaned their livelihood from the tailings of other miners. From all sides contributions flowed in, and Cataldo anticipated a frontal attack on Grant's Peace Policy.

Then the bureaucrats in Washington caved in. They reversed their former decision. Cataldo's church was built on land acquired from Slickpoo, and on September 8, 1874, it was occupied and dedicated to St. Joseph. At first two small rooms at the rear of the church housed Father Cataldo, who made regular visits there from Sacred Heart Mission. A year later Father Anthony Morvillo arrived to become St. Joseph's first resident pastor, and with him came Brother Carfagno who, as Grassi had said, was a good cook who was also good at carpentry. Carfagno used both of these talents—building a new house when he was not making venison stew. As for Morvillo, he undertook his brilliant studies in the Nez Perce language, some of the results of which were printed on the new St. Ignatius Mission Press.[51] The acquisition of this press was the second of the final events identified with Giorda. Perhaps it was his crowning achievement, for its imprints have lasted generations longer than any mission Giorda founded.

It should be recalled that Protestant missionaries had established a printing press at Lapwai on the Clearwater, May 13, 1839. Eleven days later four hundred copies of its first imprint were run off: an eight-page booklet in Nez Perce for children and other beginning readers. This was the first book printed in the Oregon country.*

The Jesuits' interest in printing came later, mostly because their methodology in forming Christian membership was different from the Protestants. The nature of the Catholic religion required not only longer preparation for adults before membership was granted but also an exactness in language in which dogma and liturgy were expressed.

The Jesuits, like the Protestants, were greatly handicapped in their attempts to communicate with the Indians without written works in the Indians' own tongue. To reduce these hitherto unwritten languages to writing was a major task and printing them without a press at hand was itself an almost insuperable obstacle. First the languages had to be learned through interpreters and the principles of grammar devised. In this, Catholic missionaries were much more exact than were the Protestants. The problem was to reproduce the Indian sounds as perfectly as possible through written symbols or words. To do

*For details on the mission presses, *see* Schoenberg, *Jesuit Mission Presses* (Portland, 1957).

this with conventional alphabets and letters was very difficult. To adapt ordinary letters to the need was obviously subject to over-simplification and loss of accuracy. Eventually the Jesuits devised their own system, using symbols from some European language, for instance, to indicate special sounds.

In one respect, at least, the Protestant missionaries were more accurate in reproducing sounds in English script. Being Americans themselves, their written syllables conformed more closely to American pronunciation of the sounds they represented. Most Catholic missionaries, on the other hand, came from Europe, and were likely to write out the Indian sounds with overtones from their own languages. This limitation in their language work was counterbalanced by the great learning they brought to their work and by the natural genius of most cultured Europeans for language. Hence the original work of the Jesuits in Indian grammars and dictionaries is much more thorough and complex, and usually more accurate, than that done by Protestants.

Once the Indian languages were reduced to writing, the problem of printing arose. Translators had to supervise printing and were thus confronted with the choice of either making a journey to St. Louis or of acquiring a mission press. For example, when Father Francis Barnum, S.J., completed his classic *Innuit Grammar* in Alaska in the late 1890s, he was forced to leave Alaska for the States to get it printed, a delay of over a year. Among the missionaries in early Oregon, the delay would have been even greater and the need for local presses was clearly apparent. If printing was to be done, a press at the mission was necessary.

In the choice of materials for printing, there was, again, a notable difference between Protestants and Catholics. The former were primarily interested in getting their writings into the hands of the Indians themselves. Accordingly, they were more concerned with readers, primers, calendars and Nez Perce-English works devised for Indian use. Lapwai's first four books were readers, its eighth was Spalding's translation of Matthew's Gospel. Though Catholic missionaries were also interested in native use of written language, they were primarily concerned with continuity, with the preparation of new missionaries. The first work from the Jesuit presses was a collection of Biblical narratives in Kalispel printed in 1876, an especially interesting production considering the historic controversy about Catholic indifference toward Scripture. But the emphasis in Jesuit printing was on works intended to help succeeding missionaries learn the language.

Next in importance were devotional pieces, catechisms, prayer books and hymnals, for the use of congregations, but even more for the use of missionaries in teaching prayers and doctrine in exact Indian idioms. The recurring use of Latin in titles and directives indicates this clearly. It should be remembered that this indoctrination in matters of religion through texts printed primarily for missionaries was not carried on without corresponding attempts at education. At St. Ignatius, for instance, the first school was established twenty years before the printing press. By the time the first books came off the press, there were, no doubt, many Indians able to read them, and many Indians received copies of them, especially of the catechisms and prayer books. Some of these are still in regular use.

There were three Jesuit mission presses, eventually, in the Northwest and Alaska, the first at St. Ignatius Mission, acquired in 1874, which was the same year that the first contract subsidy for Indian children was received from the government.* In this year, $2,100 was allowed, and the same amount was granted for each of three following years. In 1878, the annual contract sum was raised to $4,000 and so remained till 1890 when a more just policy was adopted by the government, largely through the influence of Senator

*The two other presses were at: Sacred Heart Mission, De Smet, Idaho, acquired in 1890; and Holy Cross Mission, Alaska, acquired about 1897.

George G. Vest of Missouri who visited the mission in 1883. Beginning with the fiscal year 1890, a per capital allowance of $12.50 per month for 300 boarding students was made.

It was in the mission boys' school that the St. Ignatius Press operated. Learning to set type and to operate the press was one occupation, among others, for Indian boys who attended school. The Jesuit system of education for Indians laid great stress on training in the manual arts, and it was precisely this feature that impressed Senator Vest so profoundly. Indian youths were given three hours in classroom studies; the balance of the school day was spent in manual arts—farming, carpentry, printing, painting, tinsmithing, and leather-work which was the great favorite of all the boys. Some laymen were employed to instruct in these occupations, though Jesuit brothers, and—for some skills, such as printing—the priests carried the principal burdens of instruction. Under the brothers' directions, the boys erected shops and imposing buildings like the church. They built dams, and irrigated vegetable gardens. They branded cattle and did the thousand and one other chores necessary for the support of several hundred children whose families contributed nothing more than part of their clothing.

The manual arts classes were taught in scattered buildings and sheds until 1883, when a new building called The Shops was finished. This was a three-story building about sixty feet long, very modern and solid by contemporary standards. The print shop was located on the first floor in quarters of its own, a room "larger than twelve by twelve, a little larger." It faced east and had one window about thirty inches square.

The press was purchased by Father Alexander Diomedi in St. Louis, "at an outlay of $500.00, the freight more than doubling the original cost." The actual cost of the press was $609.46 less three percent discount, or $591.18. It was ordered by Diomedi on September 10, 1874, from the St. Louis Type Foundry and Paper Warehouse. It was paid for in full that same month, but apparently was not shipped west for two months.

An entry in an account book for the superior of the Rocky Mountain Mission, marked "Printing Press" gives the following:

> 1874.   For freight (paid by Fr. Palladino) to Helena $308.71.
>   For freight (by Ravalli) to Missoula 79.50.
>   For the fabrique price of the press in St. Louis 591.18.
> 1875.   For another bill of freight pait [sic] to Kennit (?) at Missoula $30.00.

In another account book for St. Ignatius Mission, there is the following:

> Jan. 1875   Pd for freight on Print Mach to Missoula 79.50
> Feb. 28, 1875   To freight on print machine (type etc.) 12.49
> March 14, 1875   To freight on machine itself $27.00

The freight, then, via Northern Pacific, was $308.71 from St. Louis to Helena, $79.50 from Helena to Missoula, and $27 from Missoula to Ravalli, which was but a few miles by wagon from the mission—a total cost of $415.21. This seemingly high rate was standard before the coming of the railroads. What is more surprising is the total amount that the missionaries were willing to invest in a printing press. Over a thousand dollars was a fabulous amount for a poor mission. Only God knows what hardships were endured to save a thousand dollars in those impecunious years.

The long-sought press finally arrived about January, 1875. It was first set up in some building on the mission grounds, just where is not known, until The Shops building was completed. It was manually operated; the one extant photograph of it shows a large inking cylinder in the rear of the machine. Other than this little is known of the design.

Its acquisition was only the beginning. Special type for representing Indian gutturals had to be adopted and cut before the press could serve its principal purpose. Father Diomedi, who had recently arrived in America from Italy, and served an apprenticeship in printing at Woodstock College, Maryland, had to learn some English, then train Indian boys in the setting of type. This required many months. Diomedi selected only the brighter boys for the task, dusky little Benjamin Franklins, who resembled the Philadelphian in little more than their boyish mirthfulness and their final, if unexpected, triumph over the type. That Diomedi ever succeeded in training these boys is a marvel in itself.

Within the year after the press was set up, Diomedi was ready to begin the first book, which was dated 1876: *Smiimii tu tel kaimintis Kolinzute, Narratives from the Holy Scriptures.* That same year work was begun on the Kalispel Dictionary which required three years to print (1877–1879) and which is undoubtedly the most impressive item to come from the press. Also that first year an item in Latin was issued for the use of Jesuits in the Pacific Northwest: *Epistola R.P.N. Petri Beckx Ad Patres et Fratres Societatis Jesu.* Altogether sixty-six items printed on the press while it was at St. Ignatius are still extant.

It can be reasonably presumed that this is a fairly complete collection of the total output for the period. The early years were more productive; once the needs of the missionaries and the mission had been filled, there was little inducement to continue printing in Kalispel. There was no interest in producing books for the sake of books, nor for profit. Only a few books were ever sold. The expense of producing them was borne by the mission, which was in a precarious financial state. New type had to be ordered repeatedly from St. Louis to keep up with developments in written Kalispel, and this was a constant drain on the mission's Helena bank account. The paper secured for printing was usually inferior. Because of its cost and because of the mission's remoteness from manufacturing sources, scraps of all kinds were used. Newspapers and church-goods catalogues often served as supplementary paper for wrappers and it is not uncommon to find, bound in with Kalispel texts, end-sheets advertising palm trees, candlesticks, and sacred pictures. Frequently these stray pages, fortified by layering, served as covers. They date the imprint nearly as well as the title page.

The melancholy disposition of this historic press will be reported later. Like an old solider it faded away. It had served in a unique way in the history of our province as a source of erudition that has never been surpassed.

Joseph Mary Cataldo, superior of Rocky Mountain Mission 1877–93.

Jerome D'Aste who spent nearly a lifetime in the missions of Montana, much of it at St. Mary's. It was D'Aste who persuaded the Flatheads to refuse commerce with Chief Joseph's band in 1877. D'Aste died at St. Ignatius in 1910.

Philip Rappagliosi whose mysterious death in 1878 occasioned the arrival in Montana of three prominent Jesuits: Prando, Damiani, and Canestrelli.

Palladino's Church of the Sacred Hearts of Jesus and Mary built in Helena, 1875–76, at a cost of $38,413. It became Montana's first cathedral in 1884.

7

CATALDO TAKES CHARGE
1876–1884

On June 16, 1877, Joseph Mary Cataldo became the sixth superior general of the Rocky Mountain Mission.* On that same day, a tribe of Indians who enjoyed his most favored status, the peace-loving Nez Perce, killed thirty-three white soldiers in a battle that marked the formal opening of what has been called Chief Joseph's War. Like Joset, during the War of 1858, Cataldo soon became an unwilling participant in the disturbances which followed, and like Joset's, his role as peacemaker was misunderstood by some Whites who considered him a little less than a traitor.†

With his predecessors Giorda and Joset, Cataldo had been aware of the dilemma which confronted them during the early months of that year. On the one hand the Nez Perce, they knew, were being goaded into war by insensitive white settlers in a continuing dispute over reservation land. On the other they knew that if they supported the Nez Perce in their attempts to form a coalition with other tribes, the entire plateau would burst into violence. The Jesuits could not ignore what had occurred on the central plains during the previous year.‡ Every Indian warrior in the west knew that a coalition formed by the Sioux had wiped out Custer's command, the greatest defeat the American army had ever experienced. To prevent greater disaster and to contain the perimeters of the war which now appeared inevitable, the Jesuits would have to leave the Nez Perce to their fate.

One point appeared to be certain: if the Nez Perce effort to form an alliance with other tribes could be prevented, only the Jesuits could do it. No one else on the frontier had this kind or degree of influence. Neither the army nor the Indian Bureau could be counted on. The army, following the conclusion of the Civil War, had been reduced to feeble garrisons, each having 150 men or less, scattered throughout the frontier, in a line of defenses about as intimidating as a rickety rail fence. The role of the bureau was neither a happy nor a

---

*Apparently Cataldo was designated on December 27, 1876. The Turin Province Catalogue for the beginning of 1877 lists him as superior. However, according to Weibel, Cataldo "declined the high office at first." See George F. Weibel, *Rev. Joseph M. Cataldo, S.J., A Short Sketch of a Wonderful Career* (Spokane, 1928) p. 22. The earlier appointment was withheld in fact, if already announced, until Cataldo's objections had been considered. There is no doubt that Cataldo assumed his duties as superior on June 16, 1877.

†For many years Whites openly accused Joset of aiding the enemy while at the same time some Indians suspected he had manipulated the escape of Steptoe's troops. The peacemaker's lot is not an envied one.

‡The Battle of the Little Big Horn, June 25, 1876. The only American subject to escape alive was a horse.

respected one. The rising tide of public criticism, inspired by settlers who resented all bureaucracies, forced Congress to appoint a committee to investigate alleged abuses. This body, doubtlessly motivated by political advantages, excoriated the Indian service as the most corrupt branch of government.[1]

"The commissioners of Indian Affairs estimated that the preceding forty years cost the government a public charge of a half billion dollars for Indian Wars, an average of twelve-and-one-half million every year. A million dollars had been spent on every Indian killed. In fact, the Indian wars had already cost more than all of the country's foreign wars combined."[2]

Grant's Peace Policy too, had been a disaster. At times it appeared that the principal objective of most agents in compliance with national policy to Americanize the Indian was to cut his hair and put pants on him. The Yakima agent, Father Wilbur, in a statement to the government, urged the use of force to achieve Indian conformity in language, dress and life-style. "He believed the Indian should be compelled to give up hunting and to come onto one of three main reserves. Malcontents who objected should be exiled far away."[3] Monteith had expressed similar recommendations for his Nez Perce. "He wished them to cut their hair like Whites, adopt White table manners and dress and converse in English." The Reverend Henry Cowley went further. He demanded the abolition of smoking, which would have been a blow to the social and religious ceremonials cherished by Indians. Many non-Catholic agents interpreted the policy as provision for a state-established religion for each reservation, with Catholicism, if necessary, outlawed by force. Certainly they regarded Jesuits like Cataldo as being in violation of the law and therefore anti-American. Some Catholic agents who owed their appointments to members of the hierarchy, proved to be worse. Palladino commented tartly to the Catholic-Indian Bureau that he preferred an honest, liberal-minded Protestant as agent to a poor Catholic.[4]

The closest allies of the Nez Perce were the Flatheads and Coeur d'Alenes, both Catholic tribes by choice and by designation under the policy. The Coeur d'Alenes at this time were greatly disaffected by White encroachment on their lands and by the failure of the American government to make payments on money due the tribe. They were, in effect, dislodged from their lands around the Old Mission, as it was called, an area that was as dear to them as the Wallowa was to the Nez Perce.*

Father Alexander Diomedi, who had become superior of the mission in 1874, had taken the first step in the procession of Coeur d'Alene removal. In February, 1877, while pro-war policies were taking shape on the Nez Perce reservation, he had visited the camp of Chief Seltice near Spokane Bridge and persuaded him and his people to accompany him to more fertile lands a two days' journey to the south of the Old Mission. Diomedi with his reluctant Coeur d'Alenes arrived at Nilgo-Alko, "Hole in the Woods," near present De Smet, Idaho, on Shrove Tuesday. As Diomedi measured off a place for a temporary building, he continued to urge reasons for the chief's acquiescence and when he started to fell trees, the Indians joined him, probably to humor him, for many were unwilling yet to leave their homes near the Old Mission.

About this time rumors of government discussions concerning the possible suppression of the Coeur d'Alene reservation and removal of the Coeur d'Alenes to the Colville reservation reached Diomedi. To obviate further complications he insisted that his Indian families hurry along their packing and moving. The older people, especially, were dragging their feet, putting off their departures from day to day. Finally in a last desperate effort to protect the future of these people he removed from the Old Mission all the statues and

---

*There were no formalities in the removal of the Coeur d'Alenes, but the encroachment of Whites in that area persuaded the missionaries to seek removal for the sake of the Indians.

furnishings, which the Indians treasured, and dispatched them all to the new mission at Nilgo-Alko. The Indians soon followed, responding more with their hearts than with their minds.

Meanwhile, in early January Cataldo had visited Chief Joseph's camp on Captain John Creek. Joseph had listened with more than politeness to the priest's explanation of Catholic doctrine, then responded by saying that he and his band would look into it when the dispute over their land was settled.[5] At this point one of Joseph's companions craftily asked Cataldo for his opinion on the government's decision to deprive them of their land in the Wallowa Valley. Cataldo replied that he had nothing to do with government land questions. He had come on God's business.

Despite this open declaration of neutrality, which undoubtedly was conveyed to Monteith, the latter reported Cataldo to Washington, accusing him of encouraging the Indians in their rebellion.* This revealed Monteith's position, at least, and raised some fascinating questions later regarding his own acceptance by the Nez Perce Protestants.

The Nez Perce Catholics, about three hundred in number, tended to align themselves with the faction called the non-treaty Indians who objected to their removal from the Wallowa Valley and who resisted efforts to "Americanize" them by force. These Indians had become involved in a revival of the Dreamer religion, a messianic form of the old Ghost Dance religion which had flourished along the mid-Columbia a generation earlier. In its new form this nativism movement taught a mystic identification of the Indian with his land. It disapproved of agriculture, regarding it as ravishing or wounding Mother Earth. Its eclectic ritual, taken from Catholic, Protestant and Mormon sources, placed emphasis on personal testimonies, poetic-homilies on the holiness and happiness of the good old days, accompanied by continuous drumming, which eventually earned them the nickname Drummers.[6] According to Joset, most Nez Perce at this time were Drummers.[7]

A council to appease the non-treaty Nez Perce had been scheduled to begin on May 3, by General O. O. Howard, Commander of the Department of the Columbia. Howard who had enjoyed a distinguished military career, suffering the loss of one arm in battle, had the reputation of being a good soldier, but an eccentric one who used every opportunity he had to preach the Christian gospel. Known as the Bible General, who looked like an Old Testament prophet in his long white beard, Howard was not popular with his men, "owing to his ferocious religion."[8] Because of the spirit of the times, this godly preacher was quite unwilling to trust Catholics generally and "the Jesuit Cataldo" in particular. Monteith's accusations had brought out in him the darkest of his suspicions.

Howard sent word to Cataldo, inviting him to the council. Better to know where the cat is than to let him catch mice somewhere else. He even paid a visit to Cataldo's Slickpoo Mission, noting in his report that it stood midway up a choice valley, " a nicely constructed church holding perhaps two hundred people . . . but as is often the case there is considerable controversy, above and beneath the surface, between the followers of the Mission and the Protestants."[9]

Howard supported the views of Monteith and found Catholic alignment with the non-treaty Indians as very insidious indeed. He regarded Cataldo's neutrality as "equivalent to positive opposition." No wonder, then, that the Bible General was keeping an unfriendly eye on the priest. His great peace council took place on a bright sunny day at Fort Lapwai in a hospital tent, with the flaps up so that a crowd of Indians outside could participate.

"The Treaty Indians nearly all wore shirts, pants and coats," had their hair cut relatively short, and eschewed paint. The nontreaties "were very Indian looking, indeed," in clothing, hair and ornament. Father Cataldo rode up from his mission and "opened the

*Spies in Joseph's camp, reporting to Monteith, maligned Cataldo.

exercise by a short and extempore prayer in Nez Perce; many years later the participant Yellow Wolf recalled this as "prayer talk."[10]

The early sessions that followed were marked with intrigue, bickering, and frequent interruptions. The accusations against Cataldo were introduced. There was much muttering and two Indians delivered speeches on the subject. A Catholic Indian "got up and rebuked Monteith for writing a lie on the priest."[11] Monteith was required to apologize and Howard promised to correct the record in his report, but Cataldo did not trust him. Much confusion was occasioned by the presence of the Dreamers, who permitted a sullen old chief, Toohulhulsote, of the Dreamers' religion, to act as their spokesman.[12] During one angry exchange Howard arrested the old patriot and clapped him into the guardhouse. He concluded with an ultimatum which the three chiefs of the largest bands, Joseph, White Bird, and Looking Glass, were unwilling to challenge. They agreed to comply with the government's demands within thirty days. Despite the rejoicing afterwards that peace had been preserved, with or without honor, the council was a failure. Howard went off to Vancouver, complacent with his knowledge that war had been averted. The commander of Fort Lapwai boasted that he had sufficient soldiers to take care of the Indians, "if they resorted to arms," and Cataldo went back to his mission as convinced as the others, there would be no war. "I never knew nor even suspected," he said later, "that the Nez Perces would ever dare to oppose the U.S. Army."[13]

But the Dreamers thought differently. If the wise old chiefs had yielded to the white man's threats, they would act for themselves. On June 13, a small band of them, inspired by Toohulhulsote's war spirit, killed four Whites, and the undeclared war was under way. Howard sent two companies of cavalry under Capt. David Perry, and a force of about fifty volunteers joined them near Mount Idaho. Convinced that the Indians would retreat when they saw the troops, the volunteers like school-yard bullies, yearned for a fight. But the Indians had become entrenched among the stony buttes and Perry was required almost immediately to order a retreat of the Whites, during which thirty-three of the ninety soldiers were killed. Toohulhulsote's much desired war had begun, but what he had started he could not finish. Chief Joseph took command of the Nez Perce.

Cataldo learned of these developments at the Old Mission to which he had been summoned by Giorda for a routine meeting. It was Saturday, June 16. Giorda, sitting with his advisors: Joset, Diomedi, and Cataldo had just finished discussing a financial report for supporting the sisters who were to teach in the proposed school at De Smet near Nilgo-Alko. Other problems concerning the Coeur d'Alenes' removal came up. At this point an Indian entered the room with two urgent pieces of mail.[14]

One letter was from Rome. This informed Cataldo of his appointment as superior general; the other was a special dispatch from General Howard announcing the outbreak of the war. Cataldo recalled the dramatic poignancy of the moment many years later: "On the one side was the war, and on the other side the superiorship and my duties to all; poor Father Cataldo!"

First things first. Cataldo appointed Giorda as superior of Sacred Heart Mission, replacing Diomedi whom he put second in command as "Father Minister."* Completing the consultation in a manner not expected by anyone, least of all himself, he laid plans for an early departure for Nilgo-Alko where he could consult with the Coeur d'Alene chiefs.

---

*"Father Minister" in Jesuit communities is the person assigned to manage the temporal affairs of the house. He is generally second in command.

About one thousand Indians of various tribes had gathered at Sacred Heart Mission two weeks earlier for the Corpus Christi celebration and they were now gathering camas roots in the damp meadows.* On Monday the new superior left on horseback for Nilgo-Alko.

Two objectives now appeared as a challenge to Cataldo. First he had to prevent at all costs a coalition of the Catholic tribes with the Nez Perce. Secondly he must prevent non-Indians from over-reacting. The latter, in retrospect at least, seems to have been the more difficult task.

Gripped by fear many settlers were packing and fleeing to Walla Walla.† Some at Colfax were frantically throwing up stockades, while newspapers fanned the excitement with wild rumors and exaggerated reports. Nez Perce runners, it was said, were racing all over the interior, seeking allies especially among the Spokanes, Flatheads, and Coeur d'Alenes. One correspondent informed the public that ten thousand warriors would join the hostiles soon, and people who should have known better were foolish enough to believe it. "Rumors filled the air during the week with reports that the Cour [sic] d'Alene Indians had joined Joseph's band of outlaws: that they numbered several hundred warriors; and that they were marching down from Hangman Creek, killing and destroying as they came."[15] News of the war, adroitly exaggerated for sensationalism, had been flashed even to Europe "by Anglo-American cables."

The truth is that Joseph, burdened with two thousand horses and five hundred and fifty non-combatants, instead of attacking Whites, was trying frantically to escape them. He was leading his people in a strategic retreat to Canada, where Sitting Bull had gone after annihilating Custer's command. To calm the settlers, Cataldo was galloping back and forth on fast horses, one after the other. From the middle of June until late August, Cataldo "was kept afoot and literally on horseback, traveling up and down the country from Lapwai to Lewiston, from Lewiston to the Coeur d'Alenes and Spokanes, spreading everywhere a sense of security and peace."[16]

Grassi at this time was busy with tribes along the Columbia River, where he reported the Drummers were unusually active. Caruana was at the Yakima mission, using his influence to keep the Yakimas out of the war. Giorda was doing his part with the Coeur d'Alenes and Joset, though he was handicapped all summer with a bad leg, was as busy as Cataldo, mostly in dispelling rumors of alleged Indian depredations. Cataldo persuaded influential chiefs to compose testimonials of friendship and these were sent to Colfax or Lewiston for publication. "I the undersigned," Chief Seltice wrote, "testify that all my Indians, the Coeur d'Alenes, are always friendly disposed towards the whites, and we will help them as much as we can. . . ."[17]

Many Whites had left their farms unattended. In an unprecedented gesture of loyalty to the Jesuits, Seltice and his Coeur d'Alenes assumed the role of protector for the Whites who had remained, and guarded the property and livestock of those who had gone. The soldiers of the Sacred Heart—as the Coeur d'Alenes own police force was called—in details of twelve each, regularly made the rounds of these scattered homesteads "twice a day, morning and evening." Giorda also noted that these Coeur d'Alenes "took care to feed the domestic animals left behind and to see to it that existing fences were kept repaired and the gates shut."[18]

*"Corpus Christi," literally "Body of Christ," a special day celebrated each year following Pentecost and a major holiday for Catholic Indians. From the earliest times in Jesuit parishes and missions, this day was celebrated with processions in honor of the Eucharist. Catholic Indians flocked to the missions for the event and remained for some days, engaging in dancing and other social events, as well as in the spiritual celebration which replaced the old rendezvous.

†One farmer was in such a hurry that his hat blew off as he raced toward Colfax. He did not stop long enough to retrieve it.

These acts of super-patriotism, mostly manipulated by missionaries, were intended in part to convince Washington that the Catholic missionaires were not traitors and that they could be trusted despite the abuses heaped upon them as a result of Grant's Peace Policy.

The fact that they were compelled to feel suspect, indicates what kind of intolerance they experienced as Jesuits and Catholics. The frontier, a great leveller socially and economically, had also become a refuge of eccentric and bigoted inhabitants.

So Joseph was an "outlaw" and Jesuits were proving their loyalty to their adopted country by having Indians mend fences and take care of livestock. One of Cataldo's boasts was that there were no Catholic Indians in Joseph's force.* Some Jesuits, one supposes, would be embarrassed by this, for Joseph's cause surely was just, especially in view of his obvious unwillingness to shed white man's blood until he was forced.

He had led successfully his people over Lolo Pass, described by General Sherman "as one of the worst trails for man and beast on this continent," into the Bitterroot Valley where their friends and allies, the Flatheads, lived. At St. Mary's Mission there was Father Ravalli, partially paralyzed and generally confined to his bed, and Jerome D'Aste, a gentle Genoese in his fiftieth year, who, like Ravalli, was already a legend in Montana. North of St. Mary's was Missoula, a small thriving town of three hundred "as new as pine boards fresh from the mill,"[19] and fifty miles farther, St. Ignatius Mission, where Father Leopold Van Gorp was superior with Bandini and four brothers in his community. During this rainy June when Joseph arrived in Montana, Bishop James O'Connor of Omaha was the community's guest. From the Bitterroot to the east was Deer Lodge—two days by stagecoach. Another two days of hard driving beyond that was Helena, the largest town in Montana.

It was not improbable that the Flatheads, particularly Charlot's band in the Bitterroot, would join the hostiles. Certainly they had sufficient provocation, for the government had set up a puppet, Chief Arlee, whose Flathead faction had come to unjust terms with the Whites. Newspapers, prematurely alarmed, predicted a coalition. "The Flatheads Preparing To Join the Nez Perces In Their War on Whites," was announced by the *San Francisco Chronicle*.[20] The Montana Jesuits, like those in Idaho, were fully committed to peace. D'Aste, when he was not occupied with his prayers and farm chores, rode up and down the valley, more to calm the agitation among the settlers than to keep his Flatheads from forming an alliance. The Whites in their panic had been expressing their hatred for Indians openly and they refused to give credence to D'Aste's word on the peaceful intention of the Flatheads. They accused D'Aste of betraying them and even threatened to burn down St. Mary's. Ravalli had opportunities to influence his lifetime friends, the Indians. "The Bitterroot settlers would long remember 'the great debt which western Montana owes to Ravalli,' the one man who more than all others kept the Bitterroot peaceful. Without his influence in 1877 the Nez Perce passage 'would have been a very different story,' one which 'would be indelibly stamped in blood upon the pages of Montana's history'."[21]

Charlot reminded the Whites that the Nez Perce were friends of the Flatheads. "I cannot send my young men out to make war on the Nez Perces."[22] But neither would he fight against the Whites. "My hand is clean," he told Looking Glass, "and I cannot extend it to hands stained with the blood of white people; we have always been friends but not in this circumstance."[23] But Charlot bore his own grudge against the Whites for many years even to his own grave in exile.†

Refused assistance by the Flatheads, Joseph and his people purchased food and supplies at stores in the valley, feeling secure in the knowledge that General Howard was far

---

*Actually there were several Catholics among Joseph's forces, including one woman about whom Palladino writes at length. Lawrence Palladino, *Indians and Whites in the Northwest*, p. 413, et seq.

†Charlot was forced to move from the Bitterroot to Mission Valley in 1892. William L. Davis, S.J., *A History of St. Ignatius Mission* (Spokane, 1954), p. 98.

behind them and unaware that General John Gibbon with a fresh army was approaching the area from the east. The Nez Perce finally left the valley peacefully and crossed the divide into the Big Hole Basin, a lofty meadow seven thousand feet in altitude, where they made camp. The women began to gather tepee poles for use on the treeless plains.

General Gibbon, meanwhle, was in hot pursuit. He stopped at St. Mary's long enough to interview Father Ravalli, who knew more about Montana Indians than anyone else.

"The General was brought into the sick priest's tiny room. 'Here propped up in bed and *reading medicine* by the light of a dim lamp, was a charming old French man (sic) who with a skull cap on his head and a pair of glasses on his nose, received me with all the cordiality of a past age.' Gibbon found himself 'much attracted by the charms of his conversation, and sat talking to him for some time as the night wore on. When Gibbon asked him if he were not tired of the life after thirty-five years with the interior tribes, Ravalli replied that it was his ambition to stay here until he could lay his bones among the Indians. . . .

" 'How many troops' did the General have, asked Ravalli? Gibbon instinctively revealed the weakness of his force: 'About 200.' 'Oh,' said the old man, 'you *must* not attack them, you have not enough.' "[24]

It did not take long for the general to learn that Ravalli was right. During the night of August 8, Gibbon deployed his men who attacked the sleeping Nez Perce camp at daybreak. Caught off guard, the Nez Perce suffered an enormous loss. According to Joseph's statement made after his capture, two hundred-and-eight of his people were either killed in the Battle of the Big Hole or died soon afterwards from their wounds. Among the dead were two of Joseph's wives and the daughter of Looking Glass.* Gibbon, too, lost nearly half of his men as casualties, twenty-nine were killed and forty were wounded.[25] So few Americans were left after the battle that Joseph's forces easily could have destroyed them all. Joseph, instead, led his people away, leaving the dead and carrying their own wounded with them in their hopeless flight toward freedom.

Father Palladino was at Helena when news of the battle reached him on Saturday, August 11.[26] An hour later, accompanied by two Sisters of Charity, Benedicta and Mary Liguori, he left for Deer Lodge, and then "for the battle field," at which he never arrived, though he described it as horrible as the battlefield of Solferino "where some twenty-seven thousand men were killed or wounded."† The wounded were being evacuated to the sisters' hospital in Deer Lodge. "It had been impossible," Palladino wrote, "for several days to dress the wounds properly while on the road, and doing so now, they were found in several cases literally alive with maggots."

In Spokane Falls, meanwhile, on August 10, Gen. Frank Wheaton arrived with ten companies of soldiers, presumably to relieve the frightened settlers who had set up fortifications on Havermale's Island in the river above the main falls.‡ Wheaton called a general assembly of all the Indians in the area. The missionaries of Lapwai and Coeur d'Alene were urged to attend together with the principal chiefs of the tribes. "Father Cataldo, Giorda, and Joset, accompanied by a number of tribal leaders, answered the invitation. The missionaries were lodged in General Wheaton's headquarters' tent which had been pitched where Howard Street and Riverside Avenue now intersect. In the council where the military authorities urged the tribes to keep the peace, Chief Seltice expressed

*There is some doubt according to Fuller whether they were killed in this battle or later.

†The wounded had been evacuated. Palladino with countless others from Deer Lodge, Butte, and Helena, met the tattered army with buggies, ambulances, food and other requirements.

‡Now Riverfront Park in Spokane. *See* Weibel, *Short Sketch of a Wonderful Career*, p. 21.

the sentiment of the Catholic mission Indians when he declared, that if he were forced into war, he and his tribe would fight on the side of the whites."[27]

Wheaton's council was really pointless, and the loyal speech of Seltice, mere oratory. The crisis in Joseph's war had already passed. Less than two months later, on October 4, the Nez Perce leader rode into Gen. Nelson Miles' camp and surrendered his rifle. His last engagement, the Battle of the Bear Paw, had been a disaster. The power of the Nez Perce was broken forever.

After the long, tense summer, autumn that year was a welcome relief. During the crisis Cataldo had shown his mettle; now he would have a chance to expose his policies as a Jesuit superior. No one doubted that he would be demanding, perhaps even insensitive to human weakness and failures. He was like a sea captain who feels responsible for the future of those aboard his ship. Their spiritual survival depended to some extent on the discipline he required. Awareness of their dependence hardened him, made him more rigid, more attentive to the smallest particulars. Nothing went unnoticed.

Cataldo was forty years old when he became superior, still underweight, tubercular and physically as fragile as a fawn. But a strong, subborn will ruled him and dedicated him. It transformed him into an administrator whose ability could be described by only one word: awesome.

He had already indicated his attitude toward politics. Praise from some Whites, even from a United States Congressman, for his extraordinary services during the war left him unimpressed. He was especially concerned about one matter, be it Indian or White related, and that was, as he said, God's business. He knew, perhaps long before he became superior, what priorities he would set up in his pursuit of God's business. He would place heavy stress on schools. Schools were needed as badly as churches. Without schools for both Indians and Whites, churches would be like families without children. Precisely as a superior of a raw, impoverished mission, he founded directly or was directly involved in the founding of five mission boarding schools for Indians, and two prep schools and two universities for Whites. There seems to be no parallel record in the history of education in the Northwest.

But the superior had many other loose ends to tie together. Father Menetrey, who was very naive at times, had been wickedly defrauded of the land on which St. Michael's Church at Hell's Gate was located. A squatter who had settled on a corner of the church's forty acres laid claim to the entire piece. Menetrey, to get rid of the nuisance, offered the intruder a deed to all forty acres on condition that title to the land where the church stood would be deeded back. After the thief got his deed he proceeded to order poor old Menetrey off the premises. Still very indignant and somewhat bewildered by it all, Menetrey sought directions from Cataldo, who frostily ordered him to move the church, board by board, to nearby Missoula, where it was reassembled to form a classroom, pretentiously called St. Joseph's School. The Sisters of Providence, who had recently opened a hospital in Missoula taught the younger boys here. Hell's Gate, which had dwindled in population while Missoula prospered, lost its priest, aging Father Menetrey, who now lived in comfort in the hospital, serving as its chaplain and Missoula's first resident pastor. This was his reward for being a little stupid.

Not so happily resolved was the death of Father Philip Rappagliosi, the second Jesuit to die in Montana. Rappagliosi was a Roman, born on September 14, 1841, just two weeks before De Smet raised the first cross at St. Mary's. Ordained at the age of thirty, and a special favorite of Father General, he volunteered for the Rocky Mountain Mission and was soon on his way. He arrived in Helena at Christmastime in 1873, then departed for St. Mary's, about a five days' journey by stagecoach. In a brief time he learned to speak Flathead fluently, but oddly he was immediately assigned to the Blackfeet mission, where he had to start all over on a new language.[28] The superior had not made a mistake, at least he wouldn't admit to any. Like many of his subjects, he himself had learned several Indian languages, giving him the required versatility for working in any part of the mission. This was a hard way to go, but one must remember that this mission, unlike some others, was for the hardiest of souls only.

It proved to be too hardy for Rappagliosi, who soon discovered on the bleak Blackfeet mission that daily exposure to the coarseness of life was more difficult than learning Indian languages. With him at St. Peter's was Father Imoda, who had been there off and on for years and there to stay since 1874. After serving an apprenticeship under Imoda, Rappagliosi established himself in a lonely hut on the Milk River, east of Fort Belknap, where he had contact also with the Assiniboines, "Sioux of the Woods," and the Gros Ventres. He realized, apparently, that what this mission needed, more than anything else, was a martyr. In his rare contacts with other Jesuits he dropped hints. "Should I return no more," he said to one, "pray, please, for the peace of my soul."[29] He did not return.

In presenting an account of the celebrated affair, Palladino implied that some dark, insidious evil was related to the young priest's death. He spoke of an individual "unworthy of his cloth," who was "bitterly antagonistic" toward Rappagliosi because of his edifying conduct.[30] Neighboring Indians reported that this mysterious person, probably a minister or a priest, had visited Rappagliosi, who had become ill, and had persuaded him to drink a bottle of "medicine" suspected by the Indians to be poison.

Whatever it was, Rappagliosi, worn out by hunger, cold, fatigue and grief over the Indians, died on February 7, 1878. His death was a sensation in Rome, partly because of his prominent family and partly because of persistent rumors that he had been poisoned, an old-world form of murder, which always intrigued the Romans. Father General, too, was upset. "They wrote me that he had died," he exclaimed, "but they did not write that they had killed him."[31]

Though it made a good story, the report was probably false. It succeeded, however, in creating such a row that three other Jesuits immediately volunteered to take the dead *"martyr's"* place. Jesuit superiors quickly accepted all three as the will of God and they were off to the missions before they had time to change their minds.

Father Philip Canestrelli, a Roman who most resembled Rappagliosi in appearance, Father Peter Paul Prando, and Father Joseph Damiani, all had more than Rappagliosi's inspiration in common: all three devoted their lives to the Indians of Montana, all three became great masters of the various Indian tongues, and presented manuscripts in Indian to the St. Ignatius Mission Press for printing, and two of them, Prando and Damiani, were responsible for the founding of Holy Family Mission which succeeded St. Peter's as the mission center for the Blackfeet.

Prando arrived at St. Peter's in 1880, at a time when a bold, witty, and generous missionary was needed to openly challenge Grant's Peace Policy. Irrepressible, waggish to the degree of sauciness, absolutely fearless, and devoted to the Indian with a singular loyalty, he soon brought a very questionable issue to a very obvious climax in which two people lost their jobs—Prando and his adversary. He made his first safari into the forbidden land, the Blackfeet reservation, in May, 1881. Proceeding directly to the government agency at Badger Creek, twelve miles beyond the reservation line at Birch Creek, he arrived and begged the pleasure of speaking with the agent. The latter, Major John Young, received Prando with seeming cordiality, and in the course of the conversation explicitly approved of Prando's remarks about the Blackfeet school at St. Peter's, adding offhandedly that he "liked the Catholic priests," a comment which he made to sound like, "I like lepers." Prando left him with an expression of friendliness on both sides, then started his visits of the Indian camps. From May until November he covered the reservation, baptizing many children and promising to return in the spring. Before leaving for St. Peter's, he built a small hut on the off-reservation side of Birch Creek.

When Prando returned in May he baptized many adults who were well disposed, including a prominent chief with the unleader-like name of White Calf. Apparently this displeased Methodist Young, who, until then, had been undecided what to do about the priest's activities on the reservation assigned to the Methodists. He ordered Prando off the reservation and Prando, with a saucy retort, obeyed. Pied Piper-like, he was followed by many Indians to his shack on Birch Creek, where they remained as long as Prando did, in defiance of the agent. The subsequent battle between the imaginative and humor-loving Black Robe and the overly-serious, dour agent has become famous in the annals of Montana. Poor Young didn't have a chance. Not only were the Indians against him, but so was fate, for a terrible famine came upon the land; the hapless agent was blamed for everything that followed. When the smoke of battle cleared, both Prando and Young were gone, but the hut on Birch Creek was still there.

Still there, also, was the boys' school at St. Peter's, with Brother Robert Hamilton in charge. The school was housed in an almost indestructible stone building fashioned like a fortress, which stood in the grassy meadow below the buttes, where rattlesnakes dozed in the sun on hot days. Beyond Agent Young's lethal touch, the school was safe. Sometimes in the early summer afternoons, when the sun cast tiny shadows, like distortions in the fun house mirrors, the boys helped gather timothy hay for the cattle. Prando was no longer with them, nor was he attached to the Blackfeet mission. Mostly because of his indiscretions with government officials, Cataldo had assigned him to the boys' school at St. Ignatius Mission, where he spent approximately one year prefecting boys and pondering the enigmatic power of the government, which seemed to be placated only by his humiliating removal and reassignment.

The final word on Prando's achievement with the Blackfeet was expressed by Palladino. "On his rounds among these people, and in the intervals he spent in his little cabin on Birch Creek, Father Prando, as it were by contraband, baptized 686 Blackfeet and united in marriage fifty-five Indian couples."[32] It was the story of Nicolas Point all over again. He, too, had been an outcast and he, too, had baptized hundreds of Blackfeet. Not even Young, nor his vindictive bureaucracy could alter the efficacy of Prando's ministry and its final effect on the tribe.

While this lively history of the Blackfeet mission was unfolding in Montana, new schools and churches began to pop up throughout the Northwest with the regularity of the seasons. A brief reference to some of these will indicate not only the rapid growth of the church but also the energetic dedication of Cataldo and his subjects. In May, 1878, for example, Father Diomedi blessed the cornerstone of a new, very large church at St. Francis Regis Mission. Construction on this edifice dragged out for three years, not really wasted time, though seven years later, on Christmas eve, it burned to the gound.[33]

In September, 1878, another milestone was reached at St. Francis Regis. The Jesuits finally scraped together the means for a boys' school. This was five years after the Sisters of Providence had opened the girls' school in the lush valley below the mission, where there was a clipped green lawn and flowers that blossomed in profusion.[34] At this same time, Father Imoda opened the first church at Fort Benton, a rowdy Montana town at the head of navigation on the Missouri. Fort Benton needed something holy like a church dedicated to the Immaculate Conception. It had become noted mostly for its supply of booze, which flowed freely along the Whoop Up Trail to the Blackfeet who tried to consume as much as the packtrains could carry.[35]

On November 22, 1878, three Sisters of Providence arrived at Sacred Heart Mission, located permanently at De Smet that year. The sisters occupied a convent, which had been made ready, at least in part, and began instructions for the mission girls. On January 9, 1879, the first Mass was offered in this new school.[36]

Gently prompted by Cataldo, who warmly admired him, Father Grassi built a new church, sixteen by twenty feet, in the Kittitas Valley near present-day Ellensburg during the spring of 1880. His successor, Father Aloysius Parodi, curtained off the altar and also used the church for a school, the first school for white children in that valley.[37]

On June 12, 1881, Father Tosi offered the first Mass in Cheney, Washington, in a room above a local furniture store. A meeting was held after Mass to discuss the erection of a church, which was begun under Giorda's direction on September 10, on land purchased from the Northern Pacific Railroad.[38]

The pastor of Helena, Father Palladino, was occupied in Boulder Valley, Montana, on Sunday, August 21. He dedicated a new church built by Father John Vanneman, in honor of St. John the Evangelist.[39] The first church in Missoula was dedicated on December 11, 1881, in honor of St. Francis Xavier. This frame building cost $3,000, a tidy sum which was scratched together so that the Catholics of Missoula no longer would have to invade the hospital for Sunday Mass.[40] Palladino was busy again in January, 1882. In Helena he opened St. Aloysius Select School for Boys for which he had an ambitious program planned. Perhaps the founding of Gonzaga in Spokane doused his hopes, for his school struggled along for twenty-eight years before giving up the ghost.

During the year 1882, Father Joset built a small chapel in Sprague, Washington. When the first Mass was offered there on May 29 so many people appeared that a meeting was held after Mass to discuss the building of a larger church. Father Aloysius Jacquet completed this in October of the following year, and Bishop Junger dedicated it to Mary Queen of Heaven on July 15, 1886.[41]

Father Palladino, as ubiquitous as he was garrulous, offered the first Masses in Billings and Livingston, the latter being a town of tents on the Yellowstone River where it emerged from the dark mountains to the south.[42] Sometime during 1883, St. Joseph's Mission Church at Sun River, Montana, was built by Prando, and on November 1, the new Providence Academy at Sacred Heart Mission was dedicated. Built to replace the first convent, which was destroyed by fire on December 11, 1881, this second convent, too, was doomed. It burned to the ground on February 10, 1906, just after Mass had begun in its chapel.[43]

Most significant of all during this period was the founding of Gonzaga, which was a kind of Indian related epic in itself, a miracle of sorts, and a far cry from what eventually emerged.

Spokane Falls, like the Indians for which it was named, had fascinated Cataldo from the beginning. If others doubted its future, he never did, and as completion of the Northern Pacific Railroad approached this settlement both from east and from the west, he was determined to acquire a homestead or buy land from the railroad as near the falls as possible for the use as headquarters of the mission, and "a central school for Indians and perhaps for whites."[44]

The former, so far as Cataldo was concerned, deserved priority status because Grant's Peace Policy was being violated flagrantly in favor of Protestants by a new method for controlling the education of Catholic children. The plan was very bold: on February 25, 1880, a Methodist school called Training School of Indian Youth was established on four acres of land belonging to the Congregationalists' Pacific University at Forest Grove, Oregon. Subsidized by the United States' Indian Department with tax dollars, this school was directed by Melville G. Wilkinson, Captain of the Third Infantry, United States Army.*

*Captain Wilkinson enjoyed a distinguished military career, including service in the Nez Perce War. See Schoenberg, *Gonzaga University*, p. 32.

Archbishop Charles Seghers, successor of Francis Norbert Blanchet, complained bitterly to Washington, D.C. about this school, accusing Wilkinson of a raid upon Catholic reservations to find bright students who were forcibly directed to the "professedly Methodist institution." If, in accordance with the terms of the Policy, Catholics had control of a token few of all the reservations, it was now becoming clear that even these were being violated by bigoted bureaucrats who had friends in high places.[45] Eventually, because of pressure brought to bear by Seghers and others in the Catholic Indian Bureau, this infamous school was "removed" to Salem, Oregon where it became the Chemawa Training School, an entirely different kind of institution to which Catholics raised no objections.*

The immediate answer to Forest Grove as a threat to the Catholic Spokanes was a temporary school that Cataldo instructed Brother Carfagno to build at St. Michael's Mission in the summer of 1880. The Indian office in its report to the Department of the Interior for the following year, listed this school for the Spokanes, noting an enrollment of twenty-five children. What the Indian office did not report was that several children attending St. Michael's were Whites. Thus in the historic sense, St. Michael's might be considered the forerunner of Gonzaga.

In late autumn, after Carfagno's school building had been completed, Cataldo summoned Father Canestrelli from St. Francis Regis Mission where he had been uncommonly successful with Indians. As a former professor of theology in Rome, surely enough to recommend him for teaching a score of first grade Indian children, Canestrelli was directed to take up residence at St. Michael's. He was directed also by Cataldo to take the initial steps toward the acquisition of two new pieces of property, one for the relocation of St. Michael's Mission, on a site more accessible to the struggling village of Spokane Falls, and another suitable for an Indian school adjacent to the falls. In "Sketch of the Spokane Mission," Father Cataldo says, "When I left that place to visit the missions of Montana, I recommended to P. Canestrelli, who was to spend the winter 80–81 with the Spokanes, to see whether he could locate a kind of Mission-claim, to be regarded in the Land-Office as a homestead for some one of the Fathers. And also to have another claim near the Falls, because that would be a central point for our Missions where we could build a large school for Indian children, or even for white, if many should come to the country."[46]

Canestrelli, a genius in theoretical matters but timid and dilatory in the practical, procrastinated in making a decision about the land. He finally wrote to Cataldo who had spent January and February at St. Ignatius Mission, to say that homestead land was fast disappearing and none was available by the falls. He should come at once to see about the matter. There is nothing Cataldo would have liked better, but that winter was one of the worst on record. The railroad had not yet been completed. Cataldo noted that it was impossible to cross the Coeur d'Alene Mountains on horse, and he would have to wait until late spring.

When he finally arrived in Spokane Falls he found that all government land had been taken. "So I went around with Mr. Sims, the old Colville Indian agent, to see different parties, to get information in order to buy a half section of railroad land, near the Spokane Falls; and another half section near the Indian Mission at St. Michael's, which was 8 miles distant from the actual City of Spokane. We found that the place where the College is actually built, was all that we could desire for a central establishment for all our missions, being about equi-distant North and South, from Colville and Lewiston: East and West, from Helena, Montana and Yakima."[47]

---

*Ibid., p. 34, n. 7. In 1881 of the 76 children enrolled at Forest Grove only 16 came from Methodist allocated reservations; in 1882, of 91 students, only 15 came from Methodist allocated reservations. "These facts alone prove that the charges made by Catholic missionaries were not unfounded."

In these remarks Cataldo inadvertently reveals how far his thinking about the mission and the proposed school had progressed. The confines of the mission ended on the west at Yakima. The proposed school was no longer regarded as a link in a chain of schools, but rather it was the hub of a wheel, a central school for an elite selected from the missions on all sides.

Finding the two sites he wanted was only a beginning. Using all the resources of manpower and influence he had at his command, he now became as determined as a second lieutenant to secure title on what he wanted. After much coming and going by Giorda and himself, he finally purchased through Judge Lewis of Cheney, who represented the Northern Pacific Railroad, one-half section of land at $2.60 per acre. The judge immediately wrote the contract for this half-section, on which Gonzaga was built subsequently, the date being October 13, 1881.[48]

What the Jesuits had acquired for a total of 936 hard silver dollars was a 320 acre tract mostly on the north bank of the Spokane River. Approximately one mile above the Big Falls, about one acre of that tract lay on the south side of the river, a picturesque bluff jutting out into the stream, which is very swift at this point. Approximately another forty acres consisted of water surface, the river and the bay, where wild ducks and sometimes wild geese gathered in the winter months. According to the early missionaries, it was one of the most beautiful sites, not only on the river but in the inland Northwest.*

While negotiations for the Gonzaga land had been dragging on, Cataldo in his best buying mood, judged that it was time to purchase land for a church for Whites of the town. On August 8, he purchased three lots from James Glover who had laid out the townsite on the south bank of the river. On one of Cataldo's lots was an old carpenter shop, which he converted into a church, appropriately dedicating it in honor of St. Joseph, the carpenter. He himself was the first pastor traveling from St. Michael's on weekends to take care of his little flock, which started with five people. On December 5, he purchased two more lots for $400, to the east of the others. He wanted to buy more land but was strongly advised against it because, as everybody knew, the metropolis of the interior plateau was Cheney, some eighteen miles to the southwest.[49]

"A syndicate of railroad men and capitalists from Colfax saw their opportunity, laid out the townsite of Cheney . . ." wrote Father George Weibel. "They succeeded in capturing the country seat by a small majority."[50] Weibel, a stern German and rigid Jesuit historian who looked like the Kaiser after the Battle of Jutland, knew that this observation was always good for a laugh. One could not imagine a syndicate or conspiracy of capitalists coming out of Colfax, where citizens three years before had built barricades against Joseph's army, which had gone the other direction.

On Christmas day, 1881, for example, Father Van Gorp, offered Mass in St. Joseph's for twelve people, this was an improvement of 140% over the number of the first congregation, but on the same day at St. Michael's Mission three hundred Indians attended Mass and received Holy Eucharist. At this time some of the missionaries were too extravagant in their praise of the Indians, while they condemned the lack of religious fervor in the Whites.[51]

It is true that the freedom on frontiers brought out the best and the worst in men, and that some Catholics on the frontier were a disgrace to their religion. Many gave such bad examples to the Indians and other Whites that the missionaries were handicapped by their presence. It is in this context that the continuing tension between Jesuits who favored the

---

*When the property was acquired, a large bay, partly filled in later by the railroads for their tracks, extended to the north approximately 600 feet. Several islands, some with small pine trees, dotted the bay. Father Michael O'Malley, S.J. and other early missionaries who saw it in its primitive form described it as uncommonly beautiful. Father Mackin wrote that one could see the sweat baths of the Indians' along the shore of the bay below the college.

ministry of the Whites and Jesuits who favored an exclusive ministry of the Indians must be understood. Cataldo, like Giorda, whom he most admired, made no secret of his concern about Whites as well as Indians, and he was sharply criticized by both factions, each condemning him for favoring the other. A growing number of Jesuits believed at this time that more Jesuits should be assigned to work with Whites, while others—"the Old Guard," mostly veterans of the past three decades—firmly insisted that since Jesuits had been entrusted with the care of the Indians by the bishops of the United States in 1837, they should continue to work with the Indians exclusively. On the other hand, hard-pressed bishops in the Northwest, representing dioceses that did not exist in 1837, continually urged Jesuit superiors to undertake the care of Whites, since they had so few priests to do so. Most Jesuits favored a policy of compromise—a middle course that would gingerly handle commitments to both sides, no doubt hoping that the dilemma would go away.

It did not go away. One of Cataldo's subjects was a Frenchman, Father Victor Garrand, who suggested that Father General reprimand the superior "for he is pious and obedient."[52] What irked Garrand was Cataldo's constant rejoinder when new projects for Whites were discussed: *"Sumus primo pro Indianis,"* we are here primarily for the Indians. This said Garrand, "is out of date and no longer means anything." Garrand should have known otherwise, that this controversy would be an endless one, still alive a century later.

Cataldo, as a matter of record, had made his own position about Whites, as well as Indians, very clear when he dispatched an open letter "To the Very Reverend Provincials and Superiors of the Society of Jesus in America." Dated at Lapwai on April 4, 1879, this letter, now a rare St. Ignatius imprint, contained some forceful remarks about the American Church's failure to assist the Indians and the need to provide missionaries for both Indians and Whites in the west. This letter read in part:

"In the universal neglect of the Indian race in the American Republic, even by the Catholics themselves—neglect that caused a member of the Hierarchy to say, that 'The Catholic Church in America has to give a great amount to God and to man for her neglect of the Indians'—in this common neglect, I say, our Society may be proud of having continued, almost alone, the work of Christianizing and educating the Indians until the year 1870, when the Government's Indian peace policy aroused feelings of zeal and shame in many Catholic hearts, and some came forward to take a share in this Missionary work. Would to God that the same zealous feelings were now felt by many in our colleges and seminaries, and especially by young members of our Society. We stand in the greatest need of missionaries, both Fathers and Brothers, not only to establish new houses and stations among other Indian tribes in Montana, Idaho and Washington Territories. . . .

"We also stand in need of Missionaries for the whites. These are flocking into the Indian country, not by hundreds, but by thousands, and if we do not attend to their spiritual welfare, their bad example will so completely influence the Indians, even the Catholic Indians, that in a few years they will be entirely lost to the Church and become infidels."[53]

Cataldo, in fact, had come to believe by this time that in a church made up of Indian and White the former would be greatly influenced in behavior by the latter, hence there was need to develop a flourishing white church as well as a central college for white boys. He knew, also, that money for a central prestigious school "like Santa Clara" would have to come from Whites, most of whom would contribute little or nothing to an institution built exclusively for Indians.

Convinced of this, Cataldo had not long to wait for confirmation. In the summer of 1881, seven men of commerce and industry filed a formal application for incorporation of Spokane Falls, a village that could now boast of a telegraph wire and one brick building. Such heady progress prompted more lofty aspirations and after a number of lively discussions this new aristocracy, also called "the capitalists," addressed a letter to Father Cataldo on October 1, calling his attention to the need for a college. It was a long letter which flowed with such extravagant praise for their little town that today even the Chamber of Commerce would blush to read it. Unequaled advantages for a college, the letter said. The perfect climate. Unrivalled picturesque surroundings. The center of a vast territory. Students would flock here from all parts of the West, even from California.[54]

Father Cataldo, accustomed to the promotion schemes of some of his subjects, took the rhetoric in stride. He replied to the honorable gentlemen on October 20, saying that the establishment of a college had been under advisement by the fathers and that undoubtedly Spokane Falls was the place for it. He was happy the townspeople had taken the initiative. He would do all in his power to promote the proposal.

This letter was probably delivered by messenger, for on the following day, James Glover, sometimes called the Father of Spokane and prime mover for its cultural enrichment, collected his philanthropists, sixteen in number by this time, and prepared a document which was supposed to convince Cataldo that his time had arrived. Dated and signed on "this 21st day of October," the sixteen capitalists, including Cataldo's good friend Jim Monaghan, pledged $2,650 under certain conditions:

"The undersigned citizens of Spokane Falls and vicinity hereby subscribe the sum of money set opposite our names respectively to aid J. M. Cataldo in constructing a college building or rather one wing of a building to be used as a college under supervision similar to Santa Clara College, California. The wing or building now proposed to be erected will be of brick or stone and in size not less than forty feet wide by eighty feet long and three stories high. Said building to be located and built on the south half of section seventeen (17) in Township twenty five (25) north Range forty three (43) East.

"It is proposed to commence said building early in the spring of 1882, and have the same ready for use as a college in the autumn of the same year."[55]

Without questioning the integrity of the signators, one must admit that the amount of money subscribed was no bonanza. Cataldo, apparently not impressed, accepted the proposal with caution. Meanwhile, he informed Bishop Junger of the Nesqually Diocese, whose jurisdiction included all of Washington Territory in 1881, that the people of Spokane Falls had proposed a college. Cataldo had attended a meeting of the townspeople. He respectfully requested the bishop's thoughts on these matters. The bishop quickly dispelled the Jesuit's anxiety by replying on October 31:

"I received yours of the 24th instant and I was glad to read your good news in meeting such great encouragement in Spokane Falls for the erection of a College for white children near to that place. I hope you will do all you can to help that good cause along i.e. to keep up the people's courage and work to establish a College. I congratulate you on the success of having bought some land in order to build an Indian Boarding-school in order to rescue our poor catholic Indian boys from the hands of that bigoted fellow in Oregon. A few weeks ago I saw he came down with a number from the Yumatilla most likely many catholics among them who will be lost to the Church. I wish they would hurry up that establishment which is to be erected at the place."*

Bishop Junger's reference to "that bigoted fellow in Oregon" reveals his own strong feelings on the subject of the Wilkinson school. Apparently his Lordship disliked Wilkinson as much as Wilkinson disliked his Lordship.

Cataldo wrote a long letter to Rome to inform Father Beckx about current developments and to try to coax his Paternity into sending him an entire college faculty. He

*Oregon Province Archives, Provincial Papers, Junger to Cataldo, October 31, 1881. "That bigoted fellow in Oregon" is Wilkinson, of course.

presented in a very lugubrious manner the dismal facts concerning the Wilkinson school and its raid on the Spokane reservation for Catholic boys.

"Ours have been of the unanimous opinion that we ought to start a school for these Spokanes, and provide competition for that Protestant school in Oregon, i.e., a central school, and one so universal as to educate not only the Spokane youngsters but also the better boys of all the other missions. With this view we have purchased a beautiful piece of land (un bel pezza di terra) next to this town, about 8 miles from our old Spokane station.

"Hardly had the philanthropic whites learned about this purchase than they became interested and they asked me to put up a college in Spokane Falls that in addition to Indians would also admit whites, a college that would in time become a university. And they would give money toward its erection. [I told them] If only I had subjects to open a college. . . .

"And so, if we do not insist on our schools, and show the Indians that our schools are good not only for them but also for the whites, within a few years the fruit of forty years of missionary endeavor will be rotted."[56]

This was precisely the point: forty years of missionary effort would be lost if the tactics of Cataldo's opposition succeeded. But Cataldo still had hope. He urged that Spokane be designated as the center of the mission and that Father General send him men to teach in the college. "The men we desperately need at this moment [i.e. when the college opens in September or October] include: an able teacher of physics and chemistry and someone well qualified to teach English literature. If you can furnish us with others, so much the better." Cataldo would take what he could get.

This letter demonstrates at least that Cataldo had no intention of abandoning his Indians for Whites, whatever the bait. The philanthropists he noted had raised their offer to ten thousand dollars, but they had also threatened to give the money to the Methodists if the Jesuits did not produce a college within the given time. This was like waving a red flag in front of a bull, since Wilkinson's school was busy making Methodists out of Cataldo's Catholic boys. "The whites are pressing me for an answer," he warned the general. "The Methodists are going to work. . . . Let me know by telegraph."

Before receiving a response from Beckx, who was struggling with much vaster problems in revolutionary Rome, Cataldo summoned Father Van Gorp from St. Ignatius Mission and assigned to him the task of erecting a chapel and Jesuit residence on the new Spokane property. He was also instructed to attend to the ministry of the Whites in St. Joseph's Church on Main Avenue. Van Gorp, who had seen forty-seven summers, was known as a practical man. He selected a site for a residence, with a view of the river's enchanting bay, and engaged a certain Mr. Whipple to construct a two-story frame house. On December 10, Brother John Dunnigan, Caruana's former novice on Attanam Creek, arrived to assist Van Gorp and to hurry the project along. By February, 1882, the cracker-box edifice was completed and ready for occupancy, which required very little time. Brother John then built a fence around the property and began to collect an assortment of farm animals and chickens and to assemble barns and corrals for them. The north bank of the river now resembled nothing so much as a model farm or a domestic animal zoo, which is not exactly what Cataldo had in mind.

If the Jesuits thought they still had a chance to receive the ten thousand dollars, they were sorely mistaken. A deluge of protests now fell upon them. Faith in the future of Spokane Falls began to falter and even some of Cataldo's subjects demanded that the cure-everything college be located in Cheney. Some reported the superior to Rome for having spent the mission's precious dollars "on useless gravel." Cataldo was required to defend his expenditures, even while he suddenly remembered that he had not yet finalized the purchase of the second half-section of land for relocating St. Michael's Mission.

Even the bishop had got cold feet. Writing from his residence at Vancouver, Washington, he expressed doubts about the future of Spokane Falls and suggested that Sprague "would be the best place to build a college."[57] Fortunately his Lordship was not in the real estate business. Neither was Cataldo but he lost no time in purchasing that second half-section. The new property was a godsend, because Baptiste Peone, on whose land St. Michael's Mission stood, had determined to sell this. Cataldo quickly summoned Brother Carfagno from St. Ignatius, where he was cooking meals mostly, and assigned him the task of building a new St. Michael's Church on the recently acquired half-section. Accordingly Carfagno erected a new frame church, the third St. Michael's Mission, measuring twenty feet by forty feet during the summer of 1882. After it was completed he built a new missionaries' residence nearby, a one-story frame house with a loft reached by a ladder.

Meanwhile the building of the college had not ceased to be a matter of concern. Plans for it were made and discussed, but Van Gorp's heart simply was not in the project. He had little or no faith in the future of Spokane Falls. Added to these unhappy dispositions was the misfortune of poor health which had plagued him for years. Finally relieved of his duties in Spokane Falls, he left for St. Ignatius Mission on September 18, 1882. With him went the last hope for the immediate construction of the college. The financial aid offered by Spokane's pioneers was lost by default and the whole project looked hopeless. When the superior general looked about him for a builder to replace Van Gorp, he found none that could be spared elsewhere. With a heavy heart he requested seventy-two year old Father Joset to leave Sacred Heart Mission at De Smet and to take up his residence at the new St. Michael's. Though he was still technically superior of De Smet, Joset was now also in charge of Spokane Falls. To his previous responsibilities there was now added a territory as large as all of Switzerland, his native land.

Like Van Gorp, Joset lacked heart for his new job. He was not interested in a college, nor at his age, capable of producing one. He seems to have concluded that a college lacked usefulness and he very probably feared that it would work to the destruction of the missions to which he had dedicated forty years of his life. While the project was as good as dead during his year of management, sharp tongues began to wag about Jesuit deception. It was said that the Jesuits had obtained the north half of section seventeen under false pretenses. They had deceived the railroad, saying they wanted the land for a school, while in reality they wanted it for speculation. Reports on these allegations reached Cataldo at St. Michael's where he had now established his headquarters. They also reached the land agent for the railroad who refused to deliver the deed which had been promised. When Cataldo stood firmly on Jesuit rights the railroad threatened to take the matter to court. Cataldo did not back down. He occasionally inquired about the deed to section seventeen which had been promised in writing, but he received in exchange only vague replies. The railroad, as Cataldo noted later, finally made out the deeds for both half-sections on August 1, 1883, but illegally withheld one document until after the completion of the college.*

After a weary year of disappointments and threatened litigation, Cataldo finally decided to force action with regard to the construction of the college. He transferred Father Grassi from the flourishing Yakima Mission to Spokane Falls and charged him with the near impossible task of erecting a brick school. If ever there was a superman, it was Father Grassi. He arrived in May, 1883. By October of the same year, the stone foundations of the school had been laid and approximately three hundred thousand bricks and a pile of lumber were on the ground ready for spring construction.

Grassi had not produced these spectacular results alone. Upon his arrival he had the good fortune of finding a suitable architect Henry Preusse, who had arrived in Spokane

*This second deed was not delivered until late in 1886.

Falls in the preceding autumn. Preusse was engaged to make plans for a solid brick building that was to be one hundred feet by fifty feet in dimensions and two stories high. It was to have a full basement and a mansard-type roof. Cataldo wanted his school building large enough to accommodate resident students, classrooms, masters' living rooms, quarters for retired missionaries, kitchen and dining facilities, library and chapel. Apparently oblivious to the fact that one building was to serve in the capacity of a whole campus of buildings, some questioned the Jesuits' good sense in promoting so vast a building in the wilderness. To them it seemed rash to erect so large a structure, at such expense, in a place where business concerns and even banks were timid in their investments. Perhaps this was merely an excuse given for why-I-don't-donate-something-to-the-cause, but at least this is what some said, and their remarks, like their pocketbooks, contributed precious little to the progress of the project. Despite all this criticism, Preusse did as he was directed and he was paid for his efforts with certain portions of the property which the Jesuits owned.*

Since Cataldo had demanded brick for his building, there was the added problem of supply. There was no dearth of this commodity but the local brickyard, which charged the modest sum of $10.00 per thousand for brick, was located west of town on Latah Creek, a considerable distance from the college site.† Grassi decided to establish his own brickyard near the project. Monaghan knew a good brick man, Louis Adams, who lived on a ranch near Fruitland. At Monaghan's request, Adams consented to make the brick. He moved into the box-like house with the Jesuits, just a stone's throw from the project, and began at once to organize his out-of-doors factory.‡ He found the proper kind of clay in sufficient quantity on the banks of the bay about where the McGoldrick Lumber Company horse barn was located some four decades later. Day laborers were hard to find, since individualistic men live on frontiers, but Adams was able to hire five Chinese coolies.

Brickmaking began on July 2. Grassi's work schedule called for seven thousand bricks per work day, to meet the estimated need of three hundred and fifty thousand before the beginning of winter. Eighty cords of wood were purchased for burning the brick from B. M. Whiting at $3.75 per cord.[58]

During the period of brickmaking it was Grassi's quiet steady manner which set the pace for the whole crew. He worked with his men, who not only respected him, they came to revere him. One day, for example, when the water gave out in the well, a sturdy Irishman was hired to deepen it. This man, after working about twenty minutes, gave the signal to be hoisted up. When he appeared at the surface, he indignantly objected to the flimsy walls of the well and declared he would not go down again for a thousand dollars. As none of the men nearby showed himself ready to continue the work, Grassi, making the sign of the cross, stepped into the bucket and ordered the men to let him down. "Down he went," Adams reported, "and dug for four hours when every minute might have meant certain death from a cave-in."

The winter postponed further developments on the college and Grassi was reassigned to his mission. Before his departure, he totaled up his accounts on the cost of the building thus far. He recorded them in the Procurator's account book as follows: bricks—$2,400, shingles—$360, lumber—$3,635, stone work—$719, excavations—$241.50, lime—$325, cement—$300, freight for these $330, building well—$1,596, board of men—$150, laying foundations—$650, nails—$200, other mysterious costs unknown, total cost—about $14,000.

*There were certain lots between Pearl and Victoria Streets. Victoria has since been renamed Division Street.

†About six miles distant, a long way by horse and wagon.

‡Father Grassi gave Adams his room in the residence and slept elsewhere on the floor.

The components of the college soaked up the winter's rains and frosts and were still there in the spring of 1884 when Father Louis Ruellan arrived to take charge on April 15, 1884. The ceremony of installation consisted in riding with Father Cataldo, two on one poor horse, eight miles from St. Michael's Mission to the Falls. The church was opened for inspection and that was that. Father Ruellan was now pastor.

An ecstatic young Frenchman, aged thirty-eight on his next birthday, Reullan expected to transform the town into a pious Catholic enclave, like a medieval village in Brittany. He soon acquired a low opinion of American Whites. Writing home one day he complained: "This morning I said Mass in my poor little miserable cabin which is the Spokane church. For fifteen days now I have been alone."[59]

His parish consisted of about 1500 people in town, Catholic and non-Catholic included. In addition, there were as many more scattered in settlements of the immediate area. In 1884 Spokane Falls claimed five hotels, two banks, eight business blocks, two newspapers, nine manufacturing enterprises, including one which made mattresses out of logs, two livery stables, seven real-estate firms, one doctor, two architects and six lawyers. There were four Protestant churches, one to balance off each saloon, and the little Catholic church besides. The three schools in operation outnumbered by one the number of whiskey wholesale houses, though there seems to be no doubt that the latter did more business. Statistically, the town was godly. However, the temples of Mammon easily outnumbered those of God; and the newly arrived pastor, who could count numbers as well as anybody else, lost precious little time in deciding for himself how wicked it really was.

With the help of another Jesuit, Father Aloysius Jacquet, Reullan pushed construction of the college as fast as possible. A born collector of other people's money for charitable causes, Jacquet already knew the territory. He had been assigned one year earlier to cover the vast area, extending as far east as Thompson Falls, Montana, and as far south as Wallula Junction in Oregon. He had long since learned that soldiers were generous givers to religion, perhaps to make up for their excessive profanity. Two forts were among the settlements he visited, Fort Sherman and Fort Spokane. Jacquet called at each regularly, his collection basket conspicuously extended for the convenience of everyone. The priest had always served his soldier friends well and at great personal inconvenience. They were now liberal with him and with their help he kept Ruellan's debts paid.

Like a flame that grows brighter just before it goes out, Ruellan now burned with an overwhelming desire to establish the church in Spokane. He spent his days searching for fallen-away Catholics. He traveled throughout the entire area, often on foot, going from home to home in a relentless quest for souls. His nights he spent in prayer or in barns or stables, sleeping as well as he could. Never before had he suffered so many insults, never so much pain and physical exhaustion. But he was filled with contentment. He could now count one hundred at Mass. There were now two hundred Catholics in the scattered parish, whereas at his coming he was told there were "perhaps a hundred."

In mid-December, worn out and aching with pains of pleurisy, Ruellan prepared to leave the Falls to go to St. Francis Regis Mission. He arrived there on December 2. Father Canestrelli, superior of the mission at that time, said of him, "He appeared like an angel from heaven. As soon as he was among us we began to feel in a new atmosphere, one of sanctity." On January 2, 1885, Ruellan began to direct a retreat for the brothers. Five days later he was dead. His last words were, "I had come for the sanctification of my brothers, but I was not good enough." The Indians, though they had scarcely met him, offered six hundred Holy Communions for his soul. All of them wept.

At Spokane Falls, Ruellan's parishioners were filled with consternation. "Another priest has been taken away from us," they wailed. Where would it all end? Father Cataldo, far away in Rome, cordially wished he knew.

Archbishop Charles Seghers, who was murdered in Alaska in 1886.

At Yakima Mission, about 1890, left to right: John Raiberti, Joseph Cataldo and Aloysius Parodi.

St. Joseph's Church near Yakima, 1897.

Pascal Tosi, companion of Seghers in 1886 and first Prefect Apostolic of Alaska.

St. Francis Xavier's Mission for Crow Indians in Montana as it looks today.

St. Francis Xavier's School, 1888, Mission, Montana, with Bishop Brondel and Father Joseph Cataldo, left of center.

Van der Velden, as he appeared at the Cheyenne mission.

James Rebmann, first president of Gonzaga College.

Peter Barcelo was born of Mexican parentage in Montezuma in old Sonora. From 1880–85 he visited the Crow Indians of Helena and from 1885–87 he was in residence at St. Joseph Labre's. He died in 1888, fifty years old, from effects of hardships he had endured. This photograph was taken at Helena about 1885.

8

EXPANSION EAST AND NORTH
1884–1886

Joseph Cataldo sat stiffly in conference with the vicar general in Rome. The vicar, Anton Anderledy, was pinch-hitting for the general, Father Peter Beckx, who was now eighty-eight.* Cataldo's departure from America and arrival at the Eternal City had come about by chance, but there was little left to chance in taking this unexpected opportunity to present his mission's needs before the top management.

It had begun with his attendance as a religious superior at the Third Council of Baltimore on Sunday, November 9, 1884. Clad in his best cassock, a somber black, he appeared to be a blackbird among feathered creatures of many kinds: the red of cardinals, the purple of bishops, the brown of Franciscans, and the white of Dominicans. He took his rightful place in St. Mary's Cathedral where sessions continued for four weeks, closing on December 7.

During these few weeks he was as defenseless as a tethered lamb upon whom several bishops pounced at intervals, almost demanding in their pitiful appeals to have Jesuits assigned to their dioceses. The church in the Northwest was flourishing. Priests were needed everywhere, for parishes, missions, schools, administrations, and chaplains. Two bishops, both kindly but desperate men, were especially importunate: Archbishop Charles Seghers, who had resigned the See of Oregon City to return to Vancouver Island and Alaska, and Bishop Aegidius Junger of the Nesqually diocese.† They cornered Cataldo whenever opportunities prevailed, each presenting such convincing arguments for Jesuit assistance that Cataldo was almost overcome. Seghers was particularly insistent that Cataldo make arrangements to go to Europe to seek recruits. Cataldo explained repeatedly that his superiors had already refused to grant this permission. Neither prelate gave up. Finally in deference to their wishes Cataldo made one more appeal, stating specifically at Seghers's request, that the bishops of the Northwest wanted him to accompany Bishop Junger to Rome, because Junger was in such poor health he could not go alone.[1]

---

*Anton Anderledy became vicar general on September 24, 1883, and was elected general following the death of Peter Beckx, on March 4, 1887. He served as general a little less than five years.

†Charles Seghers was allowed by Leo XIII to resign the See of Oregon City on March 7, 1884. He was appointed to the See of Vancouver Island at his own request. De Baets, L'Abbe Maurice, *Msgr. Seghers L'Apotre de L'Alaska* (Gand, 1896), p. 156.

131

EXPANSION

There was something comical about this: Junger had at least three broad chins and weighed about five stones too much, while Cataldo, his proposed gentleman companion, was something less than normal in size. It would be hard, for example, to imagine Cataldo assisting the bishop in getting up from a deck chair. But this did not matter; one would expect a bishop to be larger than, say, his secretary.

The vicar general in Rome relented. He cabled Cataldo in Baltimore: *Pouvez venir.* "You may come." In company with the obese bishop, then, and Abbot Frowin of Conception Abbey, Cataldo embarked for Antwerp the same month.

It is clear from his own comments that he did not realize when he sailed out of New York harbor how fateful this journey would be. It soon became the turning point in the history of the Rocky Mountain Mission, and its influence on the history of education in the Northwest is incalculable. On the one hand, the journey did much to turn Cataldo's thinking more toward the Whites. On the other, he acquired during this journey a considerable number of distinguished Jesuits of different nationalities. These men brought with them not only an ancient cultural heritage with which they enriched a primitive frontier college but also a spirit which, in a relatively brief time, transformed a struggling mission into a well-organized province. In truth, this was the beginning of our modern province.

At Rome, Anderledy's first reaction to Cataldo's request for permission to gather volunteers from all over Europe was disappointing. For reasons best known to himself, he simply said no. At this point Cataldo received news of Ruellan's sudden death from pneumonia. Father Anderledy himself handed him the cablegram with its shocking disclosure. Anderledy waited expectantly for Cataldo's reaction. Cataldo was crushed. He had left Ruellan, a bright, promising young Jesuit in charge of the mission in his absence.

Too many had died. Father Gazzoli, the gentle friend of the pope, backbone of the Coeur d'Arlene mission had died, stone deaf and lonely, but with Joset at his side.* Father Giorda, too, had died, of a broken heart, it was said.† He and Gazzoli had been as close to one another as identical twins. Cataldo missed Giorda exceedingly. Not yet had he got accustomed to making decisions without Giorda's advice, though Giorda had been gone for over two years. Ravalli also was dead. He had passed quietly away on the feast of the Holy Angels, like a man slipping out of his home to visit a neighbor. He had died just before Cataldo left for the council. All Montana mourned. Flags were flying still at half-mast when Cataldo traveled through the territory, grim reminders that the Old Guard would soon be gone.‡

Joset was seventy-four, and Grassi, worn out with labor and frustration, was nearing the end of his years. Imoda, the one thread of continuity at St. Peter's, had to be transferred to Helena, where he was assisting the recently appointed bishop, John Brondel, in developing a new diocese. Van Gorp, who was not well, and Palladino were needed in Montana. Diomedi, stationed at a White parish in Lewiston, was trying to cover an area as wide as Belgium. Caruana, building a new church at Yakima City was in the middle of a bitter dispute. Now Ruellan was gone. Whom could Cataldo place in charge of the new college?

Sensing the depth of Cataldo's distress, Anderledy, to console him, granted the permission he had previously refused. Cataldo left Rome on January 11, four days after Ruellan's death, eager to be away, lest Anderledy change his mind again. Referring to his

*Gregory Gazzoli died at De Smet on June 10, 1882.

†Joseph Giorda died on August 4, 1882, at De Smet. He was only 59 years old.

‡Anthony Ravalli died on October 2, 1884 at St. Mary's Mission.

departure from the Roman Curia in later years, he described it "as the jump which saved the Rocky Mountain Mission."

Armed with prestigious letters of commendation from the vicar general, Cataldo visited various apostolic schools and seminaries throughout Europe and in the harvest he gathered were five future presidents of Gonzaga College, the first bishop of Alaska, and the first provincial of the California Province. There were also a few saints.

Three of the new recruits arrived in New York in September, 1885. These were Fathers James Rebmann and Herman Schuler, and one scholastic, Balthasar Feusi. All three had instructions to report to certain houses of study to complete their formation before taking up assignments in the Pacific Northwest. Of these three, Father Rebmann especially bears watching, for he soon became the first president of Gonzaga College.

Rebmann was born on June 20, 1853, in historic Speyer on the Rhine. His father, a tinsmith, left his home for America, when James was less than a year old and was never heard from again. Elizabeth Rebmann, who considered herself a widow for the rest of her life, reared her only child meticulously, sharing with him her own deep faith. When James decided to become a Jesuit, she bade him a final farewell with these sublime words: "It has cost me much to let you go. I have made the sacrifice for the love of God and you. You must never come back on account of me."[2] This was on April 8, 1872. James entered the Jesuit Novitiate at Gorheim in southern Germany two days later. After his ordination to the priesthood in 1884, at Ditton Hall near Liverpool, England, he volunteered for the missions of northwest America. Accepted with great alacrity by Father Cataldo, he was assigned to Frederick, Maryland, to complete his Tertianship. This final year of Jesuit training was concluded in June, 1886; and Father Rebmann, eager for his first apostolic work, boarded a train for the West.

Meanwhile Father Jacquet had taken Ruellan's place at Spokane Falls. He now directed his prodigious energies to the building of Spokane's new church, a poor man's "American Gothic" in red brick, facing south on Main Avenue, about one-hundred feet west of Brown Street. He put a wooden picket fence around it, mostly to keep the dogs out, because the town was overrun with all varieties, most of them half-wild. Everything was completed when Rebmann arrived via the Northern Pacific.

"I arrived in the afternoon of the Feast of Saint Peter and Paul, 1886. The building of the College was just finished but not furnished. In the room which was given me, was a strawsack, the only furniture, on the floor, without bed stead, table or chair. Sitting on that strawsack I wrote my first letters to Ditton Hall and to my mother. My knees were my desk. An empty lime barrel, which I found in the yard and cleaned, served as a wash stand the following morning. In the evening we had Benediction. An old tin tomato can served as censer fastened to some picture wire, and a small sardine can as incense boat."[3]

Though Rebmann had been assigned to Spokane Falls primarily to get the college on its feet, he was also superior of the local Jesuits and pastor of the church, relieving the overworked Jacquet of this last charge. Three days after his arrival the cornerstone of the first Sacred Heart Hospital was solemnly laid by Bishop Junger, who was assisted by the new pastor. Following this, on the Fourth of July, the new church was dedicated. Bishop Junger presided over the dedication also, but it was Rebmann who seemed to be pulled to-and-fro by the excitement of the hour.

His Lordship's blessing took care of the church; Rebmann now turned his attention to the college and the Jesuit residence nearby. He refused absolutely to share the crackerbox residence with the bedbugs, which had taken possession, so he moved into the unfinished college building, tidying it up as well as he could until something better could be done. Father Joset, back again at Spokane Falls, had no such squeamishness. He lived in the old house from which he periodically sallied forth to attend to his Indians at St. Michael's or

Sacred Heart Mission, traveling to both by buckboard. Father Jeremiah Rossi, Rebmann's new assistant, who resembled in appearance the plaintive sadness of his namesake's lamentations, lived in the new college as did two other members of the community, Brother John Donnigan* and Brother Michael Campopiano. Pierre, another occupant of the building, was a hired man. He served as the cook, though Brother John baked the bread, which was as hard as Cataldo's "useless" gravel. At breakfast one morning Joset, after several attempts to cut the bread with a knife, knocked it fiercely on the end of the table. Still no piece broke off. He handed over the loaf to Rebmann and said: "Father, *Domine dic ut hi lapsides panes fiant.*" Lord, say that these stones may be bread.[4]

Another member of the proposed college's staff arrived in the summer of 1886. This was Charles Mackin, a not-yet ordained scholastic who had been born in North Ireland on September 29, 1856. After purloining an illegal education behind hedgerows and in a Protestant college, which left him about as thin-skinned as a rhinoceros, he migrated to America and entered the Jesuit Order on October 9, 1880.

Shortly after his arrival in Spokane Falls, Joset treated Mackin to an excursion to St. Michael's in his buckboard. The old missionary, now in his seventy-sixth year, drove this like a Roman charioteer in *Ben Hur.*

"They were making new roads on Bigelow Gulch," Father Mackin recalled in his memoirs. "They had cut down the pine trees and left the stumps about two feet high. Father Josep [sic] was passing with his buckboard, one wheel on the stump and the other down below, but he didn't mind; he had made the sign of the cross when starting and he didn't mind what the bay mare or the buckboard did the rest of the way. He was boasting that he was the only one in the Rocky Mountains who had the privilege of having a buckboard."[5]

Cataldo had returned from Europe well pleased with his barnstorming raid on its seminaries. He had received literally scores of new applications for his mission, and despite much talk about selectivity and scholarship, he accepted all who were fit and willing. He took up his residence at St. Michael's again, turning the room assigned to him into a classroom. Each night he climbed the ladder to the loft, where he prayed, then slept like most Italians, as senseless as a log. Each day new appeals for help came to him from the hard-pressed bishops of the Northwest or from Jesuit local superiors who were being pulled hither-and-yon by Whites as well as Indians who wanted churches, schools, and chaplains.

One point had become clear: the pioneering mission days were past. The Indian people no longer could be segregated from the Whites in isolated missions. New methods were required, and first among these, of course, was education. More mission schools had to be developed on the reservations, like St. Ignatius, which had been praised in the U.S. Senate by Senator George Vest.† There should be resident schools where Indian children could be prepared for living in a culture foreign to them. Three resident schools, in addition to St. Ignatius, already were functioning: Sacred Heart at De Smet, St. Francis Regis and St. Peter's. The latter would have to be moved, since the Blackfeet tribal lands were now far distant. Gonzaga, designed to be the center of all, would soon be a reality.

Shortly after his return from Europe, Cataldo applied to the government in Washington through the Catholic Indian Bureau for authorization to erect buildings for schools and

*Brother Donnigan was also listed in the catalogues as Dunningham. He went by both names. His name also appears as Donnegan, Dunninham, and Dunnigan.

†George Vest, senator from Missouri, toured the West to visit all Indian schools and declared in the senate that the "only practical system for the education of the Indians was the system adopted by the Jesuits." *Woodstock Letters,* 13 (1884), p. 201.

mission work "belonging to the Blackfeet, Fort Peck, and Crow Agencies."[6] Permission was granted. Cataldo, deeply committed now to his new policy, urged the development of new missions wherever possible. This became a period of remarkable growth.

The Crow Agency, or reservation, mentioned by Cataldo, lay west of the reservation of the Northern Cheyenne, which was about seventy-five miles south of Miles City. The Crows and the Cheyennes were neighbors and they shared in a closely related history. One Jesuit, Father Peter Barcelo, had already worn himself out with four years of unrelenting travels, trying to cover both reservations, but especially that of the Crows. These Indians described by De Smet as "tall, robust and well formed, having a piercing eye, aquiline nose and teeth of ivory whiteness," had made frequent appeals for priests, but none was available until 1880 when Barcelo was assigned to visit them.[7]

"I met a camp of them," he wrote later, "on the bank of the Big Horn River and was received in a friendly manner and treated to a dinner of tough dry buffalo meat. I then told the chief, through an interpreter, that I wished to give them some religious instruction. He immediately bawled out for the people to assemble, which they did at once. I then related to them the creation of the world and found them attentive listeners; the formation of Eve from the rib of Adam caused some laughter."[8]

Barcelo baptized 114 children at this time. Meeting an Indian who was very sick, he baptized him also and conferred Extreme Unction upon him. The next day the Indian was up and around, eating with his friends and telling them what a big medicine man the Black Robe was.

Barcelo visited the Crows regularly from Helena, but after several years, when it became obvious that his state of health was becoming worse rather than better in this kind of mission activity, Cataldo dispatched Prando to replace him. Cataldo then sent Barcelo to work only with the Cheyennes, hoping a change of pace would give him a new lease on life.

Prando, whose restless, muscular body, like a pinto horse, contained a spirit as tough as a wolverine's, made his first journey to the Crows with Barcelo to learn the lay of the land and the language of its people. One of his first converts was Chief Iron-Bull, a hint of events to follow. Because of his strength and vigor, Prando appealed strongly to the masculine and powerful. Barcelo, on the other hand, though he was not timid, was sensitive and high-strung, like a poet. Born of Mexican parentage he was dark-skinned, a handicap with most Indians, who still cherished a deeply superstitious awe of white-skinned people. Barcelo had dark, piercing eyes, which seemed to burn like coals in an otherwise serene countenance. Generally credited with being a spiritual mystic, he gave much edification to his brother Jesuits, who were greatly concerned about his health problems.*

Transferring Barcelo to the Cheyennes was like moving him as chaplain from Ellis Island to Yokahama. The Cheyennes, who boasted they had never shed white-man's blood, were an uncommonly good people, at least until the corrupted Whites around them began to exercise their baneful influence. They had shared in the coalition which destroyed Custer's Command in 1876, and for this, like the Sioux, they had been punished. They were sent to Oklahoma, no doubt an attractive place to live, but for the Cheyennes it was hot and humid. They hated it and soon escaped. Regarded as hostiles, enroute to Montana many were killed. Again they surrendered and were taken to Fort Keough, near Miles City

---

*Barcelo had made his novitiate at Santa Clara under Ravalli, the novice master. It was here that he acquired his desire to work with the Indians. He was a man of continual prayer and so penitential that Palladino admits to reporting to the superior what he regarded as excessive penance. L. B. Palladino, *Indians and Whites in the Northwest*, 2d ed., p. 255, et seq.

where, fortunately for them, they found a sympathetic listener in the person of an army private, a Catholic whose name has been associated ever since with border warfare. It was George Yoakum.[9]

When the Indians were allowed to return to their reservation in 1882, Yoakum interested Bishop James O'Connor, at that time vicar apostolic of Nebraska and eastern Montana, in their welfare. Bishop O'Connor urged the Jesuits at Helena to try to do something for these forsaken and battered people, so Barcelo was dispatched to reconnoiter and to do whatever he could in the limited time allowed him.

Barcelo made his first visit to the Cheyennes in 1883 and he remained several months, writing while there the following report to Cataldo: "These Indians are well disposed; they are specially anxious about their children's schooling. We have only to be constant in our work. There is here plenty of excellent ground of pasture and cultivation. With more help from the government these Indians will be well-settled and civilized."[10] For the return address to his letter Barcelo had written: Dolours Mission, the Mission of Sorrow.

Since missionaries were few in number and the demands many, Barcelo was unable to return to the Cheyennes at that time. A mission was founded the following year by Bishop Brondel of Helena who had recently been appointed vicar apostolic of all Montana. Brondel appealed to other bishops for help; and, in response, Mother Amadeus, the almost ubiquitous Ursuline, with a little band of other ubiquitous Ursulines, arrived January 17, 1884, at Miles City. They were given a tumultuous welcome as Lady Black Robes by Indians, gamblers, cowboys, border ruffians, and the rest of the inhabitants of the "wicked little City of Montana," which was precisely the term used for Miles City in certain Eastern states. Some of the nuns remained in the wicked little city to found a school, and three others accompanied by Mother Amadeus departed for the new mission on March 29.[11]

It required four days of travel via an army ambulance drawn by mules to reach their objective; and, we are explicitly told—though it is hard to believe—that the drivers did not utter one word of profanity. The trip was very rough, up and down steep gulches, through ravines, over forbidding bluffs and along precipitous embankments. Many times the soldiers who were escorting the nuns were obliged to unload all the baggage and transport it over difficult passages, but all of them apparently kept their patience and were gallant gentlemen, at least in the presence of the nuns. Some seven miles from the mission the little caravan was met on April 2 by Father Joseph Eyler, a diocesan priest of the Cleveland Diocese, who had preceded them. By noon on this day they all reached their destination at the confluence of the Otter Creek and Tongue River.

Father Eyler had acquired a three-room log cabin for a beginning. This dwelling was designed in such a manner that the three compartments were unconnected within and all entrances were on the outside, like some modern school houses. The first compartment was on one end, sixteen by twenty-two feet, capped with a mud roof and papered with *The Police Gazette*, and was assigned to the nuns for a convent and chapel. The middle compartment was designated as the school, and the last, which had no flooring, as the rectory. Because the mission and its people were so utterly poor, it was dedicated by the bishop to St. Joseph Labre, Europe's very holy poor man who had but recently been canonized.

White settlers in the vicinity constantly made trouble for the missionaries because they did not want a mission, nor a successful Indian economy. They wanted the Indians out of the way and spared no efforts to achieve this. In a little more than a year, Father Eyler's health broke down because of the hardships of mission life and the tension between the Indians and Whites. Two diocesan priests successively replaced him for brief periods; then, in September, 1884, Father Barcelo returned.

He had scarcely got settled when, at evening time, on September 15, George Yoakum appeared to renew their old friendship. They sat in the priest's little log compartment, his kerosene lamp flickering and winking late into the night, while they chatted quietly about the reservation. When they heard a knock on the door, the priest opened it and saw four masked cowboys. They demanded that George Yoakum be brought out, saying he had sided with the Indians against the Whites. The priest parried and pleaded, then one of the masked men leveled his six-shooter and forced him aside. Three of them dragged poor Yoakum off into the darkness. Some time later Yoakum, thoroughly beaten, returned. He told Barcelo, who didn't know where to turn to for help, that they had tied him to a tree and whipped him, and that one of the men said: "This is only a foretaste of hell. If you do not hit the trail at once we will send you there."[12] Yoakum left the country and his name unjustly has been held in malediction ever since. *Miles City Daily Journal*, in its September 18 issue carried an account of the outrage. "Yoakum has been acting as an interpreter for the mission," the article stated; then it proceeded to express complacent approval for what had happened. Referring to the Indians Yoakum had befriended, it said: "In fact, the cattlemen would rather rejoice at an opportunity to inaugurate an open armed resistance against them and drive them from the country."

Barcelo soon collapsed so badly that Cataldo ordered him out of the place. He left December 18, 1884, and the three Ursulines were alone again. They had no Mass, not even the Blessed Sacrament to console them. When Christmas Eve came they prayed and waited expectantly all night, hoping that a priest would arrive. All they heard were the doleful howls of the wolves and an occasional whoop of a carousing Indian. No priest came.[13]

On February 8, 1885, Bishop Brondel arrived. He promised immediate help. He himself went on a begging tour of the East and returned with enough money to build a respectable convent and school. He also persuaded Jesuit superiors they had enough men to spare so that two could be sent to the Mission of Sorrows. Father Aloysius van der Velden and Father Peter Prando were appointed to St. Labre's in October of 1885, with the understanding that the latter would work with the Crows.[14]

For awhile after their coming, mission life went smoothly by, then its peace was shattered again, this time by a medicine man who bore the prophetic title of Porcupine. Porcupine was a young race fanatic whom the settlers' hatred had bred. He had witnessed the so-called Ghost Dance in a neighboring tribe and then introduced it among the Cheyennes. According to his contemporaries he had disappeared for while and when he returned to his people he claimed to have had conversation "with the Messiah on the West River." He brought this message: "The Indians will receive all their land back. The buffalo will increase to great numbers. The white man's guns will be harmless." All these provisions were dependent on the faithful performance of the Ghost Dance. This disturbance soon aroused most of the Indians. Even those who had been friendly to the mission gradually and quietly withdrew from all contact with Whites, the missionaries included.

Things went from bad to worse, until there were no longer children in school nor Indians for divine services. The Jesuits, under tremendous pressure from other needs, withdrew again from St. Labre's, hoping that this decision would bring the Indians to their senses. The nuns, too, were obliged to leave and on October 18, 1888, the last Mass was said at the mission by a priest from Miles City. The Indians grew so unruly that they attacked the agent who called troops to disperse them.[15]

The Cheyennes' loss was gain for the Crows. Prando now began to work with them exclusively, though for some time he continued to live at St. Joseph Labre's.

"In February, 1886," Prando wrote, as though he were speaking of someone else, "Father Prando arrived at the Crow Agency. He stopped over two months, in the Reservation, visiting Big Horn Valley, Little Horn, and the country below Fort Custer, teaching the Indians the principal truths of religion, baptizing the little ones to the number of five hundred and thirty-three, and went back to the Cheyennes."[16]

EXPANSION

In May of the following year Father Prando returned with Father Urban Grassi with the express purpose of seeking a mission site. The two Jesuits traveled in a little buckboard, drawn more or less apathetically by two Indian ponies. "They came from the Cheyennes across the country, Father Prando being the guide, driver and cook," says the modest narrator. Apparently they had scant provisions for the trip, not even any fish-bait. Since they didn't have a tent, they slept in the open, wrapped in a blanket. When they reached the Big Horn River, they regretted very much the lack of fish-bait. "But the little wagon running on the road scared an owl, which in flying, dropped its prey. It was a little rabbit the owl had just killed and started to feast upon by the neck. The rabbit supplied the missionaries a bait to fish. They called it the *providential bait,* with which they caught four catfish and about six pounds each."

At first the land-hunters considered Pryor Creek as the site for their mission, but as they talked it over, they decided that at Pryor there was "only a small remnant of the tribe far away from the others and that part of the reservation could be opened to the whites at anytime; so they thought a good place was the Big Horn valley." As soon as Father Grassi saw the mouth of the Rotten Grass River, he looked around and said: "This is the right place to build the mission." With finality Prando added, "and so it was."[17]

In July of that same year Prando again returned to the Crow camps. Traveling horseback, he journeyed 1,100 miles up and down the reservation, with nothing more than a blanket to supply his needs. He slept in Indian lodges and ate what the Indians had to eat, which was often "a piece of bread for breakfast and supper, and nothing for dinner." Riding hard, he "was sometimes eating wild cherries, and he was sometimes regaling himself with a piece of dog without salt or bread, thinking only of going ahead in evangelizing the poor rough savages." By the thirteenth of November even the sturdy Prando had endured enough. He turned his weary horse toward the Cheyenne Mission: "It was about noon; he expected to strike Rose Bud before night. But taking a north-east direction instead of due east, he was caught in the dark, while it was snowing good, and he got lost in the Wolf Mountains. He was in a summer's dress and had nothing to eat. He tied his horse to a tree, made a little fire, and laid down near the fire like a wolf. The next day, it was snowing and he went on top of a high mountain, but he could see nothing else but mountains around him covered with snow." Father Prando finally found his way out, but it was by no means the end of his hardships on the Crow Mission.

In the following year, Prando was back again and this time he came prepared. A friend in Helena had presented him with a large tent, twelve by nine feet, and additional camp equipment had been acquired through the generosity of other friends. He was accompanied by Father Peter Bandini, brother of Father Joseph, and by Eddie Dillon who had offered to come to help in the project. These three arrived at Custer Station in late January, 1887. Because of the deep snow they were forced to remain there in a hotel for almost three weeks. Then they started for the mission site at Rotten Grass, traveling for three days, over a foot of snow. They finally reached their destination on February 21 and celebrated the achievement by clearing enough snow to pitch their tent, crawled into it and warmed up for the first time since they had left the hotel. After a few days, when the weather became milder, they put up two more tents, "one for a parlor and storeroom, and another for a chapel." They started Sunday services from the beginning and "the Indians would throng and fill up the large tent." They also arranged with professional builders to erect a frame mission building, two and one-half stories high and sixty by forty feet on the ground. They then broke ground for a garden and put a fence around it to keep out wandering cattle. Iron Eyes, as the Indians called Father Prando, was in the midst of all this activity, briskly giving orders or parrying verbal thrusts of the Indians who frequently tried to get the better of him, but never did.

By September 1, the building was ready, though school was delayed because the Ursulines who were to staff it were some five hundred miles distant, and they had no money to make the journey. Some time elapsed before the elusive cash was discovered. When the Ursulines finally arrived on the first of October, they found the countryside wild with the excitement of a minor war.

It seems that a certain medicine man, modestly referred to as "The-man-who-rides-a-horse-that-has-his-tail-wrapped-up," had gone off to the mountains to fast and to find some new medicine. After visiting the Sioux, he came back to his own tribe with a sword he had discovered in the woods somewhere. He preached that by brandishing his sword he could knock down from their horses all the white soldiers in the world and that if he spread a little dust he carried in a rag he could blind them all.

It so happens that while all the Indians were camped at Soap Creek a great storm arose. The-man-who-rides-a-horse-that-has-his-tail-wrapped-up, recognizing his opportunity, quickly shouted that it was he who was causing the storm. The wind howled, the thunder clapped magnificently, and the lightening filled the sky while hail fell in such quantity that all the Indians were terrified. After the storm passed The-man-who-rides, and so on, went about shouting that he was the owner of heaven and that nothing could kill him, that he could divide the rivers with his sword—or do anything. Says Prando: "All the Crows were struck with terror, just like frogs." A number of young bucks began to follow the rascal who but itched to start a war, and one morning they all galloped off to the agency, the fanatical swordsman waving his rusty weapon, and the others, their guns. Circling the agency that very night, they shot into it, scaring the Whites half to death.

At this point the nuns arrived, bewildered by all the excitement and somewhat apprehensive about the martyrdom that appeared to be very close. But the whooping Indians espied the Black Robe with them and all but the swordsman got off their horses and came over to shake hands with the newcomers and to bid them welcome. Some of them escorted the nuns all the way to the mission twenty-three miles distant. After that, they went back to their war which ended very suddenly and quite badly for the man on the horse. Apparently when a white man shot him in the arm his medicine failed him and he began to bleed like ordinary people. Dismayed by the appearance of his own blood, he turned his horse-with-the-tail-wrapped-up into the river to escape the battle, and another Indian saw him. Suddenly realizing how great a liar the swordsman was, the Indian shot him dead and that was the end of the Crow War as well as of The-man-who-rides-a-horse-that-has-his-tail-wrapped-up.

The end of the war coincided with the beginning of the new mission school, which had taken something like forty-seven years to produce, from De Smet's first visit until 1887. No one, however, could doubt that the long wait was worth it. With fifty children living at the school by Christmastime, the mission forged ahead so fast that two new buildings were needed during the following year. Erected with the help of Mother Drexel, the new chapel—thirty-six by seventy-five feet—and the second school unit—twenty-five by one hundred feet—were ready for occupation in December, 1888. The number of pupils soon increased to 150, the United States government making a yearly allowance for 120 of them at $180 each.

Though it would be naive to suppose that St. Xavier's soon put everything on the reservation in apple-pie order, it did produce rather extraordinary results. For example, the Crow Indian Agent's report for 1893 contained the following commendation: "St. Xavier's Mission School located at the mouth of Rotten Grass Creek, on Big Horn River, had three main buildings, besides a dozen smaller ones. . . . This school was commenced not quite six years ago, and it can show already very remarkable progress in every branch of learning for Indian children. They all speak English and read and spell from the first to the fifth reader as well as any white children, and they have improved enough in arithmetic, grammar, geography, and history. They sing and play the organ very well, and the boys have a small brass band that astonishes all visitors.

"Their improvement in industrial branches is equally good. Some of the boys learn carpentry, blacksmithing, baking, farming, stock-raising and so on. The girls have been learning housekeeping, cooking, washing, ironing, machine and hand sewing and even dressmaking."[18]

Father Palladino notes in *Indian and White in The Northwest* that from its beginning to the end of 1891, the baptismal record of the mission contains 1,070 baptisms, this being nearly half of the Crow population at that time.[19] Some of these Indian converts were very fervent as Palladino observes: "On one occasion the chief, who had received Holy Communion, asked to be allowed to speak. He stood in front of the altar and spoke, or rather prayed aloud as follows: 'O God, I believe all your words, the Black Robe has been teaching me. O God! When after a long life on earth I shall die, I want you to take the key of Heaven and open the door so I can go in and see your face. O Virgin Mary! I love you; I would like to see you in Heaven. O God! pity us. We are poor people. Let the grass grow high, our ponies be fat, our cows of many calves, our potatoes big, and keep away from us the lightning and small-pox.' "[20]

Some of the Crows abstained from smoking for months, some even for a whole year, out of devotion to the Mother of God, and others abstained from meat on every Friday, even when they had nothing else to eat. A good number attended Mass and instructions every day, some of the older Indians with poor memories remaining in the Church for hours repeating the prayers until they learned them.

Undoubtedly, Father Prando, who was greatly admired as well as loved by the Crow nation, was largely responsible for this impressive initial success. But he was not alone; other Jesuits and the devoted Ursulines contributed their share, and it doesn't require much imagination to realize how magnificently great each share was. All missions were extremely trying in their beginnings, but few continued to be as arduous as the Crow Mission. One historian has observed that the Crows, with some remarkable exceptions, gave the priests cause for worry and for this reason St. Xavier's was a mission for brave and not easily discouraged missionaries. Occasional outbursts of displeasure by the Indians, opposition to the school because less freedom was allowed the children than in the physically attractive government schools, the excessively depressing nature of Crow superstitions, these and many others were the burdens which the missionaries had to bear.

In northeast Montana during this period there was another Jesuit like Prando, though he came from a very different kind of background. Frederick Eberschweiler, a Rhinelander born at Wasenwerth on June 19, 1839, had been educated by the German Jesuits during the *Kulturkampf*. He was ordained at Maria Laach, a Jesuit scholasticate which had been a renowned medieval monastery. Expelled by Bismark in 1872, despite his services to his country as a chaplain in the Franco-Prussian War, he was sent to the German province's "Buffalo Mission" in New York which became a kind of nursery for vocations to the Indian Missions.*

After an uneventful ten years in Buffalo, Eberschweiler arrived in the Northwest. Giorda, superior then, assigned him to Fort Benton where he spent two more years unhappily engaged, partly for reasons beyond his control.

---

*The so-called Buffalo Mission of the German Province maintained the Dakota Indian missions until 1909 at which time the newly formed California Province was assigned their care. The mission of Alaska Borealis, was assigned to the Lower Canadian Province. This arrangement did not work out. Alaska was returned to the California Province in 1912. The Dakota Mission was assigned to the Missouri Province.

Fort Benton on the Missouri was already an old town when Eberschweiler arrived. Jesuits and other priests had been there off and on since Nicolas Point's time. Between 1860 and 1878 nine different Jesuits had visited the place and attended to whatever was required. Finally in 1878 Father Imoda was assigned as the first resident priest of the town which had become respectable at last. During his first winter he built a frame church which he called the Immaculate Conception. Not long after this, in 1880, a secular priest took Imoda's place and remained three years. This was Father H. Camp, a warmly human priest who in a short time won the admiration and affection of his people.

It was during Camp's presence there that the townspeople built a sisters' Hospital without, however, acquiring any sisters to put into it. The building lay empty and idle until September, 1885, when a colony of Sisters of Providence arrived and opened the institution under the name of St. Clare.

When Father Camp was about to depart, he was presented with $500 in gold by the people. He gave it to his successor, Father Eberschweiler, to whom fell the little task of making a speech, which was both an introduction and a thank-you. "My name is Father Eberschweiler," he said, "E-ber-schwee-ler, but since you cannot pronounce it, just call me Father Evanston."

Despite this cordial beginning "Father Evanston" never came to like Fort Benton. He complained later that he was treated like an outcast for two years, which is probably true. Part of the fault was his own because he tended to be rather severe when he first arrived, though even those who disliked him had to admit he mellowed considerably before his departure for greener pastures.*

His departure had been contemplated for some time, because Cataldo, who was anxious to make use of the permissions he had received from the government, wanted Eberschweiler to prepare the way for a school somewhere near Rappagliosi's primitive mission for the Gros Ventres and Assiniboines.[21] To forestall opposition on the part of those ready to throw obstacles in the way, Cataldo directed Eberschweiler to undertake the construction of buildings near Fort Belknap, *any kind of buildings,* as soon as possible. This was in the general area of Rappagliosi's mission, but unsuitable for a school. There was no timber, the water was so saturated with alkali that it was a milky color, hence the name Milk River, and owing to the low bed of the river water could not be drained for irrigation. Thus, with Cataldo's approval, Eberschweiler elected to put up some temporary structures until a permanent site could be selected.[22]

Eberschweiler arrived at Fort Belknap on November 11, 1885. Going directly to the government agent, a certain Major Lincoln who was reported to be bitterly anti-Catholic, he showed him his letter from Washington, authorizing the erection of a Catholic mission. Lincoln's reaction was not recorded. This formality having been complied with, Eberschweiler then approached the local Indian trader, Mr. Thomas O'Hanlon, to make arrangements for the erection of a log cabin to serve as a residence and chapel. O'Hanlon, unlike the agent, was more than ordinarily hospitable. He assisted the Jesuit in selecting a site for the cabin on the Milk River near the present town of Harlem and secured the aid of some Indians for the labor of construction. Cottonwood trees, already becoming scarce in the area, served for logs; but no flooring other than earth was to be had. The establishment was ready by December 7. Eberschweiler moved in on the day following. He wrote about it to Cataldo: "On the 8th of December, feast of Mary Immaculate, the patroness of the United States, the solemn inauguration of my mission took place. Instead of bells, the voices of the criers in the next Indian camps announced the beginning of the divine service.

*It should be noted that Father Eberschweiler was regarded by Jesuits as a very holy man. His name was included in a list to Rome of deceased Jesuits whose cause for canonization should be examined.

I proceeded to my new Cathedral, cautiously lowering my head, entered its gate and passed through its halls. I could not place the style in which the Indians under their architect O'Hanlon had erected the edifice; it is a loghouse with two rooms, each 18 × 15. No marble altar with golden candlesticks standing there, I fixed my missionary altar on a table. Meanwhile the crowd assembled, i.e. the trader with one of his employees, the only Catholics of the place, and a few curious Indians. Then I commenced the first Holy Mass in the new Mission house, and said it with the greatest festival joy, although neither organ nor Palestrina chant resounded there."[23]

Eberschweiler's German heart for music and its need for solemnity shows through his frayed missionary vestments in numerous passages like this. An optimistic realist, he looked at the bright side, but for thirty years of frontier life he consciously sacrificed the finer things he had taken for granted in his youth.

Eberschweiler had no misgivings about the disadvantages of the location of his mission. Its most serious shortcoming was its proximity to the degenerate Whites around Forts Assiniboine and Belknap. He explained to Cataldo that since he had to choose a place in a hurry this was as good as any other until he could find a better one. He made the most of it. In subsequent letters he described the arrangements of his cabin with a dash of pride in its snugness, and he explained how he had fitted it up with a great number of colorful pictures "from Kury and Allison's in Chicago, for a very low price." He had also placed over the door a large gilded crucifix which the bishop had given him.

The Indians, powerfully attracted by this gallery, soon swarmed all over the cabin, expressing curiosity about everything they saw. Eberschweiler took great pains to cultivate their friendship. He passed the winter in entertaining them and in studying the Assiniboine language with the gratuitous help of Mr. Bent, the government interpreter. He instructed some twenty children in Catechism and hymn singing, which they loved, and when he had time for it, he visited the sick in their tepees.

On May 1, after conferring with the Indians about a permanent mission site, he saddled his horse, and in the company of Cyprian Mott, who had once been the guide for De Smet, he traveled in a southeasterly direction for forty miles into a small range of mountains called the Little Rockies. Like its neighboring Bearpaw Mountains, where Chief Joseph and his Nez Perce were captured nine years earlier, the little Rockies rose abruptly from the prairie lands, mirage-like, and from their forested crests numerous little streams of sweetwater flowed into the fertile valley that lay between the mountains and the prairie. One of these creeks was called Peoples Creek, and it was along its banks that Father Eberschweiler found that for which he had come.

So enraptured was he that he didn't feel his saddle-weariness. He wrote to Father Cataldo on May 2: "I just this evening returned from the 'Little Rockies' and hasten to write this for the mail tomorrow. I only can compare that most beautiful country with the promised land where milk and honey flows. I wished you had seen it. St. Peter's Mission is a good place for a mission, but it is just nothing in comparison with that place I have seen now. The cattle country with grazing land: the best I ever saw. Timber: that whole mountain range is thickly covered from the bottom to the top of the mountains. Water: seven beautiful creeks, running into the Milk River, clear as crystal, sweet as honey. Cultivating land: all the creeks, but especially at 'Peoples Creek'; at least 15 miles long remaining near the mountains is a deep, wide valley of the best garden land, enough to make the whole tribe here very rich and happy."[24]

The Indians, too, were much pleased with the location, apparently because it was one of their favorite resorts for buffalo hunting. At the suggestion of Father Eberschweiler, the chiefs and leading men of the two tribes petitioned President Grover Cleveland that they be allowed to move and settle on these lands. Father Eberschweiler composed the thirty-page

142

document for them. A special committee in the Senate was appointed to study the case, a technique ordinarily calculated to kill any motion for change, but in this instance the committee, prodded by Senator Vest, took immediate action. It recommended that the government accept the Indians' request. Accordingly, a commission was dispatched to Fort Belknap where a new treaty was drawn up and signed on January 21, 1887, for which Father Eberschweiler served as an official witness. According to this instrument the two tribes surrendered whatever territory they claimed by tradition and accepted in return an area of some forty thousand square miles that were adjacent to the Little Rockies.

In the summer of 1886, Father Eberschweiler, still in a hurry, rode by stagecoach two hundred miles to Fort Benton to find workers and lumber to build his mission on Peoples Creek. He found neither. It seems that a war had just broken out between the Fort Belknap Indians and the Canadian Bloods, and no one at Fort Benton, nor anywhere else for that matter, wanted to risk his scalp while freighting material for a Catholic mission. Besides, as Eberschweiler was very plainly told, there was no surplus of lumber at Fort Benton and he had better look elsewhere.

Returning to the Little Rockies, the exasperated Jesuit was surprised to find gold miners at work, apparently more interested in their luck than the loss of their scalps. He persuaded one of them, Mr. Unstet, who proved to be a diamond in the rough, to erect three log buildings with the help of his companions. One building 25' × 75' would be used as a church and priest's residence; and two smaller buildings would be used as a convent and a school. The cornerstone for the largest building was laid on September 15, 1886. Winter storms delayed activities, but the work took up again in the spring. Through the good services of Mr. O'Hanlon, Father Eberschweiler was able to buy ten thousand feet of lumber for floors, sash, and roofs for the new buildings and this, after sundry and aggravating attempts, was finally freighted out to Peoples Creek.

Father Eberschweiler was now occupied with the name for his mission. He wrote to Father Diomedi in January 1887, that he had asked for the name St. Francis Xavier Mission because "no Jesuit Indian mission has here the name of the great apostle of the heathens."[25] However, he admitted that public reports concerning the mission referred to it as St. Paul's Mission, probably because one of the men who had worked on it called it St. Paul's Mission in an article he had written for the Fort Benton paper. Others copied the reference and now, willy-nilly, it looked as though St. Paul's was going to stick. It did, and neither the mission's founder, nor St. Francis in heaven, bore a grudge. The next Jesuit mission founded in Montana among the Crows in the southeast, received Eberschweiler's designation and everybody was content.

Another circumstance favored Father Eberschweiler's plans: the Fort Belknap tribes and Bloods of Canada, after cooling off during one of Montana's coldest winters in history, smoked the pipe of peace in the summer of 1887. It was now considered prudent to bring the Ursulines to St. Paul's, though heaven knows, as far as they were concerned, a little trifle like an Indian war would never have delayed their coming. In September, 1887, Father Eberschweiler, two Ursulines, Mother Francis and Sister Martha, left St. Peter's Mission with a party of Indians bound for Fort Belknap. The group remained at the fort while the Jesuit gathered children for the mission. This was by no means an easy task and the construction of the Great Northern Railroad greatly complicated it. It seems that the construction crew had just about reached Harlem when the departure for St. Paul's was announced. The children refused absolutely to leave Fort Belknap until they had first seen the new railroad and the mysterious steam engine and cars.

Finally on the morning of September 13, after the children had been satisfied, they were rounded up and the expedition got under way. It did not reach St. Paul's Mission until one o'clock the following morning because of a series of misfortunes, including an overturned buckboard, and thus, contrary to expectations, they arrived at St. Paul's on the fourteenth, which is considered the formal date of the founding of the mission.

The Ursulines upon arrival put the children to bed; then, with characteristic vigor, set themselves to the grim business of putting their convent in order. During that same day, they organized their school and by the following day, September 15, exactly one year after the mission was begun, they opened their classroom to eighteen reluctant scholars. The government, quite reasonably we think, had allotted the sum of $100 a year for each of up to twenty-five students for their support and schooling. Though this was doubtlessly inadequate, it was as much better than nothing as life is better than starvation, and the little school prospered.[26]

While these historic events were taking place in the far-eastern end of the Rocky Mountain Mission beyond the Cascades, other new, if not young, Jesuits were kicking up dust and generally getting things done in the west. One of these was Aloysius Folchi, son of a noble Roman family, who had been born in Rome in 1834. Having become a Jesuit at the age of nineteen, he volunteered for America, where he made his novitiate and busied himself with teaching at Georgetown. Suddenly he was recalled to Rome, where he was dispensed mysteriously from his vows and directed to return to his home for some unknown emergency. This left him hurt and bewildered. One suspects that his family with Vatican connections had arranged the entire bizarre proceeding. Later he reapplied to enter the Society, but he received no encouragement. He was advised at last to seek ordination for an American diocese. Accordingly, he was ordained in Vienna for the Diocese of Charleston, South Carolina, where he worked as a missionary to the Blacks with great humility and zeal. In 1878 Cataldo accepted him for the Rocky Mountain Mission. After two stretches of formation at St. Ignatius and Sacred Heart Mission he was turned loose to work with Indians and Whites in the vast wilderness north of Spokane, which covered two counties: Stevens and Pend d'Oreille. He soon became a legend. Traveling either on his horse Jack or by the small frontier trains, which picked him up or left him off wherever he wished, he offered Mass and taught children catechism in log homes scattered all over his territory.

In January, 1885, he founded the parish of Chewelah, dedicating it to St. Mary of the Rosary. He bought an old log building which had been a trading post and converted it into a church. Less than two years later he started to build a frame church, which would not be so warm in frigid Chewelah winters, but more elegant at a cost of $1,000. Jim Monaghan, Cataldo's friend, was a member of the parish at that time and donated the land for the new church.*

They say Folchi became cranky in his old age. Perhaps he did, but it is difficult to imagine, for in middle age, when he traveled his almost endless trails through forests, bringing the Good Word and the sacraments with him, he was especially loved by the children. In his saddlebags or on his back he carried what was known as "hard candy" and this he doled out, making rice Christians, perhaps, but none of his little flock ever forgot him.†

Another apostle of the outer places, was Father Aloysius Parodi. Like Folchi he covered vast spaces, turning up here and there like a character in a Dickens's novel, always at the right time and place. In 1885 he founded the parish of Ellensburg, built the first church

---

*The Catholic Sentinel, July 22, 1886; The Chewelah Independent, June 11, 1953. It should be noted that this was Chewelah's second church, the first having been established by De Smet in 1845.

†The writer's grandfather took a homestead in 1883 in what was called Spring Valley, now the site of a large shopping center on North Division as it dips down into the Whitworth 'Y'. There he built a two-story log cabin, where the bank building now is, and Father Folchi offered Mass in this and gave instructions to the children of the area. Folchi never failed to reward the children with candy he carried in his horse's saddlebags.

there for Whites and called it St. Andrews.* A few months later he offered the first Mass in Cle Elum in the home of a Catholic family. Father Grassi was still rambling around central Washington, usually on a horse. He also visited the Okanogan country where he was preparing the way for Father de Rouge.

Father Caruana at St. Joseph's on Attanam Creek, not the personification of tact, had become embroiled in a dispute over the mission's land and Cataldo had directed him to move the mission sixteen miles to a white man's town called Yakima City. "Three years before," Parodi wrote, "Fr. Cataldo had bought 80 acres of land near old Yakima and had built a large house 46' × 30', two stories and a half high with an addition of the same length for the kitchen, pantry and dining room. And the year before, 1884, by his order, a beautiful church, roman style, had been built in old Yakima and was open for worship in 1885."[27]

As an afterthought, Parodi added: "The reason why Fr. Cataldo moved down the mission of Attanam to Old Yakima, was on account of land grabbers jumping the mission claim. An infidel from the north got a claim from the land office of 160 acres and built his house on the claim. A Catholic from the south got a claim of 40 acres and built his house on it, saying that the Gesuits have no right to get land, as they have made a vow of poverty. . . . There was not yet 40 acres of land for the mission, and Fr. Cataldo turned it over to the Bishop and moved the mission down to Old Yakima. F. Caruana had done his best to save the mission land; he had even gone to the Wallawalla land office, but it was of no use; the land is gone. The writer has the opinion that the Bishop lost the last 40 acres too, for in traveling by the mission saw a lady feeding chickens and pigs at the door of the house. The land had been given by the government for a mission but no record could be found."[28]

Later the railroad developed a new town called North Yakima, about four miles to the north of Old Yakima or Yakima City. Some Whites there demanded a church, and when they did not get one, with their noses out of joint, they started to build one for themselves. Lacking a priest, however, they soon gave up. "Father Cataldo," Parodi said, "had [the] opinion that the railroad company would not succeed to move all the town." He was mostly wrong, of course, for many of the white people in Old Town, lured by the railroad's offer of free lots and predictions of prosperity moved to North Yakima.

Caruana left the embroglio for Sacred Heart Mission and Parodi took his place briefly in Yakima. Then Father Victor Garrand appeared, sent by God, says Parodi, who seemed to think that things had got out of hand. He described what followed. "But now it was evident that the Old Yakima was condemned to death, never more to rise again. F. Garrand saw all this at a glance and found the means to get a block from the railroad company in North Yakima and the house was moved there. The few families left in the old town had contributed the most of all to build the church, and would not let Fr. Garrand move it to North Yakima. They told him if you attempt to move the church, it will be destroyed by fire before reaching North Yakima. But F. Garrand was not disheartened in the least, knowing how to get out of the difficulty. He gave [an] order to Br. Carfagno to lay the foundations of a church in North Yakima joined to the house. The church was built with a basement for the Indians. F. Garrand built the Altar. Afterwards, a small barn, the stable, the carpenter shop, the chicken house, were built by Br. Carfagno, and there [was] ground yet for a garden where Br. Carfagno planted fruit trees and grape vines. As F. Garrand said, it was a little paradise."[29]

Garrand, to be sure, could appreciate this. He had come recently—contrary to what Parodi said—from the missions of Syria and Egypt. A very blunt man, he soon joined the

*For many details concerning this, see the following, passim: OPA, Parodi Papers, Reminiscences and Reflections of Rev. Aloysius Parodi, S.J. Much of the following is taken from this source, which is one of the most accurate manuscripts by an early Jesuit.

faction of Jesuits who favored greater emphasis on work with Whites. He valued his association with Indians, however, and shortly after his arrival he built a school for Indian children at Yakima. He also built a new church for Indians twenty-five miles from town, but as their number diminished this church became almost useless. Garrand then built a new one in North Yakima, "what might be called a double church; the one upstairs for the Whites of the neighborhood, and the other a half-basement for the Indians." In other words this church had two naves, one above the other.

This was satisfactory for two years, but after the town expanded, "and American styles had been introduced," the Indians, who regarded themselves superior to the Whites, "could not bear to see those pale faces show off their finery while they themselves had nothing to drape their dignity." A well-attended meeting was convened to discuss this on Christmas, 1888, and it was decided that they would build their own church. It took six months to assemble the materials. Father Garrand drew up a simple sketch which the Indians rejected. "It is not fine enough," they said. "We want a church more beautiful than you have built for the whites." Garrand drew up new plans which pleased them and this "they executed faithfully," producing to their satisfaction a church worthy of themselves.

With Garrand included there were now four Jesuits assigned to cover the broad but sparsely settled plateau as large as Rhode Island. Parodi, whose meticulous memory was accumulating all the bits of history he personally encountered or acquired by gossip, accepted his share of the hardships cheerfully, despite his proneness to mental fatigue. High-strung like Barcelo, he was thin and short; and he looked like a modern, successful businessman in the prime of life. His worried-looking eyes and the deep furrows on his forehead suggested the appearance of one with huge responsibilities. He had the large hands of a peasant who is accustomed to working with them; but he was a bookworm, not a busy bee. Later, in Alaska, his mind was shattered by the suffering he endured, and he composed his memoirs in a mental hospital, leaving behind a lively record of Jesuit activity that has few rivals.

Father Stephen de Rouge, one of Parodi's colleagues on the plateau, succeeded Grassi in the Okanogan mission. He had come from the French nobility in a manner not likely to please the anti-clerical members of the Third Republic. Born on January 28, 1860, in the Chateau des Rues, he was the son and heir of a French count. Despite the prevailing hostility toward the Jesuit Order, Stephen was sent to the Jesuit's college where he was inspired by his teachers to become one of them. He entered the novitiate in 1879. In the following year with his companions, including George de la Motte, he was ejected by the government from the Novitiate and his father gave him shelter in the chateau, along with all of his Jesuit companions.* Some months later, French anticlerical laws forced all the Jesuits into exile, and de Rouge accompanied his novice master and companions to Aberdovey in Wales, where he pronounced his first vows as a Jesuit.

Later, still regarded as the Count Etienne de Rouge, he was requested by his government to participate in the centennial celebration of the surrender of Lord Cornwall at Yorktown. If anyone noted the hypocrisy of the French government in its two-faced conduct toward the count, it was never mentioned. De Rouge, who had already volunteered for the Rocky Mountain Mission, performed his diplomatic duties with Gallican frostiness, spent a brief time at Georgetown, then embarked by train for the west, where he completed his studies at St. Ignatius. Short in stature, his white alb and stole hanging diagonally on his breast, he approached Bishop Brondel in Helena for ordination on October 4, 1885. An amazing irony here is that this first ordination to the priesthood in Montana history in-

---

*Father Alphonsus Fletcher, who had known and worked with de Rouge in later years, frequently described his background and life at St. Mary's to the writer during the summer of 1945.

146

volved an exiled French count and an ex-patriot bishop, who had come to America only recently via Canada.

De Rouge first replaced Grassi while the latter spent time at hard labor building Gonzaga. Finally, he succeeded him when Grassi moved to North Yakima from which place he was moved later to the Umatilla Mission. Grassi had left a half-completed cabin in the Okanogan country near a place called Ellisford, and here de Rouge took up his first residence. A month after ordination, in the autumn of 1885, he completed the cabin and built a small chapel. Filled with consolation in spite of the loneliness of his life, he wrote to Cataldo: "You have heard from me at Christmastime and since then I have visited all the Indians from the whole Okanogan valley."[30] Coming from an ex-count, who had lived in a chateau with many servants, including thirty-four gardeners, this was a remarkable achievement indeed.[31]

In the years that followed, de Rouge became bald with age. From his cheeks and chin flowed a long, well-trimmed beard, which gave him the appearance of a fourth-century hermit in the desert. Though he spent many hours on horseback, crossing the deserts of central Washington where even the rattlesnakes had to carry their own water, he had developed a kind of monastic personality, almost as much Benedictine as Jesuit. Whatever one might call his spiritual ideology, he became very saintly, and his great monument, St. Mary's Mission near Omak, became the center of learning for the entire Colville reservation for nearly a century.

The seed for St. Mary's was planted by de Rouge during May 1886. At that time he purchased a log hut, a common practice in our beginnings, from the Okanogan Indians. This was described later by Father Celestine Caldi: "There is no building but a log house without a floor, window or chimney, and unfurnished. A few sticks with some wild straw served for a bed, a few boards for a table. A room added to the log house became a chapel."*

From this hovel de Rouge embarked on his endless journeys, stopping periodically at the homes of Indians and settlers to say Mass and preach, his sermons lasting nearly one hour. One white settler, who was not a Catholic, attended some of them and expressed his admiration for the priest: "He was about 30 years old, short and unimpressive in stature. Kindness, however, radiated from his eyes and he spoke in a soft mellow voice which converted somehow all that he said into a kind of poetry. His mind was always upon his mission there in the West, which was to find some goodness in the Indian's nature and in time to bring it out."[32]

During the following year, 1887, de Rouge sought new quarters because his log hut was beginning to fall apart. "Chief Smitkin," he wrote, "offered a place on his tribal possession near his wilderness home, thereby giving slight protection and encouragement. . . ."[33] Reference to protection sounded ominous, as indeed it was. This new site on Omak Creek lay in a valley that long had been a celebrated gathering place for medicine men and others engaged in superstitious practices. "Deputations of medicine men and dreamers were sent," de Rouge said, referring to himself in the third person, "to discourage the Father and make him leave the country."[34] While Smitkin protested, "This is my land," others threatened to kill the priest and no one doubted they meant it.

Undismayed, de Rouge with Smitkin's assistance began cutting and assembling logs for the new St. Mary's Mission, "while the medicine men of the tribe held a remonstrance meeting to decide whether or not they would let the white man stay among them."[35] He found a cleft in the rocky bluff south of the new mission, something that resembled a cave, and there he took refuge for safety when he was not accompanied by friends. In the cave he

---

*Fletcher seems to have been more impressed by Count de Rouge's number of gardeners than by anything else.

built an altar and arranged his bed. Apparently he told no one of its existence until years later when adventurers found remains of the altar and an improvised door. The area crawled with rattlesnakes, but history records no unfriendliness like that of the medicine men on their part, and the snakes shared the cave with the priest without ever divulging his secret.

Canonically, de Rouge was subject to the superior at St. Francis Regis Mission, but the distance to headquarters was so great he rarely made the journey. His Jesuit guests were few and when they came he wanted to celebrate. "Let us celebrate," he exclaimed when a Jesuit arrived from the Colville valley. "Will you make for me what you call some soft boiled eggs? I boil them and boil them and cannot get them soft."* Obviously his mother, the countess, had never taught him how to cook.

One of the best cooks in the entire mission was Brother Carfagno. But he was also an excellent carpenter. Whenever construction was required, Cataldo, disdaining the pleasures of the table for himself or others, assigned Carfagno to the task. The table in most missions was very plain, the food at best less than ordinary.

At Gonzaga College after the rector-president had got things organized, napkins were introduced for the use at meals. "When they appeared for the first time at dinner," Rebmann reported, "laid on the soup plates, our old patriarch, Father Joset, failed to understand why in our Indian Mission contrivances of the white people should be introduced. He crumpled his napkin up like a handkerchief and put it in his pocket."[36]

Old Joset disapproved of other innovations. "Then we decided to sleep in bedsheets instead of woolen blankets. He took the sheets which were laid also on his bed and stuck them into the remotest corner under his bed. 'Indian Missionaries,' he said the following morning to me, 'should not sleep in bedsheets.'

"Father General allowed us to open a Novitiate at De Smet Mission. Plans were drawn up of a handsome building for the Novices. When Father Joset, who was a Consultor of the Mission, saw the plans, he remonstrated saying: 'Our future Novices must learn to live in Indian teepees (tents) like the Indians, not in houses like the Yankees. Our Novitiate must consist of large tents.'

"The Father moved from Gonzaga, which was for him, after having lived over a half a century amongst the Indians in Indian fashion, too modern, to St. Michael's Mission, five miles from Gonzaga. He left, however his shaving outfit at Gonzaga. Every Saturday morning he walked the five miles from St. Michael's to Gonzaga to take his shave and to go to confession; he wanted exercise."[37]

Joset's preference for St. Michael's is a hint about its level of modernity and its primitive quality of life. Cataldo still maintained his residence there, sharing in the mission's poverty and isolation, but he moved to Gonzaga College when it was completed. At St. Michael's he received frequent letters from Archbishop Seghers, who was still pertinacious in his demand for priests for Alaska. At the council he had been very persistent, but Cataldo had advised him to look elsewhere—to other religious orders. He had found none, so he was back to Cataldo in the spring of 1886: "Let me first thank you fervently for your earnestness in the matter; you are indeed the only one to whom I made application who considers the matter of Alaska seriously," he wrote with a touch of Irish blarney to render Cataldo benevolent.

His Grace the Archbishop was probably too optimistic since Cataldo devoutly hoped he could avoid getting involved in Alaska. When he offered to compromise by loaning one priest for a year, Seghers protested in the name of all that was righteous, saying that it would be too dangerous a journey for one. He raised the ante to two priests and a brother.

*One of Fletcher's anecdotes about de Rouge.

Cataldo, worn down by such holy zeal finally surrendered but he made it clear that he would send only two priests and that they would be on loan until he received confirmation from Rome.*

In the selection of the two priests, Cataldo was very cautious. Anxious to send good men because of the obvious hazards, he was unwilling, too, to strip his own cupboard for the delectation of unknown strangers across the world. He finally decided upon sending Father Paschal Tosi and Father Aloysius Robaut, a tough little Frenchman who had come to the mission three years earlier from theology studies at Woodstock. Seghers had met both, Tosi at Sacred Heart Mission in 1883 and Robaut in July of the same year, when he was passing through Portland enroute to Spokane Falls. He approved of both, referring to Robaut as "a very fine fellow." No one seemed to object to Tosi's stubborn disposition and weak or ailing heart condition.

At St. Michael's Mission there was a volunteer workman by the name of Frank Gully, alias Fuller, whom Cataldo distrusted. His personal history was generally regarded as mysterious, but this much is known: a native of Dublin, Ireland, he had come to the United States in the 1870s and to Oregon a few years later.[38] From Oregon he drifted into the Coeur d'Alenes, bought a small farm near the mission at De Smet and subsequently applied for admission to the Society of Jesus as a lay brother. This was in January, 1883. Called "Brother Fuller" then, he was not actually a member of the Society, for Church law required a period of six months, known as "postulancy," before a brother could be admitted to the novitiate. Fuller withdrew before this trial period expired, but he continued to use "Brother" as part of his name.

For a time Fuller taught in the school at De Smet, then at St. Francis Regis Mission, but at each place he was discharged for quarrelsome and unstable behavior. On December 23, 1885, he signed an agreement at St. Michael's Mission, pledging his services to the Jesuit missions of the Northwest in return for his board and room. While there he learned of Seghers's projected expedition to Alaska and he quickly offered himself to the archbishop in place of the brother whom Cataldo could not supply.

The idea captivated Seghers despite Tosi's noisy objections and Cataldo's warnings. Tosi could not bear the sight of Fuller, with good reason perhaps, but his protests to the archbishop fell on deaf ears. The latter, an incurable romantic like De Smet, felt sure that everything would work out very well, and he went ahead with his plans, directing the two Jesuits and "Brother" Fuller to be in Victoria for departure to Alaska on July 13.

Tosi, appointed superior for the two Jesuits, with Robaut and Fuller left Spokane Falls on July 5 to meet Seghers in Victoria. Fuller enroute lived up to expectations by eccentric behavior. When the party, including Seghers, of course, left Victoria eight days later aboard the steamer *Ancon*, Seghers was jubilant, but Tosi, having witnessed the bizarre conduct of Fuller during the trip to Victoria was depressed and filled with forebodings about the future. "I had to take a revolver away from him," he wrote to Cataldo. Both Tosi and Robaut pleaded in letters to Cataldo to send reinforcements. When the *Ancon* docked at Juneau on July 15, Tosi reported: "I expect the worst."[39]

At Juneau, Seghers hired a French Canadian guide called Antoine Provost to accompany the expedition. Fuller disliked Provost and refused to help him when need arose. This, too, was pointed out to Seghers but his eyes, blinded by his Pollyanna mentality, could see nothing amiss. He brushed aside all difficulties with "God will take care," and the group now much larger than when it started, prepared to assault Chilkoot Pass to the Yukon drainage beyond. To fetch their accumulated baggage and supplies over the pass

*So far as we know Cataldo never made any pretense to anything else. Confer OPA, Cataldo Papers, Letter to Jules Jette, January 13, 1925.

about nine Indian packers had been employed, and these, together with five miners who were also headed north, led the procession up the steep incline. Seghers, bearing his own burden, struggled behind them.[40]

On July 27, while they were building a boat to cross Lake Lindeman, the first tragedy occurred: Provost disappeared. Every effort to find him for two days proved to be fruitless and the pathetic little group, badly shaken, had to leave without him. Both Jesuits were convinced that Provost was dead and that Fuller had murdered him.

Three days later the archbishop offered Mass at the headwaters of the great river. In his enthusiasm for what he regarded as making history, he seems to have forgotten about the disappearance of his guide. He nailed to a tree nearby a sign which read: "Abp. Seghers of Victoria, V.I. accompanied by Fathers Tosi and Robaut camped here and offered the Holy Sacrifice July 30, 1886."[41]

After another long month of nerve-wracking passages over windswept lakes, down rivers which crashed over rapids and through gorges, and over portages filled with brush and wilderness debris, Seghers wrote serenely to his vicar general, Father John J. Jonckau. Brother Fuller, he said, had shot a duck. In Lake Bennett they saw something swimming—a cinnamon bear—and Brother Fuller killed it with two shots.[42] He did not have to add that Brother Fuller was an expert shot with a gun.

As the expedition moved farther north, the problems increased rather than lessened. Tosi openly criticized the archbishop for bringing along Fuller who shirked his share of the work. Hostilities within the group had become intense, nerves were frayed, the weather was bad. Even good-natured Robaut had become irritable.

On September 7, the party reached Harper's Place, a trading post called Forty-Mile, where the Stewart River flowed into the Yukon. This was a winter rendezvous for miners who sought shelter here during the freeze. There were two traders, Jack Mac Queston and Jerry Harper. When Seghers asked them how things were downriver, one of them replied: "Everything is all right but at St. Michael there are two Protestant ministers, Mr. Parker and Mr. Chapman. They want to start missions among the Indians and want to come up to Nulato."[43]

When Seghers learned this "it was like a sword piercing his heart."[44] He told Tosi that they would have to leave for Nulato lest the ministers spoil his plans. Tosi opposed this, suggesting instead, that they all spend the winter at Forty-Mile, then leave by boat after the break-up of the river's ice. "No, Father, you stay here. For myself, I will go down with a couple of Indians."

Both Seghers and Tosi were stubborn. Seghers had the additional weight of rank. Overriding Tosi's vehement objections, he was determined to leave and he was determined that Fuller should accompany him.

On September 8, when Fuller shoved their boat into the current of the choppy gray waters of the Yukon, Seghers was not so much worried about his companion as he was about the Protestant missionaries who might arrive at Nulato before him. His boat disappeared down the river beyond the willows. The Jesuits never saw him again.

First Gonzaga and first St. Aloysius Church about 1893. The first residence is on the left.

Brother Carmelo Giordano, pioneer Jesuit in Alaska.

Holy Cross Mission on Yukon River, Alaska.

Sacred Heart Mission in 1963 near De Smet, Idaho, its present site.

St. Ann's Mission, Umatilla Reservation. This photograph was taken during the funeral Mass of Urban Grassi, March 25, 1890. Three years later the name of St. Ann's was changed to St. Andrew's.

9

PAINFUL GROWTH
1886–1891

The winter of 1886 was the coldest on record. Even at North Yakima the temperature dropped to fifty degrees below zero and Father Parodi almost froze to death in his bed.[1] One man did freeze to death, and one of the ranchers nearby lost approximately 1200 head of cattle. At Gonzaga College the water pipes in the new building were still somewhat exposed, and the president worried over them. When darkness fell and the temperature had dropped to twenty-four below zero, he did not go to bed at ten o'clock, as usual, nor did he go to the chapel to pray like Father Schuler. He spent the night with Brother Campopiano, "who kept a roaring fire in the lower bathroom," and Brother Alphonsus Thorain "who kept the water hot in the kitchen." All three "rubbed the pipes on the three floors with hot rags."[2]

At six in the morning, February 2, worn out from his all-night vigil, Rebmann retired to his room to pray for awhile in preparation for Mass and his final vows as a Jesuit. He heard a loud thumping on his door.

Old Father Joset, who was hard of hearing now, entered his room. "I want to say Mass right away," he said. "I was the whole night on the boat on lake Coeur d'Alene. I am nearly frozen to death. I want to say Mass right away and go to bed."

Rebmann shouted into his ears that there would be a Mass of the vows.

"Who takes his vows?" Joset asked.

"Father Schuler and I."

"You, Father Rector?" Joset said, his eyes open now, his cheeks plump and red.

"Yes, I."

Then Joset, tumbling over Rebmann and embracing him said, "I shall wait until seven o'clock with my Mass. I am so glad I came."

After the ceremony there was a special breakfast with two laymen present, friends of Rebmann's; and "Deo Gratias" was given by the rector, meaning that all were free to talk. Usually breakfast was taken in silence. There was another treat also. Mrs. Anna Sauer, a German friend of Rebmann, baked bread for the fathers and their guests. Brother Donnigan's bread that day was left in the bread box where it gave no one stomach cramps.*

---

*Mrs. Robert (Anna) Sauer was the mother of five-year-old Paul, later treasurer of Gonzaga University and procurator of the Province. In his "Reminiscences," Rebmann, who seems to have had a special interest in young Paul, provides a folksy account of his visit to the Sauer home on the day that Mrs. Sauer was making the bread. OPA, Rebmann Papers, "Reminiscences of Forty Years," pp. 14–16.

PAINFUL GROWTH

Father Diomedi from Lewiston had presided over the vow Mass. Barcelo, too, was in Spokane Falls, serving as the chaplain in the new Sacred Heart Hospital. Barcelo, it was said, already had one foot in the grave; but having a sick priest serve as a chaplain was nothing new. During the previous July he had preached at Father Mackin's first Mass in the Main Avenue Church, his eagle, dark eyes, steadily fixed on the newly ordained priest, who squirmed uncomfortably. "Father Barcelo preaching, addressed all his sermon to me," Mackin complained, "which I did not relish."[3] Barcelo, alas, soon followed Ruellan to an early grave.

In the late spring when the interior of the college was completed, the president felt assured that the school could be opened in September. Choosing the most likely date, Thursday, September 15, he arranged with the Spokane Printing Company for the production of a twelve-page catalogue announcing the opening of the long-awaited school and the terms of admission. The catalogue, a typical product of the era, heavily embellished with ornate type and artistic decorations, stated very categorically that "applicants for admission must know how to read and write and not be under twelve years of age."[4] No exceptions. It stated, furthermore, that "No one will be admitted for a shorter period than a session of ten months." Costs for board, room and tuition per student were low, even by contemporary standards: $250 for a ten-month session.

The school still lacked furnishings. A brother was dispatched to Chicago to buy furniture and equipment for faculty rooms. Then a windfall was announced: a Jesuit college in Prairie du Chien, Wisconsin, with surplus equipment on hand, offered Rebmann furnishings for his school, provided he pay the costs of transportation. Rebmann eagerly accepted the bonanza of books, students' desks, beds, bedding and other supplies. In the following year band instruments and billiard tables were thrown into the bargain.

As usual not all the news Rebmann received was good. In late spring there arrived from Helena a letter from Bishop Brondel, requesting the Jesuits to open a college in his diocese—in Montana's territorial capitol—where, the bishop added, there were many wealthy Catholics who had already pledged $25,000 in cash toward the project. Helena at this time appeared to be much more promising than Spokane Falls, where a Methodist college received such scant support it was about ready to close.

Father Cataldo took the Helena offer so seriously that he polled prominent members of the mission for their advice on the matter. He asked at least the following priests for their opinions: D'Aste, Palladino, Bandini, Grassi, Diomedi, Canestrelli, Caruana, Damiani, Van Gorp, Joset, and Rebmann. It will be noticed that only the last three were non-Italians, which was something like a majority of Italian cardinals electing the pope. Van Gorp expressed such strong arguments in favor of the Helena proposal that he deplored any other course as untenable. D'Aste, Palladino, Damiani and Bandini, all of whom had resided in Montana exclusively, favored the new school also. No one recommended abandoning Gonzaga, but neither did anyone defend it nor confirm the need for its completion. Some suggested that Jesuits withdraw from Missoula and Yakima.[5]

Reaction to the Helena petition exposed current thinking on the subject of Jesuit priorities. Whatever the Old Guard thought before, it now conceded a cautious preference for schoolwork with Whites. Champions of the white apostolate, especially Van Gorp and Palladino, could see that the trend was definitely toward their goals. No one should think, however, that the missions were ready to be boxed up and sent to the archives. None of the Jesuits, even those most ardently in favor of white schools, judged that the time had come for the dissolution of the missions. That came later.

Rebmann quite understandably, was greatly agitated during these proceedings. He knew very well that opposition to Gonzaga College was broad and deep throughout the mission, not only on the part of the Old Guard, but also by those who had been identified

154

with Jesuit institutions in Montana. He quickly perceived that a college in Helena could be used as a wedge, adroitly placed, to destroy all Jesuit activity in Spokane Falls. He might have ignored the whole affair, however, for nothing came of it. The pledged money never showed its colors. No faculty was ever appointed, no land acquired. The proposed St. John Berchmans College of Helena, eagerly sought by Van Gorp, who would succeed Cataldo as general superior, passed into history so quietly that one soon wondered what the fuss was all about.

Tosi in Alaska, whose crusty opinions Cataldo often requested, had never been consulted about the Helena college. With Robaut he had been imprisoned by snow and ice in Harper's Place where the air was so frigid it was hard to breathe. There were about forty miners at the post for the winter, a motley crowd more interested in finding gold than God, but Tosi, a very zealous priest, did what he could to change their minds.[6] Robaut had been good for him to soothe his irritation and his anger over the archbishop's naive defense of Fuller.

While the pros and cons of the proposed college at Helena were being discussed in June 1887, Tosi and Robaut prepared to leave their winter seclusion to meet with Seghers downriver. The ice of the Yukon, five or six feet thick, had broken up at last, and Harper had readied his sturdy little steamboat *Explore* for its annual descent to St. Michael for supplies. When all was ready rumors reached the migrants at Forty Mile that some tragedy had overtaken Seghers, but no one could provide particulars. When the two Jesuits boarded the *Explore* for Nulato they were still uncertain about Seghers's fate and apprehensive about their own future.

On June 5, at Fort Yukon, Harper asked an Indian in Russian if the rumor about Seghers was true. The Indian replied: "Yes, we have heard of it, but we do not know if it is true, the news came from below."[7] At each point along the river, Harper made inquiries of the natives. Gradually some details were pieced together. The Jesuits learned at last the shocking news that Seghers was dead. Of the five men who had departed from Juneau on July 20 of the previous summer, "one was dead," Robaut lamented, "another had disappeared, and a third was a killer."[8]

There was some confusion later about what precisely had occurred after Seghers and Fuller left Forty Mile on September 8 of the previous year. Many lively accounts were composed and published, especially by an aroused Catholic press, which presented Seghers as the Church's latest martyr, murdered by Fuller who was used, as the accounts related, as a cat's paw by greedy traders. Time, however, had demythologized most of these accounts. Having used Seghers's own diaries, Father Gerald Steckler has presented the most authentic report on the sequence of events.

Reduced to a party of two, Seghers and Fuller traveled by boat until the river, choked with ice, was no longer passable. On October 4, they reached Nuklukoyit where they purchased sleds and dogs, and employed three Indians to guide them to Nulato. They waited for the river to freeze solidly enough to bear their heavily loaded sleds. Seghers by this time realized that Fuller was insane. On October 16 he wrote in his diary: "Peculiar conversation with Brother in which for the third time he gives evidence of his insanity."[9] On Friday, November 19, the expedition began its final stage, with Seghers determined to reach Nulato before Sunday, November 28. The trail was difficult, however, the snow was soft and deep, and their progress was slow. In the evening of November 27, they reached a little "smokehouse," probably a summer fish camp, on the side of a bluff on the north bank of the river.[10] Seghers insisted on remaining here for the night. He was in good humor, though Fuller pouted more than usual. Seghers laughed pleasantly, making little jokes as he laid out his bearskin for a bed. Tomorrow he would be in Nulato.

During the night, several times Fuller arose and moved about in the darkened shack, barely visible in the light of the glowing coals. He remained on his bed until about six in the morning, clasping his gun, a 44 caliber, moody and restless. Shortly after six he arose again, aroused one Indian and sent him for water to make coffee. Another Indian stumbled to his feet and got up, too sleepy to realize what was taking place. Seghers stirred. He stood up from his bearskin, then bent over to pick up his mittens. Fuller fired a single shot into the stooping figure and the archbishop died instantly. His plan for Alaska died with him.

Tosi and Robaut passed the melancholy site of Seghers's death on the riverbank as they continued morosely down the river to St. Michael on the Yukon delta, where officials of the Alaska Commercial Company had taken Fuller and the archbishop's body. When they arrived at St. Michael and had set up their tents, Fuller, who was not yet in legal custody, appeared before them and said, "Well, I killed Bishop Seghers."[11]

It was not Tosi's responsibility to decide the future of the mission of Alaska. "I do not want to give up the Mission," he told Robaut. "I must go down to give the news and meanwhile I will try my best to get at least one Father and one Brother." At St. Michael, Tosi embarked on the Northern Commercial Company's ship *Dora,* reported to the United States Commissioner at Unalaska, then continued to San Francisco on the same boat, hoping to persuade his superior to keep Alaska.

News of Seghers's dramatic death had created an aura of greatness about all three of the missionaries and the Jesuits were highly complimented for their zeal and loyalty to the archbishop, a galling reminder to Cataldo that he had merely sent two Jesuits "to spy out the land. When I gave him [the archbishop] Frs. Tosi and Robaut it was only for a *visit.*" Cataldo grumbled later, "I was blamed by everybody . . . even our Fr. General wrote me *moto proprio,* now we are obliged to take Alaska. So it seems to me that the good archp. went to plead the cause of Alaska with God, as he had done with the Pope."[12]

Once Cataldo knew he was stuck with Alaska he decided to make the most of it. He agreed to send Tosi back with one more priest and a brother. What else could he do? He could not back down now, especially during all this hullaballoo about his glamorous subjects and their courage. Nor could he abandon Robaut, who was still somewhere up there, only God knew exactly where.

Tosi had left for San Francisco on June 27. The next day, since he could not persuade the captains of several boats to take the archbishop's body to Victoria, Robaut arranged for its temporary burial in the Russian cemetery at St. Michael. He was assisted at the grave by the two Protestant ministers, whom Seghers had feared and because of whom Seghers had probably died.*

A few days later, on July 6, Capt. Michael Healy of the United States Coast Guard, arrived at St. Michael aboard the cutter *Bear* with orders to take Fuller into custody. Having landed by launch with four officers and four sailors, he promptly went to the office of the trading company of the village and said, "Where is that rascal Fuller?" The trader replied, "He is in a tent over there." Healy arrested him, handcuffed him and brought him aboard the *Bear,* whence he sailed to Sitka, where the trial was subsequently held.[13] As Fuller departed from St. Michael he offered his last cynical regret: "It is really too bad I got caught, for otherwise I could have killed the two Jesuit Fathers Tosi and Robaut."[14]

Having buried the archbishop, Robaut prepared to go upriver, as Tosi had directed him. He was ordered to bring provisions for our men, Tosi had said, "for there will be myself, another Father and one Brother." Unfortunately Robaut had little experience in such matters. He packed twenty pounds of beans, two hundred pounds of flour, a few

---

*The Protestant missionaries were Dr. John W. Chapman and the Reverend Octavius Parker. Obviously they were not responsible for Seghers's death, but had they not been on the lower Yukon it is highly improbable that Seghers would have left with Fuller from Forty-Mile until the following spring.

pounds of tea, and a few pounds of coffee. "No salt, no sugar, no lard, no oil. So imagine a man with fifty pounds of flour all year!" The brother complained when he arrived later.[15]

When Robaut left St. Michael he brought with him also a box of church goods from New York, "sent by the pious Ladies' Society there." In the box were candles for the altar. The Indians on the boat had placed the box on the boiler to use it as a table for eating their meals and "the heat melted the wax. When we opened the box we found only the wicks; the vestments were all spoiled with the wax."

Robaut went upriver only as far as Nuklukoyit, where he lived with a trader who had two young sons, willing and able to teach him "Indian." There he awaited the arrival of Tosi.

The latter, meanwhile, had arrived at Spokane Falls where Cataldo formally appointed him as Superior of the Mission of Alaska, and assigned to his mission two more Jesuits, Father Aloysius Ragaru and Brother Carmel Giordano. Both were unusual personalities, what some might call characters. Ragaru was a quasi-medic who had served in a field hospital in the Franco-Prussian war. According to Giordano, he had a surgical case which went wherever he did. This contained an assortment of knives and lances, which Ragaru used whenever he got a chance. Giordano stated that he was good at medicine, the best in the mission, and that "he did not spare the knife."[16]

Giordano was especially colorful. He spent his declining years at Manresa Hall, building a massive and ugly stone shrine to the Mother of God, collecting crutches to hang above it as proof of miracles wrought there, trophies from devout believers. He was much admired by a generation of tertian fathers, and often encouraged in his harmless foibles. Short and stocky, he had one crippled leg which caused him to limp about; however, he did so not in a leisurely manner but rather like a lame dog chasing cats, for he was an active man. He had a powerful body, huge arms and hands, and an enormous head with dark, hawk's eyes that were very expressive. Sometimes they seemed sad with memories and sometimes, aglow with religious fervor. Although he could neither read nor write, he had, nevertheless, learned the dialect of the Indians at Nulato so well that he could speak Koyukon better than he could speak English and as well as he could speak his native Italian. He always prayed in Koyukon, and they say that when he was dying many years later, he spoke and prayed in Koyukon, not his native tongue. He dictated his Alaskan memoirs to three tertian fathers whom he regarded haughtily as his secretaries. Manifesting a brilliant, retentive memory and an agile mind, he related many humorous details which are often overlooked by the official keepers of diaries. Unconsciously he showed an hilarious contempt for new missionaries—young impractical priests who arrived in Alaska like innocent lambs about to be devoured by ravenous wolves. Giordano's memoirs in typescript form were read with riotous amusement in the general's curia in Rome, a delightful happening which established their author as a celebrity. The fame made him bolder. He soon began to dispense from his shrine "miracle water" as efficacious as that which came from Lourdes. No visitor at Manresa Hall, no tertian or retreatant escaped from making a pilgrimage to the shrine where he received a dose of its healing waters.

In July, 1887, Giordano was at De Smet, and Ragaru, at Colville. They met in Spokane Falls on August 1 and left by train for Tacoma where Father Hylebos, an old friend of Archbishop Seghers, presented them with gifts for the mission. The following day they left Seattle for Victoria where the Catholic captain of the steamer *Beaver* gave them free passage to Juneau. On the boat, also, were four sisters of St. Ann from Victoria, bound for Juneau.

From Juneau, leaving the sisters behind, the Jesuits continued by sea to Dyea to the Healy Place, owned by the trader John Healy. Here they spent two days purchasing mostly flour, bacon and beans for the trail. They employed ten Indians, paying each $7.50 or 15 cents per pound to carry their provisions and baggage over the pass. On August 16, they left Healy Place and began the long journey which Tosi had taken the year before with Seghers. Giordano described it all: the bears, the mountain sheep which got away, the hazardous passages through gorges that they took in their canvas boat. In danger, Ragaru sang *Ave Maria Stella*, which always got them safely by, and at night they slept on "fine mattresses, fine dry moss." Clearly they were much better organized than the missionary party of the year before.

When they reached Nuklukoyit they were greatly surprised to find Robaut there. "Why did you come up?" Tosi demanded, "Did I not tell you to get provisions for four of us and stop at Anvik?" Giordano checked the supplies Robaut had brought and threw his arms up in despair. Wicks and no candles. Fifty pounds of flour for each for a whole year! No salt, no sugar, no oil!

Tosi decided to leave Ragaru at Nuklukoyit to start a mission. "He is tired," he said. He himself would start a mission downriver at Nulato, and Robaut with Giordano would go further down to Anvik. He permitted Robaut to take with him William and George Fredericks, sons of a trader, for they were still teaching Robaut "Indian" while he, in turn, was giving them a white man's education. The Fredericks' boys were our first students in Alaska.

Ragaru was left behind with his share of the supplies. "We divided the things there," Giordano reported. "We got 18 bottles of Mass wine from Victoria, so we gave six to Father Ragaru at Nukloyet [sic] for all the year; six to Father Tosi and Father Robaut six. Also Father Van Gorp, who was a friend of Father Tosi, since Father Tosi had not a cent, gave him $80.00 in gold. Father Ragaru got $20.00, Father Robaut $20.00, and Father $40.00 for himself. This was all the money we had in starting the Alaska Mission."[17]

The other three Jesuits with the two boys and a miner left in two boats. Winter was closing in. As they passed the site of the archbishop's death, about forty miles upriver from Nulato, they "stopped there about a quarter of an hour and said some prayers for the repose of his soul, on the very spot where he had been killed. Then we went down to Nulato and Father Tosi resigned himself to pass the winter there. . . . Then we reached Anvik. The ice followed behind the boat." Characteristically Giordano added some impressive statistics:

"We reached Anvik at night, the first Sunday of October, at 11 o'clock, and our journey was from the 16th of August to the first of October. The Yukon is 2700 or 2800 miles, and we navigated with a canvas boat about 2200 miles."[18] Upon reaching Anvik, he added later, "we were so tired we just dropped in our blankets and went to bed."

Giordano began by chopping wood, "about 8 or 9 piles." He had no dogs to pull the sleigh which he had made to bring the wood home. "And I was the only dog—one with two legs."

In December over five hundred Indians at Shageluk, one day's travel from Anvik, held a great feast. Robaut recognized this as an opportunity to meet with them and possibly to convert a few to Catholicism. What followed is rather mysterious, though Giordano described it in the finest details. Coming and going from Anvik to Shageluk, Robaut drank extraordinary amounts of water. On December 3 at Anvik he became very ill, his temperature was high, and for days he was delirious. He said such peculiar and queer things that the two boys were frightened and they left the mission to live with the Protestant ministers. "I thought it was Typhoid Fever and Pneumonia" Giordano said. But no one ever knew for certain. The sickness lasted for weeks. Robaut would eat nothing. Giordano tried to persuade the Indians to get word to Nulato about two hundred and fifty miles away, so that Tosi would come to administer the last rites; however a feud between tribes along the river prevented them from reaching Tosi's mission. Then he tried to get a Russian priest from a mission downriver, but this man could not be found. On New Year's Eve, Robaut called

Giordano and said to him, "Brother, I do not think I will see the New Year Day tomorrow. You will find the old boat. Break it up and make a coffin as best you can, and next spring when there are long days and a good trail, bring my corpse to Nulato. I want to be buried where Archbishop Seghers was killed."[19]

The next morning very early, the first day of 1888, Robaut got up, wrapped a blanket around himself and sat on the steps of the hut with the door open. It was at least fifty-five degrees below zero. Giordano awakened by the sudden drop in temperature in the house, dragged the patient inside and put him back to bed.

"Brother, I am hungry," Robaut said.

Giordano had a white grouse. He cooked half of it and served it. Robaut ate ravenously. He wanted more. Giordano cooked the other half.

"I want something to eat."

Giordano described what followed:

"I had nothing, so I went outside and saw a light in the store there, the Russian Priest's brother kept a little store for the Indians, so I knocked on the door and told him if he had some meat in the store I would like to get it because Father Robaut was beginning to eat now. He gave me a hind quarter of bear meat. I brought it to our cabin, cut two steaks and gave them to Father Robaut. And sure enough after a few days he was out of danger and had a good appetite."[20]

When Robaut felt better he ordered the brother to shave off all the hair on his head, because he was afraid it would fall out. They had Mass again with candles from the trading post. It was so dark in the cabin that Robaut could not read his breviary unless he opened the door of the stove and read it by firelight, something like Abe Lincoln learning his lessons in the light of a hearth fire. Perhaps Robaut's greatest problem in his devotions then, was the children. They crowded the cabin at all hours, eager to hear the priest's bible stories and to sing hymns, for which they were extraordinarily apt.

In mid-February the Jesuits at Anvik had visitors. Two sleds arrived from Kosereffsky, down the river about fifty miles. Indian traders aboard them wanted the missionaries to come to their village. Robaut in his *History of the Holy Cross* simply wrote: "On the 23rd Feb. 1888 Fr. Robaut and Br. Giordano left again Anvick and went down 40 miles [sic] below to Kosereffsky where an Indian house had been purchased."[21] They hired a dogsled, loaded what few provisions they had along with a stove and the two Fredericks boys, and they left by trail on the frozen river for their new home. Because of bad weather the journey lasted almost three days, during which time they had to abandon their stove to lighten the load on the sled. The spent their first days at Kosereffsky in "the Cacheem" a big underground house which the natives call "Kuskuno," where only the males of the village gathered to eat and sleep. "The smell in that place was awful, and it is full of lice," wrote Giordano. "We had nothing to change, only what we had on our backs, and we were full of lice. For the Indians it is nothing, for they are used to it. Sometimes at night we took off our undershirts and put them outside in the snow to freeze those poor beasts. The next morning we went outside, took the undershirts and shook them, and those poor beasts fell down like snowflakes frozen."[22] Because of the smell, Robaut got sore eyes. "They swelled up like a bull-frog."

They went to their newly acquired shack across the river, an abandoned log cabin in which no one had lived for a long time. It was full of snow, the window panes were broken, and the only door sagged. Lacking a stove, they built their fire on the bare floor; and lacking oil or lard, they fried grouse in water. It was time to move. From the Indians they learned that three or four miles below there was a place, once an Indian village, where a good creek flowed at the foot of a hill. After a visit to the site they agreed that this was where the new mission should be built.

On April 9, Giordano left to help Tosi build the mission at Nulato which they called both Our Lady of the Snows and St. Peter Claver, as though a mission in so godless a place required two patrons. Giordano went right to work. "Father Tosi showed me the cabin there to be torn down and brought to Nulato with the dog and sleigh, and that was our future Cathedral. So I marked the logs down, North, South, East, West, tore the roof down and hired a dog and team and brought the logs to Nulato, a distance of about 2 miles. There we put it up again, and that was our first church. The first Mass was said there on the Feast of Pentecost."[23]

By mid-June, after the ice had broken up, Giordano returned to Holy Cross with Tosi and Ragaru, the latter enroute to St. Michael for supplies. The superior with Ragaru's vote of confidence, formally approved of the site Robaut had selected for Holy Cross, then departed with Ragaru, leaving Robaut and Giordano behind to clear away the trees and brush that had flourished since the village had been moved.

At first they lived in a tent on the new site. Mosquitoes were so bad that even Robaut could not tolerate them, especially when he said Mass. One morning he asked brother to build a couple of fires around the tent to smoke them out. Brother did what he was told. "As soon as he [Robaut] began the Mass, I saw one of the corners of the tent begin to burn." Father Robaut took off his vestments. With our feet we put out the fire. But the fire came back again, and we took things and threw them across the creek; some fell in the water . . . a tree near the tent caught fire but we saved the tent. When the tree caught fire, a spark of it went across the creek and started a fire across the creek so we chopped logs on which to cross the creek and save things we had thrown over. That fire worked all summer until a heavy rain came in the middle of July. It burned to Pimoot [Paimute], about thirty-five miles farther on. You must know that when dry moss catches fire, especially in the mountains, there is no way to stop it."*

So far they had done very well with their share of the $80 in gold which Van Gorp had presented to Tosi. There was one nagging problem, however, their lack of clothes. As Giordano says: "You must remember that when we left Victoria we had no trunks, no satchels, nothing except what we had on our backs. So when my pants were torn at the knees or some other place, I was obliged to cut a piece from the bottom to patch it, and so I became a young boy again in short pants."[24]

When Father Ragaru had arrived at Holy Cross he fell into the river as he left the boat. Soaked to the skin, he had to go to bed until his clothes dried. "He had only two pairs of underwear, one of course was on his back and the other he gave to me, for after a year nothing was left of mine except the seam, so he gave me the other pair of his. Hence poor Father Robaut had nothing to change."[25]

June 21, the feast of St. Aloysius, was approaching; Robaut's namesake day. Giordano had acquired one day some duck eggs from an Indian and these he had hoarded for a special occasion. "So the feast came around and I took the eggs, broke them to fry, but young ducks flew out of the frying pan. Robaut said, 'What are you going to do?' I replied, 'They are almost beginning to fly.' He said, 'That's all right, let them fly.'"[26]

Giordano waited patiently for the first steamer to arrive from the lower Yukon. At last in mid-July, he heard the whistle and rushed down to the bank. The steamer *Yukon* whose captain was Charley Peterson, pulled in and as soon as Charley saw brother he said, "Brother, I have good news for you. Three Sisters, one Father, and one Brother came from San Francisco and they are in the steamer here, Father Genna, Brother Rosati and Father Ragaru, and also there are two carpenters here hired by Father Tosi at St. Michael."

Actually, only Father Ragaru and the carpenters were aboard the *Yukon*.[27] A week later

---

*OPA, Giordano Papers, Memoirs, p. 36. Officially the first Mass on the site was August 15, 1888.

Genna and Rosati arrived, and the three sisters of St. Ann who had remained at St. Michael, disembarked from a steamer with Father Tosi as their guide on September 4. Their names should be recorded: Sister Mary Stephen, Sister Mary Joseph and Sister Mary Pauline.[28] They lived in a tent, like the Jesuits until four days later, when the father's house was ready. This they occupied like visitors, spending most of their time making the home more comfortable for the fathers. On October 8, they were able to take possession of their own house, says Father Robaut, and we can only imagine how much they broomed and scrubbed it, since it was very small and primitive.

There were now two permanent missions in the interior of Alaska, Nulato and Holy Cross, and as the years advanced, a certain rivalry developed between them. Other missions were established in bewildering succession, as Father Cataldo had men to spare for this remote part of the world.

Nearer home base there were still an endless number of demands on Cataldo's resources. In the summer of 1887, as Gonzaga College approached its venture into the more complicated business of "higher" education, the most obvious need was an adequate faculty. The school's president, at least, thought so and he continued to pester Cataldo until he received about half the number of Jesuits he had requested. In August, as preparations for the school's opening were being accelerated, the brothers finished landscaping the grounds. There was other activity in the school yard, for much to the dismay of the Jesuits, who had been forced to yield, surveyors for the Oregon Railroad and Navigation Company were staking the right of way for its tracks between the college and the bay.[29]

Father Mackin, who had been in residence at the college for some months, soon departed for his new assignment at St. Francis Regis Mission. This was a notable loss, which was corrected, alas for Rebmann, at a later date. Rebmann's first faculty now consisted of three priests besides himself: Barcelo, also chaplain at Sacred Heart Hospital in the last year of his life, Father Robert Smith, who was regarded as the territory's first native son to be ordained, though he had been born in Redding, California, and Father Francis Monroe, who would leave in due time to join Tosi in Alaska. There were four scholastics: Paul Brounts, Edward Hand, Luke Van Ree and Anthony Kolk.* All of these subsequently left the Order, Paul Brounts after ordination. There were six brothers: Lucian D'Agostino, John Schwertfeger, still a novice, Alphonsus Thorain, Joseph Koerner, Thomas Devlin and Tarsillus Garbaccio. Of these, the last three eventually left the Order. In addition to the college faculty, three other Jesuits were in residence: Cataldo as general superior of the mission, and two traveling missionaries, Folchi and Jacquet. Thus the first Jesuit community totalled seventeen members, almost one for each student in the first year.

Three boys arrived several weeks early. Their names are not given, probably to protect them from the shame of their foolishness. They were turned loose on the expansive campus where there were milk cows, chickens, and two horses named Duffy and Dick. Duffy was named in honor of the late Father Thomas Duffy of Walla Walla, who had been a staunch friend of the Jesuits. When one of the boys mounted Duffy he would lope off toward the fence along Victoria Street, which is now called Division, then walk along it close enough so that the barbed wired tore the pants off the rider. This experience would prompt the rider to get off, at which moment Duffy would walk back rather tranquilly to the barn. Dick was neither as energetic nor as vindictive. He simply walked to the gate and lay down. Then the rider would get off and Dick would walk to the barn. Though the conduct of Duffy and Dick was incorrigible and sometimes gave bad ideas to the boys, no effort was made to get rid of them. The Jesuits who demanded blind obedience from the boys tolerated open defiance from their pets.

*Anthony Kolk's original name was Amfkolk. This is the list as Rebmann gives it, at some variance with the Turin Province Catalogue. The latter, printed in Italy, may be presumed to be less accurate.

In addition to the cows and chickens on the campus, the brothers had a large garden of vegetables and grain. Beyond the fence on the northside, where Mission Avenue is now, the empty prairie stretched off into the distance, straw-colored in the late summer like an estate for hunting pheasants. It was full of prairie dogs. Occasionally an Indian family on ponies or a horse-drawn freight wagon could be seen, coming in from the Northwest, on the trail from Colville.

On September 14, the first college student was registered. This was eleven-year-old Constantine Aloysius McHugh from Helena, a winsome little fellow, characteristically Irish with that strange blend of the angelic and the impudent on his features. On the day following, three more boys registered: Richard Ganahl of Spokane Falls, who was to receive Gonzaga's first degree, Samuel Hannon of San Francisco, and Stanislaus Healy of Fort Sherman, Idaho. On September 16, the last three of the opening day student body were accepted: Frank Healy of Fort Sherman, Lawrence Corbett of Salem, Oregon, and Charles Dowd of Lewiston, Idaho. Thus on opening day, September 17, 1887, there were seven students, the oldest of whom was seventeen years of age. By the end of the first year twenty students had been in attendance, all of them Catholics, though at least two of them not exemplary. They were expelled during the year, so that the maximum number reached at any time was eighteen students. Among those not already mentioned were George and Frank Dunford, grandsons of the leader of the Mormons (Brigham Young), and Robert Monaghan, distinguished a few short years later for giving his life as a naval officer to save the lives of his men.*

A few days after the beginning of school. Father Joset appeared with two Indian boys. He informed Father President that he wanted to register them as students of the new college. "No," Father Rebmann said, "we do not receive Indian students. The school is exclusively for American boys."

"Well, you call those Americans," Joset snorted. "What about these Indian boys? Surely they are Americans."

Rebmann's response indicated that the policy of the school, originally designed to counteract the evils of Grant's Peace Policy, had been greatly altered. It also indicated that the Policy was no longer a threat. For Joset it confirmed his suspicions all along. The new college would destroy his dearly loved missions. As it grew, like a spreading tree, it would absorb more and more of the Jesuits' resources. Something had to be sacrificed. Joset thought his missions would be the first to go.

But contrary to the old priest's mournful reflections, the Indian missions were more healthy than Gonzaga and it would be many years before their demise. In central Washington, for example, three new churches for Indians were built during the early months of 1888. In February de Rouge built two, one at "Old Mission," which is now called Cashmere, and another, the second on the same site, at Ellisford.[30] Father Grassi, who now sometimes signed his letters with his new Indian name *Wakackal*, which means "Lefty" in the Yakima's language—referring to his left-handedness—built a new church at Manson, with the indispensable help of his right-handed Indians.

Cataldo, who had approved of these undertakings, was seeking Rome's approbation for his latest plan, what he referred to as the crowning achievement of his life.[31] This was his proposed novitiate, which he properly regarded as the key to continuity of the mission. On November 11, 1888, Rome formally recognized Sacred Heart Mission, De Smet, as a novitiate for brothers. This was not what Cataldo had in mind; he wanted a canonically established novitiate for scholastic novices.

---

*George and Frank Dunford, both born in Salt Lake City, were sons of Mrs. Dora Hagan, a daughter of Brigham Young and a convert to Catholicism. Robert Monaghan died in Samoa in 1899 as Spokane's first hero. His statue was placed near the Civic Center.

While this was debated by those who had the power to grant it, Sacred Heart Mission acquired a printing press, which was installed with so little fanfare that no one can date its actual arrival. In 1888, however, its first imprint appeared. This was a fifty-six page book composed in Latin and produced in a very limited edition: *Paradigma verbi activi lingua Numpu vulgo Nez Perce*. Father Anthony Morvillo had authored it with the hope that its contents would facilitate one's learning of the Nez Perce verb, not a very popular subject even then. The brother who printed the book could not understand even what the title meant, let alone its contents.[32]

Father Cataldo at this time was fifty-three years old and still in the prime of life. He had been superior for eleven years and would be superior for five more. When he took over the reins from Giorda there were thirty-nine Jesuits in the Rocky Mountain Mission, ninety-five in the California Mission, and two hundred-and-ninety in the entire Turin province which mothered both. Now there were one-hundred-and-one Jesuits in the Rocky Mountain-Alaska mission alone. The mission covered approximately the same area as the Oregon province today, except that in early 1888 there was not a single resident Jesuit in Oregon, and the Jesuit ministry in western Washington Territory had not as yet begun. However, both Oregon and western Washington would get Jesuits before Cataldo was replaced as superior in 1893.

A small corner of Oregon received them first. Cataldo had been very partial to the Umatilla, Cayuse and Nez Perce Indians in eastern Oregon, and the major reason for Jesuit hands-off prior to 1888 was that diocesan priests had served the area from the beginning. Father Louis Conrardy a close personal friend of Cataldo was presently in charge of the Umatilla Mission, called St. Ann's. Like some of the more imaginative missionaries, Conrardy had not been cut from ordinary cloth. A Belgian like De Smet, he was a man of great yearnings and impetuous actions. Also a charmer, like Accolti, and a charter member of the international set long before the jet age, he shared in all but citizenship on three continents.

In the nineteenth-century church three missionaries were especially renowned: De Smet among the Indians of North America, Constant Leivens, a Jesuit who dedicated himself to the poor in India, and Joseph Damian de Veuster, a Picpus priest who ministered to the lepers of Molokai. All were Belgians. What is so remarkable here is that Conrardy, comparatively lost in the dust of history, engaged in a career which encompassed all three: he was a missionary in India until tropical diseases drove him back to Europe; he was a missionary to Indians in eastern Oregon; and he left Oregon to serve lepers, first on Molokai with Damian, who died in his arms and then on an island near Shek-Ling, where he built a haven for the lepers of China.*

Conrardy had arrived on the Umatilla reservation in late January, 1875, prepared for the worst, and he soon had St. Ann's humming with his own energy. He was busy baptizing and instructing children within twenty-four hours. He studied the Indian's language and ate with them in their tepees. When not occupied with labors at the mission, he traveled on horseback into the remotest parts of three vast counties, Morrow, Wheeler, and Gilliam, ministering to Whites in these frontier settlements. He built the first Catholic churches in the newly pitched towns of Pendleton, Hepner, Vinson, and Condon. At the mission, he built the first Catholic school for Indian children, in 1883, and secured Sisters of Mercy from Philadelphia to staff it. During the same year, he moved the mission church to a new site below Emigrant Hill, dedicating it to St. Joseph, to whom he had a very special attraction.

*Conrardy died clutching a crucifix in one hand and a Chinese dictionary in the other, on August 26, 1914. *Extension Magazine* (October, 1961), p. 22, et seq.

PAINFUL GROWTH

As early as 1877, Jesuits visited his mission to assist him. Cataldo came in that year to preach to the Indians in their own tongue. Five years later, from November 20 to December 4, Conrardy, assisted by Archbishop Seghers, Cataldo, and Anthony Morvillo, conducted a brimstone and hellfire mission, attended by more than six hundred Indians. Cataldo wrote later that their mission had tremendous influence on the lives of the Indians and that many conversions followed it. Their point is confirmed by the baptismal book, which records twenty-three baptisms for 1881, thirty-two for 1883, but sixty for the year of the mission, 1882. Before 1887, Father Conrardy heard about the work of Damien among the lepers of Molokai, and he felt a great desire to go there "to work among the most abandoned." He offered himself to Damien, who replied: "Come, in God's name!" It was quite natural for Conrardy at this point to turn to the Jesuits to take over the Umatilla Mission. Archbishop William Gross of Portland added his own plea to that of Conrardy. The mission was accepted by Cataldo, and Urban Grassi was ordered to take over.

Grassi arrived in May, 1888. He found the school closed because of a government agent's high-handed dealings, and the sisters were gone. He began, like his predecessors, by rolling up his sleeves and moving the church, this time to a site about one-half mile eastward. Meanwhile a certain Francis Anthony Drexel, a wealthy banker living in faraway Philadelphia, passed from this world to the next, leaving to his two daughters, Katherine and Elizabeth, a vast fortune, totalling, it was said, $15,000,000.* Katherine became a nun and eventually the famous Mother Drexel, foundress of the Sisters of the Blessed Sacrament. Through the Catholic Indian Bureau in Washington the two Drexel sisters provided Father Grassi with $6,000 to build a school. Grassi then persuaded the Mother General of the Franciscan Sisters of Glen Riddle, Pennsylvania, to send four sisters to help him, and by March 10, 1890, his school was ready for business. Thirteen wide-eyed and apprehensive pupils appeared that first day. The number increased daily until so many came that an addition had to be built on the school in 1892. Mother Drexel provided another $3,000 for that purpose.

Eleven days after his school opened, on March 21, 1890, Father Grassi died from the affliction of overwork, which was complicated somewhat by pneumonia. On the previous day a telegram had been sent to Gonzaga calling for a priest to assist the dying man and Father Folchi had set out at once for Umatilla. With Folchi at his side Grassi breathed his last. He was buried under the mission church, his boots still on his feet, as though he were being prepared for harder labors elsewhere.† Father Morvillo at Slickpoo was directed to take over the supervision of the Umatilla mission, where he could continue to study his Nez Perce verbs and nouns.

Morvillo was the first in a succession of missionaries at Umatilla. Jesuit priests, scholastics, and brothers, sometimes in two's and three's, sometimes alone, often struggled against odds that would have discouraged most men, but they always gave their best. Each left his mark. Leopold Van Gorp, for example, in 1893, changed the name of the mission to St. Andrew's to honor Father J. A. Stephan of the Catholic Indian Bureau in Washington. Thomas Neate, in 1905, moved the church again. He transferred Grassi's body, also, to a nearby cemetery, where he erected a large red stone cross to mark the grave. As if rewarded for his reverence to the holy remains, he, too, died of overwork and pneumonia, not a sad ending at all if one looks beyond the grave.

*Francis Anthony Drexel died in 1885. His daughter Katherine who founded the Sisters of the Blessed Sacrament was born in Philadelphia, November 26, 1858, and died on March 3, 1955, after distributing an estimated $12,000,000 for the missions of Indians and Blacks.

†Father Grassi in his coffin with his boots still on was the occasion of much comment and some mirth among the younger Jesuits of the time. Generally regarded as very saintly, Grassi by his own efforts managed to avoid public notice of his heroic labors.

The Jesuit take-over of The Umatilla Mission coincided with a major change of location for the Blackfeet mission called St. Peter's. Cataldo's commitment to the Blackfeet had been compromised for sometime because of the shift of reservation boundaries farther north and because of Grant's Peace Policy that excluded Catholic missionaries from the reservation. But in 1885, it will be recalled, Cataldo had been granted specific permission by the government in Washington to locate a "mission school and other mission buildings" on three reservations, including the Blackfeet's.

Father Joseph Damiani, attached to St. Peter's, as had been the irrepressible Prando, occasionally slipped into the forbidden territory without protest or harassment by the new agent. Damiani, forty-three years old at this time, destined to endure like the Rock of Ages, was an Italian, dark-complexioned enough to pass for an Indian, somewhat a wag like Prando, but so impressive in his priestly demeanor that Louis Riel—the unjustly executed Métis in Canada—was inspired to compose a poem in his honor.

After permission had been formally granted for him to enter the reservation legally, Damiani lost no time in making a long tour of the reservation, alert to its potentials as a mission site. He decided to abandon Birch Creek as a residence and in the spring of 1886, he built a log cabin church and residence on the Two Medicine River, a few miles north of the Blackfeet Agency. In the following year he received from White Calf a portion of the land adjacent to his cabin. This, it was agreed, would be used for a school.

For the next three years, frustrated, weary, and preoccupied with the poverty and hardships of St. Peter's, Damiani was unable to develop the new mission. At last in 1889 the two Drexel sisters provided $14,000 for him to build his school on Two Medicine River "as soon as some government support was assured." Damiani began construction on a "two-story frame building, consisting of two distinct sections, one of which was to be occupied by the boys' school, and the other for the use of the girls." Its planned capacity was one hundred students.

When these accommodations were ready, the Catholic Indian Mission Bureau applied to the government to obtain an allowance for "the education and support of one hundred Indian children at the Holy Family Indian School at the Blackfeet Agency." A bill to that effect was introduced by T. H. Carter, Montana's delegate to Congress, and it passed the House, though the Senate Committee reported on it adversely. The bill came up for discussion before the Senate on July 25, 1890, and finally was passed by a vote of twenty-seven to nineteen.[33]

One month later, Father Damiani, accompanied by three Ursulines, left St. Peter's to occupy the new building, which was officially opened and dedicated to the Holy Family on August 25. Classes for the children were scheduled to begin the following month.

When all was ready, Damiani harnessed his horse to a wagon and started out to round up little Blackfeet children for his school. Indian affection for their children was so strong that they did not like parting with them. Even after agreeing to give up their children for the sake of their education, Indian parents might demand gifts for making the sacrifice, and then sometimes fail to keep their side of the bargain. Hence, it was almost as easy for Damiani to round up trick dogs for a circus as it was for him to gather a school full of young braves and maidens.

When, finally, Holy Family had acquired enough boys and girls for the beginning of classes, another obstacle had to be overcome, and this was not a simple matter either. Somehow, the priests and nuns had to persuade the newcomers to exchange their beaded belts, moccasins, and other Indian gear for "civilized" clothes, whatever that meant. Indian boys did not like to wear shoes, which is not surprising since white boys also prefer to do without, but, according to regulations, shoes were "civilized" and shoes had to be worn— at least to Mass and classrooms.

The discomforts and restraints of being civilized often prompted children to run away from the mission and then there was the devil to pay. Parents usually refused to force their children to return, unless, of course, the government agent stepped in and threatened to withhold the family's food rations. This got action immediately. When the same boy or girl ran away more than once during the year, the mission would not take him back, a policy that had to be kept undercover lest it encourage offenders to repeat their offense.

Despite all these annoyances, and some others I have not mentioned, the mission had an average attendance of seventy-five students the first year. They were supported by the mission which received its funds from the Catholic Indian Bureau, from the government, from the Blackfeet Tribe, and from other sources, for example, from devout Catholics. In 1892 Mother Drexel donated a small herd of cattle to the mission and an additional gift from her in 1895 made it possible to erect a new three-story building of sandstone quarried from neighboring hills.

Other Jesuits were added to the staff and two more Ursulines came from St. Peter's to assist the original three. In 1894 two scholastics arrived, John Carroll and Augustine Dimier, both of whom later spent many years as priests at Holy Family. During the same year Brother Jerome Galdos came "for a year." Born at Bilbos, southern Spain, Galdos had entered the Jesuit Order on April 16, 1886, at Ignatius Castle, Loyola, a privilege reserved to very few Jesuits. At Holy Family he was called St. Joseph because of his gentle manners and flowing white beard which made him look like an old-fashioned marble statue of St. Joseph.*

In his new headquarters, very modest ones, at Gonzaga College, Cataldo kept in touch with local superiors. He also spent a good part of the year making his "annual visitation" to each of the Jesuit institutions in his care. Despite these frequent absences he was on the scene, so to speak, as an avalanche of problems descended upon the Gonzaga community, leaving Rebmann in the position of the physician who had performed successful surgery "but the patient died." Rebmann had three positions: rector of the community, president of the college and pastor of the local church, which was across the river and had to be reached by rowboat. A very gentle, sweet-tempered aristocrat of the old German school, Rebmann was the kind of person on whom others loved to play practical jokes. He was a meticulous keeper of records and he spent many hours at his desk writing accounts in a delicate, almost ladylike hand. He kept a buggy at the parish, using it to visit his parishioners, including the Sauer family, who lived near the church. Mr. Sauer was a shoemaker, enjoying a lively trade because of the town's lumberjacks who needed boots.

Though he enjoyed his pastorship, Rebmann did not neglect the boys in the school. Only circumstances beyond his control caused his downfall there, abetted somewhat by his gentleness in handling crises. He was, perhaps, too polite—like the farmer who refuses to shoot the coyotes who eat his chickens, because he tells himself, even coyotes need food to survive. On those rare occassions when Rebmann became angry, he expressed himself in such a way that he merely evoked laughter or merriment rather than fear. He was very pious and more sentimental than most Jesuits; for instance he kept many keepsakes of his uncle, the German field general, and his mother, who made altar linens for him. Not content with possessing these, he often viewed them with longing and affection.

His first year as president had gone smoothly enough except for the aggressive land-grabbing of the railroads at Gonzaga's expense. Rebmann had gone east for a tour of Jesuit colleges and he returned on April Fool's Day after the winter frosts had been driven away by the sun.[34] Rebmann did not like cold weather. Several weeks later he planned Gonzaga's first school picnic, which was celebrated seven miles downriver from the college.

---

*Brother Jerome Galdos was born January 2, 1865. From 1889 until 1935 he worked in the Montana Indian Missions at Holy Family for 25 years. He died suddenly at Mt. St. Michael's, June 10, 1936.

Boys today would regard the affair as boring, but nobody did then. After being fenced in for seven months anything else was like a trip to Mars in a purple balloon. The boys were conveyed to the picnic site in two large farm wagons borrowed from St. Michael's Mission. Their teachers accompanied them on horseback and joined in the general banter and good-natured teasing. Though the picnic site at that time abounded in rattlesnakes, there is no record that any of the eighteen revelers returned home with snake bite. No one drowned. No one got lost. No one got intoxicated and there were no girls around to break up the party. The first Gonzaga picnic was a thumping success.

The college's first year passed into history. The president, sending his precocious little students with only vacation on their minds, back to their homes, was more concerned about the future. He was particularly involved in producing a new grade school for the parish. As usual Father Jacquet had helped raise the money. Rebmann recruited four sisters of the Holy Names from Portland. The school, when completed, comprised eight classrooms on the first two floors, each with four rounded windows which made the place look like a jail. Despite this an admiring member of the press commented that "Catholics always put up first class buildings."[35] When the sisters arrived in July it was announced that on August 27, 1888, the school for girls would be opened, but boys under twelve would also be admitted. Thus Rebmann, having founded two schools, was left yet with the problem of the "street Arabs" who were over twelve and could not read or write. He would have to start another school to provide for them.

On New Year's day, 1889, there was a partial eclipse of the sun. Some folk regarded it as an omen of evil to follow. The next day an epidemic struck the college. Even faculty members, including Brother D'Agostino—whom the boys called "Foxy Grandpa" after a popular cartoon character—were laid low with the "fever." The disease also afflicted the eyes of some of the boys. Besides the epidemic, one boy was taken to the hospital with rheumatic fever, a valuable colt died suddenly, and Father Paquin was almost killed in a runaway. Then two disgruntled boys ran away. Father Rebmann came down with the "fever" in February and was so sick a brother was at his side day and night for three weeks. The railroad surveyors were running their lines across the college property. One discouraged member of the community informed the general in Rome that a third railroad was in the planning stages and that Cataldo was being forced to build a new college several blocks distant. No wonder. D.C. Corbin's Spokane Falls and Northern was running its line only two hundred feet from the college on the west. Another line already ran only one hundred-and-twenty feet from the main entrance of the school on the south.

There was more bad news. Two prefects were causing a disturbance by their high-handed procedures. A cherished student ran away and the boy's father, Peter Ronan who had befriended the Jesuits in Montana, removed his second son in a fit of anger. At the Holy Names Convent an epidemic of typhoid broke out and one sister died. At Uniontown an isolated German settlement about one hundred miles south of Spokane Falls, whose people were at each other's throats over some dispute, pleaded for Rebmann's intervention but not even Rebmann with his sugar-sweet disposition could restore peace. A boy from Horse Plains, Montana, was dismissed and again an irate father removed a second son. The community diarist recorded this event with a caustic comment: "Another consequence of the administration of the prefect—or rather of the mismanagement of the house in general."[36] In May another boy who was so frightened by the forthcoming examinations persuaded his father to take him home. By this time the ranks of the student body had been notably lessened. From a high of thirty-five students in the second year, only twenty-seven survived to share in the commencement ceremonies on St. Aloysius day, 1889.

The next day, June 22, the boys with their frugal baggage and clad in their "travel clothes," left town, most of them by train. As they gazed out of the train windows from the

Northern Pacific depot platform, they saw a bustling new town of approximately twenty-five thousand people. From the bluffs on the south to the riverfront, new buildings, including many homes, provided a scene of lively western enterprise and opulence from the recently discovered mines. They would never see the same landscape again, for on August 4 of that year the great Spokane fire destroyed everything west of the church and parochial school that were situated on the east extremity of Main Avenue.

Most inhabitants of the city lost everything, and to them the college on the north bank threw open its doors. It was a sad time for soft-hearted Rebmann. He helped many, like his friends the Sauers, to reestablish their homes north of the river on college property that had been broken up into lots for that purpose. Thus the seeds of two new parishes were planted. Both sprung up and flourished so quickly that plans for two new churches were in the making before the year was out.

The opening of school was delayed by these unexpected happenings, and on registration day, September 17, only twelve students appeared. No one had to ask why. A week later St. Ignatius Prep was opened in a shack near the downtown church to accommodate the boys over twelve who did not qualify for Gonzaga. Thomas Purcell, a Jesuit reject for reasons of health, was put in charge. Purcell's health did not interfere with his becoming a diocesan priest, building at least nine churches in the Boise diocese, and living to a ripe old age as a faithful benefactor of Gonzaga and the Jesuits, and co-founder of a famous insurance company.*

On October 7, the first passenger train puffed and rattled over the trestle that had been built between the college and the bay, obstructing the beautiful view. It symbolized, in a way, the passage of Rebmann to a place where the view was better.

On the grounds that Rebmann was too occupied with the college to give full attention to the parish, Cataldo appointed Father Mackin as pastor of the church. Many parishioners resented this, for they felt loyal and protective toward Rebmann, who seemed to be too vulnerable in his gentleness. Mackin, nurtured in his faith in northern Ireland, possessed a temperament that was exactly opposite to the former pastor's and, as often happens, a sudden rift appeared in the parish, the majority favoring Rebmann.

Cataldo was not blind to these consequences of his decision. He called a meeting of all Jesuits in the area to discuss the future activities of Jesuits in Spokane Falls. In convening this assembly on October 6, 1889, he was setting a precedent that has been repeated on occasion, not always with the same equanimity. Under the superior's forthright influence this first assembly, or conference, agreed on some very specific resolutions. First, it was determined that the Sodality should be introduced to all classes of people from old to young. Secondly, it was agreed that Spokane Falls should be divided into four districts, that each should be presided over by one of the fathers and that Jesuits, using funds from the Order, should buy property for future parishes in all four quarters.

Mackin was resourceful. He quickly formed a pious society of the ladies, organized a choir and appealed to the men to join what he called the St. Vincent de Paul Society. Twenty-two men responded to this appeal. His position in the parish was now confirmed, but his relations with Rebmann, who was still the local superior, deteriorated to the point where neither spoke to the other except in business matters. Feelings of coldness, even hostility, developed between the two men.

In contrast to Rebmann's modesty, Mackin's great splash, his proud bearing, his flamboyant Irish sermons and civic speeches created an impression, though he never actually intended it, that Rebmann had failed to provide leadership from the beginning.

*Father Thomas Purcell died September 3, 1925 at Wallace, Idaho. He was co-founder of the Roman Catholic-Life Insurance Company, which later became the New World Life Insurance Company.

What was good for the parish was good for the college. In the minds of many arose the question of the *when* not the *if* of Rebmann's replacement.

The ax fell on January 9, 1890, without previous announcements or formalities. Mackin succeeded Rebmann as president of the college and superior of the Spokane Jesuits. Rebmann in late January was assigned to St. Ignatius Mission, Montana, a status that doubtlessly depressed him, though he accepted it with pious resignation. His departure left the college with a faculty that consisted of six priests, four scholastics and three brothers.

Father Joset, however, in his eightieth year, soon joined them. He arrived on March 5 on a stretcher, more dead than alive. After a serious fall at Sacred Heart Mission he was injured so badly that no one held hope for his recovery. Despite this, the college boys were asked to pray for his recovery, though it is difficult to see why the fathers were so eager to deprive the old man of his reward. One boy, a handsome and bright little ten-year-old from Seattle, deeply awed by the proximity of death in the college, called on Mackin one evening and asked him if Father Joset was going to die that night. Mackin knew the boy's father well. He was Malcom McDougal, a wealthy landowner whose pride and happiness was his only son Alphonsus. No doubt Mackin attempted to reassure the boy.

A few days later, on the feast of St. Joseph, Mackin declared a half holiday and gave the boys permission for an extended walk beyond the grounds. The weather was mild and the boys marched off happily under the supervision of their prefect, in the customary order of two by two. When they reached a railroad bridge downriver, young Alphonsus McDougal, for reasons never learned, opened a trap door and started down the ladder. He slipped, shouted for help, and fell eighty-five feet to the rocks below. He died instantly. The boys knelt around their mangled companion and said the rosary for him. The remains were finally gathered and brought to the college where that evening the boys sang vespers and cried all the way through. That same night Father Mackin's deep brown hair turned as white as snow. He bore this mark of his grief until he was placed in his own grave thirty-eight years later.*

Father Van Gorp was one of the six priests in residence at the college. In better health now, he served in several capacities, most of them related to business. He had been assigned to provide spiritual care of the Catholics in the northwest section of the town and he had built a new frame church which was dedicated in honor of St. Joseph on Thursday, May 15, 1890 by Bishop Junger from Vancouver. His Lordship on this occasion spent the night in the college, quite comfortably, in preparation for his meeting with Father Cataldo on the morrow. It should be added, perhaps, that on previous occasions, before the college was available for visitors, His Lordship had declined to sleep in the old residence, preferring a bed in the hay wagon in the yard. He gave as his reason the fact that there were bedbugs in the house. Bedbugs, like mosquitoes, were common nuisances on the frontier. What's more, there were no pesticides to control them. When Mackin's sister, a nun in Rome, asked her dear brother for a keepsake to remind her of his hardships on the mission, he sent her a bedbug mounted on a pin. It was Rebmann's German fastidiousness, that deserves credit for the flight of the bugs as well as for the use of sheets and napkins.

His Lordship therefore was in a good mood on May 16 when he and Cataldo as superior of the Jesuits, met in the college to discuss mutual concerns. A lot of water had gone over Spokane Falls since De Smet had met Blanchet in similar circumstances at Fort Vancouver. What occurred in 1890 has been recorded in the college diary:

"Father Cataldo arrived here last night. He came to see once more the Bishop about the question of the parish and definitively to come to some agreement.

*Mackin died on December 27, 1928, at Port Townsend, Washington. Father Rebmann celebrated the funeral Mass.

"The city of Spokane Falls has been divided into 4 sections destined to become 4 different parishes. The river is the division line east and west. Howard street is the division line north and south. The bishop will take charge of 3 parishes: the fourth one will be left to the Society: But, until the Bishop is able to send another priest to help Fr. Kautens the newly appointed Pastor, we will remain in charge of the actual old parish whilst Fr. Kautens will attend himself to St. Joseph's Church on the North Side. Father Cataldo, in the name of the Society, dispossessed himself in favor of the Bishop of all the different Church properties which of late we had acquired with our own money, namely 1) the place where the actual St. Joseph Church is built; (the building created at our own expense will also be the property of the bishop.) 2) a site in Cannon's addition lately purchased; 3) a site (blank); 4) the site of the church of "Our Lady of Lourdes" and of the parochial schools with the buildings. The only place therefore reserved to us is the site on which the St. Ignatius school is built: and this we are free to sell when we deem it most convenient. The Bishop signed this agreement with his own hand, being over glad of the conditions in which he was taking possession of this new parish."[37]

While Cataldo was giving away Van Gorp's church and a considerable amount of Jesuit property, including a big chunk the Jesuits bought for a Catholic cemetery, Van Gorp was platting the east end of what was called Sinto Addition. He gave the wide streets Indian names and along Mission Avenue on the north he provided for a park-like appearance by having islands placed down the middle of the Avenue where three rows of locust trees were planted. He might have planted oaks, had there been nurseries where oaks could be acquired.

Cataldo, still in a generous mood, provided land for the new orphanage conducted by the Franciscan sisters and for the new academy of the Holy Names sisters on Superior Street. Van Gorp sold lots like hot cakes, mostly to Catholic families, partly to create a kind of Catholic enclave, partly to raise money for the new college building to be placed at a reasonable distance from the detested railroads. Not only had the blossoms of academia been plucked away from the original college by those heartless intruders, leaving the campus a maze of tracks like a switching yard, but the facilities themselves had been outgrown. There was no debt on the first building, thank God, and if Van Gorp sold enough lots there would be little on the second. How times have changed.

Cataldo was still agitating for his "crowning achievement," the novitiate for scholastic candidates. In the summer of 1890 he arranged for Gonzaga's first summer school, which consisted of special classes in Latin for young men who had applied to enter the Order. The superior now regarded the college as a kind of nursery for vocations to the priesthood, which shows how often he could change his mind. He placed in attendance at the school an assortment of applicants who formed a substantial part of the Gonzaga student body. This became apparent when Cataldo finally got his wish. He released the good news on Easter Sunday, March 29, 1891: Rome had extended the canonical scope of the novitiate at De Smet to include scholastic novices. There was much excitement among the boys because eleven of them were directed to pack their trunks and leave for the novitiate on the following day. The keeper of the diary, overcome by spiritual sweetness of the hour, recorded the departure of the new novices with his pen dipped into honey instead of ink:

"At last the time came for our dear eleven young men to bid good bye to friends and teachers. Early in the morning, immediately after breakfast, everything was ready and time was fast approaching when they should betake themselves to the depot. They all shook hands with the students among whom they had made so many friends; then accompanied by a few larger boys who had asked for the favor of being with them to the last moment, they at last left Gonzaga College, some of them with an air of sadness and regret tempered with the joy of long cherished hope at last ready to be accomplished evidently depicted on their face. Father Cocchi, the future Master of Novices accompanied them and left Gonzaga for De Smet.

"Father Van Gorp secured for all of them half fare tickets, and saw about checking of trunks and at 8:45 A.M., the train went on puffing and smoking, in front of Gonzaga College, bringing away from us a good many friends and pupils to the new home of their choice. In them Gonzaga College loses studious, diligent and pious pupils and our dear Society of Jesus gains eleven new sons anxious to devote themselves to their own salvation and to the conquest of souls, under the banner of St. Ignatius. May they be happy and persevere in their holy vocation, is the wish of all those who have known and loved them here.[38]

Among the novices who entered that day were Alphonsus Couffrant David Duross, who died prematurely at the age of twenty four, George Kugler, Henry Adams, renowned later in a small way for his pioneering in physics at Gonzaga, and Daniel Hanly, who left the Society to become a secular priest, the first pastor of the Cathedral in Seattle, a monsignor and author of a biography of St. Joseph Pignatelli.[39] Four of this first little group fell by the wayside. Before the end of the year three other candidates entered the novitiate, only one of whom survived for ordination, Father Aemilius Boll. One of these three departed unwillingly, Mathias Jung, who lived with Gonzaga Jesuits for many years, a quasi-volunteer who was released from his vows as Jesuit because of a deformed back.*

The Master of Novices at De Smet was Father Nicholas Cocchi, a charismatic kind of priest who saw everything in a kind of happy glow. He appeared to be quite intense. Bushy eyebrows extended over his large nose, like caricatures of Harpo Marx and his small, firm mouth presented the likeness of a Garibaldi lieutenant, rather than a Jesuit. Before he died he grew a beard, very black and scrubby, and this made him look unreal, like an American stage hobo. He had a gift for languages, though it must be admitted he could not master the inconsistencies of the English usage. He often amused his merry novices with an occasional gaffe like the following: "And Jesus said to Lazarus, 'Come forth,' and Lazarus came right out of the gravey." He would say, "Be like the chickens. Get out and scratch early." He urged his charges to be zealous. "We all should have pep. We should all be undertakers."†

The new dignity for the mission at De Smet had little bearing on Rebmann's St. Ignatius, which operated Montana's first trade school, and was enjoying a golden era of its own. Its famous shops were in their prime. In addition to the shops there were three other schools, one for boys who were taught by the Jesuits, a school for older girls conducted by the sisters of Providence, and a more recently established kindergarten and nursery school opened on April 2, 1890, by the Ursulines. Priests from St. Ignatius were supplying the spiritual needs of Catholics for a vast area, including a little town like Horse Plains where a new church was dedicated in October of the previous year. Canestrelli, who ministered to the maverick Kootenais at Dayton on the west side of Flathead Lake, built a church for him in 1890 and composed his celebrated *Kootenai Grammar*, an extraordinary feat because of the complexities of this Indian language.‡

---

*Mathias Jung served for many years as a librarian's assistant and curator of the old Gonzaga Museum. He died December 9, 1938.

†These and other amusing quotations were passed on to the writer by Father Alphonsus Fletcher, one of Cocchi's novices, St. Mary's Omak, 1945.

‡*Indian Sentinel*, II, 11 (July, 1922), p. 520, et seq. The grammar, composed in Latin was printed at Santa Clara in 1894. It had a peculiar history. The edition with the exception of several copies was lost. Subsequently, the 200 copies were found unbound in the vault on the first floor of Gonzaga's Administation building.

Rebmann, too, succumbed to the itch for building, a common affliction then. In the spring of 1891, when Cataldo was counting his novices as herders count sheep, he started construction on a new St. Ignatius church which was destined, when completed, to be the largest in Montana. More than one million bricks were formed and baked on the grounds for this stupendous new undertaking, into which Rebmann threw himself with boyish enthusiasm. Two years would be required for completion and then several more for Brother Joseph Carignano to complete the fifty-eight murals, which very soon attracted so much admiration and praise that St. Ignatius became one of the great show places of Montana.*

The Indians, of course, took great pride in their holy edifice. Carignano's painting brought into their narrow world exotic realities as yet to them unheard of. They examined each and discussed its merits innumerable times. Most of the Indians took what they saw quite literally, for this was their way of creating or perceiving works of art. Carignano had included one painting on hell, and there is a quaint tradition about this that deserves a remembrance.

According to the old missionaries, Carignano's first rendition of hell contained only palefaces in the midst of flames. When this was observed by some Indians, they stopped going to church. Rebmann's inquiries about this were answered only with evasive responses at first, but eventually he received the response he considered most valid—that there were no Indians in hell. Carignano remedied this oversight by changing the features of some of his figures from those of Whites to those of Indians. As soon as this was completed the sensational news spread abroad: there *were* Indians in hell. Promptly, Rebmann's backsliders returned to church.

Cataldo, as one might expect, took great interest in the building of the church. He visited St. Ignatius frequently, arriving sometimes quite unexpectedly by train at Ravalli, which was but a half-hour buggy ride from the mission. On one of his visits he had taken note of the superior's pet, a warm wooly dog which was trained to lie on Rebmann's feet to keep them warm while Rebmann worked at his desk. Cataldo, the man of flint, regarded this as too sensual for a Jesuit, and gave the order to Rebmann, without using obscure terminology, to "get rid of the dog." Rebmann, an obedient man, found it difficult to part with his pet and he put off from day to day the unpleasant task he had been given. Then one day Cataldo arrived unexpectedly and Rebmann still had the dog. Cataldo said nothing; what he *did* conveyed a much louder message than words.

The next morning when Rebmann looked out his window to see what the weather was like, he saw the dog hanging there, as dead as last summer's flies.†

---

*St. Ignatius Church was sufficiently completed by St. Ignatius Day, July 31, 1893, for the first service within it. On that day, it was solemnly blessed. The Carignano murals were completed later. *See* OPA, St. Ignatius Mission Diaries.

†This account of Rebmann's dog was hotly contested by Father Patrick O'Reilly, who declared it "a damnable lie." A number of other reliable witnesses, however, have asserted that Rebmann himself described what occurred. One witness to the accuracy of the account was Father Francis Menager, who was generally regarded as more objective than Patrick O'Reilly.

Victor Garrand, founder of Seattle University.

Sister Kathleen Mary, S.S.A., with some of her students in class at Holy Cross Mission, Alaska.

Garden scene at Holy Cross Mission, Alaska.

10

CATALDO'S LAST YEARS AS SUPERIOR
1891–1894

Any history buff in the state of Washington can tell you that Seattle, the state's largest and most beautiful city, was named for an Indian chief who was neither large by Indian standards nor beautiful. Like many members of his tribe, the Sumquamps, he was short, almost squat with flat facial features which were crowned with a heavy mat of long coarse black hair, parted in the middle. For what he lacked in comeliness he made up in other attractive qualities which were recognized even by the dollar-chasing founders of the city. Chief Seattle, or "See-at-lee," it was said, "was the greatest personality of all the Puget Sound Indians." One should include Whites also, because at that time there were no outstanding "Bostons" in the whole western half of the territory.[1]

Chief Seattle was a great warrior. He was also an orator who could hold his listeners spellbound, but he was no demagogue. He used his talents with both vision and dignity, recognizing that the "Bostons" were here to stay and that his people had to cope with this as an irreversible reality.

When the "Bostons" settled in 1851 on a point in the sound now called West Seattle, or Alki, the chief was about sixty-five years old.[2] He died fifteen years later and some of his friends raised a monument over his grave. Carved from Italian marble, it is seven feet high and in the shape of a cross. On one side of the monument there is the inscription: "I.H.S. Seattle, Chief Of The Sumquamps And Allied Tribes, Died June 7, 1866, The Firm Friend of the Whites, and for Him the City of Seattle Was Named by Its Founders;" on the other side is the following: "Baptismal name Noah Sealthe, Age probably 80 years."[3]

The I.H.S. reminds one that Chief Seattle was a Catholic, which indicated in the context of the city's history that he had two obstacles to overcome: religion and race. A Catholic missionary summoned from God-knows-where conducted his funeral. It was Chief Seattle's last request that his friends attend the Mass, and many did, including Mr. Meigs of Port Madison, who shut down his sawmill as a mark of respect. He was "one of those who shook hands with the dead chief in his coffin."[4] This was, indeed, a great tribute to the deceased.

First called New York, then Alki, and finally Seattle, the city had its name bestowed upon it by an alleged alcoholic.[5] The university also went through a cycle of names. It was at first called St. Francis Hall, then the Immaculate Conception School, then Seattle College, and finally Seattle University. Compared to Gonzaga, which was called nothing else, the Seattle institution manifested even in its early years a more liberal spirit, which some would have called progressive and others, fickle. There is an interesting oddity, however, in the nomenclature of the two institutions: Gonzaga, originally created to serve as a college for Indian students from the mission schools, was named for an Italian saint, who had died three centuries earlier. Seattle University, on the other hand, founded specifically for white students, bears the name of a distinguished Indian Chief, whose daughter Angeline became a local celebrity.*

Like many great Jesuit universities, Seattle University can trace its beginnings to a small boys' school. In 1890, when Father Francis X. Prefontaine, Seattle's first parish priest, finally started a boys' school in the basement of his church, there were no parochial schools in Seattle. The previous year there had been one other parish church open on Christmas day. Thus in 1890 there were only two Catholic churches in Seattle: Our Lady of Good Help and Sacred Heart. That year the census disclosed that the city's population was 42,837.

An extensive fire on June 6, 1889, had proved to be a blessing; it had swept away most of the older buildings of the city, making room for the new. Our Lady of Good Help Church, a white frame structure called Gothic, resting precariously on the lofty hill at Third Avenue South and Washington, had been spared. One would have supposed the water during heavy rains would have washed it away; but Our Lady of Good Help protected her church from flood and flame alike, and the old structure stood there for many years, a monument to Prefontaine, too, who had built it well.†

Prefontaine had been around for a long time also. He had come to Seattle in December, 1867, at which time he had found only ten Catholics in a population of "about 600." He rented a small cabin for six dollars a month, converted two rooms into a chapel and installed six pews. On November 24, he blessed the chapel and offered Mass in it for a congregation of two ladies.[6] Two years later a frame church was built and dedicated to Our Lady of Good Help. It boasted of a capacity of one hundred, including children but not babies, and this indicates that the Church in Seattle was growing despite its poverty. The pastor had raised most of the $2,000 to pay for it in other places.[7]

Prefontaine, a French-Canadian priest who had been ordained by Bishop Ignace Bourget, the founder of three congregations of sisters, was in his prime.‡ "In his youth," it was said, "he was a great hunter and hunted bears even on the boulevard where the street cars now move around."[8] A large man with heavy jowls and a shock of white hair, he was regarded as "jolly." Seattle neighbors stated that "everybody loved him," and no one doubted his devotion to Seattle. He was a stubborn man, though, and he did not get along very well with his bishop. The bishop wanted a school for boys. He also wanted Prefontaine to have an assistant, which was the last thing Prefontaine wanted and he resisted. When the bishop finally sent a young priest, Father James Cunningham, Prefontaine arranged a room for him inconveniently located between the kitchen and the dining room, in the hopes that he would get discouraged and go away, which is what happened.

The Holy Names Sisters had opened a school for girls. Very well, they could also teach the boys. In 1890 Prefontaine persuaded the superior to assign sisters to his school; and in September classes for boys were begun in the basement of the church. About the same time Prefontaine made arrangements for the construction of a school building at 6th and Spring. He paid for this with his own funds and kept the deed to it in his own name.[9]

*Angeline died on May 31, 1896. Eva Greenslit Anderson, *Chief Seattle* (Caldwell, 1943), p. 331.

†The church was moved and remodeled in 1904, five years before Prefontaine's death in 1909.

‡Bishop Ignace Bourget of Montreal, Canada, founded three congregations of Sisters: Sisters of St. Ann, Sisters of the Holy Names of Jesus and Mary, and Sisters of Charity of Providence. Bourget died at Montreal on June 8, 1885.

Called St. Francis Hall, this two-story-with-attic brick building had some charming elegance about it, being not merely a monotonous, brick box like so many frugally constructed church buildings. Apparently it contained two large classrooms, each with eight elongated windows. It had a large hall on the second floor. Two nicely proportioned porches and an elaborate brick design around the top of the walls were some of its attractive features. It was topped with a gabled roof which indicated that its construction predated the change to flat roofs. Later, most of the ground surrounding St. Francis Hall was excavated and carted away, leaving it stranded on a broad base of mud. One had to enter the building by climbing up some thirty-five steps that led to either porch.

Meanwhile, in the autumn of 1890, Cataldo had dispatched Father Van Gorp, now procurator for the Rocky Mountain Mission, to Seattle to purchase property, primarily for a boys' school, which he hoped to establish at some future time. Van Gorp spent $18,000 for eight lots along Madison at Broadway, making a down payment on them at that time. The deed to this property was not delivered until February, 1891, at approximately the time Prefontaine's school building was completed and occupied.

There seems to be no doubt that Bishop Junger knew of Cataldo's interest in Seattle and approved of it. On April 11, 1891, he composed a letter to him, requesting the Jesuits to take over an already established boys school, meaning of course, St. Francis Hall.[10] He added that the building for the school was for sale, but he did not give details. His Lordship wanted the Jesuits to establish a third parish in Seattle, as well as the boys' school, hoping no doubt that the latter would develop into a college similar to Gonzaga, of which he was very fond.

The Jesuits closest to St. Francis Hall lived with their chickens and cows in North Yakima in what Father Victor Garrand, the superior, described as his "little paradise." There were four Jesuits in Yakima: Garrand, Adrian Sweere, who had recently arrived from the Osage mission in Kansas, Augustine Laure, an ecstatic Frenchman who had given his heart to the Indians, and John Raiberti, another Frenchman who was old and sickly "with only skin and bones."[11] Some people called Raiberti a ghost, and others said he had come out of the grave, which sounds like the same thing. "Once," Parodi observed, "he wrote a sermon on hell and handed it to Caruana for correction. Many words had been blocked out with black lines and the paper was spotted wtih ink. Caruana, handing it back said, 'It looks like hell itself'."[12]

Laure, the first Jesuit to work in Seattle, had arrived in Spokane Falls in 1889, fresh out of theology, and Cataldo assigned him to De Smet to complete his tertianship under Joset. In March of 1890, he was sent to Seattle to help Prefontaine during Lent. This arrangement was mutually advantageous to both the pastor of Our Lady of Good Help Church and the superior of the Jesuits, for on the one hand it demonstrated the pastor's willingness to accept an assistant, if only for seven weeks; and, on the other, it gave the superior a chance to spy out the promised land.

Laure's favorable report described what he saw: "This city is beautifully situated on hills, formerly covered with trees where men had to let in daylight with axe in hand. On the east is an immense lake of fresh water. To the west is Puget Sound which is connected with the ocean. . . . The climate is so mild the grass is green all the year round."[13]

It probably appeared unreasonable to Garrand that the Yakima fathers be assigned to take charge of another flock in Seattle, which was as far away as Paris from London. However, Garrand had been outspoken in his support of the Jesuit ministry with the Whites and Seattle offered an excellent opportunity. Even he could see that. He left Yakima without much fuss, taking Sweere with him and leaving Laure in charge of Yakima. Theoretically he was superior and pastor of both parishes, an extraordinary situation in itself. In practice he spent most of his time in Seattle while Father Laure raced about central

Washington in his buggy or on a horse, killing himself with overwork in two brief years.*

Garrand was forty-four, a slightly balding French intellectual with a showman's knack for successful processions, pageants, and magnificent altar celebrations. He had a long, thin neck, which gave him a bird-like appearance. Judging from his facial expression one might mistake his firmness of character for arrogance. There is no evidence that he was a brilliant administrator, but he certainly was a capable one. One should add, perhaps, that Garrand was also uncommonly pious. Emotional, sometimes he wept when he preached. Kind and zealous, he worked too hard for his own good.

The bishop formally established the new parish on September 12, 1891, feast of the Holy Name of Mary, dedicating it to Mary under the title of the Immaculate Conception, the name which it still bears. Garrand with Sweere arrived fifteen days later, ready if not eager to organize the parish and take over Prefontaine's school. The latter, delighted to be relieved of the burden of the school, was probably somewhat disconcerted by the mutilation of his parish boundaries for the second time in two years, but he cooperated with the Jesuits, to the extent, at least, of leasing St. Francis Hall to them for their school and temporary church. He charged the Jesuits $2,250 a year for the use of the building and furnishings, a considerable amount then, which prompted Garrand and his few parishioners to hasten the erection of their own structure. This was one problem. They had another more complex one which annoyed Garrand even more. St. Francis Hall was located within Prefontaine's parish limits even after the division was made. This was an awkward situation that required immediate attention.

Thus Garrand had his priorities set before him as he leased St. Francis Hall and built his altar and pulpit in the second floor chamber above the classrooms below. Fortunately the sisters agreed to remain as teachers for the 135 students that were registered that year, including girls as well as boys, a prototype of Seattle University. The name of the school, however, was changed from St. Francis Hall to the Immaculate Conception.[14]

Herman Goller, a scholastic at this time, and one to watch, wrote about the new parish in Seattle to the editor of *Woodstock Letters:* "Our fathers have opened a new parish and school on the sound in the beautiful city of Seattle, which later on, is likely to become a college."[15] The Jesuits had colleges on their minds even then. While this was a period of vast expansion into parish work under pressure from the bishops, Jesuits were not to deviate from either one of two ministries: Indian missions or education, until much later, when the whole world had changed. It is significant that Goller, a strong pro-college Jesuit, became the first provincial of the West Coast province.

Adrian Sweere was an excellent choice as Garrand's assistant in Seattle. Unlike the pastor, Sweere was square-jawed and heavy set. Not a forceful man, he was instead good-natured and kindly in disposition. His eyes bulged a little, though he looked a bit sleepy, and his mouth expressed great contentment with his lot. He, too, brought with him some administrative experience. He had been a superior for many years at the Osage Mission. At a critical time he would become superior and president of Seattle College.

In 1893, as Garrand struggled to provide the parish with its own church and school building, a great depression hovered over the country, not excluding Seattle. Money was hard to come by. Garrand could not even borrow the money he needed in the city, but he was able at last to establish a line of credit with a bank in Amsterdam with the help of Father Sweere. He formally incorporated the School of the Immaculate Conception on June 30, 1893, and boldly started construction of the new parish building on borrowed money.

---

*Augustine Laure of the Province of Lyons died in St. Elizabeth's Hospital in Yakima on December 19, 1892. He was only 36 years old. *Woodstock Letters*, 24 (1895), p. 472.

No one seems to have brought up the name of McDougal in these transactions. It will be recalled that Alphonsus McDougal, who was accidentally killed at Gonzaga two years earlier, was the son of a wealthy Seattle landowner, Malcom McDougal. Father Mackin had taken the boy's body to Seattle and offered Mass for him in the recently completed Sacred Heart Church.[16] Malcom, after his first feelings of anger and grief wore off, offered $20,000 and fifty acres of land in Seattle for a new college "in remembrance of the boy." Father Cataldo turned down this offer for reasons only he and God knew and God did not tell anyone. Did anybody remind Garrand about McDougal's kind proposal? Probably not. Jesuits were too naïve about money in those days. "Efficiency," as Father Leo Martin used to tell his tertians, "is not our most important norm."

Garrand and Sweere lived in a rented house. To avoid this expense Garrand took care to design the new building at Madison and Broadway for multi-purposes: church, school and rectory. It was four stories, including a basement, which had windows above ground, a foundation of hewn stones almost two stories high, and a gabled roof with three chimneys. There were four entrances. One of these was on the lowest level for the priests who lived in the basement. For the boys, there were two entrances on opposite sides leading to the main floor. The fourth entrance was on Madison Avenue at the second floor level and led to the church, there being a ramp and suitable porch. The church was two stories. This chamber of worship had three resplendent altars with enough statues for a cathedral and a sanctuary large enough to accommodate the oversized bishop, three priests, and at least twenty-four altar boys. Father Garrand blessed this church and celebrated the first Mass in it on December 8, 1894.

In Jesuit terminology, the new school was designated as *a collegium inchoatum*, an incipient college. It was designed only for boys, including in the initial year those in the seventh and eighth grades and the first two years of high school, not unlike Gonzaga's first year. The girls had been excluded, as well as the younger boys, but provision was made for them in another structure, and this too, deserves some comment.

East of the new school, less distance away than it was possible for a robust first grader to throw a stone, there was a two-story frame building owned by the very zealous and godly institution known popularly as the W.C.T.U. The proximity of this establishment to the beer and wine drinking Catholics apparently prompted its directors, in fear of some tainted association, to put it up for sale. The Jesuits tried to buy it but were unsuccessful. Later, however, through a third party they were able to complete this transaction and "the W.C.T.U. Building," so designated for some time to come, became the property of the Jesuits. Father Garrand, with a certain excusable complacency, one supposes, installed the girls with the smaller boys and their teachers in this new acquisition. The Holy Names Sisters very graciously "agreed to conduct the lower school independently of the parish, which found it necessary to withdraw support for financial reasons."[17]

Prefontaine's elegant building was not idle long. As Bishop O'Dea, who succeeded Junger, reported to the Apostolic delegate: "He leased the large fine building which he owned to the public schools. This netted him a considerable revenue for himself."[18] Eventually Prefontaine himself moved into the building; then sold it for $39,000 and retired elsewhere. Thus the source from which three great institutions were created (Immaculate Conception parish, Seattle Prep, and Seattle University) passed into history, leaving behind only traces of its existence.*

*Prefontaine with his niece Marie Rose Pauze moved into St. Francis Hall on May 31, 1903. His niece reported that: "The Jesuits acquired property of their own at present Seattle University and the building was empty so we moved there. Taxes were high and he had to get some income from the place, so he let the Hibernians, the Knights of Columbus, Catholic Foresters, and others use it for meetings. We lived in the upper part." Lucille McDonald, *Seattle Times*, April 2, 1967, p. 9.

In Spokane, which was almost as large as Seattle at that time, Gonzaga College had received its third president in five years and its students were trying to make peace with him. Father Mackin, the second president, had left for De Smet with his novices. John Baptist Rene, a rather stiff, autocratic Vendean with a European's infatuation with formality, had come from France via Ireland, where for eight years he had been founder and director of Mungret, an apostolic school for mission priests. Unaccustomed to the casualness of the American West, he was more perplexed by his charges than impatient with them. In the end he won them over by changing the time of rising in the morning from 5:30 to 6:00.

The great crisis confronting Rene was a common one: lack of space. While the campus was cluttered with buildings of all sorts: chicken coops, barns, stables, sheds, an old house and the main building, the school's ten Jesuits and fifty resident students were quartered in nooks and crannies that were either too small or too dingy, or both, for members of a reputable college which was already in its sixth year.

For some time college authorities had been fondling plans for a new school, but Cataldo had cautioned them to move slowly lest their new site be compromised by something worse than the old. As early as the autumn of 1888 architect Preuss had prepared drawings for a proposed new college and Rebmann had sent them to the general in Rome on December 18, 1888, explaining that there were two sets, one fancy and one plain, and that either could be used depending upon the amount of money available. He estimated the cost at $65,000 without explaining which of the two plans this amount could buy. In 1891, before Mackin left, there were other plans, this time only fancy ones. One projected a building that looked like the main office of an affluent insurance company—a brick monument two hundred-and-fifty-feet long with a central tower about fifteen stories high. If Rebmann could submit two plans, Mackin could provide at least one preposterous one.[19]

Nothing came of these, though much short-lived enthusiasm had been generated, and when Rene arrived to tighten up the screws, further discussion was suppressed. Like many Frenchmen, Rene lacked the ability to spend money he did not have.

Yet the problem of space remained. In September, 1891, when more resident students appeared than were expected, Rene hastily rented a neighbor's house a short distance from the college and his assistants scrambled for beds and other furnishings to accommodate two prefects and ten boys. This first boarding hall at Gonzaga was called St. John Berchman's in honor of a young Jesuit who had been canonized three years earlier. Talk of further expansion was now fashionable, especially since the brothers were still living in the original house that had been shared with the bedbugs.

In the summer of 1892 Preusse was commissioned to draw plans for not one, but two buildings, both very modest, however, and in keeping with Rene's frugal outlook. One was a frame building with a recreation hall on the first floor and a dormitory above. The other, which should have been provided earlier, was a frame church for the parish. Until this time the members of St. Aloysius parish had been using the college chapel for services. On August 6, the foundation for the church was begun. During the same month electric lights were installed in the college building, an innovation which evoked the avid interest of the young Jesuits, who had to wait, however, to enjoy the results of this investment. The power company explained that it could not supply electricity for some time.

The long-awaited power arrived on October 11. The current was turned on at 6:00 P.M., a little after dusk, and the delighted Jesuits and boys blew out the scattered lamps and stored them away with that kind of contempt that all liberated people have for the past. In the following month another step in the right direction was taken when the college water system was finally connected to city pipes, "a boon we have long been looking for," wrote Father Paul Arthuis in the minister's diary, "especially these last three weeks when the windmill has been very irregularly working on account of the want of wind."[20]

The city water arrived on November 8, election day, when Grover Cleveland was announced to be the twenty-second president of the United States. The boys, at least, toasted the new president with an abundance of water, lacking something better. It is likely, however, that the Jesuits swallowed toasts of a stronger nature, since much was expected of Cleveland for the correction of abuses in the Indian mission schools. "It is expected," Arthuis predicted, "the new administration will be fairer towards our Indian schools and will discontinue the policy of persecution inaugurated by Commissioner Morgan and his associates."[21]

Jesuit antipathy to Thomas J. Morgan was justified. Prior to his nefarious tenure in the Harrison administration, the government employed a system of contracts for the support of sectarian Indian schools. Although this system had been tarnished by Grant's Peace Policy, it permitted, at least, some government support on designated Catholic reservations. Morgan, a Utopian do-gooder at best, forced upon the Indians a new system in place of the contract schools. According to Senator Vest this system would "cost the Government millions upon millions of dollars without any appreciable result."[22] The Morgan plan was to establish among Indians non-sectarian schools, modeled on the public school system, where no religion could be taught and where the Indian was to be educated by government employees to the exclusion of all Christian denominations.[23] Whereas the Peace Policy was an overt attempt to make all Indians Protestant, the Morgan policy was designed to make all Indians secular.

In a sense the Peace Policy had prepared the way for Morgan. By destroying parental choice, Grant's Peace Policy gave the government authority to decide what religion each reservation could accept. Having determined this, it was but a short step for the bureaucrats to eliminate religion altogether.[24]

There was much opposition to Morgan's proposal, which was submitted to the Senate on July 25, 1890. "The education of the Indian cannot be accomplished," said one Senator, "but by a Sunday School which will last seven days in each week."[25] Despite the opposition, Morgan had his way. Government support of contract schools, including those conducted by Catholics, gradually declined. The Reverend Thomas Dorchester, Morgan's officious catspaw and superintendent of Indian schools, bustled about the reservations with his wife in search of Catholic employees to dismiss. Their procedure resembled a witch hunt. Unfortunately, it was as effective as it was bizarre. All mission schools declined dramatically. Arthuis's hopes for a Cleveland reform were futile. By 1901 the Golden Era of Indian missions had vanished, leaving in its wake dozens of mission schools without stable support, entirely dependent upon volunteer offerings. Most of them were destined to suffer an agonizing death. Although no one person alone could be held responsible for this, Thomas J. Morgan can be regarded as a principal villain. But Arthuis could not have known how badly Cleveland would disappoint them. The new church he was building became the center of interest. While its construction was being pushed ahead with vigor by the contractor Mr. McLafferty, the work of grading two avenues, Boone and De Smet in front and behind the college, was also rushed to meet the dedication deadline.[26] On November 13, Rene announced in the college chapel that the new edifice would be blessed by Bishop Junger on the following Sunday. A hectic week followed. Painters and carpenters, with the college president on their heels, slapped paint and pounded nails, taking care to please Preusse, who inspected everything like an old maid with a captious eye. The pews which Rene promised to rent "in the same terms as Our Lady of Lourdes," were installed on Saturday, and a wagonload of potted palms and ferns, loaned by the local undertakers, Smith and Luce, were piled in banks around the sanctuary. Two Irish lace curtains were hung back of the altar "over the two large Gothic windows."[27] Although they thought of everything as being "Gothic," they really produced Victorian. When the new St. Aloysius was ready for the bishop, it looked so perfectly Victorian that the queen herself might have emerged from the sacristy with Prince Albert beside her.

On Sunday, November 20, the solemn dedication took place. For all the excitement it might have been the Cathedral of Rheims that was being dedicated, not a frame church with fake wooden buttresses, which had been completed in three brief months. The day closed with an "entertainment," a scientific essay, among other miscellaneous offerings, on the subject of "Aerial Navigation," described by one observer as "brilliantly rendered," but at a time "when the successful conquest of the air was still a mere hope, and in the opinion of many, a foolish dream."[28] When it was all over, most Jesuits, one supposes, went to bed with a great sigh of relief.

Despite the many accomplishments of his administration, Rene's term as president lasted only two years. On March 16, 1893, he was replaced by Cataldo's right arm, Father Leopold Van Gorp. The change came suddenly, without warning or welcome. The students, who had become very fond of Rene, greeted the news with dismay. On the following day, when he left for his new post at St. Francis Regis Mission, they sent him off in a flood of tears, and then, with some resentment in their hearts, they stepped back to take a better look at Van Gorp. They had seen him on the campus for two years, a mysterious priest who appeared to be aloof and sometimes shy. Tall in stature and graceful in carriage, he looked like a worried basketball coach. His finely formed facial features with their dark, moody eyes were topped with graying hairs. His mouth turned down at the corners like Bishop O'Dea's; and, like the esteemed bishop, he was regarded as amiable in temperament by his peers, though the boys could not know that. They knew him as treasurer for the Jesuits. It is unlikely they knew much more.

Nor did many Jesuits, though it was generally believed throughout the mission that he shared with Palladino a poor impression of Spokane Falls. He had made little effort to conceal his unfavorable views about Gonzaga. At the time of the crisis over the Helena college and with Palladino, he had expressed the view that Helena was the city of the future, not Spokane Falls. Most Jesuits knew that he had been relieved of his position of local superior at least twice because of poor health. Many, too, thought he was too stingy with community money. All admitted he was a very good businessman, but it was difficult to really know him. He consciously concealed his deep spirituality so skillfully that many were astonished to hear of it after he was dead.

The Indians of St. Ignatius, where he had spent many years, called him *Kutenalko kuailks*, the Tall Black Robe.[29] With them he was usually serious and business-like, not at all like Father Bandini who loved to break wild horses. "When a wild horse is bucking and kicking, and throwing you to the ground," Bandini used to say, "you mount the horse again and again and again; if you let the horse have his own ways, you will not break him in, in 20 years."[30] Bandini was a little like that, rough and ready, but Van Gorp was just the opposite. Bandini liked to hunt rattlesnakes with a hatchet. In the end he cut the rattles off the tail and kept a can full of them in his room.[31] One cannot imagine Van Gorp with snake rattles in his room or anywhere else. He was too proper, of course, and too practical. He preferred collecting money. But Bandini and Van Gorp had something special in common: they were both excellent language scholars and they knew the Flathead language better than most Indians.

Van Gorp was a Belgian. Born at Turnhout in 1834 during the third year of the reign of Leopold I, he was educated in classical studies and entered the Jesuit Order when he was twenty-one. Influenced by the writings of De Smet he volunteered to work among the American Indians and in 1866 he came to the Rocky Mountain Mission by way of California, where he was met by Palladino at Santa Clara, the depot of departure for the north.

Cataldo had escaped from it the year before and Palladino and Bandini would escape from it in the year following.

Grassi was acting superior when Van Gorp had arrived and he sent him to St. Francis Regis for awhile to work with Indians, then to Virginia City to work with Whites. While he was at Virginia City, Montana Territory's first governor disappeared mysteriously from a boat on the Missouri and it was commonly believed that he had been murdered. Van Gorp conducted Thomas Francis Meagher's funeral in Virginia City and preached a funeral oration that Palladino regarded as so significant he included it in full in his *Indian and White in the Northwest*.[32] Van Gorp was only thirty-three years old then, a precocious age for such hifalutin prominence in the annals of early Montana. A year later Grassi made him superior at Helena, which was the hub of Jesuit activity for all of eastern Montana. For the rest of his life he occupied positions of high trust, in part because of his quiet, serene manner, but mostly because of his talent for business. His father had been a banker. Like Rene he had been taught the value of a franc.

These were the waning years of Cataldo's long superiorship. By this time he knew every town, village, and hamlet in the vast area between the Cascade Mountains and the Dakotas. He had established or helped to establish innumerable missions and parishes, and willy-nilly, the mission of Alaska. Perhaps because of his original intransigence toward Alaska, he tended to favor it in his final years. "Everybody wants to go to Alaska," he lamented to Father Parodi, when he assigned him to this mission in 1892, "and they are needed in the Rocky Mount Mission. Keep [it] secret."[33]

The problem was like the one in De Smet's time: Cataldo's Jesuits did not want to stay home and take care of the cat. They wanted to go where the glamour was and where the danger could be found. The Northwest had become too tame for many. Bandini, who had chased a bear out of his confessional in the good old days, now complained that he was expected to take baths. He used to boast that he had taken only two baths in his life and both of them by accident, when he fell into the river. Palladino supported him in this boyish aversion for bath water by stating that Queen Victoria disliked bathing and it "appears to be well authenticated history, there were no bathtubs in the royal palace."[34] Rebmann had supplied bed sheets and table napkins at Gonzaga College. At Seattle they *rode streetcars*, not horses, and at St. Ignatius Mission they built a new scholasticate with individual rooms for everybody, running water in heated bathrooms, and a library that was larger than the original mission. At De Smet, too, novices were coddled in a comfortable new house, not in tepees, as Joset had demanded. And not only the novices, but the Indians, too, were speaking Italian; Parodi, when he went there thought he was back in Italy.* No wonder, then, that many wanted to go to Alaska.

The truth is that while Garrand and Sweere were struggling to keep their college afloat, a string of hearty Jesuits passed up the coast to what Laure described as "a frightful country, where there are neither trees, nor grass, nor horses; not anything at all, except snow, ice and more snow and ice."[35] The very thought of Alaska, he said, "freezes the blood in my veins." Yet he offered to go there.

Ordinarily the missionaries departed from Spokane with little money from Van Gorp and no formalities from anyone. They took the train to San Francisco, where they embarked for St. Michael near the Yukon delta. Although Jesuit mail was addressed to Alaska through the "Northern Commercial Company, Sansone Street, San Francisco," Seattle had begun to take over the lion's share of Alaskan commerce. Eventually, when the widely publicized "ton of gold" arrived from diggings in the Klondike, Seattle established herself as the principal port for Alaskan trade, eliminating all competitors by some well-advanced

*Parodi also wrote that Cataldo learned the Eskimo language in four months. OPA, Parodi Papers, Reminiscences, p. 43.

public relations. During the brief period of the gold rush, an estimated two hundred million dollars in gold entered Seattle, and one hundred million of it was said to have remained there.[36] Thus Seattle was built on gold as Spokane had been built on silver from the mines of Idaho.

Very little of either fell into the hands of Van Gorp or Garrand. The Jesuits in early Spokane were always mortified by the pettiness of their local support and the Jesuits of Seattle soon learned they had to grin and bear it: their desperate appeals got nowhere. Nonetheless both missions survived the great depression of '93, the older one with the charisma of dedication and the younger one called Alaska, with the holy spirit of zeal. "In all my years as superior," Cataldo was wont to say later, "I never lacked for material means, but I often lacked for men." With a million square miles in his jurisdiction, half of them in Alaska, Cataldo would have lacked men even if he doubled the roster of something close to 150. Of these, when Van Gorp became president of Gonzaga College, 46 were novices or scholastics, mostly unavailable, and 36 were brothers. Alaska had its proportionate share of 8 priests and 5 brothers.

There were at this time three major missions in Alaska: Holy Cross where Tosi, delegated as vice-superior with full authority to act independently of Cataldo, made his headquarters; St. Peter Claver at Nulato, and St. Alphonsus Rodriguez at Cape Vancouver, Nelson Island, where two priests and two brothers personified Brother Giordano's contemptuous classification of "new missionaries."

Giordano has described how they had all come. During the summer of 1889, as noted above, Father Gaspar Genna, Brother John Rosati, and three Sisters of St. Ann arrived together. Like the sisters, Rosati remained at Holy Cross, but Genna joined Giordano at Nulato. Ragaru, too, had a mission near Nulato at Nuklukoyit, but he sometimes visited Giordano to help him with Genna, who was a misfit in Alaska. He should never have come there. As Giordano describes him, "He was a heavy man with a big overcoat." He was entirely incapable of taking care of himself, one of those dependents in the mission whom everyone had to succor. He could not cook, nor handle tools, nor cut wood. He could only read books, not exactly a priority occupation in the middle of nineteenth-century Alaska.

Genna had scarcely unpacked his bags when he plunged through the ice while crossing the river. "As he fell he stretched out his arms like a cross and held himself on the ice by this means."[37] Indian boys with him tried to help and one, whom Giordano called "half-crazed," ran ahead to tell Giordano what had happened. "Brother," he said, "the *wife* of Father Ragaru got drowned." Giordano modestly describes his rescue efforts, which succeeded, then adds dryly: "Father Genna wore his cassock always and Father Ragaru only at Mass." For the record he also adds: "That excitement affected his nerves."[38]

Genna, when he had been thawed out and dried off sent a hasty telegram to Cataldo, "Genna leaves or dies." Cataldo's cryptic response, which doubtlessly took some time to arrive, became an Alaskan classic, "Genna dies."[39]

There was nothing Cataldo could do, even though he wanted to, because Alaska was frozen solid. Genna would have to survive until the breakup in the spring. So when spring came and the ice broke up with a great roar and a rush toward the sea, Giordano put Genna in a row boat with a kindly miner and sent him downriver to Holy Cross, a journey of four days. From there he was sent to St. Michael and then to the states where he was reassigned to St. Mary's Mission, Montana, with Father Diomedi. He was the first, if not the last, to leave Alaska in broken health.*

Tosi demanded a replacement. In 1890 Cataldo sent two Jesuits, Father Joseph Treca

---

*After two years at St. Mary's, still in delicate health, Genna was transferred to Los Gatos. He died in Spokane on March 28, 1911.

and Brother John Negro. Tosi met them at St. Michael and directed them to start a new mission at "Cape Vancouver," in the Yukon delta.* Having got two Jesuits with one letter, Tosi tried again, explaining rather plaintively to Cataldo that Treca really should have another priest with him. He concluded his request, "Please send another Father as soon as possible." Cataldo complied with this appeal and sent Father Paul Muset, who reached St. Michael on the last boat in the fall. There he had to wait until the river and the sea froze over, and then with Eskimo guides he traveled by dogsled four-hundred miles along the coast to the Bering Sea to Cape Vancouver where he joined Treca and Negro.

At Holy Cross, meanwhile, the sisters had opened a school for girls; and the Jesuits, another for boys. The sisters had papered the interior of their cabin with newspapers to keep the cold out and the heat in. They used flour paste for an adhesive and that too created a crisis, for they soon learned that their dwelling was over-run with mice; literally hundreds of mice. "We had a mouse trap," Sister Mary Calasanctius wrote, "and ten times daily the five holes contained five mice." But there were so many they propagated faster than the sisters could catch them. In a word they had a plague.[40] One of the sisters thought of St. Gertrude "who also was of Germany," like Pied Piper, and they began at once a novena of prayer and penance. "And, astonishing as it may seem, the swarm had disappeared before the ninth day, as mysteriously as it had arrived."[41]

What is perhaps more astonishing is that the mice turned up in the fathers' house. "Sisters, do you know our house has become infested with mice," Tosi announced. After the sisters made a second novena to St. Gertrude the mice suddenly disappeared again and never returned.

The account of the mysterious mice was not recorded by Giordano, who had bigger game in his sights. "When Father Robaut was in Nulato," he reported, "Rev. Fr. Joset from De Smet mission wrote to Father Robaut and said, 'a holy missionary will come to Alaska.' He was Rev. Wm. Henry Judge. He made his Tertianship under the direction of Father Joset, and Father Joset himself was one of the first holy missionaries."[42]

At that time Joset had required his tertians to perform all the trials, or "experiments," suggested for them, including "begging from door to door." Each tertian was given a gunnysack by Joset and directed to get the sack filled. This doubtlessly was very edifying and practical in Joset's native Switzerland, but in De Smet, Idaho, where there were only Indian people, unaccustomed to such shenanigans by the black robes, it was a farce. Judge, like Mackin who described this ascetical peregrination, scarcely impressed Joset with his gleanings—mostly potatoes.

Judge arrived in Alaska in 1890 with a herd of livestock, whereby hangs a sad tale that illustrates the unexpected eccentricities of the Arctic. According to Parodi, Cataldo in one of his letters to Robaut asked him if there was grass in Alaska, and Robaut, carried away by what he probably regarded as a naive question, responded, "We grow wild grass here that can be cut to make enough hay to feed all the cattle in the United States." Impressed by this, Cataldo gave directions that when Father Judge and Brother Cunningham sailed to Alaska they were to bring cattle from San Francisco. At the last moment, just before their steamer departed, they bought four cows, two steers, three goats and three sheep. All were taken aboard the ship. At St. Michael's after they examined their stock, they ordered a bull from Unalaska, where there were other cattle. One can only imagine what frustrations Judge and Cunningham experienced in finally getting their animals to Holy Cross. On August 4, the three goats and three sheep arrived there with a cat thrown in, but the cattle did not arrive until September 12. Without approval from anybody, the village dogs soon

*This mission has been referred to variously as Cape Vancouver, Eskinole, St. Alphonsus, and, more consistently, Tununa, which later became Tununak. St. Mary's at Akulurak developed from it.

devoured the three sheep. The missionaries and children ate the two steers. From the rest "we got about 25 or 30 head of cattle, and bought three or four horses. The cows supplied with fresh milk for us and the Sisters, children and Fathers."[43]

But the experiment was not a success. Most of the cows in the end died of starvation, because they refused to leave the barn to eat. In the summer the mosquitoes were so thick and voracious that the poor brutes preferred to die of hunger than be devoured by the insects.*

"So Father Judge reached Holy Cross with Brother Cunningham," Giordano continued, "and at once we had about 150 boys and girls. The Sisters had 25 girls and the Fathers had 125 boys. They had very poor accommodations so they had to bunk just like in the steamer, one over the other, all around the house, three layer bunks, and some slept on the floor."[44]

Father Judge, the first native American Jesuit to work in Alaska, destined like Laure to die young from overexertion, might have been holy, as Joset said, but he looked very ordinary. Slightly built, but not frail, he wore his cassock whenever possible, looping a rosary over his cincture as devout Jesuits used to do. He used eyeglasses, which made him look like Prando, or as the Indians said, "Iron Eyes," and his high forehead above them was topped with thinning hair, which he parted on the left, like a very nice college boy. Judge had great compassion for the sick, and he was more practical than Genna who wanted to help the sick but did not know how. It was Judge's devotion to sick gold seekers that got him in the end, but that occurred after several brief years in indiscretions and pious excesses that some called foolish. Certainly he was not understood by other missionaries in Alaska, who had come from foreign lands and were at considerable variance with the priorities Judge had brought with him from his native Baltimore.

Another American-born Jesuit arrived from Washington, D.C. in 1891. Giordano simply reported that "Reverend Father Francis Barnum came up from Alaska with Brother (Thomas) Power and three Sisters of St. Ann from Canada."[45] The sisters had come as a reinforcement, which doubled the original contingent, and Brother Power, an excellent mechanic, had come to operate and maintain the new mission boat named the *St. Michael*. In the jargon of the Yukon it was called a steamer, but it was so small that it could carry little or no cargo aboard, though it had sufficient power to tow several loaded barges simultaneously. Tosi had purchased the boat from the Northern Commercial Company for $3,000 on the condition that the company had the first right to buying it back for the same amount, if the Jesuits decided to dispose of it.

Here a brief comment about the geography of the Yukon may be helpful. The Yukon, one of the world's great rivers, drains Alaska's vast central basin of tundra, mostly by meandering at a relatively slow pace through the willows and around the islands which block it, constantly changing its course by washing out banks and islands or forming new ones, dropping very slowly in altitude, only a thousand feet in two thousand miles, from the base of the Chilkoot Pass in the southeast to the Bering Sea. Frozen most of the year, it is heavily muddied with silt when it flows during the summer months. Its estuary which has many courses, almost like shallow tide flats, cannot bear ocean-going ships, which dock at St. Michael, on an island of the same name, eighty miles north. Here freight has to be transferred to small riverboats or steamers like the *St. Michael*. There have been many

---

*The Holy Cross Mission Diaries contain references to the death of the sheep and goats. For example, October 14, 1890, "The dogs killed one of the goats about 8:00 PM." On October 15, "The dogs tried to kill a sheep." On October 16, "Mr. Burke killed the worst of the dogs this morning." On October 30, "We killed one of the steers today." On December 1, "We killed one of the cows." When de la Motte made his visitation of Alaska in 1903, Holy Cross still had two of the cows and the bull. De la Motte stated that all the dogs at the mission had to be muzzled to keep them from killing the cattle.

such boats, most of them so small they carried little more than their own fuel and crew. They towed their cargoes and sometimes passengers behind them in barges or small boats, which lacked conveniences of every sort. For new missionaries the most tortuous of all initiations was a several day journey up the Yukon in an open boat towed by a steamer that provided no sanitary facilities, no protection from the sun, rain, or insects; and, worst of all, no privacy of any kind. In Alaska one had to "go native" to survive.

Barnum who arrived with Brother Power survived without going native, though he sipped slowly and long the heavy potions of Alaska, the nectar as well as the venom. As a well-educated and guileless American he wrote endlessly about both to his Jesuit colleagues at Georgetown and this did not set well with Tosi, his superior. Barnum had come from a wealthy, socially prominent family. Handsome in appearance, in a rugged sort of way, he had well-proportioned features with light colored eyes and thin eyebrows. In his arctic furs he looked like the hero of a Jack London movie. A convert to the church he was an extensive traveler all over the world before he entered the Maryland province for a second time, the first having been terminated by a family need, and he brought with him to the Alaska mission an urbanity and a tolerance which were incomprehensible to Tosi and other Jesuits of European backgrounds. He also brought with him a natural talent for what was commonly called the scientific method, and this, too, baffled Tosi, a rigid man who never bothered to learn English well, and never kept up with material progress in the English-speaking world.

Barnum's arrival coincided with the beginning of a certain anti-Americanism in the Alaska mission, which lasted for two generations, until the death of Crimont. In the early years the principal protagonists were, of course, Tosi and Barnum—Tosi with his stuffy, traditional complacency and Barnum with his breezy good humor. Barnum's inquisitive mind and his genius for penetrating the truth wherever he found it appeared to be an ugly threat to Tosi. Eventually it was Tosi who triumphed over Barnum because it was he who held the reigns of power; but both were destroyed, Tosi by his defects, and Barnum by his virtues.

If the sisters ever witnessed this conflict they never acknowledged it. Calasanctius, who was Flemish, wrote about Tosi in her native tongue, "His whole personality radiated the tenderness of his charity. Everywhere we went we heard him described in terms that varied little. [He was] self forgetful, patient in waiting on God and bearing the faults and limitations of others."[46]

Jesuits, and Barnum in particular, were not so generous in their judgments. Barnum wrote that Tosi "possessed a domineering and most irascible disposition and would fly into a violent temper at the slightest provocation. His sole idea of government was *sic volo sic jubeo;* and so he was in every way, a stern and harsh superior."* Later Barnum added, "He never exposed himself to any of the miseries or inconveniences which he could avoid."† Tosi wanted to make Holy Cross a great cattle ranch, Barnum said, so he would not buy a sawmill which Barnum regarded as essential to the mission's development. Tosi deliberately exaggerated things to make himself look better, and he refused to listen to advice for locating missions, along the coast, about which he knew very little. Thus the missions were poorly situated and other Jesuits had to bear the hardships. Perhaps what irritated Barnum most was Tosi's insistence that the missions should stock trade goods for bartering with the natives. Barnum expressed his sentiments:

*Georgetown University Archives, Barnum Papers, mss., "Concerning Fr. Tosi," copy in OPA. The Latin phrase may be loosely translated as follows, "This is what I think; this is what I command."

†*Ibid.*, p. 4. With due respect for Barnum's judgment, I think it should be stated that Tosi for all of his faults was a great man. He endured the hardships of Alaska willingly and for many years.

"The main cause of the most of our trouble came from the unfortunate decision of Fr. Tosi that we should accept the regular trade system of the Fur Co. This not only weakened our influence at the very start, but continued to be a continual source of annoyance and trouble with the natives . . . after all the natives could hardly be blamed for not distinguishing between trader and missionary when one had to act in both roles."*

At this time Tosi was a gaunt man with hair turning gray. His eyes, deeply resentful in appearance, were covered with rimless glasses, giving him a stern, old maid's look, which was confirmed by his tight lips and firm jaw. He seemed to be wearing dentures which pained him. No one realized it then, but he was a sick man.†

Barnum had disembarked at St. Michael on June 19. The next day Treca arrived. "He had come from Tununa in an *angiak* and having been overtaken by a storm he landed at Stebbins and made his way across the island on foot."[47] They were to return by boat, which Tosi had purchased and ordered Barnum to convert into a sailboat. They had no canvas for sails, which Tosi regarded as unimportant, so Barnum used cotton cloth they had brought for trade with the Eskimos. Then Tosi hurried them off before alterations had been completed. After a long, perilous voyage, made almost suicidal by the inadequacies of their craft, the travel-worn Jesuits landed at their mission on the northwest extremity of Nelson Island. "Our coming awoke Father Muset, and he came out of the little hut. He bowed gravely to each of us and shook hands without a word! It was the time of *'la grande silence,'* so having witnessed our arrival he retired at once."[48]

Barnum was appalled by what he found, an unprotected shack made with squared logs chinked with moss, so ill-proportioned and wobbly that four props were placed against it to keep the arctic winds from blowing it over. Tosi had been the architect, Treca "the consulting engineer, log roller and cook."

"The result of this combined efforts, impeded by several good-natured natives, is our extraordinary domicile which partakes of the features of an old Virginia smoke-house, a Harlem shanty and a native barrabora."[49]

This was home now for three Jesuits, who stretched bits of cotton cloth between them for partitions to give privacy. It contained a small stove and a few utensils; little more. For beds they placed a rug on the ground, then several blankets. Muset used a bag of rice for a pillow. Since they had only driftwood for fuel, and very little of that, they built a fire only at meal times. The room became so cold that "during the night our breath would freeze, forming ice along the edge of the blankets."[50] In winter they always slept with all their clothes on.

If the house was bad, the vermin were worse. "In Alaska," wrote Barnum, "the louse and the missionary are 'one and inseparable'; of course this intimacy is entirely due to the obstinate infatuation of the louse. In the beginning, the missionary rejects the overtures of the insinuating insect, and seeks to avoid companionship, but his efforts are in vain, the louse will not be repulsed; the intimacy is inevitable. Humiliating as the confession may sound, it is sad but true. We are all lousy, and we are lousy all the time."[51] Of the Alaska mosquito he wrote, "No description of the Yukon country is complete without some allusion to the insect plague, and it may be added that no description can do justice to this subject."[52]

No one should be surprised to hear that new residents on these inhospitable shores often succumbed to what Barnum called "Polar Anaemia," a mental illness that not only

---

Ibid., p. 9.

†Barnum expressed this opinion before Tosi went to Rome. It is quite probable that Tosi's health had been undermined by his hardships. Not only did he make no effort to take advantage of his condition but when he was finally transferred because of health, he objected.

destroyed the effectiveness of the individual, but also produced an additional hardship for others with whom he was closely confined. At the end of Barnum's first year, Treca, generally regarded as one of Alaska's most saintly missionaries, suffered Polar Anaemia. The following year Barnum described the symptoms:

"During our second winter Brother Rosati fell victim to Polar Anaemia. He became dull and listless and seemed to take no interest in anything. As he became more affected he began declaring that the devil was constantly around and that he could smell him."* Muset, too, became very ill. He had left Tununa after Christmas for a long excursion along the Bering Sea near Nunivak Island, and did not return until the end of February. He had slept fifty-two consecutive nights in Eskimo *casines* and when he arrived at Tununa his health was shattered. He never recovered, though he lived long enough to return by boat to the States. A dying man, he lived at Missoula for almost two years, then died at the age of forty-four, still pleading to be sent back to Alaska.†

Muset had left his mark in Alaska. As Father Parodi noted, "Fr. Muset composed Prayers and a catechism in verses," which the Eskimos loved to sing, sometimes all day long," and a dictionary in the Eskimo Indian language."[53]

Probably at Barnum's insistence, the mission at Tununa was moved. Crimont, who came to Alaska soon after, presented some particulars:

"In the month of March 1892 Father Tosi visited Tununa; while there he decided that the Fathers should carefully explore the inter-fluvial tract extending between the Yukon and the Kuskokwim with a view to find a site suitable for the erection of a school for Eskimo children. . . . Kanilik, on a secondary stream in the Yukon Delta region, seemed to combine some of the favorable features. Thither the missionaries moved their Tununa buildings. The new location had looked attractive as a winter abode, but it proved unsuitable for summer, as it was then discovered that an extensive mud flat lay between the house and the channel of the river. The building was again taken apart the following year and floated around to the Akulurak stream. There additional buildings were put up and four Sisters having come down from Holy Cross, the second boarding school was started in September 1894."[54]

Barnum was full of schemes for the welfare of the missions. He had discovered suitable clay for pottery and suggested that teachers and equipment be brought in to develop a pottery industry since "the Eskimos are artistic and could do this very well." This idea seemed too exotic to Tosi. Barnum urged the formation of reindeer herds. "The reindeer scheme," he wrote, "promises to work well. There were 79 calves raised at the Government station last year."[55] He tried to convince superiors to send scholastics to conduct the school at Holy Cross to relieve the priests for missionary work away from the residence. With friends in the east he organized a fund-raising program based on individual annual donations of $150 for the support of one child, explaining that this benefited the mission more than a gift of food or clothing, because the freight was so costly.[56]

This was the heart of the matter: cost. In 1889, Mother Drexel had sent Cataldo $10,000 for the support of the Alaskan mission.‡ After this was gone donations trickled in but much

---

*Georgetown University archives, Barnum Papers, ms., Tununa, Kanelik, and Akulurak," copy in OPA, 8. Brother Rosati was sent to San Francisco as soon as the ships were sailing again and he fully recovered from his breakdown.

†Muset was first sent to Holy Cross to recover. Since this proved to be inadequate he was sent to Missoula where he died on September 7, 1897.

‡OPA, Cataldo papers, letter from Cataldo to Mother Katherine Drexel, April 13, 1889. Mother Drexel had met Seghers in Rome on Christmas Eve, 1883.

of the money came from the sale of lots in Spokane's Sinto addition. Van Gorp was selling the Jesuits' cherished property in the Gonzaga neighborhood, mostly to Catholic families who wanted to live near Gonzaga and the sisters' academy. As the Alaska mission expanded, costs multiplied and Tosi was hard-pressed to make adequate provision. He expected Barnum, who had many wealthy friends, to bail out the mission by appealing to them, but Barnum, somewhat estranged from his family because of his conversion to Catholicism, was most reluctant to take advantage of his family's connections.

Since Barnum also enjoyed the reputation for being "scientific" Tosi leaned heavily on him for the completion of an Eskimo grammar. Barnum responded with gusto. After he had collected what he required along the coast, Tosi transferred him to Holy Cross where he could work on the grammar with fewer interruptions. Cataldo, no doubt, had suggested this move for he was more than determined that all the missionaries in Alaska learn the languages of the natives. He himself was a genius with language. He had learned ten Indian dialects fluently, according to Parodi, and he tended to be impatient with those who found languages difficult.[57] It appears sometimes that Cataldo's first norm for selection of missionaries was their capacity to learn languages. Parodi, who excelled in this art, was sent to Alaska despite other deficiencies. He arrived in Kanelik on August 10, 1892, having first reported to Tosi at Holy Cross. Tosi sent him back down the river with Brother Power in the *St. Michael,* with orders to deliver a special letter to Treca, and to study the Eskimo language. Barnum took note of the new arrival.

"This year," he wrote, "a new comer, Fr. Parodi, had been added to our Kanelik community. He was a saintly man with a lovable disposition but he was one who should never have been sent to Alaska for he was utterly unfitted in every way to endure such a hard life as ours. He did not seem to know how to look out for himself in any way. . . . He had neglected his feet at Kanelik and they were in such deplorable condition that he was unable to walk."[58]

Tosi's letter to Treca came as a shock. Parodi presented it and waited. Treca, who had a mortal dread of being a superior read the letter, dropped it, and turned pale. When Parodi tried to assist him he said, "Let me alone, I have to swallow the pill; it is a long time that Fr. Tosi is after me."[59] The letter read as follows: "Dear Father, by order of Fr. Cataldo I have to start for Europe; you are now acting superior in my place."[60]

Leaving Treca with his "pill to swallow," Tosi embarked at St. Michael for San Francisco, then met Cataldo in Spokane on Wednesday, August 24, 1892. Father Arthuis wrote in the Gonzaga College diary, "Father Tosi, the Vice-Superior of our mission in Alaska arrived here this morning via N [orthern] P [acific]. He has been called by Father Cataldo and will visit the States and Europe soliciting help for the missions."[61] Having visited his Indian friends at St. Michael's mission over the weekend, and after making a quick trip to Portland, Tosi left with Van Gorp on Saturday, September 3, "for St. Ignatius Mission and the East."[62] Tosi would never be the same.

A correspondent at Woodstock reported that after a sojourn in the east Tosi visited Canada, then sailed to Europe. The account continued: "His visit to the Holy See was successful in every way and he obtained all that he asked, having been appointed Apostolic Vicar with the right of giving confirmation. He returned in the spring, and on May 18, left San Francisco with Fr. Monroe and Brothers Twohig and Marchisio, of the Rocky Mountain Mission, and Brother James T. O'Sullivan, of this province, well-known as machinist and blacksmith, to those of Ours who have been of late years at Georgetown. They sailed on the steamer *Bertha,* and they were also accompanied by three sisters for the Indian schools. Brother O'Sullivan has for a number of years asked to be sent to the missions, at one time we know that he applied to go to the Zambeze."[63]

Barnum did not agree that Tosi's journey had been a success. From St. Michael's on

July 10, 1893, he wrote that "we are greatly disappointed over the result of Father Tosi's excursion, as we confidently expected greater returns. We are glad, however, that he has powers of a Prefect Apostolic."[64] Without revealing his reasons he added one detail that is reminiscent of Father Accolti in California, "We expected," he wrote, "to be coupled with some other province, and naturally each one was wishing that it would be his own. If one of our American provinces had it [the Alaska Mission], it would not prove much of a burden."[65]

From this it appears, that Barnum, at least, and probably several other Jesuits, were dissatisfied with their attachment to the Turin Province and the Rocky Mountain Mission. The latter's rather rigid regime under Cataldo and meager resources appeared by contrast with other provinces to be an unattractive sponsor. Unfortunately, the Alaskan Jesuits had little contact with their colleagues in the Northwest, for even when they became ill they went to San Francisco for recuperation, hence they felt isolated and probably resentful. Barnum expected Tosi to change all this.

Instead, Tosi came back with "powers of a Prefect Apostolic." During an audience with Pope Leo XIII, the Pope had proposed that Tosi be consecrated a bishop. According to a tradition among the old fathers of the mission, Tosi had responded, "Holy Father, in Alaska I travel with dogs. When a storm comes up I make a hole in the snow and I crawl in with the dogs and live there until the storm blows over. Please, don't bring down so low the purple of a bishop."*

Pope Leo responded, *"Andate, fate voi da Papa in quelle regione,"* that is, "Go and act as Pope in those regions."[66] On July 17, 1894, by a decree of Leo XIII, the Territory of Alaska was raised to a Prefecture Apostolic, an autonomous ecclesiastical jurisdiction which was independent, at last, of Vancouver Island.[67] One week later, on July 24, Tosi was formally appointed the first Prefect Apostolic.[68] He had come a long way with his sled dogs but not far enough to placate Barnum and a growing faction of American dissidents.

*This account was related to Wilfred P. Schoenberg, S.J., by Father Alphonsus Fletcher, S.J. at St. Mary's, Omak, 1945.

Leopold Van Gorp who succeeded Father Kuppens at Helena.

Interior of St. Francis Xavier's Church, Missoula, as it appeared in 1908. The frescoes were painted by Brother Carignano.

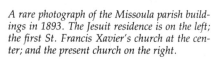

A rare photograph of the Missoula parish buildings in 1893. The Jesuit residence is on the left; the first St. Francis Xavier's church at the center; and the present church on the right.

Original log building at St. Paul's Mission, near Hays, Montana.

St. Paul's Mission. A fire destroyed the church and girls' school on the right. The building on the left, formerly the boys' building, is now used as a day school and convent.

St. Paul's Mission today.

John B. Rene, S.J., third president of Gonzaga College and second Prefect Apostolic of Alaska.

The new Gonzaga College with the new St. Aloysius Church in the background. This section of the Administration Building was occupied in 1897.

11

VAN GORP AS SUPERIOR
1894–1899

There was more than a flutter of excitement at Gonzaga College when it was announced on March 24, 1893, only eight days after he had become president, that Father Leopold Van Gorp had been appointed as the new superior of the Rocky Mountain Mission. The indestructible Joseph Cataldo had been demoted at last to the long black line of Jesuit regulars, after sixteen years of superiorship in a wilderness almost as remote from Rome as the Himalayas. To his former duties as president and treasurer of the college and treasurer of the mission, Van Gorp now added the more solemn task of religious superior over all of the Jesuits who were widely scattered across the plateau, over the mountains and along the seacoast, including those who were almost buried in the frozen tundra of Alaska. Like a one-man chancery or a corporation with one officer, the Jesuit whom the Indians called *Kute-nalko* now controlled the destiny of more men than do most contemporary bishops, a total of 136.

Though Van Gorp soon declared that the president's chair and the care of the purse would be transferred when suitable subjects could be found, many moons waxed and waned before these appointments were made. Sensibly, however, he delegated to the local assistant superior, Father Arthuis, all required authority to conduct the school, especially during his routine absences as mission superior.

Arthuis, a rare genius in his own French manner, looked like a saint and may have been one. He especially appeared to be a very patient priest. His detailed financial accounts carefully recorded in his own hand, confirm this impression by revealing an orderliness that was the secret to his prodigious productivity. He loved recitals and directed as many as time allowed. During the previous year, for instance, he had organized and directed Gonzaga's first elocution contest, which included nineteen selections of elocution and twenty of music in a program that lasted well over four hours.*

Van Gorp gave little attention to frivolous activities like recitals, though he appreciated their usefulness. He was a practical man and, as noted already, a frugal one. He was much concerned with the legal relationship between the school and the mission and one suspects that he took advantage of his duality of roles involving both to resolve certain obscurities in land ownership and jurisdiction, avoiding in this manner the possibility of a conflict. Since he was superior of both and treasurer of both there was no room for argument.

---

*June 25, 1892. The school catalogue for 1892–93 contains a copy of this program.

His bookkeeping needed no improvements. However, misunderstandings about his accounts sometimes arose and then, in his stubborness, he refused to yield and there was the devil to pay. During his second year as president there was a dispute with the electric company over a bill that Van Gorp insisted had already been paid. He was quite certain he was not going to pay that bill again. When the company's bookkeeper insisted on payment, Van Gorp dared the company to take out the lights. On June 4, 1894, the company did just that, and the mortified fathers at the college scrambled about the closets of the building seeking their cast-off kerosene lamps.[1] Three months later, before the darkness of autumn and winter enveloped the college, the president's wrath cooled and Arthuis persuaded him to reopen negotiations with the company. What followed is somewhat obscure. Arthuis may have paid the bill as requested, through the company's back door, or the company may have used a little psychology on Van Gorp. Whatever it was, when the president of Gonzaga College appeared, the company assured him that their *former* bookkeeper had made a mistake. They were all sorry, and so on. Electric lighting was reinstated in the college, the old lamps were again discarded and Van Gorp, his feelings no longer ruffled, commended the company for its honesty.[2]

The problem of the ownership of land acquired by Cataldo in his purchase of 320 acres from the Northern Pacific was not so readily resolved in Van Gorp's own carefully ordered mind. Approximately 300 acres were still owned by the Jesuits, the balance having been traded for professional services or given gratuitously to the railroads or to the sisters for the academy and the orphanage.* The question confronting Van Gorp was how much belonged to Gonzaga College and how much belonged to the Rocky Mountain Mission.

Van Gorp's official consultors were Caruana, Palladino, Garrand and Rene. The latter was superior at St. Ignatius Mission. Cataldo, who still had great influence, was superior of St. Francis Xavier's Mission for the Crow Indians, some seven hundred miles distant, where he did not have to witness Van Gorp's mistakes. Neither the consultors nor Cataldo could offer an easy solution, because both institutions, now financially independent of each other, presented a claim on the land for one reason or another.

Acting as administrator over both, Van Gorp decided to cede the college eight acres. The balance he retained as property of the mission. To establish the legal status of the latter he incorporated the Pioneer Educational Society as a non-profit corporation in the State of Washington and deeded the mission's land to the new corporation.† Some of this land was now sold and some of it was improved for selling or for an investment. Thus, Van Gorp found himself in a whirlwind of building and real estate commerce, a status which he accepted as calmly as he had accepted the position of president of the college.

In plotting the mission property, Van Gorp displayed a kind of vision that others did not share. He laid out wide streets and avenues, unlike the streets in other developments, and on the north, where the huge Heath property bordered the mission lands, he created a kind of boulevard with tree-lined islands separating traffic lanes, which he called Mission Avenue. Many of the locust trees he planted in the mid 1890s have survived ever since.

Some complained about the wide streets and one pioneer member of the parish, Michael O'Shea, who operated the Spokane Cab Company, threatened to sue Van Gorp, alleging "grave inconvenience." To placate O'Shea and other critics, Dakota street was made more narrow than the others and the threatened suit was dropped.‡

*The Jesuits had provided land for the Sisters of St. Joseph's Orphanage and for Holy Names Academy. On February 19, 1892, they gratuitously ceded a long strip along the river to the Great Northern Railroad, since the railroad demanded a free right of way as a condition for entering the city. Weibel, Gonzaga, *Silver Jubilee*, p. 134.

†The Pioneer Education Society was incorporated in 1893.

‡O'Shea was a good friend of the Jesuits. When he died on December 19, 1918, Mackin conducted his funeral.

The matter of the college's land remained unresolved. In the spring of 1894 Van Gorp undertook the legal formalities to protect the campus and to acquire a charter for the granting of degrees. The required charter suggested urgency, since two students, members of Gonzaga's first class, were expected to graduate during the following June. Richard Ganahl of Spokane and Dennis O'Rourke of Wardner, Idaho, had passed successfully through all the requirements for a Bachelor of Arts degree, according to the college catalogue, and there was considerable uneasiness in the prefect of studies' office about the procedures to be observed.

What is not clear is the delay in the application for the charter. Not until April 5, 1894, did Van Gorp assemble his staff for organizing a non-profit corporation with the power of holding property and granting degrees. A copy of the Articles of Incorporation was notarized on the same day by Judge P. F. Quinn, father of two boys in attendance at the school. Gonzaga's request for incorporation was granted by the State on April 22. It was now empowered "to give a complete collegiate education and course consisting of ancient classical, modern classical, and scientific courses, also a thorough and complete course in philosophy and theology, in accordance with the tenets of the Catholic Church."[3] If there appeared to be some incongruity regarding the state's formal permission for teaching Catholic theology, no one commented on it.

The way was now open for Gonzaga's first graduation ceremonies, which were solemnly discharged on June 28, 1894, in the presence of Bishop Alphonsus Glorieux of Boise, "and a long line of fathers of the church." It was a bang-up affair with such a large crowd and so much applause "for the heroes of the night" that even the heaps of roses wilted away.[4]

While all these events were taking place Van Gorp had been quietly pursuing another objective, which he carefully kept to himself. He had come to a decision with regard to his successor as president of the college. His choice was none other than Lawrence Palladino of Helena, who had stood by Van Gorp during the tense days of the Helena College proposal. Since Palladino had succeeded Van Gorp as pastor in Helena in 1874, no one should be surprised that Van Gorp now considered him as the most suitable successor at Gonzaga.

But there was a fly in the honey jar. In 1893, when Van Gorp became superior general, Palladino was the much cherished vicar general of the Helena Diocese. He was so cherished that Bishop Brondel resisted all efforts of Jesuit superiors to assign Palladino to other work. It finally required the intervention of the Cardinal Prefect of Propaganda in Rome to release Palladino from his office as vicar general. As soon as this was accomplished Van Gorp was free to appoint him as president of the college. Palladino formally succeeded Van Gorp on July 7, 1894.

The fifth president had recently authored what was to become a Northwest classic called *Indian and White in the Northwest*, a brisk account of the church in Montana which, so far as Palladino was concerned, comprised the entire Northwest.[5] He failed to appreciate the charms of eastern Washington, or its inhabitants, which is one reason why he did not distinguish himself as a college president. His tenure was noted for nothing spectacular and he was transferred to another position about two years later.

On October 9, 1894, ground was broken for the first of the so-called cottages which Van Gorp built on Pioneer Education Society lots. During the first year of construction he built about thirty houses ranging in value at that time between $1,600 and $3,000. Each year more homes designed by Preusse and Zittel were erected on Pioneer Education Society lots so that by 1900 approximately eighty were completed.[6] Some of these were sold to pay for the cost of others. Some were rented to supply the necessary funds for the support of Jesuit scholastics. In both cases Van Gorp made special efforts to attract Catholic families into the neighborhood so that Gonzaga College could be in fact, as well as in theory, the center of a

Catholic community. He succeeded so well in this effort that the term Gonzaga district became synonymous with Catholic. Its reputation spread far and wide as the Pacific Northwest's "Holy Land," a kind of Catholic enclave where even non-Catholics paused for the Angelus.

Some reference has been made to the support of scholastics. It should be noted, perhaps, that in the Society of Jesus, as in most religious orders, candidates are supported entirely from the moment of their actual entrance into the Novitiate. The period of the formation of Jesuits at this time covered approximately sixteen years before ordination. A typical scholastic, if he was young enough, observed the following schedule: novitiate, two years; studying humanities or juniorate, two years; prefecting or teaching in mission schools, three years; studying philosophy, three years; teaching in school another three years; studying theology, three years; then ordination. A select few spent a fourth year studying theology. After theology all spent one more year in Tertianship, or third year of Novitiate, sometimes called the *schola affectus*.*

In the Rocky Mountain Mission this schedule was honored more by exception to the rule than by observance. The lack of priests and pressing needs of the church allowed for many adaptations and it was not uncommon that scholastics were ordained within ten years, or even less, depending on their previous academic status. Whatever the schedule, the support of scholastics then, as now, occupied a prominent place in the Jesuit budget.

At St. Ignatius Mission classes for scholastics had been added to the customary missionary activities in 1891.† Three years later there were three Jesuits studying philosophy and seven Jesuits in the Juniorate studying the humanities. The philosophy that year was taught by another scholastic, the brilliant and somewhat loquacious Louis Taelman, who had been recruited by Cataldo in 1884 at the Apostolic School at Turnhout. Taelman used a commonly accepted text by the Gregorian University's Father Sanctus Schiffini, about which he complained for the next six decades. "That miserable Schiffini!" he lamented, whenever he was wont to reminisce, which was quite often, "I have had boozing [buzzing] in my head ever since."

In the following year Taelman was still teaching at St. Ignatius but there were many changes there. Paul Muset, broken in health by Alaska, had become superior. Anthony Morvillo, Jerome D'Aste and the adventurous Joseph Bandini were in possession of the mission's spiritual administration while four young scholastics attended to the teaching. Tom Meagher, the future Novice Master, who was always remembered with deep affection, was a student of the humanities, as was Ambrose Sullivan who acquired eventually the playful sobriquet of "Forever Ambie."

At Sacred Heart Mission, thanks to Cataldo's frequent raids on the Jesuit parishes in pious places like Philadelphia, there was a bumper crop of novices. In the first year there were fourteen scholastic novices and five brothers, including Edward Horwedel, who later became renowned as an exceptionally holy missionary in Alaska. Among the scholastics were seven that survived for many long years: Father Edward Griva who was, like Tosi, an Italian diocesan priest when he entered the novitiate; Alphonsus Fletcher; Augustine Dinand; Charles Greenwood; John McHugh; Joseph Malaise, who achieved some fame by producing a classic translation of *The Following of Christ*; and William Garrigan, for whom the gymnasium was named at Seattle Prep.

In the second year novitiate there were fifteen novices, all scholastics, among whom

---

*Literally "school of the heart," a time for prayer and reflection.

†St. Ignatius was not formally established as a scholasticate until 1895. At Gonzaga there were three scholastics pursuing their studies for the priesthood in 1892. The diary for September 12, 1892 states, "Today, opening of the scholasticate."

were such prominent members of the province as Joseph Piet, later provincial who helped to formalize the Oregon Province in 1932; Godfrey [Jeff] O'Shea, later president of Seattle College; James Brogan, later president of Gonzaga University; Patrick O'Reilly, the last of the Irish prophets; Nathanial Purcell, first superior at Sheridan, Oregon; and, finally, Michael Hourican, who was mostly distinguished for being very nervous and always in a hurry—even when he died.

In the entire mission in 1895, there were 154 Jesuits, of whom 73 were still in formation. This was a total of only 3 less than in the California mission. In the latter, however, there were only 64 in formation, a difference of 9 less, a rather significant percentage in such meager totals. It is clear from this that Van Gorp as superior, or Van Gorp as treasurer, was hard pressed for funds to support young priests.

Little or no money came from the missions. In Alaska where fifteen Jesuits were engaged in 1895, most expenses were borne by the Rocky Mountain Mission, where complaints about shortage of money became so commonplace that they lacked surprise. At St. Peter's among the Blackfeet, for example, the lack of funds occasioned by the government's new school policy, forced the closure of the school in June 1895, and three years later the Jesuits withdrew from the mission altogether.[7]

Father Cataldo, who had struggled desperately to develop the Indian schools, was disappointed to hear the news about St. Peter's. In the Crow mission far to the south he was still driving himself and others to keep another mission school alive. As Mackin said, "The more you would do for him, the more he would want you to do."[8] In 1895 he had sixteen Jesuits attached to St. Francis Xavier's, of which he was superior, half of them in residence at one or another of three smaller missions called stations. The largest of these was St. Charles at Pryor, some fifty horseback miles across the country from St. Xavier's, on the western side of the Big Horn Mountains and beside a small stream named for one of the lesser officials of the Lewis and Clark expedition. Today a little village is near St. Charles, a kind of sleepy backwater settlement where the only news is the arrival of a stranger and where community gossip can be exchanged without words. Isolated by its mountains and vast cattle ranches, it dozes contentedly on the banks of Pryor Creek, oblivious of the world beyond the horizon.

The Pryor Creek site had long been under consideration for the location of a mission. Writing in September, 1882, Peter Barcelo remarked that the interpreter at Fort Custer "offered himself to help me with his teams to build a church and a house and pointed out a certain place, which they called Prior [sic] Creek as most suitable for the purpose." When Grassi and Prando made their first safari together on the Crow Reservation, they examined the site before deciding on Rotten Grass Creek.*

One gets the impression that Prando was disappointed with the decision. He recognized Pryor Creek's importance as a Crow rallying point around their last great war chief, Plenty Coups, and he kept coming back to the place with more on his mind than a social call. In March, 1890, through the Catholic Indian Bureau in Washington, he secured permission from the Indian Office to erect a "chapel and school house for the accommodation of the Crow Indians." This was to be located "on Pryor Creek within the limits of the Crow reservation, on land unclaimed and unoccupied by any individual Indian, upon which to erect a chapel and a school house."

Taking his permission to Plenty Coups who was then in his prime, forty-one years old, and a great warrior among his people, he asked for the necessary land. Plenty Coups gave Prando a portion of his own, "on condition that a school be built." In October, 1891, Prando arranged for the building of a church, and while this was under way, he preached a great

*There is a considerable amount of manuscript material, including many letters of Peter Paul Prando and Peter Barcelo in the Oregon Province Archives. These and the following details appear in these sources.

mission to the Indians and baptized nearly a hundred of them. Since the building was not quite ready before winter set in, he went back to St. Xavier's. In February, 1892, he returned to Pryor, taking Brother A. Carfagno with him to help with the school project.

Later in that same month, three Ursulines: Mother Thomas Stoeckel, Mother Agnes Dunne, and Sister Patrick Brown traveled from St. Xavier's to Pryor to open the school. They started out in a sleigh loaded with provisions, but the snow was so scant in some spots that the horses had a hard time pulling it. About halfway between the two missions the sleigh tongue broke. The Indian driver unhitched his team; and after mounting one of the two animals, he led the other to the nearest ranch to borrow a wagon. This was more than a few miles distant, so the nuns had to wait throughout the remaining part of that day and a long night for his return. To keep warm they paced up and down and swung their arms the way baseball players do. When they took turns to take little naps in the heavily loaded sleigh in an effort to drive away their drowsiness, they found they were forced to use a butchered pig for a pillow.

Their driver finally returned in the morning and provisions were transferred to the wagon he brought. The journey was completed without further mishap, though it required one and one-half more days. To welcome them at Pryor, a great crowd of Indians had gathered together with Prando who began to ring a handbell vigorously as soon as the wagon came into sight.

If the clamor and noise of the welcome didn't wake up the good nuns, their first look at the school surely did. It was not really a school at all; in fact, the only building available was the church, which was a solid fifty by twenty-four feet and as clean as two bachelors could make it. In this the nuns had to establish their convent and prepare to receive their first Indian boarders. Three weeks later on March 18, they were ready for their first scholars. Three disconsolate little boys, their faces as long as their arms, were ushered in by Prando and Bandini. Since there were no accommodations for two groups, it had been decided that only small boys would be accepted. The girls, Prando said, would be taken care of later.

During the warm summer months of that year a two-story frame house was erected with funds provided by Mother Drexel. This contained a convent, quarters for the children, and classrooms. It was ready by September. The Ursulines moved into it, greatly relieved to escape their temporary habitation in the church. As soon as the church was rearranged to serve its orginal purpose, regular religious services were again provided the Indians. During this same time another building was begun, a small frame house designed for the use of the boys. For its construction $1,500 was provided by Mother Drexel, who sent a charming note to Cataldo, approving the plan. At Christmastime the first girls arrived at the school, and the boys transferred their frugal treasures to their own building. Only one other building was required and this, too, was quickly provided. The Jesuits, who had lived in tents, church sacristy, or in any other available space, now had their own house which was built of logs. It was ready for occupancy about the same time the boys' building was finished.

The Jesuit status of St. Charles Mission had never been changed since its beginnings. It remained a mission dependency of St. Xavier's and for this reason the Jesuit staff frequently exchanged places with Jesuits at St. Xavier's.

Usually there were at least two Jesuits in residence at St. Charles, one priest and one brother, but sometimes there were others, including scholastics who taught the boys and prefected them during off-school hours. Since the two missions were relatively close, there was much going to and fro by the missionaries. The Ursulines, too, frequently exchanged places with other members of their Order at St. Peter's, ordinarily because of sickness or a shuffling of personnel in their Montana schools.

In December, 1894, the Ursulines' Superior, Mother Amadeus, visited the mission from Billings to arrange for one of these exchanges. She arrived on December 3 and left on the following day with two of her nuns. The aftermath described by Mother Clotilde, O.S.U. in *Ursulines of the West,* presents an insight into the adventures of missionaries on their journeys: "The party had to ford Blue Creek, a tributary of the Yellowstone, usually small, but this time greatly swollen. The driver mistook the site of the ford and drove the horses into the raging current. There they halted abruptly, snorting and trembling. Icy water rose over the wheels and up to the waists of the nuns, while huge cakes of ice knocked against the carriage, threatening to overturn it at any moment. The driver fainted . . . Mother Amadeus succeeded in rousing the man and then instructed him to crawl out carefully over the back wheels, get to shore and go for help to a cowboy camp they had passed on the way. For three quarters of an hour the nuns sat motionless in that deathly water until aid came. Safe at last on the bank, they sang the 'Laudet' and the cowboys built a roaring fire. Before the warmth, the dripping clothes of the rescued steamed in front and at the same time froze on their backs. The good-hearted men gave up their cabin to the nuns, and they themselves spent that December night in the open. It was discovered the next day that the fore-feet of the horses had stopped on the brink of a deep hole and that the hind-legs of the poor animals had been floating in the stream."[9]

Cataldo's assistant at St. Xavier's was Francis Andreis, a promising young Jesuit of thirty-seven years who was being tutored personally by the old Master for a future position as a superior. Andreis covered the country, driving a buggy, sometimes visiting St. Charles or St. Labre's where Father Van de Velden was holding out with three scholastics, or even St. Stephens in Wyoming, where Feusi and Francis Sansone were busy learning Arapahoe. They might have spared themselves, for St. Stephens was attached to the Rocky Mountain Mission for a relatively brief period.*

While the Indian missionaries, with their backs to the wall, were fighting against the odds to stay alive, Van Gorp, strange to say, was becoming involved in a ploy to found another college. Gonzaga needed buildings desperately, Seattle's college was faltering, but Van Gorp, still fascinated with the idea of a college in Helena was moving heaven and earth and the local bishop to revive the old proposal of St. John Berchman's College, which most Jesuits thought was buried. Prior to 1897, he had purchased land in Helena for $16,000.[10] Bishop Brondel had approved the scheme in February, 1895, though it was all hush-hush, until he realized that the good Jesuit fathers would acquire by this *beneplacitum* of his the right to open a public church.† No one had to tell his Lordship what this involved in a two-horse town—state capital or not. There simply was not room for two parishes. He decided that the Jesuits, to whom he was deeply indebted, (they had turned over to him, scot-free, all the land which the Cathedral and school occupied) could have the west end of town near the railroad tracks. This, too, upon reflection, was undesirable and there followed for three years an exchange of letters between Van Gorp and Brondel, which might be described "as clearing the air."

Brondel objected to the manner in which the Jesuits had withdrawn from Fort Benton and to their projected departure from St. Labre's mission. He especially berated Van Gorp for closing the school at St. Peter's and withdrawing his Jesuits, leaving the Ursulines high

*OPA, Provincial Papers, Van Gorp correspondance. Letter of Bishop Lenihan to Van Gorp, March 30, 1898, states that he will take over St. Stephen's in July of 1899. He was very pleased with Feusi's work. Oregon Jesuits retained this mission until 1913.

†The Jesuit privilege granted by proper ecclesiastical authorities to establish churches with their colleges has been a bone of contention for a long time. Jesuit willingness, on occasions like this one, to forego the use of the privilege, has seldom been acceptable to bishops who prefer to keep firmer control on parishes and public churches. A bishop's *beneplacitum,* or approval, was in effect required for the establishment of a college; thus, Brondel was within his rights in refusing Van Gorp the required permission. He was also more astute. A college in Helena then would have been a disaster.

and dry in their huge stone novitiate building.* Van Gorp reminded His Lordship of previous Jesuit services, then complained about Brondel's violation of his promise to establish Jesuits in Billings. He insisted on the Jesuits' right, in keeping with His Lordship's permission, to develop a college in Helena. Great Falls also was mentioned, but that reference was nipped in the bud by Brondel who retorted that the priest in Great Falls didn't even have a house yet.

Nothing but hard feelings, and later, many protestations of mutual love and respect came from all this. The exchange of polemics however, revealed not so much of Brondel's plans for the future as Van Gorp's and these had little concern for Indians. It should be added, in fairness to Van Gorp, that he very much favored the support of Indian missions where Indians were responsive and available. Because of Prando's great popularity with the Blackfeet, and to compensate for the closing of the school at St. Peter's, he assigned him to Holy Family Mission in 1895.

When word spread abroad that "Iron Eyes" had come back to them, the Blackfeet flocked in from all sides. His journey through the reservation was a triumphal march and an occasion of a great religious revival. Some who had not approached the sacraments for years presented themselves to him for a spiritual scrubbing up. Prando remained five years, as quick and witty as he had been fifteen years earlier. "What's your name?" he shouted at an Indian who passed him in a wagon. "Have you had your baby baptized? Then let us take him down to the creek and get him baptized now." After baptizing the infant he discovered another mother and child in the wagon and repeated the performance.

This is why the Indians loved Father Prando. He understood them and did not scold them for failing to bring their babies to church. Very tolerant of their ways, he treated them realistically and they responded in a manner that was unique. Prando was another De Smet in this respect.

In the early weeks of 1898, fire, the voracious devourer of missions, gobbled up the original frame building at Holy Family and with it, all of its furnishings. Makeshift accommodations were quickly set up to quarter the girls with their Ursuline teachers in the upper two stories of the boys' building, until something better could be provided for them. Classes were held in the church. Cramped quarters and other inconveniences attendant upon this arrangement proved to be occasions for one epidemic after another among the children; measles, chicken pox and pneumonia followed in succession and sometimes prefects and teachers were also laid low. During one epidemic of pneumonia, Brother Galdos did the work of several people for an entire month, laboring night and day "with much cheerfulness and a maximum of patience and charity," despite the fact he himself had a weak heart.

A short time after the fire, Father Joseph Bandini was summoned to Holy Family to direct the erection of another sandstone building to replace the one lost. As soon as the building was finished, in November, 1898, Bandini went to Spokane to recuperate from exhaustion. He died there in less than three months, at the age of sixty-three.

If all this were not grief enough, the government began to cut down its appropriations for the care of the children at Holy Family in 1896 and by 1900 they were dropped entirely. The expense of mission operations was about $16,000 per year for the support of an average of 106 children in addition to the staff—an almost starvation level of operations. From the Indians themselves the mission could expect very little; they were also very poor. In 1906 the total amount for the year which the mission received in church collections and stole fees

*The Jesuits had objected to the Ursulines' proposal of building a huge Novitiate at St. Peter's, far from other churches and schools. Despite this the Novitiate was built and the Jesuits were expected to provide chaplains for the sisters there. Van Gorp regarded this as unreasonable.

was $74. Some support, almost one-fourth, came from Mother Drexel through the Catholic Indian Bureau. The Blackfeet Tribe continued to pay a little, though the amount gradually was diminished until it was nothing. Begging campaigns followed one another in dreary succession, but mission indebtedness increased year by year, while buildings and equipment deteriorated helplessly.

Father Rebmann had been superior of St. Peter's when the school was closed. Van Gorp summoned him to Spokane where he made him president of Gonzaga again, successor to Palladino on November 1, 1896. Palladino was assigned to Seattle, where progress in the school was slow and some of the staff discouraged. A new superior-pastor, Father Diomedi had replaced Garrand, who moved to St. Mary's, Montana, demonstrating as he did, the current practice of non-specialization.* In the Van Gorp years one had to be ready for anything, including starvation. But starvation required very little professional preparation.

In later years it was sometimes alleged that the retarded development of Seattle College was due to two factors beyond its control: the favored status of Gonzaga and the school's inability to accept resident students. There is evidence, no doubt, that these allegations, especially the former, are founded on fact, but this overlooks other considerations related to the historical development of the entire mission, as well as some basic differences in the population of Spokane and Seattle. Gonzaga *was* favored by superiors for many years and the reason is obvious: from the earliest years Gonzaga was identified with the academic formation of scholastics.†

It should be noted, perhaps, that precisely during this time two Catholic colleges, St. Michael's in Portland and Holy Angels in Vancouver, Washington, both founded before Gonzaga, were in the last stages of collapse for lack of students and support. Other sectarian colleges throughout the Northwest were closing their doors for the same reasons. And yet St. Martin's College near Olympia, Washington, opened on September 11, 1895, with one student, survived and prospered.[11] Significantly, St. Martin's, like Gonzaga, was a resident school.

In favoring Gonzaga college superiors had not neglected the provision of a good faculty at Seattle. Diomedi, if a bit abrupt in manner, was a very competent man, who, as Mackin said, "would rather argue philosophy and theology than take snuff, though he liked his snuff very well."[12] Sometimes called "the Renaissance Man" he looked more like a medical doctor with a paternal bedside manner. He tended to be overweight. He sometimes looked as though he had not shaved that morning and he peered through his rimless glasses with a disconcerting penetration that made honest Joes of his students. But as one of his Montana friends had said, "He was a genuine rustler," a dubious compliment in a cattle state, and no doubt intended. He was the kind of man that sowed in whirlwinds and reaped in tornadoes, and he never tried to escape from either.

Diomedi had already merited his place in history. He had set up the St. Ignatius Mission press and supervised the Indian boys in setting type and printing the nearly immortal works in Indian languages. He had produced a little known but classic account about Indians, called *Sketches of Modern Indian Life*, a kind of continuation of the De Smet narratives.[13] He was the founder of St. Augustine's parish in Florence, Montana, and finally he produced with the help of a few others, a magnificent church, which still serves the Catholics in Missoula, Montana. An account of this is included here, not only because

*Garrand had been sick with typhoid and had spent some weeks in bed. He was sent to St. Mary's in part to recuperate.

†As recently as July 6, 1981, the president of Seattle University expressed objections to alleged favoritism toward Gonzaga. He cited a similar situation in the history of favored St. Louis University and unfavored Marquette University.

St. Francis Xavier's is one of the most historic parishes in the Northwest, but also because its cathedral-like church was a personal triumph for Diomedi.

One should recall, perhaps, that Father Menetrey, a gentle old man, somewhat disillusioned by the dishonesty of others when he was cheated out of forty acres of church land, finally built a frame church in Missoula in 1881. When Diomedi arrived there in June 1888 to take Menetrey's place, he lost no time in deciding that the church was too small. He began preparations for a new one which, he boasted, would be the largest in Montana. He secured the services of a Portland architect by the name of Blanchard and a contractor with the unquestionably Irish name of Patrick H. Walsh.* He needed little else besides money, and the people were generous with that.

The cornerstone of the new church was blessed and laid on August 9, 1891, while a thousand people watched and listened. Father Diomedi read in Latin, and Father J. Neale read in English a document which was going to be placed within the stone. It read as follows: "In the year of Our Lord, 1891, on the Ninth day of August, which was the twelfth Sunday after Pentecost, Leo XIII being pope and J. B. Brondel being bishop of the Diocese of Helena, Alexander Diomedi, S.J. being rector of the church of St. Francis Xavier in Missoula, Benjamin Harrison being president of the United States, W. K. Toole being the governor of Montana and Jack Keith being mayor of the city of Missoula, the cornerstone of the new church of St. Francis Xavier in the city of Missoula was laid by the Right Reverend Bishop John Baptist Brondel in the presence of a multitude of people and assisted by Reverend Sanctus Phillippi and J. Neale."[14] If this solemn document was intended to edify the listeners it probably did. It was at least long enough.

A little over a year after the foundations were laid, on October 9, 1892, the new church was opened for use and a crowd of curious Missoulans crawled all over it and asked the delighted pastor innumerable questions. No, the interior was not finished. Frescoes were planned, and a new altar. No, the roof was higher than that, exactly seventy feet, and to the top of the cross on the belfry it was double seventy, exactly one hundred and forty-four feet. The length? One hundred-and-twenty-two feet, and the cost was $24,871. It was designed to hold six hundred persons but experiments proved that it could accommodate eight hundred when the choir loft was occupied. The large sacristy also had a loft and this was intended to be used as a parish library.

Gradually, over a period of ten years, the interior was completed the way Diomedi wanted it. Brother Carignano painted frescoes in cold weather and hot, often flat on his back, for a period of sixteen months. After that he was transferred to Gonzaga College in Spokane, where they needed a cook, but he took Missoula with him, in his heart at least. At Gonzaga, he painted fourteen large stations of the cross in the corner of his kitchen over a period of four years in his spare time. They have endured and are as impressive now as when Brother finished them.

Other furnishings of the church are equally commendable. For example, new stained glass windows were acquired for $1,600 "to protect the church's frescoes." A pipe organ costing nearly $6,000 ("the bellows are operated by a modern electric motor") was purchased from Boston's Hook and Hastings, "actually a duplicate of the organ which at Chicago's World Fair was awarded First Prize for excellence." A new bell was installed at this time, too, about which an account will appear later.

When Diomedi became superior in Seattle, he was already fifty-three years old, but young enough in spirit to adapt readily to his new position. Technically he was pastor of the parish and top administrator in the school, which was still called School of the Immaculate Conception. On his staff, besides Palladino, whose heart was still in Montana, were

*Father of Father Charles Walsh, S.J. Details regarding the Missoula Church may be found in Palladino, *Indian and White*, p. 374, et seq.

206

two other priests, Albert Trivelli, who later founded Loyola High School in Missoula, and John Nicholson. One scholastic, Conrad Brusten, carried the heaviest load in the school, and Brother Peter Rogers, like a pillar that held up the parish, was still the perennial member of the community who survived Van Gorp's purges and the passage of time. The only criticism that could be placed against this staff is that the top three were all Italians; but then so was the pope in Rome.

Palladino would have preferred to be in Montana and Father Mackin, who was now at St. Paul's Mission about two hundred leagues from nowhere, would have preferred the opposite. Mackin at heart was a city person, a kind of pious man-about-town who enjoyed a good Altar Society Social on the parish lawn. He had been transferred from the novitiate at De Smet to St. Paul's because the latter had fallen on evil days under the supervision of the too simple Father Feusi.

By 1890 Father Eberschweiler had registered five-hundred baptisms in the area. Bishop Brondel, impressed by so much progress, divided the area into two missionary districts. With his approval, the Jesuit superior assigned Father Balthaaser Feusi to St. Paul's which covered one district, and Father Eberschweiler to the Milk River area which extended all the way to the Dakotas. This meant, of course, that the latter would no longer be in residence at St. Paul's. In 1891 he established his base of operations at Fort Benton, which he heartily disliked because of the scandalous lives of certain Catholics there, and five years later at Chinook, where his old friend, Thomas O'Hanlon lived. In the years that followed he established seven new mission churches along the newly constructed Great Northern Railway. With the unflagging zeal of a saint he traveled up and down his vast mission, offering Mass, preaching, and baptizing—always fatigued, but tireless; always sad at heart (because his people neglected God and religion), but also cheerful and optimistic. For many long years after he was dead and buried, his accomplishments were legendary.

Father Feusi remained at St. Paul's from 1891 to 1894, during which time John Haupt, a mission volunteer who had helped Grassi with the construction of Gonzaga College, built a boy's school with local stone.* It was the only solid building at St. Paul's when Mackin arrived. The mission had spacious pastures secluded in the foothills of the Little Rocky Mountains and Feusi had leased these in part to several "very nice men" who, it turned out, were cattle rustlers and horse thieves. These astute outlaws, who also held up and robbed trains, were called the Curry Gang. They kept some of their stolen animals in the most unlikely of places—the mission's pasture—and, when this was at last discovered, a warrant was issued for the arrest of the mission superior for concealing stolen property. The sheriff of Harlem made plans to ride out to St. Paul's to arrest Feusi just when Mackin arrived and heard the news. Taking the fastest horse he could find, he raced out to St. Paul's, an hour ahead of the sheriff to warn Feusi. "The sheriff is coming to arrest you!" he shouted at the startled Feusi. "Pack your bag and take a horse and go east over the mountains."

Feusi was eventually exonerated, but Mackin, after he had examined the condition of the mission and its finances had few compliments to pay him.† What he complained about most was the condition of the church, and next to that Feusi's naïveté in allowing another ring of thieves to steal a flock of good sheep off the mission's pasture by exchanging it for a

---

*John Haupt later entered the Jesuit novitiate as a brother at St. Francis Regis, but soon departed. After serving as a volunteer in various Jesuit Missions throughout the world he entered the English Province in the Rhodesian Mission and built many churches there before his death in 1921. Thus he was in a sense the first Oregonian to serve in the African Mission.

†Mackin in his memoirs scarcely concealed his impatience with the way many European Jesuits conducted business. A blunt man, but not really a complainer, he suffered a certain ostracism because of his forthright manner.

flock of poor sheep. Mackin, who was practical, if nothing else, could scarcely believe how inept Feusi had been in conducting the mission's business.

Mackin had a very wealthy and generous friend, Richard Wilson of Portland. Though not a Catholic, Wilson admired Mackin very much and would give him anything he asked. He visited St. Paul's on occasion. Taking great interest in the mission he conspired with Mackin in the building of a large new church. Characteristically Van Gorp wanted a smaller church built, because it would cost less and Mackin wanted a large, expensive one, partly, one surmises, to get Van Gorp's goat. Furthermore, he wanted hard wood floors. "I had a chance of getting the hardwood in with another party that made it, cheaper than ordinary fir, and I got a man to help the carpenter to lay the floor . . . but as the Superior was putting up a large building in Spokane, in which no hardwood was used he thought I was going ahead of him."[15] If Mackin was defensive about his own accomplishments there, it was because he regarded Van Gorp as somewhat belligerent toward him. He was not the only Jesuit I'm sure, who looked forward impatiently for the appointment of a new superior general.

Mackin paid for the church at St. Paul's through his own resources. "I had kept the wool for five years and had shipped it to Boston. I sold sixty-six thousand pounds of wool at twenty-one cents, and it had increased in six thousand pounds. Four years before I had been offered only three cents a pound for what was left in 1894. I shipped four hundred muttons to Chicago getting $4.50 each for them. I shipped forty head of cattle to Chicago and got $75 net each for them, and besides I got the prize in the Chicago Stock Yards for the best bunch of cattle that went in to Chicago that year. I did relish getting the money but I did not relish having it in the papers. So the church was up and paid for, even though I asked for a three thousand dollar building, when I put up a twenty thousand dollar building. At that time the Bishop of Helena came to the Mission to give Confirmation. He had not been there for four years before, and he expected to see a number of children for Confirmation, but when he sat down on the platform he looked down the aisle and saw full grown Indians with their hands joined together and their eyes cast down coming up two by two to receive Confirmation. I was standing with the oils in my hand when the Bishop turned on me as much as to say, 'What is this?' I did not say anything, held my eyes down, and the Bishop went on and gave Confirmation. After Confirmation was over we went to the sacristy, when the Bishop in an excited mood said, 'What's this! Why didn't you let me know? This is the miracle of the age! I'm in the West forty-five years and nobody ever saw or heard anything like this. Get me an interpreter.' The interpreter was got and the Bishop went out and spoke to the Indians."[16]

The church, which was completed in 1898 and later embellished with the frescoes of Carignano, was the gem and pride of the whole region and whenever the Indians worshipped there, they gazed in awe, almost in superstition, at the painted saints around them.

Like other Jesuits, Cataldo had his eye on Alaska where the action was. He would have his chance to go there, but it would take Van Gorp several years to make up his mind to send him. Under Van Gorp, Alaska had been faring none too well in terms of reinforcements and progress. Parodi, who had come in 1892, had first gone with Treca to Tununa, the abandoned mission where Treca, Muset, and Barnum had endured a miserable winter. Parodi's nose was frozen when he arrived, but true to form, he looked at the brighter side of everything. Treca, he said, had organized a choir at Tununa. "Johnny a smart Indian boy of about 8 years of age and a little Indian girl of the same age were the leaders. They had been trained by Frs. Treca and Muset to sing the Kyrie, Gloria, Credo etc. in Latin, and every Sunday they had high Mass. They sang twice a day [the] F. Muset catechism in verses, from the principal mysteries of faith to the last Judgment. These were the last words: *Yuk Ashilinok charaiamun aiaqtok;* that is: 'the bad indian goes to the devil.' " Then he added, "It is known that F. Rabaut some time keeps the Indians 5 hours in church."[17]

Treca had brought large, colored lithographs depicting the more important truths of the church. Printed in France these vivid illustrations were used in many missions in the United States and Canada. Treca presented one showing the fires of hell. "The Indians were cheering up when they saw the fire," Parodi wrote, "and much more when they heard that there was no need of wood to keep up the fire burning."[18]

In 1893 Father Francis Monroe, one of the immortals, arrived in Alaska; another was Brother John Twohig, who replaced Brother Powers. Two other brothers also arrived that year, James Sullivan who left the following year, and Bartholomew Marchisio. In 1894 only one new Jesuit got off the boat at Holy Cross, Raphael Crimont, a pint-sized Frenchman who was greeted by Barnum when he descended the gangplank: "Is it you, poor little Crim? Oh my, we don't want you. You aren't made for this kind of country. In a few weeks you'll be dead. Stay on the boat and go back. It's the only way to do."[19]

Monroe, with whom Crimont had gone through school in France, was also on the riverbank to greet him. He looked beyond his friend toward the boat. The new missionary knew what was on his mind: "I am alone," he said.

In 1895 both Barnum and Treca left the mission, each for a year. Treca had never recovered from Barnum's *Polar Anaemia* and his face had been badly frozen during a hard trip along the frigid coast. He soon became well in sunny California, though his face was covered with ugly scars. These he concealed by raising a beard. Barnum traveled to the east to conduct a lecture tour and to publish articles about the mission, mostly to raise money and volunteers. When Barnum returned to Alaska in 1896 he was assigned to Holy Cross, but Cataldo's unexpected arrival as an official visitor during that same summer prompted Tosi to change his mind.*

This turn of events deserves some comment. First, it should be pointed out that Cataldo during the year 1896–97 retained his position as superior of the Crow Mission. He was sent by Van Gorp to inspect the missions of Alaska and to report on them upon his return. The occasion for the inspection tour was doubtless two-fold: the reoccurring complaints about Tosi's administration, and the seeming tardiness in the appearance of grammars and dictionaries in the languages of the natives. There were some in Alaska who believed that Cataldo had come to show them how to learn the languages and these were delighted to hear that Cataldo found them more difficult than he had expected.

Despite his reputation as an exacting superior, Cataldo was warmly received in Alaska, at least by the common Jesuits who found him most affable and even indulgent. He had mellowed like a bottle of wine in the course of the years. He spent the winter at Akulurak with Barnum, studying the Eskimo language. Later Barnum commented that in a weak moment Cataldo had confided to him what he thought of Tosi. "Tosi," he said, "was a hard man to manage, so he was particularly pleased to station him at a distance."[20] By contrast with Tosi, Cataldo now appeared to be as genial as a Dutch uncle.

When Treca returned north after his year of recuperation, there was still some anxiety regarding his health, so he was directed to remain at Juneau where one year earlier in 1895, Father Rene had taken over the parish from its founder, the highly respected Father Joseph Althoff of the Diocese of Vancouver Island.† Alaska had now been divided into two parts, Alaska Borealis in the north and Alaska Australis in the south, both under the jurisdiction

*Visitors were appointed from time to time to examine a mission or province and to report their findings to Rome. A visitor's task should not be judged unfavorably. Sometimes a visitor was dispatched to observe and make suggestions for change.

†Father Joseph Althoff, a Hollander, founder of the church in Juneau in 1885. He died at Nelson, British Columbia on December 30, 1925 at the age of 72. *Spokesman-Review,* December 31, 1925.

of Tosi, who still served in the dual role of Prefect Apostolic for the church and superior of the Jesuits. This division meant little in jurisdictional matters but missionary work in Alaska Australis was completely different from the activities of the north. The weather was always as wet as duck season, the forests dark and heavy and most travel was done by boat along the Inside Passage. Treca no longer needed his lousy furs or his clumsy dogsled. He now served as the stay-at-home assistant pastor while Rene visited Sitka and other rain-soaked places like Skagway and Fort Wrangel. Father Peter Bougis, another assistant, took care of Douglas Island across the Gastineau Channel from Juneau. Churches were established for Whites as well as for Indians; and though life was far from pleasant, the terrible isolation and harsh winters of the north were happily missing. At this time Juneau was the ranking metropolis of the territory with approximately two thousand inhabitants.

Juneau had been developed by miners. Another area in Alaska that was swarming with prospectors lay in the upper Yukon around Circle City and Forty Mile where Tosi and Robaut had spent their first winter. Though prospectors were not conspicuous for attending church or the sacraments, Tosi liked to think that a priest should live among them especially to administer the last rites when they tried to kill one another. He chose Father Judge, one of the Americans, for this task.

Giordano described what followed: "Father Judge then went up and it was only late in the Fall that the steamer reached Circle City on the Yukon Flat. The water was very low and so about three hundred miles from Forty Mile the Captain was obliged to leave the passengers to take their choice about returning or making the rest of the trip on foot. Meanwhile Father Judge examined his provisions and found they had forgotten to give him any Mass wine. He did not know what to do. He said to himself: 'If I do not go back to Holy Cross I will not be able to celebrate Holy Mass.' So he made up his mind and returned to Holy Cross. When Father Tosi saw him, he asked: 'What is the matter, why are you back?' and he answered, 'I could find no Mass wine among my goods so I was obliged to return.' Father Tosi replied, 'You did very well.' He then sent him to [Shageluk]."[21]

At Shageluk, Judge employed some Indians to build a church about forty-five by thirty feet, a two-part building with space for a residence. He spent the winter doing "much work there among the Indians." The memory of this reminded Giordano of an abuse by some of the Indians which captured the brother's fancy.

"An Indian with a family had a child baptized by the Russian priest. Afterwards Father Muset baptized it. It was customary to give a couple of yards of calico for making a dress for the child. When the dress was worn out the Indian had the child baptized again and got more calico. Then he took it to Mr. Chapman the Protestant minister, and got some flour as a baptismal gift. Then he returned to Holy Cross and gave the child to some other family so that it could be baptized again and he could get some more calico. I do not wish to make this story too long, but the child was baptized nine times and if that child cannot go to heaven after nine baptisms, it will be hard for anyone to go!"[22]

When summer came, Judge left for Forty Mile, this time with Mass wine in his baggage. With the help of the miners he built a log cabin, then he began his missionary work, going from cabin to cabin at night after the prospectors returned from their work. The miners were much edified by him and they soon began to attend Mass and the sacraments.

The next year, 1896, gold was discovered in the Klondike. When the miners at Forty Mile heard the news, they rushed off to the new diggings on Klondike Creek, which they named Dawson City. Judge followed the miners, somewhat reluctantly at first; then, when he saw how sorely he was needed, with enthusiasm. He built a large church there and a hospital. A reporter for the *New York Evening Post* described the church.

"The first Roman Catholic Church at Dawson City was a large structure built of logs at the north extremity of the town. The seats were merely rough boards placed on stumps.

The pastor made the altar himself, doing most of the work with an ordinary pen knife. At first there was no glass for the windows, but heavy muslin was tacked to the frames, and though the thermometer was often 60 degrees below zero, two large stoves kept the church comfortable. Like all other Catholic churches it was always open."[23]

Judge appealed to the sisters of St. Ann to staff his hospital and he was informed in the summer of 1897 that six sisters were on their way. At St. Michael's the sisters embarked on the boat *Alice* which, crowded with noisy, impatient prospectors, ascended the Yukon, too late in the season to get beyond Circle City. The captain announced that his passengers could walk the remaining three hundred miles to Dawson City or return downriver with the boat. The sisters chose the latter.

Barnum commented on conditions that summer. "The two steamers from Frisco and Seattle have come on their second trip loaded with prospectors. . . . The Yukon country is now on the verge of ruin; whiskey and bad men prevail and the old order has changed. Everybody is simply crazy over gold."[24]

It was not gold, however, that struck the Alaska mission that same year and left it in a state of shock from which it required several years to recover. This year of tragedy had begun during the winter. Father Parodi, alone at Tununa with a faithful Eskimo assistant called Loska, became violently insane. Father Barnum described what followed. "Parodi was the next one to fall a victim to Polar Anaemia, and his case proved the most serious of all. This poor man had been sent alone to Tununa, where there was really nothing to be accomplished. I have already described what a wretched place Tununa was while we were there, and being deserted for two years had not improved it any, and I have also mentioned how perfectly helpless Fr. Parodi was in managing for himself. Alone in a miserable hut with nothing but the old stove and his roll of bedding it is not surprising that a person of his temperament would have become affected by this insidious malady. The attack assumed a very violent form and developed traits that were just the opposite of the mild and gentle disposition. One day like the famous 'old monk of Siberia' in a sudden paroxysm he rushed from the house, in only his underclothes plunged into the river, crossed it and made his way up into the mountains. Loska missed him and seeing his clothes thrown around in disorder, he was alarmed and instituted a search. He spent the day dragging the river with his fish nets and then concluded that the tide had swept his body out to sea. The next day one of the sharp-eyed natives reported that he had seen some strange object on the side of the mountain. Loska used his field glasses and discovered that it was the poor priest. A rescue party was immediately dispatched, but they had immense trouble in bringing him back for he fought like a wild cat. After his return he would remain perfectly quiet and docile for a week or two and then another outburst would occur. On these occasions he would try to drown himself or to inflict some other injury so that Loska was obliged to put him under actual restraint. Finally he became so bad that Loska brought him to his house and kept him in his own room. When at last the summer came Loska brought him to Akulurak. During the journey he had to be kept securely tied to prevent him from attempting to jump overboard.

"We can never be sufficiently grateful to Loska for the care and protection he bestowed on Fr. Parodi during the dreary winter and the long journey from Tununa."[25]

The news about Parodi's breakdown was followed by the report that "Tosi had a stroke of paralysis in March and was speechless for five weeks."[26] He recovered sufficiently to travel to St. Michael's and there on June 27 he met Father Rene who took him gently aside and as tactfully as Rene could do it, informed him that he had been replaced as prefect apostolic of Alaska and superior of the Jesuits. "He was almost speechless, Rene wrote in his diary, "I told him gently why I came."[27] When Tosi, who was most reluctant to be demoted, asked Rene for his credentials the latter explained he had left them in Juneau for safekeeping. And where was his appointment by Father General? This had not yet arrived when Rene had to leave Juneau to make an inspection of the Alaska mission before winter set in.

The news was devastating. No one was eager to retain Tosi, who had ruled with Draconian severity, but neither did they want Rene, who appeared, when one first met him, to be pompous and overbearing. On June 30, after Rene had left St. Michael's, Tosi, suddenly very tired and bewildered, called for a meeting of two other Jesuits with himself. It was decided then that they should send a letter, which all would sign, to Father General in Rome. The letter was dated St. Michael's, Alaska, June 30th, 1897:

"Rev. J. B. Rene, having arrived here on the Str. *Excelsior,* announced that he was invested with full powers as Prefect Apostolic and Superior of the Missions of the Society of Jesus in Alaska, he immediately assumed entire control, giving a variety of orders, to wit: 1) For Very Rev. Fr. Tosi to retire at once to California; 2) *that all the sisters of the Akkulurak be sent to Kozyrersky;* 3) Many minor details regarding supplies, mail matter, etc. . . .

"To our great regret and embarrassment, the Rev. Fr. did not present any of the credentials usual in such cases, but contented himself by confirming the fact by word of mouth, and stated that his credentials had been left in Juneau for safekeeping.

"Under these circumstances, we the undersigned, Fathers, having accidentally met here, after consultation, reached the following conclusion, viz.: that Rev. Fr. Cataldo proceed at once to San Francisco in order to communicate with the Superiors, as this is the most speedy mode of obtaining the necessary information. Our hopes are that the Rev. Father will be able both by mail and cable to receive a positive and clear settlement of this misunderstanding, which he will bring back to us by return of the same Steamer.

"We all sincerely trust that the said Father now familiar with Alaska, will not be withdrawn to any other field.—To increase our embarrassment, not one of us have received the slightest intimation in our mail of this year of so important a change, there being no letters from the Propaganda, or his Paternity or Rev. Fr. Provincial.

P.P. Tosi, S.J. Pref. Apos. Alks
R.J. Crimont, S.J.
Frank Barnum S.J."[28]

On board the boat *Bella* Rene, filled with indignation, and more determined than ever, arrived at Nulato on July 3. The diary for the mission reveals the dismay of the local Jesuits, "*Bella* arrives on her way up. F. Rene is on board. He gives himself as Praef. Apost. and *Super. nostrorum.* He intimates, however, that he has not the least word about it from Rev. F. General or any other superior. This seems very strange. It does not seem less strange to hear the Rev. Father speak of the progress of the faith at Nulato, the good dispositions of our Indians, the plans he has already formed for the mission . . . But in the same time news arrives that Fr. Crimont has from the provincial the same powers of Praef. Ap. and Sup. Nost. May the last news be true!"[29]

To everyone's relief Rene left Nulato for Dawson City, and then another boat arrived, the *Alice,* bringing a letter from Crimont "confirming the news of his double appointment. The thing," adds the diarist, "seems most certain."

But on July 31 the *Alice* returned with Rene on board. Father Monroe, a young but not a timid man, told him that news of the appointment of Crimont had been received "and that in such a case he cannot receive him as the superior of the mission, but will, however, treat him as such before the Indians, on account of what the Rev. Father told them himself." Rene was "much put out," and demanded passage on a boat, which unfortunately

---

*Praef. Apost. and Super nostorum, abbreviated Latin for Prefect Apostolic and superior of ours, meaning Jesuits.

for all was not available. Rene returned to his room such as it was, and refused to see anybody or to eat anything. Monroe offered him a small boat which he declined. "The situation," says the chronicler, "is far from agreeable."

On August 1, the *Bella* going upriver, paused briefly during the night and left some letters, "amongst others one of Rev. F. Tosi confirms the nomination of Rev. F. Rene." After breakfast Monroe hurried to Rene to tell him this and to explain that the confusion had arisen because Crimont had been appointed superior of Alaska Borealis while Rene had been appointed prefect apostolic. Rene, refusing to accept this became very excited. "Sad day!!!" exclaims the chronicler, "who could ever believe what has been done and what has been said today!! Yet who ever had the least intention on that day to doubt the appointment of the Rev. F., or to offend him in the least?"

When Rene finally departed he left behind one nagging worry for all: they were now Rene's subjects in matters concerning the church. Would Rene be as vindictive as he had been pompous?

No one should have worried for Rene knew his own image had been tarnished as badly as anyone's. He had decided to live in Juneau, anyhow, and if communications continued to be as bad in the future as they had been during the summer of 1897, he would be powerless to disturb them. The fact is that when the dust settled Rene's better spirit emerged and he sent a letter of quasi-apology to *Woodstock Letters*:

"Perhaps Your Reverence would like to know the origin and end of the imbroglio which signalized the simple fact of the nomination of a new Prefect Apostolic of Alaska. As I am convinced it was the fault of nobody, we are free to speak plainly about it. It seems to have originated from the blunder of a copyist in Rome, who took one name for another. And as false news seems to travel far more rapidly than truth through the world, that bogus information had already spread everywhere, when the letter of Very Rev. Father General dated May 15, was journeying slowly on its way to Juneau. The true nominee had long before received the pontifical decree dated Rome, March 16, on the very eve of St. Patrick. He had been waiting for a letter of Very Rev. Father General up to the 4th of June, but then, not to lose the only chance he had of visiting our missions on the Yukon this year, he was obliged to start by the first boat sailing from Sitka to St. Michael's; trusting at the same time that the letter from Very Rev. Father General would be forwarded to him in good time to St. Michael's, as it was later on. This letter of his Paternity put an end for ever to the confusion which the false news had engendered in the minds of Ours on the Yukon. It is only fair to say that our fathers and brothers on the Yukon displayed, as a rule, great tact, discretion and good will during the short time in which uncertainly prevailed."[30]

Father Tosi, alas, could no longer give orders; he now had to take them. He begged to be left in the north, but those who always know better, thought he should live in milder climate, and so he was assigned to Juneau, where he could live in the same house as Rene. At St. Michael's he had many friends who prepared a farewell program for him, during which the commandant of the fort ordered a four-gun salute. When only three shots were heard an investigation was made and the young artilleryman, Mr. Linz by name, was found at the bottom of the rise where the guns were mounted, so seriously wounded that he had to be taken to San Francisco.[31] One shot, it appears, had accidently discharged prematurely, knocking poor Linz off his feet and burning his arm. With this melodramatic send off, Tosi, saddened but still feisty, embarked for Juneau, where he died within a few months.*

Father Cataldo, meanwhile, had returned to his mission in Montana. Rene had a passing word with him at St. Michael's on June 29. By July 3 he was sailing south, bearing

*Tosi's health, never good, had been undermined by his work in Alaska. He died on January 14, 1898.

the letter that was no longer relevant. He was probably the last to learn that Rene's "embroglio" had ended without a schism or a sacrilegious assassination. Barnum reported his departure, with some regrets, for they had become kindred spirits in the jungle of Eskimo verbs. Barnum also added a word about his own activities. His province, he said, had been trying to recall him, but he had pleaded successfully for another year to complete his grammar-dictionary. "Father Rene said he would appoint Father Crimont Superior [of Holy Cross] and leave me at St. Michael's where I can complete the Innuit Grammar and dictionary. It has all been revised, enlarged, and improved. It consists of 320 pages of foolscap, there are 7,000 words in the vocabulary and prospects are that we shall have 10,000. One more year would be well spent on this grammar and dictionary."[32]

In the autumn of that year, 1897, Cataldo was transferred to another mission. As docile as the most fervent novice, he cheerfully moved his frugal belongings to the Umatilla mission near Pendleton, Oregon. Called St. Andrew's, it lay east of the city in the rolling hills of northeastern Oregon, sheltered by the Blue Mountains on the east, where the Umatilla Indians hunted deer and elk. In the mission graveyard there was a tall metal cross which marked the place where they had buried Father Grassi. It was Cataldo himself who had sent him there—to die as things turned out. No doubt it was a comfort now for Cataldo to pray at Grassi's lonely grave.

The town of Pendleton had a church which was suffering from the rapid succession of pastors and the archbishop in Portland had recently persuaded Van Gorp to provide a Jesuit for the town as well as the mission. Father Conrardy, who lived at the Umatilla mission in the early 1880s had founded the Pendleton parish in the first place. He rode in from the mission on occasion to offer Mass in the home of Tom Milarkey on West Court Street, or at Mrs. John Murphy's on East Webb street. The Catholic population of the town was mostly Irish and they soon became too numerous for services in a home. Arrangements were made for Conrardy to use the courthouse and here on the first Sunday of each month he offered Mass and preached to his growing congregation.

In 1884 he purchased a rocky piece of ground on the east end where Court and Alta streets converged. With the willing aid of the Milarkeys, the Murphys, O'Daniels, Grogans and Reiths, Conrardy built a frame church and bell tower facing west. Archbishop Gross administered confirmation here on June 11, 1886. Favorably impressed by the fervor of these people, His Grace directed that a larger piece of property be acquired. When this was done the church was moved to the new site. In September of that year the first resident pastor was appointed. This was Father Peter De Roo, who distinguished himself later by writing learned books on the aborigines in Pre-Columbian America.[33]

For the thirteen years following De Roo's arrival, there was a succession of nine pastors, two of whom died in Pendleton; one abandoned it because "the climate was too rigorous"; and another returned to Canada to nurse his failing health. This was not a beginning to recommend Pendleton to sick or elderly priests, and, to be honest, that's about all the archbishop could spare for the struggling little parish, since he was very shorthanded everywhere.

In 1896, harassed on all sides by demands for more priests, the archbishop secured the loan of a Benedictine Father from Mount Angel for a few months. This was Father Kramer, who had the pleasure of meeting the Milarkeys and the Murphys. When he was recalled for other work, the archbishop literally begged the Jesuits at St. Andrew's to take St. Mary's parish and the rest of Umatilla County also, as he had no one to spare for any part of it.

On Wednesday, September 1, 1897, the first Jesuit pastor arrived at St. Mary's, none other than Victor Garrand who had founded the college in Seattle. Garrand made a dramatic entrance. After he had unpacked his bags and introduced himself to his flock, he hired a buggy and persuaded Father Cataldo from the mission to share a ride with him while he examined his new parish. While the two were enjoying themselves in the buggy, their horse, a most treacherous rascal, ran away with them and finally dumped them into the ditch in a very undignified manner. Besides their dignity, their bones were injured, and both had to be taken to the nearest hospital at Walla Walla.

When Garrand was released some weeks later, he arranged to have the church moved again. Now if this sounds familiar to you, you are perfectly right, for St. Mary's Church, like St. Andrew's, had been moved so often its builders would have been more clever to have put it on rollers. That is one advantage nowadays, when concrete and stone is used: the church cannot be moved.

Garrand apparently was not to be blamed because he actually had found *two* Catholic churches in different parts of Pendleton. He moved one of them next to the other and converted it into a rectory, and that settled its days of moving for, as often happens with rectories, it burned to the ground in January, 1899.

Though a very devoted Frenchman, Garrand had an eye for things Irish and also for raising money, so he arranged the first St. Patrick's Day program in Pendleton history. It was said to be a roaring success, as it raised $138, which was a fantastic sum in those times when the Sunday collection was $5. This assured Garrand of immortality in Pendleton. It was a pity he did not remain to enjoy it. Apparently, the sphinxes of Egypt beckoned him, for he returned to the romantic land of the Pharaohs and later died in Algeria.*

In 1899, Van der Velden succeeded him at St. Mary's. It was Van der Velden's good pleasure to move from a rented rectory into a new one, begun by Garrand before his departure. This two-story frame house served as St. Mary's rectory for fifty years, surviving not only all the natural enemies of houses but also many fervent hopes that it would burn down. The fact is that it lasted too long.

Van der Velden's appointment as pastor was the beginning of a quiet period of St. Mary's history, which could boast of nothing more exciting than frequent changes of pastors and assistants.

Neither Alaska's woes, nor Van Gorp's, as a superior, were over when Pendleton was occupied by Garrand. Van Gorp, however, during that year of disasters, enjoyed his own special triumph which seemed to compensate for the losses. He had begun at last to build the new Gonzaga College which was sorely needed to resolve Gonzaga's problems, as well as the mission's. If the latter appears to be obscure one should recall that the novices Cataldo had gathered during the later years of his superiority were now maturing as Jesuits, in need of courses in philosophy and theology. At the beginning of 1897 there were eight juniors at De Smet and eleven novices, eight of them in second year. At St. Ignatius Mission there were fifteen philosophers, all in second year, and nine theologians scattered over the three-year, short course.† In the following year there would be thirteen theologians and fourteen in philosophy. For the foreseeable future at least twenty-five scholastics would require teachers and living quarters, too many for the impoverished mission to send elsewhere.

While St. Ignatius, with its new steam-heated scholasticate could accommodate all of these and more, Van Gorp could not provide adequate faculties for both the scholasticate and Gonzaga. The obvious solution was to make provision for the scholasticate at Gonzaga, where it once had been on a very small scale.‡

---

*Garrand died in Constantin, Algeria, March 6, 1925.

†The short course at that time consisted of three years of theology, the long course four years. Long course graduates were candidates for solemn profession.

‡It will be recalled that there were three student scholastics at Gonzaga in 1891.

VAN GORP AS SUPERIOR

At the novitiate at De Smet the number of novices had dropped like a rock in Latah Creek, to the very bottom. Van Gorp wanted to close it, though Cataldo's feelings about it were well known. It was closed anyhow at the end of the 1897 academic year. At Los Gatos where the California Jesuits had a novitiate, there was also a sudden shortage of candidates. In September, 1898, for example, when Paul Sauer of Spokane became a novice for the Rocky Mountain Mission there were only six novices, including himself.

The most pressing need was the new college building. On July 2, 1897, Van Gorp announced its forthcoming construction. *The Review* for that morning contained the following:

"For more than a year Father Van Gorp has been conferring with Messrs. Preusse and Zittel, architects, with regard to plans for a new building, and now a definite contract has been reached. The bare building as it comes from the contractors, will cost $100,000. It will be the largest building in the city, and with the exception of St. Ignatius College, San Francisco, it will be the largest Catholic College in the West. The building and its adjacent lawns will occupy two full blocks."*

A few days later a site for the new building was selected about 300 feet east of the original college. On July 28 this was surveyed and on the following day ground was broken so casually that the diary recorded it in two words: "Excavation begun."[34]

For some months teams of horses and men employed by John Huetter, who had taken the contract for the foundations, struggled with great scoops of the Jesuits' historic gravel and boulders, until a full basement had been gouged out. It was an enormous cave, large enough to bury Spokane's thirty thousand inhabitants, provided you didn't put them into coffins.† During this operation large blocks of granite were carted to the site from quarries at Granite Lake southwest of Spokane.‡ Father Van Gorp might not have believed in grandiose buildings; he certainly believed in solid ones. His blocks of granite can be seen today, as hard and as formidable looking as the day they were quarried.

The foundations were completed during spring of the following year; and the valedictorian for the graduates of that year, Paul Sauer, practiced his speech in the bottom of the great cave, with ponderous stones piled around him. A slender, bookish-looking lad then, with a rich, musical voice, he bade his audience of stones farewell with all the boyish earnestness he could muster, but according to his own testimony he left them unmoved.

After Huetter had completed his contract and moved his blocks and pulleys elsewhere, William Rollinson and his associates moved on to the site with all the paraphernalia of the ancient industry of brick-laying. Piles of brick in a dull, rust-colored red arrived on the scene with a great clatter and probably much swearing of teamsters. Then the second phase of building Greater Gonzaga was begun. Shaped in solid brick, its massive pile was intended to survive until the day of doom. When the pile was partly assembled, a photograph was taken. From the antiquarian's point of view this is a classic. Apparently news of photography had been hurriedly noised abroad, for the unfinished beams and blocks swarmed with onlookers when the photographer clicked his shutter. One would imagine, seeing the individual faces of the crowd, that President McKinley had just been assassinated, for they all bore that grim, apprehensive appearance characteristic of early photography. Even two college boy clowns, clinging like showoffs to the beams supporting a pulley, managed to assume the same grim appearance, so painful was this business of being photographed.

*This St. Ignatius College building was destroyed in 1906 by the earthquake.

†About 8,500 cubic yards.

‡Interview with Paul Sauer, S.J., June 10, 1962.

216

By the end of 1898 the walls of the new building were entire and a wooden roof was carefully assembled over them to protect the interior from winter's rains and snows. Charles Schrimpf, the roofing contractor, then placed slate over the roof, like lead-colored shingles. Finally, Mr. Gibson undertook the completion of the interior. This required an additional six months, thus bringing the total construction time to almost two years.

As the new building neared completion, a great conference of the Jesuit administration convened in the old to discuss the new campus and its furnishings. It was eventually decided that the three buildings which originally comprised Gonzaga: the college, the hall, and the church, should all be moved to new sites. In this way, they reasoned, a three-fold objective would be realized: the college itself would be rescued from the railroad nuisance, land where the original buildings stood could be sold; finally, college facilities, now re-located, would be grouped within a convenient walking distance of one another.

Thus it was determined that the hall built in 1891 was to be relocated on the east end of the new building. St. Aloysius Church, originally located on Boone and Gonzaga Streets, was to be relocated on the west end of the new college on Boone and Astor. The old college, most complicated of all, was to be moved, after the other buildings were in use on the new sites. It was to be relocated approximately one hundred-and-seventy-five feet east, that is directly south of the church.

The first of the buildings to be moved was the hall. It was shifted without complications to the site east of the new building, with its main entrance facing Boone Avenue. Since it was no longer needed as a dormitory, the floor which divided it into stories was partly taken out, leaving a section of about sixty feet on the north end for a gallery. Then an opening of about twenty-two by sixteen feet was cut in the south wall and a forty by twenty-five stage was added. The entire structure was then renovated under the direction of Brother Carignano, who was given free scope to decorate it as he willed. Van Gorp's confidence was not misplaced. Carignano produced a worthy, if somewhat flimsy campus theatre, with a stage curtain that earned hearty applause from generations of college students. Depicting in vivid form Ben Hur's chariot race, it soon accounted for a disproportionate number of readings of Wallace's classic. Above the stage Carignano painted his concept of Shakespeare and, on the side walls, of the hall proper, Homer and Sophocles, all three of them pious enough in appearance to be taken for saints. Between the two ancient and eminent Greeks the main body of the hall was capable of seating 495 boys and 5 prefects.

By early summer, before the hall project had been completed, the new Gonzaga was ready for its occupants and the next two months were consumed by the heavy task of moving furnishings from the old college to the new. On Sunday, August 27, 1899, Open House was held for the benefit of interested persons. Our correspondent informs us that "quite a large crowd visited the building." What they found was an adapted U-shaped structure, four stories in eight above a full basement. Its front length measured 189 feet, and the wings on either end measured 90 feet. A heavy granite porch embellished the center front; and the low, granite wall with its high pillars surmounted by granite spheres softened the hardness of the overall penitentiary appearance. A broad walk had been laid along Boone Avenue to keep the shoes and stockings of Gonzaga's scholars in the proper state of tidiness; that is, provided they used it. All in all, the product of two years' construction, especially when contrasted with other building of the era, was quite acceptable; to some, even beautiful. In the passage of the eighty-four years since it was opened, it has even acquired a quiet kind of dignity which one cannot associate with most buildings, particularly modern ones. Whatever its defects then and now, it was Gonzaga's first permanent building.

On the day following Open House, the next phase of Greater Gonzaga was begun.

After the last Mass in St. Aloysius Church that morning, the Blessed Sacrament was removed to the new college chapel and work was begun on the relocation of the church. A new foundation was laid on the corner of Boone and Astor, where the present church stands. On August 30 the church bell and its tower, gifts of James Monaghan, and landmarks on the north side, were transferred to the new site, where they were installed within an hour. On the same day the church was jacked up and put on rollers. Three days later it was lowered on its new foundation. While plans were being made for doubling its capacity, it was opened for public use. Father Rebmann, in the midst of all the confusion attendant upon these historic doings, calmly inaugurated Sunday school classes which admitted 116 children on the first day.

The Jesuit community, with the exception of Van Gorp, moved into the new college on September 4. "We take dinner in the old college and supper in the new," the chronicle relates.[35] Nothing is said about where Van Gorp took supper. Judging from his lean appearance in photographs, one could presume that he often omitted it. In any case he, too, moved to the new quarters four days later. On September 23 Bishop O'Dea arrived from Vancouver to bless the new college. The ceremony was performed on the day following. "At 3:00 o'clock this afternoon," wrote Father Arthuis, "the Bishop blessed the new college visiting all the rooms from the basement to the roof." Five flights of stairs left his Excellency quite breathless, but the effort, he felt, was worth it. The building, destined for the exclusive use of boys, who are not usually inhibited by any respect for property, deserved every blessing it could get. The good bishop had walked briskly down the long halls and had sprinkled holy water generously in every room.

The final stage in campus relocation was not begun until the spring of the following year. On February 16, 1900, Spokane's *Chronicle* announced that the contract for moving the old Gonzaga college building had been awarded to the firm of Hastic and Dougan of Spokane. Estimated cost of moving was given as between $5,000 and $6,000 in addition to the cost of the new foundation, bringing the estimated total to $8,500.*

The local editor was enthusiastic about the contractor's plans. Having stated that the building weighed about 2,500,000 pounds, he estimated the need for one hundred jack screws, each capable of bearing twelve tons, to raise the building for placing a platform under it. Resting on this framework, he said, the building could be moved like any house, except that it would be pushed ahead, fifty feet a day, by hydraulic jacks.

On April 2, the east end was raised enough to place its weight on jack screws. Soon the west end was raised also and timbers were placed beneath it.

As might be expected, the Gonzaga Jesuits frequently joined the crowds of curious onlookers, who retarded the building's progress with innumerable suggestions on how it should be moved. Father Rebmann, too, trotted down to the site on occasion and reported on proceedings to his protégé, Paul Sauer, in the novitiate at Los Gatos. "The old college," he wrote, "is now already ready for being moved."†

Though the building was "already ready" all estimates in time and method for moving it proved to be overly optimistic. It made its first progress toward the new site on April 17. Only a few feet were covered that day. A week later a change in plans was announced: "The moving of the old Gonzaga college building has been delayed by the determination of the contractors to abandon the plan of pushing the building, and instead pull it with a windlass and cable. It was found that considerable more power was needed to move the structure even after it was on rollers than was anticipated. They have accordingly sent to Portland for a powerful windlass. It is not certain how many horse power will be used, but

*The actual cost was approximately $10,000.

†Interview with Paul Sauer, June 10, 1962.

it is thought that six or eight horses may be necessary to turn the windlass. The hydraulic jacks may also be brought into play for pushing the building for some portion of the distance across the campus.[36]

On June 13 the building finally reached the new site, but ten days more were required for turning it around at the required angle. To accomplish this difficult task all rollers on the seven tracks were pointed toward the center of the building. The structure was then turned by windlasses and cables attached to two corners at opposite ends of the building. All went well. The old college reached its final resting place without further complications. During July foundations were laid. These were almost ten feet high at one end, to keep the building on the same as the original level. A heating plant was then installed and by August 15, all was in readiness for its new occupants. Hastic and Dougan had achieved the near-impossible for the modest fee of ten thousand dollars.

In 1898 while Gonzaga College was still under construction, there occurred several other events which deserve recording. The first concerns the death of Father Andreis, Cataldo's promising assistant on the Crow Mission. Andreis had buggied to Pryor on June 13 and departed three days later for St. Xavier's Mission taking with him two Indian children who could not go home for their summer vacation. The St. Xavier's Mission diary briefly tells the tale: "A great misfortune has fallen on this mission and upon all of us. Fr. Andreis was drowned in attempting to cross a narrow slough on the other side of the ferry-boat landing. He reached there about 3:00 P.M. having left Pryor early in the morning. He did not realize how much the water had risen since Monday. An Indian is said to have warned him, crying out from afar that no conveyance could cross safely; but if so no one heard this. Joseph M. had accompanied Fr. A. on his trip and Angela, a girl from the Pryor school was also on the buggy, being transferred to this school by the wish of her father. Soon the team was swimming and the buggy was floating. Then it upset. Poor Fr. A. could not swim nor get hold of anything, was seen coming up a few times by Joseph, then disappeared about thirty yards from the boy. The latter managed to get hold of the wagon tongue and one of the horses so bravely escaped and rescued the girl who had succeeded in grabbing a tree branch. The dreadful news was brought us by an Indian. . . . What a terrible cross and what a gloom cast upon our lives."[37]

For days the swirling waters of the river were anxiously watched but the remains of Father Andreis seemed to have disappeared entirely. Finally on August 5 the body was discovered on an island in the river, ten miles from the slough, and on the following day it was brought to the mission, wrapped in canvas, and placed in a hurriedly made coffin. As it lay there in the mission church, with priestly vestments draped over the coffin, the priests and nuns vividly realized how few they were, a handful pitted against a raw and violent wilderness. Any one of them could be swallowed up in a moment. Father Andreis, just forty years old, had been desperately needed, now he was gone and they had to carry on without him.

The tragedy was a prelude to the closing of the school at St. Charles Mission. On July 3, 1898, the children were sent home for their vacation. The Ursulines left a short time later and the Jesuits did likewise. The school buildings were sold to the United States government in 1901 for use as a government school; the church, however, was retained for its original purpose and priests from St. Xavier's came regularly for services. Fortunately for the little children in the school, the sub-agent at Pryor fully cooperated with the Jesuits who provided as well as they could for the religious instructions. Another providential circumstance, so the father said, was the appointment of Mrs. John Keough, as the teacher in the government school.*

*Mrs. John Keough taught in the government school at Pryor from 1903–1909 and subsequently was field matron for the Crow Indians at St. Xavier, 1913–31. In both capacities she rendered the Jesuits invaluable service.

Another great loss to the mission was Barnum. He left Alaska, it was alleged, to attend to the publication of his grammar-dictionary, with the intention of returning as soon as possible. The book was published in 1901, the greatest of its kind.[38] Even before it was off the press Barnum applied to return to Alaska, but his appeal was never granted. It seems that he was too American for Tosi, now dead, and for Rene as well. One of Barnum's friends said it all, "Rev. Father Rene spoke to us about your desire to come back to Alaska. He is opposed to it for the present."[39]

Though he yearned to return, captivated like so many others by Alaska's mystique, Barnum never went back. Writing always for news of his old friends and preserving what he called his Alaskana, he died like many other Jesuits, in exile, in the land of his youth.*

The other American Jesuit, Father Judge, left the mission almost the same time as Barnum. His departure was even more final. In Dawson City he had succeeded in burning down his church. He had never intended it, indeed he was broken hearted because he had not been able to remove the Blessed Sacrament from the burning edifice.

It was June 4, 1898, Trinity Sunday, very early in the morning when this conflagration occurred. Judge, as he often did, prayed in the church during the night, lighting a candle for company as he poured out his heart before God. Called suddenly to the hospital near by, he left the candle burning, thinking he would soon return. At 1:00 A.M. the alarm was sounded, the church "was blazing like a huge furnace." Nothing was saved. "Father Judge," said Giordano, "was as if a sword had pierced his heart."

He had many friends, among whom was Alexander McDonald, a successful prospector who presented Judge with $25,000—all the money he needed for a better church, one made with lumber instead of logs.

One month later the six sisters of St. Ann arrived at Dawson City to staff the hospital. Judge's work was nearly done. The Oblate fathers would soon come to take over the administration of the Klondike, which was in Canada, outside the jurisdiction of the Prefecture of Alaska. Judge would not be there to meet them. He had predicted his own death. From his neglect of self and overwork, he contracted pneumonia. All Dawson City was aroused. No expense was spared to save the most loved man in Yukon Territory. Prayers were offered day and night. "George," the dying priest said to one of his friends, "you have got what you came for. I, too, have been working for a reward. Would you keep me from it?"[40] He died on his forty-ninth birthday, January 16, 1899. Those who prayed beside him could hear in the distance the lonely, plaintive howls of the wolves and the malemutes. It was very dark outside.

Father Judge had gone to Alaska to work "with Indians." He died among the Whites in Yukon Territory. What had happened to Jesuit priorities? Even in the mission of Alaska a mysterious force seemed to be working in favor of the Whites.

*Barnum died at Georgetown on November 21, 1921.

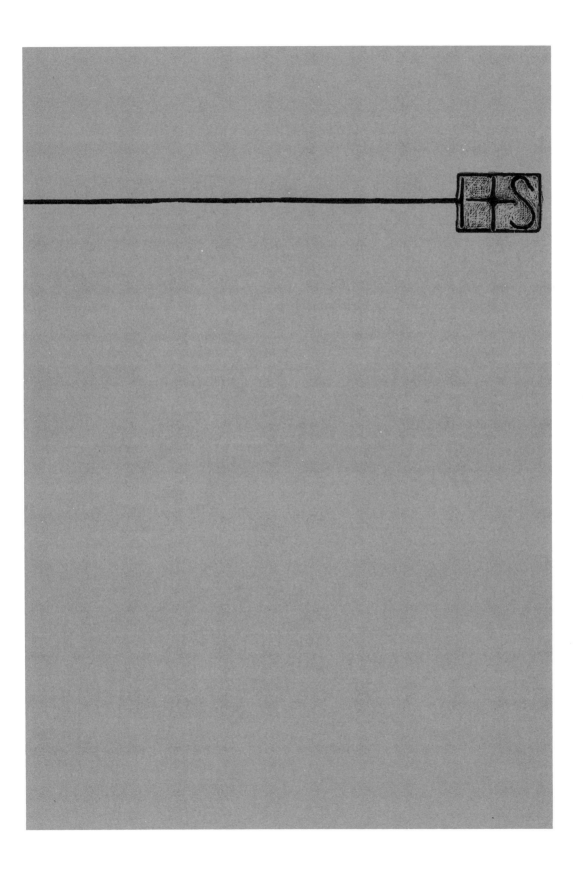

Herman Goller, tenth president of Gonzaga and first provincial of the California Province.

Lawrence Palladino, pioneer Montana Jesuit and author of Indians and Whites in the Northwest.

Bishop Raphael Crimont, eighth president of Gonzaga and first bishop consecrated for Alaska.

George de la Motte, S.J. eleventh superior of the Rocky Mountain Mission

Aloysius Robaut, S.J., companion of Seghers on trip to Alaska, 1886.

St. Stanislaus Church, Lewiston, Idaho, built in 1904.

Flour mill at St. Ignatius Mission, c. 1895.

St. Ignatius Mission about 1895. Jesuit scholasticate is at the left of the new church.

The original Garrand Building: formerly Seattle College and Immaculate Conception Church, it is now one of the science buildings on the Seattle University campus.

12

INTRODUCING DE LA MOTTE
1899–1907

Cataldo had been a builder and Van Gorp a business man. George de la Motte, who succeeded the latter, was a born diplomat. He was neither short like Cataldo nor tall like his predecessor but of average height. A man of a highly refined manner, he had a very graceful, modest appearance, almost angelic. Perhaps his physical attractiveness helped to make him popular, but it was his gentle and warmly paternal spirit that evoked the love of all. No superior in the early history of the province was more admired than George de la Motte, nor did anyone enjoy greater moral authority.

Of ancient and sturdy Gallic stock, de la Motte was born on February 18, 1861. He was endowed at baptism with a formidable title: George Henry Mary Armand Le Fer de la Motte.[1] Grandson of the personal guard of Charles X, who had abdicated thirty-one years earlier, and son of an artillery officer in the Alsatian garrison of Schlestadt, he was exposed at an early age to martial glory, but even more to the piety of both of his parents. His mother, an English convert to Catholicism only three years before her marriage, had offered him, her first-born son, "with a generous heart" to God, requesting only that some day she would have the happiness of seeing him at the altar.

An exuberant, impetuous youth, George often found himself condemned "to dry bread and water"—a punishment inflicted by school authorities. Once in adolescent anger he resolved to run away from home, "to Africa, to Asia, to America, no matter where." His father, whom he almost worshipped, talked him out of it with a kind word. "Sometime after that," George said, "I received my vocation."

De la Motte entered the Jesuit novitiate at Angers at the age of seventeen, the year after the Nez Perce War. During his second year in the novitiate, Stephen de Rouge, son of the count, became a novice also, and the two, with their Jesuit companions were exiled together, taking shelter in the de Rouge chateau until a new home was provided in Wales. De Rouge was a year older, and he was ordained first. But Madame de la Motte's prayer was finally answered; Goerge was ordained to the priesthood on July 22, 1888.

As one of Cataldo's tagalongs, gathered in the wake of poor Ruellan's death, he had volunteered in 1883 for the Rocky Mountain Mission, so a fortnight after ordination he embarked for Maryland to complete his theology at Woodstock. Here he proved to be a sensation in his studies. He was selected to perform The Grand Act, one of the last to do so. On November 30, 1890—after an intensive preparation—he defended all Catholic philosophy and theology before a solemn high audience of prelates, priests, and seminarians.

James Cardinal Gibbons himself presided. De la Motte's dazzling performance merited comment in the public press. "The audience," one reporter wrote, "could applaud in the young theologian a vast erudition, a remarkable command of his subjects, and above all else, admirable modesty and tact in the refutation of objectives."[2] Assured of a professor's chair in any Jesuit university in the world, de la Motte chose, instead, to keep his commitment to the Rocky Mountain Mission. From the comparative ease and glamor of Woodstock he traveled west to St. Ignatius Mission, a primitive frontier by contrast, and buried himself in the mountains while he prepared to work with Indians. "I never think of the Indian languages," he wrote, "without feeling a chill run in my veins. It is a good thing that the good God will be there to help me. The more I go ahead, the more I am convinced that life in the Rocky Mountains is truly a crucified life."[3]

It would be a painful crucifixion for him. A few months after he was appointed superior of St. Francis Regis Mission he fell victim to typhoid fever, to which he was exposed while he remained with a dying Indian. His health had already been undermined by fatigue; he had attempted too much to rescue his impoverished mission from the tangled mess of problems. There followed at least two years of critical sickness, during which he was at death's door three times. "I was happy to die," he said, but when he recovered he quickly added, "I am happy to be alive."

Transferred to De Smet Mission, where his burden was lighter, de la Motte promptly fell in love with the Coeur d'Alenes, who soon became his all-time favorites. "On arriving at the mission," he wrote, "I heard one old American settler say to another, 'This mission is astonishing. The Jesuit Fathers get their Indians to do whatever they wish; and they lead them as we lead horses with a handfull of straw.' That is true. Father Cataldo especially causes rain and good weather. Besides it is the same elsewhere. He is wonderful in his dealings with Indians."[4]

In 1895 after de la Motte had made his annual retreat at Lapwai, he was assigned to St. Ignatius Mission. He wrote about it to his father. "Tomorrow I shall go away from De Smet. I exchange places with the Superior of St. Ignatius Mission, which mission is to become a Scholasticate this year and Rev. Father Superior (of the Rocky Mountain Mission) has confided the charge to me. Besides my other duties I shall have to teach theology. St. Ignatius is our largest mission, our buildings alone form a village. There are four important Indian schools, besides the residence."[5]

As Cataldo had predicted, de la Motte's health was restored at St. Ignatius. He soon became robust, meaning he weighed, by self-disclosure, 185 pounds, which he had to admit was a little hard on the Indian ponies he liked to ride. They were superior to the "American horses," he said enthusiastically, because they were tougher and they liked to trot at a faster pace.

Though seemingly a trifling matter, current protocol required that superiors of theologates be solemnly professed Jesuits.* De la Motte had not yet pronounced his final vows, but this shortcoming, occasioned by his ill health, was remedied on February 3, 1896, when he became solemnly professed as required. With considerable feeling he described this to his father, "I am going to give myself to the holy Company of Jesus, which I have already done, sixteen years ago, but this time the Company is going to receive me, and give itself to me . . . on that day I shall not say holy Mass; the ceremonial of the vows requires this, that after the *Domine non sum Dignus,* [the celebrant] takes the holy Sacrament and turning to me, holds It exposed above the ciborium, I will then pronounce my vows and will immediately after that [place my vow paper] between the fingers of Rev. Fr. Superior, who in

*At this period some Jesuits when they pronounced final vows were "spiritual coadjutors," and others, a select few, were "solemnly professed." Certain offices in the Society were restricted to the solemnly professed. De la Motte pronounced his solemn vows on February 3, 1895, at St. Ignatius.

exchange, will give me Holy Communion."[6] The scholastics and Indian children were preparing a feast. "It amuses me," he said, "to see the pains they take to hide their joy."

In August, 1899, de la Motte received orders from Van Gorp to move the scholasticate to Spokane. Although this did not come as a surprise, de la Motte was distressed. Having shunned academic life when it was first offered to him, he had chosen the Indians for his portion, and now, despite this, he was being deprived of his preference. But for him all was "in the hands of the good God" and he prepared to move the scholasticate with as little fuss as possible. It was like moving a circus, for each of his subjects, as lively as trick bears and stimulated by the exodus, had a different method for getting the job done.

De la Motte arrived in Spokane on August 1, 1899, in a coach on the Northern Pacific Railway, to prepare the way for his community. The scholasticate, Van Gorp informed him, would be an integral part of the college. Since Father Rebmann, currently president of the college, did not qualify to be the superior of the theologate—he was not solemnly professed—de la Motte would have as his additional duty the presidency of the college. Rebmann, however, would be retained as pastor of the church.

The new president was followed by thirty-six scholastics, several professors of philosophy and theology (including the inimitable Father Cocchi), and a handful of brothers. This new contingent brought the total number of Jesuits at Gonzaga to sixty-five, and created one of only four formally established scholasticates in the United States and Canada.* Since the old college building, destined for relocation and use as their home, had not been moved yet, the new arrivals were placed temporarily in the top story of the new building. Here they remained until the old building was ready. The members of the Scholasticate, the faculty, and the scholastics moved on August 22, 1900. Within a short time the newly adopted quarters were gratuitously given the nickname of The Sheds, and The Sheds it remained for the duration of the scholasticate on this site.

The Sheds, as has already been noted, was supported by a ten-foot foundation, which was, in effect, a basement aboveground. Dark and cavernous, with countless timber-pillars breaking its floor space, this basement soon became a catchall of scholastic and campus activity. It was to these gloomy confines that the historic St. Ignatius Mission Press was moved, together with the works of St. Thomas Aquinas. There it rested, gathering dust for several years. Finally in 1906 another Benjamin Franklin appeared in the person of Frederic J. Williams, a Jesuit scholastic from Canada. Williams fostered many interests, photography and printing included. He discovered what he called "an ancient and dilapidated press," refurbished it, and set himself up as the campus printer. His companions referred to him as Jinks, so he became Jinks the Printer and a scroll was duly prepared and hung over his shop: *Jink's Print Shop*. Williams, with the help of several enterprising school boys, did a howling business of printing handbills, school programs, and other sundry items. In 1907 Williams's grandmother died in England, leaving him a legacy of about $950. With the approval of superiors he purchased a new printing press. After it arrived the old historic press from St. Ignatius was casually scrapped, which was almost a sacrilege. Jinks, about this time, had fallen into disfavor. He had a great weakness for pie and once too often he sneaked a pie out of the kitchen to eat at his leisure. He was sent back to Canada. Before he left he demanded, and got back, his $950 legacy.†

*These four were: Woodstock, St. Louis, Immaculate Conception in Montreal, and Gonzaga.

†The Williams Press was moved to the Mount in 1915 with the scholasticate. In 1948 Father Timothy O'Leary established a print shop at Gonzaga University in the basement of Goller Hall. The new Chandler Price was moved here again and was used until 1949 when it was replaced with a new press of the same type. This was the origin of the University Press now located in its own building on the campus. The old press was sold to the State Custodial School at Medical Lake. Eventually Holy Names Academy in Seattle acquired it.

INTRODUCING DE LA MOTTE

As president of the college, de la Motte had succumbed to one great weakness, a military program. Having survived his exposure to the barracks as an "army brat," like St. Aloysius, patron of the boys, he cherished a deep appreciation for the virtues of a soldier and the Frenchman's infatuation with the uniform.

One of his scholastic prefects in 1907 was James Kennelly from Washington, D.C., who later earned for himself the affectionate sobriquet of Big Jim. Kennelly had attended Gonzaga High School in the nation's capitol, which at that time was distinguished for its cadet corps. It would be difficult to decide which of these two, the president or the prefect, took the initiative in proposing a military program at Gonzaga. Knowing the buoyancy and resourcefulness of scholastics, however, one would probably award the credit to Kennelly.

After much discussion regarding the matter, de la Motte conferred with Major Gerhard Luhn, U.S.A. retired, on November 21, 1899. A distinguished soldier for forty-two years during which time he had served in forty different army posts, Major Luhn was a familiar figure to Gonzaga Jesuits.* His many gracious benefactions connected with Masses on army posts had endeared him to all the priests. With his great, white, flowing beard, he was easily recognizable in any congregation by anyone at the altar or in the choir loft.

The Major did not disappoint the president and the prefect. He responded with a proposal for a cadet program which he directed almost singlehandedly until his resignation in 1905. With dispatch proper to a recruiting sergeant, he summoned a meeting of the boys on that very day. He explained the end and aim of the corps and what was expected of each member, then proceeded to enlist volunteers. About sixty-five signed their names with great solemnity and ceremony; then the major lined them up in the yard for their first drill.

The Major was no ordinary soldier. The white beard, which intrigued the not-easily impressed Jesuits, awed Gonzaga's little boys and held them fast. If this were not enough to spellbind the older boys, the Major's well-known war record was. He had seen action in the Utah War of 1857 against the Mormons; in the Civil War; and in 1866 during the First Sioux Indian War which lasted from 1865–67. The spry and thundering old warrior soon commanded respect bordering on some form of worship and when he snapped his fingers, everyone jumped, as though General Grant himself had barked an order.

Both de la Motte and Luhn wanted official recognition for the corps. Accordingly, an application was filed with the United States War Department. On January 9, 1900, the college military department was formally established,[7] and could look forward to a supply of guns and uniforms from the government.

The promised guns were long in coming and when they finally arrived in mid-May, it was soon discovered that they were too heavy for some cadets who were too small to bear them. These cadets were then provided with wooden guns more suitable to their tender years, but objects of contempt and disgust. The school catalogue for 1899–1900, which was produced at the end of the academic year instead of at the beginning, contains a splendid photograph of the new corps in which seventy-seven cadets in uniform are grouped behind Major Luhn. Many of the boys looked more like drummer boys than soldiers, and most of them would have inspired pity instead of fear. A few officers with swords in their white-gloved hands have a faraway look in their eyes, as though they espied an enemy somewhere on the horizon.

During the summer of 1900 an official armory was constructed. Located "about 100 yards south of the main building," this was a frame structure for drill and storage of uniforms and drums. An inventory of the arsenal, made in 1903, showed that it contained 45 cadet rifles, 9 swords, 110 cartridge boxes, 119 waist belts, 110 bayonets and scabbards,

---

*Major Luhn was born in Hanover, Germany, on February 19, 1831; he was reared in Cincinnati, and he died in Spokane on February 16, 1920. *Spokane Chronicle*, February 17, 1920.

15 pounds of powder and 3,000 blank cartridges.[8] All in all this was scarcely enough to defend the college against a playful raid by the Spokane Indians.

Today, no doubt, such a military program would be in disfavor with some Jesuits. De la Motte, however, was very proud of it and took much pleasure in watching the boys marching on the baseball field in their blue uniforms—a sight not as inspiring as French uniforms, of course, but very stirring for their presence on an American frontier. Whatever else be said about it, it was the first military program in our province history.

Meanwhile other historic developments were taking place beneath the fine old mansard roof of The Sheds. Most important of these was the very simple inauguration ceremony on August 15, 1900, when de la Motte replaced Van Gorp as superior of the Rocky Mountain Mission. At noon on this day the Community filed into the dining room full of expectations based on rumors. After grace was recited the appointments of the house were read. As soon as the announcement of de la Motte's appointment as superior of the mission was declared, he arose and changed places with his predecessor, and that was that. There was more jubilation than usual, for Van Gorp, despite his dedication, was not a popular superior.[9]

De la Motte's first decisions were in keeping with his compassionate spirit. He soon expressed his intention to make a visitation of all communities in the Northwest and southern Alaska, "not like a steam engine," but more leisurely. "I shall spend a month or two in each mission and this will allow me to do a little good."[10] His greatest concern was the shortage of priests. While his predecessors had recognized this, they did not agonize over it like de la Motte. He wanted to be everywhere simultaneously to help his colleagues—in Yakima: "a pretty little town near the center of Washington state;" in Seattle: "It is a superb town twice as large as Spokane. We have a parish and a college there. No Indians;" in Juneau: "This journey takes three days on the Pacific Ocean. You know my pronounced distaste for ocean travel;" on the Crow Mission: "the toughest we have." When he preached to some of the Indians there, they smoked cigarettes in church, ate nuts and played with their dogs. He scolded them; they laughed and interrupted him. "Keep that for yourself," they said to him.[11]

Northern Alaska for a brief time was not under his jurisdiction. When Rene was appointed prefect apostolic and superior of the Jesuits, the mission was separated from the Rocky Mountain Mission and was attached directly to the Turin province. Only time would tell that this was no solution to Alaska's basic problem, lack of men. One gets the impression that Father General in Rome, Luis Martin, was at his wit's end, what to do about it.

Alaska's disasters never seemed to go away or dissolve with the ice and snow. The summer of 1900 was like the rest. A dreadful plague had broken out, one of those that periodically swept the arctic, and wiped out large numbers of the population, even entire villages. Ordinary mission work was disrupted. There was not time even to gather enough fish for the winter, so busy were the sisters and Jesuits in caring for the sick and burying the dead.

Brother Joseph Vincent O'Hare, not a newcomer to Alaska, was shocked by the violence of the plague. He identified it as "*la grippe,* with its kindred ailments, measles, a kind of cholera, typhus," almost everything but a broken leg.[12] He described what it was like to enter a former village, now deserted by all but the dead:

"We found the village deserted, the sick survivors having fled in terror to another place. We saw only a solitary dog on the beach, which retreated into the village as we approached, and curled itself upon the feet of its dead master. As we went up the bank and into the village, we gazed upon a sight more dreadful than any we had yet encountered. Here and there, bodies wrapped in skins and old garments, were lying about . . . lifting a tent we found the remains of a middle-aged Indian whom I used to know. The body had been left in the exact position in which it had fallen after the last agony, the head on the ground, the eyes staring, mouth wide open, the limbs turned in various directions. This body too was only half-clad, and a great rent in the shirt showed a terribly discolored side. This and several other corpses, had to all appearances remained unburied for a week or two. From another fallen tent we took a body that gave forth a swarm of blue flies and worms when disturbed. From another 'bundle' there protruded a long bony arm. Wishing to identify the victims, I uncovered the face of one of them, but such a gruesome sight met my gaze, and such an awful stench came forth, the the leader of our party told me to discontinue the identification. The whole village was reeking with filth, rotten fish, and so forth. All kinds of tools, utensils, fishing tackle, weapons, etc. were scattered about, having been abandoned by the fleeing survivors. We also came across two freshly made graves, where they had buried their first dead. Later on they had been able only to drag them outside the tent and leave them.

"Our task was to dig the grave. We made two very wide ones in the sand, each large enough to hold four bodies, lying side by side. On the bottom we placed mats and skins, then the poor, ghastly, twisted and drawn-up bodies, over them more skins and mats, then boards, and lastly mother earth. Over each of the two mounds we put a large rude cross, hastily made. Then we went away. I have yet before my eyes the sight of those poor natives, lying side by side in the big graves; they were so forlorn-looking and wretched."[13]

When the siege was over, O'Hare reported again: "Summing up the plague reports from all places heard from, and striking an average, I would place the mortality at fifty per cent of the former population. Our loss here was just that, excluding the school, whose loss was about fifty per cent, mostly girls, with one Sister, the Superioress. I think I shall never forget the dreadful scenes of the summer of 1900."[14]

There was death, too, at De Smet in Idaho. Father Joset, the ancient but still lynx-eyed patriarch of the mission, died peacefully on June 19, 1900. During autumn of the previous year and spring of this, Joset had suffered several falls that weakened him and left him more dependent on the use of his cane. In mid-May he fell heavily from his chair. This time the damage was final; the old war horse took to his bed and prepared to die. In August he would be ninety. But that did not matter any more. For eight days in June he took no food or drink, then on the afternoon of June 18, he brightened up a bit. He received Holy Communion at 5:30 on the following morning and closed his eyes in prayer. At 7:00 he quietly breathed his last.

There were many Indians at the mission for the Feast of the Sacred Heart. They solemnly passed his remains and looked upon him for the last time. In the course of one man's lifetime their entire culture had been radically changed. Joset more than any other had been responsible for this transformation. Once he had left them because of their stubbornness. He left them now for the last time and his passing made a greater impression on them than his coming. Joset's name was sent to Rome as one having died in the odor of sanctity.

The passing of Joset, despite his advanced age and infirmities, was a great loss to the work force, for he had preached frequently in Coeur d'Alene and heard confessions almost to the end. De la Motte counted every man not once but often. Demands were coming in almost daily for priests who were needed in the expanding parishes all over the Northwest.

In Havre, Montana, Father Eberschweiler had just completed another church, not the first there, and the people were demanding a resident pastor. The first Mass in Havre had been celebrated in a tent by Father Damiani of St. Peter's Mission. That was eighteen years earlier, in 1882. Father Francis Monroe, too, before his departure for Alaska, had said Mass in a railroad section house. But mostly Havre was under the zealous care of Eberschweiler, who covered the High Line all the way to the Dakota border.

On his golden jubilee in 1908, Eberschweiler referred to these early years: "I visited Havre monthly, paid with my own money for the lots which Father Superior had selected and secured them for the Jesuit Fathers. In 1894, I was just ready to build a church at Havre when Father Follet took charge of Havre for four years. A church was then built but a storm destroyed it and Father Follet left. I then resided in Chinook and again took charge of Havre by monthly visits, during which time I enjoyed the hospitality of the de Lorimer and Burke families. I said Mass in Gussenhoven's little house, which was burned in the great Havre fire, and in the West Havre school. Our new church was finished in 1900."[15]

The new church, a frame building, which cost $3,000 was erected where Father Follet's brick church had stood, on the lots Eberschweiler had purchased with his own money. According to the instructions of the bishop it was dedicated to St. Jude Thaddeus. Bishop Lenihan blessed it on September 17, 1905.

Father Eberschweiler had more history to relate. "The Catholic Havreites," he continued, "took the notion to ask Bishop Brondel to have a residing priest in Havre. Mr. P. Des Rosier presented a petition to the bishop during a great reception in Chestnut's hall, July 8, 1903. The bishop then solemnly appointed me to be the first resident priest of Havre, which was herewith made the last headquarters of the district of the Jesuit Fathers for good. Since that time a residence for Jesuit Fathers was built. We hope soon to be able to build a sister's school and a sister's hospital."[16]

Eberschweiler was no spring chicken. Nor was Van Gorp, who temporarily took Joset's place at De Smet. Caruana, the superior at De Smet, was in his sixty-seventh year—by contemporary standards, an old man—and Van Gorp was two years older. Cataldo, fortunately, was younger, by a spare year, certainly not a prime subject for moving to Alaska where such a hue and cry was being raised about reinforcements that one would assume the Battle of Waterloo were being waged again. Rene was very articulate and he possessed, besides, a thundering voice, the distinction of being a prelate, as prefect apostolic. Father General felt the pressure. He could not lean on de la Motte; the latter had no jurisdiction whatever in Alaska Borealis.

However, the General, knowing de la Motte's abundance of compassion, could get him involved by the simple expedient of appointing him official visitor with plenipoteniary powers, and this he did early in 1901. It was, in a way, a tricky maneuver, at de la Motte's expense, and Martin may have recognized this. But he knew his man, and his strategy worked well.

On May 26, 1901, de la Motte left Spokane for Alaska "to encourage and console the fathers in Alaska in their difficult ministry."[17] After a sea voyage which, as it turned out, he had dreaded needlessly because the waters were only serene, he arrived at Juneau. "There I found Rev. Father Rene and two other Fathers, all Frenchmen, old friends of mine."[18] On Trinity Sunday, he wrote, he sailed to Skagway with Rene and Jacquet, completely unaware that the latter, who had raised most of the money for the college and church in Spokane Falls, was like a time-bomb that was set to explode during the following winter. Rene and Jacquet went on to Nome and de la Motte remained at Skagway with Father Philbert Tornielli for eight days awaiting the train to White Horse. Eventually, after many adventures which were comparable in peril and jeopardy to those of De Smet, de la Motte arrived at Eagle City. There it was that Father Francis Monroe carried on heroically with a small church and a shack as a base of operations. The terrible risks continued to confront de la Motte, "but the holy Virgin protected us," and sometimes it was "the holy angels" that saved him. Leaving Eagle City, he arrived at Nulato safe but very sleepy, and he spent five days recuperating.

The kayaks intrigued him. They were like, he said, "a hollow cigar with a trough in the middle . . . as light as a straw." It was easier [to ride one] than a bicycle. As he sailed down the Yukon in various boats, with the holy Virgin coming to his aid, he gradually fell under the spell of Alaska. He was beginning to learn that once this disease got into one's blood, it was next to impossible to eradicate.

He found the Jesuits at Holy Cross, exhausted; but the mission, prosperous. Rene, despite his appearance of stiffness and a certain pomposity, had accomplished wonders there by establishing a sawmill in the nearby woods and by providing a new mission boat, the *St. Joseph*. The mill supplied lumber for all of the missions—over two-hundred-thousand board feet in the first two months.[19] The boat of forty-three tons, which could navigate in only two feet of water, had been built at St. Michael's but Holy Cross was its home port. Brother Twohig added "a house" on the deck and he was appointed its official engineer. During the summer months the *St. Joseph* was never idle and Twohig, its captain, was never happier.

De la Motte left Holy Cross on the *St. Joseph* for St. Michael's, and from there he sailed on a commercial ship to Nome and back, crossing the Bering Sea with help from "the holy Virgin and Our Lord." He returned again to Holy Cross for a meeting of the missionaries. "I have found several of our Fathers very fatigued, one especially, the superior of Holy Cross. I am probably going to take two or three of them to the Rocky Mountains. But I will have to replace them . . . I have made my choice, and called from the mountains my two predecessors, Very Rev. Fr. Cataldo and Van Gorp. A day will come, I hope when I myself will have the happiness to come here."[20]

Accordingly, in tune with inspiration of the Holy Ghost, we hope, the geriatric ward of the mission was raided for what could be spared, and Cataldo, in his sixty-sixth year, and Van Gorp in his sixty-seventh, were ordered off to Alaska, the one to become superior of Nulato and the other of Holy Cross. The latter was also "vicar-general for the prefect apostolic and vice-superior of the Alaska mission." In making these appointments, de la Motte revealed his love of titles, as well as of uniforms. He summoned three other Jesuits to Alaska: Van der Pol to assist Jacquet at Nome; Peter Pasino to Nulato for his apprenticeship; and Brother Markham of the New York-Maryland province, to replace Brother O'Hare at Holy Cross.

News of these appointments caused shock waves across the Northwest. Van Gorp, they say, liked a good joke and could tell one, but it is not likely he regarded his new assignment as funny. Nonetheless he responded with alacrity, as did Cataldo, whose principal anxiety was the gathering of enough snuff to take with him so that his supply would not run out at Nulato.[21]

The superior replaced by Cataldo was Jules Jette, with whom Cataldo now took up his residence in St. Peter's Mission, which resembled a log fortress. Jette, five-feet-ten, with blue eyes and a pink complexion, having been born to the French Canadian aristocracy in 1864, was only in his thirty-seventh year.[22] He had been in Alaska since 1898, at Nulato since 1900. Studying the language of the natives was his principal occupation, though he also visited "40 or 50 villages situated on the banks of the river within a radius of 500 miles."[23]

Cataldo snuffed, but Jette smoked a pipe. He relished the strongest Turkish tobacco he could obtain, and if that was not bitter enough, he provided his own additives from raw materials at hand. His smoke was for the pleasure of it, not to keep out mosquitoes, which swarmed around him, without his moving a muscle to fend them off. A man of long prayers, he knelt as straight as a rod, like a marble statue, seemingly without feeling, while the mosquitoes attacked. One can assume that Cataldo had finally met his match for self-dedication and discipline.

There was something remarkable in the presence of these two men in a remote little mission on the Yukon, isolated in a wilderness, unknown to all but a handful of uneducated people who were still living at the rim of the stone age. Here were two of the greatest Indian language scholars in the world, collaborating on a project of immense significance, related to our knowledge of the prehistoric migration of races. What they called Tinneh or Ten'a was an ancient language identified closely with Navaho.[24] It was also one of the most difficult languages in North America. Cataldo, who had learned other Indian languages with ready facility, found it almost impossible to master it during his two years' residence. Jette, probably the greatest language genius in our province history, not only learned to speak it better than any native, but he produced a small library of works in it: grammars, lexicons, translations of the Bible, Ten'a mythology, and other learned pieces that have no parallel in our history.

When de la Motte left Alaska, he ordered five Jesuits to leave with him, all of them replaced by others. They were: John Post, who returned to the Indian missions; Ragaru, who went back to Alaska two years later; Parodi, who had not yet recovered from his mental breakdown; Raphael Crimont, the superior of Holy Cross who was "very fatigued especially;" and Brother Cunningham, the physical giant with broad arms.*

Crimont was provided immediately with a new task that was oddly designed to furnish him with the rest he required. With ingenuous simplicity, de la Motte made him president of Gonzaga College. Perhaps he classified this position as an easy one; he had retained it along with his other duties when he became general superior. It is highly improbable, though, that Crimont entertained the same opinion. Swapping his duties as a missionary on the Yukon River for the presidency of the bustling college, however small, could be regarded as a "rest" only by a desperate superior.

Whatever Crimont's feelings, his appointment created a sensation in Spokane. On Saturday, October 12, 1901, Spokane's evening newspaper carried a banner headline which suggested that Livingston had at last escaped from the jungles of Africa. Only five words appeared in ominous bold type: "Seven Years in the Wilds." Below in smaller letters, one could see for himself who this shaggy monster was: "Rev. Raphael Crimont Emerges from the Wastes of Alaska to Become President of Gonzaga." Further details in the long sublines, characteristic of the age, confirms one's first impressions: "He Tells of the Great Scourge. Awful Scenes in the Northern Land—No One to Bury the Dead When the Plague Swept Through the Country." Finally, there appeared, like a more pleasant after-thought, "Sketch of the New President."[25]

By this bizarre announcement, Spokane learned that Gonzaga College had acquired a new president. His name was Crimont. He was a Frenchman with the appearance of a mild, genteel professor of the Sorbonne. He had spent seven years in a plague-stricken wilderness. Why on earth had they selected him to be a college president?

The new president soon relieved all doubts about the kind of administration he would have. On October 9, one day before he was officially installed as superior and president of Gonzaga, he attended a meeting of the consultors of the community to consider certain problems concerning the cadets and the school's athletic program. Without doubt his views prevailed, though de la Motte was still technically superior. The decisions formed in the meeting were made public shortly after Crimont's inauguration: (1) the military uniform was henceforth obligatory for every resident student; (2) no student who had once joined the cadets could withdraw without previous approval of the president; (3) no student would be allowed to play football against outside teams without written permission from parents or guardians.

When the new regulations were promulgated, howls of disappointment arose from all

---

*Since heavy-set, six-foot Cunningham had extraordinarily long arms, he became the clerk the Eskimos preferred whenever they traded fish for calico at St. Mary's, because the length of calico was measured by in arm's lengths.

parts of the campus. If there was displeasure over the uniform question, no one heard about it, because the noise about football drowned it out. Crimont had been informed about football's celebrated history on the campus. In October 1901, just before he took over the reins of the college, a committee of boys had appealed to de la Motte for the restoration of inter-school football. Student hopes were high at this time because the rapid expansion of the school was somehow identified in their minds with a relaxing of discipline. Thus, when Crimont promulgated his decision, their hopes were critically, if not mortally, wounded.

But boys grab eagerly for straws. There was a flurry of letter-writing home with heart-rending appeals for permission to play football, followed by anxious days of waiting. By the end of October they realized the worst. Their hopes were now dead and all but decently buried. "So far," said the director of athletics, contriving without effort the understatement of the season, "but two have received the desired permission, which is hardly enough for a good team."[26]

Crimont was much more concerned with the college's academic program than its athletics. Like his predecessor, he was an especially gifted theologian, though it must be admitted he lacked a certain kind of practical interest and know-how. Moreover, with all his charm and graciousness, he never came to fully appreciate the American personality. A European to the core, he retained certain unpleasant reservations regarding Americans, prejudices he would have been shocked to discover in himself. He never realized they were there and, because of his native sweetness of disposition, they seldom came to the surface. These were his limitations. His virtues all but annihilated them. His period of administration—almost three years—moved along serenely.

Meanwhile there was news of Nome. Brother O'Hare had written about the new church there. "At Nome a church is being built which will have the unique honor of being the most western Catholic Church on our hemisphere, or at least in North America. It takes over three months to reach Nome from Holy Cross by sled, and there is every evidence that the two fathers will have plenty to do."[27]

The two fathers also had more to do than either expected, for the time bomb, ticking away during September when navigation was still open, finally exploded in October, taking with it the peace and tranquillity of all of Nome. Stated bluntly, as the United States District Court did, Jacquet became violently insane.

At first there was an ugly dispute about which of the fathers was insane; some said Van der Pol, who had blown the whistle, and some said Jacquet, because Van der Pol said so. Jacquet, despite a colorful display of civic involvement, was behaving in a strange manner for a pious Jesuit, and letters about this reached a very perplexed de la Motte. Writing to Rene on November 28, 1901, de la Motte reported that Jacquet was certainly giving "signs of a very abnormal condition of soul."[28] Among other things he had sent "imprudent dispatches," and had disobeyed a direct order of Van Gorp. For some inexplicable reason, however, de la Motte appeared to think that it was Van der Pol who had become ill, not Jacquet. "This idea of poor Fr. Jacquet, being condemned to stay 7 months in Nome in the company of Fr. Van der Pol in such circumstances is truly calculated to fill us with apprehension," he wrote to Rene, revealing the side on which he stood. Were he in Alaska he would go to Nome himself to settle matters.

Neither Rene nor Van Gorp required prodding, for the situation in Nome had already got out of hand. Dr. Call of Nome had been summoned to care for Jacquet and probably at his recommendation Van der Pol requested Judge Wickersham's court for a hearing.[29] This was conducted on November 22, 1901, a week before de la Motte's letter to Rene. The conclusion of the court was that Jacquet had to be confined, either in jail with common criminals, because no other facilities were available, or at Holy Cross Mission. Jacquet's friends, who were many, opted for the latter without consulting Van Gorp, and the patient by court order and at government expense was shipped off by dogsled to Holy Cross. News of this appeared in the Spokane papers on March 17, 1902: "Jacquet, because of fatigue and suffering, mentally deranged, brought to Holy Cross."[30] This dispatch was correct, of course, but weeks before, Van Gorp had sent Jacquet to St. Michael's to await the opening of navigation, for the simple reason that Holy Cross had no facilities for confinement. As bad as Nome was, Holy Cross with its isolation was worse. At least Van Gorp thought so, but Frank H. Richards, the United States Marshal in Nome did not agree. When he learned that Jacquet had been sent to St. Michael's by dogsled he discharged the biggest gun he had in the form of a letter to his deputy in Koserefsky, near Holy Cross. He accused Van Gorp "of cold-blooded heartlessness" and suggested that Wickersham should put him and everyone else connected with the case in jail "for six months for contempt of court." He refused to pay for Jacquet's second trip by dogsled and ordered Van Gorp to pay it. This amounted to $525.35 for the journey which had taken twenty-four days, from December 23, 1901 to January 15, 1902.

Poor Jacquet! While they were keeping him under restraint, *The Yukon Catholic* in Dawson City, unaware of his tragic breakdown featured on the front page his splendid accomplishments in Nome: "Fr. Jacquet at Nome," the account began, "Lands Penniless, and in Two Months had built a Beautiful Church, a Parochial Residence and an Assembly Hall for Young Men." The article did not state that Jacquet, already on the skids, had borrowed $8,658 without permission to achieve these wonders. Van der Pol, still suspect to Jacquet's friends, had to raise the money to pay this. But Jacquet left a monument. He was deeply loved, and his fond desire for an illuminated cross, to serve as a beacon for people lost in blizzards, atop the church steeple "100 feet above the pavement," was realized soon after his departure from St. Michael's for a hospital in Oregon.

The harsh winter, as well as his ordeal in what de la Motte called "the Jacquet matter," was too much for Van Gorp. De la Motte relieved him as superior of Holy Cross, but still determined to use his talents, requested him to make a tour of the Alaskan Missions, since he himself could not perform this task as he had planned. Writing on April 4, 1902, he stated that the general in Rome intended to appoint him superior of Alaska Borealis, combining again the superiorship of all of Alaska and the Rocky Mountains.[31] "It is a huge responsibility because now I shall have to furnish Alaska with men and resources." The general also wanted him to come to Europe, thus he could not visit the Alaska Mission. After Van Gorp performed this service, he returned to St. Ignatius, Montana, to serve as superior of the mission.

De la Motte left for Europe in the middle of July. While he was there events in Seattle indicated that Jesuit persistence was beginning to pay off. In 1901 the school first adopted the use of "Seattle College" in reference to itself and a Loyola shield for its coat of arms and college button. "The design," a correspondent reported, "resembles that of St. Xavier's College, Cincinnati, the pot and wolves with the bars in the centre [sic] and around it Seattle College, the college colors are blue and white."[32]

The attendance at Seattle College in 1902 reached one hundred. "An idea of the progress and proficiency of the students can be obtained from the perusal of the Seattle College Journal, a neat pamphlet published at the close of last year."[33] A public elocution contest was conducted "in a large hall of the city" and two gold medals were awarded. At the closing exercises in a Seattle theatre, readings in Latin, Greek and English were presented and the faculty, if not the students, concluded that these bookish fireworks "drew a great deal of notice to our college." A successful mission had been held in the parish and Father Matthew Woods, a member of the college faculty, had built "a neat little church at Bremerton and attends the Navy Yard there. He occasionally says Mass on the warships and his visits are of great benefit to the U.S. sailors. The Church of Bremerton (called Church of the Star of the Sea) was dedicated Sunday, Sept. 28 (1902)."[34]

Jesuits were busy organizing parishes in other cities. Father Aloysius Soer, the short Jesuit from Holland who looked like the Cure d'Ars with cheeks as red as apples, built St. Augustine's Church in Russell, Idaho. At that time Soer was attached to the Nez Perce Mission at Slickpoo, where he preached in broken Dutch-English. Later, in 1905, he was transferred to Holy Family Mission and preached there in the same manner, Sunday after Sunday. The Indians said they did not mind, even if they could not understand him. They said he himself was the best sermon.

In Butte, Montana, Father Gaspar Giacaloni organized Holy Savior parish, which was predominantly Italian.[35] Construction on a church was begun, but priests from the Helena diocese took over the parish before it was completed. In Harlem, on the Montana High Line, the nimble-footed Eberschweiler built St. Stephen's Church for both Indians and Whites there; and at Barnabee, Washington, on a lonely site on the Columbia River, Father Edward Griva assembled St. Gabriel's Church. Griva, a newcomer from Italy, who had entered the Order in 1894 as a diocesan priest, suffered from two overwhelming compulsions, building churches with tin ceilings and cluttering them with many plaster statues. Each church, he built twelve of them, looked so much alike that one could tell at a glance that it was a "Griva Church." They were always made of wood, painted white and shaped like a boot, the toe being a small sacristy filled with processional paraphernalia and a primitive all-purpose room for the priest.

De la Motte was delayed in Europe, fortuitously as it turned out, for he was able, before his embarkation to attend to his mother in her dying hours. He reached home on the train which "went so fast that, at times, it seemed that it hardly touched the rails. No accident, thank God!"[36] He had brought with him six new recruits, of whom he was excessively proud, like a cat with a new batch of kittens. He left soon for a tour of the missions, encountering as he traveled a host of possible disasters, all avoided "by the holy Mother of God."

When he visited the Coeur d'Alenes he discovered that his Indian vocabulary was "rusty" but this was soon overshadowed by his admiration for the Soldiers of the Sacred Heart. "We have elected a police captain," he reported. "It was very impressive. The police to the number of fifteen are the police of the Sacred Heart. They watch over the reservation."[37] De la Motte failed to mention that the soldiers sometimes carried whips, which they used when a member of the tribe got out of hand. "The new captain," he said, "is very fervent and strong. He fears nothing; is a true Coeur d'Alene. My only worry on his account is that he acts a little too briskly. For example, about a month ago he learned that a woman had run away and was in Spokane. He set out for Spokane on horseback, rode all night without a companion, arrived in Spokane, found the woman, arrested her on the street, made her get on his horse, attached to her leg a ball thirty pounds in weight, and took her back to the reservation to the amazement of the Whites who saw him do so."[38] This was Bonaventure, "a proud Christian I assure you," a bit "too brisk," as anyone will agree.

De la Motte's headquarters were Spokane, but he was seldom home. Crimont, whom he trusted implicitly, filled in for him. Recognizing the personal ability of Crimont and the growth of the college, Father General had raised his canonical status from that of superior to that of rector. Thus on December 24, 1902, Crimont became in fact the Jesuits' first northwest rector, though the documents appointing him did not arrive in Spokane until January 13, 1903.[39]

Another form of recognition took place during the following spring. On May 26, President Theodore Roosevelt visited Spokane. When reports of the impending visit here circulated, many local organizations, eager for a little gold-plated attention, appealed to the committee in charge for a share in the day's activities. Understandably, everyone wanted to get into the act, though it was perfectly obvious that the scheduled four-hour visit could not possibly include a forty-hour round of teetotaling toasts.

Crimont, like others, applied for an opportunity to welcome the president and was informed that Roosevelt would arrive at 2:35 P.M. via the Oregon Railroad and Navigation Company train. He would leave the train at the Hamilton Street crossing at Broadway and his carriage would pass the college and the Monaghan residence on Boone Avenue where the home of the hero of Samoa would be pointed out to him. The committee in charge was not hopeful that the president's carriage would stop at the college. There was to be a parade down Riverside Avenue, a speech at Riverside and Lincoln, a visit to Fort Wright and Senator Turner's home for punch and cookies, a brief speech to the school children at Coeur d'Alene Park and finally, before departure, a ceremony of laying the cornerstone for the new Spokane Amateur Athletic Club building. Any further concessions would depend upon the president's secretary, Mr. Loeb.

Though the prospect of entertaining President Roosevelt was unlikely, Crimont made elaborate preparations to welcome him. Flags and bunting stretched from one end of the building to the other. A large painting of the president was installed over the entrance of the college. Flowers were gathered for presentation and a Latin poem was composed by Father Henry McCulloch.

When May 26 finally dawned, Spokane was all aflutter. An estimated twenty-thousand visitors poured into the city. All business stopped dead. School was dismissed. The children, six thousand of them, dressed in white suits or dresses with red sashes and blue caps, gathered in Coeur d'Alene Park to await the president. Secret service men patrolled all the streets of passage and all the bridges were placed under guard. It had been only two years since the president's predecessor, William McKinley, had been assassinated, and civil authorities were taking no chances. A special Studebaker carriage imported from Portland awaited the president, and flags were in evidence everywhere, some were even draped around dogs.

The presidential train was enroute from Coeur d'Alene to Spokane. Someone, so the fathers were told, casually remarked within the hearing of the president, that certain people in Spokane were intolerant toward Catholics. Roosevelt, an intimate friend and admirer of Cardinal Gibbons, became immediately aroused. He wanted to know if there was a Catholic college in Spokane. When informed about Gonzaga, he said he wanted to stop there. Someone protested. This would require changes in the schedule. "Then change the schedule," Roosevelt snapped.

Thus it happened that President Roosevelt's Studebaker made its first stop at Gonzaga college. The school diary describes the aftermath:

"H. [his] E. [excellency] the President arrived in Spokane about 3 o'cock P.M. He passed in front of the College, where our Cadets rendered military honors and all our pupils were lined in front of the College and the Fathers, Teachers and Scholastics with their cassocks on, were at the entrance. Fr. Rector presented him with a beautiful bouquet together with a poem of welcome, having on its first page a latin inscription, saying at the same time a few appropriate words. Fr. Rector was accompanied by the two captains of the cadets. The President rose in his carriage and said: "I thank you, Father, the Faculty and the students of Gonzaga College. I appreciate the gift you have given and I appreciate still more the words you have uttered and the sincerity of your devotion."[40]

After leaving the college, Roosevelt followed the schedule prepared by the committee, though he was forced to omit the children's speech and the cornerstone ceremony. He left the city at precisely the time arranged, flashing his brightest gold-toothed smile. "Goodby, boys," he called and his train pulled slowly eastward amid the farewell cheers of a vast crowd.

Gonzaga's student enrollment had steadily increased over the years. During the term 1900–1901 it reseached 244, which appeared in those days to be something like the Gregorian. It was admittedly the largest Catholic college in the Northwest, and among the largest Jesuit colleges in the United States. At this time even historic Georgetown had only three hundred students and Santa Clara, which celebrated its golden jubilee during this term, counted but a few more students than Gonzaga.*

With the steady increase there was proportionate concern about space. "Space fever," a kind of occupational disease for colleges, now afflicted the administration and opened the door to prolonged discussion and planning. In February, 1903, Crimont revealed to the public that plans for a one-hundred-thousand dollar addition to the new college building were being prepared in the office of Preusse and Zittel.

Crimont's estimate was modest. As the plans developed during the following months, the architects doubled the amount of the original estimate, assuring their clients in the same shocking moments that the new estimate would produce an addition worthy in every respect of the original structure.

A west wing similar in style to the east was also projected. As first conceived, this would have formed one building extending along Boone Avenue from Astor to Standard, a length of seven-hundred feet. At the west end, where St. Aloysius Church now stands, the architects placed a large collegiate church similar in design to the gymnasium on the east. Except for the church, this west annex never materialized. Plans for the east annex, when finally completed, demanded a revised estimate, which now reached $250,000, two-and-a-half times the original estimate.

This, of course, was reason for pause. Taking a deep breath, Crimont, with the approval of his superiors, borrowed the needed money and instructed the architects to proceed with construction. Ground was broken for the new addition on Monday, July 13, 1903.[41]

At this time Crimont's vice president was Father Francis Dillon, a builder like Van Gorp and an unusually astute man in matters of business. Born and raised in Maryland, he later became Gonzaga's first American-born president, succeeding Crimont, when the latter was appointed Prefect Apostolic of Alaska. Dillon took charge of the new building program and personally supervised construction with his foreman, M. C. Murphy.† Excavations to provide a granite foundation similar to the original structure required several months. The foundations, extending an additional 255 feet along Boone, were laid by the following March. The superstructure was begun during the week of March 20, 1904, and by this time Dillon was so preoccupied with his records of how many nails and screws were required that he neglected entries in the college diary. The *Spokesman-Review* for March 22 informed its readers that the brick for "the enormous addition to the college" was already on the ground, the lumber was being delivered, and the iron was expected soon. Nothing was said about the arrival of the money to build it, and, unlike our times, no campaign was waged to collect it. Crimont appealed to de la Motte for the help he needed. Though he was given substantial aid by the mission, a debt of over $100,000 was not liquidated for many years.

---

*A listing of students in U.S. Jesuit Colleges for October 1, 1901, appears in *Woodstock Letters*, 30 (1901), p. 332. At this time the College of St. Francis Xavier in New York was largest with 653 students. Santa Clara had 217 students, and St. Ignatius, San Francisco, had 249 students.

†Murphy, shortly after the completion of the new wing, mysteriously disappeared. His connections with the college were given some attention at the time.

De la Motte, taking a little time from his letter writing, had been in attendance when President Roosevelt made his appearance at Gonzaga. He sometimes complained about the piles of letters he received twice daily. "During my term of office," he wrote to his father, "I have written a few more than *3,400 letters,* in less than four years; and mind you, during my tour of Europe, which lasted four months, and my two Alaska journeys, which (together) lasted eight months, I have not so to say written such letters."[42] He composed his own correspondence by longhand, a script as dainty and tidy as a nun's, rarely keeping copies for the files.

The second trip to Alaska, mentioned above, was made in 1903. On June 9, accompanied by Van Gorp, he left for Seattle by train, then sailed to Skagway "at the foot of a terrible mountain." The two Jesuits boarded another train to take White Pass to the Klondike, then embarked again on the Yukon for Eagle City where Father Monroe was still engaged with his miners. "The poor father," de la Motte said, and using an odd expression, he went on, "is all alone for more than nine hundred miles. He sees Jesuits only once a year. . . . His house and little chapel are exquisitely neat. To fill in his free time he has built a little hospital where he himself takes care of the patients."[43]

Monroe had purchased the two log cabins, one for a church and one for a home, for $300 "from a Catholic family ready to leave the country."[44] He dedicated his mission to St. Francis Xavier, and turned several lots into a garden which mostly supported him. At the end of one year his receipts from the parish amounted to $151 and his expenses over $1,000. He himself buried his patients who died. Once every year, with a sack on his back, he visited all the miners in his care, a journey of six hundred miles, mostly on foot, through the brush that swarmed with mosquitoes.

When de la Motte visited him in 1903, Monroe requested approval for moving the mission to Tanana, where gold had been discovered during the previous winter. Most of his people had left for the new El Dorado, 350 miles distant, down the river from Eagle City. De la Motte hesitated, then responded negatively, so Monroe remained. In the following year, however, when Crimont who had succeeded Rene as Prefect Apostolic visited the mission, he closed it and took Monroe with him when he left.[45]

At Nulato, de la Motte had sad news for Jette. He had been recalled to his own mission in Canada. Perplexed by the summons, the more so because his health was excellent, Jette left Alaska "this blessed soil," for Winnipeg. He was assigned to the Jesuit College affiliated with the University of Manitoba, where he was to teach mathematics.[46] He was a rare genius in this science as well as in linguistics and he liked his subject. But Winnipeg was not Alaska, to which his heart belonged, so he consciously affected eccentricities to discourage his tenure. He wore moccasins in class and smoked a foul-smelling pipe. He refused to wear his biretta at table, saying he was only a guest in the house.* When free from other duties he prepared for the press his first work to be published in Ten'a, a little booklet of prayers and hymns called *Yoyit Rokanoga.* Having completed this, he was pleased to learn that his request to return to Alaska had been received favorably by the Canadian superior. In the summer of 1904 he left the land of his "exile," which was the land of his birth, and he never saw it again. He lost no time in racing back to the mosquitoes and the battered log residence at Nulato.

Meanwhile de la Motte continued his visitation. On July 27, 1903, at Holy Cross, he wrote again to his father, "I am very well and I admit in a whisper that I am more and more enthused over Alaska. I hope to live and die here."[47] He had succumbed at last to the dread disease, "Alaska," but he would die of something else and much sooner than he expected.

*It was customary to wear the biretta (an ecclesiastical hat which symbolized status) on formal occasions, including the principal meals. Only visitors were excused from this custom.

His visitation was half over. Impatient to be home, he hurried with the last half, spending only twenty-four hours in Akulurak and not much more at St. Michael's and Nome. In the latter he met for the first time Father Bellarmine Lafortune, a short, chunky French Canadian who was as tough as Jette, whom he replaced, was learned. Lafortune feared nothing and it was commonly known that all the animals, including Nome's countless half-wild dogs, feared him. The dogs squatted or slept where they chose on the board walk and everybody except Lafortune walked around them. When Lafortune appeared, the dogs cleared the way for him; he was that kind of man. Another French Canadian at Nome was Father Edward Devine, former editor in Montreal of the *Messenger of the Sacred Heart*. He remained in Alaska long enough, like some school teachers and government bureaucrats, to write a book about it.[48] But it was Lafortune who made history, and only sometimes wrote about it. In his first year he sent a lively report on Jacquet's cross to Woodstock Letters, "[Our church's] cross becomes more and more famous. During the long winter nights, when the poor travellers are exposed to go astray on the trail, it serves them as a light house; for the cross is covered with electric lamps, and thus illuminated it may be seen from twenty-five miles around. It has already saved a life of three or four travellers."[49]

Doubtlessly impressed by this, de la Motte preferred to comment on Nome's gold. "It is found in the streets, under the moss, everywhere."[50] Leaving it reluctantly, for the mission had many debts, he returned to Spokane in early September, where he learned from Bishop Brondel that a Gonzaga student in Helena, unable because of a fatal sickness to return to school, longed to die as a Jesuit. The bishop pleaded the cause of the dying boy so eloquently, that de la Motte permitted him to pronounce his Jesuit vows. Clad in his Jesuit cassock he died. His grave in the Catholic cemetery of Helena is adorned with a marble slab bearing the inscription, Joseph Leo Perry, S.J.[51]

There was other bad news. Young Father Sansone, superior of St. Stephen's Mission in Wyoming, had taken sick, also, and was not expected to recover for some months. De la Motte was determined to spend the winter at St. Stephen's as a substitute. This was not as altruistic as it appeared. He was eager to settle down somewhere for a spell, where Jesuits could not bother him and this he could do at St. Stephen's without a scruple about running away from his job. Besides, he had become very fond of the Arapahoe children there.

He left Spokane on Wednesday, September 30, for St. Ignatius where he arrived the same evening. There was an epidemic of measles in the school. Brother Carignano was still painting murals in the church but the weather had turned too cold for him to work. On Saturday it snowed in the hills and this made the brothers nervous because the potatoes had not been dug yet. On Monday night, October 5, de la Motte, as apprehensive as a boy who reads too much about outlaws, boarded the Northern Pacific at Ravalli and, tingling with the thrill of what might happen in "the reign of terror" on the railroad, settled down for the night. Later he wrote, "Bandits infested the state of Montana, and got the idea of terrorizing the managers of the great road-line. In [an] anonymous letter [they] made it known that if by October 1st., the sum of $25,000 was not deposited near Helena, they would blow with dynamite and destroy the property of the said company. On the day named, the locomotive set out for the appointed place with sacks filled with rocks. One mile behind another locomotive followed with a car filled with armed men and hounds raised to chase men. Unluckily the second engine made too much noise, and the bandits did not show themselves in the rendezvous. The same day they derailed three trains, and sent a new letter announcing that if on the 6th of October there were not sent to them $50,000 instead of the $25,000 in good and beautiful gold, they would wreck the railroad all along Montana: tunnels, bridges, stations, trains, everything. The railroad is managed by men who do not get scared. At the cost of great sacrifices, a skillfull defense was organized.

Armed guards were posted along the railroad (at least 1500 men). Every bridge and tunnel was guarded; every train accompanied by a locomotive which went along on reconnaissance, and hounds were in the depots ready to follow the scent of evildoers, if they should discharge dynamite."[52] In the end de la Motte admitted that he fell asleep "without being sure that I should wake up in the morning on this earth. But nothing happened. It rained all night." On the contrary, while he slept the train jumped the track near Helena, a pile of dynamite was discovered in a tunnel, and a "formidable" posse was organized to capture the bandits, who were trying to escape into Canada without the beautiful gold.

One concludes from the tone of de la Motte's narrative that he took some delight in danger. If Joset and Cataldo had survived the Indian wars, and Robaut a couple of murders in Alaska, then he, de la Motte from Britanny, had survived the war of the wicked bandits.

The Arapahoes' chief had a dozen wives. De la Motte did not like the Arapahoes' title for God: "The Pale-face on High." But the visit was a success all the same, and the children "were all weeping" when he left prematurely on December 9. By train and sleigh he went to the Crow mission. "No wolves this time. Last year we had an escort of four enormous grey wolves."[53] He hurried back to Spokane for Christmas.

News from Alaska was bad. About midnight on November 30, Robaut, alone in his mission at Okraramut on the Kuskokwim, awoke almost suffocated by smoke. Even the floor was burning under his feet when he jumped out of bed. He ran out in his nightshirt to call for help, but before anything could be done, the whole house was a mass of fire. Nothing was saved. Robaut lost all of his possessions, including his priceless language manuscripts. As he stood in his bare feet in the snow, watching many years of research and labor go up in flames, he was heard to cry, "My papers, my papers." Almost overcome with grief and anxiety about the villages he would have to abandon for some time, he borrowed enough clothes from the Indians to travel to Holy Cross.[54] Robaut recovered from this disaster and started again to compose grammars and dictionaries in the Eskimo language. These have survived, mute but inspiring testimonials not only to his industry and knowledge, but even more to his heroic sense of duty.

Thus the year 1903 ended, on a sad but stirring note. De la Motte's Jesuits had made a little history on the parish level; for example, de Rouge from Omak had built the first church in Chelan; and Folchi, still energetic at seventy, had built the first church in Wenatchee. Several milestones in local church history had been reached. In February, Bishop O'Dea had moved his residence from Vancouver to Seattle, where in October his new home burned down. His Excellency was followed by another celebrity, Mother Francis Xavier Cabrini, who descended on Seattle as lightly as a bird on October 17, to establish an orphanage. On November 11 America's first canonized citizen appeared in Superior Court Seattle, where she applied for citizenship papers. Bishop O'Dea, contrary to some accounts, was pleased to have her and her sisters, and he offered the first Mass in their new home.[55]

Meanwhile in June, the Diocese of Baker City, Oregon, was established by a decree of Pius X. Father Charles O'Reilly of Portland was consecrated as its first bishop on August 25. Bishop Brondel, old pioneer and intimate associate of Palladino, died piously in the Lord on November 3, just after de la Motte found seclusion at St. Stephens.

Archbishop Christie of Portland, who had seen two of his priests elevated to the hierarchy, O'Dea and O'Reilly, wanted to meet de la Motte in Portland in January. When the latter responded, he little realized how loaded with import this meeting might be. "I remained eight hours in Portland," he reported, "long enough to see nothing."[56] He had little to add. He would not say publicly that the Jesuits wanted to establish a school in Portland and that the archbishop favored it, but vacillated when it came time to sign the required papers.

INTRODUCING DE LA MOTTE

De la Motte went back to the missions. He began to realize "one is not made of iron," he would have to give up the idea of going to Alaska. "The poor fathers are going to grumble," he added, it was important that he spend more time in the Rocky Mountains.

One of his best friends would take his place in the north. On Pentecost Sunday, May 22, 1904, while the last of the bricks and mortar of the new addition at Gonzaga were being slapped into place, the Jesuits were startled to hear that Crimont had been appointed prefect apostolic of Alaska, succeeding Rene. On the following day a brief communication from the general superior de la Motte appeared on the community bulletin board, "Father Raphael Crimont having been called by holy obedience to Alaska, Father Francis Dillon is hereby appointed Vice Rector of Gonzaga, said appointment to last until Very Rev. Fr. General is pleased to name a new Rector."[57] Since Crimont wanted to go to Alaska anyway, the reference to "holy obedience" appears to be harsh. This was the customary expression, however, and no one took it too seriously.

Dillon's temporary assignment as Vice Rector was confirmed by Rome, without doubt to keep the way clear for another rector when the building project was completed. Rebmann, pastor of the parish, was not immediately affected by the change, but on St. Ignatius day, July 31, he was replaced by Mackin, who had succeeded him years before as president. If the first replacement of Rebmann had been embarrassing to him, this second was worse, for it seemed to be commonly understood that Mackin was brought in to solve the problem of a large church. The implications were obvious.

Dillon had a great deal to think about. Enrollment in September, 1904 had reached 353, an all time high and an increase of thirty percent over the previous year. Work on the east wing had progressed more rapidly than he had expected, which meant that in October the classroom-dormitory section could be occupied. The worst was over but Dillon, as superior of the scholasticate, treasurer for the Rocky Mountain Mission, and president of the college, was swamped with so much work he had no time to worry about the unfinished portion. All the same, by December 20, the gymnasium was finally opened to the boys, who soon demonstrated their preference for this part of the new building. No one, except the teachers, seemed to be very happy about the new classrooms and chapel.

What had happened, meanwhile, to Aloysius Parodi, whom de la Motte had sent back to Spokane? Parodi had waited at St. Michael's Mission for the superior's return, forty-three days, he said. "Five brothers were busy from morning to night, in the farm, in the garden, on the horchard [sic] and in the kitchen to supply the college in Spokane with fruits and vegetables."[58] De la Motte eventually arrived to rescue him from what he called "a rest too soon," and sent him to Yakima with the words, "I send you to your cradle."

Parodi succeeded Griva in the care of the missions for both Indians and Canadians in the Yakima Valley. Griva "the young, stout little Father" had lived in relative comfort at Fort Simcoe and buzzed about the territory in a buggy, bringing spiritual care to twelve settlements, five of them Indian. Feusi, whom Parodi especially admired, was pastor at Yakima and builder of the new church. When Taelman was pastor in 1900, he had begun construction of this new stone church, but according to Parodi, it was Feusi who gathered the materials and laid the foundation, "which is the most difficult task in the building."[59] Progress was slow. On May 22, 1904, the cornerstone was blessed, finally, by Bishop O'Dea, and by the end of November the entire structure was under roof. Father Conrad Brusten, who became a kind of permanent fixture at St. Joseph's, like Father Francis Schoenberg at a later period, offered the first Mass in the new church on May 21, 1905.*

---

*Father Brusten faithfully kept a diary for many years. In May 1946 I found one volume of the diary in use at the telephone where it served as a writing pad. Needless to say, all the diaries that survived were deposited in the Province Archives.

Parodi had his own flocks to care for, scattered over several thousand square miles. Griva had built churches in Prosser and Moxee. In other "Canadian settlements" like Belma, Parodi offered Mass in the local school or in the homes of his parishioners. Moxee was "a settlement of about 80 Canadian Catholic families, and they were large families," including the Regimbals who had fifteen children. "Two of his girls are, as Protestants say, Sisters of the Providence denomination."[60] Parodi often had dinner with the Menager family in Belma and he has left a detailed and very humorous account of what he observed.

It should be noted that the Menagers, whose three sons became Jesuits, had departed from their home in Nantes, France, because of the cruel anti-Catholic laws enforced by the government. Dr. Edouard and Madame Henriette Menager sailed from France for Montreal with twelve of their fourteen children in May 1902.[61] They first settled at Duck Lake in Saskatchewan, but the climate was too severe for Madame, and they moved to Belma in the Yakima Valley a year later. Dr. Menager tried to conduct a farm, without much success. About this time, Father Alphonsus Couffrant, "the jolly monk," came to visit them. They were later visited by Griva, and finally by Parodi. The latter, especially, made a great impression on the older boys. When de la Motte became ill in the latter part of 1904, some one suggested that he visit his countryman, Dr. Menager at Belma.

In February, 1905, he wrote, "For some months I have much to do with the family of Dr. Edward Menager from Nantes (in Brittany) who emigrated to the United States. . . . Since I am in (his) hands, I am getting much better. He understands my case, and promises me that one year from now he will have me restored to health."[62] De la Motte was whistling to reassure himself as he passed the graveyard. He had always bewailed his lack of Jesuits. He had more now, which made for him, not less, but more work. Apparently that was his problem and it would not go away.

The entire mission was bursting with energy. In Seattle, for example, the parish church had been moved from the college campus to a new site. Since the bishop had transferred his residence and built a new cathedral in Seattle, he demanded that the Jesuits reestablish their church "beyond 18th avenue" to allow room for the Cathedral parish. Not in the least miffed about it, Father Sweere purchased land on 18th and Marion, just beyond the forbidden ground, and built a huge new Immaculate Conception Church which still dominates one of Seattle's skylines. The cornerstone was laid, with some pomp and ceremony on May 15, 1904 and dedication solemnities were celebrated on December 4.[63] At this time the church boasted of a seating capacity of 950, a far cry from the Kingdome, but it was then the city's largest auditorium, or people place. Its debt was equally impressive, $65,000, a lot of cash that forecast an endless round of fund-raising entertainments, card parties and raffles. Sweere, as often happens when somebody spends a lot of money he does not have, was transferred to Yakima and Gonzaga's Father Dillon, who was already recognized as the province's unofficial trouble shooter, became pastor in his place. He became superior of Seattle College, also.

After the parish had vacated its original quarters at the college, the building was renovated to provide more classrooms. It would be sometime, however, before the school could build two floors where the church had occupied a double-high floor space. This meant, of course, that in the interim one-fourth of the college's potential floor space was unavailable.

In Alaska, too, the Jesuits were building a new parish church. When Father Monroe left Eagle City with Crimont on June 21, 1904, he accompanied him by boat to Barnette's Trading Post on the Chena River, where they arrived on July 1. A new gold strike during the previous year, 1903, had attracted hundreds of miners to the Chena, and, from the appearances of the camp, Crimont predicted that many would remain. He ordered Monroe to build a church there, then departed by boat, leaving Monroe on the bank of the Chena, penniless, landless and forlorn. The season for building in Alaska was already late.

The camp at Barnette's Landing was over-crowded, spread out along the south side of the slough. Other camps were formed, each claiming to be the best site for a permanent city. District Judge James Wickersham, however, decided to establish his court at Barnette's Landing and suggested that its name be changed to Fairbanks. Since judges have more influence than prospectors, his suggestion was adopted and Fairbanks came into being.*

Monroe now cast about for money and land. Having formed a committee to gather the one, he tramped up and down the river searching for the other. After several anxious weeks, he found and bought a site at the eastern edge of town. By this time he had $3,051 in his building fund, less than half of the estimate required. He started construction with this, encountering as he progressed, exorbitant costs and shortages of material. Only one keg of nails could be found in the whole town and it cost $50. So his carpenters, who worked for the highly inflationary cost of $1.50 per hour, used eight-penny nails through the edifice, which, alas! was on the wrong side of the river.

Finally occupied, if not completed, it had cost $6,512 "without paint." Monroe, during construction, continued to visit other mining camps, including Eagle City and Circle, where he had small churches, and Cleary, Nenana, and Iditarod, where he built churches when he was able. He continued to collect money wherever he found it, paid off the debt on the Fairbanks church, which was called the Immaculate Conception, and installed a library and reading room in its basement, where miners could take refuge during the bitterly cold winter.

Father Cataldo had left Alaska when Monroe left Eagle City. More or less frustrated in his determination to produce a grammar in the Koyukon language, he returned to Slickpoo where he found three Sisters of St. Joseph in a state of near collapse due to overwork. With de la Motte's approval he hurried to Philadelphia to make an appeal for more sisters at the motherhouse. There were none to be had, so he appealed to the Jesuits in Philadelphia for permission to preach in their church called "The Gesu." After three weeks he returned again to Slickpoo with twelve postulants, nicknamed with dull humor, "The Twelve Apostles." Michael O'Malley, a scholastic from Ireland was at Slickpoo when they arrived.

"The influx of volunteers," he wrote, "The Twelve Apostles from Philadelphia at once woke up Sleepy Slickpoo. Help came from the east, donations and food for awhile. Then a novitiate was established by proper authority. News spread in the east, and other volunteers came, and others."[64]

Cataldo's success was the envy of other missionaries and his example was not lost on some. De Rouge at St. Mary's took special note, since he needed help desperately for his recently established school.

Cataldo was already seventy-eight in years. Van Gorp would be seventy-one on his next birthday, June 11, 1905. On April 2, de la Motte was informed that Van Gorp was critically ill with pneumonia, the result of fatigue and a neglected cold. Late at night on April 7, the "Tall Blackrobe" died, and all of the rosy dreams about a college in Helena died with him. Henceforth Jesuits would look west and south, not east of Spokane, for their future.

Bishop O'Reilly in Oregon, to the south, was becoming more vocal about his need for priests and de la Motte, persuaded at last to help him, directed Feusi at Yakima to take over the beginnings of a parish at Klamath Falls. Feusi arrived on June 30, 1905, the Feast of the Sacred Heart that year. This happy coincidence prompted him to dedicate his church under the title of the Sacred Heart.

*Details about the Fairbanks church can be found in *Diamond Jubilee* by Rev. E.A. Anable, S.J. and Mrs. Margaret Crogan, (Fairbanks, 1979).

Feusi had learned a few tricks since his scrape with the Curry gang at St. Paul's. Now he lost no time in organizing his new parishioners. Five days after his arrival the new church was begun. All the material had been donated by local businessmen. Completed on All Saints Day of the same year, it was dedicated by Bishop O' Reilly on June 30, 1907.

Meanwhile Feusi busied himself with systematic visits to the outlying districts of Klamath and counties, preparing children for First Communion, rectifying marriages, saying Mass in farmhouses, and instructing the scattered sheep of his flock. In August, traveling more than one hundred miles from Klamath in a public conveyance called "the stage," he first visited Lakeview. He found many Irishmen there from County Cork, and nearly all of them were sheepherders in the adjoining range country. Some of these were very anxious to see the priest; others did not practice their religion at all, and a few belonged to forbidden societies. Feusi mustered the few he could find in town into the old courthouse, and there he shrived them and said Mass to refresh their souls.

It was Michael O'Malley who eventually took over the care of the Irishmen of Lakeview. In 1905 he was at Slickpoo with Cataldo learning Nez Perce and prefecting boys. "Then one afternoon in October of that year 1905, in the delightful season of Indian Summer, when the air was warm and still in the afternoons, and only a solitary Indian drum could be heard in the distance, Fr. Cataldo came to me in the tiny parlor and said, 'Mr. O'Malley, I want you to come to this parlor each afternoon for some time, and write what I shall dictate to you.' It was his own history. Each afternoon he dictated."[65] This was O'Malley's last year as a scholastic at Slickpoo. He left the following year to study theology in The Sheds at Gonzaga.

At Gonzaga, Dillon had been succeeded by Father Herman Goller, who became the school's tenth president on July 31, 1905. Born of well-to-do parents in Hagen, Westphalia, on September 19, 1867, Goller entered the Jesuit Novitiate at Blyenbeck, Holland, on September 30, 1886, one year before Gonzaga opened its doors. Later he offered himself for the Rocky Mountain Mission, studied his courses of philosophy at Woodstock College, then arrived in Spokane in 1891 to prefect and teach boys. He returned to Woodstock for theology in 1896 and was ordained to the priesthood there three years later. Before occupying the president's chair at Gonzaga, he had served successively as prefect of studies and vice-president. Without a doubt Goller was the most popular of all Jesuits associated with Gonzaga's early history and his popularity with his brother Jesuits was indicated by the high offices he held as a German in a peer group dominated by French and Italian Jesuits.

Very heavy, with a surplus chin or two, Goller presented the image of a genial Dutch baker. His thin eyebrows and curly hair suggested an age that flattered him and is great fondness for cigars endeared him to the older boys, who looked upon him as a kind of good-humored guru. His heart was as large as his head and accounted partly, it would appear, for his forty-four inch waistline. The weight, and perhaps the cigars, got him in the end.

Spokane newspapers were very fond of quoting Father Goller. This was doubtlessly due to his optimistic outlook on things and a certain boyish frankness that completely disarmed everyone he met. He was often involved in newspaper polemics to which he brought an amiable kind of tolerance that conceded everything except the argument.

One must not think that because of Goller's cheerfulness that he was conducting a four-ring circus for the 483 students that year. There was no indication whatever of a letup on discipline or the tortures of the classroom. Indeed, the catalogue for Goller's first year, 1905–1906, presents a no-nonsense appearance that would have frightened away any wandering school tramps who were looking for an easy college. On the other hand, the president's genial appearance was reassuring and no one, least of all himself, expected the catastrophe that almost destroyed the school.

At this time de la Motte persuaded the Menagers to move to Spokane where the doctor could establish his practice and serve as one of the medics for the college. Accordingly, they transferred cartons of their baggage, many of which had never been opened since they left France, a whole freight carload, plus their twelve children, to Spokane in the autumn of 1905 and took possession of a large frame house at 730 East Boone Avenue. Menager joined Dr. Walter Webb as a college physician, and when the great catastrophe struck, Dr. Patrick Byrne, father of Neil Byrne, assisted them.

But first there was Palladino's bell. It seems that in November 1905, during the pastorate of Father Palladino, enthusiastic parishioners at St. Francis Xavier in Missoula, presented him with $500 as a gift for his golden jubilee as a Jesuit. This wasn't all they gave him, but the money was something he had to think about. He reflected on it, consulted his superiors and the people, and finally decided to do what he wanted to do all along. He ordered a Jubilee Bell, which weighed two hundred and seventy pounds more than a ton. It was cast in St. Louis with the following inscription in Latin, "Oh ye Blessed Lawrence, Benedict, Francis, Ignatius, protect Missoula. I praise, I remind, I mourn: Praising God, The Best, The Greatest, Reminding the Living, Mourning the Dead, I willingly Spend the Life Which the Pastor's Golden Jubilee in the Society of Jesus Brought to Me." Saints Lawrence and Benedict are the saints after whom Father Palladino was named in baptism. St. Francis is the patron of the parish and St. Ignatius the founder of the Jesuit Order of which Father Palladino had been a member for fifty years.

Bishop Carroll, who had succeeded Bishop Brondel, blessed the bell on February 18, 1906, and it was mounted on a special campanile because it was thought to be too heavy for the church tower. Two years later, however, the new pastor, Father Trivelli, decided to risk it and the bell was installed in the church tower where it has been ever since, *praising, reminding,* and *mourning*. The old bell meanwhile was removed and mounted over St. Joseph's school, where its sweet tones might have sounded sour to the little boys who had to respond to its call.

The catastrophe at Gonzaga started in mid-April, 1906. A considerable number of students manifested a general physical sluggishness and complained of headaches. Somewhat alarmed, the college infirmarian, Brother Anthony Broderick, called Dr. Webb, who in turn called in Dr. Byrne for consultation. They agreed on the diagnosis: it was the dreaded typhoid fever. All of the boys were put under observation, but so far no serious cases had appeared. At the end of April three boys were sent home, and seven resident students were hospitalized in the college infirmary. Two days later, however, there were twenty-five in the infirmary. Though no one panicked, the city health officials were greatly alarmed. Attending doctors urged that the school be closed at once and that all students be sent home.[66]

Feeling helpless before this grim, invisible invasion, the usually irrepressible Goller could offer no alternative. He did what they asked. Calling together all the students who were not afflicted, he announced the termination of the school year without further formalities. There were no cheers. The students sensed the desperate nature of the situation and they left the gymnasium, speaking in hushed, excited words. That same day Goller mailed a letter to all parents.[67]

After these letters had been posted, Goller himself accompanied the Montana boys home, personally visiting as many parents as he possibly could. He returned to the college five days later, still anxious and deeply concerned about the boys in the infirmary. On May 21, Frank Fox of Nez Perce, Idaho, was the first boy to die of the disease. Father Kennelly, overcome with grief, like Goller, accompanied the body to the boy's home. A few days later Vincent Coltman died, then William Fox, brother of Frank. Thomas Desmond, a boy from Bonners Ferry, Idaho, who had entered Gonzaga with the intention of becoming a priest, was dying in his home. Taking a Jesuit cassock with him, Goller hurried to his side and wept without tears while Thomas pronounced his vows as a Jesuit. Thomas expired peacefully and was placed in his coffin, wearing a Jesuit cassock. His funeral was held at St. Aloysius Church with a choir of young scholastics chanting his requiem. Following this, two more boys died.

Then Father Prando, "Iron Eyes," the idol of the Crows, lay dying at St. Michael's Mission. At his side was Louis Taelman. "Is there anything bothering you?" Taelman asked gently. "No," Prando said, "In all of the years I've been on the mission, I have never forgotten that I am a priest. I have never done anything to dishonor my priesthood." He paused for a bit, then added, "I feel like a schoolboy going home for vacation. Though I haven't always been on my best behavior, I know that my Father will understand and will be happy to see me."* He was only sixty-one years old when he died on the eve of St. Aloysius Day. On June 22, he was buried from St. Aloysius Church. The Spokane Jesuits returned from the burial at St. Michael's with heavy hearts.

The city's germ detectives had not been idle. Every department of the college was thoroughly examined. Finally, on June 26 the City Health Department published an official statement. They had come to the conclusion that the typhoid epidemic had its beginnings in the college swimming pool, which had been constructed but three years earlier.

Though the infirmary had been sufficiently adequate for ordinary emergencies, the president was now determined to erect a separate building for the sick. He himself went out to beg for the necessary funds. He appointed the ever-resourceful Father Arthuis to supervise construction. A site was selected between the college and The Sheds, and foundations were begun immediately. The cost, first estimated to be $15,000 turned out to be almost double that. The new building, large enough to accommodate all of the casualties of a western Indian war, was occupied on February 11, 1907, much to the satisfaction of Goller, whose cheerful disposition had long since returned. He seemed to regard the new infirmary as a kind of fetish that would keep all epidemics away. Only once was it ever filled to capacity and that was during the flu epidemic of 1918. By then, Goller himself had died and was all but forgotten, except for his name on the building.†

During the typhoid epidemic the general in Rome, too, had died.‡ The newspapers made much of it, fabricating sensational accounts about the Black Pope and his alleged "influence at the Vatican."** It was all very mysterious, or worse, to most Spokane readers, who were properly informed by the local press that de la Motte would soon leave for Rome to participate in the election of Luis Martin's successor. During the late spring of 1906 province congregations were convened and the general congregation in September elected Father Francis Wernz, a noted canonist, who was destined to die "of a broken heart," because of the Vatican's distrust of him.††

De la Motte had participated in the election, then visited Pius X whom he admired almost excessively because of his position on the French "Separation Laws." Finally, before

*Related by Louis Taelman, S.J., June 1945.

†This infirmary building named Goller Hall survived many changes of function until it burned down during Easter week, March 24, 1970. Arson was suspected. *The Newsletter of the Oregon Province*, April, 1970, p. 4.

‡Father Luis Martin died in Rome on April 18, 1906.

**For example, *The Spokesman-Review*, May 22, 1906.

††Father Francis Xavier Wernz was elected general on September 8, 1906. He died on August 19, 1914 during the almost hysterical witch hunt for Modernists in Rome. On November 15, 1953, Father Leo Martin, who was in Rome at that time said to me, "Poor Father Wernz, they say he died of this or that. He didn't die of those things. He died of a broken heart. Oh, those were tense days!" From my personal journal for that day.

his return to the mission he paid his respects to his family for the last time. His father had died a few months earlier in February. Nothing, he discovered, was the same. He was impatient to be home.

In Spokane, Father Rebmann had built another church on the north side. Bishop O'Dea had split St. Aloysius parish for the second time in eight years and Rebmann had been assigned to organize the new parish, called St. Francis Xavier. Rebmann offered the first Mass in the new church on November 25, 1906, and on December 2, Father Goller, delegated by the bishop, dedicated it with appropriate speeches and blessings. On the same day the first Sunday School sessions were held. That was Rebmann's style: catechism for the children came first.

At this same time Folchi was completing another of his churches, too, one called St. Joseph, for the Austrian settlement at Jump Off near Chewelah. Folchi had most of two counties for his mission. He finally decided to make his residence at Newport, Washington, and there he built another church called St. Anthony at a cost of $35,000, which he begged from the lumberjacks. A list of his missions reads like a western guide book: Chewelah, Newport, Jump-Off, Loon Lake, Springdale, Colbert, Kulzer's Mill, Elk, Kortle's Ranch, Chattaroy, Cusick, Fan Lake, Milan, Frank's Ranch, Kalispel Indians, Scotia, Camas Prairie, Rattlesnake Prairie, Tum Tum, Everett Island, Buckeye, Schneider's Ranch, Calispel Valley, Lechner's Ranch, Wild Rose Prairie, Huckleberry Mountain, Walker's Prairie, and Chewelah Creek. He estimated that he had approximately 1,000 Catholic Whites and 180 Indians in his scattered parish. He was about seventy at this time and becoming irascible, which was unlike him, but quite understandable.

The year 1907 marked Gonzaga's twentieth anniversary and the Rocky Mountain Mission's sixty-sixth. The California mission was younger by nine years and smaller by forty-two Jesuits. De la Motte, already aware that changes were in the air, had turned his attention to the Portland area.

Father Cocchi, beloved by all, had been recalled to his province and he left The Sheds for Italy in a flood of regrets. Rene the former prefect apostolic was teaching theology in Latin with a French accent to scholastics who complained to de la Motte that they could not understand Rene. Several celebrities came to perform, including William Jennings Bryan who was riotously applauded. Griva was building another church shaped like a boot at Polson, Montana.

In Seattle on May 1 there was royal excitement when the college caught fire during classes. Only the upper floor of the Garrand building was destroyed, just enough to disrupt classes but not enough to call off school. Fortunately the basement of St. Joseph's church was available for some classes and the damaged building was made to do for the rest.

In the previous year this St. Joseph's Church had been built on Capitol Hill for the convenience of people there, as a kind of mission station of the Immaculate Conception parish. It was a sneaky way of starting another parish, but the bishop approved. Elegantly embellished by the murals of Brother Carignano, the church was formally dedicated on April 27, 1907, at which time Father Dillon sang a solemn Mass to complete the day's ceremonies. The same year the bishop declared St. Joseph's to be a new parish and Father Diomedi was appointed to be its first pastor.[68]

There was still the Portland area. Beaverton, a small town of several hundred people, mostly of German extraction, lay some ten miles west in the center of a fertile valley. The Beavertonians raised hops among other things, talked German at least part of the time, and went to and from Portland in an electric commuter train, operated by the Oregon Electric Company. The first Catholic church for these simple folk was located near Beaverton at a place called Cedar Mills. This church was begun in 1878, and was blessed on October 22,

1884, under the title of St. Anthony. Four years after the blessing, a school was also built and blessed. The Dominican Sisters, who were in charge of it, faithfully drummed the three "R's" into seventy-five little heads there every school day. In 1899, the Sisters of Mercy took over the school. By this time, there were more little heads, however, and a new convent had to be built.

In 1903, there were enough Catholics at Beaverton to arrange for a special Mass for them each Sunday, so the priest from Cedar Mills made this one of his regular "missions." This is the way matters stood on May 10, 1907, when the Jesuits took over. Father Joseph Tomkin, was the first Jesuit pastor. He found about three hundred Catholics in his parish, scattered over an area of about a five-mile radius. Within his parish and under his care, there was, also, a very fine orphanage, commonly called "the Home," which housed one-hundred-and-fifteen boys, and a diocesan congregation of sixty sisters.

After fifteen months of back-breaking labors and hardships, Tomkin, who did nothing by halves, was relieved of his burden at Beaverton, and William Deeney, was assigned to take his place. Deeney, an Irishman full of zeal and enterprise, decided the church at Beaverton was inadequate—which it was—so he started both a search for land and a building fund. A new parishioner donated a half-acre of land, the piece where the church now stands. To build up the fund, Deeney petitioned dear old St. Patrick, the saint who, today at least, summons up visions of entertainment and cheer. Deeney had a "Benefit Entertainment with *Portland* Talent" on March 17, 1909, a rather bold venture with so many Germans around. If he made any money that night, after treating his imported talent to a midnight snack, you may be sure it was the quality of the show and not the predisposed high spirits of his patrons.

Money for the fund was not easy to come by, and Deeney was having more than ordinary troubles in this way. Since he made many trips on the electric train to and from Portland, often two a day, the archbishop instructed him to apply for a pass to save expenses. The railroad declined to honor the archbishop's request, explaining that the church at Beaverton had an income and, therefore, Deeney had to pay. The archbishop's secretary, Father Thompson, retorted that Deeney was also chaplain at the orphanage. He further stated that a diocesan regulation required an institution to provide a buggy and feed for horses for the priest who came to say Mass, but how was Deeney to ask for this from the poor orphans? The Oregon Electric Company wanted everyone to know that they liked the orphans. In short, Deeney got the pass. He saved it as though it were a trophy. It is among the Beaverton papers in the Oregon Province Archives.[69]

When he first came to Beaverton, Deeney complained about the lack of fervor in his parish. In his report to superiors about a year later, he wrote that there was considerable improvement in this regard. In fact, the parish had begun to buzz with so much activity that Deeney said he needed an assistant. George Butler, pastor in Corvallis, where things were much quieter, was instructed to make his residence at Beaverton and to attend Corvallis from this place on weekends. When this was not enough help to cope with all the spiritual excitement, other Jesuits who had arrived in Portland by this time assisted in the parish on weekends.

These other Jesuits were Very Important Persons, for on August 15, 1907, an historic change had been made, the Rocky Mountain Mission and the California Mission had been merged, unlike modern corporations, without an exchange of shares of stock. De la Motte survived the shake-up; he remained the superior of both.

On July 13, 1907, he wrote to Father John Lucchesi, his vice-superior of Alaska at Holy Cross:

"I would have written you long ago, but I was waiting *daily* for the momentous decrees which are to decide the fate of our missions. They came in only yesterday.

"Upper Alaska (Alaska Borealis) is detached from the Turin Province and transferred to Canada *cum omnibus domiciliis, personis et debitis,* the transfer to take place on August 15.

"On the same day, the Rocky Mountains and California with lower Alaska are to be united under the name of 'California and Rocky Mountains Mission'. Fr. de la Motte is the new superior.

"On September 1st. the two Dakotas with all their persons, houses and debts will also join the Calif. and R. M. Mission.

"This is the tenor of the decree. As you see the *persons* are transferred to Canada, but to what extent I do not know."[70]

De la Motte further indicated that the decree was still confidential, not to be revealed until August 15, and that he would contact the provincial in Canada to arrange, if possible, for Lucchesi's attachment to his staff. "It is perfectly evident to me that I will not be able to govern efficiently the new immense mission of California and the R. M. Mission. The travelling alone will knock me over." He wanted Lucchesi to serve as his assistant in charge of the Indian missions.

De la Motte had his choice of cities for his residence. It will not be San Francisco, he said, nor Spokane. He had Portland in mind, but formalities with the archbishop there, had not yet been finalized. He had not given up on the idea of having a Jesuit school in Portland, although the Holy Cross Fathers had taken over the administration of the archdiocesan owned Columbia University in May 1902.[71] The Jesuits would settle for a parish in the city, and the archbishop was eager to give them one, perhaps to get them off his back on the school matter. The forthcoming merger of the west coast missions and the need for a residence in Portland prompted de la Motte to settle with the archbishop on St. Ignatius parish. Christie established definite boundaries for the parish, and on September 7, 1907, twenty-three acres of land were purchased for $24,000. Later another small piece was bought for $2,000. "For the time being, that is until a school and temporary church could be built, Fr. Dillon rented a hall over a store at Foster Road and Holgate. There on Nov. 24, 1907, Father Dillon celebrated the first Mass in the new St. Ignatius parish in the presence of 60 people."[72]

These are the basic facts. The account tactfully omitted the reasons for the Jesuits' huge investment, made with an eye to the future boys' school and the three-story brick residence designed and constructed at Jesuit expense for the mission superior and his administration.

Jesuits at Gonzaga reacted normally to the announcement of the new mission structure, with much speculation and unfounded rumors. The scholastics presented an entertainment for the "new" superior, a medley of songs and speeches, starting with a chorus singing "The Rocky Californians" and ending with the "Hymn of the Society."

De la Motte himself was not elated. He wrote to his sister: "I need not tell you this nomination brings me no joy, but yet it is the holy will of God. . . . Imagine a territory comprising France, England, Ireland, Spain, Italy, Germany, Austria and you will have an idea of the new mission."[73] He seemed to be more alarmed by the size of his territory rather than the number of men or the amount of its debts.

Reporters did not get wind of what the Jesuits were plotting until Wednesday, August 21. That evening the *Spokane Daily Chronicle* carried the headline: "Father De La Motte Named to Rule Four Colleges" and the front page presented a photograph of de la Motte that would confirm some Protestants in their opinions about wily Jesuits.* He appeared in steel-rimmed glasses, with piercing fixed eyes peering through and below, a mouth set straight and firm, like a judge about to hang one of his clients. De la Motte, the account concluded, had already gone to California to familiarize himself with conditions there.

---

*The four colleges were: Gonzaga, Seattle, Santa Clara, and St. Ignatius in San Francisco.

Without Alaska Borealis the proportionate number of West Coast Jesuits involved in the ministry of Indians dropped very low. Not only had the Rocky Mountain Mission lost its sense of a certain priority of interest in the Indians, but even the mission's new name reflected coming developments. The name California would suggest the general nature of the area. The four colleges in the headlines would dominate the nature of Jesuit priorities for years to come.

De la Motte, devoted missionary to the Indians of the Rocky Mountains, would never be able to change either.

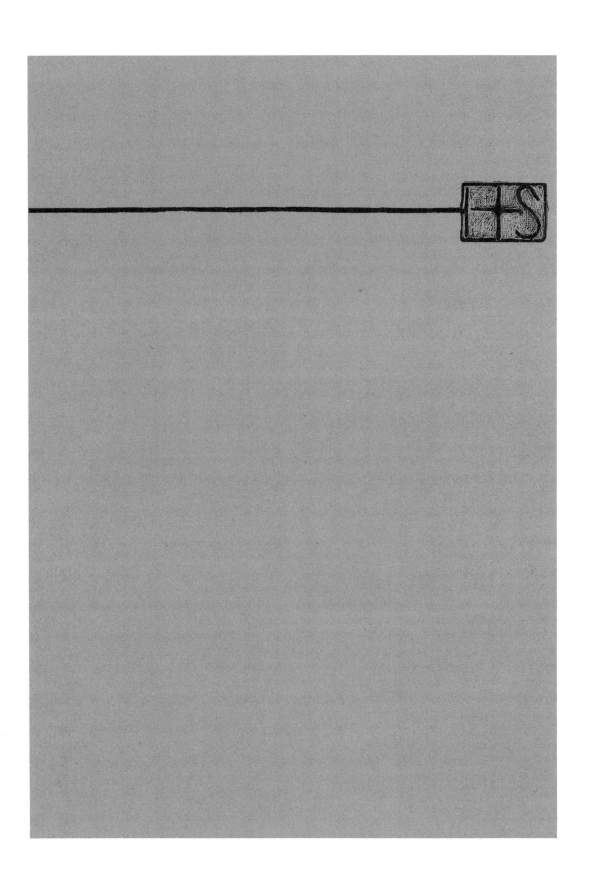

St. Mary's Mission near Omak, founded by Stephen de Rouge.

James Rockliff, S.J., second provincial of the California Province and first rector of Mount St. Michael's.

Cornelius Byrne succeeded Taelman as Dean of Indian Missionaries.

St. Aloysius Church, Spokane.

13

CALIFORNIA PROVINCE
1907–1910

When de la Motte was convalescing from illness in October 1905, he visited California for the first time to share in the golden jubilee of St. Ignatius College. San Francisco, he reported, "was the grand enchanting city of which they speak in books." It was "nearly a Catholic city" and "our holy religion is in honor there. We have a splendid church that is very devotional. This morning at 8 o'clock Mass there were 1,200 communions, and I was told this was an ordinary number. I was impressed by the evident piety of the communicants. No human respect here. Men serve Mass and genuflect before altars . . . I can say that I have remarked the same thing all over America."[1]

The church, it was commonly said, was "the most beautiful and expensive on the west coast. It was ornate in the best roccoco style, and people jammed it to capacity, (2400) every Sunday."[2] Already over their heads in debt for this grand edifice, the Jesuits of San Francisco had spent another million dollars building a college and a high school, completing what some of the diocesan clergy regarded as grandiose plans.*

Archbishop Riordan had presided at the pontifical golden jubilee Mass. He had once asked the children of the neighborhood who the visible head of the church was and they had responded, "Brother Harrick." De la Motte had met Brother Harrick during the jubilee. Formerly a gold prospector in California and Montana, where he was known as "Kid" Harrick, he had been persuaded by Brother Magri to abandon his dissipated life and to become a Jesuit. Already a legend in the city as porter for the church and college, he was remembered for his gallant piety toward the Mother of God: on his first day in the Novitiate at Santa Clara he had placed "on the finger of Our Lady's statue his last possession, a large ring of emerald stone inlaid on a golden harp."† The color of the stone and the harp gave eloquent testimony to his origins, and his brogue confirmed it. He was a small man but he was the "visible head of the church" and everybody recognized it.

Brother Harrick had been assigned to St. Ignatius in 1869, and was to remain there until 1923—years longer than the church, the college, and the high school buildings, which

---

*Many of the clergy in San Francisco deeply resented St. Ignatius Church, a "collegiate church." Because St. Ignatius Church had no parish boundaries of its own, it attracted people from all over the city, who preferred the more solemn ceremonials made possible by the presence of many priests at the college.

†This ring and other votive offering jewelry was later stolen and taken to Belgium where the thieves were apprehended; but the ring never got back to Santa Clara. E. R. Zimmers, S.J., "Better a Day," *Better a Day*, ed. John P. Leary, (New York, 1951), p. 148.

were all completely destroyed on April 18, 1906, by the most devastating earthquake in the history of the west.

The superior of the California Mission in 1906 was Father John P. Frieden, who was also the superior of St. Ignatius College where he was in residence. Frieden gathered reports on other damaged Jesuit institutions in the bay area and an account was published in due time in *Woodstock Letters* for all Jesuits to read and lament.[3] In his own community he had forty-three Jesuits, including two who would make incidental history at St. Mary's church in Pendleton: Fathers Joseph Landry and Robert McKenna. At Santa Clara College, where there were forty-nine Jesuits, including Father Richard Gleeson who was the rector, and Father Aloysius Jacquet, who had been mentally ill at Nome, the earthquake damage to the buildings had been less than substantial but serious enough to require some months for repairs.*

At the novitiate at Los Gatos it was different. The novitiate had been moved there from Santa Clara in 1888 by Father Congiato. About sixty miles south of San Francisco, but proximate to the San Andreas fault, it was shaken badly by the quake. Among the young Jesuits in the juniorate were three who became illustrious in the history of the Oregon Province, David McAstocker, Walter Fitzgerald, and Thomas Ramsay Martin. Another scholastic of note was Zaccheus Maher, a member of the California Mission.

At five o'clock in the morning on that momentous Wednesday, the bell for rising jangled as usual, and Jesuits all over the house, including the scholastics, scrambled to their feet. There was the usual rush to the chapel. At exactly 5:15 A.M. the quake started. The walls swayed, statues in the chapel tottered and fell to the floor with a terrifying crash. A large chimney buckled and a shower of brick plunged through the roof to the floor of the kitchen. As the earth continued to rock, walls groaned. It was like the crack of doom and there were some who thought it was. Most fled from the building into the open yard where they were speechless with terror. One junior, Brother August Busch, who was sick, had to be carried out. He was laid in the cloister and a priest was summoned to assist him.

All this happened in a few minutes; then there was a deathly stillness. Father Thornton, the new rector, came to reassure his community. It was all over, he said. He was going to say Mass in the chapel. Everyone should attend and receive Holy Communion in thanksgiving for his deliverance.

He started Mass at the main altar, and another priest started at the side, while members of the community pulled themselves together and opened Missals in a vain attempt to be casual. Those who had one eye on loose bricks hanging over the altar must have speculated where they would fall. Suddenly the quake started again. After a moment of hesitation the novices and juniors scurried out.

This time more serious damage was done. The two top floors were crumbling and the whole building was badly cracked. It was plainly uninhabitable, so the community began preparations to live outside. Breakfast was served in the cloister, and the rector said that everyone should relax and take a walk in the hills to calm down. The older juniors and brothers, he said, would move what was necessary out of the house, and all would take to living outdoors, as Jesuits had often done before, though seldom in such a lovely climate as California.

All day the shocks continued. Toward evening a false report arrived that a tidal wave had destroyed San Francisco. As darkness fell, the angry red sky to the north denied this piece of fiction with as bad a fact—San Francisco was burning. What had happened? How many of the forty-three Jesuits there were still alive? Los Gatos Jesuits wished they knew.

---

*One old building was destroyed and plaster fell from the walls of other buildings. Resident students moved their beds outdoors.

They went to bed that night in the cloister but did not sleep. Birds twittered in the vines above them, then settled down in silence. Not a sound disturbed the peace, but the sky in the north told of terrors.

Brother Busch, whose condition had worsened, died on Friday afternoon. As soon as it could be arranged, he was buried at Santa Clara. There was definite news now about San Francisco—it had been destroyed. A national disaster had been declared and the National Guard was on duty to prevent greater loss of life. The Jesuits at Los Gatos could scarcely bring themselves to talk about it. St. Ignatius Church was gone and St. Ignatius College; the work of fifty-five years wiped out in a single day.

On May 4, papers announced that there had been seventy-three series of shocks since April 18. There would be more, it added. As the tormented earth gradually quieted down, the Jesuits started repairs. Juniors and novices took bricks down and cleaned them, and the architect came to tell them what to do next. He said the upper floors had to be rebuilt and the rest of the building braced. It could have been a lot worse. The big loss was Brother Busch, over whose grave was a headstone and name which would forever be a reminder of a departed companion and the terrible days of the earthquake.

It was sometimes said, with tongue in cheek, that the loss of St. Ignatius, a stunning blow, was due to De Smet's curse. This was always good for a laugh. Still, there was some deeply rooted, never expressed sorrow that seemed to influence the Old Guard at St. Ignatius for many years. Both Fathers Dominic Giacobbi and Richard Gleeson, for example, who were stationed at Santa Clara during the earthquake of 1906 were closely identified with St. Ignatius College. Yet they carefully avoided all reference to the disaster. Gleeson published a life of Giacobbi, and though the quake had been one of the major events in the lives of both men, he never mentioned it.[4]

The scars of the earthquake were still visible when de la Motte arrived at San Francisco on August 21, and was introduced to the new residence at 2211 Hayes Street by Brother Harrick. A makeshift college building had been provided until a better could be built. Called The Shirt Factory, it was a huge frame structure located about a mile west of the ruins of the church, which was symbolic, some said, of the brokenhearted Jesuits in San Francisco. During the previous year there had been 240 students, even without streetcar lines, and others regarded this as proof of the school's indestructibility.

De la Motte conducted a formal visitation, as though the situation were normal. He listened to each member of the community's complaints, giving each as much comfort as he could, then left for Santa Clara College on August 31, where he started all over again. Santa Clara then was comprised of the college campus, which was surrounded by a high board fence to keep the boys from being contaminated by the evil beyond it, and large open fields where cattle grazed.[5] Compared with bustling San Francisco it was a peaceful enclave.

On September 13, de la Motte left for the novitiate at Los Gatos with its rector, Father William Thornton, who is especially remembered in the annals of the province for his intemperate zeal in collecting relics of the saints. They traveled together by buggy to an elevated salubrious shelf in the Santa Cruz foothills, "at a desirable distance from the congestion at Santa Clara."[6] De la Motte seemed to think that even Santa Clara was crowded. "On [my] reaching the place," he added, "toward 4 P.M. the whole community met me at the door, Gen'l amplexus." The hearty welcome was followed by "a grand dinner."

Originally Congiato had purchased twenty-five acres, but additional land was later acquired. Father Giacobbi, when he was attached to the community, had imported select vines which produced grapes for the novitiate's renowned wines. The novitiate was surrounded by vineyards. Within a few years the sale of altar wines completely supported the community.

Novices from the north joined their brothers in the south in a common noviceship until Sheridan was established in 1930. Among the novices at Los Gatos that September there was Francis McGarrigle, an exacting, scholarly, young man, who later produced the minor spiritual classic *My Father's Will;* and, perhaps more significantly, gathered the priceless theological library, which became the object of some exciting Jesuit in-house litigation.[7] Louis Egan, an energetic genius from Chicago was also there, about whom Father Daniel Lord later wrote a biography called *The Jesuit With the Magic Hands.* Published by the Queen's Work, St. Louis, this booklet was suppressed by the bishop in the Yakima diocese in which Egan had lived, a revealing fact about the pre-Vatican II church.[8] Also at the novitiate were Frank and Peter Menager from Spokane, sons of the doctor who used to say "children, children" when his twelve became too obstreperous.[9] Peter soon learned that being a Jesuit was not his cup of tea and returned home. Another Menager, Edward, was a Jesuit novice at Poughkeepsie, New York. A fourth, Gabriel, entered the novitiate in 1908, replacing Peter, and two of the girls became Ursuline sisters. Not bad at all for one family who, according to Parodi, "were always fighting" among themselves.

With the Los Gatos Menagers was Cornelius Valentine Mullen, a quiet, short Irish lad from the high Sierra Nevadas, where his father was engaged in mining. Older than most of the novices, almost twenty-two years in age, Mullen was introspective and shy, the only son of John and Bridget Mullen, who had lived in heavy snow country, isolated from other companions. Sturdy and well-disciplined, he kept under leash a fiery temper and appeared to be a gentle but firm young man, who was content to remain in the background until called forward to speak. He was blunt in speech and courageous. As a student at Santa Clara during the previous two years, he had come under the influence of the Jesuits and decided he could not live without them. Later he commented on de la Motte, "A very holy man, delamot [sic]. He is the one buried at St. Ignatius Mission, you know."* This brief comment indicates his fondness for reminiscing and his accuracy in recalling small details.

De la Motte, "the very holy man," his visitation at Los Gatos completed on September 21, returned to Santa Clara where he conducted business of the Order for two weeks. He disclosed in his diary the progress of the whole mission.

On September 26 there was another earthquake. Several days later Monsignor Rauw of Portland came to see de la Motte to tell him that Archbishop Christie desperately needed a priest to attend the Siletz Indian reservation on the Oregon coast. "This is not far from Corvallis," de la Motte noted. "I promised to do my best. Fr. Dimier could go there and be a sort of assistant to Fr. Butler, taking one of the stations, v.g. Monroe or two." On reflection he added, "Fr. Rauw was very pleasant."[10]

De la Motte had promised to replace Father Frieden at San Francisco with a new rector and had sent Father General Wernz a telegram urging confirmation of Father Sasia. On October 1 a cablegram arrived from Rome with nothing more than his address. There was no message. De la Motte was frustrated. Quite out of sorts, he complained bitterly about the company's service, referring to it sarcastically as being "in the OXXth century." On October 3, still without word from Rome he commented on two more earthquakes that left him with "sickening impressions." Then with Archbishop Riordan, vis-a-vis, he discussed the chronic problem of St. Ignatius as a collegiate church. De la Motte requested a parish to replace it but the archbishop chided him for not asking sooner, since no room was left for another parish. "The fathers [in San Francisco]," de la Motte argued, "are discouraged because their work has diminished." "No wonder," His Grace retorted rather tartly, "They went too far."[11] This was, of course, reference to the prestigious church, no longer standing, which was sometimes referred to as *Jesuit pride* by the clerical critics of San Francisco

---

*The inaccurate spelling of de la Motte was due to his reporter. Roger Gillis, *The Exchange,* September, 1977, p. 8.

Jesuits. The meeting produced little beyond a mutual understanding, a certain awareness of a common problem which His Grace would have sacrificed his pectoral cross to resolve.

On October 6, de la Motte was able, at last, to confirm Sasia as the new rector at St. Ignatius, and on the following day he left for The City, (San Francisco) to confer with him. Seven days later, while still in residence at St. Ignatius, he received reports that St. Joseph Church in San Jose was almost destroyed by fire. Actually, the school had burned instead and Father Sasia's precious library on the first floor had been ruined with water.

Back in Portland on October 18, de la Motte met again with Christie, who asked him to take a parish in Ashland. Things were getting complicated in Oregon, where, until recently, Jesuits occupied only Pendleton and the Umatilla missions for which Father Joseph Chianale was superior. In Spokane on November 4, de la Motte summarized the situation in a letter to Wernz: "(1) Portland, bought 20 acres, 8 enough for the church, wants to sell the rest as lots. Will build a residence there for $15,000, also a church-school building. (2) Beaverton, accepts charge of Beaverton and two convents. (3) Corvallis with Monroe, Newport and Indian reservation. Three fathers will be enough. (4) Ashland, Bishop has not offered property but will. Halfway between Portland and San Francisco. (5) Lakeview, Bishop offered property, fine place for the missionary spirit."*

The Dakota, or Sioux mission, now under de la Motte's jurisdiction had not as yet been visited. There were two missions: Holy Rosary and St. Francis, both in South Dakota and accessible by railroad from northeastern Nebraska.† On November 8, following thirty-one dusty miles in a wagon, de la Motte began his visitation at Holy Rosary. After listening to the comments of thirteen brothers, one scholastic and five priests for eight days, he prepared a *Memoriale* which suggested current mission interests as well as the general superior's tendency to control even the most minute details on the local level: The superior was to provide for the brothers a larger cellar for keeping vegetables, also a larger greenhouse for the brother who raised flowers. A band for the Indian boys was to be organized and the mission was to provide a club house for the older boys. The minister was to buy eggs for the cook during the winter months when the mission's hens were not laying. The older boys who did not like studies were to learn trades by working during the day, but they were to attend some classes at night. Finally, the *prison* was to be done away with.[12] Most missions had some form of tribal policemen who patrolled the reservation and punished miscreants for their deeds. De la Motte made it clear that the mission under no circumstances was to be the agent for this punishment.

At St. Francis Mission—named for the saint from Assisi, not for the apostle of the Indies—de la Motte listened patiently to another thirteen brothers and five priests, then prepared before his departure on November 22, a *Memoriale* like the first. Two points, especially, should be noted. He directed that the children were to know their prayers in their native languages, and that a new house for the missionaries was to be constructed. It should cost not more than $6,000 and it should have "conveniences"—doubtlessly among other amenities, inside plumbing.[13]

With this, the general superior left for St. Stephen's, the Arapaho mission, not only pleased with what he had observed, but happy with the improvements in transportation through the wilderness of Wyoming. In the past his journeys to St. Stephen's had ended after a twenty-four hour ordeal in a freezing stage coach, but now he was able to make the trip more comfortably by train.

---

*OPA Provincial Papers, de la Motte Diaries, Nov. 4, 1907. De la Motte's comment about selling part of the land to pay for the balance is at odds with other plans for the proposed school. Jesuit hopes for the school in Portland fluctuated from high to low.

†St. Francis Mission was listed as via Crookston, Nebraska; and Holy Rosary mission, via Rushville, Nebraska.

On Thanksgiving, November 28, de la Motte left St. Stephen's for Missoula, where he examined the new residence built by Father Trivelli. He declared that "it was perfect," particularly because it had "only $3,000 debt on it." He left for Spokane on December 1. The depot, he said, "was full of drunkards."

Portland by now was his official residence. For the rest of the current year, however, he remained at Gonzaga, for which he had a special predilection. A mite flippant, perhaps, revealing a modicum of vinegar in his veins, novice Connie Mullen expressed de la Motte's view. "Everything was Gonzaga." Seattle? "Well we had a post box there, not much more. The colleges in San Francisco and Santa Clara weren't that big a drawing card. Los Angeles was just a hick town."[14] Connie Mullen's comments reflected the contemporary assessment. Though Seattle had fourteen Jesuits living near the post box, no one seemed to realize it, least of all those in the novitiate at Los Gatos.

De la Motte had made Goller, rector of Gonzaga, one of his consultors. There seems to have been some idea that Goller's father in Germany was close to Otto von Bismarck, a potential obstacle to friendship which de la Motte happily overcame. Goller was a great favorite, with him as with others, and Goller's influence with the general in Rome was second only to de la Motte's. The other official consultors were Richard Gleeson, rector of Santa Clara; Joseph Chianale; and William Melchers, formerly pastor of the German church in San Jose. One could not accuse de la Motte, a Frenchman, of holding a grudge against Germans. Melchers was his assistant or Father Socius, as they used to say, very likely because he was capable of handling the superior's vast amount of correspondence. Both the superior and his socius were homeless until the residence in Portland was completed, so they drifted from one community to another, making longer visitations than normal.

Writing on December 23 to de Rouge at St. Mary's Mission in central Washington, de la Motte contributed to his cup of Christmas cheer. De Rouge was in troubled financial straits, scarcely able to keep his empire together, despite the continued support of Mother Drexel and the irregular grants from the Indian Bureau. With many dependents at the mission he was often reduced to scraping the bottom of his barrel to keep solvent. He had to beg constantly, sometimes at a distance from the mission, which required his absence from the supervision of the boys' school, the apple of his eye. He had obtained two Brothers of Christian Instruction from France to help him. Brother Rene and Brother Celestine, who had arrived in September, 1905.* Celestine, an expert taxidermist, had begun a museum with a stuffed sea gull from Omak Lake and soon the Indians became interested and brought many kinds of rare animals and birds to be mounted.[15]

The struggle for survival had changed de Rouge. He was only forty-six years old, but his long beard made him look seventy. It was said that he had become a Jesuit loner, which is not surprising. He had not lived with a Jesuit since tertianship. It was also rumored that he disliked visits from the superior and found ways to persuade him to leave the mission as soon as possible.† This had no baneful effect on his work, for in spite of the mission's great poverty it was spiritually and academically prolific.

De Rouge had fine orchards and farmland that helped to support the mission, but for lack of a skilled farmer, these did not produce as plentifully as he expected. Dependent for water on Omak Creek, which was as yet untampered with above the mission property, the land had an unlimited supply of water. It probably never occurred to de Rouge that this would change. He took the mission's water rights for granted, which was like taking for

*Northwest Progress, October 31, 1910. See also OPA D'Aste Papers, Diaries, wherein Father D'Aste comments on the brothers' visit at St. Ignatius Mission enroute to St. Mary's, Omak.

†Popular tradition notes that de Rouge used to put a log in his extra bed to indicate his preferences. This is unlikely.

granted the supply of oil in the bottom of a Texas well.

With the boys' school successfully under way, de Rouge wanted to have sisters who could supervise a girls' residence school. Cataldo's success with his novitiate for sisters influenced him to appeal to Bishop O'Dea for his approval to form a similar institution.[16] O'Dea disliked the proposal, but eventually gave his reluctant permission and de Rouge established his Lady Missionaries of St. Mary's, a society of pious ladies who devoted their lives to teaching Indian children under rather peculiar canonical conditions. Every six months these sisters pronounced "devotional vows" of religion, which bound them for a six-month period only. Madame La Londe of Tonasket, and her two nieces were the first members of this semi-religious congregation, which lasted until 1934, eighteen years after de Rouge's death.[17]

De Rouge needed money, not stuffed sea gulls. Fully aware of the situation, de la Motte informed him that he approved of his acceptance "of a pension of 8600 francs annually" left him by his recently deceased mother, "provided that it would be used for the Indian boys."[18] This was an extraordinary permission which brought at last, some financial security for the "Apostle of the Okanogans," who had less than nine years to live.

While de Rouge was holding his own against odds, three Jesuits at St. Francis Regis Mission, to which St. Mary's was attached, covered nearly seven thousand square miles of their own, with occasional help from Couffrant or de la Motte. Their mission schedule, prepared, as Schuler says, for the Catholic Indian Bureau, is contained in the mission diary for March 27, 1908.

The *Turin Province Catalogue* for the beginning of the year 1908 formally listed for the first time the "Mission of California and Rocky Mountains," and gave de la Motte's address as East Portland. Dillon, still using a public hall for a temporary church, lived in a rented home. On February 12, after completing his visitation of the Seattle Jesuits and hearing more complaints about the problems of a collegiate church there, de la Motte met with Dillon and Arthuis in Portland.[19] They decided on that same day to erect on Powell Street [sic] a brick residence, to cost "about $8,000," and a combination church-school "for about $12,000." The residence was to be built on Jesuit land and used primarily as the mission superior's permanent office-dwelling. It was to be paid for by the Jesuits themselves. Title to the land where the church was to be built would remain in the name of the Jesuits. Several proposals that the parish purchase the property never succeeded because of lack of funds.

Satisfied, de la Motte left for California. On March 10, he was in Los Angeles, "only a hick town," to see Bishop James Conaty. Things were sticky in Los Angeles. Its bishop had assumed the administration of the diocese of Monterey-Los Angeles in 1902 after concluding "a less-than-successful term as rector of the Catholic University of America" in the nation's capitol, and to compensate for his failure he was determined to establish "a center of Catholic higher education on the West Coast."[20] The Vincentian fathers, who since 1865 had conducted St. Vincent's College in Los Angeles, were under great pressure from Conaty to realize His Lordship's ambition at their expense, but they were most unwilling to go into debt for this or any other reason. Thwarted, and somewhat critical of his Vincentians, Conaty summoned de la Motte to Los Angeles to invite the Jesuits into the diocese. One suspects his ulterior motive with reason, but his initial proposal expressly ruled out the possibility of a Jesuit college. He explained to de la Motte that while he really wanted Jesuits in the city of Los Angeles, he could not allow it for the present. The Vincentians, struggling with the survival of their college, disapproved. He would see to it that the Jesuits would be invited when the Vincentians got on their feet financially. Meanwhile, His Lordship would find an available parish for the Jesuits in some other city in the diocese.

De la Motte was disappointed. He had expected more. Better, however, a half loaf than none at all, and on March 10 he recommended to his consultors that the Jesuits accept whatever parish in the diocese that Conaty offered. The consultors approved.[21]

On April 14, de la Motte completed his visitation at Los Gatos. His *Memoriale* to the rector presents another insight into his manner of government. The rector, he said, should loosen up a bit, he should give occasional holidays. Let the novices and juniors walk after meals, they needed the exercise. Cut down on some classes, there were too many. Also, get some new Latin books, something more up-to-date.[22] He left the renovated novitiate building, which resembled a four-layered wedding cake and got into his buggy. It went bumping down the road past the grey-green olive trees with his horse trotting briskly at the crack of a whip. Most decisions the superior had to make were more complicated than the Latin texts, but even these were of concern to him. They were related to the formation of his scholastics, who would become the backbone of the new province which was already being discussed. The clop-clop of the horse's hooves on the way to Santa Clara, through the prune orchards of the valley, was like the clock ticking away the last months of the mission's history. De la Motte had a keen awareness of his role in this history, and his power to influence it. Bishops often came to him because he commanded more priests than they, and their expanding dioceses needed priests more urgently than they needed money.

In June, Archbishop Christie traveled to Spokane to see him. He requested de la Motte to provide a priest for Portland's Italian parish, St. Michael's. The latter agreed, perhaps more swiftly than prudence required. Anxious about the Jesuit presence in Portland and his hopes for a school there, he would have accepted care of the archbishop's dog house.

St. Michael's was originally founded as a chapel for German immigrants by the Benedictines of Mount Angel. This was in 1890, the same year that Michael Balestra, a bright lad with the political astuteness of a Roman prelate, entered the Jesuit novitiate at Chieri. In 1894 a national church under the patronage of St. Joseph was erected elsewhere for the Germans, and the little chapel they had used was given over to the convenience of Italians who lived in the neighborhood known as Little Italy.

For several years, due to the shortage of priests, Little Italy and St. Michael's had an unstable existence. Many pastors came and went—there was no permanence at all. Then, in April, 1901, Alexander Cestelli was appointed pastor, and both church and neighborhood started to flourish. Father Cestelli built a new church. This is always a dramatic way to start things, particularly if the old one is falling apart. Bishop O'Dea of Seattle laid the cornerstone for this new edifice on the corner of Fourth Avenue and Mill Street, November 24, 1901. Seven months later, on the Feast of Saints Peter and Paul (a great day for the Italians), Archbishop Christie performed the ceremony of dedication. All went well at St. Michael's until Father Cestelli was killed in an automobile accident. This was in 1906, the same year that Father Balestra went to Alaska to be a missionary.

For two years, there was no pastor of St. Michael's, and Little Italy was in mourning. Non-resident priests continued to say Mass for the people; but no one had yet taken Father Cestelli's place. Christie appealed to de la Motte and on June 28, 1908, Father Anthony Villa arrived at St. Michael's to take over the parish for the Jesuits.[23] He did not last long, but he prepared the way, at least, for the durable Michael Balestra, who was to remain there (with his dogs) for nearly fifty years.

Meanwhile, on July 9, de la Motte met with Bishop Conaty in Santa Monica. The bishop had decided to offer the Jesuits a parish in Santa Barbara. It was Our Lady of Sorrows which had three thousand parishioners. It was an attractive parish without debt or an irremovable housekeeper. Its pastor, Father P.J. Stockman, in ill health and anxious to retire, had urged the bishop to assign his parish to the Jesuits. Although de la Motte was disappointed in its location—he preferred a parish in Los Angeles—he agreed to accept it. By mutual agreement of the bishop and the superior, Father Robert Kenna became the first

Jesuit pastor in Santa Barbara on August 23.[24] He was also the first Jesuit to be assigned to southern California.

De la Motte, by this time, was in San Francisco. He dispatched from there on August 17 letters to all Jesuit communities in his care, urging them to correct certain "abuses," which today may seem to some a comic commentary on the *enormous* problems of the pre-Vatican Church:

"P[ax] C[hristi],

"In a letter recently received from Fr. General a few abuses were called to my attention which are said to have crept into our Mission. They are the following:

"1. It is said, that Ours are too easily permitted (a) to visit externs and (b) take meals or refreshments with them.

"2. That some of Ours are (a) easily permitted to use smoking tobacco without necessity; (b) that smoking is done not privately but publicly in the Recreation Room.

"3. That some of Ours are not faithful in making annually their annual Retreat.

"4. Finally, it is said that Ours are allowed to receive and write letters during their annual Retreat.

"Before reporting to Fr. General on the above abuses, I beg your Reverence auditis consultoribus to inform me at your earliest convenience, whether and to what extent the aforesaid abuses may exist in the house admitted to your care.

"In union with your prayers and h (oly) Sacrifices

"I remain infimus in X. servus
Geo de la Motte S.J.[25]

This letter was typewritten, a kind of break with the past when circular letters were handwritten and duplicated by a primitive process, something less than Xerox. There were several other breaks with the past that were scarcely noticed, but which now appear to have been significant.

The first concerned St. Mary's, our first mission—Our Mother Mission. Once closed in the midst of a tornado of turmoil only to be reestablished by the Second Founder himself, St. Mary's had gradually outlived its usefulness. Jesuits continued to live there until Chief Charlot and the last of the Flatheads on the Ootlashoots moved to the Jocko in 1891.[26] Since the Indians were no longer in the valley, St. Mary's was classified as a mission from Missoula and Jesuits traveled there on weekends to provide Mass for a handful of Whites.

Father Jerome D'Aste, the last of the resident pastors, and normally a sweet-tempered, gentle Genoese, complained bitterly about what followed. "The property," he wrote to de la Motte on August 30, 1908, "has been *shamefully* neglected by the Fathers in Missoula, and nothing was left but the walls of the church and Father's room, and everything that could be carried away was taken to Missoula, and the church and house was going to ruin."* Fortunately Father Julian Loiseau shared D'Aste's sentiments about the old mission and he raised $400 to restore and furnish it. But when he left Missoula he said, "everything is growing wild again."

If all this irritated the poor old missionary, who had loved St. Mary's too much, the attitude of Bishop Carroll was worse. The bishop was planning a new parish in neighboring Hamilton and he had his eye on the mission. Since in the presence of Loiseau His Lordship had said, "Hereafter only American born, or Irish born priests could work in this country *for the glory of God,*"[27] D'Aste concluded "It would be better to let him have it [St.

---

*OPA, D'Aste papers, to de la Motte from St. Ignatius Mission, August 30, 1908. D'Aste died at St. Ignatius two years later on November 10, 1910, at the age of eighty-three.

Mary's] on condition that he takes care of it." The bishop soon appointed a resident pastor at Hamilton and took over St.Mary's, but his care of the place was no better than that provided by Missoula.*

For most of the Jesuits all of this was of little interest. No one bewailed the fact that another Indian mission had been closed. Preoccupation with whites had become a blinding reality. Jesuit priorities now and for some years to come would favor schools and the bailing out of bishops. In a way, the thirteen brothers and five priests at Holy Rosary signified the state of things: there was more physical labor than priestly work involved in mission activity. Besides, could the appeal of bishops for pastors in the White parishes where the demand was so great be ignored. No one bothered to say otherwise.

There was a second break, like the first, related to another Indian mission. The boys' school at St. Francis Regis Mission was officially closed on September 1, 1908, "for lack of funds."[28] De Rouge's school at St. Mary's helped to fill the void for the Colville Indian boys, but the departure of the teachers at St. Regis marked the beginning of the decline of this mission. Its days were numbered. Later there were some, like Father Paul Sauer, who regarded St. Regis sympathetically, but the hard facts of the mission's inaccessibility to the Indians exiled by the government's new reservation boundaries across the Columbia, eventually sealed its doom. Not even its rich soil, its sunny clime, nor the sisters' school in the valley could save it.

Finally, at Gonzaga too, there was a break with the past. The cadet program, begun by de la Motte with Gallican eclat, was terminated abruptly at the beginning of the school year in 1908. The corps had fallen on evil days. It had all started, of course, when the army sent official inspectors from Fort Vancouver to report on progress at Gonzaga. One inspector, Major H. E. Tutherly, in a scathing report recommended that the officer in charge be cashiered and all the arms be turned in. He regarded the corps as "a military farce," and he went back to his barracks in Vancouver in a snit. The report, as might be expected, stirred up a hornet's nest.

One aspect of the cadet corps had not been appreciated by the inspectors. This concerned its social functions which were looked upon by the fathers as indispensable and by visiting officers as ridiculous, if not downright treason. One can imagine the dismay of these officers, for example, when they were informed that the cadets did not have encampment nor overnight maneuvers, but were given picnics instead. In the casual days before the two great World Wars, and after Father Crimont replaced Father de la Motte, the fathers really didn't take military training as a serious commitment. They apparently looked upon it as a kind of disciplinary program for gentlemen-boys. It was so nice having them in uniforms, marching around on formal occasions. It gave the school status. This explains their connivance with the officer in charge when he encouraged the enlistment of smaller boys. Nothing shocked the army personnel more than the casualness with which the college authorities admitted their average cadet age was fourteen. It certainly was not the kind of program the Army had anticipated: one bewhiskered old soldier in a faded blue uniform with something like a hundred small boys bearing weapons from the United States Arsenal. If the fathers were conscious of the incongruousness of the situation, they preferred to ignore it. They were extremely proud of the boys, often justly so.

Major Luhn had resigned before the War Department had finished its martial assault. Father Dillon's request for another officer had been loftily spurned by the department, so the college employed a former student who had been in the corps and promoted him to the rank of captain. The War Department refused to have anything more to do with the school.

---

*The first resident pastor of St. Francis Assisi Church at Hamilton, built by the Jesuits in 1896, was Father M.J. Carr. Lawrence Palladino, *Indians and Whites*, p. 383.

The army now demanded that the school return its rifles and side arms. Capt. Hugh Winder, as well as the Jesuits, who were desperately determined to keep the program alive, stalled for a whole year. Two years later, after cutting enough red tape to commit high treason, Dillon finally secured an offer of sale by the government. For a total of $268.85 the college was able to secure title to the ordnance stores still in its possession.

Captain Winder instituted many needed reforms. He weeded out the younger boys and imposed an iron discipline on all who remained. For two years he generously conducted the program as a service to his Alma Mater. Then in the autumn of 1907, Captain Edmund Butts replaced him as the instructor in charge. With Captain Butts, a member of the United States Army attached to Fort George Wright, the Gonzaga cadet program was officially reinstated and for the brief time of its subsequent existence, the United States War Department provided the necessary military equipment.

It was Captain Butts's unhappy privilege to preside over the dissolution of the cadet program. Some of the teachers had complained about the amount of drill time required by the War Department alleging that it was harmful to the studies of many boys. Yielding to their remonstrances, the president, Father Goller, abolished the cadets. New compulsory courses in physical culture were provided as a compromise substitute. Though these served their purpose of bodily training reasonably well, they lacked the glamor of the former program. They were soon discontinued and the nervous energies of those lively Gonzaga boys were consumed in less formal ways, some of them quite shocking to the nice old fathers, who liked to see the little boys marching with wooden guns on their shoulders.

By this time the church and school at St. Ignatius in Portland were completed. "On September 20, 1908, at 3:00 P.M. and in the presence of a large throng of priests and the faithful, our Most Reverend Archbishop solemnly blessed the first building which contained both church and school. On the following day, the school was opened for pupils up to the fourth grade. Two Sisters of Holy Names were the teachers, and they had about forty children in attendance. During November of that year, the fathers' residence was completed. The cost of the buildings, including land and all furnishings, totaled $55,638.95 and was provided by the Procurator of the Rocky Mountain Mission of the Society of Jesus."[29]

De la Motte finally had his St. Ignatius parish, but by the end of the year he was burned out. Weariness from travel and worry about his subjects combined to undermine his fragile health. Towards the end of 1908, he was afflicted with grief. Joseph Landry whom he had recently transferred from California to be superior at St. Mary's in Pendleton, died unexpectedly from typhoid. He was only forty-four years old. Then another priest, recently ordained, a former doctor of medicine and a very talented writer, was paralyzed by a stroke. This was Father Henry MacCulloch [McCulloch], author of the life of Ensign Robert Monaghan, whose statue adorns Spokane's Civic Center.* "These are two great losses," de la Motte lamented to his sister, "at a time when I am short of priests. I have a big heart, but I am forced to repeat 'May the name of the Lord be blessed in everything.' "[30]

The new year would be better. He and Melchers were installed at last in their new residence in Portland, so he had his own hook for hanging his hat. He had been advised to take baths in Medical Lake near Spokane and this, he reported, seemed to give him strength. He knew that his ordeal as superior would soon be over.

Father Moore at the state penitentiary in Salem had requested two priests to give a mission to the prisoners. De la Motte sent Father Patrick O'Reilly, recently ordained and as fiery and threatening as Moses at the foot of Mount Sinai; and Father Vincent Chiappa, who was as gentle as O'Reilly was harsh. The mission was begun on Sunday, February 21,

---

*Father Henry MacCulloch (or McCulloch, as the Province Catalogues list him) died in Spokane on March 3, 1913. The title of his book is *Life of John Robert Monaghan: The Hero of Samoa* (Spokane, 1906).

1909, and lasted until the following Sunday. The 426 convicts, delighted to be out of their cells, attended the services, which began with appropriate music provided by the penitentiary orchestra. Only 55 prisoners claimed to be Catholics, but a much larger number were known by Irish surnames. Somewhat indignant, O'Reilly questioned many of these and reported later that there was a "mania" among convicts to assume Irish names and he was at a loss to know why.[31]

For de la Motte, O'Reilly's highly imaginative description of his holy conquests in the penitentiary was refreshing. As superior one heard so little about positive accomplishments. There were other bright spots to give him comfort during his last months as superior. The Crow Indians at Lodge Grass, Montana, had cut logs and dragged them thirty miles to build a church there. And in Spokane on June 6, four scholastics were ordained to the priesthood. One of them, Michael O'Malley, claimed by Patrick O'Reilly as "a distant cousin," has described the Spartan simplicity of the greatest event in their lives:

"We were four in number: Fr. Wm. O'Brien from Troy, New York, who was with me at the Indian Mission near Pendleton, Oregon, then Fr. James L. McKenna, native of Boston, Massachusetts, Fr. Edward Wall, native of California and myself—ordained in that order of our entrance into religious life.

"The ordination Mass began at 6 a.m. as the pastor, Fr. Charles Mackin, S.J. (native of County Armagh, Ireland) wished to have the little church free for 8 o'clock Mass. There was no singing or music, and there were no visitors, no relatives of the ordinands. It was as simple as an ordination in the Roman catacombs."[32]

Father O'Malley offered his first Mass in the orphanage, then left for the St. Regis Mission to teach catechism to the boys gathered for vacation school. The boys slept in the hay in the barn and had class on the brink of the creek, with their minds more on trout fishing than on the seven capital sins.

On Wednesday night, June 23, Seattle College celebrated the granting of its first degrees in the Social Hall on Eighteenth and East Marion. There were three graduates, sixty-six percent of whom became priests, an all time record in our province's history. Actually, it was two out of three: John Concannon, who won the premiums in all classes for excellent work, became a Jesuit; Theodore Ryan, who won the gold medal, as thin as a wafer, became a diocesan priest; the third graduate was James C. Ford, who also ran.[33]

The graduation program lasted for hours. A "Melodrama in Five Acts" called "The Hermit's Bell," was presented and six long musical selections were rendered before "Count Rudolph" was delicately murdered. The three new bachelors of art received their degrees from Bishop O'Dea, who also presented a gold medal to Francis Kane and special awards, among others, to Cyril Fairhurst for excelling in English, Latin and Christian Doctrine. The historic occasion closed with the aide-de-camp March, which ran out of marchers almost as soon as it started.

Michael O'Malley was still at St. Regis when de la Motte arrived to see him. "Father," he said, "I have received a letter from the Irish Sheepherders down in southeastern Oregon. They are asking for an Irish priest. Will you go there?" O'Malley said, "Of course," and forthwith he found himself assigned to "the pastoral care for two large counties, Klamath and Lake County. A few Jesuits were there for a few years already. Now I would be alone—the only priest in big Lake County. I did not meet the Bishop in the two years I lived in Lake County."[34]

There was still Ashland and Siletz. De la Motte had committed the Jesuits to take these churches, but keeping his promise was like a headache on Christmas. He had Father Mackin in mind for Ashland but at this point it would be awkward to change him. Mackin and Goller, whose name had been submitted to Rome for the first provincial of the forthcoming new province, were engaged in an Irish-German brouhaha over the site of the proposed new St. Aloysius Church.

Father Mackin, it will be recalled, was appointed pastor of St. Aloysius on July 31, 1904, precisely for the purpose of erecting a new church. It was understood at that time that Father Mackin counted among his many friends certain wealthy people who would have been sincerely pleased to provide some of the needed money. There is no reason to believe they were ever asked. Mackin, instead, appealed to the people of the parish to provide some of the money first. The rest he intended to gather from his friends.

Unfortunately, a news account about the proposed church contained an offhand remark which misled many and later caused hard feelings toward the college. "The Jesuit buildings," the article gratuitously stated, "are not put up by popular subscription, and it is expected the big structure will be put up without the assistance of resident worshippers." The author of this balderdash did not suggest where the Jesuits planned to get the necessary money. Perhaps from one of the many imaginary gold mines discussed by certain writers of romance.

As might be expected, certain members of the parish pounced upon the newspaper article and held it up as the reason for their neglect to support the new church project. The college, so they said, was rich enough. It could sell a million dollars worth of land and still have plenty. It did no good to explain that the college no longer had this land. Most of the Jesuits' land had already been sold to pay for the college's new buildings and the rest belonged to the Pioneer Educational Society.

Father Mackin lost no time in setting the record straight. He divided the parish into fifteen groups, dependent upon occupation or status, and announced to all of them that he had to collect $100,000 for a new church. This was in October 1908. By December 3, $20,000 had been subscribed.[35]

At this point a critical dispute arose regarding location of the new church. Mackin insisted that it be placed in the block north of the old church; that is, between Boone and Sharp avenues and Astor and Addison streets. Father Goller, who had become president of the college by this time, preferred to keep the over-all planning determined by architects, when the administration building was erected. Mackin proved to be stubborn and it is only fair to him to add that his principal argument was compelling. The parish, he said, extended entirely to the north with Gonzaga college on the southern extremity. It was to the advantage of the parishioners to place the church as close to the middle of the parish as possible. The one block difference in the proposed location meant much in terms of convenience to the parishioners, Mackin said, because the parish school could eventually be erected in the same block as the church.* The argument convinced no one, not even Archbishop Christie, who attended one of the discussions.

"I was told to get plans," Mackin wrote. "I got a sketch and they demanded of me to get another one that they might have a copy to send to the General. The plans that I wanted and the location I wanted and the kind of church that I wanted were rejected, and I could not go before my friends and say, 'This is what I want' ".[36] Though Father Mackin wrote these lines almost twenty years later, he still keenly felt the frustrations and irritations he had experienced in 1909.

As Mackin himself pointed out, no one agreed with him. One can scarcely blame superiors for supporting the majority viewpoint. In late May, 1909, Father Goller took out a building permit for a $50,000 church to be built on the southeast corner of Boone and Astor.[37] "A new foundation for the old church was then laid on the west side of Astor opposite "the Sheds" and the venerable old building now being moved for a second time,

*The St. Aloysius Parochial School is now located on the north side of Mission Avenue on the old Heath estate, which is the approximate center of the parish.

was transported to the new site.* The ground was now clear for the new church which was begun at once.

While the excavations for the basement and foundations went down into the ground, estimated costs of the building went proportionately higher. In June, Father Goller stated that the cost was placed at $150,000, adding that approximately half of this amount had been pledged and $30,000 had been collected.

At this time Goller had taken charge of the project. The rift between him and the pastor of St. Aloysius was becoming wider every day. Mackin himself suggested that he be sent elsewhere, but the president replied he should remain at St. Aloysius. In the light of subsequent developments this appears to have been the decision of Father de la Motte rather than Father Goller.

At this point some radical changes in administration were determined by the general in Rome, who signed on July 31, 1909, a decree establishing an independent "California Province,"† effective September 8. Father Goller was appointed the first provincial, giving him the upper hand, and Father Louis Taelman was appointed president of Gonzaga.

The somewhat confidential announcement came as no surprise to de la Motte. He had shared in the decision-making process, and for the most part agreed with its details, one of which proved to be a great disappointment to the Old Guard, the living members of the former Rocky Mountain Mission.‡ This concerned the name for the new province, selected by the general. After decades of struggle to establish their own identity in the Northwest, in subtle competiton with the more glamorous California Mission, they regarded themselves as the mother province and felt depressed about the oversight in the loss of their nomenclature. Their feelings had already been conveyed to Father Wernz, who responded that no one in Europe knew where the Rocky Mountains were, but nearly everyone recognized the name California. This single fact appeared to be so significant in Wernz's judgment that other details like historical precedence, larger number of Jesuits in the north, even the residence of the provincial in Portland, were brushed aside.**

De la Motte was now a lame duck superior. Working closely with the new provincial he continued to organize the new province, a project which had really begun in 1907. He still made the basic decisions, one of them to send Mackin to Ashland.[38] Mackin arrived there on August 17, 1909, marking the official date of the Jesuit take-over of the parish.

Five days later, after securing a suitable notebook from L. P. Orr's Drugstore for an announcement book, he stood in the pulpit of Our Lady of the Rosary Church and read the following announcement: "A meeting of all the members of the congregation who wish to see a Catholic community in Ashland is requested after the 10 o'clock Mass today. The

*Present site of Bea House. Used for a church until the new St. Aloysius was occupied, this building then became "the parish hall;" later, the Little Theatre for the University; and finally, a student union building. It was destroyed by fire on July 25, 1954, the day after the new student union building was occupied.

†There has been some confusion about the date on which Father Goller became the first provincial, and thus confusion about the actual date of the founding of the California Province. As notes, Father General signed the decree and made the appointment on July 31, 1909. However, these were not effective until September 8, 1909. Copies of the documents can be found in *Woodstock Letters*, 39 (1910), p. 79 et seq.

‡Father Louis Taelman often referred to this incident in the formation of the California Province. He states that the old missionaries objected to the name and that Father General promised them, when they expressed their views, that when the northern portion was made an independent province, it could have the name of the old mission. When Oregon and California provinces were separated, the matter had been forgotten by most of the people involved.

**The California mission in 1909 had 163 Jesuits, including some novices from the north. There were 178 Jesuits in the north, including some out-of-province scholastics at Gonzaga. There were 32 Jesuits in Dakota and 6 Jesuits in southern Alaska.

pastor intends to visit every Catholic family next week. Any help given to get acquainted will be highly appreciated."[39]

The new pastor's disappointment with the meeting was the first of many. Apparently, as often happens when a Catholic minority is left without adequate spiritual direction for a number of years, most had become indifferent. In writing to his superior in 1910, Mackin revealed his sadness: "We have not much to tell . . . there have been scandals, so all we could do was watch and pray. We are grateful we have been able to hold our own and to make some advances. We have only 97 Catholics (out of 2,643 people), including everyone in the parish. The hardest battle has been the monotony."

The *monotony* is revealed in Mackin's announcement book. Sunday followed Sunday with the usual Rosaries and Benedictions and meetings of the Altar Society. There were collections for Catholic U., frequent exhortations to receive Holy Communion, and an occasional burst of impatience. "Remember," he said on the 10th Sunday after Pentecost, 1910, "the collection today is for heating the church during the year. There were complaints last year that the church was not heated. I did my best. If you want it heated properly, show it by the collection." The collection was not altogether successful, and on the next Sunday, Mackin contrived from the pulpit a masterpiece of understatement; "The collection amounts to $27.50. If more "five's" instead of nickels and dimes were given, it would be all right." Perhaps it never occurred to Mackin that the tenth Sunday after Pentecost, coming in the heat of summer as it does, is scarcely a time to stimulate interest in heat.

Whatever the case, the people of Ashland gradually came to respond to Mackin's exhortations. Their devotion and fervor revived with what now appears to be remarkable suddenness. They came to love their Irish "Sogarth Aroon," and he in turn came to be greatly attached to Ashland. "I want to spend my life there," he told one of his companions. "'Tis a lovely spot." A year later, in July 1912, he made his last entry in the announcement book, little suspecting that his last words, "Wednesday, Feast of St. Ignatius," were prophetic. On Wednesday, the Feast of St. Ignatius, 1912, full of affection and memories, Mackin bade Ashland goodbye. The parish was returned to the archbishop.

There is not much to say about Jesuit activity at Siletz. Like Ashland, it was a case of a one-Jesuit show, and it lasted only four years. The one Jesuit was Augustine Dimier, S.J., a kind, middle-aged Frenchman, who had already spent some five years in Indian missions in Montana and six years in parish work. His Siletz mission territory extended from the Salmon River on the Pacific Ocean south to Cape Perpetua, about fifty miles, and included such primitive elements as reservation Indians in a state of great degeneration and such sophisticated ones as fashionable seaside resorts.

Like other priests marooned on small islands and surrounded by indifference, Dimier was greatly discouraged by the results of his labors. In a letter to Cataldo, on September 7, 1911, he complained about the hopelessness of his position: "I went from house to house, teaching children and grownups the elements of Christian doctrine. I did a good deal of that work in some families in the hope of drawing them to the church whither they very, very seldom came, but no results followed. So I give them up if Providence does not interpose miraculously in their favor.[40]

Fortunately for Dimier, there was other work to do among the Whites who lived in resort towns like Newport. Judging by human standards, his greatest conquest took place, surprisingly enough, in one of his resort chapels. His little altar boy, a student from Gonzaga in Spokane, came each summer with his family for a vacation on the beach. This good lad was so inspired by Dimier's mission spirit that he chose to follow him as an Indian missionary. He has since achieved national fame for his defense of Indian rights. His name was Cornelius E. Byrne.

In 1912, the archbishop was able to supply one of his own priests for Siletz, so Dimier was transferred to St. Paul's Mission, Montana, among the Gros Ventres and Assiniboines. Since this mission was in a flourishing state, Dimier soon recovered from the spiritual loneliness and frustrations of Siletz; but he never forgot it. It had left its mark on him. At Siletz, his name was remembered by a few, forgotten by most. Of all Oregon Jesuit foundations, none has been so obscure as Siletz and none has retained so slight a trace of the Jesuits. Ocean tides and sea mists seem to have wiped out all signs of their passage.

In the Yakima Valley, on the other hand, the original Oblate mission of St. Joseph's on the Attanam Creek had become a memorial. The spirit of Pandosy and d'Herbonez still hovered over the valley. St. Onge and Boulet, who had succeeded them, and Caruana, the first of the Jesuits there, had helped to make the place holy. In the summer of 1909, while O'Malley was counting his sheepherders in Lake County, Oregon, The Knights of Columbus in Yakima restored the old mission, a precedent that was sometimes followed in other historic missions, more often not.

Father Thomas Sherman, the famous Jesuit son of General William Sherman, had come to Yakima to preach a "mission." Introduced to the history of old St. Joseph's, he helped to create an interest in its restoration. It was reported in *Woodstock Letters:*

"The Knights of Columbus have purchased about three acres, which include all the buildings of the old mission, and will begin at once the work of restoration. Fences will be built on the place, the log buildings will be touched up here and there where decay has done its work, the old altar will be re-established, the orchard, the first in the Yakima Valley, and which is still bearing, will be trimmed and pruned."[41]

When this was printed, de la Motte, too, had undergone a major change. His last official act as general superior was the composition of a letter addressed to the mission to announce the erection of the province and the appointment of Father Goller.

St. Ignatius Church,
Portland Oregon,
Sept. 7th, 1909.

Reverend Fathers and Dear Brothers in Christ,
"Pax Christi. It gives me great consolation to inform you that by a decree which bears the date of July the thirty-first, nineteen hundred and nine, Our Very Reverend Father General has raised our dear Mission to the dignity of a Province.

"The new Province of CALIFORNIA (for such is its name) will receive its birth on the eighth of September, under the auspices of the Blessed Virgin Mary, and under the same auspices, Reverend Father HERMAN GOLLER who is appointed its first Provincial, will assume charge of his office.

"The decrees of both, the erection of the California Province and the appointment of its Provincial will be read presently.

"Thanking each and every one for the great charity and forbearance shown me during the long tenure of my office, and commending myself to your prayers and Holy Sacrifices, I remain,

"Omnium servus in Christo,
"Geo. de la Motte, S.J.,
"Sup. Miss. Calif. et Mont. Saxos."[42]

On the following day Herman Goller, the jovial Big Brother assumed his new duties. His first concern was for the new St. Aloysius Church. Father George Butler of California had taken Mackin's place as pastor. Butler, a genial mixer like Goller, found no difficulties whatever in accepting the majority's viewpoint. He agreed to undertake the raising of funds while Father Arthuis, Goller's handyman, supervised the construction work. Henceforth, Arthuis was responsible for the final plans and their execution with day labor. Throughout the month of September he devoted many long days to tedious conferences with Mr. Zittel of Zittel and Preusse, architects in charge.

The first published sketch of the new church appeared in the *Spokesman-Review* on October 10. In the caption which accompanied the large cut, the hoary old legend about Gonzaga's alleged millions was repeated with the kind of casual acceptance that defies refutation. Father Butler's Irish was magnificently aroused. "It is not true," he protested, "that the greater part of the cost of the new St. Aloysius church is to be borne by Gonzaga College. . . . This misleading statement has been made several times and I am at a loss to understand who is responsible for it. Gonzaga is by no means so financially situated as to be able to assume the greater part of the debt that must be reckoned with in the erection of our $85,000 church."[43]

Father Butler's reference to an $85,000 church added to the confusion. Since Arthuis was building it with day labor, no one really knew how much the church would cost. But indications favored Goller's figure rather than Butler's. Time proved even Goller's estimate was short. Arthuis gradually came to realize this and in his anxiety to keep costs within his budget, he made a fatal mistake. For economy's sake he ordered the total length of the church to be cut by approximately seventeen feet, though other dimensions remained as before. Thus when completed, it looked almost as tall as it was long.

With so much commotion, something was bound to get done. Father Arthuis' foundation was finally ready for the cornerstone. Father Taelman, was very fond of big celebrations. He instructed Father Butler to make the laying of the cornerstone a very solemn affair. Butler obliged with many ideas that would have put a movie director to shame. His plans included an archbishop and four bishops, representatives of the army from Fort Wright, the mayor and his City Hall flunkies, and the governor. In fact, everybody in town, if possible, but especially the clergy, the religious, the Catholic lodges, all the school children, and the orphans. There were plans for a grand parade, with bands and Gonzaga cadets.

Father Arthuis set the day. It was Sunday, October 24, 1909. A commemorative medal was struck. Also, a parchment was prepared for insertion within the cornerstone. It read in part: "The First Cornerstone of this Holy Temple, Dedicated to St. Aloysius Gonzaga, was laid and blessed, in the presence of a great concourse of clergy and people, and with due solemnity, by the Rt. Rev. Edward John O'Dea, Bishop of the Diocese of Seattle. To the Greater Glory of God."

The day dawned, one of those sparkling crisp autumn days for which Spokane is famous. Word came that Archbishop Christie had been injured in an accident and would not be able to preside. This caused no problem. With four bishops assembled in all their splendor, the ceremony was assured of a record-smashing attendance.

Long before 1:30, when the ceremony was to begin, throngs of people arrived in carriages and automobiles. Scores of photographers, both amateur and professional, established themselves in key positions. So vast was the throng that the streets had to be blocked. Spokane had seen nothing like it in its thirty-seven year history. The local press presented copious accounts of it for several days. They quoted long portions of O'Dea's sermon, described the ceremony in detail, and spilled buckets of ink in praise of the fervor of Catholics.

The new provincial, meanwhile, itching for action abroad, scheduled his visitation of California and the missions. He informed members of the press that he would like to make Spokane his province headquarters, but he would reserve judgment until he had inspected the colleges and parishes of the province. On September 15, one week after taking office, he filed new incorporation papers for the Pioneer Education Society. These were submitted as follows:

I

"The name of said corporation shall be The Pioneer Educational Society and the chief place of business of said corporation shall be in the City of Spokane, Spokane County, Washington."

II

"The corporation shall be composed of such members of the Society of Jesus as may be elected by the members of the corporation to membership therein."

III

"Said corporation is organized to further the interest of Christian education and to promote the advancement of the Christian religion through the erection and maintenance of Churches, Colleges and Schools and the preaching of the Christian Gospel. And to this end and to provide means therefore, it may acquire by purchase, may erect and construct houses, buildings, or works of every description. . . ."[44]

This document was signed by H.J. Goller, President, and P.J. Arthuis, Secretary. It should be observed that Goller in the first part declared Spokane, not Portland, to be the place of the corporation, and in the third part, he scarcely included in the purpose of the corporation the care and promotion of missions for Indians. Neither Goller nor Arthuis had ever been assigned to the missions. Their positions of influence now clearly indicated the province's priorities in favor of schools and parishes. All of Goller's circular letters to the province were dispatched from Gonzaga, where he spent most of the little time he had left. He was especially fond of the scholastics in "the Sheds," and they jumped at every opportunity to serve him.

He was enroute to Gonzaga from southern Alaska when his ship was struck by lightning. Spokane reporters, after his arrival shortly before Christmas, pounced on him for comments of any kind. What kind of trip did he have? What were his future plans? More than pleased to meet the press, as genial as a prosperous baron, he described in vivid terminology how the lightning had struck the boat with such an explosive bang that some of the passengers fainted. Delightful experience.[45]

On the same day, December 21, 1909, Santa Clara College, completely recovered from the earthquake, met with another disaster. The administration building, a four-story structure containing in part the original college, was destroyed by fire. No one was injured, but Father Neri, the blind teacher of physics, barely escaped. He had been led slowly through the smoking passageways while the fire roared overhead. All the contents of the building were lost: paintings by old masters, mission relics, books and manuscripts, even the complete plans for the new Santa Clara College.[46]

Goller was still in Spokane in January, 1910. A letter arrived from the General's assistant, Father Herman Walmesley. The General, he wrote, was very pleased to learn about "the spirit of great union and charity in the new province."[47] This revealed the extent of efforts being made by members of all sectors of the province, including the Dakotas, to create a new identity and to work together as Jesuits.

Another letter arrived from Father General. This concerned the mission of northern Alaska, which had encountered difficulties of language and citizenship in its current status as a mission of the Canadian province.[48] Both Father Wernz and Goller were sparring without revealing their true thinking on the subject. Goller wanted the mission returned to the California province and so did Wernz, but neither was willing at this point to commit himself.

In February, Goller was in Portland. While here he suffered his first heart attack which, according to Father Patrick O'Reilly, the province soothsayer, was caused by a weakness for cigars. "Don't schmoke!" O'Reilly warned succeeding generations of scholastics, "I knew a Jesuit once who wanted to be provincial all his life, but he schmoked and he died soon after he became provincial and he never had a chance to enjoy being provincial."* Neither the masters of the ascetical life nor the doctors of medicine agreed with his analysis of cause and effect, and Jesuits who were provincials laughed at it. The fact is, Herman Goller was notably overweight, and his doctor, R. J. Newell, was helpless in convincing him that he ought to lose one hundred pounds or more; preferably more.

Goller loved the good life. He had grown up in an affluent family. This accounted in part for his enormous popularity with the establishment in Spokane. It was said of him that he was the most gracious of hosts. Once when he was for an hour thrown into the company of Williams Jennings Bryan, the great populist, the following dialogue took place:

"Let us have a bottle," genially suggested His Reverence. "No thank you," stiffly replied Mr. Bryan. "Very well, I shall send down for some good cigars," continued the Father. "I do not smoke," nervously responded the Peerless One. Whereupon Father Goller, his jolly round face all aglow, arising said, "Mr. Bryan, will you have some candy?"[49]

But now Goller was a patient in St. Vincent's Hospital, Portland, and there he remained, the subject of much anxiety, for six weeks.[50] Convinced of his "complete recovery" after he was released, he began his visitation of the province, an ordeal which almost killed provincials who were as strong as mules. On May 18, he was back at Gonzaga and an old friend, Father James Rockliff, came to see him. Both Rockliff and Rebmann were prefects of the Jesuit college at Feldkirche, Austria, when Goller was a boarding student there. Rockliff with two other Jesuits had been assigned by Pope Pius X to establish Sophia University in Tokyo.† Rockliff's health was adversely affected by the humid climate, and his provincial, Father John Hanselman of New York, had recalled him back to the States. Now Rockliff stopped to see them enroute to New York, and Goller, turning on all his charm begged him to remain as his assistant or socius, while they organized the province together. He assured Rockliff that he could arrange the matter with both Father General and Father Hanselman.

On that same day, Goller drafted a long letter to the apostolic delegate, Archbishop Diomede Falconio, deploring Bishop Carroll's refusal to give him faculties for blessing a church bell unless he turned over to the bishop the deeds to two churches in Polson and Ronan, Montana.[51] These churches, Goller said, had been built on Jesuit land with Jesuit funds for the use of both Indians and Whites on the Flathead reservation. What bothered Goller most of all was the possible intention of the bishop to deprive the Jesuits of St. Ignatius Mission. Falconio responded eventually, by advising Goller to request that the

*This comment by Father Patrick O'Reilly was made to the novices and juniors during a retreat at Sheridan, August, 1940.

†Pope Pius X specifically named these Jesuits to establish Sophia. In addition to Rockliff there were Fathers Joseph Dahlen and H. Boucher, *Woodstock Letters*, 37 (1908), p. 426.

bishop state his plans and his reasons. Then, the archbishop added, Goller should again contact the apostolic delegate's office.

De la Motte was now superior of St. Ignatius Mission. Despite his disillusionment with certain Indians, the school was flourishing. The farm supported churches for both Indians and Whites elsewhere; for example in the Jocko Valley, and the two churches in Montana which the bishop wanted. Even though Griva had built both of these churches and served them faithfully, the bishop was determined. Goller's successor turned them over to the Helena diocese in 1913.

Hanselman replied to Goller's request for Rockliff's assistance on May 30.[52] He approved of the proposal on condition that Rockliff first attend the New York Province Congregation on June 25. The general, too, gave his consent, and thus it happened that James Rockliff, who had dropped in for a visit with an old friend, became socius to the provincial of the California province. Sooner than anyone expected, he would take over Goller's place as provincial.

In August, Goller was in the hospital again in Oakland, California. He returned to Spokane on August 13, accompanied by Rockliff and Father Sasia, president of St. Ignatius College, San Francisco. He announced again that he was "completely recovered," but he would remain at Gonzaga indefinitely.[53] Brother Broderick, the college infirmarian, soon took him under his wing in Goller Hall, and there he conducted the business of the province.

On Monday evening, October 16, they took him to Sacred Heart Hospital. Six days later, Rockliff sent a printed notice to all members of the province stating that the provincial had received the Last Sacraments. As his last official act the dying priest appointed Rockliff as vice-provincial, then he turned his mind completely to God. A pall of doom hovered over the still vulnerable young province, especially over the halls of Gonzaga. The president of the college, Father Louis Taelman, described Father Goller's last hours:

"What characterized the conduct of Father Goller during the last month of his sickness was complete resignation to God's holy will. About two weeks ago he said to me, 'Father, tell me to die, and I will make an act of obedience.' When flowers were sent to him by friends in the city he would request the sister in charge to put them on the altar of he chapel; and when the sister remarked, 'shall I ask Our Lord to cure you?' he answered, 'No, sister, only ask that God's will be done.'"[54]

On Saturday evening at 11 o'clock, November 5, 1910, Herman Goller, first provincial of the California province, died. He was forty-three years old.

The next day's headlines bore the news that a popular local teacher had been murderd, but prominently carried on the front page was the news of Goller's death. For days the newspapers bewailed his loss and carried long eulogies by civic leaders, and countless detailed reports about the elaborate funeral preparations.

The requiem Mass was celebrated in the old St. Aloysius frame church, which stood where Bea House is today, having been moved there for the construction of the new church on Boone Avenue. Archbishop Christie presided, Bishop O'Dea preached and other bishops, including Bishop Carroll of Helena, joined the celebrant in the final absolution. Father Cataldo was a bishop's chaplain. The Knights of Columbus served as the Honor Guard. While five hundred mourners were jammed into the church, many others outside peered curiously through the open doors.

The scholastics choir sang the Mass and the *Dies Irae* in Gregorian plain chant, which one reporter described as a great testimony of love. "No death in years," he wrote, "whether of layman or churchman, has produced so much actual grief as did that of the provincial. The funeral ceremonies several times were interrupted by sobs from the men in the audience."[55]

After the last incense blown by each bishop had drifted away, the remains were carried from the church by the pall bearers, with considerable effort, we can imagine, for most of them were elderly men, tottering on the brink of the grave themselves. The simple coffin was placed in an ornate black hearse, with black curtains, while two horses stomped impatiently. It was Tuesday, a beautiful clear day that symbolized life not death, and Goller's spirit was doubtlessly full of it, as sparkling and genial as ever. But on Astor Street there were buckets of tears and many melancholy sighs as the procession formed. The college band with muffled drums played a funeral march, leading to the cortege north on Astor Street and west on Boone Avenue to Division, with Holy Names girls and Gonzaga boys lined up stiffly on either side of the path where the hearse slowly proceeded. This was followed by the prelates, clergy, and other mourners in buggies, many of them provided by Mike O'Shea, one of the pall bearers who had once sued Van Gorp. The sad procession made its way to Fairmount Cemetery where the provincial's remains were temporarily interred, awaiting final burial at Mount St. Michael's. Father Rockliff gave the last blessing.

When the fathers returned to the college, Father de la Motte was there. He had come for the funeral but his train had arrived late. It seemed that the greatest event in the history of the new province was the provincial's funeral, and he who had really created that province, missed it altogether.

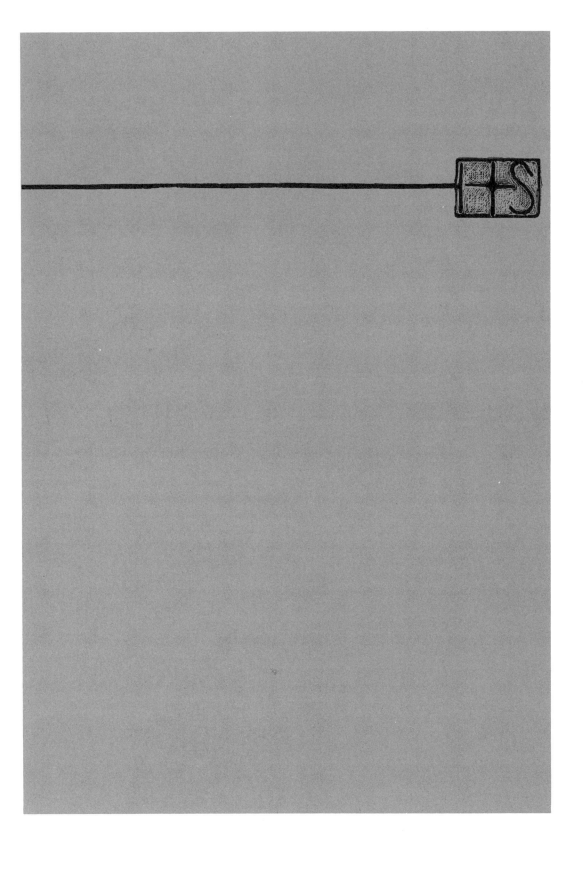

The parish buildings in Missoula. Loyola High School appears on the left, the Fathers' residence in the middle and the church on the right. Palladino's bell can be seen in the belfry of the church.

St. Jude's Church, Havre, built in 1916.

Aloysius Soer, a holy Jesuit from Holland, spoke a broken Dutch-English when he preached. The Indians said they did not mind, even if they couldn't understand him. They said he himself was the best sermon. Fr. Soer was at Holy Family and Heart Butte from 1905–32.

Eskimo hunters at St. Mary's Igloo.

Eskimo mother with children at St. Mary's Ig loo.

The present Little Flower Church at Browning, Montana.

St. Ann's Mission at Heart Butte, Montana.

Mount St. Michael's as it appeared in 1945.

Louis Taelman, eleventh president of Gonzaga and founder of the University Law School. Dean of Indian Missionaries, he served all of the bishops of the Helena Diocese until his death in 1961 at the age of 95.

14

FROM CALIFORNIA TO ALASKA
1910–1918

The new vice provincial, James B. Rockliff, formally appointed by Father General to succeed Goller on November 18, 1910, was a man of a quiet, almost hermit-like disposition, the exact opposite of his predecessor. He was not well known by members of the province, who tended to regard him with some reservations. Rockliff did not pretend to be popular like Goller, he merely did what was required in a calm, orderly manner. Perhaps it was better that way. Goller had tended to wear everyone out with his exuberant energies.

Rockliff had the appearance of a person who could do everything except play games. Among priests he looked like a bishop. Average in height, but barrel-chested, he changed little over the years. His hair did not fall out, his eyes continued to see everything in the province without the help of glasses, and his stubborn looking chin, like Rene's, gave him the same appearance of immutability whether he was the second provincial or the first rector of the Mount.

Born in England on October 4, 1852, he had studied at Stonyhurst, then at Stella Mattutina Feldkirch, Austria, where he learned the German language so well he decided to enter the German province of the Jesuits.[1] Unfortunately, Germany's May Laws obliged the Jesuits to take refuge in Holland. The novices were exiled with the others, including their novice master Father Maurice Meschler, author of the famous *Life of Christ* which has been used by novices all over the world.[2]

"When the novices first arrived at this new novitiate," Father John McAstocker wrote some years later, "the place was haunted, and they had a weird time of it. For several nights the noise was terrific. It sounded as if a squadron of cavalry galloped upstairs and then stormed down again. The house had been an old castle and human bones had been found therebye. The novices were, naturally, troubled. After some days, the novice master blessed the house and quiet was restored."[3]

Since the Buffalo mission in America was at this time a part of the German province, it benefited from the laws restricting Jesuit activities in Germany, because the exiled German Jesuits were available for staffing colleges in the United States. Thus Rockliff, like many of his colleagues, arrived here after ordination and tertianship. In rapid succession he was promoted to vice-president of St. Ignatius College in Cleveland*, then rector-president of Canisius College in Buffalo, and finally superior of the Buffalo Mission.

*Now John Carroll University.

When Father General Luis Martin died in Rome on April 18, 1906, Rockliff had been summoned to Valkenberg, Holland, for a provincial congregation to elect delegates who would choose Martin's successor. Rockliff was elected as one of the delegates and in Rome he was on hand to congratulate the new general, Father Wernz, a German. Wernz had kept him in Rome to assist in the reorganization of the provinces in eastern United States.*

If the California province knew little about Rockliff when he was appointed, he knew little about the province. He had been socius for less than a year, a year of waiting for Goller to get well or die. He had visited some of the missions, doubtlessly more than most members of the province, who were immersed in their contemporary think tanks, the colleges, which included then what we call high schools.

Rockliff had no special predilection toward Gonzaga, but very soon he was established at 3220 Forty-third Street, as the province catalogue eventually noted, with his new assistant Father Arthuis.† Gonzaga, still the largest Jesuit community on the West Coast, was also the largest of the province's colleges.‡ It had become too crowded and the rector, Father Taelman, was agitating for a new scholasticate on St. Michael's mission tract at the very edge of the bluff.

Taelman, it was said, spent too much, not too little, time with the Indians. North of Spokane, about sixty miles by railroad, there was a small reservation for the Kalispels, who had no missionary to serve them. The busy rector-president of Gonzaga happily undertook this task, along with everything else, and in the course of time it proved to be his downfall. This would prove to be a tangible reminder that the missions had fallen on evil days. Ironically, Gonzaga's failure to recognize its own identity with the missions, at least in its origins, prepared the way for its gradual loss of prestige as "the motherhouse," the center of the province.

At St. Mary's Mission, near Omak, de Rouge was still the only priest there, despite Bishop O'Dea's pleas that he have a Jesuit companion. The ex-count was killing himself with worry and labor. In November, the same month in which Goller had died, he built a hospital at the mission to provide care for the Indians who were suffering from an epidemic of tuberculosis.

"I have built lately," he wrote to Mother Drexel, "a little hospital, or the start of one, to try to save our tubercular subjects, and not to have to send them home where they (are sure to) die."[4] He needed, he said, a few things, like a microscope, to help with examinations.

Since this was the only hospital in the entire county, it was adopted by civil officials as the hospital for the care of county patients and as the only home for the aged.

Still not satisfied with his mission, de Rouge wanted college courses for the boys. His school provided the first typing classes in Okanogan County. It had a prominent track team, a baseball team and even a more famous band. To provide the college courses he could not get help from the provincial, for obvious reasons, nor from other religious orders, so he employed lay teachers whose salaries added many worries to those he already carried in his head.

Rockliff had other problems. Northern Alaska, under the supervision of the Canadian provincial, was experiencing difficulties that made de Rouge's look like petty cash. Goller, recognizing this, had fished in these troubled waters for an opportunity to take over the mission without offending the Canadians. On January 9, 1911, Father General wrote at

---

*Several provinces and the Buffalo Mission of the German Province needed reorganization because of growth.

†Arthuis became socius, or assistant to the provincial, on December 16, 1910.

‡In 1910 the following enrollments were reported: Gonzaga 417; Santa Clara 264; St. Ignatius 394; Seattle College 183. *Woodstock Letters*, 39, (1910) p. 437.

some length to Rockliff, explaining the basic complications of the language barriers the Canadian Jesuits faced, and what was involved in making the shift from Canadian to American civil jurisdiction.[5] No suggestion was made by Wernz regarding a change in status.

Finally on February 11, 1911, Father Elden Mullan, the American Assistant to the General, wrote a frank letter to Rockliff to clear the air:

"I think it would help all around if I tell Your Reverence quite unofficially and without any understanding with Father General, that he would surely be pleased if you took over N. Alaska. Certain other plans depend on it. But you will wait until Doomsday, if you expect him to impose the Mission on you!"[6]

Rockliff, not an impetuous man, favored immediate action, preferring the acceptance of Alaska Borealis and the loss of the Dakota Indian missions, to the other alternatives. For reasons not clear, however, this matter dragged on for another two years, while Rockliff negotiated with Bishop Conaty regarding the school in Los Angeles, and presided over endless meetings to resolve the scholasticate question.

On July 31, 1911, with the General's approval, he announced the appointment of Father Richard Gleeson as Vice Rector of the new community in Los Angeles. Classified originally as Los Angeles College, "A Collegium Inchoatum" at 225 W. Avenue 52, this was a high school in our use of the words, with a faculty of six Jesuits.* Three of the six, Father Joseph Tomkin and scholastics Thomas Martin, and John McAstocker, were formerly members of the Rocky Mountain Mission, and Brother Rosati formerly of the Alaska Mission. Gleeson, a Californian with deep convictions about its superiority, was especially attached to the Bay area, so it would be proper to say that Loyola University and Loyola High School in Los Angeles were founded by "foreigners," like the rest of our schools.†

Having concluded, at least for the time being, negotiations with Conaty about the school, Rockliff then turned his attention to the scholasticate problem. The last of the theologians had departed during the previous spring. There had been nine, of whom three were ordained. The others were assigned to theologates in Canada and eastern United States.‡

The Sheds could accommodate no more than thirty-five Jesuits, including the faculty, and this stretched its resources beyond comfort. In 1911 the novitiate at Los Gatos numbered thirty-one scholastic novices alone, a group which would represent only two out of three years assigned simultaneously to philosophy. It was obvious that a new building would have to be provided within a brief time. Proposals of all sorts were made, but perhaps none was more imaginative than that promoted by the pastor of Marysville, Washington.

Father P. Gard had got it into his head that the Jesuits should build "another Woodstock" in his back yard, at Tulalip on the salty beach of the Washington coast. He presented his case in a letter to Father Rene, who was teaching theology in "the Sheds," taking care to demonstrate that there was adequate land and fresh water.[7] He added many arguments and a carefully concealed hook, using the Tulalip Indian Mission for bait. Perhaps this was his greatest mistake. The Jesuits were not biting on Indian missions then and Father Gard, his plan to turn over the mission to others having been thwarted, passed from history.

*Collegium Inchoatum means literally a "college just beginning." California Province Catalogue for 1912, Spokane, 1911, p. 21.

†The two schools developed from Los Angeles College. Gleeson had almost as little use for southern California as he did for Washington.

‡The three theologates were Woodstock, St. Louis, and Immaculate Conception in Montreal.

FROM CALIFORNIA TO ALASKA

In August 1911, a meeting was held in California to discuss other proposed sites and their merits. In the light of subsequent developments, it was fortunate that Rockliff presided over this meeting. As a native Englishman who had joined a German Jesuit province, taught in a Jesuit school in New York State, and founded a university in Japan, he was certainly beyond the reproach of favoritism toward either of two factions representing sites in California and Spokane. The California Jesuits strenuously objected to the Spokane site, alleging that the weather was too severe. Apparently, some of them liked to think Spokane was somewhat near the north pole. The majority present at the meeting, nonetheless, favored Spokane. They contended that the best weather for study is not that which is temporarily pleasing to the senses, soft, equable and enticing, but one with distinct changes of seasons and enough of winter frost and snow to put tang into the atmosphere. A decision favoring Spokane was finally formed, but a minority appealed to Father General in Rome for a reconsideration of the matter. A thorough investigation of the charge revealed rather compelling reasons for locating the scholasticate in Spokane, precisely because of the weather. Taelman, one of Father Rockliff's official advisors, stated:

"Amongst the various cities that could be selected, not one surpasses Spokane in the requisites and advantages such a place should possess. From Government reports no city has more sunshine than Spokane. During the last 20 years, the average number of sunshiny days is over 200. The city of Spokane is not too northern, as some have written to Father General, and is not too cold. It seldom goes below zero here, and even then the cold is not felt much, as it is dry and bracing. The fact is that the cold is felt less here than in California or other places, according to the testimony of ours who can testify and have testified to their experiences in this matter. The scholasticate has been in Spokane for over 10 years, and during all these years the health of ours could not have been better, as the records will show. It is claimed that the Scholasticate should be in an Episcopal city. It is well known amongst the clergy, both regular and secular, that it is only a question of 2 or 3 years at most, when Spokane will have a Bishop. There is no city in the Province where we have as solid a footing and as splendid an opportunity for growth and a development as in Spokane."*

Not only did Father Taelman claim to have the ideal weather in Spokane, he also had the land. The Jesuits still owned the St. Michael's Mission property acquired by Father Cataldo in 1881. Taelman proposed it to clinch his case.

"St. Michael's has 480 acres of land. It can furnish fruit (1200 boxes this year) potatoes (800 sacks) vegetables, milk, butter, eggs. Instead of 300 chickens, there could be a 1000. Instead of 1818 scrub cows, they could have 2 dozen thoroughbreds, with plenty of milk and butter. There is a natural park there, a fine place for graveyard, etc. The place is one mile from the City limits—Roads can easily be built, with grade that is not steep. A 2 ton truck will bring all the coal in a short time. Side track could be obtained from G.N.—It can be made into a most beautiful park and Residence around Spokane. The possibilities for beautifying are exceptionally fine.—It would be the Theological & Philosophical Department of the Gonzaga University. It would be a villa for the University."†

*OPA, Mount St. Michael's papers, "Reasons for Building the Scholasticate in Spokane," p. 1. As predicted, the Diocese of Spokane was established on December 17, 1913. About three years after this, Professor Ellsworth Huntington of Yale developed a theory that there were only five centers of high climatic energy in the world. Among these was the Pacific Northwest. Area vitality was attributed to variety in weather. This seemed to confirm Taelman's remarks.

†Cataldo had acquired 320 acres by purchase. The additional 120 acres were acquired by homestead.

The general finally settled the matter by choosing Spokane. In February 1912, the actual site was approved and Mr. Zittel was commissioned to design a building for the accommodation of 80 Jesuits, to be situated on a high bluff at the southern edge of the mission property. A preliminary survey showed this to be 320 feet above the plateau. The cost of the proposed building approximated $300,000. Father Arthuis who had just completed St. Aloysius Church, was placed in charge of construction.

The church had taken two years for completion. On Monday, October 9, 1911, the last Mass was offered in the old church by Father Butler.[8] Some of the older parishioners, who attended this Mass were seen weeping. The altar boys watched them curiously, unable to understand how old people became deeply attached to a building. The boys would soon be romping gaily in the venerable building, for it was soon converted into a parish hall.

On October 12, Bishop O'Dea dedicated the new St. Aloysius Church. For two days preceding this, autumn mists had hung heavily over the city like a coastal haze, and the pessimists among the Jesuits predicted rain. The pessimists were wrong. An Indian summer came with the dawn of the twelfth. The sun was shining brightly at ten in the morning when the procession of one hundred altar boys in new red soutanes and surplices emerged from the main entrance of the college. Following them were two hundred members of the clergy and last of all, Bishop O'Dea. Thousands of people, far more than the church could accommodate, sought admission for the pontifical Mass, and J. J. Schiffner and his twenty assistant ushers were hard-pressed by the more obstreperous. But all went well.*

The new church was designed in an adaptation of the Romanesque, a style that had prevailed in western Europe from the fifth to the twelfth century. It was built in pressed brick, the same type and hue of the college. Its length was 190 feet; its width, 110 feet; and its height above the nave, 124 feet. The two lofty spires which have inspired the title of the students' yearbook, *The Spires,* rise 164 feet above the ground level and they are surmounted by crosses 10 feet high, each bearing 40 electric lights for illumination. The main floor, measuring 90' by 72', could accommodate 1,100 people comfortably while 3 galleries provided for another 300. In the broad sanctuary, elevated several feet above the nave, there were 3 altars carved from Carrara marble with columns and panels in Paonazzo, a white marble with dark veins. The center altar, presented by James Monaghan as a memorial to his deceased wife and son, measured 26' in height and 18' in width at the base. On the left, facing the sanctuary, was the Blessed Virgin altar presented by William and Bridget Codd in memory of their parents. On the right was the St. Joseph altar, presented by M. M. Cowley in memory of his wife. Mr. Cowley also donated the matching marble pulpit and communion railing, which arrived late for the dedication because the vessel on which they had been shipped was delayed in port by quarantine.

Distinct features of the interior of the church were the five private chapels which encircled the rear of the sanctuary. These were dedicated to five Jesuit saints, Stanislaus Kostka, Francis Xavier, Ignatius Loyola, John Berchmans and Alphonsus Rodriguez. A small vestry adjoined each of these altars where Masses were offered each morning by some of the fathers of the college.

The first detailed statement of the cost of the church appeared in the *Spokane-Chronicle* on December 16:

"Foundations, $19,974.62; superstructure, $108,177.20; electric fixtures, $1,294.10; insurance, interest, etc., $10,144.69; miscellaneous costs, $5,712.31; moving old church, $2,242.72; three marble altars $12,000; altar rail and pulpit, $4,000; sanctuary windows, $1,290; pews, $6,665.75; other fixtures, $4,623.95. Total cost, $176,125.34.

*The best description of the new church and its dedication ceremonies appears in *Gonzaga,* III (1911–12), p. 54.

"These figures do not include real estate, which was donated by Gonzaga college. There are now 400 families, or 3000 persons in the North Side parish. Cash subscriptions for the new church totaled $74,863.49."*

Following the dedication a banquet was served by the good ladies of the parish to the clergy and distinguished civic visitors. There were many speeches and each one was listened to attentively, if not appreciatively. Bishop O'Dea, a past master of witty after-dinner speaking, entertained his audience with appropriate banter and praise. But it was Father Cataldo who stole the show. With his dark, flashing eyes and earnest but humble manner, he reviewed the history of the church in Spokane. In the end he made a fervent plea for the Indians. It was for them, he said, that the Jesuits had come to Spokane. They were not to be forgotten at any time, least of all while the Whites were celebrating the glories of their new church and college.

After sixty years the ancient and troublesome topic of Whites versus Indians was still a delicate one. The presence of the old missionary, almost like blind Tiresias in the Greek tragedy, was a reproach to those who had forgotten the Indian. Sitting there in the banquet hall, his short, frail body dwarfed by the length of the tables and the tallness of his companions, he seemed to challenge the magnificence of the day's achievement. His eyes, confronting everyone in the room, glowed intensely, as if they were saying, "My brothers, beware lest your present preoccupations crowd out the just demands of an old responsibility!"

It must not be presumed that the Jesuits had neglected the Indians altogether. Cataldo himself, in his seventy-fifth year, was still engaged in their behalf: translating scriptures into the Nez Perce language for publication, and commuting regularly to the Umatilla mission to preach in Nez Perce.

Technically, Cataldo was pastor of St. Mary's in Pendleton. But his interests reached beyond Pendleton. Wherever Cataldo was there was action. When he came to St. Mary's he did not move the church; he built a new one, and it was made of hewn granite blocks as large and durable as tombstones.

M. P. White, who designed the cathedral at Baker, was commissioned to make plans for the new church in native stone and with a seating capacity of four hundred. White produced sketches which were adaptations of the Romanesque style, typical of American churches erected in the early 1900s. It was 167' long and 67' wide with two towers 29' × 68' high. It was precisely what Cataldo and his committee wanted.

On April 12, 1911, the contract for the erection of the church was signed by Cataldo and two builders, Messrs., Monterastelli and Perfetti. The next day, which was Holy Thursday, ground was broken for the new church. The assistant pastor, Father John Durgan performed the ceremony in Cataldo's absence. The foundations were completed, and the cornerstone laid on September 8, 1912, by Bishop O'Reilly of Baker. The event coincided with the Golden Jubilee of Cataldo's ordination to the priesthood, so the Catholics of Pendleton had more than Marian devotions to go with their Mass on that Feast of Mary's Nativity. Their mayor appeared long enough to congratulate them on their enterprise, and Governor West, of Oregon, sent a message which echoed the same sentiments. After the Bishop addressed the crowd, the hat was passed around, and the cornerstone laying was considered complete and official. The collection netted $250.

The church was finally dedicated by Bishop O'Reilly on Sunday, December 17, 1916. A number of Jesuit priests who had served the parish were present for the ceremony, but Cataldo, author of the construction program, was absent. He had been transferred to the

*Spokane Chronical, December 16, 1911. The original cost was supplemented over the years with an additional cost of approximately $75,000. These improvements included in part the following: the pipe organ installed by Michael O'Malley; the stained glass windows installed by John McAstocker; and the new lighting by Charles Suver.

Indian mission at Slickpoo, Idaho. Despite this cause for regret, the dedication was a piously gala one, with an overflow crowd and lots of fine oratory. After the hat was again passed around for the building fund, all proceeded to examine what they had dedicated. They found a remarkably solid and roomy building with furnishings in dark Cathedral oak. The fact that their money had run out before the towers were completed or new pews were installed did not greatly upset them.

When the new church was finally completed, it marked a new era for Pendleton Catholics. It could truly be said their parish life revolved around their stone church, of which they were obviously very proud. They boasted it was the finest in eastern Oregon, and it is very probable they were right.[9] Meanwhile, the old church had been sold for scrap. Its buyer paid $275 for it, which was not bad at all, considering the fact it was so decrepit that Pendleton's police had condemned it for public use.

One can see from all of this that Cataldo, even in his old age, was not one-sided in the matter of priorities. He loved his Indians and sometimes made excuses for them, but he loved others nonetheless.

At this point something should be added about two Jesuits who were isolated and lonely in the mountains of Montana, serving the Blackfeet Indians in missions attached to Holy Family. Father Aloysius Soer, the Hollander with the sweet voice and apple-red colored cheeks, dedicated a new St. Peter Claver Church at Heart Butte on August 13, 1911. In the same area, about twenty miles north and high in the Rockies, Father John Carroll had a primitive mission at Browning.

Today, Browning is a lively town with a prosperous government agency and hospital, and a Blackfeet Indian museum with an All-American fame. When Carroll arrived there in 1903 it was a scrubby looking village with shacks and tepees along muddy streets, horses grazing wherever there was grass, and innumerable barking dogs. The Blackfeet who lived in the vicinity trekked several times a year to Holy Family Mission, usually for important Christian festivals like Easter, to receive the sacraments and to renew the knowledge of their faith. This was, of course, starvation religion and Father Carroll was determined they should have more. With the approval of his superior, Father Damiani, he established specific places, like the sub-agency at Heart Butte, and Willow Creek near present Browning, as missions depending on Holy Family.

Father Carroll said Mass at Willow Creek in the tribal council hall one Sunday every month. White people as well as Indians who lived in the general area wanted a church so that they could have Mass more often. Accordingly, a Mr. Browning, who shared his name with the settlement, went about soliciting contributions. He took anything that was offered: cattle, saddles, hay, and so forth, and on a given day conducted a great auction which realized $1,200. The new St. Michael's Church was then built, in 1904, at a cost of $1,500.

During the following year Father Carroll was transferred to Alaska, where the weather was only slightly different from the Rockies. His place on the Montana mission was taken by Father Soer who visited both Browning and Heart Butte regularly and gave instruction to the children in the government school at Willow Creek.

For two years these activities sufficed, then the Indian department of the government, in a new burst of zeal for Indian education, built three new schools on the reservation, one at Cut Bank, another at Cut Finger and another at Bird. These developments complicated matters for Soer, who could not possibly attend to everything, so the provincial recalled Carroll in September, 1908.

When Carroll returned to Browning he built a shed-like annex to the church, and there he took up his residence in extreme poverty and dedication. He cut his own wood for fuel, cooked his meals, and performed all the tasks of janitor, choir director, teacher and priest.

He usually walked to the Cut Bank school for weekly Mass and instructions, often returning at night by the same means. In winter he made the trip in deep snow and sub-zero weather. Despite his efforts, his first years at Browning were bleak and seemingly fruitless. Later he wrote: "The first three years at Browning were discouraging indeed."[10]

He had introduced the Sacred Heart devotion shortly after his return in 1908. At first there had been a feeble response, but gradually, as he continued to insist on it, his mission became more spiritually awake. Before he left Browning, St. Michael's had developed into a fervent parish.

In 1910 he decided to move the church. It was still on the original site on Willow Creek, a short distance from Browning, and he wanted it on the very edge of the Indian settlement. Lacking money he did not hire a contractor, but attended to the work himself with the help of a few laborers. Thus the matter stood when Father Rockliff arrived in 1912 for his visitation. Rockliff was not a fussy man, but as an overnight guest of the missionary, he quickly recognized an impossible situation. He ordered Carroll to build a suitable residence at once. If he had no money, he was to borrow it. Under no conditions was he to continue living in the crowded, drafty shack.

Carroll did as he was directed. He built a house costing $800, surely not a palace for that, and he borrowed the money to do it. From that time until his removal in 1916, his anxiety over his debt was exceeded by only one other anxiety, the opposition of government employees to his work.

This opposition was greatest in the government resident schools, where Catholic students were in attendance. One minister, the Reverend Edward Dutchen informed the Jesuits he didn't want them *in his parish*. In 1906, during Carroll's absence, Father Joseph Bruckert, who was superior of Holy Family, came into conflict with school authorities. He prepared a petition signed by Catholic parents and two disinterested witnesses and forwarded it to the department in Washington. Soer was finally allowed to say Mass and instruct Catholic resident students once a week.

There was another change of staff in the Browning school in 1909 and the minister, the Reverend Riegan, was given a monopoly on the school's religious instructions. He was allowed to teach Protestant doctrine to all students three times weekly and Carroll was told to stay away. This continued for three years, though the Indian Bureau was trying to remedy the situation. When a certain Mr. Kelly became principal of the school in 1911, he informed Carroll that most of the children were Catholics, adding, "I don't like Catholics and I will freely cede my office when the government sends a Catholic."

Carroll tried to avoid open conflict while these abuses were prevalent, but he could not ignore the pleadings of Catholic children, who beseeched him to come as often as he could. They said the minister was trying to change their religion and they did not trust him.

Finally, a Mr. McLean, whose religion was the same as Carroll's was secured as principal of the Browning school and most of the local problems were solved. Carroll had but little time to enjoy the fruits of peace. His health had become so precarious that superiors were obliged to transfer him elsewhere. They asked the Bishop of Helena for a diocesan priest to replace him at St. Michael's but no one was available. Soer filled in until Father Thomas Daly arrived about six months later, and since this new priest did not know the Blackfeet language, Soer helped in the parish for several more years. In 1920 this aid was no longer needed, so the Jesuits withdrew entirely.

Meanwhile there had been other developments at Heart Butte. When Carroll returned from Alaska, Soer was assigned the special care of Heart Butte. He lived at Holy Family, where he did his bit in the routine work of the mission, then on each Saturday he buggied to Heart Butte where he said Mass at the sub-agency. Heart Butte had no church and its Indians were poor and scattered. Some, however, were very fervent. They tried twice to build a church but each time their beginnings were blown down by strong winds which roared along the eastern slope of the Rockies. Finally in 1910, Soer placed their need before the readers of *The Indian Sentinel:* "The Indians that live south of the Catholic mission undertook to build a church sometime ago. They manifested much good will by hauling and hewing logs, which they also set in position. Twice their work was partly undone by the wind, which sweeps over this section of the country in frequent storms; and so the Indians recently removed the material of the church and erected it on the site allotted to church purposes; there the unfinished building remains a prey to the vigorous climate, exposed to rain, blizzards and windstorms. . . .This is the proposed church of Heart Butte."

The appeal brought a response worth $500 and within a year the half-log, half-frame church of St. Peter Claver was completed. Soer blessed it and said the first Mass in it on August 13, 1911. He wrote later that it would accommodate one hundred adults but it was often overcrowded. Soon Indians began to build log cabins, in the vicinity, some of the older ones making Heart Butte their permanent residence.

This was a grand beginning and the gentle little priest from Holland took great care to nurture it. He came very regularly during all months but winter, at first in his buggy, then later with the mailman who had one of those very useful conveyances called automobiles. During Holy Week he remained at Heart Butte to conduct numerous ceremonies, his thin little voice as sweet as the early robins, and his cheeks a little more ruddy from the brisk mountain air. For twenty years Father Soer did these things and the grand beginning developed into a stable and mature mission. Though it flourished, it never existed independently of Holy Family.

Father Taelman as a province consultor had demonstrated his influence during the scholasticate site dispute. Another province consultor was Father Albert Trivelli, who will be remembered for his energetic activities in Missoula. Several of his predecessors had attempted to establish a boys' high school without much success. Trivelli, like Palladino, was very popular in Montana. In 1911, while others were celebrating the new "college" in Los Angeles, he was planning his own school in Missoula. He decided that classes could be taught in the rectory.[11] Before he had an opportunity to get things under way, however, he was appointed the new rector-president of St. Ignatius College in San Francisco, the magnificently prestigious position in a famous institution that was almost bankrupt. On September 3, 1912, his successor in Missoula, Father Gilbert, opened Loyola's doors to ten reluctant scholars. Classes were taught, as Trivelli had recommended, in the rectory until a new building was provided in 1914. This was a two-story brick box with two pillars in front, which gave it the appearance of a Carnegie Library. It was an elegant building, in a way, in tasteful contrast with the new residence Trivelli had built in 1907, which de la Motte had called "perfect."

Loyola College, as it was pretentiously called in the early years, was soon accredited as a four-year high school. It had to be closed during the school year 1918-19 because of the flu epidemic which swept the country,[12] but the following year it was opened again. What is most impressive about Loyola in Missoula is the quality of its alumni, among whom were three out of ten provincials of the Oregon Province: Fathers William Elliott, Harold O. Small, and Alexander McDonald. Two of Loyola's alumni were rector-presidents of Seattle University: Fathers Harold O. Small and Albert Lemieux.

At Gonzaga it was time for a jubilee celebration. Early in 1912, Rockliff had gone to Rome again for a procurator's congregation. He was accompanied by Father Dominic Giacobbi, who had been pining away for San Francisco while he taught philosophy in "The Sheds." Father Gleeson had found this heroic. "He was sent to Spokane," he wrote of his friend, "more than a thousand miles away and a very trying climate for one of his delicate constitution."[13] It was Gleeson, of course, who had led the opposition to Taelman's proposal for a scholasticate. Since the provincial was in Rome, Taelman, who was excessively fond of jubilees, had little to restrain him. His plans, however, included more than pious reflections.

Taelman had become a milestone president. To illustrate this it would be appropriate to relate how he made a Solomon-like decision when he was confronted by demands of the New World.

After a convincing victory over the Whitman basketball team, several members of the Gonzaga team sought an interview with Gonzaga's president. Father Taelman admitted them with characteristic warmth and briskness. They wanted to ask a favor, they explained. They would like to have a dance, a real dance with girls and all that, to celebrate their victory over Whitman. Yes, they understood very well—only too well—that dances were not permitted at Gonzaga. But what was the matter with dancing? Other schools had dances.

After a brilliant battle of wits, the Jesuit's power of analysis pitted against the students' ingenuity, Taelman finally conceded the argument. "Very well, boys," he said, "you may have a dance with girls, but the boys must dance with the boys and the girls must dance with the girls."*

From this, it appears, Gonzaga's eleventh president belonged to two worlds, the old and the new, and he shared, sometimes reluctantly, in both. Brought to manhood in the old, he was one of the few Jesuits of European background who was willing to try to bridge the gap to the new. If he did not feel at home in it, he was at least trying to understand. But no matter how much he knew about it, he could not bring himself to accept it fully. It appeared to be too simple, too innocent looking. There must be a danger lurking somewhere, so he compromised. The boys could have a dance, but the girls had to dance with the girls.

The old era at Gonzaga had been characterized by a kind of European parochialism, a ghetto-like type of education which, for all its remarkable advantages, did not benefit from contact with the accepted systems of American education. Gonzaga in its first twenty-two years existed as an isolated educational island, an island of peace and plenty, but unrealistic in some respects and ineffective in its overall influence on other schools.

Until Taelman's administration, the only official contact of Gonzaga with other schools was an occasional athletic event of minor importance. There were almost no inter-school debates, elocution contests, or academic conventions. There was little or no concern for accreditation. There was no effort to standardize its courses or to adapt its system for the accommodation of students who transferred to other schools. Almost no effort was made to seek local business support, a colossal mistake, which no other private college in the area has ever made. Though Father Taelman occasionally appeared before the Chamber of Commerce to acquaint its membership with the work of the school, not a single campaign for funds was conducted by Gonzaga until the administration of the twelfth president. Although Taelman did not bring the outside world into his college, he at least opened the door and passed through it. If his first steps were timid, he at least prepared the way for his successor.

It was fortunate for Gonzaga that Father Taelman was on hand to preside over the end of that first era. There seemed to be no reason to doubt that it would be laid to rest with all the pomp and splendor of a royal burial. As early as October, 1910, he began to lay his plans for Gonzaga's Silver Jubilee. His first project was the publication of a jubilee book, a

---

*These details were provided by alumnus John Raftis, class of 1913. A pertinent remark by Father Rebmann appears among Raftis's notes. "Sometimes subjects are talked about which go against my convictions, as for instance yesterday that one evening of this week a dance will be given in the Gymnasium. Such a thing, which was unthinkable in olden times, arouses my temper." OPA, Rebmann Papers, Daily Impressions written down during semi-blindness, November 26, 1926.

history of the school's first twenty-five years, and his choice for its preparation was Father George Weibel, the second faculty moderator of the newly established *Gonzaga* magazine.

Father Weibel was the logical choice. Under an alias, *"Historicus,"* he had produced two long articles which ran through as many volumes of *Gonzaga*. These concerned local church history, a fertile but untilled field in Weibel's day. Weibel belonged to the old school. Generally very accurate in specific details, he produced, with the assistance of his *Gonzaga* staff, a jubilee history, which was intended to edify as well as to inform. Its principal merits were numerous full-page cuts and details gleaned from the college diaries. It came off the press too late for the jubilee.

The book was only one project. Other jubilee projects were vaguely taking shape in Father Taelman's mind. Two of these were especially significant, as subsequent events proved, but they involved so many and such complex factors that even the daring young president hesitated to pursue them. Both of these objectives, the establishment of a school of law and the advancement of the college to the status of a university, had been long anticipated. In December, 1903, Archbishop Christie, in an address to the student body, predicted these and other major developments for the near future. "Gonzaga," he said, "is destined to become in the near future, a university of law, medicine and theology, in which students will have all the intellectual and material advantages of any eastern college."[14] No member of the faculty was willing to say, at this time, precisely when all of these wonders would take place. "The officers and faculty of Gonzaga College are somewhat reticent in regard to the great advancement to be made," the *Chronicle* reporter added. The school of law would "probably" be added to the curriculum when the new east wing was occupied. The school of medicine "may be realized within the next five years."

This kind of talk, as unrealistic as it was, intrigued the Jesuits. Some of them, Father Goller especially, liked to build dream schools all over the west. Gonzaga, of course, was the queen of all of these schools.

In 1908, as president of Gonzaga, Father Goller attended a meeting of Jesuit administrators in San Francisco.* Called primarily to discuss the restoration of St. Ignatius College, destroyed in the earthquakes of 1906, those in attendance proposed the relocation of Santa Clara College and the establishment of a new college in Portland. They also considered possibilities of establishing professional schools of law and medicine at both Santa Clara and Gonzaga. As Taelman explained later, they visualized Santa Clara as the center of Jesuit educational activity in the Southwest and Gonzaga in the Northwest.[15]

When Goller returned to Spokane after this very optimistic convention, he was still tingling with the kind of excitement optimism generates. Nothing seemed difficult. He announced to reporters that twenty-five acres of land had been acquired for a college in Portland and that buildings, "unpretentious" at first, would soon be erected there.[16] He confidently reaffirmed the Jesuit's previously expressed intention to develop a medical school in Spokane, saying, "The College is large enough now to support such a course, and it should come."

Father Taelman fell heir to these dream schools when he succeeded to Goller's chair. An intensely vigorous man, Taelman was not the kind to rest in dreams, nor within the comfortable embrace of the presidential chair. He began to agitate and probe for the realization of at least one objective and he used the forthcoming jubilee as a kind of whip to force the issue. In this he was aided and abetted by certain members of the local bar, especially ex-Senator George Turner, Judge J. Stanley Webster, and Attorney Edward J. Cannon. These men, as well as others in the course of the following months, volunteered their services without salaries on a part-time basis.

*Some details discussed at this meeting appear in the *Spokesman Review*, April 4, 1908.

Father Taelman presented their proposals to superiors as a practical solution to the obvious problem of support for the projected school. Without doubt, this was the deciding factor in the establishment of the law school at this time.* Father Rockliff in 1911 admitted the feasibility of Taelman's plan. His recommendation was required, at least according to ordinary practice, before the projected school would find acceptance in Rome. Taelman correctly presumed that Rockliff's approval of the plan was a reasonably sufficient guarantee for the establishment of the school. However, he also realized from the beginning that the establishment of the law school involved the larger and more difficult step of university status. He knew that Gonzaga would have to come to grips with both problems before it could solve either one. While the provincial appeared to be satisfied with the solution offered for the law school, Taelman could not predict his reaction on the university question. In fact, this point was not entirely resolved until a few days before the jubilee celebration.

One complicating factor in Rockliff's decision was the application of Santa Clara College for university status at precisely the same time. The president of Santa Clara, Father James Morissey, was in a much better position for pressing his case with the Jesuit general than Taelman. Santa Clara, already in its sixtieth year, possessed several valuable pieces of land and counted among its alumni and friends a fair number of wealthy benefactors. Gonzaga was relatively young, less than one half Santa Clara's age, and was located in a low population area. Its debt when Father Taelman assumed office was $128,000, a fabulous amount for those days. Clearly, if only one of the two schools would receive the required approval of Rome, Santa Clara would have precedence.†

Nonetheless, Taelman was confident that Gonzaga, as well as Santa Clara, would be approved. In February, 1912, he announced publicly, that preliminary steps had been taken and that it was hoped the college would be declared a university in September. He added that three new schools were under construction, schools of law, engineering, and medicine. Simultaneously, in the March issue of *Gonzaga,* a student editorial written by T. D'Arcy Brophy strongly urged that action be taken immediately. Brophy correctly placed responsibility for action on the people of Spokane: "Blessed as Gonzaga is with an enthusiastic student body, a loyal and growing alumni association and the implicit confidence and support of a great city, the task of expanding should be an easy one; and, undoubtedly, if the initiative were taken by a few citizens our hopes would soon be realized. If the people of Spokane were to show in some substantial manner that they really want a university it would be but a matter of time until Gonzaga would respond."[17]

Brophy here touched upon the delicate matter of local support. Like members of the faculty, the students were becoming more conscious of this lack of local support, and in successive issues of their magazine, they referred to it with something less than good-humored forbearance.

Currently in Walla Walla, Whitman College found itself, like Gonzaga, oppressively under debt. When its Board of Overseers threatened its removal to a larger city where it could count on additional support, the inhabitants of Walla Walla waged a desperate battle to retain it. While Catholics in Spokane anxiously awaited the outcome of the Jesuits' decision regarding the projected law school, a vast financial campaign was being organized in Walla Walla. Over $200,000 was collected and presented to Whitman to prevent its relocation elesewhere.[18] There were some who doubted Spokane's willingness to appreciate the benefits of Gonzaga College. Thus the question brought up in the early history

---

*In later years Taelman often credited these men with being co-founders of the Gonzaga University Law School.

†Santa Clara was declared a university on April 29, 1912.

of the school, whether Gonzaga College should remain in Spokane or not, still dogged the administration, though now it was reduced to the advisability of expanding the college or not.

On the evening of Easter Sunday, April 7, Taelman left Spokane via the Northern Pacific Railway for San Jose, California, to confer with the provincial who had returned from Rome. Before his departure he instructed his vice president, Father Kennelly, to announce that the law school would definitely open in the following autumn. "Members of the Spokane bar and local engineers will be called upon to take charge of the schools of law and engineering which are being arranged for next September at Gonzaga College."[19]

The sinking of the *Titanic,* carrying 1,635 people to watery graves, occupied the papers and the thoughts of everyone for the following days. When Taelman returned from California on April 18, his arrival went by unnoticed except by members of the community. He reported no developments with regard to the university status and, though his unguarded remarks revealed his own thinking on this subject, he avoided any public comments which would compromise his superior's decision.

Finally, on Saturday afternoon, April 27, after the excitement over the sea disaster had subsided, Taelman released the news everyone already expected:

"For some years there has been a desire on the part of the Gonzaga college authorities, urged by the request of many graduates of this institution and also of members of the local bar, that a law school be established, to form the law department of the coming Gonzaga university of Spokane, Wash. The time now seems ripe and propitious for such an undertaking, so that our law school will open October 1.

"Gonzaga university will consist of two departments, one an undergraduate school called the college of arts and sciences, the other a department of law. An academic or high school course as a preparation for college and a high school of commerce, besides a complete grammar school will also be conducted as in the past. It is expected that in due time the law department will be followed by other professional courses, according to the growing demands and the means that will be available. The charter of the Gonzaga University will include the power to establish various professional schools and confer degrees."[20]

The *Spokane Chronicle* for the following day carried other details:

"The first legal procedure in transforming the Gonzaga college into a university was taken this morning when President Louis Taelman, S.J., instructed Attorneys Turner & Geraghty to amend the present charter of the institution to make known the change in name and also provide for the additional colleges, such as the college of law, that are to be added.

"Article I. Section I, has been amended to read as follows: 'The name of this corporation shall be The Corporation of Gonzaga University of Spokane, Washington.'

"Henceforth the well-known educational institution that has grown up with Spokane will be known as 'Gonzaga University.' "[21]

Two weeks later, Taelman appeared in print again. Announcing plans for a law building, he said, "It is very clear that we have not sufficient facilities with our present buildings to accommodate the law school. The rooms we are now fitting up will be only temporary." The proposed building for the proposed law school was to be erected "south and a little west of the main building" in a style "similar to that of the infirmary." Father Taelman added that nothing definite regarding size, cost of construction and so forth, could be realized until Father Rockliff arrived to approve plans.

On May 18, Taelman summoned his Board of Trustees for a special meeting of Gonzaga College. He presented the new charter drawn up by Turner and Geraghty. This document was then signed by "Rev. L. Taelman, S.J., Rev. James A. Kennelly, S.J., Rev. Jos. C. Cardon, S.J., and Rev. John H. Neander, S.J."[22] It was retained in the president's files, awaiting Father Rockliff's arrival on June 2. After it had received the provincial's approval, it was dispatched to the Secretary of State at Olympia.

Taelman, during this interval, finally informed the public that the college would be formally declared a university on the last day of the jubilee celebration, June 21.[23] At the same time he gave more specific details regarding the law school, naming the first five members of the law faculty: Judges William Huneke, George Turner and J. Stanley Webster, Deputy Prosecuting Attorney R.L. McWilliams and Attorney Francis Garrecht, State Representative from Walla Walla.

With these grave matters finally disposed of, the president now turned his attention to other details of the jubilee. He appointed Father Kennelly to supervise a clean-up program for the college grounds. Kennelly had at his disposal a group of young men who were guilty of campus misdemeanors. With a little coercion they wrought wonders. Some of them, carried away by the existing optimism around them, announced their own plans. They were going to install fifteen "electroliers," campus lights on ten-foot concrete posts. Several of these were actually installed, but because of improvements in lighting methods they were eventually discarded.

Father Taelman arranged another jubilee project with a local portrait artist. John L. Peterson was commissioned to produce in oils eleven portraits of the school's presidents. These portraits, tolerably acceptable though not Rembrandts, were completed and are still extant.*

More specific plans for Jubilee Week, as it was called, gradually evolved. The President's secretary was more than ordinarily occupied with correspondence directed to high officials of church and state. Archbishop Christie and Bishops O'Dea, Glorieux and Lenihan signified their intention of participating in the jubilee. Scores of diocesan and religious priests from all over the Northwest graciously accepted Father Taelman's invitation. Governor M.E. Hay, who was running for reelection at this time, accepted an invitation with alacrity. His relations with Gonzaga had always been most cordial. The commanding officer of Fort George Wright, west of the city, agreed to be present with his staff and a detachment of soldiers. Mayor W.H. Hindley, who was also very neighborly with the Jesuits, though a Protestant minister, promised his warm cooperation and assured Father Taelman that representative groups of the city would participate in the downtown parade and final ceremonies in the Auditorium Building.

On Wednesday, June 19, Taelman's spiritual and academic fireworks began. The day was designated as Students' Day. Three major sessions were held, a Solemn Requiem Mass for deceased students, one of whom had drowned in the millpond just four weeks previously, a Solemn Distribution of premiums in the college gymnasium during the afternoon, and finally a Solemn Conferring of diplomas for commercial graduates in the evening. With Father Taelman everything was solemn, so no one should be surprised to read that all of the jubilee exercises were designated as such.

Alumni Day was arranged for June 20. This was begun at 9:00 A.M. in St. Aloysius Church with a Solemn Mass for the living members of the student body, past and present. At 11:30 there was a luncheon reception followed by athletic exhibitions. At 4:00, before the exhibitions had been concluded, one of Spokane's periodic dust storms moved in from the Palouse area and raged for three hours. It ought to be observed that this was also very solemn, for it became so violent that it blew off some house roofs. After a banquet at 5:30, attended by eighty-one graduates, the jubilee extravaganza called "Vincentius" or "Under the Shadow of the Cross" was presented by the students in a crowded downtown theatre.

*These portraits are presently hung in the Administration Building. The portrait of Van Gorp is "borrowed" periodically by collegians, but always reappears. Later presidents are presented in color photography.

Composed by Mr. Alexander Cody, a member of the faculty who subsequently published much poetry, this drama was directed by Mr. Timothy Driscoll, another member of the faculty destined for fame. "Vincentius" was a smash hit. Father Kennelly wrote in the diary, "The play was one grand success. Wearing elaborate costumes from Goldstein and Company in San Francisco, the cast included some of Gonzaga's all-time greats, John J. Weber as Corvinus, Wilfred Flood as Syrus, and Francis J. McKevitt as Torquatus. McKevitt stunned the audience with his performance of a madman."

On University Day, June 21, which was also the feast of St. Aloysius Gonzaga, Archbishop Christie preached at the Solemn Pontifical Mass of Thanksgiving offered by Bishop O'Dea. At 1:00 P.M. there was a banquet for 155 visiting celebrities who paid dearly for their meal by listening to seven long speeches. The banquet lasted until 5:00 P.M. Governor Hay was heard to remark later that it was the most intellectual assembly he had ever attended. At 7:00 P.M. the Silver Jubilee Parade formed at Bernard and Riverside. One-half hour later, to the music of the Gonzaga band, it moved down Riverside Avenue. Led by Colonel W. R. Abercrombie of Fort Wright, it was followed by a platoon of policemen, then Colonel C.W. Penrose and his staff, mounted on horses. The order of successive units was as follows: Gonzaga band, Knights of Columbus guard of honor, graduates in cap and gown, alumni, prominent officials and members of church and state, members of the Chamber of Commerce, judges, bankers, Medical Association Enakops, Bar Association, Realty Board, Ad Club, Catholic Foresters, Hibernians, Christopher Colombo Society, and so forth. The parade proceeded to Monroe Street, encircled the Monaghan monument, then went down Main to Post and thence to the old Auditorium building where a packed house awaited them. Gonzaga's Twenty-Fifth Commencement program was ready to begin.

After eight more speeches, like handicaps in an obstacle course, were delivered, the great climax of the evening was reached when Father Taelman read these words: "The name of this corporation shall be known as the corporation of Gonzaga University." A tremendous ovation filled the hall.

The feeling and hopes of every Jesuit were summed up by the editor of the *Spokane Chronicle:* "Gonzaga College was great," he wrote, "Gonzaga University will be greater."[24] It was many years before this prediction was fulfilled.

When these festivities featuring Gonzaga University were taking place, Rockliff, appreciative if not enthusiastic, was back in town, lost somewhere in the shadows. He probably felt like a fugitive, for despite his customary frank manner of responding to others, he was now reduced to defensive and non-committal replies. It seemed that everybody wanted more Jesuits. St. Ignatius College, shocked by the sudden prominence of Santa Clara, where ten thousand had marched in the parade, celebrating its new university status, wanted additional Jesuits to fill its growing need. New buildings were under construction, including the new St. Ignatius Church, as grand as the last one, and additional staff would be required for both, the church as well as the college. And, of course, the province now had two universities which were bottomless pits for all the men he could throw into them.

Los Angeles College had grown from 80 students in the first year to 149 in the third.[25] Seattle College too, had begun to expand. Father Joseph De Rop in early September, 1911, helped the Cabrini sisters with a new church and school for the Italians in Seattle. This was called Our Lady of Mount Virgin.[26]

The bishops also had countless needs and sometimes their appeals bordered on begging. Rockliff's men were now scattered in every part of the Northwest. Jesuits in Yakima supplied priests for the new church in Mabton.[27] Balthaser Feusi built a new church at Springdale near the Spokane reservation, and another in Deer Park.[28] Father Sansone who had succeeded aging Eberschweiler on the Montana High Line, built St. Thomas Church at Devon.[29] St. Mary's church for Italians in Spokane was built by Father Aloysius Roccati, and Taelman dedicated it with holy water and appropriate selections by the Gonzaga band.[30] In the summer of 1912, Sansone built another church at Hingham.[31] Then Michael O'Malley's brick church at Lakeview, called St. Patrick's, was completed and dedicated by Bishop O'Reilly.

Father Peter Hylebos of the Nesqually Diocese, Tacoma's pioneer priest, had built the first Catholic Church in Tacoma, measuring forty by twenty-four feet, at Division and Tacoma Street. This was dedicated by Bishop Junger on November 23, 1880, in honor of St. Leo the Great.[32] After four years, Hylebos produced a larger St. Leo's, forty-four by one hundred feet, at Eleventh and Market. This church had Tacoma's only bell tower to which the city police had a key so that they might ring the bell at times of disaster.

St. Leo's under Hylebos prospered and by the turn of the century, when William Jennings Bryan presented his famous Tacoma speech in a huge frame building designed for him, called "the Wigwam," Hylebos was looking for a larger church. He bought the lumber from "the Wigwam" and built the third St. Leo's at Thirteenth and Yakima. When it was dedicated by Bishop O'Dea on August 30, 1903, it was the largest church in the west, twice as large as the Immaculate Conception church in Seattle, boasting a capacity of two thousand people.[33]

This new St. Leo's made Hylebos famous among clerics from Seattle to San Francisco, but he was not happy. He cherished two great objectives: he wanted to be a monsignor and he wanted his parish to have schools. He had often said, "The Jesuits build schools." He wanted Jesuits for his parish when he was gone.

In 1910, Father Hylebos went to Europe to visit relatives and to go to Rome to secure a monsignorship for himself.[34] He had an audience with the Holy Father and discussions with the rectors of the French and Belgian colleges. He was informed that nothing could be done except through the bishop of Seattle.

During his absence Father George Weibel from Gonzaga had been assigned to replace Hylebos at St. Leo's. Weibel arrived there on August 13, 1910, and Hylebos returned shortly before Christmas of the same year.

Bishop O'Dea had not been pleased with Hylebos for reasons he did not make public. He summoned the priest to Seattle and there followed a stormy scene during which Hylebos wrote out his resignation as pastor of St. Leo's. This was in February 1911. O'Dea then sent to Weibel a telegram which read: "If you want St. Leo's, Tacoma, see me immediately."

Hylebos was never made a monsignor, but he got one of his deepest wishes; the Jesuits took over his parish in 1911 and in September, 1912, St. Leo's schools, under Father John Cunningham's supervision, were open and ready for their lofty enterprise.*

There were other churches built by Jesuits during this period. In the winter of 1911, Herman Schuler opened a new church on the Spokane reservation at Ford.[35] Thomas Grant of St. Francis Xavier mission in Montana purchased land for a church in Hardin and built a small temporary church which was replaced by a fine brick one by Taelman in 1919.[36] Father Placidus Sialm, who was attached to St. Paul's Mission, built St. Joseph's Church in Zortman.[37] Father Sansone again. He built another church called Sacred Heart at Iverness, Montana.[38] Father Frederick Ruppert of Gonzaga, who later achieved world renown by freezing to death in Alaska, built the first St. Mary's at Veradale, in the Spokane Valley.

Father Griva, like Sansone, produced churches in the way some magicians produced

---

*Hylebos died in Tacoma on November 28, 1918. On May 30, 1921, an altar monument was dedicated to his memory in Calvary Cemetery, *Northwest Progress,* December 6, 1918.

rabbits. In the spring of 1913, he opened a new St. Joseph's church for Indians at Ellis-ford.[39] At the same time Father William O'Brien from St. Andrew's Mission built St. Bridget's Church at Adams, Oregon.[40] In August Griva had another church ready for Indians at Hot Springs, Montana.[41] Father Thomas Neate, superior of St. Joseph's mission at Slickpoo, started construction on the first Sacred Heart Church at Lapwai and Father Joseph Lajoie, called "Speed" by flippant scholastics, because he walked very slowly, like an old French Abbé, offered the first Mass in it on November 16, 1913. The next month Father Louis Caramello, who became a kind of irremovable pastor like Balestra in Portland, arrived to take charge of Our Lady of Mount Virgin parish in Seattle. Young and eager, he lost no time in beginning construction of a combination church-school building on the corner of Twentieth and Massachusetts. While this was going on, he persuaded the Ur-sulines to teach in the school, which opened in 1914.[42]

Just keeping track of Griva was a part-time occupation for Rockliff. He had several Grivas to be sure, besides his routine business. In Los Angeles, for example, "the brick town" college was bursting its seams and its vice rector, Father Richard Gleeson, a quiet man who could be noisy when aroused, was demanding a larger staff. On the same night that Gonzaga proclaimed itself a university, Los Angeles College held its first commence-ment by awarding eleven high school diplomas to graduates. Father Joseph Glass, former president of St. Vincent's College, frequently referred to during the long evening as "the Reverend Doctor Glass," presented the commencement address, in which he exhorted local patrons to support the new college and urged the Jesuits to roundup the St. Vincent's alumni and use them as their own. The Reverend Doctor could scarcely do more.[43]

At Santa Clara, Father Jerome Ricard, frequently quoted in the press, for his extraordi-nary predictions of weather, was becoming somewhat controversial in certain quarters, where there was jealousy perhaps, or perhaps only resentment in the Chamber of Com-merce. Ricard's *weather* was bad for tourists. Before January, 1913, after carefully examining his sunspots, one of which he declared to be 409 million square miles in extent, he warned his fellow citizens that California would suffer four unusually violent storms. He gave the approximate dates of each.

According to his admirers in the newspaper offices, where Ricard was big news, all of these storms occurred as predicted: January 3, the worst cold wave in twenty-five years struck California. There was ice on the streets of San Francisco, and the citrus crops in southern California froze; January 9, the great and allegedly impossible snowstorm swept over California; January 14, a storm covered the entire West Coast and lightning damaged government buildings at Point Bonita; January 22, a great rainstorm. A fifth storm, perhaps not unusual for the region, occurred on January 28, when heavy fogs delayed sea traffic in the Bay.[44]

I suspect Rockliff took a lot of this with a grain of salt. He was preoccupied, anyhow, with an unusual amount of correspondence from Rome. On July 18, 1912, Father General had written to praise the zeal of our Indian missionaries for fostering devotion to the Blessed Sacrament.[45] This referred, of course, to the traditional Corpus Christi processions which early missionaries had stressed as major annual events and which de la Motte, Griva, Taelman, and others had taken great pains to perpetuate. The Indians who regarded these processions as more important than Christmas, needed no praise from Rome to encourage them, but any attention they got from abroad was regarded with a certain triumph.

The principal subject of correspondence with Rome was Alaska. When Rockliff made a visitation of southern Alaska in September 1912, he was aware of impending changes. It is not likely that he realized how drastic these changes would be. The first concerned north-ern Alaska. By solemn decree, dispatched to the three provinces of Canada, California, and

Missouri, dated in Rome on May 24, 1913, the mission of Alaska Borealis was transferred to the California province.[46] The Indian missions in South Dakota and St. Stephen's in Wyoming were transferred to the Missouri province.

The loss of the Dakota and Wyoming missions brought tears to no one's eyes. All three of these missions were at a long distance from the West Coast. The Dakota Missions, each the center of great power and influence like medieval abbeys, were staffed by nearly forty Jesuits, more than in all of Alaska and more than in all of the Indian missions of the Northwest. There were no hopes whatever, and everyone knew it, that this concentration of Jesuits could be sustained in the future by the California province. Hence there were feelings of great relief over the fact that the larger, older province of Missouri would be supplying these missions.

Northern Alaska had not changed much during its identity with Canadian Jesuits. Crimont was still prefect apostolic, and would continue to be until he became Alaska's first bishop. Ragaru and Giordano, who had journeyed over the Chilkoot Pass with Tosi in 1888, had both left the mission. Ragaru returned to Canada and lived in Montreal until his death in 1921. Giordano's departure was more sensational. He had left in 1909, after twenty-two years on the Yukon, somewhat in disgrace. As Father Segundo Llorente noted later, he would be praised today for his failings then. He was sent to the States, Llorente wrote, "in the hope that he would become 'white' again; for he had assimilated the native culture to the point that it was hard to tell him from the natives. Today this is the ideal; then it was considered less than proper."[47]

Brother Ulric Paquin who had arrived in Alaska from Canada in 1910, suffered a worse fate. In a blinding snowstorm between Stebbin and St. Michael's, on January 27, 1911, he froze to death. He had not returned to St. Michael's as expected. A search was organized, and on February 2, they found him and his dogs huddled together in the snow, dead.[48] They say it is an easy way to die, one simply falls asleep and does not wake up again. But Paquin was only thirty-six years old and he must not have wanted to die.

In the years to come, another would freeze to death, others would drown, and still others would leave Alaska to die elsewhere from wounds they had received on the mission. Alaska, before she was tamed, was an unnatural mother. She killed her children.

Father John Sifton had arrived to replace one of her other victims, in 1912.* Succeeding John Lucchesi as superior of the mission in the following year, he adapted so readily to the terrible climate that he survived for twenty-seven years.† As superior Sifton had twenty-eight subjects, some of whom had come via Canada, like Fathers Joseph Chapdelaine, Joseph Desjardin, Hormisdas Ferron and Brother Alphonsus Lemire. These four Jesuits had to be replaced within a year or two. In 1913–1914 there were thirty-one Jesuits in Alaska, the approximate number for many years to come. Of these, only six were American born. The French born prefect apostolic, who maintained his residence at Juneau at this time, seemed to have a low opinion of American missionaries. The Americans, he said, did not make good missionaries. Among other shortcomings, the Americans were not good at languages.

Crimont was wrong, of course, despite his long experience.‡ One can attribute his error in judgment to the long standing anti-Americanism in Alaska that went back to

*John Sifton is also John Sifferlen.

†Sifton died at Hooper Bay on October 20, 1940.

‡It should be remembered that Barnum, an American, produced the first, and best, to date, grammar-dictionary in Eskimo. In recent years many American Jesuits were magnificent missionaries in Alaska; for example, James Spils, John Fox and Paul O'Connor.

Barnum and Judge. There were only eight Jesuits in Alaska of French or French Canadian origin, but they were thoroughly entrenched in positions of influence.

Two of the Americans, Anthony Drathman and John Forhan, left Alaska during 1915, the one after only one year's residence at Juneau and the other after seven years. Forhan's departure was due to ill health and he died in San Francisco a year later on August 11, 1916. He was a great loss for he was extraordinarily gifted as a preacher. It was said in Nome that people waited all week to hear his Sunday sermons.[49]

In Spokane, meanwhile, Father Taelman had been removed as rector-president of Gonzaga and Father James Brogan had been appointed in his place. This occurred on August 7, 1912, while everybody was out of town. The news, which reached the new villa at Twin Lakes the same day, was disturbing to many members of the community, who looked upon the Taelman years as the best in Gonzaga history. Others, whose voices had been heard in Rome, prevailed. They had admitted Taelman's good qualities, but objected to his frequent absences to the Kalispel Indian Mission. Some, too, had been offended by his brusqueness, acquired or at least confirmed on the Indian mission where he was accustomed to order about the docile people like minors.

Taelman left Gonzaga on August 11 for his new assignment as superior of St. Francis Xavier Mission. Though he departed with just a tinge of failure clinging to his cassock, his accomplishments at Gonzaga were greater, I think, than any of his predecessors, including those who had reaped all the glory. If his preference for Indian mission work had been in a sense his downfall, it would at least bring him the respect he sought at Gonzaga. He became the greatest missionary of his times, and he served his Indians actively almost until the day of his death, fifty years later. He reached the distinguished age of ninety-four, two years longer than Cataldo.*

Decisions like Taelman's removal were painful to all superiors but especially to Rockliff, who could not share his pain as others did. He, too, was soon removed from office, after less than four years as provincial, having served less time in his position than Taelman did in his. He was certainly not in disfavor with Father Wernz, who appointed him a brief time later to the prestigious office of first rector of the new Mount St. Michael's.

Rockliff's successor as provincial was Richard Gleeson of Los Angeles, of whom it was said that he had once fallen asleep while singing the *Exultet* in San Francisco's St. Ignatius Church.† Were he here today he might deny this, but he would also laugh about it, for he never took himself too seriously. A warm, almost sentimental American, he had been born of Irish parents in Philadelphia during the first year of the Civil War. Having arrived on December 24, he was like a Christmas gift, beautiful enough to hang on the family tree. As a young boy he helped in his father's store and he read books to his old, blind pastor. Among these books was a memorable one written by a priest who had "S.J." after his name. Thinking it meant St. Joseph, to whom Gleeson had an extraordinary devotion, the boy made up his mind to join the "S.J.'s" some day. In September, 1877, when Father Aloysius Varsi visited Philadelphia on his return to California, with thirteen volunteers for the mission, he had his chance. He met Varsi, was completely captivated by his charm, and within two hours, left his home with him for California. He was only in his sixteenth year, but with his bewildered parents' blessing he entered the Jesuit Novitiate at Santa Clara on October 1, 1877.[50]

The general's letter appointing Richard Gleeson as the third provincial of the California province, arrived in Portland on March 11, 1914. The promulgation of this appointment

---

*Louis Taelman died at St. Ignatius, Montana, December 24, 1961.

†The Exultet is the ecstatic hymn sung during the liturgy on Holy Saturday.

was delayed. "I have decided," Gleeson wrote in his first official letter to the entire province, "that promulgation of my appointment should be made known to the different Communities on March 19, the feast of St. Joseph, to whose fatherly care and gracious intercession I commend the whole Province during the time of my administration."[51]

Gleeson looked like a cardinal. Being one was undoubtedly the least of his desires for he tended to be diffident in his ability and to live in the shade of his much loved companion, Dominic Giacobbi. Gleeson's hair, prematurely white and thinning, was parted sideways, on the left. His soft eyes gazed benignly through his rimless glasses and his broad mouth below his pinched looking cheeks, impressed one with its lack of firmness, Gleeson's contentment with things as he found them. He was dominated by two great concerns, his devotion to St. Joseph and his attachment to San Francisco. In other respects he was almost timid.

At home Gleeson always wore his cassock with his rosary at the cincture, a practice reserved to those who were regarded as more pious. On the street, in his worn-looking black suit and his old black hat decorously untilted, he appeared to be most properly clerical, especially with the black cord hanging around his neck like the cord for a bishop's pectoral cross. He had no cross, but rather a watch on the cord, the better to keep appointments. He was a punctual man.

Moving to the provincial's residence in Portland, dangerously near to Spokane, about which he had expressed unflattering remarks, and far from San Francisco, robbed him of the little pleasure he might have felt in assuming his new role. Portland, as beautiful as it was to the eye of de la Motte, had not changed for the worse, but there is nothing in Gleeson's writings to indicate he enjoyed being there.

Several months after his arrival in Portland, on July 29, 1914, Superiors in Rome approved the province's request to borrow money for building Mount St. Michael's. The way was now clear for construction. There was something ironic about this, Gleeson who had opposed the Mount from the beginning now became the Jesuit primarily responsible to Rome for its completion. He placed Father Arthuis in charge. Because of his experience in the dangerous arena of construction, gathered as the *de facto* contractor for St. Aloysius Church, Arthuis was presumed to be equal to the new undertaking. As it turned out, he certainly was.

The first serious problem confronting Arthuis was a practical method for raising his building materials three hundred and twenty feet to the crown of the bluff. There was a 10% grade on the wagon road that cut along the face of the hill to the top. The best bid Arthuis could get for hauling materials by wagon, merely from the base to the top of the hill, was $1.20 per ton. It was quite plain that this was beyond his means. He put his mind to work and finally solved the problem. He built a railroad, 1,100 feet in length, directly up the bluff and put a cable tram on it with a steam donkey engine at the top. The tram car carried two loaded wagons, each with a capacity of three tons. The wagons were pulled by horses on to the tram, then the horses were unhitched and led away. The tram was quickly pulled to the top where other teams were hitched to the wagons. Empty wagons were returned the same way. Arthuis now moved his material as quickly as it was needed at a saving of $1.00 per ton.[52]

Construction on the building was begun on August 24, 1914. Using from fifteen to about forty men at a time, Arthuis was able to report in March of the following year that the second-floor level of the building had been reached. All during 1915 the grim battle of the bricks, estimated at 2.5 million, was waged by the doughty builder. On March 15, the cornerstone of the building was laid. Spokane's Bishop Augustine Schinner presided over the customary ceremonies, while two hundred people, including James Monaghan and his family, listened attentively. The occasional address was rendered by the Bishop's secretary,

Father W. Metz, on the very prosaic topic, "The Importance of Education."[53] On August 15, Father Rockliff, with poetic justice, perhaps, became the first rector of the new scholasticate which had, as yet, no furnishings, not even a complete roof over it.

During September, Arthuis' health broke down, and he was assigned temporarily to St. Ignatius Mission to recuperate. Father Dillon substituted for him on the job. Dillon took up his residence in the almost-complete building and directed most of his energies toward furnishing it. More than $20,000 was required for school equipment and furniture which brought the total cost of the project to $400,000.[54]

On November 23, 1915, Gonzaga University legally transferred the property of St. Michael's Mission property, with its livestock, grain, implements and so on, to St. Michael's Hall and the old college building, technically owned by the Pioneer Education Society, came again into the possession of Gonzaga.[55] At this point Gonzaga University and the scholasticate became legally independent institutions, though the scholasticate retained its academic status as one of the schools in the university.

During the Christmas holidays the curious scholastics at Gonzaga journeyed to Hillcrest, as it was called, to examine their future home. They rode a streetcar to Hillyard, Jim Hill's railroad town below the bluff, then plowed the last two miles through snow, which was very deep that year. Accustomed to the narrow confinement of their weather-beaten "Sheds," they found the sparkling new building intriguing. Though it was certainly no Waldorf Astoria, it was the most up-to-date Jesuit building in the country and perhaps in the world. Originally built in the form of a T, it rose 100 feet from the ground level to the point of the cross which surmounted the central tower. The red brick walls with copings, cornices and battlements of mottled-white terra cotta produced a splendid example of Tudor-Gothic architecture. The main building, the horizontal bar of the T, with a length of 293' and a width of 40', was 4 stories high. The middle section of this, which projected outwards an additional 21', relieved the long straight lines of the building and created the central tower. The shaft of the T, which was one story less than the rest of the edifice, was 176' in length with a width of 59'. The gymnasium was located in the basement, the refectory and kitchen were on the first floor, and a chapel two stories high comprised the balance. The chapel especially impressed the young Jesuits, who referred to it as "cathedral-like."[56] Its eight Tudor-Gothic windows, four on each side, were the most ornate features of this wing. Though it would be thirty years before stained glass was installed, the richness of the wooden tracery relieved an otherwise vacuous-looking nave.

Understandably, the scholastics were somewhat impatient to take possesssion of their new home. January 6, 1916, the feast of the Epiphany, was designated as moving day and during the last days of Christmas vacation trunks were roped and sent ahead with other movables from the old "Sheds." January 6 dawned amid gray skies and falling snow, but hoary winter cooled no one's ardor nor dampened his enthusiasm. With their hearts beating expectantly, thirty-four scholastics set out through the storm. "Some went in autos," said the diary, "others by sleds, others took the streetcar to Hillyard and walked from there to the hill."[57] After all had arrived, Bishop Schinner blessed the building, with the assistance of Father Rockliff. Then dinner was served. Mount St. Michael's had become a home. After twenty-four years of existence, the scholasticate had come into its own.

Gleeson was not on hand for the grand debut. As soon as possible, even before permission from Rome to borrow money had arrived in Portland, he had begun his first visitation of the Indian missions. As luck would have it, he was caught in a Montana snowstorm in August, which was no more unusual than snow in San Francisco in January, but it convinced him that he was right about the Northwest after all.

After completing his inspection of St. Paul's mission, he traveled forty miles of prairie into Harlem, the nearest railroad station. The telegraph operator there handed him a telegram from Father Marcellus Renaud, provincial in Mexico. The Mexican government, Renaud said, was on the eve of expelling all Jesuits from the country. Could the California province provide shelter for the exiles and if so, how many? The priests, Renaud added, could go into hiding and take care of themselves, but he was especially anxious to find a home for the scholastics and brothers.[58]

Goller would have dispatched a telegram of welcome to everybody within a moment. It was characteristic of Gleeson, however, to ponder the matter first and to consider it from all angles before making a decision. He finally wired Renaud saying that he was free to send as many Jesuits as he deemed best, even if it meant the entire membership of the province. Gleeson then sat patiently in the train, telling himself needlessly that he would beg from door to door if necessary, to take care of the Mexican Jesuits.

On August 7, 1914, three days after the German army had crossed into Belgium, setting off the Great War, Gleeson wrote to all of the Jesuit communities of the West Coast, requesting each Jesuit to provide whatever hospitality he could, to his Mexican brothers. At this same time, on August 13, when the Germans were still driving the Belgian army before them, Bishop Conaty formally turned over Blessed Sacrament parish in Hollywood to the California Jesuits. In return, he took over St. Ignatius Parish, which Father Gleeson had been trying, unsuccessfully, to build up for three years.[59] As yet, Hollywood had not become the film capitol; it was simply a promising suburb of Los Angeles, where the Jesuits were still struggling with their college which was now called St. Vincent's. They needed all the help they could get, including parishes in the more affluent suburbs. Father William Deeney was vice rector there for a brief time. He would be succeeded in 1916 by Ruppert, who unlike Gleeson, had not fallen a victim to California's seductive charms. He was, in fact, trying to be assigned to northern Alaska.

On October 10, 1914, the feast of St. Francis Borgia, the Mexican exiles arrived at Los Gatos. Thirty priests and brothers were scattered about the province, in communities north and south. All of the novices and juniors, with their novice master and teachers were installed at the novitiate. There were thirty-seven, including two secular priests who were novices and nine brother novices. A wooden house on the hill was put at their disposal. This was a large two-story building with a wide veranda encircling the second floor. A smaller building nearby, which had served as a chapel during the tense weeks following the earthquake, was converted into additional living quarters. Here the exiled community lived with native customs unchanged and with their native language uninterrupted.[60]

Among the Mexican juniors was one called Miguel Pro. Miguel's father in more prosperous days had owned a mine in northern Mexico where the less elite of American wanderers sometimes sought employment. From them Miguel had acquired a picturesque vocabulary, said to be *American*. Now that he lived in the United States he felt compelled to make use of his American and to compare it at all times with the English-speaking scholastics in the California juniorate. Miguel, concealing his true knowledge of English, often baited his companions, creating as much confusion as merriment during recreation; to the great chagrin of some of the stuffed shirts among them. Miguel was immensely liked, even by those who were shortest on the King's vocabulary. The American juniors agreed he was the most American of the Mexicans. Their memories of him "were mainly of his infectious laughter and of his perpetual queries, 'How do say?' " Those memories later fitted perfectly into the picture of him as the "Mexican martyr for Christ the King."*

The battles in Europe, meanwhile, were raging across the continent and on the high seas, with Germany and Catholic Austria on the offensive. Most of the nations of Europe

*Father Miguel Pro was executed by the Mexican anti-clerical government. See Mrs. Melisina Mary Blount [Mrs. George Norman], *God's Jester; the Story of the Life and Martyrdom of Father Michael Pro, S.J.* (New York, c. 1930).

were involved. Gleeson, like other superiors, was deeply concerned with what might be described as the fallout in America. How long could America remain neutral? Would Jesuits in America be called to the colors as their brothers in other nations had been called? Even more serious, was there a strain on charity within province communities where Jesuits from many different nations lived together. Unintentionally, or in the heat of argument, wounds could be inflicted that would never heal.

Father Joseph Bernard in Alaska was from France. He loved his mission, Mary's Igloo, across the mountains from Nome. He knew the Eskimos and their language well. He was a very successful missionary. But he loved France more than his mission. When he was called to serve France in her need, he left his post in Alaska in 1916, to join the French army. It was a tragic mistake that he regretted for forty years. When the war was over he requested Crimont to accept him again for Alaska. Crimont said no. "Bernard left no stone unturned to be taken back to the Alaska Missions; all to no avail. For upwards of forty years he kept sending shipments of devotional literature in English to the Eskimos . . . as an octogenarian he was still writing letters to old people he had known in Alaska asking about places that existed no longer and about men that now were totally unknown. He died in France."[61]

There were two other Jesuits from France who had received a summons from their country to follow the flag. This, too, was ironic, for both had been exiled as Jesuits, declared unwelcome by their anti-clerical government simply because of their status as Jesuits. Neither was able to respond to the summons and it is likely neither wanted to. One was old Father Rene at Los Gatos, broken in health by the rigors of Alaska. He answered the final call on April 6, 1916, while the Battle of Verdun raged in his native France. The other was de Rouge, the former Count de Rouge of the Chateau des Rues.

De Rouge had been ill for some years. He suffered acute stomach pains, which he more or less ignored until early April, 1916, when he was persuaded to enter Providence Hospital in Seattle for surgery. He returned to St. Mary's at the end of the month, more dead than alive, yet he took up his work where he had left it. On the eighth of May, he wrote to Griva at Nespelem, stating that he was getting well. The next day, May 9, 1916, he was found dead on the floor of his office. He had fallen on the field of his labors, far from the chateau he had renounced, far from the Jesuits he had joined, then gladly denied himself of their companionship to enter upon a life of toil for the Indians.[62] Like Grassi, who had tutored him, he died with his boots on.

As already noted, Bishop Schinner had blessed Mount St. Michael's. The Spokane diocese, comprising all of eastern Washington, had been carved out of the Seattle diocese and on December 17, 1913, its existence had been formalized by a Bull of Pius X. Bishop Augustine Schinner, formerly bishop of Superior in Wisconsin, was appointed as the first bishop of Spokane on March 18, 1914. Having chosen Our Lady of Lourdes Church for his cathedral, he was enthroned there on June 19, just weeks before the war began.

Schinner, a very shy and sensitive person, had been born in Germany and had spent his early years there. The rector of the new cathedral, Father Verhaegen, was a Belgian, and the situation for the new bishop became very awkward, especially after Verhaegen made offensive anti-German comments to the press. Schinner in his sorrow and humiliation turned to the Jesuits at Gonzaga and Mount St. Michael's where he often retreated to find solace and peace.

One of his confidants was Father Paul Sauer, who had narrowly escaped from the Great War. He had been ordained by the Prince-Bishop Francis Egger at Innsbruck, in the church with the unpronounceable name of "Driefaltigkeitskirche," which means Trinity Church. He was still at Innsbruck on June 28, 1914, when the Archduke Francis Ferdinand was assassinated and most of Europe's rulers started to rattle their sabres. Fortunately he found passage to America, arriving in September at Gonzaga, where he served as treasurer for two years. Then he made his tertianship at Los Gatos with Giacobbi for his tertian instructor. He was back at Gonzaga in June, 1917, just after America, too, had declared war.

At Gonzaga a new spirit prevailed. It was not merely that James Brogan was different. It could be said that Taelman was the last of the old guard and Brogan the first of the new. Brogan's background, something like Mackin's, had prepared him for dialogue with the academic community. Having been born in County Clare, Ireland on Christmas Eve, in 1869, he attended Irish schools for eight years, then worked on his father's farm until he was twenty-one years old. Then he migrated to America. In 1892 he arrived at Gonzaga as a postulant for the Jesuit Order. He wanted to be a missionary to the Indians.

In five years Brogan served in four different colleges for experience, the last being St. Vincent's in Los Angeles. He was old enough, forty-four in years, to avoid the fallacy expressed in the old adage, new brooms sweep clean. If his broom left a bit of refuse here and there, at least it did not take with it the good things gathered by his predecessors. For a considerable length of time he carefully followed the path which Taelman had laid. In October, 1913, when the Catholics of Spokane celebrated the golden jubilee of the founding of the church in Spokane, he did what Taelman would have done. He organized a parade and promoted the jubilee in every manner possible. Almost a year later, on the eve of the Great War, Pope Pius X died and Father Brogan was celebrant for a very solemn requiem Mass in St. Aloysius Church. One can picture Taelman at the excessively black-draped altar more easily than Brogan. While Taelman looked more natural on an altar, Brogan looked more at home on a podium.

The effect of Brogan's quiet, almost unobtrusive entrance into the president's office, and his studied efforts to be unnoticed, lasted for better than one year. He seemed to emerge in November, 1914, when he appeared before the Chamber of Commerce to solicit membership cooperation for two projects which had been forming in his own mind: public recognition for university athletics by admission into the Northwest conference, and public recognition for the School of Law by accreditation through state law. Both proposals were as daring as they were dangerous, but Brogan felt he had no choice, especially with regard to the accreditation of the law school. He could foresee the school's first graduation in the following year. To protect his students he felt duty-bound to insist on accreditation with the state of Washington.

Brogran, at least until he got involved in war politics, was an excellent president.* Despite this, Gonzaga had ceased to be the leading community in the province, the center of influence. Speculation on reasons for this provides new insights on what might be called province politics.

First of all, the loss of the scholasticate was a greater blow than anyone realized. There had been a time when Gonzaga's rector was an *ex officio* member of the Provincial's board of consultors. Even under Rockliff, this was observed at first. However, when the Mount's independence had been determined, Dillon replaced Brogan as consultor, and Taelman's influence had evaporated. Gleeson's consultors were his socius *ex officio*, Father Henry Whittle, Trivelli now president of St. Ignatius College, Dillon of Portland and Melchers of San Jose. A closer scrutiny reveals that only one of these Jesuits was attached to a college, Gleeson's pet institution, and Trivelli had little experience on the collegiate level to recommend him. For all of our educational activity, two universities and three colleges, there was meager representation on the provincial's official council. When Trivelli was replaced,

*Brogan in his zeal for allied support in the war offended many of the German Catholics in Uniontown, Colton, and elsewhere. For many years these people disdained support of Gonzaga and sent their sons elsewhere for education.

Gleeson nominated Joseph Piet, the novice Master at Los Gatos. Not until Dillon became provincial was a college man appointed—Timothy Murphy of Santa Clara.

What this indicates is that neither the Indian nor the college ministry, top priorities in that order chronologically, were allowed the precedence of attention during the early years of the California province, a fact not lost on the province pundits. It demonstrates further that Gonzaga's history, which dominated a long period in the history of the province was on the wane, so to speak, where the western province was concerned. From Brogan's time forward, Gonzaga was no longer considered a favored community, though squabbles about it would never end.

An explanation for the new direction of interest lies, perhaps, in the recent infatuation with great parishes, where Catholic loyalties found their maximum expression for a period of a half-century. The latest acquisitions of large city parishes in southern California, at Santa Barbara and Hollywood, seemed to confirm what was going on in Oregon, where the archbishop preferred to have his Jesuits in parochial work. In a way Christie used Jesuits like Marines, for resolving crises, but always in a parish context in which he had complete control. It would be that way in Oregon for so many years that the image of the Society there could never change.

So it was parishes and the building of churches that occupied many Jesuits in Gleeson's time, as it had in his predecessor's. In some places like Havre, Montana, new churches were built to replace old ones.

As Havre had grown eastward a more central location for the church became necessary, so an entire block on Fourth Street was purchased by Father Patrick Mahoney on September 11, 1914. The county, called Hill to flatter the railroader, bought the former church property for a courthouse and began demolition on June 15, 1915. Havre, as before, when the cyclone struck, did not have a Catholic Church. Mass was said in a hall and the fathers lived in the Pepin home.[63]

Meanwhile, in accordance with the instructions of the bishop, a combination church-school building, costing $20,000 was constructed. This was completed during the summer of 1916, and classes were begun on September 5 of that year.

As soon as the temporary church and school building were occupied, Father Mahoney attacked the problem of housing for Jesuits; after all, they could not live in a borrowed home forever. During the year 1916–17 he arranged for a two-story stone building that could accommodate all foreseeable expansion for the modest sum of $8,000. When it was ready, four Jesuits moved into it, very much relieved to be back in their own quarters. Each of these four Jesuits has a distinguished place in Montana history: first there was Ambrose Sullivan, recently appointed superior and longtime missionary in Montana. Secondly there was the venerable old Father Eberschweiler, seventy-six years and deserving of all that church or state could offer him. Thirdly, there was Francis Sansone, who had joined Eberschweiler in March, 1904. A dynamo of energy, Sansone attended a vast district comprising Devon, Chester, Hingham, Guildford, Dunkirk, Grandview, Gold Butte, Fresno, Boxelder, Bear Paw, Gathair, Joplin, Inverness, Kremlin, and so on. The list is more like a railroad conductor's litany than the composition of one man's mission. Finally, the fourth Jesuit was David McAstocker, who wrote while at Havre a memorable book called *My Ain Laddie*, about the people around him, and especially about Eberschweiler.[64]

An interesting commentary on those four priests is contained in a passage which appears in one of the parish reports:

"Havre has four priests. The pastor receives a salary of $500.00 a year. One priest is assistant pastor and cares for all the places in the hill country; half a month he stays in Havre, half a month he is out on the highline; while in Havre he is ever ready to go out to the hill country on sick calls. This father makes $250.00 a year.

"Another priest is assistant pastor for the whites on the Fort Peck Reservation. He also visits the Indians for half a month, the rest of the time he works out of Havre caring for the whites. He had a salary of $480.00 last year. The fourth priest receives no salary."

This $1,230 was not much annual return for four men, but the report adds, "Because of the great poverty of our people this year, none of the fathers drew his salary."

Few, if any of the missionaries received a salary. They were supported by the Catholic Indian Bureau, the Marquette League, and their local benefactors by circulating news-letters, or as Griva did, by writing countless personal letters to acquaintances in the east. Occasionally the Extension Society of Chicago helped provide funds for churches in rural areas. When the missionaries retired or became ill, they were given care by the province, usually in the scholasticate or novitiate where younger Jesuits were inspired and sometimes bored, by their oft-repeated reminiscing, a kind of therapy for men who had lived lonely lives for decades.

In Gleeson's provincialate, as in Rockliff's, many new churches were built by Jesuits in rural areas. For example, on September 14, 1914, Father Lajoie ("Speed" to the scholastics) offered the first Mass in St. Rose of Lima Church which he had just completed at Culdesac, Idaho near Slickpoo.[65] About the same time, Celestine Caldi completed Sacred Heart Church at Fruitland, Washington on the Columbia.[66] Griva, again, built the first Holy Rosary Church at Tonasket. It was a frame church, painted white, designed like a boot and filled with statues.[67] On October 4, Bishop Schinner dedicated another Griva church at Oroville,[68] and exactly twenty-two days later Schinner dedicated St. Rose of Lima Church at Keller, which was also a Griva church.[69] On January 31, 1915, Aloysius Roccati offered the first Mass in St. Anthony's Chapel, which he had built near Priest River, Idaho.[70] In the spring of the same year, Schinner blessed another Griva church, Our Lady of Sorrows, at Cusick, Washington. Griva had completed it in 1914 and offered the first Mass in it on August 27.[71]

At St. Mary's Mission near Omak, de Rouge finally completed his fourth church, the present one, and this was blessed by Schinner on June 25, 1915.[72] In October, Griva started another church at Nespelem on the hill north of town, a stone's throw from Chief Joseph's grave. This was completed in mid-June, 1916, and Bishop Schinner, who was running low on holy water, blessed it on June 7, 1917.[73] At Lewiston in Idaho, the fathers built a mission church attached to St. Stanislaus, on Main and Twenty-third Streets, for the convenience of Catholics in that area. It was dedicated by Bishop Glorieux on October 31, 1916.[74] Father Griva again. He completed another church called St. Louis on Chicken Creek near Monroe, Washington in the latter part of 1916.[75]

This list of churches has been long. It sounds repetitive and may appear to some as trivial. Yet these are the dry facts which demonstrate the tireless zeal of a small number of men who planted the church in the boondocks of the Northwest, where finished lumber, nails, glass, shingles, doors and paint were seldom, if ever, in supply. Wagons drawn by horses were still the ordinary means of transportation. Fragile shipments like glass and plaster statues often appeared in pieces. The acquisition of bells, which were symbolic of God's voice calling the faithful to prayer, required incredible feats of begging and endless correspondence with foundries. But the solemn measure of their ringing on sweet-smelling Sunday mornings, in the hamlets across the plateau, brought a message of hope to all who heard them.

There was another kind of bell, rung by hand, for calling children to school in Spokane. St. Aloysius parish finally obtained its parochial school. Prior to 1916, four Spokane parishes had parochial schools, Our Lady of Lourdes, St. Francis Xavier's, St. Patrick's and St. Joseph's. But St. Aloysius, for over two decades, had depended upon Holy Names Academy and Gonzaga to provide parish-free elementary classes for their children. Rebmann used to say, "Gonzaga, she is a cow and everybody milks her." The Gonzaga campus and Gonzaga athletic facilities were overrun by the "St. Al's kids," who were joyfully accepted by the fathers and by the scholastics, in particular, because many were attending the Webster school, a large public institution only one block north of the university's main building. It will be recalled that both Francis Corkery, nineteenth president of Gonzaga and Bing Crosby attended Webster because there was no St. Aloysius school at that time.

In 1916, when the scholasticate was moved to the Mount, leaving vacant the old "Sheds" Father Brogan offered the parish the use of this building rent-free. On September 7, of the same year, grade school classes were inaugurated there under the Sisters of the Holy Names. The Sisters had to commute from their convent at the academy, so Brogan, using university funds, purchased a large home near the school, and this became the St. Aloysius convent.

Subsequently Gonzaga grade school classes were gradually reduced to one, the eighth grade, and this was retained for the convenience of out-of-town students. The passing of the grade school department in 1922 was generally acknowledged as a new milestone for Gonzaga. It made possible a more pronounced distinction between the college and the high school, involving independent student organizations in each department. The high school, as an independent academic unit now came into its own. It had been the largest department from the beginning, its number of students representing almost four out of five on the campus in 1920–21. Not until February 10, 1926, however, was a separate high school administration formally established.*

By this time there had been many changes. On April 6, 1917, America declared war on Germany. Father Gleeson, now talked less about progress and more about survival. Father Brogan, who was given to much flag-waving and patriotic oratory, soon antagonized certain groups of German Catholics, whose loyalty to America was unquestioned. His students, aroused by meetings and the filling out of forms for the War Department, wanted to march off at once "to make the world safe for democracy." Brogan groped frantically for ways to keep them in school, where the government wanted them.

Seattle College, too, had become a hive of war-like students, itching to enter the battle. Student enrollment, never high, dropped radically. "High wages in the shipyards," one of the teachers wrote, "have kept a great many of our larger boys, in fact it is a saying that the Seattle Dry Dock and Construction Company, one of the largest ship building plants in the country, is run by Seattle College.[76]

By the end of the year, more than 187 students at Gonzaga had enlisted for service in the armed forces. Then New Year's Day dawned, bright and clear. The temperature in the Northwest reached all time highs. It was 65° in Spokane, a reflection of America's spirit and determination.

During the spring the war garden movement got underway. Father William Bennett was designated at Gonzaga as the commander-in-chief of an army of gardeners comprised of his sophomore class in high school. The commander gave lectures in class on the care and growing of vegetables and not one of his twenty-eight students thought it funny. A sheltered slope on the southend of the campus was allocated to the patriots, and there, under their blackrobed director, "who had experience in gardening in California," the twenty-eight boys planted vegetable crops with great earnestness. "Not only boys, but the professors themselves are going to get in the game and help win the war with the hoe and spade," Brogan said. "Arrangements have not been completed, but I think we will go to

*Complete financial and physical separation of the high school from the university did not occur until 1954, when the former occupied a new campus on Euclid Avenue.

some farm near Seattle."⁷⁷ Brogan's proposal was not only impractical; it was ridiculous, and the Jesuits stayed where they belonged.

Commencements then were like war rallies. All the talk was of war, not of education or of the lofty ideals men sought. Bands played martial strains. Underclassmen, as well as graduates, demanded acceptance by the armed forces and marched away while their mothers and sweethearts wept.

On June 12, 1918, Seattle College gave up. The president Father Joseph Tomkin announced that colleges classes would be suspended until further notice, though the high school classes would continue as before. Tomkin was hopeful that Junior College classes would begin soon.⁷⁸ The provincial had approved this decision, indeed, he could offer no alternative. There was no such thing as a school without students. Other schools survived with military programs, but these too were deceptive, something to be endured for the sake of victory.

Seattle College had no military program, nor was it likely to gain one. Since 1909, when its first three degrees were awarded, only twenty-five more degrees were awarded in the nine subsequent years, a total of twenty-eight in its entire history. In 1918, the community had fourteen Jesuits, including seven priests, five scholastics and two brothers. One of the brothers was Stephen Kish, often called "Hot Dish Kish," who was regarded as one of the best cooks in the province. Seattle College might lack students, but it had, at least, a good table.

Gleeson had been busy making changes required by the war and sending special announcements to the province. Draft laws called for interpretations. The new code of Canon Law would become effective on Pentecost and certain formalities with bishops would be required for in-coming novices—if there were any. Brother William Zwak had drowned at Twin Lakes on March 20. He had gone out to the lake to gather cedar boughs to be used for Palm Sunday, and had fallen through the ice while crossing the channel. His death would be a great loss. He was only forty-two years of age.

On Good Friday, March 29, there was another death at St. Ignatius Mission. Father de la Motte, whose health had been precarious for some years, died quietly in the hospital there about 2:30 in the afternoon.

Father Arthuis, one of his closest companions, was present just before de la Motte died. On the same day he wrote, "It would be impossible to tell you what effect this death caused among the Indians whom he loved and had served so many years. Nothing but tears and lamentations all around.⁷⁹

On Easter Sunday, while the last notes of the liturgical Alleluias faded away in the brightly colored interior of the mission church, an old Indian woman could be heard in her sorrow:

"My heart fails me. I do not know where I am. I ask for George at the residence, and he cannot come to the parlor. I look for him in the church, before Our Lord, and he is not there. I inquire among the Indians, and I do not find him visiting. I go to the confessional, where he used to tell me what to do, and what not to do, and he is not there to answer me. I go down to the basement church; he is there, but when I take his hand, it is cold, and his lips cannot speak. The Indians are left orphans, and I ask myself whether he can still direct me from the height of Heaven."⁸⁰

In May there was another death. Charles Hawkins, a scholastic from the Mount, was found to be in an advanced stage of tuberculosis. He had been sent to St. Francis Regis mission "for a rest," and there he spent a very lonely year, without complaint or protest. He had grown rapidly in union with God, he said, as he brushed off expressions of regret. He said his last goodbyes to his companions at the Mount and left for Lewiston to visit his family enroute to California where, Father Gleeson thought, he might recover. On May 1, he died suddenly. His funeral was at the Mount and his classmates bore his body to the grave, chanting hymns to console themselves, for in their hearts they knew they had lost a saintly brother.

Another saintly Jesuit died soon after, but he was old and eager for life beyond the grave. Father Eberschweiler breathed his last in the odor of sanctity, as they say, at Havre, Montana on July 13, 1918. He was in his eightieth year. His name, like Joset's and de la Motte's would be sent to Rome as a possible candidate for canonization.

Before the end of 1918, three more Jesuits would die, all of them in Spokane. As Father John Dalgity would say, one had to keep his bags packed.

Meanwhile, in April, 1918, Gleeson dispatched a long newsletter to the province, the first of its kind and a forerunner of the *California Province News*. This contained in-house information to raise the spirits of the Jesuits, on whom the tensions of war were beginning to appear. Among the many tidbits of news were the following:

"Our college at Los Angeles has at last got its own Charter, and with it a new name. It is now Loyola College. This change of name was to the satisfaction of the new Bishop. He said St. Vincent's was no name for a Jesuit College. He is a Jesuit raised student, and a sincere friend of ours. He presented to the College there the whole library of the late Bishop Conaty. The library was very numerous and valuable. The Military Bishop, Bishop Hayes, sent a request for three regular Chaplains for the Army from our Province. Twenty six in all were asked from the Jesuits in the U.S. Ten each from MO. and MD., 8 each from N.O. and Cal. F. Provincial sent him the names of F. Henry Walsh, F.Bailey and F. Dinand. F. Walsh has been accepted and has gone to Ft. Mac Arthur where amongst his duties is that of teaching Geometry to his men. F. Bailey likewise had been accepted, and had gone to Camp Taylor near Louisville, Ky. He had been in the Hospital shortly before leaving, for some operation. F. Dinand being too old, was rejected as a *regular* army Chaplain. He has been for about a year acting as the K. of C. Chaplain at Camp Lewis, near Tacoma, and will so continue. He lives of course at the Camp."[81]

In mid-July, Gleeson sent out his last notice to the province.[82] In retrospect, at least, it appears to be a very incongruous one, but its subject matter had been, for a long time, an occasion of solicitude on the part of superiors. The notice concerned smoking. Gleeson repeated, as others had done before him, the admonitions of Father General about not smoking tobacco and he ended his stern directive with the remark that smoking was to be permitted *only as a medicine*. Having never read the Surgeon General's report on tobacco, he accepted what his subjects had often told him, that their doctors prescribed smoking for better health. No doubt the doctors did, but Gleeson had reservations about some of them. The letter contained no reference to snuff, nor to those who snuffed tobacco like the old Italian missionaries. The Surgeon General, like Gleeson, has never brought that up.

Two weeks later, on the feast of St. Ignatius Loyola, July 31, 1918, Father Richard Gleeson sat rigidly in the provincial's office in Portland, but he was not in command now. He had been succeeded on July 16 by Father Francis Dillon, the fourth provincial of the California province. Gleeson's biographer described the scene where the two Jesuits, vis-a-vis, discussed the future:

"Where, and in what work shall you be employed?" the newly appointed Provincial asked.

"Wherever and whatever you give me to do," Father Gleeson answered. "Only one favor I would ask, do not appoint me a Superior."

Father Dillon tapped his desk reflectively.

"What was your greatest anxiety and worry in your administration of the Province?"

"In San Francisco, the Church and the College with the enormous debt."

There was a pause seemingly ominous in the Provincial's protracted silence.

"I am sending you to San Francisco thus relieving myself of the burden."

There was a catch in Father Gleeson's throat.

"Your Reverence is not sending me there as Rector?"

"No. But as a help to the Rector."[83]

The war ended with the armistice on November 11. Gleeson was in San Francisco, scarcely prepared for what followed. Coping with the epidemic of influenza would be more demanding than the war, and more disagreeable than collecting money.

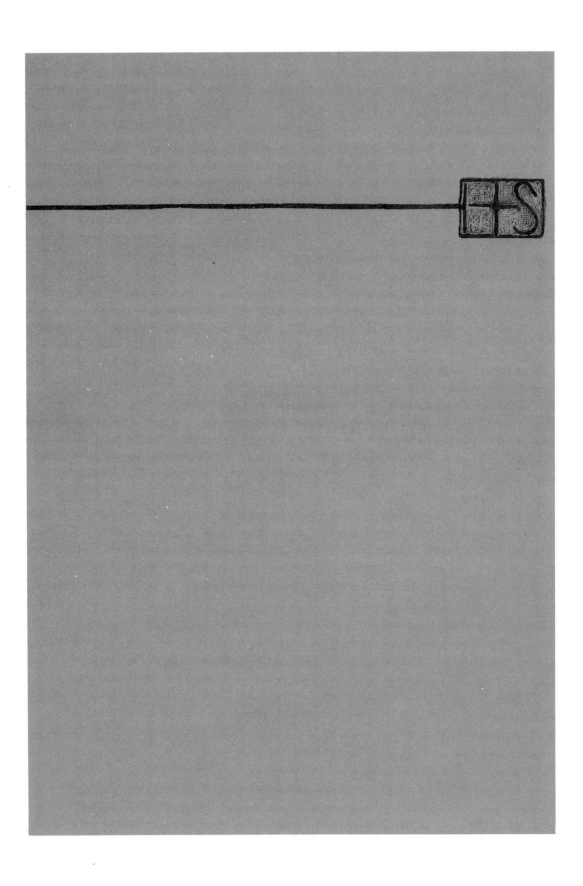

Francis Dillon, founder of St. Ignatius Parish, Portland; and third provincial of the California Province.

Mink, the famous sled dog that guarded the dead body of Father Ruppert near Pilgrim Springs, Alaska, where he had frozen to death.

Frederick Ruppert, S.J.

Seattle Preparatory School, originally Adelphia College. Garrigan Gymnasium is located to the right.

Marquette High School, St. Joseph's Parish, Yakima, Washington. Called "The Rock."

15

POSTWAR PROGRESS
1918–1923

Father Francis Dillon, the new provincial was an orderly man, who put first things first. Having just received his appointment from the new general, a Polish Jesuit with the singular name of Wlodimir Ledochowski, he sent a letter to the province to announce it.*

"V. Rev. Father General," he wrote, "has imposed upon me the burden of the Provincilate and suggested July 16th, the Feast of Our Lady of Mount Carmel, as an appropriate day for taking up the office. In conformity with the wish of his Paternity, I have assumed the burden today, under the protection of our Blessed Lady and hasten to beg your kind of cooperation, to aid me in doing my duty for the glory of God and the good of souls."[1]

Two days later he wrote the date at the top of a page in a little black book, and beneath this: "Permissions given for smoking and so forth." It was merely a memorandum book, but he confided to it his observations, as well as plans and permissions granted.

Dillon was forty-two years old, a sturdy Maryland gentleman, who would have been distressed to hear himself called a Yankee. He had been born in the border state of Maryland at Hagerstown just one year after the Civil War.† It would be inaccurate to describe him as a "Damn Rebel," but he did retain certain convictions that marked him as a true southerner in ideology, if not in armed revolt.

There was something misleading about his appearance. He stood average tall, as straight as a rod, in his black frock coat that was decorated with seven conspicuous buttons on the right. His white collar extended high above his vest. He wore a bowler hat that was as black as tar. Beneath it, his graying hair was parted in the middle. His eyes were dark. Above his square jaw his mouth formed a firm, thin line. A stubborn man, one might say, at least an uncompromising one. Dillon was both, but his stubbornness was tempered by a very personal love of Jesus Christ and His Mother. He was deeply affectionate, in his prayers as well as in his relations with other Jesuits, but he carefully concealed his feelings, sometimes leaving the superficial observer with the impression that he was cold or stern.

---

*Wlodimir Ledochowski was General of the Society of Jesus from February 11, 1915 until December 13, 1942. This was one of the longest terms in the history of the Society. Father Dillon's full name was Francis Matthew Charles Dillon.

†Born at Hagerstown on March 16, 1866, Dillon entered the Jesuit novitiate at Frederick, Maryland, on January 8, 1887, after two years of college studies at Mt. St. Mary's, Emmitsburg. He volunteered for the Rocky Mountain Mission and came to the Northwest in 1889.

He was brisk in his manner of conducting the provincial's business. He walked with a kind of lope that indicated he always knew where he was going and how to get there. But he was a good listener and in his own quiet way he conveyed a spirit of confidence in himself as well as in divine Providence.

Dillon is remembered today for a building named in his honor at Gonzaga University.* Except for that, he has joined the many Jesuits who have died and passed into an obscure history. But Dillon deserves immeasurably more. Known as the best trouble shooter the province ever had, he spent more than forty years of his life bailing out schools and missions from crises that would otherwise have inundated them. Because of his talent for resolving the most difficult problems, usually financial ones, he served briefly as rector or superior in almost every major Jesuit institution on the West Coast.

In 1918, besides the effects of the war with its strain on charity for province Jesuits from countries on opposite sides in the war, Dillon had to concern himself with the so-called Volstead Act, which was being debated in Congress. Since it provided for regulations concerning the use of alcoholic beverages for medicinal or sacramental uses, the proposed eighteenth amendment threatened the novitiate winery at Los Gatos with insurmountable obstacles. Since the novitiate until then had been supported by the winery, other means of support would have to be found. This was one problem. Another concerned the accessibility of wine for Mass throughout the province. There were some, like Patrick O'Reilly, who staunchly maintained that the Volstead Act was an attack on the Mass. Pat may have gone so far as to say it was sponsored by the devil himself.

More specifically Jesuit was another problem which the general had pointed out to American provincials more than once. This was the abuse, as some called it appropriately, of assigning young Jesuits to two periods of teaching, one before and one after studies in philosophy, or for a longer period than three years after philosophy, thus delaying their ordination and more valued services as priests by an extra two or three years. It was not uncommon for Jesuits in America to be ordained at the age of thirty-four or more years, at a time when life expectancy was considerably less than now.

Several provincials had already tried to change the system, but often pressures from local superiors, who argued that they could not spare the manpower, postponed any consistent action. Dillon, however, was not the kind of man anyone could force against his better judgment. One of his first reforms in the province was to abolish the *prolonged regency*, as it was called. Scholastics who completed their classical studies in the juniorate were sent forthwith to Mount St. Michael's and after three years of teaching during regency, they were promptly sent to theology. There was an awful wail, of course, by local superiors, but Dillon acted as if nothing had happened. Scholastics referred to Dillon's reform as the "Magna Charta," which other American provincials, taking their cue from Dillon, granted in their own provinces.

There was still another problem confronting Dillon, which not even he could resolve: the loss of government support for the children in mission schools. In 1918, there were ten Indian missions in the province. These were: Sacred Heart at De Smet; St. Mary's at Omak; St Andrew's near Pendleton; Holy Family near Browning; St. Francis Xavier's for the Crows; St. Ignatius for the Flatheads; St. Joseph for the Nez Perce; St. Paul's at Hays; Sacred Heart at Nespelem; and, St. Francis Regis near Colville. All but the last two had schools for Indian children. There were nineteen priests, fifteen brothers, and thirty sisters who conducted these missions and schools. Because of dire poverty every mission but one, St. Regis, faced certain cut backs, which at best were postponed from season to season, in the hope that something would arrive to save them.

---

*Dillon Hall houses the School of Engineering. It was built in 1948 shortly after Dillon's death.

In southern Alaska's six parishes there were seven priests, including Bishop Crimont, who had been consecrated at St. James Cathedral, Seattle, the year before.* As Vicar Apostolic of Alaska with residence at Juneau, the bishop had church jurisdiction over all of Alaska, but another Jesuit, Father John Sifton, served as the religious superior over the missionaries in northern Alaska.† Sifton also served as the resident missionary at St. Michael's. There were resident missionaries at Fairbanks and Nome, partly for white people; at Hot Springs, Pilot Station, Tanana, and St. Michael's. In addition to these there were three schools in northern Alaska at Holy Cross, Akulurak and Nulato. In all of northern Alaska there were only twenty-two Jesuits. Until this time schools had been supported in part by government-paid salaries to teachers, who were priests and nuns, but a new policy was introduced which, in effect at least, withdrew this only form of support. Thus the missions of Alaska, like those in the Northwest, faced a bleak future of survival by begging.

This was not a golden age for the missions nor could Dillon make it one. For this reason, no doubt, he did not give priority to the ministry of the missions. Having experienced administration in the missions as well as in the parishes and schools, he could not be regarded as favoring one rather than another. If he was conspicuous for anything, it was his concern for the younger Jesuits, scholastics in formation. The Mount was still a young institution. His own studies had been made at St. Ignatius where he had been in "the short course," and where structures had been loose and scholastic life somewhat permissive. All this was different at the Mount where Father William Benn, the new rector, held firm control over the natural exuberance of his subjects. The Rules of the Society were faithfully read at table every month and when Benn noted the particular relevance of one of these he would interrupt the reader. "That's a good one," he would shout. "Read it again."

Dillon's choice of his administrative staff reflected his own balanced view of the province. For his official consultors he had the following: Father Joseph Piet, the novice master, an Oregonian who had come from France to work in the missions; Father Joseph McHugh, pastor of St. Joseph's Church in Seattle, a level-headed quiet person, a perfect foil for Piet who talked too much; Father Tim Murphy, president of Santa Clara University and noted retreat master; and Father Frank Whittle the socius, or provincial assistant, who had been assistant to Dillon's predecessors for six years. Father Arthuis, after a year's sabbatical, was reappointed province procurator or treasurer.

There were two projects in the planning stages before Dillon's provincialate, and both were brought to completion shortly after he took office. Both projects, which proved to be significant developments, had their origins in the summer of 1918. These were the founding of the Laymen's Retreat Association in Spokane, taken over and changed considerably by Bishop Topel in 1959,‡ and the establishment of Marquette High School in Yakima, which, in effect at least, was forced out of existence by a diocesan high school founded by Bishop Dougherty in 1957.**

*Bishop Raphael Crimont was appointed the first Vicar Apostolic of Alaska and was consecreted bishop in St. James Cathedral, Seattle, on July 25, 1917.

†Father John Sifton was appointed Superior of Jesuits in northern Alaska on September 6, 1913.

‡In 1959 Bishop Bernard Topel established the Immaculate Heart Retreat House, which was owned and administered by the Diocese of Spokane. The Laymens' Retreat Association, as it was known, ceased to exist.

**Bishop Joseph Dougherty's decision to establish Carroll High School in Yakima provoked criticism and ultimately forced the closure of Marquette High School and St. Joseph's Academy, which had been conducted by the Sisters of Providence since 1875.

The Laymen's Retreat Association began modestly as the Knights of Columbus retreat at Gonzaga. There had been a clergy retreat for Bishop Schinner and his diocesan priests during the previous week.[2] Then from August 15 to August 18, Father Tim Murphy conducted a retreat for fourteen members of the Knights who soon formed the Retreat Association. For two years these laymen's retreats were presented at Gonzaga but in 1920 they were transferred to the Mount and scheduled during the scholastics' vacation at the Twin Lakes villa, a practice that continued for thirty-eight years.[3]

The evolution of Marquette from an elementary school to high school was similar to that of Loyola in Missoula and both schools retained certain characteristics in common, which classified them as parish high schools taught in part by Jesuits. They were subject to diocesan rather than Jesuit regulations which somehow left some with the impression they were like mulatoes, neither black nor white. This was, of course, a fickle judgment.

It will be recalled that Father Conrad Brusten, like Brother Rogers at Seattle College in the early days, was the stable ingredient at St. Joseph's parish. He had built in 1906 a new stone rectory to match the church at a cost of $11,000.[4] Both looked like strong fortresses, places where God kept His gold bullion. Three years later Brusten built another fortress, which he called Marquette College. Succeeding generations of boys, stripping it of all pretense, simply called it The Rock. Brusten reported that the three buildings, all alike in their ponderous shells of almost eternal stone, cost more than $100,000.[5]

Marquette College, of course, was only for the boys of the parish. (The education of the girls had been provided by the Sisters of Providence at St. Joseph's Academy.) Boys, aged six and over could now attend the "college" which was conducted by lay teachers. Thus matters stood in 1912 when the Jesuit provincial received a proposal from the Marist brothers in Poughkeepsie, New York, that they be permitted to establish a boys' high school "in North Yakima." The Marists, Father Rockliff reported to Brusten, wanted a foundation in the west and they hoped that they could conduct a high school.[6] Rockliff favored the idea, as did Brusten, but the latter was concerned about the brother's salary. How much would it cost for each brother per month, $35 or $40? Nothing came of this, and Marquette gradually evolved into a high school as the boys advanced in the grades. On September 30, 1918, Brusten wrote in his diary: "Our Boys school opened today. Teacher Fr. [John] Buschor 1st year high. Mr. J. Kelly of Town 7th and 8th grade. Miss Dwyer 5th and 6th grade. The number of Boys for the first day was 63."[7]

Father Buschor had fifteen freshmen. A brilliant mathematician who could evoke great admiration by multiplying large numbers in his head, he was not distinguished for his ability to keep order in class. When his lively students got out of hand, he would stomp out with threats of seeing "the superior of thish institushon." This was always followed by much merriment, then the solemn return of the teacher and the continuation of class until the teacher left again to consult "the superior of thish institushon." Despite this eccentric mannerism, Buschor managed to survive and Marquette prospered, at least in terms of boys and, eventually, more Jesuits. It would be many years before the parish could pay the Jesuits "a salary," meaning a little toward their cost of education. The fact is the province provided them at no cost to the parish, other than board and room for nine months a year, for the simple reason that Marquette had no money to pay. If this has a familiar ring, it is because the no-money bells were standard equipment in most Jesuit institutions, including those in California.

The provincial and his assistant, Father Whittle, had made an appearance in Yakima shortly after Brusten opened Marquette. They departed the same day for Seattle on the Northern Pacific, which was five hours late. Brother Rogers had waited in the depot for them until one in the morning. They had spent what was left of the night in the parish rectory because faculty quarters at Seattle College were very crowded.[8]

On the following day, October 5, the great influenza epidemic of 1918 was officially acknowledged in the Seattle College diary. In bright red ink the following appeared: "By Order of the Board of Health of the City of Seattle, all schools, churches, theatres, movies and dance halls were ordered closed today until further order on account of an epidemic of influenza."[9] Seattle College was closed.*

The wave of "Spanish influenza" had swept westward across the continent, reaching the northwest at the end of September. In Spokane both major Jesuit communities were greviously assaulted by the virus. Paul Sauer, the "father minister" at Gonzaga, was offended by this but even more by the high cost of labor. "Our workmen," he wrote in the house diary, "are clamoring for higher wages, wages that are exorbitant—but there is no way to avoid it. We are short of brothers and the whole country is offering unheard of inducements to men who are willing to work.[10] On the day following, October 4, he complained again. "Tonight 6 workmen signified their intention to quit if their wages would not be practically doubled. What can we do?"

With the arrival of the flu, Sauer's indignation was overshadowed by his anxiety. On October 5 he wrote, "a few cases of Spanish influenza appear among the Boys and the army men." No one realized the significance of this until three days later when the whole school was quarantined. On October 9, Sauer wrote, "This morning our newspapers reported 100 cases of Spanish influenza in the city. By order of the mayor, all churches, theatres and places of public amusement are closed until further notice."

The commanding officer of Gonzaga's S.A.T.C. unit ordered the university to purchase more blankets for the infirmary. "By orders of the U.S. Government, we bought 150 blankets at cost $1,312.50. They cost $8.75 now," Sauer grumbled, "where formerly the same cost less than half that amount."[11] By October 12, the epidemic at Gonzaga was at its height. "Our infirmary is filled. Officers and Dr. O'Shea have made arrangements to secure a number of Red Cross nurses to assist. . . . Masses tomorrow in church will be as on week days and not open to the public."

But business was another matter. The city's department stores "on account of bargain sales," were crowded to capacity.

Goller Hall, the infirmary, could accommodate only forty patients. Serious cases, numbering eight to ten a day, were rushed to Sacred Heart Hospital and two Sisters of Providence from the hospital, joined the staff at Gonzaga to supervise the nurses. Another ward was established on the third floor of the main building, the area later called Barbary Coast. Another ward for Jesuits was set up in "the bishop's room." By this time, October 18, there were one hundred patients on the campus, and five boys were given the last sacraments. Father John Neander, a very popular Jesuit from Sweden, who was tall, handsome, and strong as an ox, was taken by ambulance to Sacred Heart Hospital where he died three days later.† By this time one of the boys had died, just eighteen days after his arrival at Gonzaga. Then one of the nurses died, then another boy.

Reports poured in from all sides announcing deaths of friends and alumni. Also gifts poured in from neighbors. Jellies, fruits, and whatever would help the sick flowed in from kind friends in the neighborhood, and the Red Cross poured in medical supplies. Father Peter Halpin, the students' chaplain, seemed to be everywhere. "The wonder was," says an account in praise of his zeal, "how so small a frame could carry so much unobtrusive kindness and bear up under such incessant activity.[12]

---

*Closure refers only to the college department. High school classes were not discontinued.

†Father John Neander, born in Sweden, in 1877, was converted to Catholicism while visiting France. He entered the Society from the Apostolic School at Amiens in 1904 and volunteered to de la Motte for the Rocky Mountain Mission. *Woodstock Letters*, 48 (1919), p. 235, et seq.

As the atmosphere cleared at Gonzaga, matters became more serious in the city. The situation at Mount St. Michael's now became critical, thirty cases were reported in one day. The first member of the Community died on November 7. This was Edward Peacock, a third year philosopher from the Missouri province, whose gentleness and forgiving spirit had been an inspiration for the entire community.* On the day of his funeral there were forty-five Jesuits in bed, six with pneumonia. Of the one hundred and eighteen members of the Mount Community, eighty-four contracted influenza.

These were the waning weeks of the Great War. The province had six chaplains in uniform, still in the thick of it, and among these was 1st. Lt. Chaplain George M. Bailey, the most noted of them all.† A native of Belgium, Bailey had volunteered for the Indian missions, but now he was somewhere in France in the front trenches with the American infantry. He had sought the glamor of the Indian missions and found instead the bloody battlefield near his own native land. He reported faithfully to the provincial on his activities, which consisted mostly in rushing to and fro, administering the last sacraments to friend and foe alike. One gets the impression from his accounts that he loved every minute of what he was doing, though he wept for his comrades who were often killed in his presence.[13]

Rumors of peace filled the air. In Seattle on November 7, a false report ticked off a premature celebration at the college. "War ended! Thank God!" appears in the diary for that day. The deepest yearnings of hope for peace sometimes led people to grasp at straws. The minds of men were preoccupied then with only two concerns, the influenza epidemic and peace. No one seemed to notice that in all of the nation-wide confusion, Congress had passed the Volstead Act over the veto of the president on October 28. This was a great victory for the Moral Minority, surpassed only by the allied victory in war, with the unconditional surrender of Germany on November 11.

On the following day, November 12, the Washington State Board of Health ordered all bans on the gathering of people removed. The epidemic, like the war, was officially over in the State of Washington, at least, and whether they liked it or not, students returned to their classes on November 14.

Unfortunately in Alaska, the epidemic was just beginning. Father Ruppert, who had recently exchanged his palm trees in Los Angeles for the blizzards of Nome, had reasons to regret his choice after the last ship of the season weighed anchor and left the city for the south. Nome had approximately one thousand people, one civilian doctor and an empty hospital which the sisters had abandoned after the gold rush citizens had departed. The doctor had pneumonia before the ship got very far, and Ruppert found himself more or less in charge, while the epidemic raged. He opened the hospital, gathered volunteers for around the clock work of saving the Whites in Nome, as well as the Eskimos in the general vicinity. When the struggle was over, he wrote to Father Dillon:

"A kind Providence ordained that just as the first cases among the natives were detected, Father Lafortune unexpectedly came to town. I had given the last sacraments to a sick Eskimo and found three other Influenza patients in the cabin. On my way home, I was wondering what was going to happen to the natives, and how I could cope with the situation, when on arriving, there was Father Lafortune just in from the Springs, a practically three days journey away from Nome. He lost no time visiting our people, and found them sick everywhere. Day by day things got worse. The epidemic caught them unpro-

---

*Edward Peacock, born on January 28, 1890, entered the Society on July 24, 1909, at Florissant, Missouri. An obituary appears in *Woodstock Letters*, 48 (1919), p. 244, et seq.

†Father George Bailey's original name was Monballiu. Born on February 19, 1878, he entered the Society on September 8, 1897. He became a noted linguist and served as a translator during the peace conferences in Europe.

vided for, for the most part. The weather was near zero, many of them had no provision of fuel for more than two or three days, and some were even without food; and all of them were too sick to procure any. To make matters worse, the Whites were themselves either sick or half-scared to death. It was estimated that about fifty per cent, of the White population, was down with the 'Flu' before the middle of November. We had only one medical man at the post and some seventy out of eighty soldiers were down; so he could not be available at all times. Under these conditions it was not surprising if the poor Eskimos were overlooked. Father Lafortune was indefatigable in working for them. He was able to prepare nearly all for death. He was seen constantly hurrying to and fro and from one end of town to the other on his dog team. His example spurred the others into action. Soon many hands were stretched forth for relieving the deplorable conditions but the awful plague had wrought frightful ravages. Most had died or were dying, some had frozen to death; for the most part only children were left. What remained was only the wreckage. Of the Nome natives, a population of less than three hundred, about fifty children remained and fifty adults. The Catholic natives all died like Christians.

"The plague broke out at Mary's Igloo and the Springs towards the middle of November. By this time it had nearly spent its ravages about Nome. So Father Lafortune was sufficiently foot-loose to leave for a new scene of havoc. Here conditions were about the same as in Nome, except that the two or three whites were perfectly helpless. People were starving and freezing. The Catholics lost most heavily here. Nearly fifty per cent were swept away. In other parts of Seward Peninsula the epidemic worked even greater desolation than at Nome or the Igloo. A rigid quarantine prevented ingress or egress on the part of anybody and extending even to the United States Mails has saved many places from this dire scourge. The Lord's hand came down heavily on the poor Eskimos. The children have been handed over by the Government to such institutions as were ready to receive them. Our Catholic children, about twenty-five in number, are here also. I may visit them at any time, and we are at liberty to take them away whenever we are prepared for it. If only Hot Springs were ready! But without house, and without Sisters, what can we do?"[14]

Ruppert's plea for an orphanage at Hot Springs was soon realized. There was something ironic about this; the orphanage became the occasion for his own death. But that was four winters later.

The end of the war was followed by a wave of strikes and Bolshevik revolutions, which disrupted commerce in the Seattle area. Father Tomkin at the college revealed his residual Irish disposition toward the British in a letter to Dillon. "Father Roccati left two days ago for Vancouver and will take the first boat to Juneau . . . he was afraid our strike here would tie him up for good in Seattle. But there is no danger now as it is all over. They deported 36 slacker ruffians from Seattle a few days ago; law-and-order England furnished four and one-half more times of them than terrible Germany or Austria. Civilization is a fiendish dog."[15]

With tongue in cheek, he added a choice tid bit of gossip: "F.F. Meagher and O'Reilly are back from the Islands . . . [Pat] gave missions to the lepers and even risked his precious life by saying Mass and giving Benediction with leper acolytes."[16]

The barb for O'Reilly was intended to be playful but it struck the mark, elevating its nature from jest to a lofty history. The truth is O'Reilly never let anyone forget about his mission to the lepers. He had dispatched a long letter, giving complete details, to the editor of *Woodstock Letters*.[17] Later in life, when he composed a pseudo-biography of Father Tom Meagher, his companion during this mission, he dwelt at great length on the subject of his own daring zeal for the lepers' souls.* He had been granted, he testified, the great gift of

*This full-length biography of Meagher by O'Reilly was never published. It is in the Oregon Province Archives.

tongues: when he preached in English all of his hearers had understood him, each in his own tongue.

It must be admitted that Meagher and O'Reilly made a great team when they preached a mission. Meagher was a holy terror in the pulpit but in the confessional he was as gentle as a dove. O'Reilly, on the other hand, preached sweetness and light and when the time for confessions came, the timid lined up outside his confessional, expecting a soft, easy time of it. Many found, instead, an unpleasant surprise.

Father Tomkin had dispatched his remarks on February 12. A week earlier Brother Joseph Carignano, long remembered for his interior embellishments in Northwest Jesuit churches, died at Yakima.* Of his sixty-six years of life, he had given forty-six to the Order, mostly cooking and painting churches. Very lean and nearly bald when he died, he looked like an Italian produce merchant, though he had no head at all for business nor temperament for public relations. He was, in fact, quite explosive, especially after two hours on his back on a cold scaffold. He had painted more walls and canvas than many house painters, with infinitely more skill, but when he was lowered into his grave at the Mount, he was remembered more for his meals than for his art, and with reason. The scholastics liked to eat, but food at the Mount was notoriously bad. Anyone who could cook a good meal was held in high repute.

Carignano was not among the first to be buried at the Mount. Although the cemetery was only four years old, there were many rows of white tombstones marking the graves of Jesuits, some of whom had died before Carignano was born. Provision for a cemetery had been made before the Mount was occupied. "On January 6, 1916, the Feast of the Epiphany," one correspondent reported, "while Bishop Schinner blessed the house, we took possession, in the northwest corner [of the property], a large plot has been set aside as a cemetery."[18] The fact is, the cemetery was already occupied that day. There is something humorous in the observation that the first Jesuit resident at the Mount was a dead one, Brother Joseph Finello, who died in Spokane on June 24, 1915, and was buried in a temporary grave at the entrance to the new cemetery.[19]

The second burial at the Mount was a notable one, although perhaps only a few recognized the name. This was Etienne De Rouge, Count of the Chateau des Rues, whose body was buried on May 15, 1916, also in a temporary grave at the entrance. The minister's diary recorded the event very briefly: "Today the burial of Father deRouge. Matins and Lauds before Mass at 8:30, at 9 o'clock, Mass was celebrated by Father Arthuis [who had been in the novitiate with the deceased]. After that we go in procession to the cemetery. At 10:15 all was over." Just like that. No gun salutes, drums or bugles for the distinguished count.

There was one more temporary burial near the entrance. This was the body of Father Francis J. Adams who died on May 19, 1917. Adams had achieved considerable local fame before his death as Gonzaga's professor of physics. As the driver of Gonzaga's first automobile, he was often seen at the wheel in his black coat and bowler hat, chugging away on roads made for horses, enroute to science lectures for civic groups. His services were desperately needed, for most adults then feared science the way many fear it today.

There is an amusing parallel between him and one of the more recent professors of physics, Father Joseph Nealen, who often negotiated "Cowley Pass" on slippery mornings, not unlike the adventures of Adams in his automobile with skittish horses and their belligerent drivers.

In May 1910, Halley's Comet, absent since 1835, wandered back into the earth's

*Joseph Carignano was born near Turin, Italy, on February 10, 1853; entered the Society on Aguust 24, 1873; and died in Yakima on February 5, 1919, after a series of strokes.

evening atmosphere, causing so much anxiety about its alleged destructive forces that one Spokane woman committed suicide. Over the entire country there was an hysteria about the comet, which some scientists and many amateurs declared, contained a deadly cyanogen gas in its tail, which would destroy all life. Father Adams was frequently quoted in the paper, contesting these views, and there were a few, even within the Gonzaga community, who suspected he was talking off the top of his head. Eager to share his convictions that the comet was to be enjoyed, not feared, he spent many days lecturing to audiences in small towns. Time vindicated Father Adams.

The most ardent of record keepers for the Mount Cemetery was Father Anthony Drathman, who not only preserved its history but for many years in his office in San Francisco gathered information about the burial of Northwest Jesuits. Drathman had a peculiar gift: there was no safe or lock he could not open in a few minutes or less. He was often sought by the police to open stolen safes or safes in burned buildings, and they watched him with amazement, often expressing the obvious, that they were delighted he was an honest man. He was very handsome, tall, dignified, and important looking without appearing arrogant. And he loved to discover Jesuit bodies in out-of-the-way places, like under a mission church. His records, gathered like the old bones from the four directions, described the order of the burials and the methods used to maintain that order.

On "March 19, 1918, the Feast of St. Joseph," says the minister's diary, "we began to exhume the bodies of the dead at the mission preparatory to transporting them to the new cemetery."* On the following day Brother Zwak drowned at Twin Lakes and when his body was recovered a week later it was placed in its present grave. "Of all those buried in their present graves, Brother Zwak's was the first, as it was reserved for his remains because the graves in rows I, II and III preceding his, were reserved for those buried in the old St. Michael's Mission cemetery."† As far as possible, the graves were being assigned in a chronological order.

On April 1, 1918, ten bodies from the mission were buried at the Mount, the first of those that were being transferred. On April 2, nine more bodies were interred. "The scholastics, working under Father [Henry] Welch did the work, Brother [William] Coady driving the team." On April 3, the three bodies buried near the cemetery entrance were disinterred and placed in their present graves.

The next five buried in the Mount cemetery were moved on April 17, 1918, from the Catholic plot in Fairmount Cemetery, Spokane. Among these were the remains of Herman Goller; Gaspar Genna, who thought he would die on the Yukon; and Adrian Sweere, one of the founders of Seattle University. On October 8, 1920, the remains of two very special Jesuits were moved from the cathedral in Helena: Fathers Philip Rappagliosi, who had died on the Milk River, probably of starvation; and Henry Imoda. These bodies had been placed in army issue coffins, and when they were opened the body of Father Imoda was found perfectly preserved.‡ The first three to die in the Rocky Mountain Mission and to be buried at Old Sacred Heart Mission in Idaho, were re-buried at the Mount on September 27, 1922. These were Charles Huet, Francis Huybrechts and Michael McGean, all saintly heroic Jesuit brothers in the early history of the province.**

*These were bodies buried at Old St. Michael's Mission east of the Mount.

†Drathman's explanation for the postponement of burial of some Jesuits, e.g. De Rouge.

‡Several Sisters of Providence were witnesses to the fact that Imoda's body was preserved. Father Edward Kenny, Minister at the Mount, did not know about this, hence the coffins were not opened before burial in the Mount Cemetery.

**Huet, for example, died in 1858, before Giorda arrived.

In succeeding years the remains of Jesuits were moved from other missions like St. Francis Regis, but it should be remembered that many Jesuits lie elsewhere: in the cemetery at St. Ignatius; at the mission near Umatilla; at Stevensville, Montana, where Ravalli lies; and in other places. The records are complete, not only in the Great Book of Life but in Drathman's vast collection of notes and correspondence.

There is a tall cross in the Mount Cemetery and it bears the following inscription in Latin: *Societas Jesu/ Quos Genuit/ Erorum Charos/ Cineres/ Coelo Reddendos/ Sollicite/ Hiec/ Fovet*, which means "In this place the Society of Jesus carefully cherishes the precious ashes of those whom she bore. They must be given back to heaven."*

Drathman's concern for the dead had not been misplaced, but the mundane business of the province had to go on. Among its existing institutions none appeared to be more neglected than the college in Seattle, which, factually at least, had gone out of business. Its name had survived, of course, and there is no reason to believe that any of the high school students at the *college* regarded the situation as odd or irregular. Nor did the faculty. There were others in Seattle more determined to correct it than most Jesuits.

One of these was Mr. Thomas McHugh, a well-to-do man of commerce who was also more willing than most to contribute generously to the cause of Catholic education. Tom had made a promise to God to give $50,000 to charity if and when he sold his half-interest in the Deep Sea Cannery. He sold it, then consulted Father John McHugh, pastor of St. Joseph's parish, for advice on keeping his promise. Father McHugh pointed out to him the dire needs of Seattle college.† Tom had "inside information on the Adelphia situation," and on the evening of February 21, 1919, he called Father McHugh to describe this piece of available property, which could serve as the long sought Seattle College campus. Though the hour was late he offered to discuss it with the rector, Father Joseph Tomkin, and to bring both priests to the Adelphia site. There were two buildings on the property, he said, both designed for college use. Father McHugh agreed to Tom's proposal, and at 8:45 that evening the two Jesuits with their friend walked two miles or more to see the buildings on Interlaken Boulevard. All three were impressed.[20]

Four days later Father Burke reported: "Through the initiative and generosity of T.C. McHugh an option was taken today on the Adelphia College property and a telegram [was] sent to Fr. Provincial to come at once to Seattle."[21] The Provincial responded the following day that he would leave the south at once, and he arrived on the first of March to see for himself what all the fuss was about. His enthusiastic reaction prompted Seattle College officials to employ a caretaker at $40.00 a month, to put new locks on the exterior doors, and to make an inventory of the furnishings.

For the next week Father John McHugh and the Provincial "worked very hard on the transaction," which was finally concluded on the afternoon of March 12.

The Jesuits in Seattle now had two substantial, brick buildings with seven acres of land on a very desirable site overlooking Lake Union across from the University of Washington. The school building of four stories had been erected in 1905–1906 at a cost of $60,000 and the residence, in 1909–1910, at a cost of $40,000. A contemporary appraisal showed a value of $75,000 to $100,000 on the land, and $120,000 on the buildings. The question at first, taller than Tomkin's lean body in its heavy black cassock, was how much would the poverty-stricken Jesuits have to pay for it?

---

*Translation by Patrick Brannan, S.J., November 8, 1981.

†Father Joseph Tomkin was president of Seattle College. Father Francis Burke kept the community diary. It was Burke who recorded events as they occurred, but after some weeks Tomkin, who had been involved in the transaction, wrote in the diary a six-page, very detailed account of all that had happened, including the more personal facts about Tom McHugh. These are found in the 1919 diary on pages 171 to 177.

The first report which appeared in *Woodstock Letters,* stated that it had been purchased at a foreclosure sale for $65,000 of which $5,000 had been paid down by Tom McHugh.* Tomkin, however, hastened to correct this in the following number of the *Letters*: "Mr. T.C. McHugh not merely gave us the hint and $5,000, but actually purchased the property for us before Rev. Father Provincial could arrive to give a decision on the matter. He paid down in cold cash and at financial sacrifice the sum of $50,000, leaving a balance of $15,000, the full amount of purchase being $65,000, which balance he is now paying as money comes to hand. A few other good friends have joined the Roll of Honor Club with donations of $1,000 each to help towards defraying the expenses of repairs, which will probably run to $11,000.

"The gift came at our darkest hour, when it seemed that we could only pray and hope for better days. I am firmly convinced that the holy deceased Fathers who toiled here years ago brought 'God's own time' most unexpectedly."[22]

The acquisition had all been so simple and so apparently godly that no one was prepared for the storm that followed. It came from an unexpected source, the bishop's chancery. His Lordship, of course, had the worrisome problem of a new Jesuit foundation in St. Patrick's parish. Thus he had two potential Jesuit chapels or churches which *might* threaten the prosperity of his own cathedral parish and St. Patrick's. The fact that the Jesuits had two other churches in the general area, the Immaculate and St. Joseph's, added fuel to the flames.

Ironically, O'Dea once held the legal title to the land on which Adelphia College had originally been built. He had purchased fourteen acres there for a Catholic cemetery but before this so-called Holy Cross Cemetery came into general use, he had decided to establish Calvary Cemetery in a less populated area.† At that point the Swedish-Baptists, represented by Dr. Schmidt, purchased this tract "the most sightly in the city." They plotted six acres on the south, then built Adelphia Hall, the school; and Schmidt Hall, the residence, on the north. At first this school prospered, but during the war it fell on bad times and could not meet its payments. In February 1918, the Title Trust Company of New York foreclosed on a $45,000 mortgage. The local Scandinavian bank took charge, placing it on the market for $75,000.

When rumors reached the chancery that Tom McHugh was considering the purchase of the property for the use of Seattle College, there was great consternation and he was approached by members of the bishop's staff who tried to dissuade him.‡ The bishop himself was somewhat ambivalent in his attitude. While unnamed members of the Chancery were up in arms, and as the Jesuits said, "by no means friendly," O'Dea appeared to be opposed, but not hostile, As a compromise, he requested the Jesuits to turn over to him St. Joseph's parish, with all of its property purchased with Jesuit funds, offering in return a portion of St. Patrick's parish. The pastor of St. Patrick's, Father M.P. O'Dwyer, who admitted later that he had been "the goat," noisily opposed the presence of the Jesuits in his parish, including any part of it.

Father Dillon during all of this useless and unproductive bickering, remained calm and undisturbed. Insofar as he was concerned, there was no occasion for compromise. The Jesuits had not done, nor intended to do, anything wrong. He refused to turn St. Joseph's

---

*McHugh first made a $10,000 down payment, hoping that the "rich ones" would pay the balance, so that he could use his additional $40,000 gift for improvements. "Seattle, true to her past traditions," says Tomkin, "would not come forward." Thus, with his wife's approval, Tom McHugh donated his war bonds, $48,000, adding $3,100 for their depreciated value before maturity, and withdrawing the balance from his savings account.

†Tomkin states that a few burials had been made on the property before O'Dea changed his mind about the site.

‡This is stated by Tomkin in his account.

over to the Chancery and repeated at discreet intervals his request for the bishop's approval for a Jesuit school on the Interlaken Boulevard site.

"Your Lordship knows the struggles of Seattle College in the past, and now that some assistance has been offered to help the cause of education, we feel confident that our new hopes will not be blasted by a refusal to grant what we have asked, namely, to transfer our education work from the present to the new site."[23]

The bishop, after sending his vicar general to consult the apostolic delegate, withdrew his objections and finally gave his approval, at first verbally, then in writing when Dillon pressed for it.* Gradually the storm subsided and even Father O'Dwyer accepted the Jesuits, with caution, but eventually with restrained warmth. What appeared to be an insurmountable impasse, all during the last half of 1919, soon became, instead, the occasion for a renewal of friendship between the bishop and Seattle's Jesuits. "Bishop O'Dea has ever been kind," Father Francis Burke wrote in the college diary, when all differences had been worked out.[24] The bishop cheerfully blessed both buildings and gracefully accepted his role on the campus as the bishop of the diocese, the honored guest at every function.

As the Seattle crisis was gradually overcome, another appeared on Dillon's horizon. To resolve it he resorted to unprecedented measures which required Rome's formal approval. On July 8, 1919, he sent a directive to the province concerning the impending *disaster* at St. Ignatius College in San Francisco, which, like Adelphia College in Seattle during the previous year, could not meet its mortgage payments. Dillon instructed all houses of the province to help St. Ignatius by sending certain Mass stipends every month.[25] "Now in answer to our representation as to the great financial distress of our college in San Francisco," Dillon wrote, "V.R.F. General has granted us a similar favor for the benefit of that House. From September 8, 1919, we shall be permitted to receive a stipend for the weekly Mass which should otherwise be offered for F. General, and these stipends will be for the benefit of St. Ignatius, San Francisco."† There followed instructions for the procurator of each community to send a monthly report containing the number of Masses and to advance the stipends to the procurator of St. Ignatius.

San Francisco at this time had the largest and most affluent Catholic population in western United States. It was not regarded as forthright in its support of parochial schools, which were sometimes declared to be unnecessary, since many teachers in the city's public schools were Irish Catholics. Hence the need for Dillon's desperate appeal to save the city's Catholic college appears to be disheartening, especially when one realizes the poverty of some of the missions that were being asked to bail out the college.

Undoubtedly the financial dilemma of St. Ignatius College was an old one, going back to the "grandiose" church before the earthquake and the opposition of many of the clergy to religious orders in general and to St. Ignatius Church in particular. One can only speculate about it now and dwell on the happy aspects. Having been saved by the widow's mite, St. Ignatius survived and became a great university.

At Seattle the college had two separate campuses but only one high school to occupy them. No time was lost in remodeling the new one, which would provide for the first time a separate residence for the faculty. By September 1, 1919, it was reported that work on the school was nearing completion and the registration of students was set for 9:30 A.M. on September 3. Precisely at that time, one hundred and fifteen students appeared. They were

---

*O'Dea blessed the buildings on December 7, 1919, but did not give formal written permission for their canonical status until May 10, 1920.

†Mass stipends are the offerings made for the presumed expenses involved in the maintenance of the Altar and the Mass.

dismissed an hour later with instructions to appear for class on the following Monday, September 8. On that day, one hundred and thirty-four boys answered the first bell. The number of students rose gradually during the weeks that followed. The faculty, meanwhile, continued to live in the old school on Broadway, commuting each day for classes, because the residence on Interlaken was not ready for occupancy. By September 27, the residence was still unchanged, remodeling did not begin until October 7, but the eleven Jesuits moved in that day anyhow. During the morning they transferred "four big truck loads", work that proved to be so strenuous that one Jesuit was sent by the community doctor to the hospital.*

During this period Father John Laherty, another member of the community, had been serving at Bremerton as a part-time chaplain for the navy. He was also a kind of pastor-at-large for military personnel and members of the Knights of Columbus, who were promoting a program like the USO for ex-servicemen. The Knights, it will be recalled, had been very active during the late war. Laherty developed a Seattle College Alumni Association, when not engaged in his other duties, which included some teaching and the administration of the school library.

The problem for most Jesuits now was the disposal of the former Broadway campus and the Garrand building there. The secretary for the Knights of Columbus bought the old W.C.T.U. building for $200 to salvage its lumber.[26] Half-hearted attempts were made to sell the property, but nothing ever came of it. The building, remodeled after the fire with such anxiety as only fond custodians could bestow, was neglected. Broken windows soon appeared and overgrown shrubbery concealed its base and revealed the abandoned status of the structure. Occasionally high school students used it for play practice or other extra-curricular activities, but preoccupied Jesuits, happy in their possession of a new campus, cared little about what happened to it.

One could scarcely blame them. They had lived for many years in damp, musty quarters, which they called "a hole in the ground," and they had worked with inadequate equipment since the college was begun. As Tomkin noted in a letter of appreciation to Tom McHugh, "For twenty-seven years the Jesuit Fathers had labored in Seattle for the cause of Catholic education and the success of their efforts was by no means encouraging. Friends they always had who aided as best they could, but they were not in financial condition to render sufficient aid towards substantial improvement or better buildings; while those of means were not able to afford more than sympathy, advice or criticism."[27] The neglect of others, bitterly recalled, cast even greater splendor over the generosity of the McHughs.

By this time the Knights of Columbus requested the use of the old Garrand Building as part of a national program the Knights were establishing—free evening schools for war veterans to give them opportunities to catch up in the education they had missed. The Jesuits gladly shared the use of the building, rent free, and on January 8, 1920, the Knights' evening classes were begun.[28] This became a significant step toward the reestablishment of college courses, for which the Jesuits continued to probe. It would be two long years, however, before the next step could be taken. Meanwhile on the same day, January 8, Tomkin wrote to the provincial's assistant, Father Whittle, "Good Bishop O'Dea rejoices more and more every day over the educational situation. He went up to the office of Mr. McHugh as few weeks ago and said, 'Mr. McHugh, your generosity towards Catholic Education impresses me so much that I am obliged to come up here personally to thank you.' Quick as a flash, Mr. McHugh 'hoped that clerical opposition would cause no more loss, as it had already amounted to $3,000.' In astonishment the bishop [requested an explanation.]"[29] McHugh stated that during the delays occasioned by the controversy, remodeling

---

*This was Father Francis Burke.

costs had appreciated by this amount because of post-war inflation. McHugh begged the bishop 'to hear no more of it.' "

The improvements to date had cost the college $12,600. Great progress was being made. The chapel was finally occupied and the Blessed Sacrament was reserved. Litanies were recited for the first time in the new residence on March 15. On July 18, at last, the *beneplacitum* for the college on the new site arrived from Rome.[30] This concluded the ecclesiastical formalities; accreditation by the state was sought now for the pre-college courses. On October 1, 1920, representatives of the State Board appeared to conduct its examination.[31] Apparently they were properly impressed for on June 28, 1921, Seattle College High School was formally accredited by the State Board of Education. It enjoyed at this time the unique distinction of being the only strictly classical school in the state.*

The lack of college classes was still a cause of embarrassment. Comparison with Gonzaga, for example, could be invidious, though heaven knows, Gonzaga University at this time had little to crow about. In the 1920–21 school year, there were only 144 students registered in the entire university, including the School of Law, while in the high school department there were 427 students, better than three to one.

At Mount St. Michael's, which was only vaguely regarded as affiliated with Gonzaga University, there were ninety-five scholastics. They lived in their own little world, part English, part Latin, committed to the church related curriculum that had been in use for centuries. There were occasional pious diversions like the Missionary Society which sponsored lectures by visiting missionaries, and raised funds for the missions by gathering stamps, tinfoil and waste paper. At Christmastime in 1920, for instance, the Society raised $105 mostly by selling used stamps, and it sent a share of this to each of three missions, one in India, one in China and one in Africa.[32]

Shortly after Christmas, Father Benn, the Mount rector, called the scholastics together to discuss what was regarded then as a very grave matter. The doctors had informed him, the rector said, that one of the scholastics required a blood transfusion. The blood would have to be of the same type the patient had, so several volunteers would be required. Since donating blood was thought to be very dangerous, no one should offer himself without serious reflection. He, Father Rector, would return to his room, and volunteers could offer their names to him there. In the solemn stillness, Benn left the room and waited in his office on the first floor for a few brief moments. Then he peered out. The entire hall was lined up with scholastics who were eager to be the first to give blood.[33]

On the province level, there were significant changes in the provincial's board of consultors, whisperings and omens of prophecy, indicators of the future's Who's Who. In retrospect at least, one might be tempted to think that behind the scenes there were some political games in progress. The membership of the board was too illustrious to be representative. Comprising four provincials, present and to come, it appeared to be highly selective, as well as prophetic. In addition to Dillon there was Joseph Piet, his successor as provincial, and Zacheus Maher and Walter Fitzgerald, both successors to Piet when the California province was divided to form two provinces.† Whittle was still Dillon's assistant, which was living proof that Dillon was not fickle in making staff changes.

Whatever the future, these were the men who were making the decisions for the province. There had been, as always, many minor developments, both good and bad,

*Gonzaga's lower division formally designated as a high school in 1921, had a commercial department. It is interesting to note that Gonzaga did not apply for formal accreditation of the high school; however, in 1921, when the University of Washington published its first list of accredited high schools, Gonzaga was on it. At the time this was the state's most prestigious form of high-school accreditation.

†Fitzgerald and Maher were appointed as consultors on September 7, 1921. Both had been made university presidents during the previous July, one of Gonzaga, the other of Santa Clara.

another new Church by Griva not being among them. On October 5, 1919, one of those tragic mission fires had almost wiped out St. Mary's Mission near Omak.[34] Only the church was saved. The school, the museum with all of its contents, the library of over two thousand books, and all of de Rouge's precious records and diaries were consumed in the flames. An earlier mission fire on November 16, 1918, had destroyed the Ursulines' Mount Angela School at St. Peter's, and still another fire on December 9, 1920, destroyed the first mission school at St. Ignatius, which the Sisters of Providence had opened in 1864.[35]

In Alaska Bishop Crimont had nearly perished on a trip by dogsled between Nome and Hot Springs. Father Ruppert, his companion, had hurried forward to get help at the mission, but got lost in the willow swamps, after swimming the ice cold waters of the Pilgrim River.[36] Here in Oregon the Ku Klux Klan had moved in, not a battalion but an army, to promote a bill requiring all children to attend public schools. Called the "Anti-Parochial School Bill," by its opponents, this was passed on November 7, 1922, by the people of Oregon with a thirteen thousand majority vote.[37]

This was the bad news. The good news was that the Catholics, not only in Oregon, but nation-wide, formed a solid defense against the Oregon School Bill and succeeded in shooting it down in the Supreme Court of the United States.*

There were other happy developments. In the autumn of 1920, scholastics from the Mount repaired and painted Old St. Michael's Mission, north of Spokane, so that it could serve as a mission church for Catholic Whites in the district. On December 8, the fifty-fourth anniversary of Cataldo's first St. Michael's, Mass was offered again in the historic building. The scholastics taught neighboring children catechism and the future looked bright.[38]

In the summer of 1921, Father Taelman at St. Francis Xavier Mission built a new church at Wyola, near the Wyoming-Montana border. This was for the Indians. Bishop Lenihan blessed it in honor of St. Anthony on September 8. Two new churches for the Italian people were established, one called Sacred Heart in Lewiston, Idaho, built by Father Vincent Chiappa,[39] and the other St. Rita's in Tacoma, built by Father Achilles Bruno. Bruno organized this parish from scratch. On April 9, 1922, he offered the first Mass in the parish in a house which had been converted into a chapel.[40]

Father Bruno, like Griva, was a very short person. However, unlike Griva who was as nearly broad as he was tall, Bruno was so thin that he almost blew away in Tacoma's off-the-sea gales. In his black coat and hat he walked from house to house in his parish with his head down and his eyes half-closed, praying all the time. Though as delicate and frail as a little quail, he was as tough in spirit as a wild falcon. Once an irate parishioner, who had been disappointed in Bruno's refusal to compromise, waylaid him and bashed in his skull, nearly killing him. Bruno refused to identify his assailant, saying God would take care of it. He recovered from this assault. He also survived his almost starvation diet, becoming a kind of holy man. Because he spoke too low and in a kind of pidgin English that sounded suspiciously like Italian, most of us could not understand what he said.

On Tuesday, September 5, 1922, when classes at Seattle College convened, the college had a record enrollment of 75 in first-year high alone.[41] The school had a total of 210 students of whom 16 were enrolled in the *college course*, indicating that the real Seattle College was back on the road to recovery.

The community had received a new rector the previous year, on July 31. This was Father Geoffrey O'Shea, a corpulent Irishman, with Paddy's Irish features and soft, warm voice that could charm the meanest boy into saying his prayers. The voice could also be demanding, but its master seldom resorted to that. There was no need for it anyhow, since

*The U.S. Supreme Court declared the Oregon School Bill unconstitutional on June 25, 1925.

his giant body and large, expressive head were enough to intimidate the worst offender.

Tomkin, who had been a splendid administrator, was assigned to assist Father Norbert de Boynes, an English Jesuit who had been designated by Father General in Rome as an official Visitor to the California Province. De Boynes formally inaugurated his visitation on March 30, 1922, and for something like ten months, with Father Tomkin at his side, he visited each house of the province and listened to Jesuits who thought they had something to say about how the Jesuit Order should be run. On January 17, 1923, de Boynes dispatched his goodbye message from San Francisco, a letter full of hope and confidence for the future of the province. A *memoriale* was subsequently published, containing recommendations and suggestions for the conduct of the province's affairs.[42]

Meanwhile, of course, the business of the province, directed by Dillon and other superiors was pursued as usual. Father O'Shea at Seattle had strongly supported the opening of the college, though he agreed with others that the four-year program should be postponed. Offically they had begun a Junior College, which was affiliated in a loose sense with the University of Washington. Two years later the courses were expanded to cover a four-year college program. Finally, when there was a need for more space, classes were moved into a rented duplex two blocks away. This was called "the Roanoke site" in the school's saga, a period of its history soon forgotten and sometimes denied. Father Joseph Donovan was a student there, which makes it not only real and authentic, but even significant.

In Father Dillon's memorandum book there were two brief and provocative entries which revealed his deepest concerns. These were "High School in Portland," and "Province not united."[43] The first point supports the view that our Jesuit administration had never given up the idea of a high school in Portland. Hopes for the school were still alive in these waning years of Archbishop Christie's rule. Christie had given verbal approval for the proposal on several occasions, now he was in his last illness in St. Vincent's Hospital. The matter would have to be decided by his successor.

Dillon's recognition of division in the province should not be surprising. Like de la Motte, he was superior of two large groups of Jesuits who had much in common, a common heritage in the church, but whose life-styles and even local Jesuit traditions were as far apart as the Mediterranean and the North Seas. Two distinct provinces were in the making—Dillon could not overlook this. Did he already see Father Piet in the role as the last provincial of two provinces, the genial French diplomat who was attached to Oregon, but lived in California? As novice master for both, Piet formed succeeding troops of young Jesuits in his own image. This was all good, but time was running out. Both divisions of the province were growing rapidly and separation for practical reasons would have to come. It was comforting, no doubt, for Dillon to realize that he was leaving the province more united than it was when he became provincial.

Toward the end of his term, there was one more sensational event over which he had no control. On Christmas Eve, 1923, newspapers throughout the world, caught in the mystique of the Christmas spirit, carried headlines about a priest in Alaska who had frozen to death, trying to bring oranges to orphans. It was the kind of doleful news that everyone enjoyed reading. "Priest Is Frozen To Death," the *Spokane Chronicle* stated, in tall, black letters. "Former Gonzaga Chaplain Found Dead in the Arctic."* The details about Father Ruppert's dramatic death might have caused Scrooge to cry.

Ruppert was attached to the church at Nome. In early October he had left Nome with

---

*The event coming at Christmastime and involving gifts for orphans was highly emotional. Most accounts disregarded the facts indicating Ruppert's lack of prudence in undertaking the dangerous journey alone. Lafortune states that the children had plenty of Christmas candy and nuts, suggesting that Ruppert's journey was unnecessary.

Bob Ummaok, the mail carrier, and James Halpin for the Hot Springs Mission where he made his annual retreat.* He also gave retreats to the children and the Sisters and Brothers and on December 13, Thursday morning at day break, he left the mission to return to Nome, driving Father Lafortune's dog team. An hour later the mail carrier left the Springs, also by dog team; his destiny, Nome. The travelers covered about twenty-five miles of poor trail to Duffy O'Connor's roadhouse, where Ruppert found a case of oranges for the orphans at the mission. He decided, over the objections of all, to dash back to the mission with the oranges, so that the children would have them for Christmas.

This was Friday. The weather was cold, about thirty degrees below zero. He left alone with the dogs. More snow had fallen. A great silence was over the land. At the mission the brothers did their chores. Brother Wilhalm changed a door between the Sister's and the children's dining rooms. The Novena for Christmas was begun. Everyone assumed that Ruppert was safe in Nome.

But Monday afternoon, one of his dogs returned; "Mudd" was half-starved, alone and tired. Then one of the Eskimos, Old John Kakaruk arrived at the mission and reported seeing man tracks and the tracks of two dogs. It was already dark. A search party was organized for daybreak on the morrow.

On Tuesday, Old John, the two Brothers, and two others set out to investigate. Only four miles from the mission they found Ruppert's body, lying flat on its back in the snow, its arms stretched out like a cross. Beside it, almost frozen stiff, but still alive, was "Mink" the lead dog, guarding the master jealously. At first he did not recognize the visitors and he growled when they came near. When he knew them as friends he got up stiffly and walked a few feet away, watching the men place the body in the sled they had brought.

There were no clues to tell what happened. No dogsled. No oranges.† There were only Mink and the frozen corpse in all that solemn stillness. They brought the body to the mission and Brother Wilhalm described the scene. "When we got to the mission nearly all were in tears. We placed the body in a room and started to thaw the arms so we could get it into the coffin. Two days later we had the funeral and Father was laid to rest in our little graveyard at the mission."‡ Meanwhile Father Post hired Fred Topkok for $45 to take letters to Lafortune in Nome in which he related what he knew about the tragedy. Topkok arrived on the following day and by Christmas Eve news of Ruppert's death was telegraphed to the news services of the world. "Priest Dies Martyr of Charity," was the headline in the Paris edition of the *New York Herald Tribune,* summing up the judgment of the world.

Lafortune was not so sure. He was heartbroken. Ruppert, he wrote, "was not a dog driver and he knew it; he was hampered by his glasses and he knew that it was a great drawback. He knew also that there was always deer on the mountain and my dogs were wild for them." It was like an unsolved murder mystery. "What possessed him to go to the Springs any way is more than I can say. He had to die on the banks of the Pilgrim River and he could not dodge it."[44]

Thus the year 1923 ended, with a newspaper canonization and one less priest in Alaska to bear the thorny burden of the wilderness.

*Detailed accounts of the tragedy appear in the mission diaries of both Pilgrim Springs [Hot Springs] and Nome. The best published account appears in Louis Renner, S.J., *Pioneer Missionary to the Bering Stait Eskimos: Bellarmine Lafortune, S.J.,* Portland, 1979, p. 56, et seq.

†The sled was discovered in September, 1924, by Brother Hansen. The oranges were never found.

‡OPA, Frederick Ruppert Papers, Manuscript account of Father Ruppert's death by Brother Peter Wilhalm, who was with the search party, described the body as lying flat on the back with the arms extended like a cross. Father Post in the mission diary gives a different account on the position of the arms.

Manresa Hall, Port Townsend, Washington, with the original Eisenbeis mansion to the right.

St. Joseph's Church, Seattle, shortly after it was completed.

Joseph Piet, fifth provincial of the California Province; founder of Sheridan and Manresa Hall. He was provincial when the western province was divided in 1932.

Ursuline Sisters from St. Mary's Mission, Akulurak, on the mission boat about 1925.

Bellarmine High School and Faculty Residence, Tacoma, Washington.

16

PIET'S ENTHUSIASM
1924–1929

The appointment of a new provincial is often the occasion for a flood of rumors, before and after, some discussion, mostly very cautious, and a great deal of suspense. Members of the province, not unlike the bureaucrats in government, speculate on their relations with the new boss, whether they are good or bad, and whether some painful changes will be made. It always helps if the new provincial be known, then one can foresee possible threats to one's cherished kingdom, however small. It is true that Jesuits are very obedient men, but obedience to a new provincial's directives does not eliminate feelings of human attachments. One must be a very old Jesuit not to care when a new provincial is appointed.

When Joseph M. Piet took over the reigns of the province government from Dillon on May 11, 1924, he was generally recognized as a known and predictable superior, especially by the younger Jesuits. His designation, certainly, was not a surprise and there were some in the province who hailed it enthusiastically as a populist choice. Piet had been an Indian missionary, not a school man.

But that was years ago. More recently he had served as Novice Master in the formation of young Jesuits, Rector of the novitiate at Los Gatos for six years and Novice Master for nine, classifying him, willy-nilly, as a Jesuits' Jesuit, and he would never be anything else. The simple fact of his nine year tenure as novice master, considerably longer than most, who burned out after a term comparable to the provincial's, revealed more about Piet than first appears. It was, without doubt, evidence of a durability that was like Cataldo's. Piet's was the longest provincilate in province history, eight years, or as long as Rockliff's and Gleeson's put together.

One must look to his roots for an explanation. It was sometimes said, perhaps derisively by the intellectuals, that he was a "French peasant." If it were so, the church needed more "French peasants," for his family gave five sons to the church and two sons to die for France. The latter perished during the first World War. Among the five other sons, four became Jesuits, three of them missionaries, one to China, one to Brazil and one to the Indians of the Rocky Mountains. The fourth died as a scholastic before ordination and the fifth became a Vincentian priest who remained near home in southern France. One of two daughters died in young maidenhood and the second married and raised a family.

Though Piet wrote the way he talked, almost continuously—by popular demand, of course—he left little in writing about his family.* He had been born, he stated in a brief

*Piet has left a brief account of his family and an outline of his life. OPA, Piet papers, biographical notes.

sketch, on December 1, 1876, in the village of St. Etienne d'Orthe, which was near the home of St. Vincent de Paul. He was baptized, like Cataldo, in honor of "Joseph Mary," a clue, if any are required, regarding the very devout dispositions of his parents. When he was sixteen he came to America and one year later, on May 18, 1893, he entered the Jesuit novitiate at De Smet. Cocci was novice master then, with two future novice masters in his care, Piet and Tom Meagher. After the novitiate Piet "prefected," as they used to say, at St. Ignatius Mission for four years. Then he studied philosophy at Gonzaga in "the old Sheds" for three years, from 1899 to 1902, during which time he became an American citizen, on September 13, 1900.[1] Before going to St. Louis for theology in 1903 he spent another year at St. Ignatius Mission. By this time he was thoroughly "westernized," though not so profoundly Rocky Mountain Mission style that he could not become "Californiaized" at a later period. He was a little like Accolti in this respect, but he never acquired Accolti's subtle contempt for the north.

Piet had come to America for the Indians. Thus his first assignment as a priest was to St. Paul's Mission in Montana. He was made the superior there, even before tertianship, another indication of the high esteem in which he was held from the very beginning.* He often joked in later life about his long record as a superior, revealing a kind of simple vanity and the more remarkable weakness that he actually enjoyed being a superior.

At St. Paul's, where he remained four years, he earned the title "Medicine Man of the Mountains" by the simple expedient of treating his sick Indian people with hot, spiced wine. This seems to have been an effective remedy, which brought almost dying patients to his own door for another cure.[2] It was said that he had a high incidence of minor ailments among the adult males, a four-year epidemic, perhaps. Piet treated everyone, at least once, and with sly, Gallican diplomacy prevented abuses or thirsty raids on the mission's wine. He was a very young man then, at least by Jesuit norms, and this experience at St. Paul's provided him with human insights that doubtlessly proved to be useful in administration later.

As rector at Los Gatos he was the ranking custodian of the novitiate's wine vats.† This was during the pre-prohibition era, when wine was served at dinner, as part of the meal. If it was good enough for Jesus and His Apostles, it was good enough for Piet's novices and junior scholastics. These were the days when the novices picked the grapes for the winery. For something like three weeks each year ordinary novitiate routine was interrupted by grape-picking order, an hilarious time at first, when the novices were released from the drudgery of the desk. But as the days passed, the prickly heat, the heavy lifting and the persistence of the fruit flies gradually dissipated the romance of grape gathering and rendered meaningless the "Deo Gratias" on grapes, which was permission to eat as many as the novices wanted.

At this time Piet was a very attractive man, in a kind of middle-aged manner, especially to younger Jesuits who needed encouragement. He was a confirmed optimist. When Giacobbi was novice master he used to say, "I give the novices absolution and they give me poison oak." Piet with a broad smile, his blue eyes reflecting his compassion and hope, gave his novices absolution with a flash of good humor. "Three Hail Mary's," he would say cheerfully, "and plenty of entusiasm."‡ Piet's only enemy was the devil of boredom.

*Piet was ordained at St. Louis in 1906. He became superior of St. Paul's Mission in 1907 and remained there until 1911, when he began his tertianship at St. Andrew's in New York.

†Piet became rector at Los Gatos on August 1, 1913. He was also Master of Novices. In accordance with Canon Law, a religious superior could serve a maximum of six years. Hence Piet was succeeded as rector by Father Joseph Melchers on November 1, 1918, but remained as Novice Master until he became president.

‡Data supplied by Father John Thatcher, November 15, 1981. The sound *th* was difficult for Piet to say.

On a passport application, Piet described himself as being five feet nine inches tall. He had "a high forehead, normal complexion and black hair." His face was full, he said, and he had a normal mouth and a straight nose.[3] One could agree with all of this except about the normality of his mouth. This it seems to me, was notably wider than most. He had a bulldog chin, and the general appearance of a contented, well-fed mayor of a prosperous city. He regarded himself as a very practical man, which could be challanged, and like a number of other Jesuits, he was an incurable baseball fan, which he put to work by serving as umpire for the novices' games. It was commonly said, however, that his integrity as an umpire was corrupted by more lofty objectives. He deliberately called strikes balls and balls strikes to mortify his novices, which occasionally touched off unseemly disputes, doubtlessly causing much concealed mirth for Father Piet.*

Money for Piet was something you used. He never counted it and he never knew how much he or the house had. Once his mind was made up, he bought what he wanted, not minding the advice he received, for he had a great sense of fate. He would call it "divine providence," no doubt, but after forty years there are reasonable grounds to believe that Piet's many epic decisions were very human, indeed. Some of them might even be called foolish; others have been reversed, with great loss to the province.

But Piet was a very kind man eager to belong and determined to rule the province in accordance with Father General's directives. Because he took this onus so seriously, he sent out to the province more letters of instruction about duties to be performed than any of his contemporaries. Looking back on his administration one sees an almost dangerous concentration of authority in his hands, authority which he never delegated and seldom abused. He eagerly served as the father figure in the lives of all young Jesuits, who responded more often than not with good humor. For the older men, he was something else, a combination of Father Provincial and Mother Superior, who busied himself with the most trivial details of government, often missing the forest for the trees.

Piet's predecessor, Father Dillon, a man of more deliberate decisions, was no longer on the scene. On April 20, 1924, he was appointed as an official visitor to Alaska by Father Ledochowski, relieving Piet for the time being of the need to make a provincial's visit to that still French dominated mission. There were twenty-nine Jesuits in Alaska that year, including Bishop Crimont and the new superior, Father Philip Delon.† Delon, like Crimont, was from France and shared with Monroe and Piet a strong attachment to his native land.

Crimont was delighted with the choice of Piet as provincial. He wrote to him, "we have now $20,000 for the Alaska supplies. I want more."[4] The bishop, in fact, needed more. During this period about $40,000 was required annually for supplying the missions, including the three boarding schools. Over $19,000 of this was required to pay only the freight for shipping the supplies. Crimont's estimate was based on a cost of $200 annually for each priest, brother and sister, and something less for each child. Fish or caribou stew appeared often on their menus.

Comparable costs for scholastics studying theology were sent to Piet by Father Sauer, who became province treasurer in 1919, when Arthuis was recalled to France.‡ For the year

*Later when Piet was spiritual counselor at the Mount he served as umpire at ball games and often declared players to be "out" when they were "safe," mostly to test their virtue. Scholastics were not as docile to his decisions as were novices.

†Delon became superior of the mission on September 16, 1923. He was still superior when he died in the crash of the *Marquette Missionary* on October 12, 1930.

‡The health of Father Arthuis had been undermined by his many labors, especially those related to construction. For the most part, he was responsible for the construction of Gonzaga University Administration Building, St. Aloysius, and Mount St. Michael's. He died at Poitiers, France, June 13, 1923 at the age of 63.

1924, Father Sauer wrote, annual expenses at each of the scholasticates per Jesuit were as follows:

Woodstock	$600 per year plus $100 for incidentals
St. Louis	$525 per year plus $100 for incidentals
Montreal	$525 per year plus $100 for incidentals
In Europe	$468.75 per year plus $75 for incidentals

The latter, Father Sauer noted, did not include additional travel costs which came to $250 for the round trip, or one-fourth of that additional cost per year. Out-of-province scholastics at Mount St. Michael's were charged one dollar per day, less than $375 for the year, plus an unlisted amount for incidentals like clothing and medicine.[5]

"The future of the Alaska Missions hangs by a thread," Dillon wrote from the far north. "You may not have been aware that it has been largely due to the salaries paid to our Sisters by the U.S. Bureau of Education that the missions have been able to go on until this day. Now the Government has withdrawn that aid, and the deficit must be made up by the alms of the faithful. Otherwise the missions, especially the three large schools at Holy Cross, Akulurak and Pilgrim Hot Springs, may have to be closed."[6]

Like the Indian missions in the Northwest, the missions of Alaska now entered a precarious state of existence. There was one difference, however, the glamor of the missions in Alaska appealed more to donors and though the quest for funds was interminable, and a great nuisance, support was forthcoming, at least, and the missions survived in better condition than those of the Northwest.

Piet had problems which concerned him more. These were related to the province schools to which he had been exposed so superficially, while he studied philosophy at Gonzaga, that he understood very little about the schools' management and costs. For a brief period, two of his consultors were university presidents, Fitzgerald and Maher, who had a definite advantage in tilting with the provincial over disputes about available manpower. Both were Irish Americans, as were Piet's other consultors, John McHugh at St. Joseph's, Seattle, and Edward Whelan, Whittle's replacement as provincial assistant, who was just out of tertianship. All four had the gift of Irish eloquence, especially Maher, who was greatly admired as a preacher. Like Patrick O'Reilly, Maher had a streak of severity in him which, in the minds of most Jesuits at least, categorized him as "an Irish Pope."

The big crisis in education at this time was girls and/or women. Maher at Santa Clara, conforming to Father General's rigid directive prohibiting the admission of girls, opposed any change of Jesuit tradition for any school, north or south. This was all well and good for Maher and Santa Clara, located in the south where Catholic colleges were available to women. But in the north there were no Catholic colleges for women, nor could one foresee, in the near future, even the hope of one. Seattle College, for example, was languishing for lack of students while Catholic girls were forced to attend the University of Washington. Worse yet, was the absurd position in which the teaching sisters found themselves. It must be remembered that this was the period in higher education in the United States when accreditation and teacher standards were first demanded. States began to require certification, to which the sisters were denied in Jesuit colleges and universities, while Rome and the bishops bickered about whose responsibility it was to provide classes for these devoted women.

There was some flexibility in Father Ledochowski's position. This was expressed in Father de Boyne's instructions, which allowed the attendance of sisters in summer schools, provided previous permission from Rome was obtained.[7] Since the Mothers Superiors of many religious orders had appealed to Father Fitzgerald at Gonzaga for opening classes to their sisters, Fitzgerald applied to Rome for the required permission. Father General stalled, preferring to postpone his decision on this particular subject until he had studied it more carefully.

Summer schools as such were not a novel undertaking at Gonzaga. As early as 1890 summer classes had been conducted in the old college for applicants to the Jesuit Order, who lacked facility in Latin. In subsequent years, month-long courses, for which no academic credit was allowed, were presented for the benefit of Jesuit scholastics, who were teaching in high schools during the years. These informal classes served primarily as immediate preparation for the courses the scholastics were assigned to teach. Most of the old fathers regarded them as an intrusion, a useless frill which interfered with the fathers' honestly earned vacation. "In the good old days," Father Fletcher was sometimes heard to say, "we closed the school at the end of June, turned off the phones, and all went to villa for a vacation." Perhaps Fletcher was right, but expedience had its way. The informal summer classes, no longer adequate, were converted into formal academic courses in the summer of 1924 and non-Jesuit students, including women, were admitted. Since permission for participation by women had not yet arrived from Rome, this first summer school was conducted at Holy Names Academy, several blocks east of the university.

Qualified college students on all levels were eligible for admission to this first summer school, which began as scheduled on June 23. This was Monday, registration day. Classes began on Wednesday. "Summer School for Sisters began today," says the school diary for June 25. "All classes except chemistry and physics are held at H[oly] Names Acad., the Sciences at Gonzaga. There were 58 Sisters, 5 lay people, 6 scholastics and 1 priest."[8]

The ice had been broken. Things would never be the same. For its second session, begun on June 22, 1925, 72 sisters were registered out of a total of 112. This was substantial progress. Twenty-eight courses were now offered and one of them was taught by the president, who decided to take a whirl at teaching again. A born teacher, Fitzgerald taught philosophy during the session, which ended on July 30.

The increase in the number of sisters presented a housing problem this year. Provision for a limited number was made in near-by convents and Mrs. J. E. Buckly, Mother of Father Harold Buckly, acted as a committee of one for arranging other accommodations. Beginning with this summer, until Madonna Hall was erected on the campus for women students, certain family residences, otherwise vacant during the summer months, were made available to the sisters, who spent some warm, busy summers, housekeeping, studying almost frantically and praying quietly in St. Aloysius Church, where the novelty of many Masses held them for long hours. Children of the neighborhood soon became accustomed to the nun's annual invasion of Holy Land. Like the graceful swallows at San Juan Capistrano, they arrived faithfully every year and for the duration of the summer session they edified the people of the parish with their sweetness and devotion. More than one priest at the university felt they brought more to the city than they ever took away.

There were two factors now, which indicated Gonzaga's pressing need for additional student residence space, the summer school and big time football, both of which had been sneaked on to the campus somewhat surreptitiously, since the war. Everyone, especially the resident students, recognized the need for a hall. When Father Brogan, as president, organized Gonzaga's first financial drive in 1919, he presented its two objectives as debt liquidation and a new residence hall. The drive however, had been only partly successful, thirty-three and one-third per-cent successful, to be exact. When all the expenses were paid off the university had $100,000 left to pay off a $120,000 debt and to build a $150,000 residence hall, which had been offered as a kind of bait for the more sober donors. When it was all over, therefore, the university was not only $20,000 in debt, but it also had pledged itself to put up the residence.

PIET'S ENTHUSIASM

At this point Father John McHugh became the university's president. McHugh was a sick man, who had to spend most of his time in the hospital while his vice president, Father James Kennelly, dominated the campus. Kennelly was a warm supporter of the rah rah rah spirit on the campus, when the school drifted into the dangerous arena of conference-style football.

Early in 1920 an Athletic Board of Control had been created. Graduate Manager Eugene Russell, a member of this board and pardonably enthusiastic about the fortunes of the pigskin on the campus, announced on May 29, 1920, that Charles E. Dorais, former star quarterback of Notre Dame and recognized coach, had been signed up by Gonzaga University as its new coach and director of athletics.[9] Russell wanted a sensational coach and he had hired one. He now had a big lion by the tail. He and all the big brave members of the board were going to have an exciting adventure, holding onto the lion, but some of the other boards on the campus were going to starve for lack of funds, despite McHugh's expressed intention to keep football in its place. Gonzaga's problems were not unique. It was a problem everywhere and the history of the United States education during this period was characterized as the era of big stadiums and small libraries.

When Dorais arrived at Gonzaga on August 28, 1920, he found a small stadium built over a gravel bed, with a few bleachers, and a collegiate student body of about two hundred. If he was dismayed he kept it to himself and began to agitate for a new, larger stadium. A committee was formed. It recommended concrete stands in the shape of a horseshoe, designed to accommodate twenty-eight thousand fans. This was, of course, daydreaming. Eventually a scaled-down version was produced and dedicated with appropriate high jinks on October 14, 1922. The Gonzaga diary made certain observations about the day's fiscal success: "It is estimated that 5,600 people witnessed the game—the bleachers [sic] seat 5,000. Hundreds of autos were parked in the yard and many more along the avenues and streets; at the end, ten trolley cars waited on Boone St. to take away the crowd; the total sale of tickets was about $4200—half goes to W.S.C. as agreed upon. Of the Varsity's half, about $1800 netted, after expenses of the game are paid."[10]

When the 1922 season was over there was still a deficit of $7,500 against the field. However, Gonzaga was selected to play against West Virginia in the East-West bowl game at San Diego on New Year's day. Although they lost by a score of 21-13, they were hailed nationally as the Cinderella Team of the year and when they returned in a storm of adulation they were presented with a huge civic banquet and $10,290 to pay off the debt on the stadium.*

If the stadium project had ended here, in the Davenport Hotel, where everyone was cheering madly, the history of Gonzaga might have been different. The cheers were in a sense, the beginning of the end, the beginning of a sequence of events that brought the university to the brink of bankruptcy.

Of course the stadium had to be enlarged, to accommodate 10,400 persons. The university of 1925 agreed to endorse the cost of the improvements and its officers signed mortgage bonds which had a face value of $30,000. This represented in a very concrete way the Think Big motto of the Rah Rah Rahs. During the previous year, however, the team had lost its top-flight coach to the University of Detroit. Gus Dorais' departure, it should be noted, was universally regretted. Only one other person in the history of the school had placed Gonzaga before a larger public. That other person was Bing Crosby. Curiously both were at Gonzaga at the same time. Crosby graduated from the high school in June 1920, just before Dorais arrived. His two years in pre-law at the university coincided with Gonzaga's Golden Era of football, the era of Gus Dorais.

*The East-West game played on New Year's Day was a charity game. Gonzaga received only travel expenses. The money mentioned here was raised by local fans.

338

But what about the residence hall? Fitzgerald had a tendency to procrastinate in making decisions. There were embarrassing questions, though, from donors to the Greater Gonzaga Drive who had expected to see a new building by this time for the housing of the students. Like others on the campus, Fitzgerald had conceded a certain priority in favor of the stadium, not merely out of a false sense of values, but because there was a firm belief that the combination of a stadium and a winning football team would produce the necessary income for building a hall. Indeed, it would produce much more. One could look at Notre Dame to see how much prosperity football could accomplish. So the stadium came first. No wonder, then, that extraordinary interest in the community followed the gate receipts on each game. Every dollar counted was a step nearer the goal. If football during those days was really a lion devouring the school's substance, there was no one to recognize it. To its contemporaries, it looked more like a promising young colt that was going to grow into a sleek Man of War and pay off a dozen mortgages with its earnings on the turf.

But time, at least, was against everybody. After the stadium was finished, Father Fitzgerald decided he would have to come to grips with the residence hall problem. During the summer of 1923 he requested Mr. Zittel to prepare some preliminary plans for a building which encompassed classroom space on the lower floor and student living quarters on upper floors. On September 23, Mr. Zittel delivered the first drafts of his work. "Mr. Zittel brought some preliminary plans for the proposed new Senior Hall," says the diary for this day. "These will be shown the members of our community for suggestions."[11]

The plans were merely a beginning. They had to be revised several times to bring building costs within the accepted budget. In February, 1924, the architect prepared two more sets of plans. Choosing the one he favored, Fitzgerald sent it to the Provincial for approval, requesting that a decision be made as soon as possible. Mr. Zittel, estimating that it would take one month to produce more detailed plans and five months for construction, was eager to break ground before April 1. All who were involved wanted the building ready for occupancy by the fall term.

April 1 arrived and passed by. There were no ground-breaking ceremonies that day, nor that year. Required permission, loans, and other delays caused by the increasingly high construction costs of the post-war recession tied up the project for the remainder of the year. Finally in early January, 1925, D. W. Twohy of the Old National Bank and G. Hardgrove of a local investment company, met with Father Fitzgerald and his consultors "to present their plans for a loan."[12] Their proposal was the sale of a $125,000 bond issue by the firm of Ferris and Hardgrove. The fathers accepted their plan. Meanwhile, specifications on the new building, to be called De Smet Hall, were issued for bids. On February 7 the bids were opened. Two days later the general contract was awarded to the Huetter Construction Company on a bid of $130,000. The James Smyth Plumbing Company was awarded the plumbing contract for $11,506 and the Dowling Heating Company the contract for heating at a cost of $9,747.[13]

On March 4 at 2:30 in the afternoon construction on the new hall was solemnly begun before a large crowd. Bishop O'Reilly of Baker City, Oregon, presented the occasional exercise of oratory, his wit being fully equal to the occasion. According to the diary's account of the event, many diocesan priests were present to enjoy it.

Since the bids were above the estimate, arrangements were made for a $150,000 bond issue instead of the issue proposed. On March 28 the members of the Board of Trustees assembled in Father Fitzgerald's office at 9:00 A.M. Fitzgerald, Robert Shepherd, Frederick Baldus, James Brogan and Joseph Tomkin signed these bonds in the presence of Mr. Gallagher of Ferris and Hardgrove.[14] For this service, Ferris and Hardgrove received a commission of $6,250. Revenue stamps at five cents per hundred dollars totaled $75, title clearance on the property cost $196.20 and the architect's fee was $5,195.58. If the hall was finally being realized, Gonzaga would have to pay for it the hard way.

At this time, Gonzaga's debt stood at a new all-time high. The university still owed $34,500 for bonds contracted through Ferris and Hardgrove in 1917. With this and other commitments, total indebtedness was estimated at more than two-hundred-thousand.[15]

Construction on the new brick veneer building, the first to be erected on the campus since the church was completed thirteen years earlier, went ahead according to schedule. Photographs were taken at various stages and curious neighbors, as well as faculty members observed each mark of progress with an unofficial progress inspection, which served to delay matters. The building was not ready when school opened on September 8, but a month later *Open House* was celebrated. On Saturday, October 24, the first boys moved into the hall. On the same day a violent dust storm invaded the city, and a major game was played in the new stadium, which was to pay for the hall. Five thousand people that day saw Gonzaga defeat Idaho by a score of 12 to 3, which was about the ratio of the odds favoring a defunct university in ten years.[16]

The completion and occupation of the hall now cleared the way for Father Fitzgerald to give his entire attention to Spokane's forthcoming Indian Congress, in which Gonzaga's Jesuits were to play an important role. This congress, which inaugurated a new type of program for the solution of Indian problems, attracted such wide attention that a subsequent meeting, held in Spokane in July of the following year, was designated as a National Indian Congress.

The movement for this great congress had its beginnings at Gonzaga. In 1925 the university had scheduled a football game with the Haskell Indian Institute in Kansas, to be played in Spokane on October 31. Indications from Northwest tribal leadership, several months before the proposed game, showed that approximately three thousand Indians were making plans to attend the contest. Alarmed at the prospects of conflict arising from the exploitation of these Indians during their visit, Mayor Charles Fleming of Spokane called a meeting of civic officials, citizens, and prominent Indians to discuss methods for protecting the visitors. Discussion produced more than His Honor had bargained for. A plan for a vast Indian Congress gradually emerged. After consulting local railroad officials, who were pleased to encourage anything that might produce travel revenue, Fleming hastily dispatched a committee of Indians to Washington D.C. to confer with the Bureau of Indian Affairs. Railroad officials provided transportation for this committee.

President Coolidge and Indian Commissioner Charles Burke expressed their sincere regrets, saying they could not attend the congress because the invitation had come too suddenly. However, both promised their fullest cooperation. Burke summoned members of his staff to discuss plans for his department's contribution to the congress and when the plan had been exposed one of the officials exclaimed: "Why, gentlemen, this looks like an act of Providence. It is most unbelievable that a great community like that of the Northwest and a city like Spokane should lead such a humanitarian movement. If your statement is really true, then we have found the solution of the Indian problem."[17]

With the benevolent eye of the Indian department upon them, Spokane's civic officials made their plans carefully. By Friday, October 30, opening date of the congress, everything was in readiness. Newspaper reporters from the farthest parts of the country were on hand to cover the events. Seven motion picture companies had cameras ready to gather details for newsreels, while representatives of the *London Graphic* and the National Geographic Society were prepared to collect numerous photographs.[18] Superintendents of Education from many states streamed in with other government officials from Washington and from the Indian reservations. An estimated forty thousand palefaces from other areas joined the procession into Spokane to witness the historic event.[19] Members of almost forty tribes, accompanied by their squaws and innumerable babies, horses and dogs, arrived in buck-

340

boards, train coaches, busses and cars. For the most part they camped on Glover Field, along the river below Spokane's Civic Center. It was an old Indian camp ground, where the fathers had often visited Indians before. Tepees were also pitched along Riverside Avenue, near the Monaghan monument, and horses were hitched to lampposts along the same street. With marvelous efficiency, thousands of Indians were properly housed and fed as guests of the city.

Three Jesuits, in particular, entered into the activities which followed: Father Cataldo, nearing his ninetieth year, but still active and alert, Father Aloysius Soer, sometimes referred to as "the saint of the Rockies," and Father Taelman, who caused a sensation during educational conferences on November 2 and 3 by defending some very unpopular viewpoints.[20]

Three of the many scheduled events of the congress especially concerned them and their confreres at Gonzaga. The first of these was the football game, which began at 1:15 P.M. on Saturday. Thirteen thousand people, including hundreds of Indians in full tribal regalia, occupied every available seat in the stadium. Thousands more milled about, eager for a glimpse of the two Indian parades, which took place before the game and during the half-time ceremonies. The squads trotted in while the stands rocked with war whoops. The game, sometimes called Spokane's greatest, got under way. When it was over, the Indians were the victors but no scalps were taken. They had defeated the palefaces 10 to 9 in the last moment of play. The hero of the hour was Gonzaga's Art Dussault, who had scooped a wayward ball and had run twenty yards for a touchdown. Though his team had lost the game, his race down the field, with eleven Indians in pursuit, has gone down in history as one of Gonzaga's greatest moments.

Gonzaga could stand the loss, perhaps the Indians could not. There were no hard feelings. The redskins and the palefaces took their evening meal together, then joined their forces to present one of the most colorful parades in Spokane's history.

The Jesuits entered three floats in this parade. On one of these old Father Cataldo sat, in a great coat, and occupying a seat of honor made from elk and deer horns. Above him, in all their finest feathers, beads and tanned skins were a score of ancient Coeur d'Alenes, whom Cataldo had known since his coming to Spokane sixty years before. Two other floats depicted the history of Gonzaga, at least the legend on the first said so. Perhaps it was well that it did, for the almost-empty truck provided little to suggest Gonzaga's difficult beginnings. The second float, called "The Spirit of 1925," allowed scant improvement. A group of students in caps and gowns stood their ground firmly, immobile and stiff-looking, like statuary with self-conscious, strained expressions. Since the Coeur d'Alene Mission float, with its magnificent realism, had taken away the breath of the spectators, no one seemed to notice the poverty of the two succeeding units.

On Sunday, November 1, a solemn high mass was celebrated for the Indians in St. Aloysius Church by Father Taelman. After the gospel Father Cataldo preached in Nez Perce. "It was a touching sight to see the venerable missioner make his way slowly and on crutches, to the altar rails to address them in Nez Perce. But when he faced his beloved Indians, he seemed to be a new man; his clear voice easily reached every corner of the edifice, as he poured forth his heart in the sweet tongue of the Nez Perce."[21] During Cataldo's earlier years some of the Jesuits referred to him as Cast Iron Lungs. He was still Iron Lungs, despite the ravages of tuberculosis, which had cast a dark shadow on his life almost since birth. After Father Cataldo's sermon, Father Taelman, another Iron Lungs, stepped forward and spoke in Kalispel, "with his usual fluency and vigor," says an eye-witness account. The church that day was overcrowded, by curious Whites as well as Indians. Perhaps some of those present did not enjoy all three sermons which were rendered in the Nez Perce, the Kalispel and the English tongues. Neither did many understand the Latin sung in the Mass. But the extraordinary nature of the event illustrated rather dramatically the genuine catholicity of the church.

After the excitement of the Indian invasion had subsided, Gonzaga's new dean of men, Father Louis Egan, busied himself with adapting a room in De Smet Hall for a chapel. Bishop Schinner graciously gave permission to reserve the Blessed Sacrament, so that students could enjoy the presence of Holy Eucharist in their new hall. Gentle, little Father Rebmann, a living relic of Gonzaga's past, like the two Iron Lungs, had something precious to contribute to the chapel. With Father Fitzgerald's approval, he presented a beautiful chalice which he had received on the occasion of his fiftieth birthday.[22]

He had another treasure, and he offered this also. It was an altar stone, which had been used in field Masses during the Franco-Prussian war. He offered it timidly. Could his attachment for it, his love for the old country symbolized in it, offend anyone? Indeed not. Father Kennelly received it gratefully and inserted it in the altar of his chapel.

When the parade and all the hullaballoo were over, Cataldo went back to his mission. He was a sad old man now, very sad, because six Indian boys had burned to death in the latest mission fire. Mission poverty. If St. Joseph's at Slickpoo, where he spent so many years of his life, had decent support, these beautiful little Indian boys would not have died. They had lived in an old frame dormitory building, which caught fire, like many mission buildings, from cheap electric wiring or faulty flues. Then the boys had gone into the burning building to save their clothes, all they had in this world, and they never came out.[23] That had been on October 4, just weeks before the Indian Congress, and ever since Cataldo was resolved not only to have a new concrete building for the boys, but a new safe building for the girls as well.

Monsignor Hughes of the Bureau of Catholic Indian Missions in Washington, deeply touched by the old missionary's grief, published a broadside, which presented a portrait of him on his crutches, his frail body twisted and bent, but his face firmly set with determination. The Archbishop in Philadelphia, where Cataldo was well-known, wanted him to make an appearance in that city, but Piet reported that the doctor disapproved. The journey, he thought, might kill him. It was just as well. The money came in anyway, and Cataldo found peace at last. The children were housed in safe buildings.

At Akulurak in Alaska, there had been another fire. Father Dillon wired the details: "Sister's building completely destroyed. Roof caught fire from spark, fanned by a high southeast wind, building reduced to ashes in a little over an hour. No lives lost, but six nuns and 65 girls absolutely homeless. Must rebuild before September weather."[24]

Fortunately they were able to rebuild before the ice of winter nipped them in their tents, but another frame building had to be produced, another potential fire trap for the lack of something better.

News of the province, by this time, had begun to appear in a new orderly format. Piet had established *The California Province News*, which was published at Mount St. Michael's, the first issue appearing in September, 1925. Father Henry Gabriel was the editor and some thought of it as *Gabriel's Trumpet*. As spiritual father of the community, Gabriel presented monthly exhortations or sermons adapted for religious. Skillfully composed, these were published eventually in book form and received modest acclaim as excellent tracts on the pursuit of virtue.[25] Later Gabriel returned to California where, in his old age, he became somewhat irascible. He was reminded, then, of his doctrine, published for all to read. "Oh that book!" he would snort indignantly, "I wrote that for scholastics, not for myself."

In the "Brave New World," the book has fallen by the wayside and Gabriel's expertise at composition survives in the *California Province News*. Choice bits can be gleaned, our grains of history can be gathered and milled so that all might share, as our fathers did, in the bread of edification.

"Poor old Pete Enemee," the editor tells us in the first issue, revealing events at St. Ignatius Mission, "Br[other] Campo's boss-cowboy of the olden days, died suddenly during the Fourth of July celebration. This finished the feast of Pete's place and for the next two days the Fathers were kept busy in the confessional."[26]

Seattle College, Gabriel reported in the second issue, started classes with 35 students in college, and 184 in high school. In the third issue he noted that Brother Peter Buskens had arrived at Gonzaga, having left De Smet to the foibles of an impractical superior. It was Busken's contention that this superior, in the interests of monogamy, had bought twelve bulls for twelve cows.* Buskens had many other droll anecdotes about his former superior, which created in time two legendary characters, himself and the superior, the former always presented as the hero of each situation and the latter always as the villain. In those days we did not need television; we had Brother Buskens.

In the third issue of the *Province News* there also was a progress report on the new swimming pool at the Mount, with an explanation regarding its origin and need.[27] It seems that a certain water tank leaked excessively and Father Sauer had concluded, after appropriate conferences with experts, that a thirty by ninety foot concrete tank could save money and serve the dual function of both reservoir and swimming pool. Now if there was anything at all that Father Sauer liked it was to save money. He was like Van Gorp, whom he admired too much. Piet finally gave approval, provided this "tank" did not cost over $2,000, so the scholastics excavated the required area at no cost at all and Joe Tonani, Sauer's right hand, did the rest within the budget.

The Mount had a new rector at this time. On June 11, 1925, Father Thomas Martin, rector at Los Gatos was appointed rector at the Mount, succeeding Father Benn.[28] No doubt he reflected dolefully on the prospects of six more years of responsibility, but moving to the Mount had its advantages too. He would leave behind the tangled red tape of the winery in prohibition days and the serious problems of finance because of the cut in income. Not that St. Michael's was a sinecure. It, too, had problems, in fact knottier problems than Martin ever anticipated.

A New Englander, forever Boston Irish, Martin preferred the four seasons weather of Spokane to the milder climate of California, so he looked upon his return to the Northwest as a kind of homecoming. He was installed on August 4. The scholastics, fresh from villa and their annual retreat, were cordial in their welcome. They told him that the Mount building, new to the rector, was too crowded and that the swimming pool begun by Father Sauer had best be finished before the frost came. Could the rector speak to Father Sauer about speeding things up, perhaps in time for September swimming? The pool was finished on St. Michael's Day after Pontifical Mass by Bishop Schinner. As the water poured in from the Mount's own well at the bottom of the hill, Father Sauer had a crew busy leveling the fields for baseball, while Brother Giraudi and his helpers waited to see what dirt they could salvage for flower gardens.

By the time everything was settled to the satisfaction of all, the new rector began to wish he were back in Los Gatos. Like other houses of studies, Woodstock and St. Louis, the Mount was a succession of disputations, music academies, minor crises like flu epidemics or brush fires, distinguished visitors and improvements.† Martin took them in stride. There was an amazing amount of activity during his rectorate: unusual developments like

*The superior, whose name Buskens never mentioned, was Father Joseph Farrell, one of Gonzaga's first students from Thompson Falls, Montana. Joseph had lived a very sheltered life. His devoutly Catholic father was a railroad man.

†A major brush fire in August, 1926, stripped the southwestern slopes of its groves of small bull pine, leaving them barren. They have remained barren to this day.

improvements at the villa, and the building of the large new library wing, not to mention minor programs and societies, which flourished with unprecedented success. The philosophers, incorrigible pranksters that they were, had a nickname for their rector, which referred to his curly hair. They called him Kinky, which carried with it more affection than blame. If Kinky Martin ever knew his nickname, he ignored it as calmly as he ignored the snakes brought home from Pot Holes by biology majors.

At the Mount, Martin developed several trifling idiosyncracies that became legends. One was his habit of forgetting a rubric at Mass when he was on the verge of exploding about something. Sometimes he forgot the Kyrie, or the Gloria; when it was noticed, everyone took cover and waited for the storm to strike. Invariably after breakfast on such days, a culprit was summoned, queried and sentenced with great dispatch. Kinky could conduct the whole proceedings in a manner that left nothing obscure.

The duties of rector did not keep him out of the classroom. He taught Hebrew, which in those stern days was a required subject, like geology and astronomy. An expert in teaching languages, Martin developed his own grammar and most cheerfully pounded vowel points into reluctant philosophers' heads.

Indeed, Tom Martin was happy wherever he was. Not all, alas, were as contented as he. At Havre, Montana, the pastor was Father William Shepherd, an uprooted Californian, who was happy only in the Golden State. He had been exiled for several years by an unpropitious fate, first in Ketchikan where the climate would have tried Job himself, then at Holy Family Mission, where he almost starved, and finally at Havre. In 1924 he built a church there, the present St. Jude's. This was an adapted Spanish Mission edifice as solid as concrete and roof tile could make it, and as out of place in Havre as a Joshua tree.

Once, they say, Charlie Russell, the cowboy artist, paid a visit to Father Shepherd. "Father," he said out of politeness, "How do you like Havre?"

"Charlie, was the reply, "if I had a house in hell and one in Havre, I'd sell the one in Havre." As things turned out, he could sell neither, and he was not transferred from Havre until Piet got around to it, in August, 1927.

On April 26, 1925, Monday of Holy Week, Archbishop Christie died at last. With his departure from the scene went all hopes, for the time at least, of the Jesuit school he had approved, verbally, for the Portland archdiocese. Piet was not as disappointed by this lapse of opportunity as some of his subjects, who pointed to the growing number of Catholics in the province and the large increase in the number of Jesuits.* They predicted an early division of the California province and urged the need of a Jesuit school in Portland, which at that time was the largest city in the Northwest. Piet, doubtlessly due to his background, was not school-centered. His interests primarily were concerned with the formation of Jesuits, from the novitiate to tertianship, and he dedicated most of his energies to this. One suspects that schools frightened him. The noisy, robust Americans, shouting, stomping and banging books when he granted holidays during his annual visitations were like barbarians at the gates of medieval Paris. Piet was an orderly man, and these throngs of excited boys appeared to be out of control.

To create support for the Jesuit formation program, Piet established *The Western Jesuit*, a public relations type of institutional bulletin, which was published at Los Gatos. The first issue edited by Father Leo Simpson, appeared in April, 1926. Thereafter, except for the summer, *The Western Jesuit* appeared each month and carried Jesuit family news to friends and foes alike—and there were always a vocal contingent of the latter, some of them in high places. The province had two bulletins now, *The California Province News* for the

---

*At the beginning of 1925 there were 524 Jesuits in the province, an increase of nine. In the following year there was an increase of nineteen.

exclusive use of Jesuits, and *The Western Jesuit* for the general public. Both carried reports on the usual disasters, like the fires at St. Andrew's Mission and Santa Clara. On April 21, 1926, the Sisters' school at St. Andrews, the Umatilla mission, caught fire from a kerosene lamp, which exploded. The school burned completely to the ground. Fifty girls and twenty-five small boys were asleep in the building, but all were safely evacuated. One of the sisters perished in the fire.[29] At Santa Clara the Old Mission Church caught fire on Monday morning, October 25, 1926, while some of the fathers were offering Mass. No one was injured. It required three hours to bring the fire under control, and when it was all over, the original mission, in which many Jesuits had been ordained, existed no more.[30] The school and the mission church were eventually replaced.

The sister in death was joined by a number of Jesuits, who have some claim to recognition here as well as in those province bulletins. First there was Father Treca, who died in Providence Hospital, Seattle on September 16, 1926. For over a year he had been afflicted with an infection in the hip bone, which proved to be tubercular.[31] In August he left Alaska for Seattle where doctors found the disease so far advanced that they offered Treca only one alternative to eight months of agony and death, amputation of the leg at the hip. Treca consented to the latter. Before going to surgery he took his crucifix, kissed it saying, "I am in the hands of my Lord; His will be done." Father Boland, Rector at Seattle College reported other details to Piet:

"Our saintly Fr. Treca has left us. I was never so impressed at one's supreme indifference to 'life and death' as in the case of Fr. Treca. 'I'm in the Hands of God & of my Superiors,' he often said to me, 'and whatever they decide I willingly accept.' When, prior to my anointing him, I told him of the uncertainty of the outcome of the operation, he said very calmly: 'Oh, Father, that makes no difference to me.' And as he lay on the operating table, without even a quiver of fear, I blessed him and he smilingly said: 'Thank you, Father; now say the 'De Profundis' and Good-bye.' The Doctors marvelled at the heroicity of the dear old man. Before I took him to the surgery, he said to me: 'Father, I think that I shall lay my eyes for the first time upon our Blessed Mother today; and what message shall I give to Her from you?' He died two hours after the operation."[32]

A few weeks later, on October 27, 1926, Brother Terragno died at St. Regis Mission.* For over fifty years he had labored in the Rocky Mountain Mission, mostly as a cook. He was a favorite with the Indians and spoke their languages fluently. For the last thirty years he was postmaster at St. Regis Mission, as well as cook, and he served in an additional capacity as province prophet. For this he was awarded the waggish title of "Brother Provincial," the Jesuit who knew before anyone else, including the provincial, what was going to happen in the province. Perhaps he was psychic. If so, he did not look the part. Tall and plump, as good cooks are supposed to be, he appeared to be a jocular restaurant keeper, whom the patrons regarded as a kind of uncle Marcellus.

Brother Provincial died peacefully, no doubt out-guessing everybody when it would occur. Father Jules Jette, on the other hand, suffered a very painful agony before death, which was so violent that he did not recognize his Jesuit companions for some days. His superior, Father Martin Lonneux, could not offer him even aspirin to lessen the pain. They were in snowbound Alaska, at St. Mary's Akulurak, and a great blizzard was blowing across the land and sea, closing all contact with the outside. Jette, four years earlier, had nearly died at Tanana from strangulated hernia. Then, too, he was isolated by the breakup of ice on the Yukon River, beyond which was the only trail to Fairbanks, where help could be found.

---

*Roch Terragno landed in New York in 1866, where he pronounced his first vows as a Jesuit. He spent most of his life in the Indian missions. Several times he drove his oxen over the prairies from De Smet mission to Walla Walla for supplies. He died peacefully on October 27, 1926. *California Province News*, II-4 (December, 1926), p. 31.

There is a quaint anecdote about Jette's escape from Tanana on a dogsled.* The simple people of the village prayed for a miracle: a vast floe of ice that would remain stationary long enough for a dogsled to cross over to the other side. Jette was bundled up in furs and placed in the sled while the Indians watched and waited. Then lo! the ice stopped moving and Jette was rushed across and up the mushy trail to Fairbanks. His life was saved.

After a year of convalescence in Seattle, where he taught French to the mischievous boys whom he could not control, he returned to Alaska to complete his great lexicon on the Koyukon Indian language and to compose a history of the Alaska mission. At Akulurak, he had learned, there had been an ongoing dispute between the superior of the mission and the superior of the sisters for some years. The Mother Superior was a very strong-willed person who insisted on ruling the roost including such details as Mass and the administration of the sacraments. At least one Jesuit superior had left the mission in frustration. Then Father Lonneux was appointed and Jette, still convalescing, volunteered to assist him.

One evening in early February, 1927, while Jette was composing a report to Rome by lamplight, he suddenly collapsed and cried for help. The following days and nights were a nightmare for Father Lonneux, who sat beside Jette's bed and watched him in his terrible agony. In a few hours Jette's incredible mind was gone. His last days were spent in the delirium of indescribable pain. On February 7, he mercifully died, while the storm raged on. "I could not even send a telegram from one of the wireless stations," Lonneux said later, his grief still apparent after twenty years. "We placed the body in a rough box and buried it out on the tundra, covering it with blocks of ice so that wolves couldn't desecrate it. As soon as possible we buried it."† Thus ended the life of one of the greatest Jesuits in the history of the Order. A saint, many said, surely a very holy man whom everyone respected and loved, even the lively little boys at Seattle Prep. News of Jette's death did not reach the provincial until February 21.

Lawrence Palladino, noted especially for his *Indian and White in the Northwest,* was the next to go. On August 19, 1927, at St. Patrick's Hospital in Missoula, when he knew he was dying, he asked to be clothed in his cassock, the Black Robe, for the Indians. Then he asked to be laid on the floor, whence he received Holy Viaticum with profuse expressions of love and humility. And so he died, lying on the floor in his cassock, his eyes wide open, as he responded to the prayers in a firm voice, which belied his ninety years. He did not have a hair on his head, not even eyebrows, so he was like some new born babies, when he breathed his last. He was buried from St. Francis Xavier's Church, where the old bell, dedicated to St. Lawrence in his honor, tolled his passing, its mournful clamor marking the end of an era. Only Cataldo, withered in age and six months older than the deceased, remained of the early missionaries, and for him also, the bells would soon toll.

Palladino had died in August. Two other Jesuits, whose names have appeared large in our history, died in December, one following the other, seemingly with impatience. Father James Rockliff, second provincial of the California province and first rector of the Mount died at Missoula on December 4, 1927. He had made his last retreat at St. Ignatius, when a premonition of his death struck him. After making a general confession of his life to Father Dimier, a common practice in those Spartan days, he hurried back to Missoula, saying death was near. On December 1 he went to the hospital. He had only one request. He wanted to be buried at the Mount. Early morning, December 4, he sat up suddenly, turned to one side, and expired. He died as he had lived, calm and fearless.[33]

*This anecdote was told to me by Father James Conwell at Fairbanks in August, 1957. It was confirmed by people in Tanana who offered accounts of other lively episodes in Jette's life.

†These details were given to me by Father Martin Lonneux at Seattle in early December, 1952, just six weeks before he died in Fairbanks on January 21, 1953.

Later that day, in Seattle, Brother Rogers assisted Father Whittle with the death notices of Rockliff, which had to be dispatched to each house in the province. When these were ready, he mailed them, little realizing that on the following day, someone would make the same kind of journey to the post office to mail notices of his death. He retired that night as usual. About one in the morning he suffered a heart attack and was gone before the doctor arrived. He had run his last errand and served his last dinner, with quiet, unobtrusive dignity, like the faithful servant of the gospel.[34]

It was customary for Jesuits to take death in stride. When a colleague died, funeral arrangements were made with as little fuss as possible, sometimes too little. The plainest coffin in stock was ordered, some undertakers called it "the Jesuit casket," and after the funeral, the room of the deceased was cleared for another occupant, hopefully with a minimum of effort. It was always so casual that some might have thought that Jesuits lacked feeling. On the contrary, most Jesuits, whether their feelings toward the deceased were warm or not, had a strong realization that time was short and all would soon be reunited.

When a man died, the provincial usually had an empty post to fill. Other Jesuits were shuffled around. Adjustments were made until a new crop of young men appeared for assignments. Life went on.

Piet had three major projects under way in 1927. First there was the new tertianship at Port Townsend, Washington, about which Father General had been carping for years. As noted heretofore, Piet, like Dillon, gave the highest priority in the province to the formation of young Jesuits. It was characteristic of him, when he made up his mind to establish Manresa Hall as a tertianship, to nominate his favorite, Walter Fitzgerald, as the first superior there, keeping him as a province consultor and college president, with Father Leo Simpson, the new rector of the novitiate. In the long run, Piet had no high school or college Jesuits on his staff as province consultors, although in the working force more than half of his Jesuits were occupied in these activities.

Tertianship was the last year of Jesuit formal education; a year similar to the novitiate. It was intended to be a special year of prayer and reflection following the long years of study, which tended to divert the young Jesuits' interests from spiritual into secular channels. For some time tertianship had been conducted at Los Gatos where there were both novices and juniors, not an ideal situation, which Father Ledochowski took occasion to point out. Piet agreed. As novice master for nine years he understood the disadvantages of the situation. He began to search for a new tertianship.

There is a typscript account, dated June 21, 1928, and called "Memorandum—The Founding of Manresa Hall" in the house diary for this house of formation. The first part appears as follows:

"During the summer of 1926, Rev. Joseph M. Piet, S.J., Provincial, visited Port Townsend, Washington, for the purpose of inspecting the old Eisenbeis house, with a view of purchasing it for the Tertianship, which he hoped to begin in our Province the following year. At this time the Eisenbeis property was owned by the Parish of the Immaculate Conception of Seattle, Washington, as it had been bought by Father William Culligan, S.J. as a summer home for the teaching Sisters of the Seattle Parochial Schools. It seems that all the parishes had agreed to purchase this place for all the teaching Sisters, but Father Culligan found that no other parish wished to help with the financial burden of maintaining the vacation place. As he had borrowed the money to buy the place, and since he had to pay the interest alone, he was desirous of unloading the burden. At this juncture Father Provincial came to visit Port Townsend.

"The Sisters of Providence had maintained a Hospital in this City for many years and they were of course anxious that the Jesuit Fathers would come. Sister Cyrille, Superior, pointed out to Father Provincial the convenient location, three blocks from the Hospital, the wonderful healthful climate, and all the other engaging qualities of the place, so that he decided to recommend the place to his Consultors. An architect was asked to look over the building and see if it was in good condition."[35]

At this point I would like to digress for a moment to relate one of Father Sauer's most famous recollections, which he repeated frequently with considerable indignation.

After examining the old Eisenbeis property the first time, Piet, according to Sauer, directed him to go to Port Townsend, to inspect the place with a view to its proposed purpose, and to make a report. Sauer, who did not enjoy visits to the coast, did as he was told. His report was very negative. After he sent it to Piet, the latter wrote him an abrupt letter, stating with some sarcasm, that Sauer's job as treasurer, was to pay the bills, not to tell the provincial how to run the province.*

The incident bears an element of humor, but it strikes more deeply into the kind of relationship the two men experienced. Sauer was frugal, deeply attached to the Spokane area, and loyal to the missionaries, who were being sadly overlooked. Piet was just the opposite. These two men would clash again on the subject of the location of a novitiate for the north. Piet, as was proper, since he was the provincial, had his way in both cases, the tertianship and the novitiate. He was probably mistaken for both were subsequently closed and sold.

But this still lay in the future when Manresa Hall was acquired. The memorandum continues:

"In June, 1927 Father Provincial accompanied by Rev. Edward C. Menager, S.J. came to Port Townsend and purchased the Eisenbeis building and block on which it stands together with the block directly in front of it from Father Culligan. The purchase price was $7,500.00; the original cost of the place was $4,500 and Father Culligan had put in improvements to the extent of $3,000. These improvements were the renovation of the old building, the installation of electric wiring, the making of a cess pool and proper sewerage.

"Father Menager took charge of the place and began the preparation for the opening of Tertianship in September 1927. He stayed at the Hospital with Brothers Huber and McGuire and began the remodeling of the old building. Plasterers and plumbers and carpenters were engaged to work under the supervision of the Brothers and the work progressed so well that it was possible to open the House in September. In the meantime Father Menager purchased another block directly to the south of the block in front of the Eisenbeis building, and then, noticing that a sale of some twelve and one half blocks just west of the present location was being held by the County for taxes, he bid in and bought the entire amount for $708.00. The amount paid for the other block in front of the present building was $300.00.

"By the middle of August work was well completed. At this time Father Fitzgerald was appointed Superior of the new place and arrived on August 16th. Brother Johnson came a few days before and took charge of the kitchen and dining room. The Community now consisted of Father Fitzgerald, Brothers Johnson, Huber and McGuire. Father Vasta came a few weeks later as Minister of the Manresa Hall."

This tells the plain facts. In the realm of legend, perhaps, there was an additional feature of the Eisenbeis mansion that gave it a shadowy, spooky fascination, like a haunted house, immensely cherished by the tertians who regarded it as one of "the Port's" principal attractions. It was said that a former master of the house committed suicide, *self murder* (!) in the very room where the Tertian Master conducted his conferences with each tertian.

---

*Father Sauer recounted this episode many times, making certain each time that his listeners understood Piet's failure to be consistent.

This, if not the odors of the neighborhood pulp mill, was "the Port's" principal claim to fame.

On September 7, 1927, the tertianship diary begins: "About 7:30 in the evening the pioneer Tertians arrived by boat from Seattle . . . they were met at the wharf by V. Rev. Fr. Provincial (Fr. Piet) and Fr. Superior (Fr. Fitzgerald) and Fr. Instructor (Fr. Chianale) welcomed them at the home."[36]

On the following day the tertians cleaned house and assisted the new cook, Brother Kish, "the best cook in the province," prepare a grand dinner for some distinguished guests that evening. Among them were "Msgr. T. E. Ryan, Chancellor of the Diocese of Seattle, Hon. Baugauter, Mayor of Port Townsend, Fr. Klein, Pastor of Port Townsend Star of the Sea Church, Mr. C. A. Scott, President of the Chamber of Commerce, W. J. Daly, Morris Starrett, Editor of the Port Townsend Leader," besides the eighteen Jesuits. In other words, the number of people for dinner, crowded into a makeshift dining room, appeared to be about half the contemporary population of Port Townsend.

In October Father Nathaniel Purcell, the province's professional architect arrived at Manresa Hall to design an addition to the old mansion. He added a chapel, which looked like a crypt, classroom space and thirty private rooms for tertians. Piet then contracted with Father Gerald Beezer's father, a Seattle contractor, for the construction of the new wing.[37] This was ready for occupation on September 7, 1928, when twenty-two new tertians arrived. Thus with the beginning of its second year, "the Port" was more or less completed, already ancient looking, though it was half new.

Piet was so pleased with this highly superior accomplishment that he viewed with favor the proposed new "college" for Tacoma. The author and protagonist for this proposal was none other than Father David McAstocker, a sometime classmate of Piet's and currently pastor of St. Leo's. Dave was an uncommonly lovable man.[38] There was a certain wistfulness about him, a conscious dependence on others, and a warm gratefulness for anything he ever received. He often approached with empty hands and responded with a full heart. In this there was something boyish about him, in appearance as well as in manner. His wide blue eyes and applelike cheeks—flushed with the effects of tuberculosis—gave him a pink, young, innocent look despite his six-foot frame, one hundred and eighty-four pounds, and graying hair.

When appointed Tacoma's Jesuit superior and pastor of St. Leo's parish, he was forty-three years old and in as good health as he had enjoyed in a score of years. He was also spiritually and mentally fit, which is to say well qualified to serve as religious superior over seven energetic and hard-working Jesuits who were at that time trying desperately to cope with almost insuperable difficulties. One of his subjects was Father John, his own brother. John had been ordained in St. Louis in 1919 and had come to Tacoma as principal of the parish high school several years later. With his confreres he had been engaged during this time in the struggle to solve a crucial problem concerning St. Leo's church and school, the very problem for which Father Dave had been sent in—to settle it once and for all.

When the Jesuits officially took over St. Leo's in June, 1911, it will be recalled, their first concern was the establishment of a parish school. This was accomplished almost immediately, as old Father Hylebos had foreseen. What Hylebos, as well as others, had not foreseen was the destruction of the huge wooden church by fire on December 1, 1919.[39] Five thousand people had enjoyed the flames, if that is the proper word to describe people who chase fires. All that was left of the church was the charred foundation, upon which a temporary structure was improvised as soon as possible. Although parishioners planned a new permanent church, the actual building was delayed because of debts on the school, an overly crowded building which housed both grade and high schools. A new high school for boys was urgently needed. Some of the parishioners insisted that the church must come first; others, the school. There was no money for either and little likelihood of getting any, since the mortgage on the original school still remained unpaid.

As early as March, 1925, one of Dave's predecessors, Father William Boland, had evolved a plan to solve the dilemma. He proposed in a letter to Bishop O'Dea that an all-city boys' high school of the type operated by Jesuits in other cities be established. The bishop favored this plan but opposition within Tacoma prevented further developments. When Father Dave assumed full responsibilities for both church and school at exactly 5:30 P.M. on October 30, 1926, there was no visible evidence of any kind that a school was even remotely attainable. Nor was Dave at that moment so disposed to produce one.

There were other problems in addition to the above, perhaps the most crucial being the precarious state of Father John's health. High-strung like Dave, and exhausted from struggle and tension over the school, John was on the verge of a breakdown. Dave's very first order as superior was to send John to their sister Blanche's home in California for a rest.

Though this action, made by connivance of the Provincial, was calculated to be a prudent one, it was, as might be expected, misunderstood by others. Dave's open favoritism of his younger brother was well known and in some quarters at least mildly resented. Dave himself had been a favorite with certain superiors, presumably because of his affliction, and John had shared in this sentiment toward Dave. The human equation adding up to what it does, some in the St. Leo's community interpreted Dave's first order as another mark of affection or another manifestation of McAstocker solidarity.

If this were not disturbance enough, there was yet an added bug in Dave's ointment, though an attractive one that in reality Dave cherished. Father James Kennelly, a well-known favorite of Dave's, was also a member of the community. In failing health and grieving for Gonzaga where he had lost his heart, Kennelly naturally turned to Dave for understanding and sympathy, and Dave, who almost worshiped him, naturally responded. This, too, was subject to misinterpretation.

It was the beginning of another struggle, which existed principally, I think, in Dave's head. He felt obligated to stand firmly by Kennelly in his need; any other course for loyal, affectionate Dave was unthinkable. But he also considered this stand a barrier between himself and others who had disagreed with Kennelly in his alleged severity as disciplinarian at Gonzaga. Listening to Kennelly, who considered himself an outcast in any place but Gonzaga, Father Dave began to examine and re-examine his own relationships with those about him, then he, too, quite innocently lost his sense of balance. Before poor Kennelly died in St. Joseph's Hospital, Dave himself had nursed many a headache of the situation. Out of the subsequent strain, inevitable as it was foolish, Dave later produced a book called *The Joy of Sorrow*.[40]

But the headaches came first, headaches and something worse. Just four days after his arrival in Tacoma, Dave went to the hospital "for a rest," as reported by an unsympathetic diarist. It was the first of many sojourns in St. Joseph's Hospital, each in turn adding weight to the arguments of Dave's critics. He had scarcely returned to the parish when Kennelly was taken to St. Joseph's, and for the next month, while "Big Jim" hovered between life and death, Dave sat beside his bed to comfort him. Other Jesuits, struggling shorthanded against terrific odds—three priests of the community were now missing—protested vigorously, and certainly with some justification complained to higher superiors about it.*

These men, who differed with Dave and criticized him for his overfondness for an old friend, were no narrow-minded, jealous maiden aunts; they were fine priests, and aside

---

*Father Kennelly yearned to return to Gonzaga, but he was too ill to be moved. He died on March 8, 1927. *California Province News*, II-8 (April, 1927), p. 63.

from the fact that they were uncommonly weary men who might be allowed some honest grumbling to break the tension of weariness, they did have solid grounds for disapproving of their superior's vagaries of health. For whatever else transpired to weaken Dave's condition, this much is clear; the principal cause of his repeated trips to the hospital at Tacoma was overexertion, not tuberculosis. At forty-three Dave should have learned to accept his physical limitations and to abide by them, but he had not. In the spirit of all or nothing, he killed himself one week, then spent the next in bed with a taunt of absentee pastorship ringing in his ears. He resented the charge protesting that he did his work whether he was in bed or not. All that ever came from these unpleasant episodes, besides physical refreshment to take up the battle again, was Dave's oft-repeated resolution to get to bed every night by nine-thirty, a resolution that was better recognized for its violation than for its observance.

What all this added up to was a bad beginning. There was worse to come, no less than the great angry bull of the school question which Dave lost no time in grasping by both horns. Coming to a quick decision, he decided to make an all-out effort for a Jesuit-type high school, and announced it accordingly. The storm of opposition that followed nearly blew him out of Tacoma and Dave had more material to reflect on for *The Joy of Sorrow*. Some of the Tacomans interpreted his decision as an attack on the Benedictine's St. Martin's College fifteen miles distant, halfway between Tacoma and Olympia. Others were angry because he talked about new buildings when the old debt had not been paid. Still others objected to Catholic support from all parishes when the school was expected to be built in St. Leo's. Even some of the clergy joined in the general complaint and the poor pastor began to wish he were back in the little house in Arlington, California, where he heard only the laughter of the Indian children and the gentle whisperings of the palm trees.

As the storm abated, Dave set out in the company of several businessmen to discover suitable property for his school. He had no money, but he did have great confidence in the providence of God and in the righteousness of his mission. It did not take him long to find what he wanted, twenty acres on a slope facing spectacular Mount Rainier, at a price he could, he hoped, afford to pay. With the leave of superiors, he calmly bought it with eight thousand Jesuit dollars, as good as any other, though they were borrowed ones, and then announced the fact as casually as though he had just bought groceries. In the St. Leo's diary that night his assistant wrote the following: "Property acquired, of twenty acres, for Bellarmine Boys High School at S. 25th and Union Ave., Tacoma, Wash. Deal was closed today, Wednesday, December 19, 1926, by Rev. Fr. David McAstocker, Sup."[41]

Dave had reasons to believe that a storm would blow up again when his transaction was made public, and his premonitions were correct. Ridiculous, people exclaimed. He has bought a farm way out in the country! It did no good to say that the property and mortgage now belonged to the Jesuit Order, hence was of no vital concern to the parishioners, or to explain that the property was actually in the center of Tacoma, since most people, even those who lived there, did not understand how the city lay in an odd way for central high schools, and that if a school were built in a populated area, it could conveniently serve only one or the other part. There was nothing to do but let the critics thunder, which they did magnificently, so that rumblings reached even the aging ears of His Excellency in Seattle, thirty miles away. The bishop's polite inquiries were answered with an invitation to come and see for himself. "How did you ever find such a lovely site!" is what he said when Dave took him there.

So the bishop was on his side as was his provincial, Father Piet of old tertianship days. Besides money, Dave needed little more. He knew that time would vindicate his judgment as it certainly has.

On March 15, 1927, Dave received formal permission from Bishop O'Dea to go ahead with the new-school project. On the same day he organized a city-wide campaign to solicit funds and within a fortnight, he formed a building committee of men selected for their business know-how, not merely for their bank accounts or reputations for generosity. Calling them together, he made a little speech. "Gentlemen," he said, "I know a great thing about building. I know that I don't know anything. So you help me plan—you take the same blame I take and your judgment will prevail."

Out of numberless meetings presided over by Father John, who had lately returned refreshed and eager, not only a plan evolved but eighty thousand dollars, an architect, a hole in the ground, and a superintendent of construction as well. All were genuine, except perhaps the latter who was summarily dismissed when the trenches he measured for foundations were discovered to be eight feet out of line. Dave, a dreamer even when laying brick, was wrathfully indignant. He wrote to the provincial, explaining the reasons for the dismissal, "Why if that man had finished before we discovered his mistake, the whole plant would have been out of line and the view ruined!"

Though Dave kept an eagle eye on proceedings, the committee made practically all of the decisions. With the sufferance of Dave, it decided to eliminate a general contractor in the construction and to handle all subcontracts directly, thus saving a certain percentage on the building. It was asking for trouble, perhaps, but as things turned out, it ended well. Dave would have you understand, though, that it is not recommended procedure for all projects. Tacoma, like his building committee, was different. It learned to take Bellarmine to its bosom and nourish it as it might nourish a favored child.

For an architect, J. DeForest Griffin of Chehalis, Washington, an alumnus of Santa Clara, was commissioned to make plans for an adapted colonial-type school unit, something that would resemble "William and Mary." It was to consist of two stories, 160' × 200', and to be finished off in suitable brick and stone. Mr. Griffin did his part extremely well, but he too had a falling-out with Dave and the building committee. There was some misunderstanding about the amount of his fee and a few warm epithets were bandied about, ending up, as usually happens, in either the bishop's or the provincial's mailbox. Though Dave was apparently as much, if not more, to blame than the architect, he defended himself and the committee down to the last nickel. The matter was ultimately cleared up to the satisfaction of all, with the architect making more concessions than Dave.

It was Father John who did most of the scratching to get the eighty thousand dollars together. Dave made policies, wrote letters, and appealed to bankers for loans of seventy thousand more dollars to finish the two-building project, a lordly sum in those days. It was over these loans that Dave came to grief with his most steadfast supporter, the provincial. On December 16, 1927, he was summoned by the latter to Los Angeles to explain his methods of finance. A rather serious misunderstanding arose between the two men at this meeting, but Dave, as usual, took it more seriously than it really deserved. He returned home a week later, in an almost despairing mood, full of anxieties and forebodings about the future. Christmas that year was a depressing one.

Dave planned the laying of the school's cornerstone for March 18, 1928. On St. Patrick's Day, the evening before the scheduled dedication, arrangements were concluded and an Irish play directed by Dave, "Heart of Paddy Whock," was produced in St. Leo's auditorium to raise funds for the new school. While this play was going on, a meeting was held in another part of Tacoma, the purpose of which was to find ways: of preventing the cornerstone ceremony on the following day; and, if possible, to prevent the establishment of Bellarmine at any future date. Father Dave knew of this meeting and its sinister purpose. He also knew that those responsible for it were sincere men devoted to what they considered to be Tacoma's good. He was quite sure their meeting would come to naught, but the fact that this kind of sincere opposition had been carried to these lengths made his own duty to persevere all the more unpleasant. What he knew about the clandestine plot he kept to himself until years later. In St. Leo's auditorium that St. Patrick's Day, 1928, no one appeared to be more happy with the performance than its director and no one was more charmingly gracious to the patrons. All worry and anxiety about the morrow lay hidden behind the pastor's smiling face.

On the following day, a Sunday, the ceremony of dedication took place as scheduled. It is recorded in St. Leo's diary: "March 18. Rt. Rev. Bishop lays cornerstone of new college at 23rd and Union. Delightful day. Msgr. Ryan and Hanly, Mayor of town present. Celebration at 3 P.M. A large crowd [1200 people] attended."[42]

Opposition to Bellarmine gradually melted away. People no longer attacked, and many, on the other hand, came bearing gifts. Throughout the crisis Dave's building committee had remained steadfast and loyal. He had chosen them well.

But as brick was placed upon brick, and the walls of the school raised skyward, the debt went skyward, too. The superior, now badgered on all sides by bills and threats of liens, promoted every kind of church and school benefit imaginable. Card party followed card party in almost feverish succession. Spaghetti dinners, bazaars, and raffles joined the parade of benefits. Dave organized the "Monastery Players" and wrote dramas for them, then directed them and publicized them in Tacoma's newspapers. He was playwright, producer, director, public relations man, and the most enthusiastic member of the audience as well. Money only trickled in. It was never enough.

St. Leo's also had its parish school and its debts. In the parish high school during that last year of construction, only $4,000 in tuition was paid in, calculated to represent about fifty cents per day to support each member of the faculty, including two laymen and leaving about eight hundred dollars for the janitor, heat, lighting supplies, and reduction of the sixteen thousand dollar mortgage. This, of course, was absurd.

All during 1928 Dave complained in his letters to the provincial about "hard times." He reported hopefully that his "well-organized bazaar and car raffle [a snappy 1928 Dodge sedan] would net $20,000." Actually it cleared $10,000. When the roof on Bellarmine was laid, he reported that too: "I was up at the building yesterday and it looks like a million dollars. The lighting effects are especially good and the corridors are very bright and cheerful looking."

Certainly if Dave had his woes, he also had his consolations, for not every hard-working priest of his generation had the opportunity to dream about a school and see it realized. The "law of compensations," that too went into *The Joy of Sorrow.*

On September 4, 1928, less than eleven months after ground was broken for the school, one hundred and thirty-six boys answered the bell for the first class. The first boy to register was Hugh Boyle, who later entered the Society and was ordained in 1946.* Two and one-half weeks later, on September 23, the building was solemnly dedicated by Bishop O'Dea in the presence of a great concourse of people. "Father David," the diary reads, "was unable to attend."

This entry, like so many others, was ominous. In a letter to Father Piet, Dave conceded as much: "Reports will reach you from time to time about my condition but pay no attention to them unless I write to you. I know I am a sick man but I prefer to wear out than to rust out. I am getting fine attention here at the hospital, the very best in the world."

When completed, the new school had cost exactly $92,167.02 plus an architectural fee of $2,400. This amazing thrift was bettered in the next unit which Dave now proceeded to promote, a thirty-two room faculty building costing roughly $35,000. To begin this second unit there arrived on February 19, 1930, Father Purcell, who started immediately to draw

---

*Hugh Boyle entered the Society at Sheridan, Oregon, July 30, 1932.

the plans, matching as far as possible the colonial motif of the school. By March 31, he was far enough along to allow for ground-breaking ceremonies. On June 8 the building was finished and dedicated, and on August 18 the new Jesuit community took possession. This bewildering speed achieved for the most part without power equipment, by no means compromised the quality of the building. It stands today as solidly as it ever did, in up-to-the minute shapeliness, like a pretty colonial clubhouse guarding an eminence over a golf course. The picture, in fact, is a real one, for since its occupation by its energetic Jesuit schoolmasters, a public golf course has been providentially installed in the rolling meadows below. Were the panorama before it a means of livelihood, Bellarmine had never suffered from want in its five decades of existence. With the perpetual snows of Mount Rainier soaring above the golf greens, and a view of the Narrows of Puget Sound on the back side, it was quite enough to enchant Dave's poetic soul, and the bishop's, too, for every time His Excellency visited the place he kept repeating, "How did you ever find it!"

The Jesuits at Bellarmine could not be nourished by the snows of Rainier, nor their thirst slaked by the waters of the Sound. The cold fact was, it cost much more money than before to keep two groups operating, the one at the parish house, and the other up on 25th and Union. By special appointment from Rome, announced on August 19, Father Dave was made rector of the latter and since he retained his former position as pastor he was now fully responsible for both. The burden weighed very heavily after the stock-market crash. In his anxiety, he turned to writing as another means of securing money. Once he had written mainly to teach. Now he did it to earn money. He became a newspaper columnist.

This startling development is not as droll as it sounds. "It was strictly a matter of paying Bellarmine's grocery bill," said Dave sadly many years later. "I could see no other way, though I knew it would ruin me. I stayed up late every night, sometimes all night, getting my column off. I used what I got for it to pay for groceries."[43]

Dave's column, a potpourri of reflections on literature and literary celebrities, appeared first in *The Northwest Progress,* a Catholic weekly, then daily in the *Tacoma News Tribune.* For a time it ran simultaneously in both. Dropped by the *Progress,* it continued into the early 1940s in the *News Tribune,* changing its title twice, from "Literary Jottings" to "The Hour Glass of Life," and to "Life's Hour Glass." For about ten years, then, this column appeared daily, reaching the *News Tribune's* 32,000 families. Judging from letter response and the number of friendships begun, it earned its reputation for influence throughout the Puget Sound area. Dave, as always, moralized continually in his comments, good-naturedly and with an obvious sincerity that won respect even from bigots, who objected to the turn of his collar but agreed cautiously with his philosophy.

Writing to Dave after his departure from Tacoma, Mr. Charles B. Welch, editor of the *News Tribune,* urged that the column be continued: "Certainly we want to continue publishing 'Hour Glass of Life' just as long as you find time and patience to write it. We all think it is one of the cultural bits which the paper could ill afford to spare. Your inspirational articles are very fine and I hear of many who find joy and comfort in them. So go right ahead with your articles and keep them coming, for they are very much appreciated here."[44]

Either a glutton for abuse or an incurable scriptomaniac, Dave also managed to get out two books during this most trying period. He sold the first, *Flashlights,* to the Bruce Publishing Company on February 21, 1929. This brought him into contact with a publisher with whom he was subsequently associated for many years on a more than merely professional level. He found this association the most satisfying of his writing career.

The most astonishing feature of *Flashlights* is that it was produced at all. "I am amazed," wrote Bishop Cantwell of Los Angeles to Dave, "with the amount of work that you are able to do along literary lines. . . ."[45] Brought together out of the most minute crumbs of time, it did not make so bad a loaf at all, but it was not a best seller. Even Bishop Sheen's *Peace of Soul* would have languished in those indifferent times when only fiction or sentimental success-biography found a popular demand.

The happy conclusion of events in Tacoma by contrast seemed to focus attention on the failure of Seattle College. While the high school in Seattle made great strides, the college limped along with less than twenty students; this was an impossible situation. Fitzgerald on February 2, 1927, wrote to Piet from Gonzaga about his lengthy discussion on the subject with Seattle's Chancellor, Monsignor Ryan:

Monsignor Ryan, he said, "went out of his way to be extremely nice to me and many times in our conversations he referred to the fact that the rumor had it that he was opposed to the Society. He reiterated his esteem for the Jesuits and the great opinion that he has for us as teachers. He states that Bishop O'Dea had told him recently that he hoped our Society would build up a strong college in Seattle for the Catholic youth and that no other order would ever be given permission to start a college so long as we were in the field. He stated that he had heard from Father Boland that it was possible that we would separate the college from the H.S. and he took me over to the section of the city (near the Italian Sisters Home) where Bishop O'Dea had told him he hoped we would locate the College. The Bishop had bought about 50 acres near here for his future diocesan seminary for about $50,000. He also stated that he thought that it was Gonzaga that kept Seattle College so backward, but I think that I proved to him conclusively that this statement was not true. I instanced the fact that we have only a few Seattle students [at Gonzaga] about a half a dozen, and that we were as anxious as anyone to see Seattle College thrive. Secondly I told him that there was something wrong with the Catholic parishes in Seattle when we find that there are almost seven hundred Catholic students at the University of Washington and barely seventeen in the College course at Seattle College. Only by cooperation with the parishes and Catholic High Schools of Seattle could we hope to build up a strong College. I was pleased to have this opportunity to talk straight to this Msgr. whom I taught so many years ago, and I feel that some good may come of it. My impression is that Msgr. Ryan has heard that the Apostolic Delegate has made the statement that no priest who is hostile to religious may ever hope to wear the mitre. So he expended a lot of energy trying to show me that he was not hostile to the Society nor to any of the religious."[46]

On the following day, Seattle's rector, Father Boland, also wrote to Piet. His report on the monsignor was not as favorable as Fitzgerald's. According to Boland, the monsignor had revealed ["whispered"] "the attitude of the local clergy toward the Jesuits and their school (COLLEGE). He stated that the clergy were contemplating their own COLLEGE (Diocesan) since the Jesuits had done little or nothing toward College education during their stay here."[47]

Summing up the situation at this time, Seattle College owned two campuses, the Interlaken Boulevard site occupied by the high school, and the original campus on Broadway, where the old Galland building was falling into ruin. Efforts were being made to sell the latter for $65,000, without success. There were efforts also to lease the property on short terms, and negotiations for this dragged on for several years, also without success. In addition to these properties, Seattle College Jesuits had paid for the land where both Immaculate Conception Church was built, and where St. Joseph's Church was built. The St. Joseph's site had cost $30,000. Boland of Seattle College had been trying to collect this money, for the parish was not even paying interest on it. Father William Deeney, the pastor, objected to payment of either, saying that certain older members of the parish regarded it as "illegal."[48] On the other hand, Seattle College had several debts, including $26,000 owed to the province, which had been borrowed years before. Father Sauer, at last, thought the school should pay five percent interest on this and Boland, under pressure from Piet, yielded.[49]

Two decisions now triggered further developments. First Boland and his consultors agreed that a new gymnasium on the Boulevard site was essential for the welfare of the school. Secondly, the community by common consensus was determined to separate the high school and the college as soon as possible. This raised the question of the Broadway campus. Should either department be moved there? The unanimous conclusion of the consultors was that neither department should occupy the Broadway campus. This left only one option: the college would have to relocate on land as yet unknown. Boland informed Piet of these considerations and asked approval for leasing the Broadway property, for buying new property and for building a gymnasium.

In October, 1927, Deeney wrote to Boland, saying that the parish would pay the $30,000 which was owed to Seattle College.[50] He consented, he said, "after much parley." Boland had money now for the gymnasium, but Deeney was in sore financial straits. His congregation had outgrown not only the original church but also a major addition to the church. The bishop had ordered him to build a new church "to cost not over $200,000," which sounded like a lot of money then. Deeney's committee had come up with plans that reflected the parish's need, but the projected cost was $300,000. Deeney was ready to give up; however, there were several well-to-do zealots on the committee, including "young Piggot," who wanted to go for broke.[51]

During the Christmas holidays Boland met Mr. William Piggot, the patriarch. He was a very forthright man and generous patron of the Church. He preferred to lend his support to the high school. "As for colleges," Boland complained to Piet, "he said he didn't give a [damn]; they were useless. In parenthesis, let me say, that Mr. Piggot cared about as much for high schools when I first began to talk to him. When I told Mr. Piggot that the Bishop would never give his consent to our High School being placed so near the Cathedral High, he seemed to drop for the time being the idea of building on the [Broadway] site at all; and then turned his attention to the development of what he called McHugh's pet-child. For I had told Mr. Piggot that your Rev. had determined that we should remain on this Boulevard site—for one purpose or the other—High school or College. Then let it be High School, he said. Since that conversation, Mr. Piggot has been sojourning in sunny California."[52]

Father John McHugh, for reasons of health, was also sojourning in sunny California. He was at Blessed Sacrament Parish, where Piggot and Frank Sullivan, another generous patron of the church, visited him. Piggot expressed his thoughts rather bluntly and McHugh presented them by mail to the provincial. Piggot, he wrote, first asked what Seattle College was going to do. McHugh replied to him that this depended upon its friends, who ought to help by providing funds. Piggot reacted by saying that Boland was too timid. No one had asked him for funds. He added that the Boulevard site was no place for a college since there was no room for an athletic program, and that the college should acquire land below the Boulevard along the bay. He offered $25,000 as a gift on condition that Sullivan and others "like Pat Henry and T. C. McHugh" would come forward and contribute.[53]

Piet by this time was getting impatient. He had received countless reports about possible leases of the Broadway site, but never reports of anything resolved. He wrote to Boland in February, 1928: "The Broadway property situation is certainly annoying . . . I shall come north soon owing to the installation of the Bishop of Boise and the jubilee of Father Cataldo."[54]

Cataldo's Diamond Jubilee, seventy-five years in the Society, had been planned for preliminary fireworks at Lewiston, with the main attraction at Gonzaga on March 17, 1928, Cataldo's ninety-second birthday. Father Daniel Reidy had become Gonzaga's fifteenth president, succeeding Fitzgerald on August 6, 1927. Reidy was a very gracious host, and it was hoped that he would plan and supervise a program that was sufficiently elegant for the occasion.

Reidy had great faith in the scholastic value of the arts. He converted Goller Hall into a fine arts building and assembled a faculty of artists. Soon in odd corners of the campus, exotic looking people in berets were seen carrying easels and paint boxes, or sitting in front of canvases dabbing with grave, immortal strokes.

Father Michael O'Malley had become pastor of St. Aloysius Church. He loved pageantry in the sanctuary. Cataldo who had introduced him to the missions, was his greatest hero, next to St. Patrick, so he was disposed to place the resources of the whole parish at the disposal of the Jubilee committee.

In early March, 1928, the entire city of Spokane had been prepared for the great happening and all was ready. Cataldo at this time was resident at St. Joseph's Mission, Slickpoo, with the Nez Perce. Though badly crippled from a broken hip incurred several years earlier, he consented to appear in Spokane for the celebration of his ninety-second birthday and his seventy-fifth anniversary as a Jesuit. March 11 was the date chosen to bring him to Spokane for the round of ceremonies that was scheduled to continue for six days. When he arrived on schedule in the care of Father Brogan, he was met by a contingent of reporters, who asked a number of irrelevant questions concerning his opinion of Governor Alfred Smith, his assessment of present-day opportunities for youth, and others. His first public appearance for the jubilee was at the Chamber of Commerce luncheon on Tuesday, March 13. More than five hundred people rose to their feet and cheered when he entered the dining hall.

This first appearance, which proved to be a sensation for those present, was followed by a second reception at Gonzaga University on March 14. A thousand people, including students, heard at least five speeches honoring the jubilarian. Father Reidy, who delivered one of these speeches, pointed out that in the historic assembly that evening, there were the founder of Gonzaga and four former presidents, Rebmann, Taelman, Brogan and Fitzgerald. Reidy went on to say that for many years the students of Gonzaga had enjoyed a holiday on March 17 not because it was St. Patrick's Day but because in former years the cadets had presented their exhibitions on that day. Later, when the cadets had been suppressed, the holiday had survived though no one, except the Irish, had an explanation for it. Whatever the case, Reidy said that from this time forward the seventeenth day of March, the anniversary of Father Cataldo's birth, would be known as Founder's Day and, accordingly, it would be a holiday sacred to the memory of Father Cataldo.

Thus it happened that Founder's Day at Gonzaga was established on March 14, 1928, by Reidy in the presence of the founder himself. The founder had little to say that evening but he received kindly, even warmly, every person present who came to grasp his hand.

On March 16 three more public receptions were held: a jubilee Mass in St. Aloysius Church, which was attended by four bishops and scores of the clergy, not to mention the many hundreds of the laity; a festive banquet at the Davenport Hotel at six in the evening for ecclesiastical and civic dignitaries; and finally a huge civic reception in the American theatre, presided over by the mayor and Bishop White. During this reception an extraordinary incident took place. An aged Indian, every inch a chief, strode solemnly to the speaker's rostrum on the stage. It was Joseph La Mousse, the eighty-three-year-old nephew of the great Ignace La Mousse, who went to St. Louis for the Black Robe De Smet in 1837 and was killed by the Sioux. Joseph spoke to *Kaoushin* in their common tongue,

Salish or Flathead. One can ónly imagine the tenseness of this historic scene: Kaoushin, a frail, little relic of the glamorous past, sitting rigidly in his wheel chair, his dark, Sicilian eyes fixed on old La Mousse, and looking beyond him to the log cabin missions of Montana, Idaho, and Eastern Washington. De Smet's missions. The missions for which Old Ignace gave his blood. No doubt, as many times before, the words *Sumus pro Indianis,* "We are here for the Indians," again crossed his mind but he said nothing. He had already done what he could. Like Ignace he had given his life, but only a little at a time.

Old Joseph, nephew of Ignace, spoke eloquently. When he had finished, to express his happiness in action, he gave an Indian dance, a tribal rite that was as sprightly and as graceful as a supple youth would have performed it. Then Father Taelman stepped up. He interpreted the Indian's words, using the same inflection of voice and even the same kind of Indian gestures. Kaoushin and Joseph watched him intently, their faces almost impassive, as though they sensed that the drama of their lives would end with the oratory.

The last speaker that night was Edward P. Ryan, member of the university's Board of Regents. He praised Father Cataldo and suggested that a Cataldo Memorial Fund would be a practical way of honoring him. He then presented details of the plan, asking all those present to become participants in it. Eight years from now, he concluded, Father Cataldo would be one hundred years old. If everyone present pledged the required amount, the fund would reach its goal of $250,000 by that time. Ryan's proposals met with great applause and the guests departed that evening with his words fresh in their minds.[55]

Father Cataldo returned to Slickpoo to gather his meager belongings and to move to the Umatilla mission, where, it was hoped, his powerful influence would help produce a spiritual renaissance of the tribe. On March 28, the Wednesday before Palm Sunday, he set out with Father John Corbett, superior of St. Andrew's, on the journey to Pendleton, about 175 miles. All went well until they reached a point six miles east of Walla Walla, where the driver, avoiding an obstruction on the road, swerved to the right. The car rolled down the embankment and caught fire. Cataldo, jolted but uninjured, was safely extricated, as was Corbett, who had received an ugly scalp wound. Passersby took them both to St. Mary's Hospital in Walla Walla, but Cataldo insisted that they continue their journey to St. Andrew's. A friend, Frank Tierney, hearing of their plight, drove them the last fifty miles, very skillfully you may be sure, and they arrived at the mission about 7:30 P.M. Cataldo unperturbed by the day's events, demanded that Corbett must begin his classes in Nez Perce at once. So poor Corbett, half Cataldo's age and also half-dead, became on the spot the old master's unwilling disciple.

During the days that followed, Cataldo dragged himself on his crutches to the school building to teach catechism to the Indian children in their own language, and to seek suitable boys to serve Corbett as interpreters and assistants in the study of the language. A group of more talented boys he afterwards taught in his room. He supervised the preparations for the feast of Palm Sunday, conducting classes in singing as well. As the Indians began to assemble at the mission for Holy Week, he conversed with them and prepared a class of seventeen Indian children and one adult for First Communion, using his own *Life of Christ* in Nez Perce as the text for instruction. On Wednesday he heard over a hundred confessions and on Holy Thursday he offered Mass at the Sisters' Convent. After the services on Holy Saturday the Indians flocked to him, and he was kept busy giving spiritual direction and hearing confessions until 10:00 P.M.

But signs of fatigue had begun to appear. He had to be assisted to complete Mass on Easter, though afterwards he expressed himself still ready for work, and he heard more confessions. Easter afternoon, though, he was finally persuaded to go to the hospital in Pendleton. He offered Mass on Monday and when some Indians asked to see him, he had them admitted and heard their confessions. About noon he gave evidence of failing. Father

Joseph McKenna, pastor of St. Mary's in Pendleton, administered the last sacraments. For many years Cataldo, owing to his broken hip, had not slept in bed, but had taken his rest as best he could in a chair. But now he consented to being put to bed and admitted that he was comfortable. McKenna left to attend to his parish.

About five that evening the mother superior, realizing that death was near, summoned a priest patient from the next room, Father Allain, who gave the dying Cataldo a last absolution, while he held a lighted "death candle" firmly in his hand and the Sisters and doctor knelt in prayer. Cataldo peacefully breathed his last. He died as he had hoped to die, in the harness, near an Indian mission and not far from the grave of his old friend Father Grassi.

There followed two highly publicized funerals, the second in Spokane, where on Friday morning, April 13, in St. Aloysius Church, a requiem Mass was performed very solemnly by Bishop White, in the presence of Archbishop Howard, several other bishops and a congregation that filled the church to capacity. The Mount choir sang and six altar boys in black cassocks stood as an honor guard on either side of the coffin while all the people filed by to view the remains. Some touched rosaries or medals to Cataldo's cold hands. When it was all over a procession was formed and the coffin was carried to the hearse, which awaited in the middle of the street before the main entrance of Gonzaga, then the funeral cortege of fifty-seven cars proceeded to the Mount Cemetery, not far from the place where Cataldo had built his first mission sixty-two years before.

"The great missionary," the *Province News* reported, "had given his first efforts to the Indians of Peone prairie. The last public prayers at his burial were to come from the descendants of his early converts. A number of Spokane Indians had come to his funeral. When the liturgical prayers were ended, suddenly the strange accents of the Kalispel language sounded over the hill. Under the leadership of the grandson of Chief Baptist Peone, the Indians were chanting their requiem hymn for the blackrobe who had been their life-long friend, apostle and father."[56]

Three more Jesuits who had volunteered for the Rocky Mountain Mission died the same year. First there was Aloysius Parodi, the simple, gentle, priest who had survived his mental breakdown in Alaska. At the age of eighty-three, he died in Detroit on April 15, just six days after Cataldo. Brother John Schwertfeger passed away on August 24. As sacristan at St. Aloysius he had given an example of holiness to all, but especially to the altar boys. With them he was like a guardian angel, sweet tempered and patient, even when they sneaked little sips of altar wine that was left in the cruets after Mass. "So sure and regular was he at work," Father O'Malley wrote in his *Memoirs*, "that the people set their watches when he rang the Angelus bell at noon and at 6 P.M. He was a source of much edification and grace for the parish."[57] What O'Malley failed to say was that Schwertfeger, a novice then, was on the original faculty at Gonzaga College when Rebmann admitted the first students in 1887.

The fourth to die in 1928 was Mackin. Alert and saucy to the bitter end, his handsome head copiously covered with long, flowing white hair, like a mane, he died suddenly during recreation at Port Townsend on December 27. He had mellowed during his seventy-two years in his relations with brother Jesuits. No longer did he manifest that subtle Irishman's contempt for Rebmann's weakness. In the end it was Rebmann who lovingly, yet humbly, presided over the funeral obsequies for Father Mackin.[58] These, too, were conducted in St. Aloysius Church.

Reidy, like O'Malley, was from Ireland, and both agreed, for different reasons, that St. Patrick's Day should always be regarded as a special holy day in the parish. O'Malley made sure that the grade school children attended Mass as they did on days of obligation. The voices of these children, over four-hundred strong, were added to the older voices of the rest of the congregation. Father O'Malley had recently purchased a huge new pipe organ for the church, regarded at the time as one of the largest in the country.* Challenged by the roar of the new organ, every one shouted "Faith of our Fathers" so loudly that the church shook and the windows rattled. Besides the addition of the organ, O'Malley had the church *decorated*, which means painted on the inside, for the first time. The organ from St. Louis and the new decorations cost $22,000 in pre-depression dollars, but O'Malley was young then and his experience with debts had not yet made him cautious.

Sister Rita at the school was teaching the boys how to sing Vespers in Latin. The ladies of the Altar Society provided some holy-looking choir vestments for the boys, and some small, portable choir stalls arrived from somewhere, only O'Malley knew whence. The parish was ready for Vespers on Sunday nights. The new bishop, Charles D. White, "by the grace of God," as he used to say, attended as often as he could, attracted by the angelic-looking boys on each side of the sanctuary, dressed in their white tunics with large red bows and red sashes.† One of the sisters said she almost died with joy when the *Magnificat* was sung, so sweet were the voices and so pure the countenances of the little fellows, who managed all the same to get into mischief on the way home.

Piet, being French, was as impressed as Bishop White by O'Malley's choir boys. But he had become very anxious about the situation in Seattle. In July, Boland informed him that a lease on the Broadway site had not yet been signed and that the faculty building on the Boulevard had caught fire. "We ran up to the attic and found things looking bad, very bad. The fire hose attached to the main water pipe on the 4th floor was pressed into service and in a moment or two we had a fine stream of water playing into the flames. The situation was under perfect control when the fire department arrived."[59]

Piet, possibly with Boland's knowledge and approval, sent Fitzgerald from Port Townsend, to discuss the college situation with Bishop O'Dea. Fitzgerald reported to the provincial in great detail, listing points of discussion and the bishop's reaction. A new site on the north end of Seattle had been discovered, Fitzgerald said, but it was in the immediate area of the Benedictine's new parish called "The Assumption." Fitzgerald proposed to the bishop that the Jesuits trade the Benedictines the Immaculate Conception Parish for the Assumption Parish. The bishop liked the idea and said he would speak to the Abbot about it.[60]

Father John McHugh was back in Seattle in August. He reported that through a friend, Vincent D. Miller, a new and better site had been found. This was thirty-eight acres instead of forty, at a greater distance from the Benedictine's parish, and it could be purchased, probably, for $65,000.[61] It was owned by an old gentleman by the name of Thorpe, who liked the idea of a college being built on his property. A few days later, on August 12, 1928, Boland wrote enthusiastically about the "Thorpe site" and added that Miller had urged him to take an option on the property. Father Edward Menager, keeper of the House diary, wrote on August 20: "Fr. Provincial and Fr. Fitzgerald arrive from Spokane. They, with Fr. Minister, accompany Mr. V. Miller in a tour of the city inspecting possible new sites. Later they call on the Bishop at his (Bishop's) request."[62]

From subsequent correspondence several positions became known: First, Bishop O'Dea favored the Thorpe site and an exchange of parishes between the Benedictines and

---

*O'Malley's memoirs, *Flocks That I Watched*, p. 62. This organ, made by Kilgen Company of St. Louis, cost $13,000, plus $4,000 for freight and installation. It was installed in the spring of 1927.

†As one of the choir boys I recall the huge red bows and all the fuss in the basement where several sisters would supervise the vesting of about thirty of us each Sunday night. The cassocks, snow white and spotless, had wide red collars. Our sashes were worn at the waist. When we were all vested we looked like a grand advertisement for a church candle company.

the Jesuits. He did not favor a Jesuit "collegiate church."

The newly elected Abbot, Lambert Burton, suggested that "all difficulties could be avoided if the Jesuits built their college outside the present limits of the Assumption Parish," or at least "twenty or more blocks from the present site of the Church of the Assumption." He respectfully submitted several other conditions before he and the Benedictine Fathers of Lacey, Washington, could agree to the Jesuit presence there: that the bishop obtain an indult from Rome preventing the Jesuits from opening a collegiate chapel in connection with the proposed college; that the Jesuits agree not to open a high school on the property, since the Benedictines intended to establish a high school in the parish; and that the Jesuits "never be granted the permission to solicit funds, either directly or indirectly, within the limits of the Assumption Parish."[63]

The Jesuits, like the bishop, favored an exchange of parishes and an abdication of their right to a collegiate church. They were willing to accept, however, the conditions of the Benedictines by building their college at least twenty blocks from the Assumption church and by observing the Abbot's restrictions on the use of the land and fund raising.

On September 4, 1928, Fitzgerald wrote to Piet: Fr. Boland told me "that he had taken an option for thirty days and paid down $1,000.00. It seems that a man who owns some property near by, went to the old man, Thorpe, and offered him a higher price for his land, as they have found out that this property has the finest building sand about ten feet below the surface of the ground . . . and so Father Boland wrote him out a check and Thorpe signed the papers."[64]

Boland had obtained the $1,000 from Piggot, who agreed to pay the balance of the $65,000. However, Piggot died some days later without making provision for this in his will.* Boland was able to scrape together a thousand dollars each month to keep the option open, but a day of reckoning was fast approaching and the college would have to come up with some heavy cash or lose its investment.

On November 8, 1928, the house diarist scribbled a revealing entry: "The negotiations for new property are still up in the air. We of Seattle College do not yet have a clear idea of what Fr. Provincial intends to do about it. We have done everything possible to raise the money necessary to close the deal, except to rob a bank. Yet we are told we must go on. Whither . . . Fr. Fitzgerald whose status in our transaction with the Bishop is still a mystery, leaves for Lewiston."[65]

Several more months went by. Herbert Hoover had been elected President of the United States and he was sworn in. Fitzgerald in the same week wrote again to Piet. The bishop, he said, wants the Immaculate Conception parish for the diocese, as it is the largest in the city.[66] No formal approval was given yet for a Jesuit residence on the Thorpe property so the hapless Jesuits at Seattle College found themselves in a quandry, with the provincial, the bishop and the abbot all stalling to see who could or would make the first move. Finally, on May 31, 1929, the bishop formally approved of the Jesuits' erection of a religious house on the Thorpe site, with the understanding that a Jesuit parish, to be called St. Ignatius, could be established on the smaller half of a divided Assumption parish. The Jesuits agreed to transfer the administration of the Immaculate Conception parish over to the bishop, together with the title to all property there, for which the Jesuits were to receive $15,000.† On September 23, 1929, Monsignor Theodore Ryan, still chancellor of the dio-

---

*It should be noted here that the Piggot family has been very generous to Seattle College and Seattle University. The Piggot building on the present campus is a daily reminder of the family's generous patronage and its continued interest in the university.

†Piet estimated that the parish owed the Jesuits #30,000. O'Dea offered $10,000. Both compromised at $15,000. OPA, Seattle Immaculate Conception Papers, Piet and O'Dea correspondence.

cese, became the first non-Jesuit pastor of the parish.*

On the Thorpe property there was a two-story slab-veneer house, which was adapted for a chapel and dedicated in honor of St. Ignatius by Father Robert Burns. The first Mass was offered in this temporary church on November 24, 1929, by Burns before a capacity congregation of fifty persons. At last there was visible evidence of Jesuit intentions, only a primitive house but a presence nonetheless.

In the end, nothing came of this. Although the Jesuits eventually borrowed the money required to purchase the forty acres, "using the Broadway property as a back-up," they found it well nigh impossible to raise funds for the Greater Seattle College to be built there.† They gradually became disenchanted with the idea of relocating there, and returned at last to the Broadway site, where they already had a building, however decrepit, to begin anew. St. Ignatius Church was turned over to the bishop on July 31, 1940. A diocesan priest, Father Hugh Gallagher, was appointed first resident pastor of the newly established parish of Our Lady of the Lake.‡ The Thorpe property was eventually sold for less than the Jesuits had paid for it.**

Deeney and his committee, meanwhile, continued to work on plans for a new St. Joseph's Church. In the interests of promoting their collective decisions, they published what was announced to be *"The Building Beautiful,"* a parish bulletin "that will be issued at frequent intervals." On the front cover of the first issue, November 29, 1928, there appeared an architect's rendering of the new St. Joseph's, an approximate version of what was finally built, with one notable difference: the original plans called for construction in hewn granite. The church, when it finally was constructed in 1930, at a cost of over $320,000, had the same form and size as the original design in what was called then "ferro-concrete." It was something new in building style, a sensational success that soon brought it fame as one of the most beautiful churches in America.††

Fitzgerald and Piet doubtlessly approved. At Port Townsend, Fitzgerald had proved to be superfluous, a valuable administrator with little to do as along as the tertian instructor performed his tasks. He was, as Father Van Christoph would say, referring to himself, "like a doorknob on a tent." Piet recommended Fitzgerald for the rectorship of Seattle College, and he was installed there on September 4, 1929.

In due time, Fitzgerald sent Piet a brief account of the Seattle College debt. This ran as follows:

Province of California	$ 28,000 @ 5%
Sisters of Lacrosse	$ 20,000 @ 4%
Umatilla Mission	$ 6,000 @ 5%
St. Louis Mercantile	$100,000 @ 5%
Total indebtedness	$154,000

Northwest Progress, September 13, 1929. Msgr. Doogan gives the date of transfer as September 22 in *Church of the Immaculate*, p. 8.

†For many years Father John Hayes, stationed at the Seattle College residence, served as pastor of St. Ignatius Parish. Until the population increased in the area, it was like a mission parish.

‡*Northwest Progress*, February 7, 1941. It was at this time that the new Our Lady of the Lake Church was completed.

**The Thorpe property was sold in 1941 for $20,000 at a considerable loss. Provincial's archives, Portland, correspondence of Elliott with Zacheus Maher, February 12, 1941.

††*Northwest Progress*, October 10, 1930, October 17, 1930, and October 24, 1930. Only two issues of The Building Beautiful were published, copies in OPA.

Of this amount, $10,000 was in a savings account. It should be noted, also, that this was the total debt for both Seattle College and the high school, a single community then, with three valuable pieces of city property as their common heritage.[67]

For the province, two perils now lay ahead, one a complication for the other. The first, of course, was the Great Depression, which officially began in October, 1929. Its roots were deeper, in the destruction of the Great War, fifteen years earlier. The second peril was the impending division of the province, and its roots were deeper yet, in the nineteenth century. Piet and his advisors could not fail to observe that a division would have to come, sooner maybe than later, but it was not recognized as a danger, any more than was the disruption of the church following Vatican II.

The formalities of division would be complicated and tedious. It would be like the formation of two separate corporations out of one, the division of management, personnel and assets. There were certain advantages the Jesuits could count on. Any disputes, for example, could be amicably disposed of, even after a hard-fought battle, and final arbitration in Rome was not only available, it was absolute. There would be no lingering doubts or hard feelings.

Piet could see the break coming in sheer statistics. For example, there were the novices. Los Gatos could accommodate about fifty. In 1928, there were sixty-nine. One year later there were eighty-three, far too many for one novice master to direct. A second novitiate would be required by 1930. The total number of Jesuits in the province was nearing seven hundred, too many for one provincial. When all this was added up, there was only one conclusion, a divided province in fact, which would resolve the long standing difference in traditions between the north and the south. De la Motte's and, more especially, Dillon's carefully concealed conclusions would be vindicated at last.

Within the month, however, a more basic conflict remained. Would the loss of Cataldo, second only to that of De Smet, alter the declining state of the missions? Was it money only that was lacking? or was it lack of interest?

There is no evidence that Piet asked himself or his consultors these questions. Jesuit priorities in the west were no longer discussed. The Jesuits of the 1920s had thrown themselves into education and no one would challenge this for thirty-five more years. There were still some dedicated missionaries, like Father Taelman, who never gave up, nor did they ever complain. But time and death, the one by expedience, the other by default, were determining the province's course of action in this as in other respects.

Patrick O'Reilly wearing his missionary cross to which he was greatly attached.

Original farmhouse at Paradise Farm, Sheridan. Brother Vetter was the first Jesuit to occupy it. While stationed at St. Francis Regis Mission, Colville, he received a telegram ordering him "to hitch up 4 horses and go to Paradise."

The Bungalow, first novitiate building at Sheridan. This picture was taken shortly after the building was erected.

Vlodimir Ledochowski, sixth general of the new Society, from February 11, 1915 until December 13, 1942. Ledochowski established the Oregon Province in 1932.

The original building which served as a provincial headquarters from 1909–46. Brother James Wood transformed it into the first Loyola Retreat House.

Bishop Walter Fitzgerald at the time of his consecration in 1939. Fitzgerald was the first provincial of the Oregon Province and successor to Crimont as the bishop in Alaska.

17

PROVINCE STATUS AT LAST
1929–1938

On April 6, 1929, Piet mailed a brief notice to the province, requesting prayers for the success of a proposed new theologate, *somewhere in California.** This unexpected announcement was like an explosion. It had been taken for granted by many Jesuits, especially in the north, that a theologate was an integral part of the plan for the Mount.† Piet's appeal was, in effect at least, an official tip-off that changes in the province structure were already under way.

Piet would not have denied it. After all, at the beginning of the current school year the arrival of fifty new novices at Los Gatos had aroused so much publicity that everybody expected some kind of plan for expansion. Piet, it was rumored, was searching for land in the north for a new novitiate. It now appeared that his sudden eagerness for a scholasticate in the south was part of a balancing act, the provision of a novitiate and a house of studies in each of the proposed new provinces.‡ This sounded fair enough, but it ignored the long accepted plan for a theologate in the north to replace the one formerly located in "the Sheds."

This had not been a mere hope. Father Francis McGarrigle, author of *My Father's Will*, was a graduate student in Rome during the first half of the 1920s, when many European Jesuit colleges were selling off portions of their libraries for survival. McGarrigle was authorized by Dillon, and later by Piet, to purchase hundreds of sixteenth- and seventeenth-century tomes, first, and sometimes only, editions of the works of medieval philosophers and theologians. This priceless collection, gradually assembled by McGarrigle, was shipped to the Mount, where it was incorporated into the Mount library, in anticipation of the construction of an east wing for a theologate.**

*Emphasis mine. Copy of Piet letter in OPA, Provincial Papers, Piet letter to Province, April 6, 1929.

†The Mount was designed for an additional wing on the east side for the Theologate. Most Jesuit scholastics like Woodstock had faculties for both philosophy and theology.

‡Philosophy was a three-year course, tertianship one year. Added together they made four years, the length of time for theology. Hence Piet would have a balance with a novitiate juniorate of four years in each province; and a theologate in one with philosophy and tertianship in the other.

**When the California theologate was finally established, officials demanded that the books assembled by McGarrigle be sent to them. Father Ledochowski ruled otherwise, stating that the collection was an integral part of the Mount library.

No doubt Piet regarded these plans as subject to change. In the *Western Jesuit*, at this time, the following item revealed the whereabouts of the theologate he wanted for California: "Efforts are being made to secure a new site for the theologate in Santa Barbara. A generous friend in Los Angeles gave $5,000."[1]

It seemed to some by now that Piet had lost his heart to California. Though a member of the Rocky Mountain Mission originally, and thus destined to be a member of the northern province, he spent a disproportionate amount of time in the south, rather than in the Provincial's residence in Portland. There were, of course, compelling reasons for this. California was growing by leaps and bounds and with it Jesuit expansion. There were the new high school, Brophy in Phoenix and Loyola College's new site, a magnificent new church in Hollywood, the crowded conditions at Los Gatos, and the proposed theologate to require most of his attention, partly because he delegated little authority to others.

Though basically a very conservative man, Piet liked daring new ideas, and when someone suggested that the Alaska missions should have a plane "to serve not only spiritual but humanitarian needs," he favored the proposal at once. In July, 1929, he questioned Brother George Feltes about serving in Alaska as the pilot of a mission plane. The proposal appealed to Feltes and he agreed at once.

"Two weeks later," wrote Father Louis Renner, who interviewed Feltes at length, "Feltes began his flight training at the flying school at the Alameda airport across the Bay from San Francisco. On August 5, Brother took his first solo flight. It was the first time a Jesuit had ever flown a plane alone.* After ten hours of solo flying he received his Private Pilot's license. He then continued his training and instructions from the Curtis Company. Not until he had logged many more hours of solo flying in a variety of planes and only after passing numerous tests and examinations did he apply for his limited Commercial License. This license allows a pilot to carry passengers but not for hire. Brother received this license on October 31st."[2]

The choice of a plane for use in Alaska was left to the judgment of Feltes, who went to New York in January, 1930, to begin his search. After many consultations and trial runs with different planes, he chose a Bellanca Pacemaker. The Bellanca Corporation in Delaware produced a custom model with seats for six passengers. The Packard Motor Company built and presented at no cost, a diesel motor for the plane. By June, 1930, Feltes had acquired for the mission the very best plane that money could buy for this specific purpose.

Renner's report continues: "On Sunday 29, of June, 1930, at Roosevelt Field on Long Island, several thousand people were present for the presentation and blessing of the new plane. On its side in big letters, it proudly bore the name *Marquette Missionary*. This name was a "thank you" to the members of the Marquette League of New York. This lay organization had been founded for the support of Indian missions and named after the Jesuit Missionary Jacques Marquette. Bishop Crimont came down from Alaska to bless the plane and to thank the donors. After the ceremonies were concluded, Bishop Crimont and about twenty of the assembled dignitaries had the pleasure of short rides in the new plane.

"On July 19, Brother Feltes took off from New York, with Father Delon, S.J., Superior of the Jesuit Missionaries in Alaska and with Captain Pickenpack as co-pilot and headed for the West. Stopping at Detroit, Walter Kade, a mechanic from the Packard Company, joined the group. On July 30 the *Marquette* arrived at San Francisco. The Packard Company wired Brother Feltes, 'Congratulations on the first trip across the country with a Packard diesel.'

---

*A photograph of this event and an article regarding it appears in *Western Jesuit*, IV, 9 (November, 1929), p. 1, et seq.

"On August 22, Brother Feltes and Father Delon took the *Marquette* up the coast and made their landing in the continental U.S., at Seattle. The plane was put on board the S.S. Aleutian, bound for Seward. From there, it was shipped to Fairbanks by rail and on its own wheels was towed to Weeks Field where, with the help of the mechanics of the Alaskan Airways, its wings were replaced and it was ready for flight.

"Because of poor weather, it was not until September 12 that the *Marquette* made its first flight in the Alaskan skies. The plane performed perfectly. This was the first time a diesel-powered plane flew in Alaska and operated extremely well. The next day, several practice flights were made while awaiting favorable weather reports from Holy Cross. On the seventeenth, five flights were made with Ralph Wien of Fairbanks who had been engaged by Father Delon to act as co-pilot to Brother Feltes on his first tour of Alaska and to familiarize him with Alaska flying conditions. Wien was at home in Alaska and an experienced pilot. Brother Feltes had Wien do a good bit of flying so he would get used to flying diesel-powered planes.

"Finally, on September 18, word came that weather and field conditions were good at Holy Cross and the *Marquette* took off for the trip down the Yukon with Brother, Father Delon and Ralph Wien aboard. They arrived at Holy Cross in four hours and forty minutes. It was Brother's first sight of an Alaskan Mission and he was thrilled at the experience."[3]

By this time everyone, especially Delon, was enchanted with Alaska's new airplane, which would double the effectiveness of missionaries making their rounds of the villages. Like a farmer with a new tractor, Delon was eager to show everyone how well it worked. At Holy Cross old Father Robaut, the patriarch of the missions, who had never seen an automobile, was given a special ride in this new wonder machine. Taciturn and withdrawn, he had a beard now, and it was white like his hair. He wore an old coat over his cassock. The plane never had a more appreciative passenger than Robaut, who looked back wistfully upon it, after he was helped to alight on the ground.

Like other good pilots, Feltes kept a log. He recorded his trip to Nome with Father Hubert Post, the generally bad weather, and Wien's flight to Pilgrim Springs on October 7, to pick up Delon. According to Feltes, the round trip flight, a distance of 180 miles, took ninety minutes. It would have taken almost a week by dogsled.

Two days later, when the weather improved, the two pilots left with Delon for Kotzebue, where an heroic young priest, Father William Walsh of the San Francisco Archdiocese, had built a mission within the last year.[4] This was on Thursday. There was parochial work to be done over the weekend. On Sunday afternoon, October 12, there was time, finally, to go to Deering, a village near Kotzebue. The plane was readied, then snow flurries appeared, and Feltes postponed the flight. They waited for forty minutes with the plane's motor running. By the time the weather had cleared it was too late to go to Deering, but Delon wanted Father Walsh to have a short spin around Kotzebue to see his village from the air. Wien was at the controls; the two priests fastened their seat belts and Feltes remained on the ground with a group of curious Eskimos. The plane roared off, stalled, then suddenly plunged to the earth. Feltes described the tragic crash:

"Ralph took off with the two Fathers and got off nicely with some room to spare. He made a wide turn and flew in a large circle of about a mile and in doing so, got into a little snow. Some of it must have stuck to the windshield and he decided to come in to land. When he came in, he shut the motor down and when he came to the end of the field he saw that he was too high, turned and went back about a mile. In turning to the left he made a very sharp nose-high turn and stalled the plane at an altitude of about three hundred and fifty feet. It fell out of control in a wide sweeping turn, much like a spin. When he had turned back from his attempt at landing, he had turned on his motor and had shut it to about half before starting his last turn. About thirty feet from the ground he turned it on full and went into a straight dive and struck it head-on and the plane stood on its nose with the motor buried in the frozen ground, the motor mount completely collapsed back to the cabin and the front of the cockpit was even with the surface of the ground. We all ran over to the wreck as fast as we could and I was the first to get inside the cabin. I immediately saw that there was no chance of anyone being alive and we carried them out as fast as we could. Nearly all bones were broken—they had undoubtedly died instantly. The plane took the impact exceptionally well from the middle of the cabin to the tail."*

Feltes sent a telegram to Bishop Crimont at Juneau, "Father Delon, Father Walsh and Pilot Wien killed in our plane, Sunday afternoon at three forty-five. Please send a priest immediately if possible. I await instructions."

There were some who regarded the accident as a scandal, a foolish and costly gimmick from the beginning. There were many regrets, much soul searching and floods of advice by pseudo-experts. Crimont was criticized. So was Piet. Feltes had selected the wrong kind of motor, some said. Wien had tried to fly with a cold motor, said others. Most of the editorial comment was nonsense. The coronor's jury, basing its conclusions on the testimony of knowledgable witnesses gave as its verdict: "We find that all precautions were taken before the plane left the ground. We find that the plane was thoroughly tested by Brother Feltes and Ralph Wien—that a test flight was made by Wien before the passengers went up for the last flight. We find that adverse weather conditions alone, were responsible."†

Brother Feltes, whom Crimont trusted completely did not agree with this verdict. "The time—the place—the plane and weather conditions were all exonerated in the testimony. The sole cause of the accident was an error of human judgment which fault afflicts every man in every place and condition."

This is the final word on the worst accident in our province's history. The *Marquette Missionary* was taken to Fairbanks, repaired and sold by Bishop Crimont. A short time later attempts were made for the acquisition of other mission planes and a bitter dispute between the new superior, Father Francis Menager, and Brother Feltes ensued. The bishop's decision to sell the *Marquette Missionary* and a second plane prompted some Jesuits to complain about the bishop's tight control of the mission. But so distressed were superiors by the sudden loss of the *Marquette Missionary* only four months after it left the factory, that the idea of mission planes was buried for more than twenty years.‡

This was a sad time for Crimont. He had begun to show his seventy-two years of age, despite Pius XI's non-infallible pronouncement that the ice of Alaska had preserved him. Father General was beginning to wonder when he would retire. There was growing criticism in Alaska because of his obvious partiality toward French Jesuits in his administration. There were also wisps of rumor about his alleged liberality in granting dispensations from the laws of the Church, especially those regarding marriage. No one really knew what faculties from Rome Crimont had. Because of the immense problems of communication in the vicariate, numerous special privileges had been provided for the bishop. Crimont himself probably did not know all the powers that he had.

He was a very casual keeper of records, many of which were simply thrown into the basement. Though he wrote countless letters, especially when he was travelling to and

---

*Delon had a premonition of death. He had left sealed instructions at Holy Cross for the administration of the mission in the event of his death. See Louis Renner, S.J., "The Beginnings of Missionary Aviation in the Arctic: The *Marquette Missionary*" in *The Alaskan Shepherd* (July–August 1977).

†*Ibid.*

‡Today there are five mission planes in Alaska. See Provincial Archives, Portland, Fitzgerald to Ledochowski, June 24, 1932 and August 3, 1932. The latter contains a very detailed report on the controversy.

from Alaska by boat, he kept no copies. Like de la Motte, he wrote everything in long hand.

Crimont had many admirers, one of whom was Father Patrick O'Reilly. In mid-summer of 1930, while Piet was searching for suitable land in Oregon for a new novitiate, O'Reilly's first book was released by the Loyola University Press of Chicago. This was *The Light Divine In Parable and Allegory,* which sold for a modest $1.60 per copy, an extraordinary achievement by the press.[5] O'Reilly dedicated this book to Crimont. Bishop Robert Armstrong of Sacramento, a Gonzaga alumnus and a close personal friend of Walter Fitzgerald, provided the Introduction. For a frontispiece the author had arranged a full length photograph of himself, "Rev. Patrick J. O'Reilly, S.J., Missionary in Northern Alaska," as he appeared in his black cassock with his mission cross prominently displayed.

O'Reilly's identity with the two bishops in his book unwittingly demonstrated a scarcely concealed ambition: he very much wanted to be a bishop and he expected to become one. It is said that he had been given a long gold chain, which he intended to use for his pectoral cross after his consecration. Many years later, as his hopes faded away, he presented this chain to Crimont. It was probably the only genuine article Crimont possessed. As bishop even his episcopal robes were hand-me-downs from more prosperous bishops on the east coast. Whatever complaints the critics of Crimont may have had, they could never accuse him of violating poverty. No bishop in the world was poorer than he.

There is a sequel to O'Reilly's book *The Light Divine.* It seems that the first two printings had sold out earlier than anticipated, mostly because O'Reilly literally peddled them on the church steps, while he was giving parish missions. A third printing was ordered, but O'Reilly, at this time, was assigned to other tasks where potential sales were at a minimum. Eventually in 1940, when O'Reilly was assigned to Wrangell, Alaska, he arranged with Loyola University Press to ship the remainder of the third printing to Seattle. From there the numerous cartons were loaded on a freighter bound for Alaska. There is some mystery about exactly what happened, but according to a long-standing rumor in the province, the freighter struck a reef off the coast of Vancouver Island and sank. Fortunately all passengers were rescued.* Hundreds of copies of O'Reilly's *The Light Divine,* however, went down with the ship and are still on the bottom of the sea, since divers seeking treasures have never regarded it worth the risk to retrieve them.

Piet's search for land for the novitiate, meanwhile, had begun to focus on the hills and valleys south of Portland. His objective was a suitable site within convenient distance of a large city, with access to doctors and bus lines. One suspects that he was looking for another Los Gatos in the north, with the prune trees in the valley and another San Francisco fifty miles away. At last he found what he wanted. On July 28, 1930, he sent a telegram to Father General from Portland: "Ideal novitiate site found fifty-two miles from Portland very advantageous terms if immediate action taken. Consultors unanimously approve. Kindly wire permission to buy. Archbishop welcomes novitiate."[6]

The "ideal site" was a tract of eight hundred and ninety-one acres called Paradise Farm, southwest of Portland, near Sheridan, Oregon. Its owner, a retired Portland brewer by the name of G. J. Magenhiemer, who had moved to Los Angeles, was willing to sell it. On October 30, 1930, the property was purchased for approximately $36,000. Thus it came about that De Smet's dream was being realized after eighty-six years. The Jesuits would have a "motherhouse" in Oregon just forty miles from the first "motherhouse" and within sight of Mount Hood like the first one. The name given the new establishment was, of course, St. Francis Xavier's.

---

*O'Reilly often described a shipwreck in which he had been a victim. He left nothing in writing, however, to identify the time of the accident nor the name of the ship.

Determined now to bring his project to an early completion, Piet assigned Father Purcell to direct the new foundation until a rector could be appointed by Father General. Purcell arrived on Wednesday night, November 12, 1930. He offered the first Mass on the premises in a temporary chapel on the second floor of an old farmhouse on November 13, Feast of St. Stanislaus, Patron of Novices. Brother James Vetter, too, was summoned from St. Francis Regis Mission to get the farm in shape.*

The first problem to be solved was water. Though there were several springs on the property, estimates for need ran considerably more than these could furnish. The estimated need for domestic use was fifteen thousand gallons daily, a total of sixty thousand cubic feet per month. Allowing for storage, the springs could furnish only a fraction of this. Negotiations were begun with the Sheridan Water Department for permission to connect a novitiate pipeline onto the city supply. After months of discussion, in which Sheridan's pastor, Father Derouin, played a most noble part, the City Council, by a vote of five to one, agreed to allow the novitiate to tap the city line. The conditions imposed were so rigorous that, in effect, the novitiate was left to its own resources. A Portland engineer was then commissioned to make a water survey, and, after his decision was rendered, favoring an adequate supply, the matter was considered settled.

The time had now come for the first major step in the division of the province. On November 26, 1930, Father Ledochowski dispatched from Rome a long document establishing the northern division of the California province as a dependent Vice Province of California effective Christmas Day, December 25, 1930.[7] On December 20, Piet transmitted this document to the superiors of the province, directing them not to make its contents public until Christmas Day. Piet's letter, sent from Portland, contained the following: "Supplementing the enclosed letter of Our Very Reverend Father General, in which he places the northern portion of our Province under the limited administration of a Vice-Provincial, and determines that it shall be known as 'The Rocky Mountain Region', I wish to add that His Paternity has advised me that he has constituted as Vice-Provincial of the said 'Region,' Father Walter J. Fitzgerald, and has named as his Consultors: Thomas R. Martin, John J. Keep, John A. McHugh and Louis B. Fink; Father Fink has also been appointed Socius to the Vice-Provincial.

"The residence of the Vice-Provincial will be at Gonzaga University, Spokane, Wash., and that of the Provincial at 55 West San Fernando Street, San Jose, California."[8]

Fitzgerald, who had been destined for his role from the beginning, especially in the mind of Piet, took immediate charge, sending to all members of the vice-province what he called a summary of the general's letter on the division of the Province of California. This read in part:

"On account of the great increase in the number of members of the Province and the extent of labors and the difficulties of long distances to travel, it has become increasingly hard for one Provincial to administer this vast Province. Hence it has seemed good to Father General to decree a certain kind of division of the Province. This division is a provisory and administrative one for a certain length of time before a definitive and lasting division is made, and is committed to the direction of a Vice-Provincial dependent on the Provincial.

"Hence, with mature deliberation Father General has decreed the following:

"The Province of California remains for the present one and undivided, but the Northern part is committed to a Vice-Provincial which he will immediately administer from his residence which will be in Spokane. This part will comprise the States of Washington,

---

*According to province pioneers, Fitzgerald sent the following telegram to Brother Vetter at St. Francis Regis Mission: "Take four horses and go to Paradise."

Idaho, Oregon and Montana and in memory of the old Mission of that name will be called 'The Region of the Rocky Mountains.' The other part of the Province will comprise the States of California, Nevada, Utah and Arizona and will be immediately administered by the Provincial from his residence in San Jose.

"The outside Missions of Alaska and China will continue to be administered by the Provincial with this proviso that as soon as a permanent division of the Province is made, Alaska will belong to the Northern part and China to the Southern Province.

"As regards the members of the Province, a permanent distribution will be made only when the permanent division is made. The distribution will follow in general this rule: Members of the Province who have been born in either part of the Province will be assigned according to the place of origin to the part of the Province whence they came, as far as can be done. Those who have come from without the Province will belong to that part to which they shall have been destined by Superiors. Those who are in outside Missions, will be applied to that part of the Province to which the Mission belongs. If any exception is to be made, it will be considered accurately before the permanent division."[9]

While these announcements were the cause of general rejoicing in the south as well as in the north, there were some older missionaries like Taelman, who felt disappointed in the manner in which the new structures were related. There was much excitement about the new province, but which was the *new* province? The so-called new vice-province had been the mission from which the California mission had been founded. In 1930 the vice-province had ten more Jesuits than the province. The provincial, Father Piet, the vice-provincial, the novice master, and the province treasurer were all members of the vice-province. There seemed to be a little juggling of nomenclature, or an oversight of the feelings of living pioneers who were attached to their mission and its roots. Piet, I think, was capable of the latter, in part because of his own growing detachment for the north.

The differences of viewpoint on this subject did not disturb the customary spirit of fraternal love for one another by members of the two divisions. The Jesuits' traditional loyalty toward the Society and all of its members was not damaged. During the uncertain years following the division of the two provinces, there were many hard-fought battles about debts and property, but at no time did the participants forget they were Jesuit colleagues. Whatever the storm, a basic peace and harmony reigned. This was one of the benefits of the general awareness of the Society's common enemies. There were always so many outsiders willing to attack the Jesuits that the Jesuits kept their differences to themselves and presented a united front.

In 1930, no doubt the personality of Joseph Piet helped to maintain the spirit of unity. He simply imposed his decisions on a sometimes unwilling Fitzgerald, who made his own proposals, then acquiesced when Piet made the decision. On January 13, 1931, Piet wrote to Fitzgerald: "Have your cable address Zitgu registered . . . that word zitgu is an Indian compound."[10] This is hardly what Fitzgerald wanted to hear. He had proposed Manresa Hall, Port Townsend for a temporary novitiate, but Piet had ignored this.

Piet wrote again: "I hope and pray that means will soon be found so that we can begin the central portion of the new novitiate at Sheridan. The *Sheridan Sun* has written enthusiastically of the project in an article and an editorial. The picture of the novitiate to be on public exhibition in the town. They will help us with water."[11] The picture referred to here was an architect's rendering of a building that might have been a national capitol. It stood grandly on top of the hill where it could be seen across the valley many miles distant, a four-story concrete building, three-hundred-and-fifty-four feet long, with a central tower stretching two-hundred-and-forty-feet into the Oregon sky.

On February 9, Piet wrote again. He had suddenly realized that Fitzgerald was serious about using Port Townsend for a novitiate. *Keep the Tertianship,* he wrote, underlining his words.[12] The novitiate site was settled; not open to discussion.

Fitzgerald held his first formal consultation with his advisors three days later, on February 12, 1931. After discussing the nature of their authority, they took up the problem of the novitiate, agreeing on four points unanimously: there was no money to build at Sheridan. They could not borrow money. A temporary frame building would cost $14,000. All favored spending this on a permanent building.[13] Fitzgerald added arguments to those of his consultors. "Next month," he said, "the Province has to pay $16,000.00 in taxes. Father Sauer has only paid one-half of the $15,000 in bills for last month; the rest he left until some money comes in. The Alaska orders are coming in; the Procurator estimates that these will amount to $30,000 and he had not one cent in the Alaska fund he had at one time, but this account is already $9,000 in debt from last year." The province, he added, was $500,000 in debt and was throwing out of the window $30,000 in interest.[14] The ugly word "bankruptcy" came up, but Fitzgerald was more concerned with placating Piet than frightening him. What Fitzgerald wanted was a novitiate without spending any money.

Piet was not dismayed. On March 14 he wrote that "Mr. F. W. Reverman of Dougan and Reverman, Portland, sent estimates of cost of a frame building, $6,529.00." Water from the Sheridan pipeline would cost $46.25 per month and equipment for it $4,260.[15] On the same day Fitzgerald wrote to Piet a very long letter, in which he summed up:

"(1) Let the first part of our permanent building be erected at Sheridan with money available from the Province loan to Los Angeles. (2) Temporary quarters for Novices at Colville. Colton or Port Townsend are not desirable. (3) A temporary Novitiate be located at St. Michael's while [the] building is being erected at Sheridan."[16]

Somewhat annoyed by Piet's persistence in demanding a temporary building, Fitzgerald took a parting shot, which contained a veiled threat: he could take the matter to Father General:

"These suggestions, Reverend Father Provincial, are the unanimous opinion of the Consultors of the Rocky Mountain Region, and I believe that they reflect the majority sentiment of the Patres Graviores of the Region. We think, moreover, that since the question of the New Novitiate pertains vitally to our own Region, as well as to the interest of the whole Province, it is but fair that we have a voice in the arrangements for the Novitiate. Thus far, the Consultors and the Vice-Provincial have made no report to His Paternity about this matter, but we are ready and willing to present our case to His Paternity, if it will be of assistance to Your Reverence in carrying out the project of the Novitiate at Sheridan, which has always been wisely and strongly promoted by Your Reverence."[17]

Reference here was made to Colton and Colville. At both places, large, empty buildings were available, the first, having been abandoned by the Benedictine Sisters who had departed for St. Gertrude's convent, Cottonwood, Idaho, and the second, a very solid frame building formerly used by the Sisters of Providence as a school for Colville Indian girls. The latter was really in the Colville Valley near Kettle Falls, below St. Francis Regis Mission, about one hundred miles north of Spokane. Father Sauer had espoused its use, pointing out, quite reasonably many thought, that the adjoining farmland was sufficient to support the novices.* Neither Piet nor Fitzgerald favored the place, the former offering as his objection that it was too near Spokane, where there were other Jesuits.

Father Dillon, too, had a proposal. The old scholasticate building at St. Ignatius Mission was available. This could be used as a temporary novitiate without spending any money on it. Dillon, in charge of making the province inventory, the listing of all assets and

---

*This is the present convent of the Dominican Sisters.

liabilities, was appalled by Piet's optimism. There were debts everywhere. No money. Little or no credit. The country bogged down in the greatest depression in its history. But Piet would not listen. "Never mind the depression," he wrote loftily. Perhaps it would go away if you ignored it.

Father Patrick O'Reilly suddenly appeared with some happy news. "I have good hope," he wrote to Piet, "of securing a real worthwhile donation of $50,000 for a Novitiate church to be erected at Sheridan."[18] He had sent Judge D'Arcy in Salem a copy of his book *The Light Divine*. He would continue to follow up this lead, but Father Fitzgerald should visit the judge in Salem.

Fitzgerald at the moment was in no mood to visit an unknown judge in Salem who wanted a church at Sheridan, where as yet there was not even the hope of a novitiate building. On June 1 he wrote to Piet: "The auditor's report on the Gonzaga financial situation is finished and conditions are worse than anticipated. The entire indebtedness is almost $400,000; of this amount there is a sum of $60,000 in current expenses that must be paid, at once; the sum of $10,000 in salaries was due today and this amount was borrowed at the bank on a short-time loan; how the other $50,000 will be raised is a mystery. Of this amount, one half of the bills are for athletic debts, the other half for house debts. . . . If the firms and banks of the city knew our condition here, there would be only one effect for Gonzaga: bankruptcy."[19]

There was that ugly word again, bankruptcy. Father Piet considered it well. "After thoroughly considering the situation," he wrote Fitzgerald on June 20, "I finally ordered Mr. Reverman to go on in the construction of the temporary Novitiate at Sheridan. He promises to have it ready by July 25th."[20]

Two weeks later Piet reported on progress. Ninety thousand feet of lumber had been delivered for $1,100. Also some desks for $1.35 each. Kneeling benches were $14.00 for fifty, all varnished. The temporary building was costing $9,000. In a postscript he added, "I have referred an excellent boy to you. James Hess of 691 Lovejoy Street, Portland; he knows much of the history of the Society; has made up his mind to enter."[21]

The reference to this candidate for the Society reminded Fitzgerald of seven young men from Catholic Central in Butte, Montana, who had applied for admission to the Novitiate. He informed Piet that he had received a three-page complaint regarding this from Bishop George Finnegan of Helena.* Piet on July 7 responded: "I should like to have a copy of that 3 page letter on the Butte postulants. Archbishop Hanna was called upon to sign necessary letters for twenty-five postulants. . . . He has asked the diocesan clergy what they are doing for vocations to the seminary, but he is far from complaining about what we got."[22]

Fitzgerald during these tense days was in residence at Gonzaga with his assistant, Father Fink. Piet was often in Portland, reluctant after all, to give up the old spacious Provincial's residence for his new accommodations in San Jose, in the back of old St. Joseph's Church. He kept a paternal eye on developments at Paradise Farm, allowing Father Purcell little initiative and leaving nothing to chance.

The frame, bungalow-like building, under construction for only twenty-two days, was two hundred-and-seven-feet long, one storied, and shingled. It had four wings, one of which was for a chapel and another for a dining room. The front portion of the building was buried in a grove of oak trees, on the crest of the hill about four hundred feet above the Yamhill Valley. In addition to rooms for several priests and brothers, "the Bungalow" as it

---

*"Rumor says that a certain dignitary was complaining of the number of Jesuit novices coming from a Jesuit school; the sisters who heard this moan, gently suggested that he go to the high school and give the boys a rousing talk on vocations to the Diocesan Clergy." Provincial Archives, Portland, Piet to Fitzgerald, July 8, 1931.

was called, was built to accommodate fifty-one novices in small partitioned cells which the novices called "cubics," with the accent on the second syllable.*

In late July, Piet was back in Portland. With him was Father Tom Meagher, formerly novice master at Los Gatos, now assigned to the new novitiate. Piet, like Goller, enjoyed newspaper interviews, so one was arranged with a reporter from the *Oregon Journal*. Piet chattered freely about Jesuit plans for the $400,000 permanent building, including the two hundred-and-forty-foot tower "which will make the building a landmark in the Yamhill Valley." He also stated that the new Novitiate, "the first undertaking of the Northwest Jesuits since the Northern Coast region was made an independent province," was designed "to house and provide classrooms for three hundred students and the faculty."[23]

The account reveals Piet's own "plenty of enthusiasm" as well as his obvious blindness to realities like money and the state of the nation. Fitzgerald humored him. Together they made final arrangements for the opening ceremonies for what Piet regarded as his crowning achievement, the new novitiate. This represented for him the certainty of a new province in the foreseeable future.

The novitiate diary, begun on Wednesday, July 29, 1931, records the more significant details of the following days, including the arrival of the first fifteen novices. In the oral tradition of the province, these have been called "the twelve Apostles" with a deplorable lack of originality, not to mention inaccuracy in numbers.† The diary begins as follows:

"The opening of a new novitiate here at Sheridan made necessary the transfer of some novices from the Sacred Heart Novitiate at Los Gatos, California. Superiors decided to send twelve here to aid in the establishment of this novitiate. The first group of novices to arrive was composed of Brothers Earl, Toner, Ernsdorff and Weissenberg, scholastic novices, and Brothers McNally and Mahony, coadjutor novices.‡ Arriving in Salem [via the Southern Pacific] shortly before 6:00 A.M. they were met by Reverend Father Provincial [Piet], Brothers Huber and Cherpeski and Mr. Reverman [the architect]. Upon reaching their new home they were greeted by the Superior Father N. S. Purcell, S.J.; the Socius, Father Leo Robinson, S.J.; Father Keep and Brother Carroll the Infirmarian. The novices without exception expressed themselves in terms of complete satisfaction with their new home."[24]

There followed in the diary other meticulous bits of information about the day's schedule for the novices, the waxing of floors, the reading at table by Brother Paul Weissenberg and the evening recreation, which was extended until 8:25 P.M.

On Thursday, July 30, the community rose at 5:00 A.M. as was customary, and Piet met more novices at the train in Salem. "The second group of novices arrived, composed of Brothers Adams, Evoy, Twohy and Schiffner, scholastic novices, Brother Coll, a coadjutor novice and Brother Reilly a postulant."[25] After Father Robinson said Mass in the old farmhouse, as on the previous day, *Deo Gratias* was given at breakfast, an unusual event in any novitiate. This meant that instead of breakfast in silence, as was customary, the novices could talk to one another.

On July 31, the Feast of St. Ignatius, the last group arrived. "Shortly after seven o'clock Father Master [Meagher] arrived with the last group of novices composed of Brothers Dalgity, Menard, Conwell and Chapman. They went at once to the chapel where Father Master said Mass.[26] The day was a busy one for everybody. The house and grounds had to

---

*In the novitiate and juniorate, scholastic quarters were very modest, encompassing an area of approximately 9' × 14' which was set off by dividers and a curtain. "Cubic" is a shortened form of *cubiculum* which means in Latin "a little room."

†The number twelve did not include three coadjutor brother novices.

‡Their full names were: Arthur Earl, Frank Toner, Harold Ernsdorff, Paul Weissenberg, Peter McNally, and Stephen Mahony.

be tidied up, more floors waxed, and a large dinner to be prepared with what they had. There was no dearth of very important persons, since Piet, Fitzgerald and several rectors were there. Archbishop Howard arrived an hour late, about noon, the blessing of the house took place at that time instead of eleven as scheduled, and dinner was served at half-past twelve. Brother Twohy read the martyrology at the beginning of dinner for the first time in the new community.* The Archbishop's blessing and Twohy's reading made it all canonically official; the north now had a novitiate and province status was certain to follow. After the laughter of Fitzgerald's after-dinner speechmaking had subsided, "all assembled outside for group pictures. One was taken of the community and visiting clergy, one of the clergy alone and a third of the novices. Volunteer scullery followed with order for walk at 3:00. Walk companies confined their efforts to the location of a suitable place for an indoor field."[27] After all, first things first.

The next day the fifteen "apostles" rolled up their sleeves and with traditional Jesuit vigor began the transformation of the bungalow into a religious house. Twenty-five new novices arrived four days later. At last De Smet's motherhouse in Oregon was a reality. It was now filled with the laughter and song of flesh-and-blood Jesuits, as many as even the sanguine founder of the Rocky Mission ever hoped for.

Plans for a permanent building were already under way. Dougan and Reverman modified the original concept, known then as "Piet's Pride," so that a concrete shell four-hundred-and-sixty-nine feet by forty-three feet, three stories high, with an additional story in the middle, was projected for immediate construction.

Fitzgerald and Piet exchanged many letters about the actual beginnings, before there were sufficient funds to pay the bills. Reverman, Fitzgerald said, wanted to begin work not later than January 15, 1932. Purcell had returned to supervise the work.[28] But when would Piet have enough money to start?

While Piet regarded the permanent building at Sheridan as his number-one priority, he had to make countless other decisions for questions raised by the vice provincial. Fitzgerald, for example, wanted to convert the former provincial's residence in Portland into a retreat house. He regarded this as very urgent.[29] More immediately relevant was the decision of the fathers at Seattle College to return to the Broadway campus where they could use the Garrand Building. There appeared to be no other choice. They had little or no money to erect buildings on the Thorpe site, and the city was going to tax them for the Broadway property if it were not put to use. For $15,000 they were able to remodel the Garrand Building, which appeared to be a respectable beginning. Fitzgerald had consulted Father Keep, the province's prefect of studies, and it was agreed that Father James McGoldrick be placed on the Seattle College status.[30]

Dave McAstocker had got it into his head that he should expand the program at Bellarmine. He visited Fitzgerald in Spokane and presented his arguments for a sister's training school and for opening Bellarmine to college classes. Fitzgerald put him off. "I replied that he would have to wait for the division of the province, then see if enough men are available."[31] Piet was not so diplomatic. "Tacoma high school boys," he said, "could attend Seattle College. This is a distance of only one hour by machine."[32]

"We have just started Seattle College off this year," Fitzgerald reported happily, "with high hopes and we shall need more men here if the classes increase. *Per Transennam*, there are 32 in Freshmen class here, more than we had in the whole school last year."[33]

*For centuries the Martyrology was read in religious houses. This was a collection of comments about the saints who were honored on a particular day.

While John McHugh, now rector at Seattle College reported favorably on developments there, Father McNamara in Missoula was hanging black crepe over Loyola High School. "He wants to close Loyola," Fitzgerald complained, "too big a debt. [Missoula was in a] depression. 52 families had left Missoula."[34] Later Fitzgerald asked his consultors what they thought. "They are opposed to closing Loyola H.S.," he wrote simply, then added, "A new site for Marquette [in Yakima] was discussed. The parish would give $50,000 for the old Marquette building."[35]

There had been two mission fires. What was life without mission fires? No lives were lost in either, but luckily at St. Andrew's Mission in Oregon, Father "Speed" Lajoie escaped the conflagration. He could hurry when flames snapped at his backside. The fathers' and boys' building was destroyed entirely. Father John Corbett was still there, trying to follow Cataldo's advice. A new building would be erected, but the mission had to go into debt, and this occasioned, sooner, than later, a breakdown in Corbett's health.

Worse by far was the fire at St. Paul's Mission near Hays, Montana. On November 16 the sisters' large building, which also housed the girls, the dining room and classrooms, and the elegant church, built by Father Mackin, were reduced to rubble.[36] The loss of the church especially disheartened the Indians, for whom the structure had been the one visible element of stability in their lives. It would be years before either building could be replaced, but life had to go on with the meager resources left to them.

Neither Piet nor Fitzgerald, occupied with these mostly tiresome matters, had overlooked the approaching culmination of their preparations, the independent province in the north. It was like preparing for statehood; something had to be done every day. Fitzgerald and his consultors were concerned about the appointment of the new provincial, who would soon be their master. "Since the Rocky Mountain Mission [sic] is dependent," he wrote to Piet, "and [since] all consultors of the *Province* are Californians, there is danger that a California man will be appointed Provincial for the north. The Vice Provincial Consultors oppose this."[37]

Later Fitzgerald corresponded with Piet about the new province's name and the residence of the provincial:

"At the consultation in Seattle, I read several of the letters received from the Patres Graviores of the Province concerning the name of our Northern Province. The greater number of those who replied—and all were asked to give their opinion—stated that they were in favor of Oregon for the name of the Province. A few mentioned Rocky Mountain Province. Others were in favor of Seattle Province while one or two were for Spokane Province. There was a scattering of opinions for Pacific—North Western—North Pacific—Western—etc. Father Soer's vote follows: The New White Province and Indian Missions of Spokane!?! All the Consultors and myself were in favor of Oregon Province. I told them that it was Your Reverence's suggestion that it might be good to move the Provincial's Headquarters back to Portland. I think this is a good plan, since we would be nearer the Novitiate, and also nearer the houses of importance in Seattle, Tacoma, and Port Townsend. Of course, Spokane is important as a center, and I am not very set in regard to either place.

"The Monaghan Family of Spokane has offered their mansion to us for $10,000, as a Residence for the Provincial and his men. There are twenty-two rooms, counting everything; hard wood; in a good state of preservation."[38]

The Vice Provincial, meanwhile, had gone to visit the judge in Salem. He found Peter D'Arcy very pleasant and remained with him for two hours. He did not see any immediate results of his visit; however, the judge was quite pleased that he had come. "He told me the whole story of his difficulties with the Archbishop, the Pastor, the architect and the contractors. The proposed new Church in Salem, for which plans had been made and bids received, has been held up until next Spring. He told me that he thought his difficulties would be ironed out, and that the Church would be built according to his wishes. However, he stated that in case this project falls through, he wishes to give $65,000.00 to the Jesuits for Sheridan! He thinks that the Memorial to his Mother should be in Salem, as she lived there most of her life."[39]

Piet had received complaints that the novice master had been too severe with some of the novices. He asked Fitzgerald to make it a point to visit the novitiate more frequently and to persuade Father Meagher to be more gentle. Father Leo Robinson, making his tertianship there, was also the novice master's assistant. Meagher, at times, was like a dragon, without realizing it. Though he was most willing to accept correction, he preferred to do so on his own terms.

"I do not think that Father Leo Robinson would be able to help much in influencing Father Meagher," Fitzgerald wrote, "on account of the former's position as a Tertian. He told me that Father Master had been severe with him several times, telling him to remember that he was a Tertian! and still going through his own probation! The presence of Father Robinson at Sheridan is a great asset for the novices, on account of his cheerful disposition and good religious spirit."[40]

The year 1931 closed with reports of bank failures in various cities. In Portland the Hibernian bank, "a Catholic bank" closed its doors. "We had only about $1500 in that bank," Fitzgerald noted in a long report to Father Aemilius Mattern, the general's assistant in Rome. Fitzgerald had an axe to grind. He wanted specific instructions from Rome regarding the Giroux Estate, which California claimed and to which Jesuits in the north believed they had a one-half right.[41] "In the financial statement drawn up by Father Dillon, accepted by both North and South, and approved by Father General, you will note that the South will return to the North the sum of $121,000 and divide the Province debt with us evenly, taking their share of the indebtedness ($82,000). In fact the South has already made arrangements for the loan of $121,000 which will go for the new building which will be erected this month at Sheridan Novitiate." Fitzgerald felt sorry for California, because they were worse off financially than Oregon, but California had far more resources and Catholics than Oregon did. Hence Oregon should receive its just share of the Giroux Estate.[42]

Furthermore, Piet had shortchanged Oregon on the missions. "When you consider that out of the 66 men laboring on the Alaska and Indian missions over 50 are from the Northern part of the province, the question naturally arises why should the North have sent 5 out of the 9 men to China."

Fitzgerald made these complaints from Spokane on January 4, 1932. On the same day he accepted a telegram from Piet: "Received today two Roman Documents about Division." A letter followed. Addressed to Fitzgerald, it said: "Kindly inform the members of your community that on the occasion of the establishment of the Oregon Province His Paternity [Father General] has appointed Very Reverend Walter Fitzgerald the first Provincial of the New Province."[43]

The two documents had been signed and dispatched from Rome on December 8, 1931. The first one was a decree in Latin several pages in length, formally establishing the Oregon Province on the Feast of the Purification, February 2, 1932, and stating in detail what provisions were to be made by the two *new* provinces in their relations with one another. The second document was a fatherly letter addressed to members of both provinces, urging fidelity to the principles of the Society and to the traditions of each province.[44] These documents, according to custom, were to be read at dinner in the houses of both provinces on February 2, 1932.

In his decree, Father Ledochowski had mentioned specifically the name "Oregon" for the new province. In a more formal response to Fitzgerald's request regarding it, he wrote again in mid-January. At this time as Piet informed Fitzgerald, the Portland residence was presumed to be approved. Piet could not resist adding another reminder about Sheridan, though his jurisdiction over the novitiate would soon run out: "I sincerely hope that you will be able to begin the Sheridan building before Easter." Everyone, he said, assuming it to be true, favors the permanent building to be started.[45]

But not everyone did. Piet had to admit later that both Sauer and Dillon were opposed to Sheridan construction, "despite the fact that Canonical approbation had been received from the Holy See." "Do not make Dillon treasurer," Piet warned Fitzgerald. "He has the reputation of having starved Bellarmine Prep in San Jose. By way of paying off the debt he reduced the student body and filled the place with complaints."[46]

As for the residence in Portland, Piet had other advice to offer: "Father Fink will not be strong for Portland, just at present, but he is not the only one who found it hard to live with the present pastor who is by no means an irremovable one. . . . Again the Provincial's presence in Portland is not only helpful to Sheridan but to Portland also, in this sense that we ought to try to increase our influence in Portland, where Jesuit influence is a complete nothing. In Spokane, Jesuit influence is very great, while in Portland, the biggest city in Oregon, has been neglected."[47]

Time was running out for Piet. He would be Fitzgerald's Provincial only one day longer. On February 1 he wrote to say that he could not change the name of the California Province bulletin, *Western Jesuit*, to which Fitzgerald had objected, on the grounds that Oregon was "Western" also. Piet said he would add "For the California Province." He had seen Bishop Armstrong and gave him all the news about Fitzgerald's new job.[48]

Thus ended this long, intimate relationship between Piet as Provincial and Fitzgerald as his subject. Their roles would soon be reversed, for Piet was replaced as Provincial of California by Zacheus Maher on March 5, 1932. As an Oregonian, he was now subject to Fitzgerald, whose superiorship was generally regarded as more benign than Maher's.

February 2, 1932, anticipated in a sense, for ninety years, since St. Mary's mission had been founded, dawned at last. It was a Tuesday, ordinarily a class day in the colleges. At Sheridan it was a holiday in honor of Mary, whose festival day it was. The novices rose at 5:00 A.M., meditated from 5:30 until 6:45, when the candles were blessed, then attended Mass. Breakfast and scullery were in silence, though there was more noise than usual from dishes and pans. After reading the Little Office of the Blessed Virgin Mary, some novices were assigned to play handball and others to cut wood. At dinner the solemn decrees were read and a box of candy was passed around during recreation.[49]

That evening Father Dillon arrived. He was the new minister, who was to assist Purcell in the construction of the new building. Since it was commonly believed that Dillon could squeeze more out of a nickle than anybody in the province, he was now in charge of the purse strings. All he needed was the money which California had agreed to send.

In other houses of the province there was little more by way of ceremony in recognition of province status. At the Mount, for example, Father William Elliott pronounced his last vows and Brother Thorain celebrated his golden jubilee as a Jesuit. The decree was read at dinner, which by way of exception, was served in the evening, rather than at noon, in honor of the two Jesuits.[50]

At Gonzaga Father Paul Corkery pronounced his last vows. At precisely 9:00 A.M., he was presented to the students in the gymnasium, all of whom were madly excited in anticipation of a holiday. This was duly granted by the honored guest, and the students departed with a roar of delight.* Little, if anything was said about the historic establish-

---

*The writer was present. This was a customary practice. When Last Vows were pronounced by Jesuits, a reception followed and a holiday was granted.

ment of the new Oregon Province. This was taken care of at dinner, over which the new provincial himself presided. The decree was read and the General's letter also. That was that, the province was finally a province, the fortieth in the Society. It was all very simple. Jesuit formalities were barely explicit.

Three days later, on February 5, the provincial and his assistant left Gonzaga to establish their residence in Portland. Though western Oregon is damp and misty at this time of the year, the appearance of flowers and the brilliant green of the grass raised Fitzgerald's spirits. Spring was the season of hope. Although the finances of the new province appeared to be hopeless, and the plight of the new novitiate, desperate, Fitzgerald knew that somehow, in God's mysterious Providence, they would survive. The daily worries about money would go away. But when? Fitzgerald would ask himself this for many years.

Like Piet, he wanted an informed province, and the support of friends. He established at once *The Oregon Province News*, which first appeared in March, 1932, and *The Jesuit Seminary News* for friends of the Jesuits, to secure their continued support. Father Gerald Beezer was the editor of the latter, which also appeared for the first time in mid-March.

The first notice in the *Province News* concerned the appointment of Zacheus Maher as Provincial of the California Province. Not much was said about the retiring provincial, Father Piet, who, despite his faults as an administrator, had directed more changes for western Jesuits than any other superior, with the possible exception of Cataldo. During his eight years as provincial he had established Manresa Hall and the new novitiate at Sheridan. He had approved and supported the establishment of Bellarmine and Brophy prep schools. He had been involved in the erection of three of the West Coast's most distinguished churches, St. Joseph's in Seattle, Our Lady of Sorrows in Santa Barbara, and Blessed Sacrament in Hollywood. He had supervised the construction of new additions on buildings at Mount St. Michael's and Sacred Heart Novitiate in Los Gatos. He had participated, at least as provincial, in the construction of new buildings on three campuses: Gonzaga, Santa Clara and St. Ignatius College, San Francisco. He had also shared as provincial in the acquisition of a new campus by Loyola College, Los Angeles, and the restoration of the old campus of Seattle College. Finally, he had presided over the division of the California Province, into two provinces, each of which was as large, when he left them, as only one had been when he became its superior in 1924. There would be criticism of Piet, justified criticism in a way, but also some that was unreasonable. Those who indulged in the latter, including Fitzgerald, were like Sunday morning quarterbacks.

The time had come for Piet to return to his province, which was Oregon. He wrote to Fitzgerald on March 13, announcing that he would arrive in Portland on the following Friday morning to receive his new assignment.[51] Fitzgerald's response indicates that he had no inhibitions about his former superior. He appointed Piet a "local superior" for the residence in Portland, with the special task of preparing the building for its new function.

"It is planned to open a Laymen's Retreat House at this residence. For the present, according to the directions of Father General, the matter of Laymen's Retreats will have to be looked into, whether all the requisites for opening such a house are at hand, etc. After I receive your report on this matter, I shall obtain the necessary permission. Father General stated that he will have no objections to opening this house, provided all the above things are attended to. In the meantime, I would like you to renovate the building somewhat, in accordance with our limited means. I am sending you Brother Huber who will assist in installing plumbing &. It would be good to get estimates of the cost of fixing up the place, renewing the rooms, putting in running water, putting down linoleum && so as to make the house habitable for retreatants. Before proceeding to the work, get the estimates of all the proposed improvements, and submit the same to me for approval."[52]

Piet, like a good religious, went to work at once. He secured the required permission from the Archbishop for the establishment of the retreat house, and began renovations in the building. He had got things scarcely under way, however, when Father General appointed him as the new Tertian Master at Port Townsend. Here he took up his own residence in May, becoming in due time the arbiter in disputes between Fitzgerald and Maher, as well as Instructor for many Jesuits whom he had trained as novices fourteen years earlier.

The disputes were almost chronic because the two new provincials had chronic money problems. Neither province could pay its honest debts and Fitzgerald, in sheer desperation, I presume, complained to the general that Piet was to blame. He had spent too much money on credit.[53]

Fitzgerald also nagged Maher until he obtained some of the money for building the novitiate. He finally received it and on April 11, 1932, Reverman arrived to stake out the lines for the new building. Two days later, Father Meagher turned over a shovelful of reddish clay, the native soil of Paradise Farm, and read a number of pages from the ritual, while novices sang a hymn to St. Joseph, "Bleak sands are all around us, no home can we see." When they had finished, workmen, who had been standing curiously by, reached for their tools, and the project was under way.

On the following day, Fitzgerald wrote a long letter to the general, enclosing a copy of the financial report on the province. The province, he said, "is on the verge of bankruptcy." That word again. The annual revenues were only $73,550 leaving a deficit of $111,552. Total liabilities in the province, he said, were $443,868.04 and total assets only $271,758.23. True, he added, there were many other stable assets like land and buildings, but these could not be reduced to cash to pay the importunate banks, which would not extend further credit. Father Sauer, he also said, could not borrow money to buy supplies for Alaska and Bishop Crimont was coming to see him to probe for a solution.

But if California would pay Oregon its debts, all would be well. "I have tried to make this plain to the California Province, so as to get the money at once. You might say: But has not California given Oregon $120,000 for the Novitiate? I reply, No, they have made a loan in San Francisco and they pay by small installments as needed for the work at Sheridan."[54]

The burr under Fitzgerald's saddle was called "the Giroux Estate," and if Fitzgerald's horse needed spurs, Dillon was on hand to apply them. If, as Dillon demanded, California paid Oregon $88,000 as its share of the Giroux Estate, all could be resolved happily. But Zacheus Maher did not have any money. The Giroux Estate had been spent (or most of it) on land at Santa Barbara for a theologate. California was in worse shape financially than Oregon, even Fitzgerald admitted that.

The most basic problem, as Fitzgerald saw it was: "the indebtedness of Oregon has remained the same after the separation as it was under the united Province, and the revenues have been cut in two."[55]

Fitzgerald wrote again to the general. Since Oregon did not have money to pay other provinces for theologians, and since California was unable to pay Oregon for the philosophers at the Mount, could Oregon send its theologians to the Mount?[56]

To this, Father General simply said, "No."

Fitzgerald wrote again. It would be necessary he said to make some provision for the Juniors. During the summer, twenty-six novices would pronounce their vows, ready to begin their classical studies. There was no room for them at Sheridan. Their places in the bungalow would be taken soon by the incoming novices and the new building would not be ready for nine or ten months. Arrangements could be made to send them to the Mount, only for one year, when the new building would be habitable.

To this Father General said, "Yes."

Thus it happened that on July 26, 1932, eleven new Juniors who had just pronounced their vows as Jesuits, left Sheridan in the old novitiate bus driven by Brother Aloysius Laird.[57] In late afternoon of the same day they arrived at the Umatilla Mission where they slept in the new boys' dormitory. On the following afternoon they arrived at the Mount, more bewildered than tired, but ready at last for the studies they had entered the Society to pursue. On the same day eleven more new Juniors left Los Gatos for the Mount, accounting for a total of twenty-two. Later three more from Los Gatos and one from Sheridan, joined their companions.

This crisis had been resolved but Fitzgerald had many others. All during autumn of 1932 and during the year that followed, he returned again and again to the "Giroux Estate" hopeful that Maher would wave a magic wand and suddenly produce the money. Maher, too, complained to the General. He was ashamed of making his visitation at the Mount because the California Province could not pay for its scholastics there. Fitzgerald, Sauer and Dillon were all demanding money. The cry of bankruptcy was in the air all the time. And everyone pounced on poor old Piet.

Father Mattern wrote to Piet from Rome on November 10, 1933. "We knew, of course, before Fr. Dillon came [to Rome] the critical condition of the finances of the Oregon Province, and he could only confirm our fears. California is not much better off, but it has greater resources. The hardest thing we did during the stay of the two procurators was the settlement of the interminable controversy of the Giroux Estate, which the two provinces had not been able to agree upon."[58]

Somehow, during this bleak time, Father Sauer managed to scrape together enough to pay a little on bills here and there to keep creditors satisfied. He was generally credited with being a financial wizard. If Dillon could squeeze money, Sauer could hoard it. There seems to be no doubt that he more than anyone else was responsible for survival and the Provincial never hesitated to give him the credit, though he often teased about it. "What's the matter with the Procurator? Please send me some more money!" Father Sauer would take this teasing with mock German seriousness. "I'm the Province goat," he would write back. "You see the Great Northern's freight cars with the goat? Well that's the Great Northern goat and I'm the Oregon Province goat." Then he would draw the picture of a goat at the end of his letter, and sign it "Oregon Province Goat."

One cannot say, as perhaps one would like to, that the Provincial faced these disturbances with an unfailing equanimity. Yet he met them cheerfully and with characteristic Jesuit detachment. Often enough he could even laugh at his woes. He seemed to enjoy his provincial visitations. He liked travel and, no less, liked to meet people.

He was very approachable, so much so that whenever he came to the house, everyone beat a path to his door for an informal visit. He laughed a lot, a nice airy "ha" (pause) "ha" (pause) "ha" with his head back and face radiating pleasure.

Always on visitations he had a heart-to-heart talk with brother cook. "Brother," he would say, gravely nodding his head, "do the best you can in the kitchen. On you depends the happiness of the whole house. A well-fed community is a happy community."

"Well fed" then did not include dessert, for if the province was on "the verge of bankruptcy," so were the individual communities. When Father Sauer submitted his financial report on March 30, 1933, the province then owed $537,855.89. Gonzaga still owed $400,000, Seattle College $175,000 and Bellarmine in Tacoma $68,000. Total indebtedness at that time for the province and its institutions was $1,764,855.89.*

---

*"Their Province [California] is in splendid financial shape." Provincial Archives, Portland, Sauer to Fitzgerald, March 30, 1933. Only Oregon's property was in danger of foreclosure, some of it mortgaged for loans to California schools.

A few weeks later a ray of sunshine appeared. Fitzgerald wrote to the General: "There has been so much sad and distressing news, particularly financial, that I have had to write to your Paternity of late, that it gives me great pleasure to share with you our great joy and happiness in accepting the donation of the chapel for our new Novitiate at Sheridan, Oregon."[59] Judge Peter D'Arcy, he said, "had come on March 12, at the close of the Novena of Grace to St. Francis Xavier, the Patron of our Novitiate." There are two brothers and one sister in the D'Arcy family, he explained, all over seventy. They had visited the novitiate and had been so impressed by the novices they wanted their mother's memorial chapel to be built there. Peter, older than John or Theresa, made the proposals, but all three would pay for the chapel. They themselves would make the contract with the architect and builder and pay both directly. Construction was to begin immediately.

This was late April. On the Feast of the Sacred Heart, June 24, 1933, the first Mass was celebrated in the new novitiate in a temporary chapel on the third floor. The novices moved in on the same day, though the building was little more than a damp concrete shell. Finishings, even furnishings, except for bare necessities were put off to a later day. The principal merit of the new building, besides its simplicity, was its relatively low cost. At $2.40 a square foot, it represented a great bargain. This did not allow for furnishings, nor for the brick veneer, which was twenty years in arriving, nor for the chapel wing and kitchen facilities. The bungalow was retained for the latter and served in various capacities besides, such as a storage area for the dried prunes.

As a consultor of the province, Father Tom Martin, Rector of the Mount, knew all that was going on at the Novitiate, but he could scarcely have guessed that he would be Sheridan's first rector. That fact was not revealed until November 16, 1932.[60] When the news was broken to him, he could hardly console himself with the reflection that very few Jesuits have the opportunity to become rectors of two different novitiates. So it will be Sheridan, he thought grimly, recalling the countless consultations during which the subject of Sheridan's poverty had been weighed. One might just as well be appointed president of an insolvent bank, as be made rector of Sheridan, for there were many debts and few resources.

Father Martin did not make the trip to his new residence till July, 1933. As he rode through the little town of some fifteen hundred which had been named for an Indian fighter of considerable fame in the region, he could see the novitiate building in bold relief against the western sky. It crowned an eminence, something like a fort, overlooking a highway and small river running along Yamhill Valley. It appeared to be massive. A large cross clearly seen for many miles surmounted the concrete structure. Like Los Gatos, when he first saw it, it was box-like and plain, a supermarket without lights.

The road to the building crossed novitiate hayfields and Rock Creek bridge, passed a prune-dryer and an assortment of prune trees, then ascended the hill abruptly at an angle, coming onto the novitiate from the rear. It was a picturesque ride, particularly on a July day. Mountain ridges farther west, bordering on the Pacific, glowed with the sun along their crests, and deep forests darkened their slopes. Near at hand, cattle grazed in the shade of old oaks; and the last quarter-mile between two rows of windswept apple trees ended suddenly on the summit, where one could look out across grain fields and orchards far to the east where peaks of the Cascades were covered with eternal snow. "Most beautiful view from any Jesuit house in America," one Eastern Jesuit had said, a lovely place to retire in old age. But Father Martin was not retiring.

We do not know what he thought that day when he stepped out of the car that had brought him. We do know he was not afraid, not even of the poverty. In fact, he often said in later years, "Poverty is Sheridan's greatest blessing." It took a brave man to face what he had to face on July 13, 1933. As superior he was responsible to the Society and the Church for approximately fifty young men with another fifty due in a matter of two weeks. He had no means to support them except the few cows, the orchard and about eight hundred acres of poor soil that turned into gumbo during wet seasons whereas in dry seasons it cracked wide open in little cakes like those you see around sulphur springs. He had no adequate water supply, no furnishings for the house, no books for scholars, no credit to borrow on, and it was just five months after the bank holiday. One thing he knew for certain; he could not expect his community to live on the view, which for all its charms, would not put a single loaf on the table.

Fortunately for all concerned, Sheridan had many friends. Mothers' clubs in Missoula, Spokane, and elsewhere hurried to its aid with clothes and furnishings. Father Peter Brooks of the Missouri Province shipped books. St. Ignatius Mission sent cattle. Friends in Yakima donated loads of potatoes, carrots and apples. The D'Arcys of Salem provided holiday dinners. Perhaps most touching of all was a truck-load of groceries gathered at Christmastime by boys of Seattle Prep.

Meanwhile the Jesuits at Sheridan were not idle. The brothers were working hard, trying to make the most of the farm, while novices cut firewood in the forests and juniors stripped forms from the building and made furniture with the lumber. De Smet and his companions on the Willamette had never worked harder and lived more simply than the pioneers of Sheridan. More than one crisis arose, when the rector's faith was sorely tested and there was talk of sending the novices to their homes. Though each time the disaster was averted by the arrival of additional help, all could see clearly how slender was the thread on which the fate of the house hung.

One can easily understand how, in the circumstances, Father Martin developed a rather strict view of poverty. It became a critical issue with him, and he punished offenders with some rigor. When he saw waste or when someone asked for an unusual permission, he bristled. Yet he was not a stingy man. He was simply conscious of his personal poverty and the community's indigence.

Martin's term as Sheridan's first rector was not all worry. He taught Greek which he loved, and he filled boxes with notes on the authors he explained. He became an authority, though he published nothing. "If things had been different," he told a junior, "perhaps I'd know some Greek today. But they made me a superior. There has been no time for study and I know very little." Greek could interest him so intensely that if a junior went to his room anytime during the day, Father Martin would give a long dissertation on the subject. He taught Greek in Latin, using English only rarely to explain some difficult construction, and when a junior failed to answer questions in Latin, he snapped, *"Male sonat! Proximus frater!"** We have his grade book for the Greek classes, a treasure for the painstaking record it is. Father Martin took his Greek very seriously, much more so than the juniors did.

The juniors returned to Sheridan in the summer of 1933. Fitzgerald had written recently to the general, reporting this fact, as well as another: Father Maher, he said, intended to send twenty-two scholastics to Santa Clara for philosophy. There would be ample room at the Mount for the Oregon theologians. This would save a considerable amount of money which the province lacked.[61] Father General relented and approved the plan. However, he added, this was permission granted "for the first year theologians only."

On May 28, Fitzgerald wrote to Father Mattern to say how much he appreciated this concession. "We shall have nine theologians. Of course, the opening of theology means that the schools must make sacrifices of men; but they all do it willingly. There is great rejoicing especially among the older Fathers, the Mountaineers, that we have again the

*Literally, "That sounds badly. The next brother [respond to my question]."

course in theology. It will be a big savings financially to have our own men at St. Michael's and the vacancy caused by the withdrawal of the California philosophers will gradually be supplied."

"There is no let-up in our financial difficulties," he added grimly. Some thought had been given to closing temporarily the new novitiate building, but further discussion revealed this would save little in costs.[62]

If the "Mountaineers," as Fitzgerald called them, expected the Mount to endure as a theologate, they would be sadly mistaken. Fitzgerald's action helped to change Zacheus Maher's mind about keeping his philosophers in California and quickened his efforts to establish his own theologate.

The general had announced "a meeting of Procurators" to be held in Rome on September 26, 1933. This required a province meeting, or, as it was called, "Congregations," to elect a representative or "procurator" to attend the Roman meeting. Accordingly, Fitzgerald summoned the Professed Fathers of the new Oregon Province for its First Province Congregation to be held at Gonzaga on June 13 and 14, 1933. This meeting convened at 10:00 A.M. on the first day in room 221 of the administration building.[63] Three events of note should be stated here: First, Father Dillon was elected to serve as the province's representative in Rome, a frank admission of concern about its fiscal status. Secondly, Father Taelman submitted a *postulatum*, that is a formal request for the beatification of Kateri Tekakwitha, the so-called "Lilly of the Mohawks."* Another member of the province congregation urged that the Society request the Holy See to define as dogma the doctrine of the Assumption of Mary. This meeting adjourned at 5:40 P.M. on June 14, and some of its membership in a hurry to get home, departed from Spokane the same evening.[64]

Father Dillon began work on a sixteen-page report which included such provocative subjects as "the involved property relations between the bishops and our Province at Spokane, Missoula, Lewiston, Portland, Pendleton, Holy Family Mission, St. Xavier's Mission, etc."[65]

The existence of problems of this nature should surprise no one, because the Pacific Northwest church was still in a transition stage. The extent of the problem, however, is a little shocking. Because so many parishes and missions were involved, it would take years before solutions would be found. Fitzgerald's successor, Father William Elliott, would inherit "the involved property relations," and in some cases, so would Elliott's successors.

The general, meanwhile, was most solicitous about the embattled province. He understood Oregon's problems and he regretted California's inability to pay its share of the interest on the old California Province debt, which was in the form of mortgages on property in the north. The general wanted to commend Father John Fox at Hooper Bay in Alaska, for establishing "the Sisters of Our Lady of the Snow," an Eskimo sisterhood.[66]

There had been some criticism of the Jesuits for not developing a native clergy in Alaska and elsewhere—China, for example. None of the critics had ever been to Alaska or China; nonetheless, their criticism had a certain validity, and it was widely accepted. It was common knowledge that Pius XI, "the Pope of the Missions," strongly favored a native clergy wherever possible.

Until this time there had been only one Eskimo Jesuit whose tragic experience discouraged others.† Joseph Prince had been baptized as a child by a Russian Orthodox priest,

---

*Kateri Tekakwitha was born at Auriesville, New York, in 1656. She died at Caughnawaga, Canada in 1680 after a life of heroic virtue. Pius XII declared her "Venerable" in 1943 and John Paul II beatified her on June 22, 1980. See Provincial Archives, Portland, First Provincial Congregation, 1933.

†There is a brief biography of Brother Prince in print: *Out of the Northland*, (New York, 1931), by Arthur D. Spearman, S.J.

but later, when he was ten years old, he met Father Ruppert in Nome and he asked to be received into the Catholic Church. Ruppert, with his parents' permission, sent him to Holy Cross Mission for an education.

At Holy Cross Joseph became strong and attached to his religion. When he was nineteen-years-old, in 1928, he asked the superior Father Philip Delon, if he could become a Jesuit, like Brother Paquin, whom he had known and admired at St. Michael's. Delon said to him: "I will take you to visit your parents at St. Michael's. You must tell them what you wish to do and see how you can stand a long separation from them. If you still wish to go, I will take you to Seattle."[67]

Joseph agreed. He spent three happy days with his parents in their igloo on the Bering Sea. They were not Catholics and could not understand his decision to leave them. The hour came for him to leave. His mother clung to him. "Joseph," she screamed, as he stepped on the runners of the sled. "Come back! Stay with us!" Full of anguish, with his Mother's cries in his ears, he left her. He never saw her again.

For six months Joseph lived at Manresa Hall, Port Townsend to fulfill the canonical requirement called postulancy. Then on December 20, 1928, he arrived at Los Gatos to begin his novitiate. He was very happy, but he was cold all the time, even in the summer. Huddled in blankets he slept by the furnace. During the winter of 1929 he suffered a lingering attack of influenza, which soon developed into tuberculosis. He was sent back to Port Townsend with the hopes of improvement, and then to the sisters' hospital at St. Ignatius, Montana, where it was thought the mountain air could help him. Instead his condition got worse.

In December, he received news of his family. They had all become Catholics. Father Sifton wrote: "The grace, I believe, came to them in no small measure through your prayers and your immolation to God."[68]

When death appeared to be close, Fitzgerald sent instruction that Joseph should be allowed to pronounce his vows as a Jesuit. At ten minutes to nine on the evening of January 6, 1931, Joseph, in a feeble voice, repeated the holy words. The next day he died. He was buried at St. Ignatius Mission, near the graves of the old missionaries. It would be many years before another Eskimo would become a Jesuit, though the example of Joseph Prince was an inspiration for all.

Father Fox's experiment with his native sisterhood had the approval of Bishop Crimont. It appeared to be successful, so Father Fox established a similar congregation of men.* This did not work out, however, and the plan was quietly dropped. The sisters, too, were eventually disbanded. There were some who said that the project was premature. Perhaps it was. But when these sisters were gone there was a kind of emptiness in the Alaskan Church, and no one felt it more keenly than Father John Fox.

In August 1933, the Oregon Provincial was back on his favorite subject, poverty:

"On July 10," he wrote to superiors of the province, "the Sheridan Novitiate was mortgaged to satisfy the claims of our creditors who had not received complete compensation for work on and materials for the new building, and were about to file liens on the building. "On July 15, the First National Bank of Portland threatened legal action to recover $10,000.00 which was borrowed by the Pioneer Educational Society to purchase the neces-

*Father Fox had about five brothers in his little congregation. These were sent to his mission stations as "prayer leaders" during Fox's absence. They were suppressed by Fitzgerald after he became the bishop of Alaska. If they were regarded as premature, they were also the forerunners of the current deacon program. See *Jesuit Seminary News*, III, 5 (September, 1934), p. 1.

saries of life for our Province houses. These are only some of our financial difficulties.

"The big problem that is facing our Province now, is whether we can still continue to operate our three Province houses, Mount St. Michael's, Port Townsend, and the Sheridan Novitiate. We are facing the alternative of being forced to send home our Novices, or of raising enough money to support the Province houses. At present it costs the Province $6,000.00 per month to buy the necessaries of life for the Tertianship, Scholasticate, and Novitiate. The income to meet these expenses is less than $2,000.00 per month."[69]

According to Fitzgerald's estimate in this letter, it was costing the province about $20.00 per month to clothe, house, feed, and educate each Jesuit. This was scarcely high living on the hog, but it represented a deficit of almost $50,000 per year.

There was much talk on the streets about "prosperity around the corner" and some little joking about which corner and when would we find it. Though the Jesuits did not know it yet, the worst was over. It would be years before things would be normal, but the ugly threats of bankruptcy gradually faded away, except, perhaps, at Gonzaga. At Seattle College the rector, Father John McHugh, noted a healthy improvement. There were some who said from what? The Jesuit faculty of seven members were still commuting daily from the Seattle Prep residence,* sharing one old car, which was always somewhere else, when it was needed. Most ended up walking home each night, several monotonous miles, often in the rain.

But the sweet fragrance of progress was in the air. The college had become coeducational in fact, if not in theory, when students were accepted for the fall term 1933.† It has been generally admitted, since it is not regarded as morally reprehensible, that this school's struggle to admit women students on the undergraduate level, has influenced Catholic education and the cause of women's equality for a long time to come, perhaps forever. This is strong language.‡ The sequence of events at Seattle College, however, will demonstrate how intransigent the opposition to coeducation was and how chauvenistic some members of the Church could be.

Fitzgerald bore this shocking innovation with silence, which was interpreted favorably, putting him on the good side of the dispute. He bragged to Rome how well Seattle College was doing, without revealing why, and then proceeded to other matters like Father McGoldrick's conquests at the University of Washington. McGoldrick had recently been awarded his doctorate and was now occupied with the formalities of placing Seattle College before the public and acquiring accreditation for the school. The College library was in a lamentable state, so McGoldrick started there. He advertised for donations of books and the first one he received was from his old friend at Manresa Hall, Father Peter Halpin. The name of the book was: *The Diseases of the Horse.***

In October, Fitzgerald reported to Father Mattern that Judge D'Arcy had died on the sixth, some weeks after he was reconciled to the church. Father Patrick O'Reilly, with Fitzgerald and a Benedictine as assistants, celebrated a Solemn High Requiem Mass, which was sung by the Juniors' choir.[70] O'Reilly preached also, "a splendid sermon," said Fitzgerald, and six Juniors in cassocks were pall bearers. The church in Salem was crowded

---

*The high school division of Seattle College was officially designated as Seattle Preparatory School on December 7, 1933.

†One hundred freshmen were registered that fall term which opened on September 25. OPA, Seattle University Papers, Diaries, September 25, 1933.

‡Seattle College's struggle and final status as coeducational influenced almost every Jesuit College and University in the United States.

**Interview with James McGoldrick, S.J., July 6, 1981.

with non-Catholics who had never witnessed such a Roman spectacle in their lives.

There were rumors now that Father William Dunne, rector of the Novitiate at Los Gatos, had found a new site for a Theologate which had suitable land, also, for vineyards. Now that President Roosevelt and his rubber stamp Congress had lifted Prohibition, the wine business was profitable again. Father Maher, still under pressure from Oregon, was taking a second look at Dunne's discovery.

In April 1934, Father Maher wrote to Piet: "Doubtless the news has reached you ere this of the purchase of the Tevis property for the Theologate and of the decision to begin theology there next September. Many motives prompted us to take this action, most potent of all being the impossibility of doing any building at Santa Barbara just now, the uncertainty of the oil situation there."[71] Richfield Oil Company had purchased an oil lease on the property for $50,000 some years prior to this. Maher was rather apologetic to Piet for departing from the original plans for the use of the property.

"We secured the estate of 1000 acres," he added, with 200 more to come when a retainer passes away, together with building for $75,000, most of which money came to us by way of the insurance on the wine at the Novitiate when the winery burned. We will have to erect some private rooms; but the present building will readily care for refectory, chapel, professors' rooms, etc."

This letter ended with "What shall we call it?" and Piet responded by saying, "I am delighted, of course, that you will start a theologate in September in California." He did not want to suggest a name, as that would be determined by Maher and his consultors.[72]

On May 30, Maher dispatched a letter to the California province announcing the theologate's name. "It was decided," he said, "to name the theologate ALMA COLLEGE, whose post office address is Alma, California. "In dedicating the theologate to St. Joseph, we are not unmindful of Joseph Giroux, the great benefactor of the Society, whose connection with the Santa Barbara site is so well known to all."[73]

To some, perhaps, the reference to Giroux smacked of self-righteousness in the wake of the prolonged controversy. Maher, whatever his faults, was incapable of this. The fact is he was too outspoken, a kind of not-so-benevolent czar, who could dramatize his orders with such ferocious expressions that no one dared cross him. There was nothing subtle about him. This is one reason why he was regarded as one of America's greatest preachers.

Bishop O'Dea had died on Christmas Day, 1932, and his successor, Bishop Gerald Shaughnessy, a Marist priest who kept a well-clipped beard, which he sometimes stroked, was appointed to the see of Seattle on July 1, 1933. Consecrated, or as they say today "ordained" bishop on September 19, in Washington, D.C., he was installed by Archbishop Howard on October 10. Fitzgerald attended the installation ceremonies, but it was some months before he was able to have a leisurely discourse with him to determine his pleasure in matters of mutual concern. The new bishop, he reported to the general, was pleased to see him, but he raised many objections about the Jesuits' schools. Bellarmine in Tacoma, for example, was too close to St. Martin's in Olympia, threatening the Benedictine's school there. On the other hand, the Jesuits had not established a Catholic college in Tacoma, where it was badly needed. His Excellency, apparently, did not see any conflict of Benedictine interests here, though a Jesuit College in Tacoma would be a greater threat than Bellarmine.[74]

Coeducation at Seattle College was brought up. Shaughnessy belonged to the old school, like Zacheus Maher and the general, and Fitzgerald responded to his question about it at great length, as much for the general's ear as for the bishop's. Following McGoldrick's line of argument and using his carefully defined distinctions, Fitzgerald wrote: "I explained that in our regular College classes, there is no co-education, but that in the School of Extension both men and women are admitted to the classes which are held during the afternoon and the evening. The reason why women are admitted to these classes, is the great need of Catholic education for those who take up the profession of nursing, school teachers and the like. Besides, over fifty Sisters of various sisterhoods of Seattle come to the College classes."

The "afternoon and evening classes in the School of Extension" bit seems to have mollified the bishop and most other critics of co-education. What they did not know could not hurt them. But the truth is McGoldrick's "afternoon" began at ten o'clock in the morning, and classes following this were carefully designed for full attendance by women, who were in "the School of Extension." This technicality, adopted somewhat reluctantly, was nonetheless worthy of a Roman moral theologian.

One remark made by the bishop vis-à-vis Fitzgerald, alarmed the latter who quoted it verbatim twice. "I do not know," the bishop said, "whether Seattle College will solve the problem of Catholic education in Seattle or not." Fitzgerald saw in this a subtle threat, a kind of peek into the bishop's schemes for another Catholic college if Seattle College did not develop more rapidly. Significantly, Fitzgerald noted in his letter that the bishop "will not go out of his way to help us in our work," but if the Jesuits did not make progress, he would "cast them aside and take another Order."[75]

At the end of April, 1935, McGoldrick himself wrote to Father General in support of "the Extension School." He commented at length on Shaughnessy's expressed approval of the program and of Seattle College in general and pointed out that until the bishop succeeded in getting a college exclusively for women, Seattle College was providing "*indispensable* aid to the diocese." McGoldrick's was a desperate plea with the general to allow the college to pursue the only course that would permit it to survive.* No one knew that better than he, and no one struggled more valiantly than he to save Seattle College at the final turning point of its history.

McGoldrick's letter failed to convince Ledochowski, but the latter was willing, at least, to wait and see. Thus matters stood when Father Zacheus Maher was appointed as the general's assistant for America, which was, in practice at least, the most influential American Jesuit in Rome—the advisor to the general on American affairs, including higher education.† The importance of this development in terms of survival for Seattle College was not lost on Oregon Jesuits. If the future looked black, when Maher's appointment became public, it was because most Jesuits underestimated James McGoldrick. The year and the appointment were only beginnings and when the smoke of battle cleared "the Extension School" was still there, more openly promoted now as "Co-educational." By this time, to Maher's dismay, it was an accepted practice in nearly every Jesuit College in the country.

Other events meanwhile were shaping the history of the young, still vulnerable Oregon Province. On May 11, 1934, by an act of the Board of Trustees, a School of Engineering was added to the existing faculties of Gonzaga University.[76] This step had not been unexpected, for Gonzaga had introduced a pre-engineering course of two years in 1920. The time was now opportune for establishing the school, since the region was humming with dam-building activity that indicated its future as the center of a vast hydro-electric system. This would demand surveyors, bridge-builders, construction engineers, and electrical engineers.

All that was required at Gonzaga, besides money, was a catalyst, someone to acceler-

---

*See Copy of McGoldrick's letter to Ledochowski, April 29, 1935, Provincial Archives, Portland. McGoldrick was convinced then and still is that without coeducation Seattle College would have been forced to close. Interview July 6, 1981.

†Zacheus Maher became the Assistant for America on September 14, 1935.

ate the course of events for bringing the matter to a decision. Precisely when construction on Coulee Dam was begun this catalyst appeared in the person of Edmund McNulty, a gifted Jesuit scholastic who was attached to the teaching staff at the Mount. McNulty also taught physics at Gonzaga, where he had organized a group of students for the construction of an elaborate electric machine.

McNulty's own enthusiasm was contagious. Even the university's heavily burdened president, Father John Keep, felt its influence. When McNulty proposed the school in the early spring of 1934, Keep's reaction was favorable, though he was greatly concerned about the amount of money required to establish it. McNulty reassured him that the costs would be minimal and that equipment would be gathered at the expense of local business men. Keep was wary. While McNulty continued to urge the matter, Keep referred it to Portland, where Fitzgerald supported it.

Keep at this time was worried over debts and over-worked for lack of an adequate staff. He became ill and spent periodic sessions in the hospital. He returned from the hospital, however, long enough to conduct a meeting of the Trustees, during which McNulty submitted arguments for his proposal. The Trustees approved the plan and so advised the president, with whom the final decision rested. His decision was favorable and on May 8, 1934, *The Gonzaga Bulletin* announced the innovation with a banner headline. This was the first really big news that the student paper had carried in three lean years.

Though student and civic reaction was very enthusiastic, Keep began to regret his decision. During the summer he insisted so strongly on retaining liberal arts courses for majors in engineering that the required professional training could not be provided. Father Dillon, currently a member of the Gonzaga staff, jumped into the fray to rescue it from financial disaster. An uncommonly practical man, as his previous record had indicated, Dillon strongly favored the school. Because of his efforts the required courses in engineering were introduced in September according to schedule.

At last, after so many vicissitudes, the school registered thirty-one students on September 3, 1934. Four days later the first classes in the new school were conducted in the administration building. The weather that week was extremely warm. On Friday, September 7, after a hot, muggy day, rain fell and cooled the air. By September 16, when the new Jesuit professor of sociology, Leo Robinson, arrived from St. Louis, the weather was actually chilly.

The air in the president's office was chilly also, when a bill for some of McNulty's new engineering equipment arrived. The bill which contracted for several electrical meters totaled thirty-two dollars. Keep was alarmed. He summoned McNulty, questioned him about the alleged extravagances and dismissed him with a caution that he must be less extravagant in the future. In retrospect, the incident, which reveals Keep's vigilance over the university's frugal treasure, is almost humorous. It was not funny, however, in September 1934, when the engineering school's founder realized the extent of his resources, short of literally begging for everything he would need.

During that autumn, Keep, in a state of total collapse, was taken to the hospital again where he hovered between life and death for weeks. Dillon, who replaced him as vice-rector, was prepared to make any sacrifice to keep the school of engineering in operation. He greatly encouraged McNulty in his labors, and when a visiting member of the Jesuit Educational Association suggested that the school should be discontinued, Dillon firmly refused. With a touch of fierceness, like a desperate warrior defending a fort, he protested that the school would not be closed under any circumstances. Thus he saved what McNulty founded.*

*As noted previously, Gonzaga's engineering building is called Dillon Hall.

One consequence of this was not predicted: the founding of the School of Engineering was one of two identifiable events which saved the university from certain bankruptcy. Spokane's support, substantially withheld until then, gradually began to make itself felt. In time it became an effective factor in the university's financial stability and growth.

A second consequence appeared later. Father Robinson succeeded to the president's chair on December 27, 1935. He spent the first day in office with Father Dillon. "We are bankrupt," Dillon told him, "Let us be honest. We should take down our shingle, close our doors and pay off our creditors as well as we can." This was the doughty Marylander speaking, Francis Dillon, who had battled for Gonzaga for more than two decades. He could see no way to pay off the infamous Gonzaga bonds.

Many other famous schools gave up during the depression years. They had closed their doors and paid off creditors, as Dillon suggested. St. Mary's College in Kansas, immortalized in the books by Father Finn, had been a victim of the depression and lack of public support. Perhaps Gonzaga could do the same, go down into history as another martyr-college, a witness to the grave injustices of the American school support system.

The bonds had been due on March 1, 1935. With the interest they represented an immediate liability of $335,500, with an additional $143,000 with interest due later. For years the school's operations had shown deficits. In 1932, for example, there was a total loss of $66,514.95. In June of the following year, the assistant treasurer, Harold Wagner, whose services to Gonzaga were beyond reckoning, reported an overall loss of $38,200.92. This was some improvement, like a condemned man being told he would not lose his head but only his ears. At the end of the following year, mostly because of the government's student aid program, the total operating loss was only $9,577.52.[77]

Robinson's appeals to Fitzgerald were fruitless, since the province itself was still floundering financially. In September, 1935, Fitzgerald reported to the General that the Oregon Province was falling behind at the rate of $4,000 a month.[78] The California Province, he said, still owed Oregon over $150,000, but was unable to pay even the interest on it.* "God's will be done," said Fitzgerald piously at the end of his letter. Only God Himself could liquidate the fiscal embroglio in which the Oregon Jesuits had found themselves since becoming a vice-province.

Fitzgerald did not have the gift of prophecy, and for him the struggle would never end. He plodded along, concealing his anxieties behind spontaneous Irish laughter, revealing his true feelings only to those, who like himself, were responsible for the welfare of the province.

He saw during these last years of office many of "the Mountaineers" die. Old Father Rebmann, Gonzaga's first president, died peacefully in Spokane on November 5, 1935. He was eighty-four in years. Not so old was Father Tom Meagher, the novice master, who died on March 16, 1936 in Portland. He was only sixty-seven, still in the saddle and deeply loved by everyone who knew him.

Another old-timer to go was Brother Peter Janssen, and with him many amusing anecdotes about his performance as the Mount's telephone receptionist. Janssens was eighty-eight when he left his post for the last time. He died on November 26, 1936.

Finally one of Alaska's most distinguished missionaries, Father John Lucchesi, whose heroic deeds during the great epidemic on the Yukon have been revealed by Alma Savage in *Dogsled Apostles,* died on November 30, 1937.[79] Born to Italian nobility, Lucchesi had renounced great honor and wealth to serve the poor in Alaska for thirty-nine years. "To his holiness and to his extraordinary talents for the job of Superior," wrote Father Llorente,

*The exact amount of the debt was $153,014.26. The last payment on this debt to Oregon was paid off by California on May 8, 1952.

"we must add his indefatigability on the trail, forever running ahead of his dogs breaking trail for them.Today we shudder when we are told that he used to row from Nulato to Akulurak. He suffered much in his last five years from a hernia and a suffocating asthma that brought him many times to the point of death . . . I annointed him once at night. Next morning he got up and ate five hot cakes for breakfast."[80]

The final word on Father Fitzgerald as Oregon's first Provincial was composed by himself. Ignoring his own worries about money, in a gallant gesture of appreciation, "since the Society of Jesus is deeply indebted," he presented a valuable block of land to the sisters of the Holy Names for their new Normal School.

"For this purpose," he wrote Mother Francis Xavier, the Provincial Superior, "we should like to offer the block of property which lies across the street from the Orphanage, as a gift to help you in your work. Moreover, the Oregon Province has paid in taxes and street assessments about $16,000 during the period of ownership. The only amount that we ask to be paid us is $6,000.00. The entire block and the $10,000.00 in taxes we would consider as our contribution to your noble work."[81]

Three weeks later, on November 21, 1938, Father William Elliott succeeded Walter Fitzgerald as Provincial of the Oregon Province.

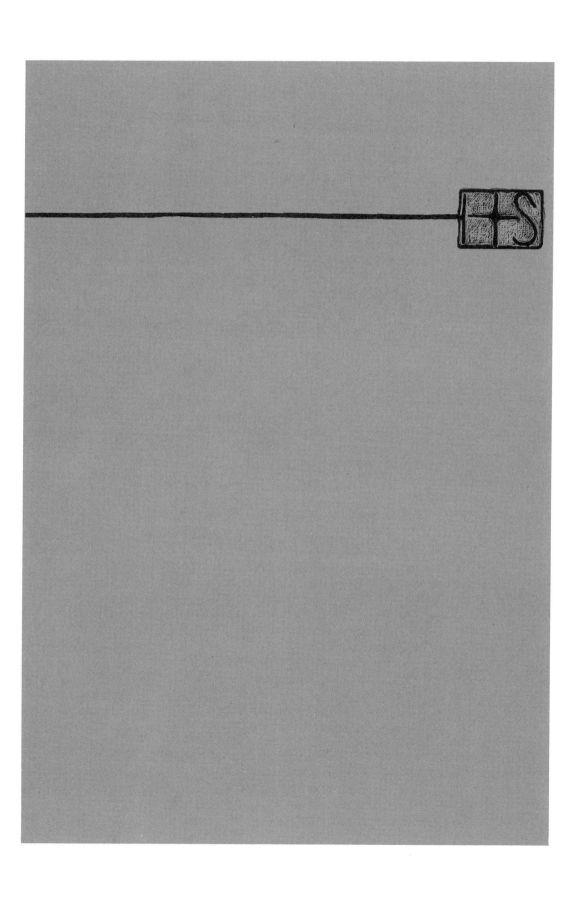

Bronze statue of Christ the King on King Island, between Siberia and Alaska, an emblem of peace between the two hemispheres. This was erected by Father Bernard Hubbard and his assistants.

Province delegates to General Congregation in Rome, 1946. Left to right: Leo Martin, noted as tertian instructor; Leopold Robinson, third provincial of the Oregon Province and provincial at the time; and William Elliott, second provincial of the Oregon Province.

The Liberal Arts Building at Seattle University. This building, constructed when Frank Corkery was president, was the university's first major building.

John Kelley, seventh provincial of the Oregon Province

Holy Family Mission, Montana, 1981.

18

ELLIOTT'S SURVIVAL SKILL
1938–1942

William Gregory Elliott was one of a kind. Tall like Abe Lincoln and slim as a cedar sapling, his head tilted a little to the left as he walked quietly about his business, and like a young curate, he was eager to serve. His dark, almost black eyes, contained a soft glow of sadness. One noticed them first. They might have been the eyes of a French mystic who possessed the virtue of reading souls.

Elliott had such a full head of black hair that his face, by contrast, appeared to be thin, like his neck and arms. Had he been twenty years younger, he might have been a basketball star, but he was in his early forties now, not only in the prime of life but in the prime of his priesthood, an inspiring model for the young Jesuits he directed in the mundane business of the Novitiate. He was Father Minister at Sheridan, second in authority to the rector, Tom Martin. He supervised the care of the farm, the gathering and drying of the prunes and the more meticulous business of keeping the house clean and the kitchen supplied with food and dishes.

There seemed to be a problem about both. The food, no matter how great the supply, disappeared, like rice in India. And the dishes were broken at an alarming rate. The fact is that the novices who washed them, always in too much haste, dropped them sometimes a stack at a time, or ran into each other, breaking two stacks instead of one. It was once reported that the dish supply company regarded the Novitiate as its second best customer in the whole state. Only the mental hospital at Salem broke more dishes.

Father Minister accepted his novices and juniors as he found them. There was nothing more characteristic of him than his serene gentle acceptance of reality, including its limitations. In practice this indicated one obvious mannerism, his ever-present kindness. This was partly due, no doubt, to his broad streak of compassion for the underdog, an inherited quality, I suspect, but honed to a singular perfection by personal suffering.

Though he appeared to be reticent about his ancestors, Father Elliott was too kind to ignore questions about them. So he noted their identities in a detached fashion, revealing a modest pride in his origins, combined with the lofty detachment that leaves one knowing they are already in heaven.* Oddly enough his background was very much like his predecessor's, Walter Fitzgerald. Both were a youngest child in their families and both were reared on homesteads in isolated rural areas, the one in southeastern Washington, the

*Interview with Father Elliott, Portland, May 21, 1981.

other in western Montana. And like Zacheus Maher, who was a native Californian, they were the first native sons to administer the high office of provincial.

Elliott's father, George, was Irish American. His parents had come from Bandon, County Cork. His mother, Jane Elliott, nee Amiraux, was French, and her mother's maiden name, Cyr, was an old one in the history of France. After their marriage in Helena, the Elliotts homesteaded near Potomac, Montana, a forlorn wilderness thirty miles east of Missoula, where William was born on October 24, 1895, the fourth child and last in the family. His two sisters had died before his birth and his brother Ralph was five years older than he.

In 1909, the younger Elliott was sent to Missoula for high school, two years in the public school, then two years with the Jesuits, after Loyola was established in 1911. Having graduated in 1913, he entered the Society at Los Gatos on September 7 of the same year. His novice master was Joseph Piet.

Seven years later the Provincial, Father Dillon, assigned Elliott to teaching in the high school division of Seattle College, which had recently been relocated on the Boulevard site. There, for three hectic years he threw himself into work with boys, for whom he had a special charisma, with such energetic abandon that his health was shattered.

"I wore myself out," he admitted later, "I corrected every paper I received. It was too much, with everything else. The third year almost killed me. That's when the headaches started. When I went to Rome for theology, I was dead tired. At Rome it was too much, new language, theology; I couldn't study."*

He left for Rome with a companion, Francis Altman, known mostly for certain eccentricities, which included a rather odd sense of humor. Altman, basically a very kind person, and a dedicated one, later became Gonzaga's eighteenth president. In Rome he kept a brotherly eye on Elliott, whose headaches did not cease even during siesta or the summer outings. Somehow Elliott managed to survive two years of the rigors of Rome. It had become obvious however, that a change would have to be made. Thus it happened that, with his somewhat enigmatic confrere, he was transferred to the theologate in Milltown Park, Ireland, where Elliott was ordained on July 31, 1927. He completed the long course in theology, a remarkable triumph for common sense, but he was unable to undertake the study required for the *Ad Gradum* examination.†

After making his tertianship at Manresa Hall, he became the Father Minister at the Mount, where his talents were put to the test. There were 107 scholastics at the Mount that year, some of them known to be mischievous. Most were very lively, imaginative young men, whose daily demands of the minister exceeded those in the rector's office. Father Tom alias "Kinky" Martin was still rector and when he left the Mount to be rector at Sheridan, he found Elliott there. The Novice Master, Tom Meagher, needed a new socius because Robinson had departed for St. Louis to earn a doctorate in sociology. Elliott, it was hoped, could serve as socius and recover from his illness in the more placid atmosphere of the novitiate.

No doubt the change was good for him. The gentle rolling hills surrounding the Yamhill Valley, like his own tranquil spirit, enclosed this little world and sheltered him from the harshness of the big city battle, in which he had been a casualty. Although his headaches remained, he grew stronger, and Fitzgerald, doubtlessly with higher goals in mind, appointed him minister of the community, keeping him as socius to the novice

---

Ibid.

†The *Ad Gradum* examination, a difficult ordeal for a healthy man, covered all of philosophy and theology, seven years' class matter. Those who did not take it, or did not pass it, could be "solemnly professed" later for other reasons.

master as well. He was now back to a very busy schedule. He was minister, procurator for an impoverished institution, socius to the novice master, prefect of health and director of reading at table, an examiner for candidates to the Society, writer of the house history and a house consultor.

One member of the community was Father Joseph Farrell, whose principal assignment was spiritual advisor to the juniors. "Father Farrell," the minister said to him one day, "I have to read the Litanies every night. You should read them once in awhile to spell me off."*

"Oh no," Farrell replied cheerlessly, "I can't. I get stiff in the joints at that time of the night."

Elliott's facetious reply and Farrell's indignation provide some humorous insights for both. "You shouldn't go to places like that," Elliott remarked, with a perfectly straight face.

In 1937, Elliott was replaced as socius by Father John Moffatt, a tertian, who had already garnered considerable fame for his devotional books, one of which, *Sanity of Sanctity*, had appeared as early as 1929 before Moffatt was ordained.[1] Moffatt succeeded Meagher in 1938 as novice master when Meagher died unexpectedly. The influence of Zacheus Maher appeared in this appointment, which was very controversial from the beginning.

It was common knowledge that the novice master and the minister held very different views on the formation of young Jesuits. Moffatt, raised very strictly by a widowed mother whose two sons became priests and three daughters nuns, was rigid and often coldly aloof. He had favorites under the mistaken theory that this was required for the formation of leadership. He was severe on others as well as on himself. On one point especially he disagreed with Elliott: the place of sports in the lives of young Jesuits. Elliott who had suffered much from excessive work supported a reasonably strong program of athletic activity, including swimming. Mofatt firmly forbade all swimming in the Novitiate and repeatedly urged his novices to forgo swimming for the rest of their lives. For him, somehow, swimming appeared to be sensual. Most other forms of sports were barely tolerated. Moffatt himself was an ascetical, monkish man, and he expected his novices to be like himself. If Elliott calmly accepted each as he found him, sometimes being too tolerant, Moffatt went to the opposite extreme. He seemed to have a univocal concept of what a good Jesuit should be and he tried to force everyone into that mold. One of his own novices identified the fatal flaw: Father Moffatt, he said many years later, not only tried to provide guidance for the novice period, but he also tried to provide the kind of guidance, even in practical matters, that excluded later forms of directions. Thus Moffatt unintentionally prepared his novices for future misunderstandings with spiritual directors and superiors who had the advantage of knowing current circumstances. As a consequence of all this, Moffatt's novices were sometimes regarded as "stubborn."† On the other hand, superiors frequently praised "the New Legion" as Moffatt novices were sometimes called, not always with honor. In the upheaval of the 1960s, the New Legionaires accredited themselves well, and some of the credit for this should be given Father Moffatt.

One of Moffatt's novices was John Kelley, an outgoing young lad with many attractive qualities like Elliott's. He was the athletic type in a moderate sense, certainly not a feature to endear him to the novice master. He was conspicuously kind and open-hearted like Elliott, and like Elliott he was sometimes too honest for diplomacy or politics. Strange as it seems, here in the small world of the novitiate were two men remarkably alike, yet so

*Litanies were a common prayer recited every night in Jesuit communities throughout the world.

†Interview with Father Charles Weiss, Spokane, December 21, 1981. Weiss attributed these observations to Father John P. Leary.

unlike a third that personality conflicts were inevitable. Kelley sensed the novice master's hostility toward him and feared the consequences. One suspects that Moffatt, subconsciously, of course, expressed the resentment he felt toward Elliott as his rival in the formation of the scholastics by making things difficult for Kelley.

This detailed account of Elliott's personality is useful, I think, for an understanding of the years that followed, years that left their mark on him and on the province. Despite his own, too modest opinion, it appears that he had been selected for important administrative posts long years before he was suddenly plucked from the bucolic serenity of Sheridan to undertake the provincial's duties in a very stormy period of the province's history. His own version of what happened is characteristically simple: "Zac wanted Robby [Robinson] for provincial but Robby was too young. He had me appointed for filling in the time until Robby was ready."*

Admirable self-effacement. Who would know more about it than Father Elliott? Only one person of course, Zacheus Maher, and there is no record of his opinion of the matter. We know, however, that there were scores of Jesuits in the province, any one of whom could have been useful "for filling in the time."

Old Brother Varaldi at Gonzaga had died that summer.† He had been the gardener as long as any one could remember, a silent, meek old man who loved the flocks of birds on the campus so much that they perched on his shoulders while he clipped the lawns and hedges. Varaldi, it was said, took a peculiar delight in writing letters to Father General, a harmless hobby that occasioned much amusement and a few anxieties.

Father Fitzgerald had not been amused by them mostly because the general did not find Varaldi's advice useful. Fitzgerald, at this time, was especially occupied with two important successions, his own successor as provincial and a bishop to succeed Crimont in Alaska. Both required formal *ternas;* that is, lists of three recommended candidates in the order of preference. Preparing a terna for provincial was relatively simple, but one for the bishop in a vicariate involved enough red tape to clothe a cardinal.

The subject of Crimont's successor was especially touchy, because the still feisty old Frenchman had no intention of resigning his vicariate. If a coadjutor were assigned, a most deplorable alternative for him, he wanted another Frenchman, and he was ill-disposed to accept anyone else. Under Ledochowski's specific directives, Fitzgerald had candidly addressed the matter by urging Crimont to resign. He was in his eightieth year, time Fitzgerald said, to take his rest.[2] Crimont, however, made it clear he was a bishop and he would die as the bishop. He refused to resign.

But Rome was adamant. Am American born coadjutor with the right of succession was to be appointed. Fitzgerald, accordingly, submitted two ternas to Rome during the late summer of 1938. In the autumn, as his term of office was nearing its end, everyone was wondering who would succeed him and where he would go. Though he suspected the answers to both, he would never know for sure until final word was received from the general.

Father Michael O'Malley, who had served his share of time in debt-ridden parishes, jokingly appealed to him for a new status. "As a last favor," he said, "Not much, just a nice *little* parish with nothing to build and no debt."

"If I knew of a place like that," said the Provincial, "I would go there myself."

November 20, 1938, was the last day for Fitzgerald as provincial. He suddenly experienced a massive hemorrhage, which some doctors believed, saved him from a fatal stroke.[3]

---

*Elliott interview, May 21, 1981.

†Aloysius Varaldi, S.J. died on July 28, 1938, in his 53rd year in the Society.

For years his blood pressure had been abnormally high. Fortunately he recovered quickly from this crisis, and on the following day, November 21, Father William Elliott was formally "read in" as the second provincial of the Oregon Province. With his baggage and his headaches he moved into the provincial's residence in Portland. A few days later Fitzgerald moved out. He went to Port Townsend "for a rest, as light-hearted as a bird."

Rumors were flying now that Fitzgerald was going to be named bishop. He dismissed them casually with one word, "Nonsense," but when he began to make his retreat just before Christmas, he had more on his mind than the *Spiritual Exercises*. On the third day he got the jolt he half-expected, a cable from Rome: "Congratulations my prayers assured. Ledochowski." So it would be Alaska.*

He had not long to wait for the public announcement. "New Bishop of Alaska," said *The Inland Catholic*, "To Be Consecrated Here Next Month."[4] Relations back in Peola, Washington were saying, "I told you so," and fellow Jesuits were claiming gifts of prophecy, too. Each had seen it coming a long time ago.

It did not take long for the bishop-elect to recover his poise and native wit. "I hope the mitre fits after all this hullabaloo," he wrote one of his clerical friends. And to another,"If at the consecration Mass the wine barrels for the offering are very heavy, I shall recommend that you handle one of them!"

Meanwhile the new Provincial, Father Elliott, got things humming for the consecration. Because Bishop White of Spokane had extended a most cordial invitation, offering his diocese for any need whatever, St. Aloysius Church, Spokane, was selected. Old Brother Broderick, often referred to as "the bishop of St. Al's," gave his "Placeat," which made it all "official," and other arrangements like printing and choir were concluded.

Of course, photographs had to be taken, especially a formal one. In this the bishop sits stiffly, just as the Titular Bishop of Tymbrias should sit, from behind his glasses the familiar bright eyes of Walter, prefect of Holy Angels' Sodality, shine out, softer now with a touch of sadness and perhaps reluctance to assume the new dignity. But the curve in the mouth is the same. There is the same alertness in the tense position of his hands and in the hunch of his shoulders. One expects him to jump up and offer his chair to the photographer.

By February 24, 1934, feast of St. Matthias, Apostle, everything was ready.† St. Aloysius Church was resplendent with lights and red tulips and even the dingy main building at Gonzaga looked brighter with some two hundred and fifty surpliced clergymen standing around, waiting for the signal. Bishop Crimont was radiant, too; the ice had preserved him. Perhaps it had preserved him just for this, the day his power of consecrating would manifest itself.

All Catholic Spokane was in a flutter, especially the convents. Though the day was a blustery one, crowds lined Boone Avenue from Gonzaga to the church to see the many bishops in all their splendor. Among the many bishops there were Spokane's Bishop White and Bishop Armstrong of Sacramento, who had been reared a block away and who had been consecrated in the same church. There were abbots, monsignori, Franciscans, Benedictines, Dominicans, Redemptorists, Servites, Holy Cross Fathers, Oblates, Sulpicians, and many, many Jesuits and diocesan priests. Archbishop Howard of Portland was there, too, last in the procession. The bishop-elect walked gravely; he already had the solemnity of a bishop if not the indelible character, and he kept his head down, so that no one could see what he was thinking.

*Elliott's appointment was dated November 1, 1938. He assumed office on November 21.

†Pope Pius XI had just died and earlier that morning funeral obsequies were conducted in his memory. The Altars were draped in black for the early Masses. By 10:00 A.M., when the Mass of the Consecration began, the church was completely transformed.

ELLIOTT'S SURVIVAL SKILL

For the Pacific Northwest the occasion was historic; it meant that the region had reached its majority. A large and influential hierarchy now marched in procession where so recently Indians had struck their wigwams and built campfires. In the span of the bishop-elect's life, Washington had passed from Indian Territory to Statehood, Spokane from an Indian village to a modern city, and Gonzaga from nothing at all to an important regional university. Bishop Fitzgerald was the first native-born son of the state to be elevated to the episcopacy. He had been associated with Gonzaga as a student, teacher, rector. As rector he had welcomed Bishop White to Spokane. As vice-provincial at Gonzaga he had organized a Jesuit Province. He had pioneered in more ways than one, and now the Northwest was pioneering with him.

The epic nature of the occasion was not lost on Bishop Crimont. He proudly used historic vestments and took care that all details concerning the same were duly publicized. The Pontifical and pectoral cross he used had once been Archbishop Segher's; the crozier, Cardinal Farley's which had been a gift from the Cardinal on his deathbed to Bishop Crimont. The bishop-elect's pectoral cross had been presented in 1873 to Archbishop Gross by Savannah's diocesan priests. From Archbishop Gross the jewel had passed down to Archbishop Christie of Portland, Oregon, who gave it to Bishop Crimont for his consecration in 1917. There was at least one element of modernity. The crozier Bishop Fitzgerald carried was brand new, a gift to him from Father Felix Geis, a diocesan priest from Lakeview, Oregon.* Bishop Fitzgerald had no other more intimate friend than Father Geis. They had been boys together at Gonzaga with "Smiling Bob" Armstrong, and the friendship of the three had strengthened over the years.

And so the historic procession streamed into St. Aloysius while the organ boomed. It was a little after ten, a few minutes late. The choir, nearly a hundred voices from the Mount and Gonzaga, sang as never before and the ceremonies went along smoothly. When the picture taking came at the end, everyone was laughing. Especially the new bishop.

That evening, in a rousing reception, the bishop met his friends, an army of them. Some had been boys under his supervision when he was teacher or rector. Some had been boys *with* him, and these had gay stories to tell. Dr. John O'Shea, who was responsible for the adage: "Everyone leaves his heart or his appendix at Mount St. Michael's," got up to say he had been present when the Gonzaga boys had tossed Walter into the Spokane River. Those *naughty* boys! (Loud laughter.) "That was forty-one years ago, when Walter was a slender, curly-haired boy." More laughter, and the Fitzgerald family, who were present, beamed with pleasure. The main speaker for the evening, Mr. Charles P. Moriarity of Seattle, got very serious. "Bishop Fitzgerald," he said, "labored in the vineyard of the Lord and as his burdens increased the same gentle spirit of the humble Jesuit characterized his every act." And then he went on to talk about the war brewing in Europe's dark cauldron and about men who, more than ever, were looking to the message of the Church.

On the surface, at least, the succession of these events was thought to be glorious. But there had been two carefully kept secrets about the new bishop and the very few who were aware of their nature had reason to be worried. In the first place, contrary to appearances, Fitzgerald's health was precarious and it would not be long before it became a subject of an immense amount of correspondence between Juneau and Rome. He had suffered one massive hemorrhage, a grave matter which had been discretely withheld from the public; arterial sclerosis was already beginning to appear in the patient.

This was bad enough. The second problem, involving Crimont, aggravated the situation rather than relieved it. Deeply disappointed in the selection of his coadjutor, Crimont

---

*Felix Geis had been a Jesuit scholastic who changed his status to be a brother, and then left the Jesuit Order. Cataldo encouraged him to be a secular priest. He was ordained for the Diocese of Baker City in 1920, and remained a close friend of the Jesuits all his life.

could not bring himself to accept Fitzgerald graciously at Juneau. Totally out of character, he received his coadjutor coldly, gave him directions that appear to have been harsh, and assigned him to the unpleasant task of begging in order to dig the vicariate out of debt.[5] It is to Fitzgerald's everlasting credit that he kept all this to himself, though he was profoundly hurt. Tensions thus created tended to accelerate Fitzgerald's deterioration. Hence the administration of the Church in Alaska, instead of acquiring continuity, got an almost irremovable, slowly dying bishop who outlived eighty-two year old Crimont by less than two anguish-filled years.

Fortunately the new provincial was spared the knowledge of these dour developments. He had a generous assortment of problems of his own to cope with, not the least of these being debts. "You are undertaking the government of the Province," Zacheus Maher wrote to Elliott from Rome, "at a critical time; but you should know, for your own encouragement, that you have the confidence of the Province, and this is a tremendous asset."[6] It was an asset that Maher himself soon overlooked. "Rumors," he continued, "claim that Father Dillon, for whom I have the highest respect, is running the Province." "Do not worry," he added, "he is not running the Province."*

If Maher's reference to the "rumors" about Dillon had surprised Elliott, they certainly did not alarm him. Only a few regretted Dillon's influence, which had been very great in Fitzgerald's administration. Elliott's official consultors were Tom Martin, rector at Sheridan, Frank Corkery, president of Seattle College, Robinson, president of Gonzaga University, and John Dougherty, the provincial's socius who had been appointed by Fitzgerald. Two new officials appeared on Elliott's roster: Leo Martin, who was also rector at the Mount, was now the "Director of the Jesuit Seminarian Aid" and John Keep was "Prefect of Studies of the Province." Keep was still convalescing, after two years, from his close scrape with death, so one can judge how seriously this office was taken at first.

And where was Dillon? As usual poor Dillon was trying to bail out a sinking ship. All he had was a leaky bucket, so his cause was doomed before he started. Specifically he was superior of Holy Family Mission in Montana, which was so close to bankruptcy the creditors had already taken legal action. His was the unpleasant task of presiding over the final solution to the stickiest mess in the history of the Oregon Province. Called "the Holy Family Mission Case" it involved litigation for several years and helped to tarnish in the eyes of many, the good name of the Jesuit missionaries who had nearly starved and frozen to death for a half century.

On October 27, 1938, several weeks before his departure from the provincial's office, Fitzgerald composed a detailed report regarding this case for Father General. This was as follows:

"A serious financial problem has arisen at Holy Family Mission for which the Society may be held accountable. I have given Father Assistant all the information regarding the matter and I have received his advice as to what should be done.

"First of all, I shall give a short history of the difficulty. In the summer of 1936, Father Tennelly, Director of the Catholic Indian Bureau, visited Holy Family Mission with Father Provincial, and stated that on account of the large number of orphan and dependent Indian children on the Blackfoot reservation, the Federal government would approve of the use of Indian tribal funds, provided the Mission would improve the buildings and make them sanitary and habitable for the Indian children. The Superior of the Mission, Father John Prange, was asked to prepare plans for the necessary improvements. The Indian Council approved of using their Tribal funds for 50 children at $125.00 per year ($7,500.00) for the

*Dillon's influence as a fiscal conservative was very great, hence sometimes those who differed with him for their own reasons criticized him for "running the province."

first year with the promise of raising the number to 80 children if the Mission could properly care for them. At once the boys' building was renovated at a cost of $8,000.00. Next the plan to renovate the Sisters' and girls' building was considered. More extensive repairs would have to be made here as these buildings housed the service building, i.e. kitchen, laundry &. The Superior of the Mission, who had done quite well in renovating the boys' building, began to prepare plans for the new building. Since the properties and buildings of this Mission belonged to the Catholic Indian Bureau and since the Bishops of the Diocese of Helena had taken a direct administration of the Mission (similar in the manner in which Parishes are administered by a Bishop), the Jesuit Provincial wrote to the Superior of the Mission, when asked about a loan of money to be made for this plan, (copies of this letter were sent to the Director of the Catholic Indian Bureau and to the Bishop of the Diocese of Helena), that since the Society owned nothing at the Mission, the Province of Oregon would not be obligated by any indebtedness, and the Superior was warned to make no indebtedness without the formal approbation of the Bishop. This the Superior carried out. In May 1938, when the repair work was completed and a new church (for which funds were donated) erected, a total indebtedness of over $47,000.00 had been incurred. Things stood in this manner, when I returned from Rome on June 1, 1938, and I sent Father Dillon to report on the financial situation at the Mission. When Father Tennelly (Head of the Catholic Indian Bureau) came to the Province in July 1938 to visit the Indian Missions, I told him of the imminent danger which threatened to close this Mission for lack of funds to settle the obligations, and both of us with Fathers Dillon and J. Prange went to Helena to confer with Bishop Gilmore. This meeting was held July 17, 1938 at the Bishop's Residence. The bishop stated that he did not wish the Mission to be closed and that the Diocese of Helena would endorse the loan, if the Catholic Indian Bureau would make the loan in the east at a low rate of interest. The Superior of the Mission was advised to tell the creditors that in a short while a loan would be made and all the bills would be taken care of. On Father Tennelly's return to Washington, D.C., he approached the Chairman of the Board of Directors of the Catholic Indian Bureau, Cardinal Dougherty, concerning the loan. The Cardinal refused to have anything to do with the matter, as the Bureau was in no wise obligated. When Bishop Gilmore was told of this, he wrote to the Superior of the Mission that he did not consider the Diocese of Helena obligated to meet the indebtedness. These decisions left the Superior of the Mission in a very unpleasant position, viz. with many debts and no money to meet them. Owing to the fact that one of the creditors had begun a law suit to obtain payment, it seemed imminent that all the other creditors, about twelve, would do likewise, with the danger of selling out the Mission to obtain their payment. This would be a scandal to the Church, since it was evident that someone (either the Bishop, the Bureau or the Society) was obligated to meet the indebtedness. Hence, I determined to place the matter before the Apostolic Delegate and I went to Washington, D.C. First, I went to see Father Tennelly, who informed me that Cardinal Dougherty had already directed him to place the matter before the Delegate, which he had done. I went to see the Delegate the following day, September 20, and I presented a Memorandum of the position of the Society concerning the case. The Delegate told me that he had already made his decision, viz. that he had written to Cardinal Dougherty that the Catholic Indian Bureau should make the necessary loan of money and that the Bishop of the Diocese and the Jesuit Provincial should endorse it. He moreover stated that he believed that the Bishop of the Diocese was the responsible party, since he had authorized the local Superior to go ahead with the repairs of the buildings, but also the Jesuit Superior was responsible partly in as much as he had contracted an indebtedness in excess of what it should have been. I thought that the matter had been settled and I returned to the Province. A few days after my arrival home, I received a letter from the Apostolic Delegate announcing that he had received more information on the case, and had decided that neither the Catholic Indian Bureau nor the Bishop of the Diocese was obligated to take care of the indebtedness of the Mission. The reasons given in this letter for the decision were, first the Catholic Indian Bureau was not obligated because, although the properties belonged to the Bureau, it only held these properties in trust; then, the Bishop is not obligated since he exercised only a supervisory part as *Ordinarius Loci;* finally, the Jesuit Fathers are obligated since they have the canonical ownership of the Mission, though not the legal. After Consultation I wrote the Delegate that the Society had not the legal nor the canonical ownership of the Mission, since the bishop of the Diocese had exercised for years more than a supervisory direction of the Mission, a fact sustained by several acts of the Bishop. I have received no answer as yet from the Delegate. Copies of the letters have been given to Father Assistant, who was here when the matter was discussed. After Consultation I received a confidential letter from Father Tennelly in which he advised me to comply with the Delegate's advice and made the necessary loan to liquidate the Mission and afterwards to make an appeal. I have not answered this letter until I have a meeting of my Consultors in a few days. However, I did have a meeting of the Proc. of the Province, Father Sauer, Father Dillon, with Very Reverend Father Assistant a few days ago, and Father Dillon suggested that each of the parties concerned, viz. the Bishop, the Bureau and the Society, would share the indebtedness. I am placing this before my Consultors and if they approve, I shall make the offer to the Delegate. Father Assistant approved of the compromise. I shall keep Your Paternity informed as to the outcome of the deal. . . ."[7]

This was the situation when father Elliott succeeded Fitzgerald. Elliott in a letter to Maher proposed a compromise on payment of the debt.[8] Assuming it to be $75,000 as estimated before all the chattels, that is motors, pumps, trucks, auto, grain, hay and so forth, were disposed of Elliott suggested that the province pay $35,000 and that the Catholic Indian Bureau and the Diocese of Helena split the balance at $20,000 each. This proposal was rejected. At any rate the proposal was premature because Elliott, who had been appointed, had not yet been read in as provincial. Besides, Elliott was to change his mind about a compromise.

During the following months, at Elliott's request, a complete survey of the Indian missions, their histories, debts and sources of revenue, was prepared by a committee under Dillon's supervision. According to this report, only one diocese out of seven in the Northwest, contributed anything at all to the Jesuit Missions.

"They [the bishops] leave the whole burden to us," the report states, "as though it were not part of their diocese as well.

"Much of this is our own fault. We have taken it for granted that the Indian problem is our own, not the Bishop's. We have never called on them for money to educate these children of the Diocese. We have too easily surrendered small parishes to them, and then taken these places back again too quickly.

"Except for the Bishop of Spokane, who has given approximately $1,000 a year for the past two years, none of the Bishops give anything to our Missions. They do give something to secular Priests engaged in the same work."[9]

The committee was shocked to learn that each of these seven dioceses had received approximately $5,000 in 1938 from the Board of Catholic Missions and from the Indian and Negro Collections throughout the United States. "Note well," the report continued, "these monies are given for the Missionary Bishops and their Dioceses [annually]. We get nothing for the Indian work."[10]

At Father Maher's request Taelman, the most professional of the missionaries, submitted a special "Report on the Present Status of Indian Missions." One paragraph in particular, sums up what was happening at Holy Family Mission and elsewhere:

"On the part of the Catholic education of the Indian children, the last 40 years have seen a steady diminishing and disappearing of our Mission boarding schools, which experience showed to be most important for the spiritual success of the Missions. Lack of financial help mostly forced the sad situation. That situation exists today more than ever, with no prospect for improvement, so that the boarding Mission schools, with a rare exception like at St. Ignatius, are doomed. For 40 years, there has been no help for the schools from the Federal Government. The contributions from the Catholic Indian Bureau have steadily diminished, being wholly insufficient for Boarding schools. Mother Catherine Drexel has withdrawn her help. And where, here or there, the Tribal Council of the Indians are giving some help, the future is unreliable, since these Councils are liable to change their mind and drop further appropriations. Unless a mission has unusual resources to practically support its own boarding school, it can no longer reasonably keep it up. Such is apparently the case with Holy Family Mission and with other Missions facing financial difficulties."[11]

Taelman took a parting shot at his Jesuit adversaries, who believed that it was a waste of time to learn Indian languages for use on contemporary missions.

"The sad fact," he said, "criticized by local Bishops, that for a number of years past, no Jesuit Father has been trained or made to learn the Flathead language, reveals a lack of proper interest in the spiritual welfare of the old Indians and the right administration of the Sacraments. There seems to be no justification for the said neglect."[12]

It sounded as though Joset's ghost were scolding from the grave.

Unresolved, the dilemma of Holy Family Mission was postponed until the beginning of the new school year in 1939. All Catholic support had been withdrawn. The Blackfeet Tribal Council decided "to allocate the sum of $5,000 to Holy Family pending settlement of Mission financial affairs."[13] This was only half of the funding required for opening school, and even this was dependent upon irredeemable conditions. Dillon expected the chattels to be seized before the end of November, and if this were not bad enough, he could get no word of help or direction from the bishops, though he tried repeatedly. "So in brief," Elliott wrote to Maher, the school has not opened. The Fathers, of course, are still there."[14]

At this point the Mission owed $57,682.40, not including interest, of which $24,387.01 was due to ecclesiastical or religious institutions. Until then the Chancery of the Diocese of Helena had insured the mission buildings for $85,540.00. The mission, by way of money, lacked even a dime, but $962.00 was due from certain funds. Elliott loaned Dillon $150.00 to provide food for the two Jesuits still in residence for maintaining services in the mission church.[15]

The closing scene of this sorry imbroglio was a dramatic one. His Eminence Cardinal Dougherty presided over it. Present were Archbishops Spellman and Curley, Bishop Gilmore of the Helena Diocese, Father Tennelly of the Catholic Indian Bureau, Father Zacheus Maher and representatives of the creditors. Though very tense the meeting was orderly, said Father Maher in his letter to Elliott. The Bureau was exonerated of any responsibility for the debt. After much discussion the blame was placed on Bishop Gilmore, who had given explicit permission for the expenditures, and on Father John Prange, the Jesuit superior, when the debts were incurred. Father Prange, in the mind of the board, was guilty "of mismanagement of large sums of money spent by him and his failure to keep accounts."[16] When the dust had settled it was agreed that "of the remaining indebtedness after the sale, the Bishop of Helena was to pay half and the Oregon Province the remaining half."

Elliott, typing on the train enroute to Alma, California, responded to the news contained in Maher's report. "Your letter about the settlement of the Holy Family situation has rather stunned us . . . but apparently it is over and we will be the first to obey."[17] To this

Maher replied: "I am so sorry that you are disappointed at the settlement arrived at with regard to the Holy Family Mission . . . by this agreement the Bureau will contribute the results of the sale, less costs, and the Bishop will pay the balance on a fifty-fifty basis with the Province."[18]

Regretfully this was not the end of the Holy Family Mission case. With the approval of higher superiors, Elliott withdrew the Jesuits still there in September, 1940, and for many years to come the odium of debt and closure was identified with the Jesuits and no one else. Father Egon Mallman, meanwhile, was assigned the care of Holy Family as a mission station from Heart Butte where, like a watchful eagle in his lofty nest, he had been in residence for over five years. His dedication to this difficult mission had already inspired the whole province. "You certainly describe a giant's work as being done by Father Mall-mal," Maher wrote to Elliott, "particularly in catechizing the children."[19] It could be said, perhaps, that Mallman's catechism classes were a poor substitute for what the Jesuits and the Ursulines had provided at Holy Family Mission for fifty years. His services, however, were the only ones available.

He described his program for the readers of *Jesuit Missions*: "My territory covers 1500 square miles, and I have about 1500 Catholic Indians and four whites. I say Mass at Heart Butte one Sunday, Holy Family the second, Little Badger the third, and Old Agency the fourth. But the schedule is upset in winter: last year I was snowed in 50 days, but had better luck this year. I have no schools but teach Catechism in 11 county schools once a week, and we have a vocation school financed by the Marquette League.

"I live in an extension to the old church. When I first arrived I had to shovel snow out of the house all winter. The second year the tempeature got to 54 below zero, and the chalice froze to my lips in the morning; but I have insulation now. Of course our places are old, and require unending repairs, which I have to do myself for there is just never enough money to hire labor. But the people ae good, God bless them; and are honestly glad to have a priest."[20]

This is where Mallman lived for forty years. A brilliant and scholarly priest, he no doubt found its isolation a hardship. He spoke a soft, very English kind of speech. It sounded refined and rich and summoned up faint images of English cathedrals and Ann Hathaway's thatched cottage beside an English hedge lane. His words appeared, at first, to be in strange contrast with the place where they were heard, like a professor's lecture in a tepee, but no one could doubt their sincerity and effectiveness.

In a sense Mallman's was the last word on the Holy Family Mission case. His successors on the reservation, inheriting the legacy of Imoda, Prando and Damiani, were no longer embarrassed by it. Mallman had long since demonstrated that the Jesuits, whatever their mistakes, have been steadfast in their loyalty to the Blackfeet Tribe as De Smet himself would have it.

The Jesuit committee report had noted that "we too easily surrendered small parishes to bishops." It would not be difficult to document this as a fact, though arguments could be introduced in favor of the alleged abuse involved. On September 2, 1939, for example, the day that Nazi Germany invaded Poland, Elliott wrote to Ledochowski that the bishop in Seattle wanted St. Ignatius Church back. Father John Hayes had been the pastor there, commuting from Seattle College. The bishop argued that "No college would be built there," as the Jesuits had once promised. Besides, the Jesuits had one parish already, St. Joseph's.*

*Provincial Archives, Portland, Elliott to Ledochowski, September 2, 1939. The Bishop never had St. Ignatius Parish, so it seems incongruous that he should have asked for it "back". The Jesuits had two other parishes in Seattle: St. Joseph's and Monte Vergine for the Italian people.

There were several oversights in this simplistic demand, but Father Maher, without quibbling, replied simply, "Give it to him."[21]

Nine days earlier, Maher had dispatched a letter to all Jesuits in the United States stating that because of the current war and Rome's isolation from America, the General had requested him to remain in the United States *with powers of Visitor for the Assistancy*. He added that he would establish his residence at St. Andrew's on the Hudson, that is at Poughkeepsie, next door to Roosevelt's Hyde Park.[22] In his own mind Maher was now acting general for America, though there is reason to believe he was partly mistaken in this.*

Elliott took Maher at his word. He felt compelled to report on another major dispute-in-the-making with the bishop of Helena. This concerned the unilateral decision of the bishop to require certain formalities of Jesuits before giving them the faculties of the diocese. In the course of time this rather arbitrary action of Bishop Gilmore became a celebrated case in Canon Law called "The Helena Promises." Elliott discribes the sequence of events which culminated in Gilmore's famous "Promises":

First, he admitted to Maher, there had been "unfriendly relations with the Bishop" following the closure of Holy Family Mission. Then he explained that sometimes members of the Gonzaga faculty gave retreats in the Helena Diocese and used these opportunities to seek football players and other students for the university. Gilmore demanded that hereafter any Jesuit coming to the diocese was required to report first to him in Helena and state his business in the diocese, before he could receive faculties. Elliott wrote to the bishop to point out the inconvenience and extra cost of this procedure, but the bishop did not reply. Finally a tertian father was sent to Missoula for helping in the parish during Lent. He contacted the Chancery in Helena to secure faculties and was told to report to Father Dennis Mead, the pastor of the diocesan parish in Missoula, who was also the head of the deanery. Prior to this the pastor of St. Francis Xavier's parish was the head of the deanery. The Jesuits had not been informed of the change. When the tertian father applied to Father Mead for faculties he was required to sign a statement from the bishop, whereby:

(1) he was required to profess the nature of his business in the diocese and the time he was to remain in it;
(2) he was not to sollicit students for any Jesuit Colleges;
(3) he was not to sollicit [or "rope in"] any members of the Helena Diocese for the Society, and he was to refer any who came to him to discuss vocation to his confessor or the Bishop; 4) failure on his part to live up to the conditions under which the faculties were granted means *ipso facto* their removal.†

This was only the beginning of the saga about the infamous "Promises." It was also a classic example of the kind of friction which existed between some bishops in the Northwest and the Jesuits at this period. Bishop White of Spokane was a notable exception. While he held his ground firmly as bishop, he was regarded as just and even supportive of Jesuit spiritual activities; for example, the Sodality of the Blessed Virgin Mary. Most bishops then barely tolerated the Jesuits and at least one seemed "to be a confirmed enemy of the Society of Jesus."‡ On the one hand, appeals by province superiors for help from

*It was subsequently stated that "Rome was appalled by the authority Father Maher exercised."

†Provincial Archives, Portland, Elliott to Maher, March 2, 1940. This is the first form of the so-called Promises. Later they were revised and made more simple, though their content remained substantially the same.

‡*Ibid.*, report to Rome, no date, but compiled about 1941. The bishop referred to was, of course, Gilmore.

Rome, in cases where there were obvious violations of Canon Law, were usually acknowledged with a "Don't rock the boat" response; on the other, Father Maher was critical of the province because there were difficulties. "You certainly have fallen heir to a pack of Canonical trouble," he wrote to Elliott by way of a greeting.[23] He never seemed to realize that Rome itself was part of the problem because of its failure, at times, to defend Jesuit rights "for the greater good elsewhere."

One should expect conflicts where honest men think and act differently; and all of them will never go away because there are honest men. However, in recent years these unpleasant exchanges, as common then as they are painful, seldom occur. Perhaps the Jesuits as well as bishops, have come to a deeper realization of their common cause.

On March 13, 1940, Elliott wrote to Maher again, this time about problems in the novitiate. Taking the bull by the horns, he presented a frank commentary on Moffatt, who, as has already been noted, was Maher's protege. Moffatt, he said, placed too much emphasis on externals. There seemed to be no difference between substantials and accidentals. His mannerisms grated on some, he added. He had told him not to allow novices to sleep on the floor or make holy hours at midnight.[24]

There was another matter also. The Provincial of the Holy Names Sisters had requested "college affiliation" with Gonzaga, since the academy could not grant degrees.

Maher, who was prompt in his correspondence, replied during the following week. He said that Father Robinson had already requested that Holy Names girls be allowed to attend science classes at Gonzaga.[25] He rejected both requests, indicating his continuing rigidity on the subject of coeducation.

He complained to Elliott about Seattle College's year book: "The whole book is so completely a girls' book that I wonder if the Editors have given a thought to how much pain it would cause His Paternity [the general] were it ever to reach him? Dances, dances, dances, girls' sports (by classes in badminton for girls in the Casey Courts?), basketball for girls, bowling for girls . . . all these in the name of Jesuit education, that these young ladies might have a Catholic philosophy of life." It was time, he added, that the Sisters opened a college in Seattle!*

One gets the impression that Elliott was determined to stay out of the fight. McGoldrick had skin thick enough for both and he was eager to expose it. If he had confounded Rome by bringing the girls in, there was no need for Portland to get them out. Fitzgerald had said, "I can't give permission, but I won't block you," and Robinson had recommended that Seattle College be transformed into a junior college. "Send the upper division students to Gonzaga," was his solution to the impasse between McGoldrick and Maher.[26] When the latter visited McGoldrick in his office, to make a final attempt to dislodge the coeds, McGoldrick snapped, "That's settled and I'm not reopening that question."

"Zac," McGoldrick said later, "became as quiet as a mouse."[27]

McGoldrick's introduction of lay professors caused another disturbance, especially with the bishop, who complained about "the irreligious staff" at Seattle College. "Let's go for a walk," said McGoldrick to the bishop. They walked and the bishop argued. McGoldrick presented his bellicose monologue in a brogue thick enough to confuse his Excellency and that was the end of the matter. They remained the best of friends.

The new president, Frank Corkery, like Elliott, allowed McGoldrick to take the heat. Corkery, scarcely out of tertianship, was the new "wonder boy" in education. If McGoldrick liked to fight, Corkery liked to make honeyed speeches, and he soon acquired fame for his sweetness and light, as well as support for a new building, which everyone demanded for an obvious reason: space. McGoldrick's aggressiveness had paid off; Seattle

*The exclamation point is Maher's.

College's enrollment in the fall of 1940 was "1400 students in all departments." Corkery commissioned a young, relatively unknown architect by the name of John Maloney to design a so-called Liberal Arts Building.

Elliott favored the project. However, he intended to spend the summer of 1940, making a visitation of the missions of Alaska. Bishop Crimont had brought up the subject of Father Bernard Hubbard, "The Glacier Priest," who was no longer welcome in many missions of the north. Some of the missionaries had complained to Crimont for years that Hubbard's lectures, presumably in support of the missions, had done more harm than good. People who used to support the mission, a little here and there, no longer sent this help, because, it was said, Father Hubbard's lectures took care of everything. The truth is the missions received little or nothing from Father Hubbard's lectures because there was no money left after his expenses were paid. Crimont, who had an old man's weakness for sturdy doers like Hubbard, wanted to give him another chance.[28] He assured Elliott that Hubbard's work "could take care of the Missions of King Island, Diomede, Kotzebue and Pilgrim Springs, by itself alone."*

Hubbard wanted Elliot's support, because Fitzgerald, influenced by the missionaries' reports, preferred to keep him out of Alaska. Father Maher, too, was unsympathetic, "adducing to me," said Hubbard, "that there are clouds on the horizon. Clouds never did bother me."[29]

Fitzgerald's views had been gathered first hand. In July after his consecration, he began an extensive tour of the missions and by autumn he had covered five-thousand frozen miles. He had visited thirty-seven missions and confirmed a total of 330 people. In October he was back in Spokane for the consecration of another Gonzaga alumnus, Bishop Condon of Great Falls. Then in Chicago for a bishops' meeting. Then Fairbanks again, where he generally laid the mitre when not traveling.

After a peek into his mail-box to retrieve what was there, he left for another tour of the missions. "I took the mail plane out of Fairbanks, connected with the Unalakleet mail plane, and then on to St. Michael's on Norton Sound. At St. Michael's Father Lonneux met me and I confirmed thirty-one in his church there. Next day we took a dog team to Stebbins, fifteen miles from St. Michael's, and I confirmed thirty more there. Then we took a long hike by dog team seventy-two miles to Chaneliak, where Father has a congregation of two hundred and fifty Eskimos. I had a good 'musher' and he pushed the dogs right along. We made this trip in ten hours flat. We skirted Bering Sea on the ice and then up the river to home base. At Chaneliak I confirmed forty more Eskimos. The Eskimos are a wonderfully fine people, patient, with great faith and devotion. The whole village came to Mass and Holy Communion for the week that I spent with them.

"Then a plane appeared over our village and whisked me away, back to McGrath, where I stopped overnight in a roadhouse. The next morning, Sunday, I left by plane for Fairbanks, fasting, hoping to get there by noon. But our plane ran out of gas and we had to make a forced landing on a river and await another plane from Fairbanks which answered our radio call for help. I began Mass at 1:45 p.m. . . . I am going to Kodiak (on the Aleutians) on tomorrow's train which connects with the boat at Seward."[30]

The bishop wrote this in April, 1940; in June he was in Los Angeles, begging. During July he made his retreat at Sheridan, and soon after he left for Eastern United States. More begging for Alaska. He talked and preached from any platform respectable enough for a bishop. He wrangled, cajoled, bargained. "By this time," he wrote, "I feel as though I could hold up a policeman and take his money."

---

*Provincial Archives, Portland, Crimont to Elliott. September 30, 1940. Crimont was rather naive in believing that Hubbard was going to get the money for this from Henry Ford "and other philanthropists."

He got to St. Paul in September and was ready to drop from exhaustion. "But," he says, "I spoke in St. Paul cathedral six times to nearly ten thousand people who attended Mass on that Sunday, and got a fine honorarium. That quickly restored my strength." He called himself "a peripatetic mendicant missionary," which had a fine ring to it, if no great dignity.

In his comings and goings he often stopped at Mount St. Michael's and regaled the Scholastics with an account of his wanderings. While he calmly smoked a big black cigar, pausing now and then to survey the ash on the end of it, he would describe the Eskimos, his favorite subject of conversation. And one of his favorite stories, he repeated it often, was about Eskimos kissing.

"I told the Eskimos," he would say, "that special indulgences were granted for kissing my bishop's ring. So they came up, one by one, and rubbed their noses on it—that's the way they kiss." A big Irish grin. "Now do you suppose they got the indulgence?"

"Did the bishop find his begging tours disagreeable?" a scholastic would ask.

"Well, now," he would answer, grinning from ear to ear, "I never thought I would live our rule so literally . . . beg from door to door, should need or occasion require it."

"How about life on the trail, did he find that difficult?"

"Remember when you were boys? No matter how hard it was you enjoyed camping trips. Well, I just pretend I'm on a camping trip, and the hardships are not so hard."

And then, without realizing he was paying himself a tribute, he would say, "Those men up there, they are the real heroes in that bleak and desolate land. They are spiritual giants and I feel very small when I meet them."

According to Crimont there were not enough "spiritual giants" up there and in his letters to Elliott he pleaded for more. On May 2, 1940, he wrote, "Do I understand rightly that sailing on the Alaska May 18, Your Reverence plans to stay with the boat until you reach Seward . . . .? Father McElmeel is to be replaced in Nome to be more free to attend to his duties as Superior in the North. Father Joseph McHugh would be in charge of Nome, and would have Fr. Thomas Cunningham's experience to initiate him in his work.

"If it is true that Father Lafortune does not leave King Island, and does not accompany the Islanders to Nome, Father Thomas Cunningham will take care of them during their stay in town. He now speaks their language very well.

"I was told by Fr. Fox that Father Sifton at Hooper Bay had a slight stroke recently. If he was to get worse, Father T. Cunningham should go there in the Fall to help Fr. Fox.*

"The remark regarding Fr. T. Cunningham having too small a field of work at Diomede for a man of youth and vigor, is certainly true, but it does not take account of all the results of his station at that place."[31]

This letter, only a part of which is quoted, not only reveals the kind of control the old bishop still held over the missions but also, more incongruously, the number of superiors to whom each missionary had to respond. There were two bishops, the provincial and the mission superior. Fortunately the missionaries were so isolated they were happy to see any of the four when they did appear—which was not often.

If Crimont had advice for Elliott's journey, Fitzgerald had more. On May 8, 1940, he typed out "Some Suggestions Concerning Father Provincial's Trip to the Alaska Missions." These filled a crowded page which included many homey details and ended as follows: "In your travels in Alaska, remember the story which Mr. Dave Brown told me in Spokane. He said, 'Father, you will have to change your notions as to time and space, when you get to Alaska. If you miss a boat on the Yukon, don't get excited. Sit down on the bank, light your pipe; another boat will be along in two weeks! Nuff said!"[32]

*Father John Sifton died suddenly at Hooper Bay, Alaska, on October 20, 1940, in his 52nd year in the Society.

ELLIOTT'S SURVIVAL SKILL

One cannot imagine Father Elliott sitting on the slimy bank of the Yukon, smoking a pipe. He survived his famous visitation though, and was back in Portland by September. A barrage of letters soon began to arrive from Zacheus Maher. He was at Yakima. "Birettas," he said indignantly, "should be worn at all meals." At Gonzaga the Fathers kept their birettas on hooks outside the dining room and wore them only when they had too. Goodness! Some Jesuits were getting lax.*

Maher had noticed that Arthur "Nate" Green was listed in the catalogue as a scholastic preparing for ordination. He did not think that Green should be ordained. Elliott replied that Bishop White spoke very highly of Green and wanted to ordain him.† Maher did not give up. "Father General authorized me to make the decision and that is, as I informed you orally, Green is not to be ordained."[33]

A week later Elliott dispatched a very polite, but spunky response to Maher. He reminded Maher that Father Mattern, Maher's predecessor as assistant to the General, had already approved of Mr. Green when he interviewed him at the time of his application to the Society in 1926.[34] By this time Maher was very exasperated. Green, he repeated, was not to be ordained. He should become a brother.[35] At this point Elliott reported that he was appealing the matter to the Vicar General. The province, he said, wanted Green ordained.

For "Nate" Green, Elliot's struggle on his behalf was not a trivial one. As for Elliott, Maher's clash over Green appeared to be less than gallant, perhaps even meddlesome. According to church law, after all, it was Elliott, the *ordinarius personalis*, who was designated to make the decision regarding a man's fitness for ordination. Elliott knew this and did not yield on the point. Green was eventually ordained, much to the chagrin of Maher, who by this time apparently had begun to regard Elliott in a less favorable light.

"The Oregon Province," he wrote sonorously, while the dispute raged, "is bristling with difficulties by reason of the multiplicity and variety of demands made upon it, by reason of the lack of manpower and of the material resources needed to properly carry on the various works of the Province itself. The spirit of the Province, however, merits great praise, for in spite of these difficulties, the Rectors particularly and many of the men are devoting the best efforts to master the various problems which must be faced."[36] He wrote also to say that the General wanted the Province to take on another job. He wanted Father Joseph Ledit to infiltrate Russia, which was at war, "to work with the dispersed Poles."[37] Later he added that Ledit, presently in Rome, was trying to find a method for sneaking into the forbidden land.

This was not Ledit's first godly assault on Communist Russia. He had managed to survive there for some years earlier, until he was discovered and incarcerated with famished rats which gnawed on his feet while he slept.‡

Father Elliott reported at the same time on progress at Seattle College. A plenipotentiary meeting had been assembled to discuss the new Liberal Arts Building. "Father Corkery, Rector of the College," he said, "made the following report on the financial situation:

"There is on hand at present $110,000.00 in cash. This represents the amount saved by

*The biretta was initially an academic hat worn by clerics as a symbol of their status. Jesuit priests and scholastics were expected to wear their birettas when they attended meals in the community refectory. The custom disappeared in the 1950s.

†Bishop White said to Elliott: "He is a wonderful little man." Green was very short, almost a dwarf and had a deformed back. His ordination was on June 3, 1943 and he died prematurely on December 3, 1955 at Bellingham, Washington.

‡Joseph Ledit had joined the Oregon Province originally to be a missionary in Alaska. His genius for languages, however, caused him to be assigned to the difficult Russian mission. When he returned to the Province after being a Russian prisoner he spoke to students of Gonzaga High School.

the Society over the period of the last few years (about $30,000) plus the returns from the present financial drive which is being carried on in Seattle for the benefit of the College. Included in this $110,000 is $10,000 of a gift of $40,000 provided by a certain Mrs. Hamback. The remaining $30,000 of her gift seems to be secured and with this there will be actually $140,000 available for construction. Moreover, this would still leave a deficit of at least $10,000, since the total construction cost of the entire building would be $150,000.

"Consequently, it was agreed upon that due to the want of sufficient funds only one half of the building including the central tower would be built at present; the remainder to be constructed when and if the remaining deficit should be supplied. This one half of the building and tower will cost approximately $130,000."[38]

Members of the College faculty were living in temporary frame buildings, mostly old houses acquired in the immediate neighborhood. This problem, too, had been addressed in the meeting and Father Corkery "was advised to look into the question of acquiring a suitable building. The Marne Hotel, a spacious and apparently satisfactory house nearby was mentioned and Father Corkery was asked to inquire into the possibilities of such a purchase."*

The required $150,000 was finally obtained and the architect was directed to construct the entire shell of the building, but to complete only one-half of the interior. While this was one of the greatest bargains in province history, cost over-runs brought the initial investment to $165,000. Maher was quick to complain to Elliott that Corkery had spent more than he was authorized to spend.[39] The new Liberal Arts Building was solemnly blessed by Bishop Shaughnessy on June 22, 1941. A vast building, larger in actual size than it appeared to be, it could accommodate at that time eleven hundred students. The old Garrand Building was renovated for use as a science building.

At Sheridan, meanwhile, there was an ugly crisis about water. Despite Piet's optimism and the normally heavy coastal rains, the lack of water had been a matter of grave concern from the very beginning. In the first year, for example, this entry appears in the House Diaries: "Due to lack of water there was no scullery." In other words, the novices could not wash the dishes that evening. The situation became more critical, and by September, 1939 it was necessary to haul water by truck from the town of Sheridan.[40]

Father Leo Gaffney, a tertian in 1938, had offered his services to Fitzgerald for finding a solution. "There was a lot of talk about it then," Gaffney explained, when he related his memories about it.[41] "There were hopes for wells and things, but the novitiate was dependent on reservoirs filled with rain water." After tertianship, Gaffney was assigned to Sheridan to teach Latin and French, but his principal job was to solve the water problem. He started prospecting on Bell Mountain, nine miles distant, where he found "lots of water, the sources of Rock Creek at an altitude high enough to bring by gravity all the water needed into the reservoirs without pumps."

He began his survey for the pipeline with the aid of juniors during the summer of 1940; then in September, with novices. The order of the day for the lucky novices went like this: Rise at 5:00 A.M. Meditation, then Mass at 6:30 A.M. Breakfast at 7:00 A.M. In the truck at 7:45 A.M. and on the pipeline at 8:30 A.M. All day in the hot sun, cutting brush, pulling the surveyor's chain along a steep mountainside covered with loose shale, with only apples and peanut-butter jelly sandwiches for lunch. The juice of the apples was all they had to quench their thirst. Brother Charles Spalding, an uncommonly pious old man who had to live in the guest house because he sang hymns all night in his sleep, in his loud, fervent Kentucky voice, drove Gaffney and his six-man crew to the site. He also drove them home,

---

*The Marne Hotel was formerly St. Rose Academy. Father Frank Logan, S.J. attended grade school there and later lived in the temporary residences at Seattle College while the Marne Hotel was discussed.

if he did not get lost while saying his rosary. On one historic occasion the crew had to walk nine miles home in the moonlight, carrying the surveying equipment, because Spaulding was saying his rosary, parked at the wrong place high on the mountain. He had been waiting for the crew to appear for five hours before he was discovered. For Gaffney this was bad enough, but Brother Costello's recitations of poetry irritated him even more. Costello always recited poetry when he became fatigued and light-headed.*

The Gaffney plan was ambitious, an eight inch steel pipeline for nine miles from the source, a waterfalls on Bell Mountain, to the Novitiate's "resevoir hill," where the storage tanks were in place. The water, plentiful in winter, "when we needed the heat," would be used for operating a hydro-electric generator to produce heat for the novitiate. God knows we could have used it! The huge concrete shell, heated by sliver-covered slabwood from the plywood mill at Willamina, was always cold in the winter. "There was also enough water to irrigate the Novitiate's eight hundred gumbo acres, and enough grass could be grown (the county agent predicted) to feed 120 head of cattle. Estimate cost? "Up to $100,000."

Where would the money come from? Gaffney's cousin Nellie had a large legacy left by her father. He wrote to her requesting a loan at a favorable rate of interest. There was great jubilation when she wired that she would lend the money. Jack D'Arcy heard about the project and he came to Sheridan to see the rector, Father Francis Gleeson. "What's this about a water project?" he asked. "What are you going to use for money, washers?" Later he told Gleeson: "If you can be sure of the project, I may be able to help you."

Gleeson took up the matter with Elliott to secure the required permissions. Elliott wrote to Maher on January 11, 1941, to brief him on developments.[42] There had been a meeting at the Mount, he said.† Father Gleeson made a report. According to this there was $39,000 on hand. The pipe would cost $28,000. That left $11,000 for labor, machinery rental, road making and whatever incidentals would be required. Another $800 would have to be paid for additional rights of ways. If we put the project out at contract, it would cost even more. Father Dillon thought that we lacked sufficient data for approving the project. Elliott had another objection: the future upkeep of the line. "The Sheridan Water Company," he said, "considers it necessary to patrol their line. How about costs for ours?" Our friends wanted us to have water, he added, but not necessarily one million gallons a day. The money donated for the purpose, he felt, should be returned, but he would wait before making a decision until Father Gleeson had time to provide additional data.

When the decision was finally made to abandon the Gaffney proposal, it was generally believed that Zacheus Maher was responsible for it. His unpopularity rose to new heights, Gaffney was transferred to Seattle College to teach mathematics and Gleeson began to look for another source for water. But Maher had not made the final decision. Elliott with his consultants unanimously opposed the project, and Maher assured Elliott on January 20, 1941, that he heartily approved of the decision.[43]

Much relieved, Elliott wrote again to Maher on February 12. Seattle College, he said, had received $20,000 for the land in north Seattle. The school was refinancing its debt at 3% interest. Father Corkery would like permission to buy the Madison Street Cable Terminal Building for $8,500.[44]

---

*Other members of the novice surveying crew, besides Frank Costello were Joseph Danel, Lewis Doyle, Charles Wollesen, and Wilfred P. Schoenberg.

†Father Joseph Chianale had died that very week. Called "Kee-eye" he was regarded as the "dean of western philosophers." One claim to province fame rests on the circumstances of his arrival. In 1890 while he was in Italy, through a mix-up in names, he received sudden orders, meant for someone else, to go to the Rockly Mountain Mission. Cheerfully and without protest or question, he left his homeland and relatives, never to see them again. He died on January 4, 1941.

The latter, though Elliott preferred to remain mum on the subject, until Corkery was ready to reveal his plans, was intended for the use of a School of Engineering, which McNulty, now back from graduate studies, and Leo Gaffney had suggested.*

By this time, rumors had reached Maher that Elliott was "exhausted." He ordered Elliott to California for a rest and made Tom Martin Vice Provincial. From this point on a kind of cat-and-mouse game about Elliott's alleged illness developed in Maher's watchful mind. One gets the impression from his correspondence that he was seeking an opportunity to replace Elliott, using sickness as an excuse. In mid-July, 1941, he hinted broadly that Elliott should request a successor. "Father General," he wrote, "is willing to release a provincial from office, if health requires it."[45]

Elliott calmly ignored comments like these. With admirable indifference he reasoned that the General would replace him if he wanted to, and until then he would carry on. He reported in late July that Father Edward Flajole, rector at the Mount had a serious car accident. Tormented by a bee, while he was driving, he had gone off the road and had broken his left arm rather badly. Also Father Robinson was in the hospital with the flu. He had been ordered to take a vacation. Bishop White, he added, wanted to take over the parish in Colville and the consultors said give it to him.[46] Five days later Maher wired: "Transfer of Colville parish approved."†

Robinson went to St. Ignatius for a rest and Maher wrote to Elliott: "You have a disproportionate number of problems in Oregon, and hence my sympathy goes out to you. . . ." He then brought up the health issue, Elliott's not Robinson's, reinforcing his "sympathy" with another not-very-subtle suggestion: "His Paternity will not take it amiss if Your Reverence were to ask to be relieved upon the completion of your triennium."[47]

Elliott replied by reporting on Robinson's health which, unlike his own, had deteriorated dramatically while he was at St. Ignatius. He was in the Sisters' hospital there "He staggers a good deal at times."[48] No final diagnosis had been made.

Elliott had been concerned about the province archives. Piet, when he moved to San Jose from Portland in 1930, had taken all the records with him, assuming California to be the mother-province and quite oblivious to the understanding that records related to the north were to remain here. Since the missions had all been located in the north, Elliott insisted that everything related to them should be preserved in the archives at Portland or the Mount, where a room in the rear of the library wing had been set aside for this purpose. Father Weibel had already gathered a few boxes of mission materials there. Father Sauer, whose hobby was mission history, had also contributed his bit, as did Father John Sullivan, known then as "Honest John." Elliott's pursuit of data about Loyola High School in Missoula, with an eye on the chances of reopening it, led him to the Provincial's residence in San Jose. On September 15, 1941, he wrote triumphantly to Maher: "One good thing has come out of our correspondence with San Jose in trying to unearth some documents about Missoula. Eventually we get either the letters or extracts from letters of the Fathers General to the Provincial of these parts from the very beginning to the division of the Province. These had been taken to San Jose when this part was made a vice-province and have been there since with no copies or records left up here. I can hardly praise Father [Leo] Simpson enough for the big work he has done for us in going over all that correspondence. He has copied out many things and sent excerpts onto us, and on the other hand has sent us most of the original letters and has made excerpts for the California files."[49]

Maher was also pleased. A week later he commented on Elliott's letter: "It is good to

*The School of Engineering was established on September 22, 1941, with Dr. Harry T. Drill as the first dean.

†This telegram was confirmed by Maher's letter to Elliott on July 29, 1941.

know you received so much which now properly belongs to Oregon, and which will be helpful for your own archives. What you need now is someone to index the Oregon Archives and make them more readily available for reference."[50]

At this time Robinson's health had become so critical Elliott sent him away for a rest and appointed the ubiquitous Dillon as vice-rector. When Maher wrote to Elliott on November 1, he took note of Elliott's previous comment "that Robby was reaching the breaking point." There seemed to be no known explanation for Robinson's illness. It was generally believed that his problem was fatigue. It was not worry about the university, as one might expect, for Gonzaga by this time had recovered and was enjoying the greatest prosperity in its history. Several government programs including the very popular Civilian Pilot Training program, had brought a record number of students to the campus. During the last year before the war, 1940–1941, the university counted a total of 1,213 students, including 121 students in the Law School and 91 Jesuit scholastics at Mount St. Michael's. Approximately one-fifth of Gonzaga's students came from Idaho, Oregon and Montana, indicating its regional centeredness at this time. As might be expected the professional schools of education, law, engineering and nursing drew the largest number of students from outside the states.

This was Gonzaga on the eve of the greatest war in history. Financially stable at last, after ten critical years, it barely existed on its meager income. Recently remodeled, painted and re-equipped after so many years of unavoidable campus deterioration, it was soon a shambles from a tragic fire. Its student enrollment, highest in its history, was about to drop to the level of its pioneer years. Little wonder that its baffled president, Father Robinson, could exclaim with fervent conviction: "God has His arms around Gonzaga! If He did not, it would have long since perished."

The 1941 fire was the occasion for Robinson's fervent exclamation. This was the Gonzaga's greatest of many fires, a ruinous holocaust which swept away many improvements and acquisitions the president had laboriously built or gathered, like the law library and the many new science laboratories. It started during the night of December 10, 1941, three days after Pearl Harbor.[51]

At 2:22 A.M. the Spokane Fire Department answered an alarm telephoned from Gonzaga by the night watchman. In a few minutes fire engines were coming in from all directions, and so were the neighbors. The center wing of the building, housing, libraries and chemistry laboratory were all ablaze. The flames could be seen from all parts of the city and even from some points many miles distant. Hundreds, if not thousands, came to witness the free show.

One can only imagine the noise and confusion within the cloistered residence of the building. Jesuit members of the faculty appeared one by one, startled-looking and bedraggled, their clothing hastily arranged and their hair uncombed. A check showed that one was missing. Father Jules LaMotta, vice-president and professor of Latin had begun his annual retreat twenty-four hours earlier. While some were speculating concerning his whereabouts, he suddenly emerged, dressed in his cassock, which was neat and proper, and carrying his suitcase and telephone. He wore a black coat over his cassock and a hat on his head, as though he were ready for a journey, and he was calmly smoking a cigarette on the end of a holder.*

Elliott reported details of the fire to Maher on December 12. His letter entered hopefully, "Father Robinson holds up well," he said.[52] When Maher responded on December 17

---

*OPA, Gonzaga Papers, ms. "The Gonzaga Fire," December 10, 1941. The total loss in the fire was given at $131,461.10 in pre-war dollars. It was covered completely by insurance. OPA, Gonzaga Papers, Financial Reports for July 1, 1942–June 30, 1943.

he suggested that Robinson be removed as president-rector, because of the hardships he had borne.[53]

Bishop Fitzgerald, Elliott's predecessor and Robinson's too, was also "bearing hardships." In his fifty-ninth year that December, he was burning the candle at both ends. After a summer of fund raising he had rushed back to Fairbanks to change his summer clothes for winter: fur cap, parka and muckluks. Northern Alaska had only two seasons. He left on December 3 for "a real trip;" he wanted to visit the missions at their worst. "I have spent the winter visiting the missionaries in the front-line trenches," he wrote to his friend Father Geis in Oregon, "and it has been a wonderful experience for me. I arrived at Akulurak on the south mouth of the Yukon, close to the Bering Sea, on December 11 and remained there for Christmas. Akulurak is the central mission for about one thousand natives scattered from the Yukon south to the Bering Sea. From all over the tundra Eskimos came with their families for the Christmas celebration at the mission. On Christmas Eve there were over one hundred sleds in the village, and as each sled has an average of seven dogs, you can easily imagine how the midnight air was rent with the howling of the Malemutes. Of course the mission supplies the dried salmon for the dogs and the Eskimos get one good meal, so many come for Christmas and the meal. It was a great sight to see the great number of teams leaving the mission after dinner on Christmas, scattering in all directions that require two or three days' trip by dog team."[54]

The bishop makes no mention of a very painful accident which occurred on this trip. With a "musher" and dog team he had been following the Yukon trail. They came to one point where an abrupt portage had to be made and the musher tried to stop the sled to let the bishop out. But he could not stop the dogs.

"Jump, Big Priest!" he shouted.

The bishop jumped, landed on the brink and fell over the bank. Fifty feet down his chest hit a block of ice. Minutes later his trip took up where it had suddenly stopped and no one was to know till six months later he had broken the breast bone and several ribs.

Meanwhile the problems of war had occupied Father Maher. On December 22 he wrote to Elliott requesting his approval on the text of a letter to be sent to President Roosevelt in support of the war. Then, on January 8, 1942, he dispatched from West Baden College in Indiana, a circular letter to all American Jesuits, which reads as follows:

"Reverend Fathers and Dear Brothers in Christ:

"Pax Christi.

"With the knowledge and unanimous approval of the Very Reverend Fathers Provincial of the American Assistancy, the following letter was sent to the President of the United States:

December 29, 1941

"His Excellency
Franklin D. Roosevelt
The White House
Washington, D.C.

"My dear Mr. President:—

"As representative of the 5,552 American members of the Society of Jesus, it is my privilege and high honor to reaffirm at the outset of the new year, so pregnant with danger for our beloved land, our pledge of devoted loyalty to you, our President, and to our Country.

"We realize that this is a time of danger. With you we are ready to face it. We know well that it is a time for sacrifice. We are prepared to make it. We understand fully that it is a time when more than ever before the citizens of our land must intimately appreciate the priceless possession which is theirs in the Constitution and the Bill of Rights. To safeguard these guarantees the nation finds itself at war. In all modesty and in all truth, we who are the sons of a Soldier Saint, will not be found wanting in their defense.

"During the previous World War, all the Jesuit Universities and Colleges in America served the country, not only by continuing their normal educational activities whereby patriotic citizens and high minded leaders were supplied to the nation; they assisted the Government in other fields as well. Should you, Mr. President, deem it necessary or useful to the defence of the country or the promotion of the common welfare to employ again the facilities of these institutions in the present danger, you have but to make your wish known. I can assure you of our wholehearted, our devoted, our glad cooperation.

"By our training and our calling we are men of prayer as well as men of action. Be assured, Mr. President, that no day passes but we are mindful of you before the altar of God. Even as you, so we, too, put our confidence and our trust in Him. May our heavenly Father give you health and strength to bear the heavy burden He has placed upon you. May His Holy Spirit be with you in the council chamber. And under your brave leadership may God in Whom we trust, bring our dear country safely through the dangers that beset us to the happy haven of peace and the retention and consolidation of those cherished liberties which are now imperilled.

"I remain, Mr. President, with sentiments of profound esteem,

"Respectfully yours

[signed] Zacheus J. Maher, S.J.
Assistant General of the Society
of Jesus for America"

To this letter the president replied as follows:
"The White House
Washington

December 30, 1941

Dear Father Maher:

"My courage to face the heavy tasks in the New Year now at hand is strengthened by the splendid pledge of support which you give in behalf of all American members of the Society of Jesus.

"The times are indeed pregnant with danger for our land for those cherished institutions to which we owe all our happiness as a nation. We are at war with unscrupulous adversaries who employ unspeakable means; but in national unity we shall find the strength to carry on to victory.

"The assurance that the government can rely upon you and your fellow Americans, who are spiritual sons of a Soldier Saint, will give new determination to our effort to continue this war until we have vindicated for all time an order of society which shall recognize the dignity of human nature in accordance with immutable laws laid down by the King of Kings who is Lord and Master of us all.

Very sincerely yours

[signed] Franklin D. Roosevelt"[55]

By this time Father Maher had convinced the general in Rome that Elliott should be replaced as provincial. On January 17, 1942, he wrote to Elliott that Father General "requests you to lay down the burdens of your office." He directed Elliott to prepare a terna for a new provincial.[56] There were many rumors at this time and later that Maher's decision to replace Elliott had been greatly influenced by Robinson and Frank Corkery. Both, apparently, regarded Elliott's health as too fragile. He has outlived both by at least twenty years. Elliott's explanation for his removal before the customary two terms were over is very simple: "Zac put me in until Robby was ready. When Robby was ready Zac took me out. I have always been convinced of this."

On April 10, 1942, Father Leo Robinson became the third provincial of the Oregon Province. Father Elliott had once said, "He staggers a good deal at times." Father Maher had got his way finally; Robinson was provincial. But it was, in a way, a hollow victory. The new provincial had a dreaded disease called multiple sclerosis and nobody, as yet, even suspected it.

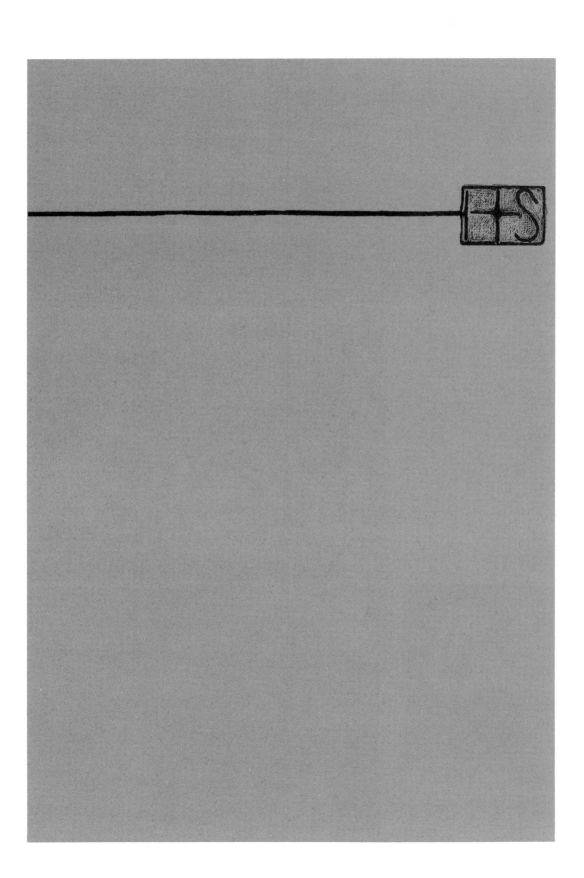

*Father Clifford Carroll, Gonzaga University
Librarian who foiled the prison plot.*

Cornelius Mullen, S.J.

*Father Charles Suver saying Mass atop Mt.
Suribachi on Iwo Jima during World War II.*

*Father Leopold Robinson, third provincial
of the Oregon Province 1942–1948.*

Campion Hall, Portland

19

"PRAY FOR THE SWEDES"
1942–1948

Whenever anyone offered to help Father Robinson, he responded with a wistful smile. "Pray for the Swedes," he would always say, in a roguish manner, his voice wavering a little. He talked the way he walked, with the hint of staggering in both.

He was of Swedish extraction, of course, born "Rasmussen," which had become "Robinson." Some wags of the province playfully called him "Leopold Ragnor Rasmussen Robinson." This brought a warm, amused grin to his face, which usually looked sad or pensive. His parents, devoted Catholics who had been converted to the Church by the good example of the Sisters of Providence in the local hospital, lived in Astoria, Oregon, where "Robby" was born on August 20, 1899. His father operated a furniture store there and served as Chairman of the Republican Party in that precinct.* Despite this political affiliation, the elder Robinson was mostly liberal in his views, which accounted in part for the liberal views of his children, especially Robby's.

Robby spent many years on the Gonzaga campus before becoming its president. He had been a resident student from 1911 to 1916, when the Gonzaga family spirit had produced some great men. After seven years of earlier Jesuit studies, he spent another four years on the campus, teaching philosophy, prefecting the boys and directing one of the brass bands. Having completed theology at St. Louis, where he acquired his interest in work with the deaf people, he returned to the campus, a priest and doctor of philosophy in sociology. Though a little older and much wiser, he had retained the same jaunty disposition which had marked him as a scholastic. He soon knew all the boys on the campus by their first names. His memory amazed them and his candor completely disarmed them. He became one of the most popular priests in Gonzaga history.

His appointment as provincial arrived on April 6, 1942,[1] and four days later he was formally installed, doubtlessly awed by his new responsibilities, but also determined to enjoy the opportunities they would give him. He had been a Province consultor for six years and was entirely familiar with all the details of Elliott's administration, with which he and his fellow consultor Frank Corkery had been somewhat out of tune.

In retrospect, his predecessor, Father Elliott, appears to have been a quiet, steady organizer, directing his energies toward stability in the province, by pulling things to-

---

*One of Robinson's favorite stories is about his father's politics. Before his death the elder Robinson said to his son, "You remember how I was chairman of the Republican Party? All those years I voted Democrat. I had to be a Republican. It was good for business."

425

gether, paying off old bills, pacifying bishops and clearing away canonical snags that had accumulated during the pioneering mission period. A moderate man in all particulars, Elliott doubtlessly retained the respect of most members of the province, but his views, especially on higher education seemed to alienate a few, his successor included.

Robinson's background at this time was unique. Though he was not the first American-born provincial, nor the first native of the northwestern part of the United States to become provincial, he was the first provincial who had gone through the mill of doctoral studies on an American campus. At St. Louis University, where he had pursued his theological studies for four years, he had returned for another three in graduate work. St. Louis left its mark upon him. For long years he shrewdly observed one of America's most influential Catholic universities at close range and he departed from it with some very definite ideas about what to do and what not to do in an expanding academic society. One point, especially, had been deeply impressed upon him; Jesuits could not operate their universities without non-Jesuit professional assistance.* In this view he was far in advance of most of his contemporary Catholic educators, who conceived of their schools as a kind of family affair. They seemed to resent the presence of lay professors on their staffs and fostered a ghetto-like mentality toward all externs, Catholic as well as non-Catholic. Robinson, perceiving the folly as well as the barrenness, of this policy, was determined from the very beginning of his presidency at Gonzaga to repudiate it. But years passed before he was able to modify the thinking of his provincial, Fitzgerald. Despite his efforts, as previous remarks have already indicated, Fitzgerald refused to permit a layman dean in the engineering school. Fitzgerald belonged to the old school. Gonzaga was a Jesuit family business, and so far as he was concerned, it would remain that way.

There is no evidence to suggest that Elliott supported Fitzgerald in his view. Elliott, in fact, made it clear that he had no objections to the appointment of James McGivern as dean of the School of Engineering. Indeed, all the records indicate that Elliott gave Robinson at Gonzaga and Corkery at Seattle College, a free hand in the administration of their presidencies. Their differences with Elliott seem to have centered on the kind of stress, or lack of it, that was placed on contemporary intellectualism. All three regarded current trends differently. Even Robinson, who held the most extreme views of these three, criticized the superintellectualism of professors at the Mount as "metaphysical constipation." The new Thomistic movement sweeping the Church helped to create as many positions on the subject of Catholic education as there were Catholic educators. Elliott simply attached less importance to academic achievements than his successors did, an accidental difference that was probably much exaggerated during this period of growth and self-criticism.

Appropriately one could say that Father Fitzgerald had plowed the fertile land of the province. Elliott had harrowed it, making it level and preparing it for the seed. Robinson now appeared to plant it. Each was the right man at the right time, though each suffered from the limitations imposed by his own academic origins.

Robinson, like his predecessors, was unpretentious and down to earth. His informal manners and contempt for stuffy traditions helped to endear him to young Jesuits, who not only felt at perfect ease with him, but took great pleasure in his company. He made them feel important. Indeed, he was sometimes criticized for trusting the young too much and for giving young men assignments which older Jesuits claimed for themselves.

But Robinson was no pushover. He was very perceptive, and he made demands proportionate to his trust. He was openly concerned about spiritual values and each year,

---

*James McGoldrick in Seattle had arrived at the same conclusions. He and Robinson received their doctoral degrees about the same time.

when he made his regular visitations, he sharply prodded each Jesuit to pray often and well. For the younger Jesuits, he provided instructions and books on affective prayer, convinced that it was superior to meditation, easier to practice and more conducive to fidelity in prayer.

Elliott had left some unfinished business. What bothered him most was his failure to assign a priest to Fairbanks, where the parish was short one man. "Now that I am out of a job," he told Robinson, "I will gladly go to Fairbanks." Without much reflection Robinson sent him. When Father Zacheus Maher heard about it he dispatched a firm protest to Robinson, directing him to recall Elliott at once. It appeared, he explained, to himself and others, that Elliott had been sent to Alaska to get him out of the way.* Perhaps Maher felt defensive about his decision to replace Elliott with Robinson. If Elliott were back in the province, Maher's critics could no longer complain.

Robinson, too, had left some unfinished business at Gonzaga. Ten days before he moved to Portland, the faculty exodus to the fields of war had begun. The first to go was Father James McGuigan, principal of the high school, who had received his appointment as an army chaplain on May 27, 1942. The ranks of the students, also, thinned out quickly despite defense officials' preference for a sit-tight policy in colleges. School routine, which had maintained its balance during the tense, uncertain months before the war, was gradually shifting into new grooves. Campus life, formerly carefree and buoyant, had now become desperately earnest. The ghosts of war occupied many chairs in classrooms, and other occupants, sensing their presence, felt awkward and unpatriotic unless they were doing something directly concerned with the war effort.

In these circumstances certain extra curricular activities required modifying. The first of these to receive a blow from the administration's axe was football. It was no secret that Robinson had always regarded football at Gonzaga with an unfriendly eye. As president he had barely tolerated it. According to Robinson's reasoning, the war was a better excuse than any to dispose of football so on the day before his departure, with the approval of his new vice-president, Father Altman, he released the news that Gonzaga University had dropped intercollegiate football for "the duration of the war."† When this news appeared in the *Gonzaga Bulletin*, Robinson was already in Portland.

"In his public announcement of the change," the Bulletin article stated, "Father Leo J. Robinson, president of the university, gave as the principal reason for the decision of the board of trustees the 'dissemination of the ranks of football caused by the wartime emergency'."[2]

Among the students this decision caused less consternation than it did elsewhere, perhaps because they were more willing to make sacrifices for the war effort than some of their elders. It was difficult to see how the university could do anything else, no matter what pressures were brought to bear to retain the sport. Robinson, who was 400 miles away, took whatever criticism there was in stride. The excitement about Gonzaga's football, which was soon smothered by the war, could not have mattered less to him.

For most Americans 1942 was a dismal year. Axis-Power victories on most fronts created a pall of anxiety throughout the country, which only the fireside chats of the president could dispel temporarily. Applications for the Novitiate dropped off. Scholastics like other seminarians, were classified as "4-F," the last of the categories to be summoned for military service. At Alma the theologians became sky-watchers for enemy planes and at

---

*Interview with William Elliott, Portland, May 21, 1981.

†Robinson was opposed to the return of football at Gonzaga at any time, but spoke of its temporary deferment "until after the war" to appease those who differed with him. Subsequent correspondence shows that he would allow it on the campus under certain conditions.

the Mount, Father Sauer was appointed to command a Civil Defense unit made up of scholastics. The philosophers contributed their blood, one pint at a time, to prove their patriotic dispositions.

At Seattle College the effects of the war had not been so drastic. The wisdom of McGoldrick's insistence on coeducation appeared in a new context. There is an undocumented account of an interchange of correspondence between McGoldrick and Zacheus Maher, during McGoldrick's gallant battle for the girls. "Seattle College," said Maher, according to this possibly apocryphal but delightful narrative, "must not have *both boys and girls.*" McGoldrick is credited with this saucy reply, "Then we'll get rid of the boys."

That is what the war did; it got rid of the boys.

On June 22, 1942, Seattle College adopted what was called "the emergency quarter-system program," which was an acceleration method of studies "for the duration of the War."[3] At this time McGoldrick was still dean and one suspects that his excellent relations with the University of Washington, also on the quarter system, had some influence on his decision.

There were nineteen Jesuits at Seattle College that year, some living in the improvised frame housing on the campus and some at the residence on the boulevard. One member of the community, Father Robert Dachy, had a leave of absence for studies in England, where he was trapped by the war. Eager to return to his post in Seattle, he attempted a crossing of the Atlantic in February, 1943. He was never heard from again. It is presumed that he was among the eight-hundred-and-fifty victims lost on a torpedoed Cunard ship, which according to the Associated Press went down with all on board.

Thus far, except for the war, Robinson's provincialate had been rather dull. Few of his progressive plans for the province could be realized because of the national emergency. Determined to bring higher education in the province into the twentieth century, he gave top priority to graduate studies, for scholastics as well as priests. The need for war chaplains, however, forced him to modify his schedule for what might be called his Six-Year Plan for the Production of Doctorates. In his first year as provincial there were twelve Jesuits assigned to "special studies," that is graduate work: William Bischoff, John Dempsey, William Gaffney, James Goodwin, Clifford Kossel, Albert Lemieux, Alex McDonald, Timothy O'Leary, James Royce, Leo Schmid, Harold Small, and John Taylor. During the same time, there were six Jesuits assigned to service in the Armed Forces as chaplains: Maurice Flaherty, Harold Greif, Eugene LeGault, James McGuigan, Curtis Sharp, and Raymond Talbott.

Gradually Robinson became conscious of an insolvable dilemma facing him and the province: on the one hand the Oregon province had the poorest record for the proportionate number of doctorates in the American Assistancy, and on the other hand the best candidates for doctoral studies were the younger Jesuit priests who also made the best chaplains. Should he prepare for the future of the province's colleges at the expense of young men in the services, who deserved the best chaplains possible? There was always the temptation to say, "Let others provide the chaplains," and in view of Oregon's poverty, this was not altogether unreasonable.

No one doubted where Zacheus Maher stood on this matter. Somewhat conservative and very traditional in his views, he tended to regard doctoral studies as unnecessary luxuries. He wanted chaplains, "ten percent," he eventually decided, of the priest members of the province.

On December 13, 1942, while Robinson wrestled with his priorities, Father Ledochowski, the General in Rome, quietly died, after appointing Father Alex Magni, the Assistant for Italy, as the vicar general.[4] Maher immediately informed all Jesuits in the United States of the General's death, cautioning all to keep the news confidential until the new vicar general made it public.[5] Ledochowski's death had been expected for sometime, and on December 10, 1942, four days earlier, Pope Pius XII had personally approved the designation of all Jesuit Assistants as Visitors, giving them additional jurisdiction in their own assistancies.[6] Thus the normal administration of the Society was provided for, despite the fact that a new general could not be elected for some years, due to the war.

The Oregon winter that year seemed to be colder than usual. Freezing rains west of the Cascade Mountains coated the highways and country roads with enough ice to skate on, and the heavy vegetation as well, snapping the tops of the alder trees encased, as they were, like crystal figurines. The provincial received reports that one of his newly appointed chaplains, Father Curtis Sharp, was in critical condition in the Army hospital at Camp Carson, Colorado. Sharp had been in surgery, for an appendectomy, and complications had arisen. Robinson left immediately for Colorado. Because, as Elliott said, he staggered a little, he carried a cane. As he walked through the entrance of the hospital grounds he overheard a young woman behind him say, "Mother, look! that priest is drunk." It was a depressing experience.

Father Sharp died on January 20, 1943. He was fifty years old, almost too old to be a chaplain, but young enough to be one of the most popular high school principals in province history. He and Joseph Keep had been inseparable for years. Both had had mischievous streaks, along with a boundless supply of energy. When they were scholastics, summer vacation was spent for three weeks on Robinson Island on Spirit Lake in northern Idaho. They persuaded the superior, so it was often said, to permit them to rent a farm horse on the mainland, for digging a pit for garbage on the island. Getting the startled horse on and off the raft proved to be more difficult that they anticipated, and the horse broke its leg in the process. They had to shoot it, pay for the horse, and spend the greater portion of their vacation digging a hole on the island to bury it. This had been a quarter of a century before. Now Sharp was dead, and Keep was to die on December 14, 1947 at Portland when he was only fifty-six. Theirs was not the generation to resolve Robinson's dilemma, but their loss in terms of province tradition, the passing on of the province heritage, was not insignificant.

Robinson, who knew that he had multiple sclerosis, returned to Portland somewhat shaken by the unfortunate disclosure of his public image. He seldom took a drink, though he could use one everytime he reflected on the subject of his continuance as provincial. He realized, of course, that he could never drink in public, and seldom, if ever, in private. Most men, I think, would have opted by this time to request a successor. Not Father Robinson. He was shrewd enough to know that this apparent vulnerableness gave him the strength of independence. If Zacheus Maher wanted to retain him as provincial as he was, he could afford to be audacious, almost to the point of impudence. Like Elliott, for different reasons, he became fearless in his decisions, and one of these, formed as time progressed, was to participate more fully in the non-Jesuit academic community, though Maher strongly disapproved of it. Robinson permitted members of the province to attend professional meetings around the country. To this Maher objected, and every time someone attended a meeting, Robinson received a crusty letter scolding him for permitting it.*

It is difficult to demonstrate the enormous influence that Robinson had on American Jesuit higher education, following this decision. From this point on he encouraged not only his own subjects to earn professional degrees and to participate as members in professional associations, but also many Jesuits of other provinces, who admired him as much as young

---

*At first Robinson could not understand how Maher always knew about these meetings. Then he realized that news of those travelling appeared in the *Province News*. Robinson said, "So I suppressed it!" Interview with Robinson, Spokane, autumn, 1962.

Oregonians did. He became renowned as "Robby" the great guru, who sometimes talked like a buffoon to amuse his colleagues, but whose will was formed with such granite determination to change the prevailing system that within five years his was the accepted ideology. He was not the only Jesuit to bring about this vast change nationwide, but as a provincial, he had a leading part in it.*

Meanwhile, he had no time for self-pity. In late January he left Portland for Gonzaga to make his visitation. Negotiations there were underway for a U.S. Navy training program, which was formally begun on July 1, 1943.† Spokane's was typical weather for February; sunny days and cold nights. John McAstocker, current pastor of St. Aloysius Church, lived with his assistants Father Louis Geis and John Prange, in the old Heath residence on Mission Avenue, in back of the new St. Aloysius School, which had been built by Father Sauer three years earlier. Paul Sauer had been assigned to supervise the construction of the first unit of the new St. Aloysius School because of his experience in the building of the wing at the Mount. This first unit was erected in 1940. The Sheds, occupied by the grade school from 1916 to 1940, had been converted again, this time into a chemistry building, which was called Cataldo Hall.

Father Connie Mullen was now the principal in the high school, succeeding McGuigan. Mullen was running a no-tomfoolery enterprise at a new location. In 1941 the Spokane School Board announced that the old Webster Grammar School, one block from the Gonzaga campus, would be discontinued. They did not add that the Gonzaga district had developed into an almost universally Catholic neighborhood, "the Holy Land," with a large parochial school, an academy, an orphanage, a boys' high school, a university, two convents for nuns and a home for the aged. Negotiations for rental of the Webster school had been started at once by Gonzaga officials. By August 14, 1941, an agreement was concluded, the school board leased the building for a thrifty $3,800 per year. On the second of September, Gonzaga High School had begun classes in this hastily adapted building.

Thus it happened that in a very brief period the Gonzaga campus had been cleared of the lesser schools, from which the university itself had originally sprung. No one seemed to recognize the irony of this situation, least of all the provincial himself. It was sometimes said, with at least a grain of truth, that his strength in supporting higher education left him weak in supporting anything less, especially the high schools and the missions.

At Sheridan and at the Mount, major crises had arisen, partly because the upheaval associated with Vatican II was already in the making.‡ The most urgent crisis was at Sheridan, where Moffatt's novices and the juniors were going to extremes in their practice of asceticism. The new rector, Father John Forster, was appointed during the previous summer to replace Father Gleeson. Forster, whose German antecedants and training in theology at Valkenburg left him as rigid in some respects as the novice master, believed in regimentation. He wanted complete control at all times. To serve his ends he had decreed that all novices were to wear one kind and color of jacket, juniors another and brothers a third. They were to wear these jackets at all times outside the house, so that Forster could identify students at a glance even from a distance.

*The provincial of the New England province at this time, Father John McEleney, also had great influence in the same manner. He experienced obstacles similar to those that Robinson faced.

†Navy programs had been previously conducted on the Gonzaga campus. See Gonzaga House Diaries, July 6, 1942: "6 Navy men arrived to begin their CPTC training, 75 army and navy men were to start on July 1, but the course is slow in getting under way. Too much red tape." Eventually Gonzaga conducted the V-5 and the V-12 programs. The Gonzaga V-12 program trained 686 Navy officers. *Gonzaga Bulletin*, May 18, 1962.

‡The conditions for Vatican II had been in the making for decades before the Council. At Mount St. Michael's, for example, pressures for greater academic freedom brought about the complete "open use" of the library in 1943. This was regarded as a significant step toward the new spirit of intellectualism moving through the Church.

Forster was a good Jesuit, but despite his fidelity to the rules, he had some irritating idiosyncracies, like his suppression of sports on the one hand, and, on the other, his preference for presenting weighty lectures on world architecture as a special treat for students during Thanksgiving. He also went overboard on the subject of paths, which under his direction were being constructed through the poison oak all over Paradise Farm.

His Prefect of Studies was Father Oscar Auvil, a very thin diabetic with watery eyes and bald head, who called all the juniors together on New Year's night and announced, "Well, I have visited every juniorate in the United States and I'm happy to report that ours has the longest school year in the Assistancy. We have at least five class days more than any other juniorate." Auvil was the kind who thought that more always meant better. He taught in Latin and Greek in a dry, cracked voice, entirely without humor or concession to human frailties. He was as wooden as a broomstick, but a kind and just man, who performed all his works with a strong sense of duty.

John Forster, just the opposite of Robinson, who was so uninhibited in speech that he evoked huge gales of laughter when he addressed groups of Jesuits, wanted to keep everything secret. He was greatly distressed when one junior wrote home that Brother Lacey had caught twenty rats in his trap. One windy day the minister Father Jules Hermans, parked the one and only community car on the crown of the hill, and carelessly left off the brake. The wind, a few moments later, blew the car over the top of the hill. As it bounced off the cloister walk it gained momentum, racing down the steep precipice, crashed through the fence, and into the ravine several hundred feet below, where it still rests today. The juniors having heard the first crash, witnessed what followed from a class room on the third floor. It was the biggest and funniest event of the year and the subject of much merriment, which Forster did his best to suppress. Robinson thought Forster would mellow, with a little help, but he had long since decided that Moffatt would have to go.

On March 17, 1943, Robinson had written to Maher, requesting permission to hold ordination of Oregonians up north, but had received a negative reply, as usual, on this delicate subject. For many years Rome had insisted that ordinations be conducted "in the theologate." Because Alma's chapel was too small for ordinations, however, Oregon and California province priests were ordained first at Santa Clara, and then in St. Mary's Cathedral at San Francisco. Year after year Oregon provincials requested that since the ordinations were not *de facto* in the theologate, they be conducted for Oregonians in the north, which would make it more convenient for families and friends to attend. The struggle went on for years.[*] Robinson was more successful, however, in having the novice master removed. To this, Maher finally yielded. He appointed Father Mark Gaffney, professor of psychology at the Mount, on May 7, 1943.[7] Moffatt withdrew promptly from all contact with young Jesuits and offered himself for retreat work with sisters, an occupation for which he was eminently qualified. Soon he was in demand by convents all over the United States and Canada, and his retreat schedule was made out for years in advance. It was while he was giving a retreat in Cleveland, Ohio, that Moffat suffered a stroke. At their insistence, the Little Sisters of the Poor cared for him until he died on April 12, 1969. He was 74 years old. He had published nine books for the sisters—all of them spiritual treatises.

Mark Gaffney, who was like a saint, changed the spirit of the novitiate from one of almost excessive penance and fasting to another of the direct opposite. Moffatt, for example, had forbidden singing except for the singing of hymns in the chapel or at the shrine. Gaffney enjoyed singing and his novices joined him for hours at a time for the sheer delight

*Provincial's Archives, Portland, Robinson to Maher, March 17, 1943. In 1952 Father Janssens finally yielded when he learned that it was farther from the Oregon Province to San Francisco than from London to Rome. In that year Oregon ordinations were held in St. Aloysius Church, Spokane, with Bishop White as the ordaining prelate.

of it. The singing symbolized something more, a kind of let-up in more serious matters, which eventually proved to be Gaffney's downfall.

At the Mount another German was at the bottom of a noisy disturbance, which displeased Robinson so much that he imposed a penance on all the scholastics in the community. Although first-year philosophers, including myself, had not been involved in the dispute, the provincial scolded us all and imposed the saying of one rosary for our lack of humility in class. Father Edward Flajole, the same who had broken his arm when a bee got into the car, was rector. Flajole loved nothing more than being left alone to complete his doctoral dissertation in German. He simply wanted peace, but there was no peace, because a Father Francis Müller of the Lower German Province, cut off in America by the war, was teaching a kind of philosophy that the scholastics refused to accept. The Mount's "house doctrine," as it was called, was very strictly Thomistic, a reflection of the scholastics at the time who were enthusiastic Thomists. Müller, on the other hand, was a Suarezian, if anything, though he was so disposed to a pious kind of skepticism that the only truths he held as absolute were explicitly defined by the church. He was a very kind, sensitive man, but in the classroom he was stubborn and defensive, and each class was a donnybrook between him and his more aggressive students. In time the daily battles evolved into a declaration of war, a situation which Flajole could no longer contain by advising everybody to be patient. In retrospect it is all very humorous, like the battles Suarez himself had with those who reported him to the general for giving scholastics candies and jam to win them over.* But in 1943 the war within the house was almost as real as the war in Europe, at least until Robinson arrived, called all scholastics together in Bellarmine Hall, and scolded them for lack of docility to their teachers. He reported the matter to Maher, stating that "the scholastics seem uppish."[8] In view of his own attitude toward academic professionalism, this appeared to be a strange way to act. Actually it was a true indication of Robinson's kind of intellectualism, which contained a certain contempt for the purely abstract, and too much respect for the empirical, which was popular in secular universities. When applied, Robinson's kind of scholarship was related to social reform, not the real distinction between essence and existence, about which the scholastics argued with more spirit than they brought to games.

A review of the Mount's activities at this time would be incomplete without a description of the twice-a-year triduum for the "renovation" or renewal of vows. This lasted three days and consisted of a meditation in the late afternoon, for which points were given by some celebrity, in addition to the morning meditation, points for which were given at night after Litanies. The triduum was made more or less in silence, so there was no hour of recreation after lunch or dinner. Usually you used this extra time for polishing your shoes, scrubbing and waxing your room and removing all superfluous articles, which you brought down to the common shelf, where you picked up other superfluous articles for dumping during the next triduum.

On the last day of the triduum at the evening meal the "Beadle," a kind of scholastic gopher, took over the pulpit and read out several defects of each scholastic, which had been submitted for the occasion by each. These were composed in Latin. This ceremony began with the words *"Aliqui defectus Fratris so and so,"* and there followed Latin phrases, most of which had been used a hundred times each year. For example many accused themselves of failing to sweep their rooms twice a week as required, or of not jumping out of bed at exactly five in the morning at the first sound of the bell.

---

*Francis Suarez (1548–1617) one of the greatest theologians in the history of the church was a Jesuit. He differed in certain philosophical matters from St. Thomas Aquinas (c. 1225–1274) a Dominican. For centuries the battles between their followers raged in ecclesiastical classrooms.

There were always some enterprising sinners who used some of their extra time during the triduum to sift through the Latin dictionary for exotic words or idioms that would startle all of us, even though we expected it. There was greatly suppressed merriment during this exercise, not only because of the wags who produced these creative confessions, but because of the frequent incongruities of the self-accusations.

The renewal of the vows took place the next morning at Mass. Although a Jesuit's first vows are perpetual; that is, for keeps, they are renewed twice each year until final vows are pronounced at the end of the long years of training. The purpose of this public renewal is intended, of course, to remind one of his obligations and to motivate each to seek greater perfection in the observance of the vows. A very elaborate schedule was posted. Mass was begun much earlier than usual, and each scholastic marched up to the altar in order of seniority, and pronounced the three vows in the same way he said them the first time in public. The ceremony was very long and really quite dull to the observer, and tempers were usually short, because of the fatigue from extra meditations and extra efforts to be devout and edifying during the triduum. It was not uncommon that one violated half his resolutions made with gusty fervor, before the day was over. There was one compensation, however, for all of this effort: *Deo Gratias* or talking was allowed at breakfast and Vow Day was always a holiday. Sometimes there was an extra bonus, like a visit by the provincial, who would entertain members of the community with a narrative of his recent travels on official business, and his discreet but hilarious editorials on prominent church personalities.

Father Maher had continued to nag the provincial for more chaplains. He sent Robinson a list of 155 American Jesuit Chaplains already commissioned in the Armed Forces, 14 awaiting commissions and 49 as auxiliary chaplains.[9] Robinson responded that the Oregon Province had 9 commissioned chaplains, 1 awaiting commission and 6 as auxiliary chaplains. He could not, he wrote, assign the "ten percent" Maher demanded. By January 1, 1944, though, he would have four more priests to be assigned. Actually Robinson assigned only two more priests to be chaplains. He had many volunteers but reasoned that the province needed the graduate degrees more than the army needed chaplains. However, many Jesuits who were not regarded as chaplains were teaching classes for the armed forces or were serving in other semi-military capacities. Most priests in the Oregon province were badly overworked during World War II.[10]

In Alaska Bishop Fitzgerald was the military vicar-delegate under Cardinal Spellman and responsible for the supervision of all Catholic chaplains in that area. He regularly visited every military post, making a difficult journey all along the route of the Alcan Highway, which was still under construction. He visited the Aleutian Islands and landed near Kiska when American troops recovered this island from the Japanese. "The Japanese had, like the desert Arabs of old, folded their tents and stolen away."[11]

Wartime travel was difficult, but all through 1944 Fitzgerald was on the road visiting army posts and missions. He attended endless meetings, and participated in squabbles with American Legion posts where too much Presbyterianism was mixed with patriotism. The hard pace was beginning to tell. Photographs of the bishop which were appearing periodically in *Jesuit Missions* and other publications showed the strain. The bishop was much thinner and his forehead was furrowed with lines of weariness. There was either no smile or a wan one, a sure sign that the bishop was nearing the end of his rope.

"I have asked Bishop Crimont to excuse me from attending the meeting of the bishops in Washington this fall," he wrote at this time. "His health is fine and I would not be surprised if he would bury his coadjutor! He is a marvel."

After Anchorage, the bishop visited Sitka and Father Patrick O'Reilly, who was an auxiliary chaplain as well as pastor of the local parish.

"You will sleep in the bedroom," said Father Pat, his brogue thick with eagerness and welcome.

"And where will you sleep?"

"Oh, outside on the coffin. I often sleep there."

"On the what!"

"The coffin. Let me show you."

They went out on the porch. "You see," said Father Pat, "the army shipped too many coffins up here—couldn't ship 'em back, so I got this fine aluminum one for a dollar." He patted it fondly. "Beautiful, isn't it?"

"Yes," said the bishop. "For a dollar?"

"For one dollar. This army fellow said he couldn't *give* it to me. So one dollar."

"You sleep here?"

"Oh often, very peacefully."

"Ha ha," said the bishop. "That's very funny."

"I'll tell you what, bishop, whichever one of us dies first gets the coffin," said Father Pat gallantly. "It's yours if you die first."

"Do you think it will fit either of us?"

"Undoubtedly. And come, let me show you where I want to be buried."

They proceeded outside.

"Under that tree," said Father Pat, his eyes misty now. "I've thought about it a lot."

"It's a nice tree," said the bishop.

"Yes," said Father Pat, "the best tree in Sitka."

The bishop left a couple of days later. The coffin was still there, and there it remained for years. As it turned out neither the bishop nor Father Pat were buried in it.*

In early March, 1944, another appeal was made for chaplains. Maher, in a very confidential letter to Robinson informed him that Bishop O'Hara had sent him a telegram stating that "four hundred units are to be sent overseas immediately." They desperately needed chaplains.[12] The landings at Normandy were only three months away.

Meanwhile a curious and little-known event occurred which had no precedent in the history of the province. Altman had been removed as rector-president of Gonzaga University at the end of his first three-year term, and Father Frank Corkery of Seattle College was appointed to replace him. This left a vacancy at Seattle. On March 25, 1944, Father Arthur Dussault was formally named as rector-president of Seattle College, but the appointment was not made public. There followed such a storm of protest from Corkery and his consultors, who insisted Dussault's loss would be catastrophic at Gonzaga, that Maher rescinded the appointment. Father Harold Small was assigned as rector-president instead.[13] Small, only thirty-seven years old, was one of the youngest rectors in our history. Like Robinson he had earned a doctorate in sociology which McGoldrick blissfully interpreted as an omen. Small's appointment was the beginning of a trend, a commitment to the new order: the social sciences instead of the humanities; social justice instead of the gross national product. God save the underdog! Small himself, however, had no comment.

In April, 1944 the Allied Forces were fighting their way north on the Italian peninsula. It would be June before they were to enter Rome. The vicar-general, Father Magri, died before this on April 14. His death, however, did not create a crisis; Norbert de Boynes was chosen immediately to replace him and Maher was firmly in control in Poughkeepsie. There was nothing more relentless than that. Robinson wrote to him about the leaks the

---

*Another corpse had the use of this coffin, which presently lies in the Ketchikan cemetery.

novitiate building had sprung.[14] It had been designed for exterior walls of brick veneer, but the bricks had never arrived. Robinson had consulted architect John Maloney, who recommended covering the exterior with black tar. At a cost of $11,000 the building was literally tarred, but unfortunately it was not feathered. Anything over the tar would have improved its appearance. Tourists passing along the highway below were greatly startled that autumn to look on the hill above the Yamhill Valley and see a sinister black building, three stories high, higher in the middle for cannons, perhaps, like a fortress dominating the main route from Portland to the sea. If the building had looked like a supermarket before, it now looked like a huge bat roost in twentieth-century concrete. The Jesuits laughed about it. Now they would have to get bricks to cover it, lest some neighbors, who already had misgivings about the crafty occupants, became more alarmed.

Robinson wrote again to Maher to report: "Thank God the building no longer leaks."[15] He did not mention bricks, which could not be had for the gossip about them. There was no point in going into debt to buy them unless the water problem were solved. In other words, the old twin problem of money and water had become a triple problem: *bricks* were now an added subject for the provincial's consultation.

Old Father Griva, in his eighties now and no longer building mission churches for Indians, had sent Maher a copy of his memoirs consisting of 383 typed paged. These revealed an heroic but uninteresting life of repetitious journeys to Indian villages where he had baptized, shrived and offered Mass. Maher was impressed. "Father Griva," he wrote, "has just sent me the history of his 50 years. Haven't you someone in the Province who could throw this into a sprightly book? Maryknoll is sweeping the country with its productions."[16]

The subject of mission memoirs prompted Robinson to take another look at the province archives. Like Elliott he was genuinely concerned about the preservation of records. He wrote to Maher at the end of 1944. He was worried, he said, about the archives. An addition [to the residence] would cost $25,000 to $30,000. It would be better to get another place and use this one for retreats. The archbishop was friendly. He would probably consent.[17]

So Robinson was back to the concept of a retreat house in Portland, partly to resolve his space problem at the provincial's residence. Archbishop Howard, who had given formal permission for a retreat house when Piet was assigned to Portland, was still chugging along, still "thinking" about that high school for boys that the Jesuits wanted to build. When he first arrived in 1926 the Jesuits had reminded him that his predecessor had approved the proposal but had not produced the written documentation required by Rome. Howard had replied that he himself would provide a school for boys, but it had taken him thirteen years to get Central Catholic off the ground.[18] It finally opened on September 5, 1939, as part of the Archdiocesan Centennial Celebration. As time progressed the archbishop mellowed toward the Jesuits. He really did want a Jesuit school in the city, but some on his chancery staff opposed the idea. The retreat house was another matter. No one objected to this. In fact, the archbishop welcomed it. What Robinson needed, however, was a new provincial's residence. For the moment he had to postpone action, but he knew now how he would proceed as soon as the war was over.

At Gonzaga there were two decisions to be resolved, one of which concerned his pet interest, the social order. Corkery wanted to start an adult labor relations school. Father James Linden, long time regent of the Law School was willing to undertake the direction of the school, which would consist of evening classes in public speaking, procedures in meetings and labor law. With Robinson's hearty acquiescence, classes were begun on March 12, 1945.[19]

The second decision concerned the high school. The old Webster School building, occupied on a rental basis by the high school, had come up for sale. Robinson appealed to Maher for permission to buy it "for forty thousand dollars." The province, he said, would finance the venture until Gonzaga could raise the money.[20] Maher was unavailable then, but he eventually cabled Robinson to give his approval, "provided that no external debt would be incurred."[21] Because the final price was higher than that expected, this deal fell through. Perhaps it was better after all; on April 9, one month later, the building was practically destroyed by fire.[22]

Three days after the fire, which forced the high school back into the university's administration building, President Roosevelt suddenly died at Warm Springs, Georgia. Harry Truman, who succeeded him as president, declared May 8, 1945 as VE Day, following definitive Allied victories in Germany. The war in Europe was over.

As for the war against Japan, the Allies were closing in. The island of Iwo Jima, like a Maginot Line, lay between the Allies and Tokyo. A massive invasion of the island was planned, and in February, 1945, the assault was begun. With the invading Marines was chaplain Charles Suver, a member of the province. The ship on which he approached the island was crowded. Looking up at the summit of Mount Suribachi on the island, Suver said to his companions: "If you put the flag on top of that mountain, I will say Mass under it."

There followed days of bitter fighting, during which Chaplain Suver served in an emergency hospital near the base of the mountain. But when the Marines fought their way up the steep slopes, Suver was with them. One of the most renowned war-time photographs in history was taken when the Marines planted the American flag on the summit of Mount Suribachi. Within hours, Suver was offering Mass beneath it, on the back of a Jeep, surrounded by battlescarred Marines. A famous photograph of this, too, was taken, and it appeared in newspapers and magazines throughout the world, as an inspiration for men of all faiths.*

Later Suver, sometimes called "Second Spring" because of his enthusiasm for innovative causes, achieved fame in the course of another feat during the war.† In "Believe It or Not" by Ripley, the following appeared: "Rev. Father C. Suver, Chaplain 5th Div. U.S. Marines Was Buried Alive In a Foxhole By An Exploding Shell—Only His Hand Was Exposed! By Wiggling His Fingers He Attracted Attention And Was Rescued Unharmed!" Only Suver's fingers appeared in the illustration which accompanied this bizarre text.[23]

In Alaska, which was a long way from Iwo Jima, there had been some criticism of the provincial for his failure to make a visitation of the missions. Since he himself made such little fuss about his illness, few if any Jesuits talked about it, and those in remote places like Alaska never heard of it. They complained without understanding the real situation. One could hardly blame them; the war had brought many changes, and they felt considerable dependence upon the provincial's approval, even though Bishop Crimont was making most of the decisions.

It was rumored that Bishop Fitzgerald, too, had begun to make decisions respecting the Society's internal affairs, like giving orders to scholastics at Holy Cross regarding their spiritual formation, matters related to their Jesuit superiors alone. It was unlike Fitzgerald to act this way. He, too, was a sick man, though he denied it or laughed it off. In March, 1945 he had experienced another sled accident. As usual he joked about it.

*In *Newsweek*, March 19, 1945, for example, the following caption accompanied it: "Faith Lives on Iwo Jima: Roman Catholics among Marines who fought their way to the summit of Mount Suribachi on Iwo Jima attend Mass conducted there by a Navy Chaplain." The photo also appeared as the front cover of *Jesuit Missions*. XIX, 9 November, 1945).

†Father Louis Sauvain who is very adept at bestowing nicknames was responsible for "Second Spring Suver."

"I had an interesting experience on my last lap of the trip from Nelson Island to Bethel, a three day trip by dog team. On the last day my sled turned over on the Kuskokwim River and I was spilled with the rest of the contents over the ice. I was merrily skidding along on my parka head-foremost, when I struck a protruding ice pack. My face was struck with the result that I got a beautiful 'shiner' a bloody nose and a cut and swollen mouth. Since it was sub-zero weather, the bleeding stopped quickly and as I had discovered no broken bones, I got back on the sled, which the Eskimo 'musher' had righted, and within four hours we reached Bethel. Forgetting my gory appearance, I went to the roadhouse, where I was known, for a room. The woman in charge gave me a look and sternly told me that there was no vacancy. Evidently she took me for a Saturday evening roisterer. I told her that if Father Menager had returned from the up-river district, I could possibly find a room at his place. She gave me another look and inquired if I were Father Fitzgerald. On realizing how I must have looked, I humbly replied that it was what was left of him. At once she gave me the best room in the house and invited me to dinner. The latter interested me most so after removing the clotted blood, which began to run again, but still with my right eye closed and blackened, I put my feet under the dinner table and I lay to. She was celebrating her thirty-second wedding anniversary with turkey, ice-cream and everything, which rapidly disappeared under my scientific approach. I had not eaten a meal for two days; we only had tea and hardtack on the trail. The Eskimo ate some of the dried dog fish, but that was too much for me. I lost twenty-six pounds on my visit to the missions and when I got home I tipped the beam at one hundred and fifty exactly. The following of a dog team is guaranteed to reduce the avoirdupois. As it was close to St. Patrick's Day, it was hard to convince the people there that I got my wounds legitimately! I had an Eskimo 'musher,' but he could not speak a word of English in my defense."[24]

With a big patch on his eye, the bishop said Mass the next morning, preached, and confirmed as if nothing had happened.

Two months later, on May 20, 1945, Bishop Crimont died, eighty-seven years old and active to the last. He was buried on "Shrine Island" in a crypt beneath the chapel. Father William Levasseur, a pious dreamer, but *French,* had "conceived the fantastic idea of erecting a national shrine to St. Teresa on an island some twenty-three miles distant from Juneau by car," Robinson reported. "With the consent of the Bishop he expended approximately $75,000 on erecting a handsome chapel . . . . while the Church, home and school were falling into a state of decay in town."[25] The site, enclosed by windswept trees, through which ocean breezes sighed in a mournful way, like an unseen choir, was pure poetry, and the burial recalled the mysterious ritual of placing a deceased pope in a sarcophagus beneath St. Peter's.

Fitzgerald took over with a heavy heart. There would be more desk work now and not so many accidents on the ice. The end of the war did not end problems. In a way it increased them. There were still chaplains, soldiers, missions to be visited, hungry missionaries. Many parishes had to be reorganized, larger churches built, schools planned if not established. New missions had to be started. All this in the face of rising costs in Alaska where carpenters got thirty dollars a day.

The provincial had made up his mind to visit the missions of Alaska. He left Portland as soon as he was able to leave, in early September, 1945, and he spent almost two very painful months flying from village to village, but making light of it. His first stop was Juneau. "Bishop Fitzgerald," he wrote in his twenty-seven page report to Rome, "has undertaken the arduous task of reorganizing the diocese along canonical lines. His Chancellor is renovating and repainting the Church, home and school. The disordered, neglected condition of the diocesan files and documents baffles description. There were in the files but thousands of letters and papers tied in bundles and stored here and there. The whole staff has been laboring diligently to straighten things out. Some order is beginning to appear. The former Chancellor or Pastor and his assistant have both been removed. They should have been changed years ago, but the old Bishop would not consider it."[26] Crimont was regarded as a saint, but like some saints before him, he had left his office as vicar apostolic in a tangled mess.

If Robinson's report on Juneau had been guardedly negative, it glowed with praise for the other missions of Alaska. For Holy Cross, Robinson reserved his highest compliments. In part he wrote: "But the mission has done and is doing a tremendous spiritual work. All along the line at Bethel, Hooper Bay, Tununak, Chiniliak etc. I heard of this. At all these places I heard how the graduates of our two mission schools were everywhere the mainstay of the Church and a help to the missionaries. A detailed study of this influence might help much. Perhaps I am exaggerating somewhat, but not very much. Certainly without our mission centers at Akulurak, Holy Cross this district would be a great spiritual wilderness."[27]

Later in the report Robinson added: "The mission operated a very profitable truck garden and farm and has maintained a herd of milk cows.* Father [James] Spils, the Superior, is a farmer and tells me the garden does very well. Ordinarily it serves not only to furnish the mission with much necessary food but they sell much produce to the local natives and stations along the river. I was astonished at what they are able to do considering the great length of the winter, from October to any time in May. All the plants are begun in a large green house and as soon as possible in the spring transplanted to the garden. . . . The net cost of operating this huge plant last year was $2,000, the gross expense about $12,000. In other words, the mission last year only cost the procurator $2,000."[28]

Robinson had called Spils a "farmer" because he had come from Colton, Washington, a farm community. It would be more accurate to describe him as a "mechanic" because he had been shifted from mission to mission, all over Alaska, to erect buildings or renovate them. He specialized for a brief time in installing inside plumbing in the larger missions, for which reason the toilets were often referred to as Spilways." The missions received considerabe quantities of hand-me-downs, including machinery, and Father Spils, for many years, exercised heroic patience in keeping this machinery in operable condition. In one mission, for example, where the Sisters had an old washing machine, Spils had to stand by on wash days to repair the machine three or four times.†

When Robinson returned to the province his first words of advice were: "If you go to Alaska, be sure to bring mosquito netting. Any kind of good chicken wire will do." He related his adventures for the benefit of the scholastics at the Mount, keeping them in hysterics for two hours. The climax in his performance was reached when he described, and demonstrated, his encounter with a narrow boardwalk over the tundra marsh to the church at Bethel. As he staggered along, using his cane to steady himself, he fell into what he called "tobacco juice" twice, before he was rescued by Father Frank Menager, of whom he reported: "I cannot speak too highly of this Father."

In late autumn, 1945, an uneasy peace had descended over the world. Father Maher informed all American provincials that he had been recalled to Rome, where the Society's routine business henceforth would be conducted.[29] He sailed on December 7, 1945, leaving behind him the much relieved American Jesuits, who had never been comfortable with his

---

*This was not the original herd ordered by Tosi. It was a second attempt made to keep cattle at Holy Cross. Crimont ordered this herd to be terminated.

†This was at Copper Valley where there was some doubt about who was more heroic, the sisters of St. Ann or Spils.

rather autocratic rule. When he departed, most passengers were coming from Europe, not going there. Maher was the kind of person who liked it that way; he had often used the expression, "Go against the crowd."

Robinson's principal concern now was the realization of his plan for a new provincial's residence, with adequate quarters for archives, and the renovation of the old residence for a retreat house. In June, 1946, he sent one of his scholastics, Wilfred Schoenberg, to Washington, D.C. to be trained in the National Archives for subsequent professional care of the province's records. He wrote to the vicar general, Father De Boynes on July 14, urging at considerable length the need of the retreat house, hence the related necessity of a new province curia. He had in mind one similar to that occupied by the provincial in Chicago, which would cost about $30,000.[30] De Boynes approved of the retreat house by cable on July 29.[31] Robinson wrote to Father Sauer in Spokane the next day. He stated that he had received permission to open the retreat house and to purchase a new residence. He wanted Sauer to send $30,000 to "Father Charls [sic] Chapman," acting procurator in Portland. Chapman would prepare the new curia during the provincial's absence in Rome for the general congregation.[32] Finally on July 31, Robinson wrote to De Boynes, advising him that the cable had arrived and that Father Mark Gaffney would be acting provincial during his absence in Rome.

De Boynes had announced that the Congregation for electing a new general would take place in Rome in September. Robinson, as provincial, would be required to attend this. In addition there were two elected delegates representing the Oregon province, William Elliott and Leo Martin. It was reported, without confirmation by the electors, that Elliott had been selected unanimously to demonstrate the province's respect, and disapproval, that he had been removed as provincial by Maher. Whatever the truth may be, Elliott went off to Rome to help elect Father John Baptist Janssens, a Belgian, as the new general, on September 15, 1946. Following this the delegates elected Father Vincent McCormick of the New York Province as the American Assistant, replacing Zacheus Maher, who returned to the ranks for the rest of his life.*

Chapman in Portland was delighted with his own assignment. It was the sort of thing he could do well. He had been the provincial's secretary since spring of that year and Robinson had instructed him to find "a suitable old house that would be conveniently placed for visiting Jesuits." Within a few days Chapman casually mentioned this particular to a real estate agent, Mr. McGuire, who recommended the purchase of the former McKenzie property.

The McKenzie home was on the corner of 20th and Hoyt in the northwest section of Portland. It was an old-fashioned greystone mansion, castle-like with one rounded tower, many chimneys and countless little gables covered with slate. It looked more like a fortress. Had it been one, its score of wide and gleaming windows would, forsooth, expose its occupants to various and sundry missiles, and no one builds a fortress that way. The fact is, it was a residence, a primly kept and inviting one, for despite its heavy features, there was an air of hospitality about it that one associated with the gracious living of late nineteenth-century America.

The furnishings of the grounds around the mansion confirmed its lived-in apearance. Vines and low-clipped evergreens enlivened the drabness of the building's lead color. A low wall and laurel hedge, neither of them high enough to obscure the lowest window, surrounded the place like an inverted moat, and a lone pink dogwood tree, which was cared for meticulously for 20 years by a former owner, stood meekly at the entrance, dominated, no doubt, by the hardness of the stone around and above it. The lawn was as

---

*Zacheus Maher died in San Francisco on October 1, 1963. He was 81 years old.

439

green as any turf in Ireland, a little island of velvet within its boundaries, a carpet where, in bygone years, some grand lady might have stood while she admired her castle.

The house has had a peculiar history. It was built in 1890 by a certain Dr. McKenzie. According to a rather dubious tradition, this wealthy medic had sprung from Scottish folk of the Highlands and, after finding success in America, wanted to build for himself and his family a home like a castle in the land of his boyhood. What is certain is that Mrs. McKenzie was Scottish, and, at her insistence, a Scottish motif of thistles was carried out in carvings on fireplaces and panels.

The house cost Dr. McKenzie $100,000, and another $100,000 was expended to furnish it. Though placed on a corner, its lavish gardens extended over the whole block. These were the showplace of Portland.

Mrs. McKenzie was a Catholic. During her last illness, Father Balestra of St. Michael's Parish, brought Holy Communion to her, and, when she lay dying in her palatial home, he administered for her the last rites of the church. After her death and the death of Dr. McKenzie, the furnishings were sold and the property passed into other hands.

For thirty years ownership of the building changed frequently. Being too large to be used as an ordinary family home, it was put to other uses, and not all of them noble. It was, at various times used as a speakeasy, a convalescent home, and a rooming house. An elderly lady who owned it was anxious to dispose of it. She asked $30,000 for it. The property was suitable. After careful examination, it was purchased for $27,500, considerably less than the cost of an addition to the older building. Chapman was ordered to have it renovated and prepared for its new function.

Chapman found it to be a fourteen-room house with seven fireplaces, a billiard room and an unfinished basement, except for a wine cellar at one end. By removing many of the frills, adding walls here and there, and finishing off the basement, he converted the place into a twenty-five room residence and office building which retained a certain air of warmth but also acquired a no-nonsense appearance which would have startled Mrs. McKenzie if she could have seen it. The wine cellar was converted into a vault for records; the billiard room, into a sacristy and chapel; and the window which had "WAIT FOR THE SHOT" inscribed upon it was exchanged for a plainer one which bore a simple cross to designate the new use. Where an elaborate knocker had once decorated the front door, a new brass plaque was placed for the dual purpose of covering the gap after the knocker had been pilfered and of announcing to the public that this was now "Campion Hall, Jesuit Provincial's Residence."

When the provincial returned from Rome the new residence was ready and he took possession with characteristic eclat, giving Old Testament names to the carvings, and commenting playfully on the fussy designs in some of the chambers. So Dr. McKenzie's old greystone mansion brooded no longer over the past like a rooming house full of aristocratic ghosts but echoed with the clatter of the present: an office and a clearing house for seven hundred busy Jesuits. The grounds, too, were alive, and Mrs. McKenzie's lone dogwood tree, the last remnant of one of Portland's garden showplaces, blushed meekly every spring and yielded its branches for altars instead of tea tables. The occupation of Campion Hall cleared the way for the establishment of the retreat house, but due to the enormous postwar boom at Seattle College and Gonzaga University, there was a shortage of available Jesuits to get it under way. The provincial had other, more immediate, problems to cope with, and one of these was Bishop Fitzgerald. After the death of Crimont, Fitzgerald's health deteriorated rapidly. Like his predecessor, he refused angrily to consider retirement or the appointment of a coadjutor.

Robinson wrote to the new general: "I must represent to Your Paternity immediately the rather distressing state of affairs now existing on the mission. From a number of sources, especially Father [James] Conwell the recently appointed Chancellor of the diocese, I have learned that Bishop Walter Fitzgerald is far from well. He is suffering from ever increasing spells of high blood pressure that are extremely dangerous and have already made inroads on his ability to carry on.

"This condition creates lapses of memory that appear even in important matters. He has temporary hallucinations that induce the severity of his high blood pressure. His doctor has given absolute orders to retire from his office for at least 3 months to take a rest. . . . The diocese is upset, disorganized and confused."[33]

On March 13, 1947, Janssens wrote to Fitzgerald urging him to appoint a vicar to be in charge, and to return to the states for a rest. Two weeks later, although no vicar had been appointed, Fitzgerald was in Oakland, California, in a hospital, where the doctor said he must remain indefinitely.[34] In a few days he left the hospital and was found unconscious on the streets of San Francisco. The archbishop had sent data to the apostolic delegate, but Rome was moving slowly. Juneau's chancellor was in an agony of helplessness.

On May 16, 1947, Robinson addressed another desperate plea for help to Father Edward Goulet, secretary to the general. The situation in Juneau had grown more critical, yet the bishop refused to resign.[35]

There had been other subjects of correspondence between Portland and Rome. Robinson, while he was in Rome for the Congregation, had persuaded the general to approve the release of microfilm of the Rocky Mountain Mission records in the Curia Archives. The film was ready, but Brother Phillip Sullivan could not find a legal way to ship it.* Robinson again requested permission for ordination of Oregon candidates to be held in the north.[36] He was acting chairman, Robinson said, of the American provincials and he would host the provincials' annual meeting in Gonzaga from the first of May to the eighth.[37] He wanted to open the retreat house which was to be called Loyola by June 1, 1947, if possible. He intended to put Father Joseph Grady in charge.[38]

Father Corkery from Gonzaga had appealed for permission to open all university classes to women. There it was again: coeducation. But Father Maher was no longer making the decisions. Besides, Seattle College had been formally coeducational since 1935. It was a powerful precedent, as Maher had predicted.

During the war years and immediately after, girls attended some classes on the daytime campus at Gonzaga, apparently without comment about it being unusual or unacceptable. Boys had too much on their minds to quibble about the invasion of girls, especially since the invaders appeared to be so helpless and pretty. In Corkery's early years as president the subject arose regularly in discussions of the faculty, among whom there was a consensus favoring it. But it was Bishop White who took the initiative in promoting coeducation. "The Bishop of the diocese of Spokane," Robinson reported to Janssens, "Most Reverend Charles White, is a [sic] apostolic zealous man and is a friend of the Society."[39]

Usually Bishop White got what he requested of the Jesuits. After making an accurate survey among Catholic girls on non-Catholic campuses in the region, he concluded that a coeducational university was essential to his diocese. At his Excellency's request, Father Janssens weighed the reasons for a change at Gonzaga, then gave his approval in the summer of 1948. By September Gonzaga was officially coeducational.

Among Gonzaga's more outspoken faculty members at this time was Father Clifford Carroll. One of Robinson's successful protégés, he had received his doctorate at St. Louis.

*Provincial Archives, Portland, Sullivan to Chapman, February 24, 1947. The film eventually arrived in Portland. Robinson directed me to come to Portland to hand carry it back to the Archives in Spokane.

Among other offices held by him at the university was that of librarian. There is a fascinating little anecdote about his cleverness in foiling a prison-break plot, the story of which was widely publicized in *Coronet* magazine.[40] Written by Stuart Whitehouse, the article was titled "The Case of the Curious Convicts." Whitehouse wrote, "In the cloistered seclusion of a college campus, a librarian uncovered and foiled a strange plot unfolding many miles away."

It so happened Father Carroll became aware that the book *Among the Wild Tribes of the Amazons* had gone more than once through inter-library loan to the Washington State Penitentiary at Walla Walla. Father Carroll thought this was odd. When the book was returned, he sat quietly at his desk and flipped the pages casually. Then recalling how books usually open at their most perused pages, he set the volume on his desk and released both hands. Each time he repeated this the book fell open to pages 210 and 211. Reading these pages Carroll's eyes grew wide with amazement, for on these two pages there was a detailed description of how-to-make blow guns and poison darts. Suspecting that inmates might be plotting a jail-break, he contacted the warden at once. Upon investigation, deadly tubes and improvised nail-bullets, capable of being used effectively on guards seventy-five yards away, were found by the shocked prison officials. As described in the book, "the darts were thin, sharp and poisoned."

Father Joseph Grady arrived in Portland on June 4, 1947. A moderately thin man with a heavy head of hair and thick-looking glasses, he appeared to be a sales representative for sporting goods rather than the founder of a house of prayer. On the same day Brother James Wood joined him to supervise renovations in the old building. Neither was afraid of hard work. After twenty-three days of whirlwind activities, on June 27, Father John Mc-Astocker arrived to direct the first retreat, which began on that day at 6:30 p.m. Twelve men attended this first three-day retreat.

Since several months were required, even for dynamic Brother Wood, to provide more rooms for retreatants, no other retreat was given at Loyola during that summer. On September 26, the second retreat began and lasted three days. It was attended by seven men. Another gap in schedule occurred because Grady was required to direct the parish during the illness of its pastor, Father Keep. By November, however, details were sufficiently worked out so that a regular schedule of weekly retreats could be maintained.

According to the arrangements made, Grady supervised the operations, scheduled retreats, paid the bills, secured supplies, and attended to other chores like a business manager. McAstocker conducted the retreats and Wood took charge of remodeling and repair work. In December two novices from Sheridan joined the staff to prepare rooms and to wait on retreatants at table. This was part of novitiate training and novices were rotated each week.

In the first full year, 1948–1949, twenty retreats were conducted at Loyola with an average attendance of eight. If this appears to be a small beginning, it must be remembered that in retreats large numbers are not so important as the intense effect produced on those who make them. The large numbers would come as soon as the good word spread by the retreatants themselves. In the following year, for example, thirty-nine retreats were given, with an average attendance of twenty-one, an overall increase of five hundred percent.

These dry facts are the bones of history that relate to the Loyola Retreat House. But retreat houses, like monasteries, shelter within them the deepest of human experiences, the experiences of earnest men groping for God. Not all retreatants at Loyola were Catholics. In fact, many were not, but all had this in common: they were there because they felt a deep need for a more intimate knowledge and love of God. Many went through spiritual crises, which were, at the same time, the most painful and the most consoling of human experiences. Hidden away in lovely wooded isolation, just a hundred yards from Portland's busy streets, these men in their silence came to grips with the basic problems of life. They prayed, they heard the eternal principles expounded, they sought counsel, some of them wept. After the third day they departed, renewed in spirit, refreshed. Only the retreat master knew how much had changed in three days.

While the first retreat was being given, on June 27, 1947, Robinson wrote to Janssen regarding the canonical attachment of St. Ignatius Mission to Mount St. Michael's. "All property," he said, "belongs to the Society; 2,521 acres in all." Legally it was in the name of Montana Catholic Missions, S.J. "The title is clear. There can be no doubt about this."[41]

As for Bishop Fitzgerald, no word had been received regarding a successor. When he returned from California to Juneau on June 9, 1947, he looked haggard and worn, his step unsteady, his mind confused. He wrote to friends, however, that he was completely cured. On July 5, he was persuaded to go to the hospital in Juneau. There his condition worsened and doctors advised that he be removed to Providence Hospital in Seattle, where he would get more specialized care. On Monday, July 14, he went by plane to Seattle. Finally on Saturday of the same week, July 19, the sisters called Father Small at Seattle College. Small went at once to Providence, reaching there about ten o'clock in the morning. He annointed the bishop and remained with him until he passed away quietly just before noon. The cause of death was cerebral hemorrhage.[42] He was only sixty-four years old and he had lived only twenty-six months beyond his predecessor, Bishop Crimont.

Father Robinson, too, was near the end of his term as provincial. When he stood by the grave of the bishop at Mount St. Michael's, he looked gray and forlorn. His jaws sagged, his face bore heavy wrinkles, giving him the appearance of a man twenty years older; with his cane he steadied himself. He pondered the bishop's coffin, as it rested on the straps above the empty grave. The next grave was Brogan's who had died in March. Brogan, like Fitzgerald, had been president of Gonzaga before him. Brogan dead. Fitzgerald dead. John Dougherty's grave was there, too. John had been his assistant, and Elliott's before him. He had never felt comfortable with John, a matter he never discussed. Robinson himself was under sentence of death from multiple sclerosis. The general wanted him to serve as provincial one extra year, but that would be impossible.

It was a warm day, rather muggy for Spokane. The philosophers would leave soon for the villa at Twin Lakes. When they returned it would be the beginning of a new school year.

Was there something we could do for Robby?

Yes, pray for the Swedes.

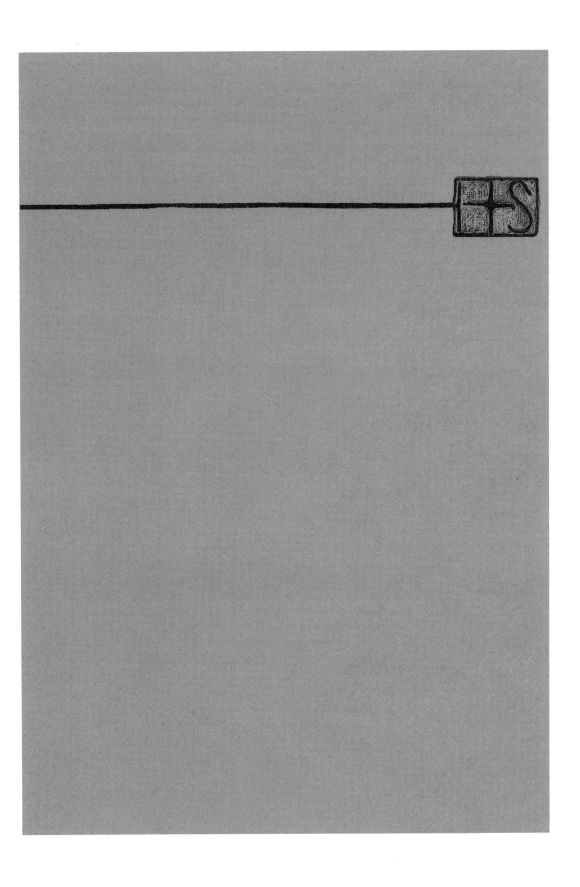

Jesuit High School, Portland, on a rainy day.

Front view of St. Francis Xavier's Novitiate after completion in 1956. The architect for the renovation program was John W. Maloney of Seattle who designed the entire middle section.

Bishop Francis Gleeson as cook for the construction crew building St. Mary's Mission, Andreafski, Alaska. . . . . . .

. . . .and Bishop Francis Gleeson assisting in construction of St. Mary's Mission, Andreafski, Alaska.

Harold O. Small, fourth provincial of the Oregon Province and American Assistant to Father General for many years.

20

A STABLE PROVINCE
1948–1954

Francis Dillon was not of Swedish descent, nor did he know many people who were. He was the last of the old California province provincials and a much admired curiosity to the young Jesuits because of his gusty resistance to attacks on his simplistic theology. He was not only the last of the provincials; he was one of the last of the Neanderthal theologians, and he defended his positions with such earnest sincerity that everyone respected and admired him.

In January, 1947, he celebrated his sixtieth anniversary as a Jesuit. At a reception after Mass in St. Aloysius Church, Bishop White presented him to the noisy students, who sniffed a holiday in the wind, and then the university's quartet sang "Dear Old Girl." The music was excessively loud, but Dillon did not seem to mind. He stood up to thank the boys for their performance. An old man now, he radiated warmth and love, and above all holiness. He said he had a girl, too. "My Girl," he called her, adding brightly, "What a fine girl she is." How beautiful! How pure! His girl was the Blessed Mother, he said, and he recommended every boy to turn to her on all occasions.[1] That evening the scholastics sang all the old songs he liked. It was a kind of last hurrah.

Like an old war horse he began to fade away. He shuffled around, his mouth still firm and his eyes direct and unflinching. He read "the funnies," as they were called then, holding the paper high above him, his head tilted back to look at it, an amused expression on his aging face. Then, while a doctor was examining him on Sunday, October 5, 1947, he died suddenly, still convinced that the world was a little over six thousand years old.

Dillon's death had been expected. In Alaska another Jesuit pioneer died the same month, leaving, like Dillon, a legacy of inspiration. Father Bellarmine Lafortune died in Fairbanks on October 22, 1947, in his seventy-eighth year. He had been with the Eskimos for forty-four years. One of his Jesuit companions composed a stirring testimonial:

"With the death of Fr. Lafortune, one may say that an era came to an end. It was the era of the giants; Tosi, Robaut, Treca, Lucchesi, Jette, Monroe, Sifton, Lafortune . . . to name the greatest. God sent them to Alaska as He did the Fathers of the Church at the turn of the Fifth Century to serve as luminaries in the darkness of paganism. He endowed them with great physical resistance, an uncontaminated faith and much zeal for the salvation of souls, and they cooperated well with God's gifts. No other name ever became such a password 500 miles beyond Nome as Lafortune's. When he died, everybody knew that there was a new saint in heaven."[2]

In the summer of 1923, Dillon had accepted for the novitiate a young man from Missoula, Montana, who resembled him in many ways. This was Harold Osmane Small, rector-president of Seattle College, currently being considered by Father General as successor to Robinson as provincial.* When Harold entered the novitiate at Los Gatos on August 14, he had the well-scrubbed, rosy complexion of a lively Irish school kid. He was shorter than average and somewhat timid then, but to compensate for these limitations, he was gifted with a quick, facile mind and an uncommonly strong backbone. Unlike many shorter-than-average people, he did not express aggressiveness in his manner. He appeared to be almost passive at first, but he soon outgrew this, when he understood his companions. A naturally orderly man, with an inquisitive mind and an extraordinary memory for names and people, he quickly learned when to speak and when not to. He had great inner strength, doubtlessly derived from his antecedents on both sides of the family, Irish Americans who had arrived in Montana at one time or another via Canada.†

Like Father Elliott, who had entered the novitiate ten years earlier, Harold was the product of Loyola High School, a benefit he regarded so highly that he was determined in later years to open it again. He would get his opportunity some day, for he was destined to occupy chairs in high places. This could have been predicted by anyone who knew him, except himself, because as a philosopher and theologian he had the manner and voice of at least a bishop, perhaps a cardinal. He sometimes served as Master of Ceremonies in the sanctuary on solemn occasions, and his calm, measured behavior blended in so perfectly with the pomp and splendor of the ceremonies that one hardly noticed it. Despite these splendid examples of talent, he was still diffident as a tertian, and when Father Elliott appointed him to be principal of Gonzaga High School, he begged off on the grounds that he lacked confidence in himself.‡ As one might have expected, he was appointed as dean of Seattle College almost as soon as he had unpacked his trunk there.

Graduate studies had not changed him, but had helped to bring out what he already was. As dean and president he became more so. He now possessed self assurance. He made quick decisions without hesitation, but not without an awareness of the political implications of his actions. In one respect especially, he demonstrated his superior administrative ability: he could keep many balls in the air without becoming ruffled or flustered. He appeared to be altogether unflappable.

No one, I think, was surprised when the general appointed him provincial on February 2, 1948. Father Hugh Geary, a diminutive Irishman from eastern Montana, with thick black hair and roguish grin, like a Gaelic leprechaun, had succeeded John Dougherty as the provincial's assistant. He dispatched notices to the members of the province on March 29, 1948, informing them that on this day Father Small had been formally installed as the new provincial.[3] Father Robinson returned to Gonzaga University to teach sociology.

The timing was inopportune, perhaps, because one of the members of the province, Father Francis Doyle Gleeson, was scheduled to be consecrated as the Titular Bishop of Cotenna and Vicar Apostolic of Alaska, on April 5, 1948, just one week later. Since Fitzgeralds' death, almost seven months had gone by, before his successor was selected, and then, by some fickle trick of fate, Gleeson was informed of his appointment by the newspaper.

*Provincial Archives, Portland, Janssens to Robinson, Feb. 2, 1948. Father Small's middle name was bestowed upon him to honor a Sister of Charity of Providence, a very dear friend of the family. Interview with Small by Schoenberg, July 6, 1981, Seattle.

†Small's great grandfather on his father's side came from Ireland via Germany and Canada. His mother was a native of Stratford, Ontario. She was of Irish descent.

‡Interview with Small. He first convinced Father Dougherty, Elliott's assistant, that he should not be principal.

Since leaving his position as rector at Sheridan, Gleeson had been pastor of St. Stanislaus Parish in Lewiston, Idaho, and then superior of St. Mary's Mission near Omak, the latter being his residence on February 8, 1948, when he sent the following telegram to Hugh Geary: "Received telegram from Denver Registrar [sic] congratulating on appointment and asking for biograpical data. Is this a joke or should I take it seriously. F. Gleeson."[4]

It was no joke. He had been selected to be bishop.

In the province he had been regarded as very talented, especially as a cook. When he was rector of Sheridan, he often cooked for the entire community, one hundred or more, to spell off the brother who had to cook every day, and these times were always memorable: the meals were excellent and every pot and kettle in the kitchen had been used in their preparation. He could bake pies that would merit blue ribbons in the county fair. Needless to say, as a community man, he was very popular.

There is an interesting document in Gleeson's file. On May 2, 1912, when he applied to enter the novitiate, he received a physical examination by Dr. Jobic Audic, son-in-law of Dr. Menager. Audic examined five Jesuit candidates that day, Charles Owens, Curtis Sharp, Edgar Taylor, Hugh Geary and last of all, Francis Gleeson. He reported that the first four were in "A-I" condition. He had reservations about Gleeson, nothing serious, he said, but he wanted to make another examination. Gleeson, like the others, was finally approved with comments about a small irregularity. Oddly, he has outlived all the others by at least two decades.

The choice of Gleeson for Alaska was very popular. He was known as a humble, unobtrusive priest, with a deep commitment to religious poverty. When he made his preparation for his consecration, this became increasingly obvious. Father Augustine Ferretti, a member of the Mount's teaching staff and one of the province's most able organizers was placed in charge. The time was short and things began to hum. To save costs, one of the scholastics, Neill Meany, a gifted artist who applied himself to the study of heraldry to accomplish his assignment, designed the bishop's coat-of-arms.* Father Leo Yeats of Gonzaga made the official portraits, taking the bishop-elect's photograph in his dingy fourth-floor studio, using a war surplus bedspread as a background. Archbishop Howard was invited to be the consecrating prelate, with Bishop White of Spokane and Bishop Martin Johnson of Nelson, British Columbia, as co-consecrators. Travel expenses, someone noted, could not have been less. The ceremony was conducted in St. Aloysius Church in Spokane on a sunny spring day, with dignity and holy prayers but also with simplicity—the trademark of the new bishop.

It would be appropriate, I think, to describe three other photographs of Bishop Gleeson, which are in the files. All of them were taken of his Excellency in 1950, when he assisted other Jesuits and workmen in the construction of the new St. Mary's Mission on the Andreafski River in Alaska.† In one the bishop is shown, standing in front of the cook-shack, wearing his chef's hat and broad white apron. He cooked all the meals for the crew as they built the mission. The second shows the bishop in war surplus army coveralls, military olive green, at the controls of a bulldozer, which he operated part time, when he was not busy in the kitchen. The third shows him wearing the same apparel using surveyor's instruments, while others were driving stakes. Even one of these is sufficient commentary on the kind of bishop Rome had presented to the rugged mission of Alaska. Leo

---

*Neill Meany designed coats of arms for other bishops and schools as well as book jackets. He served for a time as cartoonist for *The Homiletic and Pastoral Review*.

†St. Mary's Mission at Akulurak was being relocated at Andreafski. The new St. Mary's was built before the staff and children were transferred on August 2, 1951. They arrived at Andreafski at 9:45 P.M. the following day.

Kaufmann, a perceptive young Jesuit, said "My faith in the Holy Spirit's choice has been greatly confirmed."

Father Small was doubtlessly relieved when the new bishop had been consecrated. Such highfalutin fireworks marked a hard beginning for a new provincial, who had been away from the province for several years, and who was only forty-one years old. He had his first status, or list of assignments, to make out, which included for August, 1948, an unusually large number of scholastics—sixteen—to be assigned to theology: thirteen to Alma, one to West Baden and two to Ireland. He also had to process and approve thirty-five young men who were coming into the novitiate, an unusually large number.

He had left Seattle College somewhat hurriedly, in the midst of paper work for securing a university charter, and though the new rector-president, Father Albert Lemieux, former dean at Gonzaga, was perfectly capable of conducting his office, there were many loose ends to tie and a certain paternal care to exercise in Seattle, where Jesuits were suffering from growing pains.

The new university charter became effective on May 28, 1948.[5] On that day Seattle College, almost fifty-seven years old, became Seattle University by formal declaration of the sovereign State of Washington. Having suffered almost everything except martyrdom, this institution had finally, and deservedly, reached the top rung of academic designation, largely because of the struggle of a few devoted Jesuits who had faith in the Catholics of Seattle, as well as faith in themselves. Only ten years earlier these Jesuits had one small building and a handful of students. On May 28, 1948, Seattle University had 2,793 students.[6] This was a kind of triumph never before experienced by Jesuits in the Pacific Northwest and those that shared in it relished it to the full. One can easily understand this spirit of triumph, this new awareness which now swept the campus and brought with it a new sense of maturity.

No longer could it be said that Gonzaga's status as a university implied more prestige than Seattle's. Seattle's former dean was now provincial and Gonzaga's was now president of Seattle University. Under Lemieux, the old veterans there told one another that the university would leap forward. And so it did. Soon, almost twice the size of Gonzaga, it was the largest Catholic university in the west. Could it be true that Robinson had suggested only a few years before that Seattle College should be attached to Gonzaga as a junior partner!

Seattle University's greatest crisis lay ahead, but the strength gathered during the Lemieux Administration and several subsequent years would ultimately save what had been celebrated in 1948 from disaster. When that final test came, the glorious transition of 1948 would not only be remembered, it would be one of the principal life rafts on which the university was preserved.

At Gonzaga, Father Corkery, who had helped to pave the way for all the excitement at Seattle was much worried about new quarters for the high school, which occupied some temporary barracks acquired from the government. These barracks leaked so badly that holes had to be drilled in the floor to let the water drain off. There was one drinking fountain for four hundred boys, and the barracks got so hot when the sun came out that some of the boys threatened a riot.

Bishop White had been agitating for over a year for the construction of a new high school on a new campus. Whenever occasion offered itself, he publicly stated that this was his number one priority. He was aging now. He had been bishop for over twenty years and he was anxious for the Jesuits to take advantage of his friendship in securing the canonical erection of a new community for the high school before he died.

450

Because of the opposition of the bishops, there really was in Seattle only one canonical Jesuit Community, Seattle Prep, and Seattle's only Jesuit rector served in this position for both the university and the prep school. All efforts to change this met with firm resistance.* Bishop White, who was familiar with this situation, reminded the Spokane Jesuits that his successor might not permit a second Jesuit community with a rector for each, and he urged that action be taken as quickly as possible. As far as the Jesuits were concerned, there was no problem that Mr. Money could not solve. But Mr. Money was elusive.

When Father Gordon Toner became principal of the high school in 1948, he brought with him all of his Toner get-it-done spirit, and one of his first objectives was to find suitable land for a new campus. He persuaded a friendly pilot to fly him on a tour of the city, so that he could single out from the air larger parcels of open land that might be available. In this manner he discovered the large open space on east Euclid Avenue. Father Small reported this to Father General.

"Unexpectedly, "he wrote, "they [officials at Gonzaga High School] located a large unoccupied piece of land about one mile from the present campus, the main part of which belonged to the County and which, therefore, they felt could be purchased at public sale for a low price. They acquired 28 lots for $1,800. When the date of sale approached they realized, once the public learned that Gonzaga might build their high school here, that all the surrounding property would rise in price. Upon the advice of the consultors, I, therefore, presumed permission to allow Gonzaga to purchase other surrounding lots for a sum of $11,700.

"Through silent and quick action Gonzaga acquired about four blocks for the unbelievably low price of $13,500. When Bishop White was informed of the purchase he commented that it was the best news he had heard in a long time. The money was all at hand from a drive which the Bishop sponsored for a new Gonzaga High School several years ago. I ask Your Paternity to ratify this purchase.

"In order to round out this property we would like to buy another block and one half which is owned by a lumber company and upon which they intend to pile lumber.

"The Great Northern Railway in gratitude for our giving them a right-of-way into Spokane through our property many years ago seems willing to trade a piece of their property for that owned by the lumber company and then sell us the desired land. Father Francis Corkery thinks that we may be able to purchase the property for as low as $5,000."[7]

Eventually the Great Northern property was acquired in the manner in which Small had described, and Gonzaga High School proudly held in the university's name, something like twenty-three acres for a future school. This was progress.

Father Corkery had been making mysterious remarks during this time about a new endowment in the making, which would stabilize Gonzaga's finances, so he thought, for the foreseeable future. In other words, Corkery implied that he was coming to terms with Mr. Money. He frequently asked prayers for this inscrutable purpose which kept the community on edge, as though news would suddenly arrive that Gonzaga had been presented the long-sought formula for making gold.

Father Small had inherited the contents of this secret, with some other headaches, from the Robinson administration. Realizing the need for continued reticence, he shared Corkery's concern and did all he could to expedite the mysterious project and to secure for Corkery the required permissions from Rome.

When Jesuits at Gonzaga finally discovered what was in the wind, there were mixed reactions, with the majority admitting their ignorance about matters so indecently techni-

---

*Seattle University's Jesuit Community was directed by "a superior" appointed by Rome. In time this superior became independent of the rector at Seattle Prep.

cal, and hoping that Corkery's optimism were justified. They soon learned that correspondence regarding the project had been flying back and forth between Portland, Rome, Washington, D.C., and Spokane since 1946. Robinson had dispatched to Rome a report in August of that year and Father de Boynes, just before the election of Janssens as the new general, responded with caution, accusing Robinson, in polite language, of exaggeration or gullibility. Robinson had merely quoted Corkery's figures on costs and profits and de Boynes mostly said, "I don't believe them," and time proved he was right. The General Congregation delayed further action, more correspondence containing opinions piled up, and finally the matter, quite sticky by this time, was dumped into Small's lap.

All these preliminaries had focused on one transaction, the acquisition of Spokane radio station KGA. Station KGA belonged to Louis Wasmer, one of Gonzaga's regents. In June, 1946, Wasmer offered to sell the station to Gonzaga on terms that were reportedly equal to an endowment income worth $300,000 annually.[8] According to current reports the total net profits of the station were approximately $400,000 per annum.* Wasmer offered to sell KGA for approximately $500,000, the payments to be made over the years out of the station's income. Gonzaga had nothing to lose.

The offer appeared too good to be true. Without a doubt, ownership of KGA would solve the endowment problem for some time to come, if Wasmer's offer was a firm one and if the station's income was as high as estimated. Corkery prudently examined all aspects of the proposal and sought both legal and business advice. KGA, he was informed, had been in operation for twenty years. Its first broadcast took place on January 8, 1926. The Northwest Radio Company had built and was operating it, with a twelve-hour daily program, over a wave length of 240, using ten kilowatts of power. In 1929 it was sold to E. E. Pierce, a Seattle banker. Wasmer, who also owned KHQ for some time, purchased KGA in 1933 and gradually built it up as one of the Northwest's most powerful stations.[9] At a reported cost of $250,000 he modernized it throughout the mid-1940s, and in 1947 raised its power to fifty kilowatts.[10] Three possible threats to the best interests of the university appeared in Corkery's first scrutiny of the offer: (1) financial liability; (2) identification of the university with doctrines expressed in routine broadcasts; for example, on non-Catholic religious programs; (3) the antagonism of local businessmen, who would consider the university, a tax-exempt institution, as an unfair competitor. To protect against the university's financial liability, every possible threat was explored. At this time tax-exempt public corporations, like colleges and universities, were allowed the ownership of profit-making corporations with continued exemption on federal taxes, provided the income was used as an endowment. Other universities had taken advantage of this form of tax structure for many years. Besides Jesuit universities there were other universities which, like Baylor, either owned commercial radio stations or other forms of profit-making businesses; for example, hotels, lumber yards or oil wells. So long as Gonzaga University was tax-exempt in its operation of KGA, there could be no financial risk whatever in its ownership.

To further safeguard its financial interest, it was proposed that legal counsel for the corporation of Gonzaga University, as new owner of the station, file a petition with the Federal Communications Commission for a more favorable broadcast channel or for a "clear channel." Since it was commonly known that the FCC was on the verge of making channel adjustments, it was hoped, perhaps with unwarranted optimism, that fifty-kilowatt-station KGA would be awarded a change. If this were accomplished the value of KGA would be notably increased.

*According to these estimates the station's net profit would be $400,000 which meant that the university would be able to make $100,000 payments annually for five years, and to retain $300,000 for endowment. The actual income for the first year was $249,555.96. OPA, Gonzaga Papers, KGA, CPA Report, June 15, 1949.

The second possible threat to the interests of Gonzaga University—identification with doctrines expressed on broadcasts—proved to be less complex than it seemed at first. Two other Jesuit-owned stations: Loyola of the South's WWL in New Orleans, a clear channel station; and St. Louis University's WEW, had operated for many years on the principle that station ownership in no way implied agreement with doctrinal views expressed in broadcasts.

These precedents, as well as the accepted attitude of the public toward radio or newspaper ownership, convinced Corkery that Gonzaga had nothing to fear.

The possibility of opposition of some local businessmen was more precarious and Corkery examined it carefully. Perhaps those who shared the view that tax-exempt schools should stay out of business failed to realize Gonzaga's predicament, as well as the amount of its contribution to the community. Tax-exemption was but a form of a partial government subsidy, more or less large, depending on the university's ability to invest money. Surely no one could reasonably object to Gonzaga's efforts to acquire this legitimate subsidy, especially in view of its advantages to students, as well as to tax-payers, whose taxes were considerably lower because these students attended a private university. It was clear, then, that probable opposition to Gonzaga's ownership of KGA, while regretted, had to be disregarded for the greater good. At the same time, Corkery made it plain that the university was determined to maintain the most cordial relations possible with all of Spokane's businessmen.

The Wasmer proposal now became a rosy-bright hope for the future, a solution to the most baffling of Gonzaga's riddles. It was also a subject of numberless conferences as well as the stacks of correspondence between Gonzaga and Washington, D.C., Portland and Rome. Out of the whirlwind, which was carefully shielded from the public because of the interests hostile to Gonzaga, conditions of the sale of the station and transfer of its license gradually became clear.

During the spring of 1949, the terms were agreed upon. Corkery requested that the agreement be executed and dispatched to his office with a CPA report on the station's financial operations. The report did not arrive until June 15, 1949. On the following day the contract between Wasmer and the university was signed. Notice of it, announced jointly by Father Corkery and Mr. Wasmer, appeared in the evening's *Chronicle*, stating simply that the station had been sold to Gonzaga for a consideration in excess of $400,000. More than three months were required to work out all of the details of transferring management of the station, as well as the ownership. Finally, in the last week of September, Father Corkery posted the following notice on the Jesuit community's bulletin board:

"Today final details were completed for the transfer of Radio Station KGA from Mr. Louis Wasmer to Gonzaga University. As of midnight Friday, September 30th, the station belongs to our community. With God's help this station can go a long ways in solving many of our major problems of the future. All the members of the community are asked to keep this intention frequently in their Masses and prayers so that our hopes may be realized."[11]

At the time appointed, October 1, 1949, Gonzaga took possession of KGA. Harvey Wixson, acting manager of the station under Wasmer, was employed as station manager for the Jesuits and little evidence of any kind appeared on the surface to indicate the change of ownership.

Contrary to expectations the acquisition of KGA did not solve Gonzaga's chronic financial problem. For one thing, competition with television forced radio's advertising rates down so that KGA's monthly income dropped substantially below previous figures. In 1951 income was $248,515.87 and costs were $242,134.87.[12] In addition to this, an historic new tax law swept away Gonzaga's exemption on the station's profits. Father Corkery's persevering efforts to secure an improvement in KGA's frequency assignment, or a clear channel, met with repeated failures.

In November, 1950, Father Corkery, somewhat anxious and discouraged by the obstacles which confronted him on every path, wrote to the provincial, Father Harold Small. "In general, with costs rising daily and enrollments definitely decreasing," he said, "the economic picture is bad—very bad—and we're all going to tighten our belts, cut expenses wherever we can, and look for outside sources of income."[13] The war in Korea had alarmed college administrators everywhere and Gonzaga's president was no exception. As matters turned out, his anxiety about decreasing enrollment was not groundless. Full-time day-campus enrollment dropped from 1649 in 1949 to 1415 in 1950. A year later there was another drop of one hundred and seventy-four students, not a disastrous decrease, by any means, but an ominous one, leading to financial insecurity and uncertainties about the scheduling of classes.

If Father Corkery's fears regarding enrollment had been well-founded, it would appear, in retrospect at least, that his anxiety about money was not. While financial reports for the period of 1946–1951 do not show any sensational gains, they indicate stability and a modest measure of progress. During these five years, for example, Gonzaga received a total of $817,788 in gifts, the largest of which was $201,000 from Bing Crosby for the library. Disposition of funds included $539,444.31 for the construction of Dillon Hall and $15,000 for the remodeling of the old canteen for a temporary student union building. In 1951 there was $405,300 in the various building funds.[14]

It would be pertinent at this point to add that during the year 1950–1951 Gonzaga made grants in aid totaling $12,326.75. In addition to this it awarded one hundred and twenty-eight scholarship grants totaling $50,897.11. These were distributed as follows: thirty-six for basketball players, totaling $15,562.48; twenty-one for members of the boxing team, $10,117.38; eight for athletic managers, $5,256. Thus athletic scholarships amounted to $30,935.86. Forty-two academic scholarships, including fourteen for the Cataldo Memorial fund, five for law students, nineteen for music students and the balance in other schools, totaled in value $19,961.25.[15]

During this same year, 1950–1951, unsalaried Jesuit faculty members contributed to the university a donation in services estimated at $131,372.82 plus another donation of $18,244.03, which Jesuits had received for religious services not directly connected with the university. The average annual contribution of the Jesuit staff for a ten year period, 1944–1954, was $126,475.31.[16] This figure, representing an income of five percent would require a total investment of $2,529,506.20. This was Gonzaga's principal endowment. And this, not station KGA, was, of course, Gonzaga's hope of survival.

Corkery soon directed that, in view of the change in tax laws, it was time to dispose of the station. On October 29, 1952, he informed Father Small that a party interested in KGA had offered $50,000 a year for a ten-year lease, which included an option to buy it for a total of $500,000.[17] Small wrote three days later to assure Corkery that permission from Father General for the sale would arrive and that Gonzaga should proceed with negotiations. On January 20, 1953, Corkery signed a contract with Bankers Life and Casualty Company of Chicago for a ten-year period. In a letter to Small a few days later, Corkery revealed details of the contract.[18] When all of Gonzaga's remaining obligations were satisfied, Corkery added, the university would count approximately $250,000 profit on the investment.

Approval for the transfer of the license to Bankers Life was received on May 28, 1953. About three days later the actual transfer was made and Gonzaga University was pleased to recognize that it was no longer in the radio broadcasting business.

This ended the saga of KGA. The provincial in Portland, who was relieved that Gonzaga had survived without losing its shirt, could turn his attention to other matters.

At Sheridan and at the Mount, during the earlier period in Small's provincialate, there was an interminable debate about what kind of clothing was appropriate for swimming. Father Zacheus Maher had promulgated two very unpopular decrees, the first that "uppers"—some form of shirt like a tank top—had to be worn by Jesuits when they went swimming, and the second that titles of Jesuits were to be used at all times, even when they were engaged in sports. Nicknames and first names were strictly forbidden. Thus in the novitiate and juniorate "Brother" was to be used, later at the Mount "Mister." Since gym shirts or tank tops were unavailable, the scholastics used T-shirts instead. The more daring, having experienced the soggy, bedraggled appearance of wet T-shirts, found ingenious reasons for disposing of "uppers" while others continued to wear them, more or less under protest. What might be described as the "War of the Uppers" dragged on for years, because no superior was willing to dispense from anything so hallowed as a decree of Zacheus J. Maher. It was almost like abolishing one of the Ten Commandments.

At this point Small visited the juniors while they were having a holiday at Nestucca Bay on the ocean. He saw for himself how wretched they looked in wet T-shirts, "like wet rats." He wrote to the rector, Father John Dalgity: "From my visit to the Juniors' Villa yesterday, I have formed the judgement that religious modesty and discipline is not improved by the wearing of white T-shirts with the swimming trunks . . . As far as I am concerned, there is no need to continue to wear them."[19]

Time took care of the titles. Robinson, who had always favored the use of first names, pretended not to notice when they were used and Small regarded the fuss about them as beneath his attention. The good old American custom of addressing one another fondly by first names, or some colorful appellation, was gradually restored. Peace reigned until other pecadillos could be found for the scholastics to argue about.

Father Small had more serious reservations about other adversities. At Sheridan, Mark Gaffney had proved to be too soft-hearted to serve longer as Novice Master, and he was replaced by William Elliott, former provincial. Oscar Auvil, for reasons of health, had been replaced as dean. His flip little "not exact" in class recitations had given way to Father John Taylor's silent cold glare and an atmosphere of considerable tension, about which the juniors complained when the provincial made his visitation. Taylor, a frostily professional dean-teacher, with an apparent reluctance to allow humor within earshot, was also an articulate member of the provincial's board of consultors, where the question was raised about continuance at Sheridan. Piet, who had founded the novitiate, had been dead for about seven years, surely long enough, some of the wags jocosely remarked, for him to get out of purgatory and into heaven, so the provincial could count on his help in solving the dilemma.

Taylor was also librarian. He had provided a glass case containing some relics of classical antiquity at the entrance of the very proper library on the fourth floor. One of the juniors, whose sense of humor was more active than the dean's, added two items to the exhibit, a gunny sack labelled "The Sack of Rome," and a discarded remnant of a boot, which was labelled "Achilles' Heel."* Taylor was not amused.

---

*The imaginative junior was Frank Case, present rector at Seattle University.

In a letter to Janssens, Small listed six reasons why the Sheridan property should be abandoned. Since these reasons contain an authentic account of the over-all situation at Sheridan, they are presented here in full:

Reasons for Moving

"1. There is not an adequate supply of water at Sheridan. During the latter part of July and the months of August, September and into October, the use of water must be drastically curtailed. One year the water had to be hauled by truck to the house. There can be no lawns or flowers and no irrigation of fields.

"One shallow well supplies the drinking water. A little creek which almost dries up each summer, and did one summer, supplies water for other uses. Deep wells have been sunk in vain. The United States Geodetic Survey told us that in this area there is a hard clay about 30 feet down which prevents water from going deeper. They recommend sinking a series of shallow wells. This we are doing. Their worth would not be known until next fall, but judging from the one in operation they would never guarantee an adequate supply of water for household use and certainly would never supply enough for *any* irrigation.

"It was suggested to save winter water for irrigation but we learned from professionals that irrigation takes about one million gallons per acre. We could not store that much. The town of Sheridan is short of water and, therefore, refused to share any water with us.

"Nine miles from the Novitiate is an abundant source of fresh water which could be carried to the house by gravity flow and would care for all household needs and irrigation. We would be practically assured of a perpetual supply for the Portland General Electric has taken steps to effect this. According to engineers this project would cost between $165,000.00 to an outside figure of $200,000.00

"There is, however, a possible site for a novitiate 25 miles from Portland, where some of the richest soil in Oregon is located, which has a well that gives 435 gallons a minute. Within five to ten years this valley will be irrigated by water from a dam.

"2. Although there are 800 acres at Sheridan only about 40 acres are arable soil. Other land can be used for grazing but most of it is poor even for this. We graze 75 head of cattle but need twice this number. This farm should earn 5 to 10 thousand dollars a year, at the most, not charging the labor of three Brothers against the profits. This would be very little support in hard times for now the Arca Seminarii is giving Sheridan about $4,000.00 a month in addition to the $1,500.00 a month from the D'Arcy Estate. A new place with fertile soil would be more encouraging to the Brothers and more promising for the future.

"3. The present building is poorly planned and expensive to finish. *Poorly planned:* There are no class rooms, the center section is too wide for any normal use. Although strongly reinforced, yet the steel is not building but ship steel without any "give" and, hence, one architect thinks that in a severe earthquake the building would suffer serious damage. The building is extremely noisy because, they say, it was poured in one piece.

Expensive to finish: (a) Brick for building $235,000.00
                     (b) Refectory wing.................. 250,000.00
                     (c) Finish interior 100,000.00

(a) The building leaked seriously until a water proofing substance, looks like tar, was placed on the building. If this dries and cracks, the walls will leak again. The building must be bricked, therefore, to prevent leaking.

(b) The present refectory is an old wooden shell which was erected 20 years ago as a temporary structure for one year. Class rooms and perhaps an infirmary should be placed on the second floor of a new refectory wing.

(c) The pipes in the water and heating system were cheap so that they will soon have to be replaced. The floors are simple cement without a covering. Much of the plaster was spoiled by the leaking building. Much painting was never done. The top center floor was never finished.

"4. There is very little level ground. The building sets on a high hill where it can be beaten by vertical wind blown rains from the ocean. This makes the back of the building difficult to heat in the winter.

"5. The Novitiate is 55 miles from Portland. This distance makes it hard to get hired help and skilled technicians must be paid from the time they leave Portland. Contractors say that it will cost an extra $5.00 per day per man to build at Sheridan. There is extra cost in purchasing food, etc., and transporting men to the doctors. Intellectual and cultural advantages for faculty and juniors suffer.

"6. Some business men think it is foolish to sink more money into the present location."[20]

While Small's six reasons for moving appear to be compelling, his reasons against moving seemed to outweigh them. As he noted, an adequate supply of water was obtainable, the scholastics were happy and healthy at Sheridan, and improvements could be made on the novitiate building as money was available, without the need to borrow a great sum at any one time. "The consultors unanimously judge," he added, "that if we had the money we should move the Novitiate to a more fertile area—and with this I whole-heartedly agree." Since, however, there was no money, all agreed that the present building should be retained.

These prophetic deliberations were concluded in March, 1950. In May Gonzaga was in the news again. Harry Truman, President of the United States, had agreed to accept a "Citation of Merit" from the university. This auspicious event had its roots in *America,* the Jesuit national weekly, in which an editorial praising the president "as one of the great moral leaders in the history of the presidency," had appeared on March 4, 1950. Especially praiseworthy, the editorial stated, was the president's firm support of "natural law," and rejection "of legal positivism taught in most of the American law schools."[21]

A few days after this editorial appeared, it was read with no little pleasure by John Patrick Leary, who was nearing the completion of his second year of theology at Alma

College in California, where he had kept in close touch with two of his pet themes, politics and Gonzaga. Perceiving a sudden natural relevance between these two themes, otherwise not particularly related, he reread the editorial, then wrote a long letter to Corkery on March 24, 1950. The letter is no longer extant but its contents are well remembered.* Leary referred to the *America* editorial, praising its timeliness and insight. He also referred to press notices that President Truman was scheduled to appear in Spokane in May following, for the dedication of Coulee Dam. It seemed to him, Leary added, that this would be a grand opportunity for Gonzaga University to present an honorary degree to the president precisely because of his stand with regard to the natural law. The university's law school, already high in national prestige, would benefit from the occasion, but this was less significant than Gonzaga's rather dramatic repudiation of legal positivism and its expression of encouragement to the president for his courageous position.

The proposal was brilliant and Corkery recognized it immediately. There was no time to lose. A conference via short wave radio was arranged between Gonzaga and Alma, and Leary, who had more leisure for considering all practical aspects of the matter, presented, through the Alma operator, detailed plans for the proposed ceremony. During the weeks that followed other discussions were held by the same means. Leary was informed that the president was reluctant to accept an honorary degree from any university except his own alma mater, but he would be pleased to accept a citation. With the assistance of Father Edward Shipsey of Santa Clara University, Leary composed the citation which was concluded as follows:

> "NOW, THEREFORE, we, the President and Faculty of Gonzaga University, inspired by love of country and devotion to freedom under God, do hereby confer upon the Honorable Harry S. Truman, President of the United States of America, this Citation of Merit.
> Given at Spokane, Washington, on this eleventh day of May, in the year of Our Lord, one thousand nine hundred and fifty."

At the president's request, news of the impending ceremony was withheld from the press until eleven days before the event. It was released simultaneously by the president's press secretary in Washington and Father Corkery in Spokane on May 1, 1950. The *Chronicle* for that evening carried a disaster-size headline: "Gonzaga Will Honor Truman," and there followed, in smaller print, a detailed account of the now famous citation, presented in cautiously phrased diplomatic language, lest someone be offended by a presumed political alliance between the university and Truman's party. Father Corkery, realizing the possible implications, worded his own statement very carefully:

> "President Truman has graciously accepted our invitation to appear on our campus and give an address. As President of the United States, he is one of the vitally pivotal figures of the world today. Upon his shoulders rest responsibilities that may well affect the future of all mankind. We feel the people of Spokane, regardless of political affiliation, will be anxious to hear the President of the United States."

This statement appeared in the *Spokane Chronicle* on May 1, 1950, ten days before the arrival of the president. Since no president of the United States, previous to this, had made an

---

*My journal for that day contains this entry: "This a.m. Jack Leary came with a letter to Father Corkery at Gonzaga. He asked me to read it and tell him what I thought of it." There followed a report in detail on the contents of the letter.

address on a Northwest college or university campus, Gonzaga officials were much concerned about protocol and appearances. A committee, with Joseph Drumheller as chairman, was quickly formed. Campus renovations were begun under the direction of Father Dussault, who was also in charge of public relations. Press rooms were installed in De Smet Hall. New phone and telegraph lines were connected. Mr. Truman, who had recently come into sharp conflict with the Southern Democrats on the civil rights issue (the latter now called themselves Dixiecrats) was expected to present a major speech concerning civil rights and the Dixiecrats. Scores of reporters, not to be caught off guard, indicated their needs to cover the speech and the university administration cheerfully offered to provide more than was required. Father Dussault turned out pages of data for them, including an advance copy of Father Corkery's own speech of welcome.

Members of the ROTC and its commanding officer, Colonel Tabscott, were particularly diligent in their preparations for their commander-in-chief's arrival. Helmuts and guns were shined until they gleamed. Uniforms were pressed until the pleats looked as flat as cardboard. Band instruments were cleaned and flags carefully checked to make sure that all was in order.

It so happened that about one year earlier, Colonel Tabscott had requested the assistance of the university's public relations office for designing an ROTC standard which would represent Gonzaga in a unique manner. After a conference or two a flag with the university's coat of arms in the center was decided upon and the public relations' office then undertook a research program to gather authentic details on the coat of arms, since its use in the flag would set an official precedent.

Colonel Tabscott dispatched this data to the army's quartermaster depot in Philadelphia, where the standard was made. The embroidery work in color, for the coat of arms and the legend "Gonzaga University Reserve Officers' Training Corps," required six months to complete. Providentially, the standard was finished a few days before President Truman's arrival. With the approval of Mr. Truman, the university scheduled the presentation of this standard to the ROTC unit during the campus ceremony. This, too, was a precedent, for it was reported that no American president, previous to this time, had presented a military standard to an ROTC unit.

May 11 finally dawned. If the arrangements committee had been anxious about the weather, their fears were groundless. The sun shone brightly and the huge platform, erected on the north end of the quadrangle, facing the new engineering building, was swathed in golden sunlight.

A slight breeze continued to blow from the southwest, across the quadrangle, tempering the warm, spring sunshine. The crowd continued to gather quietly, as though they were entering a church.

What followed is described by Father Corkery in a letter to the provincial:

> "The President's motorcade coming through town went North on Division to Mission, and over Mission to Addison, and down Addison toward the main entrance of the University then around in the back of the church into the quadrangle. The R.O.T.C. boys flanked the line of march for six solid blocks and then the crack Honor Guard in white hats, white scarves and white puttees, led the President's motorcade into the campus while the R.O.T.C. band played a thrilling march.

> "On reaching the platform a reception was held for the local Civic Committee who shook hands with the President and his party which included Mrs. Truman and Margaret, and Secretary of Agriculture Brannon, and many other dignitaries. On the platform was all the faculty in

academic garb, Bishop White and the President's party. It really made a colorful show. You will note we had none of the local politicians on the stage at Gonzaga. We kept it a purely academic affair. The ceremony went off beautifully and the President and Senator Magnuson seemed highly pleased.

"The President took time out of the middle of his speech to praise the extraordinary work of the R.O.T.C. Unit. He then presented personally the Unit Flag with the Gonzaga seal on it. He was delighted with the Citation given him, as a matter of fact the whole ceremony went off beautifully and in a highly dignified manner."[22]

At Alma, California, that evening, Leary waited impatiently for the news of the day via San Jose radio. At 9:40 he dialed the station. Five minutes later the "message" of the sponsor seemed longer than usual. At last the announcer got down to current business. The feature news of the day, Leary was pleased to note, was the president's speech, the "Gunzaegoe" speech, said the announcer. There followed a prolonged description of the event, during which the "Gunzaegoe" speech was described as an offer to the dixiecrats "of the olive branch of peace."[23] The speech the announcer concluded, had been delivered in the bright sunshine of the "Gonzaegoe" campus in the presence of approximately four thousand people.

Many newspapers and at least one periodical, *The Catholic Mind*, published the full text of the president's Gonzaga address.[24] A more significant sequel, however, was the final destiny of the university's citation. President Truman arranged to have it framed and placed on the wall of his office in the White House. When Corkery visited him there some twelve months later, it was the first object he noticed. "Father Corkery," said President Truman, noticing the visitor's glance, "that citation from Gonzaga is one of my proudest treasures."

In the euphoria of the president's visit to the campus, another matter was not overlooked; it merely got less attention. In his letter about Truman's reception, Corkery included a paragraph about this.

"The major donation which was recently received, and about which I spoke to you, came at a time of such high excitement that it didn't have the 'solemn octave' of rejoicing that it normally would have had but you can imagine how pleased everyone was. The cheque for $100,000 passed through nearly every hand in the Community before it finally got to the Bank. I only hope that this is the harbinger of good things to come for the High School. We really have to get to work on that now, but this donation was of course a tremendous 'shot in the arm'."[25]

The money had been given by "dear Johanna Mahoney," as Father Frank Masterson often referred to her in the years to come. She was an elderly spinster who had inherited great wealth, but lived simply, almost frugally, and gave it all away to charity. Her generosity to the high school, exceeding that of all others, extended even to the grave, for she provided that most of the residue of her estate was to become the property of the high school at the time of her death, avoiding even the formalities and cost of probate.* Her gift, of course, not only inspired others, but became the occasion for a major fund drive, city wide, except for one parish where the pastor objected.

Father Small was much gratified with the Mahoney gift, since the relocation of Gonzaga High School was one of the most pressing needs of the province. Other pressing needs were bricks and water at Sheridan, of course, and a new library at Gonzaga Univer-

---

*Johanna Mahoney passed, we trust, to an enviable reward in 1963.

sity. Members of the history department had been insisting that the Province Archives, still at the Mount, be transferred to Gonzaga where they would be more available for research. Even if he consented to these sometimes irritating demands, there was no space at Gonzaga to accommodate the archives. This situation, Father Corkery often stated, would be corrected when his old classmate, Bing Crosby, completed arrangements for financing a library building.

In Portland, Small was pleased to note, Father Henry Schultheis, who had cleared up Bellarmine High School's debt with some hard-nosed frugality, was transforming St. Ignatius Parish spiritually as well as physically. The parish staff had shared the original residence with the provincial's staff, but this residence had been transformed into Loyola Retreat House. Schultheis purchased the VanHoomissen home on 45th and Powell and converted it into a rectory. In May, 1950, ground was broken for a new church, sadly needed for forty years. This was completed and dedicated by Archbishop Howard on May 20, 1951.[26] Designed by John Maloney in contemporary ferro-concrete, the church had a capacity for 650 people. It soon earned some modest fame for what a parish church ought to be, for it represented the best features of permanence, dignity and economy in building and maintenance.

Schultheis, while he enjoyed the new church and loved to show it off, could not relax and stretch in the sun for a bit. His idea of a vacation was a fast trip to California on business with the provincial. He was an excellent driver, but a fast one, the kind that cannot bear to see a car in front of him, nor a speed cop behind him. His Jesuit confreres generally said that he could not sit long enough to be photographed. As soon as the church was dedicated he began his campaign to build a new school. He had very ambitious plans for the parish.

Small also had very ambitious plans for him. These did not appear yet, partly because the provincial had other irons in the fire, and partly because he was doing such a good job the general intended to keep him for another triennium. Mark Gaffney had become his socius, after leaving the post of novice master, replacing Hugh Geary, whose health had begun to fail.* Mark was sent to Rome in September of 1950 to represent the province at the procurator's congregation, a rather significant honor which indicated the high esteem in which he was held. He carried with him certain *postulata* or requests made by the province, including one for the general's intervention in the now infamous case of the Helena Promises.[27] The Promises, so far as the provincial was concerned, was still "unfinished business."

Janssens did not think the bishop was right, but he preferred to let matters stand as they were, "because Rome did not like to condemn a bishop."[28] Officially Janssen's response was as follows: "With caution and patience we ought to proceed."[29] In effect this preserved the *status quo,* and the Promises continued to be regarded as "unfinished business." Perhaps the best word that can be said about them is that they were finally buried with the bishop after his sudden death in San Francisco in 1962. It should be noted, also, that subsequent relations between the Bishop of Helena and the Jesuits have been unusually cordial, indicating perhaps, that the past with its misunderstandings has been buried too.

Shortly after Gaffney returned from Rome, Small wrote to the general about Mount St. Michael's alleged status as a *Collegium Maximum,* which ecclesiastical designation literally means "the greatest college." There are only several in the United States in addition to Mount St. Michael's. From 1918 to 1921, the Mount had been listed as a *Collegium Maxi-*

---

*Hugh Geary died in the train enroute to Spokane on July 4, 1953. He had finally consented to move to the Mount for better care. Father Michael McHugh was with him.

mum, but "we are told," Small explained, "that opposition arose from Jesuits in San Francisco to designating the Mount the *Collegium Maximum* of the Province, and, therefore, the term was no longer used."[30]

Father Janssens responded favorably to Small's request and the Mount was formally declared a *Collegium Maximum* in 1951. Most members of the province were unaware of it and the new honor meant so little to the rest that they did not bother to learn what it represented. It was common knowledge that the Mount had been a Pontifical Institute for many years, and the story had often been told of Ledochowski pointing out Spokane on a map, where the Mount was located, to Pope Pius XI. Later in September 1970, when Mount St. Michael's was closed as a scholasticate, it was moved to the Gonzaga campus under the title of St. Michael's Institute. There it retained both designations, which were regarded as highly desirable by ecclesiastical institutions.

The church in the Pacific Northwest at this same time received additional recognition from Rome. For over a century there had been only one archdiocese in the entire Northwest and Alaska. This was Portland in Oregon, successor to Oregon City the second archdiocese in the United States, established in 1846. Then on June 23, 1951, the Diocese of Seattle was created, an archdiocese with a metropolitan area comprising the dioceses of Seattle, Yakima, Spokane and Juneau, which heretofore had been a vicariate.* Bishop Thomas Connolly, who had succeeded Bishop Shaughnessy on May 18, 1950, was promoted to the Archiepiscopal dignity as the first Archbishop of Seattle. On the same day the Diocese of Yakima was established, and two weeks later, on July 9, Joseph Dougherty, former chancellor in Seattle, was appointed Yakima's first bishop.

This was a giant step forward for the church but the creation of more bishops and dioceses brought additional complications to religious superiors with subjects in all of these dioceses. Old disputes still existed; for example, in Yakima, the Jesuits' ownership of Marquette High School, had to be transferred to less experienced chanceries and new bishops who were reluctant to make decisions.

Shaughnessy's death had prepared the way for a rapport with the new bishop Thomas Connolly. Hopeful that he would understand the Jesuits' awkward position at Seattle University, its canonical dependence on the high school community, Small continued to press him for a *beneplacitum* to erect the university as a separate religious house. Connolly adamantly refused, even when Janssens wrote to assure him that the Jesuits would never open a collegiate church. The collegiate church was, of course, the crux of the problem for the Archbishop and his predecessors. The fame of the collegiate church in San Francisco, continued to exercise a baneful influence on the relations between the Jesuits and bishops.

On August 10, 1951, Janssen enacted a decree which classified the new Diocese of Juneau as part of the Oregon Province.[31] In other words, the territory once designated as *Alaska Australis* was no longer regarded as a mission. For those who disliked living in Alaska it was now discomforting to learn that one need not volunteer to go there to be assigned by the provincial. This was a surprise for some in the province and for others a fair warning: there were lonelier outposts to be feared than Heart Butte or Hays, Montana.

Father Tom Martin, alias "Kinky" was growing old and mellow at Sheridan. Forthright and delightfully inquisitive, he was always the center of interest, whether saying graces before meals one step ahead of the community, or recreating with the Fathers by simultaneously carrying on conversations, slitting pages of new books, and working crossword puzzles. "It's a sin to miss recreation with him," one Father remarked. "He tones us up for a whole day."

*The Vicariate of Alaska comprised all Alaska until the Diocese of Juneau was erected on June 23, 1951. On August 8, 1962, the Vicariate became the Diocese of Fairbanks, and on February 9, 1966, the Archdiocese of Anchorage was established.

The novices and juniors during this period saw much of him. Wrapped in a tarnished green-black coat that seemed to defy all efforts to destroy it, he stepped briskly about, interested in everything that was going on. In one hand he carried his breviary and at intervals he paced back and forth, saying his Psalms with relish. When he approached a group he paused to inquire as to the state of things, what, why, and who knew how. Then with a smile of satisfaction he was off again, on the lookout for another project. Projects amused him immensely, especially those that were highly imaginative. One got the impression sometimes that the wilder the schemes, the more pleased he was. Perhaps most of his satisfaction in these sometimes bizarre discoveries derived from his own relief at no longer being responsible for them.

Despite his wit, his Greek, and his gift for government, Father Tom's fame really rests on his community exhortations. Looking back, one is inclined to wonder why he was so popular as a speaker. He was not a rhetorician, like Bishop Sheen, and he had no great gift of eloquence. In a church pulpit he would have been listened to, though probably soon forgotten. But in a Jesuit chapel he belonged. He was effective. He reached the heart by his unobtrusive simplicity and directness. The time when we were most aware of him as Father Martin was when he gave his exhortations, and even then, somehow, we were aware of Father Martin speaking rather than Father Martin. And when we discussed his remarks the next day, we were seldom conscious of the personality, but only of his message. Yet his remarks were very personable. It would be a mistake to think they could have been effective without the warm personality behind them.

In November, 1952, much against his will, he assisted at a celebration for his golden jubilee. For the occasion, Father General sent congratulations, a printed program announced, "Happy 12½ Olympiads," and a banquet was spread. After the strawberry sundaes were consumed, songs were sung and spiritual bouquets were presented. Then there were speeches. Father Tom accepted all the praise, perhaps *suffered* is the right word, and then he himself rose to speak. In a moment he adroitly turned all the praise and attention from himself to the Society. As he went along, one no longer thought of him; one thought of the Society, and of thanksgiving to God for St. Ignatius.

Father Tom aged before our eyes: his hair, still bushy, turned gray; his step lost a little of its sureness; his trips around the grounds became less frequent. Always afflicted by the effects of the appendectomy years before, other minor ills befell him. In July, 1953, he developed throat trouble. He went to Portland to have it cared for, the first time he had been away from the house for three years. He seems to have suspected at once what it was, for in August he started keeping a medical diary, which he called "Data". His entry for Sept. 21st says this: "Saw Dr. Bailey who tells me what it is." It was cancer.[32]

When he was brought to the hospital he was quite a celebrity. A cancer specialist brought young doctors to examine the peculiarities of his case and Father Tom greeted them cordially. On his hospital chart there was a special notice: "Question the patient closely. He won't ask for anything."

When the doctor exhausted all known means to stop the cancer, he went to tell Father Tom. "I went to his room very depressed," he said later, "wishing I could think of something encouraging to say. You know, Father Martin cheered me up. He laughed and joked about the future." But the future was not long. He died, fully conscious, on May 8, 1954. A remarkable thing happened then, at least Mark Gaffney who was present, said it was so. As death came to claim him, his countenance suddenly brightened. He tried to raise his hands. "Mary!" he exclaimed. "How beautiful." His voice trailed off and then he died.[33] Mark never doubted that Father Tom had seen a vision of the Mother of God.

Father Pat O'Reilly, battle-scarred and weary, took Martin's place at Sheridan. He had been badly shaken some time before by a storm he had created in St. Patrick's Parish in

Spokane. It had started so innocently that Father Pat could not understand why it backfired. All he had done was to say in the pulpit at Sunday Mass, that there was *no Santa Claus*, and that it was a *sin* to tell one's children there was. What followed is not difficult to describe, but it should be left to everyone's imagination.

After some days, before the storm had abated, Father Dumbeck, mounting the pulpit at Mass, announced the following: "Maybe Father O'Reilly doesn't believe in Santa Claus, but I believe in him. Brother Kordich believes in him and all the other fathers believe in him." This helped to restore order, but it reduced the hapless O'Reilly to the level of an outcast, at least until the children forgot about him when they saw Santa Claus in the department stores.

Father Joseph Logan was now rector at the novitiate, replacing John Dalgity, the province's self-proclaimed "Holy Man" who was, indeed, very spiritual, but somewhat erratic in government. Logan's skill in diplomacy was required to keep O'Reilly and Father Frank Menager apart. They often quarrelled about whether Cataldo had actually killed Rebmann's dog. O'Reilly insisted that the account was "a damnable lie." Menager had retired because of old age and bad health, the latter mostly caused by very bad food in the missions of Alaska. He had ulcers, but this didn't keep him from eating raw oysters with heavy doses of vinegar.

O'Reilly celebrated his diamond jubilee as a Jesuit on July 8, 1953. He made a royal tour of the province, ready and willing to recite the more edifying details of his life for each community, at Mass or dinner, but preferably both. Before he arrived at Manresa Hall, the tertianship, several lengthy conferences had been conducted to determine if Pat should talk at all. The tertians all voted against it, so the rector, Father James Kiely informed the distinguished visitor that he was welcome; however, his speech making was not required. Having rendered this decision, Kiely got cold feet. He always had found it difficult to make up his mind, one way or another, so now he vacillated until the tertians threatened to make a formal protest. All this palaver was useless anyhow, for Pat, contrary to instructions, wheeled around at Mass and delivered a twenty-minute exhortation on the wonderful graces he had received in the last sixty years.

The Jesuit staff at Port Townsend during this period consisted of Kiely as rector, Leo Martin as tertian instructor, Tom Maher as minister and Peter Halpin as former minister, now semi-retired. Halpin collected stray dogs which barked all night. One of his many dogs, called "Hero" was an arrogant creature that instinctively knew he had a privileged existence under Halpin's patronage. He seemed to defy others to dislodge him as the community's favored guest. When he rode in the only car of the house, he sat upright occupying the front seat next to the driver, who was usually Brother John Connors, the cook. John, it must be admitted, had a quick temper, "Hero" was too much for him to handle and he was determined to get rid of him. Then one day he had his opportunity. With Hero at his side he drove into the forests, and came out without him. In fact, Hero was no more. The next day Halpin said to Connors: "Brother, Hero is lost. I know he is somewhere. Drive me around so that I can find him." The two drove up and down the streets of Port Townsend, stopping at vacant fields and parking lots. Halpin walked up and down, shouting: "Hero, Hero." But Hero never appeared again. A week later Halpin had another dog.

Kiely, who was already old, spent much of his time worrying, and part of the rest looking for something to worry about. Leo Martin, however, more than compensated for whatever deficiencies "The Port" might have had. He was the most authentically humble man most of us ever met. When he presented the Long Retreat of thirty days, required as part of tertianship, his strong, homely face, creased with lines of compassion and fatherly sollicitude, was etched in our minds to last, hopefully, forever.

Leo was already a legend in the province and many were the stories about his guiless-ness in a wicked world. As grandson of T. C. Power, he belonged to the aristocracy of Montana pioneers, and of this he was inordinantly proud. As a young candidate for the priesthood he had been sent by Bishop Carroll to the North American College in Rome to prepare for ordination. While there he decided to become a Jesuit. When he returned to Montana and informed Carroll of his decision, Carroll reacted with anger and determina-tion. He assigned one of his priests, Father William O'Maley, to persuade Leo to change his mind. For months O'Maley attempted to convince Leo he should return to Rome and be ordained for the diocese, but Leo declined. Instead, he entered the novitiate at Los Gatos.

Once he said to me: "Put out your hand." He placed a medal in it and spoke very solemnly, like a prophet of God. "Pope Pius the Tenth put that medal in my hand. I have known four popes, and if you ask me which is the greatest, I would say the one we have right now, Pius the Twelfth."*

For a priest who "knew four popes" not to mention his other lofty ecclesiastical con-nections, Leo manifested so little awareness of his own self-importance that a stranger could mistake him for a pensioned servant. "Everyone that has gone through Port Town-send while Father Martin was there recalls with amused and at times uproarious glee what a wonderful, abstract, forgetful, impractical devout, thoughtful, mysterious, un-selfconscious person he was," wrote John Leary. "On even first impression, one noticed his remarkable reverence for everyone, even the old hound dog that annoyed others at the Port got respect from the instructor. His whole demeanor was shy. When he walked, often he shuffled, half apologetically. This was all the more remarkable in the light of powerful convictions that shot forth now and then from his deep lamp-light eyes. Once he saw where the right lay, few tried to dislodge him. If he were wrong, as at times he was, he said so, not with any great surprise but as if it should have been expected."[34]

It will be remembered that Father Small was more than casually concerned with the re-establishment of his old Alma Mater, Loyola High School in Missoula. On May 20, 1952, he wrote to Janssens, proposing that it be opened in the following September as a parish high school. At the same time he informed Janssens that efforts were being made to convince the new bishop in Yakima to make Marquette a Jesuit high school.

There was some evidence to believe that Father Coudeyre, once paster in Missoula, was so opposed to the existence of Loyola that he had given away its library, reasoning, foolishly, that this would eliminate further discussion on the subject.[35] One of Small's consultors, also an alumnus of Loyola, opposed reopening the school presumably because of limitations on man power. As president of Seattle University, Lemieux could foresee endless needs for Jesuits to keep pace with the university's prolific growth. On the other hand, Father Louis Geis, present pastor in Missoula, urged that Loyola be reopened, and he continued to place some discreet pressure on Small to make it possible.

With the General's approval, Small sent Father Robert Rebahn, one of the province's most capable priests in this kind of work, to reopen Loyola High School in the original building on September 3, 1953. Thirty-two freshmen were enrolled on the first day.[36]

In Seattle, where Father Christopher ["Christy"] McDonnell was "Head Master" of the prep school, there was considerable pressure for additional space. At Christy's request, Small had appealed to Janssens for permission to make a substantial addition to the old school building. With the exception of the Garrigan Gymnasium, no improvements had

---

*This occurred following an exhortation Martin had given the terians, during which he presented some personal observations on Rome in the time of Pius X.

been made on the building since it was occupied by the Jesuits some three decades earlier. The Jesuit residence, which had minor renovations after an earthquake, required upgrading or replacement rather desperately. The last of the university faculty had long since departed and Christy was engaged in prolonged negotiations with the university regarding the division of community goods. These were finally concluded by the end of 1951 and Small dispatched a complete report to Janssens for approval on January 17, 1952. To complete the separation of the two now legally independent institutions, Christy filed for separate incorporation. On September 18, 1953, he reported to Small: "As of today we are incorporated under the title of Seattle Preparatory School."[37]

The new wing had been occupied in September of the previous year. Sufficient funds for it had not arrived, so the new addition was left partly finished, and this became an occasion of some playful jesting, but not in Christy's presence.

The backbone of the Seattle Prep administration at this time was as follows: Father McDonnell, rector and principal; Father Ralph Sudmeier, minister; and, Father Paul Weissenberg, vice-principal. McDonnell and Weissenberg had been there over twenty years. McDonnell was generally regarded as the most colorful of our high school principals, an office which he contrived to endure for twenty-six years, including seven at Bellarmine, and Weissenberg was equally respected as the most dedicated of high school vice-principals.* Among his duties during his long tenure was the care of the furnace, which he took very seriously. Since he was a thrifty man, the building was cold on weekends, and on Mondays, too, for it required a day to warm it up. On occasion the more vocal students carried blankets and huddled in them on Mondays to make their point.

At last in Spokane there was action, also, on the proposed new Gonzaga High School. A formal fund drive under Bishop White's special patronage, was begun on November 13, 1952, three years after the property was acquired. Cautious plans had been laid. Organized by Lawton Associates, hundred of volunteers canvassed the city. When the returns were in one month later, it was announced that $835,840 had been collected or pledged. Of this amount $685,000 was finally realized, approximately eighty-five percent of the total. Added to the almost $250,000 previously gathered, the total amount assured the construction of the new school. Plans for this were drawn by architect John Maloney, who worked especially close with three of the Jesuits: Gordon Toner, Michael Kunz, and Harry Jahn. The latter, in particular, scrutinized each blue print with a loan shark's eye, and counted each bolt and brick with his own computor, in his heavily thatched head, and guarded every penny spent until the architect shouted, "Help!"

At this point some loyal opposition appeared, under the leadership of Father William Keating, who protested that the new property owned by the high school was unsuitable for that purpose. It bordered on an industrial area, Keating said, that was located in northeast Spokane in the low-income neighborhood; but, he pointed out, city growth was extending into the more affluent northwest section of the city, whence most of the high school students would come. A new site on Garland Avenue in northwest Spokane had been identified as available at relatively low cost; however, there were those who said it was unsuitable because it was the wrong shape for school property; besides, it was covered mostly with basaltic rock.[38] The discussion, rather heated at times, raged for weeks until the provincial called a meeting to settle it. Christy McDonnell was asked his opinion. With others he examined both sites and wrote: "If you wish an expression of my preference of sites, I feel that *all things considered*, the Nevada site gets my vote."[39] As an opinion of the majority, Father Small adopted it and by dispatching a solemn order of cease and desist

---

*In 1960 Gonzaga University awarded Father McDonnell an Honorary Doctor of Pedogogy degree for his distinguished service in secondary education. He was principal at Bellarmine High School at that time.

further discussion, he resolved the matter finally and forever for better or worse.[40]

The way was now clear for construction. On June 27, 1953, bids for the building were opened in the president's office at Gonzaga University. Gordon Toner, who had been the ever-ready spark plug for the campaign's success, was ecstatic when Corkery awarded the contract to the Bouten Construction Company of Spokane on the lowest bid of $1,207,000 including alternates, for a modern fireproof building to accommodate eight hundred boys. On July 3, 1953, Bishop White presided over ground-breaking ceremonies and construction was begun with a great clatter and the roar of bulldozers.

It was Father Small's last year as provincial. He had planned for some time to attend a meeting of the Alaskan missionaries at St. Mary's Mission on the Andreafski, which had been built to replace the aging and unsuitable St. Mary's at Akulurak. The meeting was scheduled to convene on February 10, 1953. Small arrived at Dillingham on Bristol Bay, Alaska, enroute, on February 2. Of Holy Rosary Mission at Dillingham he wrote: "After a fire in 1950, which totally destroyed the combination church and residence in Dillingham, Fr. Endal constructed a two-story building about two miles outside of town on the road to the Government Hospital. The building has a full but unfinished basement, where Fr. [George] Endal and Fr. [Harold] Greif cook and eat their meals; a large classroom on the first floor, where Fr. Endal teaches 16 children in the first four grades; and on the top floor, where there is a living room for the Fathers and a chapel. I counselled Fr. Endal to put a floor and heat in the basement to safeguard their health. There is a small chapel in town."[41]

The provincial was most concerned about the recent controversy involving labor unions and the fishing industry in which three of his Jesuits had participated. Sometimes referred to as the Bristol Bay Controversy, this was nothing less than a jurisdictional dispute of three labor unions, the CIO, AFL and the alleged communist dominated ILWU for the control of the lucrative fishing trade in Alaskan waters. Owners of the industry with headquarters in Seattle arranged for seasonal employment of Eskimos from the villages, including many Catholics. Hence the bishop was deeply concerned regarding the spiritual care of these Eskimos who were periodically uprooted from their natural environments and thrown together in an alien town, where temptations abounded. The bishop was also concerned about the influence and possible take-over of the unions of the communist ILWU, and the misuse of labor by industry, in paying a just wage. With his approval, two Jesuits, George Endal and Jules Convert joined the Cannery Union to help the Eskimos in their struggle on the one hand against a communist union and on the other, against an industry that would take advantage of the turmoil to pay less wages.[42]

Father Clifford Carroll of Gonzaga University, who had earned his doctorate in economics at St. Louis University, and had considerable experience in labor relations, joined these two Jesuits in Dillingham at the request of Convert, who also had abundant labor experience on the docks of Marseilles, France. Carroll served as a consultant all during the summer of 1951. Largely due to the efforts of the Jesuits, the ILWU was rejected by the Eskimos, who ultimately created a major crisis for the industry by voting unanimously to strike.

Repercussions were felt in Seattle, even at Seattle University where pressure was brought to bear for the removal of the two union Jesuits from Dillingham. Other forms of coercion were used to eliminate the two priests from their positions, without results. When Father Small visited Dillingham in 1953 the controversy had been resolved but two of his Jesuits still bore scars from their wounds in battle.

Father Small arrived at St. Mary's on February 7. "Andreafski," he wrote, "which is the new location of the old Akulurak Mission, is situated near the confluence of the Yukon and

Andreafski Rivers on low rolling hills which are slightly wooded. The children from the flat tundra were fascinated by the trees when they moved there. The large new building, to which this summer is being added the fathers and boys wings is so well insulated that the heat can be turned off most all day. The building is certainly a tribute to Fr. Spils who planned and constructed it. The Church is large and beautiful, but with the added facilities for children and a fast growing village, it will soon be necessary to have a separate mass for the village. The fathers will regulate the development of the village in order to organize a model village both materially and spiritually."[43]

The missionaries' meeting began on February 10. The subject of Jesuit membership in labor unions was challenged by some of the more traditional missionaries. "Fr. Endal gave an explanation of the work which he and Fr. Convert were doing in the canneries during the summer. This dispelled some misunderstandings among the missionaries, and resulted in an expression of encouragement for the two Fathers from the Meeting. Fr. Convert continues to work with the Natives, as a union laborer, striving to protect them against drink, gambling, and immorality, and cooperates with them in seeking just wages and good working conditions. Fr. Endal does not work in a cannery, but takes a very active part in the union activities. It was the hope of the Fathers that he would try as soon as possible to withdraw from professional union activities. Last Spring Fr. Endal, with Bishop Gleeson present, met with company officials in order to achieve greater mutual understanding, so that Father would help toward the formulation of a workers' contract. It achieved favorable results."

One of those present for the meeting was Father Tom Cunningham whose dramatic exploits could fill volumes. Born in New Zealand of Irish parents, he entered the Irish province of the Jesuits, but switched to Oregon, later, to devote his life to the Eskimos. In 1935 he began his missionary work in Nome and for the next quarter of a century he scoffed at arctic dangers. For many years he lived on a rocky mound in the Bering Straits, called Little Diomede Island. This was scarcely more than a rifle shot from Big Diomede, Russian territory. During those days the American Eskimos and Russian Eskimos visited freely with one another. But in 1939, when Cunningham took a walk across the boundary, he was snatched "by Soviet soldiers and locked in a subterranean room" on Big Diomede. When the ice broke up, his Eskimos diverted the Soviet sentries and he leaped from an icy cliff to safety on an ice floe and was rescued by his friends. "Later he learned that the Soviets had a price on his head, 4000 rubles, or $122.87 in the currency they used on Little Diomede."[44]

Craggy-looking with eyes of cold glacier blue, Cunningham was lean and muscular, like a tank commander. He spoke with an Irish brogue, rather than in the broad dialect of down under. Most of the year he wore a caribou-hide parka, which was as natural to him as his skin and the Eskimo language he had adopted. "As a hunter he excelled all, even the best of the Eskimos. He had mushed with his dog sled as much as 2500 miles in a winter, often in weather that kept the Eskimos indoors."[45]

As a result of his assistance to the United States Air Force, including the compilation of a small pocket dictionary in Eskimo for use in emergencies, he became widely known as "Father Tom" to the military all over Alaska. He served as a chaplain during the war, and remained at the Air Force's insistence in the reserves with the rank of Major. Regarded as one of the greatest authorities on the Arctic, he was often consulted by officials, but he always remained a shy, reticent priest.

During the missionaries' meeting, Father Tom had not spoken often, but when he did, all took notice. Father Small included his thoughts about the Jesuit's relations with his flock:

"Fr. Cunningham, who lives very simply and whom all respect for his knowledge of the Natives, insisted that missionaries should not live according to the standards of the

Natives because they do not expect it or respect you for it. The missionary should have the tidiest house in the village as an example to the Natives. Natives should not be allowed to visit before Mass, during meals, while you are reading the office, or after a certain hour in the evening unless an emergency arises. Your bed room should be private and all, even the simplest residence, should allow for this."

The whole range of missionary activities was covered during the eleven days of the meeting; the alleged shortage of missionaries, which the bishop himself disputed, native vocations and catechists, the use of native languages, contact with the natives in daily service, management problems, relocation of missions, and so on. Alaskan missionaries are noted for their candor. Like many other missionaries, and the people they serve, they enjoyed nothing more than a good argument, which would be endless as well as insolvable. After eleven days of this, they all agreed to at least this much: not more than two of them should leave in any one plane, lest more be lost in the event of an accident.

Father Small continued his visitation. At Mountain Village he noted that Father Fox, "a saintly man," provided closed retreats for the Eskimos in the district, "still given annually with much fruit." Father Paul O'Connor at Hooper Bay, a member of the Territorial Housing Bureau, "who commands the highest respect from the Territorial and Federal officials," had been responsible for new housing in the village. The Hooper Bay Eskimos had abandoned their igloos for the new houses, and it was hoped the rate of tuberculosis would decrease as a result. At Holy Cross there was talk of moving the mission site, and at Nenana a recent fire had destroyed the combination church and house, taking with it "two historical pectoral crosses, one of which belonged to Archbishop Seghers, who was killed near Nulato, the other of Archbishop Gross of Portland."* At Fairbanks two young priests, George Boileau and Henry Hargreaves "work zealously in this parish, which is filled with many young married people. The grade school attended by about three hundred children is very well equipped and has acquired an excellent reputation in town. The Charity of Providence Sisters teach in the school and conduct a hospital."

When he returned to Portland, the Provincial composed and dispatched a letter of commendation to the missionaries. "It was an inspiration," he wrote, "for me to visit the missions in Alaska and observe the enthusiasm, zeal and self sacrifice with which you labor for the spreading of Christ's kingdom in this northern land."[46] The mission of Alaska, he concluded, was in excellent condition.

In March, Stalin died and some said he had been murdered. During the same month the provincial made his visitation at Seattle Prep, which had more than its share of problems that year, then at Seattle University, where he felt more at home than anywhere else. He had begun to feel the weight of office. His hair had thinned out, his laughter which made others feel comfortable in his presence, was less spontaneous now. He had been shaken by a doctor's report, which gave him only six months to live. A heart condition, it was said. Fortunately he had kept this prediction to himself, awaiting additional data. The diagnosis had been wrong, of course, but things were never the same.

He was taken for granted now. He had become so perfectly integrated within the province that Jesuits did not think of one without the other. He had also become so adept at governing that no one ever doubted the meaning of his orders when he gave them. He could be abrupt, and when he raised his eyebrows, one knew he meant business. On the other hand, he usually acted with great restraint, always sensitive to the needs of others

*Bishop Gleeson, in addition to serving as the Ordinary of the Vicariate also served as pastor of this modest little parish at Nenana. Hence most of his clothes and personal possessions were also destroyed by the fire.

and always willing to provide without being asked. He came to know the province as well as it knew him, partly because he sought good advice and received it. He would go down in our history not only as a very capable administrator, but as an uncommonly kind one, a superior who gently demanded obedience and returned for it comfort and encouragement.

Time ran out before he resolved the question of Sheridan. On October 8, 1953, Father Logan, reported to Small on the progress of the well-digger who had been employed to solve the problem of water. "The well is now down 375 ft. with no sign of water at the bottom. The driller will go down another 50 ft. or so before giving up."[47] At the one hundred and twenty foot level a pocket of water had appeared, "perhaps 25 gals a minute," but it had been sealed off by the casing. In conclusion, Logan said, it was "none too bright a picture, but at least we are still pumping some water."

Four days later Logan wrote again. "We didn't call in the 'witcher' on the present bore because we didn't think it necessary. . . . The 'witcher' is reported to have told the digger *some days after operations had begun* that he was digging four feet in the wrong direction." The witcher pointed out a place thirty feet from the bore. "It seems to me," Logan added, "on the strength of his last year's success, we should consult the witcher again."[48]

Eventually adequate water was assured. The greater question of completing the novitiate at Sheridan or seeking a new site had to be faced, and somehow resolved. The temporary coating of tar on the building could last no longer. While Father Small held many consultations regarding this, he left the final decision for his successor, who was appointed on February 9, 1954.[49] This was Henry Joseph Schultheis, pastor of St. Ignatius in Portland, known throughout the province for his thrifty management of Bellarmine High School and for sometimes singular demands he made on his subjects.

Henry had deep roots in the Northwest. His paternal grandfather, Michael Schultheis and the Niebler brothers were "the Germans" who bought the Jesuit farm on the Willamette in 1868. Michael, out-numbered three to one by the Nieblers, sold his share to the brothers in 1875 and then took up a homestead in the fertile Palouse country south of Spokane, near present Colton, Washington. His rude home became the first church on occasion, when missionary priests like Cataldo passed through the area, travelling from Spokane Falls to Lewiston. Henry was born at Colton on October 25, 1900, when his grandfather was one of the most highly respected and wealthy patriarchs in the state. Unlike his brothers who took up farming, Henry went to college; he was a student at Gonzaga from 1919 to 1922. He entered the novitiate at Los Gatos on July 16, 1923, about one month before Harold Small entered.

Schultheis did not take office immediately. On March 23, 1954, the general appointed Father Michael Kunz of Gonzaga as the first rector of the new high school community.[50] At the same time the new community was canonically established as Gonzaga High School, and though Kunz as yet lacked any assigned subjects, he was formally installed as rector, the province's only *abbas nullius* in its entire history. Kunz was almost too gentle for the tough job ahead of him. Fortunately, he received in due time a faculty of twenty-eight priests and scholastics, among whom were Gordon Toner and Joseph Perri, two outstanding administrators to whom Kunz delegated almost complete control.

On April 20, 1954, Schultheis, also, was formally installed. Small, at his own request, was assigned to Sheridan for some months to recuperate from the rigors of his provincialate and to serve as spiritual director for the scholastics.

Like Small, Schultheis was regarded as a strong "company man," an organization component temporarily in command. He was a good provider and he enjoyed festive occasions, like special dinners and picnics, and he liked nothing more than robust beer drinking songs shouted merrily by the crowd during and after a noisy but dignified party. One could be at ease with him when he felt like celebrating togetherness, but most Jesuits, I think, did not feel comfortable with him when they met him alone, vis-a-vis. To some he appeared unpredictable or volatile and perhaps he was. But he was basically a very dedicated and kind man, who sometimes found it necessary to speak plainly, even harshly. But he was also the kind of man who willingly washed up the dishes and cleaned up after a party. This alone was a high recommendation in a society of confirmed bachelors.

"Schultie," as he was usually called, inherited the unformed decision regarding Sheridan. He gave it immediate priority, commissioned John Maloney to design three new wings to complete its facilities, a kitchen and refectory wing to retire the old bungalow which had been "temporary" for a quarter of a century, and wings on either end of the main structure to accommodate additional novices and juniors. Veneer bricking was specified for the entire plant.

Once more, the decision to move forward without resources at hand required great courage. Credit for making that decision must be awarded to Schultheis. He ordered the architect to proceed and appointed Father Dan Lyons to serve as the principal fund raiser for the project. On November 19, 1954, Schultheis wrote to Janssens that the water supply with the new well was "the best ever;" indeed, he added, "up to now the novitiate had an abundance of water." Plans for the bricking and the additions were under way. The province had been able to gather $200,000 for the project, but about $600,000 more was required.[51]

With Schultheis in the driver's seat, wheels began to spin. He liked quick results the way he liked fast cars. The surveyors began their tasks on November 23, 1954. Finally, on June 13, 1955, at four in the afternoon, bids for the new construction were opened at Campion Hall, Portland. Present for the event were Schultheis, Logan, Hubert Adams, Minister at Sheridan, and two representatives from each firm submitting bids. The Ross Hammond Company of Portland offered the lowest bid and was awarded the contract on the estimated construction cost of $700,000. Fifteen days later, at eleven in the morning the historic project was begun. Sheridan at last, was scheduled for completion, after twenty-four years of use.

No one could see the future. No one could possibly predict that the novitiate's days were numbered, and that the Jesuits would have far less time to enjoy the fruits of their labors there than they had endured in the cold, drafty house on the eminence above the Yamhill Valley.

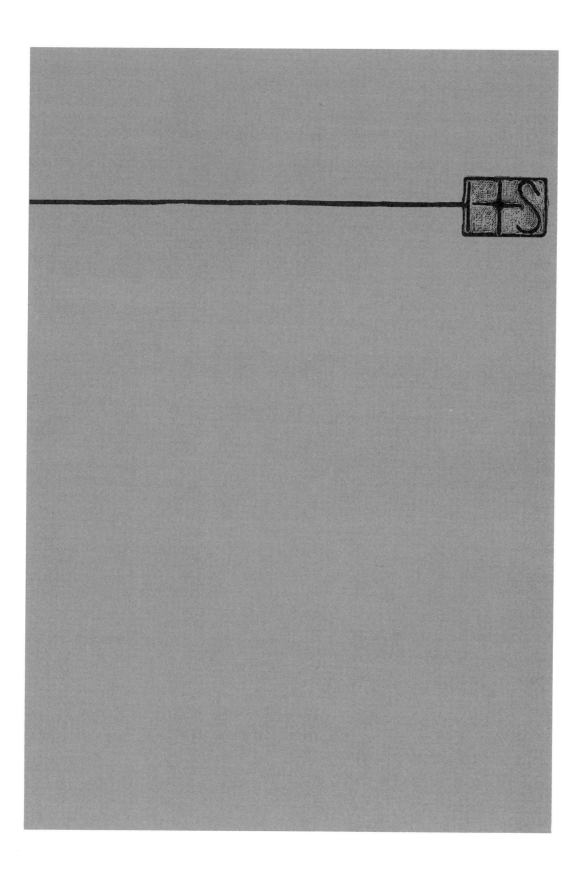

The Piggott Building on the Seattle university Campus which was named for generous benefactors of the university.

Henry J. Schultheis, S.J., fifth provincial of the Oregon Province, directed the completion of the building program at Sheridan and was one of the founders of Jesuit High, Portland.

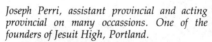

Joseph Perri, assistant provincial and acting provincial on many occassions. One of the founders of Jesuit High, Portland.

Copper Valley School in Alaska

21

BRICK AND MORTAR
1954–1959

During the early months of the Schultheis regime, the rank and file became aware of their new superior as what might be charitably called "controversial." There were those who liked his blunt candor, his bustling hyperactive manners, and his loyalty and trust in his appointees. Others, accustomed to the suave, sophisticated methods of his predecessor, found him harsh and unwilling to listen. He sometimes stepped on toes to get things done. This was almost inevitable for a person of his temperament. He knew it and sometimes fell over backwards to compensate for it.

Non-Jesuits, perhaps, would have found this hard to believe, for among the Jesuit communities in the Northwest, no one enjoyed a better rapport with them than Schultheis. Wherever he went, in whatever position he found himself, he maintained a deep, warm-hearted relationship with "externs," as non-Jesuits were frequently called, and they responded with their respect and generosity. He never hesitated to ask them for help and they never disappointed him. This is one reason why he was willing to go into debt for the completion of Sheridan.

But Schultie's relationships with his subjects were more complex. As an energetic and naturally curious person he was highly visible. He was also vocal. At a critical time, when change was beginning to be felt, his strong uncompromising voice was heard and some-times resented. But nothing, perhaps, was resented more by his critics than his support of one of his assistants, and his obstinate unwillingness to discuss a middle course in the dispute. This assistant was Father William Weller, the unpopular Prefect of Studies of the province.

To understand the nature of the discord occasioned by Father Weller, one must realize that this was but a small part of a much larger battleground within the American Assistancy. It involved the Jesuit Educational Association (JEA) under the direction of a very dedicated but somewhat autocratic professional whose name was Father Edward Rooney. The JEA had been established to serve not only as an accrediting agency for Jesuit schools but also as a clearing house for Jesuit Colleges and high schools. JEA was also a powerful means for raising standards. These lofty objectives were especially required by western Jesuit schools because of the rapid expansion taking place in the west. Rooney and the JEA were under the direct supervision of the provincials of the United States, taken collectively.

Each province, including Oregon, had a Prefect of Studies, charged during this period with the task of coordinating the schools and the JEA. For years the Prefect of Studies played a minor role in the Oregon province, but as the provincial's work increased, the more detailed direction of the schools was delegated to the prefect.

During this same postwar period the universities, nation-wide, were developing, slowly but effectively, more and more independence from the provincial's control. Many saw this as a disaster, others as a natural trend toward the ideal of university autonomy. As the professional schools in the universities prospered, there was less direct Jesuit management and a corresponding decrease of influence of the JEA on policies and standards. Rooney and the JEA turned to a more aggressive role in standardizing the high schools.

In 1951, during the early period of these enlargements, Weller was appointed as Prefect of Studies of the Oregon Province by Father Small. This appeared to be a wise choice, since Weller was known to be self-motivated, capable of detailed desk work, and fearless in making decisions. As the former dean at Gonzaga he had insisted on higher standards of teaching and grading. He seemed to think, however, that standards of teaching could be improved by lowering grades, a rather strange fallacy for one who held the humanities in such high regard. His battle cry for some time had been: "A 'C' is a good grade."

In the course of time Weller introduced the notorious "province exams," that is standard exams for all of the province's high schools based on Syllabi provided by him and his innumerable committees. The exams were not resented so much as the publicized reports following them, in which each class in the province was graded on the basis of a ratio between its performance and its median I.Q. In other words, this expose of the teachers' standings disregarded many basic factors related to the secondary teachers and their students, for example the questionable objectivity of the I.Q. grades. Despite a hue and cry that was raised by the teachers, loud enough to be heard in Timbuctoo, Weller persisted in forcing these examinations on the schools until the bitter end.

If this made him unpopular with teachers, his "C is a good grade" made him absolutely anathema with the students. The fact is 'C' was not a good grade for students who had been selected, for the most part, from the upper fifty percentile of their age levels in the United States. In 1955, for example, due to this grading which had influenced the younger teachers, one student from Gonzaga Prep graduating in the Honor Classical Course, with a grade point average of 1.98, occupied the median position in his class. In other words, one student above half of the graduating class left Gonzaga Prep with a grade point average that did not qualify him for college, though Gonzaga Prep, by its express assertion, was a college preparatory school. This was an injury, of course, and it focused the attention of the province on the basic flaw of "C is a good grade," but Weller himself never changed his mind. This would appear to have been a disaster. However, two factors favored the students: the administration of Gonzaga Prep provided letters of recommendation to all who deserved and needed them. Secondly, class rank or standing was stressd and found to be an acceptable norm for the institutions of higher learning.

Father Weller was not an unjust or foolish person. On the contrary, he was intelligent and very dedicated to the welfare and progress of students in Jesuit schools. His efforts were entirely directed to the improvement of teaching and discipline, precisely for the benefit of the student. He was courageous in his determination to achieve the very best in province high schools, and he suffered bitter criticism without resentment or backing down on his ideals.

One could write, perhaps, a chapter on why he failed as a Prefect of Studies, or why he failed to convince most teachers in the province that his were the correct procedures. Was it because, as some said, he refused to accept advice from others? Or was he carried away by the ideals of the JEA and believed that ideals could be reached by force? In one sense he served the province very well. He had succeeded in at least making the province conscious of the need for quality in teaching and discipline. One wonders, however, if the turmoil he created was worth it.

It was characteristic of Father Schultheis to give Weller his uncompromising support, since he was instinctively very loyal to his assistants. At the same time he was diffident about his own judgment in school matters. His unwillingness to discuss the so-called "Weller System" proved to be his own undoing, for in the end his attempts to retain Weller as Prefect of Studies prompted the general to replace him.*

This would be later. Meanwhile, however, Father Weller was in a position to influence province priorities. It would be unfair, I think, to accuse him of an almost complete disregard for the missions. He did not exclude them, he merely concentrated on his own field, which he was determined to plow in his own way. In effect, the missions were scarcely considered as a significant factor in province planning, at least until steps were taken for Oregon involvement in Africa.

This was not intended. Certainly the provincial, like those before him, was diligent in making his visitation of all the missions, bringing with him a fresh, breezy kind of encouragement, which most missionaries understood. among the latter there were few, if any, critics of Schultie.

When the one hundreth anniversary of St. Ignatius Mission on its present site was celebrated, Schultie gave it his best shot. First he appointed Father Ferretti to take charge of it, giving him at least five full months to prepare. This could not have been a better choice. Ferretti raised many thousands of dollars from businessmen, who said he was in the wrong profession. They said he should have been the president of an industrial conglomerate.

Ferretti wanted the province Archivist as his assistant. The Archives were still at the Mount in 1954, under my direction. I was teaching at Sheridan that summer.† Schultie appeared one evening, called me out of recreation and assigned me to St. Ignatius Mission as soon as summer school was over. Two rather significant events followed. First, Ferretti requested me to prepare and present a program with Indian boys on television, which had just been introduced in Montana. This program was presented "live" as they now say, in the studio on top of a mountain northwest of Missoula, the first of its kind.

The second project initiated by Ferretti was a mission history exhibit in the basement of the church, a-do-it-ourselves museum, organized for temporary use, but on a grand scale. This, too, was delegated to me as part of my duties. With materials from the Archives and the old Gonzaga Museum, and considerable help from the Ursuline Nuns at the mission, a major exhibit was assembled. Favorable comment appeared in Montana papers and magazines, but most important of all, the provincial himself was greatly impressed. When the exhibits had been taken down he said to me: "The museum was excellent and we should have a permanent one somewhere in the Province. I want you to think about it and make plans for a museum that the Province can build and maintain. Let me know how we can do this." In this directive of Father Schultheis there lies the very beginnings of The Museum of Native American Cultures in Spokane, one of the nation's greatest depositories of Indian relics and art, founded eleven years later.

The St. Ignatius Centennial celebrations commenced on September 24, 1954. Bishop Gilmore was celebrant of the festive Mass, with Francis Cardinal Spellman among the

---

*This was not the only reason for the early replacement of Schultheis as provincial. A major reason was, oddly, too much Schultheis kindness and patience in the matter of discipline. Provincial Archives Portland, correspondence, Janssens and Schultheis, from Nov. 14, 1958–February 18, 1959.

†I succeeded William Lyle Davis as Archivist in 1954. Between 1944 and 1954 I had been assistant to Davis. Other assistants at various times were Richard Sisk, Robert I. Burns, William Laney, and William N. Bischoff. The latter undertook the first formal organization of the files. Three other Jesuits were involved in the early stages of gathering province records: George Weibel, John Sullivan and Paul Sauer.

visiting prelates. Father Schultheis was celebrant at an evening Mass for deceased missionaries and members of the tribe. Countless other attractions—pageants, war dances, and processions—were scheduled to entertain and edify the thousands of visitors who came to Mission Valley to acknowledge the one hundred years of dedicated service the Jesuits had freely rendered to the tribe. There was something ironic about the praise heaped upon the missionaries for their contribution. It would not be long before much of this was repudiated, and the missionaries were bitterly assailed and their contribution to the tribe either denied or minimized. Fortunately in 1954, these un-historical condemnations had not yet surfaced.

I was not present for the centennial festivities. Lately assigned to Gonzaga Prep, I was summoned to Spokane by Father Kunz who, not unlike a mother hen, was trying to Father his chickens from assorted locations into his new chicken house, for that's what the barracks-residence looked like. I was the fourth member of the Jesuit faculty to arrive there, soon enough, indeed, to sleep on the floor, since the community had no beds.

Two other Jesuits had already moved into the partially completed residence, the old high school barracks, which had been moved in June, for the second time. They were Gordon Toner and Joseph Perri.* The rickety doors of the one-floor, no-basement building had been bolted inside, so Toner, no longer a sylph-like stripling, crawled through a window to gain entrance. Perri was younger, but as a former member of Sheridan's "Domi Club," he was less athletic.†

As construction on the school building neared completion, Father Kunz wrote to the Provincial that the State of Washington had approved the name of the new institution.[1] Legal incorporation in the state was completed on July 29, 1954, under the title of Gonzago Preparatory School, Inc. On August 22, Kunz offered the first Mass in the school chapel. The rest of the building, though unfinished, was occupied the same week. Finally, on Sunday, September 5, with Bishop White happily performing the ceremony of blessing, the formal dedication of the school took place. Classes were begun on Monday, when 646 students reported to their teachers. After sixty-seven years of existence, at least thirteen of them as an orphan, Gonzaga Prep had at last come into its own. It had its own building and its own campus.

There was only one sour note: since all of the contracts for the construction of the school had been undertaken legally by Gonzaga University, with Father Mathias Wilhelm in charge, Gonzaga Prep's administration had no jurisdiction whatever over the satisfactory completion of the contracts or over necessary additional expenditures that arose after changes in plans had been made. Any changes, even very small ones, in construction plans had to be approved by Gonzaga University. Oversights—for example, water pipes to the fields—were not approved out of consideration of reducing the university's share of the debt remaining on Gonzaga Prep. It would be some long, frustrating months before the community owned and controlled its own building and during those months Wilhelm made arbitrary decisions which benefited the university, not the prep school.

On the other hand certain unfavorable circumstances actually turned out to be an advantage to the prep school. Cash pledges which had not been honored required attention and Father John Hurley was assigned the distasteful task of collecting them. He proved to be so successful he was designated as the full-time fund raiser, or, as later designated, Development Director, becoming within a short time a prototype of what other

---

*Toner was the principal and Perri both vice-principal and minister of the new community. Perri had just completed tertianship at Port Townsend.

†The "Domi," or "at home," club in the novitiate was comprised of certain novices whose special talents kept them indoors when other novices were assigned to handball or cleaning the duck pens.

high schools, not only in the province but in the whole country, eventually adopted. Hurley developed an "Associates Program" which in time placed Prep on a solid financial base. Without Hurley and his counterparts in other schools — for example, Father Tom Sexton at Bellarmine — our high schools would either not have survived, or would have survived with extreme difficulty, when the supply of Jesuit teachers ran short in the 1970s.

Father Schultheis had kept a fatherly eye on Prep, somewhat solicitous about its finances during the first year of its independence. A strong advocate of the art of begging, he regarded fiscal solvency as something like sanctifying grace in the natural order. He could appreciate John Hurley's talents, for example, more than the instructor of history's, but he really was trying to rule the province in a manner of kindness for everyone.

One of his Jesuits, Father James Royce, was on loan to the Bishop of Nelson, as president of Notre Dame. Schultie aware of his isolation paid him a visit and reported on the situation to Janssens:

"Desiring to see for myself the work that Father was performing, Father John Dunne, the Rector of the Mount, and I made a trip to Nelson, British Columbia. Nelson is some 150 miles from Spokane, and is practically the only contact that Father Royce would have with Jesuits at any time. . . . We found him working hard under great difficulties.

"I think it proper, at this time, to inform Your Paternity how we became associated with the school. The school had been operating for some five years under the leadership of a layman. Early this summer the Bishop launched a campaign for money for the college. Shortly after, the layman quit and was very critical of the Bishop. The Bishop appealed to Gonzaga University for help. He was looking for a head for his school in order that the drive for funds would not be a complete failure. The authorities at Gonzaga represented to this office the great urgency of the situation, the great things which could be expected from this College for the Church in British Columbia. . . . We then made Father Royce available. From the very beginning we had insisted that he would remain for but one year. Nor has the Bishop ever approached us for the extension of his stay. Instead, he appealed, it seems, directly to Cardinal Leger, who then appealed to Your Paternity."[2] Later Schultie added that he and Father Dunne discussed the matter and decided that Royce should not remain. "Canadian Provinces should handle the situation."

Bishop Johnson wanted to keep Royce, which is not surprising. He was getting, for next to nothing, a hardworking Doctor of Psychology who was on the way to becoming one of the leading experts in the United States on the subject of alcoholism. Many universities more prestigious than Notre Dame College in Nelson would have grab-bagged Royce at any price.

Providing Notre Dame with a president, who also served as dean, full time professor, and part-time janitor, was only one of the province's benefactions to the college. With the provincial's approval, Gonzaga provided Notre Dame with temporary accreditation by classifying it as an affiliated college, a most generous gesture on the part of Gonzaga in view of certain academic risks involved. Gonzaga also furnished some of the teachers, who commuted to Nelson, and Gonzaga's librarian Father Carroll, shipped truckloads of duplicate books, at no cost, to bolster the fledgling college's own library.

Royce remained only one year, despite the insistence of His Eminence Cardinal Leger that he remain five. The college became affiliated with St. Francis Xavier University in Nova Scotia, and thus passed out of the province's history.*

*In 1963 Notre Dame was given a university charter by the province of British Columbia. Because of insurmountable difficulties, the province took it over in 1977, establishing it as the David Thompson University Center. It is currently offering courses through the University of Victoria. See *Commonwealth Universities Yearbook,* 1980.

BRICK AND MORTAR

Father Royce returned to Seattle University when Arby Lemieux was on a building rampage. A new student union building called "The Chieftan" in honor of Chief Seattle, had been dedicated on June 23, 1953. This had cost something like $407,000, a mere trifle contrasted with things to come.[3] A new residence for girls, called "Marycrest," built to accommodate 210 students, came next. It was completed and occupied in 1954.[4]

At Gonzaga, too, the skies-the limit era of bricks and mortar had suddenly begun. On October 24, 1954, Father Corkery dedicated two new buildings, the student union building called The Cog, and a residence for 156 girls, called Madonna Hall. There is a curious footnote regarding the occupation of The Cog and the exodus from the former student union building, called The Canteen. The latter was the original St. Aloysius Church, a frame building which had been moved twice and basically remodeled three times, first to enlarge it, secondly, to convert it into a parish social hall, and thirdly, to convert it into The Canteen. It was abandoned by Gonzaga on June 25, 1954, in favor of The Cog and that very night burned to the ground, taking with it an irreplaceable collection of photographs belonging to the Spokane Civic Theatre.[5] Without the old church, which had been on the site of present Bea House, the campus was left with seven major buildings, described by one coed as "the prettiest little campus of any college in the Northwest.[6]

In the fall semester of 1954, Gonzaga had a total of 1,435 students: 986 men and 449 women. Of these, 938 were Catholics. Seattle University that autumn had a total of 3,361 students, of whom 2,833 were full-time, day students, of these, 1,612 were Catholics.[7] Under construction or in the planning stages at Seattle University were three more major buildings, a men's residence to be called Xavier Hall, a Jesuit residence to be called Loyola Hall, and a large building for Commerce and Education, eventually completed in 1958 and named the William Piggott Building. At Gonzaga a supreme effort was being made to get the Crosby Library under construction. Groundbreaking for the Crosby Library finally took place on Wednesday, September 12, 1956. Bing Crosby turned over the first shovel full of dirt. The building was dedicated with Crosby in attendance on November 3, 1957.[8]

At Bellarmine in Tacoma the building bug also had bitten the faculty. Father Frank Toner, one of the four Jesuit Toners, was rector there. As personable as Gordon, but less addicted to practical jokes, he had embraced Bellarmine as his very own. There was a Booster's Club at Bellarmine, a group of promoters who had no equals for their zeal and generosity. With Frank Toner's ever-ready blessings, the Boosters erected two buildings on the campus in three years: a cafeteria in 1955 and a new gymnasium in 1957.[9]

Meanwhile there were stirrings in Portland. Though Schultie had been born and raised in eastern Washington, he had, by this time, adopted Portland as his Promised Land. So far as he was concerned, only one thing was wanting, the existence of a Jesuit high school in Portland, a Jesuit objective since the early years of the century. As pastor of St. Ignatius parish he had won the confidence and respect of Archbishop Howard, which gave him an entree to discuss a subject that had become, by this time, a painful one.

In June, 1954, the Holy Cross Fathers, privately revealed that Columbia Preparatory School, conducted by them since 1902, would be closed. At this time it was suggested that the Jesuits take over the Columbia prep campus in the West Hills, but certain difficulties involving school jurisdiction, stood in the way. The matter was dropped. Columbia Prep was closed in June, 1955, and the Holy Cross Fathers sold the campus to a real estate agent for subdivision.

But neither the Archbishop nor the Jesuit provincial was satisfied. The Archbishop made it clear to the provincial that he favored a Jesuit school on the west side of Portland, but he had grave reservations regarding the Jesuit's right to establish a collegiate church. The provincial reassured him verbally that the Jesuits would not exercise this privilege, but under no circumstances would the Jesuits yield the right to control their own school. This

480

exchange of views took place during the mid-summer of 1955.

In August, information regarding an ideal piece of land for the school turned up. Father Schultheis, having examined the property, was determined to buy it for the use of the proposed school. On Saturday, August 14, 1955, he persuaded the Archbishop to accompany him to the site. Howard was delighted because the site was outside the city of Portland and would be, therefore, open to less criticism from priests who were especially opposed to the Jesuits having a school in Portland. He gave his consent for the school on the spot contingent upon the conditions that had been verbally approved.

On Tuesday, August 16, both the provincial and the Archbishop wrote letters. Schultheis wrote as follows: "We will not open a collegiate church or make the chapel available to others than staff and students.[10] Howard wrote that he hereby gave permission for the Jesuits "to open a school in Portland on the site examined last Saturday." He added that he would aid the school substantially by allowing a financial drive and by making a contribution.[11]

Schultie was elated. He already had an option on the land, which was a fifty-six acre tract on the Bertha-Beaverton Highway, fifteen minutes from downtown Portland. Known locally as the Hillsdale Dairy Farm, this property had a one-half mile highway frontage. It was a family estate of an industrious Swiss farmer, turned businessman, Fred Zwahlein. When this worthy gentleman learned the purpose for which the Jesuits wished to use his farm, negotiations were quickly completed and announcements of the purchase appeared in the papers, in the *Oregon Journal* on August 18, and in the *Oregonian* on the following day. The sale price of the property was $165,000 and this was advanced by the province, pending the formation of the new community and the establishment of the school.

On August 18, Schultheis sent a detailed report to Father General: "Shortly after negotiations for taking over Columbia Prep ended unsuccessfully, His Excellency and I discussed the question. He has been ready, indeed anxious for us to open a school here. The restrictions he then placed, we felt, were never his, but those of one strong advisor. Last week he invited me to see him, and formally asked us to open a school. I called together the consultors, and after again carefully going over all aspects of the problem, we felt we could assure the Archbishop that we could proceed, relying on your consent as given in April."[12]

The Provincial then listed the conditions of the Archbishop: There could be no collegiate church, on the other hand Jesuits would control the school and have no diocesan inspection of students. The Archbishop hoped "we would not be too selective," but he left the matter to the Jesuits.

There were fifty-six acres, he added, and we would be required to buy it all at once. The cost was $2,700 per acre. We have paid $35,000 down, with four percent interest on the balance. The province was short of cash because of Sheridan and we would have to borrow to close the deal.*

A few hours later, after signing papers for the purchase, Schultheis embarked by plane for Montana to keep another appointment. On the same plane was Mr. Albert V. Fonder, whose grandson had recently graduated from St. Thomas More's Parish School in Portland. When he heard reports on developments, he immediately made a verbal application to Schultheis to enroll his grandson in the new high school. This boy, John O'Phelan, was the first student registered. His grandfather's application was made official in writing in January, 1956.

It would be pleasant to note that the announcement of the new school was received with universal jubilation. Such, however, was not the case. There were those even among

---

*Jesuit High eventually returned this money to the province.

the priests who, for reasons of their own, disapproved of the new foundation. In heart-warming contrast to these was Father Willis Whelan, the Principal of Central Catholic, for whom the Jesuits had considerable respect. When Whelan received reports on the new school, he wrote to the Provincial:

"Please accept our best wishes for the new high school in the southwest Portland area. Although we know that we are in for some top-flight competition, both scholastically and athletically, we are glad to have you working for the cause of Catholic Secondary Education in this locality.

"If we can be of assistance, let us know."[13]

Steps for organizing the new prep school were begun at once. Father Dan Lyons was assigned by the Provincial to supervise a building drive and John Maloney of Seattle was commissioned to design building plans for a school with a capacity for six hundred boys and residences for boarding students and Jesuit faculty. On January 8, 1956, Father Wilhelm of Gonzaga University was appointed the first superior of the community and in April Father Perri of Gonzaga Prep was designated as the first principal.

Schultheis' choice of principal was excellent. Basically a very practical man, Joe Perri had a strong sense of order and a singleness of purpose, which made him a fearless administrator. At Alma, when he was a theologian, he was called "Big Neat" because of his fondness for a tidy room.* True to his Italian forebears Perri had an elegant manner which prompted Jack Leary to refer to him as "Joseph Cardinal Perri." Once at the Mount Leary persuaded Perri to don the bishop's costume, which was kept with our stage props, and to sweep about the house giving his blessing to the newly arrived and unsuspecting Californians, who dropped to their knees in confusion and awkwardly kissed Joe's fake ring. That he could pull this off with a train of giggling attendants following him, indicates his skill in the management of school boys. At Gonzaga Prep where he was vice-principal, he really ran the school, because Gordon Toner deferred to his judgment in practically everything. They were a great team, where Gordon was the heart and Joe the head. As Joe said, "There was nothing petty about Gordon. He was genuinely interested in the kids and he did anything the Society asked him to do."[14] Gordon, if anything, was too docile to Father Weller, and it was Joe Perri who kept a happy balance at Gonzaga as long as he was there. When the rector, Father Kunz, learned that he was leaving, he wept bitter tears.†

Perri left Spokane at once and moved into a basement room of Campion Hall, where Dan Lyons was also in residence. Meanwhile the papers of incorporation "Jesuit High School, an Oregon Corporation, not for profit," were drawn up by the school's attorney, John T. Casey, and filed in Salem in the first week of February.

It was time to talk about money. At a luncheon meeting held in the Congress Hotel on January 10, J. Stuart Leavy was selected as the general chairman for the city-wide drive for funds. An abundance of brochures was produced, all the proper names were listed, and scores of solicitors were motivated with appropriate pep talks. Finally, on Sunday, March 11, twenty-one Jesuit priests and two Holy Cross Fathers, who had gathered from all over the province, invaded the pulpits of Portland to present the needs of the new school. Canvassing for funds began during the following week. By Wednesday of that week, $117,000 had been pledged.

Three days earlier, bids on the first unit of the project—a service building with kitchen, cafeteria, heating plant, and miscellaneous rooms for temporary classrooms—had been submitted. On the same day, the contract for grading and drainage were awarded to the

*Harold Free, another very orderly Jesuit, was called "Little Neat," because he was younger than Perri.

†The provincial notified Kunz of Perri's departure from Gonzaga Prep on a Saturday afternoon in April. After the provincial departed, Kunz and I discussed the news, then notified Perri, who was at Hayden lake.

John L. Jersey Construction Company for its bid of $32,767. The Ross B. Hammond Company won the building contract for the first unit with its bid of $222,422. On Tuesday, April 10, 1956, ground-breaking ceremonies were held on the building site with His Grace, the Archbishop, presiding, and with Mayor Fred Peterson of Portland and Mayor A. H. Rossie of Beaverton in attendance.

Other developments kept apace. An official coat-of arms, designed by Father Andrew Vachon, was adopted, and the official motto, "Age quod agis," which means "Do well whatever you do," was included at the base of the shield. Vachon, who had won wide respect for his illustrations in *Jesuit Missions* and the *Western Jesuit*, had designed a similiar coat-of-arms for Bellarmine High School.

The fund drive soon petered out far short of its goal. Undismayed the Provincial assigned ten Jesuits to beg from door-to-door during the summer of 1956. These unlucky men deserve to be remembered. They were: Jim Poole, Charles Wollesen, Frank Walsh, Harold Free, Michael McHugh, Frank McGuigan, Gene Toner, Len Kaufer, Earl Lariviere, and Frank Mueller. To their number must be added that of Lee Kapper, who assisted on a part-time basis while he was attending classes in library science at the University of Portland. These men collected in hard cash a total of $186,540.[15] Poole, as might be expected, for he has a knack for begging, topped the list with $28,579. But it was Mike McHugh who won the booby prize for the most unique contribution.

Mike, it appears, had approached the father of a large family for a pledge. This chap replied that because of his large family he could spare no money. He was busy, he said, giving them all a haircut. Mike said, "Well, I need a haircut. Give me a haircut and that will be your contribution!" And so it was.

By August 4, 1956, Jesuit High reported a total of $622,193 received, approximately half of what was required for building the entire school, which based on 1957 estimates was expected to cost $1,200,000. The campus was developed, however, at a much higher figure. Facilities for boarders, as originally planned, were never provided. With the debt for land to be liquidated, the Jesuits could ill afford to provide funds from their own resources.

As work on the first unit of the building progressed, Perri organized the academic structure of Jesuit High. Entrance examinations were administered on April 14, 1956, at the Cathedral grade school. The first faculty, consisting of eight members, was announced in June. Among them were five priests, two scholastics and one layman, hired to teach and coach. The public was advised that only freshmen would be admitted during the first year and that each succeeding year another division would be added. Books, typewriters, desks, (discarded from another school), chalk, and a thousand other items large and small, had to be acquired for the opening of school.

By September 9, 1956, all was in a more-or-less state of readiness, and the faculty assembled for the first teacher's meeting. Though historic, it was dull, like most teachers' meetings. There was, however, a strong spirit of enthusiasm. An undercurrent of nervous excitement lent itself to all proceedings, and made them more than tolerable. All knew very well that, during the next few months, they would be under Portland's demanding scrutiny, not to mention that of their brother Jesuits through the Northwest, who were carrying greater loads in other schools to make Jesuit High possible.

The next day, September 10, 1956, the great climax was reached. The doors of Jesuit High, forty-third among Jesuit preparatory schools in the United States, were opened wide, and ninety solemn little freshmen trooped through. Portland's Jesuit High School, a mere hope for exactly forty-nine years, was now a reality.

Father Earl La Riviere, one of the teachers, wrote about the eventful day: "Deluges of rain came on Sunday, Sept. 10th, and our apprehension mounted. The area surrounding the school was a quagmire. If the boys stepped from the boardwalk, which Brothers Wood and St. Marie had built all the way from the highway to the school door, their feet would be heavy with wet, adhesive mud—and of course, they would drag this into the classrooms and onto the newly tiled and waxed office floors. . . .

"In the front of the school the intercom system on the back of the gas company's truck was blaring instructions to a gang of workers digging a ditch for the school's gas line. Next to another room, the cement mixer was going. On the side of room 3 a crew of workmen was drilling into the wall and another crew was riveting on a boiler. Outside of this room a portable welding machine was in full operation.

"In room one, during class, a large milk vending machine was installed, then later on it was filled with milk, after this, the overhead ventilating machine was turned on and the resulting noise forced Fr. O'Dea to cease speaking for a time.

"Besides this, the workmen next door were laying terraza flooring amid shouts for more materials mingled with the howling of another mixer."[16]

Beginnings, as Joset used to say, are always hard and Jesuit High was no exception. Wilhelm proved to be a rather reticent superior, more interested in the buildings than in the community and Father Perri found it necessary to serve as a surrogate superior, as well as principal.

Dan Lyons, who supervised the fund raising, assembled a collection of old cars as gifts, most of which could not be operated. Misunderstandings with neighbors on zoning created needless anxieties. The cost of water for developing athletic fields appeared to be so excessive that a well and a pump house had to be provided on the property. The one ace in the hole they had, twenty-five acres of prime land, was managed badly and funds expected from its development were not forthcoming.

But they survived and grew strong. The ninety freshmen advanced in due time to seniors and Jesuit High became a full four-year high school with a Jesuit faculty of eighteen priests and scholastics. New buildings had arisen, like new additions to a home, with painful apprehension and thrift. The first classroom unit and multi-purpose gymnasium building was completed in 1957; the second classroom unit and football stadium in 1958; and a section of the faculty residence in 1959.

By this time Jesuit High had achieved a modest measure of fame. In competitive tests it ranked at the top. Its debating teams, like teams from Jesuit prep schools the country over, participated in the most important tournaments, taking more then their share of trophies. Its athletic teams won more than they lost. Its speakers, despite the disadvantage of their younger ages, placed in the state finals oratorical contests. Its dramatic productions and speaking contests for grade-school students attracted city-wide attention.

When Perri arrived at Jesuit High he found an abandoned cow pasture. When he departed in 1965, ten years later, he left a well-established four-year prep school with 511 selected students and a developed campus of nearly thirty acres. While the labor of many hands and the gifts of many noble donors were required to produce all this, there can be no doubt that Joe Perri, more than any one else, should be regarded as the founder of Jesuit High. Commenting on his departure he said, "I feel good about Jesuit High. The direction I gave it is essentially good."[17]

The provincial would certainly agree. He treated Jesuit High like a spoiled pet, and it was commonly alleged in the Province, much to the chagrin of the Jesuits there, that the Provincial was sending them only "race horses," the best men. "To get the place started right," was Schultie's principal defense, not a very convincing argument, when the also new Gonzaga Prep was provided with four scholastics in one year who left the Order, a bizarre kind of record for those relatively happy times.

If the provincial detected the subtle beginnings of the slaughter less than a decade in the future, he did not reveal it. He liked what he saw, a province, like himself, occupied with feverish activity, careening along at something like sixty miles per hour, with everyone enjoying the ride. Few, if any, were aware of the disasters ahead. Surveys had been made. Had not the prefect of studies predicted that by 1960 there would be so many Jesuits in the province there would be a shortage of beds to accommodate them? Seattle Prep and Gonzaga Prep should build new faculty residences. God knows they needed them. The wind rattled through the Seattle residence like an old hay barn. Someday it would probably slide off the hill in one of Seattle's occasional cloudbursts.

There was one other ambition Schultie cherished, a new tertianship. Almost everyone recognized the need for that. Not only was Port Townsend "at the end of the world," as the Greyhound Bus clerk informed a desperate passenger, but its air had become polluted by a paper mill, with such sulphurous odors that tertians lost sleep. Halpin's barking dogs had been quite enough, but they were heard only on one side of the house. The odor aroused everyone. Hopes for a change had been entertained for years.

But impending changes in Alaska required more immediate attention. Bishop Gleeson, of course, had moved to Fairbanks in 1951, when the new bishop, Dermot O'Feanagan from Ireland, was assigned to Juneau. His Chancellor, the indefatigable Father James Conwell, had begun the almost endless task of transferring title to every scrap of mission property from the Jesuits to the bishop. Fairbanks would soon be a diocese. Monroe High School was opened on September 6, 1955, with thirty ninth-grade students and with Father Bernard McMeel as its first principal.[18] The bishop was also planning a new church, which would become the cathedral. The decision to close the boarding school at Holy Cross had also been made, and a new school, reportedly in a better location, was under construction to replace it.

This was the highly publicized Copper Valley School project. Father Jack Buchanan, who was called "The Pack Rat Priest" by *Newsweek Magazine*, was its founder. Buchanan, like Jim Poole, had great powers of persuasion and he used all of them in begging materials for this colossal project in the wilderness, a kind of super school for developing a high degree of leadership among the Eskimos and Indians of Alaska. There were some who thought it was being built on the wrong location, and there were others who thought it should not be built at all. But Bishop Gleeson, like Buchanan, had great faith in its future and he loaned it all the available resources of the Vicariate. Father Spils, the builder, was transferred from St. Mary's, where he had completed the impressive new mission, to take charge of construction. Father Buchanan was assigned full-time to the procurement of materials and labor, most of which were being donated, and Brother Feltes was assigned to the supervision of the trucks to be used to haul the materials from Anchorage or Fairbanks.

The new school was built on a 640 acre site located at the junction of the Tazlina and Copper rivers, a mere thousand yards from the place where the historic Valdez Trail crossed the Tazlina, and about eight miles from the village of Copper Center. The Valdez was the trail that led gold seekers north to the Klondike.

Construction on the mission was begun in 1955. Father Erwin Toner in *The Oregon Jesuit* described the wheel-like design and its progress:

"The buildings at Copper Valley fan out from a circular enclosure, 150 feet in diameter. This central structure will have a steel and glass roof above the blacktopped court, thus providing recreation space for the students during inclement weather.

"First building under roof was a T-shaped dwelling for the convent. The 30-foot wide building extends 220 feet from the central court and has a side wing 120 feet long. The buildings are made of concrete block with full cement basements, excavated to half their depth.

"The second building put up was the kitchen and dining rooms. This building, located between the Sisters' convent and the Fathers' and Brothers' wing, is 52 feet wide and extends 120 feet out from the center court. Alongside it, the Fathers' and Brothers' building is 36 feet wide and 160 feet in length. Putting in the room and hall partitions in these buildings will keep Fr. Spils and his carpenters busy during the winter months.

"When springtime weather permits, the girls' dormitory, a 30 by 140 foot building directly behind the convent, will be built. Across the center court, directly opposite from the kitchen and dining room, will be a building 52 feet wide and 130 feet long. Part of it will house the boiler and laundry rooms. The rest of it will be used as a gymnasium. Between the gymnasium and the girls' dormitory is a 50 by 140 foot building, which will be divided into necessary classrooms. The final building, for which no cement foundations have been poured as yet, will be the church. This building will extend out from the center court between the Fathers' wing and the gymnasium."[19]

Most of the lumber for the project came from Sandpoint, Idaho, from Jim Brown, Buchanan's former classmate at Gonzaga, who had a mill there. At first Buchanan himself trucked this lumber to the port of Seattle. "On one 14-day job he made seven 400 mile round trips from Sandpoint, Idaho to Seattle's docks," wrote Toner, "the eight-hour trip when empty and 16-hour drive when loaded, driving a 3½ ton truck and trailer with an 11-ton load, left few hours for rest."[20]

"We have been very blessed in getting materials," Feltes observed, "about 95% of everything as a result of begging." The completed building, it was estimated, would have cost over two million dollars, had it been paid for in cash. "The school is expected to be completed in five years at a cost of $3,000,000, and a Catholic University of Alaska is already being planned."[21]

By late autumn of 1956 it was sufficiently completed for use. With temperatures dipping to thirty degrees below zero, twenty-six orphan children, Sisters of St. Ann, Brother Hess and Bishop Gleeson, were shuttled by bush plane from Holy Cross to Anid, where an Alaskan Airlines plane, gratuitously provided, awaited them. When all were aboard, they were flown the five hundred and forty miles to Gulkana, Alaska, and the final stage of the journey was made by bus. Thus on a typically frigid day in the north, the painful history of the Holy Cross residential school came to an end, and the roseate history of Copper Valley school began. There was no time to weep over one or to celebrate the other.*

The tertianship issue had begun to take form. On January 8, 1957, the provincial wrote to the general to summarize developments.[22] Suitable property, he said, had been found on the south side of American Lake, thirty minutes drive from downtown Tacoma. Father Leo Martin at first had objected to the site, but when he visited it a second time he said, "I withdraw all opposition to the fitness of the proposed place." One of the principal objections to this new site was that it lay in "a district where homes of the wealthy are, and for this reason the Bishop may not grant permission for us to open a tertianship there."

On January 18, Father Janssens replied that the provincial should "see what the ordinary [the archbishop] says about the new site." Then he added a point probably overlooked by Schultie, "There are other dioceses in this region."[23]

Committed to action, Schultie now wrote to Archbishop Connolly, who responded immediately by requesting more information. Schultie wrote again on February 22. He identified the proposed tertianship location as 8601 Thorneland, Tillicum, Washington, known, he added, as Thornwood. It was on the south side of American Lake. Like Manresa Hall, it would be used as a retreat house on occasion only. The present tertianship at Manresa Hall would be sold.[24]

---

*Holy Cross was still regarded as a school, but it did not have resident students.

It soon became apparent that Connolly did not like the idea of having Jesuits at Thornwood. Father Leo Gaffney was assigned then to Port Townsend as the minister, charged with the additional task of finding a new site. In due time Gaffney located several contiguous parcels of property between Seattle and Everett. He was able to negotiate the acquisition of all of these by purchase. This required several years, however, and by this time changes within the church rendered further developments here as unlikely and the property was sold.[25]

Two years remained for Henry Schultheis as provincial. They were not happy years for him. As time had progressed, under Weller's influence, he had become more engrossed with the high schools and Jesuits in formation, and more detached, even isolated, from the universities. When Father William Armstrong, for example, returned from Europe with two earned doctorates in foreign languages, expecting to be assigned to Seattle University, he was sent to teach at Gonzaga Prep. Father Leo Kaufmann, completing doctoral studies in philosophy at St. Louis was tentatively appointed as principal of Gonzaga Prep, and Father Richard O'Dea returning from the University of Louisiana with a doctorate in English was assigned to Jesuit High.* This seeming waste shocked and irritated administrators in the universities, who protested with appropriate indignation.

Meanwhile academic excellence, especially in the high schools, replaced more pious priorities, and competition in such national examinations as the merit exam became so keen that the high schools' sense of solidarity suffered. Weller's visitations turned into local donnybrooks much dreaded by administrators and teachers. "Pray pray!" pleaded the principal of Seattle Prep to Father Frank Falsetto one day. "Pray that we get out of this morass!"

Some progress was made. At St. Aloysius in Spokane, Father John Prange built an almost indestructible new parish residence—a brick and concrete block that lacked only guards and a logo to turn it into a branch of the Old National Bank. On February 21, 1957, five Jesuits moved in. Father Erwin Toner, so crippled with arthritis that he was compelled to abandon his brothers' macho image and become an editor, developed his Jesuit Seminary association so extensively that he had to buy his own building to accommodate it. This was next to Campion Hall on Hoyt Street. Erwin with his eager staff moved in during February, 1957.[26] At Gonzaga the Patrick Welch Hall was under construction and at Seattle University plans for a new Sisters' Formation Program were being scrutininzed. Father General commended Father Schultheis for completing the novitiate.[27] He also sent his approval for the Formation Program "provided adequate teachers are available, who are apt in teaching what is required."[28]

In May the provincial reported to Rome that Bishop Dougherty of Yakima had announced he was opening his own high school in September. Thus the Jesuits' Marquette High School was in jeopardy and Schultie expressed doubt that it could survive.[29] A month later, on June 10, the Jesuits departed from Juneau. It was all very simple: members of the parish held a reception for Fathers Robert Whelan and Emmet Buckley. The next morning they turned the parish over to the new bishop and left, after sixty-two years of Jesuit presence.†

The bishop of Yakima kept his word. On September 3, 1957, Central Catholic High School opened on one floor of St. Paul's grade school. Sooner or later, Yakima's two pioneer high schools St. Joseph's Academy and Marquette, would have to go. The small

---

*Armstrong was soon transferred to Seattle University. O'Dea replaced Gordon Toner as principal at Gonzaga Prep in 1958, and subsequently left the order.

†Whelan remained in Alaska and became Coadjutor Bishop to Bishop Gleeson on December 6, 1967 and succeeded Gleeson on November 30, 1968.

City, as everyone knew, could not support three Catholic high schools.

This was not our best year, and the following year, 1958, was not much better. There were a few hopeful signs. The Province Archives were moved from the Mount into new quarters in the Crosby Library on February 14, 1958. Ten scholastics from the Mount, using two large trucks assisted me. The six hundred archive boxes, twelve files, map cases, reference library, and other miscellany required the entire day to move. Gonzaga University's new rector-president, Father Edmund Morton, had succeeded in filling Corkery's shoes, a feat not to be despised. A new rector, Father Alexander McDonald, was assigned to replace Father Joe Logan, one of the most popular rectors Sheridan ever had, and Logan was appointed rector of Bellarmine. Some called it "musical chairs," but no one objected to it. Anything else would have been an abuse of talent.

Three distinguished members of the province died within weeks of one another, leaving the province bereft of some of its favorite characters. Father Leo Martin, after a very painful illness, died in Providence Hospital in Seattle on April 12, 1958. John Leary's remarks characterize the event: "No lengthy obituaries or shock at his going, no floral pieces or wordy eulogies attended him. He just slipped away like the soft-touched, downbeat man he was. He probably shuffled in before the Divine Presence, sneaking a wondrous look now and then, curious, but head still bowed with reverence to the end."[30]

Several weeks later Father Patrick O'Reilly breathed his last. His were eighty-seven humorless years, but years of heroic dedication. Pat never asked anything for himself, except an audience. He loved to talk. When at last his remains, laid out in a plain "Jesuit coffin," were balanced on straps above his grave, the scholastics sang In Paradisum. There was a sudden lull and Mike O'Malley whispered, "Perhaps Father Pat would like to say a few words." Laughter followed this, then another sudden silence. "No words?" asked O'Malley. "He's dead."

On July 13, 1958, Father David McAstocker was finally dead also. One ought to say "finally" for he had been dying for fifty years, the only Jesuit we know who had a golden jubilee of dying. He had composed his many books on his deathbed. Every day we expected him to die, since he had only a small portion of lungs left and despite doctor's orders, smoked strong cigars. Life for him had been a battle in more sense than one, but he died peacefully at Monrovia, California, where a saintly Maryknoll nun, Sister Mary Godfrey, had cared for him with tender Christ-like love. He had survived his younger brother John by six months, almost to the day, a strange twist of fate that confirms one's belief that God calls each in His own time, not ours.

For the provincial the months following McAstocker's death were very discouraging. Apparently he did not realize that a subtle change was taking place in the province. A new spirit he neither recognized nor understood was beginning to appear in the younger Jesuits. A new freedom was expressing itself and he was subconsciously uncomfortable with it. Weller's methods were under attack on all sides and the provincial underestimated its bitterness. On October 10, 1958, Janssens informed him that Weller was to be relieved of his office and be reassigned to another position in the province. The general's reasons were understood, if not fully expressed.

Schultie was dismayed. Still somewhat naive about the province's attitude toward Weller policies, he sent a three-page defense to the general, giving reasons why Weller should be retained in his present position.[31] Then a week later he wrote to the general to say that Father Kunz, whose health was poor, had asked to be relieved as rector of Gonzaga Prep.[32]

Father Schultheis, they say, was a stubborn man, not a disobedient one. He simply lacked understanding of the Weller situation, or was too soft regarding it. He was hurt and bewildered by it; one can only imagine how he felt when he received two letters from

Janssens on February 18, 1959, one informing him that Father Alexander McDonald had been appointed as the new provincial, replacing him, and the other a stern order to reassign Father Weller without further delay.[33] Schultie responded the same day, expressing his willing obedience in all things. From this point on he never criticized the decision of his superior, nor did he manifest in even the slightest degree self-pity or arguments to justify himself. He closed the door and never looked back.

When Father McDonald was informed of his appointment he requested Schultie to remain in office for the meeting of missionaries in Alaska. It was agreed that he would take up the reins of the provincialate on March 10, 1959.[34]

News of Weller's removal was too good to keep. It swept the province like a prairie fire, and there was much rejoicing that the system everybody disliked was finally being terminated. Mostly, the province felt relieved, for tension had taken its toll. It was time for peace and reconciliation after a hard struggle between factions that were sincere and devoted to truth. As Jesuits, both Schultheis and Weller were highly respected, and by some admired. They had performed valuable services for the province and neither should be regarded as a failure. Evidence to the esteem in which Schultie was held can be demonstrated by the fact he was soon appointed as treasurer of the province. As province treasurer he completely reorganized the province's fiscal office with notable success.

Father McDonald was a dark horse. He had so little opportunity to share the public's attention that he was little known by outsiders and not much better known by the members of the province. If one word could describe his predecessor, it would be impulsive. For Alex it would be the word gentle. Schultie seldom listened to anybody; Alex seldom spoke. When he did, however, he used the king's English, for he was an Oxford man.

With his trunk and his degree from Oxford, he moved into Campion Hall in Portland, and from this moment a new spirit in the province prevailed.

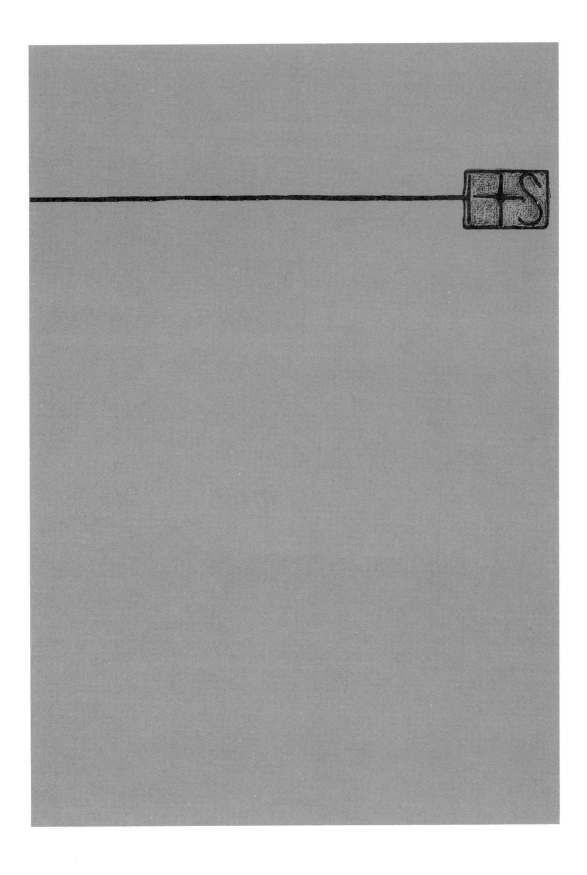

Alexander McDonald, sixth provincial of the Oregon Province.

Present St. Mary's Mission at Andreafski, Alaska, successor to St. Mary's Akulurak. Present St. Mary's is the scene of missionary meetings and retreats.

Henry Hargreaves, S.J. superior of Alaska Mission 1956–63

Francis Corkery, S.J., nineteenth president of Gonzaga University

John Baptist Janssens, S.J., general of the Soci-¹ ety of Jesus from 1946–64

22

THE DARK HORSE
1959–1964

Gentle, even shy, and an Oxford man are accurate designations for the second son of a western cowboy, who came to Fort Washakie, Wyoming in 1874. Angus J. McDonald, whose roots were in Scotland took special pleasure in his ability to speak Gaelic, but foregoing opportunities of showing it off, he accepted service in the United States government on an ox team train in the unsettled wilderness. "The outfit consisted of 4 teams of oxen of 8 yokes each," he explained in his memoirs, "the crew, 4 drivers and one wagon boss. We hauled corn and oats for cavalry horses and commissary supplies for soldiers. I walked back and forth beside those four teams, seeing that each did his share. Made six trips one summer, 300 miles round trip. . . . There were no white people from Landor north to the Montana line. Killed buffalo, deer, elk and antelope, wolves, cayotes, bobcats, bears. Later, after one of my favorite horses was bitten by a rattler, I started in on them, but gave up after killing 150."[1]

At the time of the Custer Battle, Angus was on the road to Fort Washakie. He slept on the open plains, without a tent, once when it was 54° below zero. Eventually he got his own spread one hundred miles from the nearest store. And after that civilization moved in and he owned the local bank, too.

The history of Angus is like a popular television show, *The Virginian*. He was the doting father of his two sons, Angus and Alexander, who were born after he had become wealthy and famous in that part of Wyoming.[2] Unfortunately, he died before his sons knew him very well—Alex was only six. His widow was defrauded of most of his wealth. When the boys reached the proper age she brought them to Missoula to be educated by the Jesuits. Both were bright, conscientious students at Loyola, but natural non-athletes, and conspicuous for wide-eyed innocence. Alex, who was a favorite with all, even the nuns, spent many long hours practicing on his violin, a delicate young virtuoso, who was gradually losing his interest in the violin, and gaining interest in the priesthood.

When Alex completed his sophomore year, Loyola was closed. The three McDonalds moved to Spokane, where Angus and Alex then attended Gonzaga. In 1934, when he was twelve days older than seventeen years, he entered the novitiate at Sheridan. He was ordained in San Francisco before he was thirty, and he became rector of Sheridan when he was only forty. Destined for higher things, he set a kind of record for brevity of rectorship, eight months and thirty-four days, during which he greatly improved his ability to operate a car by running errands for the community.

There was nothing soft about Alex, nor submissive. His gentleness could be deceptive, like a young buck's. While he still looked as boyish as a Mount scholastic, he acted with caution and maturity, like an old senator. When he said something, which was not often, he got immediate attention. He seems to have had one weakness, he asked more of his friends than of others. This was his solution perhaps, to what he regarded as a problem, his lack of knowledge about most men in the province. But not for long. Alex governed the way he studied Greek in high school or played the violin, with undivided attention.

He quickly mainfested his philosophy of government by his choice of assistants. He appointed no-nonsense John Taylor as vice-rector of Sheridan, pending the general's decision.* He retained John Monahan as his socius and assigned Leo Kaufmann to the position formerly held by Weller. All three of these men were respected as intellectuals, and they had one more characteristic in common: they were traditionalists. Monahan was justly regarded as brilliant and Kaufmann was generously endowed with common sense and a sharp wit, which he used to regale his colleagues in their more solemn moments. One could always count on Kaufmann to say something witty, bordering on irreverent, when our cause appeared to be lost. He did this with such artless spontaneity that one sensed he was both realistic and perceptive.

The new provincial had inherited a large province, not in size but in numbers. On March 10, 1959, the Oregon Province had 670 Jesuits, an increase of 59 during the Schultheis administration. The province staffed 2 universities, and 9 high schools, including the 2 new ones in Alaska, Monroe in Fairbanks, and Copper Valley. There were 41 Jesuits in northern Alaska and 23 working on the Indian missions.[3] There were 23 parishes administered by Jesuits in the province, and 3 houses of study: Sheridan, the Mount, and Port Townsend.

Despite the impressive increases in personnel, Jesuits were still spread as lightly across the province's one million square miles as before. As manpower increased, needs increased. Alex doubtlessly realized that this could not go on indefinitely without enormous disadvantage to the province and certain high risks. Monahan's voice was raised frequently in favor of what might be called a policy of containment, that is a policy of maintaining student levels, especially in the universities, at that point of maximum ratio of Jesuits to students. Some, on the other hand, like John Leary, then academic vice president at Gonzaga and Lemieux at Seattle University, favored expansion of student levels and services, foreseeing, as they did, far more dependence on non-Jesuit staff members, even as they exerted additional pressure on the provincial for an ever-increasing number of Jesuits. The lack of men to supply the demands made on him proved to be very painful to the provincial, who sometimes took these importunate claims too seriously.

This could explain, for example, Alex's tendency to postpone decisions. He sometimes left one with the impression that he was waiting for a better deal, a plan that would provide fifteen men instead of fourteen for a given need. Under the circumstances one could scarcely blame him.

In the course of time Alex determined to retrench in the area of parishes and Indian missions, some of which were like parishes anyhow. While this tended to centralize, rather than scatter Jesuit activities, it produced few, if any, suitable candidates for the faculties of our burgeoning schools. The few who were gained were soon lost in the shuffle and our manpower was spread as thin as before. In 1959, for example, when McDonald became provincial, there were thirty-one houses, including parishes, and thirty missions. In 1964, when Kelley succeeded him, there were twenty-eight houses and twenty-eight missions.

---

*Some members of the community, like Brother John O'Brien, still speak of Taylor's "hundred days," when Taylor's favorite breakfast of soft-boiled eggs and toast was served every morning.

Alex recognized a dilemma when he saw one. This one dogged him to the end, as it had his predecessors. Unfortunately his successors would feel the full impact of this long-time conflict between supply and demand. Some harsh realities would have to be faced then, not in the manner of Alex's rather dainty touches here and there, but in the manner of bulldozers and demolition bombs.

Meanwhile Alex ruled the province, normally with gentle but firm directives and many common letters composed in the king's choicest English. Like Father Small, he was a steady desk man, who preferred regularity to adventure.

In March he received a lengthy letter from Henry Hargreaves, the recently appointed superior of the Jesuits in northern Alaska. The letter was long and comprehensive, containing two subjects especially that should be noted here.

"Father Tom Cunningham," he wrote, "will be with the group of military men starting a new Ice Skate Project on floating ice in the Arctic. Father Tom will help out only at the beginning and then will resume work at Barrow."[4]

Hargreaves' letter included this remark on another subject: "The Bishop has been studying the possibilities of starting a Secular Institute for some of the lay apostles who come up to teach or do other work at Holy Cross and Copper Valley and Dillingham. The lay workers are most helpful and zealous, but there is no permanancy about the system. They stay only a year or so then 'rotate.' By the way, Gonzaga U. sent up some excellent young people. This volunteer work reacts on the young people and really makes them interested in studying and furthering their Faith. This movement is one of the best things to happen to the Missions in a long time." This was the seed from which the now worldwide Jesuit Volunteers Corps grew.[5]

Father Tom had experimented on ice floes before. "In the winter of 1951 the Air Force, long reluctant to hazard men's lives on the pack ice (as the Russians were doing,) tried an experimental camp on an ice floe 200 miles off Barter Island, Alaska. It called in Father Cunningham as consultant and he was one of a party of eight. They were there just 22 days when the ice broke. The men scrambled to safer ice and watched their camp ground to bits. A plane made a perilous ski landing to take them off." In September, 1958, he was back on the ice. One of his subsequent adventures was described in the national newspaper supplement *The American Weekly:*[6]

"Last October an ice cake in the Arctic Ocean hundred of miles from land was being lashed by polar gales and was cracking up.

"Twenty men were on this island, but nobody panicked, despite the fact that all except one of the group were rank amateurs in the Arctic, that 24-hour darkness had clamped down, and no rescue plane could reach them for a month.

"The major credit for inspiring that amazing morale was given to a quiet, indomitable Jesuit priest—the only man there who really knew the ice pack and had lived through such a breakup. . . .

"In his part-time capacity as civilian ice consultant to the Alaska Air Command, Father Tom was on the floe which was the insecure home of Station A, a floating camp of the International Geophysical Year scientists. He had predicted the breakup of the floe, almost to the week—but the scientists had disregarded his warnings.

"Whenever the marooned men heard a noise like the roar of a hundred freight trains they knew it meant a new crack in the ice cake. At each boom, the priest would pull his caribou-skin parka over his grizzled head and remark: 'Well, let's get out and see how much real estate we have left.'

"It was Father Cunningham who had pinpointed the ice floe for Station A camp in the beginning.[7] He was the first to set foot on it—and he was stubbornly resolved to be the last to leave it.

"The rescue plane from Thule, Greenland, was on the ice cake only 17 minutes. Father Tom lingered behind as the rest of the men scrambled aboard. With a triumphant grin on his seamed face, the priest in the white parka was last aboard—carrying his chalice and his folding altar."[8]

The plucky scientists and their priest-advisor had been on the floe from September 23 until November 7, 1958. Father Tom was awarded the Air Force Commendation Medal for his meritorious service. This was presented with a long citation describing "Chaplain (Major) Thomas P. Cunningham AO 929 942," and his heroic exploits.

The chaplain annotated a carbon copy of the citation: "I am enclosing this as an interesting piece of information, albeit somewhat distorted. They pinned the medal on me in the presence of four generals and eleven Colonels and then took it back, saying, 'It is the only one we have—might need it again.' I think this ranks fourth from the bottom in AF decorations."[9]

On April 4, 1959, Father Tom was back on an ice floe, "650 miles north of Pt. Barrow," he wrote Erwin Toner. "We are drifting northwest approximately one mile per day. This is the Air Force Geophysical Year Camp, where I am on loan for 90 days." In May he wrote again to say that his work was nearly finished. The runway for C-124's was completed and six of these planes were landing every day, each with a cargo of 120 tons. The camp, he added, was officially opened on May 21, and the commanding General presented him with another Commendation Medal "for meritorious achievement under difficult and hazardous conditions." Father Tom's letter concluded with a provocative statement, "I earned this medal."[10]

If medals are awarded in the Great Beyond, he soon earned another one. He had returned to his church, St. Patrick's at Point Barrow, in June. On September 3, 1959, he was found dead, a victim of a heart attack, in his little hut. He died as he had lived, alone in the vast emptiness of the Arctic silence.

It will be recalled that Hargreaves, in his letter to McDonald had mentioned the work of lay volunteers. Father Jack Morris, who modestly declined the honor of having founded the Jesuit Volunteer Corps, wrote about his first contact with the volunteers. "I went to Copper Valley School in June, 1957, taking the place of Bill Dibb. I was the first scholastic to go directly to Copper, joining Tom Gallagher, who had one year [of regency] left. Larry Haffie was working the Seattle [mission] office. He put me on the plane to Fairbanks, from there I drove to Copper. It was the Feast of the Sacred Heart. I recall that because there was a party in progress and one kid said, "You decide to come because we have a party."[11]

When Morris arrived at Copper "the volunteers had been there for one year. . . . There was no corps as it were, but rather a loosely unorganized procession of volunteers coming to our mission—Copper, Fairbanks, Dillingham. Bishop Gleeson was handling the thing."[12]

In 1957 there were fourteen lay volunteers in the Alaskan Mission. In the following year there were more than double that number, thirty-eight; and as the years passed, more, and still more came, until structure was finally provided.[13] Jack Morris not only designed this structure, but gave it a soul, which made it an effective spiritual reality.

It was precisely during this period that Father Theodore Hesburgh, President of Notre Dame University, one of the self-appointed spokesmen for Catholic education in the United States, and Monsignor John Treacy Ellis, highly esteemed Church historian at Catholic University, were publically critical of contemporary Catholic education. Their belittling remarks were exactly what Paul Blanshard and his Protestants and Others United for Separation of Church and State (PAOU) wanted to hear. Many Americans were already defensive about the public schools. There were deep-rooted misgivings about them and the school system which either was recently integrated and undergoing shock, or was preoccupied with resisting integration. Parochial schools, on the other hand, had acquired the image of the traditional American school with growing numbers of bright-eyed children and cool attractive nuns teaching them in plain but adequate classrooms.

But the price Catholics were paying for their schools was getting higher every year, not, God forbid, because of increased expenditures by the nuns who lived on forty or fifty dollars a month, but because of the ever-increasing cost of public schools, which they had to support first. Thus, when Mary Perkins Ryan published her now almost forgotten book, suggesting, it was said, that parochial schools were no longer needed, or were obsolete, even some Catholics who favored the parochial school system, wavered in their loyalty.[14] What the Ku Klux Klan in the Oregon School Bill had failed to do, Catholics themselves began to do. With the confidence of the public in their school system gradually undermined, they began to dismantle the system. The dedicated sisters, who had made the system possible, felt the brunt of the criticism and the loss of faith in it. During the years that followed, there were many other causes related to the decline of the Catholic grade schools of America, but none, it seems to me, had a greater impact than the tragic events of the late 1950s and the early 1960s.

The sisters in the teaching orders, accepting the criticism meekly, renewed their determination to up-grade their own educational standards. In Seattle, Father Lemieux, the president of Seattle University, pledged his full support to assist them.[15] The university's College of Sister Formation, referred to as "the most significant movement in Catholic education today," was established in the summer of 1956.[16] During the 1957–58 school year the university served as one of two national demonstration centers for the program. The other was the College of St. Teresa in Winona, Minnesota.

> "Until completion of a separate campus by the Sisters of Providence, at Providence Heights on the east side of Lake Sammamish in 1961, Seattle University will furnish faculty and facilities for the college. The Providence Heights College will become an institutional branch of the university with its own faculty and facilities, but with degrees granted by the university.
>
> "The 4 religious orders now participating in the program are: the Sisters of Charity, Providence; the Sisters of St. Joseph, Newark; the Dominican Sisters of the Congregation of St. Thomas Aquinas, Tacoma; and the Dominican Sisters of the Congregation of the Holy Cross, Edmonds."[17]

The Sisters Formation Program attracted widespread interest throughout the United States and even abroad. Even the Secretary of the Sacred Congregation of Religious at the Vatican took note. He called it "a significant undertaking . . . making an invaluable contribution to the good of the church."[18] In October, 1959, a million readers of The Catholic Digest learned how the sisters were fighting back. With Seattle University they were facing head-on the greatest challenge to Catholic education since the Oregon School Bill and they were doing it, not with political lobbies and back-to-the-wall desperation, but with eclat and some feminine charm.[19] Had there been no upheaval in the church in the next decade, which no one really predicted, they would have succeeded beyond their wildest dreams.

Father McDonald was a silent, patient observer of these two promising movements, the Sisters' Formation and lay volunteers in Alaska. Though he was naturally given to profound literary tastes, his was a bread-and-butter life. Administration, which must have been boring for him, occupied most of his attention. In March, 1959, he wrote to Janssens that Weller had been assigned to teach juniors at Sheridan, in part to reassure the province that he was not in disgrace. A month later he wrote to Rome again to report that there had been serious trouble with the Bishop of Yakima, who had demanded the removal of the pastor of St. Joseph's and the principal of Marquette. He had also refused without giving reasons, to accept the former president of Gonzaga University as pastor. Father Corkery was known then all over the nation, as a distinguished churchman, and there appeared to be no reasonable grounds for rejecting him as a pastor in Yakima.[20]

In June, Alex wrote again, saying that he had a conference with Bishop Dougherty on June 5. The Bishop, he said, wanted the Jesuits to remain at Marquette. He absolutely opposed a proposal to move Marquette to the Tri-City area, where Catholics were pleading for a Catholic high school. He suggested that the Jesuits keep Marquette in Yakima, at least for a time, then close it.[21]

Later in June, Alex reported to Father Janssens that the Bishop of Great Falls had taken over the parish at Big Sandy, Montana. Bishop Topel of Spokane, he said, was taking over the churches at Springdale, Clayton, and Wellpinit, all of which had been attended from the Mount. In Portland, Archbishop Howard was taking over St. Michael's Italian parish which the Jesuits had directed "on a temporary basis for forty years."[22] Mr. and Mrs. Frost Snyder, old friends of the Jesuits at Bellarmine in Tacoma, wanted to build a new chapel for the boys. This would make Bellarmine the most complete high school campus in the province.

On the other hand, St. Mary's Mission near Omak was in deep financial trouble. There were 3 Jesuit priests at St. Mary's, 7 Dominican sisters and 140 Indian children in the mission grade school. When Father Joseph Balfe became superior after the death of Father Paul Corkery, there were debts amounting to $33,000. A loan was made to pay off all outstanding bills, thus a fresh start was made. The real problem at St. Mary's was two-fold: ordinary income from the tribe and the bishop fell far short of what was required to support 140 children, whose parents could not afford to pay for them, and secondly, over a period of years, Paul Corkery had accepted $140,000 from a benefactor in Yakima on demand notes. This friend or his heirs could legally press for the money from the mission at any time.[23] Not even the province could raise that kind of money on short notice. "For a long range program," Alex added, "we are counting on a meeting of our Indian Missionaries next spring at Gonzaga to provide a plan to make our work among the Indians more effective."

Oregon in 1959 was celebrating its hundreth anniversary of statehood, and the centenary committee had requested civic and religious groups to publish booklets relating their histories. Alex, who had a strong sense of history, requested me to comply with the committee's request. Thus *Jesuits in Oregon* was written. Erwin Toner undertook its publication and through the resources of *The Oregon Jesuit* he printed and distributed thirty-thousand copies which contained illustrations by Andrew Vachon. The booklet also contained a photograph of Alex that shows him as a young monsignor in rimless glasses with his eyes partly closed and his lips parted in a broad, toothy smile. Creases along his cheeks are visible reminders of his ability to remain slim, despite his almost all-day desk work. Looking at this portrait, no one could doubt that our provincial was a benign and scholarly priest.[24] Poor Alex! He was almost too gentle for what lay ahead.

In January his mind was made up about Marquette. There were too many needs for

Jesuits to tie up a high school faculty that was no longer required. He conveyed his decision to Father Janssens, who agreed. On February 3, 1960, he wrote to Bishop Dougherty:

"My superiors in Rome have reached a decision which affects the position of Jesuits in Yakima. I am anxious that you should be the first to hear of it to allow in good time for any adjustments that have to be made.

"In the hope of leaving the field clear for the full development of Yakima Central Catholic, we are to withdraw our Jesuit staff from Marquette High School at the close of the current school year."[25]

The bishop was in California. No doubt he was informed of McDonald's letter, but he did not reply until one month later. "Thanks to the Jesuit Staff," he wrote, "Marquette has a rich tradition which must be continued for the good of the Church. Accordingly, I have made arrangements to maintain the school with another faculty. I am confident that with the dedicated support of the parish priests and people of St. Joseph's Parish, Yakima, and with the assistance of others from outside the parish whose sons will attend Marquette, the school will remain in operation."[26]

This was not exactly what the provincial had expected. He had been to Alaska and back since writing the bishop and problems related to the mission occupied his thoughts, not the future of Marquette.

No one questioned the bishop's right to do what he said he was going to do, keep Marquette open. Jesuits had long since conceded that Marquette was a parochial, not a Jesuit school. For example, Fitzgerald in May, 1932, proposed to Bishop O'Dea of Seattle that we have a regular Jesuit High School in Yakima. O'Dea objected, however, "because of the uncertainty of the times."[27] The Jesuits, however, owned the property and building, and there was not the slightest doubt about that. However, another ugly uncertainty reared its head. The bishop had taxed all the parishes, including St. Joseph's for the support of Central Catholic. Marquette, on the other hand, which had a majority of students from parishes other than St. Joseph's, was partly supported with an inadequate tuition fee set by the bishop, with the deficits made up by only the parish. In other words, St. Joseph's had to contribute to Central Catholic located elsewhere, and then pay for the support of outside students attending Marquette. The school had survived because of indirect Jesuit support. What would happen now? And there was the larger question, should Jesuits leave Yakima entirely, not only Marquette, but St. Joseph's as well?

Alaska, too, presented questions. The provincial had arrived on February 17 and remained there nine days, most of which had been spent at St. Mary's, attending a meeting of missionaries. On February 29, 1960, he dispatched a detailed account of his observations to Rome, The meeting included twenty-seven men, he said. Bishop Gleeson was present but Father Hargreaves, the Superior, presided over all sessions. As usual, "the discussions were frank, lively and penetrating and they revealed the high caliber and the earnest zeal of the missionaries who took part."[28] An ancient protest was heard again.

"One complaint by a few of the missionaries was that they thought the Province was not interested in Alaska. This sentiment was voiced particularly by several of Ours of foreign extraction, who based their judgment largely on the proportion of members of the Province on the mission as compared with certain European countries. In answer to this complaint, it may be pointed out that in addition to the forty-two Jesuits on the Alaska missions, we have twenty-two among Indians at home, eight in Japan, and six in the Juneau Diocese in Alaska.[29] Moreover, we have educational commitments in our two universities and six province high schools to an extent that has no parallel in some of the European provinces which were used as a basis of comparison. It is nevertheless true that we could show more interest in missionary activity. Some reasons may be adduced which explain this reserve even if they do not excuse it. Some of Ours at home feel that the need for missionaries is greater in South America, Asia, and Africa than in Alaska. Others, seeing the run-down state of our home Indian missions, doubt the value and lasting effect of work for Eskimos and Indians. Since Alaska is now one of the fifty states of the union, it does not have the same appeal as a foreign mission (though it does have this appeal to European Jesuits)."[30]

These remarks reveal not only Alex's own sincere interest in the missions, but also his grasp of the mission situation worldwide. He recognized for example, that Father John Baud's presence at Nulato, serving less than eight hundred Catholics, only half of whom came to Mass, for twenty-five years,was difficult to defend against the bleak statistics about Central America which sometimes counted one priest for thirteen thousand Catholics. Without suggesting the abandonment of Alaska, Alex clearly recognized greater needs elsewhere, and Father Janssens did not miss the point. The Oregon Province, he understood, was more or less willing to undertake a new mission.

Father McDonald had requested the bishop in Yakima to publish a statement regarding the Jesuit's departure from Marquette in the diocesan paper. When this appeared a month later, on March 4, 1960, there was, as the bishop expected, a great hue and cry. A group of the lay people wrote to the Apostolic delegate in Washington, Archbishop Egidio Vagnozzi, who then wrote to McDonald for an explanation. McDonald responded, informing Janssens about it on March 13.[31] By this time, letters began to arrive from Yakima, one of them from an attorney, Mr.J.W. McCardle, who summed it all up: "These people are stunned and shocked, upset beyond belief."[32]

Judge Robert Willis of Yakima was an old friend of the Jesuits. He, too, was shocked. "Undoubtedly," he wrote, "I am not aware of all the problems that you have encountered in recent years at Marquette, although I do know that things have not always progressed with ease and smoothness. I do know, however, that there is a substantial percentage of the members of our community, non-Catholic as well as Catholic, who are most distressed to learn of the Jesuits'decision to divorce themselves from Marquette. I am sure, also, that most of these people, including myself, would be willing to make substantial sacrifices in order to keep the Jesuits here."[33]

The noisy protest prompted the provincial's assistant, John Monahan, whose head contained a most remarkable collection of information on almost every subject imaginable, to comment in jest about some inevitable "law"; it was always easier, he said, to get into a public enterprise than it was to get out of one. So far as Yakima was concerned, there was worse to come.

Other news that was less than welcome arrived in 1960. Father Harold Small, former provincial and currently tertian instructor, was appointed on May 18, to be Father General's Assistant for American, with residence in Rome. The province was already short of men who could serve as administrators, so that the loss of Small was difficult to accept. To replace him as tertian instructor, Father Edward Flajole, rector at Sheridan, was moved to Port Townsend and Father Michael McHugh was made rector at Sheridan. Both were appointed by Father General on June 22 and assumed office on July 3. Thus within sixteen months Sheridan had four different superiors: McDonald, Taylor, Flajole, and McHugh.

Sheridan with its tan-colored bricks and snappy new wings seems to be in its prime thanks in part to Father Francis Bisciglia, who conducted his horticultural activities like a tireless landed gentleman. He supervised novices and juniors until they transformed the primitive grounds into park-like gardens. One could say the hill top literally blossomed. Never had the novitiate been so prosperous. There were forty-four novices, forty-nine juniors, and an excellent staff of twenty-three Jesuits and brothers. One would imagine that these flourishing conditions, just two years before Vatican II would provide reassuring evidence that all was well, that basically we had nothing to fear.

Such was not the case. Cracks had begun to appear in the system which had endured since the Council of Trent. As early as 1960 Father McDonald wrote to the general that among the juniors there was widespread discontent about the studies. Something very fundamental was wrong, but Alex could not as yet identify it.

There was, for example, smoking. According to the letter of the rule, smoking was forbidden unless one received permission from the provincial to smoke.* Some of those in this new generation of Jesuits smoked without bothering to seek permission. When Alex tried to enforce the rule he was criticized. Gradually the rule, which was concerned with accidentals only, passed out of existence, unnoticed and unmourned. But some aberration, which was very basic to the system, had taken place. Subconsciously the young men had ignored legitimate authority, without being formally aware of anything wrong. To them the rule, which did not apply in some countries, was meaningless. To many observers their response had been "sincerity." This precedent would soon manifest itself in other matters. Clearly the system could not be salvaged with a little tinkering.

Discontent surfaced again when the provincial made his visitation at Alma. He reported this to Janssens: "There is a great deal of ferment and criticism among the theologians about the course of studies in the Society—not destructive or necessarily unhealthy criticism. . . . In general they feel that our training does not produce results in professional competence of academic standards or degrees commensurate with the time devoted to our years of study. Among the causes for this trouble—in addition to the usual complaints about poor teachers—they mention a certain lack of integration and progression and the intellectual isolation that comes from the separation of the juniorate and philosophate and their situation away from large university Centers."[34]

The provincial added that he did not regard the critical attitude of these scholastics "as dangerous or harmful." They reflected a wholesome desire to remedy the situation. It seems that Alex, subconsciously at least, had already accepted the premise that "the situation" needed a remedy.

These young Jesuits who complained to Alex about the studies—what happened to them? Of the forty-nine juniors at Sheridan when Alex made his visitation in 1960, eighteen only were finally ordained as priests, and only ten of these priests have survived as Jesuits. In other words, approximately one out of five of this group, *who had already taken vows as Jesuits,* survived. By pre-Vatican standards, this was a very poor showing. Most classes prior to this, after taking vows, lost three or four before ordination and in a few cases only a similar number after ordination.

It was still too early for anyone, even the provincial to understand what was happening. Even now opinions will differ on not only the *why* but even the *what* of events taking place that is the real nature of the collapse of old structures. Was it in the Jesuit system, in the social backgrounds of the discontented young men, or in both?

In 1960, who could say? What is significant is that at this point the provincial recognized a change. When he visited the general in Rome about this time, Father Janssens had inquired of him about the disproportionate loss of vocations.[35] Was it due to lack of counseling, the general asked. There is no record of the provincial's response. He doubt-

*Pope Pius XII had requested the Jesuits to forego smoking, though it was well-known that his canonized predecessor, St. Pius X, smoked after dinner each day.

lessly provided one, and the subject of change in the young Jesuits was probably aired, without either priest being aware of the dragon's teeth that had already been sown.

Meanwhile, one should not take the complaints of scholastics too seriously. Complaining was a kind of occupational hazard of isolated young men who did not have more substantial troubles to worry about. Father Hilary Wertz, rector at Alma, had once playfully remarked that the community table was too good, that is why the theologians complained about their teachers. The solution, he opined, was to hire some new cooks.

Alex, I'm sure, did not think so, but he had weightier matters to consider. In October he received a long letter from Hargreaves at Bethel, mostly about Father Segundo Llorente's admirers, who wanted him to serve in the Alaska legislature as on official, elected by a write-in vote. The proposal explicitly stated that Llorente would not have to campaign for office. Many voters in his district wanted him to represent them and intended to write in his name on the ballot. Hargreaves found it "hard to decide" whether or not he should permit this, but the Bishop noted there had been precedents.[36] On October 24, 1960, Janssens gave Llorente permission to run for civil office. Llorente merely permitted himself to be elected in a write-in vote with full approval of Bishop Gleeson. He was elected and was duly sworn in as a representative of his district in the State Legislature at Juneau. Bishop O'Flanagan of Juneau, however, did not approve and he forbade Llorente to serve as a priest in any capacity as long as he was in the diocese. Llorente was permitted only to say Mass privately early in the morning.[37]

Hargreaves had some other news. Father Paul Linssen, a competent but hard-headed young Hollander, had probably drowned while freighting supplies for his mission at Chifornak. "His boat was found empty on a sand bar at [the] mouth of the Kuskokwim River where the river opens out in a wide delta. Apparently he got stuck on the bar and a storm came up, which swamped the boat. His native guide may have been inexperienced at that part of the coast and in handling a large boat."[38]

A few days later Hargreaves wrote again:

"This is the story of Fr. Linssen as much as we know. On Sept. 16th, in the morning, Fr. Linssen and a pilot, Bernard Nevak of Chifornak, left Bethel for downriver. It was a calm, clear day, and the weather remained the same for several days. His boat the Klutch was loaded heavily with stove oil plus some drums of kerosene and gas, intended for Fr. Deschout at Tununak. On top the drums was a load of lumber being sent by the Dept. of Aviation to build plane docks at several villages.

"Some men who came upriver in the next day or so mentioned seeing the Klutch on sand bars. Other than that the boat appeared in good shape. They should have reached the town of Kwigillingok one or two days after leaving Bethel. On the 20th and 21st heavy winds with gusts up to 40 and 50 miles per hour hit the coast. And for the next two weeks the weather very unsteady. Plane pilots were asked to check on the boat, and on the 23rd it was sighted by Don Murphy flying a Cessna 180.

"During the next three days planes searched the coast and bay, but found no trace of persons or debris. Stormy weather prevented searches at varying intervals. On Oct. 3rd the teacher at Platinum while walking along the beach spotted a body floating near the shore. It was recognized, but with difficulty due to immersion and stone bruises, as that of Fr. Linssen. The men at Platinum made a coffin, next day the body was shipped to Bethel. Requiem Mass was offered on Oct. 5th, in packed church. Father was buried in Catholic cemetery in Bethel.

"A man searching around the Klutch found some Stations of the Cross on the sand, overshoes and pants and fur cap. There is the possibility that Father tried to swim or make it to shore from the boat since he had nothing on when body was discovered. The Klutch unfortunately had no life boat, and we don't know if there were any life preservers. In that cold water, however, a person couldn't live for more than five minutes or so.

"To date the body of the pilot, Bernard Nevak had not been found. Debris was found for about ten miles along the shore near Platinum."[39]

Thus the life of another young Jesuit was snuffed out by the subtle forces of nature in Alaska. Linssen was only forty years old. And without his strong, able assistance, Deschout, too, would have to leave Tununak and even Alaska, because the years in the Arctic had been unkind to him. Without Linssen's help, Deschout was unable to cope with the labors in his vast district. He was transferred to Sheridan, where he suffered a major stroke and died February 12, 1966 at the age of sixty-six.

There was still a new mission for Oregon on the general's mind. It had been suggested that a mission in South America would be appropriate. Janssens, however, had other ideas.* The Polish Province, because of repressive travel regulations, could no longer staff the mission of Lusaka in Northern Rhodesia. He requested Oregon to consider this. McDonald responded generously, but with the problem of money on his mind:

"All the Consultors were in agreement that we could and should undertake to help the Lusaka Mission on the basis of a long range program, even though we felt that we could not very well do much by way of a 'crash' program of sending many men or large financial aid in the immediate future. Our plan would include the following stages of action. First, we shall get in touch with the Archbishop of Lusaka and possibly send a man to the Mission to survey the situation sometime during the coming year. Within two years we would begin a program of sending some Fathers and scholastics to the Mission each year. Within about four years we could undertake the staffing of some sort of educational institution.

"It is understood that in the beginning our men would operate within the framework of authority of the Polish Province Fathers. But it would seem that eventually our work would prove more effective if we were given full responsibility for a section of the Mission territory or a specific project like a school. We likewise realize that if the Polish Fathers are not permitted to send new recruits from their home country, we would face the possibility of gradually replacing them and assuming full responsibility for the whole Jesuit work in the area.

"In view of the uncertain political future of the region, we doubt the wisdom of investing large sums of money in school buildings that might at any moment be confiscated and taken from our care. There would also be serious difficulty in raising such sums of money. If we are to inherit the fund raising organization of the Polish Jesuits in the Midwest and the East, we may encounter friction from those Provinces where the operations take place. Our own Province could not provide large amounts.

"Our educational traditions and practices may not be easily transplanted to a country where the English system is in possession, but per-

*On June 11, 1960, Janssens wrote a commentary to McDonald on the latter's proposal for a Jesuit mission in South America. On September 20, he wrote McDonald again, requesting him to take Lusaka, instead. Both letters in Provincial Archives, Portland.

haps we would encounter no greater difficulty than the Polish Fathers have met with in the past.

"Geographically, we are the most remote of all the American Provinces from the African scene. In the jet age this may not be such an important factor, except for expense of travel and freight. The full significance of our position must be learned from experience.

"To sum up our answer to Your Paternity, we accept the Mission which is being offered to us, with the resolve to do our best with the resources at our disposal. We realize that our present limitations and commitments are fully known and that we will not be expected to produce results beyond our capacities. We think that the challenge is good for us. With God's help we will do our best to meet it."[40]

On November 8, 1960, the provincial notified the province about the new mission: "According to word recently received from Very Reverend Father General, the Oregon Province has been entrusted with the responsibility of helping the Lusaka Mission in Northern Rhodesia. . . . It should be remembered that we are still entrusted with Alaska and the home Indian Missions. Work in these places should be esteemed as no less pleasing to God than work in Africa, and no less a responsibility of the Province."[41]

Father Louis Haven, teaching at Gonzaga University, was the first to respond to the news about the new mission. Having heard about it via one of the province's most productive rumor mills, he hastily sought Rhodesia's mysterious whereabouts in an atlas, and without further delay, composed his letter to the provincial, volunteering to go to the new mission. Within the hour he posted his request to Portland. His was the honor of being the first Oregonian to be assigned to Africa.

On the last day of 1960, Alex wrote to Janssens to say that the number of volunteers for Lusaka "was most gratifying." He wanted to send Father Joe Logan during April to scout the land.[42]

There was an ancient link between Oregon and Rhodesia, though few knew about it. John Haupt, a master carpenter who had assisted Father Grassi in the construction of the first Gonzaga College, "The Sheds," first entered the brothers' novitiate at St. Francis Regis Mission in 1887.[43] A restless wanderer by nature, he soon left, and traveled throughout Asia, then Africa, serving at intervals as a volunteer in Jesuit missions wherever he found them. He finally entered the English Province in Rhodesia in 1909, becoming famous in both North and South Rhodesia as the talented and dedicated builder of mission churches. Oddly, too, he died of blood poisoning in 1921 with Brother John Buskens at his side. John was a blood brother of Brother Peter Buskens alias "Mr. Gonzaga" who had left his own claim to fame in the Oregon Province.

In 1960 the members of the province knew little or nothing about Lusaka. Most of us realized that this part of America harbored the unwelcome tse-tse fly and some had heard that a Jesuit brother there had been killed by a lion, which sounded very biblical. When Father Monahan, our walking encyclopedia, was consulted about the bugs in Africa, he quipped, "The bugs own Africa."

Father Erwin Toner in *The Oregon Jesuit* presented some basic details, without dwelling on the missions long, complicated history or the tse-tse flies:

"The Lusaka Mission has been cared for by Jesuits from Poland and is part of the original Zambezi Mission. This mission was confided to the fathers of the Society of Jesus by rescript of the Sacred Congregation for the Propagation of the Faith on February 7, 1879. Since the Communist government of Poland prevents reinforcements reaching Lusaka Mission, the Oregon Province will receive the assignment of assisting in staffing the mission.

"Lusaka, the capital of Northern Rhodesia, has an estimated population of 68,000 Africans and 12,000 foreigners. Although located 15 degrees south of the Equator, the climate is mild. Most of the territory is a plateau. 3000 to 4500 feet above sea level, with some sections reaching an altitude of 5000 to 6000 feet. In the area is located one of the great copper-producing centers of the world. Work in the copper mines is the greatest source of jobs for native labor, and copper is the principal export of the country. The fertile upland plains, where cultivated, produce good crops of maize, rice, tobacco, sugar, and tea. Teakwood is the main lumber export of the area."[44]

There was little to add about Lusaka at first. The provincial and Joe Logan* left Portland on Monday, March 27, 1961, for Northern Rhodesia to survey the special needs of the mission, leaving John Monahan in charge of the province. Alex returned about a month later, bringing with him the impression that Lusaka's superiors wanted a "high school, a million dollars and a staff."[45] During the summer of 1961 they got two Jesuits instead, Louis Haven and Neil McCluskey. Both had shared in several formal "Departure Ceremonies," wearing white cassocks, which made them look glamorous, and large mission crosses, which made them look like Pat O'Reilly. They finally arrived in Africa in the autumn. McDonald reported on progress in January 1962: "From the letters we have received from Lusaka in Northern Rhodesia, we have reason to believe that there is a future for the Oregon Province on that Mission. . . . Father Haven seems to have taken root and is happy in his work at the minor seminary in Mpima."[46]

McCluskey, it seems, did not think his talents and training would find adequate scope in Northern Rhodesia, Alex explained, so he was expected to return to the province. Alex continued, "Our first objective will be to staff the seminary. Next summer we hope to send one or two priests and some scholastics there."

Other changes in the province required the general's approval. The Mount's villa at Twin Lakes, Idaho, had become unsuitable because of an influx of postwar lake settlers who denied us privacy. Father Francis McGuigan, the minister, wanted to sell the Twin Lakes property and buy a very attractive lodge called Linger Longer on Priest Lake.[47] The province would like to turn over St. Mary's Parish in Pendleton and St. Andrew's Mission near by to the Bishop of Baker City. The bishop was eager to receive St. Mary's and he had agreed to take the mission also, since Alex did not want to leave one Jesuit in the area without companionship. At Gonzaga, Father Leary requested permission to borrow more money. The new chemistry building under construction, projected at a cost of $700,000, required an additional $128,000 to complete it.[48]

Leary's building engine, like Lemieux's at Seattle University, had a full head of steam and appeared, at times, to be out of control. Lemieux had recently completed the Bannon Building, large enough to swallow three of Gonzaga's recent acquisitions. But Leary was not impressed. Even before the chemistry building had been contracted for, he announced a drive to secure one million dollars for a student's athletic pavilion and $228,000 to reconstruct the old gymnasium into an auditorium theatre. Scarcely had the pleasant shock

*Enroute home, Logan made a pilgrimage to Lourdes, where he mysteriously became very ill. Providentially an Irish priest from Africa happened to be at hand. He brought Logan to Ireland and placed him in a hospital there. Logan never fully recovered from the illness but he returned to Africa as a missionary until he was recalled in 1969. He died in Seattle on December 19, 1981. *The Oregon Jesuit*, (new series), 1, 5 (January, 1982), p. 17.

of this worn off, one month later, when he informed the students that three new men's dormitories would be built during the spring and summer along Boone Avenue. Contracts for the construction of these small residences, designed to accommodate a total of 130 students, were awarded early in May, and during the same month Leary revealed plans for the new $600,000 faculty residence. A substantial part of its cost, $50,000, had already been pledged by the much-esteemed class of 1912. In making the announcement, Leary indicated that an additional $250,000 would be sought to remodel the former faculty quarters in the administration building into fourteen new offices and twenty classrooms.[49]

Crater-like holes in the ground in several places, ditches here and there, mud, bulldozers, interrupted electricity and blocked-off streets were signs of the times. Leary was on a building rampage. "It is a terrible thing to fall into the hands of the living Leary," Father Jerry Diemert had jested one day, referring with droll finality to Leary's powers of persuasion.

Leary had an acquisitive eye on the old Webster School, which had been restored by School District 81 after the fire of 1945. The Webster School had been built in 1900 for $38,000. When fire destroyed the building in 1945, it was rebuilt at a cost of $149,600. Between 1952 and 1957, it was used as a school for retarded children. Gonzaga tried to buy it, when it was vacated, without success. The school board announced on July 19, 1962 that the building would be sold.[50] Leary's negotiations got nowhere. The school board of Webster finally decided to auction off what they regarded as a white elephant and on July 30, 1962, Leary occupied the front seat at the auction. He sat stiffly attentive. When the auctioneer said, "Father Leary, will Gonzaga University bid on this property?" Leary stood up, his face cherry red with excitement. "Gonzaga bids $115,000. I . . . ah . . . . "he hesitated and sat down. There were no other bids. "Sold to Gonzaga University for $115,000." Later Leary announced that the fifty-year-old Law School would be housed in the Webster building.

At Gonzaga Prep, the new rector, Father Frank Masterson, was also spear-heading a new faculty residence to replace the old barracks. A dynamo of energy like Leary, Masterson was trying to cope with the mysterious behaviour of a few of the scholastics. One had rented Spokane's huge new Coliseum for a student party without bothering to inform the principal about it. Some were ridiculing the sacrosanct Epistle on Obedience by St. Ignatius, which was read in the dining room every month. Others were leaving the premises in the evenings without customary permissions. And still others were handing out books, allegedly "great literature," to boys who were unprepared for them. Permissiveness had not yet reached the point where scholastics counseled students that they did not have to attend Mass unless they felt like it, but that would come also, before the authentic reform began.

Masterson was rector at Prep for six full years, during which there was a total of fifty-two scholastics in his community.* Of these, twenty-two left the Order before ordination and thirteen left as priests, after ordination. This left seventeen, or one out of three, who survived. Masterson was generally regarded as an excellent superior, if anything a little left of the middle of the road. What was happening at Gonzaga Prep, I think, was indicative of what was going on in province, and in the Church, when the impact of the 1960's was finally recognized.

It was during this period, also, that the flow of "vocations" or candidates for the Society, began to dry up. "Gonzaga," Father Janssens had once exclaimed, when the name came up in a conversation, "that's the school from which we have received so many

*Masterson was rector of Gonzaga Prep from February 5, 1959 to June 21, 1965. He was subsequently rector at Sheridan and at Jesuit High in Portland.

vocations." But in 1963 Father McDonald asked, "Why are there no vocations at Gonzaga Prep?"

But life went happily on. Leary had another brainstorm: he wanted to establish Gonzaga abroad. He wanted a Gonzaga-in-Florence, the art center of Europe. The provincial, cautiously agreeing with him, wrote to the general in January, 1963.[51] Janssens approved and the new program was begun in the following autumn under Neil McCluskey, who had returned from Africa.

Alex had other concerns. Bishop Topel of Spokane had shown interest in acquiring St. Patrick's parish for the diocese. In February Alex corresponded with Janssens about it and arrangements were made for the transfer of the parish to the bishop of July 1, 1963.[52] Bishop Topel then sent the provincial a check for $9,000 in payment for Jesuit-owned land there, a gracious gesture on the part of his Excellency and a rare treat for the Jesuits.[53]

At this same time, Archbishop Howard requested the return of the Sheridan Parish, which had been served from the novitiate. This, too, was turned over to the Archbishop with a certain alacrity, because the provincial, by this time, was hard-pressed to find men for Africa. This was not for lack of volunteers. But many who brought up the subject were informed that their Africa was in the Northwest. The Archbishop of Lusaka, however, was getting desperate and his Jesuit counterparts, the provincials of both Polish provinces, appealed to Father Janssens, who in turn, deposited their entreaty at McDonald's embattered door.

"The Fathers Provincial of both Polish Provinces," Janssens wrote sweetly, "have earnestly requested that their Provinces be relieved of the responsibility for the Lusaka Mission, because the Society in Poland is not and, in the foreseeable future, will not be permitted to supply men or money to the Mission from Poland itself, nor will it be able to exercise any administrative supervision. Archbishop Adam Kozlowiecki has recently urged the same action."

Janssens went on to say that Jesuits from Poland and Ireland would remain in Lusaka. Structures would remain the same. "The Oregon Province would send, for instance, one or two fathers and two scholastics each year to the Mission." Archbishop Adam would solicit funds. He would also like to visit the province and discuss matters like the appointment of an Oregonian as superior of the Mission.[54]

Alex had a stickier problem close at home. Father Edward Flajole simply had not worked out as a tertian instructor. He was still wound up in German literature, and as brittle in his thinking as some of the diehards in the Vatican Council. A delightful person when he had no responsibility, Flajole tended to take matters too seriously when he became a superior. He was like John Forster in this respect. But all this no longer mattered. A new tertian instructor had to be found as quickly as possible, and as the provincial and his consultors looked around, they could not find one. The Consultors finally pointed their fingers at Alex, which was just too bad. Suddenly he found himself appointed to this exalted office, which seems to have become a haven for ex-provincials. In the spring of 1964 he proposed the name of John Kelley, for his successor as provincial.[55] Janssens agreed. On May 24, Alex wrote to Janssens. Father Kelley, he said, would take over the provincial's position on June 10. Meanwhile he was keeping him informed on province matters.[56]

Three days before the new provincial took office Father William Bichsel, stationed at St. Aloysius Parish, pulled a little boy out of the Spokane River and pumped the water out of him. The police and newspaper reporters arrived when it was all over. They wanted to know Bichsel's name. For the sheer fun of it he replied that he was Father William Lyle Davis of Gonzaga. The next morning, June 8, 1964, Father Davis was reading the paper.

His eye fell on the article about the little boy's rescue from the river. He was an old man and an eccentric one. When he walked around the campus with his cane, and a flower in his button hole, he looked like a retired parson with dyspepsia. He peered with disbelief at the article. "Gawd Almighty!" he exclaimed. "How could they make a mistake like that!"

This incident, too, was important. It illustrated the traditional spirit of the province. We did not take ourselves too seriously.

Lee Kapfer, first American superior of Lusaka Mission, with students.

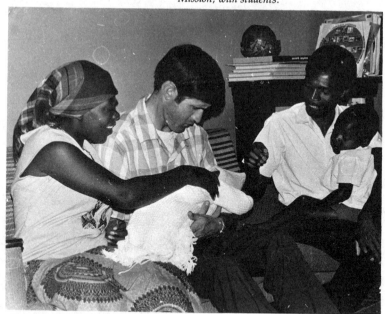

Kevin Maxwell in Matero Parish, Lusaka, with the Catechist and his family. The baby's name is Maxwell, Jr.

Pedro Arrupe, General of the Society of Jesus.

Brother Robert Calouri, secretary to many provincials.

John Murray, who died in Zambia in 1966 in an effort to save his altar boys.

23

VIOLENT WINDS OF CHANGE
1964–1970

No one could doubt that John Joseph Kelley was a priest, even when he was wearing mufti. With his sharp, refined features and trimmed black hair, graying at the temples, his willowy slender body which created an illusion of tallness, and his easy grace in walking, despite a back affliction, he appeared quite naturally to be Irish, while his dark eyes, filled with mystery, betrayed his professional preference. His eyes, like Father Elliott's, caught one's attention. Aloof and disciplined, they sometimes sparkled with compassion, revealing a loving soul that was generous but guarded. When he spoke, his voice was soft, with the lilt of the Irish male in it, almost like a song.

Judging from appearances only, one would say that Kelley was a seminary rector or a professor of moral theology. It has been said, sometimes, that moral theologians used their energies to break bonds created by canon lawyers. If this sounds simplistic, perhaps even slanderous, one must at least allow for the fact that most moral theologians are very compassionate men who struggle mercifully to justify as much human freedom as possible under the law.

This was, I think, Kelley's most obvious tendency in his attitude toward law. Gifted like Leo Kaufmann, with a rich endowment of common sense, he also had an Irish breezy tolerance which allowed for change and adaptations. He was uncommonly kind, at least until someone double-crossed him, then his easy going flexibility became a reprimand, like that of an angry Moses returning from the mountain. Most of us liked this Kelley anger. It gave him credibility and character. His kindness was seen as strength, not sentiment. No one wanted a Pollyanna provincial, least of all at a time like this.

Jack Kelley was only forty-eight when he assumed office at exactly twelve noon on June 10, 1964. Born in Helena, Montana, on July 20, 1916, he was the province's third native Montanan to become provincial.* His father, William L. Kelley, and his mother, Clara Kelley, nee Gendreau, had six children. Their two daughters entered the convent and three sons, Jack, Dan and Bill, became priests. The fourth son, Francis, who dared to be different, was a Jesuit for one year before becoming a policeman and a detective.

The family lived in various places, for example, in Missoula, where William Senior was Sheriff, and in Spokane, where he was secretary-treasurer in the Federal Land Bank. In Spokane they lived in Holy Land, St. Aloysius Parish on the corner of Astor and Sinto, an

*The first two were Elliott and Small. McDonald, often claimed by Loyola of Missoula, was a native of Wyoming and entered the Society from Spokane.

especially holy place, because later the Holy Names Convent was built there and this became the Mater Dei Seminary. When Jack was twelve the family moved to Glendale, California, but he returned to Spokane in 1933 to complete his high school at Gonzaga.[1] He entered the novitiate at Sheridan in 1934. Many years later, after he had completed all of his studies, he was assigned to Seattle University where he spent many more years, six of then as superior of the Jesuit community.

It is difficult at this point to continue. The Second Vatican Council had left the Church in turmoil and the War in Vietnam was slowly escalating until there was utter confusion in the United States, especially in the universities and colleges where most of the Jesuits were involved. "Today we live in the most catastrophically revolutionary age the world has ever seen" one observer noted, referring to this specific time. "There is not simply one but ten to fifteen revolutions going on simultaneously."[2] Indeed, most of the world was engaged in the greatest upheaval in modern times, and our little part of that world was as volatile as the rest. Trying to relate this part of the province's history is like trying to put a hurricane in a paper sack.

In the madness, which one sees at first, one point gradually becomes clear: no other provincial in the history of the province was required to face the kind of crises that confronted Kelley when he became the top man in the Oregon province. "I felt overwhelmed at times," he admitted later. "I was aware of the cataclysm."[3] No other provincial was forced to make so many and such crucial decisions as John Kelley. His influence proved to be proportionate to the risks he faced—no other provincial has left so lasting a mark.

"The dam broke loose," Brother Robert Calouri, the genial secretary for five provincials, remarked during an interview on April 10, 1981. "All structures suddenly were swept away, traditions were disrupted. Many priests left the Society. The provincial could not, as others before him, send out a regular status. Everything had to be discussed. We had to have assemblies. I think, and others have said the same, Father Kelley was the right man at the right time."*

Calouri, or "Cal," as he was usually called, was an excellent judge of the times, for he typed and circulated throughout the province more letters, more announcements and more minutes of meetings during the Kelley Administration than during any two administrations before it.

There was a lull at first, a brief period of peace. As Jack explained it, "the west was a year behind the east in making changes. At provincial meetings I learned what was going on in the east, for example, picketing of the provincial's residence by scholastics. The Congresses started in the east in New England and Chicago. We got on the band wagon."[4]

There were other reasons for the quiet before the storm. The younger Jesuits who favored what they called "reforms" in the Order, looked to Father Janssens and a forthcoming general congregation to make the revisions they demanded. But Janssens had a massive stroke and then a heart attack. Fully aware of the growing impact of Vatican II on the Society, he died on October 5, 1964, worn out and apprehensive, like a Pius X before the Great War. Planning for the Congregation was already under way. Within the province top priority was given to the selection of two delegates and the consideration of postulata to be submitted to the larger body in Rome.[5] Elected as delegates were Arby Lemieux and Jack Leary, who joined the provincial for the first session of the Thirty-First General Congregation in May 1965. On May 22, Father Pedro de Arrupe y Gondra, a Basque, like Ignatius Loyola, was elected general, and meetings continued until mid-July when the Jesuits were driven from Rome by the heat.

---

*Father Harold Small wrote to Kelley when he left office. "The Province was blessed because you were a man who could read the signs of the times."

Kelley, before leaving for the Congregation, had postponed his major decisions, awaiting like everyone else, directives from the Congregation to come. On October 21, 1964, he wrote to the vicar general Father John Swain, that Father Gordon Keyes had completed a new church at Nespelem, Washington, at a cost of $25,000, much of which had been raised by a loyal Jesuit friend, Mary Milla.[6]

In April, 1965, Kelley wrote again to Swain, apologizing for the intrusion, since the vicar-general was swamped with preparations for the congregation. "As you can see by the enclosed letter, Bishop Condon of the Great Falls, Montana, Diocese, is asking that we relinquish our missions on the Crow Reservation to the Capuchin Fathers. He wishes to take over St. Joseph's Church in Hardin and St. Xavier's Mission at Xavier, Montana, now, and Our Lady of Loretto parish at Lodge Grass, Montana, and St. Charles Mission in Pryor within a year or two. My consultors and I are in favor of relinquishing these missions according to the Bishop's request. We are quite short on Indian Mission personnel and this will help us to better staff the remaining missions that we have."[7] There seems to have been more to the matter than the provincial reported. The Capuchins, who had taken over St. Joseph Labre's Mission, were making a great success of it. Condon made no secret of his admiration for them.

We owned about 250 acres of land connected with these missions, Kelley explained, and he suggested that we donate the land to the bishop, who wanted a decision by May 15. Hence the urgency in seeking the vicar-general's approval.

By a curious happenstance, Father Swain, too, had written about the same time to Kelley. His was a provocative letter. "So much emphasis," he wrote, is put on education in the Province that work in the mission field occupies a low place in priorities. Even in the Mission itself, too much manpower and money is devoted to schools."[8]

This was certainly a straightforward criticism of the province's priorities, which had long since ceased to be a subject of discussion, let alone contention. An examination of the Oregon missions, however, compared to those of other provinces, seemed to contradict Swain's assertion. Oregon, for example, with 109 fewer members in the province than California, had 20 more Jesuits in the missions. Oregon had almost three times as many Jesuits in the missions as the New Orleans province, which was about the same size in numbers.*

At Hardin there had been a Jesuit pastor whom everyone there especially loved. He was Father John Murray, a very shy young priest, who took particular care of the poor and the children in his parish. John had been pleading to go to the mission in Africa and his people were most unwilling to let him go. They had many stories about him: how, for example, he read his breviary while driving out to Yellowtail Dam for Mass. Bishop Condon's request was a godsend. John got his wish at last and he flew off to Lusaka, as happy as a lark.

Father Weller, too, wanted to go to Africa. He was already fifty-nine years old, but he thought he could be useful. He had heard that Archbishop Adam required a secretary. Weller explained that his Latin was a little rusty, but he could get it up in a brief time. He really wanted Africa and he was prepared to give up whatever was required. Like Murray, he finally was assigned to Lusaka, which was, no doubt, as pleasing to Father Swain as it was to himself.

But Father Kelley was in Rome then. "Before the end of my first year," he said later, "I was at the General Congregation. There were 2400 postulata, which covered everything. I witnessed the arguments the pros and cons."[9] He returned to an anxious province with the

---

*In 1967 the number of Jesuits in the Missions for some provinces was as follows: California, 74; Detroit, 55; New Orleans, 36; Oregon 94. It is difficult to explain Father Swain's letter.

news that the Congregation would convene again on September 8 of the following year, 1966. Meanwhile, he added, it was business as usual. He began to make his visitation of the communities in the province.

In February, 1966, the new Father General, who had been a missionary in Japan, wrote to Kelley to say that the administrative status of Lusaka was still undetermined. "I think we have to work towards unity of planning in Lusaka, which could lead to a vice province in the future."[10] Characteristically Arrupe included a little bouquet: "The Oregon Province continues to be very generous in Lusaka."

Two days later Kelley wrote to Arrupe. A province committee on studies had recommended the integration of juniorate studies with philosophy.[11] This concept of "collegial" instead of successive programs of concentration, first on the classics, then philosophy, had gradually evolved in other American provinces as well as in Oregon, partly because of the additional years of study required for doctorates in specialized fields. For some years, not without reason, there had been complaints by Jesuits who were required to begin doctoral studies after fifteen years of traditional Jesuit formation. Jesuit students in graduate studies were usually ten years older than their classmates. A hope was commonly expressed that a collegiate program combining the juniorate and philosophy would reduce the ordinary course by one year, and secondly, that selected scholastics could be assigned to graduate work during regency; that is, in the time usually occupied by teaching in high school. As simple as these proposals looked, they were historic departures from a system that had been regarded as almost sacred for centuries. Kelley's request was a kind of trial balloon. What would the new general decide?

The new general had already decided to visit America. He announced that he would leave Rome for the United States on April 2 and would visit the Oregon Province on Thursday and Friday, April 14, and 15. In over four hundred years no Jesuit general had ever set foot in America. On March 30, 1966, Kelley dispatched a copy of particulars to members of the province. Father General's main purpose in coming to the country at this time, he wrote, was to visit the major scholasticates. He would arrive in Seattle at 10:12 A.M. on Thursday, hold a press conference, then attend a luncheon for Seattle Jesuits at Seattle University. Later he would speak to students, alumni and friends for one hour before leaving Seattle for Spokane. He would arrive in Spokane at 5:15 P.M., hold a press conference, then attend a reception for Jesuits only at Gonzaga University. At 7:30 there would be a dinner for Spokane Jesuits, then Father General would leave for the Mount. On Friday he would address the Mount faculty and scholastics, then attend a brunch at the Davenport Hotel for students, alumni and friends. He would leave Spokane at 12:20 P.M.[12] No young executive would get as much done in so brief a time.

The general's visit went so well it was over before anyone fully realized it had begun. He returned to Rome, and on April 29 wrote to Kelley: "My memories of my visit to America are still fresh and vivid. It was heartening to meet so many American Jesuits."[13] He approved of the proposal to move the juniorate to Mount St. Michael's, and Kelley informed him on May 8 that the juniors would move there in the first part of June. Kelley also requested approval for another innovation. Since the Mount would now provide a four-year collegiate program, scholastics working on their master's degrees would require housing at Gonzaga University.[14] First, would Father General approve the construction of a province-owned dormitory to be called Bea House, to honor Cardinal Bea? Secondly, the new rector at the Mount, Father Lemieux would like permission for the construction of a gymnasium-swimming pool building.* There was adequate money for it in the Johanna

---

*Father Arby Lemieux became rector of the Mount on January 10, 1966. *The Jesuit*, March–April, 1966.

Mahoney fund, if our own brothers were assigned to assist in its construction.*

Lemieux had been president of Seattle University for seventeen years. His successor as president was Father John Fitterer, a hale, well-met fellow who showed promise of becoming one of the university's most capable executives. Lemieux succeeded Father Joseph Donovan at the Mount. Joe, a calm, scholarly historian, had been riding out the post Vatican storm, which had left him wounded and all but dead. Most of the scholastics then were World War II babies, who seemed to think they had identity crises which required psychiatric care. Concepts like freedom, authority and obedience were bandied about lightly with new meanings that older Jesuits could not recognize. Some young Jesuits openly stated that they were remaining in the Society only to change it, while others, more modest in their demands, explained they were checking out the Order to see whether or not they should remain. The placid, serene Mount of the 1940s had become a kind of psychological battleground, with the traditionalists and innovators on opposite sides, the former being the older men or faculty, and the latter the scholastics.

It was Father Lemieux's task to resolve these differences. Building a new gymnasium doubtlessly would help, but in the end it would solve nothing. What is perhaps more enigmatic about it was the proposal in the first place. During its construction there was considerable, and not irresponsible, discussion about moving the scholastics from the Mount to an urban campus, where neither the gymnasium nor the swimming pool would help either faction.

But Kelley's major concern at this point was the acquisition of another building in Portland for a curia. Campion Hall with its two ancient annexations, frame houses used for the *Oregon Jesuit*, the mission procurator and others, had long since become inadequate. A search had revealed the availability of a vacated estate called Dunthrope. The price was right and architects' reports on renovation and additions were favorable. Kelley wrote to Arrupe on June 29, 1966, requesting his permission to buy and remodel Dunthrope. Arrupe responded on July 28, saying that he had given "careful consideration" to the request for buying and enlarging a house to serve as a residence. Though Dunthrope might be a "good business," this was not the only consideration; *appearances* and *location* were also important.[15]

The problem, though the general did not elaborate on it, was that Dunthrope had the appearance of a rich man's estate, a no-no in the brave new world where saving money was not the ideal, but the appearances of it was. Unfortunately, this is the way people judged us, and there was really not much anyone could do about it.

Before leaving for Rome for the second session of the Congregation, Kelley reassured the general that he had accepted his decision, and other plans for a curia would be formed.[16]

One week later news arrived from Lusaka. John Murray was dead. An obituary which appeared later contained the following:

> "Just a month before his death he was appointed Superior of the Chingombe Mission, a remote place in the mountains about 140 miles east of Broken Hill. It is probably our most difficult mission.

> "On Monday, August 15th, Father John left the mission with an African priest and six schoolboys in a Land Rover on the way to Broken Hill. About 9 miles from the mission he began the very steep ascent of the mountain.

---

*A group of six brothers under the leadership of the very capable James Wood formed what was called the Brothers' Construction Crew. In addition to Wood, there were Lloyd St. Marie, Drew Maddock, Vic Ortmann, Andy Schantz, and Marion Melius.

The car had practically reached the last turn when it lost its power. The brakes would not hold. Father ordered his companions to jump. They did, and were unharmed. The car left the road. Father jumped. He didn't make it.

"On August 17th, the Archbishop of Lusaka officiated at the Solemn High Mass at Sacred Heart Church, Broken Hill, Zambia. He rests in the Broken Hill cemetery alongside the other religious pioneers of the Lusaka Mission. Father Murray died on the Feast of Our Lady's Assumption, August 15th. By God's planning, it was also Father Murray's feast day, his 25th anniversary as a Jesuit. He celebrated it in heaven."[17]

When Kelley departed for Rome, he left Father Frank Costello, who was a province consultor, in charge of the province. Three major developments were pending: first a new curia; secondly, the use or disposition of Sheridan, now that it was more than half empty; and thirdly, construction of Bea House at Gonzaga, where a near-score of scholastics lived in temporary housing awaiting a permanent residence. The novitiate dilemma, I think, interested Costello most. He had never liked the country and like many others in the province, thought that the novitiate should be in an urban setting. Kelley and the other consultors had already agreed that the novitiate should be sold.

There was a little ditty that was being quoted at the time, something Father Tom Meagher had included in his novitiate commentary:

> Bernardus valles, colles Benedictus amabat,
> Oppida Franciscus, magnas Ignatius urbes.
>
> In sheltered valleys Bernard loved to dwell,
> Saint Bennet chose the mountain's lonely crest,
> In towns Saint Francis fixed his peaceful cell,
> But mighty cities pleased Ignatius best.[18]

"The new novitiate has its bricks and greatly expanded facilities," Father Joseph Conyard. "But the site is still a long way from 'Main Street' and the modern seminary is moving to the center of action."*

At the congregation in Rome, where most of Jesuit action was taking place, not all was hard labor and crusts of bread. On Sunday, October 23, a chartered bus bore some of the delegates to Florence. Father Kelley, writing on the following day, reported the adventure:

"I still feel a little punchy and I was one of the lucky ones, thanks to Father Small. But I'll get to that later. As guests of Jack Leary and Gonzaga-in-Florence, 25 of us left Rome yesterday morning by charter bus for Florence. About half way there we stopped for lunch at a restaurant at the edge of a beautiful little lake in the Umbrian hills. We arrived at Florence at 5:00 P.M. Fathers Regimbal, Dussault, Murray and the students were there to greet us. As we had half an hour before festivities were to begin, Father Small and I took a brief stoll about town. We had an enjoyable social hour from 5:30 to 6:30, then dinner, and after that the students entertained us, very well I would say, with songs, group and solo. We departed from Florence at 9:00 P.M. surrounded by serenading students."[19]

The bus, new and comfortable, travelling sixty-five miles an hour, bore its passengers through the lovely autumn night. After the first hour, many began to doze. Small and

---

*Father Joseph Conyard had replaced Erwin Toner in November, 1963. Conyard's remarks appeared in *The Jesuit*, which had replaced *The Oregon-Jesuit*, at the same time, November–December, 1966, p. 5.

Kelley ensconced comfortably in their seats near the front, continued to chat in a low voice. Suddenly Small sat us in his seat and shouted: "Look at that truck ahead! We're going to hit it." The bus was only two hundred feet away, its driver dozing too. The truck and trailer were loaded with thirty tons of sheet metal, which projected three or four feet over the back. The driver recovering consciousness too late, drove into the back of the truck. "I'll never be able to forget that sound of shattering glass and crunching, twisting steel as the front of our bus was ripped to pieces. . . . The bus was filled with smoke and it was very dark initially until the headlights of the cars coming up to the scene began to light the interior of the bus. It was a shambles. Several were slumped in their seats in shock, the majority were bleeding, some profusely from facial cuts and smashed noses. I've never seen so much blood. Father Small sitting next to me had smashed his mouth against the seat in front of him and was bleeding copiously from cuts inside and outside his mouth, and was very faint from the shock. Father John Connery, provincial of Chicago, who was sitting in front of me, was one of the worst of those injured. His nose was all smashed with the bridge protruding through the skin. His face was bathed in blood. . . . Jack Leary had several lower front teeth smashed and it was feared his jaw was broken."

It was hours before the seriously injured were taken to a hospital. The other, battered but ambulatory, arrived back in Rome at five o'clock in the morning in a nondescript caravan of police cars. Providentially, perhaps miraculously, no one was killed.

This was as close as our province came to losing in one shot our general's assistant, our provincial, and one rector.*

On November 4, 1966, Costello wrote to Arrupe, requesting permission to sell the Novitiate.[20] There was still a debt of $165,372.46 on the place, in which the Jesuits had initially invested something like $165,000, then added an approximate million when Schultheis was provincial. A religious group which preferred to remain anonymous had already expressed interest in buying the property. The general did not respond to this request until the Congregation had adjourned on November 17. Writing to Kelley, who was back in the province, he simply said that he disapproved of the proposal to sell the Novitiate.[21]

The provincial, after his return to the province from the Congregation, was in a sense, a changed man. He now supported the liberal groups within the province, mostly the younger men, who soon quoted the motto: "Don't trust anybody over forty."

The Church Fathers in Vatican II had laid heavy stress on new freedoms from antiquated laws or practices and new procedures for subjects sharing in the decision-making processes of superiors. These were monumental breakthroughs, but obviously subject to such broad interpretations that the concept of authority lost all meaning for some. "When the dam broke," Kelley said, "structures, for example, the rules, were placed in abeyance. There was a flood of demands. Superiors were no longer in command."[22]

With the new cult of youth in western society and the prevailing practice in religious orders to give the young, even novices, a preferential voice in all decision making, "for the young are the hope of the future," there was a corresponding demotion of older members, many of whom over-reacted. As the latter developed their own "litany of negativism," the breach between the old and the young widened, leaving youth, inexperienced, but vocal and often ruthless, in control. Novices, it was said, had more influence than an older Jesuit who had spent forty years in religion.

One of the key words was "communication." It seemed for a time that Society no longer needed Jesus the Savior, or prayer or the sacraments, but only *meetings*, where all

*Father Arby Lemieux, another delegate at the Congregation, had remained in Rome that day because of a cold.

521

could communicate. Thus the new "democratic" methods were introduced and countless committees were formed and very costly province assemblies were held. The provincial's official board—the province consultors—meanwhile fuctioned as usual, but with so many opinions and pressures forced on them that their burden was doubled.

Doubled, too, was the burden of the provincial. Doubled and more. "I hated meetings," Kelley said but he not only supported them in principle, he attended most of them with humility and the kindest of dispositions.

This marathon of meetings and re-evaluations and self-studies did not get under way formally until August, 1967, and did not pick up steam until the following year. This allowed time for some subtle collective changes in attitude regarding the so-called democratic processes in decision making and the gradual polarization of sides. Most older Jesuits wanted to retain the traditional system of government as it was, largely monarchical, or as some wags said "monarchical but limited by insubordination of its subjects." Many younger Jesuits at first favored modification of the system, but gradually shifted to something else, which was neither Jesuit nor common sense. "Discernment" was another key word. Discernment as a term was as old as the Society, but new stress was placed on its use and new interpretations were introduced to guide the provincial in government. In its grosser form, one *discerned* in favor of what he wanted, the binding force for his decision coming from his own insights rather than from the decision of the superior or law. The latter became a popular view of many young men, leaving not only the superior defenseless in their respects but also older Jesuits who grew up in another tradition and were incapable of adopting these subjective norms of "obedience." They were equally incapable of forming political parties for expressing collective views and when the point was finally arrived at wherein young Jesuits were given advisory votes on fundamental principles, older Jesuits found themselves at a distinct disadvantage.

"The tension," said the provincial of the California Province, "is felt more by the older people than by the younger. There certainly seems to be some kind of unspoken fear among the older men that with all the changes they're being talked into a situation which they never opted for which the young are pushing."[23]

No one should be surprised about all this. What was taking place in religious orders, like the Society, was taking place in the Church at large. Post counciliar periods are always torn by controversies. There was a spectacular difference, however, within the Church as compared to the orders: defections of Catholics, that is drop-outs of active membership, achieved a high rate among older members, as well as younger ones. Concessions made to appease the younger in certain matters, e.g., the liturgy, drove out many of the old, but failed in their purpose. On the other hand, defections in religious orders appeared mostly, though not exclusively, among younger members. For example, of the thirteen Jesuits ordained in 1966, nine eventually left the priesthood. Of the twelve ordained in 1967, eight left the priesthood. Of the fourteen ordained in 1968, eight left, and of the twelve in 1969, seven left. During the year 1967 the provincial received eighteen requests for permission to leave the Society from priests and scholastics. During the same year twenty-four novices entered, of whom six survived as Jesuits. In 1968 the number of novices entering the novitiate dropped dramatically. Of the eight who entered that year, six left the Society.

This record did not improve with time. For example, in 1974 twenty-one Jesuits requested permission to leave the Society and eight others requested leaves of absence, which almost invariably ended in final departure. Two years later, in 1976, twenty-one scholastics requested permission to leave the Society and eight priests applied for laicization, meaning dispensation from their vow prohibiting marriage.

There is a bright side to all of this. Although each request for permission to sever one's relationship with the Society was like a painful stab in the heart of the provincial, Father

Kelley, and Father Kenneth Galbraith, who succeeded him, manifested the greatest kindness and concern for those departing. Normally everything possible was done to assist them, some of them displaying less than noble sentiments in return. One scholastic on his departure circulated a letter among his friends. Included in this letter were the following remarks: "I don't so much feel I've been ejected from the Society, as that, like a no-longer needed clay mold, the Society somehow has cracked and fallen away from me. Born free." Others left letters, justifying themselves and blaming the church and the Society for their failures.

Father Arrupe, who understood human weakness in a high degree, repeatedly counseled the provincial not to be depressed, or anxious, but to express the Society's most gentle kindness to those who depart, giving them an alms to help them start a new life and an assurance of our blessing and prayers.

Perhaps of the greatest concern during this period was the *cause* of what was happening. Why the unprecedented loss of "vocations," not only of those who were preparing for the priesthood, but of priests themselves? Father Kelley, when he was interviewed, responded in this way: "Our permissive atmosphere, the lack of protection. People got careless. They stopped praying. They lacked appreciation for the Mass. They lacked maturity because of our over-protective training program."[24]

This about tells it all. Elaborate surveys by the professionals have said less. The last point Kelley makes, however, would be challenged by some. Precisely because of it, the system of studies was about to be overhauled, and to this there were many objections in the province. One crucial decision had already been made and implemented. The juniors were in residence at the Mount. Four more steps would follow, perhaps you would call them one: move everything to the city, the novitiate, the Mount, the theologate at Alma, and the tertianship. No one could dispute the fact that Ignatius loved the City. Incredibly, all of this was accomplished within a brief span of time.

Meanwhile there were Jesuits who persevered. No one, least of all the general or the provincial, lacked interest in their welfare, though some still felt threatened and abused. They shared rumors among themselves about the dire consequences of change, one of them being that the province was going bankrupt. In early January, 1967, the provincial responded to the latter: "With the advent of what promises to be a new and exciting year for the Oregon Province there is an important matter which I wish to clarify. I refer to unfounded rumors about the financial status of the province. I am pleased to report that we finished the year 1966 with a balanced budget. In the realm of extraordinary expense Bea House cost approximately $430,000. This was somewhat more than we anticipated, but we were able to pay all but $45,000 from a special fund set aside for construction."[25]

The new general was a good correspondent and most of his letters contained a message of hope along with his approval for appointments or changes within the province. On January 9, 1967, he gave his approval for a new faculty building at Seattle Prep, and two weeks later he sent a required rescript permitting Seattle Prep to borrow one million dollars.[26] On March 2, he approved of transferring the parish at Hardin and St. Francis Xavier's Mission to the Bishop of Great Falls.[27] On March 19 he appointed Father Lee Kapfer as the superior of the Lusaka Mission. Kapfer was a very popular choice. A tall and slender man, with handsome, contented features, topped by a full head of wavy hair, he spoke with a soft voice, seldom in demand and never in anger. His deceptively sly wit sometimes evoked gales of laughter. As an American representing a minority among missionaries from several countries, he was capable of consummate diplomacy simply by being himself.

Kelley with good reason was still preoccupied with finding a new residence. In April he reported to the general that a suitable site had been selected in north-west Portland "on the old St. Vincent [Hospital] property, "which could be acquired for $50,000. Cost of construction for the new residence was estimated to be $335,000.[28] The general approved the acquisition of the property on May 20, but complications of zoning appeared to be imminent, and for the second time the provincial's hopes were dashed.

By this time, however, there was so much excitement about the new province committees and the forthcoming conferences, that some members talked of little else. Hope was running high. In February Kelley had exchanged one committee for another, enlarging it in the process. The first of these, chaired by Father Cliff Kossell, and called the Juniorate-Philosophy Integration Committee (JPI), had outlived its usefulness.[29] It was replaced by a new one called the Provincial's Advisory Committee (PAC) a title bestowed upon it by its chairman, Father Edward Morton. PAC held frequent meetings at first, and one wonders why, since the provincial already had one advisory board, his consultors, who served in the same capacity.

There followed, also, three all-province "Conferences." One should keep in mind that the *Conferences* were held in 1967, the *Congresses* in 1969, and the *Assemblies* after 1970. Basically they were all the same, endless talk and not much action, but they served the immediate purpose of presenting an orderly review of changes sought by many in the province. The first of the Conferences was held between April 28 and April 30, at Seattle University; the second, at Gonzaga University between July 7 and July 10; finally, the third, at Seattle University between December 27 and December 29.

In 1967 a sensational conference of sixty-five representatives of both the Oregon and California provinces was held at Santa Clara from the sixth of August to the fifteenth. Its report was published as *Proceedings of the Conference on the Total Development of the Jesuit Priest*. It seems that the representatives gathered at Santa Clara, carried away by the new spirit of love-thy-neighbor, came perilously close to indiscretion in its pronouncements on the relationship of "mature Jesuits" with certain women. Father Arrupe was quick to respond.

> "Your letter has served to confirm previous reports that the consensus of the Santa Clara Conference on 'Relationships with Women' has been interpreted, or misinterpreted, by some of Ours to approve, even advise, what is colloquially called 'a third way.'
>
> "If there be a new way to observe the religious vow of chastity, one would expect to find it in the decrees of Second Vatican Council, for the counsels are a divine gift which the Church received from her Lord and which Church authority has the duty, under the inspiration of the Holy Spirit, to interpret and regulate in their practice (GP 43). 'Perfectae Caritatis,' however, gives no basis for 'a third way.'
>
> "The decree on chastity of the last General Congregation does not call for isolation from the feminine half of the human family. On the contrary, it foresees that mature, simple, anxiety-free dealing with the men and women to whom we minister can be the apostolic fruit of genuine human love and friendship arising from a love; consecrated by chastity to Christ our Lord. Thus St. Ignatius by his personal friendship and affability led countless men and women to God."[30]

Thus "the third way" became a motto of contempt for reform by those who opposed it. But one should think better of the incident. It not only reaffirmed traditional Jesuit concern regarding the value of the vow of chastity, but provided evidence, if any is required, that contemporary Jesuits took this matter seriously.

The Santa Clara Conference had involved both Oregon and California, two provinces who were discovering anew their common ground. Changes at the Mount had involved California and Father Edmund Smythe of the University of San Francisco had served on Kossell's JPI Committee to represent that province's interests. Now it was Oregon concern regarding the relocation of the theologate at Alma. Needless to say, the young men favored it, and so did many of the older men, some of whom supported the University of San Francisco as the appropriate place for it. But the younger men rejected this. "Theological education today," wrote one of them, "must go on within an *ecumenical university* and *urban* environment if it is effective to prepare a priest to minister to the contemporary world."[31] Father Kelley agreed and he wrote to the general in support of moving Alma College to Berkeley. The general in July gave his approval for Seattle University to build a new pavilion to replace its war surplus frame gymnasium, and the following month acknowledged Kelley's recommendation on Alma.[32] Construction on Seattle University's Pavilion, later known as the Connolly Center, was begun in February, 1968. It was completed in 1969.

The general was requested, too, for permission for another innovation that startled the old guard. Bellarmine in Tacoma had changed its name to Bellarmine Prep during the previous year, 1966.[33] Now a year later there was considerable discussion about coeducation; partly because of a decline in the number of students. In a sense Bellarmine had overexpanded its facilities, and though one could foresee a notable decline in the number of Jesuit teachers that would be available, its management opted for a broader school base to support the school. While this would not be a precedent for Catholic schools in general, since many diocesan schools were coeducational, or as they said co-instructional, it would be a notable break from the past for Jesuit high schools, especially since it would be undertaken on the basis of expedience rather than principle. For the present the subject was hypothetical, for other than sounding out Rome's position on the matter, no action was taken at this time. It would be seven years yet before girls invaded Bellarmine and longer than that before they made beachheads at Seattle and Spokane. All Oregon Province high schools, except Jesuit High in Portland, eventually became coeducational.

On October 4, the provincial appointed two more advisory committees: one on buildings and one on finance. These were planily useful additions to administration, particularly when the province was engaged in the sale of property and the constuction of buildings for the new order of things. One of the new buildings, the gymnasium-pool complex at the Mount was dedicated on Sunday, October 8, in memory of Johanna Mahoney. The so-called "Brothers Construction Crew" shared in the honors of the day, for they had provided most of the labor for the building at a savings of $70,000. During the same month, after the general had finally given approval, the novitiate was put up for sale. There was considerable discussion, also, about selling the cattle ranch at St. Ignatius Mission and the lately acquired summer camp at Priest Lake.

While the provincial was not indifferent to some of these suggestions, he was open to decisions made by his committees and conferences, and he seldom failed to take the action they recommended. At this time he was somewhat preoccupied with the mission in Alaska, partly because of the forthcoming decree of Father General, making "the Mission of Alaska coterminous with the geographical boundaries of the State," but mostly to bring the generally more conservative missionaries into the swim of the post Vatican waters.* Reports on Alaska had always been contradictory. One of the best of these, presented by Father Jack Lawlor in 1960, pinpointed the key problem, which seemed to defy solution:

*The decree of the general was dated October 10, 1967, but instructions given required it to be read on October 29, 1967, the Feast of Christ the King.

"The weakest link in the Alaska mission unity chain is the three-branched superior link. This had been brought to your attention before and seems to be the personal lament of almost every Jesuit in Alaska."[34] The "three branched superior" referred to the Jesuits' three superiors on the mission: the bishop, the provincial and the mission superior. Problems related to this appeared from the very beginning.

Since meetings were presumed to resolve most things, including the unlikely, an especially grand one was conducted in mid-October, 1967. Present on this occasion were the provincial, his socius, Jack Lawlor; his consultors Frank Costello, Cliff Kossell, and Joe Showalter; and Joe Conyard of the Jesuit Seminary Association, all representing the province. From Alaska were the superior Jules Convert and his consultors, Rene Astruc, Bill Dibb, Lom Loyens and William McIntyre, also known as "OO", which was pronounced Oh-Oh.[35] One positive result of the meeting is that the missionaries got a square meal, no small benefit since they all looked as lean and hungry as the sled dogs. Loyens was an urban missionary, teaching anthropology at the University of Alaska, but he might as well have been at remote Kaltag on the Yukon, for all the flesh on his bones. He smoked his pipe interminably, filling the air, which was peaceful, with the sweet aroma of his tobacco.

Kelley was determined to examine the mission himself. On October 17, following the meeting, he announced his departure for Alaska on October 23, and the assignment of Jack Lawlor as acting provincial in his absence. He included in the announcement his agenda and a map of the missions, twenty-six in number, which he hoped to visit before his return on December 11.[36] Subsequently he regaled the province with three folksy reports on his peregrinations. "Father Neil Murphy proved a warm and genial host," he wrote. "His culinary talents were equalled only by his hospitality. For my future travels in colder and less hospitable regions, weatherwise, he literally gave me the parka off his back."[37]

At Bethel he was so bored for three days while waiting for the plane, he "even went so far as to see 'Batman' at the local theatre." When he finally landed at Tooksook Bay, coming out of the fog, he was met by Father Frank Fallert. "As we edged to the side of the field practically all the children in the village swarmed up the little hill and were there, with Father Frank Fallert, to greet me. After extricating myself from my seat—believe me, that's a real feat in these small planes—I dropped to the muddy ground, shook hands with Father Fallert and several of the natives and, surrounded by half the village, marched down to the church. As we passed their huts the natives would come out and Father Fallert would introduce them to me, we would shake hands and march on. I felt like some conquering hero returning from the battles. The natives, all Eskimos, are very friendly and unsophisticated.[38]

Later, Father Bernard McMeel, one of the missionary pilots, picked up Kelley at St. Mary's and accompanied him to missions throughout the interior, including Holy Cross.

"Holy Cross, Father McMeel's home base, has about 250 souls," Kelley reported. "To take care of about 75 youngsters of gradeschool age there are three Sisters of St. Ann and three lay volunteers."

Because of the unusually good weather and time saved in McMeel's plane, Kelley returned to Portland two weeks earlier than scheduled. He was beginning to feel the weight of office, but his two most difficult years lay ahead.

The first of these years, 1968, was deceptively quiet, at least in terms of open confrontation. But it was the quiet of imminent violence, not in the physical order but in the minds of men who cared one way or another. The years of the too readily tolerated "self-fulfillment" were bearing bitter fruit, while the years of "discernment" and "get out of Vietnam" mostly dominated by a noisy discontented youth, were really just beginning.

Many significant appointments were made during this year. On March 21, Joseph Perri, personnel director for Seattle's Archbishop, was appointed as a province consultor.

Frank Masterson became the new rector of Jesuit High on May 17, and on the following day Gordon Moreland became the rector of the novitiate and the new novice master, replacing Frank Mueller.* At Bea House in Spokane, Alfred Morrisette replaced Dave Clark as superior, and in Woodburn, Oregon, at St. Luke's Parish, Frank Duffy became the first Jesuit pastor. Woodburn, an old parish dedicated by Archbishop Christie in 1901, had become the center of Mexican-American Agrarian workers. Father Duffy had long experience with Mexican-Americans in the Yakima Valley. That same autumn Joseph Showalter became the director of the Jesuit Seminary Association, replacing Joseph Conyard, who was assigned as Director of the International Educational Development Corporation in New York. Finally, Patrick Hurley was appointed rector of the Mount in October. He replaced Arby Lemieux who was worn out with frustration and confusion. All of these new appointees soon played a major role in the grand new design of things that gradually began to take shape.

The provincial still had on his hands some bits of unfinished business, all of which were related to the presence of Jesuits in "the right place." These were steps in the relocation process, to place Jesuits in urban areas, and the relocation of the provincial's own residence. For two days, April 21 to April 22, 1968, Kelley met with his Building Committee in Portland to discuss the latter. He informed the committee that this had become a crucial matter because the province had sold Campion Hall to an insurance company, which expected to take possession of it in the near future. In other words, our provincial was in the awkward position of being dispossessed, if he did not move out in a reasonably brief time.[39]

There was other favorable news. The general had approved purchase of an old apartment building contiguous to the Seattle University campus, for a new tertianship.[40] Later (on October 28, 1968), he also approved of the sale of Manresa Hall at Port Townsend. On September 1, 1968, twenty-six tertians reported to their instructor, Father Alex McDonald, in the renovated apartment building, which could easily be classified as a residence on the poverty level. It looked like a tenement on New York's east side, not a tertianship for studying ascetical and mystical theology. The most surprising feature about it was that when it caught fire one day, it did not burn to the ground. But it was in the city where the action was; who cared about the house? When Manresa Hall was put up for sale it sold within a couple of months, confirming the belief of some of the older Jesuits that there still were people who preferred a small town. The ancient, spooky mansion fetched $50,000 in cash for building and lot, and the new owners announced that it would be renovated again, this time to serve as an old-world inn. Called Manresa Inn, it experienced hard days before it became established. As an inn it makes much of the glamor of its former residents, the Jesuits. For example, bits of history are perpetuated by appropriate signs, such as, "This was the Beadle's Room" and "This was the Jesuit's Dining Room," and so on.

Another tidbit for the Building Committee's delectation was the news that plans for moving Alma to Berkely were going forward. Arthur D. Little Company had been commissioned to investigate the financial advantages of relocation and the Arthur Johnson Company had been engaged to take charge of funding and development.[41] The former's announcement that it would cost $150,000 more per year to conduct the theologate at Berkeley rather than Alma did not frighten anyone.[42] Zacheus Maher, who would have objected, was in his grave.†

*Father Frank Mueller had taken Father Elliott's place as Novice Master in September, 1961. Like Kelley, Mueller had a stormy term of office, sharing in Kelley's frustrations over the departure of the young Jesuits. After leaving Sheridan, Mueller, trained in Canon Law, became Chancellor for the Bishop of Fairbanks.

†Maher died on October 1, 1963, in San Francisco.

VIOLENT WINDS OF CHANGE

Kelley wanted to visit his missionaries in Africa. On June 25, he embarked, arriving in Lusaka seventy-two hours later. Lee Kapfer, the superior, and Bill Weller met him at the new airport, which was Africa's second largest. For three weeks Kapfer escorted him by car throughout the mission, both of them getting lost occasionally on the hot, dusty roads of the Zambian plateau. One of their first stops was at the parish of Matero, a suburb of Lusaka. "Our timing was good," Kelley reported, "we arrived just as the pastor, Father Kokalj, was beginning to baptize seventeen black babies. The mothers were in a line spread across the back of the church with the sponsors standing behind each one. Contrary to our custom, the mother, not the sponsor, holds the baby. With that many babies, of course, there was a good deal of wailing and commotion. About half the mothers solved the problem by giving their lunch straight from the tap. These were baptized, smiling and contented, receiving at the same time both spiritual and material sustenance."[43]

"Having seen all of our mission stations," Kelley wrote at the end of his report, "and having talked to all of our Fathers there, what do I think of it all? I think we have a great future in Zambia provided we get moving *now*. As in all of Africa, so in Zambia—time is running out for the Church. For centuries Africa was a sleeping giant and it is just in our lifetime that it has shaken off its somnolence and is rising to stand on its own two big feet. Nations are still coming into being. Others are developing with cyclonic speed. They don't have time for the usual gradual acculturation process. If the Church doesn't move with them it will be left behind. There is still time for the Christianization process but not much. The seeds of nationalism in some countries are budding in rapid and unexpected ways.

"The Church must be a part of the Africanization process. Like it has all too often been in the past in other countries, and with notable failure, it cannot superimpose its European culture and ways on the Africans. It must become one with them, with their thoughts, their hopes, their ways. Simply put, it must become African to succeed. This demands an African clergy, an African liturgy, an African church."[44]

The provincial was happy to state, he said, that "most of our Fathers in Zambia would concur with the above." He was also happy to return to Portland on July 26, "thus ending another of my odysseys as Provincial."

Two weeks later, on August 8, 1968, Bill Weller was dead. He had not been killed by a lion, like the Brother at Katondwe who had been dragged off while he was working in the garden. Nor by the tse tse fly. He simply died suddenly of a heart attack in the customary American way.[45] He was buried in Africa, which doubtlessly would have pleased him. The wounds of Wellerism had long since healed in the province and he was regarded as a great hero for having his heart attack in Africa instead of in America.

Towards the end of this same year the voices for "revolution" were being heard. Pope Paul VI had published his encyclical *Humanae Vitae*, which was openly challenged by many Catholic theologians. It was also challenged by Gonzaga's Dean of Men in the school paper. Tom Grief was known to be liberal, but a full page article in the *Gonzaga Bulletin*, authored by him, shocked many on campus and even a few in Rome.[46] His article entitled "Revolution, What is the Cause, and the Consequences?" contained three basic thoughts:

"I think the first key to understanding the revolution is the realization that freedom is an intoxicant. A taste only whets the appetite and stimulates an insistent drive for more . . . .

"The second key to understanding the revolution is to see where this drive for freedom is going, and what it is fighting against . . . .

"Within institutionalized religion the battle is against behavior controls such as the puritan social ethic."

528

One needs no considerable background to recognize this hodgepodge of jargon of contemporary radicals. Father Arrupe wrote at once to say he was "troubled by the views attributed to Thomas H. Grief," and added that "fortunately his remarks were countered by Father Kenneth W. Baker."[47]

Baker tore Grief's high voltage nonsense to shreds. "The first thing to note," he wrote, "is that the essay seemed to be an objective presentation of the case of modern young radicals. We are exposed in rapid succession to the opinions of contemporary upsurgents with regard to society, church, state, family, schools and industry. We are given no obvious evaluation of these opinions."[48]

Grave conflicts within the Gonzaga Community had already raised barriers to understanding. "The fear has been expressed," Arrupe wrote, "that Father John P. Leary is inordinately de-emphasizing the public image of Gonzaga as a Jesuit and Catholic university."[49] Leary, it seemed to some, had united with the more liberal students against the Jesuit faculty in such disputes as parietal hours, student drinking, and especially the recognition and acceptance of radical speakers on university platforms.*

One other area of controversy involved the trusteeship. Leary had sought and obtained the provincial's approval for the addition of three lay men to the Board of Trustees. It was generally recognized that this was certainly a move in the right direction. Indeed, it was a move already taken by other Jesuit universities. Problems arose, however, when Leary failed to observe guidelines demanded by the Jesuit Community in the selection of these trustees. Some Jesuits complained to the provincial that Leary, despite the spirit of Vatican II for dialogue and open-mindedness, had acted arbitrarily and contrary to the expressed preferences of the community.

Recognizing the gravity of the situation, the provincial hurried to Spokane during mid-December 1968, to confer with Leary and members of the Community. Having heard the arguments of all sides, he returned to Portland, summoned a Consultor's meeting for December 21, then dispatched a detailed report to Arrupe. In this he strongly urged that a "freeze" be imposed on the transfer of any authority from the old Jesuit Board of Trustees [appointed by the provincial] to the new board composed of Jesuits and lay men.[50]

Leary's position, in keeping with the growing numbers of university administrators, was that Gonzaga, as a state-chartered institution, retain a certain independence. The provincial revealed his misgivings about this situation in a letter on January 24, 1969:

"Jack Leary, of course, is convinced that I am interfering in a situation that is none of my business. I am convinced otherwise. Unfortunately, one of the sources of the entire problem is that fact that Jack (through no fault of his own) is wearing two hats, that of President of the University and that of Rector of the Jesuit community. Thus they have no one with authority to represent them. As a result I must step in and do so . . . .

"The old Board of Trustees is working on a set of bylaws somewhat similar to Boston College, Georgetown and Scranton which provides for a board of Jesuits, seven or nine or any number which will be the controlling board of the University. This will be one of the plans proposed at the big meeting. This Board in turn would meet annually and delegate authority to

*"Parietal hours" was one of the battle cries of the liberal students in the late 1960s. It granted boys and girls permission to visit each other's rooms during scheduled hours. Leary predicted a revolt at Gonzaga if parietal hours were not granted. During the dispute over parietal hours, Father Arthur McNeil, distinguished Jesuit chemist at Gonzaga and former Academic Vice President, resigned in protest. He accepted a teaching post at Seattle University.

the new Board of Trustees who then would run the University. The controlling board of Jesuits would interfere *only* in matters of faith or morals or if the goals of the University are not being met. Jack Leary is dead set against this and I fear that he and I are on a collision course in this matter."[51]

Leary at this point suggested that he resign, but Kelley thought the timing was poor and asked him to remain.[52] Then on January 18, 1969, Van Christoph, a member of the Gonzaga Community was appointed rector by the general.[53] Quite properly the community expected Christoph to represent them, but this he was reluctant to do and John Taylor, one of the Jesuit trustees, took the initiative and led an all-Jesuit drive to retain the control of Gonzaga.

"The pot continues to boil," wrote Kelley in early February, "[Christoph] should be invaluable in helping to work out the sticky mess still to be faced. We are having a meeting at G.U. Thursday, February 7, with the old and new boards of trustees, Jack Leary, the lawyers, myself, and Cliff Kossell to try and come up with some compromise solution to the restructuring problem. My principal worry is not to antagonize the three laymen who are good and influential men.

"As you can see from the clippings many of the issues are confused. There was never any question about having laymen on the Board of Trustees. Not one person at Gonzaga is against that. The real question is the handling of the ultimate authority.

"From the clippings you will notice that Jack Leary appears as the conquering hero and the Jesuit Community are constantly labeled 'old Guard'. I am the mysterious force hovering in the background."[54]

Kelley received a letter about this from Alma: "The NCR makes it look like you are scurrying behind the scenes at Gonzaga like the phantom of the opera. Maybe you are. All I can say is that you have my sympathy."

The meeting of the two boards went well. It was agreed to postpone changes in Gonzaga's legal structure until after July 1, 1969, when a new model non-profit corporation act adopted by the State of Washington was to become effective. In the interim the new Board of Trustees had delegated authority to conduct day-to-day management of the university. When Gonzaga's new legal structure was finally adopted it was so satisfactory to all that Seattle University also adopted it.[55]

Meanwhile, in April, Father Leary left Gonzaga for a prolonged rest at Cranwell Prep in Massachusetts.* Father Richard Twohy was appointed as acting president by the trustees to replace him, and on May 16, 1969, the general formally approved of this action. On June 8, it was publicly announced that Twohy had been designated as the twenty–second president of Gonzaga University.[56] Peace descended finally on the campus in Spokane and the new president with his new board of trustees began the long, often precarious battle of restoring fiscal stability to the university.

During the unpleasant struggle at Gonzaga, the provincial had proved his ability to maintain a certain cool detachment from the disagreeable decisions he had to face. He neither held grudges nor did he take out on the province the frustration he felt within. More than twice each month he received requests for departures from the Society, some from young priests, whose positions required immediate replacements. In 1969 for example, there were twenty–two requests for permission to leave the Society and ten other petitions for leaves of absence which ended in departures. While the needs continued to rise, the number of men at his disposal declined. In the midst of it all, he retained a most

---

*Leary subsequently founded New College in Sausalito, California, then Old College in Reno, Nevada.

cheerful optimism that, at times, appeared to be almost indifference.

During the previous December he had disposed of a thorny problem that had annoyed provincials for decades. This concerned the St. Ignatius Mission ranch, that had its origins in the mission's foundation in 1854. Over the years the ranch had grown in size, land having been added by purchase or grant. When the school was flourishing it had supported the mission, but in recent years, despite good management at times, it had brought in very little income.

When Kelley became provincial he paid a courtesy visit to Bishop Hunthausen in Helena, during the course of which His Excellency requested him to consider the disposal of the St. Ignatius ranch. Despite the fact that the province had received little or no income from it, the impression was given that Jesuits, with so much land and cattle, were wealthy. The bishop also did not think it proper for priests at the mission to spend their time in the management of a ranch.[57]

Kelley considered the matter for a year, then proposed its sale to his consultors, who approved. The ranch was put up for sale for $450,000, its current value, and the Flathead Tribe was offered the first chance to purchase it. For one year Kelley waited, and since the tribe showed no interest, put it on the market at $460,000. Soon after, in November 1968, a buyer, Mr. James Brown from Sandpoint, Idaho, appeared and offered to meet the requested price by paying $100,000, the balance to be paid in ten years, with eight per cent interest.[58] On November 30, 1968, Kelley wrote to the general, giving the history of the case and requesting the required permission to sell the ranch. The general consented to this by letter on December 9. Brown's Pack River Lumber Company took possession and Kelley, like others in the province, thought this was the end of the matter.

But is was not. The pastor of St. Ignatius Mission, Robert Tanksley and Thomas Connolly, the province's director of the Social Apostolate, which included the missions, objected quite strenuously to the province's possession of the money. They demanded it for the use of St. Ignatius Mission. Tanksley consulted civil and canon lawyers, who disagreed with our lawyers.[59] Soon the Flathead Tribe entered into the dispute, contending that the money belonged to the tribe because of certain changes in the original grant from the government. Thus the St. Ignatius Mission Land Case came into being. It would be many years before it was settled, gratuitously on our part in favor of the tribe.

Meanwhile there were meetings. Members of PAC met in January at Gonzaga Prep, in February at the novitiate at Sheridan, and in March at Bellarmine Prep in Tacoma. Somewhat influenced by committee member Pat Hurley, also rector of the Mount, their principal item of discussion was the sale of the Mount. For some in the province this was like a proposal to sell the altar vessels, but Hurley had a bone in his teeth and he would not let go. In the February meeting there was some unrealistic talk about how much money they could get for the Mount and how they would use it. A resolution was passed to explore the possibility of having all collegiate scholastics in residence somewhere else by September, 1969. Wishful thinking. In March committee members, having heard a report from a representative of the Arthur D. Little Management Company, recommended, among other things, that their company prepare a feasibility study for the relocation of the Mount.[60]

No doubt these heavy decisions pleased the provincial who was busy organizing another committee. "I have appointed an ad hoc Province Commission on Ministries which, I think, will be one of the most important assignments in the thirty-eight year history of the Oregon Province."[61] Louis Gaffney of Seattle University was appointed the Commission's Chairman. This commission was busy in a twinkle. In its first declaration, not to be taken lightly it seems, the following appeared: "We encourage the prayerful support of this project as the most significant in the history of the province."[62]

My, my, we were beginning to take ourselves seriously.

At the suggestion of the provincial another representative of Arthur D. Little Company, Robert J. Fahey, met with the commission to explain procedures used "in directing the New England, Chicago, Detroit and Maryland Provinces through their ministries' study. He made such a fine impression that it was proposed to Father Provincial that he be engaged for our Province Planning Program."[63] This was the great thrust of 1969.

Before it got under way, another of the provincial's priorities was finally resolved. Two lots were purchased at Twenty-second and Hoyt in northwest Portland for the new provincial's residence and office building. In January, 1969, architects Maloney, Herrington, Freeze and Lund of Seattle were commissioned to design a building which was to be constructed by the Brothers Construction Crew as soon as they completed their work on the bishop's house in Fairbanks. The brothers arrived in Portland at the end of March and on May 12, 1969, ground-breaking ceremonies were celebrated with discretion and the hope that the labor unions would not butt in and prevent our brother's crew from doing the job. The ground had already been softened up, because the previous night Brother Lloyd St. Marie had been digging for worms to take on a fishing trip.[64]

The provincial was a bit defensive about his new house, though, Lord knows, he had to have one. He could not run the province from a vacant lot. There were rumors about it, he wrote the province in mid-April 1969. We are going to build, he said.

> "To avoid having a white elephant on our hands at any time in the future we are building the new Curia as an office building. It will be of very simple construction with brickbearing walls. It will be efficient and yet will have pleasant working surroundings. It is an investment. With the Brothers' Crew doing all the work it will be worth at least $150,000 more than our initial investment on the day of completion. Its location is convenient to downtown just two blocks from the present Curia. The area is being renewed with many new clinics and apartment houses abuilding in it. We received $96,000 for the old Curia which will provide approximately one third of the total cost of the new one."[65]

Father Schultheis, former provincial, would have been pleased to hear this. A tough man in business he had always served as a good counselor for his successors. But he was gone now. He had died in Tacoma only a few days before, on March 22, 1969. His last years, unlike his provincialate, were very happy years for him at Bellarmine, where he had begun his ministry. He had mellowed. No one, they say, was more gentle or more thoughtful of others than he. His death was merciful, for it spared him from some of the harsh realities of the changing world, for example the decision to abandon Sheridan.

PAC, bored with its own meetings, soon voted themselves out of existence, much to the relief of the provincial. His hopes were with the Commission on the Ministries, which published in April, 1969, an impressive report called: *NOW The Jesuits of the Oregon Province have a contingent proposal for the future.* This was a proposal for a five-phase program:

I. Planning, elections of delegates, April 25–July 25
II. First Province Congress, July 25 to July 27
III. Task Force Studies, Recommendations, July 27 to November 26
IV. Second Province Congress, November 26 to November 30
V. Decisions, November 30 to January 1, 1970.

Undoubtedly the best part of *NOW* was Section III, "Data for Planning," a fifty-seven page summary of "Manpower prospects" and finances of the Oregon Province, probably the best document of its kind in our history. Produced on a Seattle University computer under the direction of Louis Gaffney, it makes for very dull reading, but in the modest opinion of the commission's chairman, it is the only good that came out of the project.

There were other publications, one following the other in rapid succession: For Phase I *Oregon Province Planning Program Collected Province Plans* appeared in July, 1969. This contained eighty-nine proposals, some of which were so far out that they tended to bring ridicule upon the rest. One plan, for example, pre-occupied with an allegedly imminent revolution of the blacks, proposed concentration of Jesuits in the inner cities of Seattle and Tacoma, almost to the exclusion of all else. The author "did not deem the Spokane area important," so Jesuits there, he suggested, should phase out St. Aloysius Parish, Gonzaga Prep and Gonzaga University. We should also retreat from Missoula and Yakima, and the mission in Africa as well. The Mount, he added, should be moved to Seattle.

For Phase II another publication appeared: *The Jesuits of the Oregon Province Plan for the Future Proceedings of the Province Congress First Session July 25–27, 1969*. This was followed by *Plan For the Future Task Force Plans Phase III November 15, 1969 Oregon Province Society of Jesus*, a compendium of reports of twenty-seven task forces.

Meanwhile in California members of the province with Oregonians were conducting multiple sessions in "Self Study" which produced another twelve published reports between 1969 and 1971.

At the Second Province Congress there was a controversy on the so-called "Principle of Attraction." On November 2, 1968, Kelley had sent a letter to all Jesuits in special studies. "We have decided," he said, "on a procedure of early assignment of our men in special studies as an aid to institutional planning. We would welcome candid expressions of opinion on where you wish to be assigned when you return from studies . . . all this, of course, is in the context of sincere Ignatian indifference."[66]

This was an implicit rejection of the Principle of Attraction which "required that the Provincial cooperate with the process, that he agree as a general policy to assign men to the apostolates that have attracted them."[67]

After a heated discussion the Second Province Congress passed a resolution favoring the Principle of Attraction.* One who dissented was Leo Kaufmann, who was persuaded by some of his playful colleagues to compose a spoof containing the key words and memorable phrases used by the intent young men of the congress:

> "As a necessary preamble,
> Don Davis disavows all this and more, sight unseen: I Move the following, not for the permanent record, but that the chair may now declare the opposition permanently out of order. . .

> "Give me even one house cynic who would not like to hitch a ride on that—at least hop along on the same idea. We have given the massive no-no to the no-bite, the no-muscle, the no-thrust. Everthing on-going and germain to the gut level of the cutting edge. Even the very exigencies of the moment, in eye-ball contact with the life-style of custodians of empty institutions with warm bodies filling every empty slot in man-to-man replacement.

---

*At the Congress one young Jesuit presented an impassioned plea for acceptance of the principle. On the following day he contradicted his position by demanding that one of five Jesuits in the province be assigned to the missions.

"Unlike democratic tyrants, putting their blood into the mortar, we took the bull by the tail, and looked reality in the face, without avoiding the issues. We called a halt to the population explosion of province prefects. Who could say we have not prioritized all our over-riding urgencies?

"The local sheriff, it is true, was hard put to acquaint some scouts with the inner workings of their wagon train. But with a single soft stroke thirty years of pseudosocial work was pastoralized. A lone objection to prayer did come through loud and clear, but that one alcoholic superior we sought in vain.

"Finally we brought even pre-tridentine theologians back from the drawing boards, re-tooled and re-tread, banished the daughters of Priam—casting fear to the future—and updated even the old prophets all the way back to what is going on right now.

"Thus I move that the young men be kind to the old men too."[68]

The impish glint in Leo's eye, his deep voice croaking uncertainly with suppressed mirth, brought the Congress back to its senses, to the safe and sane position, a sacred province tradition, of not taking itself too seriously.

Not all went well with the construction of the new provincial's residence. The basic problem was the unions' refusal to permit the Brothers to construct the building, hence the cost was much higher than Father McNulty, the province treasurer in charge of the project expected it to be.* By this time cost was no longer the first consideration. We suddenly had to face the realities of the business world and accept them despite the hue and cry about "the sinful structures."

Kelley, by this time, no longer worried about it. He had other "happenings" as they said then, to keep him occupied. On April 17, 1969, Arrupe had approved his request to close tertianship and to postpone the assignment of Jesuits to tertianship until Rome sent new directives regarding it. The fad for wearing beards and long hair appeared about this time. Unfortunately in its earlier period it was identified with the hippie types, so Kelley opposed them. He wrote a letter to the province on July 5, 1969, strictly forbidding either beards or long hair, but he was forced to back down when these new hirsutish styles were approved in other provinces.[69]

On September 12, a new young English scholar emerged as an influential member of the province. This was Kenneth Galbraith, who had recently returned from doctoral studies in North Carolina. He was appointed a province consultor on this date. On October 7 another significant appointment was made. Joe Perri, whom many expected to succeed Kelley, became Superior at Seattle University.

Alma College, meanwhile was finally closed on September 30, 1969. Transferred to Berkeley, it opened on the following day, October 1, as the Jesuit School of Theology at Berkeley, "JSTB" one of several similiar theologates in the United States, located in urban areas. Finally on Christmas Eve, December 24, Kenneth Baker was appointed president of Seattle University, replacing Jack Fitterer, who was subsequently made "chancellor," a new title at the university. Baker was not inaugurated as president until June 7, 1970, at which time he announced that the expected deficit of Seattle University for that fiscal year, would not be $1,400,000 as predicted, but only $700,000. In other words the university had not broken both legs, but only one, which was supposed to be very comforting to all.

---

*McNulty replaced Schultheis as treasurer in 1966.

534

This was Kelley's last year as provincial. He had been immersed for over five years in highly emotional discussions, surrounded by bitter dissent and sometimes betrayed in his trust of younger men, who had long since gone their own way. Yet he was unbowed, unbroken. Like a supple young birch tree he had bent with the wind. Had he been brittle and unbending, he would be, by now, a broken man.

There were many rumors about his successor. Some were saying it would be Leo Kaufmann, and others Joe Perri. On February 10, 1970, the general appointed Kenneth Galbraith, a younger man than either. Kelley, who still regarded himself as a middle-of-the-roader, made no attempts to conceal his pleasure with the choice, though it was commonly believed that the new appointee was quite liberal in his views. But this was Kelley's genius. He could accept everyone with kindness.

Now a lame duck administrator, he began his own preparations for a new life. On March 3, 1970, he informed all Oregon Jesuits in Zambia that the Missions of Lusaka and Chikuni had been merged to form one vice-province. On March 24, he took note of the fire that had destroyed Goller Hall at Gonzaga during the night, taking with it all the earthly possessions of Father Tom Royce.*

He noted, too, with some annoyance, the occasional barbs in the province *Newsletter* edited very conscientiously by Neill Meany. "That back fence gossip rag," one critic had called it.[70] Few, if any would agree with that. Meany quoted the *California Province News*, which had presented a text from the Book of Judges at the end of a long list of those who had left the Society: "Let anyone who is frightened or fearful go home," the text read. "So two and twenty thousand men went away from Mount Galaad, and only ten thousand remained."[71] One of the young Jesuits at Alma found this very offensive and he dispatched to Meany a blistering note of protest, which Meany printed. But an old Father at the Mount diagreed with the critic, saying, "Not all have left, what about us who remained?"

The incident revealed how wide the gulf between the young and old had become, and how dangerously politicized. No one, not even Jack Kelley, could predict how it would all end.

---

*Arson in this fire, which demolished the building and its contents, was suspected but never proved. Royce, away at the time, lost everything.

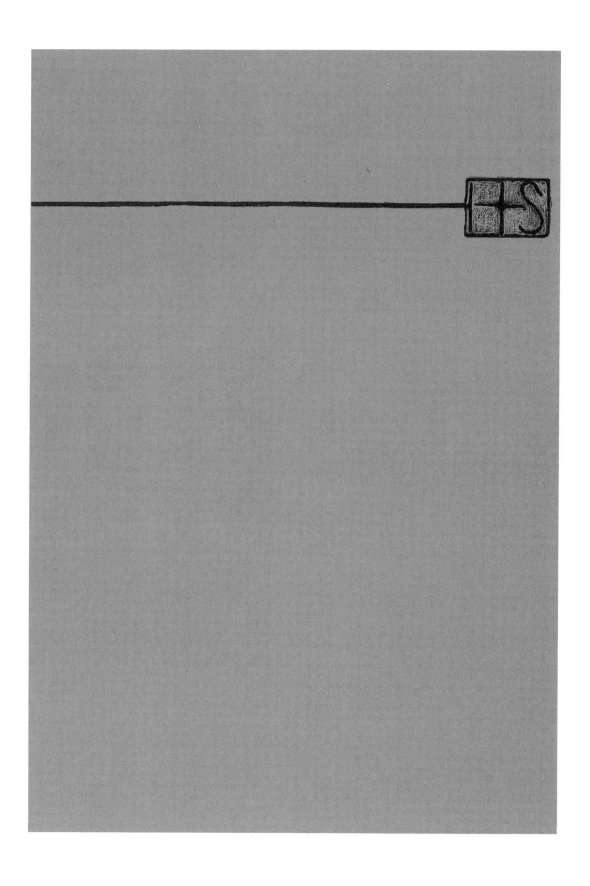

Kenneth Galbraith, eighth provincial of the Oregon Province.

Lom Loyens, ninth provincial of the Oregon Province.

24

THE DIVIDED PROVINCE
1970–1976

It was common knowledge in 1970 that not all of the Jesuits of the province were saints. If the truth were known, some of them were not disposed to take the decrees of the Second Vatican Council and the 31st General Congregation as wholeheartedly as Father Arrupe expected. No one should have been surprised at this, for the old saying is wise: you cannot teach old dogs new tricks. It should be added, perhaps, that superiors, fully aware of this, applied new and sometimes painful pressures to the older Jesuits, anticipating a ready response which was, in the circumstances, somewhat unrealistic. Only unprincipled men change overnight.

The older men, I think, should have regarded the demands made on them as a compliment. Their obedience had been tried often and not found wanting. If superiors expected much of them, as they did, they had reason to believe that much would be rendered. "Nothing impressed me more when I was provincial," Father Kelley once said, "than the way members of the province were obedient. I was never disappointed, not once."[1]

To some there appeared to be a double standard. More was demanded of the older Jesuits than of the young, so it seemed, and as long as this alleged imbalance was credited, superiors had an additional hardship in governing the province. Polarization of attitudes, tradition versus reform, was the actual *status quo*, not the oneness of hearts and will that everybody talked about. Thus ready obedience for which the Society of Jesus was noted, became more difficult and the process of healing, already at work, went unperceived. There was nothing new in all this, Church history provided many examples. But no one seemed to be interested in precedents, and the gap between the provincial and some members of the province widened rather than narrowed with the passage of time.

This unhappy situation prevailed when Kenneth James Galbraith became the eighth provincial of the Oregon Province on June 10, 1970. Father Kelley, intrigued with the prospect of having been provincial for exactly six years, had arranged for Galbraith to be "read in" as his successor at twelve o'clock noon on the dot. The community in the curia had gathered for lunch, the formalities of succession were concluded as planned, in a very brief ceremony, then the phone rang. The call made from some distant city was for Father Kelley. He responded by informing his correspondent that he was no longer provincial. Galbraith was summoned, and there at the phone, two minutes after taking on the burdens of the office, the new provincial had to make his first difficult decision. It was an unpleas-

539

ant one, but he never hesitated for a moment. This, the province learned, was characteristic of him, an occasion for praise as well as for criticism depending upon whom you consulted.

This new provincial was, some said, an incurable idealist, a generous man with a full, loving heart, who always believed the best in everybody. His simplicity and fervor in challenging his subjects to throw themselves into Spiritual Renewal, as Father General frequently demanded, did not always produce the response he expected. Perhaps he was not surprised at this, but his persistence in pursuing this practice implied to others that he did not realize what storms he was creating, or if he did, that he regarded the results he received as worth the risk.

Young Jesuits idolized him. He was their guru. Some older Jesuits, on the other hand, wary yet of the vast changes taking place around them, somewhat resentful of the loss of customs to which they had become endeared, tended to drag their feet when he prodded them. One should not condemn them, for there was much confusion in the Church, occasioned mostly by conflicts of traditional doctrine emanating from Rome on the one hand and on the other, of some very liberal doctrine from certain theologians, who attributed it falsely to the Second Vatican Council. While Galbraith was not involved in these doctrinal disputes, he appeared to some as anti-traditional and thus somewhat suspect in his repeated efforts to promote change, or "renewal," as he envisioned it.

For better or worse, this was his chosen task as provincial: spiritual renewal. When he received notice of his appointment he released the following statement:

> "The turbulent spirit prevading so many areas of our modern society has made itself felt within religious life too. While some members, especially the younger ones, search for new meaning and direction in religious life, others choose to deepen the significance of what has long played a part of our apostolate.

> "Reconciling the resulting polarization that springs from these divergent viewpoints, while forwarding the work and meaning of the Society of Jesus within the Church and through the Church within the Society, becomes the chief task of a Provincial Superior today. The burden upon him, then, is the task of being a listener, sensitive to the needs of his men and of the Church in the Northwest. Our Province Congress, which met last November, set a course of renewal in several dimensions. I welcome the opportunity to aid in that renewal in the capacity of Provincial Superior."[2]

These were brave words. The older men who read them hoped for the best. They were not sure, then, that they knew "Kenny" Galbraith. He had not even received his doctorate in English from one of the customary universities. University of North Carolina, why North Carolina? He had little executive experience and not much as a teacher in the university. He was regarded as an excellent teacher, though, and his appointment to administration would deprive the universities of a strong academic man.

He was also a pleasant man to engage in conversation. His youthful enthusiasm, somewhat tempered by a natural reticence, was reflected in his facial expressions, which appeared to be open and genial. Years before his Jesuit classmates had rated him as "sincere, courteous and tactful." They said he had a "good sense of humor," but that he was also "shy and aloof." No one said he was a good listener, perhaps because this rare and delicate virtue is often mistaken for bashfulness. From observations in later years one could add to these the judgments of his peers. As provincial, Kenny was usually firm, even uncompromising, a bold and determined lion instead of a race horse like his predecessor.

Born in 1928 and raised as the oldest of six sons of Maurice Frederick Galbraith and Evelyn Smith Galbraith, he had become quite naturally the leader of the pack, the surest of the lions. One got the impression at once that he knew he was in command and was making no apologies for it. He was not arrogant. Simply stated, he was the boss.

One may doubt that he retained this position within the family without challenge, for all of his brothers became distinguished. When Kenny was appointed provincial, the Seattle University Alumni Association laid first claim to the six sons of Maurice Galbraith of Tacoma. "Seattle University graduates," the Association noted, "included Dr. Charles J., '48, Tacoma surgeon; William R., '51, Portland engineering corporation vice president; Dr. Richard F., '53, Minneapolis neurologist; Maurice F., Jr. '57, San Diego sales training manager; and Patrick E., '58, Air Force captain in the Pentagon. . . . Mr. and Mrs. Maurice F. Galbraith in 1961 received the SU Alumni Distinguished Service Award."[3] The list did not include Kenny, obviously, because he entered the Jesuit novitiate at Sheridan in 1947, after an indifferent performance at Seattle University for only one year.* Academically the maverick in the family, Kenny received his B.A. from Gonzaga University.

As provincial, Galbraith lost no time in communicating with the province. On the very day of his inauguration he dispatched to its members a three-page letter containing particulars about "Restructuring the Provincial Curia Administration."[4] Having noted that during the previous November the Province Congress had voted overwhelmingly for a new plan of administration, he proceeded to announce details of the new structure. "The men comprising this staff and their titles are as follows:

1. Executive Assistant—Father Jack Lawlor
2. Provincial Assistant for Education—Father Ed Morton
3. Provincial Assistant for Apostolates—Father Jack Morris
4. Provincial Assistant for Missions—Father Bill Davis

There followed a job description of each, and another one of his office. "The Provincial," he said, "still retains his official position, holding full authority (I use this word here for clarity rather than emphasis) in the province." No other Doctor of English Literature could have expressed more clearly the relationship he was establishing between himself and the province. He had made it clear, certainly on two controversial issues regarding province government: the influence province congresses or assemblies would have on his administration; and, secondly, the form and extent of his delegating authority.

While he declared this to be his structure, he had only one theme: renewal, not only in spirit, but in other structures within the province. It had not become clear yet, but in retrospect one detects it: Galbraith had his feet set on a course of change that meant much more then renewal. For some it was liberation, but for others, who were anxious, it was destruction. For better or worse, Galbraith would never leave the province as he found it.

In the beginning there was routine work to be done. The new Campion Hall located at 2222 N.W. Hoyt was nearly completed and plans were formed for its occupation on St. Ignatius Day, July 31, 1970 three weeks after Father Kelley, who had labored so zealously to acquire it, left office.† On July 6, Galbraith requested permission from Rome for Gonzaga

---

*Interview with Galbraith, September 12 and September 13, 1981, Spokane. Galbraith described this period as one of growing pains.

†Thus Campion Hall was located in the old Mackenzie Mansion from 1947 until 1970. After the departure of the Jesuits the Episcopal Church purchased the property from the insurance company and restored it, adding a clever addition and dedicating it on Palm Sunday, April 4, 1971, as the William Temple Mission House. *Newsletter of the Oregon Province*, May, 1971, p. 6.

University to build an addition to the Law School. He explained that following the Goller Hall fire the insurance company offered to settle for a cash loss of $107,000, but in accordance with the policy, to pay $195,000 to replace the building. This, with what the university held in a trust fund, $90,000, would cover the cost of the addition, which was required to retain accreditation.[5] The general responded on July 23, approving Galbraith's request.[6]

A few days later, on July 16, Galbraith wrote again to Arrupe, proposing this time that the collegiate program at Mount St. Michael's be moved to Bea House on the Gonzaga Campus. His arguments were many and compelling. Another ad hoc committee appointed by the last province congress had studied the question long and carefully. Seattle had been considered as a possible new site for the program. Costs at the Mount had multiplied. Scholastics there felt isolated, and it had cost the province over $30,000 each year for transportation of teachers and scholastics to Gonzaga for classes. The Mount should be vacated and sold. The new rector, Father Patrick O'Leary was hopeful that the collegians could be in residence on the campus for the beginning of school in September as the ad hoc committee had recommended.[7]

Father Arrupe was wary. "The Arthur D. Little Report on finances makes the move and sale seem imperative," he wrote, "but I have some reservations about the conclusions of this report since experience proves that in every other case where a house of formation moved to a campus, e.g., Woodstock, Weston, St. Louis, Loyola in Los Angeles, the per diem cost for the living and education of scholastics rose."[8] He requested more information, which was posted to him on August 11. Time was running out. On August 29 Arrupe wired Galbraith: "Move from Mount to Bea approved, lease preferred to sale of the Mount."[9] Finally on September 3, 1970, Arrupe sent formal permission for the innovation, including in his letter some solemn admonitions regarding the proper spiritual formation of the young Jesuits, who would be placed in a new, untried environment for Oregonians.[10] On September 12, 1970, the historic migration was made. "For the first time in fifty-four years," *The Chronicler* noted, "the Mount stood empty." *The Chronicler* was inaccurate. A number of older fathers and brothers remained at the Mount until its sale in 1978.

The thirty-eight philosophers and three priests of the California and Oregon provinces began the 1970–71 school year at Cardinal Bea House on the Gonzaga University campus. Father Patrick O'Leary, the new rector, in true biblical fashion, led his people down from the mountain to the opportunities and challenges presented by this new location.

"The move was precipitated by the need in Jesuit formation for closer contact with the people to whom our service is directed."[11]

Though much was made of this "need" by the scholastics, who seemed to think they were returning from exile in Siberia, many older Jesuits felt betrayed. The Mount had replaced Gonzaga as a kind of motherhouse for the province and there was no discussing its abandonment without emotional feelings one way or another. Attachment to the Mount for most was deeper than that for Sheridan, which so far had escaped "the renewal." Thus it was that the gulf between the factions within the province was widened, instead of being improved by the latest change.

Meanwhile Father Michael O'Malley died. He had made his philosophy at Gonzaga, too, in the old sheds, before the Mount was built. A widely known legend in the Northwest, he had danced an Irish jig on his ninetieth birthday. He was still active then in St. Aloysius Parish in Spokane, where one could see him hurrying about the parish, calling on old people to comfort them, bringing them Holy Communion on First Fridays, and passing out books and leaflets to foster piety. For many long years he opened the church at five-thirty in the morning, or even earlier. He heard an almost infinite number of confessions, offered daily Mass for the people and supervised countless funerals. When he was over ninety he still dragged out the six large candles that, in those days, were placed beside the coffin. He visited the patients in the hospital and when his own turn came to be a patient, he confounded doctors by refusing to stay in bed. He used the opportunity to visit other patients. Whatever he did, he was always in a hurry and always oblivious to himself and his own comfort. When parishioners gathered a purse for him to return to Ireland for the first visit in a score of years, he was not given his ticket or his money till he boarded the plane, lest he give it away before he got there. He was always anxious about being "a trouble" to others and he never sat still long enough for anyone to wait on him or scarcely even to take his picture. On August 20, 1970, still active at the age of 95, he stopped a Jesuit companion at Gonzaga and asked why the lights had gone out. The lights had not gone out. An ambulance took him to Sacred Heart Hospital and an hour later he responded to his last call in this world.[12] Without him the province would never be the same.

The funeral for Father O'Malley was held on August 24. On the day preceding this, a five-day orientation program for the lay volunteers in the Jesuit Volunteer Corps [JVC] was concluded at Copper Valley Mission in Alaska. It had been, according to its Jesuit directors and volunteer participants, a profoundly spiritual experience which prepared the volunteers for a difficult year in the isolated missions of Alaska. Unfortunately, Joseph Ryan, archbishop of Anchorage, in whose diocese Copper Valley School lay, did not agree with what he had observed. In an extremely critical memorandum to Jesuit Fathers William Davis and John Morris, the archbishop expressed his opinion that the Orientation Program was "the type of thing which is insidiously undermining our Church."[13] There followed another celebrated skirmish, first regarding the procedures observed during the Orientation Program and secondly, regarding the existence of the Copper Valley School.

First, a flurry of letters to the archbishop followed in the stormy wake of his charges. Each Jesuit accused responded with respectful but lively denials of wrong-doing. Galbraith supported his subjects valiantly. There were more letters of criticism, then the furor died down for awhile, but broke out again when the archbishop announced the closure of the school. This had not been done without appropriate preliminaries. The archbishop presided over a meeting at the school on January 28, 1971, "to discuss the school's future." He had already replaced the Jesuit superior of the mission with one of his own diocesan priests, under whom the Jesuits continued to labor for the benefit of the mission. To some Jesuits the results of the meeting were already a foregone conclusion, termination of the mission, but surprisingly, the archbishop offered the Jesuits "the opportunity to take over the complete operation of the school."[14] When the Jesuits agreed, however, the archbishop withdrew his offer and announced to the public on March 11, 1971, the closing of the Copper Valley School. This was greeted with amazement and dismay wherever the mission was known. In Gonzaga's school paper *Signum,* a full-page article expressed indignation in terms that were uncommonly blunt.

"A shock wave," said the paper's correspondent, "passed through a large segment of the Gonzaga community last spring when the harsh news reached the campus that the remote Jesuit mission at Copper Valley on the Alaskan tundra had been arbitrarily closed by the Diocese of Anchorage. The initial reaction to the news among the more than 100 former Zags who had contributed one or two years of their lives to Copper Valley and its young residents ranged from disbelief to outrage."[15]

Gonzaga had been a nursery for the Jesuit Volunteer Corps which had grown, by this time, into a national organization involving hundreds of candidates each year. "Be poor among the poor for one year. For once in your life, be the Church," was the motto on campus.*

*Gonzaga had been one of the founding institutions of both the Corps and Copper Valley School. In 1971 twenty-two Gonzaga students joined the Corps.

"And it was certainly time," the *Signum* correspondent observed, "that no one got rich at Copper Valley. The Jesuits' paid the volunteer's transportation to and from the mission and gave him $10 a month for spending money, which was actually more than enough for the simple reason that there was no place to spend it. Those who went, well knew that a year at the mission was substantially more than fun and games. . . ."

"Fr. John J. Morris, S.J., the vice-provincial for apostolates of the Oregon Province of the Society of Jesus and a man who takes almost violent exception to the closing of Copper Valley, says the job description goes something like this: 'You teach, you build, you scrub floors, you wash clothes, you fix broken boilers, you drive a broken-down truck to Elmendorf Air Force Base to pick up a load of reject coal and before you leave you try to thaw out the oil in the engine of the truck which has congealed to the consistency of lard in 60 degrees below zero.' "[16]

Only God knew what hardships and sacrifices had gone into Copper Valley School. Now it had been abandoned, a more than million dollar school in a seldom traveled area, swept by arctic winds, which moaned through it like the ghosts of the happy children educated there for fifteen years. "A tragedy of church politics," Morris called it.

"In the peak years, there were about 175 young Alaskans in the mission school. A third of them were white, and the rest were Indians and Eskimos who came hundreds of miles from Point Barrow, the Seward Peninsula, Kodiak Island, even Little Diomede Island, which is Alaska's closest point to the U.S.S.R. They stayed for the school year as boarders and the volunteers worked with them."[17]

The phenomnal success of Copper Valley School before its closure was due, of course, to the volunteers. "This is the only area of the American Church," said Bishop Francis Gleeson, "where volunteers outnumbered the priests. They have become an absolute necessity."[18]

During the excitement following Ryan's final announcement regarding the school, Galbraith kept a discreet silence. The Alaska Mission Superior, Father Bernard McMeel, kept him informed, occasionally referring to "a white wash" or rigged meetings which confirmed decisions already made.[19] McMeel, unlike Morris, was calm and realistic about it all and he helped to heal the wounds on both sides of the fracas by closing the door on it, as Ryan had closed the door on the school.

The truth is Galbraith had a more serious problem to address. This, too, involved a painful confrontation, in which it must be presumed that everyone involved was prompted by the highest motives. Father Kenneth Baker, brilliant, young, and agressive, had returned from successful doctoral studies at Marquette University and had attracted considerable notice in the Religious Studies Department at Gonzaga University following the departure of Father Joseph Conwell.* Baker, who had a keen sense of the ironic, frequently commented on abuses in the Church, much to the delight of older Jesuits who took from his sometimes heavy banter much comfort. Baker, it was often noted, had courage. If sometimes he appeared to be too critical, he at least was vocal, like James Hitchcock in St. Louis, and witty, like William Buckley in New York.

Seattle University was in deep financial trouble. Over-expansion had caught up with it and the university which had begun to use this year's tuition to pay last year's operating costs found itself confronted with possible bankruptcy. At this point, in December, 1969, Baker was appointed president, replacing Jack Fitterer, who became Chancellor. It was hoped that Baker, who possessed great moral strength, not to mention youthful zest and energies, could lead the university out of the morass.

*Conwell had resigned in a dispute over administration policies and had been given a sabbatical year of study on the religions of Asia.

But Baker had firm ideological views, a philosophy of education that demanded more stress on "Catholic" and resisted all compromise. When he refused to grant a holiday in honor of Martin Luther King, his office was invaded by a group of bullies who held him captive and threatened him for some time, while they tore apart the president's office. Though threatened with great physical harm, Baker did not yield. Later there were two bombings on campus, minor incidents, more or less, during which windows were shattered and the original Garrand Building was damaged.

Bombs and threats were one thing; the debt quite another. The banks refused Seattle University additional credit without collateral. Almost everything the university owned was already mortgaged. The university payroll for October 1, 1970 could not be met until $500,000 in a Ford grant, set aside for a rainy day, was pledged to establish a line of credit. There was money left to operate only until October 15. Baker requested a meeting with the provincial, his staff and advisors, and this took place in the Chinook Hotel in Yakima on October 10.*

At the meeting Baker presented four possible options: voluntary bankruptcy, lease of the university property to the state, sell to the state for the use of community colleges, or finally, a holding operation, that is retrenchment. After much discussion, the latter was agreed upon as a course of action.

But this required compromise on Baker's part. The Board of Regents, influential and generous civic leaders, some Catholic and some not, agreed to save the university on certain conditions, the principal one related to Baker's public projection of the nature of the university. The regents, in other words, made it clear "that their support as well as any kind of support from the city in general, required that the Catholic dimension be played down and the Christian humanism aspect be played up."[20]

The provincial reported to Father General: "The crisis," he said, "was not lost on the Jesuit community. As the crisis grew, so did fear and tension among the Jesuit faculty members. Hard thinking and equally strong emotion fell generally into two camps: (1) those who felt the Board of Regents was putting undue pressure on a President to resign and therefore was to be resisted at all costs; and (2) those who felt the President should resign for the sake of the university's survival. Feeling on the issue ran so strong that I was urged to step into the picture and settle the issues immediately lest we not only lose the University but a Jesuit Community as well."[21]

Galbraith arrived in Seattle on October 27. Subsequent discussion with members of the community and members of the Board of Trustees, all Jesuit at this time, revealed that a consensus wanted Baker to resign. When presented with this view, "Father Baker, in a generous fashion typical of him, accepted their decision and tendered his resignation."[22]

This experience, like the one at Gonzaga two years earlier, was very painful to all who were involved. And like Gonzaga also, when the crisis was resolved, Seattle University still faced years of painful adjustments and trials, before, at last, it became stable and even prosperous. Credit for the latter must be allowed to those who deserve it, Bill Boeing, Thomas Bannon, Bob O'Brien and Les Sheridan, all regents and especially Father Arby Lemieux, who succeeded Fitterer as Chancellor, and Father Louis Gaffney who succeeded Baker as President. Under Gaffney peace was restored, confidence in the university was confirmed, and only minor retrenchments made. When it was all over, the university was stronger than ever.

Galbraith had demonstrated a dynamic leadership in this Seattle University crisis. He turned his attention now to one of his pet projects, the province meetings. In September, 1970 he had announced the formation of an Oregon Province Assembly, a semi-permanent

*A point here should be stressed: Baker had not created this situation, but had fallen heir to it.

body with officers and by-laws. The first assembly, he added, would be conducted in Loyola Retreat House, Portland, on November 27 and November 28, 1970. "The importance of such a body as the Province Assembly cannot be overestimated. As no Provincial today can hope to forward the apostolic work of his Province without the genuine and candid cooperation of his men, so no Province can hope for solid impact upon the world without an ongoing discernment concerning the significance of its efforts. Such 'grass roots' representation as the Province Assembly structure provides can furnish the Provincial an invaluable advisory source for furthering our apostolates. Because the Assembly will be a permanent body with representatives duly elected for terms of three years and meeting at least semi-annually, the entire Province can hope for a continuing effort toward renewal."[23]

It is not "just another meeting," he wrote to an elected member, "the continuing assemblies have all the significance of a Congress." His executive assistant, Father Lawlor, in a memorandum to all Oregon Jesuits noted that "the Province Assembly has become the ordinary means by which corporate discernment of the Province is put before the Provincial."[24]

These were high-sounding phrases, but there were penetrating questions within the province about the difference between discernment of the provincial with his official consultors and the discernment of the provincial with his new assembly. Was it better to have a few well-informed advisors or many ill-informed ones? Or both, as Galbraith desired it? Most members of the province did not agree with Galbraith.

For Father Brad Reynolds, Editor of *The General Exchange,* the first assembly was a great success. "Life began to have meaning for the Assembly," he wrote, "and it grew in wisdom and understanding." Later he added: "But in subsequent meetings, more and more difficulties arose. It began with ballotbox stuffing while voting for delegates and ended at the final Province Assembly with personality conflicts in a 'fish bowl.'

"The second Province Assembly was held at Waikiki Retreat House in Spokane on April 23-25, 1971. The Novitiate at Sheridan hosted the third Assembly on November 26-28, 1971. The fourth and final Assembly convened on April 14-16, 1972, at the Loyola Retreat House in Portland. All the superiors and administrators in the province were asked to join what would end up as the final Assembly."[25]

The last of these assemblies in 1972 produced three comments by delegates, which should be recorded here. The first by Brad Reynolds described what they *were doing.* "What we are doing here," he said, "is simply what we used to do at Villa, except that we would shut up when the Provincial came into the room."[26]

Father Jim Powers contributed a remark that suggested they *discontinue* what they were doing. "I don't suppose it is any secret by and large, the Province does not take the Assembly seriously."[27]

Finally, Brother Thomas O'Shea, who had cared for the sick at Mount St. Michael's for forty years, made his impassioned appeal, referred to by some, as the only important contribution ever made by the Assemblies. "I am really upset," Tom said, "a little angry and a little afraid of the fact that we have come down to 1972 and we don't have any preparation for the infirm of the Province."[28] Thus Tom pointed out what they were *not doing.*

After that the Central Committee decided there was no need for an Assembly. On January 9, 1973, Galbraith consulted with members of the Central Committee over the phone by conference call. Father Mike Merriman, chairman then, reported that the assembly was dead.

"What can you say about a two-year old assembly that died?" Reynolds asked. "That it was beautiful. And brilliant. That it loved coffee and parliamentary procedure. Once, when it was preparing for its third meeting, the Chairman of the Central Committee wrote: 'It is interesting to note that the key issues listed on the agenda for the previous two assembly meetings . . . are still among the key issues that face the Province.' The beginning of the end, don't you know?"[29]

The Provincial's obituary was not quite so ecstatic.

"My Brothers," he wrote, "At the conclusion of the Oregon Province Congress in November 1969, the assembled members of the Congress resolved that the efforts so well begun at that time should continue. As you well know, the resolution took the form of the Province Assembly.

"However, the history of the Province Assembly has shown that the Congress resolution never really took."[30]

There seems to have been no serious effort to discover why not. The answer, perhaps, would have been embarrassing. More likely than not, had a poll been taken, the vast majority of the ordained members of the province would have opposed the assemblies in the first place. Hence their demise, in the eyes of many, marked a turning point. The new, so called "more democratic" action had failed. Most Jesuits preferred the traditional manner of government which was, in effect, a great tribute to Ignatius of Loyola.*

The assembly was one experiment. *The General Exchange*, another. One often heard during these transition years that communication was the means of reform and lack of it the flaw in the mechanism of society. Meetings as one form of communication had been undertaken with the zeal of unemployed politicians. Our province paper or bulletins should be combined, it was said, to form one good professional paper, useful for circulation to Jesuits and non-Jesuits. Father Pat Twohy, a happy-go-lucky, hobo philosopher type, a combination mystic and Will Rogers, agreed to serve as the first editor of the new publication. Thus *The General Exchange*, Volume I, Number 1, appeared on November 16, 1971. The new editor had interviewed Father Van Christoph, the impulsive and peppery rector at Gonzaga, mostly because he knew that Christoph would respond in the way he did.

> " 'I don't want a paper lecturing to me," said Father Van Christoph recently when he was asked to comment on the new Province paper. He further exclaimed that no one had asked him whether he wanted the paper, and he was sure that no one in the province was out soliciting subscriptions. . . .' If it's a service for Jesuits they should ask Jesuits if they want the service.' There's no choice whether you want it or not, he concluded.
>
> "He further questioned how this unasked for service could in any way serve the interests of unity, in a way that couldn't be achieved by other less expensive means. Fr. Christoph felt that unlike secular readers of print Jesuits are not in awe of the printed word. 'A simple mimeographed newsletter would do.' "[31]

Christoph, I might add, had a very strick sense of poverty. After he was sixty years old, he refused to have his teeth repaired. "No sense to it," he snapped. "It's just money you put into your head, then bury it in the ground."

*Father Edmund Morton former Assistant Provincial for Education has frequently pointed out that the new administrative structures "work very well *horizontally* because of the frequent meetings at this level; but not *vertically*, because there is too little communication from one level to another. The old system was better, when the provincial came and gave a general rec'. He gave us all the news in the province and kept us informed."

Twohy interviewed another member of the Gonzaga community, who played God in one of Roger Gillis' hilarious, home-made dramas. This was Father Gerald Kohls. Kohls, for some reason always tan and rugged looking, like a model in a *New Yorker Magazine* ad, was professor of philosophy, not of physical ed. He spoke with a voice that was very low and solemn sounding. Perhaps that is why he was selected for the role of God. Wrapped in a white sheet, his arms outstretched with droopy long white sleeves, he was less convincing as God than Mike Pope in a quarter acre of black cloth as Mother Superior. "For many of you, I imagine," Kohls admitted, "I am not what you pictured God would look like." On the subject of "What is the major problem confronting Jesuits today?" Kohls had this to say: "That's a dumb question . . . seriously [it is] polarity."[32]

So it was still the gulf between the old and the new, between tradition and renewal.

For one of the new Jesuits the matter had become moot. Like Paul Linssen, he had drowned in the cold waters of Alaska. On October 8, 1971, Brother John Huck with Jim Churbuck, a member of the Volunteer Corps, George Tyson and George Taller, Alaskan natives, were involved in a boating accident near the confluence of the Andreafski and Yukon rivers. The boat evidently capsized on the storm-whipped waters. Only one body was found; the other three were presumed dead.

> "The four had been at Marshall and Pilot Station for several days, and were anxious to return to St. Mary's. They set out, but the water became so rough that they put to shore on an island where two other men had already sought refuge from the cold, wet weather. These tried to persuade John and his companions to stay, but the urge to go home was too strong. The St. Mary's crew launched out into the river and was gone. About an hour later the two men on the island judged that it would be safe to leave their haven. Down river they found the overturned, drifting boat and the body of George Taller. The heavy news reached the mission and was flashed to the lower forty-eight; and the Province waited in sorrow and shock for several days while all attempts to recover the other bodies failed."[33]

Huck, only thirty-three years old when he died, had been in charge of building and construction throughout the Alaskan Mission. His accomplishments read like a schedule on the pipe line. He built churches at Um Kumute, Tununak, Kaltag, Emmonak and living quarters at Sheldon's Point, Marshall, Aniak and Barrow. He installed a heating plant at Bethel, renovated the Church at Aniak, the bishop's house at Fairbanks and the Radio Station KNOM at Nome. His last project was the construction of a two-story residence for eighteen volunteers at St. Mary's where he also completed the girls' dormitory and installed a heating plant.

The Radio Station KNOM was Father Jim Poole's renowned achievement. With the assistance of the Volunteer Corps, as disc jockeys, Poole started broadcasting sixteen hours a day in the summer of 1971. "We're short of priests. We're getting shorter. That's why I got into this. I get into people's living rooms every day."[34] Close to twenty thousand Eskimos and Indians living in the ninety villages within the KNOM coverage area are hearing not only the music provided by KNOM, but five fifteen-minute news summaries a day, brought up to date by Associated Press teletype, clicking away most of the time. Some of the broadcasting each day is in Eskimo. With $70,000 per year, all from donations, and his seventeen volunteers, who received $5.00 a week for spending money, Poole operates one of only two radio stations in the entire western half of the state.

John Huck's was a great loss to the Mission, but there were many more losses to the province during this period when religious life was as stormy as the waters of the Yukon.

During Galbraith's first year as provincial, there was an over-all decline of thirty-four Jesuits, due to death or departures. In the following year the decline was twenty-eight, then in 1972 it was sixteen. In the six years that Galbraith was in office the province dropped from 608 members to 515, a fact of life then that alarmed everyone and prompted in-depth studies like Father Ivan Hutton's, which revealed the inevitable: a fast decreasing number of younger Jesuits and a gradually increasing median age for members of the province. Two grave consequences of this began to appear. First, the pool of Jesuits in the proper age-level for selecting young superiors, had almost disappeared, leaving higher superiors with no other alternative than appointing older Jesuits as local superiors. Where people were still sensitive to "the generation gap," this tended to alienate young Jesuits even more. Secondly, the province's high schools had depended largely on younger Jesuits. Many of those who would have staffed the high schools had departed, leaving an almost-vacuum in the schools that had been for a century the principal source of vocations.

Deeply conscious of this crisis, Galbraith declared 1972–73 "The Year of the High School", intending not only to focus attention on the gravity of the problem, but also to find a method for retrenching or consolidating without offending the high school administrators. To even attempt this was unrealistic, because no principal would suggest the annihilation of his own school. But Galbraith was getting desperate. In *The General Exchange* on October 10, 1972, he released his proposal.

This issue of *The Exchange* was produced by Brad Reynolds, as Assistant to the Editor, Pat Twohy having opted to work in the Indian Missions. In late October, however, Reynolds was appointed editor and remained in this position until June, 1974, producing a lively paper that was really too good for the limited audience it reached.

During the same month Senator George McGovern was campaigning for president of the United States. Something like one hundred Jesuits of the Oregon Province signed an endorsement for him in a Jesuits for McGovern move. Two members of the Gonzaga University faculty appeared with McGovern in photographs, which were widely circulated in the press. These were Father Bernard Tyrrell of the Gonzaga University Philosophy Department and Father Frank Costello, chairman of the University's Political Science Department. Details about this and one-half page photograph appeared in *The General Exchange* for November 1972, and the fat was in the fire. Feelings ran high in this presidential campaign, but within the province, partly due to what Kohls called "polarity," the emotions of some got out of hand and a few exciting, but not bloody confrontations occurred. The newspapers made the most of it. Reynolds, too, like a reporter with a hound dog's nose, presented views of many Jesuits. When *The Oregon Journal* asked Father Frank Masterson, Rector at Jesuit High, what he thought, he responded with uncharacteristic diplomacy: "Political and moral stands may and must be taken by individuals," he said somewhat sonorously, "we expect our students to take their own stands. But as an educational institution dedicated to free inquiry and objectivity we remain neutral."[35] It was not often that Masterson declined to say what he really thought.

The incident marked the beginning of a period of open unpopularity for the provincial with the more conservative Jesuits. This culminated finally in his stance on the 1973 grape and lettuce strike, during which he directed members of the province to boycott these items, in solidarity with the strikers.[36] While older Jesuits made sincere efforts to comply with his directive, and younger ones demonstrated at stores selling the allegedly non-union lettuce and grapes, angry outbursts indicated deep feelings on the subject, which was highly controversial even for those less involved.

The noise and excitement was good therapy. As the smoke of battle cleared the healing process, which had long since started, began to appear more brightly, the provincial's popularity improved, and peace began to settle at last over the province. In retrospect, it appears, we had reached the bottom with "wicked lettuce and sinful grapes." The cry of "sinful structures" still had to be dealt with, and whether the provincial knew it or not, it was on his agenda. It was a hot item.

It all began in 1973 when Galbraith held a meeting from February 23 to February 25 at the retreat house in Portland to which he invited high school administrators in order "to discern with them" methods for resolving the manpower problem. In effect Galbraith wanted these Jesuits to make a decision to determine which school or schools should be closed. After a weekend of discussion he was informed very candidly that it was impossible to enter into discussion on this matter because each administrator was identified with a particular institution. This told Galbraith, as he stated later: "I had to do it."[37] He began a careful scrutiny of the five high schools, "evaluating things even hypothetically." He was making an effort, he said, "to prioritize the province's activities on this level."

The high school in Missoula, he decided, "could have four Jesuits for three years. After that it will be up to my successor." The privileged status of Jesuit High in Portland seems to have been taken for granted. In Spokane and Tacoma, where Gonzaga Prep and Bellarmine Prep were the only Catholic schools for boys, there were special considerations. Tacoma had two schools for girls, St. Leo's and Aquinas, but it was common knowledge that both were in the latter stages of decline in enrollment. In Spokane, likewise, there were two schools for girls, Marycliff and Holy Names Academy. Although no one was admitting it openly, both schools were declining quite rapidly and there were hopes expressed by some of the Holy Names Sisters that the diocese would combine all three schools, including Gonzaga Prep, and operate one coeducational school, using the Prep campus. In Galbraith's judgment "both Spokane and Tacoma had to move toward consortiums, that is each city should have a single Catholic high school." He assumed that these would be Bellarmine and Gonzaga Prep.

At Seattle Prep since 1969, the rector was Father Emmett Carroll, sparse and ascetical looking, with weak eyes and a quick impulsive laugh. He was a middle-of-the-road thinker, who saw virtue in sticking to his guns, no matter who was offended. The principal was Father Robert Goebel, a popular Pied Piper, who could get along with anybody. He had recently been in a serious car accident, so he was replaced by Father John Kindall, a brilliant innovator with the chest of a weight lifter and eye glasses as thick as the bottoms of pop bottles. This was the Prep administration, which was now under siege.

Among Galbraith's more influential counselors were three who regarded Seattle Prep as "a sinful structure" because a large percentage of its students came from prosperous families. We were committed to work for the poor, they said. Renewal for them meant that: commitment to the poor. Seattle Prep, they said, must be the first school to go. A "showdown meeting" was conducted, during which the provincial, who was caught in the middle, carefully presented his premises and conclusions, one of which was: Seattle Prep ranked below Bellarmine and Gonzaga, because in Seattle there were three other Catholic high schools. Carroll took exception to this and other conclusions and appealed to Rome.* By this time there was wide-spread anxiety about the future of the school; faculty, students, parents, and alumni were aroused. Kindall asked to be relieved as principal, and Galbraith, after convincing him to remain, met with a group of faculty and parents, numbering eighty, for a two-day conference, April 30 and May 1, 1973. According to Reynolds, Galbraith's position was: "If the people don't want the game plan, then the people don't want the value system of the Jesuits."[38] Galbraith finally agreed to keep Seattle Prep open on one condition: Prep had to come up with a new program, "a radical change."[39]

---

*Carroll wrote to Rome on June 5, 1973. Some of the details contained in this passage were gathered during an interview with him on December 3, 1981, Seattle.

By this time Kindall had already worked out "a radical change" a program which would in effect convert academically high ranking Seattle Prep into a minority school, or as some unjustly concluded, a remedial school for minorities.[40] Called "the Hex Kindall Plan" this was openly challenged by some members of the province, and Kindall for at least a second time, requested a new assignment.* The provincial appointed Father Tom Healy as the new "President-Principal" and announced that for the forthcoming school year "a new thrust" would be attempted at Seattle Prep, for which five young Jesuits, "some of the finest young talent in the province," would be assigned to Prep to carry out this mandate.[41]

Tom Healy was not only conscientious, but competent. Small in stature, well-groomed and energetic, he left one with the impression that he kept his foot on the brake, lest he get out of control. He had the appearance of a corporate president who knew everything that was going on, but discreetly kept his peace. Fortunately he was readily acceptable to the supporters of Seattle Prep, who had been alienated by the provincial's tough talk. During this very year he and his bright young think tank would have to invent "a radical change."

Superiors in Rome preferred that Emmett Carroll remain as rector, but differences of opinion between himself and the provincial convinced him that he should resign. The general accepted his decision. Father Dennis Dennehy, was appointed to replace him, and Carroll was assigned to Seattle University, where, on August 27, 1973, he received a letter from the provincial in which the following appeared: "the future of Prep is far from certain."[42]

Battered but still standing straight, Galbraith soon released another unpopular decision, which shocked many members of the province. He had determined, he said, in keeping with province renewal and required coordination, that teaching scholastics, henceforth, would be assigned to two schools only, Jesuit High and Bellarmine.[43] This was understandably, a deep disappointment to administrators at Seattle Prep and Gonzaga, from which, in the past at least, the majority of vocations to the province had come. The fact that Galbraith had graduated from Bellarmine and Father Terry Shea, one of his most trusted advisors, was president there, seems to have had no influence on the decision. When the smoke of this skirmish had cleared, Galbraith had relented just a little and Gonzaga Prep was allowed two scholastics, only one of whom survived.

It was during this period that the novitiate was finally sold. Galbraith had first approached the general on the subject, in a cautious manner, and having received some encouragement, formally applied for his permission to sell on December 19, 1973. He informed Arrupe that the novitiate building, formerly occupied by one hundred and fifty men, now housed only thirty-two, that the province had a buyer for the property and that a suitable complex for relocating the novices had been found in Portland.[44] The Archbishop had already given his approval for the establishment of another Jesuit community in that city. Since the purchaser of the property had requested the Jesuits to move out before January 1, there was some need for a hurried response to this appeal.

Arrupe, always considerate of others, conveyed his approval of the sale, and all else, by phone on December 28. A formal approval with the proper rescript for the canonical erection of novitiate in Portland was dispatched from Rome on January 14, 1974.[45] Before this, on January 11, 1974, Galbraith notified the province of current developments with the following letter:

> "On January 2nd negotiations were concluded with the Delphian Foundation, a branch of the Church of Scientology, for the sale of our novitiate at Sheridan, Oregon. Ownership will become effective February 1st.

*Kindall became principal of the diocesan high school, Central Catholic in Billings.

"The sale price was settled at $1,100,000.00, an amount the Province Financial Advisory Board and the Province Consultors judged to be excellent in light of all the circumstances. Revenue from the sale will go to the Province Arca Seminarii.

"As for the novitiate program, it has already relocated to the site of the former Holy Child Academy in Portland. In place of purchase, which at this time seems unwise for a number of reasons, the province has chosen to lease the site. Novices will now carry out their collegiate experiment at either Mt. Hood Community College or Portland State University.

"The passing of landmarks like the novitiate reminds us of the changing structures affecting all levels of Society life. Whatever response such a passing begets in you, I surely hope that gratitude toward all who helped to shape the novitiate's history, as well as gratitude that the province has been relieved of a heavy burden, will be one of them."[46]

So that was that. Only the Mount was left and it was on the block for sale, like a treasured heirloom that we could no longer afford to keep. "The passing of landmarks," as Galbraith had noted, was an understatement. These had been our happy homes, our hopes for a secure and peaceful retirement, where we would be surrounded by young Jesuits and familiar sights. The haunting words of the poet, "never more, never more," passed through the minds of some Jesuits who suddenly felt their roots had been pulled out and burned. Whom to blame? No one. We were living in a world that was being born anew.

Galbraith made some changes in his staff. James Meehan became the Provincial Assistant for Education, replacing Morton, and Roy Antunez became Provincial Assistant for Apostolic Works, replacing John Morris. About the same time, on August 15, 1973, William J. Loyens became Superior of the Alaska Mission.

Affectionately called "Lom" which is the equivalent of "Bill" in Belgium, whence he had come many years earlier, Loyens proved to be a popular choice for an office that still lacked perimeters of jurisdiction. It was the same old story: Jesuits in Alaska had at least three superiors to whom they reported, despite all efforts of the bishop and Jesuits to resolve ambiguities. Seemingly the matter was insolvable. The new superior, however, was optimistic. "We are here for the bishop," he said simply, and later he added, "We own nothing in Alaska, nothing at all. That gives us freedom."[47]

Lom was interviewed by Reynolds. He was living in a small apartment near the University of Alaska, where he was a highly respected professor of anthropology. Sitting back comfortably in a big chair, a cigarette in his right hand, he spoke in a soft musical voice with just a hint of an accent in it. "I studied English like blazes while I was supposed to be studying tropical medicines." Behind his rimless glasses his facial features belied his forty-seven years; he looked like a young reporter on vacation. His sparkling eyes, dimples, wavy dark hair, and straight ivory-white teeth all conveyed the impression of youthful health and vigor. He made quick, graceful gestures as he talked and he turned his head easily like a bird. He enjoyed a good joke, and even one badly told. "You know," he said, "the best definition of Alaska is one, big, little town. You cannot do anything in Fairbanks that will not be known very quickly throughout the bush."[48]

Lom had struggled valiantly to get there. Born on December 22, 1926 at Vlijtingen, Limburg, Belgium, son of Matthew Loyens and Marie Loyens, nee Biesmans, he was baptized an hour later by the doctor, indicating, perhaps, that he was too frail to await the customary ceremonies. He was christened Willem Jan, that is William John. In due time he entered the Apostolic School at Turnhout, which Father Paul Deschout attended. Then on

February 2, 1947, before he had studied English "like blazes," he wrote to the Oregon Province Vocation Director at the Mount. "This Rev. Father [Deschout] made me bold enough to write you. As I will make myself a Jesuit and follow the example of Father de Schout, a big difficulty arises: How could I see my vocation realized, if I have to enter the Flemish Province. . . . There is no how to push away this problem. I am ready to leave yet this country. What have I to do, Father?"[49]

Through the intervention of Father Robinson, provincial then, Loyens was accepted for the novitiate of the Oregon Province and Father Small arranged for his transfer to Sheridan in January 1950. Within five months he was sent to the Mount. "I am so happy here in America," he said to me, "that my Mother would be disappointed to know I could be as happy away from her."

About the Mount he said, "They were talking about a Ph.D. in philosophy or something. At the last minute it changed and I went to Alma. At Alma I was appointed to get a Ph.D. in theology to teach at Alma. I got that mess unscrambled and I came up here. At a meeting in Copper (Valley), where I wasn't present, the boys decided I should get a doctorate . . . in economics!"[50]

His dilemma was simple, he seemed to be a genius at everything he studied. The faculty at Alma was determined to have him in theology and wrote to Father General about him. A great struggle followed with Father Schultheis siding in with Loyens and urging the general to assign him to Alaska. For his ordination in 1958 the general sent him a present: his appointment to Alaska. He was allowed first to obtain his doctorate in anthropology at the University of Wisconsin.

"Congratulations," Provincial Alex McDonald wrote to him on March 18, 1964, after he had won a National Science Foundation Graduate Fellowship. "The province is proud of the academic honor awarded to you."[51] A year later Father Kelley gave him permission to print his article: "The Koyukon Feast of the Dead."[52] When he received his doctorate on May 25, 1966, his faculty voted him the Bobbs-Merrill award as the outstanding graduate student of the year.

The University of Alaska lost no time in drafting him to teach there, because his specialty concerned the cultural anthropology of the Eskimos in the Arctic. His popularity as a teacher was confirmed by another award in the following year, "Outstanding Service to Students." Though his smile could charm a shaman's stick to light up, he doubtlessly earned this, for he worked day and night on the students' behalf.

Life would be different now. Taking a leave of absence from the university, he devoted his time and energies to the problems of the mission of Alaska.

At Seattle Prep, meanwhile, time was running out. At the end of the school year 1973, the race horses under Healy had no prospects for a "radical change." Healy, determined to save the school, reminded them, "We have only six more months." In desperation he went, at last, to the files. He found there a plan formed in early 1972, during a meeting at Lake Sammamish, with Father James Powers of Seattle University. This conference had been called by Powers to study a Carnegie Foundation idea for speeding up the high school program.

Jim Powers, gifted with an extraordinary talent and desire to express himself, also enjoyed the happy facility of being quite pragmatic about means to an end. When he selected his graduate school for his doctorate in English he said, with an enigmatic smile all over his features, "I want a good school without a lot of fooling around. Get the degree and get it over with, that's what I think." Influenced by "a fellow" at the Batelle Institute, Dr. Matt Cullen, who had placed in his hands the Carnegie plan for "Less Time More Options," Powers espoused its cause and called Prep's attention to it. At the Lake Sammamish Conference he reported on a similar program at Gonzaga in 1946–48, when he had been a student there. Results for this earlier experiment for an accelerated high school program were discussed and Powers pointedly called everyone's attention to the differences between the Carnegie Plan and Gonzaga's. The Carnegie Plan, he said, was not a structure of three years in high school and three in college, suggesting simply a shortening of both courses, but a six-year continuum using entirely new teaching concepts on the lower level.

Nothing came of the conference, but Powers, who also had great vision, despite his ever-present need for eye glasses, did not give up. On January 28, 1974, addressing a group at Seattle University as Acting Dean of Arts and Sciences, he said: "Two years ago at Lake Sammamish a group of interested faculty and administrators of Seattle University hosted a small contingent from Seattle Prep to explore in a germinal way this proposal and although it became clear at that time that the idea was, because of a variety of circumstances, premature, nevertheless, it now would appear to be on target. I, for one, am delighted at the prospect and anxiously await its fruition."[53]

Healy now had his plan for Prep's "radical change." Since it was tied in with Seattle University there was little chance that the provincial would reject it.

Almost immediately, in February, 1974, Father Louis Gaffney, president of Seattle University, appointed a steering committee, chaired by Father William Le Roux, to work out details with Seattle Prep. This committee, with the cooperation of 125 persons serving on sub-committees, members of both faculties, administrators, parents, and experts submitted the final outline of the proposed program on November 18, 1974.[54]

While all these learned people drank their coffee, smoked cigarettes, or puffed on pipes, and talked endlessly, other events were going on in the province where things still held firmly together in spite of all the grumbling. The general had solemnly announced "in the name of the Father and of the Son and of the Holy Spirit," the opening date of the 32nd General Congregation in Rome, hence a Province Congregation to select delegates was duly convened by Galbraith at Seattle University on February 15, 1974. During its four-day sessions, Leo Kaufmann and Gordon Moreland, both of them generally regarded at "traditional" rather than "reformers," were elected to accompany the provincial to the Roman meeting, scheduled to begin on December 1, 1974.

Galbraith planned an early departure to visit enroute members of the province in sundry locations. He had been engaged in two pet projects, which were gradually taking shape: the Tri-School Program at Tacoma, and the restructuring of administration and ownership of St. Mary's Mission near Omak.

On January 9, 1974, Arrupe consented to the first of these, and to some extent, the second. Writing to Galbraith he said: "This approval of coeducation at Bellarmine High School [sic] should not be considered as introducing a policy for Jesuit high schools, but rather a constructive response to a critical local situation."[55]

The Omak proposal had been submitted by Father Tom Connolly, who had served for a brief time as Province Director of the Social Apostolate and special consultant to the provincial. Connolly with Shea, John Morris, and Bill Davis shared Galbraith's confidence, particularly in matters related to renewal. Partly because of Connolly's tenacious and aggressive dedication, the Indian missions were enjoying a revival, which to some extent influenced the new nativism sweeping the country. One product of the latter was the Indian's desire to control his own destiny, as well as other aspects of tribal life, including his schools. Connolly urged that the Indians on the Colville reservation be given the opportunity of owning and controlling the school at St. Mary's. Galbraith agreed to this and sought the general's permission.

In his letter of January 9, Arrupe added: "By this same letter I wish to approve in general the three-phase plan of turning over to the Colville Tribal Council the administration and ownership of the Indian school at St. Mary's Mission in Omak, Washington."

The three phases had been described by Galbraith as follows:

Phase I: The establishment of a School Board, the majority of which would be tribal members. Such an act can be seen as giving responsibility to the tribe for school policies, financing and direction.

Phase II: Relinquishing approximately 20 acres of unusable mission land to the tribe so that government funds can be acquired by Indians for erecting two new class buildings.

Phase III: Relinquishing all property on which the present school building now stands and for the same reason. The school and buildings would yield to control of the Tribal Education Board. Church property and farm land would still be under Jesuit ownership.[56]

Connolly's plan, having been adopted, the school passed under the control of the Colville Tribal Council which renamed it in 1973 for the recently deceased Paschal Sherman, an Indian alumnus of St. Mary's who had gone on to earn five college degrees, eventually becoming an attorney for the Veteran's Bureau in Washington, D.C.[57]

Before leaving for Rome, Galbraith approved the so-called merger of Seattle Prep and Seattle University, meaning the "radical change," directed the Jesuits at Loyola High School in Missoula to merge with Sacred Heart Academy, and approved the new President at Gonzaga University, Father Bernard Coughlin of the Missouri Province.* He also appointed Father Ken Krall as the new editor of *The General Exchange* and Father Jack Lawlor as the Vice-Provincial during his absence. Galbraith embarked by plane for eastern United States on September 14, 1974.

Before this, six Oregon Jesuits who had joined the Horizons for Justice Program for the summer of 1974, returned to their regular assignments. Among them was Father Tom Williams, commonly called "Tiger Tom" because he was as gentle as a kitten. He had spent the summer in Mexico, assisting in parishes and keeping a diary which amused all of us when it was printed. I have included here a fragment, which I would like to call "The Bus."

"July 22, Monday: Went by bus to the metro. The driver stopped for everyone no matter where they were. Very polite and kind. We worried about being on time and went in hurry and worry Got to the bus station 45 minutes early for the 10:30. 10:30 came, but no bus. Asked a young mother of a blond rascal about the bus. She said to relax as the bus hadn't come yet, let alone left. An hour later we were on our way. The driver had a rosary hanging from the mirror. The way he drove I felt like hopping on the dashboard and saying Mass."[58]

Williams was not our only writer at the time. In addition to those already mentioned, Bernard Tyrrell of Gonzaga University had recently published a best-seller called *Christotherapy*, which was translated into many languages and published throughout the world.[59] John Evoy had just completed *The Rejected*, published by the University of Pennsylvania Press,[60] and William Bischoff of Seattle University was completing *We Were Not Summer Soldiers: The Indian Diary of Plympton J. Kelly, 1855–1856*, which was published in

---

*Unfortunately the Sisters of Providence who conducted Sacred Heart Academy did not regard this as a merger, but a takeover. See *The General Exchange,* April, 1974, p. 1.

1976.[61] One of our most prolific producers was Michael J. Taylor, also at Seattle University. Another was James Royce an authority on alcoholism, whose latest book *Alcohol Problems and Alcoholism* was regarded as a kind of classic on the subject.[62] William Armstrong established his own publishing house, which printed his booklets in the lighter vein, and Kevin Waters composed music for the more solemn occasions in churches all over the United States. Finally there was J. J. Mueller. Father J. J. of Gonzaga University, on loan from the Missouri province, has always been very serious about writing. He spends each summer with other young Jesuits, equally dedicated, in some sweltering house in Massachusetts, writing articles and planning books. J. J., despite his tender years and boyish looks, has already published one book with a high-powered title: *Faith and Appreciative Awareness.*[63]

This list is suggestive, not comprehensive, indicating only generally that Jesuits in Oregon, far from the centers of high culture, have not forsaken the example of Peter Canisius and other scholars, whose singular "martyrdom" was wrought by a pen.

Members of the 32nd General Congregation had other ways to suffer. They completed their sessions on March 7, 1975, and hurried to their homes, eager to be active again after long and tedious meetings. In Galbraith's absence Lawlor had not been idle. On January 10, 1975, he dispatched a seven-page letter to Arrupe, requesting approval for the coeducational six-year program at Seattle Prep, as proposed by the New College Steering Committee's Report of November 18, 1974." Presented like Thomas Aquinas' arguments for God, For and Against, the letter left little unanswered and nothing for the general to quibble over.[64]

On February 3, Lawlor wrote to Arrupe again. This time, because the Academy had been closed, he requested approval for coeducation at Gonzaga Prep. Only five pages were required, including a report of Father Meehan, and this, too, with its suggestion of sounding trumpets and call for desperate actions, appeared to be so compelling that not even Cardinal Ottaviani himself could turn it down.[65] The fact is, the general promptly granted both requests, one for Seattle Prep on February 6, and the other for Gonzaga Prep on February 28. The province now had only one all-boys school, Jesuit High in Portland. If the critics were right, this would become the principal source of vocations.*

The way was now clear for the radical change. In February, 1975, both Prep and Seattle University announced the new six-year plan. Father Gaffney, aware of its advantages to Seattle University, commended Powers for his vision and persistence. Calling him the "Godfather of all of the planning," he wrote: "The idea was yours and I am grateful for the persistence you had in holding to it even when it would seem that no one was willing to listen to the plan seriously. . . . and as I have mentioned to you in conversation an important fringe benefit of the whole operation is that I believe Matteo Ricci College will insure support from the [Portland] Curia for continuing Jesuit manpower at Seattle University."[66]

Under the new title of Matteo Ricci College, the Prep program was inaugurated in September, 1975, with freshmen, sophomores in the revised curriculum, and juniors and seniors in an adapted one.† While many Jesuits in the province withheld their judgment, or openly criticized the innovations, students, parents and other observers reacted favorably. Sustained by a grant of $236,000 from the Carnegie Foundation, which put its money where it made recommendations, the new school was able to employ a large staff of lay

*In the past, most candidates entering the Society applied from the high schools. In more recent years, however, this is not the case. Despite this, some still think that an all-boys school should be the best nursery for vocations.

†Matteo Ricci was a seventeenth-century Jesuit in China who was very successful but controversial within the church. The name is appropriate for Ricci used innovative methods, "the radical change" in the missions.

teachers to supplement the meager Jesuit community of fifteen.* Healy's burden was not less but more. Fortunately he had the confidence of the provincial, who appeared, by this time, to be as enthusiastic about the experiment as anybody.

During these last months several Jesuits had passed from this life to the next, and there are at least two of them who should be especially remembered. The first of these was Father Raymond Nichols of Seattle University who died on October 24, 1974. According to Father James McGoldrick, Nichols should be regarded as one of the founders of modern Seattle University together with Father Howard Peronteau, who died in 1949. Nichols was in his eighty-first year, a pioneer until the hour he died. During the difficult early years, in the 1930s, he did the work of three men: he taught a full schedule, he supervised the installation of the gardens, which made Seattle University a sylvan paradise, and he served as pastor of a country parish. He enjoyed a hearty appetite and each morning he assembled on a platter such an assortment of eggs, sausage and pancakes, that a visitor, when he saw it unguarded, assumed it was the serving dish for the whole table. He helped himself to part of it, while others cheered him on and Nichols watched, fascinated by the bold plundering of his breakfast.

Like Nichols, Father Tim O'Leary of Gonzaga had been a zealous worker. For many years he taught chemistry and directed the premedical program with such professional integrity that his signature became an open sesame to a medical school. For years he offered the early Mass in St. Aloysius Church and spent the rent of the period until class time, hearing confessions either there or in the student chapel. Known as "Terrible Tim" he was prefect of De Smet Hall and generations of Gonzaga students left the campus with enormous love and respect for him. For the last ten years of his life he suffered from shingles, but he continued his work as always. He was only sixty-five when cancer was discovered. A week before he died, he sent a message to his fellow Jesuits:

> "I have talked things over with Father Rector [Father Beuzer] and he approves of my decision. The doctor, when I asked him, said I could live 'probably six more months' with blood transfusions and drugs. Without these he thinks I will die 'in about a week.' I have asked him to pull all the plugs and discontinue medication. If you have time to see me, I would like you to come to say goodbye. I beg your pardon for all my faults and I promise to say 'hello' to our Lord and Our Blessed Mother when I meet them for each of you. I will always pray for Gonzaga. Tim, SJ."

He died on May 10, 1975.

Galbraith was in his last year as provincial. Like most of his predecessors he had begun to falter. He experienced times of depression and doubt about his acceptance. Though "renewal" in its deepest spiritual sense urged him constantly forward, he often felt weary. Sometimes he had been tempted to anger and he was afraid of that. Like the rest of us in those dismal days, when we were climbing out of the pit of confusion and controversy, he needed encouragement and above all, understanding. He would, instead, be deeply hurt.

---

*"A Fast Trip Through High School, College" in *Seattle Post-Intelligencer*, November 9, 1975, presents a positive account of the school. The amount of the Carnegie grant variously stated appears there as in my text. There were twenty non-Jesuit teachers the first year.

This happened in autumn. During the summer he reestablished tertianship again, in a rented home on East Mission in Spokane.* Father General attached this canonically to St. Michael's Institute and appointed Father Joseph Conwell as the first tertian instructor in the new order of things.[67] Galbraith also recommended a new rector for St. Michael's, Father David Leigh, a young, scholarly Jesuit who had earned his doctorate in English, like himself. Leigh, quiet and unobtrusive, grew a beard to identify with the scholastics, harped on poverty to his subjects, and practiced it, and wrote articles when he was able, for exotic literary magazines. His almost black eyes, sometimes glazed over when he was deep in thought, seemed to bear some profound reproach. For me they held the sorrows and injustices of the world which he felt keenly, but kept to himself. On the surface Leigh appeared to be relaxed and brimming with humor.

One of the most famous of Oregon Jesuits was Father Dan Lyons. He had founded *Twin Circles*, a national Catholic weekly and for a period of at least ten years had been a strong voice raised in behalf of traditional or conservative Catholicism. Though a highly controversial personality, well known in this country and abroad, he retained the respect of many and the love of most. Dan had always been a selfless Jesuit with deep compassion for the poor. A biography of him was published in 1973.[68]

But Dan, too, was human. On September 17, 1975, he appeared at Galbraith's office and requested laicization with freedom to marry. No one had to tell Galbraith how this would be received by a cynical world. One week later the provincial sadly dispatched a report to Father General:

"In a news release dated September 12, 1975, the Religious News Service here in the United States stated that 'Father Daniel Lyons, S.J., a well-known Catholic newspaper columnist, and a prominent spokesman for conservative Catholicism, has requested an indefinite leave of absence from the Jesuits.' A later article found in *Time Magazine* this week adds the further note that Father Lyons has formally requested laicization with intent to marry. In substance both of these sources are correct."[69]

Father Galbraith that year had received eleven requests for departure from scholastics, and six from priests for laicization. Some of the latter, who had been approved for ordination by himself, had brought him grief, but none so much as the highly publicized case of Dan Lyons, who had been an inspiration to countless thousands for his eloquent defense of priestly celibacy.

---

*This was called Leo Martin House. Later tertianship was moved to 525 East Sinto, the former home of Father William Codd, which the province purchased in 1981. This, too, has been called Leo Martin Tertian House.

Thomas Riley Royce, tenth and present provincial of the Oregon Province.

Bronze statue of Bing Crosby, alumnus of Gonzaga University. This was dedicated on May 3, 1981.

Cornelius Mullen, patriarch of the province, the oldest Jesuit in our history. Born November 13, 1885, before Gonzaga University opened its doors.

Mater Dei Institute, Seminary for delayed vocations to the priesthood. Opened on Gonzaga University campus in 1981. On the right is Father John Evoy, Superior.

25

THE GOLDEN YEARS
1976–1982

It was appropriate that Father Lom Loyens, a naturalized citizen and as patriotic an American as any native, should become provincial of the Oregon Province during the Bicentennial Year. He was appointed to this office by Father General on March 8, 1976, and on June 15, he replaced Galbraith at the provincial's residence 2222 N.W. Hoyt Street.*

The mood of the province, like America's, had already changed. The bitterness of Vietnam and the Nixon scandals were behind us and the Boston Pops were entertaining wildly excited tens of thousands on the Commons with patriotic renditions like "Battle Hymn of the Republic" and "God Bless America."

Loyens eased into the scene so quietly that one moment he was not there and the next he was. He was warmly welcomed, and though he was handicapped somewhat for his lack of personal knowledge about membership, he was quick to learn. Within a few months he knew everyone by their first names, and each of us had come to think that we knew him as well. In the beginning he practiced one tiny little deception: he patted everyone on his back and told him that he was doing "a wonderful job." No one found fault with this and in the end, it brought much peace and joy to the province.

Frequently during those early months, Loyens approached the local paisano and asked, "How do I handle this?"

The local paisano was Brother Robert Calouri, secretary to many provincials and party to their secrets for the last decade. Also called "Cal" he was the confidante for many others and because of his great efficiency, his services were much sought by other communities, even the curia in Rome. He himself would make a good provincial, but for that he would have to be ordained, and he frequently said "I prefer to be a brother. That's what I like."

Cal has exercised so much influence on the province that I felt I should contemplate him at work. As I watched I wrote "Typical Pose of Brother Calouri," which reads as follows:

> "He sits at his typewriter, his job partner, with an electric bug in his
> ear, its string-like wire hanging beside him, like the cord of a hearing aid.
> He bounces one leg over the other in the manner of one who is using his
> hands so expertly he need not pay attention to them. His head scarely

*Father Galbraith subsequently became rector of the Jesuit School of Theology in Chicago.

561

moves. His lips form a firm line, indicating his no-nosense disposition at work, but his eyes are almost always deep pools of laughter, a kind of amused mocking in their mysterious depths. But they are honest eyes and they are truly windows of a gentle, understanding soul.

"Some would say his eating habits are eccentric. Left over zucchini or cheese for breakfast is, perhaps, noticeable. But he enjoys good food and he knows the difference between the good and the bad. He is as poetic in his tastes at the table as he is in the selection of a knit shirt. Uncommonly imaginative, one would have to say, but Cal is not a tempermental artist. He has the wisdom and the compassion of a good priest."[1]

Calouri had entered the Society by answering an advertisement in *The Sacred Heart Messenger*, which prompted a playful sally by Alex McDonald: "We should close our schools," he said, "and put ads in the *Messenger*." Cal had gone to Seattle University without knowing it was Jesuit related. He wasted his money there, he admitted, in two-bit gambling. Then he worked for a theatre while he went to business college, worked for a railroad, fought for the flag in Korea and finally decided he would rather work for God.[2]

Father Schultheis responded to his inquiry about the Jesuits. "Come see me," Schultie wrote. While they visited, Schultie twirled his rosary and periodically sighed, "Oh my, think it over." Schultie called Cal again and this time Cal was ready to sign up. He sold his Ford and entered the novitiate, so sure of himself that he burned all his bridges behind him.

He reminisced about the last provincial: "Ken would have done *anything* for his subjects," he said. "He was a very kind person. He went to dinner once and I said, 'You would give your life for any one of your guys,' and he answered, 'Bob, I would.' When he made his visitation he asked each one 'What is your relationship to the Lord?' and some who did not want to be challenged by renewal were not prepared for that."[3]

Perhaps the deadlock was terminology. There are words for most of us that have emotional undertones and sometimes we tend to resent new words or terms. "Renewal" was a word that some Jesuits did not like when it was used alone. They had become accustomed to "renewal of vows," a festive occasion with subtle, gut memories of fervor and the *Suscipe*, "Take me, Oh Lord." They had grown up with "reform Sundays," when the novice master or minister read off a list of our collective faults, which put us in stitches of laughter. But the naked word "renewal" had become associated with many unpleasant realities, like the loss of Sheridan and the Mount. No wonder some shunned it.

Loyens, like his predecessors, had to cope with the age-old problem, priorities in our ministries. During Kelley's administration, education, which had been taken for granted for over forty years as our most important apostolate, was openly challenged by those who regarded it as too structured. "Education ties us down," they said. They favored less structured activity, like social activism and missions, though some of them would not be caught dead in a difficult mission. During the Galbraith period, at least until the 32nd General Congregation, education, especially on the high school level, attracted very few of the younger Jesuits. Our university administrators, too, had more to worry about than others realized, for they were beginning to feel the bind, not only over escalating costs but over cutbacks in Jesuit availability. The future looked bleaker yet, as deanships and department heads passed from low-cost Jesuits to non-Jesuit teachers who were salaried. There had been a gradual shift in this direction, and by 1976 in both universities, the actual Jesuit teaching force was much less than half of the Jesuit communities. The number of younger Jesuits on these faculties had diminished shockingly, and this produced a morale problem, at least for those who bore the unpopular burden of teaching.

Fortunately, another trend appeared which worked to the advantage of both Oregon province universities. The influence of the Principle of Attraction, and the growing practice of inter-province cooperation in staffiing our institutions, brought a number of out-of-province Jesuits into our universities, profoundly influencing them both. When, for example, Father Bernard Coughlin of the Missouri Province was selected to be president of Gonzaga University, not only Gonzaga but the province gained an exceptionally competent administrator who was able to influence other Missourians, such as, Marty O'Keefe and J. J. Mueller to join his faculty. In like manner other young Jesuits arrived: from Maryland, Patrick Brannan and Michael Williams; from India, Aloysius Michael; from New York, Michael Siconolfi; and from California, James Arenz. An increment of eight young Jesuits, professionally competent and active, in one community like Gonzaga, helped to create a spirit which attracted other youthful members of our own province.

This new nationalism in Jesuit outlook and practice had been a primary objective of the Jesuit Conference established by the American provincials in 1972 and located in Washington, D.C. This new "Way of Jesuit Service" projected a three-phase development of Jesuit collective activity, presented as follows:

> *Phase I (1965 and before):* We had lived within a stable and very successful structure which had worked well for so long we tried to keep it. Its critics said that it was "sluggish in providing a grass roots feed-back."
>
> *Phase II (1965–1975):* According to the Conference this was a holding period.
>
> *Phase III (1975–   ):* Discernment, a common plan for our ministries growing out of discernment, a corporate mission responsibility of one Jesuit for another and of one community for another. Thus the Jesuit Conference was said to be six thousand Jesuits in union of minds and hearts, for a corporate mission. Not six to ten Jesuits in the office, nor the provincials who made up the board; but a communication or feedback with voluntary participation, designed to know what is going on in the world, in the church, and in the Society by "shared" experience.

The nationalist, or even internationalist, nature of this final innovation of structure is included here because it placed the Oregon Province in a new perspective. The province's singular isolation in a relatively unknown part of America, which is still a religious frontier after 140 years of Jesuit presence, had been altered in a subtle but positive manner. With administrative barriers breaking down, the future of the Oregon province was certain to benefit more than the heavily populated provinces.

Galbraith had helped to create the new structure; Loyens invited province participation in it. Thus its influence was being felt within the province without meetings, confrontations, or hard feelings.

"When a person becomes a provincial," Loyens said later, "he comes obviously into an operation that is ongoing, where directions pre-exist, where commitments have been made with a number of works in place and also with a staff and the ongoing apparatus of the Society's government in place."[4] Like other provincials, he faced what the Jesuit conference called the lack of clarity regarding his role. Did the prudent provincial give priority to *cura personalis*, the care of individuals in the province, or to *cura apostolica*, the care of apostolic works? "It seemed to me," he reflected, gazing absently into space, "there was need to allow some time for settling resentments, disappointments, and especially to foster greater union of minds and hearts."

"Out of this came several conclusions. One was the importance of my stressing *cura personalis* through the visitations. . . . Secondly, I became convinced that the *cura apostolica* for our works could be delegated to the Provincial Assistants for Formation, Social and Pastoral Ministries and Education, who then could act as observers, as facilitators, as gatherers of input, as well as advisors to me, and to provide relevant material for staff meetings."

Thus Loyens placed priority on visitations with the willing acceptance of the vast amount of time required to conduct them as he preferred to do. It seems to me this brings into focus the tone and rhythm of his entire provincialate. He was like the captain of a ship, giving comfort and strength to its crew after a passage through a dangerous storm.

In his concern for each he urged the taking of "sabbatical years," years for reviewing modern theology, and what he called, in one of his first letters to the province, "alternative experiences." Among these he listed a few recommendations:

—Visiting hospitals
—Visiting jails and prisons
—Matt Talbot Center
—Community Organizers
—Northwest Indian Missions
—Spanish speaking apostolate
—Clinical pastoral education
 program

—Community Day Care Center
—Alaska bush work
—Family planning counseling
—Working with mentally
 handicapped
—Horizons for justice
—Visiting the elderly
—Blanchett House[5]

Loyens never doubted the healing powers of alternative experiences and he encouraged and sometimes ordered his subjects to share in them. Though his term of office was brief, due to health as we shall see, he also made several difficult decisions that might have been classified as unfinished business for some years. He had gradually reorganized the provincial's staff. Ivan Hutton, who had been the provincial's executive assistant for several years, eager to complete his doctoral studies at Stanford University, was replaced by Joseph Perri, who seemed to fit into any slot they found for him. Perri was appointed on July 15, 1977. Peter Davis, a young, blonde Jesuit with blue eyes and a contagious laugh, replaced Roy Antunez, who became pastor at St. Joseph's in Yakima. Davis was appointed on August 11, 1977. Peter, preoccupied with the poor, got around the province by hitchhiking, even with strangers, which did not seem to worry anybody. Like Father Pat Carroll, who often did the same, he had a permissive guardian angel who allowed these adventures and protected both of them from disaster. Jack Fitterer, who had been President of the Association of Jesuit Colleges and Universities in Washington, D.C. since leaving Seattle University, replaced James Meehan, who became president of Jesuit High. Finally, Jack Kelley, former provincial, was drafted to replace Father McNulty on January 1, 1977 as province treasurer. Kelley inherited a well-organized office, an impressive Financial Committee composed of five laymen and three Jesuits, including McNulty, and the province debts.*

By this time, William Sullivan, a Wisconsin Jesuit, had replaced Edmund Ryan as president of Seattle University. Ryan, after the most grandiose inauguration in province history, served as president for less than one year. He became ill and had to be relieved of his duties in May, 1976.

One can imagine that Loyens felt very pleased with his new staff, and he had reason to be. However, as often happens in human affairs, there was one flaw. Jack Fitterer, who

*The members of the Province Finance Committee were: Mr. Louis L. Barbieri, Mr. William Boone, Mr. Richard De Donato, Mr. Leo Sherry, Jr., Mr. Ford Watkins, Father Frank Case, Father Gordon Moreland, and Father Edmund McNulty.

had been appointed to his position on August 27, 1977, quietly left the Society three months later. Brad Reynolds made it province news:

"Fr. Jack Fitterer left the Oregon Province on Saturday morning, November 26th. He was granted an official leave of absence by the Provincial, Fr. Lom Loyens, and was relieved of his post as Provincial Assistant for Education.

"According to Bishop Morris Arnold, Suffraget Bishop for the Episcopal Diocese of Massachusetts, Fr. Fitterer has requested to be accepted into the Episcopal priesthood. Bishop Arnold told the EXCHANGE that Fr. Fitterer has already been accepted into Trinity Church, an Episcopal Church in Boston, by Rector Dr. Thomas Blair. 'He has been received, I understand, by the Rector of Trinity Church in Boston,' Arnold said, 'as a baptized member of the Church.'"[6]

Capable only of gentleness, though he was deeply hurt, Loyens bade Fitterer farewell with kind words. In the months that followed he could not bear to discuss the subject.

Several weeks later Mount St. Michael's was finally sold. Father Kelley reported the details to his Financial Committee on January 16, 1978:

"Mount Saint Michael's was sold to the Pillar Corporation on December 30, 1977. The terms of the sale were as follows: Sale price, $1,500,000. Downpayment $255,000. Contract balance, $1,185,000 with interest at 8% per annum from December 30, 1977, payable as follows: $121,700 or more on or before June 1, 1979, and a like sum or more on or before June 1 of each and every year thereafter until paid in full. Commission, $90,000, with $30,000, paid on signing and a $60,000 note from buyer in lieu of commission. Real Estate Excise Tax, $15,000. Title insurance $3,083.63. ½ closing fee, $525.50. ½ attorney's fees for drafting Security Agreement, Financing Statement and Bill of Sale, $75.00. Revenue Stamp Fee, $1,500. Real Estate Tax adjustment ($7.82)."

To this Kelley added some practical details. "The Jesuits living at the Mount may remain until March 30, 1978, and three acres with water rights were reserved for the Jesuit cemetery."[7]

Kelley also wrote to the general, reminding him that in its present condition the Mount would require more than one million dollars investment to bring it up to the safety code, and that the income from the sale was badly needed for the support of scholastics and retired men in the province.[8]

There were sixteen Jesuits in residence at the Mount at this time, most of them retired, or ill, under the care of Brother Tom O'Shea. Each was given his choice of community in the province for his future residence. Jesuit personal belongings were gathered and packed, and then on February 18, 1978, an auction was conducted. Some five hundred people swarmed over the place, inspecting the old desks, chairs, pitchforks and other miscellanea, looking for a bargain. About six thousand dollars was raised, enough to relocate all the Jesuits, if not to take care of them.[9] All was well on Sunday night, March 4. The Jesuits had moved out the previous day, leaving some baggage behind, with the intention of retrieving it on the following day. Packed in the boxes were a tabernacle, a number of ciboria, chalices and a very large collection of first-class relics of the saints with related documentation. On the next morning, March 5, all had mysteriously disappeared. Reynolds reported this too.

"The Superior of the Fatima Crusades group, now living at the Mount told F. Paul Luger, the Jesuit rector that someone called Sunday evening, claiming to be from the Jesuit Novitiate, and asked that a door to the Jesuit portion of the building be left unlocked."[10]

These precious Jesuit heirlooms have never been recovered and to this day this mystery is a subject of much speculation. An inside job? an iconoclast? members of a cult? Whatever or whoever, there is something insidious about this theft of holy things. Only one point is clear: the thief knew all about the contents of those boxes left behind.

Loyens was not the kind to cry over lost causes. He had received word in this same month of the archbishops' and bishops' approval for his pet project, common faculties for Region XII. This incredible breakthrough achieved largely through the efforts of the Oregon Provincial, requires some explanation. Priests, by church law, must have the local bishop's permission to work in his diocese. This permission is called "faculties." In Alaska for some years, because of a shortage of priests and the uncertain boundaries of the dioceses, it was a practice for all bishops there to give faculties to all priests of each diocese. In other words, when one priest obtained faculties in Juneau, he automatically had them for both Anchorage and Fairbanks. It was Lom Loyens' hope to extend this practice to all of Ecclesiastical Region XII.* Notice of the bishop's approval of this was conveyed to the priests of the province in May 1978:

> "All priests in the diocese of Region XII who have received faculties for preaching and hearing confessions in one diocese now have the same faculties, applicable in all the dioceses of the Region. The policy of reciprocity was agreed upon by the Bishops of the ten dioceses at a meeting in early April.

> "The request for reciprocal faculties was initiated by Fr. Lom Loyens, the Oregon Jesuit Provincial, at the Regional meeting of Bishops and Religious Superiors held last fall. 'I'm happy the bishops have reached this agreement,' Loyens said, 'as it indicates the type of cooperation we support in the Region. It's too bad we couldn't get something like it for the whole United States.'

> "The agreement, which covers the dioceses in the five northwestern states, goes into effect immediately. The directive issued by the Bishops read: 'All diocesan and religious priests who are on a residential assignment in any diocese of Region XII, that is, within the States of Alaska, Idaho, Montana, Oregon and Washington, and who have the faculties for preaching and hearing confessions in that diocese or residence, thereby also enjoy the same faculties in each of the dioceses of Region XII."[11]

By this one stroke, the administration of bishops' chanceries and the provinces of all religious orders were greatly simplified, in keeping with the objectives of Vatican II.

On April 24 of this same year, Loyens dispatched a significant letter to the province, which marked a new beginning of the Society's long-time commitment to education. As noted above, as a priority this had fallen into disfavor with many. Fortunately the staff of

---

*Region XII was coterminus with The Oregon Province.

the Jesuit conference, alarmed by the crisis which had begun to threaten the Jesuits' activity, especially in higher education, published a report which had been four years in the making. This report, "The Jesuit Mission in Education" was sponsored by all of the American provincials.

> "In this letter," the report began, "we provincials are writing directly to our brother Jesuits serving the twenty-eight Jesuit institutions of higher education in the United States. We will speak frankly of our Jesuit aims in higher education, and we hope thus to foster, as fully as possible, our cooperation and common identity in this apostolate.
>
> "This letter is an expression of our corporate commitment to that apostolate. For our part, we pledge ourselves to continue preparing and assigning young Jesuits to this important apostolic work."[12]

Loyens in his own correspondence with the province regarded the report as "a conclusion to a painful period of evaluation and self-examination." He stressed the need for the province's support of higher education and requested that "our men in formation, as an invitation, to consider that specialized work and to remain open to the call of the Lord in genuine availability."[13]

The provincial's words were carefully chosen. He had no desire to create a sudden rush to the colleges, leaving the high schools and the missions high and dry. A dedicated missionary, struggling in a difficult mission like northern Alaska, was still an ideal. There were some like Father Charles Saalfeld who had gradually moved from high-school teaching in the province to teaching in Fairbanks, then to mission work in the bush. The Laudwein twins, too, Fathers Jim and Joe, a pair of zealous, down-to-earth Jesuits from Spokane, had followed the same route. Another was Father John Gurr, who was in a sense an escapee of the classroom. Gurr, known as the absent-minded professor, despite his learned manner and doctorate in philosophy, took to the bush like a horse to clover.

Charlie Saalfeld, as Father Frank McGuigan of Fairbanks noted, died in the bush at about this time.

> "His body," said McGuigan, "was found on the shore of the Yukon River just outside the village of Nulato three days after he had been left off by Fr. Jim Sebesta. Because of darkness and high winds Jim had dropped Charlie off there in the event he needed help in taking off again on his continued flight to Kaltag. Jim had brought Fr. Saalfeld to Koyukuk, and was returning him to his parish at Nulato. Father never reached the village, and due to the high winds, the villagers never heard the sound of the plane as it landed and took off again. His frozen body was found a hundred feet from where he stepped out of the airplane and waved 'goodbye' to Fr. Jim. As the autopsy confirmed, Fr. Charles Saalfeld had died of a massive heart attack, Sunday, March 5, 1978. His body was discovered three days later by one of his devoted parishioners. . . . After the funeral services which were offered at Sacred Heart Cathedral in Fairbanks, the people of Nulato asked Father Frank Fallert, the Jesuit Superior of Alaska, to return Saalfeld to their village for burial. Bishop Whelan and Fallert concurred that Charlie should be returned to 'his people.' It was their gentle, yet firm persistence that brought Saalfeld's three sisters, Bishop Whelan, and Fallert all back to Nulato for the final liturgies for this Jesuit priest.

"Despite the snowy frozen ground of Nulato's hillside cemetery, the grave for the Pastor of Nulato was finished to exact dimensions for an outer box. At the burial, Father's three sisters watched as the unadorned casket was placed on birch poles across the grave and gently lowered."[14]

Jesuit deaths, as the province aged, became more commonplace. They seldom occasioned little more than comment and on obituary by faithful Neill, who sometimes signed himself "the Old Meany of the Province." Neill's obituaries, like his cartoons and poetry (?) usually contained some forthright comments about the deceased, which only proved they had been human; but there were those who held fast to the thesis that history is intended only to edify. They objected to Neill's candid presentations and for awhile, drove him out of business. But popular demand brought him back. As before, he made it a point, taking pride in his profession, of interviewing those more likely to die, while he still had an opportunity. A few members of the province, it was said, intimidated by the awesome burden of truth, conveyed by Meany's obituaries, were praying for longer lives than his, which is to say, they wanted him to die before they did.

Even Meany's resources were stretched when three Jesuits at Seattle University died within three days. James Cowgill died on Monday, January 8, 1979 at 10:30 p.m. Arthur Earl died on Wednesday, at 2:00 a.m., and Arby Lemieux followed the latter into eternity fifteen minutes later.

The funeral for all was held simultaneously in St. James Cathedral which needless to say, was as crowded for the ceremony as it would have been for the obsequies of an archbishop or a rock singer. In Spokane the weather was so severe that the burials had to be postponed for some days. Father Leo Kaufmann, one of the province's most vocal wags and Seattle's new rector, expressed some concern about this, for, he stated, with mock seriousness in such a delicate matter, that it cost more to keep the coffins at the undertakers than the *per diem*.* In other words, it cost more to be dead than alive.

Kaufmann became rector on June 29, 1978. Just one year later Father Thomas Royce became rector of the Gonzaga University community.[15] He replaced Vincent Beuzer, who had survived six years. Like Armand Nigro, his associate in the Department of Religious Studies, Beuzer frequently overextended himself by conducting innumerable retreats and lectures all over the western hemisphere. Armand included Australia and New Zealand as well. Beuzer's assistant, the Father Minister of the Community, was Father Emmett Painter, commonly called "E.B." Beuzer enjoyed talking and E.B. got his kicks by putting up signs and smoking cigars.

The new rector, Tom Royce, was energetic, but uncontentious, a kind of well-oiled dynamo of activity that never squeaked. Though he had lived in Rome two years, acquiring his doctorate in philosophy, he walked and talked with the simplicity of a novice. There was a homespun meekness about him, a kind of early-American plainess that suggested a Tom Sawyer or a Huckleberry Finn in his manhood. Mark Twain would not have approved of this, because Royce's origins were mostly Irish. On festive occasions Tom may reluctantly admit that his esteemed paternal grandfather, a well-known medic, was of English descent. His father, however, implacably committed to his Celtic purity, conveniently interpreted English as "Welsh" which gave him much comfort and a benign kind of self-delusion which he carried to his grave.[16]

The full name of Tom's father was James Emmett Royce, as Irish as he could make it, and for his mother Lucy Riley Royce. Both were from Chicago, where they were married in 1911. James Emmett, as determined regarding his occupation as he was about his origins,

---

*The *per diem* is the cost per day in Jesuit communities.

spurned an opportunity to follow his father in medicine and travelled west instead. In time he became a trusted confidante of Bishop White and for some years served as editor and publisher of the diocesan weekly called *The Inland Catholic*.

Tom was born on March 5, 1926, the fourth child in the family and the second from the last of five. His older brother James entered the Society ten years before him, in 1933, and set a pace which might have made Tom "Jim's brother" if Tom had not made his own paths.

When Tom was read in as rector on July 1, 1979, he sat in front of the altar in Jesuit House, watching the reader of the Roman documents with great curiosity and a wide grin on his face, apparently much amused by what the general was saying about him.

At Gonzaga that summer, there was considerable discussion about an infirmary for the use of the community. E.B., who liked making plans the way he liked making signs, had got it into his head that an infirmary *had to be built* in Jesuit House and he would not let anyone forget it. He employed an architect, called meetings and wrote reports. In a word, he nagged everyone until this infirmary or "Health Center" was built. Everybody was happy about it once the war was over. The project was finally completed on February 4, 1980, when the first nurse, Dana Brainerd reported for duty. Dana, with a head of radiant golden hair and a heart as soft as wax, ordered supplies and checked in her first patient on February 12, 1980.[17] This was Father Tom Larkin, who had taught at Gonzaga since anybody could remember. Her next patient was Father John Fox from Alaska, who had lived alone for forty years and resisted every effort of Dana to baby him.

During the same summer of 1979, the novitiate was moved again. It had been decided that the Convent of the Holy Child was too large for the foreseeable future. Its cost, too, $500,000, was prohibitive. Some consideration had been given to the purchase of St. Leo's Convent in Tacoma, no longer used.[18] At this point another convent near at hand, belonging to St. Ignatius parish in Portland, attracted the novice director's attention. Father Pat O'Leary thought it was perfect, but the pastor of St. Ignatius, Ken Krall, reported that this convent was not as yet available. Several retired Sisters of the Holy Names, who had taught at the parish school, lived there and were reluctant to move. Two large residences in the parish were available, however, and these were purchased for temporary use. One, which was designated as Xavier House, bordering on the Loyola Retreat House grounds, was occupied by six novices and Pat O'Leary. The assistant to the novice master, Father John Fuchs, was housed in a wing of the retreat house, and the rest of the community occupied Faber House on Tibbets street. These were the minister, Edmund McNulty, the patriarch Connie Mullen, and three faithful brothers who had been at the novitiate for many years, Frank Mauer, Steve Karpinski and Larry Bies.[19]

For two years the novitiate survived in this fashion. But plans were gradually worked out with the Holy Names Sisters by Father McNulty, who remodeled Faber House to their complete satisfaction. A deal was then struck with the parish. Finally approval was granted by the parish council and a half-dozen other officials, and O'Leary took possession of the St. Ignatius convent. In the summer of 1981 he gathered his community under one roof.[20] This was the ninth site for our novitiate, compared to the fourth site only for our scholasticate.* Either one or both confirmed our faithful observance of the rule that we should be willing and ready to live in any part of the world where necessity required it.

---

*The nine novitiate sites were: St. Francis Xavier on the Willamette River; St. Joseph's Mission, Yakima Valley; St. Francis Regis Mission; Sacred Heart Mission; Sacred Heart Novitiate at Los Gatos; Sheridan, Oregon; Portland Site I; Portland Site II; and, finally, Portland Site III. The scholasticate was first located at St. Ignatius, Montana, then Gonzaga, Mount St. Michael's, and finally Gonzaga.

GOLDEN YEARS

In December, 1979, there was good news and bad news. The good news, announced by Brad Reynolds, who missed nothing as he raced about the province with his camera slung over his shoulder, was that Matteo Ricci College, having attracted national attention, received a major award. "A Certificate of Achievement from the Academy of Educational Development" was presented by former president Gerald Ford to both Father Thomas Healy and Father William Sullivan, who went to New York for the occasion. With the award was a ten thousand dollar cash prize from the Atlantic Richfield Corporation.

Though a rector of a long standing community of ninety years, Healy, by this time, had only eight Jesuits as his subjects, one of whom, Father James Hess, was in retirement at Mount St. Vincent. Another, Father Robert Pospisil was an artist in residence, and a third, Father Thomas Sullivan, was destined to die in the following July. That left two priests Tom Bunnell and John Foster, and three scholastics including David Thomas and Michael Treleaven. The other scholastic left the Society. The rest of the faculty, thirty-three in number, were non-Jesuit.

The bad news was Portland. It was twofold, and I suspect one helped create the other. First, there was the St. Ignatius Mission land case which had been dragging on for ten years. You will recall that Father Kelley as well as Pedro Arrupe in Rome, approved the sale of the mission ranch land to the Pack River Lumber Company in 1969. The sale was challenged by the Flathead Tribe, who contended that this land reverted to the tribe when it was no longer used for the purpose for which it was given, the education of the Indians. Because of the litigation, Pack River withheld further payments on the land. Thus we found ourselves in a three-way dispute, willing to settle with the parties of both sides but unable to obtain an agreement with either one.

On December 21, 1978, Mr. Leo Sherry, Jr., our attorney in the case, and member of our Financial Committee, informed Father Kelley that the Indians had rejected a cash settlement and wanted nothing but the land, and that the lumber company "was unwilling to sell the land [back to us] at an acceptable figure." Sherry recommended adjudication as the only current solution.[21]

There seems to have been no doubt that, despite the tribal objections, the Jesuits had full title to this land. While it was true that the original grant of the controversial thousand acres contained a reversion clause, the Federal Government in 1910 *issued deeds in fee simple* granting to the Montana Catholic Mission, S.J. 640 acres of land, the Providence Sisters 320 acres and the Ursuline Sisters 320 acres. As time passed additional pieces of land were presented as gifts, or were acquired by purchase by Montana Catholic Missions. Thus 240 acres were purchased from the Ursulines and in 1959 Mount St. Michael's purchased 240 acres from the Providence Sisters for $34,000.* By 1965 the total acreage owned by Montana Catholic Missions had increased to 3,100 acres, of which one thousand acres were contested.

While we negotiated, the tribe changed its position several times. The Society, meanwhile, set up a fund to settle this claim, which was a constant source of anxiety to the entire province. This money has been destined for a retirement fund to pay for the care of old and sick Jesuits, who could no longer be cared for at the Mount or Sheridan. Now there were grave doubts regarding the province's ability to provide what was required.

In November, 1979, Kelley made a final offer to settle with the tribe, a half-million dollar certified check or judication in court. Reynolds tells us what followed:

"While the tribe did not respond to the letter, they did file a legal suit against the Society, claiming the land as theirs. However, a short time later

*The province purchased this 240 acres from the Mount.

570

the Tribal Council reversed its earlier decision to sue and in a 6 to 4 vote, decided to drop the lawsuit, and accept the settlement of $500,000.

"The final settlement with the tribe was reached at the end of November, when a check for the full amount was delivered to a representative of the tribe in Missoula, Montana.

"According to Fr. Jack Kelley, the Society will now seek a final settlement from the Pack River Lumber Company, asking for the $180 thousand still owed, plus approximately $85 thousand on accrued interest. A deadline, established by the original contract with the company, is set for January 17 of this year. Kelley said that if Pack River is unable to pay the amount, then the land reverts back to the Society of Jesus.

"Kelley added that some settlement must still be reached for the money received from the sale of land which the tribe did not lay claim to, approximately 2,100 acres. Some members of the province maintain the money should be set aside for Indian missionary activities in the Oregon Province.

"Once the financial settlement has been reached with Pack River Lumber Company, the final disposition of the remaining money will eventually be settled by the Provincial and his consultors."[22]

Kelley said later: "The decision of the Provincial and his consultors to compensate the Indians with a gift of $500,000 was based not on any legal obligation but simply on good will and the desire to provide a more amenable climate in which our missionaries could work."[23]

"The cool one-half million dollars," as Reynolds called it, was one of the toughest decisions an Oregon provincial ever made. This decision, ultimately, was from Loyens who had to choose: this money will be used for retired and sick Jesuits who had given their life's work, trusting in the Society for the future, or to the Flathead Tribe, which had no legal claim to it. Once Loyens had made his choice, not a voice was raised to oppose it. It was a choice, which, as Kelley said, "we could all be comfortable with." It was also a great act of faith in God's providence.

By this time Loyens had succumbed, somewhat, to serious health problems. In 1973 he had contracted "London flu" and there were some in Alaska who said he had never recovered. Tests revealed that he had a serious case of stomach ulcers, which surprised no one, since he seldom ate breakfast or lunch, and even at dinner, ate very little. On December 7, 1979, he appointed Father Perri as acting provincial, then left for Belgium to breathe his native air, which he hoped would cure him. When he departed, he left behind him a united province. Not everyone was a saint yet, but there was peace and harmony. Jack Kelley had paved the way for this be accepting change and by directing the province into new grooves. Ken Galbraith had made spiritual renewal a reality by providing special retreats and spiritual institutes and by encouraging new forms of community liturgies. Lom Loyens, too, had done much by reviving burned-out Jesuits with his "alternative experiences." He had called more than fifty to solemn vows, had released many to make tertianship, and had assigned those formerly living at the Mount in isolation to new communities where they were happier.

In the immediate future there was one complication: a meeting of all of the American provincials with Father General was scheduled for the week of May 18, 1980, in Spokane. Perri, of course, was at his best in organizing this seven-day event, which required perfect timing. Humanly speaking, Perri performed perfectly, but a great surprise in store for everyone, shattered his well-laid plans.

First there was Loyens. After returning to the province he left again for Rome on March 19, 1980, to consult with Father General on the following day. He returned to Portland on March 26. In a letter to the province on April 7 he wrote: "I am deeply sorry to inform you that my health remains poor and that I must continue with medication and rest to solve the gastro-intestinal problems.

"Upon the advice of the doctors and after consultation I have approached Father General to acquaint him with my situation. He has agreed that I should not continue as Provincial and he has asked us to present him with a terna as soon as possible. . . . As for myself, I shall follow the medical advice and continue to rely on Father Joseph E. Perri, as Acting Provincial to handle the ordinary affairs of the Province."[24]

A week later Perri announced Lom's departure for Belgium for an indefinite period of rest. He called off a scheduled meeting of province superiors, and girded himself for the week of May 18.

The meeting was to be conducted at Gonzaga's retreat center, Waikiki, which was, ordinarily, an ideal suburban haven for privacy. Joe had arranged for Tom Royce and myself to join him in meeting Father General on his arrival at the Spokane Airport at 11:30 on that Sunday morning. The weather was ideal as we entered the terminal, fifteen minutes before Arrupe's plane was due. Joe, having coffee with several novices, greeted us and I went up the ramp alone, just as our guest appeared with other Jesuits from New York. As I took Father General's baggage he said to me: "Your mountain, what is its name, St. Helens, has erupted! How far is that from here?"

"Too far," I said complacently, and soon we were all inspecting the quarters at Waikiki, which was brilliant in the late spring sunshine.

Mount St. Helens was about 250 miles southwest of Spokane. About 3:30 in the afternoon that Sunday, the sun was gradually blotted out and Spokane's sky became as black as midnight. Two hours later the ash began to fall, an estimated hundred million tons of it fell over the Spokane region, closing all roads and streets and even the railroad lines. Planes could neither come nor go. Spokane was isolated. Washington was declared a disaster area.

Some Jesuits never arrived for the meeting. Others arrived late, after a hectic round-about trip by car, coming in from the north, instead of the west. Father General cancelled his public appearances. Fortunately, clean-up work in the city had progressed sufficiently for him and his assistant Father Gerry Sheehan to spend Friday afternoon and evening with Gonzaga Jesuits at Jesuit House. First he spoke to us in Hughes Hall, fervently, energetically, affectionately, like an aroused messiah, whose hours are numbered. He described his recent audiences with the Pope, John Paul II, and explained, when we asked, why Jesuits in more recent years had not made elaborate plans for the future. "The world," he said, "is changing too fast. We are only a small part of it, we cannot control it nor foresee where it is going. *We have to make our paths by walking on them.*"

Then he had dinner with us and spent the evening in our familiar recreation room as casually as any visitor, waving his arms as he talked and charming us all with his warmth and simplicity. The next morning the planes were flying again and he left us all with reflections about a thin, little Basque, who was called the Black Pope.

There were rumors concerning our new provincial. Some said it would be Perri and others that it would be Royce. Perri it was reported, had diabetes. Besides, Royce was younger. On June 2, 1980, Perri dispatched a notice to all members of the province: "Today," he said, "Very Reverend Father General, Pedro Arrupe, appointed Father Thomas R. Royce Provincial of the Oregon Province, effective immediately. Father Royce will take up his office on Friday, June 13th, the Feast of the Sacred Heart."[25]

In his first letter to the province, Tom issued a "call for love of Jesus and dedication to

Him and in His Spirit an appeal to work together."[26] In the same letter he announced his priorities: "two of the most important immediate issues facing this province," he wrote, were "the issue of new vocations to the Society and the care for the infirm of the province." No one could dispute either.

It was clear from this that Royce intended to be a provincial who placed *cura personalis* first. This was heartening news for a large silent minority who had borne the burdens of controversy without having formal opportunities to represent their views. There were Jesuits like Joe O'Connell, who had his doctorate in French literature from the Sorbonne, yet he served as a hospital chaplain for years without a murmur or protest. Fred Kohler spent decades, supervising the maintainance of buildings. John V. Murphy, known as "V. Rev." served in administration and marriage counseling and Raymond Talbott was a chaplain on skid row in Seattle, where he was beaten three times by inebriates younger then he. There were Armed Forces chaplains, also, like Frank Walsh and John Graisy, both Lieutenant Colonels in the Air Force for twenty years. There were teachers like "Fearless Frank" Falsetto who taught physics in high school and college for over thirty years, with only (let us say) an occasional comment about the system. Dave Olivier, Charles Weiss and John McDonald were three other teachers, whose quiet, unsung labors in the classroom, hidden from view, deprived them of opportunities to make speeches in province assemblies. Provincials in times of stress had listened to these men, and scores of others like them, but those who raised stronger voices in favor of, or against, were the ones who got his attention. Now that peace had come and most controversies were forgotten, everyone got attention, some, perhaps, more than they wanted.

John McClusky had lamented that there are no more characters in the province. Almost bald, but with a heavy white, straggly beard, John looks like a hard-rock prospector until, wearing red trousers, he rides his bicycle around the campus, the epitome of an eccentric professor. He is no character, of course. Steve Kuder in his black beard and Dutch boy's cap, peering through his rimmed, thick glasses with a Rip Van Winkle look of surprise, is no character either. Neither is Don Sharp, who takes snuff like Cataldo seventy years ago, and laughs with a booming voice that identifies his whereabouts in the house as soon as he enters. Don cooks pork roasts for the scholastics and diets on grapefruit. Another no-character is Jim Wilson of Woodburn, who draws cartoons and writes like this: "Frs. Tim Kaufman and Pete Davis are cruising late at night the Willamette Valley looking for a pig. Lock your doors! Keep an eye on your neighbor! This might be the last time you will see your neighbor. Tim and Pete's 'Jesuit Pig Out Dinners' went on the auction block on Feb. 20."[27] These young men are not characters nor is Brother George McMonagle, whose room has so many shrines and holy pictures he can scarcely crawl into bed.

There will always be characters, thank God, and in a way the new provincial is one of them. With his pixylike smile, his fascination with exotic people, like those he met on "Night Walk" and his serene acceptance of anything, anything at all to wear, eat or sleep in, he qualifies to rank with some of our greatest characters, those that rose to the top, like Joseph Piet.

As he would say now, there were two issues which he himself would have to resolve. First he had to organize his own team. The initial problem here, he wrote, was that Peter Davis, Pastor at Woodburn and Provincial Assistant for Social and Pastoral Ministries had too much to do.[28] He preferred his work at Woodburn, where he was presently preoccupied with his youth group and the acquisition of the old train depot for a youth center. He needed one dollar to buy this, and $20,500 to move and remodel it.[29] To facilitate this and other activities at St. Luke's parish, Royce appointed Tom McCarthy as Assistant

Provincial for Pastoral Ministries, leaving the rest for Peter. Joe Perri was retained in his dual role of Executive Assistant to the Provincial and Assistant for Education, which he had undertaken when Jack Fitterer disappeared from the scene. Father Jim Wyse, the Assistant Provincial for Formation, had about two hundred Jesuits in his care. "I am more and more amazed at this staff and the amount [of work] that they do; this especially includes Jack Kelley, Bob Calouri and their lay assistants."[30] In charge of the Jesuit Seminary Association was Frank Masterson, still as enthusiastic for his difficult work as he had been for several years, with phenominal success.* Lee Kapfer, on leave from Africa, was his docile assistant. Finally there was Tony Harris fresh from graduate studies, whom Royce appointed "Vocation Director." Masterson would produce money and Harris would recruit many Jesuits; then we would all sail into the sunset singing "Ave Maria Stella."

Less pleasant, in a way, was Royce's decision regarding the final disposition of the St. Ignatius Mission Land Case. This involved approximately $200,000 remaining from the sale of the mission ranch to the Pack River Lumber Company. By this time members of the province no longer felt emotionally disturbed about the matter, though some expected the decision to favor the province's ownership of this money. The province had received $460,000, plus interest for the total sale to Pack River. Of this, the province paid $500,000 to the Flathead Tribe to clear the title of one thousand acres. This was more than the province had received for the acreage involved, so it was obvious that if the $200,000 were paid to the mission, the province would lose over $100,000. This would have to come from some other sources. In other words, to sell the ranch, the province would lose over $100,000 if the mission were awarded the $200,000.

After careful and candid consideration, the provincial and his consultors decided in favor of the mission.[31] Thus the balance of money from the sale was turned over to St. Ignatius and the province took the loss. In a memorandum to superiors of the province, Father Kelley later presented a brief report on the provinces' finances, as a result of this decision. "Our total net loss for the year 1980–1981 was $153,663," he said. "Here again we should note that this year we had to make good the St. Ignatius Mission Claim of $198,742."[32]

Since Royce as rector at Gonzaga had been plucked, so to speak, to become provincial, a new rector was required. Frank Costello was appointed and Patrick Ford replaced "E.B." as Minister. By this time Marcia Renouard secretary to both, had become so efficient in conducting the community's routine affairs, like visitors and health insurance, that both the rector and minister were free for other employment. Pat, who had his doctorate in education from Stanford, was assigned by the university president to organize and direct a kind of continuing doctoral program in education, which Seattle University had adopted several years before.

Frank Costello, too, was given a special assignment. On August 31, 1980, the provincial appointed him chairman of the Golden Year Committee. "I wish," Royce wrote to him, "to give the committee a clear charge. The committee will study and present a plan for steps leading to, and events to be coordinated as part of, Our Golden Year. I would like to see a plan presented to my consultors by January 9, 1981."[33] In this committee there was broad province representation: Peter Ely, Pat Flannigan, Roger Gillis, Tony Keaty, John Kindall, Gordon Moreland, Joe Obersinner, Joe Perri, Louie Renner and Harold Small.

"The objectives," Royce continued, "we have outlined for 'Our Golden Year' celebration are (1) an appreciation of our heritage, the sources and strengths of our spirit as a

*In a memorandum to the province in October, 1980, Father Masterson reported on results of the Seminary Association's fund raising. Added to the Scholarship Fund for the year 1979–80 was $164,783.46. Average cost per year in Jesuit training had gone up to approximately $8,500, a noticeable increase from the three-to five-hundred dollars in the good old days.

province; (2) a realistic assessment of the challenges and resources today in the light of the Christ of the Gospel message and the General Congregation 32; and, (3) the stimulation of hope in our common response to the call of the Church in the Northwest and throughout the world for a deeper faith in the Christian enterprise."[34]

It is plain from this directive that the provincial and his advisors did not have in mind an ordinary golden jubilee banquet with chicken a la king and long speeches. His call, as he noted, was for a spiritual renewal, which drew strength from the past, as well as the present.

The committee met three times and submitted an eleven-page proposal to Royce which contained the "Golden Year Statement of a Theme":

"Celebration of the Golden Year of the Oregon Province of the Society of Jesus is an act of gratitude and an act of hope. Grateful for all that God has accomplished in our history, we are moved with confidence toward the future. This celebration focuses on our heritage in order that we might recognize, and in our own time emulate the vision, courage, and generosity of men who saw apostolic opportunities and responded to them.

"By dwelling on our history, we deepen the realization that it is truly *our* history. It is not *they*, but *we*, who have experienced these fifty years. The union of minds and hearts that we desire emerges out of our corporate experience.

"While we confess to failures in vision, in courage, in generosity, our attention is drawn especially to the action of God's grace, not to its absence. Humbled by this awareness, we celebrate what is good in order that we may find courage and inspiration. We are willing to risk some 'triumphalism' in the spirit of the *Contemplatio ad Amorem*. Saint Ignatius, himself, has taught us that gratitude is past, we cannot have hope for the future. Hope, rather than nostalgia, is our theme. We do not look at the past to lament its passing. We attend to our roots because they remain the permanent, vital source of the Ignatian charisma which nourishes our personal life in Christ and our apostolic labors with *Christ ad Majorem Dei Gloriam*."*

At one time along the way there was a proposal made that we should add to this sublime manifestation something about our being sinners, but since everyone already knows that, this public confession was voted down.

The recommendations of the committee, then, were as follows:

    I. *History of the Province* by Wilfred Schoenberg.
    II. *Priesthood Days, at ordination in Seattle,* June 13, 1981.
    III. *Jesuit Spirituality Days at Novitiate* in December 1981.
    IV. *Seattle-Wide Celebration* with a Concert Mass composed by Kevin Waters, to be held in Seattle about February 2, 1982.
    V. *Video Tape: Interviews with Older Jesuits,* Bob Lyons with help from Tim Kaufman, Mark Hoelsken, Gary Uhlencott and Ted Fortier.
    VI. *Travelling Slide Show* to be prepared by Brad Reynolds, Gary Uhlencott and Mark Hoelsken.

---

*Originally drafted by Gordon Moreland, the Statement of a Theme was revised and approved by the committee on November 6, 1980, by telephone conference.

This program, as proposed, was formally accepted by the provincial and his consultors, and in May 1981, Father Robert Grimm of Seattle University was appointed "Coordinator for the Oregon Province Jubilee Celebration slated to run from June 1981 to July 1982.[35]

Another major event, meanwhile, occupied the province. On February 26, 1981, for the first time in history, a Pope visited the Province, or at least touched down upon it. Pope John Paul II, having visited the Philippines, Guam and Japan, made a brief three-hour stop in Anchorage, Alaska, while his plane was scheduled for refueling. Alighting there at 10:40 a.m. the Holy Father was met at the airport by appropriate dignitaries, including some cardinals, and was taken by motorcade to the cathedral in downtown Anchorage. Mass in a former air strip, made into a park, followed. This open-air liturgy was attended by forty thousand eager Alaskans, who defied the Arctic winds and below freezing weather. Concelebrating Mass with the Pope was Archbishop Francis Hurley, Bishop Robert Whelan and a large number of priests, who flocked in from remote missions to share in one of the greatest events of their lives.

Harold Grief was there, a coat over his alb. Jim Sebesta was there also, grinning from ear to ear and carrying his coat. Jim Laudwein, one of the twins, his face as broad as an Eskimo's, and lighted up by a happy smile, hurried through the crowd to be on time. One surprise visitor was Bob Rekofke, of Big Sandy, Montana. He appeared with a polar bearskin rug, not for warmth, but as a gift from the Alaska Polish Community to the Pope. Purchased for $3,500 in Lakeside, Montana, where there are no polar bears, this rug was hand carried to the Holy Father by Rekofke at the request of the donors. Thus Rekofke's face appeared to be as complacent as any of the Jesuits, who admitted great admiration for his ingenuity in getting around. Brad Reynolds was there, too. It was not often one could take pictures of the Pope with his forgotten Jesuits on the rim of Christianity. Finally, there was Tom Royce himself, to greet the Pope for members of the province.[36] Royce had already made an impressive impact on the province. He had appointed Joe Maguire, "The Marrying Parson" who conducted innumerable weddings, as the rector of Bellarmine. He named Frank Case as rector of Seattle University to replace Leo Kaufmann who had undergone open heart surgery, and Gerard Chapdelaine as the rector of Gonzaga Prep to replace Pat Kenny, who became the new president of Jesuit High. In his first two years Royce appointed or submitted names for approval in Rome for twelve superiors, almost half the total number in the province.

At Gonzaga University, meanwhile, two major developments were taking place. The university had acquired a television channel and Bob Lyons, initially sponsored by the province in graduate studies in communications, arrived on the campus in late spring, 1981, with a large truckload of sophisticated television equipment. Under Lyon's supervision, all major buildings were connected by cable, so that broadcasts could be made from every corner of the campus. When Dussault's ambitious project, Bing Crosby's immortal pipe on his bronze statue was dedicated, Lyons supervised a live broadcast of the event, which appeared on Spokane's major television station. While all this might appear to be trivial in the over-all context of our history for one hundred and forty-one years, it illustrates at least, the slow steady progress of the Jesuits, from the ox carts of St. Mary's to a television broadcast that was seen and heard in many parts of the United States and Canada, including a few where the oxcarts had passed. Like Nicolas Point, Lyons produced pictures in color, enough to dazzle every Indian in America.

The second project on the campus was more daring, but one of an ancient kind, as old as cable television was new. The provincial announced its existence in a letter to the province on August 21, 1981. "This is to notify you," he said, "of a new province apostolic undertaking. The Mater Dei Institute of Priestly Formation began on August 21, 1981. It is located two blocks north of St. Aloysius Church, Spokane, in what has been St. Aloysius Convent. Sixteen students have been admitted."[37]

This proposal had been one of Armand Nigro's innumerable dreams. Vincent Beuzer shared in it, and with Al Carroll as the third member of a committee, these three Jesuits prepared a detailed report for Bishop Lawrence Welsh, the Spokane Diocesan Priests' Senate, and the provincial. During the early months of 1981, the bishop, the senate and the provincial with his consultors, approved the plan and the province made available the necessary funds.

> Royce's letter continued: "In it carefully selected men over 30 years of age possessing a Bachelor's degree or equivalent will begin a five academic-year course (taken in four calendar years, plus four summer sessions) in theology under Gonzaga University professors. At the end of this course, they will be candidates for ordination to the priesthood. Each must be sponsored by a Bishop or a religious superior before beginning their second year. Their training will thus be integrated into that apostolate."

Father Jack Evoy was appointed Director, Father Charles Suver his assistant. Nigro received more than five-hundred inquiries and processed over one-hundred applications. The sixteen candidates who were accepted came from many parts of the United States and Canada, indicating, in a verifiable sense, the new nationalism of the American church and with it the Oregon Province.

What better place to end this history? A new seminary to provide priests for the church, and eager anticipation of an all-province Congress.

> "You will declare this 50th year sacred," the provincial wrote on August 27, 1981, quoting the Book of Leviticus. "The Jubilee is to be a holy thing to you, you will eat what comes from the fields. The land will give you its fruit.[38]
>
> "Mary was the patron of the first mission in the Northwest," he added. "I am dedicating this jubilee to her under the title of Madonna of The Way. May she show us the way to direct our efforts . . ."

And so we will make our paths by walking on them, into the next decade and into the next century, comforted by the Madonna of The Way, and led by the Holy Spirit.

"The Rocky Mountain Mission Madonna" by an unknown nineteenth-century artist was brought to the Rocky Mountains by Father Gregory Gazzoli in 1847. According to tradition it was presented to Gazzoli by Pope Benedict XIV, his great uncle, as a gift to the mission. For many years it was displayed at Sacred Heart Mission near Cataldo, then at De Smet, where it acquired the title "Madonna of De Smet."

Pacific Ocean

Bellingham
Republic
Kettle Falls
Priest Lake

Omak
Inchelium
Colville
Sandpoint

Everett
Nespelem
Pend Oreille L.
Flathead

Port Townsend
Coulee Dam
Wellpinit
Hayden Lk.

Bangor
Seattle
Spokane
Coeur d'Alene Lk.

Wenatchee
Desmet

Olympia
Tacoma
Ellensburg
Moses Lk.

WASHINGTON
Pullman

Yakima
Richland
Pasco
Lewiston
Lapwai
Culdesac

Astoria
Kennewick
Walla Walla

Vancouver
Portland
Pendleton

Nestucca Villa
Sheridan
The Dalles

Woodburn
Salem

Baker

Eugene
Bend

OREGON

Crater Lk.
Boise

Cave Jct.
Medford
Ashland
Lakeview
Klamath Falls

ID

Heart Butte

Lk.

St. Ignatius

Great Falls

Havre

Harlem

Hays

M O N T A N A

Missoula

Helena

Anaconda

Butte

Bozeman

Billings

Pryor

St. Xavier

Hardin

Miles City

U.S.

× Custer Battlefield

Lodge Grass

AHO

N

W — Oregon-Province — E

of the Society of Jesus

S

Neill R. Meany, S.J.
1982

Pocatello

Twin Falls

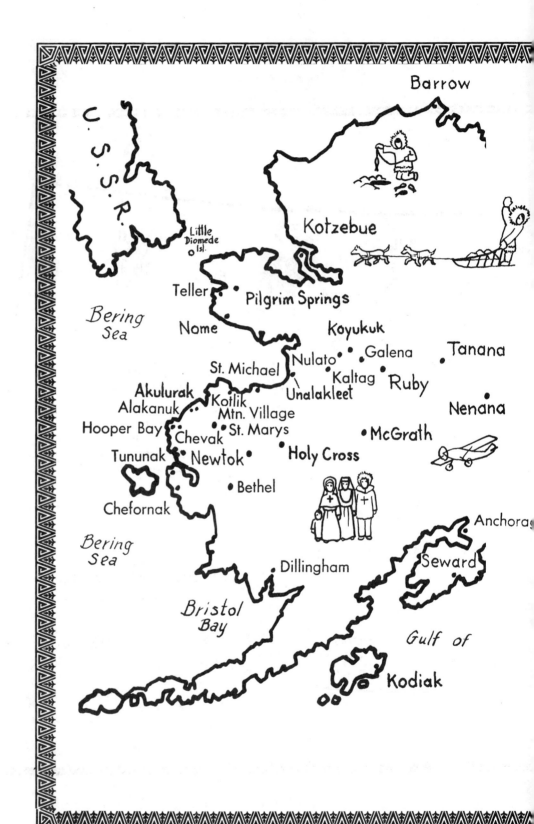

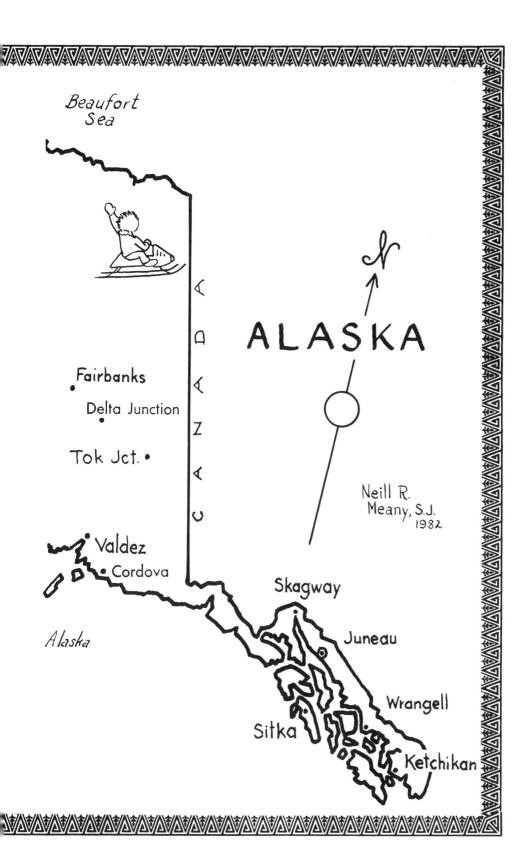

Beaufort
Sea

ALASKA

N

CANADA

Fairbanks

Delta Junction

Tok Jct.

Neill R.
Meany, S.J.
1982

Valdez

Cordova

Skagway

Alaska

Juneau

Wrangell

Sitka

Ketchikan

APPENDICES

by
Gregory C. Rathbone, S.J.

APPENDIX A

GENERALS OF THE SOCIETY OF JESUS (1820–1982)

Luigi Fortis . . . . October 18, 1820–January 27, 1829
John Roothaan . . . . July 9, 1829–May 8, 1853
Peter Beckx . . . . July 2, 1853–March 4, 1887
Anthony Anderledy, (Vicar General) . . . . September 24, 1883
Anthony Anderledy. . . . . March 4, 1887–January 18, 1892
Luis Martin . . . . October 2, 1892–April 18, 1906
Francis Wernz . . . . September 8, 1906–August 19, 1914
Vlodimir Ledochowski . . . . February 11, 1915–
                                                                              December 13, 1942
Maurice Schurmans (Vicar General) . . . . April 11, 1938
Alex Ambrosius Magni (Vicar General) . . . . December 14, 1942
Norbert de Boynes (Vicar General) . . . . April 19, 1944
John Baptist Janssens. . . . . September 15, 1946–
                                                                              October 5, 1964
Pedro Arrupe . . . . May 22, 1965

APPENDIX B

SUPERIORS AND PROVINCIALS OF THE OREGON REGION (1841–1982)

Superiors of the Rocky Mountain Mission
Peter John De Smet 1841
Joseph Joset. . . . . August 6, 1845
Michael Accolti. . . . . February 17, 1849
Nicholas Congiato (also Superior of California Mission) . . . . August 1, 1854
Nicholas Congiato . . . . March 1, 1858
Joseph Giorda. . . . . January 21, 1862
Urban Grassi, Vice Superior . . . . September 11, 1866
Joseph Giorda. . . . . September 12, 1869
Joseph Cataldo. . . . . June 16, 1877
Leopold Van Gorp. . . . . March 24, 1893
George de la Motte . . . . August 15, 1900
George de la Motte (also Superior of California Mission) . . . . August 15, 1907

California Provincials
Herman J. Goller . . . . July 31, 1909
James A. Rockliff . . . . November 18, 1910
Richard A. Gleeson . . . . March 19, 1914
Francis C. Dillon . . . . July 16, 1918
Joseph M. Piet . . . . May 11, 1924

Oregon Provincials
Walter J. Fitzgerald, Vice Provincial. . . . . December 25, 1931
Walter J. Fitzgerald . . . . February 2, 1932
William G. Elliott . . . . November 21, 1938
Leopold J. Robinson . . . . April 10, 1942
Harold O. Small. . . . . March 29, 1948
Henry J. Schultheis . . . . April 20, 1954
Alexander F. McDonald . . . . March 10, 1959
John J. Kelley . . . . June 10, 1964
Kenneth J. Galbraith . . . . June 10, 1970
William J. Loyens. . . . . June 15, 1976
Thomas R. Royce . . . . June 13, 1980

APPENDIX C

JESUIT ECCLESIASTICAL SUPERIORS IN ALASKA 1894–1982

Paschal Tosi (prefect apostolic) 1894–1897
John B. Rene (prefect apostolic) 1897–1904
Joseph Crimont (prefect apostolic) 1904–1917
Joseph Crimont (vicar apostolic) 1917–1945
Walter J. Fitzgerald (coadjutor bishop) 1939–1945
Walter J. Fitzgerald (vicar apostolic) 1945–1947
Francis D. Gleeson (vicar apostolic) 1948–1962
Francis D. Gleeson (bishop of Fairbanks) 1962–1968
George T. Boileau (coadjutor bishop of Fairbanks) 1964–1965
Robert L. Whelan (coadjutor bishop of Fairbanks) 1968–1969
Robert L. Whelan (bishop of Fairbanks) 1969

APPENDIX D

GENERAL SUPERIORS IN ALASKA 1886–1982

Paschal Tosi (vice-superior) 1886–1894
Paschal Tosi 1894–1897
John B. Rene 1897–1902
George de la Motte 1902–1907
Joseph Perron (vice-superior) 1907–1909
John L. Lucchesi 1909–1913
John B. Sifton 1913–1923
Philip Delon 1923–1930
John L. Lucchesi 1930–1931
Francis M. Menager 1931–1933
John B. Sifton 1933–1936
Francis B. Prange 1936–1938
Joseph McElmeel 1938–1944
Paul C. Deschout 1944–1950
Norman E. Donohue 1950–1956
Henry G. Hargreaves 1956–1963
George T. Boileau 1963–1964
Jules M. Convert 1964–1968
Bernard F. McMeel 1968–1973
William J. Loyens 1973–1976
Francis J. Fallert 1976–1982
Michael J. Kaniecki 1982

APPENDIX E

RECTORS

Gonzaga University, Spokane, Washington
George de la Motte (superior) .... August 9, 1899
Raphael Crimont (vice-rector) .... October 10, 1901
Raphael Crimont .... January 27, 1903
Francis Dillon (vice-rector) .... May 23, 1904
Herman Goller (vice-rector) .... July 31, 1905
Herman Goller .... October 10, 1905
Louis Taelman (vice-rector) .... September 8, 1909
Jacob Brogan .... August 7, 1913
John McHugh .... March 11, 1920
Walter J. Fitzgerald .... July 21, 1921
Daniel J. Reidy .... August 6, 1927
John Joseph Keep .... July 31, 1930
Francis C. Dillon (vice-rector) .... November 1, 1934
Leopold J. Robinson .... December 21, 1935
Francis J. Altman .... May 30, 1942
Francis E. Corkery .... April 15, 1945
Edmund W. Morton .... August 6, 1957
John P. Leary .... July 19, 1961
Vincent J. Beuzer .... August 15, 1973
Thomas R. Royce .... July 1, 1979
Frank B. Costello .... August 24, 1980

Seattle Prep School and Seattle University, Seattle, Washington
Hugh Gallagher (last superior) .... August 1, 1907
Carol Carroll .... June 15, 1911
Joseph Tomkin .... August 15, 1914
Geoffrey O'Shea .... July 31, 1921
William M. Boland .... August 24, 1925
Walter J. Fitzgerald .... September 4, 1929
John A. McHugh .... February 16, 1931
John J. Balfe .... April 4, 1934
Francis E. Corkery .... June 11, 1936
Harold O. Small .... April 13, 1945
Albert A. Lemieux .... May 20, 1948
Christopher J. McDonnell .... September 29, 1950
John V. Murphy .... June 14, 1956
Louis A. Sauvain .... August 3, 1962
Richard S. Bradley .... June 21, 1965
Emmett H. Carroll .... June 21, 1969
Denis P. Dennehy .... August 27, 1973

Seattle Prep School
Denis P. Dennehy .... August 15, 1975
Thomas F. Healy .... June 11, 1979

Seattle University
L. John Topel . . . . August 15, 1975
Leo B. Kaufmann. . . . . June 29, 1978
Francis E. Case . . . . September 14, 1981

Bellarmine Preparatory School, Tacoma, Washington
David P. McAstocker . . . . August 19, 1930
Francis Gleeson . . . . May 13, 1933
Henry Schultheis . . . . June 25, 1939
Leo T. Eckstein. . . . . February 5, 1947
Francis A. Toner . . . . May 31, 1953
Joseph P. Logan. . . . . June 11, 1958
Joseph L. Showalter . . . . June 17, 1963
Thomas G. Williams . . . . June 1, 1968
L. Patrick Carroll . . . . July 1, 1970
Robert N. Byrne. . . . . August 14, 1977
Joseph A. Maguire. . . . . July 31, 1980

Gonzaga Preparatory School, Spokane, Washington
Michael B. Kunz. . . . . April 9, 1954
Francis D. Masterson . . . . February 5, 1959
Daniel C. Weber. . . . . June 21, 1965
L. Paul Fitterer . . . . July 31, 1971
Patrick J. Kenny . . . . July 17, 1977
Gerard E. Chapdelaine . . . . August 25, 1980

Jesuit High School, Portland, Oregon
Mathias I. Wilhelm (superior) . . . . January 8, 1956
Louis E. Haven, (superior). . . . . July 31, 1957
Thomas J. Sexton . . . . June 21, 1959
Gordon E. Toner . . . . June 21, 1965
Frank D. Masterson. . . . . May 17, 1968
James M. McDonough . . . . August 15, 1974
Joseph H. Small . . . . July 31, 1978

Jesuit Novitiate, Sheridan, Oregon/Portland Oregon (1974)
Francis Dillon, superior . . . . July 31, 1932
Thomas R. Martin . . . . July 13, 1932
Francis D. Gleeson . . . . January 27, 1939
John S. Forster . . . . June 4, 1942
John A. Dalgity . . . . January 27, 1947
Joseph P. Logan. . . . . July 19, 1952
Alexander F. McDonald . . . . June 6, 1958
Edward S. Flajole. . . . . June 21, 1959
Michael J. McHugh . . . . July 3, 1960
Francis D. Masterson . . . . June 21, 1965
Edward S. Flajole. . . . . June 9, 1966
Gordon Moreland . . . . May 18, 1968
Patrick B. O'Leary . . . . May 23, 1976

NOTES

1. These were the Skelsa-ulk; the Kootenai, or Water People; the Spoge'in, or Sun People; the Spokanes; the Kalispel, or People-Who-Had-Canoes, also called the Pend d'Oreilles; the Skitswish; the Coeur d'Alenes, or Camas People, and many others. John R. Swanton, *The Indian Tribes of North America*, Smithsonian Institution, Bureau of American Ethnology, Bulletin 145, Washington, 1953, passim.

2. *Ibid.,* pp. 393–94. The Flatheads' primeval rights and use of the buffalo hunting grounds have been disputed, but weighty opinion favors the Flatheads' view expressed here. Note also that the Blackfeet acknowledged these prior rights in the Blackfeet Treaty of 1855. Cf. Albert J. Partoll, "The Blackfoot Indian Peace Council," in *Frontier and Midland*, vol. 17, #3 (Spring, 1937), pp. 199–207.

3. Gregory Mengarini, S.J., *Recollections of the Flathead Mission;* edited and translated by Gloria Ricci Lathrop, this has appeared as *Recollections of the Flathead Mission Containing Brief Observations both Ancient and Contemporary Concerning This Particular Nation* (Glendale, 1977). *See* chapter two, "The Religion of the Flatheads," pp. 149–59 (hereafter cited as *Recollections*).

4. *Ibid.,* p. 119, et seq.

5. Harry Holbert Turney-High, "Flathead Indians of Montana," *American Anthropological Association Memoirs,* No. 48 (1937), p. 78. Also, Sister Providentia Tolan, S.P., Providence Mother House (Montreal, 1980), pp. 8–15. Sister Providentia has interviewed many old and informed Indians about alleged predictions of the coming of the Black Robes.

6. Reuben Gold Thwaites, ed., *The Jesuit Relations and Allied Documents; Travels and Explorations of the Jesuit Missionaries in New France, 1610–1791,* 73 vols. (Cleveland, 1896–1901) 68:334. Also, Francis Parkman, "Discovery of the Rocky Mountains" in *The Atlantic Monthly,* 61 (1889), pp. 783–93. Also, Charles E. De Land, "The Verendrye Explorations and Discoveries," *The South Dakota Historical Society Collections,* 7 (1914), 218 et seq.

7. This exact date, avoided even by Father Lawrence Palladino, is confirmed by De Smet who states that in 1839 "on the 18th of last September two Catholic Iroquois came to visit us. They had been for twenty-three years among the nations called the Flatheads and Pierced Noses (Nez Perce) about a thousand Flemish leagues from where we are (Council Bluffs.)" Hiram Martin Chittenden and Alfred Talbot Richardson, *Life, Letters, and Travels of Pierre-Jean De Smet, S.J.,* 4 vols. (New York, 1905) 1.29 (hereafter cited as *Life, Letters, and Travels*).

8. Gilbert J. Garraghan, S.J., *The Jesuits of the Middle United States,* 3 vols. (New York, 1938), 2:238 (hereafter cited as *Jesuits of Middle U.S.*). Also Lawrence B. Palladino, S.J., *Indians and Whites in the Northwest: a History of Catholicity in Montana 1838–1891,* 2d ed. (Lancaster, Pa., 1922), p. 8. Note that this is the corrected edition (hereafter cited as *Indians and Whites*).

9. Palladino, *Indians and Whites,* p. 8. Palladino got carried away in his geography. Jogues was not martyred on the banks of the St. Lawrence, but on the Mohawk River at Auriesville, New York, forty-two miles west of Albany.

10. *Ibid.,* p. 9 and pp. 13–19. According to Palladino, this first delegation was composed of two Flatheads and two Nez Perce who had been adopted by the Flatheads. There has been a celebrated dispute about the matter. The best Protestant version appears in Clifford Merrill Drury, *Henry Harmon Spalding,* (Caldwell, Idaho, 1936), pp. 72–90. Professor Drury in comments to me noted that his principal source was "the McBeth Sisters." Drury had not consulted Palladino's second edition, which contains a full chapter on the subject, chapter three, "A Correction." Palladino, whose version is very probably correct, arrived among the Flatheads in 1867, six years before the McBeth sisters who arrived in 1873. The most complete treatment of the subject appears in Garraghan, *Jesuits of Middle U.S.,* 2:236-44.

11. Bishop Joseph Rosati in a letter of December 31, 1831, which appeared in the *Annales de la Propagation de la Foi. See* Palladino, *Indians and Whites,* pp. 11–12.

12. George Catlin, *Letters and Notes on the Manners, Customs and Condition of the North American Indians* (London, 1841), 2 vols., plates 207 and 208 opposite 2:108.

13. Palladino, *Indians and Whites,* p. 20.

14. Garraghan, *Jesuits of Middle U.S.,* 2:247. There is a tradition, as delightful as it is errone-

ous, that Old Ignace left the boys in the Jesuit school in St. Louis and returned to his lodge in the Bitterroot without them. His wife was so distressed, says the legend, that she herself went to St. Louis and brought them back. The fact is, the Jesuits at St. Louis persuaded Old Ignace to take his sons home with him.

15. W. H. Gray, *History of Oregon 1792–1849*, drawn from *Personal Observation and Authentic Information* (San Francisco, 1870), p. 173. Gray, "one of the whites present," was not molested. The Sioux inquired of Gray about the origin of the five Indians. Gray replied, "Snakes" [Shoshones], not realizing the hatred which the Sioux held for these Indians. This response unwittingly condemned the five to death. Gray in his account of the tragedy tends to cover up for himself. Mengarini and Palladino have different versions. See also Palladino, *Indians and Whites*, p. 27 for additional details.

16. E. Laveille, S.J., *The Life of Father De Smet, S.J.* (New York, 1915), p. 17.

17. Mengarini, *Recollections*, pp. 182–83.

18. *Ibid.*

19. Palladino, *Indians and Whites*, footnote on p. 29. Rosati said Young Ignace would spend the winter at the mouth of the Bear River. Garraghan has him waiting at Westport for De Smet.

20. Garraghan, *Jesuits of Middle U.S.*, pp. 249–50 has full text of the letter.

21. *Ibid.*

22. *Ibid.*, p. 26.

23. *Ibid.*

24. Chittenden and Richardson, *Life, Letters, and Travels*, 1:220. Succeeding details are taken from De Smet's letters contained in the same source.

25. *Ibid.*

Chapter 2
THE FIRST ROCKY MOUNTAIN MISSION

1. This was the date of Father Roothaan's formal letter. The letter was not received or promulgated in St. Louis until February 26,

1831. There were fifteen members of the vice province. Cf. Gilbert J. Garraghan, S.J., *The Jesuits of the Middle United States*, 3 vols. (New York, 1938), 1:314–15 (hereafter cited as *Jesuits of Middle U.S.*).

2. *Ibid.*, 2:256.

3. Point's memoirs appeared under the title of "Recollections of the Rocky Mountains," in *Woodstock Letters*, vol. 2 (1882), p. 298 et seq., vol. 12 (1883), p. 3 et seq. and vol. 13 (1884), p. 3 et seq.

4. Garraghan, *Jesuits of Middle U.S.*, 2:259.

5. *Ibid.*, p. 256.

6. *Ibid.*, p. 257.

7. *Ibid.*

8. *Ibid.*, p. 258.

9. From Bidwell's Journal for May 19, "A Journey to California," reproduced in *John Bidwell: Pioneer, Statesman, Philanthropist*, quoted in Gilbert J. Garraghan, S.J., *Chapters in Frontier History* (Milwaukee, 1934), pp. 139–40.

10. John Bidwell, "The First Immigrant Train to California," in *The Century Illustrated Monthly Magazine*, 41 (Nov. 1890), pp. 103–6.

11. Hiram M. Chittenden and Alfred T. Richardson, *Life, Letters and Travels of Pierre-Jean De Smet, S.J.*, 4 vols., (New York, 1905) 1:297 (hereafter cited as *Life, Letters and Travels*).

12. Gregory Mengarini *Recollections of the Flathead Mission*, ed. and trans. Gloria Ricci Lathrop, *Recollections of the Flathead Mission Containing Brief Observations both Ancient and Contemporary Concerning This Particular Nation* (Glendale, 1977), chapter two, "The Religion of the Flatheads," pp. 149–59. (hereafter cited as *Recollections*).

13. E. Laveille, S. J., *The Life of Father De Smet, S.J.* (New York, 1915) p. 121 (hereafter cited as *Life of De Smet*).

14. Oregon Province Archives located in the Crosby Library, Gonzaga University, Spokane, Washington (hereafter cited as OPA), ms. Mengarini, *Memoirs of the Rocky Mountain Mission*.

15. Laveille, *Life of De Smet*, p. 123.

16. Garraghan, *Jesuits of Middle U.S.*, 2:262.

17. Laveille, *Life of De Smet*, p. 124.

18. OPA Ms. Mengarini, "Personal Memoirs."

19. *Ibid.*

20. L. B. Palladino, S.J., *Indians and Whites in the Northwest: a History of Catholicity in Montana 1838–1891*, 2d ed. (Lancaster, Pa., 1922), p. 39 (hereafter cited as *Indians and Whites*).

21. *Ibid.*, p. 43.

22. OPA Ms. Mengarini, "Personal Memoirs."

23. Luigi Antoine Muratori, S.J., *A Relation of the Mission of Paraguay*. The "reductions" of Paraguay were founded at the beginning of the seventeenth century. Spanish Jesuits converted the natives, taught them to till the soil and developed a kind of theocratic state comprising thirty-two cities, inhabited by approximately forty thousand families. In 1767, when the Jesuits were expelled from Spanish dominions, the reductions were gradually destroyed.

24. Palladino, *Indians and Whites*, p. 52.

25. Garraghan, *Jesuits of Middle U.S.*, 2:269.

26. *Ibid.*, 2:273 et seq. Garraghan presents a detailed account of the correspondence at this period related to church government.

27. Pierre-Jean De Smet, S. J., *Letters and Sketches with a Narrative of a Year's Residence Among the Indian Tribes of the Rocky Mountains.* (Philadelphia, 1843), p. 229 et seq. The letter was dated 28 September 1841.

28. Palladino, *Indians and Whites*, p. 50.

29. Chittenden and Richardson, *Life, Letters and Travels*, 1:402.

30. Wilfred P. Schoenberg, S.J., *Jesuit Mission Presses in the Pacific Northwest: A History and a Bibliography of Imprints 1876–1899*, p. 71 (hereafter cited as *Jesuit Mission Presses*).

31. Two of these occasions are described by Father William Bischoff. *See* William N. Bischoff, S.J., *The Jesuits in Old Oregon* (Caldwell, 1945), p. 43 and p. 129 et seq. (hereafter cited as *The Jesuits*).

32. Schoenberg, *Jesuit Mission Presses*, p. 72, n. 6.

33. These paintings have survived and have, in part, been published: Joseph P. Donnelly, S.J.,

ed., *Wilderness Kingdom: Indian Life in the Rocky Mountains 1840–1847. The Journal and Paintings of Nicolas Point, S. J.* (New York, 1967).

34. Garraghan, *Jesuits of Middle U.S.*, 2:315.

35. Bischoff, *The Jesuits*, p. 40.

36. Garraghan, *Jesuits of Middle U.S.*, 2:279.

37. *Ibid.*

38. *Ibid.*, pp. 281–83.

39. This was the controversial "Whitman Ride to Save Oregon for America," which was balderdash. Cf. William I. Marshall, *Acquisition of Oregon and the Long Suppressed Evidence about Marcus Whitman*, 2 vols. (Seattle, 1911).

40. Garraghan, *Jesuits of Middle U.S.*, 2:291.

41. Hubert Howe Bancroft, *The Works of Hubert H. Bancroft*, 29 vols. *History of Oregon* (San Francisco, 1886), 1:398.

42. OPA Ms. Mengarini, "Personal Memoirs."

43. Mengarini, *Recollections*, p. 76.

44. Garraghan, *Jesuits of Middle U.S.*, 2:292.

45. *Ibid.*, p. 294.

46. Palladino, *Indians and Whites*, p. 57. Soderini, when he left Fort Hall for Vancouver to join Blanchet, unexpectedly met De Smet along the way. De Smet persuaded him to remain in the Society and he remained with De Smet throughout the winter at St. Ignatius on the Clark Fork. On account of misunderstandings, Soderini left the mission in the spring, returned to St. Louis, and soon went to Rome where he left the Society. *Woodstock Letters*, 30 (1901) 207.

Chapter 3
THE EARLY YEARS

1. Gilbert J. Garraghan, S. J., *The Jesuits of the Middle United States*, 3 vols. (New York, 1938), 2:295 (hereafter cited as *Jesuits of Middle U.S.*) Garraghan has the vessel's name as *Infatigable*, as does Laveille. Bancroft, on the other hand, has it as *L'Indefatigable*, which I think is correct. The Methodists, in whom Bancroft had a special interest, chartered the same ship to leave Oregon. *See* Hubert H. Bancroft, *The Works of Hubert H. Bancroft*, 29 vols., vol. 1, *History of*

Oregon (San Francisco, 1886) p. 325 (hereafter cited as *History of Oregon*).

2. Sisters of Notre de Namur, *Notice Sur Territoire, et Sur La Mission de L'Oregon* (Brussels, 1847), p. 107.

3. Francis Norbert Blanchet, *Historical Sketches of the Catholic Church in Oregon During the Past Forty Years* (Portland, 1878), p. 143.

4. Blanchet had already been appointed a bishop. On December 1, 1843, he was named vicar apostolic of Philadelphia *in partibus*. This was subsequently changed to vicar apostolic of Drasa to avoid confusion. News of his appointment did not reach Oregon until November 1844. He was consecrated in Montreal on July 25, 1845. Archives of the Archdiocese of Portland in Oregon, Blanchet Correspondence, Book I. Also Edwin V. O'Hara, *Pioneer Catholic History of Oregon* (Portland, 1911), p. 98. (hereafter cited as *Pioneer Catholic History*).

5. O'Hara, *Pioneer Catholic History*, p. 87.

6. Hiram M. Chittenden and Alfred T. Richardson, *Life, Letters, and Travels of Pierre-Jean De Smet, S. J.*, 4 vols. (New York, 1905), 2:448 (hereafter cited as *Life, Letters, and Travels*).

7. Garraghan, *Jesuits of Middle U.S.*, 2:299.

8. Chittenden and Richardson, *Life, Letters and Travels*, 2:449.

9. Bancroft, *History of Oregon*, 1:224.

10. Garraghan, *Jesuits of Middle U.S.*, 2:354. Accolti wrote [1846]: "The prices of articles of commerce are exorbitantly high. A pair of French shoes—$5.00; a pair of water-boots—$10.00; a blanket—$6.00."

11. High costs and bills plagued the mission from the beginning. It was soon learned that the best system for payment was through Father George Jenkins, procurator for the English province, who received money from Father General, $8,000.00 per year in the early years; then paid the bills in the Hudson's Bay Company office in London. In time, however, Father General, who received the money from The Association for the Propagation of the Faith, could provide only $1,200 per year. This was for the entire Rocky Mountain Mission considerably less than what was required. In Garraghan, *Jesuits of Middle U.S.*, there is an extended presentation of the mission's finances, 2:351 sq.

12. Chittenden and Richardson, *Life, Letters and Travels*, 2:468.

13. *Ibid.*, 2:474, New Manresa, which has been preserved as a shrine, is across the river from present-day Cusick, Washington.

14. Garraghan, *Jesuits of Middle U.S.*, 2:326.

15. Chittenden and Richardson, *Life, Letters and Travels*, 2:471.

16. Garraghan, *Jesuits of Middle U.S.*, 2:301.

17. *Ibid.*, 2:270. Mengarini in his memoirs describes the journey in some detail. Icicles, he said, formed on the horses and mules and helped bring them down. The millstones had been presented to Ravalli in Antwerp. *See* Oregon Province Archives, Mengarini *Personal Memoirs*.

18. L. B. Palladino, S. J., *Indians and Whites in the Northwest: a History of Catholicity in Montana 1838–1891*, 2d ed. (Lancaster, Pa., 1922), p. 60 (hereafter cited as *Indians and Whites*).

19. Oregon Province Archives, Ms. Mengarini, *Personal Memoirs*.

20. Palladino, *Indians and Whites*, p. 58.

21. Gregory Mengarini, S. J., *Recollections of the Flathead Mission*, ed. and trans. Gloria Ricci Lathrop, *Recollections of the Flathead Mission Containing Brief Observations both Ancient and Contemporary Concerning This Particular Nation* (Glendale, 1977), chapter two, "The Religion of the Flatheads," pp. 149–59 (hereafter cited as *Recollections*).

22. Palladino, for example, reports on Ravalli's use of artificial respiration at St. Paul's Mission near Kettle Falls in 1857. L. B. Palladino, *Anthony Ravalli, Memoir* (Helena, 1884), p. 8.

23. Palladino, *Indians and Whites*, p. 61.

24. Garraghan, *Jesuits of Middle U.S.*, 2:307.

25. Now called Priest Lake, this lake's nomenclature has had a curious history. In May 1846, De Smet named it "Lake Roothaan" in honor of Father General. Cf. Chittenden and Richardson, *Life, Letters and Travels*, 2:550. The Indians who could not pronounce Roothaan, called it "Blackrobe Lake," and its river drainage, "Blackrobe River." Later the Northern Pacific Railway changed the latter to "Priest River," and the lake took its final name from this.

NOTES

26. One letter dated in Rome in August 8, 1845, was received in the mission on July 5, 1847. De Smet did not receive mail from his family for a period of over three years. One Jesuit complained to the general, "It ordinarily requires two years to get an answer, very often three or four years." Garraghan, *Jesuits of Middle U.S.*, 2:358. I can think of some modern Jesuits who would prefer this to the current means of communications.

27. Garraghan, *Jesuits of Middle U.S.*, 2:327.

28. *Ibid.*, 2:319.

29. E. Laveille, S. J., *The Life of Father De Smet, S. J.*, (New York, 1915), p. 186 (hereafter cited as *Life of De Smet*).

30. *Ibid.*, p. 196.

31. Nicolas Point, S.J., *Wilderness Kingdom: Indian Life in the Rocky Mountains 1840–1847: The Journals and Paintings of Father Nicolas Point.* Translation and Introduction by Joseph P. Donnelly, S. J. (New York, 1967).

32. A detailed history of the publication of Point's memoirs has appeared. *See* Wilfred P. Schoenberg, S. J., "Review of Wilderness Kingdom: Indian Life in the Rocky Mountains: 1840–1847," *Montana: The Magazine of Western History*, vol. 18, no. 1 (Jan. 1968), p. 88.

33. Garraghan presents a long treatment of this subject. He gives Ravalli's long report to the general and other pertinent documents. *See* Garraghan, *Jesuits of Middle U.S.*, 2:375 et seq.

34. *Ibid.*, 2:427.

35. Mengarini, *Recollections*, Appendix B., p. 233 et seq., contains this long letter of Mengarini to the general.

36. Henry Harmon Spalding's mind apparently became unbalanced by his discovery of the massacre. He charged the Jesuits with the bloody deed and carried his vendetta so far that he had the following inscription engraved on his wife's tombstone: "She always felt that the Jesuit Missionaries were the leading cause of the Massacre." *See* Clifford Merrill Drury, *Henry Harmon Spalding* (Caldwell, Idaho, 1936), p. 361. The Jesuits were a hundred miles away at the time of the massacre. *See also* Garraghan, *Jesuits of Middle U.S.*, 2:345.

37. Garraghan, *Jesuits of Middle U.S.*, 2:336.

38. *Ibid.*, 2:302 et seq. Accolti wrote later at great length about the farm and its products. Wheat was selling then at $3.00 per bushel, oats for $1.50.

39. *Ibid.*, 2:394.

40. *Ibid.*, 2:401. It has been stated that between 1847 and 1854, 4,200 persons were murdered in San Francisco, an average of 600 a year for seven years. This beats any record known of modern American cities.

41. *Ibid.*, 2:408.

42. *Ibid.*, 2:331.

43. Palladino, *Indians and Whites*, p. 66.

44. *Ibid.*, p. 67.

45. Garraghan, *Jesuits of Middle U.S.*, 2:383.

46. *Ibid.*, 2:385.

Chapter 4
THE GATHERING STORM

1. Lawrence B. Palladino, S.J., *Indians and Whites in the Northwest: A History of Catholicity in Montana 1838–1891*, 2d ed. (Lancaster, Pa., 1922), p. 54 (hereafter cited as *Indians and Whites*). *Also*, Hiram M. Chittenden and Alfred T. Richardson, *Life, Letters, and Travels of Pierre-Jean De Smet, S.J.*, 4 vols. (New York 1905), 4:1470 (hereafter cited as *Life, Letters and Travels*).

2. William N. Bischoff, S.J., *The Jesuits in Old Oregon* (Caldwell, 1945), p. 62 (hereafter cited as *The Jesuits*).

3. Gilbert J. Garraghan, *The Jesuits of the Middle United States*, 3 vols. (New York, 1938), 2:432 (hereafter cited as *Jesuits of Middle U.S.*).

4. General Archives of the Society of Jesus (hereafter, GASJ), Letter of Roothaan to Elet, December 6, 1849.

5. GASJ, Letter of Elet to Roothaan, February 14, 1850.

6. GASJ, Letter of Accolti to Father Joseph Simmen, assistant to Roothaan for the German Assistancy, n.d.

7. Garraghan, *Jesuits of Middle U.S.*, 2:419.

8. Missouri Province Archives of the Society of Jesus (St. Louis), Accolti to De Smet, November 8, 1852.

9. GASJ, Letter of Demers to Propaganda, November 30, 1853.

10. Joseph W. Riordan, S.J., *The Half Century of St. Ignatius Church and College* (San Francisco, 1905), p. 43.

11. The Oregonians never had reason to complain about their dependency on the Turin Province. The Jesuits in California, however, appeared to be disappointed, and Accolti continued to agitate for California's annexation to an American province. *See* Garraghan, *Jesuits of Middle U.S.*, 2:420.

12. GASJ. Letter of Congiato to Beckx, December 24, 1861.

13. Oregon Province Archives, Crosby Library, Gonzaga University, Spokane, Washington (hereafter, OPA), Joset Papers, Ms. "Sketch of Sacred Heart Mission Church;" *also*, Bischoff, *The Jesuits*, p. 131.

14. Palladino, *Indians and Whites*, p. 69.

15. John Mullan, *Report of a Construction of a Military Road from Fort Walla Walla to Fort Benton* (Washington, 1863). *See also* George W. Fuller, *A History of the Pacific Northwest* (New York, 1931), p. 316, et seq. (hereafter cited as *Pacific Northwest*).

16. Palladino, *Indians and Whites*, p. 95.

17. OPA, Joset Papers, Ms. "Origin of St. Ignatius Mission."

18. Chittenden and Richardson, *Life, Letters, and Travels*, 4:1232, et seq.

19. *Ibid.*, p. 1233.

20. OPA, Joset Papers, "Account of '58 War." *Also*, William N. Bischoff, S.J., "Documents: Yakima Campaign," *Mid-America*, 31 (1949) p. 88.

21. Isaac I. Stevens, *Narrative and Final Report of Exploration for a Route for a Pacific Railroad*, vol. 12, bk. 1, p. 201 of *Reports of Explorations and Surveys to Ascertain the Most Practicable and Economical Route for a Railroad from the Mississippi River to the Pacific Ocean*, 12 vols. (Washington 1855–1860).

22. Robert Ignatius Burns, S.J., *The Jesuits and the Indian Wars of the Northwest* (New Haven, 1966), p. 82 (hereafter cited as *Jesuits and Indian Wars*).

23. Palladino, *Indians and Whites*, p. 96.

24. *Ibid.*

25. *Ibid.*

26. Garraghan, *Jesuits of Middle U.S.*, 2:360.

27. Missouri Province Archives of the Society of Jesus, De Smet to Thomas O'Neil (Rector of Bardstown) May, 1860.

28. Chittenden and Richardson, *Life, Letters, and Travels*, 3:836.

29. Joseph La Barge died in St. Louis on April 2, 1899. *See* Hiram M. Chittenden, *History of Early Steamboat Navigation on the Missouri River: Life and Adventures of Joseph La Barge*, (Minneapolis, 1962), p. 440.

30. E. Laveille, *Life of Father De Smet, S.J.* (New York, 1915), p. 385 (hereafter cited as *Life of De Smet*).

31. OPA, Joset Papers, Ms. "Notes on Colville Mission."

32. Fuller, *Pacific Northwest*, p. 273, et seq.

33. OPA, Joset, Ms. "Notes on Colville Mission."

34. Burns, *Jesuits and Indian Wars*, p. 169 et seq.

35. Letter of Vercruysse to Father Broeckaert, November 13, 1857, quoted in Laveille, *Life of De Smet*, p. 273.

Chapter 5
A SECOND START

1. Complete details regarding this and other Indian battles in which Jesuits were involved appear in Robert Ignatius Burns, S. J., *The Jesuits and the Indian Wars of the Northwest* (New Haven, 1966), passim (hereafter cited as *Jesuits and Indian Wars*).

2. Oregon Province Archives (hereafter cited as OPA) Joset Papers, Ms. "Account of '58 War." (Letter to Giorda).

3. *Ibid.*

4. Lawrence B. Palladino, S.J., *Indians and Whites in the Northwest: A History of Catholicity in Montana 1838–1891,* 2d ed. (Lancaster, Pa., 1922), p. 190 (hereafter cited as *Indians and Whites*).

5. E. Laveille, *The Life of Father De Smet* (New York, 1915), p. 284 (hereafter cited as *Life of De Smet*).

6. General Archives of the Society of Jesus, Rome (GASJ), Congiato to Beckx, December 10, 1858. For a complete account of the Blackfeet Mission, see Wilfred P. Schoenberg, S.J., "Historic St. Peter's Mission," in *Montana, the Magazine of Western History,* Vol. 11 (1961), p. 63, et seq; also Wilfred P. Schoenberg, S.J., *Jesuits in Montana* (Portland, 1960), p. 35, et seq.

7. Sacred Heart among the Coeur d'Alenes moved five times, as did St. Ignatius among the Kalispels. St. Peter's among the Blackfeet moved four times in its first eight years. *See* Burns, *Jesuits and Indian Wars,* p. 53.

8. Palladino, *Indians and Whites,* p. 458.

9. *Ibid.,* p. 194.

10. *Ibid.,* p. 194 et seq.

11. *Ibid.*

12. [George F. Weibel, S.J.] "Fifty Years of Peaceful Conquest, *The Gonzaga Magazine,* Vol. 5 (1913–14), p. 299.

13. Meriwether Lewis and William Clark, *History of the Expedition under the Command of Lewis and Clark to the Sources of the Missouri River, etc.,* ed. Elliot Couse, 4 vols. (New York, 1893), entry for July 3, 1806, 3:1066, et seq.

14. Palladino, *Indians and Whites,* p. 357, et seq.

15. *Ibid.,* p. 297.

16. *Ibid.,* p. 138, et seq. Palladino gives a detailed account regarding the arrival of "The First Sisters in Montana."

17. *Ibid.,* p. 306, et seq. These and following details are taken from Palladino's account.

18. *Ibid.,* p. 206, et seq.

Chapter 6
PROGRESS THROUGH ADVERSITY

1. Gilbert J. Garraghan, *The Jesuits of the Middle United States,* 3 vols. (New York, 1938), 2:128.

2. *Ibid.*

3. Archives of Archdiocese of Portland, Blanchet correspondence, folio 4:1, 2, 13; R. De Martins, *Juris Pontificis De Propaganda Fide, Pars Prima, Complectens Bullas Brevia Acta SS,* Romae, 1894; Edwin V. O'Hara, *Pioneer Catholic History of Oregon* (Portland, 1911) p. 211.

4. Grassi became vice-superior on September 11, 1866. The Turin Province Catalogues for the three following years refer to him as general superior. Some of the older catalogues, however, were notoriously in error because of the problems of communication between the mission and Europe. On the other hand, Lawrence Palladino definitely states Grassi was vice-superior. *See* his *Indians and Whites in the Northwest: a History of Catholicity in Montana, 1838–1891,* 2d edition (Lancaster, Pa. 1922), p. 465 (hereafter, *Indians and Whites*). *Also,* William N. Bischoff, *The Jesuits in Old Oregon* (Caldwell, 1945) p. 223, Biographical Appendix compiled by William Laney.

5. John Owen, *The Journals and Letters of Mayor John Owen, Pioneer of The Northwest 1850–1871, Embracing His Purchase of St. Mary's Mission; The Building of Fort Owen; His Travels; His Relations with the Indians; His Work for the Government; and His Activities as a Western Empire Builder for Twenty Years,* ed. Seymour Dunbar and Paul C. Phillips, 2 vols. (Helena, Mont., 1927) 2:31.

6. *Ibid.,* p. 35.

7. George F. Weibel, S.J., *Rev. Joseph M. Cataldo, S.J., A Short Sketch of a Wonderful Career,* (Spokane, 1928) p. 5 (hereafter, *Cataldo*). About himself, Cataldo wrote that he had gone to Santa Clara and "there instead of dying he finished his theology." Oregon Province Archives (OPA), Cataldo Papers, "Autobiography 1912."

8. OPA, Cataldo Papers, "Sketch of the Spokane Mission," p. 10 (hereafter, "Sketch of Spokane").

9. *Ibid.,* pp. 11–12. The Mullan Road was completed in 1862. Durham gives a description of its course from Walla Walla to Fort Benton via Spokane. Also, N. W. Durham, *History of the*

City of Spokane and Spokane County, Washington, 3 vols. (Spokane, 1912) 1:297.

10. Weibel, *Cataldo*, p. 10.

11. Hiram M. Chittenden and Alfred T. Richardson, *Life, Letters, and Travels of Pierre-Jean De Smet, S.J.*, 4 vols. (New York, 1905) 2:480, 561. De Smet's first impression of the Spokane Valley was not favorable, but later he changed his mind and praised what he saw there.

12. Nicolas Point, S.J., *Wilderness Kingdom: Indian Life in the Rocky Mountains 1840–1847: The Journals and Paintings of Father Nicolas Point,* tran. and ed. Joseph P. Donnelly, S.J. (New York, 1967) p. 81.

13. Woodstock Letters, vol. 18 (1889), p. 355.

14. OPA, Caruana Papers, "Notes on Early Missionary Labors in Spokane" (hereafter, "Missionary Labors in Spokane").

15. *Ibid.*

16. OPA Cataldo Papers, "Sketch of Spokane," p. 16.

17. *Ibid.*, pp 34–35.

18. Weibel, *Cataldo*, p. 10.

19. Palladino, *Indians and Whites*, p. 157.

20. OPA, Grassi Papers.

21. *Ibid.*

22. Palladino, *Indians and Whites*, p. 151.

23. Weibel, *Cataldo*, p. 14. Weibel's account is taken directly from Cataldo's manuscript history of the Nez Perce Mission in the Oregon Province Archives.

24. *Ibid*, p. 15.

25. J. M. Cataldo, S.J., *The Life of Jesus Christ from the Four Gospels in the Nez Perce Language* (Portland, 1914).

26. OPA, original contract.

27. H. Lueg manuscript, Schultheis family history contained in *From St. Paul Minnesota to Portland Oregon in 1867,* (Portland, Ore. 1868) by H. Lueg.

28. Palladino, *Indians and Whites,* p. 181, et seq.

29. Francis Paul Prucha, S.J., noted authority on government Indian policy in an address at Gonzaga University, March 26, 1981, as quoted by Alice Feinstein in the *Spokane Chronicle,* March 28, 1981.

30. George F. Weibel, S.J., "Fifty Years of Peaceful Conquest," in *Gonzaga Magazine,* vol. 5 (1913–1914), p. 300.

31. OPA, Grassi Papers.

32. George M. Waggett, O.M.I. "The Oblates of Mary Immaculate in the Pacific Northwest, 1847–1878," *The Records of the American Catholic Historical Society,* 63 (1952) p. 187.

33. *Ibid.*, 64 (1953) p. 74.

34. *Ibid.*, 64 (1953) p. 75.

35. T. Ortolan, O.M.I., *Cent ans d'Apostolat dans les deux Hemispheres Les Oblates de Marie Immaculee.* 4 vols. (Paris, 1914) 2:318, et seq.

36. U.S. House Executive Document, 41st Congress, 3rd Session, No. 1449, 497.

37. OPA, Manuscript history of the Yakima Mission by J. B. Boulet.

38. *Ibid.*

39. Weibel, "Fifty Years of Peaceful Conquest," p. 125.

40. E. Laveille, S.J., *The Life of Father De Smet, S.J.* (New York, 1915) p. 362 (hereafter, *Life of De Smet*).

41. *Ibid.*, 363.

42. *Ibid.*, 364.

43. *Ibid.*, 366.

44. *Ibid.*, 367–69.

45. *Ibid.*, 369–70 for this English version. *See* OPA, Sacred Heart Mission Papers, for the original letter of Pius IX in Latin.

46. Laveille, *Life of De Smet*, p. 369–70.

47. Weibel, "Fifty Years of Peaceful Conquest," vol. 5, p. 184 et seq.

48. Palladino, *Indians and Whites,* p. 469.

49. Laveille, *Life of De Smet*, p. 386.

50. *Ibid.*, p. 388. In a letter to Father Adolph Petit in Belgium, from Colville in October 1873.

51. Anthony Morvillo, S.J. *A Dictionary of the Numipu or Nez Perce Language by a Missionary of the Society of Jesus in the Rocky Mountains*, Part I. English-Nez Perce, St. Ignatius, 1895. *Also*, Anthony Morvillo, *Grammatica Linguae Numipu. Auctore Presbytero Missionario E Soc. Jesu In Montibus Saxosis.* De Smet, 1891. *Also*, Anthony Morvillo and Joseph Mary Cataldo, *Parodigma verbi activi lingua Numpu vulgo Nez Perce studio P.P. Missionariorum S.J. in Montibus Saxosis*, De Smet, 1888.

Chapter 7
CATALDO TAKES CHARGE

1. Robert I. Burns, *The Jesuits and the Indian Wars of the Northwest* (New Haven, 1966) p. 365 (hereafter *Jesuits and Indian Wars*).

2. *Ibid.*

3. *Ibid.*, p. 366.

4. Archives of Bureau of Catholic Indian Missions, letter to Giorda to John Baptist Brouillet, February 25, 1876.

5. George Weibel, *Rev. Joseph M. Cataldo, S.J.* p. 20 (hereafter, *Cataldo*). *Also*, Burns, *Jesuits and Indian Wars*, p. 372 fn.

6. Click Relander, *Drummers and Dreamers*, (Caldwell, Idaho, 1956)

7. Oregon Province Archives (OPA), Joset Papers.

8. Burns, *Jesuits and Indian Wars*, p. 376.

9. *Ibid.*, p. 377

10. *Ibid.*

11. *Ibid.*, p. 378

12. George W. Fuller, *A History of the Pacific Northwest* (New York, 1931), p. 265 (hereafter, *Pacific Northwest*).

13. OPA, Cataldo Papers, ms. Address of Cataldo at Jubilee Banquet, Lewiston, Feb. 20, 1928.

14. OPA, *Historia Domus S. Cordis Jesu.*

15. Burns, *Jesuits and Indian Wars*, p. 383. The official name of Hangman Creek is Latah Creek.

16. Weibel, *Cataldo*, p. 21.

17. Burns, *Jesuits and Indian Wars*, p. 384.

18. Alexander Diomedi, S.J., *Sketches of Modern Indian Life*, reprint from *Woodstock Letters* (1894), p. 75.

19. Burns, *Jesuits and Indian Wars*, p. 421.

20. *Ibid.*, p. 434.

21. *Ibid.*, p. 425.

22. *Ibid.*, p. 438.

23. *Ibid.*, p. 446.

24. *Ibid.*, p. 450.

25. Fuller, *Pacific Northwest*, p. 269.

26. Palladino, *Indians and Whites*, p. 411.

27. Weibel, *Cataldo*, p. 21.

28. Palladino, *Indians and Whites*, p. 221.

29. *Ibid.*, p. 219.

30. *Ibid.*, p. 218.

31. *Ibid.*, p. 219.

32. *Ibid.*, p. 223.

33. Weibel, "Fifty Years of Peaceful Conquest," p. 347.

34. *Ibid.*, p. 344.

35. Palladino, *Indians and Whites*, p. 304.

36. Mother M. Antoinette, F.C.S.P., *The Institute of Providence: History of the Daughters of Charity, Servants of the Poor, Known as the Sisters of Providence*, 5 vols. (Montreal, 1937–1949), 5:338.

37. Weibel, "Fifty Years of Peaceful Conquest," p. 459; *The Catholic Sentinel*, Portland, May 13, 1880.

38. *The Catholic Sentinel*, September 22, 1881.

39. *Ibid.*, September 15, 1881.

40. Palladino, *Indians and Whites*, p. 374.

41. Archives Diocese of Spokane, Record Book of Dedications, p. 54; *The Catholic Sentinel*, June 15, 1882.

42. Palladino, *Indians and Whites*, p. 447.

43. OPA, ms. Sisters of Charity of Providence; *The Indian Sentinel*, vol. 3, 2 (1923), 63.

44. Weibel, *Cataldo*, p. 23. For the history of Gonzaga University, *see* Wilfred P. Schoenberg, S.J., *Gonzaga University* (Spokane, 1963).

45. On Grant's Peace Policy, *see* Peter J. Rahill, *The Catholic Indian Missions and Grant's Peace Policy, 1870–1884.* (Washington, 1953).

46. OPA, Cataldo Papers, Ms., "Sketch of Spokane Mission."

47. *Ibid.*

48. *Ibid.*

49. *Ibid.*

50. Weibel, *Cataldo*, p. 23.

51. *Woodstock Letters*, vol. 18 (1889) p. 358.

52. Archives of the Society of Jesus, Rome. Microfilm in Oregon Province Archives, undated letter of Victor Garrand to Luis Martin, general from 1892–1906.

53. *Ibid.*, Original in OPA, Provincial Papers.

54. *Ibid.*, copy in Gonzaga University Papers. The original copy was sent to Bishop Junger.

55. *Ibid.*, Gonzaga University Press, original letter dated "21st day of October 1882." This should read 1881.

56. *Ibid.*, Gonzaga University Papers. Copy of the letter in Italian in Cataldo's hand. The original sent to Rome does not appear on the microfilm. The text presented here is a translation by Gerard Steckler, S.J.

57. *Ibid.*, Provincial Papers, Junger to Cataldo, Feb. 6, 1882.

58. *Ibid.*, Procurator's account books, 1881–1884.

59. After Ruellan's premature death, a book containing his letters was published in France (anonymous), *Louis et Auguste Ruellan Pretres de la Compagnie de Jesus*, Angers, 1885. Trans. Michael O'Malley, S.J.

Chapter 8
EXPANSION EAST AND NORTH

1. George F. Weibel, *Rev. Joseph M. Cataldo, S.J.: A Short Sketch of a Wonderful Career* (Spokane, 1928), p. 27.

2. Oregon Province Archives (OPA), Rebmann Papers, Reminiscences of Forty Years.

3. *Ibid.*

4. *Ibid.*

5. OPA Mackin Papers, Memoirs.

6. Lawrence B. Palladino, S.J., *Indians and Whites in the Northwest: A History of Catholicity in Montana 1838–1891*, 2d ed. (Lancaster, Pa., 1922), p. 228. (hereafter, *Indians and Whites*).

7. Hiram M. Chittenden and Alfred T. Richardson, *Life, Letters, and Travels of Pierre-Jean De Smet, S.J.*, 4 vols., (New York, 1905) 3:1035 (hereafter, *Life, Letters, and Travels*).

8. OPA Prando Papers, St. Xavier's Mission.

9. William Bischoff, *The Jesuits in Old Oregon* (Caldwell, 1945), p. 124, et seq. (hereafter, *The Jesuits*).

10. OPA, Barcelo Papers, Letter to Cataldo, July 21, 1883.

11. [Mother Clotilde, O.S.U.] *Ursulines of the West*, (Seattle, 1936), p. 34, et seq. *Also* (anon) *Ursulines of Alaska: Life of the Rev. Mother Amadeus of the Heart of Jesus* (New York, 1923).

12. William Arendzen, S.S.E., "The Cheyennes and Their Catholic Mission," in *The Indian Sentinel*, II (1920), p. 63.

13. Emmanuel Roets, O.M. Cap., and Alexis Gore, O.M. Cap., *Historical Sketch: St. Labre's Catholic Indian Mission*, (Detroit, 1927).

14. Bischoff, *The Jesuits*, p. 126, et seq.

15. Arendzen, *op. cit.*, p. 70.

16. OPA, Prando Papers, St. Xavier's Mission, p. 2.

17. *Ibid.*

18. Joseph Bandini, letters to M. P. Wyman, July 6, 1893, printed in *The Report of the Commissioner of Indian Affairs*, 1893, p. 181.

19. Palladino, *Indians and Whites*, p. 261.

20. *Ibid.*, p. 262.

21. *Ibid.*, p. 230, et seq.

22. OPA, St. Paul Mission Papers, Eberschweiler's Foundation of St. Paul's Mission.

23. *Ibid.*, Eberschweiler letter to Cataldo, April 1, 1886.

24. *Ibid.*, Eberschweiler letter to Cataldo, May 2, 1886.

25. *Ibid.*, Eberschweiler letter to Alexander Diomedi, January 23, 1887.

26. Palladino, *Indians and Whites*, p. 233.

27. OPA, Parodi Papers, Reminiscences and Reflections of Rev. Aloysius Parodi, S.J., p. 30.

28. *Ibid.*

29. *Ibid. Also, Woodstock Letters*, 17 (1887), p. 196.

30. Sister Maria Ilma Rauffer, O.P., *Black Robes and Indians on the Last Frontier: A Story of Heroism* (Milwaukee, 1963), p. 173, et seq. This book contains a history of St. Mary's Mission, Omak, and a rather complete biography of de Rouge. De la Motte's presence in the de Rouge chateau is narrated in P. d'Herouville, *Vingt-Cinq Ans Chez Les Peaux-Rouges, Vie du P. de la Motte, S.J.*, Paris and Tournai, c. 1924. Manuscript translation by Michael O'Malley, S.J. in OPA, de la Motte Papers.

31. Rauffer, op. cit., p. 175.

32. *Ibid.*, p. 180.

33. *Ibid.*, p. 178.

34. *Ibid.*, p. 181.

35. *Ibid.*, p. 182.

36. OPA Rebmann Papers, Reminiscences of Forty Years, p. 18.

37. *Ibid.*

38. Gerard Steckler, S.J., "The Case for Frank Fuller," in *The Pacific Northwest Quarterly,* vol. 58 (Oct. 1968), p. 190, et seq. This is the best material published on Fuller and has been used extensively. Another important work on Seghers and Fuller is Steckler's unpublished doctoral dissertation: "Charles John Seghers, Missionary Bishop in The American Northwest 1839–1886," University of Washington, 1963. *Also,* OPA, Giordano Papers, Memoirs of an Alaskan Missionary, p. 3, et seq. Carmel Giordano, S.J., was in Alaska for 25 years from 1887–1912. At Bishop Crimont's request he dictated these memoirs to three tertians: Joseph J. King, Egon Mallman, and Joseph H. Johnson. Five copies were made; the fifth was taken to Rome by Norbert de Boyne, S.J., following his official visitation of the American Assistancy. Giordano's manuscript contains many details on the Seghers's missionary journey of 1886 and on early Alaskan history not found in any other source.

39. OPA, Tosi Papers, letter to Cataldo, July 19, 1886.

40. OPA, Giordano Papers, Memoirs, p. 4.

41. OPA, Jette Papers, Notes for *History of Alaska Missions*.

42. OPA, Seghers Papers, Letter to John J. Jonckau, August 31, 1886.

43. OPA, Giordano Papers, Memoirs, p. 4.

44. *Ibid.*, p. 5.

Chapter 9
PAINFUL GROWTH

1. OPA, Parodi Papers, "Reminiscences and Reflections of Rev. Al Parodi, S. J.," p. 28.

2. *Ibid.*, Rebmann Papers, "Reminiscences of Forty Years," pp. 14–16.

3. *Ibid.*, Mackin Papers, Memoirs, 2:2.

4. *Gonzaga College* (Spokane Falls, 1887), p. 104.

5. OPA, Provincial Papers related to proposed college at Helena.

6. *Ibid.*, Giordano Papers, Memoirs, p. 9.

7. *Ibid.*

8. Gerard G. Steckler, S. J., "The Case of Frank Fuller," p. 197.

9. *Ibid.*, p. 195.

10. *Ibid.*, p. 197.

11. OPA Giordano Papers, Memoirs, p. 10.

12. *Ibid.*, Cataldo Papers, letter to Jules Jette, January 13, 1925.

13. *Ibid.*, Giordano Papers, Memoirs, p. 10.

14. *Ibid.*, p. 11.

15. *Ibid.*, p. 19.

16. *Ibid.*, p. 88.

17. *Ibid.*, p. 20.

18. *Ibid.*

19. *Ibid.*, p. 23.

20. *Ibid.*, p. 24.

21. OPA, Holy Cross Mission Papers, Diaries, Introduction I:1. This volume contains a brief manuscript history of Holy Cross Mission by Robaut.

22. *Ibid.*, Giordano Papers, Memoirs, p. 28.

23. *Ibid.*, p. 25.

24. *Ibid.*, p. 39.

24. *Ibid.*

26. *Ibid.*, p. 37.

27. *Ibid.*, Holy Cross Mission Papers, Diaries, Introduction I:2.

28. Sister Mary Joseph Calasanctius, *The Voice of Alaska*, (Lachine, Quebec, 1935) p. 57.

29. A detailed account of railroad activity in the vicinity of the college can be found in N. W. Durham, *History of the City of Spokane and Spokane County Washington*, 3 vols. (Spokane, 1912), I:413.

30. OPA, de Rouge Papers, correspondence.

31. George F. Weibel, *Rev. Joseph M. Cataldo, S. J., A Short Sketch of a Wonderful Career* (Spokane, 1928), p. 31.

32. Wilfred P. Schoenberg, S. J., *Jesuit Mission Presses* (Portland, 1957), p. 56, et seq.

33. Lawrence B. Palladino, S. J., *Indians and Whites in the Northwest: A History of Catholicity in Montana, 1838–1891*, 2d ed., (Lancaster, Pa., 1922), p. 228, et. seq.

34. [George F. Weibel, S. J.] *Gonzaga's Silver Jubilee, A Memoir* (Spokane, 1912), p. 80, et seq. Weibel closely followed the college diary for this book. Subsequent details in the text are also taken from the college diary, presently filed in the Oregon Province Archives.

35. *Ibid.*, p. 43.

36. OPA, Gonzaga University Papers, Diaries, May 12, 1889.

37. *Ibid.*, May 16, 1890.

38. *Ibid.*, March 30, 1891.

39. Daniel Aloysius Hanly, *Blessed Joseph Pignatelli (of the Society of Jesus), A Great Leader in a Great Crisis* (New York, 1937).

Chapter 10
CATALDO'S LAST YEARS AS SUPERIOR

1. Cornelius Holgate Hanford, *Seattle and Environs 1852–1924*, 2 vols. (Chicago, 1924) 1:143. The name of Chief Seattle has been given variously, e.g., "Sealth."

2. *Ibid.*, p. 148.

3. *Ibid.*

4. *Ibid.*

5. *Ibid.*, p. 143. Dr. David C. Maynard proposed the name Seattle and the Oregon Legislature adopted it; *see also*, William C. Speidel, *Sons of the Profits* (Seattle, 1967), p. 25, et seq.

6. W. J. Metz, *Life Sketch of Monsignor F. X. Prefontaine*, (Seattle, 1908), p. 12, et seq.

7. *Ibid.*, p. 15; also, *The Catholic Sentinel* (Portland), September 16, 1871.

8. Victor Garrard, S. J., *Augustine Laure, S. J.*,

NOTES

Missionary to the Yakimas, ed. E. J. Kowrack (Fairfield, 1977) p. 15 (hereafter, *Augustine Laure*).

9. Lucille McDonald in the *Seattle Times*, April 2, 1967, an interview with Prefontaine's niece Marie Rose Pauze; *see also*, Edmund Long, *Church of the Immaculate 1891–1966.* (Seattle, 1966), p. 5, for early history of St. Francis Hall.

10. OPA, Provincial Papers, Letter of Junger to Cataldo, April 11, 1891.

11. OPA, Parodi Papers, Reminiscences, p. 24.

12. *Ibid.*

13. Garrand, *Augustine Laure.*

14. Long, *Church of the Immaculate,* p. 5.

15. *Woodstock Letters,* 20 (1891), p. 477.

16. Wilfred P. Schoenberg, S.J., *Gonzaga University,* p. 106.

17. Long, *Church of the Immaculate,* p. 5.

18. Archives of the Archdiocese of Seattle, Letters of Bishop O'Dea, January 16, 1903.

19. Schoenberg, *Gonzaga University,* p. 119.

20. OPA, Gonzaga University Papers, Diaries, October 29, 1892.

21. *Ibid.,* November 9, 1892.

22. Lawrence B. Palladino, S. J., *Indians and Whites in the Northwest: A History of Catholicity in Montana 1838–1891,* 2d ed. (Lancaster, Pa., 1922), p. 109 (hereafter *Indians and Whites*).

23. *Ibid.*

24. *Ibid.,* p. 110.

25. *Ibid.,* p. 111.

26. Weibel, *Gonzaga's Silver Jubilee* p. 136.

27. OPA Gonzaga University Papers, Diaries, November 19, 1892.

28. Weibel, *Gonzaga's Silver Jubilee,* p. 139.

29. Palladino, *Indians and Whites,* p. 477.

30. OPA, Parodi Papers, Reminiscences, p. 21.

31. *Ibid.,* p. 20.

32. Palladino, *Indians and Whites,* p. 310, et seq.

33. OPA, Parodi Papers, Reminiscences, p. 22.

34. Palladino, *Indians and Whites,* p. 477.

35. Garrand, *Augustine Laure,* p. 28.

36. Speidel, *Sons of the Profits,* p. 338.

37. OPA, Giordano Papers, Memoirs, p. 40.

38. *Ibid.*

39. Segundo Llorente, S. J., *Jesuits in Alaska,* (Portland, 1962) p. 15.

40. Sister Mary Joseph Calasanctius, *The Voice of Alaska* (Lachine, Quebec, 1935) p. 93, et seq.

41. *Ibid.*

42. OPA Giordano Papers, Memoirs, p. 46.

43. *Ibid.*

44. *Ibid.,* p. 47.

45. *Ibid.,* p. 49. The best published work on Barnum is Leo B. Kaufmann, S. J., "Whom the Lord Loveth," in *I Lift My Lamp,* ed. John P. Leary, S. J. (Westminster, Maryland, 1955) pp. 236–69. An account of Barnum's attractions to Alaska appears on pp. 243–44.

46. Kaufmann, "Whom the Lord Loveth," p. 261.

47. Georgetown University Archives, Barnum Papers, ms., "Account of a Journey from St. Michael's to Tununa 1891." Copy in OPA.

48. *Ibid.,* p. 11.

49. *Woodstock Letters,* 22 (1893), p. 43.

50. Georgetown University Archives, Barnum Papers, ms., "Tununa Kanelik and Akulurak." Copy in OPA.

51. *Woodstock Letters,* 22 (1893) p. 50, et seq.

52. *Ibid.,* p. 435.

53. OPA, Parodi Papers, Reminiscences, p. 37.

54. OPA, Alaska Mission Histories, ms. "Catholicism in Alaska," by Raphael Crimont, S. J., p. 17, et seq.

55. *Woodstock Letters*, 22 (1893), p. 515.

56. *Ibid.*

57. OPA, Parodi Papers, Reminiscences, p. 34.

58. Georgetown University Archives, Barnum Papers, ms. "Tununa Kanelik and Akulurak." Copy in OPA.

59. OPA, Parodi Papers, Reminiscences, p. 39.

60. *Ibid.*

61. OPA, Gonzaga University Papers, Diaries, August 24, 1892.

62. *Ibid.*, September 3, 1892.

63. *Woodstock Letters*, 22 (1893), p. 327.

64. *Ibid.*, p. 515.

65. *Ibid.*

66. Llorente, *Jesuits in Alaska*, p. 9.

67. OPA, Prefecture of Alaska Papers, original decree.

68. *Ibid.*

Chapter 11
VAN GORP AS SUPERIOR

1. OPA, Gonzaga University Papers, Gonzaga Diaries, June 4, 1894.

2. *Ibid.*, August 28, 1894.

3. *Ibid.*, Book of Articles of Incorporation and Meetings of the Board of Trustees, 1894–1934, p. 2.

4. *Ibid.*, Gonzaga Diaries, June 28, 1894.

5. Lawrence B. Palladino, S.J., *Indians and Whites in the Northwest: a History of Catholicity in Montana.* 1st ed. (Baltimore, 1894).

6. *Spokesman Review*, January 27, 1900.

7. OPA, Holy Family Mission Papers, Ms., Holy Family Mission. For details concerning St. Peter's, *see* Wilfred Schoenberg, S.J., "Historic St. Peter's Mission" in *Montana Magazine of Western History*, 11 (1961) p. 68, et seq.

8. OPA, Mackin Papers, Wanderings, 2:18.

9. [Mother Angela Clotilda, O.S.U.] *Ursulines of the West 1535–1935; 1880–1935,* (Everett, 1936), p. 53.

10. OPA, Provincial Papers, Van Gorp correspondence with Bishop Brondel, June 4, 1897.

11. Demetrius Jueneman, O.S.B. and Sebastian Ruth, O.S.B., *Between the Years 1895–1945, St. Martin's College* (Lacy, 1945), p. 14.

12. OPA, Mackin Papers, Wanderings, Part II, p. 4.

13. Alexander Diomedi, S.J., *Sketches of Modern Indian Life,* (Woodstock, 1884).

14. *The Sunday Missoulian*, October 4, 1942, p. 4.

15. OPA, Mackin Papers, Wanderings, Part II, p. 49.

16. *Ibid.*

17. *Ibid.*, Parodi Papers, Reminiscences, p. 39.

18. *Ibid.*

19. Leo Kaufmann, S.J., "Whom the Lord Loveth" in *I Lift My Lamp*, ed. John P. Leary, S.J. (Westminster, Md., 1955), p. 268 (hereafter, "Whom the Lord Loveth").

20. OPA, Barnum Papers concerning Father Tosi, p. 1.

21. *Ibid.*, Giordano Papers, Memoirs, p. 69.

22. *Ibid.*, p. 70.

23. Quoted in Rev. Charles J. Judge, S.S., *An American Missionary: a Record of the Work of Rev. William H. Judge, S.J.* (Ossining, New York, 1907) p. 203, et seq. (hereafter, William H. Judge).

24. *Woodstock Letters* (1897), p. 496.

25. Georgetown University Archives, Barnum Papers, ms., "Tununa, Kanelik and Akularak," p. 18, et seq. Copy in OPA.

26. *Woodstock Letters*, 26 (1897) p. 496.

27. OPA, Rene Papers, Diaries, June 27, 1897.

28. OPA, Copy of original in Prefecture Apostolic of Alaska Papers.

29. OPA, St. Peter's Mission Papers, Nulato, Diaries, July 3, 1897.

30. Woodstock Letters, 26 (1897) p. 523. Rene's letter was dated San Francisco, October 31, 1897.

31. *Woodstock Letters*, 27 (1898), p. 67, et seq.

32. *Woodstock Letters*, 26, (1897), p. 496.

33. Peter De Roo, *History of America Before Columbus: According to Documents and Approved Sources* (Philadelphia, 1900).

34. OPA, Gonzaga Papers, Diaries, July 29, 1897.

35. *Ibid.*, September 4, 1899.

36. *Spokane Chronicle*, April 25, 1900.

37. OPA, St. Francis Xavier Mission Papers, Diaries, June 16, 1898.

38. Rev. Francis Barnum, S.J., *Grammatical Fundamentals of the Innuit Language as Spoken by the Eskimo of the West Coast of Alaska* (Boston, 1901).

39. Kaufmann, "Whom the Lord Loveth," p. 265.

40. Judge, *William H. Judge, S.J.*, p. 257.

Chapter 12
INTRODUCING DE LA MOTTE

1. OPA ms. "Life of Rev. George de la Motte, S.J. 1861–1918, Last Superior of the Rocky Mountain Mission," translation by Michael O'Malley, S.J. of P. D'Herouville's *Vingt-Cinq Ans Chez Les Peaux-Rouges, Vie Du P. de la Motte, S.J.*, (Paris and Tournai, c. 1924.)

2. *Ibid.*, p. 6.

3. *Ibid.*, p. 7.

4. *Ibid.*

5. *Ibid.* p. 17.

6. *Ibid.*, p. 18.

7. OPA, Gonzaga Papers, Gonzaga Cadets, official documents (20).

8. *Ibid.*, (24).

9. *Ibid.*, Gonzaga Diaries, August 15, 1900.

10. OPA, ms., "Life of de la Motte," p. 22.

11. *Ibid.*

12. *Woodstock Letters,* 29 (1900) p. 422.

13. *Ibid.*, p. 425, et seq.

14. *Ibid.*, 30 (1901), p. 299.

15. OPA, Eberschweiler Papers, Notes and Clippings on his Jubilee; also, *The Register,* Eastern Montana Edition, October 16, 1932.

16. *Ibid.*

17. OPA, ms., "Life of de la Motte," p. 23.

18. *Ibid.*, p. 24.

19. OPA, Parodi Papers, "Reminiscences," p. 60.

20. OPA, ms. "Life of de la Motte," p. 30.

21. Michael M. O'Malley, S. J., *Flocks that I Watched: Memoirs of Father Michael O'Malley, S.J., 1875–1970*, ed. Timothy O'Leary, S.J. (Spokane, 1971), p. 22 (hereafter, *Memoirs*).

22. The best published material about Jette is "Julius Jette: Distinguished Scholar in Alaska," by Louis L. Renner, S.J., in *The Alaska Journal,* 5 (1975) p. 239, et seq.

23. OPA, ms. "Life of de la Motte," p. 60.

24. *Woodstock Letters,* 31 (1902), p. 79, et seq.

25. *Spokane Chronicle*, October 12, 1901.

26. *Ibid.*, October 26, 1901. The director of athletics was Thomas Meagher, S.J.

27. *Woodstock Letters,* 30 (1901), p. 300.

28. OPA, Provincial Papers, de la Motte letter to Rene, November 28, 1901.

29. *Ibid.*, Jacquet Papers, Letters, etc. of Government Officials and Doctors.

30. *Spokesman-Review*, March 17, 1902.

31. OPA ms. "Life of de la Motte," p. 34.

32. *Woodstock Letters*, 30 (1901), p. 165.

33. *Ibid.*, 31 (1902), p. 320.

34. *Ibid.*

35. Archives Diocese of Helena, Scrapbooks IV, p. 95.

36. OPA ms. "Life of de la Motte," p. 41.

37. *Ibid.*, p. 43.

38. *Ibid.*, p. 44.

39. OPA, Gonzaga Papers, Gonzaga Diaries, January 13, 1903.

40. *Ibid.*, May 26, 1903.

41. *Ibid.*, July 13, 1903.

42. OPA ms. "Life of de la Motte," p. 76.

43. *Ibid.*, p. 57.

44. OPA, Eagle City Papers, "History," p. 5.

45. *Ibid.*, p. 7. Crimont left with Monroe on June 21, 1904.

46. Renner, "Julius Jette," p. 241.

47. OPA, ms. "Life of de la Motte," p. 61.

48. Edward J. Divine, *Across Widest America, Newfoundland to Alaska with the impressions of ten year's sojourn on the Bering Coast*, (Montreal, 1905).

49. *Woodstock Letters*, 32 (1903), p. 135.

50. OPA ms., "Life of de la Motte," p. 66.

51. [Weibel] *Gonzaga's Silver Jubilee*, p. 203.

52. OPA ms., "Life of de la Motte," p. 67, et seq.

53. *Ibid.*, p. 72.

54. *Woodstock Letters*, 33 (1904) p. 105.

55. *The Catholic Northwest Progress*, December 24, 1948.

56. OPA ms., "Life of de la Motte," p. 73.

57. OPA, Gonzaga Papers, Gonzaga Diaries, May 23, 1904.

58. OPA, Parodi Papers, "Reminiscences," p. 79.

59. *Ibid.*

60. *Ibid.*

61. Francis Menager, S.J., *The Menager-Charvet Saga*, (Spokane, 1965) p. 1, et seq.

62. OPA ms., "Life of de la Motte," p. 79.

63. Msgr. John Doogan, *Church of the Immaculate, 1891–1966*, p. 4.

64. O'Malley, *Memoirs*, p. 25.

65. *Ibid.*

66. OPA, Gonzaga Papers, Gonzaga Diaries, May 2, 1906.

67. OPA, Gonzaga Papers, Goller correspondence, May 1, 1906.

68. William J. Deeney, S.J., *The Building Beautiful*, I (1928), p. 2, et seq.

69. OPA Beaverton Papers, ms., "History in Misc. Papers."

70. OPA, Provincial Papers, de la Motte to Lucchesi, July 13, 1907.

71. *The Catholic Sentinel*, June 19, 1902.

72. OPA, St. Ignatius Parish, Portland Papers, Residentia et Schola Sancti Ignatii pro Statu Oregon, p. 1, et seq.

73. OPA ms., "Life of de la Motte," p. 83 et seq.

Chapter 13
CALIFORNIA PROVINCE

1. OPA, ms. "Life of de la Motte," p. 80, et seq.

2. E. R. Zimmers, S.J., "Better a Day," in *Better a Day*, ed. John P. Leary, S.J. (New York, 1951), p. 148.

3. *Woodstock Letters*, 35 (1906), pp. 119 and 258, et seq. One report was sent in by Landry.

4. Richard A. Gleeson, S.J., *Dominic Giacobbi, A Noble Corsican* (New York, 1938), hereafter cited as *Giacobbi*.

5. OPA, Provincial Papers, de la Motte's Diary, August 31, 1906.

6. *Ibid.*, September 13, 1906.

7. Francis J. McGarrigle, S.J., *My Father's Will* (Milwaukee, 1944).

8. Daniel Lord, S.J., *The Jesuit With the Magic Hands* (St. Louis, 1948). Louis Egan had experienced a period of dependency on alcohol without creating scandals for anyone. He overcame the problem entirely. Bishop Joseph Dougherty of Yakima objected to the revelation of this part of Egan's past and suppressed the booklet.

9. OPA, Parodi Papers, "Reminiscences," p. 80.

10. OPA, Provincial Papers, de la Motte Diaries, September 29, 1907.

11. *Ibid.*, October 3, 1907.

12. *Ibid.*, November 16, 1907.

13. *Ibid.*, November 22, 1907.

14. Roger Gillis, S.J., "Profile: Fr. Cornelius Mullen, S.J." in *The Exchange,* September, 1977, p. 8.

15. Sister Maria Ilma Rauffer, O.P., *Black Robes and Indians on the Last Frontier* (Milwaukee, 1963), p. 262.

16. *Ibid.*, p. 269, et seq., concerning "The Ladies Catechists Missionaries of St. Mary's Mission."

17. Archives of the Diocese of Spokane, correspondence regarding St. Mary's Mission. De Rouge died May 9, 1916.

18. OPA, Provincial Papers, de la Motte Diaries, December 23, 1907.

19. *Ibid.*, February 12, 1908.

20. Gerald McKevitt, S.J., *The University of Santa Clara: A History, 1851–1977,* (Stanford, 1979), p. 158.

21. OPA, Provincial Papers, de la Motte Diaries, March 10, 1908.

22. *Ibid.*, April 14, 1908.

23. OPA, Portland, St. Michael's Parish, ms. history of the parish.

24. Gleeson, *Giacobbi,* p. 138, et seq. Also, *Woodstock Letters,* 37 (1908), p. 403.

25. OPA, Provincial Papers, de la Motte correspondence: to Rectors from San Francisco, August 17, 1908.

26. Lawrence Palladino, *Indians and Whites in the Northwest,* p. 77.

27. OPA, D'Aste Papers, from St. Ignatius Mission, August 30, 1908, to de la Motte.

28. OPA, St. Regis Mission Papers, Diaries, September 1, 1908.

29. OPA, Portland, St. Ignatius Parish Papers, "History in Latin," trans. Wilfred Schoenberg.

30. OPA, ms., "Life of de la Motte, p. 84.

31. *Woodstock Letters,* 38 (1909), p. 273. Also *Catholic Sentinel,* March 4, 1909.

32. Michael M. O'Malley, S.J., *Flocks That I Watched: Memoirs of Fr. Michael O'Malley, S.J. (1875–1970),* ed. Timothy O'Leary, S.J. (Spokane, 1971), p. 26 (hereafter, *Memoirs*).

33. Seattle College Catalogue, 1909.

34. O'Malley, *Memoirs,* p. 27.

35. *Spokane Chronicle,* October 15, 1908.

36. OPA, Mackin Papers, "Memoirs," p. 76.

37. *Spokane Chronicle,* May 28, 1909.

38. OPA, Ashland [Oregon] Diary, August 17, 1909.

39. *Ibid.*, August 23, 1909.

40. OPA, Dimier Papers, Dimier to Cataldo, Newport, September 7, 1911.

41. *Woodstock Letters,* 38 (1909), p. 421.

42. OPA, Provincial Papers, de la Motte correspondence from Portland, September 7, 1909.

43. *Spokesman Review,* October 10, 1909.

44. Provincial Archives in Portland, Papers, de la Motte.

45. *Spokesman Review,* December 21, 1909.

46. *Woodstock Letters,* 39 (1910) p. 114.

47. OPA Provincial Papers, correspondence with Rome, Walmesley to Goller, December 18, 1909.

48. *Ibid.*, Wernz to Goller, December 20, 1909.

49. *Inland Herald* [Spokane], November 8, 1910.

50. *Spokesman Review*, November 6, 1910.

51. OPA, Provincial Papers, Goller to Falconio, original draft of letter, May 18, 1910, in Goller's hand.

52. *Ibid.*, Goller correspondence with Rome, Hanselman to Rockliff, from New York, May 30, 1910.

53. *Spokane Chronicle*, August 17, 1910.

54. *Spokesman Review*, November 6, 1910.

55. *Ibid.*, November 9, 1910.

Chapter 14
FROM CALIFORNIA TO ALASKA

1. John McAstocker, S.J., in *Western Jesuit*, II (April, 1927), p. 1, et seq.

2. Maurice Meschler, S.J., *The Life of Our Lord Jesus Christ, the Son of God*, trans. Sister Mary Margaret, O.S.B. (St. Louis, 1913).

3. McAstocker, *Western Jesuit*.

4. Sister Maria Ilma Rauffer, O.P., *Black Robes and Indians on the Last Frontier* (Milwaukee, 1963), p. 304.

5. OPA, Provincial Papers, correspondence with Rome, Wernz to Rockliff, January 9, 1911.

6. *Ibid.*, Mullan to Rockliff, February 11, 1911.

7. OPA, Province Histories, Gard to Rene, August 1, 1908.

8. *Spokane Chronicle*, October 10, 1911.

9. OPA, St. Mary's Pendleton Papers, McKenna Diaries, passim.

10. OPA, Browning, Montana Papers, manuscript history.

11. OPA, Loyola High School Papers, "Loyola, a Heritage," Mimeographed history by Patrick Stewart, S.J., and others (Missoula, 1974).

12. *Ibid.*

13. Richard A. Gleeson, S.J., *Dominic Giacobbi, A Noble Corsican* (New York, 1938), p. 118.

14. *Spokane Chronicle*, December 2, 1903.

15. *Spokesman Review*, April 24, 1912.

16. *Ibid.*, April 4, 1908.

17. *Gonzaga*, III (1911–1912), p. 310.

18. *Spokesman Review*, June 20, 1912.

19. *Spokane Chronicle*, April 11, 1912.

20. *Spokesman Review*, April 28, 1912.

21. *Spokane Chronicle*, April 29, 1912.

22. OPA, Gonzaga Papers, Book of Meetings of Trustees, p. 19, et seq.

23. *Spokane Chronicle*, May 25, 1912.

24. *Spokane Chronicle*, June 20, 1912.

25. *Woodstock Letters*, 44 (1915), p. 121.

26. *Northwest Progress*, October 27, 1911, and December 29, 1911.

27. Archives of the Diocese of Spokane, Correspondence previous to 1914, O'Dea-Charvet.

28. Archives Diocese of Spokane, Record Book of Dedications, p. 54; *Catholic Sentinel*, July 30, 1914.

29. [Joseph H. Gerharz], *Fifty Years of Growth: Golden Jubilee, Diocese of Great Falls, 1904–1954* (hereafter, Gerharz, Golden Jubilee of *Great Falls, 1904–54*); *The Eastern Montana Catholic Register*, XXX, 49 (December 3, 1954), p. 73.

30. OPA, Gonzaga Papers, Diaries, May 19, 1912.

31. OPA, Hingham, Montana, manuscript.

32. Charles M. Smith, editor, *The Centenary, 100 Years of the Catholic Church in the Oregon Country; Supplement to the Catholic Sentinel*, May 4, 1939, p. 86.

NOTES

33. OPA, St. Leo's Parish, Tacoma Papers, ms. history.

34. *Ibid.*, Memorandum of Father George Weibel, S.J.

35. OPA, Griva Papers, Diaries.

36. Gerharz, Golden Jubilee of *Great Falls, 1904–54*, p. 59.

37. *Ibid.*, p. 76.

38. *Ibid.*, p. 77.

39. OPA, Griva Papers, Diaries.

40. Dominic O'Connor, O.F.M. Cap., *A Brief History of the Diocese of Baker City*, (Baker, 1930), p. 79.

41. Patrick Casey, ed., *1841–1941, A Centenary of Catholicity in Montana: Souvenir Centenary Edition; The Register Diocese of Helena*, XVII, 35 (August 27, 1941) III, p. 2.

42. Andrew Prouty, ed., *1850–1950 Centennial of the Diocese of Seattle; The Catholic Northwest Progress*, LIII, p. 36, (September 8, 1950), p. 63.

43. *Woodstock Letters*, 42 (1913) p. 109.

44. *Ibid.*, p. 248.

45. *Acta Romana Societatis Jesu, 1912*, 74, July 18, 1912.

46. *Ibid.*, 1913, p. 54, et seq., May 24, 1913.

47. Segundo Llorente, S.J., *Jesuits in Alaska*, (Portland, 1969), p. 27.

48. *Woodstock Letters*, 40 (1911), p. 386.

49. Llorente, *Jesuits in Alaska*, p. 31.

50. *St. Ignatius Church (San Francisco) Monthly Calendar*, February, 1946, p. 56.

51. *Ibid.*, March 1949, p. 106.

52. *Spokesman Review*, May 30, 1915.

53. *Spokane Chronicle*, March 22, 1915.

54. *Ibid.*, December 1, 1915.

55. OPA, Gonzaga Papers, Diaries, November 23, 1915.

56. *Woodstock Letters*, 45 (1916), p. 185.

57. OPA, Gonzaga Papers, Diaries, January 6, 1916.

58. *St. Ignatius Church, Monthly Calendar*, March, 1949, p. 106, et seq.

59. *Woodstock Letters*, 44 (1915), p. 121.

60. *St. Ignatius Church, Monthly Calendar*, March 1949, p. 108.

61. Llorente, *Jesuits in Alaska*, p. 32.

62. Rauffer, *Black Robes and Indians on the Last Frontier*, p. 263, et seq.

63. OPA, Eberschweiler Papers, Eberschweiler's memoirs on his Golden Jubilee.

64. [David McAstocker, S.J.], *My Ain Laddie*, edited by David Dorley (alias), (Milwaukee, 1922).

65. OPA, St. Joseph Mission Papers, Diaries, September 13, 1914.

66. Archives of the Diocese of Spokane, Correspondence previous to 1914, O'Dea–Extension correspondence.

67. OPA, Griva Papers, Diaries.

68. Archives of the Diocese of Spokane, Record Book of Dedications, p. 54.

69. *Ibid.*

70. OPA, Priest River, Idaho, Manuscript.

71. Archives of the Diocese of Spokane, Record Book of Dedications, p. 54.

72. *Ibid.*, p. 55.

73. OPA, Griva Papers, Diaries.

74. OPA, St. Stanislaus Church, Lewiston, Diaries.

75. Archives of the Diocese of Spokane, Record Book of Dedications, p. 56.

76. *Woodstock Letters*, 47 (1918) p. 113.

77. *Spokane Chronicle*, May 27, 1918.

78. *Seattle College Bulletin*, Seattle, (1919).

79. OPA, ms. "Life of de la Motte," p. 92.

80. *Ibid.*, p. 93.

81. OPA, Provincial Papers, Gleeson News-letter to Province (April, 1918).

82. *Ibid.*, Gleeson to Province, July 13, 1918.

83. *St. Ignatius Church, Monthly Calendar,* June, 1949, p. 220.

Chapter 15
POSTWAR PROGRESS

1. OPA Provincial's correspondence, Dillon to the province, July 16, 1918.

2. OPA, Gonzaga University Papers, Diaries, August 15, 1918.

3. OPA, Mount St. Michael's Papers. Papers related to the Laymen's Retreat Association. There is a considerable amount of material here, including copies of various bulletins and prayer manuals published by the Association.

4. OPA, Marquette, Yakima Papers; Conrad Brusten ms., "Origin and Progress of the Church in the Yakima District."

5. *Ibid.*

6. *Ibid.*, Rockliff to Brusten, January 27, 1912.

7. OPA, Brusten Papers, Diaries, September 30, 1918.

8. OPA, Seattle College Papers, Diaries, October 4, 1918.

9. *Ibid.*, October 5, 1918.

10. OPA, Gonzaga Papers, Diaries, October 3, 1918.

11. *Ibid.*

12. *Gonzaga* X (1918–19), p. 13.

13. *Woodstock Letters,* 48 (1919), p. 106, et seq.

14. Letter of Frederick Ruppert, S.J., to Francis Dillon, S.J., Provincial, February 24, 1919, copy in *Woodstock Letters,* (1919), p. 264, et seq.

15. OPA, Provincial Papers, Tomkin to Dillon, February 12, 1919.

16. *Ibid.*

17. *Woodstock Letters,* 48 (1919), p. 109 et seq.

18. *Ibid.*, 45 (1916), p. 181.

19. OPA, Mount St. Michael's Papers, Minister's Diaries, *passim.* Some of Father Drathman's material which is related to the history of the Mount cemetery is in the Oregon Province Archives; some, in the care of Father Hubert Adams, cemetery custodian, who has made it available.

20. OPA, Seattle College Papers, Diaries, February 21, 1919.

21. *Ibid.*, February 25, 1919.

22. *Woodstock Letters,* 48 (1919), p. 406.

23. OPA, Provincial Papers, Dillon to O'Dea, May 16, 1919.

24. OPA, Seattle College Papers, Diaries, May 10, 1920.

25. OPA, Provincial Papers, Dillon to the province, July 8, 1919.

26. OPA, Seattle College Papers, Diaries, May 20, 1920. This refers to the building purchased by Mr. O'Keefe of the Knights of Columbus as the former "Protestant Orphanage."

27. *Ibid.*, Tomkin to T. C. McHugh on March 12, 1920.

28. *Northwest Progress,* January 9, 1920.

29. OPA, Seattle College Papers, Tomkin to Whittle, January 8, 1920.

30. *Ibid.*, Diaries, noted under August 31, 1920.

31. *Ibid.*, October 1, 1920.

32. *Woodstock Letters,* 50 (1921), p. 229.

33. *Ibid.*, p. 90, et seq.

34. *Northwest Progress,* October 17, 1919.

35. OPA, St. Ignatius Mission Papers, Diaries, December 9, 1920.

36. *Woodstock Letters,* 50 (1921), p. 83.

37. A. B. Cain,, *The Oregon School Fight: A True and Complete History,* (Portland, 1924), p. 3.

38. *Indian Sentinel*, II, 7 (1921), p. 304.

39. OPA, Lewiston, St. Stanislaus Church Diaries, February 29, 1920.

40. *Northwest Progress*, April 25, 1924.

41. OPA, Seattle College Papers, Diaries, September 5, 1922.

42. Memoriale *Visitationis Provinciae Californiae Relictum a R. P. Norberto de Boynes Visitatore Eiusdem Provinciae, N.P.*, [1923].

43. OPA, Provincial Papers, Dillon's notebook.

44. OPA, Nome Papers, Diaries, under December 14, 1923.

Chapter 16
PIET'S ENTHUSIASM

1. OPA, Piet Papers, Citizenship documents.

2. Edgar Dowd, "Bull-Head-Mental Case," in *Inland Catholic*, IX, 13 (February 23, 1940), p. 3.

3. OPA, Piet Papers, Passport.

4. OPA, Provincial Papers, Piet correspondence with Crimont, from Seattle, June 4 [1924].

5. *Ibid.*, Sauer to Piet correspondence [no date].

6. *Indian Sentinel*, January, 1925, p. 14.

7. Norbert De Boyne, S.J., *Directiones Relictae Reverendo Patri Provinciali Provinciae Californiae*, p. 5.

8. OPA, Gonzaga Papers, Diaries, June 25, 1924.

9. Spokesman Review, May 30, 1920.

10. OPA, Gonzaga Papers, Diaries, October 4, 1922.

11. *Ibid.*, September 23, 1923.

12. *Ibid.*, January 10, 1925.

13. *Ibid.*, De Smet Hall account book.

14. *Ibid.*, Diaries, March 28, 1925.

15. *Ibid.*, Treasurer's General Statement, May, 1925.

16. *Ibid.*, Diaries, October 24, 1925.

17. *Gonzaga Quarterly*, XV (1926), p. 18.

18. *Ibid.*, p. 19.

19. *Ibid.*

20. *California Province News*, I-4 (December, 1925), p. 30.

21. *Ibid.*

22. *Ibid.*

23. *Indian Sentinel*, VI (1925), p. 5.

24. *California Province News*, I-1 (September, 1925), p. 7.

25. Henry Albert Gabriel, S.J., *Ascetical Conferences for Religious*, St. Louis, 1939.

26. *California Province News*, I-1 (September, 1925), p. 8.

27. *Ibid.*, I-3, (November, 1925), p. 10.

28. For a lengthy obituary on Father Thomas Martin, *see* Wilfred Schoenberg, S.J., "Father Thomas Ramsay Martin 1881–1954," in *Woodstock Letters*, 5, 2 (1957), pp. 133–62.

29. *California Province News*, I-9 (May, 1926), p. 71.

30. *Ibid.*, II-3 (December, 1926), p. 28.

31. *Western Jesuit*, I (January, 1927), p. 4.

32. OPA, Seattle College Papers, Boland to Piet, October 2, 1962.

33. *California Province News*, II-5 (January, 1927), p. 39, et seq.

34. *Ibid.*, p. 40.

35. OPA, Port Townsend Manresa Hall Papers, Diaries, enclosure in first volume. Details about this also appear in the *California Province News*. III-2 (October, 1927), p. 10.

36. *Ibid.*, September 7, 1927. Manresa was named in honor of the cave in Spain where St. Ignatius wrote his renowned *Spiritual Exercises.*

37. *Oregon Jesuit*, XX, 2 (February, 1951).

38. For a full-length biography of David McAstocker, see *Father Dave* (Milwaukee, 1950), by Wilfred P. Schoenberg, S.J.

39. *Tacoma Daily Ledger*, December 2, 1919.

40. David McAstocker, *The Joy of Sorrow* (Milwaukee, 1936).

41. OPA, Tacoma, St. Leo's Parish Papers, Diaries, December 29, 1926.

42. *Ibid.*, March 18, 1928.

43. David McAstocker interview with Wilfred Schoenberg, S.J., California, May 19, 1952, Schoenberg journal for that date.

44. OPA, David McAstocker Papers, correspondence with *The Tacoma News Tribune*, Welch to McAstocker, March 28, 1935.

45. *Ibid.*, Author's Portfolio of Books for *Flashlights*, letter of Cantwell to McAstocker, August 14, 1929.

46. O.P.A., Seattle College Papers, Fitzgerald to Piet, February 2, 1927. The Apostolic delegate mentioned here was Archbishop Pietro Fumasoni-Biondi.

47. *Ibid.*, Boland to Piet, February 3, 1927.

48. OPA, Seattle College Papers, Deeney to Boland, October 25, 1927.

49. *Ibid.*, Boland to Piet, April 3, 1927.

50. *Ibid.*, Deeney to Boland, October 25, 1927.

51. *Ibid.*, Fitzgerald to Piet, October 6, 1928.

52. *Ibid.*, Boland to Piet, February 15, 1928.

53. *Ibid.*, McHugh to Piet [Winter of 1928].

54. *Ibid.*, Piet to Boland, February 21, 1928.

55. Details regarding Cataldo's jubilee can be found in many sources. See the *California Province News*, III-4 (December, 1927), p. 25, et seq. For the occasion Father George F. Weibel contributed a biography of Gonzaga's founder that occupied the full issue of the *Gonzaga Quarterly* for March 15, 1928. This was reprinted under the title *Rev. Joseph M. Cataldo, S.J., A Short Sketch of a Wonderful Career.* In the next issue of the *Gonzaga Quarterly* there appeared very complete details of the jubilee celebration.

56. *California Province News*, III-9 (May, 1928), p. 97, et seq.

57. Michael M. O'Malley, *Flocks That I Watched: Memoirs* (Spokane, 1971), p. 62.

58. *Western Jesuit*, February, 1929, p. 4.

59. OPA, Seattle College Papers, Boland to Piet, July 15, 1928.

60. *Ibid.*, Fitzgerald to Piet, July 23, 1928. This first proposed site in north Seattle was on 32nd Ave. N.E. and 70th St. East.

61. *Ibid.*, McHugh to Piet, August 4, 1928. This proposed site "was bounded on the South by East 80th St., on the North by East 85th Street, on the West by 30th Ave. Northeast and on the East by 35th Ave. Northeast." Vincent D. Miller to Piet, August 7, 1928.

62. *Ibid.*, Diaries, August 20, 1928.

63. *Ibid.*, Copy of letter from Lambert Burton, O.S.B. to O'Dea, September 18, 1928.

64. *Ibid.*, Fitzgerald to Piet, September 4, 1928.

65. *Ibid.*, Diaries, November 8, 1928.

66. Provincial Archives in Portland, Fitzgerald to Piet, March 8, 1929.

67. OPA, Seattle College Papers, Fitzgerald to Piet, July 9, 1930.

Chapter 17
PROVINCE STATUS AT LAST

1. *Western Jesuit*, IV, 4 (April, 1929), p. 3.

2. Louis Renner, S. J., "The Beginnings of Missionary Aviation in the Arctic: The *Marquette Missionary*," in *The Alaskan Shepherd*, 15 (July–August, 1977). This is a reprint of an article that had appeared in *Eskimo* (Spring–Summer, 1976), p. 8, et seq.

3. *Ibid.*

4. A biography of Father William Walsh has been published: *A Shepherd of the Far North* (San Francisco, 1934), by Robert Glady.

5. Patrick J. O'Reilly, S.J., *The Light Divine in Parable and Allegory*, (Chicago, 1930).

6. OPA Provincial Papers, Piet correspondence with Ledochowski, telegram, July 28, 1930.

7. Copy in OPA, Provincial Papers, Documents. Also *Catholic Sentinel*, January 1, 1931.

8. OPA, Provincial Papers, Piet letter to Superiors, December 20, 1930. The letters and decrees appear in the *California Province News*, VII, 6 (February, 1932).

9. Provincial Archives, Portland. Fitzgerald to members of the Vice Province, included with documents relative to the establishment of the Vice Province.

10. *Ibid.*, Piet to Fitzgerald, January 13, 1931. "Zitgu" is a Kalispel word meaning "house or lodge" according to Mengarini.

11. *Ibid.*, Piet to Fitzgerald, January 28, 1931.

12. *Ibid.*, Piet to Fitzgerald, February 9, 1931.

13. *Ibid.*, Minutes of first meeting of consultors, February 12, 1931.

14. *Ibid.*, Fitzgerald to Piet, February 17, 1931.

15. *Ibid.*, Piet to Fitzgerald, March 14, 1931.

16. *Ibid.*, Fitzgerald to Piet, March 14, 1931.

17. *Ibid.*

18. *Ibid.*, O'Reilly to Piet, April 27, 1931.

19. *Ibid.*, Fitzgerald to Piet, June 1, 1931.

20. *Ibid.*, Piet to Fitzgerald, June 20, 1931.

21. *Ibid.*, Piet to Fitzgerald, July 3, 1933.

22. *Ibid.*, Piet to Fitzgerald, July 7, 1931.

23. *Oregon Journal*, July 27, 1931.

24. OPA, Sheridan Novitiate papers, Diaries, July 29, 1931.

25. *Ibid.*, July 30, 1931. The full names were: Hubert Adams, John Evoy, Richard Twohy, Robert Schiffner, Thomas Coll and Phillip Reilly.

26. *Ibid.*, July 31, 1931. The full names were: John Dalgity, Ernest Menard, James Conwell, and Charles Chapman.

27. OPA, Sheridan Novitiate Papers, Diaries, July 31, 1931.

28. Purcell had gone to Spokane to consult Fitzgerald.

29. Provincial Archives, Portland, Fitzgerald to Piet, July 10, 1931.

30. *Ibid.*, July 17, 1931.

31. *Ibid.*, Fitzgerald to Piet, September 24, 1931.

32. *Ibid.*, Piet to Fitzgerald, September 26, 1931.

33. *Ibid.*, Fitzgerald to Piet, September 24, 1931.

34. *Ibid.*, Fitzgerald to Piet, August 11, 1931.

35. *Ibid.*, Fitzgerald to Piet, September 3, 1931. Despite this, Loyola High School in Missoula was closed in September, 1932. See *Oregon Province News*, I, 5 (September, 1932), p. 2.

36. *Jesuit Missions*, XI, (1937), p. 175, et seq.

37. Provincial Archives, Portland, Fitzgerald to Piet, July 31, 1931.

38. *Ibid.*, Fitzgerald to Piet, September 30, 1931.

39. *Ibid.*

40. *Ibid.*

41. *Ibid.*, Fitzgerald to Mattern, January 4, 1932.

42. *Ibid.*

43. *Ibid.*, Piet to Fitzgerald, January 6, 1932.

44. Both documents appear in *Acta Romana Societatis Jesu*. The Decree of erection appears in VI (1931) p. 869, et seq.; the letter is in the same volume, p. 926.

45. Provincial Archives, Portland, Piet to Fitzgerald, January 14, 1932.

46. *Ibid.*, Piet to Fitzgerald, January 19, 1932.

47. *Ibid.*, Piet to Fitzgerald, January 21, 1932. The removable pastor was Father Augustine Coudeyre, who was transferred to Missoula in June, 1932.

48. *Ibid.*, Piet to Fitzgerald, February 1, 1932.

49. OPA, Sheridan Papers, Novices Diaries, February 2, 1932.

50. OPA, Mount St. Michael's Papers, Minister's Diaries, February 2, 1932.

51. OPA, Provincial Papers, Piet to Fitzgerald, March 13, 1932.

52. *Ibid.*, Fitzgerald to Piet, March 14, 1932.

53. Provincial Archives, Portland, Fitzgerald to Ledochowski, April 12, 1932.

54. *Ibid.*

55. *Ibid.*

56. *Ibid.*, April 15, 1932.

57. OPA, Sheridan Novitiate Papers, Diaries, July 26, 1932.

58. OPA, Piet Papers, Mattern to Piet, November 10, 1933.

59. Provincial Archives, Portland, Fitzgerald to Ledochowski, April 26, 1933.

60. *Ibid.*, Ledochowski to Fitzgerald, November 16, 1932.

61. Provincial Archives, Portland, Fitzgerald to Ledochowski, May 5, 1933.

62. *Ibid.*, Fitzgerald to Mattern, May 28, 1933.

63. OPA, Gonzaga Papers, Diaries, June 13, 1933.

64. OPA, Gonzaga Papers, Diaries, June 14, 1933.

65. Provincial Archives, Portland, Dillon to Ledochowski, September 26, 1933, "Oregon Province [Report]."

66. *Ibid.*, Ledochowski to Fitzgerald, June 30, 1933.

67. Arthur D. Spearman, S.J., *Out of the Northland*, (New York, 1931), p. 28.

68. *Ibid.*, p. 39, et seq.

69. Provincial Archives, Portland, Fitzgerald to Superiors, August 5, 1933.

70. Provincial Archives, Portland, Fitzgerald to Mattern, October 17, 1933.

71. OPA, Piet Papers, Maher to Piet, April 14, 1934.

72. OPA, Piet Papers, Piet to Maher, June 27, 1934 [copy].

73. *Ibid.*, Copy of Maher's letter to members of the California Province, May 30, 1934. Alma College was formally dedicated on October 19, 1934.

74. Provincial Archives, Portland, Fitzgerald to Ledochowski, April 5, 1935.

75. *Ibid.*

76. A detailed account of the School of Engineering appears in Wilfred Schoenberg, S.J., *Gonzaga University Seventy-Five Years*, p. 365, et seq.

77. OPA Gonzaga University Papers, Financial Reports, July 1, 1933 to June 30, 1934.

78. Provincial Archives, Portland, Fitzgerald to Ledochowski, September 15, 1935, *"De Statu oeconomico valde periculoso totius Provinciae,"* which means "Concerning the very dangerous financial condition of the whole province.

79. Alma Savage, *Dogsled Apostles* (New York, 1942), p. 89 et seq.

80. Segundo Llorente, S. J., *Jesuits in Alaska* (Portland, 1969), p. 48.

81. Provincial Archives, Portland, Fitzgerald to Mother Francis Xavier, October 30, 1938.

Chapter 18
ELLIOTT'S SURVIVAL SKILL

1. John E. Moffatt, S.J., *The Sanity of Sanctity: Simple Reflections on the Common Sense of Devotedness*, (New York, 1929) Moffatt was ordained in the same year.

2. Provincial Archives, Portland, Crimont to Fitzgerald, April 14, 1937, refers to Fitzgerald's letter to Crimont.

3. *Ibid.*, Elliott to Maher, November 22, 1938. "You will be surprised to hear we almost lost Father Fitzgerald on the very last day of his Provincialate." Fitzgerald described the incident in a letter to Father Felix Geis. OPA Alaska Vicariate, Papers, Fitzgerald to Geis, December 14, 1938.

NOTES

4. *The Inland Catholic,* VIII, 9 (January 27, 1939).

5. There is a lengthy, published account of Bishop Fitzgerald's life by Wilfred P. Schoenberg, S.J., entitled "Beggar Bishop" which appears in *Woodstock Letters,* 81 (1952), p. 203, et seq. Crimont's attitude toward Fitzgerald gradually improved.

6. Provincial Archives, Portland, Maher to Elliott, December 2, 1938.

7. *Ibid.,* Fitzgerald to Maher, October 27, 1938.

8. *Ibid.,* Elliott to Maher, November 10, 1938.

9. OPA Provincial Papers, Histories, Report "Foundations of the Missions of the Oregon Province" [19].

10. *Ibid.*

11. Provincial Archives, Portland, Taelman to Maher, October 28, 1940.

12. *Ibid.*

13. *Ibid.,* Elliott to Maher, October 15, 1939. It should be noted that this tentative proposal of a grant by the tribe was designed to support Indian children, not the mission or its debt. The tribe contributed nothing to the mission.

14. *Ibid.*

15. "Liabilities of Holy Family Mission, October 15, 1940, a report included with the above.

16. Provincial Archives, Portland, Maher to Elliott, November 16, 1940.

17. *Ibid.,* Elliott to Maher, November 25, 1940.

18. *Ibid.,* Maher to Elliott, December 4, 1940.

19. *Ibid.,* August 11, 1941.

20. *Jesuit Missions,* 22 (July–August, 1948), p. 3.

21. Provincial Archives, Portland, Maher to Elliott, October 27, 1939.

22. *Ibid.,* Maher to all Jesuits of the American Assistancy, October 18, 1939.

23. *Ibid.,* Maher to Elliott, July 9, 1939.

24. *Ibid.,* Elliott to Maher, March 13, 1940.

25. *Ibid.,* Maher to Elliott, July 13, 1941.

26. Interview with Father James McGoldrick, Seattle, July 6, 1981.

27. *Ibid.*

28. Provincial Archives, Portland, Crimont to Elliott, May 2, 1940.

29. *Ibid.,* Hubbard to Crimont, May 18, 1940.

30. OPA, Alaska Vicariate Papers, Fitzgerald to Geis, April 8, 1940.

31. Provincial Archives, Portland, Crimont to Elliott, May 2, 1940.

32. *Ibid.,* Fitzgerald to Elliott, May 8, 1940.

33. *Ibid.,* Maher to Elliott, October 31, 1940.

34. *Ibid.,* Elliott to Maher, November 6, 1940.

35. *Ibid.,* Maher to Elliott, November 13, 1940.

36. *Ibid.,* November 7, 1940.

37. *Ibid.,* November 20, 1940.

38. *Ibid.,* Elliott to Maher, November 20, 1940.

39. *Ibid.,* Maher to Elliott, December 18, 1940; *Seattle Times,* June 22, 1941.

40. *Jesuit Seminary News* VIII, 6 (October, 1939), p. 1.

41. Interview with Father Leo Gaffney, S.J., Spokane, September 15, 1980.

42. Provincial Archives, Portland, Elliott to Maher, January 11, 1941.

43. *Ibid.,* Maher to Elliott, January 20, 1941.

44. *Ibid.,* Elliott to Maher, February 12, 1941.

45. *Ibid.,* Maher to Elliott, July 14, 1941.

46. *Ibid.,* Elliott to Maher, July 23, 1941.

47. *Ibid.,* Maher to Elliott, August 11, 1941.

48. *Ibid.,* Elliott to Maher, August 29, 1941.

49. *Ibid.,* September 15, 1941.

50. *Ibid.,* Maher to Elliott, September 22, 1941.

51. OPA, Gonzaga Papers, ms. "The Gonzaga Fire," December 10, 1941.

52. Provincial Archives, Portland, Elliott to Maher, December 12, 1941.

53. *Ibid.*, Maher to Elliott, December 17, 1941.

54. OPA Alaska Vicariate Papers, Fitzgerald to Geis, Easter Sunday, 1942.

55. Copy in OPA Provincial's Papers, Letters from Zacheus Maher.

56. Provincial Archives, Portland, Maher to Elliott, January 17, 1942.

Chapter 19
"PRAY FOR THE SWEDES"

1. *Jesuit Seminary News XI*, 2 (April, 1942), p. 9.

2. *Gonzaga Bulletin*, April 10, 1942.

3. *Northwest Progress*, June 5, 1942.

4. Provincial Archives, Portland, telegram Maher to Robinson, December 14, 1942. "Cable just received announces death of Father General."

5. *Ibid.*, Maher's Notice to all Provinces, December 15, 1942.

6. *Ibid.*, Maher to Robinson, December 10, 1942.

7. *Ibid.*, May 7, 1943.

8. *Ibid.*, Robinson to Maher, October 31, 1943.

9. *Ibid.*, Maher to Robinson, November 18, 1943.

10. *Ibid.*, Robinson to Maher, November 22, 1943.

11. OPA Vicariate of Alaska Papers, Fitzgerald to Geis, September 22, 1943.

12. Provincial Archives, Portland, Maher to Robinson, May 10, 1944.

13. *Ibid.*, May 3, 1944.

14. *Ibid.*, Robinson to Maher, November 2, 1944.

15. *Ibid.*, December 13, 1944.

16. *Ibid.*, Maher to Robinson, December 11,

1944. The Griva Memoirs were never published.

17. *Ibid.*, Robinson to Maher, December 29, 1944.

18. OPA ms., Central Catholic High School.

19. *The Inland Register*, March 16, 1945.

20. Provincial Archives, Portland, Robinson to Maher, March 4, 1945.

21. *Ibid.*, Maher to Robinson (cable), March 29, 1945.

22. OPA Gonzaga University Papers, Diaries, April 9, 1945.

23. *San Francisco Examiner*, August 3, 1945.

24. OPA, Vicariate of Alaska Papers, Fitzgerald to Geis, April 15, 1945.

25. Provincial Archives, Portland, Robinson report on visitation to Alaska. No date (probably January, 1946).

26. *Ibid.*

27. *Ibid.*

28. *Ibid.*

29. *Ibid.*, Maher to all Provincials, October 26, 1945.

30. *Ibid.*, Robinson to de Boynes, July 14, 1946.

31. *Ibid.*, de Boynes to Robinson [cable] July 29, 1946.

32. *Ibid.*, Robinson to Sauer, July 30, 1946.

33. *Ibid.*, Robinson to Janssens, no date [probably January, 1947].

34. *Ibid.*, Janssens to Fitzgerald, March 13, 1947.

35. *Ibid.*, Robinson to Goulet, May 16, 1947.

36. *Ibid.*, Robinson to Janssens, February 11, 1947.

37. *Ibid.*, February 28, 1947.

38. *Ibid.*, no date [probably March, 1947].

39. *Ibid.*, November 28, 1947. Also Small to

Janssens, July 10, 1948, regarding Bishop White's request.

40. *Coronet*, October, 1949, p. 87, et seq.

41. Provincial Archives, Portland, Robinson to Janssens, June 27, 1947.

42. OPA, Vicariate of Alaska Papers, mimeographed letter of James Conwell, Chancellor, to Fitzgerald's friends, August 30, 1947.

Chapter 20
A STABLE PROVINCE

1. OPA, Dillon Papers, manuscript on Dillon by Wilfred P. Schoenberg, S.J.

2. Segundo Llorente, S. J., *Jesuits in Alaska* (Portland, 1969), p. 56.

3. OPA, Provinical Papers, general notice, Dougherty to the Province, March 29, 1948.

4. OPA, Vicariate of Alaska Papers, Gleeson, consecration papers.

5. *Northwest Progress*, May 14, 1948.

6. *Catalogues Provincial Oregoniensis Anni 1948*, p. 22. Gonzaga University at that time had 1,700 students. *Ibid.*, p. 29.

7. Provincial Archives, Portland, Small to Janssens, October 17, 1949.

8. OPA, Gonzaga Papers, correspondence regarding KGA, Robinson to de Boynes, June 30, 1946.

9. *Spokane Chronicle*, June 16, 1949.

10. OPA, Gonzaga Papers, correspondence regarding KGA, Blackburn to Corkery, March 22, 1949.

11. *Ibid.*, original copy inserted in diaries.

12. *Ibid.*, KGA, CPA report for December 31, 1951.

13. *Ibid.*, Corkery to Small, November 5, 1950.

14. *Ibid.*, Financial Reports, 1946–1951.

15. *Ibid.*

16. *Ibid.*, *Gonzaga University Institutional Self-Analysis*, Secton C., pp. 87–98

17. *Ibid.*, Corkery to Small, October 29, 1952.

18. *Ibid.*, February 23, 1953.

19. Provincial Archives, Portland, Small to Dalgity, August 1, 1949.

20. *Ibid.*, Small to Janssens, February 21, 1950.

21. *America*, March 4, 1950, p. 630.

22. Provincial Archives, Portland, Corkery to Small, May 15, 1950.

23. *Spokesman Review*, May 12, 1950.

24. *The Catholic Mind*, October 1950, pp. 577–580.

25. Provincial Archives, Portland, Corkery to Small, May 15, 1950.

26. [Henry J. Schultheis, S.J.] *Dedication of the New St. Ignatius Church* (Portland, 1951).

27. Provincial Archives, Portland, Janssens to Small, September 27, 1950.

28. Interview with Small, July 6, 1981, Seattle.

29. Provincial Archives, Portland, Janssens to Small, September 27, 1950.

30. *Ibid.*, Small to Janssens, February 24, 1951.

31. OPA, Provincial Papers, Small to members of the Province, August 17, 1951.

32. *Ibid.*, Thomas Martin papers, data on his last illness.

33. Reported by Mark Gaffney to me, summer, 1954, Portland.

34. *The Oregon Jesuit*, 26, 7 (September, 1958), p. 10.

35. Interview with Small, July 6, 1981, Seattle.

36. OPA, Loyola High School papers, Missoula, "Loyola—A Heritage," p. 6.

37. Provincial Archives, Portland. McDonnell to Small, September 18, 1953.

38. *Ibid.*, Gordon Toner to Small, January 3, 1953.

39. *Ibid.*, McDonnell note at end of Memo for Consultors, January 13, 1953.

40. *Ibid.*, Small to Corkery, January 14, 1953.

41. *Ibid.*, Small to Janssens, "Visitation of the Mission of Northern Alaska, February 2 to March 10, 1953.

42. OPA, Convert Papers, "Concerning the Situation at Bristol Bay, 1951," dated Dilling-ham, Alaska, July 26, 1951.

43. This and following selections are from Small's "Visitation of the Mission of Northern Alaska."

44. *Fairbanks News—Miner*, September 4, 1959.

45. *American Weekly*, January 18, 1959.

46. Provincial Archives, Portland, Small letter to Missionaries in Alaska, July 22, 1953.

47. *Ibid.*, Logan to Small, October 8, 1953.

48. *Ibid.*, October 12, 1953.

49. *Ibid.*, Janssens to Small, February 9, 1954.

50. *Ibid.*, March 23, 1954.

51. *Ibid.*, Schultheis to Janssens, November 19, 1954.

Chapter 21
BRICK AND MORTAR

1. Provincial Archives, Portland, Kunz to Schultheis, July 21, 1954.

2. *Ibid.*, Schultheis to Janssens, November 19, 1954.

3. *The Oregon Jesuit*, 24, 1(January, 1955), p. 1.

4. *Northwest Progress*, October 15, 1954.

5. *Spokesman Review*, June 26, 1954.

6. *Gonzaga Bulletin*, October 23, 1953.

7. *The Oregon Jesuit*, 24, 1(January, 1955), p. 1.

8. *The Oregon Jesuit* 25 8(October, 1956), p. 5.

9. *The Oregon Jesuit*, 24 2(February, 1955), p. 1.;

"Origins of Bellarmine Boosters," by Francis B. Costello, S.J., in *The Oregon Jesuit*, 60, 5 (May, 1960), p. 6.

10. Provincial Archives, Portland, Schultheis to Howard, August 16, 1955.

11. *Ibid.*, Howard to Schultheis, August 16, 1955. Howard made a contribution of $5,000.

12. *Ibid.*, Schultheis to Janssens, August 18, 1955.

13. *Ibid.*, Whelan to Schultheis, August 24, 1955.

14. Interview with Joseph Perri, May 1, 1981, Portland.

15. Provincial Archives, Portland, Jesuit High Financial Drive, 1957. During the following summer another group of Jesuits was assigned to beg for Jesuit High. These two unprece-dented fund drives by Jesuits indicate the pro-vincial's priorities of interest.

16. *The Oregon Jesuit*, 25, 8(October, 1956), p. 6.

17. Interview with Joseph Perri, May 1, 1981, Portland.

18. *The Oregon Jesuit*, 24, 8 (October, 1955), p. 2.

19. *Ibid.*, 9 (November, 1955), p. 1.

20. *Ibid.*

21. *The Oregon Jesuit*, 25,10(December, 1956), p. 2.

22. Provincial Archives, Portland, Schultheis to Janssens, January 8, 1957.

23. *Ibid.*, January 18, 1957.

24. *Ibid.*, Schultheis to Connolly, February 22, 1957.

25. Interview with Leo Gaffney regarding ter-tianship, December 15, 1981.

26. *The Oregon Jesuit*, 26,2(February, 1957), p. 1. Prior to this, Toner rented offices in a nearby building. These had become inadequate.

27. Provincial Archives, Portland, Janssens to Schultheis, February 28, 1957.

28. *Ibid.*, March 14, 1957.

29. *Ibid.*, Schultheis to Father Severian Azcoma, May 2, 1957.

30. *The Oregon Jesuit*, 26,7(September, 1958), p. 11.

31. Provincial Archives, Portland, Schultheis to Janssens, November 14, 1958.

32. *Ibid.*, November 22, 1958.

33. *Ibid.*, February 18, 1959.

34. *Ibid.*

Chapter 22
THE DARK HORSE

1. OPA, McDonald Papers, ms. "A Few Notes For Our Boys About Their Daddy, A. J. McDonald of the Quarter Circle Y."

2. *Ibid.*

3. *The Oregon Jesuit*, 28,4 (April, 1959), p. 1.
4. Provincial Archives, Portland, Hargreaves to McDonald, May 24, 1959.

5. See "Wilfred Schoenberg, S.J., "Lay Apostles on the Alaska Mission," *The Oregon Jesuit*, 27,1 (January, 1958), p. 10.

6. *The American Weekly* (in the Pittsburgh *Sun-Telegraph*), January 18, 1959, p. 2.

7. Article in *The Oregon Jesuit*, 27,10 (October, 1958), p. 7, described the ice field, which measured 8,000 feet by 6,500 feet.

8. *The American Weekly*, January 18, 1959, p. 2.

9. OPA, Cunningham Papers, Citation to Accompany the Aware of the Air Force Commendation Medal.

10. Letter to Father Erwin Toner, May 27, 1959, in *The Oregon Jesuit*.

11. OPA, Jesuit Volunteers Corps, ms., "An Account of the Beginnings of the Jesuit Volunteer Corps," by John Morris, S.J.

12. *Ibid.*

13. *Ibid.*, "Number of Volunteers in JVC: NW" by Larry Gooley, S.J.

14. Mary Frances Perkins (Mary Perkins Ryan), *Are Parochial Schools the Answer: Catholic Education in the Light of the Council* (New York, 1964).

15. *The Oregon Jesuit*, 28:2 (February, 1959), p. 5.

16. *Ibid.*

17. *Ibid.*

18. *Ibid.*

19. *Ibid.*, 28:10 (December, 1959), p. 2.

20. Provincial Archives, Portland, McDonald to Janssens, April 29, 1959.

21. *Ibid.*, June 10, 1959.

22. *Ibid.*

23. OPA, St. Mary's Mission Papers, "Report on St. Mary's Mission, Omak, Washington," November 3–4, 1959.

24. Wilfred P. Schoenberg, *Jesuits in Oregon*, 1844–1959 (Portland, 1959) p. 51.

25. Provincial Archives, Portland, McDonald to Doughterty, February 3, 1960.

26. *Ibid.*, Dougherty to McDonald, March 2, 1960.

27. Provincial Archives, Portland, O'Dea to Fitzgerald, May 20, 1932.

28. *Ibid.*, McDonald to Janssens, February 29, 1960.

29. Former Oregonians were also in the Chinese Mission, now attached to the California Province.

30. Provincial Archives, Portland, McDonald to Janssens, February 29, 1960.

31. *Ibid.*, March 13, 1960.

32. *Ibid.*, McCardle to McDonald, March 8, 1960.

33. *Ibid.*, Willis to McDonald, March 10, 1960.

34. *Ibid.*, McDonald to Janssens, December 6, 1960.

35. Interview with McDonald, July 5, 1981.

36. Provincial Archives Portland, Hargreaves to McDonald, October 3, 1940.

37. OPA Llorente Papers, Letter to Schoenberg regarding his civil service in Juneau.

38. Provincial Archives Portland, Hargreaves to McDonald, October 3, 1940.

39. OPA, Linssen Papers, circular letter of Hargreaves regarding Linssen's death, October 17, 1960.

40. Provincial Archives, Portland, McDonald to Janssens, October 23, 1960.

41. OPA, Provincial Papers, McDonald letter to the Province, November 8, 1960.

42. Provincial Archives, Portland, McDonald to Janssens, December 31, 1960.

43. OPA, Haupt Papers, Signed application form to enter the Society.

44. *The Oregon Jesuit*, 30:1 (January, 1961), p. 1.

45. Interview with McDonald, July 5, 1981, Seattle.

46. Provincial Archives, Portland, McDonald to Janssens, January 16, 1962.

47. *Ibid.*, February 27, 1961.

48. *Ibid.*, Leary to McDonald, April 23, 1962.

49. *Spokesman Review*, May 4, 1962.

50. *Ibid.*, July 20, 1962.

51. Provincial Archives, Portland, McDonald to Janssens, January 30, 1963.

52. *Ibid.*, February 18, 1963.

53. *Ibid.*, Topel to McDonald, June 12, 1963. Bishop White had offered to pay the Jesuits for the land for St. Aloysius Church but the Jesuits declined the offer.

54. *Ibid.*, Janssens to McDonald, October 30, 1963.

55. *Ibid.*, McDonald to Janssens, no date [Oregon 64/9]

56. *Ibid.*, May 24, 1964.

Chapter 23
THE VIOLENT WINDS OF CHANGE

1. Interview with Father John Kelley, April 21, 1981, Portland.

2. Barbara Ward, *Rich Nations, Poor Nations*, quoted in *The Jesuit*, September–October, 1966, p. 4.
  3. Interview with Kelley, April 21, 1981, Portland.

4. *Ibid.*

5. A Province Congregation was held at Gonzaga University in January, 1965.

6. Provincial Archives, Portland, Kelley to Swain, October 21, 1964.

7. *Ibid.* April 21, 1965.

8. *Ibid.*, Swain to Kelley, April 10, 1965.

9. Interview with Kelley, April 21, 1981, Portland.

10. Provincial Archives, Portland, Arrupe to Kelley, February 14, 1966.

11. *Ibid.*, Kelley to Arrupe, February 16, 1966. This was called the Juniorate Philosophy Integration Committee (JPI) under the chairmanship of Clifford Kossell.

12. OPA, Provincial Papers, Kelley to the Province, March 30, 1966, with an account of the general's schedule in the province.

13. Provincial Archives, Portland, Arrupe to Kelley, April 29, 1966.

14. *Ibid.*, Kelley to Arrupe, May 8, 1966.

15. *Ibid.*, Arrupe to Kelley, July 28, 1966. The two words were underlined by Father Arrupe.

16. *Ibid.*, Kelley to Arrupe, August 8, 1966.

17. *The Jesuit*, November–December, 1966, p. 17.

18. OPA, Sheridan Novitiate Papers, Commentary on the Rules, originally included by Father Thomas Meagher.

19. OPA, Provincial Papers, Kelley to the Province from Rome, October 24, 1966.

20. Provincial Archives, Portland, Costello to Arrupe, November 4, 1966.

21. *Ibid.*, Arrupe to Kelley, December 13, 1966.

22. Interview with Kelley, April 21, 1981, Portland.

23. Father Patrick Donohoe was the provincial for California. *The Jesuit,* spring, 1969, p. 1.

24. Interview with Kelley, April 21, 1981.

25. OPA, Provincial Papers, Kelley letter to the province, January 6, 1967.

26. Provincial Archives, Portland, Arrupe to Kelley, January 9, 1967.

27. *Ibid.,* March 2, 1967.

28. *Ibid.,* Kelley to Arrupe, April 19, 1967.

29. OPA, Provincial Papers, Kelley to the province, February 4, 1967.

30. *Ibid.,* December 21, 1967. This included a copy of Arrupe's letter to Connolly, December 12, 1967.

31. Peter J. Henriot, S.J., in *The Jesuit,* winter, 1969.

32. Provincial Archives, Portland, Arrupe to Kelley, August 29, 1967.

33. *The Jesuit,* March–April, 1966, p. 17.

34. Provincial Archives, Portland, J. W. Lawler to McDonald, December 8, 1960.

35. *The Jesuit,* November–December, 1967, p. 5.

36. OPA, Provincial Papers, Kelley to the province, October 17, 1967.

37. *Ibid.,* St. Mary's, Alaska, November 5, 1967.

38. *Ibid.*

39. *Newsletter to the Oregon Province,* May, 1968.

40. Provincial Archives, Portland, Arrupe to Kelley, January 22, 1968.

41. *Newsletter of the Oregon Province,* May, 1968.

42. Provincial Archives, Portland, Kelley to Small, January 23, 1969.

43. OPA, Provincial Papers, Kelley to the province, July 29, 1968. This is a nine-page account of his visitation in Africa.

44. *Ibid.*

45. OPA, Provincial Papers, Kelley to the province, August 13, 1968. This is taken from a letter of Kapfer to Kelley.

46. *Gonzaga Bulletin,* November 8, 1968, p. 8. Grief left the Society soon after this.

47. Provincial Archives, Portland, Arrupe to Kelley, December 9, 1968.

48. *Gonzaga Bulletin,* November 22, 1968, p. 5.

49. Provincial Archives, Portland, Arrupe to Kelley, December 9, 1968.

50. Provincial Archives, Portland, Kelley to Arrupe, December 15, 1968.

51. Provincial Archives, Portland, Kelley to Small, January 24, 1969.

52. *Ibid.*

53. *Ibid.,* Arrupe to Kelley, January 18, 1969. Christoph took office on February 13, 1969.

54. Provincial Archives, Portland, Kelley to Small, February 2, 1969.

55. OPA, Provincial Papers, Kelley to the province, February 11, 1969.

56. *Spokesman Review,* June 8, 1969. The Trustees acted on June 6, and Kelley sent formal notice to the province on June 17.

57. Provincial Archives, Portland, Kelley to Arrupe, November 30, 1968.

58. *Ibid.*

59. Provincial Archives, Portland, Kelley to Arrupe, December, 6, 1969.

60. OPA, Minutes of the Second PAC meeting at Sheridan, February 21 to February 22, 1969.

61. OPA, Provincial Papers, Kelley to the province, February 1, 1969.

62. OPA, Provincial Papers, Letter of the Ad Hoc Commission on the Ministries to the province, March 17, 1969.

63. OPA, Minutes of the Third PAC meeting at Tacoma, March 28 to March 29, 1969.

64. *Newletter of the Oregon Province,* June, 1969.

65. OPA, Provincial Papers, Kelley to the province, April 19, 1969.

66. OPA, Provincial Papers, Kelley to Special Students, November 2, 1968.

67. The best explanation of the Principal of Attraction appears in *The Attraction Principle in the Chicago Province,* by R. F. Harvanek, S.J., np., nd.

68. OPA, Minutes of the Second Session of the Oregon Province Congress, November 26 to November 30, Spokane. Leo Kaufmann's Resolution at the End of the Congress.

69. Interview with Kelley, April 21, 1981, Portland.

70. *Newsletter of the Oregon Province,* January, 1970.

71. *Ibid.,* December, 1968.

Chapter 24
THE DIVIDED PROVINCE

1. Interview with Kelley, April 21, Portland.

2. OPA, Provincial Papers, Letter of Galbraith sent out from the Provincial's office as a News Release, March 1, 1970.

3. *Newsletter of the Oregon Province,* April, 1970, p. 10.

4. OPA, Provincial Papers, Galbraith to the Province, June 10, 1970.

5. Provincial Archives, Portland, Galbraith to Arrupe, July 6, 1970.

6. *Ibid.,* Arrupe to Galbraith, July 23, 1970.

7. *Ibid.,* Galbraith to Arrupe, July 16, 1970.

8. *Ibid.,* Arrupe to Galbraith, July 31, 1970.

9. *Ibid.,* August 29, 1970.

10. *Ibid.,* September 3, 1970.

11. *The Jesuit,* spring, 1971, p. 16.

12. Memoirs of Michael M. O'Malley, S.J., *Flocks That I Watched,* (Spokane, 1971), epilogue, p. 119.

13. Provincial Archives, Portland, correspondence with Archbishop Ryan, August 28, 1970.

14. Provincial Archives, Portland, McMeel to Lawlor, April 6, 1971.

15. *Signum* (Gonzaga University) September, 1971, p. 3.

16. *Ibid.*

17. *Ibid.*

18. *The Jesuit,* winter, 1968, p. 1.

19. Provincial Archives, Portland, McMeel to Lawlor, April 6, 1971.

20. Provincial Archives, Portland, Galbraith correspondence with Seattle University, Emergency Meeting, Seattle University Crisis, October 10, 1970, Chinook Hotel, Yakima.

21. Provincial Archives, Portland, Galbraith to Arrupe, November 21, 1971.

22. *Ibid.,* Baker accepted the editorship of the *Homiletic and Pastoral Review* in New York.

23. *The General Exchange,* February, 1973, p. 3.

24. Provincial Archives, Portland, Lawlor to the Province, January 15, 1971.

25. *The General Exchange,* February, 1973, p. 3.

26. *Ibid.,* April, 1972, p. 3. In the experience of older Jesuits discussions at Villa did not cease when the provincial came in the room; they usually became more lively.

27. *Ibid.,* March, 1972, p. 13.

28. *Ibid.,* April, 1972, p. 8.

29. *Ibid.,* February, 1973, p. 3.

30. *Ibid.*

31. *Ibid.,* November 16, 1971, p. 4.

32. *Ibid.,* p. 5.

33. *Ibid.,* p. 7.

34. *Ibid.,* October, 1973, p. 7.

35. *The Oregon Journal*, October 10, 1972.

36. OPA, Provincial Papers, Galbraith to the Province, November 29, 1973.

37. Interview with Galbraith, September 13, 1981, Spokane.

38. *The General Exchange*, June, 1973, p. 1.

39. Interview with Galbraith, September 13, 1981, Spokane.

40. The Kindall Plan is presented in *The General Exchange*, March, 1973, p. 8.

41. *Ibid.*, June, 1973, p. 2. Two of these young men left the Order within a relatively brief time.

42. Interview with Carroll, December 3, 1981, Seattle.

43. *The General Exchange*, April, 1973, p. 1.

44. Provincial Archives, Portland, Galbraith to Arrupe, December 19, 1973.

45. Archbishop William Dwyer had approved both the sale and the relocation of the novitiate in Portland. The rescript for the canonical erection in Portland is dated January 10, 1974. Provincial Archives, Portland, Arrupe to Galbraith, January 14, 1974.

46. OPA, Provincial Papers, Galbraith to the Province, January 11, 1974.

47. *The General Exchange*, October, 1973, p. 1, et seq.

48. *Ibid.*

49. OPA, Loyens papers, Loyens to Director of Vocations, February 28, 1947.

50. *The General Exchange*, October, 1973, p. 1, et seq.

51. OPA, Loyens Papers, McDonald to Loyens, March 18, 1964.

52. William John Loyens, S.J., "The Koyukon Feast of the Dead," in *Arctic Anthropology*, II:2.

53. OPA, James Powers papers, "A Presentation," January 28, 1974.

54. Provincial Archives, Portland, Lawlor to Arrupe, January 10, 1975.

55. *Ibid.*, Arrupe to Galbraith, January 9, 1974.

56. *Ibid.*, Galbraith to Arrupe, December 21, 1973. The Oregon Province handed over to the tribe the first two parcels of land in April, 1974.

57. *The General Exchange*, June, 1974, p. 3.

58. *Ibid.*, October, 1974, p. 2.

59. Bernard Tyrrell, S.J., *Christotherapy: Healing Through Enlightenment*, (New York, 1975).

60. John Joseph Evoy, *The Rejected: Psychological Consequences of Parental Rejection* (University Park and London, 1981).

61. William N. Bischoff, S.J., *We Were Not Summer Soldiers: The Indian Diary of Plympton J. Kelly, 1855–1856*, (Tacoma, 1976).

62. James E. Royce, *Alcohol Problems and Alcoholism* (New York and London, 1981).

63. J. J. Mueller, S.J., *Faith and Appreciative Awareness* (Washington, D.C., 1981).

64. Provincial Archives, Portland, Lawlor to Arrupe, January 10, 1975.

65. *Ibid.*, February 3, 1975.

66. OPA, James Powers Papers, Gaffney to Powers, March 3, 1975.

67. The Tertian House was attached to St. Michael's Institute on June 24, 1975. Provincial Archives, Portland, Galbraith to Arrupe, June 24, 1975.

68. John D. McCallum, *The Story of Dan Lyons, S.J.*, New York, 1973.

69. Provincial Archives, Portland, Galbraith to Arrupe, September 24, 1975.

Chapter 25
THE GOLDEN YEARS

1. Composed April 28, 1981.

2. Interview with Brother Robert Calouri, April 29, 1981 at Portland.

3. *Ibid.*

4. *The Alaska Northwest Exchange*, formerly

called *The Province Exchange,* December, 1979, p. 5, et seq.

5. OPA, Provincial Papers, Loyens to the Province, September 7, 1976.

6. *The Alaska Northwest Exchange,* December, 1977, p. 3. Reynolds became editor of *The Exchange* for the second time in May, 1977.

7. Provincial Archives, Portland. Kelley Memorandum to Financial Committee Members, January 16, 1978.

8. *Ibid.,* Kelley to Arrupe, June 22, 1978.

9. *The Alaska Northwest Exchange,* March, 1978, p. 7.

10. *Ibid.,* p. 1.

11. *Ibid.,* April–May, 1978, p. 1.

12. The Jesuit Conference, "The Jesuit Mission in Education" (Washington, 1978).

13. OPA, Provincial Papers, Loyens to the Province, April 24, 1978.

14. Father Frank McGuigan in *The Alaska Northwest Exchange,* April–May, 1978, p. 8.

15. OPA, Provincial Papers, Loyens to the Province, May 15, 1979, announcing Royce as the new rector of Gonzaga University, effective July 1, 1979.

16. Interview with Father Thomas Royce, May 28, 1981, Portland.

17. From manuscript records in the Jesuit House Infirmary

18. OPA, Provincial Papers, Memorandum of Father Clifford Jones to Superiors and Administrators, January 16, 1978.

19. *The Alaska Northwest Exchange,* September, 1979, p. 1.

20. *The National Jesuit News,* October, 1981, p. 15.

21. Treasurer's Archives, Portland, Sherry to Kelley, December 21, 1978.

22. *The Alaska Northwest Exchange,* January, 1980, p. 1, et seq.

23. *Ibid.*

24. OPA, Provincial Papers, Loyens to the Province, April 7, 1980; also, *The Alaska Northwest Exchange,* April, 1980, p. 1.

25. *Ibid.,* Perri to Province, June 2, 1980.

26. *Ibid.,* Royce to Province, June 24, 1980.

27. *The Oregon Jesuit,* February, 1982, p. 10.

28. OPA, Provincial Papers, Royce to the Province, September 5, 1980.

29. *The Alaska Northwest Exchange,* November, 1980, p. 6.

30. *Ibid.*

31. *National Jesuit News,* December, 1980, p. 15.

32. OPA, Provincial Papers, Kelley to Superiors of the Province, September 11, 1981.

33. Provincial Archives, Portland, Report to Father Provincial and the Province Consultors from Frank B. Costello, Chairman, Golden Year Committee, January 16, 1981, p. 1, et seq.

34. *Ibid.*

35. *National Jesuit News,* May, 1981, p. 14.

36. *The Alaska Northwest Exchange,* May, 1981, p. 4. Also, *The National Jesuit News,* April, 1981, p. 24.

37. OPA, Provincial Papers, Royce to the Province, August 21, 1981.

38. *Ibid.,* August 27, 1981. The quotation is from the Book of Leviticus 25:8–11.

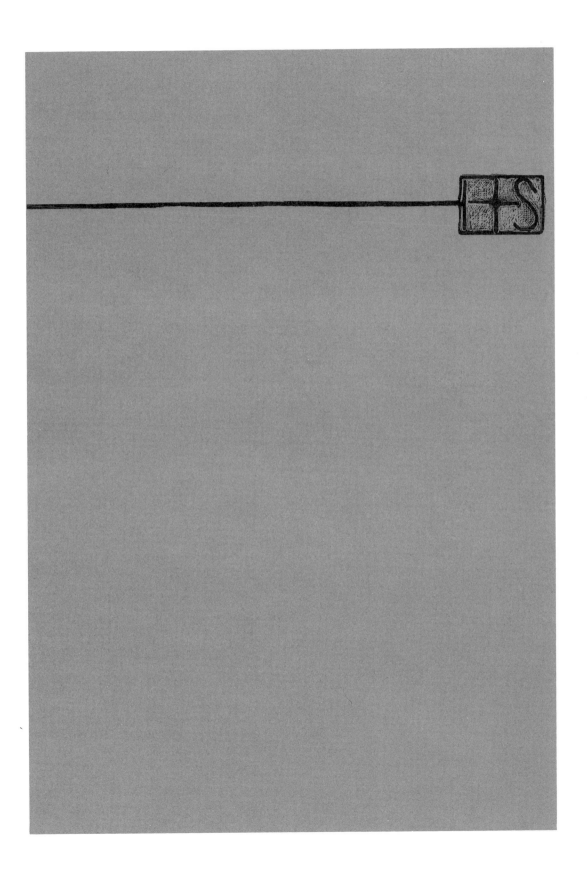

ILLUSTRATIONS

ILLUSTRATIONS

ILLUSTRATIONS

Note: The design element used throughout the
book originates from the branding iron that was
forged in the Jesuit Mission shops on the Willamette, probably in 1845. This brand was used
on the cattle of St. Francis Xavier's Mission.

INDEX

INDEX

641

INDEX

INDEX

INDEX